Fodor's Road Guide USA

California

First Edition

Fodor's Travel Publications
New York Toronto London Sydney Auckland
www.fodors.com

Fodor's Road Guide USA: California

Fodor's Travel Publications
President: Bonnie Ammer
Publisher: Kris Kliemann
Executive Managing Editor: Denise DeGennaro
Editorial Director: Karen Cure
Director of Marketing Development: Jeanne Kramer
Associate Managing Editor: Linda Schmidt
Senior Editor: Constance Jones
Director of Production and Manufacturing: Chuck Bloodgood
Creative Director: Fabrizio La Rocca

Contributors
Editing: Harriot Manley, Andy Moore, Marty Olmstead, and Bobbi Zane, with Michele Bloom, Victoria Caldwell, Laurel Carroll, Angela Casey, Lisa Cole, Yvonne Daley, Michael de Zayas, Jobie Fagans, Robert Fleming, Hannah Fons, Anna Halasz, Holly Hammond, Gail Harrington, Amy Hegarty, Jay Hyams, Laura Kopp, Fran Levine, Eric Lucas, Christa Malone, Harriot Manley, Pat Hadley-Miller, JoAnn Milivojevic, Elizabeth Minyard, Candy Moulton, Elizabeth Nash, Virginia Rainey, Eric Reymond, Laura Scheel, Kelly Sobel, Barbara Stewart, Susan Walton, Kirsten Weisenberger, and Ethan Young
Writing: Cailin Boyle and Chiori Santiago, with Gary Chandler, Sarah Cupp, Vanessa Lazo Geares, David Mandel, Paula Margulies, Kirsten Masick, Sidharth Murdeshwar, Amanda Robinson, Brian Rohan, and Mary Woods
Black-and-White Maps: Rebecca Baer, Robert Blake, David Lindroth, Todd Pasini
Production/Manufacturing: Robert B. Shields
Cover: Mary Altier (background photo), Bart Nagel (photo, illustration)
Interior Photo: Photodisc

First Edition
ISBN 0–679–00494–7
ISSN 1528–1434

Special Sales
Fodor's Travel Publications are available at special discounts for bulk purchases for sales promotions or premiums. Special editions, including personalized covers, excerpts of existing guides, and corporate imprints, can be created in large quantities for special needs. For more information, contact your local bookseller or write to Special Markets, Fodor's Travel Publications, 280 Park Avenue, New York, NY 10017. Inquiries from Canada should be directed to your local Canadian bookseller or sent to Random House of Canada, Ltd., Marketing Department, 2775 Matheson Boulevard East, Mississauga, Ontario L4W 4P7. Inquiries from the United Kingdom should be sent to Fodor's Travel Publications, 20 Vauxhall Bridge Road, London SW1V 2SA, England.

PRINTED IN THE UNITED STATES OF AMERICA
10 9 8 7 6 5 4 3 2 1

CONTENTS

MAPS

COLOR ATLAS

Great Road Trips

Of all the things that went wrong with Clark Griswold's vacation, one stands out: The theme park he had driven across the country to visit was closed when he got there. Clark, the suburban bumbler played by Chevy Chase in 1983's hilarious *National Lampoon's Vacation*, is fictional, of course. But his story is poignantly true. Although most Americans get only two precious weeks of vacation a year, many set off on their journeys with surprisingly little guidance. Many travelers find out about their destination from friends and family or wait to get travel information until they arrive in their hotel, where racks of brochures dispense the "facts," along with free city magazines. But it's hard to distinguish the truth from hype in these sources. And it makes no sense to spend priceless vacation time in a hotel room reading about a place when you could be out seeing it up close and personal.

Congratulate yourself on picking up this guide. Studying it—before you leave home—is the best possible first step toward making sure your vacation fulfills your every dream.

Inside you'll find all the tools you need to plan a perfect road trip. In the hundreds of towns we describe, you'll find thousands of places to explore. So you'll always know what's around the next bend. And with the practical information we provide, you can easily call to confirm the details that matter and study up on what you'll want to see and do, before you leave home.

By all means, when you plan your trip, allow yourself time to make a few detours. Because as wonderful as it is to visit sights you've read about, it's the serendipitous experiences that often prove the most memorable: the hole-in-the-wall diner that serves a transcendent tomato soup, the historical society gallery stuffed with dusty local curiosities of days gone by. As you whiz down the highway, use the book to find out more about the towns announced by roadside signs. Consider turning off at the next exit. And always remember: In this great country of ours, there's an adventure around every corner.

HOW TO USE THIS BOOK

Alphabetical organization should make it a snap to navigate through this book. Still, in putting it together, we've made certain decisions and used certain terms you need to know about.

LOCATIONS AND CATEGORIZATIONS

Color map coordinates are given for every town in the guide.

Attractions, restaurants, and lodging places are listed under the nearest town covered in the guide.

Parks and forests are sometimes listed under the main access point.

Exact street addresses are provided whenever possible; when they were not available or applicable, directions and/or cross-streets are indicated.

CITIES

For state capitals and larger cities, attractions are alphabetized by category. Shopping sections focus on good shopping areas where you'll find a concentration of interesting shops. We include malls only if they're unusual in some way and individual stores only when they're community institutions. Restaurants and hotels are grouped by price category then arranged alphabetically.

RESTAURANTS

All are air-conditioned unless otherwise noted, and all permit smoking unless they're identified as "no-smoking."

Dress: Assume that no jackets or ties are required for men unless otherwise noted.

Family-style service: Restaurants characterized this way serve food communally, out of serving dishes as you might at home.

Meals and hours: Assume that restaurants are open for lunch and dinner unless otherwise noted. We always specify days closed and meals not available.

Prices: The price ranges listed are for dinner entrées (or lunch entrées if no dinner is served).

Reservations: They are always a good idea. We don't mention them unless they're essential or are not accepted.

Fodor's Choice: Stars denote restaurants that are Fodor's Choices—our editors' picks of the state's very best in a given price category.

LODGINGS

All are air-conditioned unless otherwise noted, and all permit smoking unless they're identified as "no-smoking."

AP: This designation means that a hostelry operates on the American Plan (AP)—-that is, rates include all meals. AP may be an option or it may be the only meal plan available; be sure to find out.

Baths: You'll find private bathrooms with bathtubs unless noted otherwise.

Business services: If we tell you they're there, you can expect a variety on the premises.

Exercising: We note if there's "exercise equipment" even when there's no designated area; if you want a dedicated facility, look for "gym."

Facilities: We list what's available but don't note charges to use them. When pricing accommodations, always ask what's included.

Hot tub: This term denotes hot tubs, Jacuzzis, and whirlpools.

MAP: Rates at these properties include two meals.

No smoking: Properties with this designation prohibit smoking.

Opening and closing: Assume that hostelries are open year-round unless otherwise noted.

Pets: We note whether or not they're welcome and whether there's a charge.

Pools: Assume they're outdoors with fresh water; indoor pools are noted.

Prices: The price ranges listed are for a high-season double room for two, excluding tax and service charge.

Telephone and TV: Assume that you'll find them unless otherwise noted.

Fodor's Choice: Stars denote hostelries that are Fodor's Choices—our editors' picks of the state's very best in a given price category.

NATIONAL PARKS

National parks protect and preserve the treasures of America's heritage, and they're always worth visiting whenever you're in the area. Many are worth a long detour. If you will travel to many national parks, consider purchasing the National Parks Pass ($50), which gets you and your companions free admission to all parks for one year. (Camping and parking are extra.) A percentage of the proceeds from sales of the pass helps to fund important projects in the parks. Both the Golden Age Passport ($10), for those 62 and older, and the Golden Access Passport (free), for travelers with disabilities, entitle holders to free entry to all national parks, plus 50% off fees for the use of many park facilities and services. You must show proof of age and of U.S. citizenship or permanent residency (such as a U.S. passport, driver's license, or birth certificate) and, if requesting Golden Access, proof of your disability. You must get your Golden Access or Golden Age passport in person; the former is available at all federal recreation areas, the latter at federal recreation areas that charge fees. You may purchase the National Parks Pass by mail or through the Internet. For information, contact the National Park Service (Department of the Interior, 1849 C St. NW, Washington, DC 20240-0001, 202/208—4747, www.nps.gov). To buy the National Parks Pass, write to 27540 Ave. Mentry, Valencia, CA 91355, call 888/GO—PARKS, or visit www.national-parks.org.

IMPORTANT TIP

Although all prices, opening times, and other details in this book are based on information supplied to us at press time, changes occur all the time in the travel world, and Fodor's cannot accept responsibility for facts that become outdated or for inadvertent errors or omissions. So always confirm information when it matters, especially if you're making a detour to visit a specific place.

Let Us Hear from You

Keeping a travel guide fresh and up-to-date is a big job, and we welcome any and all comments. We'd love to have your thoughts on places we've listed, and we're interested in hearing about your own special finds, even the ones in your own back yard. Our guides are thoroughly updated for each new edition, and we're always adding new information, so your feedback is vital. Contact us via e-mail in care of roadnotes@fodors.com (specifying the name of the book on the subject line) or via snail mail in care of Road Guides at Fodor's, 280 Park Avenue, New York, NY 10017. We look forward to hearing from you. And in the meantime, have a wonderful road trip.

THE EDITORS

Important Numbers and On-Line Info

LODGINGS

Adam's Mark	800/444—2326	www.adamsmark.com
Baymont Inns	800/428—3438	www.baymontinns.com
Best Western	800/528—1234	www.bestwestern.com
	TDD 800/528—2222	
Budget Host	800/283—4678	www.budgethost.com
Clarion	800/252—7466	www.clarioninn.com
Comfort	800/228—5150	www.comfortinn.com
Courtyard by Marriott	800/321—2211	www.courtyard.com
Days Inn	800/325—2525	www.daysinn.com
Doubletree	800/222—8733	www.doubletreehotels.com
Drury Inns	800/325—8300	www.druryinn.com
Econo Lodge	800/555—2666	www.hotelchoice.com
Embassy Suites	800/362—2779	www.embassysuites.com
Exel Inns of America	800/356—8013	www.exelinns.com
Fairfield Inn by Marriott	800/228—2800	www.fairfieldinn.com
Fairmont Hotels	800/527—4727	www.fairmont.com
Forte	800/225—5843	www.forte-hotels.com
Four Seasons	800/332—3442	www.fourseasons.com
Friendship Inns	800/453—4511	www.hotelchoice.com
Hampton Inn	800/426—7866	www.hampton-inn.com
Hilton	800/445—8667	www.hilton.com
	TDD 800/368—1133	
Holiday Inn	800/465—4329	www.holiday-inn.com
	TDD 800/238—5544	
Howard Johnson	800/446—4656	www.hojo.com
	TDD 800/654—8442	
Hyatt & Resorts	800/233—1234	www.hyatt.com
Inns of America	800/826—0778	www.innsofamerica.com
Inter-Continental	800/327—0200	www.interconti.com
La Quinta	800/531—5900	www.laquinta.com
	TDD 800/426—3101	
Loews	800/235—6397	www.loewshotels.com
Marriott	800/228—9290	www.marriott.com
Master Hosts Inns	800/251—1962	www.reservahost.com
Le Meridien	800/225—5843	www.lemeridien.com
Motel 6	800/466—8356	www.motel6.com
Omni	800/843—6664	www.omnihotels.com
Quality Inn	800/228—5151	www.qualityinn.com
Radisson	800/333—3333	www.radisson.com
Ramada	800/228—2828	www.ramada.com
	TDD 800/533—6634	
Red Carpet/Scottish Inns	800/251—1962	www.reservahost.com
Red Lion	800/547—8010	www.redlion.com
Red Roof Inn	800/843—7663	www.redroof.com
Renaissance	800/468—3571	www.renaissancehotels.com
Residence Inn by Marriott	800/331—3131	www.residenceinn.com
Ritz-Carlton	800/241—3333	www.ritzcarlton.com
Rodeway	800/228—2000	www.rodeway.com

Sheraton	800/325—3535	www.sheraton.com
Shilo Inn	800/222—2244	www.shiloinns.com
Signature Inns	800/822—5252	www.signature-inns.com
Sleep Inn	800/221—2222	www.sleepinn.com
Super 8	800/848—8888	www.super8.com
Susse Chalet	800/258—1980	www.sussechalet.com
Travelodge/Viscount	800/255—3050	www.travelodge.com
Vagabond	800/522—1555	www.vagabondinns.com
Westin Hotels & Resorts	800/937—8461	www.westin.com
Wyndham Hotels & Resorts	800/996—3426	www.wyndham.com

AIRLINES

Air Canada	888/247—2262	www.aircanada.ca
Alaska	800/426—0333	www.alaska-air.com
American	800/433—7300	www.aa.com
America West	800/235—9292	www.americawest.com
British Airways	800/247—9297	www.british-airways.com
Canadian	800/426—7000	www.cdnair.ca
Continental Airlines	800/525—0280	www.continental.com
Delta	800/221—1212	www.delta.com
Midway Airlines	800/446—4392	www.midwayair.com
Northwest	800/225—2525	www.nwa.com
SkyWest	800/453—9417	www.delta.com
Southwest	800/435—9792	www.southwest.com
TWA	800/221—2000	www.twa.com
United	800/241—6522	www.ual.com
USAir	800/428—4322	www.usair.com

BUSES AND TRAINS

Amtrak	800/872—7245	www.amtrak.com
Greyhound	800/231—2222	www.greyhound.com
Trailways	800/343—9999	www.trailways.com

CAR RENTALS

Advantage	800/777—5500	www.arac.com
Alamo	800/327—9633	www.goalamo.com
Allstate	800/634—6186	www.bnm.com/as.htm
Avis	800/331—1212	www.avis.com
Budget	800/527—0700	www.budget.com
Dollar	800/800—4000	www.dollar.com
Enterprise	800/325—8007	www.pickenterprise.com
Hertz	800/654—3131	www.hertz.com
National	800/328—4567	www.nationalcar.com
Payless	800/237—2804	www.paylesscarrental.com
Rent-A-Wreck	800/535—1391	www.rent-a-wreck.com
Thrifty	800/367—2277	www.thrifty.com

Note: Area codes are changing all over the United States as this book goes to press. For the latest updates, check www.areacode-info.com.

Fodor's Road Guide USA

California

California

California celebrated its sesquicentennial as a state in the year 2000. The most populous state in the Union boasts the highest peak in the continental United States (Mt. Whitney) and the world's tallest trees (redwoods). Its Death Valley desert is the deepest (282 ft below sea level), and from its Sierra peaks spills the continent's highest cascade, 2,425-ft Yosemite Falls.

Just 150 years ago, when New York was a first-class seaport, California was a quiet, rural expanse with a only few haciendas and a couple of tiny settlements along the Pacific shore. That changed quickly, of course, after gold was discovered in a Coloma millrace in 1848, but the descension of what seemed to be the entire world on California didn't add any polish. One visitor, Hinton R. Helper, summed up the place in 1855 as an "abominable land of concentrated rascality [which] can and does furnish the best bad things that are obtainable in America." California, he concluded, would "never become a great State."

From these inauspicious beginnings, the Golden State evolved. Engineers built complex systems to carry mountain water to the desert and created Los Angeles. They carved roads into the most inaccessible places—including the treacherous Sierra pass that claimed the lives of the pioneering Donner Party—and made possible a fervent car culture and unshakeable wanderlust. Californians redirected rivers and plowed valley land to plant what became "the nation's produce basket," then told the rest of the country how to eat its harvest by reinventing American cuisine, embracing global flavors, and touting Zen diets, tofu burgers, and vegan restaurants. In most urban areas you can sample Afghanistan shish kebobs, chiles rellenos stuffed with shrimp, Vietnamese pho, and many culinary delights in between.

Thankfully, the builders couldn't tame all of the state's monumental natural beauty. Today the beauty of its rocky coastline, its moody forests, frosted mountain-

CAPITAL: SACRAMENTO	POPULATION: 32,063,000	AREA: 158,693 SQUARE MI
BORDERS: AZ, NV, OR, MEXICO, PACIFIC OCEAN		TIME ZONE: PACIFIC
ABBREVIATION: CA	WEB SITE: GOCALIF.CA.GOV	

tops, sunny beaches, and the sculpted grandeur of Yosemite National Park are a magnet for outdoors lovers (or anyone who's tired of the surfeit of museums, theaters, galleries, and cultural offerings that seem to spring from California soil as easily as its pear orchards and artichoke fields).

The sheer diversity of California's terrain, culture, and people is difficult to grasp. In a way, this is a state made up of lots of little states. The rugged northern coast has an extremely different character from the laid-back south; the agricultural Central Valley seems a stranger to the urbanized mid-section; and some folks in the northeast corner wouldn't even blink if the rest of the state crumbled into the sea. Every few years, some group of activists revives a plan to secede the southern half of the state from the northern. So far none of these schemes got off the ground.

And so California endures, an unpredictable romance full of pleasures and surprises. It's a place where many a visitor arrives to spend two weeks, and then never leaves. Watch out. You've been warned.

History

For thousands of years before the arrival of Europeans, more than 500 independent groups of indigenous people lived in California. They had little reason to quarrel; the land was bucolic and rich, the weather benign, and there was plenty of territory to go around. Far from "primitive" hunter-gatherers, many of these bands—Ohlone, Pomo, Miwok, Maidu, Hupa, Yurok, among others—lived in permanent settlements governed by complex hierarchies of chiefs and assembly houses. They used agricultural techniques to cultivate meadows, control acorn pests, and regenerate woodlands to ensure a food supply. They had little idea that, in the meantime, bands of ragtag explorers were claiming their ancestral homes for Spain.

The earliest Europeans began arriving in the mid-1500s, seeking a mythical land called Califas. The first European may have been Portuguese explorer João Rodrigues Cabrilho. Historians still argue whether Englishman Sir Francis Drake dropped anchor in San Francisco bay in 1579 (a famous brass plaque marking his visit was deemed a hoax). Not until 1769 did Spanish settlers from Mexico, led by Padre Junípero Serra, establish the first of a chain of some 21 missions at what is now San Diego, stretching as far north as Sonoma.

The mission system decimated Native Americans; disease and overwork laid waste to the population and the onslaught of European culture meant the demise of old ways. Settlers radically altered the physical environment, too. As natural as they may appear, California's golden hillsides and woodlands are composed mostly of introduced species. Little of the native prairie survived the influx of great cattle herds after the Mexican government took over the missions in 1834, awarding vast amounts of land to ranchers, known as "Californios," who were willing to settle the new territory.

Huge demand for beef and hides made the Californios wealthy—and lazy. They tolerated the occasional European or American arrival who asked to share the wide-

CA Timeline

2000 BC	1300 BC	1000 BC	1542
Awaneechee tribe comes to the area now known as Yosemite.	Miwok tribe comes to site of present-day Marin County.	Giant sequoias that now flourish in Sequoia National Parks sprouted.	João Rodrigues Cabrilho may be first European to sight the California coast.

INTRODUCTION
HISTORY
REGIONS
WHEN TO VISIT
STATE'S GREATS
RULES OF THE ROAD
DRIVING TOURS

open spaces. One such was John Augustus Sutter, a shrewd Swiss man who began building his own fiefdom in the Sacramento River in 1839. In 1846 a group of rowdies took advantage of Californio hospitality by marching onto General Mariano Vallejo's land in Sonoma, hoisting a handmade flag embellished with a grizzly bear, and declaring the territory part of the American republic. Within two years, the Treaty of Guadalupe Hidalgo turned the rest of Mexican California over to the United States.

In January 1848, carpenter James Marshall was inspecting the new sawmill he'd built for Sutter when he noticed something glinting in the streambed. The two men tried to keep the discovery secret, but in a few months the cry of "Gold!" echoed around the globe. In the words of historian J. S. Halliday, "the world rushed in," and with it an onslaught of pleasure-seeking, entrepreneurial, no-holds-barred characters.

California's rapid economic growth depended on actively exploiting its considerable resources. Although the Gold Rush lasted less than 10 years, it was followed in the 1860s by a quest for silver in the Comstock Lode. Burgeoning travel and trade made the need for a transcontinental railway obvious by the time businessmen Charles Crocker, Mark Hopkins, Collis Huntington, and Leland Stanford (known as The Big Four) invested $1,500 each to found the Central Pacific Railroad of California. Built mostly by Chinese labor, the railway joined East and West coasts at Promontory Point, Utah, in 1869.

During the first half of the 20th century, the frenzied development continued—rivers were dammed, mines dug, redwoods logged, and levees built to expose the rich riverbed farmland in the Sacramento Valley. But with prosperity came fear. Laws excluding Chinese immigrants had been passed in the 1880s; similar laws prevented Japanese, who prospered as Central Valley farmers, from owning land. In 1945 the vigilantes attacked Mexican-Americans in the notorious "Zoot Suit" riots in Los Angeles. Ethnic tensions remain.

But the pioneering sensibility and the spirit of restlessness that created the Golden State endure as well, and along with them, a willingness to change the status quo. Development of natural resources has proceeded at a slower, more thoughtful pace in the wake of environmental activism (California launched the original Earth Day celebration); planners continue to confront suburban sprawl, freeway congestion, and urban decay. At the westernmost rim of the contiguous states, where Spanish is the unofficial second language with Cambodian, Vietnamese, and Urdu not far behind; where a thousand ideologies push up against the endless Pacific, anything seems possible.

Regions

The state can be divided geographically to make matters—and trip planning—less complicated.

1769	1825	1848	1850	1851
Father Junípero Serra and followers establish San Diego de Alcalá, the first of a chain of 21 missions along the El Camino Real (now Route 101).	California becomes a territory of the Mexican Republic; Monterey is the territorial capital.	Gold is discovered at Johann Sutter's mill in Coloma.	California joins the Union.	Chinese immigrants are established in San Francisco and the gold fields.

1. SOUTH COAST

Stretching from San Diego north along the coast to Oxnard and east to San Bernardino and Palm Springs, the South Coast region combines big-city attractions of Los Angeles with the surf-and-sun culture for which California is famous. Further inland, the geography is diverse, from desert communities to snow-topped mountains, exquisite alpine scenery, and a citrus-growing tradition. Disneyland, in Anaheim, is one of the biggest draws.

Towns listed: Anaheim, Arcadia, Arcata, Avalon (Catalina Island), Beaumont, Beverly Hills, Big Bear Lake, Borrego Springs, Brea, Buena Park, Burbank, Calabasas, Calexico, Camarillo, Carlsbad, Catalina Island, Cathedral City, Cerritos, Channel Islands National Park, Chula Vista, Claremont, Corona, Corona Del Mar, Coronado, Costa Mesa, Crestline, Culver City, Dana Point, Del Mar, Desert Hot Springs, El Cajon, El Centro, Encino, Escondido, Fallbrook, Fullerton, Garden Grove, Glendale, Glendora, Hemet, Hollywood, Huntington Beach, Idyllwild, Indian Wells, Indio, Irvine, Julian, Laguna Beach, La Habra, La Jolla, Lake Arrowhead, Lancaster, La Quinta, Long Beach, Los Angeles, Malibu, Manhattan Beach, Marina del Rey, Mission Viejo, Newport Beach, North Hollywood, Oceanside, Ojai, Ontario, Orange, Oxnard, Pacific Beach, Pacific Palisades, Palmdale, Palm Desert, Palm Springs, Pasadena, Pine Valley, Pomona, Port Hueneme, Rancho Bernardo, Rancho Cucamonga, Rancho Mirage, Rancho Santa Fe, Redlands, Redondo Beach, Riverside, San Bernardino, San Clemente, San Diego, San Fernando, San Gabriel, San Juan Capistrano, San Marino, San Pedro, Santa Ana, Santa Monica, San Ysidro, Seal Beach, Sherman Oaks, Simi Valley, Studio City, Temecula, Thousand Oaks, Torrance, Universal City, Valencia, Van Nuys, Venice, Ventura, Victorville, West Covina, West Hollywood, Westwood Village, Whittier, Woodland Hills, Yucca Valley.

2. EASTERN CALIFORNIA/HIGH SIERRAS

Eastern California encompasses Death Valley and the Mojave Desert, stretching past the eastern slope of the Sierra Nevadas to Mammoth Mountain. The town of Barstow, in the Mojave Desert, still reflects the area's mining past. Further west, the fertile Central Valley (in the San Joaquin and Sacramento Valleys) produces 25 percent of the country's food. This rich agricultural zone spans from Bakersfield north to Fresno—which is the center of the San Joaquin Valley and the gateway to Yosemite, Kings Canyon and Sequoia National Parks—and up to Stockton and Modesto. In the High Sierras you'll find spectacular views, awe-inspiring granite peaks, and the world's largest living things—the giant sequoias.

Towns listed: Bakersfield, Barstow, Bishop, Blythe, Death Valley National Park, Fresno, Hanford, Joshua Tree National Park, Kernville, Lone Pine, Madera, Mojave National Preserve, Needles, Porterville, Selma, Sequoia and Kings Canyon National Parks, Tehachapi, Three Rivers, Twentynine Palms, Visalia.

1854	1861	1890	1906	1932
Sacramento becomes the state capital.	The Central Pacific Railroad Co. begins building eastward to complete a transcontinental rail system.	Yosemite National Park is established.	The great earthquake and fire level San Francisco.	Last known full-blooded Miwok Indian, Tom Smith, dies.

INTRODUCTION
HISTORY
REGIONS
WHEN TO VISIT
STATE'S GREATS
RULES OF THE ROAD
DRIVING TOURS

3. CENTRAL COAST

The Central Coast, from Santa Barbara north to Santa Cruz, has some of the most beautiful coastline in the world. California Route 1, also known as Highway One, winds down the coast in a twisting and turning ribbon of ocean vistas. Extending between the two economic centers of the state (LA and San Francisco) the Central Coast offers a peaceful way of life amid some of the most scenic views on the globe.

Towns listed: Aptos, Atascadero, Big Sur, Cambria, Capitola-by-the-Sea, Carmel, Carmel Valley, Coalinga, Gilroy, Hollister, King City, Lompoc, Los Olivos, Monterey, Morro Bay, Pacific Grove, Paso Robles, Pebble Beach, Pismo Beach, San Simeon, Santa Barbara, Santa Cruz, Santa Maria, Solvang.

4. WINE COUNTRY

America's answer to Tuscany, California's Wine Country—Napa and Sonoma counties—resembles its Italian counterpart, with rolling hills and a gentle Mediterranean climate. Wines made here have long won awards, and, with a number of superb restaurants, this region is an exciting destination for food-and-wine lovers. Year-round tours and wine tastings keep locals and visitors coming back.

Towns listed: Calistoga, Fairfield, Guerneville, Healdsburg, Napa, Oakville, Petaluma, St. Helena/Rutherford, Sonoma, Vacaville, Yountville.

5. SAN FRANCISCO, SILICON VALLEY, AND THE REDWOOD AREA

This region incorporates a broad range of first-class sights and regions. San Francisco and the Bay Area are a magnet for many visitors, with their must-see, world-famous landmarks—the Golden Gate Bridge, Alcatraz, and the Transamerica Pyramid. The state's third-largest city, San Jose, is the heart of Silicon Valley, birthplace of the tiny chips and circuits that support the Information Superhighway. And not to be overlooked is the mighty Redwood Area, which runs along the coast north of San Francisco, from Marin to Mendicino and Fort Bragg and on to the Oregon border. Wilder and rockier than its southern neighbor, this part of the coast is distinguished by a craggy coast-line, beautiful redwoods, and character-filled towns. Stretching inland, the sparsely populated Shasta Cascade area owes its roots to mining, lumber, and ranches; outdoor sports rule today.

Towns listed: Albion, Antioch, Berkeley, Bodega Bay, Booneville, Campbell, Cazadero, Clear Lake Area, Concord, Corte Madera, Crescent City, Cupertino, Elk, Eureka, Felton, Ferndale, Fort Bragg, Foster City, Fremont, Garberville, Geyserville, Gualala, Half Moon Bay, Hayward, Hopland, Inverness, Jenner, Lafayette, Lake County, Larkspur, Little River, Livermore, Los Altos, Los Gatos, Martinez, Mendocino, Menlo Park, Millbrai, Mill Valley, Milpitas, Mountain View, Oakland, Olema, Palo Alto, Pleasanton, Point Arena, Point Reyes Station, Princeton-by-the-Sea, Redwood City, Redwood National Park, San Fran-

1935	1942	1964	1965	1969
Boulder Dam is completed, backing up the Colorado River.	After the U.S. enters World War II, Japanese-Americans are removed from California to internment camps.	The Free Speech Movement at University of California, Berkeley, begins an era of political protest.	Led by Cesar Chavez, the National Farm Workers Association wins its first strike. The Watts Riot in Los Angeles claims 32 lives.	A coalition of Native American nations claims Alcatraz Island as historic territory and occupies it for more than 18 months.

cisco, San Jose, San Mateo, San Rafael, San Ramon, Santa Clara, Santa Rosa, Saratoga, Sausalito, Scotia, Sea Ranch, South San Francisco, Sunnyvale, Tiburon, Trinidad, Ukiah, Union City, Vallejo, Walnut Creek, Weaverville, Willits.

6. GOLD COUNTRY

The Gold Country is where California as we know it began. It was here, in 1848, that James Marshall discovered gold along the American River. Within three years, the state's population swelled from 15,000 to 265,000. And California has drawn people in search of a new life ever since. From Oakhurst in the south, through Sonora, Jackson, Placerville, Coloma, and Nevada City, the region was fueled and overfueled by the promise of riches. Today, many museums and historic sites in the area document the search for yellow nuggets.

Towns listed: Auburn, Bear Valley, Bridgeport, Colfax, Coloma, Davis, Grass Valley, Jackson, Jamestown, June Lake, Lake Tahoe Area, Lee Vining, Lodi, Mammoth Lakes, Marysville, Merced, Modesto, Murphys, Nevada City, Oakdale, Oakhurst, Placerville, Rancho Cordova, Roseville, Sacramento, Santa Nella, Sonora, South Lake Tahoe, Squaw Valley, Stockton, Sutter Creek, Tahoe City, Tahoe Vista, Truckee, Yosemite National Park.

7. THE FAR NORTH

Ancient volcanic activity shaped the landscape of the Far North. The most notable feature is Mount Shasta, a dormant volcano that tops 14,000 ft and can be seen for miles around. Less dramatic but more extensive is Lassen Volcanic National Park at the southern end of the Cascade range, with its sulfur vents and bubbling mud pots. The 10,457-ft Mount Lassen and 50 wilderness lakes are the park's highlights. Shasta Dam is an enduring manmade feature. Plentiful access to uncrowded wilderness is the hallmark of the Far North. Here you will find some of the best hiking and fishing in the state.

Towns listed: Alturas, Chester, Chico, Dunsmuir, Lassen Volcanic National Park, Mt. Shasta, Oroville, Quincy, Red Bluff, Redding, Susanville, Willows, Yreka.

When to Visit

The timing of your visit depends on your destination. Southern California stays relatively warm in winter, but summer brings a "June Gloom" to San Diego and smog to Los Angeles. If you want to explore the southern deserts, spring and fall are ideal. Winters are cool even in Palm Springs, and summer heat forces people to stay indoors for much of the day. Inland, winter brings snow to the Sierras, and summer temperatures regularly climb above 100° Fahrenheit. While Northern California can be cool and wet in winter, the other three seasons usually offer beautiful weather. But be prepared— summer temperatures can be bizzarely low. Anyone who's made an excursion to the City by the Bay in July knows to dress warmly when fog settles in. Visit San Francisco

1970	1989	1994
California is the most urbanized and populated state in the nation.	The Loma Prieta earthquake causes extensive damage to the Bay Area of northern California.	Southern California is struck by the major Northridge earthquake, prompting predictions of a "Big One" in the next century.

in October, however, and you may be wearing shorts. Go figure. The microclimate of the Bay area makes dressing a challenge. You may begin your day wearing a T-shirt in Palo Alto, one hour south of San Francisco, and end your day reaching for a scarf, an umbrella, or both. Check forecasts before you pack.

INTRODUCTION
HISTORY
REGIONS
WHEN TO VISIT
STATE'S GREATS
RULES OF THE ROAD
DRIVING TOURS

CLIMATE CHART

Average Monthly Temperatures (in °F) and Monthly Precipitation (in inches)

	JAN.	FEB.	MAR.	APR.	MAY	JUNE
LOS ANGELES	68/49	69/51	70/52	72/54	74/58	78/61
	2.9	3.1	2.6	1.0	.19	.03
	JULY	AUG.	SEPT.	OCT.	NOV.	DEC.
	84/65	85/66	83/65	79/60	72/54	68/49
	.01	.14	.45	.31	2.0	2.0
	JAN.	FEB.	MAR.	APR.	MAY	JUNE
SAN DIEGO	66/49	67/51	66/53	68/56	69/59	72/62
	1.8	1.5	1.8	.79	.19	.07
	JULY	AUG.	SEPT.	OCT.	NOV.	DEC.
	76/66	78/67	77/66	75/61	70/54	66/49
	.02	.10	.24	.37	1.5	1.6
	JAN.	FEB.	MAR.	APR.	MAY	JUNE
SAN FRANCISCO	56/46	60/49	61/49	62/50	63/51	64/53
	4.0	3.0	3.0	1.3	.25	.15
	JULY	AUG.	SEPT.	OCT.	NOV.	DEC.
	65/54	66/55	69/56	69/55	63/52	56/47
	.04	.07	.26	1.3	3.2	3.1

FESTIVALS AND SEASONAL EVENTS

WINTER

Dec.   **Newport Harbor Christmas Boat Parade.** For this event in Newport Beach, more than 200 festooned boats glide through the harbor nightly during the days leading up to Christmas. | 714/729–4400.

Miner's Christmas Celebration. For this Columbia event there are costumed carolers and children's piñatas as well as a Victorian Christmas feast at the City Hotel, lamplight tours, and a Nativity Procession. | 209/536–1672)

El Teatro Campesino. The internationally acclaimed company annually stages its nativity play *La Virgen Del Tepeyac* in San Juan Bautista. | 831/623–2444.

Jan.   **East-West Shrine All-Star Football Classic.** This Palo Alto annual is America's oldest all-star sports event. | 415/661–0291.

Tournament of Roses Parade and Football Game. Every year Pasadena does itself proud on New Year's Day, with lavish flower-decked floats, marching bands, and equestrian teams, followed by the Rose Bowl game. | 626/449–7673.

Feb.   **AT&T Pebble Beach National Pro-Am Golf Tournament.** The legendary golf tournament begins in late January and ends in early February. | 831/649–1533.

Chinese New Year Celebration. San Francisco's Chinatown is the scene of parades and noisy fireworks, all part of a several-day event. | 415/982–3000.

Chinese New Year Parade. Los Angeles also has its noisy, festive holiday. | 213/617–0396.

Riverside County Fair and National Date Festival. Indio's big deal is an exotic event with an Arabian Nights theme; camel and ostrich races, date exhibits, and tastings are among the draws. | 800/811–3247.

SPRING

Mar. **Snowfest.** This event in North Lake Tahoe is the largest winter carnival in the West, with skiing, food, fireworks, parades, and live music. | 530/583–7625.

Nabisco Dinah Shore Golf Tournament. The finest female golfers in the world compete for the richest purse on the LPGA circuit at this event in Rancho Mirage. | 760/324–4546.

Mendocino/Fort Bragg Whale Festival. Whale-watching excursions, marine art exhibits, wine and beer tastings, crafts displays, and a chowder contest fill up the calendar for this event. | 800/726–2780.

Apr. **Cherry Blossom Festival.** This elaborate presentation of Japanese culture and customs winds up with a colorful parade through San Francisco's Japantown. | 415/563–2313.

Toyota Grand Prix. This event in Long Beach, the largest street race in North America, attracts top competitors from all over the world. | 562/436–9953.

May **Bay to Breakers Race.** Thousands sign up to run the 7½-mi route from bay side to ocean side—a hallowed San Francisco tradition. | 415/777–7770.

Feats of Clay. Running throughout the month of May, this national ceramics competition and exhibition is held in Lincoln. | 916/645–9713.

Jumping Frog Jubilee. Inspired by Mark Twain's story "The Notorious Jumping Frog of Calaveras County," this event in Angels Camp is for frogs and trainers who take their competition seriously. | 209/736–2561.

Sacramento Jazz Jubilee. This four-day late-May event is the world's largest Dixieland festival, with 125 bands from around the world. | 916/372–5277.

Great Monterey Squid Festival. The squirmy squid is the main attraction for this Memorial Day weekend event. You'll see squid-cleaning and -cooking demonstrations, you can sample the chewy seafood, and take in entertainment, arts and crafts, and educational exhibits. | 831/649–6544.

June   **Chalk It Up Festival.** During the first weekend in June, in Pasadena City Hall Plaza, artists use the pavement as their canvas to create chalk masterpieces that wash away when festivities have come to a close. There are also musical performances and exotic dining kiosks. The proceeds benefit arts and homeless organizations of the Light-Bringer Project. | 626/440–7379.

Napa Valley Wine Auction. St. Helena stages open houses, a wine tasting, and an auction. Pre-registration by fax in early March is required. | 707/942–9775 | fax 707/942–0171.

Classical Music Festival. During the latter part of June, Ojai hosts a noted outdoor concert series. | 805/646–2094.

July   **Carmel Bach Festival.** The works of Johann Sebastian Bach and his contemporaries are the focus of three weeks of concerts, recitals, and seminars. | 831/624–1521.

Gilroy Garlic Festival. During the last full weekend in July, Gilroy, the self-styled Garlic Capital of the World, celebrates its smelly but delicious product. Don't miss the garlic ice cream. | 408/842–1625.

Aug.   **Cabrillo Music Festival.** Santa Cruz hosts one of the longest-running contemporary orchestral festivals for two weeks early in the month. | 831/426–6966.

California State Fair. Agriculture is the reason for this event, with high-tech exhibits, a rodeo, horse racing, a carnival, and big-name entertainment. It runs 18 days from August to Labor Day in Sacramento. | 916/263–3000.

Old Spanish Days' Fiesta. The nation's largest all-equestrian parade is part of this Santa Barbara event with riders on horses and horses pulling 19th-century carriages as well as two Mexican marketplaces, free variety shows with costumed dancers and singers, a carnival, and a rodeo. | 805/962–8101.

FALL

Sept.   **Russian River Jazz Festival.** Jazz fans descend on Guerneville for this jam at Johnson's Beach. | 707/869–3940.

San Francisco Blues Festival. Fort Mason is the venue for this late September annual. | 415/826–6837.

Los Angeles County Fair. The world's largest county fair, this event in Pomona means entertainment, exhibits, livestock, horse racing, food, and more. | 909/623–3111.

Oct.   **Grand National Rodeo, Horse, and Stock Show.** San Francisco's Cow Palace hosts this 10-day, world-class competition straddling the end of October and the beginning of November. | 415/469–6057.

Pismo Beach Clam Festival. In Carmel, speakers and poets gather for readings on the beach, seminars, a banquet, and a book signing, and restaurants along Pomeroy Avenue engage in a competition for the best clam chowder.

Tor House Poetry Festival. The late poet Robinson Jeffers lived in this area for many years and is honored by this event held in Carmel. | 831/624–1813.

Nov.   **Death Valley '49er Encampment.** Furnace Creek commemorates the historic crossing of Death Valley in 1849, with a fiddlers' contest and an art show. | 760/786–2331.

Doo Dah Parade. During Pasadena's fun-filled spoof of the annual Rose Parade, the Lounge Lizards dress as reptiles and lip-synch Frank Sinatra favorites, and West Hollywood cheerleaders come out in drag. | 626/440–7379.

State's Greats

Natural beauty and technological wonders vie for attention in a state that offers plenty of both. Any visit to California should include at least an afternoon's drive along the coast and a stop at one of the many state beaches and parks or at a vineyard in the wine country—and there are many small wine regions in addition to the famous Napa Valley. After taking in the magnificent scenery, head to one of the state's urban centers, where you'll find a spectrum of high-tech entertainment, from movie-studio theme parks to interactive museum exhibits to hands-on science centers.

High on a list of scenic attractions in northern California is the winding route along **Route One** from Big Sur to the Lost Coast; the **redwoods** of Humboldt County, the **sacred Native American sites** of Mts. Shasta and Lassen, and Yosemite National Park. For dazzling edutainment, you can't beat the **Monterey Bay Aquarium, the California Science Center** in Los Angeles, **the Tech Museum** in San Jose or **Metreon,** and the shopping and entertainment complex in downtown San Francisco.

In Southern California art lovers are making tracks to the **Getty Center** in the foothills of the Santa Monica Mountains. **Disneyland** continues its expansion and the face of Anaheim is being transformed. And for exquisite views, you can't beat a sunset drive down the Pacific Coast Highway, also known as Route One. And no trip to Southern California would be complete without at least one visit to **Los Angeles,** where 75 percent of all movies made in the Unites States are produced. San Diego's beautiful beaches are a must-see. Inland, breathtaking desertscapes await in **Death Valley** and **Anza-Borrego** parks. And no trip to California would be complete without marveling at the stunning **Yosemite National Park.**

Beaches, Forests, and Parks

If it's beaches you want, you've come to the right place. California has 1,264 mi of coastline. Consider **Zuma Beach** in Malibu, or **La Jolla** in San Diego. Further north, Santa Barbara has stretches of water that are warm and quiet. Big Sur boasts hidden beaches that offer some solitude with your sun, sea, and views. Santa Cruz is a surfer's dream. And even in San Francisco you can dip your foot in (albeit chilly) waters. North of San Francisco, in Marin County consider **Stinson Beach.** Accessible from a windy road off U.S. 101, it's worth the trip.

If you're interested in trees, then just look up. **Muir Woods** north of San Francisco has beautiful forest. The redwood forests of Northern California are the only native home to these beautiful trees. And the large parks inland—**Yosemite** and **Kings Canyon and Sequoia National Parks**—protect hundreds of thousands of acres of forest. Trees don't get any larger than the giant sequoias that grow in the Sierras.

INTRODUCTION
HISTORY
REGIONS
WHEN TO VISIT
STATE'S GREATS
RULES OF THE ROAD
DRIVING TOURS

The country's largest municipal park is in LA—**Griffith Park** spans 4,100 acres. And it's perched right above Hollywood. San Francisco has the **Presidio,** as well as **Golden Gate Park.** Then there are the otherworldly desert parks such as **Death Valley** and **Anza-Borrego.**

Culture, History, and the Arts

Alcatraz Island is best known for its federal penitentiary, home of the BirdMan and Al Capone. And for more than 20 years, it's been a symbol of Native American civil rights. The occupation of the former prison by an intertribal group of protesters, who moved onto the windy island for almost two years beginning in 1969, is regarded as a turning point in the recognition of Native Americans in California. Today "The Rock" is part of the Golden Gate National Recreation Area, and tours take place throughout the year.

Century-old architecture can be found in dozens of California's small towns, from Cayucos to Woodland. Visiting north coast lumber towns including Elk and Mendocino, Bodega and other fishing towns, and Gold Rush towns gives you a feel for the state as it used to be. One such place is **Columbia,** near Sonora, a quaint restored Gold Rush town that's also a state historic park. Here, costumed musicians strum banjos in the streets and the saloon serves ice-cold sarsaparilla. Kids enjoy riding an open stagecoach and panning for gold dust in a wooden flume. For another view of the boom-and-bust mining legacy, visit **Bodie,** a decaying mining settlement near Burney in the Sierras.

Albert Bierstadt and Carelton Watkins put California on the map with their paintings and photographs of its spectacular scenery. Generations of artists followed, literally, in their footsteps—plein-air painters such as the Society of Six and photographer Ansel Adams, the great chronicler of Yosemite. In the visual arts, the state produced the sculpture of Douglas Tilden; the iconoclasts of the San Francisco Art Institute, which spawned the Bay Area Figurative style; the Funk artists; and within the past five years, a whole realm of high-tech animation and digital art.

Some of the great places to see fine art are the **Getty Center,** perched on a Los Angeles hillside; the **Los Angeles County Museum of Art;** and the **Norton Simon Museum of Art** in Pasadena, with its sculpture garden designed by Frank Gehry. History buffs enjoy the collections of the **Huntington Library** and, in San Francisco, the **California Historical Society.** Downtown are the **Yerba Buena Center for the Arts,** the **San Francisco Museum of Modern Art,** and the **Ansel Adams Center for Photography.** The **Mexican Museum** (presently in Fort Mason Center) also plans to break ground for a new facility downtown.

Los Angeles is a center for film and theater; campy **Mann's Chinese Theater** offers three screens and the footprints of cinema stars in the concrete out front. For live performances, check out the **Ahmanson Theatre, Dorothy Chandler Pavilion,** or **Mark Taper Forum.**

Music enticed a generation to join in the 1960s Summer of Love, and outdoor concerts are one of the best excuses for a visit. The venerable **Monterey Jazz Festival** in September features world-class artists on several stages. Other notable outdoor venues are the **Hollywood Bowl, Berkeley's Greek Theater,** and the **Concord Pavilion.**

The capital city of Sacramento has both urban amenities and sleepy charm. The restored Old Town along the river is crowded and touristy, but the **California State Railroad Museum** is definitely worth a visit. The restored **Capitol** rotunda is impressive, and you are welcome to sit in when the assembly is in session. Central Sacramento is shady and extremely walkable, especially in spring and fall when the weather cools. In late summer, visit the **State Fair** for an overview of agriculture, economy and down-home oddities from each county.

Sports and Other Activities

Mention California and most people think of beaches, **surfing,** and the surfer culture. The Los Angeles area beaches are famous for their surf. South of LA, in San Diego, you can catch waves in La Jolla. North of LA you'll be packing your wet suit as you try the waves at Rincon Beach near Santa Barbara. Around Santa Cruz and north you'll also find massive waves trying to pull you down into the frigid water.

Santa Cruz and north to San Francisco is huge for **windsurfing.** The truly devoted log on to www.callofthewind.com for the latest updates on what's blowing where. In San Francisco, devotees drag their board to the Presidio's Crissy Field and battle the elements under the Golden Gate Bridge.

Sailing enthusiasts get a taste for their passion around the San Francisco Bay. Then there's the rest of the coastline waiting to be discovered.

In Southern California, Santa Catalina Island is a popular **boating** area. Another favorite option here is **scuba diving,** as it is in La Jolla in San Diego and in the Monterey Bay area. Northern California waters are COLD. Just because the license plates say "California" doesn't mean the water is warm.

Mountain biking was invented in Marin County, at the north end of the Golden Gate Bridge. One visit and you'll see why. Mount Tam as it's known (Mt. Tamalpais, more formally) and the Marin Headlands are begging to be explored.

The 600-mi-long California Coastal Trail and the Pacific Crest trail (which has one end in Mexico and the other in Canada) meander through pristine woodlands, inviting **hiking** and **backpacking.** For day trips, consider Topanga State Park in Los Angeles, Mount Tam and Angel Island in the San Francisco area, Torrey Pines State Reserve in San Diego, the Tahoe Rim trail in Lake Tahoe, or pretty much the entire park also known as Yosemite.

If you're visiting between late fall and early spring, **skiing** is everywhere. Lake Tahoe hosts five great resorts. And in the LA area, Big Bear will get you traveling downhill at the requisite speed.

And if your idea of a workout is having Helga massage out your aches and pains, look to California's **spas,** from the mud baths and natural hot springs of Calistoga to Ojai and Palm Springs.

Then of course, there is the **wine.** Napa Valley, only an hour or so from San Francisco, is the most celebrated wine area, yet its neighbor, Sonoma County, is challenging its better-known cousin for viticulture voice. Take a drive up to Napa for the day. Most wineries have tasting rooms and are really happy to sell you wine directly. And because food is critical to good wine, there are some fabulous restaurants in Napa.

Rules of the Road

License Requirements: You must be at least 16 years of age to get a driver's license in California. Persons with valid driver's licenses from other U.S. states and foreign countries are permitted to drive in California.

Right Turn on Red: Unless otherwise posted, right turns on red are permitted after a full stop.

Seatbelt and Helmet Laws: All passengers are required to wear safety belts in the state of California. Children under 4 years of age or weighing less than 40 pounds must travel in an approved child safety seat. Motorcyclists must wear helmets.

Speed Limits: The maximum speed limit on California highways is 70 mph, unless otherwise posted. Always follow posted speed limits.

For More Information: California Highway Patrol | 916/657–7202.

North Coast Driving Tour

FROM SAN FRANCISCO TO REDWOOD NATIONAL PARK

Distance: 250–275 mi   Time: 7 days

Breaks: 1 overnight in Inverness; 2 overnights in Mendocino; 1 overnight in Ferndale; 1 overnight in Eureka; 1 overnight in Redwood National Park

Exploring the northern California coast is easiest by car. Route 1 is a beautiful, though sometimes slow and nerve-racking, drive. You'll want to stop frequently to appreciate the views, and there are many portions of the highway along which you won't drive faster than 20–40 mph. You can still have a fine trip even if you don't have much time, but be realistic and don't plan to drive too far in one day.

The north coast is a year-round destination, though the time of your visit determines what you'll see. The migration of the Pacific gray whales is a wintertime phenomenon, roughly from mid-December to early April. In July and August, views are often obstructed by fog. The coastal climate is quite similar to San Francisco's although winter nights are colder than in the city.

❶ Depart from San Francisco and head north over the Golden Gate Bridge for approximately 10 mi, then proceed west (take the Mill Valley/Stinson Beach exit off U.S. 101 and follow signs) to **Muir Woods National Monument.** This is the world's most popular grove of old-growth *Sequoia sempervirens* (redwoods). The coast redwoods that grow here are mostly between 500 and 800 years old and stand as tall as 236 ft. Live oak, madrone, and buckey trees and numerous wildflowers grow along Redwood Creek. Spend an hour or so hiking around before leaving for Stinson Beach.

❷ **Stinson Beach,** approximately 8 mi north of Muir Woods National Monument on Route 1, has the most expansive sands in Marin County and is as close as you'll get to the stereotypical southern California beach. If you're traveling in summer, allow extra time because the roads are jammed. Have lunch and spend the afternoon strolling the coastline.

❸ **Bolinas,** north on Route 1 about 5 mi, is the southern entry to the **Point Reyes National Seashore,** which borders the northern reaches of the Golden Gate National Recreation Area. It's a great place for hiking and viewing wildlife, full of rugged, rolling grasslands. The ½-mi Earthquake Trail passes by what is believed to be the epicenter of the 1906 quake that destroyed much of San Francisco, and the late-19th-century Point Reyes Lighthouse is a good spot to watch for whales. The towns of Olema, Point Reyes Station, and Inverness, all in or near the national seashore area, have dining, lodging, and recreational facilities.

❹ Head north to the town of **Olema,** 15 mi north of Stinson Beach on Route 1, and the Point Reyes National Seashore's **Bear Valley Visitor Center,** which has exhibits of park wildlife. The rangers here can advise you on everything from whale-watching to hiking trails and camping. A reconstructed Miwok village, a short walk from the visitor center, provides insight into the daily lives of the region's first human inhabitants.

❺ From Olema continue north, 5 mi on Route 1, to **Inverness,** a town that boomed after the 1906 earthquake, when wealthy San Franciscans built summer homes in its hills. Today many of the structures serve as full-time residences or small inns. The **Point Reyes Lighthouse Visitors Center** is between 10 and 20 mi southwest, about a 45-minute

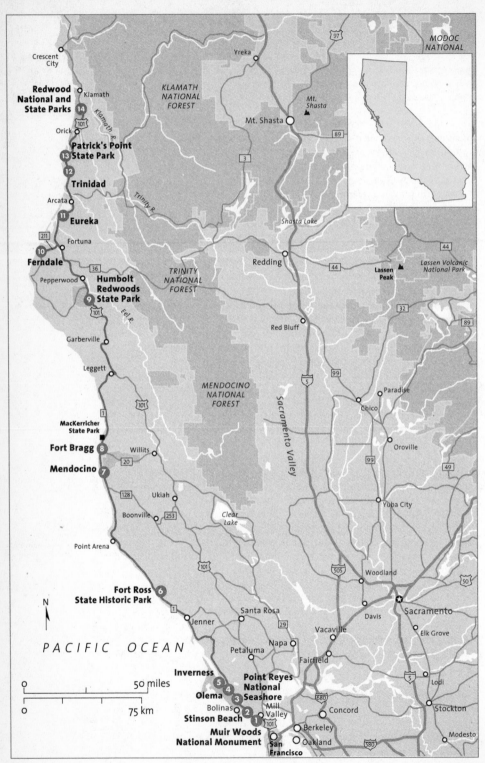

MODOC
NATIONAL

Crescent
City

Redwood
National and
State Parks 14 Klamath

KLAMATH
NATIONAL
FOREST

Yreka

Mt.
Shasta

Mt. Shasta

Orick

Patrick's Point
State Park 13

12

Trinidad

Arcata

11 Eureka

Fortuna

Ferndale 10

Pepperwood

Humbolt
Redwoods
State Park 9

TRINITY
NATIONAL
FOREST

Shasta Lake

Redding

Lassen
Peak

Lassen Volcanic
National Park

Garberville

Eel R.

Leggett

MENDOCINO
NATIONAL
FOREST

Red Bluff

Paradise

Chico

Oroville

MacKerricher
State Park

Fort Bragg 8 Willits

Mendocino 7

Ukiah

Boonville

Clear
Lake

Yuba City

Point Arena

Sacramento Valley

Woodland

Fort Ross 6
State Historic Park

N

Jenner

Santa Rosa

Davis

Sacramento

Elk Grove

PACIFIC OCEAN

Petaluma

Napa

Vacaville

Fairfield

Inverness 5

4

Olema 3

Point Reyes
National
Seashore

Bolinas

2 Mill
Valley

Concord

Stockton

50 miles

75 km

Stinson Beach

Muir Woods
National Monument

Berkeley

Oakland

San
Francisco

Lodi

Modesto

drive, from Inverness, across rolling hills that resemble Scottish heath. There are hundreds of steps from the cliff top to the lighthouse below, but the views are worth it. Stay overnight in Inverness.

INTRODUCTION
HISTORY
REGIONS
WHEN TO VISIT
STATE'S GREATS
RULES OF THE ROAD
DRIVING TOURS

⑥ Next you'll come to **Fort Ross State Historic Park,** 50 mi north of Inverness via Route 1. Completed in 1821, Fort Ross was Russia's major fur-trading outpost in California. By 1841 Russian settlers had depleted the area's population of seals and otters and sold the post to John Sutter, later of Gold Rush fame. The state park service has reconstructed Fort Ross, including its Russian Orthodox chapel, a redwood stockade, the officer's barracks, and a blockhouse. The excellent museum here documents the history of the fort and some of the the North Coast.

⑦ Continue 72 mi north on Route 1 to **Mendocino.** Logging created the first boom in this windswept town, which flourished for most of the second half of the 19th century. As the timber industry declined in the early 20th century many residents left, but the town's setting was too beautiful for it to remain neglected for long. Artists and craftspeople flocked here in the 1950s, and in their wake came entrepreneurial types who opened restaurants, cafés, and inns. By the 1970s, a full-scale revival was under way. A bit of the old town can be seen in dives like Dick's Place, a bar near the Mendocino Hotel, but the rest of the small downtown area is devoted almost exclusively to contemporary restaurants and shops.

The restored **Ford House,** built in 1854, serves as the visitor center for Mendocino Headlands State Park. The house has a scale model of Mendocino as it looked in 1890, when the town had 34 water towers and a 12-seat outhouse. Guided history walks leave from Ford House on Saturday afternoon at 3:00. The park itself consists of the cliffs that border the town; access is free.

The **Mendocino Coast Botanical Gardens** offer something for nature lovers every season. Even in winter, heather and Japanese tulips bloom. Along 2 mi of coastal trails, with ocean views and observation points for whale-watching, is a splendid array of flowers. You can have lunch or dinner at the on-site Gardens Grill. Stay 2 nights in Mendocino.

⑧ **Fort Bragg,** about 5 mi north of the botanical gardens on Route 1, has changed more than any other coastal town in the past few years. The decline in what was the top industry, timber, is being offset in part by a boom in charter-boat excursions and other tourist pursuits. The city is also attracting many artists, some lured from Mendocino, where the cost of living is higher. This basically blue-collar town is the commercial center of Mendocino County.

MacKerricher State Park includes 10 mi of sandy beach and several square mi of dunes. Canoeing, hiking, jogging, bicycling, camping, harbor-seal watching at Laguna Point, and fishing at two freshwater lakes, one stocked with trout are popular. You can often spot whales between December and mid-April from the nearby headland.

⑨ **Humbolt Redwoods State Park,** 85 mi north of Fort Bragg on Route 1, is home to the giant redwoods. The Avenue of the Giants begins about 7 mi north of Garberville and winds north, more or less parallel to U.S. 101, toward Pepperwood. Some of the tallest trees on the planet tower over this stretch of two-lane blacktop. The Avenue follows the south fork of the Eel River and cuts through part of the more than 53,000-acre Humboldt Redwoods State Park.

At the Humboldt Redwoods State Park Visitor Center you can pick up information about the redwoods, waterways, and recreational opportunities. Brochures are available for a self-guided auto tour of the park. Stops on the auto tour include short and long hikes into redwood groves.

⑩ The town of **Ferndale** (20 mi north on U.S. 101 and 8 mi west on Route 211) has some of the most well-preserved Victorian homes in California, built by 19th-century Scandinavian, Swiss, and Portuguese dairy farmers who were drawn to the mild climate.

The main building of the **Ferndale Museum** hosts changing exhibitions of Victoriana and has an old-style barbershop and a display of Wiyot Indian baskets. In the annex are a horse-drawn buggy, a re-created blacksmith's shop, and antique farming, fishing, and dairy equipment. Stay overnight in Ferndale.

⑪ From Ferndale, drive north to **Eureka** via Route 211 and U.S. 101 for approximately 10 mi. With a population of 28,500, Eureka is the North Coast's largest city. It has gone through cycles of boom and bust, first with mining and later with timber and fishing. Many of the nearly 100 Victorian buildings here are well preserved.

The most splendid is the **Carson Mansion,** built in 1885 for timber baron William Carson. A private men's club occupies the house. Stay overnight in Eureka.

⑫ The town of **Trinidad,** 23 mi north via U.S. 101, got its name from the Spanish mariners who entered the bay on Trinity Sunday, June 9, 1775. The town became a principal trading post for the mining camps along the Klamath and Trinity rivers. As mining, and then whaling, faded, so did the luster of this former boomtown. Development has overlooked this scenic spot for now, making it one of the quietest towns that still has inns and dining spots. Picturesque Trinidad Bay's harbor cove and rock formations look both raw and tranquil.

⑬ **Patrick's Point State Park,** 5 mi north of Trinidad via U.S. 101, is the ultimate California coastal park. On a forested plateau almost 200 ft above the surf, it has stunning views of the Pacific, great whale- and sea-lion-watching in season, picnic areas, bike paths, and hiking trails through old-growth forest. There are tidal pools at Agate Beach and a small museum with natural history exhibits.

⑭ **Redwood National and State Parks** are less than 20 mi north of Patrick's Point State Park. After 115 years of intensive logging, this 106,000-acre parcel of tall trees came under government protection in 1968, marking the California environmentalists' greatest victory over the timber industry.

At the **Redwood Information Center** you can get brochures, advice, and a free permit to drive up the steep, 17-mi road (the last 6 mi are gravel) to reach the Tall Trees Grove, where a 3-mi round-trip hiking trail leads to the world's first-, third-, and fifth-tallest redwoods. Whale-watchers will find the deck of the visitor center an excellent observation point, and birders will enjoy the nearby Freshwater Lagoon, a popular layover for migrating waterfowl.

Within **Lady Bird Johnson Grove,** off Bald Hills Road, is a short circular trail to a grove of redwoods that was dedicated by, and named for, the former first lady. For additional views, take Davison Road to Fern Canyon. This gravel road winds through 4 mi of second-growth redwoods, then hugs a bluff 100 ft above the pounding Pacific surf for another 4 mi.

To reach the entrance to **Prairie Creek Redwoods State Park** take the Prairie Parkway exit off the U.S. 101 bypass. Extra space has been paved alongside the parklands, providing fine vantage points from which to observe an imposing herd of Roosevelt elk grazing in the adjoining meadow.

To return to San Francisco drive south on U.S. 101/Route 1 for approximately 250 mi.

Sierra National Parks Driving Tour

*FROM THE YOSEMITE VALLEY TO KINGS CANYON AND
SEQUOIA NATIONAL PARKS*

INTRODUCTION
HISTORY
REGIONS
WHEN TO VISIT
STATE'S GREATS
RULES OF THE ROAD
DRIVING TOURS

Distance: 390 mi   Time: 5 days

Breaks: 2 nights in Kings Canyon; 1 night in the Yosemite valley area; 1 night in Bodie ghost town area

Yosemite, Kings Canyon, and Sequoia national parks are famous throughout the world for their granite peaks, towering waterfalls, and giant sequoias, among other natural wonders. Yosemite, especially, should be on your "don't miss" list. Unfortunately, it's on everyone else's as well (the park receives about 4 million visitors annually), so lodging reservations are essential. During a week's stay you can exit and reenter the parks as often as you wish by showing your pass.

Summer is the most crowded season for all the parks, though things never get as hectic at Kings Canyon and Sequoia as they do at Yosemite. During extremely busy periods—when snow closes high-country roads in late spring or on crowded summer weekends—Yosemite Valley may be closed to all vehicles unless their drivers have overnight reservations. Avoid these restrictions by visiting from mid-April through Memorial Day and from Labor Day to mid-October, when the parks are less busy and the weather is usually hospitable.

The falls at Yosemite are at their most spectacular in May and June. By the end of summer, some will have dried up. They begin flowing again in late fall with the

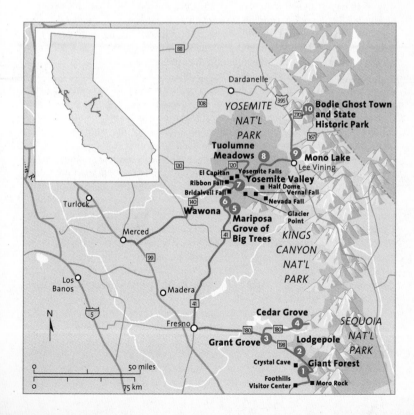

first storms, and during winter they may be hung with ice, a dramatic sight. Snow on the floor of Yosemite Valley is never deep, so you can camp there even in winter (January highs are in the mid-40s, lows in the mid-20s). Tioga Road is usually closed from late October through May; unless you ski or snowshoe in, you can't see Tuolumne Meadows then. The road to Glacier Point beyond the turnoff for Badger Pass is not cleared in winter, but it is groomed for cross-country skiing. In parts of Kings Canyon and Sequoia snow may remain on the ground into June; the flowers in the Giant Forest meadows hit their peak in June or July.

❶ Begin your tour in the **Giant Forest** at **Sequoia National Park.** The Giant Forest is known for its trails through a series of sequoia groves. You can get the best views of the big trees from the park's meadows, where flowers are in full bloom by June or July. The most famous sequoia in the area is the General Sherman Tree, off the Generals Highway 3 mi south of Lodgepole and about 1 mi north of the Giant Forest. Benches allow you to sit and contemplate the tree's immensity: weighing in at 2.7 million pounds, it has the greatest volume of any living thing in the world. The first major branch is 130 ft above the ground.

    Moro Rock, an immense, granite monolith, lies along Moro Rock–Crescent Meadow Road. It rises 6,725 ft from the edge of the Giant Forest. Four hundred steps lead to the top; the trail often climbs along narrow ledges over steep drops. From the top you look southwest toward the Kaweah River to Three Rivers, Lake Kaweah, and—on clear days—the Central Valley and the Coast Range. To the northeast are views of the High Sierra. Thousands of feet below lies the middle fork of the Kaweah River.

    Crystal Cave is the best known of Sequoia's many caves, formed from limestone that metamorphosed into marble and decorated with stalactites and stalagmites of various shapes, sizes, and colors. To visit the cave, you must first stop at the Lodgepole Visitor Center or the **Foothills Visitor Center** at Ash Mountain to buy tickets—they're not sold at the cave. Drive to the end of a narrow, twisting, 7-mi road off the Generals Highway, 2.2 mi south of the old Giant Forest Village. From the parking area it's a 15-minute hike down a steep path to the cave's entrance.

❷ Within Sequoia National Park, **Lodgepole,** 5 mi north of the Giant Forest via Route 198, is in a canyon on the Marble Fork of the Kaweah River. Lodgepole pines, rather than sequoias, grow here because the U-shape canyon directs air down from the high country that is too cold for the big trees but is just right for lodgepoles. A pizza stand, an ice cream parlor, and showers are open in summer.

    The **Lodgepole Visitor Center** has the best exhibits in Sequoia or Kings Canyon and a small theater that shows films about the parks. You can buy tickets for the Crystal Cave, get advice from park rangers, and purchase maps and books.

❸ From the Lodgepole Visitor Center, continue north on Route 198 for 20 mi to **Kings Canyon National Park** and **Grant Grove,** King Canyon's most highly developed area, the original grove that was designated as General Grant National Park in 1890. Here you can pick up several trails and visit the **Gamlin Cabin,** an 1867 pioneer cabin that's listed on the National Register of Historic Places. Also within Grant Grove is the **Centennial Stump,** the remains of a huge sequoia cut for display at the 1876 Philadelphia Centennial Exhibition.

    Grant Grove Village has a visitor center, a grocery store, campgrounds, a coffee shop, overnight lodging, and a horse-rental concession.

❹ Drive 20 mi east on Route 180 to **Cedar Grove.** This area is in a valley that snakes along the south fork of the Kings River. It takes about an hour to travel the spectacular 30-mi length down from Grant Grove along the Kings Canyon Highway (usually closed from mid-October to April). At road's end you can hike, camp, or turn right around for the drive back up. Built by convict labor in the 1930s, the road clings to some dramatic cliffs along the way; watch out for falling rocks. The highway passes the scars where large groves of sequoias were logged at the beginning of the 20th century and runs along the south fork and through dry foothills covered with yuccas that bloom in the summer. There are amazing views into the deepest gorge in the United States, at the confluence of the two forks, and up the canyons to the High Sierra.

Cedar Grove was named for the incense cedars that grow in the area. You can rent horses here, a good way to continue your explorations; and there are campgrounds, lodgings, a small visitor center, food, and a gas station.

Spend a night or two in the Kings Canyon National Park.

INTRODUCTION
HISTORY
REGIONS
WHEN TO VISIT
STATE'S GREATS
RULES OF THE ROAD
DRIVING TOURS

⑤ Proceed north from Cedar Grove to **Mariposa Grove of Big Trees.** (It's 58 mi west on Route 180 and then 50 mi north on Route 41.) Mariposa is Yosemite's largest grove of giant sequoias. They can be visited on foot—trails all lead uphill—or, in summer, on one-hour tram rides. The Grizzly Giant, the oldest tree here, is estimated to be 2,700 years old. If the road to the grove is closed (which happens when Yosemite is crowded) park in Wawona and take the free shuttle; passengers are picked up near the gas station. The access road to the grove may also be closed by snow for extended periods from November to mid-May. You can still usually walk, snowshoe, or ski in.

⑥ From Mariposa proceed northwest to **Wawona** approximately 5 mi on Route 41. The historic buildings in **Pioneer Yosemite History Center** were moved to Wawona from their original sites in the park. From Wednesday through Sunday in summer, costumed park employees re-create life in 19th-century Yosemite in a blacksmith's shop, a Wells Fargo office, a jail, and other structures. Ranger-led walks leave from the covered bridge on Saturday at 10 AM in summer. Near the center are a post office, the Wawona General Stores, and a gas station.

⑦ Continue 22 mi north via Route 41 to the **Yosemite Valley area.** At the **Valley Visitor Center** you can see exhibits, obtain information, and pick up local maps. The staff at the **Wilderness Center** provides trail-use reservations (recommended for popular trailheads on weekends or from May–September), permits ($3), maps, and advice to hikers heading into the backcountry. When the Wilderness Center is closed, ask at the Visitor Center.

Waterfalls and mountain peaks are scattered liberally throughout this area. Be sure to see **Yosemite Falls**—actually three falls that combine to a height of 2,425 ft—the highest waterfall in North America and the fifth-highest in the world. **Bridalveil Fall,** a filmy fall of 620 ft that is often diverted as much as 20 ft one way or the other by the breeze, is the first view of Yosemite Valley for those who arrive via the Wawona Road. At 1,612 ft, **Ribbon Fall** is the highest single fall in North America, but also the first valley waterfall to dry up in summer; the rainwater and melted snow that create the slender fall evaporate quickly at this height. Fern-covered black rocks frame 317-ft **Vernal Fall,** and rainbows play in the spray at its base. The 594-ft **Nevada Fall** is the first major fall as the Merced River plunges out of the high country toward the eastern end of Yosemite Valley.

El Capitan, rising 3,593 ft above the valley, is the largest exposed granite monolith in the world, almost twice the height of the Rock of Gibraltar. Astounding **Half Dome** rises 4,733 ft from the valley floor to 8,842 ft. **Glacier Point** yields what may be the most spectacular vistas of the valley and the High Sierra—especially at sunset—that you can get without hiking. The Glacier Point Road leaves Wawona Road (Route 41) about 23 mi southwest of the valley; then it's a 16-mi drive, with fine views into higher country.

All this exploring is sure to leave you tired and hungry, so plan to spend the night in one of the campgrounds or lodges in the park.

8 After a good night's rest, start your 55-mi drive to **Tuolumne Meadows**; you'll travel west on Big Oak Flat Road to Route 120/Tioga Road east. Tioga Road, the scenic route to Tuolumne Meadows, stays open until the first big snow of the year, usually about mid-October. Tuolumne Meadows is the largest subalpine meadow in the Sierra and the trailhead for many backpack trips into the High Sierra. Numerous ponds and streams crisscross the meadows and grasslands, which are carpeted with brightly colored wildflowers in spring. There are campgrounds, a gas station, and store (with limited and expensive provisions), stables, lodge, and a visitor center.

9 Twenty miles east of Tuolumne Meadows on Route 120 to U.S. 395, you'll come to **Mono Lake.** Eerie tufa towers—calcium carbonate formations that often resemble castle turrets—rise from the impressive lake. Since the 1940s the city of Los Angeles has been diverting water from streams that feed the lake, lowering its water level and exposing the tufa. Millions of migratory birds nest in and around Mono Lake. Stop at the **Scenic Area Visitor Center** for information on trails and activities in the area.

10 From Mono Lake and Lee Vining, continue north on U.S. 395, then east on Route 270 for 23 mi to **Bodie Ghost Town and State Historic Park**—the last 3 mi of this drive are on unpaved roads, and snow may close Route 270 in winter and early spring. Odd shacks and shops, abandoned mine shafts, a Methodist church, the mining village of Rattlesnake Gulch, and the remains of a small Chinatown are among the sights at fascinating Bodie Ghost Town, elevation 8,200 ft. The town boomed from about 1878 to 1881 as gold prospectors, having worked the best of the western Sierra mines, headed to the high desert on the eastern slopes. By the late 1940s, the strikes were over and all the residents had departed. A state park was established in 1962, with a mandate to preserve but not restore the town. There's an excellent museum, and you can tour an old stamp mill (where ore was stamped into fine powder to extract gold and silver) and a ridge that contains many mine sites. Spend a night in the Bodie area before returning west on Route 120 through Yosemite to Route 140 west to Merced, approximately 110 mi away.

ALBION

MAP 3, B5

(Nearby towns also listed: Elk, Little River, Mendocino)

The steep coastal cliffs reminded Captain W. A. Richardson of his English home, so when he decided to settle down and build the area's first lumber mill in 1853, he dubbed the area Albion after an ancient name for Britain. The mill was established on the river flats below the bridge that now spans the Albion River; the settlement became official with the opening of its first post office in 1859.

Beneath a picturesque trestle bridge, the Albion River meets the sea against a backdrop of rocky coastline. A small beach with sheltered coves is perfect for walking, wading, and exploring the tide pools. Never turn your back on the ocean, however; the heedless are sometimes struck by sudden "sneaker waves." Today, Albion is little more than a settlement but the open space is very appealing. Head up to Albion Ridge Road, east of Rte. 1, to watch red-tailed hawks, turkey vultures, and migratory tundra swans, or hole up in a cabin, light a fire, and listen to the surf.

Information: Fort Bragg Mendocino Coast Chamber of Commerce | 322 N. Main St. (P.O. Box 1141), Fort Bragg 95437 | 707/961–6300 or 800/726–2780 | fax 707/964–2056 | chamber@mcn.org | www.mendocinocoast.com.

Attractions

Van Damme State Park. Once part of a redwood lumber port, this park has 1,831 acres of beach and upland trails including Fern Canyon and the Pygmy Forest, where mature pine trees and cypress stand from six inches to eight ft tall. It's 2 mi south of Mendocino, 5 mi north of Albion. | Rte. 1 | 707/937–5804 | $2 per car | Daily 8 AM–sunset.

Dining

Albion River Inn. American. The ocean views are as captivating as the food in this glassed-in dining room. Duck, fresh pasta, and local wines and cheeses are its trademarks. | 3790 Rte. 1 N | 707/937–1919 or 800/479–7944 | $25–$40 | AE, D, DC, MC, V.

Ledford House. Mediterranean. From this blufftop location just north of Gualala in the town of Albion, you'll have panoramic views of sunsets over the Pacific Ocean. The food has a strong Mediterranean influence but draws subtly on Asian and Latin flavors. Entrées include rack of lamb and ahi tuna. | 3000 N. Rte. 1 | 707/937–0282 | ledford@ledfordhouse.com | www.ledfordhouse.com/ | $35–$45 | MC, V.

Lodging

Albion River Inn. New England-style cottages overlooking the bridge and seascape where the Albion River empties into the Pacific. Duplex and single cottages, all with private baths, some with hot tubs. Decks look out to spectacular views of the rugged coastline. Restaurant, complimentary breakfast. No air-conditioning, refrigerators, some in-room hot tubs. No TV in rooms. Business services. No smoking. | 3790 Rte. 1 N | 707/937–1919 or 800/479–7944 | fax 707/937–2604 | ari@mcn.org | www.albionriverinn.com | 16 rooms, 4 cottages | $180–$220 rooms, $220–$280 cottages | AE, D, DC, MC, V.

Fensalden Inn. Once a stagecoach stop, the inn is housed in several buildings perched on a hill on 20 acres of lawns bordered by cypress trees. The buildings include two barns, in which rooms are furnished with antiques and original art. Water tower suites have fireplaces, cathedral ceilings. The main house feels like a cozy log cabin; the bungalow has a loft and redwood-lined shower. Fireplaces. Complimentary breakfast. No air-conditioning; refrigerators. No TV in rooms. No smoking. | 33810 Navarro Ridge | 707/937–4042 or 800/959–3850 | fax 707/937–2416 | www.fensalden.com | 8 rooms | $120–$195; 2–night stay minimum in summer, 3–night stay minimum holiday weekends | MC, V.

Watertower Farm. You may be greeted by a sheep or a goat at this three-story, wood-shingled water tower surrounded by meadows and redwood trees. The ground floor of the converted water tower has two walls of windows and a wood stove; the second floor has a tree-shaded balcony, and the third floor has a loft. There is a two-night minimum (three-night for holidays), and a separate room cleaning fee of $60. In-room VCR. Hot tub. | 32371 Middle Ridge Rd. | 415/381–4499 | 1 room | $95 | No credit cards.

ALTURAS

(Nearby towns also listed: Clear Lake Area, Susanville)

The population of remote Alturas could fit easily into a normal-size auditorium in one of California's big cities. Nevertheless, the town plays a big role as the Modoc County seat. When the first European settlers, the Dorris family, arrived in 1874, there wasn't much here. The family built Dorris Bridge over the Pit River, from which the original town took its name. They later opened a small wayside stop for travelers.

Some of those wanderers stopped and stayed, and today Alturas is a market center where ranchers come to cash in their crops and livestock.

Information: Chamber of Commerce | 522 S Main St, 96101 | 530/233–4434 | fax 530/233–4434.

Attractions

Modoc County Museum. Exhibits explore the development of the area from the 15th century through World War II. Featured are American Indian artifacts, firearms, and a steam engine, which is located right outside. | 600 S. Main St. | 530/233–6328 | Donations accepted | May–Oct., Tues.–Sat. 10–4.

Modoc National Forest. With nearly two million acres, the forest is home to 300 species of wildlife. In spring and fall, look for migratory waterfowl, as the Pacific Flyway crosses directly over the forest. Hiking trails lead to Petroglyph Point, one of the largest panels of rock art in the U.S. No reservations needed for 43 campsites; no showers, gas, or store. | 800 W. 12th St. | 530/233–5811 | fax 530/233–8709 | www.r5.fs.fed.us/modoc | Free | Daily.

Lava Beds National Monument. More than 450 lava tube caves, the greatest concentration in North America, are found at this location that borders Modoc National Forest. During the 1872 Modoc War, California's last war that involved a Native American tribe, the caves were hideouts for the Modoc Indians, allowing them to sustain fighting with the U.S. Calvary for several months. You can access about two dozen of the lava tubes. Morning walks and cave tours are offered during the summer. The monument is 50 mi north of Alturas just of Route 139. | Off Rte. 139, Tulelake | 530/667–2282 | fax 530/667–2737 | www.nps.gov/labe | $5 per vehicle | Daily dawn–dusk.

Modoc National Wildlife Refuge. Canada geese, mallards, teal, wigeon, and pintail can be found everywhere in summer and fall within this 6,280-acre refuge, established to protect migratory waterfowl. In summer, white pelicans, cormorants, and snowy egrets arrive. The park is open for hiking, bird observation, and photography. A portion of the refuge is set aside for hunters; regulations and seasons vary. | 530/233–3572 | Free | Daily dawn to dusk.

ON THE CALENDAR
JULY: Lost River. Every year the Modoc County Arts Council performs a historical drama representing the story of the Modoc Indian War, which took place in 1872. | 530/233–2505 | www.lost-river-drama.org.

Dining

Black Bear Diner. American. You can't miss the big black bear that stands menacingly in front of this roadside spot. The menu is basic, from spaghetti to porkchops to prime rib. | 449 N. Main St. | 530/233–3332 | Breakfast served. Open daily 6AM–10PM | $5–$10 | AE, D, DC, MC, V.

Brass Rail. Continental. Formerly a whiskey distillery, this restaurant offers hearty meals in a comfortable setting. Try the Basque lamb. Also known for rib-eye steak and shrimp and scallops. Kids' menu. | 395 Lakeview Hwy. | 530/233–2906 | Closed Mon. | $15 | MC, V.

Lodging

Best Western Trailside Inn. This is the only lodging in town with a swimming pool. If you're looking for outdoor entertainment, this hotel is 2 mi north of Rachael Doris Park, 3 mi south of Devils Garden, and 5 mi north of Modoc Wildlife Reserve. It's also 5 blocks south of the Modoc County Museum. There is a courtesy car to and from Alturas Airport, 1 mi west. Cable TV. Some kitchenettes. Outdoor pool. Business services. Some pets allowed. | 343 N. Main St. | 530/233–4111 | fax 530/233–3180 | 38 rooms | $55–$75 | AE, DC, MC, V.

Frontier Motel. This quiet motel in the heart of town is family operated (even the youngest members help by answering the phone) and can be found next to the high school.

It's about 5 mi north of Modoc Wildlife Reserve. The adjoining restaurant serves Thai and American food. Restaurant. Some kitchenettes, some microwaves, cable TV. | 1022 N. Main St. | 530/233–3383 | 11 rooms | $35–$50 | MC, V.

Hacienda. In the heart of farm country, this motel is marked with a large 19th-century wagon wheel out front. A gas station, fast-food restaurants, and a supermarket are all within 5 blocks. Cable TV. Some kitchenettes, some refrigerators. Pets allowed. | 201 E. 12th St. | 530/233–3459 | simcity@hdo.net | 20 rooms | $31–$49 | AE, D, DC, MC, V.

ANAHEIM

(Nearby towns also listed: Buena Park, Corona, Costa Mesa, Fullerton, Garden Grove, Santa Ana)

Anaheim was a small rural community with a focus on citrus crops until Disneyland was constructed in the 1950s, launching a period of enormous growth. Soon the city had changed its emphasis from oranges to tourism, building the Anaheim Convention Center and homes for Major League baseball's California Angels and the NHL's Mighty Ducks.

In 1878 Anaheim was founded with 881 residents, today the population exceeds 266,000. The city's name is a hybrid of the Santa Ana River and the German word for home.

Information: Greater Anaheim Chamber of Commerce | 100 S. Anaheim Blvd., #300, 92805 | 714/758–0222 | www.anaheimchamber.org.

Attractions

Arrowhead Pond. The Mighty Ducks of Anaheim, a professional hockey team, take to the ice at this arena. | 2695 Katella Blvd. | 714/704–2500 | fax 714/704–2447 | www.arrowheadpond.com | $15–$75 | October to April.

★ **Disneyland.** The snowcapped Matterhorn, the centerpiece of the Magic Kingdom, dominates Anaheim's skyline. There's plenty here that you won't find anywhere else.

Start your visit with a stroll along **Main Street,** a romanticized image of small-town America, circa 1900. Trolleys, double-decker buses, and horse-drawn wagons travel up and down a quaint thoroughfare lined with rows of interconnected shops selling everything from Disney products to magic tricks, crystal ware, sports memorabilia, and photo supplies.

Disneyland is divided into theme lands. **Fantasyland,** its entrance marked by Sleeping Beauty Castle, is where you can fly on Peter Pan's Flight, go down the rabbit hole with Alice in Wonderland, take an aerial spin with Dumbo the Flying Elephant, twirl around in giant cups at the Mad Tea Party, bobsled through the Matterhorn, or visit It's a Small World, where robot children representing 100 countries sing the well-known song.

In **Frontierland** you can take a cruise on the steamboat *Mark Twain* or the sailing ship *Columbia.* Children of every age enjoy rafting to Tom Sawyer Island for an hour or so of climbing and exploring. Some visitors to **Adventureland** have taken the Jungle Cruise so many times that they know the operators' patter by heart. Special effects and decipherable hieroglyphics entertain guests on line for the Indiana Jones Adventure, a don't-miss thrill ride through the Temple of the Forbidden Eye. Also here are the animated bears of **Critter Country; Splash Mountain,** Disney's steepest, wettest adventure; and the Enchanted Tiki Room.

Tomorrowland has the futuristic Astro Orbitor rockets, Rocket Rods, Space Mountain, and toys of tomorrow at Innoventions. The twisting streets of **New Orleans Square** are for shopping and browsing in the company of strolling Dixieland musicians. Also here is the Pirates of the Caribbean ride. The Haunted Mansion, populated by 999 holographic ghosts, is nearby.

At **Mickey's Toontown** children can climb up a rope ladder on the *Miss Daisy* (Donald Duck's boat), talk to a mailbox, and walk through Mickey's House to meet Mickey. Here is also where you'll find the Roger Rabbit Car Toon Spin, the largest and most unusual black-light ride in Disneyland history. The Magic Kingdom's crowd-pleasing live-action and special-effects show Fantasmic! features exhilarating music and just about every animated Disney character ever drawn.

The box office opens a half hour before the park's scheduled opening time. Brochures with maps, available at the entrance, list show and parade times. You can move from one area of Disneyland to another via the Disneyland Railroad. In addition to touring all the "lands," the train travels through the Grand Canyon and a prehistoric jungle.

If you're planning on staying for more than a day or two, ask about the Flex Pass, which gives you five-day admission to Disneyland for roughly the same price as a two-day passport. The passes are not sold at the park itself, but you can buy them through travel agents and at most area hotels. | 1313 Harbor Blvd. | 714/781–4565 | $39 | Daily. Hours vary with season.

Edison International Field. This baseball stadium is the Anaheim Angels' home turf. The Los Angeles climate practically guarantees perfect weather on game days. | 2000 E. Gene Autry Way | 714/634–2000 | fax 714/940–2001 | www.angelsbaseball.com | $10–$22 | April to September.

ON THE CALENDAR

JULY: *Anime Expo.* Every year thousands of Japanese Anime and Manga Comics fans gather to celebrate this burgeoning art form. Held annually at a designated convention center. | 626/582–8200 | www.anime-expo.org.

Dining

Angelo's. American. Waitresses on roller skates bring your food to your car at this flashback burger and fries joint. You can also step inside for a sit-down meal. | 511 S. State College Blvd. | 714/533–1401 | $5–$10 | No credit cards.

Cattleman's Wharf. Steak. There are five individually designed dining rooms in this large complex—a unique building that looks like a lighthouse and is often cited as a landmark. Signature dishes include prime rib and lobster tails. Entertainment Tues.–Sat. Kids' menu. | 1160 W. Ball Rd. | 714/535–1622 | Closed Sun., no lunch | $21–$36 | AE, MC, V.

Cuban Pete's Caribbean Grill. Cuban. Whole roast pig and other exotic dishes are part of the adventure at this colorful restaurant and bar, where the nightlife heats up with live entertainment Thursday through Saturday. The restaurant is brightly decorated, but not garish, and you'll find mainstream dishes on the menu to appease conservative eaters. | 1050 W. Ball Rd. | 714/490–2020 | fax 714/635–8220 | lunch Sun. Closed Mon. | $12–$25 | AE, D, DC, MC, V.

Foxfire. Continental. Rack of lamb, Northern halibut and lobster stuffed with shrimp and crab are a few of the specialties at the elegant Victorian-style restaurant. You can dine outdoors under umbrellas on the heated, partially-covered patio. Entertainment. Kids' menu. | 5717 E. Santa Ana Canyon Rd., Anaheim Hills | 714/974–5400 | $15–$22 | Sunday brunch | AE, DC, MC, V.

Gustav's Jägerhaus. German. Authentic hearty German dishes and German breads, beer, and wine distinguish this friendly neighborhood restaurant. Open-air dining is available. Kids' menu. | 2525 E. Ball Rd. | 714/520–9500 | fax 714/520–9597 | Breakfast also available | $11–$16 | AE, D, MC, V.

Hansa House Smorgasbord. Scandinavian. The specialty here is the Swedish buffet, but there are American dishes as well. It hasn't been redecorated since it opened in 1962, but that just adds to the charm. Open-air dining is available. Salad bar. Kids' menu. | 1840 S. Harbor Blvd. | 714/750–2411 | Breakfast available | $9 | AE, D, MC, V.

VACATION COUNTDOWN Your checklist for a perfect journey

Way Ahead

- ❏ Devise a trip budget.
- ❏ Write down the five things you want most from this trip. Keep this list handy before and during your trip.
- ❏ Book lodging and transportation.
- ❏ Arrange for pet care.
- ❏ Photocopy any important documentation (passport, driver's license, vehicle registration, and so on) you'll carry with you on your trip. Store the copies in a safe place at home.
- ❏ Review health and home-owners insurance policies to find out what they cover when you're away from home.

A Month Before

- ❏ Make restaurant reservations and buy theater and concert tickets. Visit fodors.com for links to local events and news.
- ❏ Familiarize yourself with the local language or lingo.
- ❏ Schedule a tune-up for your car.

Two Weeks Before

- ❏ Create your itinerary.
- ❏ Enjoy a book or movie set in your destination to get you in the mood.
- ❏ Prepare a packing list.
- ❏ Shop for missing essentials.
- ❏ Repair, launder, or dry-clean the clothes you will take with you.
- ❏ Replenish your supply of prescription drugs and contact lenses if necessary.

A Week Before

- ❏ Stop newspaper and mail deliveries.
- ❏ Pay bills.
- ❏ Stock up on film and batteries.
- ❏ Label your luggage.
- ❏ Finalize your packing list—always take less than you think you need.
- ❏ Pack a toiletries kit filled with travel-size essentials.
- ❏ Check tire treads.
- ❏ Write down your insurance agent's number and any other emergency numbers and take them with you.
- ❏ Get lots of sleep. You want to be well-rested and healthy for your impending trip.

A Day Before

- ❏ Collect passport, driver's license, insurance card, vehicle registration, and other documents.
- ❏ Check travel documents.
- ❏ Give a copy of your itinerary to a family member or friend.
- ❏ Check your car's fluids, lights, tire inflation, and wiper blades.
- ❏ Get packing!

During Your Trip

- ❏ Keep a journal/scrapbook as a personal souvenir.
- ❏ Spend time with locals.
- ❏ Take time to explore. Don't plan too much. Let yourself get lost and use your Fodor's guide to get back on track.

Hasting's Grill. Contemporary. Heavy on sushi, the menu reflects a fusion of Pacific Rim, Pan-Asian, Indian, and Scottish cuisines. The restaurant is in the Hilton Anaheim, and rotates operations with the hotel's other fine dining restaurant, Pavia, so call to see which one is open on any given week. | 777 Convention Way | 714/740–4422 | fax 714/740–4252 | No lunch | $20–$30 | AE, D, DC, MC, V.

JW's Steakhouse. Steak. Filled with antiques and dark-wood furnishings, this upscale steak-house exudes old-world charm. All kinds of cuts are served, from filet mignon to porter-house. | 700 West Convention Way | 714/703–3187 | fax 714/750–9100 | $25–$40 | AE, D, DC, MC, V.

La Casa Garcia. Mexican. Enchiladas and tacos of all kinds are the recommended fare. The style is distinctly southwestern. | 531 Chapman Ave. | 714/740–1108 | Breakfast also served | $5–$15 | AE, MC, V.

Luigi's D'Italia. Italian. Old-fashioned southern Italian favorites like spaghetti Bolog-nese (pasta with a thick sauce of meat, vegetables, wine, and cream) and scampi fra diavolo (pasta with shrimp and mushrooms in tomato sauce) are the norm here. Luigi's also has an impressive beer list featuring imports like Peroni and Moretti. | 801 S. State College Blvd. | 714/490–0990 or 714/533–1300 | $7–$20 | AE, D, MC, V.

Mr. Stox. Contemporary. California-influenced dishes like mesquite-grilled lamb and fresh seafood with pasta and home-grown herbs are served at this elegant early-Cali-fornia manor house with intimate booths and Oriental rugs. | 1105 E. Katella Ave. | 714/634–2994 | $18–$30 | AE, D, DC, MC, V.

Overland Stage. American. In the spirit of nearby Disneyland, theme restaurants like this Old West surf-n-turf (complete with spittoons at the bar) abound in Anaheim. Traditional beef and seafood dishes are served with hearty vegetable plates. | 1855 South Harbor Blvd. | 714/971–4570 | fax 714/971–3626 | No lunch | $15–$25 | AE, D, DC, MC, V.

Pavia. Italian. Rather than the typical spaghetti and meatballs, you can expect dishes with goat cheese, capellini, portobello mushrooms, and seafood. This restaurant's signature dish is cioppino, a fish stew made with fresh seafood, including lobster and shrimp, and vegetables. In addition to many light pasta and seafood dishes, such as grilled mahi mahi, you can try one of the nightly specials, which always include a seasonal white fish. Wall-to-wall murals and Italian marble complement the Northern Italian menu, and piano accompaniment adds an old-world touch. Pavia rotates operating hours with the hotel's other restaurant, Hasting's. | 777 Convention Way | 714/740–4419 | fax 714/740–4252 | No lunch | $18–$30 | AE, D, DC, MC, V.

Taqueria Garcia. Mexican. Potent freshly ground spices make traditional dishes like que-sadillas and burritos especially flavorful. Fruit juice concoctions are popular, but don't come thirsty for margaritas or tequila—the Taqueria doesn't serve alcohol. | 500 S. Euclid Ave. | 714/772–6862 | Reservations not accepted | Breakfast also served | $8–$12 | No credit cards.

Thai and Thai. Thai. Traditional favorites like pad Thai are superb, but you can experi-ment with more daring dishes like whole fish deep fried and covered with spicy Thai red curry sauce (don't be afraid to alert your waiter if your palate prefers a more mild ver-sion). | 150 E. Katella Way | 714/635–3060 | fax 714/635–2741 | $10–$20 | AE, D, MC, V.

Wahsing. Chinese. The food is Americanized, but good. Recognizable favorites like Gen-eral Tso's chicken and won ton soup make up the menu. Take-out and delivery are avail-able. | 575 Chapman Ave. | 714/740–1888 | fax 714/663–8888 | $8–$15 | AE, MC, V.

White House. Italian. Chef David Libby has been named a Chef of the Year in southern California for creating classic and innovative dishes with ahi tuna, Sonoma rabbit, chicken en papillote (baked inside parchment paper), and Norwegian salmon. Built in 1909, this mansion-turned-restaurant maintains its original elegance. There is an enclosed carpeted patio. | 887 S. Anaheim Blvd. | 714/772–1381 | No lunch weekends | www.anaheimwhite-house.com | $18–$29 | AE, MC, V.

Yamabuki. Japanese. You can sit in a tatami room or a take a seat at the full sushi bar in this stylish Japanese restaurant. The decor features original artwork, and the menu includes traditional Japanese dishes. Don't miss the plum-wine ice cream. Kids' menu. | 1717 Southwest St. | 714/239–5683 | No lunch weekends | $14–$30 | AE, D, DC, MC, V.

Yogiraj Vegetarian Restaurant. Vegetarian. The absence of meat hasn't made for an absence of flavor. Indian spices and sauces abound in both the traditional and exotic legume and rice dishes. Yogiraj skimps on ornaments, opting for the simplicity of clean, white surroundings. | 3107 W. Lincoln Ave. | 714/995–5900 | $8–$12 | No credit cards.

Lodging

Anaheim Best Inn. Across from Disneyland's main gate, this two-story hotel has large rooms with marble-topped vanities. There's a Denny's on the property. Complimentary Continental breakfast. Microwaves, refrigerators. Pool. Hot tub. Laundry facilities. | 1604 S. Harbor Blvd. | 714/635–3630 | fax 714/520–3290 | www.daysinn.com | 58 rooms, 8 suites | $99 rooms, $139–$159 suites | AE, D, DC, MC, V.

Anaheim Hilton and Towers. Next to the Anaheim Convention Center, this busy Hilton is the largest hotel in southern California; it even has its own post office. Rooms are bright, and you can either walk a few blocks or take a shuttle to Disneyland. 4 restaurants, 2 bars (with entertainment). Some refrigerators, room service, cable TV. 2 pools (1 indoor). Beauty salon, hot tub. Gym. Shops. Video games. Kids' programs. Business services. Parking fee. Some pets allowed. | 777 Convention Way | 714/750–4321 | fax 714/740–4460 | www.hilton.com | 1,567 rooms | $119–$179 | AE, D, DC, MC, V.

Anaheim Maingate Inn. Five hundred feet from the Disney Tram Station, the hotel has free shuttle service to the park and discounted passes to Disneyland, Sea World, and Universal Studios. Rooms are modest but respectable. Restaurant, complimentary breakfast. In-room data ports. Hot tub. Laundry facilities. | 1211 S. Disney West Drive, 92802 | 714/533–2500 or 800/654–6175 | fax 714/520–0578 | maingateaha@stayanight.com | www.stayanight.com | 40 rooms | $69–$85 | AE, D, DC, MC, V.

Best Western Stovall's Inn. Next door to Disneyland and half a block from the Anaheim Convention Center, this large motel has a free shuttle to Disneyland. There is a topiary garden on the premises. Videos and video games are available. Bar. Cable TV. 2 pools, wading pool. Hot tubs. Laundry facilities. Business services. | 1110 W. Katella Ave. | 714/778–1880 | fax 714/778–3805 | www.bestwestern.com | 290 rooms | $96–$115 | AE, D, DC, MC, V.

WHAT TO PACK IN THE TOY TOTE FOR KIDS

- ❏ Audiotapes
- ❏ Books
- ❏ Clipboard
- ❏ Coloring/activity books
- ❏ Doll with outfits
- ❏ Hand-held games
- ❏ Magnet games
- ❏ Notepad
- ❏ One-piece toys
- ❏ Pencils, colored pencils
- ❏ Portable stereo with earphones
- ❏ Sliding puzzles
- ❏ Travel toys

Brookhurst Plaza Inn. Disneyland is 2 mi southeast of this motel. The restaurant and bar are touristy, with Astroturf and hanging plants; the rooms are without ornamentation, but adequate. Knott's Berry Farm is 2 mi southeast. Tickets to Disneyland are available at the desk. Some kitchenettes, some in-room hot tubs. Pool. Hot tub. Laundry facilities. Business services. | 711 S. Brookhurst St., 92804 | 714/999–1220 or 800/909–1220 | fax 714/758–1047 | yun@stayhere.com | www.stayhere.com | 91 rooms | $70–$195 | AE, D, DC, MC, V.

★ **Candy Cane Inn.** Lush gardens, a gazebo and courtyard make breakfast on the lawn a great way to start the day. Rooms are spacious, with dark oak furniture and shuttered windows. The inn is one block from the gates of Disneyland. Complimentary Continental breakfast. Some in-room safes. Pool. Hot tub. Laundry services. | 1747 South Harbor Blvd., 92802 | 714/744–5284 | fax 714/772–5462 | www.travelx.com/candy | 172 rooms | $75–$130 | AE, D, MC, V.

Carousel Inn and Suites. Location is key here. The inn is just across the street from Disneyland and minutes from shopping centers, theaters, and restaurants. Free Disneyland shuttles are available. Restaurant, complimentary Continental breakfast. Microwaves, refrigerators. Pool. Video games. Laundry facilities. Business services. Free parking. | 1530 S. Harbor Blvd. | 714/758–0444 or 800/854–6767 | fax 714/772–9965 | 131 rooms, 26 suites | $69–89 rooms, $109–$149 suites | AE, D, MC, V.

Castle Inn and Suites. Perhaps inspired by Disneyland, this hotel has a castle-like exterior with faux stone and towers. It is directly across from the park's front gates and offers a free Disneyland shuttle. There are video players in guest rooms. Microwaves, some refrigerators, cable TV. Pool, wading pool. Hot tub. Laundry facilities. Business services. Free parking. | 1734 S. Harbor Blvd. | 714/774–8111 or 800/521–5653 | fax 714/956–4736 | www.castleinn.com | 197 rooms, 46 suites | $72–$82 rooms, $82–$112 suites | AE, D, DC, MC, V.

Comfort Inn–Maingate. Disneyland is 1 mi south and a 24-hr Jack-In-The-Box is right next door to this modern motel. There is a complimentary Disneyland shuttle. Complimentary Continental breakfast. Cable TV. Pool. Hot tub. Laundry facilities. Business services. Free parking. | 2200 S. Harbor Blvd. | 714/750–5211 | fax 714/750–2226 | www.comfortinn.com | 66 rooms | $49–$69 | AE, D, DC, MC, V.

Comfort Park Suites. Only 3 blocks from Disneyland, this hotel has shuttle service to and from the Magic Kingdom. The convention center is 2 blocks away, several restaurants are within 4 blocks and Knott's Berry Farm is 10 mi away. Complimentary Continental breakfast. Microwaves, refrigerators, cable TV. Pool. Hot tub. Laundry facilities. Business services. Disneyland shuttle. | 2141 S. Harbor Blvd. | 714/971–3553 | fax 714/971–4609 | www.comfortsuites-anaheim.com | 93 suites | $64–$129 suites | AE, D, DC, MC, V.

Conestoga at Disneyland. Pint-sized cowboys will love this Old West-style hotel with swinging doors and a Bonanza-style lobby, and the restaurants look like saloons. The residential location makes for quiet evenings. A complimentary shuttle heads to Disneyland every hour. Restaurant, bar. Some microwaves, some refrigerators, room service, cable TV. Pool. Hot tub. Video games. Laundry service. Business services. Free parking. | 1240 S. Walnut St. | 714/535–0300 | fax 714/491–8953 | www.ramada.com | 254 rooms | $79–$89 | AE, D, DC, MC, V.

Days Inn. A block and a half from Disneyland, complimentary shuttles can transport you to the park. Complimentary Continental breakfast. Some refrigerators, cable TV. Pool. Hot tub. Laundry facilities. Business services. Free parking. | 1030 W. Ball Rd. | 714/520–0101 | fax 714/758–9406 | www.comfortinn.com | 45 rooms | $69–$99 | AE, D, DC, MC, V.

Days Inn at Convention Center Maingate. Two blocks from Disneyland and across the street from the Anaheim Convention Center, this motel has a free Disneyland shuttle. The tile roof, stone lobby and room accents lend southwest appeal. Room doors open directly to the outdoors. Complimentary Continental breakfast. Some in-room safes, refrigerators. Pool. Hot tub. | 620 W. Orangewood Ave. | 714/971–9000 or 800/999–7844 | fax 714/

740–2065 | anaheim@daysinn-maingate.com | www.daysinn-maingate.com | 63 rooms | $70–$90 | AE, D, MC, V.

Desert Palm Suites. Though only a few hundred yards from Disneyland, business people visiting the convention center down the block tend to frequent this hotel. The rooms here are clean and spacious. Complimentary Continental breakfast. Microwaves, refrigerators. Pool, sauna. | 631 W. Katella Ave. | 714/535–1133 or 800/635–5423 | fax 714/491–7409 | 105 rooms | $69 | AE, D, DC, MC, V.

Embassy Suites. Every contemporary room here has a private balcony with a separate living room, and the grounds are beautifully landscaped. The hotel is a cool 6 mi from the hubbub of Disneyland, and offers a free shuttle to the park. Restaurant, bar, complimentary Continetal breakfast. In-room data ports, microwaves, refrigerators, cable TV. Indoor pool. Hot tub, sauna. | 3100 E. Frontera St. | 714/632–1221 | fax 714/632–9963 | www.embassy-suites.com | 222 suites | $179 suites | AE, D, DC, MC, V.

Fairfield Inn by Marriott. Quick service and check-out for busy travelers are this hotel's specialties. Palm trees give a tropical look; furnishings are modern. There is a free Disneyland shuttle. Refrigerators, room service, cable TV. Pool. Hot tub. Shop. Laundry facilities. Business services. Free parking. | 1460 S. Harbor Blvd. | 714/772–6777 | fax 714/999–1727 | www.marriott.com | 467 rooms | $94–$104 | AE, D, DC, MC, V.

Four Points Hotel Anaheim. One block from Disneyland and half a block from the Anaheim Convention Center, this is a futuristic, mirrored-glass hotel with modern rooms. 2 restaurants, bar with entertainment, room service. In-room data ports, some in-room safes, in-room VCRs. Pool. Hot tub, sauna. Video games. Laundry facilities. Gym. Business services. | 515 W. Katella Ave. | 714/991–6868 | fax 714/991–6565 | www.fourpoints.com | 105 rooms | $100–$170 | AE, D, MC, V.

Granada Suites. Boasting rooms that are "40 percent larger than a standard," this hotel is 3 mi northwest of Disneyland and has free shuttle service to the Magic Kingdom, Knott's Berry Farm, and other local attractions. Restaurant, complimentary Continental breakfast. Kitchenettes, microwaves, cable TV. Pool. Business services. Disneyland shuttle. Free Parking. | 2375 W. Lincoln Ave. | 714/774–7370 or 800/648–8685 | fax 714/774–8068 | 80 rooms | $69–$89 | AE, D, DC, MC, V.

Fairfield Inn by Marriott Anaheim Hills. In the heart of the North Orange County corporate business area, this modern hotel is next door to a shopping center with restaurants and a health club. There is a shuttle ride from area theme parks, including Disneyland which is 15 mi away. Restaurant, complimentary Continental breakfast. Cable TV. Pool. Hot tub. Exercise equipment. Laundry facilities. Business services. Free parking. | 201 N. Via Cortez, Anaheim Hills | 714/921–1100 or 800/324–9909 | fax 714/637–8790 | 163 rooms | $69–$79 | AE, D, DC, MC, V.

Holiday Inn Anaheim at the Park. Families frequent this Mediterranean-style hotel. Complimentary shuttle service brings you to nearby attractions, including Disneyland, Knott's Berry Farm, the Movieland Wax Museum, Medieval Times, and two shopping areas. Restaurant, bar. Microwaves, room service, cable TV. Pool. Hot tub. Video games. Laundry facilities. Business services. Free parking. | 1221 S. Harbor Blvd. | 714/758–0900 | fax 714/533–1804 | www.holiday-inn.com | 254 rooms | $109 | AE, D, DC, MC, V.

Holiday Inn Express. Disneyland is only 3 blocks away from this hotel. Bathrooms are lined with marble tile and gold-framed mirrors. Complimentary Continental breakfast. Some in-room hot tubs. Pool. Hot tub. Refrigerators, in-room VCRs. Laundry facilities. | 435 W. Katella Ave., 92802 | 714/772–7755 or 800/833–7888 | fax 714/772–2727 | service@holiday-anaheim.com | www.holiday-anaheim.com | 72 rooms, 32 suites | $99 rooms, $150 suites | AE, D, DC, MC, V.

Howard Johnson Plaza Hotel. The main entrance to Disneyland is about 2 blocks away, but you can also take a shuttle provided by the hotel. The atmosphere here is generally peaceful and quiet. The rooms are divided among six buildings. Some refrigerators, room service, cable TV. 2 pools, wading pool. Hot tub. Video games. Laundry facilities. Business services. Free parking. | 1380 S. Harbor Blvd. | 714/776–6120 | fax 714/533–3578 | info@hojoana-heim.com | www.hojoanaheim.com | 318 rooms | $69–$99 | AE, D, DC, MC, V.

Hyatt Regency Alicante. Towering palm trees fill the 17-story atrium at this luxury chain hotel. Disneyland is 1 mi north and the nearest beach is 20 mi south. Disneyland shuttles are available. Restaurants, bars. Cable TV. Pool. Hot tub. Driving range, tennis. Exercise equipment. Shops. Video games. Business services. Parking fee. | 100 Plaza Alicante | 714/750–1234 | fax 714/740–0465 | www.hyatt.com | 396 rooms | $99–$144 | AE, D, DC, MC, V.

Jolly Roger Hotel. With a ship-like design and a pirate theme, this hotel lives up to its name. It is across the street from Disneyland, and shuttles are available. Restaurants, bar (with entertainment). Cable TV. Pool. Video games. Laundry facilities. Business services. Airport shuttle. Free parking. | 640 W. Katella Ave. | 714/772–7621 or 800/446–1555 | fax 714/772–2308 | www.tarsadia.com | 58 rooms | $59–$119 | AE, D, DC, MC, V.

Marriott. Rooms on the north side of this hotel have good views of Disneyland's summer fireworks shows. Discounted weekend and Disneyland packages are available, as are shuttles to the theme park. 3 restaurants, complimentary Continental breakfast. In-room data ports, refrigerators, cable TV. 2 pools (1 indoor-outdoor). Beauty salon. Hot tub. Exercise equipment. Shops. Video Games. Laundry facilities. Business services. Airport shuttle. Parking fee. | 700 W. Convention Way | 714/750–8000 | fax 714/750–9100 | www.marriott.com | 1,033 rooms | $189 | AE, D, DC, MC, V.

Park Vue Inn. Family-owned since 1963, this inn is across the street from the main pedestrian entrance to Disneyland. A shuttle to the park is available. Restaurant, complimentary Continental breakfast. Microwaves, cable TV. Pool, wading pool. Laundry facilities. Business services. Free parking. | 1570 S. Harbor Blvd. | 714/772–5721 | fax 714/635–0964 | res@parkvueinn.com | www.parkvueinn.com | 88 rooms, 25 suites | $69 rooms, $89–$120 suites | AE, D, DC, MC, V.

Peacock Suites. Two blocks from Disneyland, this hotel only has suites. Complimentary Continental breakfast. Microwaves, refrigerators, cable TV, in-room VCRs and movies. Pool. Hot tubs. Exercise equipment. Laundry facilities. Business services. Disneyland shuttle. | 1745 Anaheim Blvd. | 714/535–8255 or 800/522–6401 | fax 714/535–8914 | www.shell-vacationsonline.com | 140 suites | $139 suites | AE, D, DC, MC, V.

Penny Sleeper Inn. A good choice for the budget traveler, this two-story hotel is one block from Disneyland Park and one block from I–5. Restaurant, complimentary Continental breakfast. Cable TV. Pool. Laundry facilities. Business services. Disneyland shuttles. Free parking. | 1441 S. Manchester Ave. | 714/991–8100 or 800/854–6118 | fax 714/533–6430 | www.pennysleeperinn.com | 192 rooms | $79 | AE, D, MC, V.

Quality Hotel Maingate. Three blocks south of Disneyland, this hotel offers a shuttle to the park. 2 restaurants, lounge. In-room data ports, room service, limited cable TV. Pool. Beauty salon. Video games. Laundry facilities. Business services. Disneyland shuttle. Some pets allowed, fee. Parking fee. | 616 Convention Way | 714/750–3131 | fax 714/750–9027 | www.qualityinn.com | 284 rooms | $119 | AE, D, DC, MC, V.

Radisson Maingate. This hotel, practically on Disneyland's 'front porch,' offers friendly service. Some rooms in the hotel's two buildings have pull-out sofas as well as beds. Regular shuttles can zip you 1 block to Disneyland or 10 mi west to Knott's Berry Farm. Restaurant, bar. In-room data ports. Room service, cable TV. Pool, wading pool. Game room. Video games. Laundry facilities. Fitness room. Business services. Free parking. | 1850 S. Harbor Blvd. | 714/750–2801 | fax 714/971–4754 | www.radisson.com | 314 rooms | $99–$109 | AE, D, DC, MC, V.

Ramada Limited. This modern chain motel is a 10-minute drive from Disneyland and just 1 mi from Knotts Berry Farm. Complimentary Continental breakfast. Microwaves, refrigerators, some in-room hot tubs, cable TV. Pool. Hot tub. Laundry facilities. Business services. Disneyland shuttle. Free parking. | 800 S. Beach Blvd. | 714/995–5700 | fax 714/826–6021 | www.ramada.net | 74 rooms | $50–$75 | AE, D, DC, MC, V.

Ramada Limited–Disneyland Park. One and a half blocks from Disneyland, this hotel changed management and decor in 2000. A Disneyland shuttle is available. Restaurant, complimentary Continental breakfast. Microwaves, cable TV. Pool. Laundry facilities. Business services. Free parking. | 921 S. Harbor Blvd. | 714/999–0684 | fax 714/956–8839 | www.ramada.com | 92 rooms | $79–$89 | AE, D, DC, MC, V.

Ramada Maingate Saga Inn. You can take the shuttle to Disneyland, though it's right across the street. Built in 1960, remodeled in 1993, this inn is 5 mi from Knott's Berry Farm and around the corner from the Anaheim Convention Center. Restaurant, complimentary Continental breakfast. Microwaves. Pool. Hot tub. Laundry facilities. Business services. Free Parking. | 1650 S. Harbor Blvd. | 714/772–0440 | fax 714/991–8219 | www.ramada.com | 186 rooms | $89 | AE, D, DC, MC, V.

★ **Sheraton.** A standout among the commercial atmosphere of hotels surrounding Disneyland, this Sheraton is a sprawling replica of a Tudor castle. The flower- and plant-filled lobby has a grand fireplace where you can sit by the indoor fish pond. New "Smart Rooms" have copier-printer machines, and include a daily Continental breakfast and evening hors d'oeuvres. Some first-floor rooms open onto interior gardens and the pool area. Disneyland shuttles. Restaurant, bar. In-room data ports, room service, cable TV. Pool. Hot tub. Exercise equipment. Video games. Laundry facilities. Business services. Airport shuttle. Parking fee. | 1015 W. Ball Rd. | 714/778–1700 | fax 714/535–3889 | www.sheraton.com/anaheim | 491 rooms | $190 | AE, D, DC, MC, V.

Super 8–Anaheim Park. Rooms are modern and economical for the area. Disneyland is ½ a block away. Disneyland shuttle. Complimentary Continental breakfast. Cable TV. Pool. Hot tub. Laundry facilities. Business services. Disneyland shuttle. Free parking. | 915 Disneyland Dr. | 714/778–0350 | fax 714/778–3878 | www.super8.com | 111 rooms | $65–$75 | AE, D, DC, MC, V.

Travelodge. This lodge is across the street from Anaheim Stadium. Disneyland is 1 mi away. Complimentary Continental breakfast. Microwaves, cable TV. Pool. Hot tub. Laundry facilities. Business services. Refrigerator. Disneyland shuttle. Free parking. | 1700 E. Katella Ave. | 714/634–1920 | fax 714/634–0366 | www.travelodge.com | 72 rooms | $79 | AE, D, DC, MC, V.

WestCoast Anaheim Hotel. This 14-story hotel is one block south of Disneyland. The lobby has a hardwood floor, there's a heated Olympic-size pool, an espresso bar, and all rooms have balconies that look out onto the park. A pool bar is open in the summer. Restaurant, bar, room service. Pool. Hot tub. Laundry facilities. Business services. | 1855 South Harbor Blvd. | 714/750–1811 | fax 714/971–3626 | 500 rooms | $100–$160 | AE, D, DC, MC, V.

APTOS

MAP 4, D9

(Nearby towns also listed: Capitola, Fenton, Gilroy, Santa Cruz)

Aptos was named by the American Indians who lived here for centuries before Mexico colonized the area; later it became an extended cattle ranch. In the 1850s, when the first general store, lumber mill, and leather tannery were built, the town became more industrialized. Around the turn of the century, the city became a boomtown for redwood timber harvesting, but within 40 years the hills were bare, and apples became the next industry.

Now Aptos is a bedroom community of Monterey, and its main business is tourism. The trees grew back and this "sunny side" of Monterey Bay can boast the beautiful Forest of Nisene Marks State Park and some incredible stretches of sandy beach.

Information: **Aptos Chamber of Commerce** | 7605#A Old Dominion Ct., 95003-3818 | 831/688–1467 | fax 831/688–6961 | commerce@got.net | www.aptoschamber.com.

Attractions

Aptos Museum. You can tour a collection of artifacts and photographs from the early days of Aptos. | 7605 Old Dominion Ct | 831/688–1467 | Free | Weekdays 10–4.

De Laveaga Disc Golf Course. Also known as "Frisbee golf," this is a distinctly Western sport in which players try to flip a plastic disc into metal cages arranged like holes on a golf course. De Laveaga, ranked among the world's best courses, has 27 holes and hosts a Master's Cup Pro-Am Tournament each April. Bring your own discs. | 401 Upper Park Rd. | 831/423–7212 | Free | www.delavelaga.com | Daily dawn to dusk.

Forest of Nisene Marks State Park. Hiking, jogging, and biking trails are available at this 10,000-acre redwood forest park. There is a picnic area with barbecue pits. Directions are tricky: From Route 1 N exit at State Park Dr., turn left and follow the signs. From Route 1 S exit at State Park Dr., turn right and follow signs. | Aptos Creek Rd. | 831/763–7062 | $1 per vehicle | Daily dawn–dusk.

Seacliff State Beach. The half-submerged cement hull of the WWI tanker Palo Alto, now a fishing pier, is a local landmark. It was a dance hall and amusement center in earlier times. Visitor center. Swimming allowed. | 201 State Park Dr. | 831/685–6500 | Free | Daily dawn–dusk.

ON THE CALENDAR

JULY: *Aptos Fourth of July Parade.* Billed as "the World's Shortest Parade," it covers all of 2 blocks along Soquel Drive and includes nearly every Aptos resident, human and animal. | 831/688–1467.

Dining

Bittersweet Bistro. Contemporary. Formerly a whiskey distillery, this bistro now has a bright, sleek, black-and-white decor set off by warm ochre walls. Fresh, local ingredients are featured, along with organic produce and fabulous desserts. Open-air dining. Sunday brunch. | 787 Rio Del Mar Blvd. | 831/662–9799 | Closed Mon. | $15–$26 | AE, MC, V.

Britannia Arms. English. Darts, dominoes, and live soccer broadcasts from the UK and around the world recreate a British pub. Live music Tues.–Sat. after 9 PM. Be prepared for heavy traditional foods like bangers and mash, steak and kidney pie, and chicken curry, along with your choice of 16 imported draft beers. | 8017 Soquel Dr. | 831/688–1233 | $7–$19 | AE, MC, V.

Southern Exposure Bistro. Comtemporary. Among the French- and Italian-influenced dishes you'll find at this 1925 California bungalow are lavender peppercorn filet of beef, rack of lamb, maple-glazed duck with peaches, hoppin' john (a classic Southern dish with black-eyed peas and ham hocks), and southern bread pudding. Seasonal desserts include pumpkin crème brûlée and fresh organic berries with zabaglione (custard of egg yolks, wine, and sugar) made with local wine. Open-air dining. | 9051 Soquel Dr. | 831/688–5566 | southexp@pacbell.net | Closed Mon., Tues. No lunch | $28–$39 | AE, MC, V.

Lodging

Apple Lane Inn. Set on a three-acre hillside and surrounded by apple orchards, flowerbeds, and a barn with livestock, this four-story 1870 farmhouse has an ocean view. Rooms have an eclectic country style, and are complemented by fresh flowers. The attic suite offers a view of the meadows. The wine cellar room has cedar paneling, a beamed ceiling, and a private entrance. Complimentary breakfast. Some pets allowed. No smoking. | 6265 Soquel Dr. | 831/475–6868 or 800/649–8988 | fax 831/464–5790 | www.applelaneinn.com | 5 rooms | $110–$180 | AE, DC, D, MC, V.

Bayview Hotel Bed and Breakfast. Local art hangs in the library and other common areas of this Victorian-Italianate B&B, built in 1878 of old-growth redwood and noted for its second empire mansard roof. The rooms have period furniture, feather beds, and book-lined alcoves. Seacliff State Beach and Park and the Nisene Marks State Forest are ¼ mi away. Some rooms have fireplaces and two-person soaking tubs. Complimentary Continental breakfast. Cable TV, some in-room VCRs. No smoking. | 8041 Soquel Dr. | 831/688–8654 or 800/422–9843 | fax 408/688–5128 | lodging@bayviewhotel.com | www.bayviewhotel.com | 11 rooms | $150–$250 | AE, MC, V.

Best Western Seacliff Inn. Seacliff State Beach and Park is 3 blocks west of the inn (across the highway) and Monterey Bay Marine Sactuary is ¼ mi. A shopping center with a cinema is across the street. At the inn's Restaurant Severino, you can dine on prime rib, the house specialty, on a garden patio near the koi pond and waterfall. Restaurant. Some in-room hot tubs, in-room VCRs. Outdoor pool. | 7500 Old Dominion Court | 831/688–7300 or 800/367–2003 | www.seacliffinn.com | 133 rooms, 7 suites | $119 rooms, $159–$229 suites | AE, D, DC, MC, V.

Seascape Resort. Views of the ocean are superb from these one- and two-bedroom condos tucked into a pine grove on a bluff above the beach. Rooms have gas fireplaces. Restaurant, bar. No air-conditioning, some kitchenettes, in-room VCRs and movies. Pool. Massage, spa. Golf course, tennis. Gym, volleyball. Bicycles. Kids' programs. Business services. | 1 Seascape Resort Dr. | 831/688–6800 or 800/676–1684 | fax 831/685–0615 | www.seascaperesort.com | 285 rooms | $220–$429 | AE, D, DC, MC, V.

ARCADIA

MAP 9, H3

(Nearby towns also listed: Glendora, Pasadena, San Gabriel, San Marino, West Covina)

This Los Angeles bedroom community of 48,300 once served as the backdrop for the opening sequence of the popular TV show "Fantasy Island," but is probably best known today for the Santa Anita Park.

Information: Arcadia Chamber of Commerce | 388 W. Huntington Dr., 91007 | 626/447–2159 | arcadiacc@earthlink.com | www.ci.arcadia.ca.us.

Attractions

The Arboretum of Los Angeles County. The park has 127 acres of shrubs and trees, organized by continent of origin. Highlights include the historic Queen Anne Cottage and coach barn, the Santa Ana railroad depot and the Hugo Reid Adobe. The grounds also contain a research center, reference library, and bird sanctuary. | 301 N. Baldwin Ave. | 626/821–3222 | fax 626/445–1217 | www.arboretum.org | $5 | Sept.–May, daily 9–5, June–Aug., weekdays 9–6:30, weekends 9–4:30.

Santa Anita Golf Course. This well-established 18-hole course was designed by Billy Bell, Jr. and is a sprawling, lush, tree-lined property nestled in the valley crevice, shaded by rolling hills. The clubhouse is a Spanish pink-stucco building, with a terra-cotta tiled roof. | 405 S. Santa Anita Ave., 91006 | 626/447–2331 | fax 626/447–6813 | Yearround.

Santa Anita Park. Famed thoroughbred racetrack founded in 1934 and the location of many motion pictures since. Santa Anita developed and introduced the photo finish, electrical timing and magnetically controlled starting gate. Highlights of a day at the track include the morning workouts during the racing season, and the regular attendees. High-rolling youths take note: minimum betting age is 18. | 285 W. Huntington Dr. | 626/574–7223 | fax 626/446–1456 | www.santaanita.com | $5–$20 | Wed.–Thurs. 10:30–4:30, Fri., Sat. 11:30AM–11:30PM, Sun. 10–4:30.

ON THE CALENDAR

SEPT.: *International Festival of Food.* This one-day annual event at the LA County Arboretum celebrates foods from around the world, with cooking demonstrations, tastings, and interactive entertainment that involves the entire family. | 626/447–2159 | www.arcadiachamber.com.

Dining

Cabrera's. Mexican. This Arcadia favorite is homey and warm, with dark-wood paneled walls, red leather booths, and colorful woven rugs. You can enjoy traditional dishes like enchiladas, or try some great Mexican twists on American classics: the filet mignon wrapped in bacon with a tamale is a zesty adventure. Sip on margaritas or choose from a long list of imported beers. | 625 E. Live Oak Ave. | 626/445–5327 | fax 626/445–9774 | www.cabreras.com/index | Breakfast served | $10–$25 | AE, MC, V.

Chez Sateau. Continental. Fish, in general, and sushi and oyster-veal mousses, specifically, are the specialties. Mr. Sato, who has over 20 years experience as a chef, has created a Japanese-influenced menu for the Continental French bistro setting. Early-bird suppers. Sunday brunch. | 850 S. Baldwin Ave. | 626/446–8806 | Closed Mon. | $10–$20 | AE, D, DC, MC, V.

The Derby. American. The name of this cozy family-owned restaurant with its beamed ceiling and private booths is carried out in a decor that features jockey and racehorse memorabilia. It's primarily a clubby-feeling steak house, but it gets jumping on the weekends with music and dancing. Kids' menu. | 233 E. Huntington Dr. | 626/447–8173 | No lunch weekends | $12–$28 | AE, D, DC, MC, V.

La Parisienne. French. Notable country-style specialties include bouillabaisse, warm pheasant salad, and salade Niçoise. The restaurant is known for its service and intimate, pastel dining space. | 1101 E. Huntington Dr., Monrovia | 626/357–3359 | fax 626/357–9649 | No lunch Sat. | $17–$28 | AE, DC, MC, V.

Lodging

Embassy Suites. A modern all-suites hotel featuring two-room suites with private bedroom, queen size sofa bed, full kitchen with bar. A waterfall splashes into a koi pond in the tropical-style atrium. Pool. Laundry service. Business services. | 211 E. Huntington Dr. | 626/445–8525 | fax 626/445–8548 | 194 suites | $154–$164 suites | AE, D, DC, MC, V.

Extended Stayamerica. One mile from the Santa Anita Race Track, this three-story chain hotel is ideal for a longer stay. All rooms are attractive studios with a queen-size bed, full kitchen, and work area. Front desk is only open 7 am to 11 pm and there is no restaurant. In-room data ports. Laundry facilities. business services. | 401 E. Santa Clara St., 91006 | 626/446–6422 or 800/EXT-STAY | fax 626/446–6533 | 122 rooms | $69–$89 | AE, D, DC, MC, V.

Hampton Inn. This is a comfortable family hotel built in 1991, with traditional decor. Seven blocks from the mall and within 4 blocks of more than 25 restaurants. Pool. Exercise gym. Laundry service. Business services. | 311 E. Huntington Dr. | 626/574–5600 | fax 626/446–2748 | 131 rooms | $89–$109 | AE, D, DC, MC, V.

Residence Inn by Marriott. Many of the attractively decorated guest rooms have fireplaces. This hotel is 7 mi from Old Pasadena, 1 mi from Santa Anita Park and within walking distance of 12 restaurants. Pool. Hot tubs. Exercise equipment. Business services. Airport shuttle. | 321 E. Huntington Dr. | 626/446–6500 | fax 626/446–5824 | 120 rooms | $132–$158 | AE, D, DC, MC, V.

Santa Anita Inn. Just a few blocks from the Santa Anita Race Track, this hotel has beautiful grounds with curving jogging trails, flower gardens and lush foliage. A series of two-story buildings feature spacious rooms done in cool pastels, all with balconies and some with kitchenettes and fireplaces. Complimentary Continental breakfast, room service. Some kitchenettes, some in-room safes. Pool. Hot tub. Video games. Laundry facilities. Business services. | 130 W. Huntington Dr., 91006 | 626/446–5211 | fax 626/445–1241 | 114 rooms | $65–$90 | AE, D, DC, MC, V.

ARCATA

(Nearby towns also listed: Eureka, Trinidad)

Arcata began life as Union Town in 1850, serving as a depot and base camp for gold miners and lumberjacks. The area remains dotted with lumber mills and a sturdy mix of self-sufficient folk. Today this town of 15,000 people is home to 7,500-student Humboldt State University. It's become something of an artists' colony as well; one of the main attractions in May is the Kinetic Sculpture Race, a wacky competition of moveable sculptures instituted by sculptors Hobart Brown and Jack Mays in 1969.

The town's activity centers around Arcata Plaza. Once a cow pasture, it's now mostly paved and surrounded by several restored buildings, including stone-and-brick Jacoby's Storehouse, built in 1857, and the Hotel Arcata. For contemporary nightlife, nearby Humboldt State University offers a program of theater, dance, and music. The old-fashioned Fourth of July is a truly hometown event, with the populace turning out for barbeque, baseball, and a fireworks display.

Information: Arcata Chamber of Commerce | 1635 Heindon Rd., 95521-5800 | 707/822–3619 | chamber@arcata.com | www.arcata.com/chamber.

Attractions

Arcata Ballpark. Home to the semipro Humboldt Crabs baseball team. You can watch them play most nights and some afternoons during the summer. | F and 9th Sts. | 707/826–2333 | http://www.crabsbaseball.org | $4; $60 season passes and $30 10-ticket strips available | Mid-June–July.

Arcata Community Forest/Redwood Park. A 620-acre "living museum" of second-growth redwoods, with 10 mi of roads and trails open to bicyclists, hikers, and horseback riders. Dedicated in 1955, it was the first city-owned forest in California. The park has a playground

KINETIC SCULPTURE RACE

The Kinetic Sculpture Race, held during Memorial Day weekend, is one of the wackiest and most visually memorable competitions in the state. The event covers 3 days and 35 mi; up to 100 zany people-powered sculptures roll out of Arcata's town square, across sand dunes, through Old Town Eureka, plunge into Humboldt Bay, float (if all goes well) across the Eel River, and end up at the Ferndale Fairgrounds.

The whole thing started in 1966 when Ferndale sculptors Hobart Brown and Jack Mays challenged each other to a duel, which they settled by racing a couple of non-motorized contraptions they'd pieced together out of odds and ends in their studios. Today, the race draws thousands of spectators, and the surviving contraptions are exhibited as fine art in California museums and galleries. And rightly so: the vehicles are huge, wildly inventive machines powered by bicycle gears and equipped with Styrofoam for flotation. Entrants spend a year or more turning the simple armatures into oversized lobsters, space capsules, dinosaurs or, in one case, a giant mangy dog. The race starts at noon, preceded by a Kinetic Kickoff Party and crowning of the Rutabaga Queen. Learn more by calling 707/786–9259.

© Corbis

and picnicking, and is on the eastern edge of town. | Off 11th Street and 14th Street | 707/822–8184 | Free | Daily dawn to dusk.

Arcata Marsh and Wildlife Sanctuary. This 154-acre refuge on the edge of Arcata Bay is home to more than 200 species of waterfowl, including ducks, osprey, herons, grebes, and egrets. You can watch them foraging for food on the mud flats at low tide. Four and a half miles of trails lead through an interpretive center, Arcata Salt Marsh, Butcher's Slough, and "Mt. Trashmore," a now-grassy hill covering the old garbage dump that operated during the 1960s and '70s. Following major restoration efforts, Arcata Bay now produces more than half of the oysters grown in California. | 569 S.G. Street, Arcata 95521 | 707/826–2359 | Free | Daily 9–5.

Arcata Skatepark. This park designed for skaters features three bowls with rails, a 4-ft-tall "fun box," a snake run with vertical edges. You must furnish your own safety equipment (it's required). | 1062 G St. | 707/822–3619 | Free | Daily dawn to dusk.

Humboldt Light Opera Company. This opera company offers an annual December program, plus musicals in spring and summer. | 1482 Buttermilk Ln | 707/445–4310 | $10 | Showtimes vary.

Humboldt State University Natural Histories Museum. Five-hundred-million-year-old fossils, a 60-gallon tide pool tank filled with local fauna, a saber-toothed cat skeleton, butterflies, and Pacific seashells are among the features of this museum. | 1315 G St. | 707/826–4479 | $1 suggested donation; members free | Tues.–Sat. 10–5.

Victorian Walking Tour. Pick up a map at Arcata Chamber of Commerce and plan your own drive or stroll to 15 notable Victorian homes located on quiet neighborhood streets. | 1635 Heindon St. | 707/822–3619 | Free | Daily.

ON THE CALENDAR

MAY: *Kinetic Sculpture Race.* A popular three-day, 38-mi race of human-powered wheeled sculpture. | 707/786–9259 | Free | Daily.

Dining

Café Tomo. Japanese. Casual atmosphere, and great sushi and sashimi on the ground floor of historic Hotel Arcata. You can also find tempura dishes and seafood specials. Live music and dancing. | 708 9th St. | 707/822–1414 | fax 707/444–2797 | Reservations recommended | No lunch weekends | $7–$16 | MC, V.

Humboldt Brewing Co. American. A laidback watering hole catering mostly to a college crowd. Live music on weekends. Burgers, sandwiches, salads, and microbrewed ales. | 856 Tenth St. | 707/826–2739 | Reservations not accepted | $7–$16 | AE, D, MC, V.

Jambalaya. American. This spacious, modern bistro with a full bar is known as an artist's hangout. The owner is the head of the Art Department at Humboldt State University and displays modern art from local artists for sale. Popular dishes include roasted chicken, stuffed layered portobello mushroom, smoked pork chops, and the fresh seafood. Occasional live music. | 915 H St. | 707/822–4766 | Closed Sun. | $10–$20 | MC, V.

Lodging

Best Western Arcata Inn. This standard chain hotel, built in 1992 and furnished traditionally, has extra-large rooms. It is within half a block of a family-style Mexican restaurant, 15 min. from the ocean, and 5 min. from Humboldt State University. Complimentary Continental breakfast. Cable TV. Indoor pool. Spa. | 4827 Valley West Blvd. | 707/826–0313 or 888/646–6514 | fax 707/268–8002 | www.bwarcatainn.com | 58 rooms, 4 suites | $82 rooms, $103 suites | AE, D, DC, MC, V.

Hotel Arcata. Arcata's history as a timber town is reflected at this 1915 hotel on the plaza. Sundrenched rooms with antique accents, floral curtains and clawfoot tubs are small, but quaint, and minisuites with sitting rooms are well-appointed. The tiled lobby with gold chandeliers houses a beauty salon and a Japanese restaurant. Restaurant. Beauty salon. Business services. | 708 Ninth St. | 707/826–0217 or 800/344–1221 | info@hotelar-cata.com | www.hotelarcata.com | 32 rooms | $66–$132 | AE, D, DC, MC, V.

ATASCADERO

(Nearby towns also listed: Cambria, Morro Bay, Paso Robles)

This is one of several Central Coast towns equidistant from both San Francisco and Los Angeles. First the home of the Salinas Indians and then of Franciscan missionaries, the community was officially founded in 1913 as a planned, utopian colony by magazine publisher Edward Gardner Lewis. It may not be perfect, but it is a pleasant city of 25,000 residents, the second largest city in San Luis Obispo County. Atascadero is far enough from the coast to bask in the dry valley sunshine, but just close enough to taste morning fog and ocean breezes.

Information: Atascadero Chamber of Commerce | 6550 El Camino Real, 93422 | 805/466–2044 | http://atascaderocofc.com.

Attractions

Charles Paddock Zoo. The Charles Paddock Zoo is home to over 100 species of animals in 5 acres of naturalistic habitat. In addition to housing native and exotic animals, the zoo also rehabilitates injured birds and animals, and participates in preservation and breeding programs for endangered critters from around the world. The zoo also boasts a petting zoo and a knowledgeable staff. | 9305 Pismo, Atascadero | 805/461–5080 | www.caza.org/cpzoo/cpzoo.htm | $3 adults, $2 children | 10-6 (June–Aug.), 10-5 (Sept.–May).

Historic Templeton. Founded in 1886 when the southern Pacific Railroad came through the area, this pleasant rural community has retained much of its historical character. Many of the old buildings have been restored, and most new construction follows the rustic style. The rich agricultural land surrounding Templeton supports large almond, cherry, and apple orchards, and several wineries. Rodeo is big here too, with competitions and horse shows held yearly. | U.S. 101, 5 mi north of Atascadero | 805/434–1789 | Free.

Santa Margarita Lake Regional Park. Nature lovers will enjoy an array of hiking and riding paths, and thousands of acres of open space in this diverse and enormous park. Anglers will find black bass, striped bass, trout, catfish, crappie and bluegill—and no jetskiers or waterskiers. In fact, swimming isn't allowed either, since the reservoir provides drinking water for San Luis Obispo. Swimmers can use the park's pool, open Memorial Day to September. | 15 mi south of Atascadero, on El Camino Real | Main phone 805/788–2415, Marina 805/438–4682 | $5 day use, $4 boat launch.

Dining

Genie's Steak House. Steak/Seafood. If you're here on Thursday through Sunday, you'll likely get to meet the owner and namesake—she's the one singing up at the piano. Thus you can enjoy show tunes and jazz standards as you dig into steak, ribs, and seafood at this classy, but casual, eatery. | 7030 El Camino Real | 805/466–6515 | $15–$30 | AE, D, MC, V.

Players Restaurant. Italian. Players Restaurant has been providing Atascadero with good sturdy Italian cuisine for over 15 years. Come here for family-syle meals, local wines, and both indoor and patio seating. | 8845 El Camino Real | 805/466–5664 | fax 805/466–5706 | $10–$15 | AE, D, MC, V.

Tia Juana's Mexican Restaurant. Mexican. *Sunset Magazine* touted the food here as some of the best Mexican fare on the West Coast. That's a tall order in this part of the state, but you won't find many detractors. Authentic recipes, super-fresh ingredients, and pleasant indoor and outdoor seating have earned Tia Juana's a reputation among locals and visitors alike. | 9159 El Camino Real | 805/462–9036 | $6–$10 | No credit cards.

Lodging

Best Western Colony Inn. This three-story hotel is a block off U.S. 101, and features modern rooms with microwaves, refrigerators, and hairdryers. The pool is quite big, and free passes for the fitness gym next door are available at the front desk. Pool, sauna, fitness room. | 3600 El Camino Real | 805/466–4449 | fax 805/466–2119 | www.bestwestern.com | 75 rooms | $65–$139 | AE, D, DC, MC, V.

Lakeview Bed and Breakfast. This quiet, comfortable inn offers panoramic views of Atascadero Lake. Rooms have simple, elegant decor, and a bottle of wine and full breakfast comes with a night's stay. The innkeeper has bikes and boats for his guests, as well as complimentary passes to the Charles Paddock Zoo and the Monterey Bay Aquarium. | 9065 Lakeview Dr. | 805/466–5665 | www.innaccess.com | 3 rooms, 2 with shared bath | $92–$175 | No credit cards.

Oak Hill Manor Bed & Breakfast. This English Tudor-style inn sits atop an oak-covered hill and commands spectacular views of the Santa Lucia Mountains. Featuring various European accents, most rooms have fireplaces, large beds, whirlpool baths, private balconies, and/or sitting rooms. Sauna, library, English pub (billiards, darts, game table). | 12345 Hampton Ct | 805/462–9317 | fax 805/462–0331 | www.oakhillmanorbandb.com | 8 suites | $145–$225 suites | AE, MC, V.

AUBURN

MAP 3, E6

(Nearby towns also listed: Colfax, Coloma, Placerville, Roseville)

Auburn's first residents were Nisenan Indians who arrived around 1400 BC and managed to live a peaceful life apart from Mexican missionaries and European settlers until that moment when California catapulted into the world's consciousness with the discovery of gold. By the end of 1849 their bucolic land was overrun by miners, and the town of Auburn was established as a jumping-off spot to remote gold fields. The transcontinental railroad rolled through in 1865, and the town grew.

One of the best-preserved towns in the Sierra foothills, Auburn is known for its historic central section, which has many restored 19th-century buildings, including the oldest California post office in continuous operation.

Information: Auburn Area Chamber of Commerce | 601 Lincoln Way, 95603-4803 | 530/885–5616 | infor@auburnarea.com | www.auburnchamber.net.

Attractions

Folsom Lake State Recreation Area. The most popular multi-use, year-round unit in the California State Park System, this 18,000-acre park is two-thirds water. You can fish, hike, camp, picnic, ride horseback, water-ski, swim, and study nature. Folsom Lake is formed behind Folsom Dam and has 120 mi of shoreline. | 916/988–0205 | folsom.parks.state.ca.us | $6 per vehicle ($6 if paying kiosk is staffed) | April–Sept. 6am–10pm, Oct.–March 7am–7pm.

Gold Country Museum. Old mining equipment, a stamp mill, and a period saloon illustrate life and work during Gold Rush days. Try panning for gold at a small stream nearby. | 1273 High St. | 530/887–0690 | $1 | Tues.–Sun.; closed holidays.

Bernhard Museum Complex. You'll find displays on blacksmithing, coopering, and winemaking in this restored Victorian house and outbuildings. Tours available. | 291 Auburn-Folsom Rd. | 530/889–6500 | $1 | Tues.–Fri. 10:30–3, Sat.–Sun. 12–4. Closed one week in Jan.; week varies, call ahead.

Placer County Museum and Courthouse. This classic gold-domed building houses a museum documenting the area's history—Native American, railroad, agricultural, and mining—from the early 1700s to 1900. The courthouse features a restored turn-of-the-century sheriff's office and a collection of American Indian artifacts from around the country. | 101 Maple St. | 530/889–6500 | Free | Tues.–Sun. 10–4.

ON THE CALENDAR
MAY: *Auburn Symphony's Annual Outdoor Concert.* On the Saturday of Mother's Day weekend, music is performed by the local high school band, as well as local jazz performance, and followed by a performance by the Auburn Symphony, all on the fair ground lawns. Enjoy the food vendors, and be sure to brings blankets and lawn chairs. | 530/823–NOTE.
JUNE: *Placer County Fair.* A wholesome county fair incorporating educational and entertaining family activities. The fair is put on by the Placer County Fair Association. Carnival, vendors, animals, a destruction derby, and the Enduro Race— 200 laps around a wet and soapy track. | 800 All-American City Blvd., Roseville 95678 | 916/786–2023 | www.placercountyfair.org.

Dining
Bootleggers Old Town Tavern. Continental. Exposed brick walls, a vaulted wood ceiling, and a huge stone fireplace in the dining room make this rustic restaurant in Old Town Auburn a favorite with locals, families, and tourists stopping through on their way to Lake Tahoe. The Korean skirt steak, marinated in a spicy teriyaki sauce, is a house specialty, as is the succulent grilled chicken. Nightly seafood specials are also available. Year-round open air dining in an all-brick courtyard. | 210 Washington St. | 530/889–2229 | Closed Mon. No lunch Sun. | $12–$22 | AE, MC, V.

★ **Latitudes.** Eclectic. You can select from a diverse menu, ranging from vegetarian dishes like East Indian curried tofu and teriyaki tempeh to country fare like cider chicken or lasagna with spinach noodles. Housed in a three-story Victorian, the restaurant has a sweeping porch and full bar. | 130 Maple St., | 530/885–9535 | No dinner Mon. or Wed. Closed Tue. No lunch Sat. Breakfast Sun. | $15–$40 | AE, D, MC, V.

Lou La Bonte's. Continental. This casual family style 160-seat dinner house has been in business since 1945. On the north side of town right off I-80, it's homey, with a fireplace, and sports photographs on the walls. This standby is known for prime rib and pan-seared salmon. Piano bar. Dinner theater. Kids' menu. | 3460 Lincoln Way | 530/885–9193 | fax 530/885–4378 | Breakfast also available | $15–$25 | AE, DC, MC, V.

Pasquale T's. Italian. A wall-sized mural of a Mediterrenean seascape and grapevine-strung lattices remind you of the southern Italian influences at this family restaurant. Try the homemade ravioli, the linguine in red clam sauce, or the excellent rigatoni al fredo with prosciutto. | Grass Valley Hwy. | 530/888–8440 | $10–$20.

Lodging
Auburn Inn. The lobby of this Victorian-style inn features a dramatic curved staircase. Though a short distance from the freeway, the inn is fairly quiet. Complimentary Continental breakfast. Cable TV. Pool. Hot tub. Laundry facilities. | 1875 Auburn Ravine Rd. | 916/885–1800 or 800/272–1444 | fax 916/888–6424 | 81 rooms | $54–$65 | AE, D, DC, MC, V.

Best Western Golden Key. This chain hotel has a rose garden and flowerbeds in front of all rooms. Built in the 1960's on the outskirts of town, this two-story motel with exterior entrances is next door to Lou La Bonte's restaurant. Restaurant, picnic areas, complimentary Continental breakfast. Some refrigerators, room service, cable TV. Pool. Laundry facilities. Some pets allowed. | 13450 Lincoln Way | 530/885–8611 | fax 530/888–0319 | www.hotelswest.com | 68 rooms | $56–$76 | AE, D, DC, MC, V.

Holiday Inn. While the hotel might look imposing on the outside, it is full of country charm on the inside. Rooms are appointed with cherry-wood furniture. The hotel's restaurant, Marie Callender's, is a part of a chain that serves American fare, breakfast, lunch and dinner; its pies are the big draw. Restaurant, bar, room service. In-room data ports. Pool, hot tub, gym. Business services. | 120 Grass Valley Hwy. | 530/887–8787 or 800/814–8787 | fax 530/887–9824 | hiaubca@neworld.net | www.holidayinn.com | 90 rooms, 6 suites | $99 rooms, $109 suites | AE, D, DC, MC, V.

AVALON (CATALINA ISLAND)

MAP 4, I16

(Ferries to Catalina Island leave from Dana Point, Long Beach, San Pedro)

Avalon, Santa Catalina Island's only port, lies 22 mi off the Southern California coast and services four different passenger ferries from the mainland. A one-time pirate's cove during the Spanish-Mexican settlement period, Avalon was first developed by the Banning family, then by the chewing gum magnate William Wrigley, Jr. A small but bustling resort and fishing center, Avalon has happily seen nearly 90% of the area extending beyond its immediate borders set aside as a nature preserve.

Information: **Catalina Island Vistors Bureau and Chamber of Commerce** | 1 Green Pleasure Pier, Box 217, 90704 | 310/510–1520 | catalinainfo@ispchannel.com | www.catalina.com.

Attractions

Catalina Island Museum. Housed in a 1929 casino, the museum displays artifacts and records of the island's 7,000-year history. | 1 Casino Way | 310/510–2414 | fax 310/510–2780 | www.catalina.com/museum.html | $2 | Daily 10:30–4.

Catalina tours and trips. Santa Catalina Island Company's Discovery Tours Center has information on a number of different tours run by various companies. Some highlights include the Casino tour, Catalina Adventure Tours on glass-bottom boats, and the Catalina Interior Safari, which offers guided motor tours through the interior of the island. | 150 Metropole Ave., Avalon | 800/322–3434 | fax 310/510–7254 | www.catalina.com/scico/html/discovery_tours.html | $10–$36, depending on tour | Daily 8–5, tour schedules vary.

Two Harbors. At Catalina Island's isthmus, 23 mi west of Avalon, this part of the island is a refuge from upscale civilization, with spectacular views, hiking, boating, scuba diving, kayaking, moutain biking and adventure touring. | 310/510–0303 | www.catalina.com/twoharbors.

Wrigley Memorial and Botanical Garden. William Wrigley, Jr., of chewing gum fame, developed Santa Catalina into a resort. The Wrigley Memorial and Botanical Garden, about 2 mi south of Avalon, contains a memorial to him, and a garden featuring indigenous plants. | 1400 Avalon Canyon Rd. | 310/510–2288 | $1 | Daily 8–5.

ON THE CALENDAR

APR.: *Annual Underwater Cleanup.* Since 1981, Catalina Island has hosted this day-long event to collect litter at the ocean floor of Avalon Bay, where scuba diving is prohibited except on this one day. Prizes are awarded for the most interesting piece of trash. | 310/510–2595 ext. 123 | www.ccd.org.

Dining

Antonio's Pizzeria and Catalina Cabaret. Italian. You can enjoy this vintage pizza-joint diner at a table with an old-fashioned jukebox or sit outdoors on the patio or deck, outfitted with umbrellas for day and heaters for nighttime. Try the Catalina calzone and soak up the water view. Entertainment Thurs.–Sun. | 230 Crescent Ave. | 310/510–0008 | Breakfast also available | $8–$12 | AE, MC, V.

Armstrong's Fish Market and Seafood. Seafood. Your best bet is to check the chalkboard for the day's specials and select from local favorites such as mesquite-grilled swordfish, fresh lobster, and abalone as you dine on a deck overlooking the harbor at Avalon Bay's only exclusively seafood restaurant. | 306 Crescent Ave. | 310/510–0113 | $16–$28 | AE, D, MC, V.

Blue Parrot. Seafood. This surf-n-turf hot spot serves traditional grilled dishes like New York rib eye and Louisiana chicken, fish and chips and fresh locally caught seafood like mahi mahi. Also look for their spicy cajun selections. The Coconut Bar inside is a fun nighttime spot with live entertainment and great ocean views. | 205 Cresent Ave. | 310/510–2465 | fax 310/510–2039 | www.blueparrotcatalina.com | $12–$18 | AE, D, MC, V.

★ **Channel House.** Continental. This long-time family-owned restaurant serves Catalina swordfish, coq au vin, and pepper steak with a continental flair. You can dine on a romantic patio with umbrella-shaded tables and a bay view, or in the quiet interior. Open-air dining. Pianist Fri., Sat. Kids' menu. | 205 Crescent Ave. | 310/510–1617 | $16–$22 | AE, D, MC, V.

Rick's Café. Contemporary. On the second floor of the Hotel Vista del Mar, Rick's has a bird's-eye view of the bay. Known for local seafood, top sirloin, and pasta. | 417 Crescent Ave. | 310/510–0333 | $15–$36 | AE, MC, V.

Lodging

Casa Mariquita Hotel. This stucco, tiled roof hotel is nestled among lush gardens with curving walkways. Some balconies offer ocean views, others look out onto the lavish island homes and rolling hills. Rooms are cozy and sundrenched, with antique portraits, floral spreads and dark-wood furniture. Large penthouse is romantic and indulgent. Refrigerators, in-room VCRs. | 229 Metropole Ave. | 310/510–1192 or 800/249–1197 | fax 310/510–8358 | casamarq@juno.com | 22 rooms | $130–$180 | AE, D, DC, MC, V.

Edgewater Hotel. If you're lucky enough to snag a room at this family-run beachfront hotel, you'll get luxury with character. Rooms are all different, some with hot tubs, ocean views, swinging French doors, or fireplaces, all with light-oak furniture, candles, cheery bedspreads and curtains. Complimentary Continental breakfast. Microwaves, refrigerators, hot tub. | 415 Crescent St. | 877/334–3728 or 310/510–0347 | edgewater@ispchannel.com | 8 rooms | $195–$395 | AE, D, MC, V.

Glenmore Plaza. This historic structure is in the heart of Avalon, only steps from the harbor boardwalk and all its restaurants, shops and galleries. The hotel is also only ⅓ of a block from the beach. Guest rooms offer either mountain, ocean, or city views. The owners serve wine and cheese every evening. Complimentary Continental breakfast. In-room hot tubs, cable TV. | 120 Sumner Ave. | 310/510–0017 or 800/422–8254 | fax 310/510–2833 | glenmore@catalinas.net | www.catalina.com/glenmore.html | 47 rooms, 3 suites | $155–$190 rooms, $290–$450 suites | AE, D, MC, V.

Hotel Metropole. This romantic hotel could easily be in the heart of New Orleans' French Quarter. Some guest rooms overlook a flower-filled courtyard of restaurants and shops; others have ocean views. Adding to the romance are fireplaces and hot tubs (in some rooms only). For a stunning panorama, head for the rooftop deck. Complimentary Continental breakfast. Minibars, some in-room hot tubs, cable TV. Hot tub. Shops. Laundry facilities. Business services. No smoking. | 205 Crescent Ave. | 310/510–1884 or 800/541–8528 | fax 310/510–2534 | metropole@catalinas.net | www.catalina.com/metropole | 44 rooms, 4 suites | $135–$259 rooms, $335–$375 suites | AE, MC, V.

Hotel St. Lauren. While it looks like a Victorian structure original to the neighborhood, this replica was actually built in 1987. Each room features Victorian decor and contains rosewood furniture and a ceiling fan. The 6th-floor patio offers a panoramic view of the city and the Pacific Ocean—which is only one block away. Complimentary Continental

AVALON
(CATALINA ISLAND)

INTRO
ATTRACTIONS
DINING
LODGING

breakfast. Cable TV. Some hot tubs. | 231 Beacon St. | 310/510–2299 | fax 310/510–1369 | saint-laur@aoc.com | www.stlauren.com | 42 rooms | $90–$225 | AE, MC, V.

Hotel Villa Portofino. The proprietors of this hotel operate in the tradition of a European seaside resort with very high standards. Ocean-facing guest rooms have fireplaces and marble baths. A private sundeck overlooks the beach. Restaurant, bar, complimentary Continental breakfast. Cable TV. | 111 Crescent Ave. | 310/510–0555 or 888/510–0555 (for reservations) | fax 310/510–0839 | hotelvp@catalinas.net | www.catalina.com/vp.html | 34 rooms, 8 suites | $125–$145 rooms, $250–$335 suites | AE, D, DC, MC, V.

Hotel Vista Del Mar. Contemporary guest rooms furnished in rattan and greenery open onto a skylit atrium. Two larger rooms have ocean views. Complimentary Continental breakfast. Refrigerators, some in-room hot tubs, cable TV, in-room VCRs. Beach. Business services. | 417 Crescent Ave. | 310/510–1452 or 310/601–3836 (for reservations) | fax 310/510–2917 | www.catalina.com/vista_del_mar/ | 15 rooms | $95–$325 | AE, D, MC, V.

Inn on Mt. Ada. Occupying the former Wrigley mansion, the island's most exclusive hotel has all the comforts of a millionaire's home—at millionaire's prices; however, all meals, beverages, and snacks (as well as golf cart usage) are complimentary. Guest rooms are traditional and elegant; some have canopy beds and overstuffed chairs. The hilltop view of the Pacific is spectacular, and service is top-notch. Complimentary breakfast. Cable TV. No smoking. | 398 Wrigley Rd. | 310/510–2030 or 800/608–7669 | fax 310/510–2237 | www.catalina.com/mtada | 6 rooms | $330–$620 | MC, V.

Las Flores and La Paloma. These cottages, 2 blocks from the beach, are quaint and hidden behind overgrown flowers and vines. The cottages have New Orleans-style architecture and design and some have balconies. Some kitchenettes, microwaves, refrigerators, some in-room hot tubs, in-room VCRs. | 326 Sunny La. | 800/310–1505 | fax 310/510–2424 | lapaloma@ispchannel.com | 16 cottages | $59–$189 | AE, D, DC, MC, V.

Pavilion Lodge. Across the street from the beach, this popular motel has simple spacious rooms. There's a large, grassy courtyard in the center of the complex. TV, cable, refrigerator, no phones, complimentary Continental breakfast. | 513 Crescent Ave. | 800/851–0217 | 73 rooms | $219 | AE, D, DC, MC, V.

BAKERSFIELD

MAP 4, H12

(Nearby towns also listed: Kernville, Tehachapi)

At the San Joaquin Valley's southern end, 112 mi north of Los Angeles, stands the Nashville of California. Besides being the state's country music mecca, Bakersfield (pop. 175,000) serves as a vibrant hub for the region's oil and natural gas industries and produces a wealth of agricultural products.

Information: **Bakersfield Chamber of Commerce** | 1725 Eye St., 93301 | 661/327–4421 | chamber@bakersfield.org | www.bakersfield.org/chamber.

Attractions

Bakersfield Museum of Art. This colorful 17,800-square-ft building overlooks Bakersfield's Central Park. The museum houses an eclectic collection of works by regional artists, as well as some works of Georgia O'Keeffe and other internationally known painters and sculptors. | 1930 R St. | 661/323–7219 | fax 661/323–7266 | www.csub.edu/bma | $4 | Tue.–Sat. 10-4, Sun. 12-4.

★ **California Living Museum.** Plants and wildlife native to California dominate here, with a focus on conservation. Endangered-species exhibits feature the kit fox, bald eagle, mountain lion and desert tortoise. There is also has a reptile house and an extensive fossil display. | 10500 Alfred Harrell Hwy. | 661/872–2256 | fax 661/872–2205 | bizweb.light-speed.net/calm/ | $4 | Tues.–Sun. 9–5.

★ **Kern County Museum.** On 16 acres, 56 historic buildings have exhibits on local history and culture between 1865 and 1945. Also on-site is the Lori Brock Children's Discovery Center, which focuses on interactive learning experiences for children 12 and under. | 3801 Chester Ave. | 661/32–EVENT or 661/861–2132 | fax 661/322–6415 | www.kruznet.com/kcmuseum | $5 | Weekdays 8–5, Sat. 10–5, Sun. 12–5.

Tule Elk State Reserve. This park is named for the herd of elk that roams its 965 acres. Also known as dwarf elk, the animals are best seen from the viewing area near park headquarters. The visitor center offers information about the Tule Elk and features natural history displays. | 8653 Station Rd., Buttonwillow | 559/822–2332 | Free | Daily.

ON THE CALENDAR
APR.: *Kern County Scottish Gathering and Games.* Since 1995, people of Scottish descent have been invited to celebrate their heritage with pipe bands, sheep dogs, celtic arts and crafts, and traditional Scottish food. | 661/366–3469 | www.kernscot.org.
SEPT.: *Kern County Fair.* This is a big old-fashioned country fair complete with livestock shows, pie-eating contests and amusement rides. | 1142 South P St. 93307 | 661/327–4421.

Dining
Bill Lee's Bamboo Chopsticks. Chinese. Modern and spacious dining rooms with bamboo chairs and recessed lighting distinguish this busy restaurant. From Kung Pao chicken and ginger beef to a vegetarian and American menu, you'll have plenty of choices here. | 1203 18th St. | 661/324–9441 | fax 805/324–7811 | www.billlees.com | $7–$15 | AE, D, DC, MC, V.

Buck Owens' Crystal Palace. American. As you soak in the memorabilia at the country crooner's museum, restaurant and bar, you'll find a comforting menu offering creative appetizers, burgers, steaks and pizza, and a long list of domestic and imported beers to wash it all down. | 2800 Buck Owens Blvd. | 661/328–7560 | fax 661/328–7565 | www.buckowens.com | No lunch | $8–$25 | AE, D, MC, V.

Café Med. Mediterranean. You can be seated outside on the lush garden patio, and order from a large and unique menu of Mediterranean and California specialties. There's something for virtually every taste, whether it's an avocado and shrimp salad, veal parmesan, or bouillabaisse. | 4809 Stockdale Hwy. | 661/834–4433 | fax 661/834–0188 | www.cafemed.com | $8–$30 | AE, D, DC, MC, V.

Chateau Basque. Basque. If you've never had traditional Basque cuisine before, this family-owned restaurant is a good place to try it. Dishes range from garlic chicken and braised beef to catfish, all served with hearty portions of soup, pink beans, salad, vegetables, pickled tongue and french fries. | 101 Union Ave. | 661/325–1316 | www.chateaubasque.com | $15–$20 | AE, D, MC, V.

Rosa's. Italian. This homey restaurant's dark-wood and red tablecloths create an intimate, Old World atmosphere. In warm weather, you may choose to dine alfresco on the adjacent tiled patio. Favorite menu items include cannelloni and manicotti. | 2400 Columbus | 661/872–1606 | $9–$17 | MC, V.

Uricchio's Trattoria. Italian. This downtown restaurant draws everyone from office workers to oil barons—all attracted by the tasty food, trendy open kitchen, and indoor and outdoor seating. Panini (Italian sandwiches, served at lunch only), pasta, and Italian-style chicken dishes dominate the menu, but the chicken piccata outsells all other offerings. | 1400 17th St. | 661/326–8870 | Closed Sun. No lunch Sat. | $9–19 | AE, D, DC, MC, V.

Wool Growers. French. Established in 1954, this casual, family-style restaurant with country decor specializes in cooking from the Basque region of southern France. Photographs and Basque country artwork adorn the walls of the restaurant's two dining areas. Try the hearty homemade vegetable soup, or maybe the roast leg of lamb. Kids' menu. | 620 E. 19th St. | 661/327–9584 | Closed Sun. | $12–$18 | AE, DC, MC, V.

Lodging

Best Western Hill House. Catering primarily to business travelers, this property is in downtown Bakersfield, just across the street from the Convention Center and Centennial Garden. The courthouse and other government buildings are within easy walking distance of the hotel, as are the downtown area's restaurants and shopping opportunities. Restaurant, bar, complimentary Continental breakfast. Refrigerators, cable TV. Pool. Exercise equipment. Some pets allowed (fee). | 700 Truxton St. | 805/327–4064 | fax 805/327–1247 | 99 rooms | $50–$54 | AE, D, DC, MC, V.

Best Western Inn. This two-story hotel with outside access to rooms is pleasant and respectable, spotted with palm trees and potted plants. Oversized rooms wrap around a courtyard with a large pool and patio area. A jogging path winds around the property. Restaurant, bar, complimentary Continental breakfast. Some in-room safes. Pool. Hot tub. Laundry facilities. Business services. | 2620 Buck Owens Blvd., 93308 | 661/327–9651 or 800/424–4900 | fax 661/334–1820 | www.bestwestern.com | 195 rooms | $60–$80 | AE, D, DC, MC, V.

California Inn. This modest, three-story motel was built in 1990 just 1 mi from downtown. The immediate neighborhood is well-stocked with popular chain and independent restaurants. Complimentary Continental breakfast. Cable TV. Pool. Hot tub, sauna. Laundry facilities. | 3400 Chester Ln. | 661/328–1100 | fax 661/328–0433 | 74 rooms | $41 | AE, D, DC, MC, V.

Clarion Hotel. This five-story chain hotel looks outdated from the outside, but is well-appointed and attractive inside. A pleasant lobby with peach stone tiles and overgrown potted plants greets guests. Rooms are spacious, with dark-wood furnishings. Restaurant, bar, complimentary Continental breakfast, room service. Some in-room safes. Pool. Hot tub. Laundry facilities. Business services. | 3540 Rosedale Hwy., 93308 | 661/326–1111 or 888/326–1121 | fax 661/326–1513 | www.choicehotels.com | 122 rooms | $80–$100 | AE, D, DC, MC, V.

Courtyard by Marriott. Just to the northwest of the downtown area, this business-oriented hotel is within walking distance of three sit-down restaurants. The Bakersfield Convention Center is just 2 mi away. Restaurant, bar. Pool. Exercise equipment. Laundry facilities. Business services. | 3601 Marriott Dr. | 661/324–6660 | fax 661/324–1185 | www.marriott.com | 146 rooms | $89 | AE, D, DC, MC, V.

Doubletree Inn. Easily accessible from Rtes. 99, 58, and 178, this hotel was built in 1985 and is popular with business travelers. The exterior combines elements of both Californian and Spanish Mission-style architecture, including terra-cotta roof tiles and Mediterranean landscaping. Restaurant, bar, coffee shop, no-smoking rooms, room service, pool, hot tub, dry cleaning, business services, in-room data ports. Free airport shuttle. | 3100 Camino Del Rio Ct. | 661/323–7111 | fax 661/323–0331 | www.marriott.com | 248 rooms, 14 suites | $99–$109 rooms, $150–$1,000 suites | AE, D, DC, MC, V.

Four Points by Sheraton. At just 6 mi from the Kern County Airport and 1½ mi off Route 99, this hotel is a gathering point for vacationers and business travelers. The property surrounding the hotel is beautifully landscaped with tall palm trees and flowerbeds. Restaurant, bar. In-room data ports, some refrigerators, room service, cable TV. Pool. Exercise equipment. Business services. Airport shuttle. | 5101 California Ave. | 661/325–9700 | fax 661/323–3508 | www.sheraton.com | 198 rooms | $135–$145 | AE, D, DC, MC, V.

La Quinta. Built to resemble an adobe Spanish Mission building, this three-story hotel 3 mi from the airport has a terra-cotta tiled roof, exposed wood beams, and a covered circular drive. Restaurant, complimentary Continental breakfast, cable TV. Pool. Business services. Airport shuttle. Some pets allowed. | 3232 Riverside Dr. | 661/325–7400 | fax 661/324–6032 | 129 rooms | $49–$65 | AE, D, DC, MC, V.

Oxford Inn. This modest motel is about 12 mi west of downtown Bakersfield, and the Kern County Airport complex is 3 mi away. Some guest rooms overlook the property's tropical courtyard. Refrigerators (in suites), cable TV. Pool. Laundry facilities. Business services. Airport shuttle. Some pets allowed (fee). | 4500 Buck Owens Blvd. | 661/324–5555 or 800/822–3050 (California) | fax 661/325–0106 | 208 rooms | $55 | AE, D, DC, MC, V.

Quality Inn. Just a mile from the airport, this motel is also close to the town's main shopping mall and the Bakersfield Convention Center. The immediate area offers several dining options, and there is a restaurant right next door to the motel. Complimentary Continental breakfast. Some refrigerators, cable TV. Pool. Hot tub, gym. Laundry facilities. | 1011 Oak St. | 661/325–0772 or 800/221–6382 (California) | fax 661/325–4646 | www.qualityinn.com | 90 rooms | $56–$66 | AE, D, DC, MC, V.

Quarter Circle U Rankin Ranch. This family-owned working ranch produces cattle, hay, and row crops. Since 1965, it's also operated as a guest ranch that allows guests to experience the traditions of the Old West. You can choose from seven rustic, dorm-style cabins and enjoy recreational activities amidst the pines and wildflowers that dot the property. Dining room. No room phones. Pool. Tennis. Hiking, horseback riding. Boating. Kids' programs, playground. | 23500 Walker Basin Rd., Caliente | 661/867–2511 | fax 661/867–0105 | www.rankinranch.com | 14 rooms in 7 buildings | $310 | Closed Oct.–mid-Apr. | AP | AE, D, MC, V.

Ramada Limited. Though it doesn't have a restaurant, this attractive four-story chain hotel has an inviting lobby with a shiny marble floor. All rooms are suites with sitting rooms. Complimentary Continental breakfast. In-room data ports, some in-room safes, microwaves, refrigerators, some in-room hot tubs. Pool. Hot tub. Gym. Laundry facilities. Business services. | 828 Real Rd., 93309 | 661/322–9988 or 888/298–2054 | fax 661/322–3668 | www.ramada.com | 80 suites | $60–$80 suites | AE, D, DC, MC, V.

Rio Bravo Resort. At this hotel, with its sprawling campus on Lake Ming, it's hard to be bored. You can choose from water skiing, boating, hiking, tennis, swimming, golf and white water rafting, to name a few of the activities. The grounds are spectacular, with walking trails through gardens, gazebos at the edge of the lake and fountains. Restaurant, bar. Pool. Hot tub. Gym. Tennis. | 11200 Lake Ming Road, 93306 | 805/872–5000 or 888/517–5500 | relax@riobravoresort.com | www.riobravoresort.com | 110 rooms | $80–$130 | AE, D, DC, MC, V.

Super 8. Just across the street from a family fun-park and within easy walking distance of more than 30 restaurants and a multi-screen movie theater, this particular motel is a convenient choice for traveling families. Cable TV. Pool. | 901 Real Rd. | 661/322–1012 | fax 661/322–7636 | www.super8.com | 90 rooms | $65 | AE, D, DC, MC, V.

BARSTOW

MAP 4, J13

(Nearby town also listed: Victorville)

This bustling high-desert town of 21,500 marks the westernmost point of the East Mojave National Scenic Area. (Maps, guidebooks, and friendly advice on desert travel are available at the California Welcome Center.) Barstow was a thriving mining center in the late 1800s, but today it's the U.S. Army's mammoth Fort Irwin National Training Center that drives a substantial percentage of the town's economy.

Information: California Welcome Center | 2796 Tanger Way, Suite 106, 92311 | 760/253–4782 | fax 760/253–4814 | www.gocalif.ca.gov/WelcomeCenters/barstow/index.html.

Attractions

Afton Canyon. In this canyon, considered the "Grand Canyon of the Mojave," the river surfaces here after flowing underground for more than 50 mi. The canyon is designated as a watchable wildlife area and is excellent for rockhounding, hiking, photography, horseback riding, and for touring the historic Mojave Road. | 40 mi NE of Barstow on I–15 off Afton Rd. S | 760/253–4782 | fax 760/253–4814 | www.gocalif.ca.gov/WelcomeCenters/barstow/index.html | Free | Daily.

★ **Calico Early Man Archaeological Site.** Part research project, part open-air museum, this site offers you the opportunity to explore Pleistocene geology and the origins of humankind. The complex consists of two master pits—where most of the finds have been made—one training trench, and four test pits. The discoveries made here have extended knowledge of human activity on this continent back by at least 50,000 years. The site is 15 mi northeast of Barstow off of I–15. From the Minneola exit, follow signs north about 2 mi on graded dirt roads to the site. | Off I–15, Yermo | 760/252–6000 (Bureau of Land Management) | $5 | Wed.–Sun. 9–4:30, Wed. 12–4:30.

Calico Ghost Town Regional Park. Calico is one of the West's few remaining original mining towns. Founded in 1881, it boomed with silver, borax, and gold mining activity. When silver prices dropped and the borax mines moved to Death Valley, Calico became a ghost town. It was preserved by Walter Knott (founder of Knott's Berry Farm and a relative of the owner of one of the town's silver mines) and eventually donated to the County of San Bernardino. Today Calico is part of the 480-acre County Regional Park. Seasonal events and living history reenactments illustrate the area's heritage. | 36600 Ghost Town Rd., Yermo 92398; 10 mi west of Barstow on I–15 | 760/254–2122 or 800/862–2542 | fax 760/254–2047 | www.co.san-bernardino.ca.us/parks | $6; special rate for children | Daily 8 to dusk.

Factory Merchants Outlet Mall. 95 outlet stores, including Calvin Klein, Nike and 9 West, draw regular bargain hunters and back-to-school shoppers. There is Chinese food, pizza and even a pretzel shop if shopping makes you hungry. | 2552 Mercantile Way, lower level suite #A | 760/253–7342 | fax 760/253–7368 | Free | Daily 9–8.

Mojave River Valley Museum. Documenting the history of the Mojave river and its surrounds, this museum maintains exhibits illustrating the Gold Rush, the rise and fall of boomtowns, and the region's rich archeological heritage. | 270 E. Virginia Way | 760/256–5452 | www.admenu.com/mvm/ | Free | Daily 11–4.

★ **Rainbow Basin.** Brilliantly colored bands of minerals and the fossils of prehistoric mammals are all that remain of the lake that covered this area between 10 and 30 million years ago. Erosion by wind and water have exposed different layers of sedimentary rock, giving the basin its name. North America's oldest mastodon and pronghorn antelope remains were found here, and the entire area is heaven for rockhounds and fossil-seekers. Be advised, however: Rainbow Basin is remote and arid, and it is imperative that you come armed with good maps and plenty of drinking water. Heading north towards Fort Irwin the basin is off Fort Irwin Rd., about 8 mi from Barstow. | Fort Irwin Rd. | 760/253–4782 | fax 760/253–4814 | Free | Daily.

Roy Rogers and Dale Evans Museum. 33 mi south of Barstow, this museum celebrates the history that made these two a famous team in Western movies of the 1950s. | 15650 Seneca Rd., Victorville | 760/243–4547 | www.royrogers.com/museum | $7 | daily 9-5.

ON THE CALENDAR

MAR., APR.: *Calico Hullabaloo.* On Palm Sunday weekend, locals get together for a big dance to celebrate the coming warm weather. | 36600 Ghost Town Rd. | 760/254–2122.

MAY: *Calico Spring Festival.* Held Mother's Day weekend, this event heralds the arrival of springtime with music, food, dancing, and a variety of other diversions. | 36600 Ghost Town Rd. | 909/254–2122.

SEPT.: *Main Street USA.* Every year, residents of Barstow gather on their 7-mi strip of Rte. 66 to celebrate with old cars, antiques and a drive-in theater. | 888/4–BARSTOW.

OCT.: *Calico Days.* Columbus Day weekend, Barstow celebrates its mining boomtown history with a wild west parade, National Gunfight Stunt Championships, Old Prospectors Burro Run and other 1880's games and contests. | 760/254–2122.

NOV.: *Calico Fine Arts Festival.* This pre-Thanksgiving event features local and regional artists displaying their wares for browsing and buying. Vendors run the gamut from oil-painters to wood-whittlers. | 909/254–2122.

Dining

Carlos and Toto's. Mexican. For a touch of Mexico, head for this popular restaurant. The must-try fajitas are famous in the area, and on Sunday there's a buffet brunch between 9:30 to 2. If you're really hungry, you can try the "Munchies", an appetizer special combining tacitos, flautas, and tasty chicken wings. Sunday brunch. | 901 W. Main St. | 760/256–7513 | $7–$15 | AE, D, MC, V.

Idle Spurs Steak House. Steak. Since the 1950s, this wooden roadside ranch has been a Barstow staple, with a menu of choice cuts of meat, lobster, ribs and a great microbeer list. Covered in cacti outside and Christmas lights inside, it's a colorful and nostalgic place popular with both locals and tourists, who gather around a big wooden bar. | 690 Rte. 58 | 760/256–8888 | $12–$25 | AE, D, MC, V.

Lodging

Best Western Desert Villa. A mere 8 mi from the Calico Ghost Town, this modest motel was built in 1984. The shores of Lake Dolores are only 12 mi away, and—for those less interested in nature—a shopping mall is within close driving distance. Restaurant, complimentary Continental breakfast. Some kitchenettes, some refrigerators, cable TV. Pool. Hot tub. Laundry facilities. | 1984 E. Main St. | 760/256–1781 | fax 760/256–9265 | www.bestwestern.com | 95 rooms | $74 | AE, D, DC, MC, V.

Comfort Inn. This light-blue, two-story chain hotel is set against a barren desert backdrop, within 3 blocks of a movie theater and 3 mi from a golf course. Rooms are pleasant, in shades of green with floral bedspreads, and are very spacious. Restaurant next door. Complimentary Continental breakfast. Microwaves, refrigerators. Pool. Laundry facilities. Business services. | 1431 E. Main St. | 760/256–0661 or 800/228–5150 | fax 760/256–8392 | www.comfortinn.com | 64 rooms | $80–$90 | AE, D, MC, V.

Days Inn. All the aquatic fun of Lake Dolores is within 5 mi of this motel, and there are more than a dozen popular restaurants within walking distace of your room. Cable TV. Pool. Some pets allowed. | 1590 Coolwater Ln. | 760/256–1737 | fax 760/256–7771 | www.daysinn.com | 113 rooms | $44–$54 | AE, D, DC, MC, V.

Good Nite Inn. Rooms at this California-based hotel are nicely furnished in pink floral prints with light-wood furniture and ceramic lamps. Rooms with king- or queen-size beds have a small eating area as well as a desk. Outdoor pool is heated. Some in-room data ports. Pool. Hot tub. Laundry facilities. | 2551 Commerce Parkway, 92311 | 760/253–2121 or 800/NITE–INN | fax 760/256–3850 | www.goodnite.com | 109 rooms | $50–$80 | AE, D, DC, MC, V.

Holiday Inn. Situated on a commercial lodging strip, this Spanish Hacienda-style hotel is one of the nicest in town and attracts mostly business travelers. The Calico Ghost Town is only 12 mi away, but if you're more into shopping than exploring, there's an outlet mall 5 mi away. Restaurant. Pool, hot tub. | 1511 E. Main St. | 760/256–5673 | fax 760/256–5917 | 148 rooms | $95 | AE, D, DC, MC, V.

BEAR VALLEY

MAP 3, H7

(Nearby town also listed: Bridgeport)

Though not really considered a town in its own right, Bear Valley attracts scores of skiers and nature enthusiasts every year with its natural beauty and collection of resorts, condominiums, ski lodges, and private homes. Two miles north of the village is Lake Alpine, at 7,000 ft, on the Sierra's western slope. Though busiest in the winter months when powder is plentiful, Bear Valley is a year-round destination, and a few hundred people make it their full-time home.

Information: **Bear Valley Mountain Resort** | Rtes. 4 and 207, 95223 | 209/753–2301 | fun@bearvalley.com | www.bearvalley.com.

Attractions

Bear Valley Mountain Resort. Off Routes 4 and 207, this ski area has 25 cross-country and downhill courses, multiple lifts, and a 2,000-ft. vertical drop. Slopes range from beginners to advanced, and there's a restaurant and lounge to warm up in after a long day on the slopes. | Junction of Rte. 4 and Rte. 207 | 209/753–2301 | Half-day lift pass $29; full-day $38 | Daily, but hours vary depending on snow conditions.

ON THE CALENDAR

JULY/AUG.: *Bear Valley Music Festival.* Tune in to jazz and more at this two-week-long event. Top musicians perform at various venues in the village. | Junction of Rte. 4 and Rte. 207 | 209/753–2574 or 800/458–1618.

Dining

Basecamp Restaurant and Pub. American. The rustic, rough-hewn wood paneling and mountain views from the windows of the dining room here serve as a fitting backdrop for hearty pub sandwiches, hot wings, burgers, and a wide selection of Napa and Sonoma Valley wines and microbrews. | 148 Bear Valley Rd. | 209/753–6556 | $6–$10 | MC, V.

Lodging

Bear Valley Lodge. A massive stone fireplace and soaring stained-glass panels in vibrant, abstract patterns make the "Cathedral Lounge" at this year-round lodge a spectacle worth checking out. The lodge itself has a cedar-shingle exterior and is surrounded by acres of evergreen trees and mountain vistas. Guest rooms are comfortable but frill-free, and most have excellent views of the mountains. In the winter, you can practically ski to your room. Restaurant, bar. Cable TV. Pool. Skiing. | 3 Bear Valley Rd. | 209/753–2327 | 51 rooms | $129–$249 | AE, MC, V.

Tamarack Pines Inn. Some 7,000 ft up in the Sierras on a spit of land between the Mokelumne and Stanislaus River valleys, this bed-and-breakfast doesn't stick to any one theme; some rooms are furnished with antique pieces, some with more contemporary accoutrements, and still others have beds tucked half-way up the wall in alcove-lofts accessible by ladder. All rooms have excellent mountain views in common, however, and the surrounding wilderness makes for some exciting exploring opportunities for nature-lovers. Complimentary Continental breakfast. Some kitchens, some microwaves, some refrigerators. In-room TV/VCRs, no cable. No pets. No smoking. | 18326 Rte. 4 | 209/753–2080 | 6 rooms | $60–$135 | D, MC, V.

BEAUMONT

(Nearby towns also listed: Hemet, Palm Springs, Redlands, Riverside)

Beyond the main drag's fast-food stops and gas stations waits a friendly small town in the shadows of the San Bernardino Mountains. This largely residential, ethnically mixed community of 9,700 is enjoying a civic revival of sorts as prime antique-hunting territory.

Information: Beaumont Chamber of Commerce | 450 E. 4th St., 92223 | 909/845–9541 | bmtch@wmn.net | www.beaumontcachamber.com.

Attractions

Edward-Dean Museum of Decorative Arts. This museum space is dedicated to Asian and European decorative arts and furniture from the 17th to the 19th centuries. The museum also presents changing displays of international art in various media. | 9401 Oak Glen Rd. | 909/845–2626 | fax 909/845–2628 | www.pass-area.com/chervaly.htm | $3 | Sept.–July, Tues.–Fri. 10–5, weekends 10–4:30.

Oak Valley Golf Club. Dwarfed by the mountains that wall it in, this well-established 18-hole, par-72 course is one of Beaumont's treasures. Since 1991, it's sloping fairways are considered among the best in southern California. | 37-600 14th St. | 909/769–7200 or 877/OAK–CLUB | fax 909/769–1229 | www.oakvalleygolf.com | Yearround.

ON THE CALENDAR

SEPT.: *Oktoberfest.* Since 1989 Beaumont's hosted this food and beverage festival at Noble Creek Regional Park. It's a weekend-long event with beers from around the state and around the world, live bands, arts and crafts and local food. | 909/845–9555 | www.the-pass.com/bcvrpd.

Dining

El Rancho Restaurant. American. The bright and open restaurant at the Best Western, done in pinks with floral accents, serves steak, lobster and other standard dinner fare. The breakfast menu is hearty, and lunch is sandwiches, salads and soups. | 480 E. 5th St. | 909/845–2176 | fax 909/845–7559 | Breakfast served | $6–$13 | AE, D, DC, MC, V.

Lodging

Best Western El Rancho. A classic American motor inn, this Best Western is on the west side of town, 5 mi from the local outlet mall and about 25 mi from the Palm Springs airport. There's a Tex-Mex restaurant adjacent to the motel and plenty of other dining options nearby. Restaurant, bar. Some refrigerators, cable TV. Pool. | 480 E. Fifth St. | 909/845–2176 | fax 909/845–7559 | www.bestwestern.com | 52 rooms | $50–$80 | AE, D, DC, MC, V.

Highland Springs Resort Center. On 900 acres of woodland backcountry, this conference center and hotel is sheltered by tall trees so close to the property that bears are sometimes sighted. Rooms are respectable and spacious. Restaurant open only for conferences. Refrigerators. Pool. Hot tub. Gym. Business services. | 10600 Highland Springs Ave. | 909/845–1151 | 28 rooms, 55 cottages, 2 suites | $70–$130 | AE, D, DC, MC, V.

BENICIA

MAP 6, D2

(Nearby towns also listed: Concord, Vallejo, Walnut Creek)

This community on San Pablo Bay was founded in 1848—the first California city settled by Anglo-Americans. The state's third capital (from 1853 to 1854), Benicia is now home to about 28,000 and is known for its old military sites, historic homes and First Street antique shops.

Information: **Benicia Chamber of Commerce and Visitor Center** | 601 First St., 94510 | 707/745–2120 | bencosc@aol.com.

Attractions

Benicia Capitol State Historic Park. The Greek Revival capitol, restored and furnished in period style, is the centerpiece of this complex dedicated to the town's brief stint as the third state capital. Nearby is the Fischer-Hanlon House, a Gold Rush-era hotel surrounded by a Victorian garden, as well as a small park. | First and West G Sts. | 707/745–3385 | $3, ages 6-12, $2 | Daily 10–5.

Benicia Glass Studios. Glassblowers in three separate workshops can be seen hard at work, heating glass, gathering it onto blowpipes, shaping it and reheating it and shaping it again. The end products of their toil include distinctive vases, bowls, goblets, figurines and soap dishes, which can be viewed—and purchased—on site. | 707/745–5710 | Free | Mon.–Sat., 10–4.

Benicia Camel Barn Museum. The colorful name of this attraction dates back to the 1850s, when the U.S. Army housed a herd of Middle Eastern camels here in the hope they would help in the exploration of the western desert. Now the old barn displays historical exhibits and artifacts relating to the town and the U.S. Army arsenal. | 2060 Camel Rd. | 707/745–5435 | fax 707/745–2135 | Wed.-Sun.1–4.

Dining

Sala Thai. Thai. Thai-dyed in red and gold, this storefront restaurant dishes up fresh-made choices like lively yum nuer steak salad with chili, garlic-sauced calamari and Thai eggplant with spicy prawns. After removing your shoes, you and your party settle at low tables and dangle your feet into the hollow below—a suprisingly comfortable way to eat. The best bargains here are the lunch specials that allow patrons to mix and match for about $7. | 807 First St. | 707/745–4331 | No lunch weekends | $13–$22 | MC, V.

Sandoval's. Mexican. Gussied up with a faux balcony to evoke a desert pueblo, the dining area here is casual—a laid-back, economical choice for families. Selections are traditional, offered in dinner combinations rather than a la carte. The house specialty is chili verde and steak a la Mexicana with a cheese quesadilla; there are also choices for vegetarians and kids. | 640 First St. | 707/746–7830 | fax 707/746–7309 | Closed Sunday | $9–$11 | AE, D, DC, MC, V.

Union Hotel. Continental. Once a true destination restaurant, this ground-floor dining room in an 1882 hotel is still extremely popular for brunch and holiday dinners. Though almost all ingredients are fresh, especially the seafood, the combination of old-fashioned Continental dishes and oppressive Victorian furnishings makes almost everything taste heavy. | 401 1st St. | 707/746–0100 | Reservations essential for weekends | No dinner Monday | $12–$18 | AE, D, DC, MC, V.

Lodging

Best Western Heritage. You'll need a car if you stay at this three-story hilltop motel, but it is away from downtown and interstate traffic congestion. Guest rooms are larger than average and decorated mostly with red, white and blue. Some microwaves, some refrigerators, cable TV. Pool, hot tub. | 1955 E. 2nd St. | 707/746–0401 | fax 707/745–0842 | 95 rooms, 3 kitchenettes, 2 suites | $89 rooms, $99 kitchenettes, $120 suites | AE, D, DC, MC, V.

BERKELEY

(Nearby towns also listed: Concord, Emeryville, Oakland, San Rafael, Walnut Creek)

Although the University of California dominates Berkeley's history and contemporary life, the university and the town are not synonymous. The city of 102,000 facing San Francisco across the bay has other interesting attributes. More than 50 cafés surround the campus, without which the city might very well collapse. Students, faculty and other Berkeley residents spend hours nursing coffee concoctions of various persuasions while they read, discuss and debate. But for all Berkeley's liberal Bohemianism, the townspeople are known as epicureans and support a lively dining scene augmented with lots of specialty food stores.

Information: **Berkeley Convention & Visitors Bureau** | 2015 Center St., 94704 | 510/549–7040 | www.berkeleycvb.com.

JULIA MORGAN

California's foremost female architect was born in San Francisco in 1872, raised in Oakland, and in 1894 became the first woman to graduate with a degree in civil engineering from the University of California, Berkeley. In 1898 she also became the first woman admitted to the Ecole des Beaux Arts, where she studied classical architecture. At a time when upper-middle-class women could barely venture out of the house unaccompanied, Julia Morgan was determined to become a designer of homes. Morgan's touch, along with that of her mentor, Bernard Maybeck, is evident throughout northern California and as far south as San Simeon, where she helped shape the outrageous architectural fantasy of newspaper king William Randolph Hearst. But it's in Berkeley that she's remembered most fondly. Her designs of the Berkeley City Club on Durant Avenue, the Greek Theater on the UC Berkeley campus, and the Julia Morgan Center for the Arts, now a community theater on Berkeley's College Avenue, reflect her vision of airy, serene public spaces.

Originally St. John's Presbyterian Church, this was one of Morgan's first public commissions. It was built in 1908 for $2 a square foot, which was all the congregation could afford. It's an example of the First Bay Tradition, which influenced architectural design from 1890 to 1935. The style involved the use of natural materials, open-beam ceilings, and rustic detail. Among Morgan's 700 designs are Asilomar, the YWCA Conference Center in Pacific Grove, near Monterey, and numerous buildings on the UC Berkeley campus. Morgan died in 1957.

Attractions

Bade Institute of Biblical Archaeology. Part of the Graduate Theological Union of seminaries, the institute has a library open to the public and changing art exhibitions. | Pacific School of Religion, 1798 Scenic Ave. | 510/848–0528 | Free | Mon–Fri; closed holidays.

Berkeley Art Center. This city-owned gallery, tucked away in Live Oak Park, highlights the work of local artists. The center also hosts lectures, readings and a national juried show. | 1275 Walnut St. | 510/644–6893 | Donation accepted | Wed.–Sun. noon–5 pm.

Berkeley Marina. This outdoor café-and-fruit stand at the marina's entrance is a great place to nab a quick lunch while you watch the boats. Adjacent Shorebird Park is a favorite spot for kite flying and strolling. | 201 University Ave. | 510/644–6376 | Free.

Berkeley Repertory Theatre. This top-notch theater group regularly presents ground-breaking programs of new works as well as Shakespeare and venerable American classics. | 2025 Addison St. | 510/845–4700 | Varies | Tues.–Sun.

Berkeley Rose Garden. Home to hundreds of species of roses, this historic garden is gradually being restored to its original splendor by city volunteers. The garden's hillside perch is a great vantage point for admiring the sunset. Just across the street is Cordonices Park, with a playground featuring a curving, WPA-era cement slide, the only one left in the city. | Euclid Ave. and Eunice St. | Daily; best blooms mid-May–Sept.

Charles Lee Tilden Regional Park. This sprawling park with 2,077 acres in the Berkeley hills has picnic areas, nature programs, and 31 mi of hiking trails. You can swim in Lake Anza, or take a spin on the vintage merry-go-round. There's also a miniature steam train, pony rides, the Little Farm with barnyard animals, a public golf course, and a botanical garden. | Canon Dr., off Grizzly Peak Blvd. | 510/562–7275 | Free, fee for golf, rides | Daily.

Judah L. Magnes Museum. An impressive collection of Judaica and exhibits honoring Jewish culture, literature and art are housed in this former residence. The surrounding grounds are beautifully landscaped and a pleasant place to stroll. | 2911 Russell St. | 510/549–6950 | Donation accepted | Sun.–Thurs. 10–4 PM, tours by appointment.

La Peña Cultural Center. In the tradition of the Chilean penas, or small musical gatherings, the center offers poetry readings, live music, films, and performances and is a venue for local artists. Adjacent are a small restaurant and a shop that sells items from South America, Mexico and the Caribbean. A mural outside depicts activists and artists from local history. | 3105 Shattuck Ave. | 510/849–2568 | Admission prices vary | Tues.–Fri., 10–5 PM, event schedule varies.

University Of California. The oldest in the statewide, 9-campus UC system, Berkeley was founded in 1868. It's responsible for the city's cosmopolitan flavor and its reputation for innovation and progressive politics; the Free Speech Movement generated by students in 1964 made Berkeley a mecca during the era. It's also renowned for its research departments, law school and sports teams. The parklike campus is a good place to stroll, and Telegraph Ave., at Bancroft St. on the south side of campus, remains a magnet for skateboarders, students and graying flower children. | At end of University Ave. | 510/642–5215.

Extensive collections of Native American artifacts and exhibitions of art by indigenous peoples dominate **Phoebe Apperson Hearst Museum Of Anthropology.** | On Bancroft Way, at end of College Ave. In Kroeber Hall | 510/642–3681 | $2 | Wed.–Sun., 10–4:30pm.

The well-respected **Berkeley Art Museum,** housed in a monumental "brute art" concrete building, plays host to major touring exhibitions throughout the year and maintains its own substantial permanent collections of Contemporary and Asian art. Café on ground floor; also houses Pacific Film Archive and a theater. | 2626 Bancroft Way | 510/642–0808 | $6 | Wed–Sun. 11–5; Open til 9 Thurs.

Public lectures and readings are held at **International House,** which also serves as student housing. The cafeteria has global fare at rock-bottom prices. | Bancroft Way and Piedmont Ave. | 510/642–9490 | Free | Daily.

KODAK'S TIPS FOR TAKING GREAT PICTURES

Get Closer
- Fill the frame tightly for maximum impact
- Move closer physically or use a long lens
- Continually check the viewfinder for wasted space

Choosing a Format
- Add variety by mixing horizontal and vertical shots
- Choose the format that gives the subject greatest drama

The Rule of Thirds
- Mentally divide the frame into vertical and horizontal thirds
- Place important subjects at thirds' intersections
- Use thirds' divisions to place the horizon

Lines
- Take time to notice lines
- Let lines lead the eye to a main subject
- Use the shape of lines to establish mood

Taking Pictures Through Frames
- Use foreground frames to draw attention to a subject
- Look for frames that complement the subject
- Expose for the subject, and let the frame go dark

Patterns
- Find patterns in repeated shapes, colors, and lines
- Try close-ups or overviews
- Isolate patterns for maximum impact (use a telephoto lens)

Textures that Touch the Eyes
- Exploit the tangible qualities of subjects
- Use oblique lighting to heighten surface textures
- Compare a variety of textures within a shot

Dramatic Angles
- Try dramatic angles to make ordinary subjects exciting
- Use high angles to help organize chaos and uncover patterns, and low angles to exaggerate height

Silhouettes
- Silhouette bold shapes against bright backgrounds
- Meter and expose for the background illumination
- Don't let conflicting shapes converge

Abstract Composition
- Don't restrict yourself to realistic renderings
- Look for ideas in reflections, shapes, and colors
- Keep designs simple

Establishing Size
- Include objects of known size
- Use people for scale, where possible
- Experiment with false or misleading scale

Color
- Accentuate mood through color
- Highlight subjects or create designs through color contrasts
- Study the effects of weather and lighting

From *Kodak Guide to Shooting Great Travel Pictures* © 2000 by Fodor's Travel Publications

The **Greek Theatre,** an outdoor amphitheater, is the setting for concerts and performances throughout the summer. | At East Gate | 510/642–9988 | Varies.

Numerous plant species are arranged at the **Botanical Garden** by geographic and climate zones. The garden includes a redwood grove and a rhododendron grove, as well as hundreds of tropical plants, a waterfall, and the California natives garden. The Botanical Garden is in Strawberry Canyon. | Centennial Dr. | 510/642–3343 | $3 | Daily 9 AM–7 PM.

Hands-on exhibits at the **Lawrence Hall Of Science** use computers, telescopes, and real lab equipment to teach about plant and animal life, physics, and astronomy. Exhibits change regularly, and there are different shows at the planetarium throughout the year. Gift shop. | Centennial Dr. | 510/642–5132 | $6 | Daily, closed university holidays.

Thanks to the efforts of Cal Performances, which books internationally touring dance companies and musicians, **Zellerbach Hall** is often referred to as the Lincoln Center of the West. The facility is also home of an acclaimed music festival and an annual production of the irreverent "The Hard Nut" by New York choreographer Mark Morris, a spoof on "The Nutcracker Suite." | 510/642–9988 | Bancroft Way, off Telegraph Ave. | Ticket prices vary | Events schedule varies.

ON THE CALENDAR

APR.: *Cal Day.* The UC Berkeley campus invites the public to its annual open house with performances, lectures, exhibits, tours, sports events and balloons for all. | 510/642–5215.

SEPT.: *How Berkeley Can You Be? Parade.* This hilarious homegrown parade on University Avenue embraces all entrants, including nudists, tokers, "art cars," women on stilts, and the "Fashion Police," who write citations for onlookers clad in polyester. No, Dorothy, you're not in Kansas anymore! | 510/849–4688.

OCT.: *Indigenous Peoples Day.* An official holiday declared by the City Council as an alternative to Columbus Day, this event at Civic Center Plaza features a powwow and Indian market. | 510/615–0603; 525–3048.

Dining

Ajanta. Indian. This restaurant has won praise from the local press for its regional Indian cuisine and elegant subcontinental decorating scheme. Specials change monthly, but always popular are the pork vindaloo and galina shakooti, a chicken curry dish. | 1888 Solano Ave. | 510/526–4373 | $10–$15 | MC, V.

Café De La Paz. Contemporary. Occupying a second-story perch overlooking a busy North Berkeley corner, this friendly spot has ethnic art on the walls and abundant plants surrounding a small fountain in the center of the dining area. The café is especially well-known for its fresh vegetarian fare, and also popular and tasty are the mole poblano and jumbo prawns. Consider washing it all down with a sparkling glass of sangria. Weekend brunch. | 1600 Shattuck Ave. | 510/843–0662 | $8–$17 | AE, MC,D, DC, V.

Café Rouge. American. An airy space looking out on the bustling Fourth Street shopping district, this casual restaurant features perfectly grilled chops, crisp fries and burgers the regulars swear by. Other popular menu items include slow-roasted chicken and steak frites. If you'd rather people-watch while you eat, you can sit under an umbrella at a bistro table on the small patio outside. | 1782 Fourth St. | 510/525–1440 | Reservations accepted | Daily lunch 11–3; Tue.–Thur. and Sun. 3:30–9:30; Fri.,Sat. 5:30–10:30; Sun. 5–9:30. Closed most major holidays | $17–$24 | AE, MC, V.

Cesar's. Spanish. This North Berkeley tapas restaurant has a cozy, rustic interior and sidewalk tables. It's an echo of Spain with a changing menu of salads, sandwiches, and other small plates to go with a large selection of wines and beer. You might consider ordering a number of dishes and sharing with your companions. The Spanish cheeses are well-recommended, as are the grilled shrimp, codfish, and fig pastries. | 1515 Shattuck Ave. | 510/883–0222 | $5 | AE, MC, V.

★ **Chez Panisse Restaurant & Café.** Contemporary. This is the restaurant that put California cuisine on the map. The upstairs café is relaxed and casual, with lots of blonde wood and light—it's the place for a glass of wine and wood-oven pizza. Downstairs dining is a bit more formal with an open kitchen and ever-changing prix-fixe menu. Fresh, organically grown vegetables and fruits are hand-picked daily. Delicious home-baked desserts. Beer and wine. | 1517 Shattuck Ave. | 510/548–5525 | Reservations essential | Closed Sun. | $20–$25 café, $45–$75 restaurant | AE, D, MC, V.

Ginger Island. Contemporary. In the heart of Berkeley's vibrant Fourth Street shopping district, Ginger Island has two main dining rooms lit by skylights. Windows look out onto the sidewalk and are flung open in warm weather. The menu's predominant theme is pan-Asian islandy, with original dishes made from fresh, often organic ingredients. The savory, slightly sweet barbequed baby back ribs are a hit, and the pasta dishes work well as a light meal. Daily seafood specials. Sunday brunch. | 1820 4th St. | 510/644–0444 | $15–$20 | AE, DC, MC, V.

Homemade Café. American. Irreverent service, old-fashioned breakfasts and hearty lunches characterize this Berkeley institution. Expect a line out the door on weekend mornings, but you can wait at a sidewalk table with a mug of hot coffee. Unpretentious, elbow-to-elbow seating and a tiny counter inside make for a novel dining experience. The café is particularly known for two-egg breakfasts with homefries and the "Mexican Scramble." | 2454 Sacramento St. | 510/845–1940 | Breakfast and lunch only | $4–$9 | MC, V.

La Note. French. Golden walls, sage trim, and rustic pottery provide a bit of Provence in downtown Berkeley. You can dine out on the patio in fine weather and enjoy live music with dinner on Sunday. The forte here is French country dishes, beautifully presented. Try the ginger pancakes for breakfast, or the beef medallions for dinner. | 2377 Shattuck Ave. | 510/843–1535 | Mon.-Fri. 8 AM–2:30 PM; Fri.–Sat. 6–10 PM; Sat.-Sun. 8 AM–3 PM. Closed most major holidays | $8–$17 | AE, MC, V.

Mazzini Trattoria. Italian. The Florentine-style woodwork, mustard-colored walls, trompe l'oeil murals of Tuscany and marble tabletops here suggest a real Italian trattoria. The menu emphasizes traditional Tuscan and Umbrian home cooking, with items like fennel fritters, orecchiette with bitter greens, risotto with porcini mushrooms, and Tuscan fish stew. The Trattoria also has a full-service bar and extensive wine list. | 2826 Telegraph Ave. | 510/848–5599 | $10–$20 | MC, V.

Pyramid Brewery. American. Cheering sports fans, families with crying babies, inebriated college students and entreprenuers gather to watch onscreen sports at the bar here or relax over hearty pub food, making the environment cheerful, if a bit noisy. There's not much to absorb sound between the hardwood floors and the high ceilings, but the excellent brewer's burgers and chicken pub sandwiches make up for the din. You can also order pizza and some very feisty chicken wings. Tours of the adjacent brewery are conducted daily, and the palm-shaded patio is a great place to sample the house brews. Kids' menu. | 901 Gilman St. | 510/528–9880 | $8–$15 | AE, MC, V.

Rivoli. Continental. A large window in the rear of the dining room here overlooks a lush garden, and the interior is classic California, with lots of blonde wood, breeze, and soothing colorwashes. The grilled local halibut is an excellent menu choice, as are the portobello mushroom fritters. The restaurant also maintains a wide selection of wines, many of them from the nearby Napa Valley. | 1539 Solano Ave. | 510/526–2542 | Reservations accepted | Dinner only | $15–$17 | MC, V.

Santa Fe Bar & Grill. Contemporary. One of the first restaurants to promote "California Cuisine," this establishment carries on in a turn-of-the-century Santa Fe Railroad depot that's a historic landmark. The Grill is known for imaginative dishes based on fresh available produce, like Chilean sea bass, salmon grilled in parchment, and rack of lamb. The dining area is graced with large brightly colored canvasses and live piano music. | 1310 University Ave. | 510/841–4740 | $14–$23 | AE, DC, MC, V.

Skates on the Bay. Contemporary. Right on the Berkeley Marina with a sweeping view of the Golden Gate and Bay bridges, this restaurant's cocktail lounge is popular with locals, who pack the place on weekend evenings. The dining area has a working fireplace that's stoked up on cool nights, and the menu features such novelties as honey peppercorn salmon and "cowboy steak." Kids' menu. | 100 Seawall Dr. | 510/549–1900 | No dinner Sun. | $18–$25 | AE, D, MC, V.

Lodging

Bancroft Hotel. This 1928 Craftsman building was originally constructed as a woman's dormitory residence. The guest rooms are small, but the hotel is just off the Berkeley campus and around the corner from Telegraph Ave. Some rooms have spectacular views of the bay. Complimentary Continental breakfast. No air conditioning, cable TV, in-room VCRs. No smoking. | 2680 Bancroft Way | 510/549–1000; 800/549–1002 | fax 510/549–1070 | reservations@bancrofthotel.com | www.bancrofthotel.com | 22 rooms | $89–$190 | AE, DC, MC, V.

Berkeley City Club. Julia Morgan, the architect for Hearst's San Simeon, designed this landmark Gothic-style hotel, with its gardens and inner courtyards, in 1927. The high arched ceilings, many-paned leaded glass windows, and abundant chandeliers have earned it the nickname "Little Castle." You can walk 3 blocks north or south to downtown Berkeley's shops and restaurants. Restaurant. Complimentary breakfast. TV in common area. Indoor pool. Exercise equipment. Laundry facilities. | 2315 Durant Ave., 94704 | 510/848–7800 | fax 510/848–5900 | berkeleycityclub.com | 18 rooms, 2 suites | $110–$180 rooms, $155–$185 suites | MC, V.

Berkeley Marina Radisson. Right on the marina, at the foot of University Avenue, the Marina Radisson has some spectacular views of the San Francisco skyline across the bay. It also has access to Shorebird Park's winding, tree-shaded walking paths. Restaurant, bar, room service. In-room data ports, cable TV. 2 indoor pools. Exercise equipment. Business services. | 200 Marina Blvd., 94710 | 510/548–7920 or 800/243–0625 | fax 510/548–7944 | www.raddison.com | 375 rooms, 6 suites | $119–$198 rooms, $350–$750 suites | AE, D, DC, MC, V.

Berkeley Travel Inn. From this garden-encircled motel, you can walk 7 blocks west to the University of California's West Campus or 2 blocks north to a BART station. The restaurant serves Thai food; other restaurants and a grocery store are across the street. Restaurant. Laundry service. | 1461 University Ave. | 510/848–3840 | fax 510/848–1480 | 42 rooms | $50–$90 | AE, DC, MC, V.

Campus Motel. Built in 1952, this two-story motel is 5 blocks from the UC Berkeley campus in a quiet, mostly residential area. Cable TV. | 1619 University Ave., 94703 | 510/841–3844 | fax 510/841–8134 | 23 rooms | $65–$119 | AE, MC, V.

Claremont Resort Spa & Tennis Club. Built in 1914, this landmark hotel looks like a sugar-frosted castle in the Berkeley hills. Twenty-two landscaped acres overlook the San Francisco Bay and skyline. The Claremont maintains an extensive art collection. Restaurants, bar (with entertainment), room service. In-room data ports, some microwaves, refrigerators, cable TV. 2 pools, hot tub. Beauty salon, spa. Tennis. Gym. Business services. | 41 Tunnel Rd. | 510/843–3000 | fax 510/843–6239 | www.claremontresort.com | 279 rooms, 13 suites | $245–$375 rooms, $400–$900 suites | AE, D, DC, MC, V.

French Hotel. A small European-style hotel with an espresso bar and quaint café in the lobby, the French enjoys prime real-estate in the middle of north Berkeley's "gourmet ghetto". It's across the street from Chez Panisse and within 2 blocks of an excellent bookstore and other shops, and a short walk from downtown and the UC campus. Room service. Free parking. | 1538 Shattuck Ave., 94709 | 510/548–9930 | fax 510/548–9930 | 18 rooms | $78–$130 | AE, D, DC, MC, V.

Gramma's Rose Garden Inn. Five buildings dating back to 1899 make up this inn, headquartered in an old farmhouse surrounded by English-style country gardens. Some guest rooms have private patios with small gardens of their own, but all visitors are welcome to stroll around the property and take in the sights and aromas that abound. An oasis in the middle of the city, Gramma's is within walking distance of the UC campus and Telegraph Ave., as well as a number of acclaimed restaurants. Complimentary Continental breakfast. No air conditioning, cable TV. | 2740 Telegraph Ave., 94705 | 510/549–2145 | fax 510/549–1085 | www.rosegardeninn.com | 40 rooms | $115–$265 | AE, D, DC, MC, V.

Hotel Durant. Just a block from the UC Berkeley campus, this six-story, 1928 hotel is a favorite of visiting professors and parents. The surrounding area is mostly quiet residential streets and tree-lined avenues. Rooms accented with dark woods and stately plaids are small without feeling cramped. Restaurant, bar. Some refrigerators. No air-conditioning, cable TV. Airport shuttle. | 2600 Durant Ave., 94704 | 510/845–8981; 800/238–7268 | fax 510/486–8336 | durant@sfo.com | www.hoteldurant.com | 140 rooms | $155–$400 | AE, D, DC, MC, V.

BEVERLY HILLS

MAP 9, D3

(Nearby towns also listed: Culver City, Hollywood, West Hollywood, Westwood Village)

Swimming pools and movie stars are a couple of the images that spring to mind at the mention of this iconic L.A. subdivision. Among the world's most elite addresses, Beverly Hills' Rodeo Drive lures visitors from around the globe to its art galleries, boutiques, salons, and jewelry shops. Since Mary Pickford and Douglas Fairbanks, Sr. set up house here some 80 years ago, Beverly Hills has been home to countless movie and television stars.

Information: Beverly Hills Visitors Bureau | 239 S. Beverly Dr., 90212 | 310/248–1015 | admin@bhvb.org | www.bhvb.org.

Attractions

Museum of Television and Radio in California. Paying homage to "The Box," this museum maintains a collection of over 95,000 historical and contemporary advertisements and programs. You can view programs on individual consoles or at programmed screenings. | 465 N. Beverly Dr. | 310/786–1000 | www.mtr.org | $6 | Wed.–Sun. 12–5, Thurs. 12–9.

★ **Rodeo Drive.** Famous long before the shopping scenes from "Pretty Woman" took place here, this area is home to posh galleries, jewelry stores, exclusive salons, hip restaurants, and top-shelf retailers like Giorgio Beverly Hills. | Along Rodeo Drive to Wilshire Blvd. | www.bhvb.org | Free.

ON THE CALENDAR

SEPT.: *Beverly Hills Summer Arts Festival.* Every year at the Civic Center Plaza, Beverly Hills gathers to celebrate arts, food and drink, music and fashion. | 310/550–4796.

Dining

The Belvedere. Contemporary. Located within the Peninsula Beverly Hills Hotel, the Belvedere serves some of the best food in L.A. to some of the town's most powerful movers and shakers. Amid elegant French Renaissance surroundings or out on the open-air terrace, producers, agents and "civilians" dine on contemporary American dishes, like cobb salad or warm lobster and brioche bread pudding. Guitarist, harpist Sun. Kids' menu. Sunday brunch. | 9882 Little Santa Monica Blvd. | 310/788–2306 | Breakfast also available | $20–$35 | AE, D, DC, MC, V.

Crustacean. Pan-Asian. Inventive Vietnamese cuisine is in keeping with this 1930s French Colonial estate-style setting. Some of most popular dishes include Dungeness crab simmered in sake, chardonnay, and cognac. The décor is as inspired as the menu—you won't forget the beautiful aquarium filled with rare koi or the bamboo garden verandas. Three patios open off the main dining area, shaded with large umbrellas and heated on chilly evenings. Pianist. | 9646 Little Santa Monica Blvd. | 310/205–8990 | Reservations essential | Closed Sun. | $55–$65 | AE, DC, MC, V.

Da Pasquale. Italian. An affordable meal in this neighborhood is hard to find—Da Pasquale might be the exception, and the pizza might be worth the trip anyhow. You can dine on pies topped with fresh tomato, garlic, and basil, or three cheeses and prosciutto al fresco on the restaurant's small covered patio. | 9749 Little Santa Monica Blvd. | 310/859–3884 | Reservations essential weekends | Closed Sun. No lunch Sat. | $15–$20 | AE, DC, MC, V.

★ **Dining Room at the Regent Beverly Wilshire.** Continental. Business people and well-heeled locals head to this formal dining room for elegant breakfasts, power-lunches, and impressive dinners. Grilled swordfish with barbecued shrimp sometimes appears on the prix-fixe menus; other choices are the Chilean sea bass with bok choy and lemongrass essence, and grilled Angus steak with fries. There's a pianist, ballroom dancing, and three-piece jazz band on weekends. | 9500 Wilshire Blvd. | 310/275–5200 | Reservations essential | Jacket required | Breakfast also available. No supper Sun. | $17–$36 | AE, D, DC, MC, V.

Ed Debevic's. American. Waiters and waitresses in 50s costumes—and sometimes on roller-skates—serve staples like meatloaf, hamburgers, and hot wings, all sided with major helpings of tongue-in-cheek attitude. If you're in the mood for something quiet and low-key, this ain't it. | 134 N. La Cienega Blvd. | 310/659–1952 | $7–$12 | AE, D, MC, V.

Il Pastaio. Italian. This sunny corner restaurant has a Tuscan feel and has been lauded for its innovative pasta dishes like rich garganelli with broccoli and sausage and creamy wild mushroom and mascarpone risotto. | 400 N. Canon Dr. | 310/205–5444 | No lunch Sun. | $25–$30 | AE, DC, MC, V.

Lawry's. Steak. Established in 1938, this family-run place is the home of Lawry's Seasoned Salt, which has flavored many a hamburger the world over. The atmosphere is friendly, with the main dining area decked out in old English fashion—lots of dark, polished wood and low light. The main items here have always been four cuts of aged prime rib, but over time, seafood dishes and generous salads have been added to the menu. | 100 N. La Cienega Blvd. | 310/652–2827 | No lunch | $22–$32 | AE, D, DC, MC, V.

Maple Drive. Contemporary. Thanks to an eclectic menu, you can try traditional-turned-sophisticated dishes like steamed chicken with matzo-ball soup or the aptly-named "kick ass chili," a signature dish. A terrace overlooks a garden with modern sculptures. Consider a post-dinner stroll to help work off the chili. Jazz Mon.–Sat. | 345 N. Maple Dr. | 310/274–9800 | Closed Sun. | $19–$34 | AE, DC, MC, V.

Matsuhisa. Contemporary. Chef/owner Nobu Matsuhisa came here from Japan by way of Peru. A seafood master, he creates unusual and imaginative dishes by combining Japanese flavors with South American salsas and spices. Consider the caviar-topped tuna stuffed with black truffles, or the sea urchin swathed in *shiso* leaves. The restaurant is popular with celebrities, so reserve early and keep your eyes peeled for recognizable faces. | 129 N. La Cienega Blvd. | 310/289–4925 | Reservations essential | No lunch weekends | $50–$60 | AE, DC, MC, V.

Natalee Thai. Thai. Approachable and affordable in a chic, contemporary setting. Try conservative dishes like pad Thai or the Outrageous Beef Salad, or get lost in ruby curry or Siamese shrimp. The building is open and airy, with polished blond oak tables and geometric artwork. | 998 S. Robertson Blvd. | 310/855–9380 | www.nataleethai.com | $7–$15 | AE, D, MC, V.

Nate 'n' Al's. Delicatessen. This is a famous gathering place for shoppers and Hollywood comedians who banter with the waitresses. The huge deli sandwiches, cheese blintzes, potato pancakes, and lox and scrambled eggs are first rate. | 414 N. Beverly Dr. | 310/274–0101 | Breakfast also available | $11–$18 | AE, MC, V.

ObaChine. Pan-Asian. With its hammered-copper bar, mahogany tables, and etched glass, this restaurant is truly a jewel in the crown of chef-turned-restaurateur Wolfgang Puck. The creative pan-Asian menu includes Cambodian-style shrimp crepes and sizzling whole catfish with ginger-*ponzu* sauce made of Japanese radishes and citrus juices. | 242 N. Beverly Dr. | 310/274–4440 | Closed Sun., Mon. No lunch | $16–$24 | AE, DC, MC, V.

Polo Lounge. Contemporary. Inside the legendary Beverly Hills Hotel, this landmark restaurant, with its distinctive banana-leaf wallpaper, has been a meeting place for Hollywood heavy-hitters since 1912. The Lounge serves a menu of modern Asian/Californian cuisine, which you can enjoy in a private booth or out on the expansive patio. Sun. brunch. | 9641 Sunset Blvd. | 310/276–2251 | Reservations essential | Jacket required | Breakfast also available | $25–$40 | AE, DC, MC, V.

Prego. Italian. Part of a small, stylish chain of Italian restaurants, Prego is as consistent as it is comfortable, with roomy wooden booths. Regulars praise the baby lamb chops, large broiled veal chop, bruschetta Toscana, and agnolotti filled with lobster and ricotta. | 362 N. Camden Dr. | 310/277–7346 | No lunch Sun. | $10–$20 | AE, DC, MC, V.

Stinking Rose. Italian. Named after one of garlic's less-pretty nicknames, this fun-loving restaurant seasons everything from appetizers to desserts with potent garlic cloves. Consider trying Lucifer's garlic steak alla Dante—and remember to bring the breath mints. | 55 N. La Cienega | 310/652–7673 | $12–$30 | AE, DC, MC, V.

Lodging

Avalon Hotel. Well-appointed rooms are painted avocado, lavender, or peach, with retro furniture, hip knick-knacks, big screen TVs and minimalist artwork. Free standing sinks with bamboo fixtures, in-room stereos and cell phone rentals are just a few reasons this chic, small hotel is so popular among visitors. Restaurant, bar, room service. some in-room data ports, minibars. Pool. Massage. Gym. Laundry services. | 9400 W. Olympic Blvd. | 310/277–5221 | fax 310/277–4928 | www.avalonlosangeleshotel.com | 76 rooms, 12 suites | $190–$250 rooms, $475–$525 suites | AE, D, DC, MC, V.

Best Western Sunset Plaza Hotel. The sunny lobby of this charming chain hotel is warm and inviting, with peach ceramic tile, blossoming potted plants, brass fixtures and plush mauve carpet. Rooms are likewise rosy, with pink carpets, curtains and bedspreads. Restaurant, bar, complimentary Continental breakfast. Refrigerators, in-room VCRs. Pool. Laundry facilities. Business services. | 8400 Sunset Blvd. | 323/654–0750 or 800/421–3652 | fax 323/650–6146 | www.bestwestern.com | 97 rooms | $120–$160 | AE, D, DC, MC, V.

★ **Beverly Hills Hotel and Bungalows.** An area landmark since its construction in 1912, the luxe, opulent "Pink Palace" is steeped in Hollywood legend. Greats like Greta Garbo and Howard Hughes have spent discreet holidays here, as have luminaries like Cecil B. DeMille. The Polo Lounge has long been a meeting place for the industry elite. Restaurant, room service. In-room data ports, some kitchenettes, cable TV, in-room VCRs and movies. Pool. Beauty salon, hot tub. Tennis. Exercise equipment. Shops. Business services. | 9641 Sunset Blvd. | 310/276–2251 or 800/283–8885 | fax 310/887–2887 | 203 rooms, 37 suites, 22 bungalows | $355–$410, $600–$2800 suites, $600–$4,700 bungalows | AE, DC, MC, V.

Beverly Hills Plaza Hotel. Overstuffed sofas and lots of potted plants in the black-and-white lobby provide excellent screens for people-watchers. Guest suites are done in bright white with lots of light and glass. Restaurant, bar with entertainment. In-room data ports, safes, some kitchenettes, minibars, refrigerators, cable TV. Pool. Hot tub. Exercise equipment. Business services. Some pets allowed. | 10300 Wilshire Blvd. | 310/275–5575 or 800/800–1234 | fax 310/275–3257 | 116 suites | $160–$495 suites | AE, D, DC, MC, V.

Beverly Hilton. Celebrity-spotting is a popular pastime at this centrally located luxury hotel. The Hilton's marble-and-glass–filled public areas are in contrast to the guest rooms, which are decorated in warm desert colors. The Hilton stands in the heart of Beverly Hills, 2 blocks from Rodeo Drive's shops and galleries. Restaurant, 3 bars, room service. In-room data ports, refrigerators, cable TV. Pool, wading pool. Beauty salon. Exercise equipment. Shops. Business services. Some pets allowed. | 9876 Wilshire Blvd. | 310/274–7777 | fax 310/285–1313 | www.hilton.com | 581 rooms, 90 suites | $175–$395 rooms, suites $250–$1,100 | AE, D, DC, MC, V.

Carlyle Inn. Named after the 19th century English poet Thomas Carlyle, this contemporary European-style inn has easy access to Century City, Restaurant Row, and Rodeo Drive. Rooms occupy four levels of circular terraces that overlook a lush courtyard. Restaurant, complimentary breakfast. In-room data ports, cable TV/VCRs, movies. Exercise equipment. Business services. | 1119 S. Robertson Blvd., Los Angeles | 310/275–4445 or 800/322–7595 | fax 310/859–0496 | www.carlyle-inn.com | 32 rooms, 16 suites | $115 rooms, $135 suites | AE, D, DC, MC, V.

Luxe Hotel Rodeo Drive. Just north of Wilshire Blvd., this creation of New York designer Vicente Wolf echoes the refinement of Beverly Hills. Sophisticated guest rooms and public spaces feature rich mahogany, polished silver and gilded detailing. Guest rooms have contemporary furnishings and designer linens, and penthouse suites have private sundecks. Restaurant. In-room data ports, some refrigerators, minibars, cable TV. | 360 N. Rodeo Dr. | 310/273–0300 or 800/HOTEL–411 | fax 310/859–8730 | 86 rooms | $195 | AE, D, DC, MC, V.

★ **Peninsula Beverly Hills.** Done in opulent French Renaissance style, the interior of this local fixture seems far removed from the buzz of activity outside its walls. Guest rooms resemble luxury apartments, some with marble floors, antique furnishings, private terraces, and hot tubs. The Peninsula also maintains a Rolls-Royce for fetching weary shoppers back to the hotel. Restaurant, bar, room service. In-room data ports, safes, minibars, cable TV, in-room VCRs (and movies). Pool. Hot tub, massage. Driving range, putting green. Exercise equipment. Business services. | 9882 Little Santa Monica Blvd. | 310/551–2888 or 800/462–7899 | fax 310/788–2319 | pbh@peninsula.com | www.peninsula.com | 160 rooms, 36 suites | $395–$525, $600–$3,000 suites | AE, D, DC, MC, V.

Raffle's L'Ermitage. Euro-Asian design has made this luxury hotel a favorite among returning guests. Spacious rooms have a living area, work area, bedroom and sitting area, all richly decorated with silk, maple-wood screens and French doors; all rooms are technologically equipped with stereos, 40" screen TVs, a copier/printer/fax machine, and cell phones. Restaurant, bar, room service. Pool. Gym. Business services. | 9291 Burton Way | 310/278–3344 or 800/800–2113 | fax 310/278–8247 | info@lermitagehotel.com | lermitagehotel.com | 121 rooms | $330–$400 | AE, D, DC, MC, V.

★ **Regent Beverly Wilshire.** Built in 1927, this landmark Italian Renaissance-style hotel is known for its exemplary service and celebrity clientele. Strategically located at the intersection of Rodeo Dr. and Wilshire Blvd., the hotel is within 2 blocks of dozens of fabulous shops, restaurants, and galleries. After a hard day of shopping, you can unwind with a beverage at a poolside cabana, or snooze in one of the Regent's famously comfortable beds. Restaurant, bar with entertainment, room service. In-room data ports, refrigerators, cable TV. Pool. Beauty salon, hot tub, massage. Gym. Business services. Some pets allowed. | 9500 Wilshire Blvd. | 310/275–5200 or 800/545–4000 | fax 310/274–2851 | www.rih.com | 395 rooms, 69 suites | $385–$545, $570–$750 suites | AE, D, DC, MC, V.

Renaissance Beverly Hills Hotel. A covered, flower-filled patio and large bright atrium give this elegant hotel an airy California feel. Guest rooms are done in warm tones of salmon and burnished gold, and have private balconies with views of Los Angeles and easy access to Rodeo Drive. Restaurant, bar, room service. In-room data ports, minibars, cable TV, in-room VCRs. Pool. Exercise equipment. Business services. | 1224 S. Beverwil Dr., Los Angeles | 310/277–2800 or 800/421–3212 | fax 310/203–9537 | www.renaissancehotels.com | 137 rooms, 21 suites | $199–$260, $350–$900 suites | AE, D, DC, MC, V.

BIG BEAR LAKE

(Nearby towns also listed: Lake Arrowhead, San Bernardino)

Located in the wooded mountains about 30 mi northeast of San Bernardino, the village of Big Bear Lake and its eponymous valley offer stellar year-round recreational opportunities. The San Bernardino National Forest beckons to hiking and camping enthusiasts, and at 6,754 ft above sea level, the area's seven resorts attract cold-weather legions of skiiers, snowboarders and sledders.

Information: Big Bear Lake Resort Association | 630 Bartlett Rd, 92315 | 800/4BIGBEAR | bblra@bigbearinfo.com | www.bigbearinfo.com.

Attractions

Alpine Slide and Recreation Area. With a multitude of winter sports activities, Alpine appeals to all levels of athletes. | 660 Cherry Ln | 909/866–4626 | fax 909/866–9482 | $12 | Sun.–Thurs. 10–6, Fri., Sat. 10–9, Sun. 10–dusk.

Moonridge Animal Park. Special features include noon-time presentations about the injured and displaced animals who live here and the 3 PM feedings of grizzly bears, snow leopards, cougars, wolves and other wild creatures. | 43285 Moonridge Rd., 92315 | 909/866–0130 | $2.50 | daily 10–5. Nov.-Apr. weekends only.

Big Bear Queen. You can take a relaxing cruise across the waters of Big Bear Lake on this tour boat during summer months. | Paine Rd. at Lakeview Dr. | 909/866–3218 | $10 | May-Oct., daily tours: 10, 12, 2, 4.

PACKING IDEAS FOR COLD WEATHER

- ❏ Driving gloves
- ❏ Earmuffs
- ❏ Fanny pack
- ❏ Fleece neck gaiter
- ❏ Fleece parka
- ❏ Hats
- ❏ Lip balm
- ❏ Long underwear
- ❏ Scarf
- ❏ Shoes to wear indoors
- ❏ Ski gloves or mittens
- ❏ Ski hat
- ❏ Ski parka
- ❏ Snow boots
- ❏ Snow goggles
- ❏ Snow pants
- ❏ Sweaters
- ❏ Thermal socks
- ❏ Tissues, handkerchief
- ❏ Turtlenecks
- ❏ Wool or corduroy pants

*Excerpted from *Fodor's: How to Pack: Experts Share Their Secrets*
© 1997, by Fodor's Travel Publications

Skiing. During the winter months, Big Bear Mountain becomes a busy ski town crowded with vacationing Angelenos. For more information on resorts and lodging, contact the Chamber of Commerce. | 630 Bartlett Rd. | 909/866–4608 or 909/585–2519 | fax 909/866–5671 | www.bigbearinfo.com/ | Big Bear Mountain Resort: $35 weekends, $46 holidays | Weekdays 8–5, weekends 9–5.

Bear Mountain. Bear Mountain overlooks the lake and claims the best vantage point for the surrounding countryside. | 43101 Goldmine Dr. | 909/585–2519 | fax 909/585–6805 | www.bearmtn.com | May–Nov., daily.

Snow Summit is the best-known peak in the Big Bear area. | 880 Summit Blvd. | 909/866–4621 or 909/866–5766 | fax 909/866–3201 | www.snowsummit.com | May–early Sept. Winter hours from mid-Nov.–mid-Apr.

ON THE CALENDAR

OCT.: *Oktoberfest*. Every year more than 22,000 visitors from across California, Arizona, Las Vegas and even Germany gather at the Convention Center over six weekends beginning in mid-September to celebrate with food and drink. Beer tasting, demonstrations, games and contests for the whole family. | 909/585–3000 | www.bigbearlakeoktoberfest.com.

Dining

Blue Whale Lakeside. American. Big Bear's only lakeside restaurant is a great place to watch the sun set, and dine on prime rib, steaks, and seafood. Large windows in the main dining area have panoramic views of the water and surrounding hills, and the open-air deck gives you the opportunity to dine alfresco while taking in the brisk mountain air. Salad bar. Pianist weekends. Kids' menu. Sunday brunch. | 350 Alden Rd. | 909/866–5771 | $13–$19 | AE, D, MC, V.

Captain's Anchorage. Seafood. This beautiful log-and-stone cabin was opened in 1947, and serves mostly seafood, and also steak and chicken dishes. Recommended choices are the jumbo shrimp teriyaki, the red snapper durango, and the prime rib. | 42148 Moonridge Way | 909/866–3997 | No lunch | $12–$25 | AE, MC, V.

Hungry Bear. American. A quirky combination of food and fun makes this country kitchen and bakery a pleasant pit stop. You can order a burger, meatloaf or honey-dipped fried chicken, and pick up a collector's plate or a Beanie Baby or Puffkin doll at the shop. | 40191 Big Bear Blvd. | 909/866–7337 or 909/866–8167 | www.hungrybear.com | Dinner on weekends only. Breakfast served | $6–$9 | DC, MC, V.

Ingrid's Deli. Deli. This small, stone, roadside deli serves up great, overstuffed sandwiches on homemade bread. Eat on the patio or take it to go. A full-service deli offers take-out: sliced meats, cheeses and baked bread. | 41234 Big Bear Blvd. | 909/866–8122 | $4–$7 | MC, V.

Mandarin Garden Chinese. Chinese. With one of the largest menus in Big Bear Lake, there's plenty to choose from. You can order traditional Chinese dishes like moo goo gai pan or try your hand at the American menu, with orange roughy or top sirloin. | 501 Valley Blvd. | 909/585–1818 | Sunday brunch | $8–$15 | AE, MC, V.

Pineknot Coffeehouse. Continental. Serving a hearty breakfast menu, great lunch sandwiches, and dozens of gourmet coffee and tea drinks, this popular spot is warm and inviting with oversized couches and lounge chairs and a wood-paneled ceiling. | 535 Pine Knot Ave. | 909/866–3537 | fax 909/866–2537 | www.pineknotcoffeehouse.com | No dinner | $3–$6 | AE, D, DC, MC, V.

Southwest Station. Mexican. This colorful casita nestled among looming pine trees serves mostly Mexican favorites like chimichangas, tamales, and fajitas, but also some American favorites like filet mignon, ribs, lobster and pasta. The long margarita menu is as colorful as the drinks themselves. | 41787 Big Bear Blvd. | 909/866–8667 | $7–$15 | AE, D, MC, V.

Lodging

Alpine Village Suites. At this plain, two-story lodge choose from a suite, a cabin or a condo, all very spacious with fireplaces, full kitchens, and some with hot tubs. Suites are 100 yards from Big Bear Lake. Kitchenettes. | 546 Pine Knot Ave. | 909/866–5460 or 877/224–4232 | fax 909/866–0031 | alpine@pineknot.com | www.alpinevillagesuites.com | 6 suites, 2 cabins, 1 condo | $89–$199 suites, $129–$259 cabins, $389 condo | AE, MC, V.

Big Bear Lake Inn Cienega. Right on the lake and close to the village and local ski resorts, this inn is popular with families. The hotel was built in 1989 as both a vacation destination and a conference center. Children under 17 stay free. Complimentary Continental breakfast, picnic area. Some kitchenettes, refrigerators, cable TV. Pool. Hot tub. | 39471 Big Bear Blvd. | 909/866–3477 or 800/843–0103 | www.bigbearlakeinn.com | 50 rooms | $69–$119 | AE, D, MC, V.

Eagle's Nest. This Ponderosa-pine log cabin B&B is just ½ mi from Snow Summit and 2 mi from Big Bear Mountain Ski Resort. Guest rooms are named after Western movies, and are decorated with Old West–themed antiques. Cottage suites have fireplaces, some with adjacent hot tubs. Complimentary breakfast for lodge guests. Microwaves (in cottages), refrigerators, cable TV. Some in-room hot tubs. Some pets allowed. | 41675 Big Bear Blvd. | 909/866–6465 | fax 909/866–8025 | www.bigbear.com/enbb | 5 rooms, 5 cottages | $85–$120 rooms, $130–150 cottages | AE, MC, V.

Escape for All Seasons. At the base of Snow Summit, Escape is a popular destination for winter ski enthusiasts. In the warmer months, the inn offers a variety of sun-and-fun activities in the Big Bear area. Kitchenettes, microwaves, cable TV, in-room VCRs (and movies). Bicycles. Business services. | 41935 Switzerland Dr. | 909/866–7504 or 800/722–4366 | fax 909/866–7507 | 60 suites | $120–$330 suites | AE, D, MC, V.

Forest Shores Inn. These three-story lake-front condos are suited to long stays. Studios and one- and two-bedroom units have homey, wooden furnishings, stone fireplaces, big backyards and boatslips. Kitchenettes. Pool. Hot tub. | 40670 Lakeview Dr. | 909/866–6551 or 800/317–9814 | fax 909/866–6406 | frontdesk@forestshoresinn.com | www.forestshoresinn.com | 13 condos | $135–$215 condos | AE, D, MC, V.

Goldmine Lodge. Built in the 60s amid a pine forest in the San Bernardino Mountains, this intimate, rustic lodge is 1½ mi from both the Bear Mountain and Snow Summit ski areas. All accommodations have mountain views, and all suites have fireplaces. Picnic area, complimentary Continental breakfast. Some kitchenettes, cable TV. Hot tub. Playground. | 42268 Moonridge Rd. | 909/866–5118 or 800/487–3168 | fax 909/866–1592 | 5 rooms, 6 suites | $79–$129 rooms, $129 suites | AE, D, MC, V.

Holiday Inn Big Bear Chateau. Built to resemble a European chalet, this hotel is about 1 mi from the closest ski slopes. Some rooms have fireplaces and hot tubs to warm you after a long, cold day in the snow. Restaurant, bar (with entertainment), room service. Cable TV. Pool. Hot tub. Business services. | 42200 Moonridge Rd. | 909/866–6666 or 800/232–7466 | fax 909/866–8988 | www.holiday-inn.com | 80 rooms | $109–$159 | AE, D, DC, MC, V.

Inn at Fawnskin. At this contemporary log home you can stay in one of four cozy rooms upstairs, each with quilt-covered beds and antique fixtures. A master suite has a full private bath, a stone hearth and a lakefront balcony. The downstairs common area is quaint with country comfort, including a stone fireplace and a cathedral ceiling. Complimentary breakfast. | 880 Canyon Rd. | 909/866–3200 or 888/FAWNSKIN | fax 909/878–2249 | TMurphy@bigbear.net | www.fawnskininn.com | 4 rooms | $90–$170 | AE, MC, V.

Knickerbocker Mansion Country Inn. At the edge of the San Bernardino National Forest, this historic 1920s mansion is moments away from Big Bear Lake. Original cedar panelling and antique furniture give the rooms a warm glow, and the four-poster and sleigh-style beds are fitted with quality linens. Some rooms have fireplaces. Complimentary breakfast. Some in-room hot tubs, cable TV, in-room VCRs. | 869 Knickerbocker Rd. | 909/878–

9190 or 800/388–4179 | fax 909/878–4248 | knickmail@aol.com | www.knickerbocker-mansion.com | 11 rooms | $110–$280 | AE, D, MC, V.

Marina Resort. Perched on the edge of Bear Lake, this log cabin–style resort has panoramic mountain views and a private white-sand beach. The shops and restaurants of the village of Big Bear Lake are less than 1 mi away. Guest rooms have high, beamed ceilings and contemporary furnishings. Restaurant, picnic area, complimentary Continental breakfast. Refrigerators, some in-room hot tubs, cable TV. Pool. Hot tub. Putting green. Business services. | 40770 Lakeview Dr. | 909/866–7545 or 800/600–6000 | fax 909/866–6705 | www.marinaresort.com | 42 rooms | $105–$125 | D, MC, V.

Northwoods Resort. Situated in Big Bear Lake proper, this log cabin inn is convenient to ski resorts and area shops. The enormous lobby contains a stone fireplace surrounded by hunting and fishing gear, and cozy guest rooms are decorated with hand-crafted wood furniture; some have hot tubs and fireplaces. Restaurant, bar, room service. In-room data ports, refrigerators, some in-room hot tubs, cable TV. Pool. Hot tub, massage. Exercise equipment. Bicycles. Business services. | 40650 Village Dr. | 909/866–3121 or 800/866–3121 | fax 909/878–2122 | info@northwoodsresort.com | www.northwoodsresort.com | 138 rooms, 9 suites | $149–$239 rooms, $199–$499 suites | AE, D, DC, MC, V.

Our Secret Garden Mountain Retreat. Whether you're in the rose, tulip, lilac or sunflower cottage, you'll have a cheery, homey room, a fireplace, and maybe an in-room jacuzzi. Fragrant flowers and winding vines wrap around each free-standing white-and-green cottage, minutes from Snow Summit and Bear Mountain. Microwaves, refrigerators. No kids. | 784 Berkley La. | 909/866–0966 | info@bigbearsecretgarden.com | www.bigbear-secretgarden.com | 4 cottages | $100–$140 cottages | MC, V.

Robinhood Inn. Popular with families, this inn is right across the street from Big Bear Lake and close to ski resorts. The country-style lobby area has phenomenal mountain views, and guest rooms face a courtyard with a hot tub. Most rooms also have fireplaces. Picnic area. Some kitchenettes, some refrigerators, some in-room hot tubs, cable TV. Hot tub, massage. Business services. | 40797 Lakeview Dr. | 909/866–4643 or 800/990–9956 | fax 909/866–4645 | www.robinhoodinn.com | 27 rooms, 3 chalets | $59–$149 rooms, $159–$399 chalets | AE, MC, V.

Switzerland Haus. This intimate inn is nestled in a grove of pine trees and features Swiss-style architecture and decorative elements. Area shops and attractions are nearby, and both cross-country and downhill skiing are available about 200 ft from the front door. Restaurant, complimentary breakfast. No air-conditioning, some microwaves, refrigerators (in suites), cable TV, in-room VCRs (and movies). No room phones. Sauna. Cross country and downhill skiing. | 41829 Switzerland Dr. | 909/866–3729 or 800/335–3729 | www.switzerlandhaus.com | 6 rooms (4 with shower only) | $140–$200 | AE, D, MC, V.

Wildwood Resort. Ideal for families or groups, the country-rustic cottages and rooms at Wildwood are uphill about four and a half blocks from several shops. Cottages have full kitchens, and the whole resort is just a ½ mi from the lake and nearby ski slopes. Most rooms and all cottages have fireplaces. Restaurant, picnic area. Kitchenettes (in cottages), cable TV. Pool. Hot tub. Playground. Some pets allowed, fee. | 40210 Big Bear Blvd./Rte. 18 | 909/878–2178 or 888/294–5396 (for reservations) | fax 909/878–3036 | www.wildwoodresort.com | 5 rooms, 14 cottages | $75–$195 rooms, $100–$250 cottages | AE, D, MC, V.

BIG SUR

MAP 4, D11

(Nearby towns also listed: Carmel, Carmel Valley)

The appeal of Big Sur lies not in the tiny town (although it's a worthwhile stop), but in the dramatic coastline running from Carmel to San Simeon—90 mi of jaw-dropping cliffs, pine groves, and expanses of sea gleaming beneath endless sky. As writer

Henry Miller put it, this is "the face of the earth as it was intended to look." Route 1 hugs this magnificent stretch of scenery; just south of Point Sur, the road approaches the Big Sur Valley and Molera State Park. The former ranchland and adjacent Pfeiffer Big Sur make a pretty backdrop for the Big Sur River, part of which is designated a "Wild River" under the federal Wild and Scenic Rivers Act.

The region also is the home of the endangered California condor. To explore the Big Sur Coast and support the condor repopulation efforts, pick up the audio tape tour "Unsurpassed," which narrates the history and ecological details of the area, with an introduction by longtime local resident Clint Eastwood. You can order the tape from the Big Sur Land Trust (408/625–5523; $12 includes shipping and handling). The proceeds are used to preserve the land and wildlife.

Information: **Big Sur Chamber of Commerce** | PO Box 87, 93920 | 831/667–2100 | info@www.bigsurcalifornia.org | www.bigsurcalifornia.org.

Attractions

Andrew Molera State Park. The largest state park in the Big Sur area, most of it is accessible only to hikers, bicyclists and equestrians. There are three bike trails, 20 mi of hiking trails, guided horseback tours, and a walk-in campground ½ mi from parking lot, with fire pits, and toilets. The park is 5 mi north of Pfeiffer Big Sur State Park. | Rte. 1 | 831/667–2315 or 831/667–2316 | $3 | Daily.

Garrapata State Park. Situated in the northernmost section of Big Sur, these 4 mi of gorgeous coastline encompass a ½-mi stretch of sandy beach, coastal vegetation, and tidal pools. Sea lions, harbor seals, and sea otters frolic offshore. Possible sightings of gray whales from December to March. (For whale-watching territory, take the Soberanes Point Trail, a 1.7-mi loop.) No amenities, no parking lot, no crowds. The park is 20 mi north of Pfeiffer Big Sur State Park. | Off Hwy. 1 | 831/667–2315 | Free | Daily.

Pfeiffer Beach. A short trail leads from the parking lot through a grove of cypress trees to a spectacular white beach marked by large, jagged rock formations and natural rock tunnels. Be careful of "sleeper" waves around rocks and near tidepools; unsuspecting tourists have been washed out to sea. There are no amenities except a restroom at the parking lot. | Sycamore Canon Rd., off Rte. 1 | 831/667–2315 or 831/667–2316 | $6 per vehicle | Daily.

Pfeiffer Big Sur State Park. Monumental redwoods fill 821 acres on the Big Sur River. There are swimming holes, year-round camp sites, plenty of hiking trails, and ranger-led nature walks available Memorial Day through Labor Day. Showers and RV hookups are available. | Rte. 1 | 831/667–2315 or 831/667–2316 | $6 per vehicle | Daily.

★ **Point Sur Lighthouse.** Perched atop the 361-ft rock of Point Sur, the lighthouse and adjacent buildings were constructed in 1889. The number of people allowed into the lighthouse is limited, and you must take a three-hour volunteer-led walking tour offered on a first-come, first-served basis. | Rte. 1 | 831/625–4419 | www.lighthouse-pointsur-ca.org | $5 | Tours offered Sat. 10 and 2, Sun. 10; Apr.–Oct. Wed. 10 and 2; Jul.–Aug. Thurs. 10.

Dining

Cielo. Eclectic. Sitting at the top of a bluff overlooking the Pacific, this restaurant at the Ventana Inn has open-beam, vaulted ceilings supported by massive timbers. Windows provide views of the ocean and the surrounding hills and open-air dining (at lunch only) gives you a front-row seat. Known for creative Mediterranean/Californian food, many of the herbs and fruits come from the inn's own gardens. | Rte. 1 | 831/667–2331 | No breakfast | $24–$30 | AE, D, DC, MC, V.

Nepenthe. American. Set 800 ft above the ocean with a superb view from outdoor terraces, a meal at this restaurant can be a spectacular experience. The American food—burgers (fresh from the firepit), sandwiches, and salads at lunchtime—is overpriced, though worth it for the amazing location. | Rte. 1 | 831/667–2345 | $30–$35 | AE, MC, V.

Lodging

Big Sur Campground and Cabins. Rent a cabin, including three A-frame units in a tall stand of redwoods, a tent-cabin, or pitch your own tent at one of the camp sites with public restrooms and hot showers. The 13 cabins have heat and private bathrooms. RV sites with water and electric are available. Hot showers, telephones, fishing, playground, volleyball, basketball, beach and trail access within 10 mi drive. | Rte. 1 | 831/667–2322 | www.caohwy.com/b/bigsurcg.htm | 81 camp sites, 4 tent-cabins, 13 cabins | $26 camp site, $50–$62 tent–cabins, $90–$235 cabins | AE, MC, V.

Big Sur Lodge. In Pfeiffer State Park, this old lodge has cottage-style units, some with two bedrooms, fireplaces, and/or kitchens. A general store is on the property, and the lodge offers free day passes to five local state parks. Restaurant. No air-conditioning, some kitchenettes, no room phones, no TV. Pool. | 47225 Rte. 1 | 831/667–3100 or 800/424–4787 | fax 831/667–3110 | www.bigsurlodge.com | 61 rooms | $169–$199 | AE, MC, V.

Big Sur River Inn. An operating inn since 1934, the accommodations are divided among separate wood-frame buildings with standard rooms on the east side of Rte. 1 and more expensive suites to the west. Some rooms have views of the Big Sur River. Restaurant. No room phones, no TV. Pool. No smoking. | Rte. 1 | 831/667–2700 or 800/548–3610 | fax 831/667–2743 | www.bigsurriverinn.com | 14 rooms, 6 suites | $70–$110 rooms, $125–$190 suites | AE, D, DC, MC, V.

Deetjens Big Sur Inn. One of the area's most popular inns, the Deetjens Big Sur Inn built by hand in the 1930s by Norwegian immigrant Helmuth Deetjens. Spread out among five one- and two-story buildings, rooms within are filled with the kind of old furniture that gives the inn a sense of rustic charm. Restaurant. No room phones, no TV. | Hwy. 1 | 831/667–2377 | 20 rooms | $125–$180 | AE, MC, V.

★ **Post Ranch Inn.** Gaze out at the ocean or the mountains without leaving your individually designed "house." Each unit has a wood-burning fireplace and private balconies and exudes a different theme—try staying 9 ft high in the treehouse. At the inn you can take yoga class, go on an herb garden talk and guided nature hikes, stargaze, and indulge in the Saturday afternoon wine tasting. Dining room, complimentary Continental breakfast, room service. Mini-bars, refrigerators, in-room hot tubs. Pool. Massage. Exercise equipment. Business services. | Rte. 1 | 831/667–2200 or 800/527–2200 | fax 831/667–2824 | www.postranchinn.com | 30 rooms | $455–$755 | AE, MC, V.

★ **Ventana.** At an elevation of 1200 ft with great views of mountains, forest, and ocean horizon, this inn lies on 240 acres. Wood-paneled rooms in 12 separate one- and two-story buildings have stone fireplaces, wicker furnishings, and are designed with country contemporary and natural furnishings. Dining room, bar, complimentary Continental breakfast. Cable TV, in-room VCRs. 2 pools. Massage, spa. Exercise equipment. Business services. | Rte. 1 | 831/667–2331 or 800/628–6500 (in California) | fax 831/667–2419 | www.ventanainn.com | 59 rooms, 3 houses | $340–$975 rooms, $850 houses | AE, D, DC, MC, V.

BISHOP

(Nearby towns also listed: Death Valley National Park, Kings Canyon National Park, Sequoia National Park)

Wonderfully bucolic, Bishop is bookended by some serious range, with 11,278-ft Blanco Mountain to the east and 13,652-ft Mt. Tom to the west. For throngs of backpackers, climbers, fishermen, and campers, this town near the Nevada border exists as both supply point and point of departure for the Sierras, Inyo National Forest and Death Valley. With a population of 3,800, Bishop is the largest city in Inyo County.

Information: **Bishop Area Chamber of Commerce and Visitors Bureau** | 690 N. Main St., 93514 | 760/873–8405 | info@bishopvisitor.com | www.bishopvisitor.com.

Attractions

Ancient Bristlecone Pine Forest. This unusual park makes up 28,000 acres in Inyo National Forest. Some of the gnarled and majestic trees are more than 4,000 years old, making them a millennium older than the oldest redwoods. There are self-guided trails through the forest. | 873 N. Main St. | 760/873–2400 or 760/873–2500 | fax 760/873–2458 | mammothweb.com/sierraweb/sightseeing/bristlecone.html | Free | July 4–Labor Day, weekdays.

Laws Railroad Museum and Historical Site. Once an active railroad community, this site combines both railroad artifacts and general town history. The museum is built around the original narrow-gauge railroad depot and Locomotive No. 9, complete with a string of cars. Surrounding the depot are Owens Valley exhibit buildings, such as an agent's house, a carriage house, and a doctor's office. Take the exit at Silver Canon Rd. | Rte. 6 | 760/873–5950 | mammothweb.com/sierraweb/bishop/laws | Donations accepted | Daily 10–4 (weather permitting).

ON THE CALENDAR

MAY: *Mule Days.* Approximately 700 mules compete in more than 155 events, during the Nation's Premier Mule Show each Memorial Day weekend. Since the Mule Days' beginnings in 1969, crowds have grown to an excess of 50,000 fans. Country stars appear on Thursday night and the nation's largest non-motorized parade takes place Saturday morning at 10 in downtown Bishop. | 760/872–4263 | www.muledays.org.

AUG.–SEPT.: *Tri-County Fair, Wild West Rodeo.* Rodeo shows, livestock displays, and live entertainment grace this Labor Day weekend fair at Sierra Street and Fair Drive. | 760/873–3588 | fax 760/873–8874.

Dining

Bishop Grill. American. A meat-and-potatoes diner where the waitress calls you "hon" while refilling your coffee for the 10th time, this homey spot is Americana to the core. A burger and fries or a turkey sandwich will set you back $3.50. | 281 N. Main St. | 760/873–3911 | Breakfast also available | $8–$12 | No credit cards.

Firehouse Grill. American. This simple country restaurant serves hearty meals like prime rib, teriyaki chicken, and fettuccine Alfredo. A selection of seafood is also available. | 2206 N. Sierra Hwy. | 760/873–4888 | No lunch | $11–$36 | AE, D, DC, MC, V.

Lodging

Best Western Holiday Spa Lodge. Anglers and nature enthusiasts often make this lodge their home base while taking advantage of the area (the hotel even offers fish cleaning services). There are fireplaces in the suites. Mammoth Mountain skiing areas are 45 mi northwest. Some microwaves, refrigerators, cable TV. Pool. Hot tub, spa. Laundry facilities. Some pets allowed. | 1025 N. Main St. | 760/873–3543 | fax 760/872–4777 | www.bestwestern.com | 89 rooms, 1 suite | $75–$82 rooms, $94 suite | AE, D, DC, MC, V.

Comfort Inn. Surrounded by the High Sierra, this Swiss-style motel is central to many hiking and fishing locales. Mammoth Mountain skiing resorts are 45 mi northeast. The hotel is ½ mi south of U.S. 6 and U.S. 395. Picnic area, complimentary Continental breakfast. Microwaves, refrigerators, cable TV. Pool. Hot tub. Laundry facilities. Some pets allowed. | 805 N. Main St. | 760/873–4284 | fax 760/873–8563 | www.comfortinn.com | 54 rooms | $79–$89 | AE, D, DC, MC, V.

El Rancho Motel. In a valley surrounded by mountains that rise over 13,000 ft, this wood-framed single-story building was built in 1962 and is near the downtown area. The Greyhound bus station is one block north. Some kitchenettes. | 274 Lagoon St. | www.bishopweb.com/elrancho.html | 760/872–9251 | 16 rooms | $48 | MC, V.

Matlick House. This turn-of-the-century farmhouse is now a B&B that has been restored and filled with period antiques. The parlor contains a hand-carved hardwood fireplace, and every bedroom has a private bath. A big country breakfast is served in the morning, and wine and hors d'oeuvres are available in the evening. Restaurant, complimentary breakfast. | 1313 Rowan La. | 760/873–3133 or 800/898–3133 | matlickb@gte.net | www.thesierraweb.com/lodging/matlickhouse | 5 rooms | $75–$85 | AE, MC, V.

Motel 6 Bishop. The motel is 15 mi from a water-skiing area and 45 mi from the Mammoth Mountain snow skiing area. Some kitchenettes, refrigerators, cable TV. Pool. Hot tub. Laundry facilities. Business services. Some pets allowed. | 1005 N. Main St. | 760/873–8426 | fax 760/873–8060 | www.motel6.com | 52 rooms | $59–$69 | AE, D, DC, MC, V.

Thunderbird. This is an economic choice if you wish to stay near the High Sierras. It's 45 mi from the Mammoth Mountain skiing and sports area. Refrigerators, cable TV. Some pets allowed. | 190 W. Pine St. | 760/873–4215 | fax 760/873–6870 | 23 rooms | $44–$80 | AE, D, DC, MC, V.

BLYTHE

MAP 4, N15

(Nearby town also listed: Joshua Tree National Park)

Ninety-three miles south of Needles and 172 mi east of San Bernardino, this Mojave Desert town hugs the Colorado River on the border with Arizona. Like the world-famous swallows of Capistrano beach, Blythe welcomes back its own snowbirds in wintertime—RVers and second-home owners primarily from the Midwest and Canada.

The town was incorporated in 1916, but was likely inhabited for thousands of years before that by Native American tribes, namely the Mojave. These cultures left their mark in the giant geoglyphs that grace the mesas in the area surrounding Blythe.

Information: Blythe Chamber of Commerce | 201 S. Broadway, 92225-2564 | 760/922–8166.

Attractions

Blythe Intaglios. The Blythe Intaglios are probably the most famous anthropomorphic geoglyphics (giant prehistoric rock carvings on the mesas), or "Intaglios" as early Italian settlers called them. One of the geoglyphs portrays a 167-ft human figure, and all can be seen most completely from the air. The Intaglios, 15 mi north of Blythe, are a good starting point for a self-guided tour of the Native American Indian history of the area. | Rte. 95 | 760/922–8166 | Free | Daily.

Cibola National Wildlife Refuge. Over 17,000 acres encompass this peaceful park area, home to wintering Canada geese and sandhill cranes. Here you can fish, hike, canoe, raft, kayak, bike, or picnic. | 66600 Cibola Lake Rd., Cibola | 520/857–3253 | fax 520/857–3420 | southwest.fws.gov/refuges/arizona/cibola.html | Free | Weekdays 8–4:30.

ON THE CALENDAR

JAN.: *Colorado River Country Music Festival.* National and local country music artists perform at outdoor concert venues. | 760/922–8166.
APR.: *Colorado River Country Fair.* On the banks of the Colorado river this is an annual old-fashioned country fair. | 760/922–8166.

Lodging

Best Value Inn. This chain hotel is within walking distance of area fast food restaurants, movies and shopping. The quieter shores of the Colorado River are just 4 mi distant. Restaurant, bar, complimentary Continental breakfast. Cable TV. Pool. Some pets allowed (fee).

| 850 W. Hobson Way | 760/922–5145 | fax 760/922–8422 | 50 rooms (34 with shower only) | $45–$49 | AE, D, DC, MC, V.

Best Western Sahara. Flanked by palm trees and topped with terra cotta tiles, this comfortable chain motel is 4 mi from the Colorado River and just 2 mi from recreational activities such as fishing, boating, skiing, and golfing. Restaurant, complimentary Continental breakfast. Microwaves, refrigerators, cable TV, in-room VCRs. Pool. Hot tub. Some pets allowed. | 825 W. Hobson Way | 760/922–7105 | fax 760/922–5836 | www.bestwestern.com | 46 rooms | $62 | AE, D, DC, MC, V.

Hampton Inn. In the town's hotel square area, this hotel allows easy access to various restaurants and stores and a movie theater. I–10 is little more than a block away. Restaurant, complimentary Continental breakfast. In-room data ports, microwaves, refrigerators, cable TV, in-room VCRs. Pool. Hot tub. Exercise equipment. Laundry facilities. Business services. Some pets allowed. | 900 W. Hobson Way | 760/922–9000 | fax 760/922–9011 | www.hampton-inn.com | 59 rooms | $65–$72 | AE, D, DC, MC, V.

Legacy Inn. Built in the 1950s, this moderate-size inn is right in the heart of the commercial district and is within walking distance to area restaurants and shops. Complimentary breakfast. Microwaves, cable TV. Pool. Some pets allowed. | 903 W. Hobson Way | 760/922–4146 | fax 760/922–8481 | 48 rooms | $54–$85 | AE, D, DC, MC, V.

BODEGA BAY

MAP 3, B7

(Nearby towns also listed: Guerneville, Inverness, Jenner, Santa Rosa)

The claim to fame of Bodega Bay is its role as the backdrop for Alfred Hitchcock's thriller *The Birds* (1963) about the plight of rural residents plagued by an invasion of vengeful birds. After visiting in 1961, Hitchcock decided the local weather and skyline were perfect for shooting. He also decided that the old Potter Schoolhouse, which was slated for demolition, was exactly what he wanted for a scene where Tippi Hedren saves screaming children from a vicious feathered flock. Hitchcock had the school rebuilt—it still stands, and is now a private residence.

Scenic Bay Hill Road allows a nearly unchanged view of the town since it was filmed more than thirty years ago. The Tides Wharf Restaurant and parking lot in Bodega Bay played the part of a gas station, café, and boat dock that goes up in flames in the movie (the conflagration was simulated on a Hollywood set).

Today, sea creatures are the object of attention for residents and visitors, and the town is a busy commercial fishing port known for its catch of Dungeness crab.

Information: Bodega Bay Chamber of Commerce | 850 Rte. 1, 94923-0146 | 707/875–3422 | www.bodegabay.org.

Attractions

Bodega Landmark Studio. This gallery displays the work of Sonoma coast artists and craftspeople. | 17255 Bodega Hwy. | 707/876–3477 | Free | Thurs.–Mon. 10:30–5:30 | AE, V.

Chanslor Ranch. A full-service riding stable, the ranch rents horses for riding along the beach or over coastal hills of its 700 acres. There are horses for all levels of riders, and guides are available. | 2660 Rte. 1 | 707/875–3333 | fax 707/875–3030 | www.chanslor.com/ | $25–$50 group guided ride; $35–$60 private guided ride | Daily 9–5.

Ren Brown Gallery. This is the largest collection of contemporary Japanese prints in northern California. Original prints, ceramics, and sculpture by local artists are also available together with antique furniture, including Japanese tansu and netsuke carvings. | 1781 Rte. 1 | 707/875–2922 | Free | Wed.–Mon. 10–5; closed Tues.

APR.: *Annual Fisherman's Festival.* Live music, wine tasting, clam chowder, and nearly 100 booths offering crafts items are all part of this celebration of Bodega Bay's fishing town legacy. A high point is the Blessing of the Fleet, at 11 AM on Sunday, when decorated fishing boats sail in procession to receive benediction on the bay. | 707/875–3422.

Dining

Breakers Café. American. Sweeping bay views can be seen from the glass-enclosed café or from the outdoor patio. Breakers uses fresh fish delivered daily from local docks. The menu includes fish and chips, jambalaya, pasta primavera, mushroom and rosemary chicken, and some vegetarian dishes. | Pelican Plaza, 1400 Rte. 1 | 707/875–2413 | $10–$20 | MC, V.

Lucas Wharf. Seafood. The windows overlook the bay, and the menu reflects what comes in on the fishing boats. Friendly staff. Known for fresh local seafood. Kids' menu. | 595 Rte. 1 | 707/875–3522 | Reservations not accepted except for parties of 6 or more | $13–$24 | D, MC, V.

Sandpiper Restaurant. Seafood. Fresh fish and shellfish await you at this bayside grotto. The menu includes seafood lasagne, shark, crab cioppino, clam chowder, and daily specials. | 1410 Bay Flat Rd. | 707/875–2278 | www.sandpiperrestaurant.net | $10–$20 | D, MC, V.

Tides Wharf Restaurant. Seafood. The 150-seat dining room has a rustic feel, with sweeping ceilings and exposed beams. The complex encompasses a fresh fish market, oyster bar, bait and tackle shop, even a fish-processing plant. Docks and picnic area are nearby. As should be expected, the menu features fresh seafood, but also includes grilled steaks. | 835 Rte. 1 | 707/875–2751 | fax 707/875–3285 | $18–$37 | D, MC, V.

Lodging

Bodega Bay Lodge. Built in the 1960s, the five two-story buildings that make up the lodge have exceptionally large rooms, lofts, and views of the ocean below. Doran beach is a brisk 10-min. walk. Restaurant. In-room data ports, refrigerators, some in-room hot tubs. Cable TV. Pool. Exercise equipment. Sauna, spa. Business services. | 103 Rte. 1 | 707/875–3525; res: 800/368–2468 | fax 707/875–2428 | www.woodsidehotels.com | 79 rooms, 5 suites | $200–$250 rooms, $400–$425 suites | AE, D, DC, MC, V.

Bodega Coast Inn. This resort sits along the bay ½ mi from the beach, allowing views of the water from patios or upper-level balconies of most rooms. Room styles vary according to theme—for example, the bird, whale, or Jack London room—and some have fireplaces. Complimentary Continental breakfast. Refrigerators, some in-room hot tubs, cable TV, in-room VCRs. Hot tub. Business services. | 521 Rte. 1 | 707/875–2217 or 800/346–6999 (in California) | fax 707/875–2964 | wwww.bodegacoastinn.com | 44 rooms | $179–$329 | AE, D, DC, MC, V.

Bodega Estero. A geodesic building with open-beam cathedral ceilings, this B&B is nestled against a hillside, and is 1 mi north of Bodega. The guest rooms and common living room are uniquely furnished in contemporary style, and each has a view of the Pacific coastal hills. Complimentary Continental breakfast. No room phones, TV in common area. No kids under 16. No smoking. | 17699 Rte. 1 | 707/876–3300 or 800/422–6321 | bodegabb@sonic.net | www.bodegaestero.com | 4 rooms | $90–$155 | AE, MC, V.

Bodega Harbor Inn. Bodega Bay and the Pacific coastline provide the scenery for this blue-and-white 1940s-era clapboard hotel. From some rooms you can see the bay or the Bodega Headlands. A public golf course and beach are 1 ½ mi away. Complimentary Continental breakfast. Cable TV, no room phones. | 1345 Bodega Ave. | 707/875–3594 | fax 707/875–9468 | www.bodegaharborinn.com | 14 rooms, 2 suites | $55–$77 rooms, $85–$100 suites | MC, V.

Chanslor Ranch Bed and Breakfast. Horses are provided at this full-service, working ranch B&B for horseback rides along the Sonoma coast. There are also miles of nature trails from mountain tops to coastal dunes to white sand beaches. Rooms are in two separate buildings and can be joined to form suites. Some rooms are without private baths. The ranch is 1 mi north of town. Complimentary Continental breakfast. Cable TV, some in-room VCRs, no room phones. Hiking, horseback riding. | 2660 Rte. 1 | 707/875–2721 | fax 707/875–2785 | www.chanslor.com | 5 rooms, 3 suites | $99–$169 rooms, $158–$258 suites | MC, V.

Inn at Occidental. Situated among grand redwoods atop a secluded knoll above the small village of Occidental, the original structure was built in 1877. With a nod to its Victorian design, the inn is filled with antiques, family heirlooms and works by local artists. Afternoons feature Sonoma wine and hors d'oeuvres. Complimentary breakfast. In-room hot tubs. Business services. No pets. No kids under 12. No smoking. | 3657 Church St., Occidental | 707/874–1047 or 800/522–6324 | fax 707/874–1078 | www.innatoccidental.com | 16 rooms, 2 suites | $175–$270 rooms, $270 suites | AE, D, MC, V.

Inn at the Tides. Built in the 1980s, this condominium-style complex resort is nestled between green hills and the bay. The rooms benefit from high ceilings and the display of various works by local artists. 2 restaurants, bar, complimentary Continental breakfast. In-room data ports, refrigerators, cable TV. Pool. Hot tub, sauna, massage. Business services. | 800 Rte. 1 | 707/875–2751 or 800/541–7788 | fax 707/875–3023 | 86 rooms | $159–$239 | AE, MC, V.

Sonoma Coast Villa. A secluded country estate set on 60 acres with terraced gardens, red-tile roofs, terra-cotta stucco and a columned veranda create an ambience reminiscent of the Mediterranean. Rooms within the three single-story buildings all have fireplaces. Some rooms have showers only. Dining room, complimentary breakfast. Minibars, refrigerators, some in-room hot tubs, in-room VCRs. Pool. Spa. Putting green. Business services. No smoking. | 16702 Rte. 1 | 707/876–9818 or 888/404–2255 | fax 707/876–9856 | reservations@scvilla.com | 18 rooms | $245–$350 | AE, D, MC, V.

BOONVILLE

BOONVILLE

INTRO
ATTRACTIONS
DINING
LODGING

(Nearby towns also listed: Elk, Hopland, Point Area, Ukiah)

This apple-growing, sheep-raising ranch town in the Anderson Valley may be the only one in America with its own language—Boontling. According to local lore, the indigenous dialect got its start among town gossips. In 1888 the unmarried daughter of a San Francisco family became pregnant; to avoid scandal, they sent the girl to stay with friends in then-remote Boonville. Naturally, the ladies of Boonville were dying to discuss this deliciously naughty situation, but they couldn't indulge without offending the mother-to-be. So they made up a few secret words. They shared the gossip with their husbands, who invented more words to enliven the clandestine conversation. Eventually, the Boontling vocabulary grew to some 1,300 words shared by 200 families.

Each word had a history. "Syke," meaning horse, was derived from a horse named Cyclone. "Shaggy," meaning clumsy, is the legacy of a clumsy guy named Shag. "Charl," meaning to milk a cow, imitates the sound of the milk hitting a bucket. Only a handful of people, now in their seventies, can "harp" Boontling these days, but that's okay—there just ain't that much to talk about in Boonville, anyway. A quiet, close-knit rural community surrounded by vineyards, it's still a place of hard work and few words.

Today the town has adapted to a more urbane crowd, and has wineries, a couple of excellent restaurants, and even a microbrewery. It still can't shake off that small town charm, though.

Information: Anderson Valley Chamber of Commerce | Box 275, 95415 | 707/895–2379.

Attractions

Anderson Valley Brewing Company. Locally known as the Boonville Brewery, this brewery moved to its 30-barrel facility, 1 mi from the center of Boonville, when demand for the ales exceeded the capacity of the 10-barrel space in the basement of the Buckhorn Saloon. You can try Boont Amber Ale, High Rollers Wheat Beer and Hop Ottin' India Pale Ale or shop for gifts for your ale-loving friends. | 17700 Rte. 253 | 707/895–BEER | Free | Tours daily 1:30 and 4:30 except holidays | MC, V.

ON THE CALENDAR

APR.: *Anderson Valley Brewing Company Annual Boonville Beer Festival.* Food vendors, crafts booths, live music are the staples of this festival; you can sample craft-brewed beers from northern California and Oregon. | 707/895–2337.

JULY: *Boonville Art Walk.* Visit restaurants to see work by regional artists and enjoy food and music. | 707/895–2204.

Dining

Boonville Hotel. Contemporary. The small, sunny country dining room overlooks the gardens. The lunch menu features authentic Mexican fare, including camarones rancheros, carne asada, and chiles rellenos. The imaginative dinner menu changes daily. Try smoked trout salad, fresh corn cakes, curry roasted Petaluma duck. On Friday night there's an oyster bar. Kids' menu. Open-air dining on deck. | 14050 Rte. 128 | 707/895–2210 | Closed Tues. and Weds | $14–$24 | MC, V.

Buckhorn Saloon. American. This brew pub was built on the original site of an old saloon. In its present incarnation, it is a 3-story cedar structure with redwood decks, valley views, vaulted ceilings, a loft, and a beer garden. Known for beer, of course—Boont Amber Ale, High Rollers Wheat Beer, and Winter Solstice Seasonal Ale to name a few. Try the veggie burger, sausage sampler, vegetable jambalaya, or the ribs. | 14081 Rte. 128 | 707/895–3369 | Reservations not accepted | $7–$14 | AE, D, MC, V.

Horn of Zeese. American. A friendly one-room diner with a concrete patio with tables and umbrellas. Known for salads, soups, burgers, sandwiches, vegetarian dishes. Sunday brunch. | 14025 Rte. 128 | 707/895–3525 | Reservations not accepted | Breakfast also available, no dinner, closed Tues. Labor Day–Memorial Day | $6–$12 | No credit cards.

Lauren's Café. American. This cozy eatery is a favorite among locals. There's a play area for kids and live music twice a month on weekends. You can try the burgers, soups, or Caesar salad. | 14211 Rte. 128 | 707/895–3869 | Closed Sun.–Mon., no lunch | $10–$20 | No credit cards.

Otto's Ice Cream. American. There are only a couple of tables in this tiny, old-fashioned ice-cream parlor, but you'll find an intriguing selection of ice cream and yogurt desserts, such as smoothies made with spirulina or bee pollen. | 14111 Rte. 128 | 707/895–3994 | daily | $1–$5 | No credit cards.

Lodging

Anderson Creek Inn. Set on 16 acres overlooking Anderson Creek, the inn offers views of the wine country, expansive gardens, and ancient oak trees. Cozy reading spots include a hammock perched in a private treehouse. Rooms have king-size beds and some have fireplaces. Complimentary breakfast. Pool. | 12050 Anderson Valley Way | 707/895–3091 or 800/LLAMA–02 | fax 707/895–2546 | 5 rooms | $110–$170 | MC, V, D.

Boonville Hotel. The 8 rooms in this old but upgraded hotel are furnished with elegant handmade beds and tables from local artisans. Bungalow and studio rooms set beside a creek have country decor, porches and private entrances. Restaurant, complimentary

Continental breakfast. No TV in rooms. No smoking. | 14050 Rte. 128 | 707/895–2210 | fax 707/895–2243 | 10 rooms | $95–$200 | MC, V.

Philo Pottery Inn. Built in 1888 as a stagecoach stop on the road to the north coast, this redwood B&B is one of the oldest inns in the Anderson Valley. Guest rooms are furnished in turn-of-the-century style with patchwork quilts, antiques, and lots of pillows. Some rooms are without private baths. The inn is 5 mi north of Boonville. Complimentary Continental breakfast. No room phones, no TV. | 8550 Rte. 128, Philo | 707/895–3069 | philoinn@pacific.net | www.innaccess.com/phi | 5 rooms | $100–$130 | MC, V.

BORREGO SPRINGS

MAP 4, L16

(Nearby towns also listed: Julian, Temecula)

A stopover by Juan Bautista de Anza on his way to Monterey put this adorable low-desert hamlet of 2,200 on the map in 1774. Yet settlers with more permanent designs didn't arrive for another 100 years. Thirty miles west of Salton Sea, 85 mi east of San Diego, the 600,000-acre Anza-Borrego Desert State Park (largest in California) encircles the town.

Information: Borrego Springs Chamber of Commerce | 622 Palm Canyon Dr., 92004-0420 | 760/767–5555 or 800/559–5524 | borspcoc@znet.com | www.borregosprings.com.

Attractions

Anza-Borrego Desert State Park. The Anza-Borrego Desert State Park encompasses 600,000 acres of the Colorado Desert and includes Borrego Springs. Check with the visitor center first, and note the displays which explain geology, history, desert plants and wildlife. The desert blooms with colorful annuals in the spring. Also of interest are the fossil-laden Carrizo Badlands, the Butterfield Overland Stagecoach Road, and Seventeen Palms Oasis. | 200 Palm Canyon Dr. | 760/767–5311 | www.anzaborrego.statepark.org | $5 per vehicle | Daily.

Dining

Bernard's. Continental. In a single large room with a wall of windows overlooking the mall, chef-owner Bernard offers casual dining with a unique Alsatian flavor. Try sauerkraut Alsatian style, plus daily regional Alsatian specialties like bouillabaisse and roast leg of lamb. | 503 The Mall | 760/767–5666 | Closed Sun. | $7–$16 | AE, D, DC, MC, V.

La Casa del Zorro. Continental. The dining room has white linens, silver, original Marjorie Reed oil paintings, and a huge fireplace. The menu changes regularly; examples of the type of dishes you'll find are buffalo tenderloin, rack of Colorado lamb, and horseradish-encrusted salmon. Open-air dining on the side deck among fragrant roses is a treat. Kids' menu, early-bird suppers. | 3845 Jackie Pass Rd. | 760/767–5323 | Breakfast also available | $25–$45 | AE, D, DC, MC, V.

La Pavillion at Rams Hill. Contemporary. Colorful original paintings add to the Southwestern style of this spot, known for prime rib and filet mignon. Open-air dining on the deck looks out to mountain views and the adjacent golf course. Sunday brunch. | 1881 Rams Hill Rd. | 760/767–5000 | Closed July, Aug. No supper Sun.–Thurs. | $14–$22 | AE, MC, V.

Lodging

La Casa Del Zorro. Surrounded by the desert beauty of Anza-Borrego Desert State Park, this very luxurious and stylish resort was built in 1937. You can choose to stay in a standard room, suite, or in single or multiple bedroom casitas (or cottages), some of which have fireplaces and private pools. Restaurant, bar, room service. Cable TV. 5 outdoor pools, 6 cottage pools. Beauty salon, hot tubs, massage. Tennis. Exercise equipment. Bicycles.

Kids' programs. Business services. | 3845 Yaqui Pass Rd. | 760/767–5323 or 800/824–1884 | fax 760/767–4782 | www.lacasadelzorro.com | 75 rooms, 2 suites, 19 casitas | $225–$295 rooms, $305–$375 suites, $295–$880 casitas | AE, D, DC, MC, V.

Palm Canyon Resort. From the outside, this luxury hotel looks like an Old West town; once inside however, the property is completely modern. Many of the rooms have ceiling fans and outdoor spaces where you can sit back and take in the surrounding desert. Restaurant. Refrigerators, cable TV. Gym, 2 pools. Hot tub. Laundry facilities. | 221 Palm Canyon Dr. | 760/767–5341 or 800/242–0044 | fax 760/767–4073 | 60 rooms, 1 suite | $85–$120 rooms, $115–$185 suite | AE, D, DC, MC, V.

Palms at Indian Head. Spectacular desert views of the surrounding Anza-Borrego Desert State Park can be had from this small romantic hotel. Large guest rooms are decorated in hand-crafted Southwest lodgepole furniture. When it was called the Old Hoberg Resort, celebrities Marilyn Monroe, Bing Crosby, and Lon Chaney, Jr., among others, vacationed here. Restaurant, complimentary Continental breakfast. Cable TV, no room phones. No smoking. | 2220 Hoberg Rd. | 760/767–7788 or 800/519–2624 | fax 760/767–9717 | thepalms1@juno.com | www.ramonamall.com/thepalms.html | 10 rooms | $159–$190 | D, DC, MC, V.

BREA

MAP 9, I5

(Nearby towns also listed: Fullerton, La Habra, Pomona)

A former oil boom town, tar was one of the first discoveries of early settlers (the word "brea" means tar in Spanish). Brea straddles the Los Angeles-Orange County divide. The quiet suburban city of 32,900 is characterized by a well-maintained commercial area, shopping centers, and its family-oriented community.

Information: Brea Chamber of Commerce | #1 Civic Center Cir., 92821 | 714/529–4938 | breachamber@breachamber.com | www.breachamber.com.

Attractions

Brea Mall. The main attraction in downtown Brea, this ever-growing shopping center has movie theaters and food. | 1065 Brea Mall | 714/990–2732 | Free | Mon.–Sat. 10–7, Sun. 11–7.

Richard M. Nixon Presidential Library and Museum. Next to the former president's birthplace, the museum has exhibits featuring Nixon's career, with an emphasis on foreign policy during his White House tenure. There is a 75-seat amphitheatre, reflecting pool, and First Lady's Rose Garden. | 188001 Yorba Linda Blvd., Yorba Linda | 714/993–3393 | Free | Mon.–Sat. 10–5, Sun. 11–5.

Dining

★ **La Vie en Rose.** French. It's worth a detour even if you're not heading for Brea to eat at this restaurant in a reproduction Norman farmhouse. The food, which includes salmon, lamb, and veal, is stylishly presented; for dessert try the crème brûlée or the Grand Marnier soufflé. | 240 S. State College Blvd. | 714/529–8333 | Reservations essential | No lunch on weekends | $25–$38 | AE, MC, V.

Lodging

Embassy Suites Hotel. Decorated in an Egyptian motif, the hotel boasts a seven-story central atrium with tropical gardens and a reflecting pool stocked with multi-colored koi. Walk to the Brea Mall or head to Disneyland, just 15 minutes away. Restaurant. Pool. Hot tub, sauna. Gym. Laundry services. Business services. | 900 E. Birch St. | 714/990–6000 | fax 714/990–1653 | 229 rooms | $159 | AE, D, DC, MC, V.

Homestead Village. A modern three-story hotel with exterior corridors, this spot caters specifically to longer-staying guests—many of whom head straight to Disneyland, 10 mi away. Gym. Laundry service. Some pets allowed. | 3050 E. Imperial Hwy. | 714/528–2500 | fax 714/528–4900 | 133 rooms | $52–$89 | AE, D, MC, V.

Woodfin Suite Hotel. This all-suite hotel is divided among five two-story buildings. Complimentary shuttle service is provided to any destination within a 5 mi radius and also to Disneyland. All rooms have full kitchens. Complimentary breakfast. Pool. Gym. Laundry service. Business services. Some pets allowed (fee). | 3100 E. Imperial Hwy. | 714/579–3200 | fax 714/996–5984 | 88 suites | $79–$199 suites | AE, D, DC, MC, V.

BRIDGEPORT

MAP 3, H7

(Nearby towns also listed: Bear Valley, Lee Vining, Yosemite National Park)

Thirty minutes from Yosemite National Park's east entrance, historic Bridgeport (pop. 500; elev. 6,465 ft) lies within striking distance of a myriad of alpine lakes and streams, and both forks of the Walker River. Located at the split of U.S. 395 and Rte. 182, Bridgeport sits astride the Toiyabe National Forest, and roughly 20 mi south of Bodie State Historic Park, a well-preserved ghost town which served as backdrop for Clint Eastwood's *Man with No Name*.

Information: Bridgeport Chamber of Commerce | Box 541, 93517 | 760/932–7500.

Attractions

Bodie State Historic Park. Notorious for saloons, brothels, opium dens and gambling halls, Bodie was a bustling mining town with nearly 10,000 residents at its peak. Today, Bodie is a ghost town on the State Historic Park of 1,000 acres. The buildings are not restored, they are simply prevented from decaying any further. The town is often inaccessible during winter months. | Off Rte. 270 | 760/647–6445 | www.ceres.ca.gov/sierradsp/bodie.html | $1 | June–Aug. 9–7. Sept.–May 9–4, weather permitting.

Dining

Bridgeport Inn. American. White linen tables grace the dining room at this clapboard Victorian inn, built in 1877. The prime rib and Alaskan crab legs are complemented by homemade soups, pastas, and a large wine list. Victorian appointed rooms are also available. | 205 Main St. | 760/932–7380 | Closed Dec.–Feb. Breakfast also available | $10–$25 | MC, V.

Lodging

Best Western Ruby Inn. Near the courthouse and in an area known for its prime angling, this motel offers fish cleaning and freezing facilities. Built in the early '60s, two single-story buildings rest in the high country valley of the eastern High Sierra. Cable TV. Some pets allowed. | 333 Main St. | 760/932–7241 | fax 760/932–7531 | 30 rooms | $80–$165 | AE, D, DC, MC, V.

Cain House. This old home has been refurbished as a B&B in an elegant California style with some European touches. Complimentary breakfast. Some refrigerators. Tennis courts. | 340 Main St. | 760/932–7419 | fax 760/932–7419 | 7 rooms | $90–$140 | AE, D, MC, V.

Redwood Motel. In the Sierras just over 1 mi from many lakes and streams, this is a popular spot with anglers. Fish cleaning and freezing facilities are provided at this modest hotel built in the early 1950s. Bodie Ghost Town is 20 mi away; Yosemite is 45 mi east (when the passes are open; otherwise you will have to drive north almost as far as Lake Tahoe). Some pets allowed. | 425 Main St. | 760/932–7060 | 19 rooms | $75–$90 | AE, MC, V.

Silver Maple Inn. Next to the Mono County Courthouse (1880), this inn is centrally located in Bridgeport on attractive wooded grounds with views of the nearby Sierras. Built in the 1940s, the motel provides fish cleaning and freezing facilities and BBQ pits to cook your catch. Cable TV. Some pets allowed. | 310 Main St. | 760/932–7383 | 20 rooms | $70–$90 | AE, D, MC, V.

Walker River Lodge. Right in the center of Bridgeport, this hotel's lobby doubles as an antiques shop. Many of the rooms overlook the East Walker River. Picnic area. Pool, hot tub. Gym. Some pets allowed. | 100 Main St. | 760/932–7021 | fax 760/932–7914 | 36 rooms | $80–$125 | AE, D, DC, MC, V.

BUENA PARK

MAP 9, H6

(Nearby towns also listed: Anaheim, Cerittos, Fullerton, La Habra)

A former agricultural area gone industrial, Buena Park counts on the Movieland Wax Museum and Ripley's Believe It or Not! Museum as its principal draws. It was in Buena Park that Walter Knott and Rudolph Boysen created the boysenberry by grafting together blackberry, red raspberry and loganberry. The hybrid preserves were sold at Knott's roadside stand, which eventually grew into today's other main attraction, Knott's Berry Farm amusement park.

Information: **Buena Park Convention and Visitors Office** | 6601 Beach Blvd., Suite 200, 90621 | 714/562–3560 or 800/541–3953 | tourbp@buenapark.com | www.buena-park.com.

Attractions

★ **Knott's Berry Farm.** Family theme park, focused on the atmosphere of the Old West, including cowboys and indians, gun fights, ghost towns, and stagecoaches. There are six theme areas to the park, and Camp Snoopy is designed especially for younger children. Live entertainment is freqently scheduled and the ongoing theatrical production "Mystery Lodge" dramatizes the history of North American Indians. | 8039 Beach Blvd. | 714/220–5200 | www.knotts.com | $36 | Daily, hours vary.

Movieland Wax Museum. Wax effigies of over 300 film and television celebrities, from John Wayne to Barbra Streisand. The complete scene displays are from productions such as "Wizard of Oz," "Star Trek," and others. | 7711 Beach Blvd. | 714/522–1154 | www.movieland-waxmuseum.com | $13 | 10–7:30 weekdays, 9–8:30 weekends.

Ripley's Believe It or Not! Museum. A Los Angeles landmark, Ripley's museum features humorous, often bizarre, and always interesting items collected from around the world. | 7850 Beach Blvd. | 714/522–7045 | www.movielandwaxmuseum.com | $9 | Weekdays 11–5, weekends 10–6.

Dining

Medieval Times Dinner and Tournament. American. Medieval games, fighting and jousting exploits entertain while standard chicken-and-ribs dinners with plenty of sides are served just as they were in the Middle Ages: with no utensils. | 7662 Beach Blvd. | 714/521–4740 | Reservations essential | Show times vary | $24–$37 | AE, D, MC, V.

Mrs. Knott's Chicken Dinner Restaurant. American. This restaurant at the Knott's Berry Farm park's entrance serves fried chicken, along with tangy cole slaw and Mrs. K's signature chilled cherry-rhubarb compote. The meal price includes three courses. | 8039 Beach Blvd. | 714/220–5080 | Sun. brunch. Breakfast also available | $11 | AE, D, DC, MC, V.

Lodging

Best Western Buena Park Inn. Set smack within the business area, this two-story chain motel is a short walk to Knott's Berry Farm, the Movieland Wax Museum, and Ripley's Believe It or Not Museum. Restaurant, complimentary Continental breakfast. Some refrigerators, cable TV. Pool. Laundry facilities. Business services. | 8580 Stanton Ave. | 714/828–5211 | fax 714/826–3716 | www.bestwestern.com | 63 rooms | $69–$110 | AE, D, DC, MC, V.

Colony Inn. The closest motel to Knott's Berry Farm's south entrance, this chain motel has large guest rooms and modern décor. Complimentary Continental breakfast. Cable TV. Pool, wading pool. Laundry facilities. | 7800 Crescent Ave. | 714/527–2201 or 800/982–6566 | fax 714/826–3826 | 90 rooms | $49–$65 | AE, D, DC, MC, V.

Courtyard by Marriott. Two blocks from Knott's Berry Farm, this chain is highly geared toward business travelers and is in the thick of the commercial district. Walk to area restaurants and attractions. Restaurant, bar. In-room data ports, some microwaves, refrigerators, cable TV. Pool. Exercise equipment. Laundry facilities, laundry service. Business services. | 7621 Beach Blvd. | 714/670–6600 | fax 714/670–0360 | www.marriott.com/courtyard | 145 rooms | $69–$89 | AE, D, DC, MC, V.

Dynasty Suites. As the name implies, large suites make up the offerings at this business-oriented motel chain. Knott's Berry Farm is 5 mi away. Complimentary Continental breakfast. Microwaves, refrigerators, some in-room hot tubs, cable TV. Pool. Hot tubs. Laundry facilities. Business services. | 13530 E. Firestone Blvd., Sante Fe Springs | 562/921–8571 or 800/842–7899 (for reservations) | fax 562/921–2451 | www.dynastysuites.com | 49 rooms, 2 suites | $49 rooms, $69–$110 suites | AE, D, DC, MC, V.

Embassy Suites. Large suites have a separate living room with sofa beds. The free shuttle to Disneyland makes this motel popular with families. Knott's Berry Farm is just one block away. There is a two-hour complimentary open bar. Restaurant, bar, complimentary breakfast. In-room data ports, kitchenettes, microwaves, refrigerators, room service, cable TV. Pool. Hot tub. Video games. Laundry facilities. Business services. | 7762 Beach Blvd. | 714/739–5600 | fax 714/521–9650 | www.embassy-suites.com | 201 suites | $159–$179 suites | AE, D, DC, MC, V.

Fairfield Inn by Marriott. Part of the reliable national chain, this three-story hotel is within the main commercial area of town, 6 mi from the Anaheim Convention Center, 1 mi from Knott's Berry Farm and 6 mi from Disneyland. A shuttle takes guests to Disneyland free of charge. Complimentary Continental breakfast. In-room data ports, some microwaves, refrigerators, cable TV. Pool. Business services. | 7032 Orangethorpe Ave. | 714/523–1488 | www.marriott.com | 134 rooms | $59–$89 | AE, D, DC, MC, V.

Holiday Inn–Conference Center. Two blocks from Knott's Berry Farm, this large chain outpost claims the area's largest outdoor heated pool. For other frolics, the hotel sits within the entertainment zone where you'll find Movieland Wax Museum and the Middle Ages dinner show among others. Free shuttle to Disneyland. 2 restaurants, bar. In-room data ports, room service, cable TV. Pool, wading pool. Hot tub. Exercise equipment. Video games. Laundry facilities. Business services. | 7000 Beach Blvd. | 714/522–7000 | fax 714/522–3230 | www.holiday-inn.com | 245 rooms | $99–$139 | AE, D, DC, MC, V.

InnSuites. This all-suites hotel is 1 ½ blocks from Knott's Berry Farm and provides shuttle service to Disneyland. Some in-room perks include popcorn, juice, and a social hour on the ground floor. Picnic area, complimentary breakfast. Microwaves, refrigerators, cable TV. Pool. Hot tub. Basketball, exercise equipment. Shops, video games, library. Playground, laundry facilities. Business services. | 7555 Beach Blvd. | 714/522–7360 | fax 714/523–2883 | buenapark@innsuites.com | www.innsuites.com | 185 suites | $79–$149 suites | AE, D, DC, MC, V.

Marriott. Equidistant to Los Angeles and Anaheim, this 8-story chain hotel is just 11 mi from Disneyland and 5 mi from Knott's Berry Farm. Restaurant. In-room data ports, refrigerators, cable TV. Pool. Hot tub. Exercise equipment. Business services. | 13111 Sycamore

Dr., Norwalk | 562/863–5555 | fax 562/868–4486 | www.marriott.com | 171 rooms, 27 suites | $69–$124 rooms, $139 suites | AE, D, DC, MC, V.

Radisson Resort. Towering nine stories above Buena Park's commercial district, this chain provides complimentary shuttle service to Disneyland and special discount vacation packages to the theme park. Knott's Berry Farm is within walking distance. Restaurants, bar, room service. Some refrigerators, cable TV. Pool. Hot tub. Tennis. Gym. Video games. Laundry facilities. Business services. Airport shuttle. | 7675 Crescent Ave. | 714/995–1111 or 800/422–4444 | fax 714/828–8590 | www.radisson.com/buenapark | 320 rooms | $89–$179 | AE, D, DC, MC, V.

Red Roof Inn. Choose from standard rooms or larger suites at this chain hotel that sits 1 mi from Knott's Berry Farm and 6 mi from Disneyland. Restaurant, complimentary Continental breakfast. Cable TV. Pool. Hot tub. Business services. Some pets allowed. | 7121 Beach Blvd. | 714/670–9000 or 800/633–8300 | fax 714/522–7280 | www.redroof.com | 127 rooms | $50–$58 | AE, D, DC, MC, V.

Sheraton Cerritos at Towne Center. This large modern chain rises eight levels above the commercial center of town. Disneyland, by car or hotel shuttle, is 10 mi away, and Knott's Berry Farm is 4 mi away. Restaurant, bar. In-room data ports, some minibars, cable TV. Pool. Hot tub, spa. Exercise equipment. Shops. Business services. Some pets allowed. | 12725 Center Court Dr., Cerritos | 562/809–1500 | fax 562/403–2080 | 203 rooms | $79–$139 | AE, D, DC, MC, V.

Super 8. Part of the budget-conscious chain, this two-story motel is next to Knott's Berry Farm and 6 mi from Disneyland. Picnic area, complimentary Continental breakfast. Some

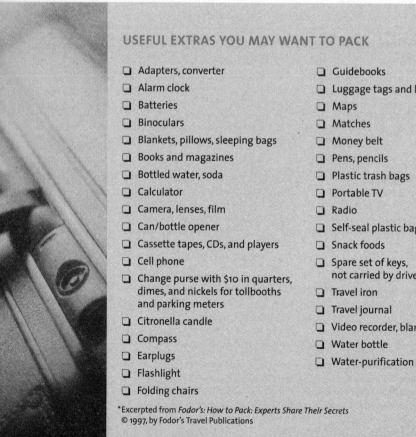

USEFUL EXTRAS YOU MAY WANT TO PACK

- ❏ Adapters, converter
- ❏ Alarm clock
- ❏ Batteries
- ❏ Binoculars
- ❏ Blankets, pillows, sleeping bags
- ❏ Books and magazines
- ❏ Bottled water, soda
- ❏ Calculator
- ❏ Camera, lenses, film
- ❏ Can/bottle opener
- ❏ Cassette tapes, CDs, and players
- ❏ Cell phone
- ❏ Change purse with $10 in quarters, dimes, and nickels for tollbooths and parking meters
- ❏ Citronella candle
- ❏ Compass
- ❏ Earplugs
- ❏ Flashlight
- ❏ Folding chairs
- ❏ Guidebooks
- ❏ Luggage tags and locks
- ❏ Maps
- ❏ Matches
- ❏ Money belt
- ❏ Pens, pencils
- ❏ Plastic trash bags
- ❏ Portable TV
- ❏ Radio
- ❏ Self-seal plastic bags
- ❏ Snack foods
- ❏ Spare set of keys, not carried by driver
- ❏ Travel iron
- ❏ Travel journal
- ❏ Video recorder, blank tapes
- ❏ Water bottle
- ❏ Water-purification tablets

*Excerpted from *Fodor's: How to Pack: Experts Share Their Secrets*
© 1997, by Fodor's Travel Publications

kitchenettes, refrigerators, cable TV. Pool. Hot tub. Laundry facilities. Business services. | 7930 Beach Blvd. | 714/994–6480 | fax 714/994–3874 | www.super8.com | 78 rooms | $58 | AE, D, DC, MC, V.

Travelodge. A chain hotel in the commerical area, this two-story complex provides free shuttles to both Disneyland and Knott's Berry Farm. Picnic area, complimentary Continental breakfast. Many kitchenettes, some microwaves, refrigerators, cable TV. Pool. Hot tub, sauna. Game room. Laundry facilities. Business services. | 7039 Orangethorpe Ave., | 714/521–9220 | fax 714/521–6706 | www.travelodge.com | 100 rooms, 12 suites | $64–$128 | AE, D, DC, MC, V.

BURBANK

MAP 4, I14

(Nearby towns also listed: Glendale, North Hollywood, Universal City, Van Nuys)

Burbank got its big break in the 1920s when First National Pictures (later acquired by Warner Bros.) started its movie studio here. In 1939, The Walt Disney Company followed suit and, in 1951, NBC made its move. While one side of Burbank is a film and TV mecca, the other is but a quiet San Fernando Valley bedroom community.

Information: Burbank Chamber of Commerce | 200 W. Magnolia Blvd., 91502 | 818/846–3111 | fax 818/846–0109 | burbankchamber@worldnet.att.net | www.burbank.acityline.com.

Attractions
Media City Center. This outdoor shopping center has department stores, an IKEA, Virgin Megastore, Chevy's and a restored 1895 carousel. | 201 E. Magnolia Blvd. | 818/566–8617 | Free | Mon.–Fri. 10–9, Sat. 10–8, Sun. 11–7.

Dining
Dalt's Classic American Grill. American. A stylish, vintage 1950s restaurant that covers all menu basics—the cheeseburger is classic. The restaurant is a favorite with kids. Kids' menu. | 3500 W. Olive Ave. | 818/953–7750 | Reservations not accepted | $10–$15 | AE, DC, MC, V.

Lodging
Anabelle Hotel. Sister hotel to the Safari Inn, this sibling is a bit more refined with special touches like complimentary bathrobes and room service. It's just 1 mi from NBC Studios and 3 mi from Warner Bros. Studios. Restaurant, room service. In-room data ports, refrigerators. Pool. Gym. Laundry facilities, laundry service. Airport shuttle. | 2011 W. Olive Ave. | 818/845–7800 or 800/782–4373 | fax 818/845–0054 | 47 rooms, 6 suites | $174 rooms, $190–$215 suites | AE, DC, MC, V.

Hilton–Burbank Airport. Right across from the Burbank-Glendale-Pasadena Airport, this eight-story hotel is geared towards the business traveler. Ask for a room with a mountain view—unless you would prefer to observe the airport activity. Courtesy shuttles will transport you 4 mi to Universal Studios and the Universal Ampitheatre, among other nearby attractions. Restaurant, bar, room service. Some in-room refrigerators, cable TV. 2 pools. Hot tub, sauna, spa. Exercise equipment. Laundry facilities. Business services. Airport shuttle. Some pets allowed. | 2500 Hollywood Way | 818/843–6000 | fax 818/842–9720 | 403 rooms, 83 suites | $159–$179 rooms, $180–$210 suites | AE, D, DC, MC, V.

Safari Inn. The movie *True Romance* was shot here, but you won't find the characteristic leopard print décor from the film. Instead, rooms are clean and plain with a home-away-from-home feel. Movie buffs can head to Universal Studios and Hollywood just 4 mi away. Restaurant, Refrigerators. Pool. Hot tub. Business services. Airport shuttle. | 1911

W. Olive Ave. | 818/845–8586 or 800/782–4373 | fax 818/845–0054 | 55 rooms | $104 | AE, D, DC, MC, V.

BURLINGAME

MAP 6, C7

(Nearby towns also listed: Half Moon Bay, San Mateo, South San Francisco)

Anson Burlingame, U.S. Minister to China under Abraham Lincoln, was visiting California as a guest of banker William C. Ralston in the 1860s when he fell in love with the oak-dotted rolling hills of his host's estate. He promptly chose 1,100 acres, where he would settle after his retirement from his service in China. In an expansive gesture, Ralston not only presented Burlingame with the land, he named the new town site after his guest.

The little colony didn't become a town until after the Burlingame Country Club was built in 1893, with its own railroad station completed in 1894. The first two stores opened for business on Burlingame Square in 1901. After the 1906 earthquake in San Francisco, the little town boomed. Having attained critical mass early in the century, Burlingame hasn't changed much since. It's known mainly for its auto dealerships, a downtown lined with antique stores, and its proximity to San Francisco International Airport.

Information: Burlingame Chamber of Commerce | 290 California Dr., 94010-4117 | 650/344–1735 | BgameCofC@aol.com | www.gtnp.com/burlingame.

Attractions

Burlingame Museum of Pez Memorabilia. Here you'll find the largest known collection of plastic Pez candy dispensers in the world. | 214 California Dr. | 650/347–2301 | www.burlingamepezmuseum.com | Free | Tues.–Sat. 10–6.

Dining

Gulliver's. Continental. This is the typical businessman's working-lunch spot, with an English pub atmosphere. Known for prime rib and seafood. Kids' menu. | 1699 Old Bayshore Hwy. | 650/692–6060 | $25–$35 | AE, D, DC, MC, V.

Kuleto's Trattoria. Italian. It's one of the several Kuleto's restaurants in the Bay Area; watch chefs at work over the oakwood grill. Kids' menu. | 1095 Rollins Rd. | 650/342–4922 | No lunch weekends | $8–$17 | AE, D, DC, MC, V.

Lodging

Hyatt Regency San Francisco Airport. Famous for its 10-story atrium lobby complete with native plants and thundering waterfalls, this large chain hotel is about 5 mi from the airport. Some rooms have views of the bay and hills. Restaurant, bar. Cable TV. Pool. Hot tub, massage, sauna. Business services, airport shuttle. | 1333 Bayshore Hwy. | 650/347–1234 | fax 650/347–5948 | 793 rooms | $150–$385 | AE, D, DC, MC, V.

Sheraton Gateway. This well-maintained chain hotel is a good choice for business travelers. Many rooms have a view of the surrounding waterways and the San Francisco International Airport is a mere 3 mi away. Restaurant, bar. Refrigerators, cable TV. Indoor pool. Exercise equipment. Business services, airport shuttle. | 600 Airport Blvd. | 650/340–8500 | fax 650/343–1546 | 404 rooms | $199–$299 | AE, D, DC, MC, V.

CALABASAS

(Nearby towns also listed: Encino, Malibu, Woodland Hills)

This burgeoning and attractive upper middle-class residential town of 16,600 is well situated for outdoors types. It's close to Malibu, the Santa Monica Mountains Recreation Area, and Topanga State Park.

Information: **Calabasas Chamber of Commerce** | 23564 Calabasas Rd., 91302 | 818/222–5680 | www.sfvalley.org/calabasas.

Attractions

Leonis Adobe. This restored 1844 ranch house was once the home of Miguel Leonis, a prominent and colorful local figure. On the grounds are outbuildings, farm animals, and the Plummer House—relocated from Hollywood and furnished with period costumes and dioramas. | 23537 Calabasas Rd. | 818/222–6511 | Donations accepted | Wed.–Sun. 1–4.

Dining

Gaetano's. Italian. No jeans allowed at this semi-formal spot specializing in dishes from the northern region of Italy. Try the osso buco (veal shanks cooked in olive oil, tomatoes, and white wine) or the seafood pasta. | 20536 Calabasas Rd. | 818/223–9600 | Reservations essential | No lunch weekends, closed Mon. | $13–$26 | AE, MC, V.

Saddle Peak Lodge. Contemporary. If you like fresh, wild game on your plate, this is the place to be. The simulated hunting lodge is cozy and has unusual furniture and decorations. | 419 Cold Canyon Rd. | 818/222–3888 | Reservations essential | No lunch, closed Mon.–Tues. | $20–$50 | AE, MC, V.

Lodging

Country Inn at Calabasas. In the commercial heart of Calabasas, this motel is within walking distance of restaurants. Some rooms have gas fireplaces. Pool. Exercise equipment. Laundry service. Business services. | 23627 Calabasas Rd. | 818/222–5300 | fax 818/591–0870 | 122 rooms | $99 | AE, D, DC, MC, V.

CALEXICO

(Nearby town also listed: El Centro)

This diminutive sister-city of Mexicali, which lies 7 mi over the International border is a port of entry to the US. Standing at sea-level, Calexico (pop. 18,600) is reached by east-west Rte. 98, or the north-south Rte. 111.

Information: **Calexico Chamber of Commerce** | 1100 Imperial Ave., 92232 | 760/357–1166 | www.calexico.com.

ON THE CALENDAR

WED.: *Las Palmas Swap Meet.* Weekly throughout the year vendors from southern California, neighboring states and even Mexico gather to sell their goods. This market, held in an empty lot across the street from the chamber of commerce, is open from 6AM to 3PM. You can find everything from vegetables to clothing to shoelaces. | Calexico Chamber of Commerce, 760/357–1166.

Dining

Yum Yum Chinese. Chinese. This restaurant, up the street from the Quality Inn, is considered to be so good and so authentic that it's frequently full of visitors from out of town and out of state. | 845 Imperial Ave. | 760/357–6000 | $7 | MC, V.

Lodging

Quality Inn. The Mexican border is 8 blocks from this motel. The lounge area has light music on the weekends. Restaurant. Some refrigerators, room service, cable TV. Pool. | 801 Imperial Ave. | 760/357–3271 | fax 760/357–7975 | www.qualityinn.com | 60 rooms | $53–$74 | AE, D, MC, V.

CALISTOGA

MAP 3, C6

(Nearby towns also listed: Geyserville, Rutherford/St. Helena, Yosemite)

Its proximity to an inactive volcano, Mount St. Helena, and the dozens of underground hot springs the volcano helped spawn is what has brought Calistoga fortune. Indians called the area "Colaynomo," or "oven place," and built sweat lodges over the bubbling springs. When forty-niner Sam Brannan saw the mineral-laden geysers in 1859, he recognized the region's potential to lure health-seekers and decided to develop it as a resort. He gathered a group of investors, wined and dined them, and according to legend ended the evening with a toast to his vision of "the Saratoga of California!" The imbibing of too many spirits tangled his tongue, however, and he ended up drinking to "the Calistoga of Sarafornia"—and thus the town was christened.

Wining and dining remain the main pastimes (Calistoga is strategically located in the Napa Valley wine-producing region), along with spa treatments that include mud baths, soaks in mineral pools, massage and such esoteric delights as chakra-balancing and aromatherapy.

Information: Calistoga Chamber of Commerce | 1458 Lincoln Ave. #9, 94515-1449 | 707/942–6333 | execdir@napanet.net | www.napavalley.com/calistoga.

© Corbis

TAKING THE MUD

Whoever decided that a cure for one's ills consists of sitting naked in a tub full of hot dirt was either a genius of holistic health care or a brilliant con artist. In any case, the mud-and-mineral baths of Calistoga are California's Lourdes, a pilgrimage for generations of tourists seeking physical relief (or mental retreat). Certainly, a day spent soaking and steaming at one of the town's many spas is an excellent restorative.

A typical treatment begins with a stint in a mud bath. After disrobing, you step into a tub of thick, black, slightly fetid stuff; you sink into the depths while an attendant shovels more on top of you to make sure you're evenly braised. The "mud" actually is local volcanic ash, a grainy concoction that will make you think you've been submerged in a giant vat of hot oatmeal. Relax. If you don't pass out from the heat, you'll find the experience wonderfully soothing. After 10 min or so, your limp body is dug out and you're escorted to the shower, followed by a steam bath or a soak in a mineral tub. Next, swaddled in a cotton blanket as snugly as a babe-in-arms, you're allowed to melt into a cot while your mind drifts into transcendental territory. Top it off with a massage, and you may not even recognize yourself.

Attractions

Robert Louis Stevenson State Park. In the summer of 1880, the author of *Treasure Island* spent his honeymoon here in the hills northeast of Calistoga, in an abandoned bunkhouse of the Silverado Mine. The experience inspired his short story "The Silverado Squatters." *Treasure Island*'s Spyglass Hill is supposedly modeled after Mount St. Helena. If you hike to its top, you'll get a great view of the valley. | Rte. 29 | 707/942–4575 | Free | Daily 8 AM–dusk.

Old Faithful Geyser of California. One of the few regularly erupting geysers in the world, Old Faithful is fed by an underground river. The water heats to 350° Fahrenheit and erupts about every 40 minutes for one to two minutes on average, spewing 60–150 ft into the air. Earthquake activity can disrupt normal eruption patterns. Self-guided geothermal tours are available. | 1299 Tubbs Ln | 707/942–6463 | fax 707/941–6898 | www.oldfaithfulgeyser.com | $6, special kids' and senior citizens' rates | May–Sept., daily 9–6; Oct.–Apr., daily 9–5.

Petrified Forest. Mount St. Helena erupted 3.4 million years ago, covering this redwood forest with ash that petrified the giant trees. The grounds contain a museum and picnic facilities. | 4100 Petrified Forest Rd. | 707/942–6667 | fax 707/942–0815 | www.petrifiedforest.org | $4, special kids' and senior citizens' rates | Daily 10–5:30.

Sharpsteen Museum and Sam Brannan Cottage. Artifacts, photographs, and dioramas depicting 19th-century Calistoga, and a scale model of Calistoga Hot Springs Resort are on display here. The exhibits were created by Ben Sharpsteen, a Walt Disney studio animator. Next to the museum is one of the resort's 1860s cottages, built by developer Sam Brannan. Exhibits change every three months and include an interactive geothermal display. Tour guides are available. | 1311 Washington St. | 707/942–5911 | Donations accepted | Apr.–Oct., daily 10–4; Nov.–Mar. noon–4.

Wineries. On the northern-most edge of the Napa Valley, Calistoga wineries reap the benefits of the moderate, balmy climate and fertile soil to produce award winning varietals. Most of the area wineries are open for tours and tastings. | Dunaweal Ln | 707/942–6333 | Daily.

★ **Clos Pegase Winery.** Designed by architect Michael Graves, this elegant winery is noted for its extensive collections of art, including many sculptures displayed in unexpected places such as out in the vineyard and in underground tunnels. | 1060 Dunaweal Ln | 707/942–4981 | Free | Daily 10:30–5; tours at 11 and 2.

Sterling Vineyards. A tram takes guests to the hilltop winery, with its Greek-style architecture. There are wine tastings, self-guided tours, and good views of Napa Valley—especially at sunset. The admission price covers the tram ride, a tour, and wine tasting. | 1111 Dunaweal Ln | 707/942–3344 or 800/726–6136 | fax 888/231–5024 | www.sterling.com | $6 | Daily 10:30–4:30.

ON THE CALENDAR

FEB.: *Napa Valley Mustard Festival.* Throughout Calistoga and Napa Valley there are tours, tastings, special restaurant menus, and live entertainment during this celebration, which extends into March. | 707/942–6333.

JUNE–JULY: *Napa County Fair.* At the fair you'll find rides, entertainment, arts and crafts, livestock competitions, and food booths. | 707/942–5111.

JULY: *Silverado Parade.* The city celebrates Independence Day with this classic small-town parade, which sends fire engines, floats, clowns, marching bands, and a beauty queen with her court along Lincoln Avenue downtown. | 707/942–6333.

Dining

Alex's. American. The service is friendly and the cooking is home-style at this restaurant known for prime rib and beef, fresh seafood, and pasta. Kids' menu. | 1437 Lincoln Ave. | 707/942–6868 | Closed mid-Dec. through mid-Jan. and Mondays. No lunch | $12–$20 | AE, D, MC, V.

All Seasons Café. Contemporary. You can order seasonal specialties here, from artichokes to winter squash. The restaurant is also known for house-smoked poultry and fish as well as an outstanding wine list. | 1400 Lincoln Ave. | 707/942–9111 | fax 707/942–9420 | No lunch Wed. | $8–$20 | MC, V.

Bosko's Ristorante. Italian. In an old stone building with wine-country art on the walls, this casual restaurant is known for fresh pasta, seafood, and wood-oven-cooked pizza, and it has a good selection of local wines. | 1250 Lincoln Ave. | 707/942–4101 | fax 707/942–4914 | Reservations essential | $25–$35 | AE, MC, V.

Café Sarafornia. American. This homey café has an earthy decor reminiscent of the 1970s. It serves hearty breakfasts like eggs and home fries, along with pastries, sandwiches, and burgers. | 1413 Lincoln Ave. | 707/942–9111 | fax 707/942–4914 | Reservations not accepted | Breakfast also available | $12–$25 | MC, V.

Calistoga Inn. Contemporary. Grilled meats and fish for dinner, and sandwiches, soups, and salads are served at this microbrewery with a tree-shaded outdoor patio. | 1250 Lincoln Ave. | 707/942–4101 | $20–$35 | AE, MC, V.

★ **Catahoula.** Southern. You can try the spicy seafood gumbo or the pork quarterhouse steak with grits at this casual, contemporary eatery specializing in Cajun cuisine. It's named for the state dog of Louisiana. | 1457 Lincoln Ave. | 707/942–2275 | Closed from early to mid-Jan. No lunch Sun.–Thurs. | $12–$24 | D, MC, V.

Checkers Restaurant. Contemporary. The extensive menu at this chain of diners includes sautéed sea scallops with artichoke hearts, "firecracker" chicken in a spicy Asian sauce, salads, and pastas. | 1414 Lincoln Ave. | 707/942–9300 | www.sterba.com/checkers | $8.95–$12.95 | MC, V.

Hydro Bar and Grill. Contemporary. 20 draft beers are on tap at the lively bar of this red-brick restaurant. Try seared salmon on buckwheat noodles or spinach salad with roasted shallots. | 1403 Lincoln Ave. | 707/942–9777 | fax 707/942–9420 | $5–$15 | MC, V.

Pacifico. Mexican. Tamales, chicken mole, fish tacos, and ceviche are some of the favorite dishes at this casual restaurant. Kids' menu. Sunday brunch. | 1237 Lincoln Ave. | 707/942–4400 | $8–$16 | MC, V.

Wappo Bar Bistro. Contemporary. An eclectic menu of food from around the world, particularly the Mediterranean, makes this the most interesting restaurant in town. On weekend afternoons, you can order tapas at this family-owned restaurant, which has a brick patio with a grapevine arbor for outdoor dining. On Sundays, there's entertainment. Kids' menu. | 1226B Washington St. | 707/942–4712 | Reservations essential on weekends | Closed Tues. | $15–$20 | AE, MC, V.

Lodging

Brannan Cottage Inn. This charming Victorian country cottage is the last remaining structure built by Sam Brannan, the city's original developer. Listed on the National Register of Historic Places, the 1862 inn features five graceful arches in front and a broad wrap-around porch. Rooms are furnished with antique pine and wicker furniture. A full buffet-style breakfast is served in the garden. On weekends, there's a two-night minimum stay. Complimentary breakfast. Refrigerators, cable TV, no room phones. No kids under 12. No smoking. | 109 Wapoo Ave. | 707/942–4200 | www.bbinternet.com/brannan | 8 rooms (5 with shower only) | $90–$170 | MC, V.

Calistoga Country Lodge. Southwestern-style bleached pine furniture and Native American artifacts fill the rooms at this lodge. Although secluded, it's only 1½ mi from downtown. Some rooms have private baths. Complimentary Continental breakfast. No room phones, no TV. Outdoor pool. Outdoor hot tub. | 2883 Foothill Blvd. | 707/942–5555 | fax 707/942–5864 | cowgirl@countrylodge.com | www.countrylodge.com | 6 rooms (4 with private baths) | $155–$175 | AE, MC, V.

Calistoga Inn. This circa-1882 European-style inn is surrounded by flower-filled gardens. This downtown site is shared with a microbrewery. Restaurant, complimentary Continental breakfast. No air-conditioning, no room phones. No smoking. | 1250 Lincoln Ave. | 707/942–4101 | fax 707/942–4914 | calistoga@napabeer.com | www.napabeer.com | 18 rooms (all with shared bath) | $65–$90 | AE, MC, V.

Calistoga Spa Hot Springs. Some of the pretty, motel-style rooms here have kitchenettes (a supermarket is nearby) and coffeemakers, so the spa is popular with families and budget travelers. You can have mineral baths and mud baths here. On weekends, there's a two-day minimum stay. Picnic area. Kitchenettes, cable TV. Two pools, wading pool. Hot tub, massage, spa. Exercise equipment. Business services. | 1006 Washington St. | 707/942–6269 | fax 707/942–4214 | www.napavalley.com/calistoga | 57 rooms (55 with shower only) | $100–$150 | MC, V.

Christopher's Inn. Many of the antique-furnished rooms at this 1910 Georgian country inn have sunken hot tubs, garden access, and fireplaces. One even has an outdoor fireplace and fountain. From here, you can walk to town or bike to the winery. A conference room is available. Complimentary Continental breakfast, room service. Some in-room hot tubs, cable TV, some in-room VCRs, room phones. Business services. No smoking. | 1010 Foothill Blvd. | 707/942–5755 | fax 707/942–6895 | www.christophersinn.com | 22 rooms (5 with shower only) | $155–$395 | AE, MC, V.

Comfort Inn Napa Valley North. This hotel has hot mineral-water pools, and many of its rooms have views of the hills. Complimentary Continental breakfast. In-room data ports, cable TV. Hot tub, sauna, steam room. Business services. | 1865 Lincoln Ave. | 707/942–9400 | fax 707/942–5262 | www.comfortinn.com | 55 rooms | $85–$179 | AE, D, DC, MC, V.

Cottage Grove Inn. These chic individual cottages have skylights, fireplaces, and front porches with wicker rockers. You can borrow CDs and videos from the inn's library. Downtown spas and restaurants are 2 blocks away. Complimentary Continental breakfast. Minibars, refrigerators, in-room hot tubs, in-room VCRs. | 1711 Lincoln Ave. | 707/942–8400 | fax 707/942–2653 | www.cottagegrove.com | 16 rooms | $215–$275 | AE, D, DC, MC, V.

Culver Mansion. You'll have views of the Napa Valley, Palisades, and Mt. St. Helena from the veranda of this Victorian bed and breakfast. Rooms are furnished in period style and feature hand-made mattresses; most have private baths. Complimentary breakfast. Outdoor pool. Outdoor hot tub, sauna. No kids under 16. No smoking. | 1085 Foothill Blvd. | 707/942–4535 or 877/281–3671 | fax 707/942–4557 | jacrose@culvermansion.com | www.culvermansion.com | 6 rooms | $160–$190 | AE, MC, V.

Dr. Wilkinson's Hot Springs. The oldest family-run spa in the Napa Valley, is synonymous with northern California relaxation. Guests can indulge in a series of spa treatments based on the mud baths, mineral baths, and therapeutic massage, and have access to one large indoor warm mineral water whirlpool and two outdoor warm mineral pools. Accommodations are in individual bungalows in quiet garden surroundings or in a handsomely restored Victorian house. The spacious rooms are near sundecks, lounges, and garden patios. Cottages with full kitchens are also available. Some kitchenettes, refrigerators, cable TV. Massage, steam room. Business services. | 1507 Lincoln Ave. | 707/942–4102 | fax 707/942–6110 | www.napavalley.com/drwilkinson.html | 42 rooms | $119–$149 | AE, MC, V.

The Elms. The last of the "Great Eight" original homes in Calistoga, the Elms was built in Second Empire style in the late 19th century. Its garden holds old elm trees and a hammock. The inn's theme rooms include "Nouveau Dream," with a lace-covered, king-size canopy bed; "Palisades Garden," with a mountain view; and "Victorian Fantasy." Six rooms have fireplaces. Complimentary breakfast. Some in-room hot tubs, cable TV, no room phones. No smoking. | 1300 Cedar St. | 707/942–9476 or 800/235–4316 | fax 707/942–9479 | 10370243@compuserve.com | www.theelms.com | 7 rooms (5 with shower only) | $115–$225 | MC, V.

CALISTOGA

INTRO
ATTRACTIONS
DINING
LODGING

Foothill House. At this remodeled circa-1900 bed and breakfast, originally a farmhouse, all the antiques-furnished rooms have fireplaces or wood-burning stoves. Complimentary breakfast. In-room data ports, refrigerators, some in-room hot tubs, cable TV, some in-room VCRs. Laundry facilities. No smoking. | 3037 Foothill Blvd. | 707/942–6933 or 800/942–6933 | fax 707/942–5692 | www.foothillhouse.com | 3 rooms, 1 cottage | $165–$250 rooms, $325 cottage | AE, DC, MC, V.

Golden Haven Hot Springs. Couples can enjoy a mud bath together or refresh themselves with a dip in the mineral pool at this contemporary motel and spa. Seasonal specials and discount coupons are available on the Web site. Some refrigerators, some in-room hot tubs. Outdoor pool. Massage, spa. No kids under 16. | 1713 Lake St. | 707/942–6793 | www.goldenhaven.com | 27 rooms | $75–$165 (2–night minimum weekends, 3–night minimum holidays) | AE, MC, V.

Indian Springs. Three geysers have been pumping out 212° water at this old-time spa for more than a century. You'll find some of the best bargains on mud baths, massages, and facials. A huge mineral-water pool is reserved for hotel guests. The spa is open daily from 9 to 7. Outdoor pool. Massage, spa. | 1712 Lincoln Ave. | 707/942–4913 | fax 707/942–4919 | www.indianspringscalistoga.com | 16 bungalows, 2 houses | $175–$225 bungalows, $315–$500 houses | D, MC, V.

Meadowlark Country House. A 20-acre country estate just north of downtown, this inn breeds and shows horses and lets guests feed them (carrots and apples provided). All rooms have breathtaking views. The main house, built in 1886, has a separate guest wing with flagstone terraces and French doors. The country-style rooms have four-poster beds and English country antiques. Complimentary breakfast. Cable TV, in-room VCRs. Pool. Hot tub, sauna. Business services. Some pets allowed. No smoking. | 601 Petrified Forest Rd. | 707/942–5651 or 800/942–5651 | fax 707/942–5023 | www.meadowlarkinn.com | 7 rooms | $185–$250 | AE, MC, V.

Mount View Hotel. This landmark hotel, built in 1917 and furnished in French country decor, is one of the valley's most elegant. The resort, which is within a block or two of more than 15 restaurants and 20 shops, also rents out three cottages that have private redwood decks and hot tubs. Restaurant, bar, complimentary Continental breakfast. Some in-room hot tubs, cable TV. Pool. Hot tub, spa. Business services. | 1457 Lincoln Ave. | 707/942–6877 or 800/816–6877 | fax 707/942–6904 | 32 rooms, 8 suites, 3 cottages | $145–$190 rooms, $230–$275 suites, $240–$275 cottages | Closed most of Jan. | AE, D, MC, V.

Pink Mansion. Each room at this restored 1875 Victorian home has been decorated with angels, cherubs, and Victorian and Oriental treasures, many of them collected by Alma Simic, the inn's last and longest resident-owner. It was under her care that the mansion was repainted pink, and rechristened, in the 1930s. Most rooms have fireplaces, and there's also a garden on the property. Complimentary breakfast. Some in-room hot tubs, in-room VCRs. Indoor pool. Hot tub. Library. No smoking. | 1415 Foothill Blvd. | 707/942–0558 or 800/238–7465 | fax 707/942–0558 | pink@nappanet.net | www.pinkmansion.com | 6 rooms | $145–$295 | D, MC, V.

Scott Courtyard. All the accommodations here are suites that have a living room, bedroom, bathroom, and private entrance. Picnic area, complimentary breakfast. No room phones. Pool. Business services. No smoking. | 1443 Second St. | 707/942–0948 or 800/942–1515 | fax 707/942–5102 | Jcourtyard@aol.com | www.scottcourtyard.com | 3 rooms (1 with shower only) | $165–$175 | D, AE, MC, V.

Silver Rose Hot Springs and Spa. Vineyards, fed by hot springs, surround this 20-room inn, which has a winery and tasting room on the grounds. Spa facilities and treatments, including mud baths and bodywraps, are reserved for guests, who can choose to stay at either of the inns here: Inn on the Knoll, with its rose gardens, or the newer Inn at the Vineyard, which has a wine-bottle-shaped pool. Complimentary Continental breakfast. In-room data ports, some in-room hot tubs. Two pools. Hot tub, massage, spa. Putting green, two tennis courts. Gym. Business services. No smoking. | 351 Rosedale Rd. | 707/942–9581 or 800/995–9381 | fax 707/942–0841 | silvrose@napanet.net | www.silverrose.com | 20 rooms | $160–$280 | AE, D, MC, V.

Wine Way Inn. Handmade quilts adorn the beds at this traditional inn, and George the Wonderdog entertains new arrivals with tricks. The building dates to 1915. Complimentary breakfast. No room phones. No smoking. | 1019 Foothill Blvd. | 707/942–0680 or 800/572–0679 | fax 707/942–2636 | 6 rooms (4 with shower only) | $90–$165 | AE, D, MC, V.

CAMARILLO

MAP 4, H14

(Nearby towns also listed: Oxnard, Port Hueneme, Simi Valley, Thousand Oaks, Ventura)

Roughly midway between Los Angeles and Santa Barbara, this Ventura County corridor town (pop. 52,300) off U.S. 101 offers proximity to outlet shopping, the City of Oxnard, Port Hueneme, and Point Mugu.

Information: Camarillo Chamber of Commerce | 632 Las Posas Rd., 93010 | 805/484–4383 | www.camarillochamber.org | info@camarillochamber.org.

Attractions

Confederate Air Force/World War II Aviation Museum. At the Camarillo Airport you can join a 90-minute tour through an extensive collection of aviation memorabilia, artifacts and World War II aircraft (some in flying condition), including a Japanese Zero fighter, a Grumman F8F-2 Fighter and a North American B-25 Mitchell Bomber. The history of flight from the Wright brothers to World War II is showcased and depicted in films. | 455 Aviation Dr. (Eubanks airport entrance) | 805/482–0064 | $5 | Tues.–Sun. 10–4.

Dining

California Grill. American. You can get pan braised chicken breast in port wine sauce, lobster tails, mushroom ravioli and dinner salads such as the special Asian turkey salad at this casual eatery located in a shopping plaza. Daily specials including prime rib Mondays ($12.95). Early-bird suppers. Weekday lunch. No dinner Mon.–Wed. | 67 Daily (corner of Las Posas) | 805/987–1922 | $12–$18 | AE, MC, V.

Ottavio's. Italian. Basic, but tasty, meals of pasta, veal, and pizza are served at this restaurant, family-owned and operated since 1969. Early-bird suppers. | 1620 Ventura Blvd. | 805/482–3810 | $8–$17 | AE, D, MC, V.

Lodging

Best Western Camarillo Inn. This terra-cotta-topped motel is 10 mi from the Pacific Ocean and the scenic Rte. 1 that runs beside it. Complimentary Continental breakfast. Cable TV. Pool. Hot tub. Business services. | 295 Daily Dr. | 805/987–4991 | fax 805/388–3679 | www.bestwestern.com | 58 rooms | $69–$79 | AE, D, DC, MC, V.

Country Inn and Suites by Carlson. This hotel is 1 mi from the Camarillo outlets and 8 mi from the ocean. Complimentary breakfast. In-room data ports, some microwaves, some refrigerators, cable TV. Pool. Hot tub, spa. Laundry facilities. Business services. | 1405 Del Norte Rd. | 805/983–7171 or 800/447–3529 | fax 805/983–1838 | 100 rooms | $119 | AE, D, DC, MC, V.

Country Inn Holiday Inn Express. This hotel, 2 mi from Camarillo Mall, has a country decor. It's equidistant to Santa Barbara, 45 mi to the north, and Magic Mountain, 45 mi to the northwest. Complimentary Continental breakfast. In-room data ports, microwaves, refrigerators, cable TV. Outdoor pool. Hot tub. Laundry facilities. Business services. | 4444 Central Ave. | 805/485–3999 or 800/523–5536 | fax 805/485–1820 | 107 rooms, 23 suites | $69 rooms, $79–$149 suites | AE, D, DC, MC, V.

CAMBRIA

(Nearby towns also listed: Atascadero, Morro Bay, Paso Robles, San Simeon)

First it was Slabtown. Then, the city was renamed Rosaville, in an apparent bid to imbue its moniker with slightly more class. Next it became San Simeon, and then Santa Rosa, before residents settled on the name Cambria. But even now, this mining-town-turned-artists'-colony is plagued by identity confusion: residents pronounce it "Cam-bria;" visitors usually dub it "Came-bria."

Settled in the early 1860s, Cambria was the county's second largest town by the 1880s, a center of shipping, mining, dairy farming, logging, and ranching. In 1894, railroad lines were extended from the south to San Luis Obispo, and Cambria lost its dominance as a shipping port.

This hidden jewel has beautiful coastline views, towering pines, and charming restaurants; it's become an isolated, but happy, refuge for about 3,000 city-weary creative types and countless road-weary tourists meandering down Rte. 1.

Information: Cambria Chamber of Commerce | 767 Main St., 93428-2825 | 805/927–3624 | info@www.cambriachamber.org | www.cambriachamber.org.

Dining

Bistro Sole. Contemporary. From the outside, you might mistake this Main Street restaurant for an old home. Inside, its brightly lit rooms are simply and elegantly adorned with white tablecloths, cloth napkins, candles, flowers, and local artists' works (for sale). A covered, heated patio is available for outdoor dining. Try the nut-crusted pork loin. Sunday brunch. | 1980 Main St. | 805/927–0887 | $13–$25 | MC, V.

Brambles Dinner House. Continental. Built in the late 1800s, this restaurant looks like a charming English cottage. Try the prime rib, grilled salmon, or rack of lamb. You can eat outdoors on a two-level heated patio overlooking a creek. Kids' menu. Early-bird suppers. | 4005 Burton Dr. | 805/927–4716 | www.bramblesdinnerhouse.com | Reservations essential | No lunch | $12–$30 | AE, DC, MC, V.

Old Stone Station. Contemporary. The owner and his father built this quaint wooden two-story restaurant by hand. It's known for steaks, prime rib, and seafood grilled or blackened. You can eat outdoors on a covered heated patio. | 713 Main St. | 805/927–4229 | $15–$35 | MC, V.

Robin's. Contemporary. Vegetarian specials, like Thai red curry with tofu, are available every night at this charming restaurant, which has a Spanish-style exterior and gardens and a cozy interior with a fireplace and an alcove. Also offered are dishes like grilled salmon, tandoori prawns, and garlic rosemary chicken. There's a flower-decked heated patio for outdoor dining. | 4095 Burton Dr. | 805/927–5007 | www.robinsrestaurant.com | $10–$15 | MC, V.

Sea Chest Oyster Bar and Restaurant. Seafood. Just a stone's throw away from the beach, this quaint New England cottage-style restaurant serves fresh seafood from local waters and from around the world. It's been popular with tourists and locals for over 20 years. Try the John D's oysters Rockefeller, steamed clams, or *cioppino*. A game room with checkers, chess, cribbage, and cards keeps you occupied while you wait for a table. | 6216 Moonstone Beach Dr. | 805/927–4514 | www.cambria-online.com | Reservations not accepted | No lunch. Closed mid-Sept.–May 1 and Tuesdays | $20–$35 | No credit cards.

Sow's Ear. American. An elegant wooden house with a fireplace is the setting for this restaurant. Try chicken-fried steak or baby-back pork ribs. | 2248 Main St. | 805/927–4865 | No lunch | $15–$30 | D, MC, V.

Tea Cozy. Tea. This English tea room in a century-old Victorian house serves afternoon tea with scones, cake, and double Devon cream. You can also order classic British lunches here, like Cornish pasties or a Ploughman's lunch of sharp cheese, sausage, and crusty bread. There's a gift shop stocked with teas, British grocery items, and antiques. | 4286 Bridge St. | 805/927–8765 | No supper | $8–$30 | MC, V.

Lodging

Best Western Fireside Inn by the Sea. This inn near Hearst Castle overlooks Moonstone beach. It has a cozy lobby and spacious rooms, many with fireplaces. Complimentary Continental breakfast. No air-conditioning. Refrigerators, cable TV. Pool. Hot tub. Business services. | 6700 Moonstone Beach Dr. | 805/927–8661 | fax 805/927–8584 | www.bestwesternfiresideinn.com | 46 rooms | $129–$189 | AE, D, DC, MC, V.

Burton Drive Inn-Sylvia's. Each of the 600-square-ft suites has a unique design at this inn in the heart of old Cambria. Complimentary Continental breakfast. Microwaves, refrigerators, cable TV. | 4022 Burton Dr. | 805/927–5125 | fax 805/927–9637 | www.burtondriveinn.com | 10 suites | $95–$165 | AE, D, DC, MC, V.

Cambria Shores Inn. From the central lawn of this waterside inn, you can enjoy spectacular ocean views, particularly at sunset. Complimentary Continental breakfast. No air-conditioning. Refrigerators, cable TV. Business services. Some pets allowed (fee). | 6276 Moonstone Beach Dr. | 805/927–8644 or 800/433–9179 (in CA) | fax 805/927–4070 | www.cambriashores.com | 24 rooms | $115–$135 | MC, V.

Castle Inn by the Sea. The rooms at this inn, which has access to hiking trails, have ocean views. It's minutes from Hearst Castle, and if you drive 10 mi north, you can observe elephant seals in their natural habitat. Complimentary Continental breakfast. In-room refrigerators, cable TV, room phones. Heated pool. Hot tub. | 6620 Moonstone Beach Dr. | 805/927–8605 | fax 805/927–3179 | www.cambriaonline.com/castleinnbythesea/ | 31 rooms | $75–$135 | AE, D, MC, V.

J. Patrick House Bed and Breakfast Inn. The rustic log home and guest house that make up this B&B sit on beautifully landscaped, tree-shaded grounds in a residential area. Most of the antiques-decorated rooms have fireplaces, and one has a wood-burning stove. Homemade quilts lie on the beds. Complimentary breakfast. No room phones. No smoking. | 2990 Burton Dr. | 805/927–3812 or 800/341–5258 | fax 805/927–6759 | jph@jpatrickhouse.com | www.jpatrickhouse.com | 8 rooms | $125–$180 | AE, D, MC, V.

Mariners Inn. A deck overlooks the ocean at this inn 5 minutes from downtown; it's particularly appreciated in whale-watching season. Restaurant, complimentary Continental breakfast. No air-conditioning; in-room data ports, some refrigerators, some in-room hot tubs, cable TV. Hot tub. Business services. No smoking. | 6180 Moonstone Beach Dr. | 805/927–4624 | fax 805/927–3425 | 29 rooms | $55–$210 | AE, D, MC, V.

Moonstone Inn. Breakfast, which might include maple pecan cereal, is delivered to your door on a silver tray at this inn just 200 ft from the ocean on Cambria's east end. Rooms are furnished in Queen Anne style. Complimentary Continental breakfast. Refrigerators, cable TV, in-room VCRs (and movies). Hot tub. No smoking. | 5860 Moonstone Beach Dr. | 805/927–4815 or 800/821–3764 | fax 805/927–3944 | www.cambriasbest.com/moonstoneinn | 10 rooms | $110–$155 | AE, D, DC, MC, V.

Squibb House. The beautiful garden at this well-preserved 1877 farm house has bloomed since the early 1900s; its rose bushes and plum trees can be enjoyed from a gazebo on the grounds. The inn, in the center of the east village and 7 mi south of Hearst Castle, has period furnishings and a gas stove in each room. Complimentary Continental breakfast. No room phones. No smoking. | 4063 Burton Dr. | 805/927–9600 | fax 805/927–9606 | www.cambria-online.com/thesquibbhouse | 5 rooms | $135–$145 | MC, V.

CAMPBELL

MAP 3, D9

(Nearby towns also listed: Cupertino, Los Gatos, San Jose, Saratoga)

In 1851, Benjamin Campbell came West with his family and bought 160 acres here, planting them with crops. This farm would later become the core of the historic downtown. By 1887, the town had become a fruit shipping center, and later, it prospered from its fruit drying grounds and canneries. Today, the city of 38,000 exists primarily as a bedroom community for the techies of Silicon Valley.

Information: Campbell Chamber of Commerce | 1628 W. Campbell Ave., 95008-1535 | 408/378–6252.

Attractions
Campbell Historical Museum and Ainsley House. You can tour the 1935 Tudor Revival Ainsley House with all of its original furnishings, as well as the Campbell Historical Museum which displays changing exhibits illustrating aspects of Santa Clara Valley life, like the agriculture of prunes and apricots, historical toys, and the evolution of laundry. | 51 N. Central Ave. | 408/866–2119 | fax 408/379–6349 | $6 | Thurs.–Sun., noon–4.

ON THE CALENDAR
OCT.: *Oktoberfest.* German food and beer, live music, and arts and crafts make up this Campbell Historical Museum event. | 408/866–2119.

Dining
King's Head. English. Leek and potato soup, beef Wellington, steak and mushroom pie, and other dishes from across the pond fill the menu in this British pub where nightly entertainment ranges from karaoke to Celtic to medieval to blues. | 201 Orchard City Dr. | 408/871–2499 | $8–$22 | MC, V.

Lodging
Campbell Inn. A roaring fireplace in the lobby welcomes you to this two-story hotel where rooms are pink and some have fireplaces and separate sitting rooms. Complimentary Continental breakfast. In-room data ports, refrigerators, some in-room hot tubs, in-room VCRs. Pool. Lake. Hot tub. Tennis. Bicycles. Laundry service. | 675 East Campbell Ave. | 408/374–4300 or 800/582–4449 | fax 408/379–0695 | sales@campbell-inn.com | www.campbell-inn.com | 95 rooms | $190–$250 | AE, D, DC, MC, V.

CAPITOLA

MAP 3, D9

(Nearby towns also listed: Aptos, Felton, Santa Cruz)

California's oldest seaside resort was founded in 1869 as Camp Capitola, in a river valley between two bluffs on the north side of Monterey Bay. Now a town of 10,000 that's 1½ hours from San Francisco, Capitola's "downtown" might remind you more of a village in the south of France or on Italy's Mediterranean coast. A regional magazine named its beach one of the state's best.

Information: **Capitola Chamber of Commerce** | 716G Capitola Ave., 95010-2777 | 831/475–6522 | www.capitolachamber.com.

Attractions

Capitola Historical Museum. Changing exhibits including photographs, uniforms, and other artifacts illustrate town history in this museum in a 1920 residence. | 401 Capitola Ave. | 831/464–0322 | www.capitolamuseum.org | Free | Fri.–Sun., noon–4.

ON THE CALENDAR

SEPT.: *Capitola Begonia Festival.* A parade of begonias floats down the lagoon in this half-century-old event. | 831/476–3566.

Dining

Ostrich Grill. Casual. Wood-fired steaks, grilled ostrich, pastas, and grilled seafood are served to your booth in this dining room lined with children's art from the local Kim Harden Art School. | 820 Bay Ave. | 831/477–9181 | www.ostrichgrill.com | $16–$30 | AE, MC, V.

Lodging

Inn at Depot Hill. A former Southern Pacific railway depot, this 1901 inn is now a Santa Cruz County hallmark, with individual theme rooms that are decked to the hilt. Luxury is in the rich details: the Paris room has walls upholstered in handmade toile fabric; the Railroad Baron room evokes an 1800s Pullman car with damask and silk curtains and red velvet chairs; the Delft room has a 10-ft coffered ceiling, a feather bed, and a fireplace surrounded by Dutch tiles. Breakfast is often served on the brick courtyard surrounded by plants, or in your own room; a nightly reception includes wine and hors d'oeuvres. Two blocks from a sand beach. Complimentary breakfast. In-room data ports, some in-room hot tubs, cable TV, in-rooms VCRs. No pets. No smoking. | 250 Monterey Ave. | 800/572–2632 | fax 831/462–3697 | lodging@innatdepothill.com | www.inatdepothill.com | 11 rooms, 1 suite | $220–$325 rooms, $325 suite | AE, D, MC, V.

Monarch Cove Inn. Built on the cliffs in 1911, this white-walled bed and breakfast has breath-taking ocean views. Complimentary Continental breakfast. Some in-room hot tubs. No pets. | 620 El Salto Dr. | 831/464–1295 | monarch@infopoint.com | 8 rooms, 8 cottages | $185–$225, $205–$275 | AE, MC, V.

CARLSBAD

MAP 4, J16

(Nearby towns also listed: Escondido, Oceanside, Rancho Santa Fe)

Simply put, the strong suit of this small beach spot in southern Orange County is loca-tion, location, location. Gently sloping hillsides—covered each spring with buttercups—give way to vibrant wetlands at Batiquitos Lagoon, then to a stunning shoreline. This is a major flower-producing area and an antique-hunters paradise.

Information: **Carlsbad Convention and Visitors Bureau** | 400 Carlsbad Blvd., 92018 | 760/434–6093 or 800/227–5722 | www.carlsbad.org/.

Attractions

★ **Legoland.** A 9-ft-tall red Lego brick dinosaur greets you at the entrance to this roller coaster and retail-filled Lego toys theme park, the first one of its kind in the country. The park is designed specifically for children ages 3–12. | 1 Lego Dr. | 760/918–5346 | www.legolandca.com | $34 | Daily 10–5.

South Carlsbad State Beach. Joggers and skaters flock to the smooth, six-block prome-nade behind the seawall on the beach. On warm summer nights, couples like to stroll here, admiring the gorgeous sundowns. There's also a sidewalk on the bluff above. This beach is narrow like City Beach, but it's noted for surfing and swimming. Parking is free along the street, or you can use an ample pay lot at the beach's south end. A wheelchair-accessible rest room is available, but there are no showers or concessions. | 760/438–3143 | $4 per vehicle | 24 hours daily.

ON THE CALENDAR

FEB.: *Andersen Consulting Match Play Championships.* The La Costa Resort and Spa hosts this annual PGA event on one of its two championship 18-hole courses. | 760/ 931–8400.

MAR. AND APR.: *Flower Fields at Carlsbad Ranch.* Spring's arrival is celebrated in the blooming ranunculus in yellow, white, salmon, pink, red and gold. | 760/431–0352.

MAY AND NOV.: *Carlsbad Village Fair.* The first Sunday in both November and May brings nearly 900 vendors and 100,000 people to town to meander through the booths and shops in the old village area. There is food, music and even a rock climbing wall. | 760/931–8400.

Dining

Bellefleur Winery and Restaurant. Contemporary. Tuscan-inspired archways and photographs of vineyards complement white table cloths at this stylish spot that has occasional live jazz. Pan-seared white sea bass with olive tapenade and oak-grilled rack of lamb are favorites. | 5610 Paseo Del Norte | 760/603–1919 | fax 760/603–8465 | www.bellefleur.com | $15–$23 | AE, MC, V.

Neiman's. Steak. Tables line the walls in a carousel-like manner in this round 1922 Victorian dining room. Views of downtown and the beach fill picture windows and live entertainment, from blues to salsa, is in the air. Filet bearnaise and prime rib are on the menu. | 300 Carlsbad Village Dr. | 760/729–4131 | fax 760/729–6131 | $10–$20 | AE, D, DC, MC, V.

Spirito's. Italian. This cozy restaurant serves fresh pasta and pizzas with interesting toppings. Outdoor seating. No smoking. | 300 Carlsbad Village Dr. | 760/720–1132 | $6–$13 | MC, V.

Tuscany. Italian. Three dining areas with frescoed walls and names like the "Renaissance room" complement the Northern Italian, mainly Tuscan, cuisine. Try *spezzatino di pollo e falsiccia* (chicken and sausage with capers and portobella mushrooms) or *vitello di Riviera* (the house-specialty veal). No smoking. | 6981 El Camino Real | 760/929–8111 | fax 760/ 929–0421 | No lunch weekends | $12–$24 | AE, DC, MC, V.

Vigilucci's Trattoria. Italian. Unpretentious and casual, this place is reminiscent of a Milanese trattoria, and it's a comfortable choice for families. Try *osso bucco* (veal) or *cippino* (mixed seafood on a bed of linguini). You can eat outdoors on a covered patio. Kids' menu. No smoking. | 505 First St., Encinitas | 760/942–7332 | $10–$25 | AE, D, DC, MC, V.

Lodging

Beachwalk Villas. These nine spacious beachfront units with simple light wood furnishings have full kitchens, and up to three bedrooms. In-room data ports, kitchenettes, cable TV, in-room VCRs. Pool. Laundry facilities. No pets. | 3100 Ocean St. | 760/720–1400 | bchwlk@beachwalkvillas.com | www.beachwalkvillas.com | 9 rooms | $120–$220 | AE, MC, V.

Carlsbad Inn Beach Resort. Set on a wide landscaped lawn in the center of town, this picturesque European-style inn is convenient to the beach. Some rooms have fireplaces. Picnic area. Some kitchenettes, cable TV, in-room VCRs (and movies). Pool. Hot tubs. Exercise equipment. Kids' programs. Laundry facilities. Business services. | 3075 Carlsbad Blvd. | 760/ 434–7020 or 800/235–3939 | fax 760/729–4853 | www.carlsbadinn.com | 62 rooms | $178–$250 | AE, D, DC, MC, V.

★ **Four Seasons Aviara.** This luxury hotel sits on 30 acres of coastline in a residential area, 5 mi from Legoland. Its rooms, with linen drapes and custom-designed bedding, have private balconies or landscaped terraces with views of the hotel's golf course, the lagoon or the mountains. Restaurants, bar (with entertainment), room service. In-room data ports, minibars, cable TV. Pool, wading pool. Beauty salon, hot tub, massage. Driving range, 18-hole golf course, putting green, tennis. Gym. Business services, airport shuttle. Some pets allowed. | 7100 Four Seasons Pt | 760/931–6672 or 800/332–3442 (for reservations) | fax 760/931–0390 | www.fourseasons.com | 276 rooms, 44 suites | $375–$485, $595–$645, $825–$4,100 suites | AE, DC, MC, V.

Holiday Inn Carlsbad by the Sea. Each spacious room has a private balcony at this seaside hotel. From I–5 take the Palomar Airport exit. Restaurant, bar (with entertainment). Refrigerators. Cable TV. Pool. Hot tub. Laundry facilities. Business services, airport shuttle. | 850 Palomar Airport Rd. | 760/438–7880 | fax 760/438–1015 | www.holiday-inn.com | 145 rooms | $129–$149 | AE, D, DC, MC, V.

Inns of America. Some rooms have ocean views at this hotel within seven blocks of Carlsbad beach and accessible from the Poinsettia exit off of I–5. Restaurant, complimentary Continental breakfast. Cable TV. Pool. Laundry facilities. Business services. Some pets allowed. | 751 Raintree Dr. | 760/931–1185 | fax 760/931–0970 | www.innsofamerica.com | 126 rooms | $77–$82 | AE, MC, V.

La Costa Resort and Spa. This 400-acre luxury resort has two PGA championship golf courses, a 21-court racquet club, and an award-winning spa. Restaurants, bar, room service. In-room data ports, minibars, cable TV. Two pools. Hot tub, spa. Gym. Driving range, two golf courses, putting green, driving range, tennis. Bicycles. Kids' programs. Business services, airport shuttle. | 2100 Costa Del Mar Rd. | 760/438–9111 or 800/854–5000 | fax 760/931–7585 | www.lacosta.com | 470 rooms, 75 suites, 5 rental homes | $325 rooms; $550–$2,400 suites; $1,400–$1,950 homes | AE, D, DC, MC, V.

Ocean Palms Beach Resort. This 1940s hotel offers beachfront studios and suites. It's in the west part of town close to 30 restaurants and 20 antique stores. Picnic area. Kitchenettes, cable TV. Pool. Hot tub. Playground. Laundry facilities. | 2950 Ocean St. | 760/729–2493 or 888/802–3224 (for reservations) | fax 760/729–0579 | www.ocean-palms.com | 56 rooms | $80–$195 suites; $80–$95 studios | AE, D, DC, MC, V.

Pelican Cove Inn. Two blocks from the beach and surrounded by palm trees, this two-story inn's rooms have gas fireplaces and feather beds. Complimentary breakfast. No air-conditioning, cable TV, some room phones. No smoking. | 320 Walnut Ave. | 888/735–2683 | pelicancoveinn@sandcastleweb.com | www.pelican-cove.com | 8 rooms | $100–$180 | AE, MC, V.

Ramada Suites. Each unit has a fully-equipped kitchen at this hotel ¼ mi from the beach and 1.5 mi from Legoland. On Wednesdays, you're offered a complimentary barbecue dinner. Complimentary Continental breakfast. In-room data ports, kitchenettes, refrigerators, cable TV. Pool. Hot tub. Laundry facilities. No smoking. | 751 Macadamia Dr. | 760/438–2285 | fax 760/438–4547 | www.ramada.com | 121 suites | $99–$139 suites | AE, D, DC, MC, V.

Surf Motel. This two-story roadside motel is across the street from the beach. Restaurant, complimentary Continental breakfast. Some kitchenettes, refrigerators, some in-room hot tubs, cable TV. Pool. | 3136 Carlsbad Blvd. | 760/729–7961, 800/523–9170 | fax 760/434–6642 | surfm@dknhospitality.com | www.surfmotelcarlsbad.com | 28 rooms | $80–$140 | AE, D, DC, MC, V.

CARMEL

MAP 4, D10

(Nearby towns also listed: Big Sur, Carmel Valley, Monterey, Pacific Grove, Pebble Beach)

Carmel became an artists' colony after the 1906 San Francisco earthquake, when writers, artists, and musicians migrated here seeking the serenity of this coastal town bordered by redwood groves and the crashing sea. As more people came, Carmel got a little citified—so the artists fought back, battling paved streets, street lights, and other annoying intrusions. Many strange regulations remain on the books, including an ordinance against wearing high-heeled shoes.

Carmel natives can be a bit curmudgeonly toward tourists, who arrive in droves each summer. There are no street addresses on the buildings, perhaps a vain attempt to foil outsiders. It's an expensive city, too, with some of the coast's priciest real estate – all of which tends to keep the riffraff at the border.

Still, Carmel, which encompasses just one square mi, is irresistible. It has a delightful small-town quality yet an undeniably commercial cachet. The downtown streets are lined with galleries and restaurants, and the town will probably never get over the fact that actor Clint Eastwood was once mayor.

Information: **Carmel Business Association** | San Carlos St. between 5th and 6th Sts., PO Box 4444, 93921 | 831/624–2522 | www.carmelcalifornia.org.

Attractions
The Barnyard. "Carmel's shopping village" is an outdoor shopping venue surrounded by beautiful gardens. All of the 50 shops and restaurants are housed in a beautiful collection of barns. | Carmel Rancho Blvd. | 831/624–8886 | Free | Mon.–Sat. 10–5:30, Sun. noon–4; restaurants open until 8:30 daily.

★ **Mission San Carlos Borromeo Del Rio Carmelo.** Father Junipero Serra established this mission, also called Carmel Mission, at Monterey in 1770 and moved it to its present site the following year. It was Father Serra's residence and headquarters until his death in 1784. He is buried beneath the church floor in front of the altar. Relics of the mission's early days and some of Father Serra's books and documents are displayed. A fiesta is usually held the last Sunday in September. | 3080 Rio Rd. | 831/624–3600 | $2 | Daily.

Pacific Repertory Theatre. In the historic Golden Bough Cinema building, you can see plays, improvisation, kids' programs, music, and poetry at this theater. As show times vary, it is best to call for specific information. | Monte Verde between 8th & 9th | 831/622–0100 | fax 831/622–0703 | www.pacrep.org | Closed Jan.

★ **Point Lobos State Reserve.** Covering 1,225 acres of land and water along the rugged seacoast, the reserve is traversed by 10 mi of trails. Wildlife from deer and rabbits to harbor seals, gray whales, and California sea lions can be seen. Many sea birds, including cormorants and pelicans, nest along the coast. You'll also find coastal plants like Monterey cypress and Monterey pine. Nature walks. Diving by permit only. Some pets not allowed. Maps available at the entrance station. | Rte. 1, Box 62 | 831/624–4909 | $7 per vehicle | Daily dawn–dusk.

Rancho Cañada Golf Club. The two 18-hole par 71 golf courses here are open to the public. Both courses require you to traverse the Carmel River many times. With mature and deceptively long fairways, generous bunkers and many water obstacles, these courses will challenge even the best of them. | 4860 Carmel Valley Rd. | 831/624–0111 | $65–$80 | Daily.

Robinson Jeffers Tor House. The late poet and playwright Robinson Jeffers built this Tudor-style cottage on Carmel Bay for his wife and himself in 1911. The house, modeled after a barn, has a 40 ft high garret with thick granite walls. | 26304 Ocean View Ave. | 831/624–1813 | fax 831/624–3696 | www.torhouse.org | $7 | Closed Mon.-Thurs.

Seventeen-Mile Drive. This scenic route from Pacific Grove to Carmel is the highlight of any trip to this area. You can bike the route during daylight hours when no major sporting event is scheduled (there are six golf courses on the route), though you must sign a release form. The admission fee includes a map listing 21 points of interest. | Gatehouse at Hwy. 1 | 831/625–8426 or 831/624–6669 | fax 831/625–8411 | $8 | Daily dawn–dusk.

JULY: *Carmel Bach Festival.* Vocal and instrumental performances of Bach's works take place at venues throughout the city all month during this festival, held every year since 1935. | 831/624–2046 | www.bachfestival.org.

Dining

Anton and Michel's. Continental. This sophisticated restaurant looks like a bit of Provence transported to the Monterey peninsula. You can order rack of lamb or ahi tuna or one of several other seafood dishes, but should save room for one of the flaming desserts. Courtyard seating is available in summer. No smoking. | Mission St. at 7th Ave. | 831/624–2406 | www.carmelsbest.com | $17–$30 | AE, D, DC, MC, V.

Britannian Arms. American. A favorite among locals, this authentic British pub has a daily happy hour from 4–7 and serves classic pub food like fish and chips. Outdoor dining on a garden patio. Kids' menu. No smoking. | Dolores St. | 831/625–6765 | $9–$20 | AE, D, DC, MC, V.

Caffe Napoli. Italian. Grapevine lights twinkle on the ceiling at this cozy, family-owned café. Try cannelloni, the grilled artichoke or roasted garlic appetizers, and tiramisu. No smoking. | Ocean Ave. and Lincoln St. | 831/625–4033 | www.littlenapoli.com | $7–$16 | MC, V.

★ **Casanova.** Eclectic. Exposed beams, stucco walls and simple chandeliers set the stage for Provençale and Northern Italian dishes like pan-seared salmon with citrus sauce, ratatouille and potato gnocchi, and grilled veal with sautéed morel mushrooms and potatoes au gratin. | 5th Ave. between San Carlos and Mission Sts. | 831/625–0501 | fax 831/625–9799 | www.casanovarestaurant.com | Reservations essential | $16–$28 | AE, MC, V.

The Cottage. Casual. This country-cozy restaurant downtown serves soups, salads, and sandwiches. Kids' menu. No smoking. | Lincoln St. at 7th | 831/625–6260 | Breakfast also available. No supper Sun.–Wed. | $10–$25 | MC, V.

Flying Fish Grill. Pan-Asian. This small family-owned restaurant is a homey and romantic spot. Favorite entrées include peppered ahi tuna and almond-crusted sea bass. | Mission St. at the Carmel Plaza | 831/625–1962 | Closed Tues. No lunch | $14–$22 | AE, D, DC, MC, V.

French Poodle. French. Popular dishes at this elegant restaurant include filet mignon and fresh crab legs served with hot champagne sauce. No smoking. | Junipero Ave. at 5th Ave. | 831/624–8643 | Closed Sun. No lunch | $40–$57 | AE, DC, MC, V.

General Store. American. A medieval European village is evoked in the group of historic buildings that make up this landmark restaurant. The central fireplace was once used to forge metal as part of Carmel's original blacksmith shop; its dining area was the former general store. This dog-friendly restaurant is known for rotisserie meats, duck, and huge steaks. For dessert, you'll probably be tempted by the chocolate chip cookie served warm in a skillet with vanilla ice cream and chocolate sauce. Open-air dining on a large brick patio with a garden. Kids' menu. | 5th Ave. at Junipero Ave. | 831/624–2233 | $11–$28 | AE, D, DC, MC, V.

Grill on Ocean Avenue. Continental. A long wooden bar stretches across the front of this quaint and comfortable restaurant with adobe arches. Popular dishes include filet mignon, salmon, and rack of lamb. | Ocean Ave. between Dolores and Lincoln | 831/624–2569 | $18–$40 | AE, D, DC, MC, V.

La Bohême. French. The three-course, prix fixe dinners change nightly at this romantic Parisian restaurant. Past menu items include *tournedos forestière* (beef, forest mushrooms, bacon, and wine sauce) and *escalope de veau aux poireaux* (range veal with leeks and cream sauce). There's only one entrée each night, so plan ahead. Call for a schedule, or check the restaurant's web site for menus for upcoming months. | Dolores St. at 7th Ave. | 831/624–7500 | www.laboheme.com | No lunch | $26 | MC, V.

Le Coq d'Or. Continental. Try the filet mignon, sirloin of lamb, or scampi Provençale at this homey restaurant. There's a heated outdoor dining area. Kids' menu. No smoking. | Mission St. between 4th and 5th Sts. | 831/626–9319 | www.lecoqdor.com | No lunch | $18–$25 | AE, MC, V.

Little Napoli. Italian. This family-owned restaurant prides itself on its friendly atmosphere and dishes cooked from family recipes. No smoking. | Dolores St. near Ocean Ave. | 831/626–6335 | $15–$20 | MC, V.

Lugano Swiss Bistro. Swiss. Swiss artwork on the walls sets the stage for an Alpine culinary adventure. Try the farmer's sausage platter or thin-sliced veal with wild mushrooms. Italian specialties are also served. There's a heated patio for outdoor dining. Some pets are allowed on the patio. Entertainment on Fridays. | 3670 The Barnyard | 831/626–3779 | Reservations essential on weekends | $15–$17 | AE, DC, MC, V.

Mission Ranch. American. Great views of the surrounding meadows and the ocean can be had from this restaurant, a popular meeting place for locals. The building dates to the mid-1800s. There's a heated patio for outdoor dining. Kids' menu. Sunday brunch. No smoking. | 26270 Dolores St. | 831/625–9040 | No lunch weekdays | $10–$29 | DC, MC, V.

Mondo's. Italian. Copper pots hang from the ceiling in this tile-floored dining room, anchored by a stone fireplace. Pastas and pizzas with toppings like pesto, goat cheese, prosciutto, and vegetables fill the menu. | Dolores St. between Ocean and 7th Aves. | 831/624–8977 | fax 831/624–4102 | www.mondos.com | $9–$17 | AE, MC, V.

Pacific's Edge. Contemporary. There is a Pacific Ocean view from the elegant dining room at this restaurant. Chefs use fresh local ingredients in preparing health-conscious meals that can include Colorado rack of lamb, Pacific salmon, and lobster. Kids' menu. Sunday brunch. No smoking. | 120 Highland Dr. | 831/622–5445 | $40–$65 | AE, D, DC, MC, V.

Patisserie Boissiere. French. This quiet and intimate candlelit restaurant is known for prawn pasta, lamb dishes, and salmon. | Mission St. between Ocean and 7th Aves | 831/624–5008 | No supper Mon.& Tues. | $9–$17 | AE, MC, V.

Raffaello Restaurant. Northern Italian. The beautiful candlelit Florentine dining room seats just about 12 people. Homemade pastas are a must here, as well as any of the dishes made with wine sauces. No smoking. | Mission St. between Ocean & 7th Aves | 831/624–1541 | No lunch | $18–$28 | AE, DC, MC, V.

Rio Grill. Contemporary. This restaurant has an upbeat, contemporary look and a creative menu with a western flair. It's known for oakwood-grilled chicken, fish, and beef. The wine list is exceptional. Outdoor patio dining is available for lunch only. No smoking. | 101 Crossroads Blvd. | 831/625–5436 | www.riogrill.com | $7–$24 | AE, MC, V.

Robata Restaurant. Japanese. Monterey Bay salmon, sukiyaki, and sea bass are a few of the specialties at this cozy spot on the lower level of a popular shopping complex. | 3658 The Barnyard | 831/624–2643 | Reservations essential for parties of 5 or more | No lunch | $12–$20 | AE, DC, MC, V.

★ **Robert's Bistro.** French. The rustic beams, intimate booth seating, low lights, and wood-burning fireplaces create a cozy, romantic atmosphere here. | 217 Crossroads Blvd. | 831/624–9626 | No lunch | $21–$34 | AE, D, DC, MC, V.

Rocky Point. Steak/Seafood. The only oceanfront restaurant in Monterey County, this casual spot is known for its breathtaking views of the coastline. A large heated terrace seats 100. No smoking. | Rte. 1, 10 mi south of Carmel | 831/624–2933 | Breakfast also available | $20–$32 | AE, D, MC, V.

Sans Souci. French. The atmosphere at this candlelit restaurant, which is known for its seafood dishes, is cozy, warm, and quiet. Try grilled salmon or oven-roasted Chilean sea bass. Kids' menu. | Lincoln St. between 5th & 6th Sts. | 831/624–6220 | Closed Wed. No lunch | $20–$30 | AE, MC, V.

Thunderbird Bookshop Café. Casual. This restaurant is in a bookstore, and it overlooks a beautiful garden. Menu items include soup and salad, turkey pot pie, and macaroni. You can eat outdoors on a covered patio. | 3600 The Barnyard | 831/624–1803 | $6–$9 | AE, D, DC, MC, V.

Toots Lagoon. American. Informal, relaxed, and old-fashioned, this eatery has polished mahogany floors and a sweeping bar with comfortable seating. It's known for comfort food—the menu includes steak, baby back ribs, fresh seafood, pasta, and pizzas. | Dolores St.&7th Ave. | 831/625–1915 | $10–$30 | AE, D, DC, MC, V.

Lodging

Adobe Inn. The beautifully furnished, spacious rooms at this inn a block from Ocean Avenue have fireplaces and private decks. Some have ocean views. Complimentary Continental breakfast. In-room data ports, cable TV, in-room VCRs. Pool. Sauna. Business services. | Dolores St. at 8th Ave. | 831/624–3933 or 800/388–3933 | fax 831/624–8636 | www.adobeinn.com | 19 rooms, 1 suite | $175–$298, $315–$400 suites | AE, MC, V.

Best Western Carmel Bay View Inn. Rooms at this cozy and friendly inn in the heart of downtown have fireplaces, and some have spectacular ocean views. Complimentary Continental breakfast. Some refrigerators, cable TV, some in-room VCRs. Pool. Business services. No smoking. | Junipero Ave. between 5th and 6th Avenues | 831/624–1831 | fax 831/625–2336 | www.bestwestern.com/carmelbayviewinn | 58 rooms, 6 suites | $159–$269, $169–$249 suites | AE, D, DC, MC, V.

Best Western Town House Lodge. In the heart of Carmel, this tidy chain motel is within 2 blocks of shops and restaurants. In-room data ports, cable TV. Pool. | San Carlos St. at 5th Ave. | 831/624–1261 | fax 831/625–6783 | 28 rooms | $95–$175 | www.bestwestern.com/carmelstownhouselodge | AE, D, DC, MC, V.

Briarwood Inn. All the rooms in this charming country inn in downtown Carmel have fireplaces. Art galleries, shopping, restaurants, and golf are nearby. Complimentary Continental breakfast. Refrigerators, cable TV, in-room VCRs (and movies). No smoking. | San Carlos St. at 4th Ave. | 831/626–9056 or 800/999–8788 | fax 831/626–8900 | 12 rooms, 1 suite | $95–$250, $350–$500 suite | AE, MC, V.

Candle Light Inn. Centrally located, this friendly inn features large rooms with sitting areas. Some rooms have platform hot tubs facing the fireplace. The building is surrounded by beautiful gardens. Complimentary Continental breakfast. Some kitchenettes, refrigerators, some in-room hot tubs, cable TV. Spa. Business services. | San Carlos St. between 4th and 5th Aves | 831/624–6451 or 800/433–4732 | fax 831/624– 6732 | concierge@carmelinns.com | www.innsbythesea.com | 20 rooms | $169–$219 | AE, D, MC, V.

Carmel Garden Court Inn. This small inn in the heart of Carmel has a country manor feel, with wicker furniture, flowers, and fireplaces. Breakfast is served on a private, flower-covered patio. Complimentary Continental breakfast. Refrigerators, cable TV, in-room VCRs. Business services. No smoking. | 4th Ave. and Torress St. | 831/624–6926 | fax 831/624–4935 | 10 rooms, 7 suites | $150–$170, $190–245 suites | AE, MC, V.

Carmel Mission Inn. This modern inn on the edge of Carmel Valley has a lushly landscaped pool and hot tub area and an indoor pool. Some rooms have views of the valley. Restaurant, bar. In-room data ports, refrigerators, cable TV. Pool. Hot tubs. Laundry facilities. Business services. Some pets allowed (fee). No smoking. | 3665 Rio Rd. | 831/624–1841 or 800/348–9090 | fax 831/624–8684 | 163 rooms, 2 suites | $149–$189; $189–$359 suites | AE, D, DC, MC, V.

Carmel Resort Inn. Each of the 31 cozy cottages here, complete with popcorn maker, is nestled in pines and surrounded by colorful gardens. There's a pond and a waterfall on the grounds. Complimentary Continental breakfast. Microwaves, refrigerators, cable TV. Hot tub, sauna. No smoking. | Carpenter St.&1st Ave. | 831/624–3113 or 800/454–3700 | fax 831/624–5456 | 31 cottages | $79–$275 cottages | AE, D, DC, MC, V.

Carmel River Inn. Trees and gardens surround this quiet inn, 1 mi from downtown, where rooms have wooden bed frames, and many have fireplaces. Some kitchenettes, cable TV, room phones. Pool. | 0.5 mi off Carpenter St. exit from Hwy 1 | 831/624–1575 or 800/882–8142 | fax 831/624–0290 | carmelriverinn@hotmail.com | www.carmelriverinn.com | 19 rooms, 24 cottages | $110–$140, $140–$170 | MC, V.

Carmel Sands Lodge. The sunny rooms at this two-story downtown motel have light oak furniture and pastel upholstery. Pool. Laundry facilities. No pets. | San Carlos St. at 5th Ave. | 831/624–1255 or 800/252–1255 | innkeeper@carmelsandslodge.com | www.carmel-sandslodge.com | 38 rooms | $90–$180 | AE, D, DC, MC, V.

Carmel Tradewinds Inn. All rooms at this two-story hotel have a pool or ocean view, high ceilings with exposed beams, and many have fireplaces and balconies. Complimentary Continental breakfast. In-room data ports, some minibars, some in-room hot tubs, cable TV, room phones. Pool. | Mission St. at 3rd Ave. | 831/624–2776 or 800/624–6665 | fax 831/624–0634 | info@carmeltradewindsinn.com | www.carmeltradewindsinn.com | 26 rooms, 2 suites | $100–$150 | AE, V.

Carriage House. This brown-shingled inn has spacious, raftered rooms with down comforters on the beds and gas-burning fireplaces. Complimentary Continental breakfast. Refrigerators, some in-room hot tubs, cable TV, in-room VCRs. Business services. | Junipero Ave. between 7th and 8th Aves | 831/625–2585 or 800/433–4732 | fax 831/624–2967 | www.webdzine.com/inns | 13 rooms | $279–$339 | AE, D, MC, V.

Coachman's Inn. Inside the Tudor-style building, afternoon sherry hour and cozy fireplaces at this downtown inn are reminiscent of old England. Complimentary Continental breakfast. Some in-room hot tubs, cable TV, room phones. | San Carlos St. between 7th and 8th Aves, | 831/624–6421, 800/336–6421 | info@coachmansinn.com | www.coachmansinn.com | 30 rooms | $100–$160 | AE, MC, V.

★ **Cobblestone Inn.** Stones from the Carmel River completely cover the lower level of this inn, and they surround the fireplace in each guest room. Local artisans' works are featured throughout. Beautiful gardens surround the building, and each window is decked with flowers. Complimentary breakfast. Refrigerators, cable TV. Business services. | Junipero St. between 7th and 8th Aves | 831/625–5222 or 800/833–8836 | fax 831/625–0478 | www.foursisters.com | 24 rooms | $105–$240 | AE, DC, MC, V.

Colonial Terrace Inn. Flower gardens join the seven buildings of this 1925 inn with plush, floral rooms, some of which have fireplaces and ocean views. Complimentary Continental breakfast. Some kitchenettes, refrigerators, some in-room hot tubs. No pets. | San Antonio St. between 12th and 13th Aves. | 831/624–2741 or 800/345–8220 | fax 831/626–2715 | www.colonialterraceinn.com | 25 rooms | $110–$200 | AE, MC, V.

★ **Cypress Inn.** When Doris Day became part owner of this inn in 1988, she added her own touches, such as posters from her many movies and photo albums of her favorite canines. The 1929 inn, a block south of Main Street, has a courtyard with fireplaces and serves afternoon tea. Guests are greeted with complimentary sherry, fresh flowers, and a fruit basket. Bar, complimentary Continental breakfast. Some refrigerators, cable TV. Business services. Some pets allowed. | Lincoln St. and 7th Ave. | 831/624–3871 or 800/443–7443 | fax 831/624–8216 | info@cypress-inn.com | www.cypress-inn.com | 34 rooms, 1 suite | $125–$350, $350 suite | AE, D, MC, V.

Dolphin Inn. Many of the rooms at this 1940s inn, in the heart of the village, have gas-burning fireplaces and king-size beds. The balconies are laced with flowers. Complimentary Continental breakfast. Refrigerators, cable TV. Pool. Business services. | San Carlos St. and 4th Ave. | 831/624–5356 or 800/433–4732 | fax 831/624–2967 | concierge@carmelinns.com | www.ibts-dolphininn.com | 26 rooms, 3 suites | $129–$189, $229–$239 suites | AE, D, MC, V.

Green Lantern. This 1927 inn, which has a soothing fireplace in the lobby and dining area, is in a residential neighborhood. Restaurant, complimentary Continental breakfast. Refrigerators, cable TV. Business services. No smoking. | 7th and Casanova Aves | 831/624–4392 | fax 831/624–9591 | 21 rooms | $129–$209 | AE, D, DC, MC, V.

Happy Landing. Rooms in this 1926 Comstock Hansel-and-Gretel style cottage have high ceilings and stained-glass windows. The grounds are covered with flowers. Complimentary breakfast. No room phones, cable TV. No kids under 13. | Monte Verde St. & 6th Ave. | 831/624–7917 | 5 rooms, 2 suites | $90–$130, $165 suites | MC, V.

Highlands Inn/Park Hyatt Hotel. You may enjoy stunning views of the Pacific and coast from this luxury hotel, nestled in a Monterey Pine forest at the edge of Big Sur, on 12 wooded acres. The one- and two-bedroom suites have hot tubs, fireplaces, double spa baths, and ocean-view decks. Restaurants (*see* Pacific's Edge, *above*), bar (with entertainment). In-room data ports, some kitchenettes, minibars, cable TV, in-room VCRs. Pool. Exercise equipment. Bicycles. Business services. Airport shuttle. Baby-sitting. Some pets allowed (fee). | 120 Highland Dr. | 831/624–3801, 831/620–1234 or 800/682–4811 | fax 831/626–1574 | gm@highlands-inn.com | www.highlands-inn.com | 37 rooms, 106 suites | $315–$415, $450–$600 suites | AE, D, DC, MC, V.

Hofsas House. The comfortable rooms here have partial ocean views, and some have balconies and wood-burning fireplaces. Rooms have showers only. Restaurant, bar, complimentary Continental breakfast. Some kitchenettes, cable TV. Pool. Sauna. | San Carlos St. | 831/624–2745 or 800/221–2548 | fax 831/624–0159 | 33 rooms, 5 suites | $90–$200; $250–$280 suites | AE, MC, V.

The Homestead. This downtown inn, where all rooms have private baths, is full of antiques. Some kitchenettes, cable TV, room phones. | Lincoln St. at 8th Ave. | 831/624–4119 | fax 831/624–7688 | 8 rooms, 4 cottages | $65–$90, $95–$120 | AE, V.

Horizon Inn. Some rooms in this recently remodeled inn offer spectacular ocean views, and many have gas-burning fireplaces. Complimentary Continental breakfast. Refrigerators, cable TV. Spa. Laundry facilities. Business services. | Junipero Ave. between 2nd and 3rd Avenues | 831/624–5327 or 800/350–7723 | fax 831/626–8253 | www.monterey.com | 31 rooms, 6 suites | $139–$189, $180–$259 suites | AE, D, MC, V.

La Playa Hotel. This 1904 mansion is decorated with oil paintings and has ornate fireplaces and hand-carved wooden furniture. Its rooms have views of gardens, the ocean, or Carmel. Cottages with brick fireplaces are available. Restaurant, bar. Some kitchenettes, cable TV. Pool. Business services. | Camino Real at 8th Ave. | 831/624–6476 or 800/582–8900 (in CA) | fax 831/624–7966 | www.laplayacarmel.com | 75 rooms, 5 cottages | $139–$265, $265–$575 cottages | AE, DC, MC, V.

Lobos Lodge. Gas fireplaces and sitting areas are found in each room at this inn four blocks from the beach. Complimentary Continental breakfast. Some kitchenettes, refrigerators, cable TV. | Ocean Ave. and Monte Verde St. | 831/624–3874 | fax 831/624–0135 | 30 rooms, 2 suites | $99–$135, $165–$195 suites | AE, MC, V.

Mission Ranch. Sheep graze in the oceanside pasture near the two buildings of this 19th-century farmhouse. Off the entry way is a Victorian parlor; the entire inn is furnished with antiques, and handmade quilts, stuffed mattresses, and carved wooden beds lend the rooms a country ambience. In a secluded area 1 mi from downtown. Restaurant, bar (with entertainment), complimentary Continental breakfast. Cable TV. Tennis. Exercise equipment. Business services. No smoking. | 26270 Dolores St. | 831/624–6436 or 800/538–8221 | fax 831/626–4163 | 31 rooms | $95–$275 | AE, MC, V.

Normandy Inn. This romantic getaway in the heart of Carmel is surrounded by lovely gardens. The rooms at the 1921 inn have feather beds and some have wood-burning fireplaces. The beach is four blocks away. Complimentary Continental breakfast. Some kitchenettes, refrigerators, cable TV. Pool. | Ocean Ave. between Monte Verde and Casanova | 831/624–

3825 or 800/343–3825 | fax 831/624–4614 | 45 rooms, 4 suites, 3 cottages | $98–$200 | AE, MC, V.

Pine Inn. The town's first inn, this has been has been a favorite of Carmel visitors for generations. Built in 1889, the three-story property takes up the entire block. Antique tapestries line the walls and rooms have canopy beds. It's four blocks from the beach and close to shopping. Restaurant, bar. Refrigerators, room service, cable TV. Business services. | Ocean Ave. and Monte Verde St. | 831/624–3851 or 800/228–3851 | fax 831/624–3030 | info@pine-inn.com | www.pine-inn.com | 49 rooms, 6 suites | $105–$250, $250 suites | AE, D, DC, MC, V.

Quail Lodge Resort and Golf Club. Five minutes from Carmel and the beach, this sprawling resort is practically surrounded by the golf course. Rooms are comfortable and pleasant with rattan armchairs, glass-topped tables, and floral drapes and spreads. Restaurants, bars (with entertainment). Cable TV. Two pools. Hot tub. Driving range, 18-hole golf course, putting greens, tennis. Baby-sitting. Business services. Pets allowed (fee). | 8205 Valley Greens Dr. | 831/624–2888 or 800/538–9516 | fax 831/624–3726 | info@quail-lodge-resort.com | www.quail-lodge-resort.com | 84 rooms, 15 suites | $295–$550, $395–$550 suites | AE, DC, MC, V.

Sandpiper Inn. This Prairie-style inn was built in the 1920s and is located on a quiet corner one block from the beach. Exposed-beam ceilings, skylights, fireplaces, canopy beds, and antiques contribute to the inn's charm. Complimentary Continental breakfast. No room phones, TV in common area. Business services. | 2408 Bay View Ave. | 831/624–6433 or 800/633–6433 | fax 831/624–5964 | www.sandpiper-inn.com | 16 rooms | $145–$220 | AE, MC, V.

Stonehouse Inn. This inn was built in 1906 and is furnished with a mixture of antiques and modern pieces. Some rooms have ocean or garden views. Some rooms have shared baths. Complimentary breakfast. No room phones. No kids under 12. | 8th Ave. between Monte Verde and Casanova Sts. | 831/624–4569 or 877/748–6618 | www.carmelstonehouse.com | 6 rooms | $159–$207 | AE, MC, V.

Stonepine. The oldest thoroughbred racing farm west of the Mississippi, this inn has an illustrious history. It was built in 1928 as the Crocker banking family's country estate and sits on 300 park-like acres. The inn has a hand-carved limestone fireplace, 18th-century tapestries, oak paneling, and sweeping garden views. Bathrooms have sunken marble hot tubs. Dining room, complimentary breakfast, room service. Refrigerators, in-room hot tubs, cable TV. Pool. Tennis. Exercise equipment, horseback riding. Business services, airport shuttle. | 150 E. Carmel Valley Rd. | 831/659–2245 | fax 831/659–5160 | stonepine@worldnet.att.net | www.stonepinecalifornia.com | 12 suites, 3 cottages | $375–$900 suites; $750–$2500 cottages | AE, MC, V.

Sunset House. A small B&B three blocks from Carmel Beach, this inn has cozy rooms with fireplaces and cathedral ceilings, and some with ocean views. Complimentary Continental breakfast. Refrigerators, some in-room hot tubs, no TV. Some pets allowed. | Camino Real near Ocean Ave. | 831/624–4884 | fax 831/624–4884 | www.sunset-carmel.com | 4 rooms | $150–$190 | AE, D, MC, V.

Svendsgaard's Inn. This two-story, horseshoe-shaped inn has a country decor and extensively landscaped grounds with a courtyard. It's two blocks from Main Street. Restaurant, complimentary Continental breakfast. Some kitchenettes, refrigerators, some in-room hot tubs, cable TV. Pool. Business services. | 4th Ave. and San Carlos St. | 831/624–1511 or 800/433–4732 | fax 831/624–5661 | www.webdzine.com/inns | 35 rooms | $125–$139 | AE, D, MC, V.

Tally Ho Inn. In an English garden in the heart of Carmel, this two-story hillside inn has nice ocean views. The penthouse units have fireplaces. Complimentary Continental breakfast. In-room data ports, cable TV. Business services. | 6th Ave. and Monte Verde | 831/624–2232; 800/652–2632 | fax 831/624–2661 | info@pine-inn.com | www.tallyho-inn.com | 14 rooms, 2 suites | $115–$250, $250 suites | AE, D, DC, MC, V.

★ **Tickle Pink Inn at Carmel Highlands.** Crashing waves, seagulls, and sunsets are the views from every room at this seaside inn atop a cliff. A private, country-style two-bedroom cottage is also available. Don't miss the outdoor hot tub, which also has ocean views. Complimentary Continental breakfast. Refrigerators, some in-room hot tubs, cable TV, in-room VCRs. Hot tub. Business services. | 155 Highland Dr. | 831/624–1244 or 800/635–4774 | fax 831/626–9516 | www.ticklepink.com | 34 rooms, 13 suites | $249–$279; $299–$359 suites | AE, MC, V.

Vagabond's House Inn. Each room is uniquely furnished at this early-1900s inn, but all overlook the courtyard garden's flowers, oak tree, and waterfall. Many rooms have fireplaces. Complimentary Continental breakfast. Cable TV. No kids under 12. Some pets allowed (fee). | 4th Ave. at Dolores | 831/624–7738 or 800/262–1262 | fax 831/626–1243 | 11 rooms | $95–$165 | AE, MC, V.

Village Inn and Annex. This adobe-style inn with French country decor was built in 1954, and is in the heart of downtown. The suites have fireplaces. Complimentary Continental breakfast. Cable TV. | Ocean Ave. and Junipero St. | 831/624–3387 | fax 831/626–6763 | info£carmelvillageinn.com | 48 rooms, 5 suites | $135–$175, $189–$385 suites | AE, MC, V.

Wayside Inn. This two story motel is just one block off of Ocean Avenue. Perks include a picnic basket breakfast and a free newspaper delivered to your door every morning. Restaurant, complimentary Continental breakfast. Some kitchenettes, refrigerators, cable TV. Business services. Some pets allowed. | 7th Ave. and Mission St. | 831/624–5336 or 800/433–4732 | fax 831/626–6974 | www.webdzine.com/inns | 31 rooms | $99–$259 | AE, D, MC, V.

CARMEL VALLEY

MAP 4, D10

(Nearby towns also listed: Big Sur, Carmel, Monterey, Pacific Grove, Pebble Beach)

Though horse ranching is still common, wine making has become the predominant industry in this tiny village. Remember not to confuse Carmel Valley with the town of Carmel; the latter is 9 mi west at the ocean.

Information: Monterey County Convention and Visitors Bureau | Box 1770, Monterey, 93942 | 831/649–1770 | www.gomonterey.org.

Attractions

Chateau Julien. Maker of fine chardonnays and merlots, the winery offers a tasting room and daily tours by appointment. | 8940 Carmel Valley Rd. | 831/624–2600 | fax 831/624–6138 | www.chateaujulien.com | Weekdays 8–5, weekends 11–5.

Garland Ranch Regional Park. This multi-use park has picnic tables, horse and hiking trails, and guided walks on Saturdays. | Carmel Valley Rd., 9 mi east of Carmel | 831/372–3196 | fax 831/372–3917 | www.mprpd.org | Free | Dawn to dusk.

Holman Ranch Trail Rides. Take a one- or two-hour guided tour on horseback, and see the Valley's stuning views from atop the ridge line. Riding lessons are also available. | Box 149, 93924 | 831/659–6054 | fax 831/659–6056 | www.holmanranch.com | $40 for a one-hour guided ride, $60 for two hours | Tours by appointment only.

Dining

Caffe Rustica. Contemporary. Wood-beamed ceilings and river-rock walls adorn the dining room, where guests feast on a variety of European-inspired California cooking, from roasted meats to house-made gourmet pizzas from the wood-burning oven. | 10 Delfino Pl | 831/659–4444 | fax 831/659–4666 | Reservations essential | Closed Weds | $13–$17 | MC, V.

Corkscrew Café. Contemporary. Inspired by French provincial cooking, the short menu at this charming restaurant changes daily, based upon the produce available from their garden; most of the wine selections are from local vintners. | 55 West Carmel Valley Rd. | 831/659–8888 | Reservations essential | Closed Mon.–Tues. | $15–$22 | MC, V.

★ **Wagon Wheel Coffee Shop.** Casual. Cowboy and rancher memorabilia hang from the wood-beamed ceiling at this bustling breakfast and lunch spot, long a favorite with locals. | Valley Hill Center, Carmel Valley Rd. next to Quail Lodge | 831/624–8878 | No supper | $6–$9 | No credit cards.

Lodging

★ **Bernardus Lodge.** Exposed beams, dark wood floors, and large windows welcome you to this lodge in the woods run by the owners of the Bernardus Winery where wine is complimentary and some rooms have stone fireplaces. Restaurant, room service. Some kitchenettes. Pool. Beauty salon, hot tub, massage, sauna, spa, steam room. Tennis. Gym, hiking, horseback riding. Laundry services. Business services. | 415 Carmel Valley Rd. | 888/648–9463 | www.bernardus.com | 57 rooms | $245–$375 | AE, D, DC, MC, V.

Blue Sky Lodge. Operated by the same congenial family since 1953, this motel offers simple accomodations and off-site apartments. There is a shared library and piano room for use by all guests. Some kitchens, pool, hot tub. | 10 Flight Rd., Box 233, 93924 | 831/659–2256 or 800/549–2256 | fax 831/659–1632 | www.blueskylodge.com | 15 rooms, 12 duplex apartments | $89–$105, apartments $103–$113 | AE, D, MC, V.

Carmel Valley Lodge. The rooms at this attractive inn surround a landscaped patio. There are several one- and two-bedroom cottages with fireplaces. Complimentary Continental breakfast. Some kitchenettes, some refrigerators. Pool, hot tub, sauna, exercise room. | 8 Ford Rd., at Carmel Valley Rd. | 831/659–2261 or 800/641–4646 | fax 831/659–4558 | info@valleylodge.com | www.valleylodge.com | 19 rooms, 4 suites, 8 cottages | $149–$189, $219 suites, $239–$319 cottages | AE, MC, V.

★ **Carmel Valley Ranch.** Every room at this luxury, all-suites resort has a cathedral ceiling, wood-burning fireplace, and large deck. The grounds are superbly tended. 2 restaurants. 2 pools, 2 hot tubs, 2 saunas, 18-hole golf course, 13 tennis courts. | 1 Old Ranch Rd., 93923 | 831/625–9500 or 800/422–7635 | fax 831/624–2858 | www.grandbay.com | 144 suites | $425–$1200 | AE, D, DC, MC, V.

★ **Quail Lodge.** Guests at this resort on the grounds of a private country club have access to golf, tennis, and an 850-acre wildlife preserve frequented by deer and migratory fowl. Modern rooms with European decor are clustered in several low-rise buildings. Each room has a private deck or patio overlooking the golf course, gardens, or a lake. Restaurants, bars, pools, hot tub, sauna, golf, tennis courts, bicycles. | 8205 Valley Greens Dr. | 831/624–1581 or 800/538–9516 | fax 831/624–3726 | 86 rooms, 14 suites | AE, DC, MC, V.

CATALINA ISLAND

MAP 4, I16

(Nearby town also listed: Avalon)

Twenty-one miles long by eight miles wide, this island was first settled by Gabrielino Indians in 500 B.C. In 1542 A.D., Catalina was discovered by Europeans. Also known as Santa Catalina, the island served as a base for smuggling and pirating operations during the Spanish-American period. A private company once owned by chewing-gum magnate William Wrigley, Jr. developed it into a resort area catering to fishermen. Today, Catalina is a haven for swimming, tennis, horseback riding, hiking, camping, and fishing.

Information: **Catalina Island Visitors Bureau and Chamber of Commerce** | 1 Green Pier, Avalon, 90704 | 310/510–1520 | www.catalina.com.

Attractions

Crescent Beach. The water is calm at this narrow, pebbly beach at Avalon Pier. There are restrooms, showers, and dressing rooms, and lifeguards are here from Memorial Day to Labor Day. Volleyball and basketball courts are nearby. You can walk to fast-food spots on Crescent Avenue. | 310/510–1520 | Free | Daily.

Descanso Beach Club. A private, pebbly beach with almost no surf, clear and clean water, and a bar and grill with sandwiches and other food. Nearby concessions rent kayaks, snorkeling gear, and will arrange kayak outings. No lifeguards. | 310/510–7408 or 310/510–7410 | $1.50 | 10–dusk, Easter–end of Oct.

Dining

Café Prego. Italian. An extremely popular spot, this restaurant's specialties are pasta, seafood, and steak. Kids' menu, early-bird suppers. No smoking. | 603 Crescent Ave. | 310/510–1218 | Reservations essential | $9–$26 | AE, D, DC, MC, V.

El Galleon. Seafood. Eat while surrounded by harbor and beach views. Microbrews are available, and so is karaoke entertainment. Kids' menu. No smoking. | 411 Crescent Ave. | 310/510–1188 | Reservations not accepted | $12–$25 | AE, MC, V.

Landing Bar and Grille. Steak. The harbor view and dancing on summer weekends attract the party crowd. You can eat outside on the patio. Try the filet mignon, baby back ribs, or pineapple-ginger chicken. Kids' menu. No smoking. | 101 Marilla | 310/510–1474 | Reservations not accepted | Closed Mon. No dinner Tues. | $13–$18 | AE, DC, MC, V.

Ristorante Villa Portofino. Italian. Choose from veal, seafood, and pasta dishes listed on a Continental menu at this Mediterranean-style villa, complete with pink stucco walls. Kids' menu. No smoking. | 111 Crescent Ave. | 310/510–0508 | Reservations essential | No lunch | $15–$30 | AE, DC, D, MC, V.

Lodging

Banning House Lodge. The summer home of the Banning brothers who own Carmel Island, this 1910 lodge is a quaint and rambling white-boarded house overlooking Two Harbors. Some rooms have views of Isthmus Cove and Catalina Harbor. Complimentary Continental breakfast. No air conditioning, no room phones. | Box 737, Avalon | 310/510–2800 | fax 310/510–0244 | www.catalina.com/scico | 11 rooms | $139–$149 | AE, D, MC, V.

Best Western Catalina Canyon Resort and Spa. In the foothills above Avalon Bay, this multi-level resort has a lush garden courtyard and Mediterranean-style architecture, minutes from downtown. Free shuttle to boating and shopping. Restaurant. Cable TV. Pool. Spa. Laundry service. | 888 Country Club Dr. | 310/510–0325 or 800/253–9361 | fax 310/510–0900 | www.catalina.com/canyon.html | 73 rooms | $161–$214 | AE, D, DC, MC, V.

Catalina Island Seacrest Inn. This Victorian B&B has rooms with four-poster or canopy beds. You can have breakfast in the lace and wicker sun room. The third-floor sun deck has views of Avalon. Complimentary Continental breakfast. Refrigerators, some in-room hot tubs, no room phones. No smoking. | 201 Claressa Ave. | 310/510–0800 | fax 310/510–1122 | 8 rooms | $105–$195 | D, DC, MC, V.

Hotel Atwater. Built in the 1920s, the 2-story hotel 1½ blocks from the beach, has rooms with run-of-the-mill furnishings. You can walk to Avalon's restaurant and shopping district. Refrigerators, no room phones. | 125 Sumner Ave. | 310/510–1788 or 800/626–1496 | fax 310/510–2073 | 92 rooms | $86 winter, $125 summer | AE, D, DC, MC, V.

Hotel Mac Rae. This 1920 Mediterranean 2-story, family-owned hotel is in downtown and has some rooms with ocean views. Walk to shops, restaurants, and bars. Complimentary

Continental breakfast. Cable TV, in-room VCRs (and movies). No smoking. | 409 Crescent Ave. | 310/510–0246 | fax 310/510–9632 | 24 rooms | $155–$190 | MC, V.

Pavilion Lodge. A large, grassy courtyard is the centerpiece of this 2-story motel complex, across from the beach. Rooms are simple and spacious. Refrigerators, cable TV. | 513 Crescent Ave. | 310/510–1788 | fax 310/510–2073 | 73 rooms | $219 | AE, D, DC, MC, V.

Seaport Village Inn. This multi-tiered inn, built in the 1980s, is on a southern hillside 300 steps from the beach, shops, and restaurants. It has special dive group rates and gear transport from the hotel to Casino Dive Park (a gear washdown area). Some kitchenettes, refrigerators, some in-room hot tubs. | 119 Maiden Ln. | 310/510–0344 | fax 310/510–1156 | 34 rooms | $99–$199 | AE, MC, V.

Snug Harbor Inn. At the beach, overlooking Avalon Bay, this small 2-story inn has rooms with ocean views, gas fireplaces, and fine furniture. You can help yourself to complimentary wine and cheese in the afternoon. In-room safe, in-room hot tubs, cable TV. | 108 Sumner Ave. | 310/510–8400 | fax 310/510–8418 | www.snugharbor-inn.com | 6 rooms | $195–$325 | AE, D, MC, V.

CATHEDRAL CITY

MAP 4, K15

(Nearby towns also listed: Palm Desert, Palm Springs, Rancho Mirage)

South of Palm Springs on East Palm Canyon Drive, Cathedral City is a middle-income multicultural community of 30,000 people with eclectic and civically progressive businesses and shops.

Information: **Cathedral City Chamber of Commerce** | 68845 Perez Rd. #6, 92234 | 760/328–1213 | fax 760/321–0659 | www.cathedralcitycc.com.

Attractions

Desert Princess Country Club. Lakes and wide, flat fairways against a backdrop of mountains make up this David Rainville-designed golf course. Tennis courts and spa facilities are other attractions. | 28555 Landau Blvd. | 760/322–0441 | www.desertprincesscc.com/ | Daily.

ON THE CALENDAR

MAY: *FountainWorks Festival*. Food, drinks, arts & crafts and live entertainment help celebrate town spirit around the downtown fountain. | 760/328–1213 | www.cathedralcitycc.com.

Dining

LG's Prime Steak House. Steak. White table cloths and candles keep company with cacti in this white stucco place that serves porterhouse steaks, prime rib, and king crab legs. | 74-225 Rte. 111, Palm Desert | 760/779–9799 | fax 760/779–1979 | www.lgsprimesteakhouse.com | $25–$50 | AE, D, MC, V.

Lodging

Cathedral City Travelodge. The 2-story hotel has a maroon exterior, affordable rates, and is across the street from the Camelot Amusement Park. Cable TV. Pool. | 67–495 Rte. 111 | 760/328–2616 | fax 760/328–0577 | 43 rooms | $82 | AE, D, MC, V.

Comfort Suites. Enjoy a complimentary barbecue every Wednesday here. The 3-story building has one, two, and three bedroom suites and has extended stay rates. Pool. Laundry service. Business services. Some pets allowed. | 69151 E. Palm Canyon Dr. | 760/324–5939 | fax 760/324–3034 | 97 suites | $95–$105 | AE, D, DC, MC, V.

Doral Palm Springs Resort. This four-story luxury resort and hotel sits on a golf course and lush grounds, 345 acres in all. Rooms are modern and well-appointed, each with plush upholstery and unique furniture. Some rooms include a wrap-around balcony and pool view. Restaurant, bar, room service. Refrigerators. Pool. Beauty salon, hot tub, massage, sauna, steam room. Golf courses, tennis. Gym, bicycles. Laundry services. Business services. | 67967 Vista Chino | 760/322–7000, 888/386–4677 | fax 760/322–6853 | truhs@doralps.com | www.doralpalmsprings.com | 285 rooms | $110–$190 | AE, D, DC, MC, V.

CERRITOS

MAP 9, G6

(Nearby towns also listed: Buena Park, Garden Grove, Long Beach, Seal Beach, Whittier)

A largely unknown area on the 605 Freeway to the west and the 91 Freeway to the north, Cerritos (pop. 53,200) attracts a growing Indian population, providing outlets and services geared toward a South Asian culture.

Information: Cerritos Chamber of Commerce | 13005 Artesia Blvd., #A-110, 90703-1357 | 562/404–1806 | www.cerritos.org.

Attractions

Cerritos Center for Performing Arts. Symphonies from across the country, pop and country-western singers, and nationally known comedians perform in this downtown venue. As shows change frequently, call for exact shows and showtimes. | 12700 Center Court Dr. | 800/300–4345 | fax 562/916–8514 | www.cerritoscenter.com | $40–$120.

ON THE CALENDAR
OCT.: *Hilarious Halloween Haunt.* A Halloween puppet show performed at the Cerritos Public Library. | 562/916–1350 | www.library.ci.cerritos.ca.us.

Dining
Arte Café. Pan-Asian. An elegant dining room with a patio that seats up to 50, the menu here has crab and spinach ravioli in a champagne cream sauce, and seared rare ahi tuna served over wasabi mashed potatoes topped with crispy wontons. Kids' menu. No smoking. | 12741 Towne Center Dr. Rd. | 562/403–1080 | Reservations essential | $11–$19 | AE, D, DC, MC, V.

Lodging
Sheraton Cerritos Hotel at Towne Center. Close to shopping, restaurants, and attractions, there is easy highway access from this hotel to Los Angeles and Orange County. The glass building is in park-like Towne Center, next to the Cerritos Center for Performing Arts. Cable TV. Pool. Gym. Video games. Laundry service. Business services. Some pets allowed. | 12725 Center Court Dr. | 562/809–1500 | fax 562/403–2080 | 203 rooms | $135–139 | AE, D, MC, V.

Travelodge. This two-story roadside motel is 1½ mi southeast of town. Cable TV. Pool. | 11854 Artesia Blvd., Artesia | 562/402–0070 | fax 562/402–0070 | 49 rooms | $50–$60 | AE, MC, V.

CHANNEL ISLANDS NATIONAL PARK

MAP 4, H15

(Nearby towns also listed: Oxnard, Port Hueneme, Santa Monica)

From the Santa Barbara horizon you can often see the five major Channel Islands. The most popular, Anacapa Island, is 11 mi off the coast. Its remoteness combined with unpredictable seas protect the island from development and create a nature-lover's paradise. On a clear day you can see seals, sea lions and bird life. Migrating whales can be seen up close from December through March.

ON THE CALENDAR

DEC.: *Channel Islands Harbor Parade of Lights.* A celebration of the islands' beauty, this night-time parade on the water has been a tradition since 1965. | 805/966–7107 | www.cinms.nos.noaa.gov.

CHESTER

MAP 4, E4

(Nearby towns also listed: Quincy, Susanville)

When the Feather River was dammed in 1926 to form Lake Almanor, the tiny logging town of Chester found itself poised near the shore of a major watersport attraction. Today Chester, with a population of 2,500, serves as the commercial center for the entire Lake Almanor area, and as a kicking-off point for visitors to the nearby Lassen National Forest and Lassen National Park.

Information: Chester Chamber of Commerce | 529 Main St., 96020 | 800/350–4838 | almanor@chester-lakealmanor.com | www.chester-lakealmanor.com.

Attractions

Lake Almanor. This 52-square-mi lake in the shadow of Mt. Lassen was created by the Pacific Gas and Electric Company for hydroelectric power, but it's also a popular draw for campers, swimmers, boaters, waterskiiers and fisherman. Despite its altitude (4500 ft), the lake warms to above 70 degrees in summer. | Almanor Ranger District headquarters: 900 W. Highway 36 | 530/258–2141 | Campgrounds closed mid-Oct.–mid-May.

Lassen Scenic Byway. Beginning west from Chester on Highway 36, this 172-mi scenic drive loops through the forests, volcanic peaks, geothermal springs, and lava fields of Lassen National Forest and Lassen National Park. It's an all-day excursion into dramatic wilderness, but along the way you'll pass through five small communities where refreshments and basic services are available. | Almanor Ranger District headquarters: 900 W. Highway 36 | 530/258–2141 | http://www.r5.fs.fed.us/lassenbyway/lassenbyway.html | $10 admission per car within Lassen National Park | Partially inaccessible in winter; call for current road conditions.

Dining

Benassi's. Italian. For dinner, the area's most popular Northern Italian eatery offers steaks and seafood in addition to homemade pasta specials. Quick lunches are also available, including carry-out delicatessen sandwiches. | 159 Main St. | 530/258–2600 | Closed Mon. No supper Sun. | $10–$18 | MC, V.

Creekside Grill. Contemporary. On the banks of a bubbling brook near the center of town, this California-style restaurant serves light meat dishes as well as pastas and salads, all made with fresh seasonal ingredients. Wine and microbrew bar. As the hours change frequently, you should call before you go. | 278 Main St. | 530/258–1966 | Recommended | No lunch | $8–18 | MC, V.

Peninsula Station Bar and Grill. American. Golfers and boaters alike can enjoy big meals of steak, prime rib, and seafood at this traditional establishment next door to the Almanor Country Club. Patio seating and full bar available. | 401 Peninsula Dr., Lake Almanor Peninsula | 530/596–3538 | Closed Mon. No lunch Sun. | $10–20 | MC, V.

Lodging

Bidwell House. This two-story 1901 wooden ranch house is situated at the east end of town on two-acres of aspen studded lawns, and gardens. The front porch, outfitted with chairs and swings, commands a view of Lake Almanor. Separate cottage available. Complimentary breakfast. No air conditioning, cable TV, room phones. No pets. No smoking. | 1 Main St. | 530/258–3338 | bidwellhouse@thegrid.net | www.bidwellhouse.com | 14 | $75–150 | MC, V.

Chester Manor Motel. All rooms in this 50s-era one-story motel have been remodelled since new owners took it over in 1999. The motel is located near the center of town within easy walking distance of restaurants, and offers picnic tables among the pine groves on its two-and-a-half acre lot. Picnic area. No air conditioning, some mircrowaves, some refrigerators, cable TV, room phones. No pets. No smoking. | 530/258–2441; 888/571–4885 | fax 530/258–3523 | chestman@psln.com | 18 | $55–78 | AE, MC, V.

CHICO

MAP 3, E5

(Nearby towns also listed: Oroville, Red Bluff, Willows)

Settled in 1843 by General John Bidwell, a 19th-century agriculturalist, gold miner, and U.S. congressman, Chico is now the home to a campus of the California State University system. The city of 40,000 owes its vibrancy to the Cal State students who patronize the many cafés and several ethnic restaurants in town.

Information: Chico Chamber of Commerce | 300 Salem St., 95928 | 530/891–5556 or 800/852–8570 | fax 530/891–3613 | www.chicochamber.com.

Attractions

★ **Bidwell Mansion State Historic Park.** The park's centerpiece is a 26-room Victorian home built between 1865–1868 for city founder General John Bidwell. | 525 the Esplanade | 530/895–6144 | $1 | Weekdays noon–5, weekends 10–5; last tour daily at 4.

Bidwell Park. With more than 3,000 acres, this is the second-largest city-run park in the nation, spanning from downtown to the foothills of Sierra Nevada. It has hiking and bicycling trails, a playground, sports facilities, and picnic areas. | 411 Main St. | 530/895–4972 | fax 530/895–4825 | www.ci.chico.ca.us | Free | Daily 9AM–dusk.

California State University, Chico. Big Chico Creek winds its way from the hills under a canopy of trees through Bidwell Park and the 130-acre Chico State campus downtown. | 400 West 1st. St. | 530/898–4428, 530/898–6322 or 530/898–4636 | www.csuchico.edu | Free | Daily, tours by appointment.

Chico Museum. Permanent and changing exhibits display local history and art. Check out the Chinese Taoist temple that was in use from 1860–1939. Guided tours are available. | 141 Salem St. | 530/891–4336 | Donation | Wed.–Sun. 12–4.

★ **Sierra Nevada Brewing Company.** One of the pioneers of the microbrewery movement, this sparkling brewery offers tours and tasting. You can eat lunch or dinner in the brew pub. | 1075 E. 20th St. | 530/345–2739 | Free | Tours Tues.–Fri. at 2:30 and Sat. noon–3 on the ½ hr. Sun. 2:30

ON THE CALENDAR

OCT: *Nowhere X Nowhere.* Dozens of bands and films from all over the world draw 30,000 pop-culture fans to this four-day rock and roll festival. | 530/345–3697 | www.nowherexnowhere.com.

Dining

Black Crow Grill and Taproom. Contemporary. You can watch the chef prepare lemon roasted chicken with garlic mashed potatoes, fresh grilled fish, and burritos in the open kitchen. Several local microbrews are on tap, and the local contemporary art on the walls changes often. | 209 Salem St. | 530/892–1391 | fax 530/892–1393 | $8–$16 | AE, MC, V.

Red Tavern. Contemporary. Hot-smoked golden trout, roast quail with apple salad, and couscous-stuffed chicken with almond sauce and chanterelle mushrooms are on the menu. The restaurant is lined with black and white photographs of food and is just outside of downtown, surrounded by historic homes on a tree-lined street. | 1250 The Esplanade | 530/894–3463 | www.redtavern.com | Reservations essential | $14–$20 | AE, MC, V.

Lodging

Best Western Heritage Inn. This 3-story hotel is 1 mi north of downtown, a short drive from movies and a mall, and a 5-minute drive to Bidwell Mansion and Bidwell park. Complimentary Continental breakfast. In-room data ports, some refrigerators, some in-room hot tubs. Pool. Hot tub. Business services. | 25 Heritage Ln | 530/894–8600 | 101 rooms | $60–$85 | AE, D, DC, MC, V.

Esplanade Bed and Breakfast. Wine is served every evening on the garden patio or in the parlor of this 1913 bed and breakfast. Complimentary breakfast. Some in-room hot tubs, cable TV, some room phones. | 620 The Esplanade | 530/345–8084 | esplanade@now2000.com | 5 rooms | $80–$100 | MC, V.

Holiday Inn. The hotel is 2 mi from CSUC, the historic area downtown, Bidwell Park, Bidwell Mansion, and Sierra Nevada Brewery. Restaurant, bar (with entertainment), room service. In-room data ports, some refrigerators, cable TV. Pool. Hot tub. Video games. Laundry facilities. Business services. Airport shuttle. Free parking. Some pets allowed. | 685 Manzanita Ct | 530/345–2491 | www.holiday-inn.com | 171 rooms, 6 suites | $66–$85, $110–$150 suites | AE, D, DC, MC, V.

L'Abri Bed and Breakfast. Barnyard animals and hay bales create a country theme at this ranch bed & breakfast on 2 ½ acres 7 mi northwest of town. Complimentary breakfast. No room phones, no TV. No pets. No smoking. | 14350 Rte. 99 N | 530/893–0824 | 3 rooms | $80–$100 | MC, V.

Vagabond Inn. This 1970s 2-story inn, designed with natural colors, is near restaurants, shopping, and historic homes. Complimentary Continental breakfast. Cable TV. Pool. Business services. Some pets allowed (fee). | 630 Main St. | 530/895–1323 | www.vagabondinns.com | 43 rooms | $50–$63 | AE, D, DC, MC, V.

CHULA VISTA

MAP 4, K17

(Nearby towns also listed: Coronado, San Diego, San Ysidro)

This suburban San Diego satellite of 135,000 has bayside parks, a harbor with two marinas, and coastal wetlands, indicative of the town's name, which means "beautiful view" in Spanish. It is one of several towns along I–5 that link downtown San Diego with Tijuana, just across the Mexican border.

Information: Chula Vista Chamber of Commerce | 233 4th Ave., 91910 | 619/420–6603 | www.chulavistachamber.org.

Attractions

Arco Olympic Training Center of the United States Olympic Committee. The visitor center at this 152-acre facility tells the history of the Olympics. You can take a tour of the training facility. | 2800 Olympic Pkwy. | 619/482–6222 | Free | Mon.–Sat. 9–5, Sun. 12–5.

Chula Vista Nature Center. You can walk the 1 1/2 mi path and view native flora, fauna, birds, and their marshland habitat. The center is accessible by a shuttle bus that leaves every 25 minutes from a parking lot at E. St. on the west side of I–5. | 1000 Gunpowder Point Dr. | 619/409–5900 | $4 | Tues.–Sun. 10–5.

ON THE CALENDAR
AUG.: *Lemon Festival.* Food, live music, and arts and crafts at this street fair celebrate the town's history. | 619/420–6602.

Dining

Bob's on the Bay. American. You can watch boats come in and out of the marina while you eat on an indoor/outdoor patio. House specials are seasonal lobster, catfish, mahi mahi, halibut, and king crab legs, or pasta. Kids' menu. Sunday brunch. No smoking. | 570 Marina Pkwy. | 619/476–0400 | $10–$25 | AE, D, DC, MC, V.

Buon Giorno. Italian. Eat on tables decked with white tablecloths and candlelight. The restaurant has wine racks on the walls and specializes in veal chop, osso bucco, and seafood. You can eat outside on a canopied patio with a view of the golf course. Music, Thurs.–Sun. Kids' menu. No smoking. | 4110 Bonita Rd., Bonita | 619/475–2660 | No lunch Sun. | $9–$29 | AE, MC, V.

Butcher Shop. Steak. This dimly lit 1979 restaurant has walnut paneling and wrought-iron chandeliers. You can order corn-fed beef from Nebraska, a shrimp feast, Alaskan king crab legs, or prime rib. Entertainment Wed.–Sat. No smoking. | 556 Broadway | 619/420–9440 | $11–$18 | AE, D, DC, MC, V.

Lodging

Good Nite Inn. You can walk to the bay, restaurants, and the Chula Vista Nature Center from this 2-story hotel, built in 1982. It's 10 mi from the Mexican border and 12 mi from San Diego. Restaurant. Some Microwaves, refrigerators, cable TV. Pool. | 225 Bay Blvd. | 619/425–8200 | fax 619/426–7411 | www.goodnite.com | 118 rooms | $55 | AE, D, DC, MC, V.

Holiday Inn Express. This southwest-style motel is 2 mi from the Mexican border and 20 mi from SeaWorld. Restaurant, complimentary Continental breakfast. In-room data ports, refrigerators, cable TV. Pool. Hot tub. Laundry facilities. Business services. | 4450 Otay Valley Rd. | 619/422–2600 | fax 619/425–4605 | www.holiday-inn.com | 118 rooms | $89 | AE, D, DC, MC, V.

La Quinta Chula Vista. Surrounded by trees and gardens, this three-story hotel with a Spanish tile roof is 10 mi from downtown San Diego. Complimentary Continental breakfast. Cable TV. Laundry facilities. | 150 Bonita Rd. | 619/691–1211 | 142 rooms | $70–$90 | AE, D, MC, V.

Ramada Inn. Just 15 mi south of San Diego and 8 mi north of the Mexican border, the 4-story building was constructed in the 1908s. Restaurant, bar. Cable TV. Pool. Hot tub. Business services. | 91 Bonita Rd. | 619/425–9999 | fax 619/425–8934 | www.ramada.com | 97 rooms | $72–$95 | AE, D, DC, MC, V.

Rodeway Inn. The Mexican border is 6 mi south, and San Diego International Airport is 7 mi from this motel. Restaurant. Microwaves, cable TV. Pool. Hot tub. | 778 Broadway | 619/476–9555 | www.comfortinn.com | 49 rooms | $50–$60 | AE, D, DC, MC, V.

Vagabond. This 2-story motel is 3 mi from the beach. Complimentary Continental breakfast. Pool. Hot tub. Laundry facilities. | 230 Broadway | 619/422–8305 | 91 rooms | $50–$80 | AE, D, DC, MC, V.

CLAREMONT

MAP 9, K3

(Nearby towns also listed: Glendora, Ontario, Pomona, Rancho Cucamonga)

Claremont was a citrus oasis around 1900, but today it's a college town, home to the Claremont College and the School of Theology. Claremont has been a winner of the National Arbor Day Association's Tree City USA award for 13 consecutive years, and is home to the Rancho Santa Ana Botanic Gardens, a vast display of native California plants.

Information: **Claremont Chamber of Commerce** | 205 Yale Ave., 91711-4725 | 909/624–1681 | www.claremontchamber.org.

Attractions

Montgomery Art Gallery at Pomona College. You can see temporary exhibitions and permanent collections of The Claremont Colleges. The week before commencement there is a display of the work of the senior-class art majors. | 330 N. College Ave. | 909/621–8283 | Free | Sept.–May, Tues.–Fri. 12–5, weekends 1–5.

Rancho Santa Ana Botanic Garden. You can stroll 85 acres of native California plants and flowers here. The garden has three areas arranged by climate and plant type. Plant Communities has native specimens; East Alluvial Gardens has plants from coastal dunes, channel islands, and the deserts; and Indian Hill Mesa has wild species. | 1500 N. College Ave. | 909/625–8767 | www.cgu.edu/inst/rsa | Donation | Daily 8–5.

ON THE CALENDAR
NOV.: *Pilgrim Place Festival.* Pilgrim Place, a community of retired church professionals, hosts this festival including a bazaar, a craft fair, an outdoor luncheon, and activities for children. | 909/621–9581 | www.pilgrimplace.org.

Dining
Pizza 'N Such. Pizza. All the dough is hand-thrown in this 24-seat place downtown with art from the owner's gallery on the walls, and an open kitchen. You can also get soup, salads, and Italian standards like chicken parmigiana. | 273 W. 2nd St. | 909/624–7214 or 909/624–5431 | $6–$14 | AE, MC, V.

Yiannis. Greek. The dining area has cedar walls with Greek plates and paintings. You can also eat outside on the sidewalk. The menu has shish kebob, braised lamb shanks, and lots of desserts. No smoking. | 238 Yale Ave. | 909/621–2413 | Closed Mon. | $13–$20 | AE, MC, V.

Lodging
Howard Johnson Express Inn. This two-story motel is surrounded by palm trees and is accessible from the Indian Hill exit off of Rte. 10. Restaurant. Pool. Beauty salon, hot tub. Gym. Laundry services. Business services. | 721 S. Indian Hill Blvd. | 909/626-2431, 800/406-1411 | fax 909/624–7051 | www.hojo.com | 62 rooms | $55–$70 | AE, D, DC, MC, V.

Ramada Inn and Tennis Club. This 2-story motel is on seven landscaped acres, off "the 10" freeway. There's a free shuttle to the LA County Fairplex, Ontario International Airport, and all local colleges. You can walk to restaurants and shops. Complimentary Continental breakfast. Refrigerators, cable TV. Pool, wading pool. Hot tub. Tennis. Laundry facilities. Business services. Some pets allowed. | 840 S. Indian Hill Blvd. | 909/621–4831 | fax 909/621–0411 | www.ramadaclar.com | 122 rooms | $65–$89 | AE, D, DC, MC, V.

CLEAR LAKE AREA (LAKE COUNTY)

(Nearby town also listed: Alturas)

You'll find the state's largest natural lake here, with boating, water-skiing, swimming, and fishing for crappie, catfish, and largemouth bass year-round. There are also plenty of quiet inlets for bird-watching, and hiking and biking. There is a town called Clearlake on the south end of the lake, but the most developed area is the west shore, around Lakeport. Long a quiet place for retirees, this part of Lake County is becoming popular with homebuyers squeezed out of the markets in nearby Sonoma and Napa counties.

Information: **Clear Lake Chamber of Commerce** | 4700 Golf Ave., 95422-0629 | 707/994–3600 | www.clearlake.ca.us/chamber.

Attractions

Clear Lake State Park. You can hike the Indian Nature Trail, a self-guided path, and visit Pomo Village to learn how the Pomo people lived for centuries. You can also stop by the visitors' center to see nature and cultural displays. There are 147 camping sites on the western edge of the lake. | 5300 Soda Bay Rd, Kelseyville | 707/279–4293 | www.parks.ca.gov | Day use per vehicle.

Outrageous Waters. The water slides are open Memorial through Labor Day but the batting cages, race track, arcade and games are open all year. | Rte. 53, Clearlake | 707/995–1402, 877/932–3386 | fax 707/994–1759 | www.outrageouswaters.com | $14 | Wed.–Fri. 3–8, Weekends 12–8.

ON THE CALENDAR

JUNE: *Middletown Days.* You can enjoy a pancake breakfast, barbeque, parade, junior rodeo, and square dancing in Middletown Park on Central Park Ave. | 707/987–0359.

Dining

Anthony's. Continental. White table cloths and small, shaded lamps are on each table in this floral dining room with garden and lake views. House specialties include rack of lamb, lobster and prime rib. | 2509 Lakeshore Blvd., Lakeport | 707/263–4905 | fax 707/263–6276 | Closed Tue. Wed. | $15–$25 | AE, MC, V.

Jan's Kitchen. Eclectic. Large-portions of veal marsala, chicken in puff pastry, rack of lamb and Mexican specialties mark the ever-changing menu. Four large wooden tables fill the dining room. The 5-course prix fixe includes wine and dessert. | 3315 Lakeshore Blvd.,Lakeport | 707/263–4905 | fax 707/263–6276 | Reservations essential | Closed Mon.—Wed. | $25 | AE, MC, V.

Ma'Shauns Rainbow Restaurant. Continental. The seasonal menu in this dining room overlooking Clear Lake changes often, and includes dishes like filet mignon with port and

Stilton blue cheese sauce, and veal with white wine sauce and chantrelle mushrooms. | 2599 Lakeshore Blvd.,Lakeport | 707/263–6237 | $14–$28 | AE, D, MC, V.

Lodging

Anchorage Inn. At Clear Lake, this single-story 1970s inn near downtown has a flower garden and lake views. Picnic area. Some kitchenettes, cable TV. Pool, lake. Hot tub, sauna. Dock. Laundry facilities. | 950 N. Main St. | 707/263–5417 | fax 707/263–5453 | 34 rooms, 20 suites | $54–$115, $69–$115 suites | AE, D, DC, MC, V.

Best Western El Grande Inn. Built in 1985, this 4-story Spanish-style hotel has suites with lake views. The lake, shopping center, grocery store, and restaurants are all nearby. Restaurant, bar. Some refrigerators, cable TV. Indoor pool. Hot tub. Business services. | 15135 Lakeshore Dr. | 707/994–2000 | fax 707/994–2042 | www.bestwestern.com | 68 rooms, 24 suites | $66–$115; $125 suites | AE, D, DC, MC, V.

Highlands Inn. Most rooms have lake views at this two-story building built in 1992. There's a private pier for fishing and boats. Picnic area. Cable TV. Pool. Laundry facilities. | 13865 Lakeshore Dr. | 707/994–8982 | fax 707/994–0613 | www.highlands.com | 20 rooms, 2 suites | $75–$165, $125–$185 suites | AE, D, DC, MC, V.

Kristalberg. The two-story B&B has rooms with lake views. You can go biking, hiking, boating, and take quiet walks here. The staff speaks English, German, French, and Spanish. The breakfast is made from organic vegtables and fruit. Complimentary breakfast. No smoking. | 715 Pearl Ct., Lucerne | www.virtualcities.com | 707/274–8009 | 3 rooms, 1 suite | $60–$90, $125–$150 suite | AE, D, MC, V.

Mallard House Inn. Each of the rooms in this 4-building motel cluster are simply done in pastel colors with light wood furnishings. Some kitchenettes. Spa. Dock, boating. No pets. | 970 N. Main St.,Lakeport | 707/262–1601 | fax 707/263–4764 | mallardhouse@pacific.net | www.mallardhouse.com | 13 rooms | $60–$90 | AE, D, MC, V.

Skylark Shores Motel and Resort. Some rooms have lake views in the three buildings and four cabins which make up this motel on Clear Lake. Some kitchenettes, some microwaves, some refrigerators, cable TV, room phones. Dock, boating. | 1120 N. Main St.,Lakeport | 800/675–6151 | fax 707/263–7733 | skylarkshores@pacific.net | www.skylarkshoresmotel.com | 40 rooms, 4 cottages | $50–$80, $75–$130 cottages | AE, MC, V.

COALINGA

MAP 4, F11

(Nearby towns also listed: Hanford, King City)

This oil, gas, and livestock center off I–5 (pop. 8,200) began as a coal transfer point for the Southern Pacific Railroad. Short-hand for "coal loading station A," the name "Coalinga" stuck and the area burgeoned into a permanent oil-boomer settlement. It's not much to look at now but for those driving between Los Angeles and San Francisco, it's a popular stop for gasoline and steaks at Harris Ranch.

Information: Coalinga Area Chamber of Commerce | 380 Coalinga Plaza, 93210-1709 | 559/935–2948 | www.coalingachamber.com.

Attractions

R.C. Baker Memorial Museum. See American Indian artifacts, ranch hand equipment, fossils, and oil-field equipment. | 297 W. Elm St. | 559/935–1914 | By donations | Mon.–Fri. 10–12, 1–5 Sat. 11–5 Sun. 1–5 Holidays 1–5.

DEC.: *Christmas Craft Fair.* Local arts and crafts prepare for the holidays at this fair at the beginning of month. | 559/935–2948 | www.coalingachamber.com.

Dining
Harris Ranch. Steak. Crowds of couples and families are drawn to this Mexican-style hacienda with fountains and a patio. Try the prime rib and steak from Harris Ranch. You can also eat in the coffee shop or lounge. Kids' menu. No smoking. | 24505 W. Dorris Ave. | 559/935–0717 | Breakfast also available | $9–$23 | AE, DC, MC, V.

Lodging
Big Country Inn. This inn is located right off I–5 on the west side of town. Four cottage-style, one-story buildings make up the inn complex. Pool. Some pets allowed. | 25020 W. Dorris Ave. | 559/935–0866 | fax 559/935–0644 | 48 rooms | $52–$86 | AE, D, DC, MC, V.

Harris Ranch. An inn, a private 2,800-ft airstrip, a restaurant, and service stations can be found on this ranch 35 mi west of Hanford. The hotel is built in the tradition of an early California hacienda, featuring a red-tiled roof, stone columns, archways, and surrounding manicured lawns and gardens. Light pine furniture and country floral prints accentuate guest rooms. Restaurant, 2 bars, room service. Cable TV. Heated pool. Hot tubs. Laundry facilities. | I–5 and Rte. 198 | 559/935–0717 or 800/942–2333 | fax 559/935–2839 | www.harrisranch.com | 123 rooms | $99–$250 | AE, D, DC, MC, V.

Motel 6. This two-story motel is on the east side of town, accessible by taking Exit 198 (Hanford) off of I–5. Outdoor pool. Cable TV. Laundry facilities. | 25008 W. Dorris Ave. | 559/935–1536 | fax 559/934–0814 | www.motel6.com | 122 rooms | $40–$55 | AE, D, DC, MC, V.

COLFAX

MAP 3, E6

(Nearby towns also listed: Auburn, Nevada City)

Named for Ulysses S. Grant's Vice President, Colfax was intended to be a temporary, segregated camp for Chinese laborers laying tracks over the Sierra Nevada, and for miners trading wares in Gold Country. Today, Colfax, off I–80 in the foothills of the Sierra, is a quiet town, where manzanita and oaks give way to high-mountain conifers. Part of downtown, across I–80, has historical buildings.

Information: Colfax Chamber of Commerce | 2 Railroad St., Box 86, 95713 | 530/346–8888 | www.colfaxarea.com.

Attractions
Stevens Trail. Travel down American River Canyon to the water's edge, and you can see one of California's most important waterways. | I–80 past Colfax Cemetery | 916/985–4474 | Free | 24 hours.

Colfax Cemetery. Important figures in the town's history are buried under moss-covered gravestones at this 19th-century cemetery. | 180 N. Canyon Way | 530/889–4000 | Free | Daily.

Colfax Theatre. You can see current films in this 1930s theater, wherein the carpets, fixtures and curtains have all been restored to their original grandeur. | 49 S. Main St. | 530/346–8424 | $6.

Dining
Dinghus McGee's. American. This is a roadhouse with steak and three-course dinners in the main dining room, and limited menu at the bar. | 2121 South Auburn St. | 530/346–6368 | fax 530/346–7052 | No lunch | $11–$18 | AE, MC, V.

Giovanni's. Italian. Owned by the same family for 60 years, this trattoria which is greatly influenced by northern Italian cuisine has a menu of pastas and entrées. | Rte. 174 and Rollins Lake Rd. | 530/346–7400 | No lunch Sun.–Weds | $9–$18 | AE, D, DC, MC, V.

Madonna's. American. Primarily a lunch spot, this small café serves prime rib at dinner on the weekends. Open air dining available. | 42 North Main St. | 530/346–8213 | No dinner weekdays, breakfast also available | $5–$23 | AE, MC, V.

Lodging

Colfax Motor Lodge. Rooms are simple and affordable at this motel, nestled among a plethora of dining facilities, and accessible by taking the Colfax Grass Valley exit off of I–80. | 550 South Auburn St., 95713 | 530/346–8382 | 18 rooms | $30–$45 | MC, V.

Rollins Lakeside Inn. The knotty pine cabins at this water-side resort that caters to boating enthusiasts have kitchens and outdoor barbecues. Microwaves, refrigerators. Outdoor pool, lake. | 18145 Rollins View Dr., Box 152, Chicago Park 95712 | 530/273–0729 | fax 530/273–0729 | www.rollinslake.com | 9 cabins | $105–$175 | MC, V.

COLOMA

MAP 3, F6

(Nearby towns also listed: Auburn, Placerville)

Coloma boasts the South Fork of the American River, where James Marshall found gold in 1848, triggering the 1849 California Gold Rush. The actual site is in the Marshall Gold Discovery State Historic Park. The town is 50 mi northeast of Sacramento off Route 49.

Information: El Dorado County Chamber | 542 Main St., Placerville, 95667 | 800/457–6279 | www.eldoradocounty.org.

Attractions

★ **Marshall Gold Discovery State Historic Park.** A statue of Marshall pointing toward his gold discovery, only ½ mi away, overlooks the park grounds. You can also see Marshall's 1860 cabin, a replica of Sutter's mill, and a museum, or go fishing. | 310 Back St., Coloma | 530/622–3470 | fax 530/622–3472 | www.windjammer.net/users/isg/coloma | $2 per vehicle | Daily; museum, 10–4:30; park 8–sunset.

Pioneer Cemetery. You can view the graves of over 600 pioneers in this cemetery. Call to arrange a tour. | 310 Back St. | 530/622–3470 | fax 530/622–3472 | free | daily.

ON THE CALENDAR

JAN.: *Gold Discovery Day.* James Marshall's 1848 discovery of gold at Sutter's Mill, which led to the California gold rush, is reenacted each year. | 530/622–3470.

Dining

Eppies Restaurant. American. Burgers and fried chicken are on the menu of this casual restaurant with landscapes on the walls. Eppies is 8 mi south of town. | 6850 Greenleaf Dr., Placerville | 530/622–2303 | fax 530/622–9376 | $14–$22 | AE, D, DC, MC, V.

Lodging

Coloma Country Inn Bed and Breakfast. The inn is a restored 1852 two-story grey and white clapboard farmhouse on five acres inside State Historic Park. Rooms have antique double- and queen-size beds, handmade quilts, stenciled friezes, and fresh flowers. Complimentary breakfast. Business services. | 345 High St. | 530/622–6919 | www.colomacountryinn.com | 7 rooms, 2 suites | $95–$120, $145–$200 suites | No credit cards.

Shafsky House Bed and Breakfast. Antiques, relief wallpaper, intricate woodwork, and oriental rugs fill this Victorian B&B, 6 mi south of town. Complimentary breakfast. No room phones, TV in common area. No smoking. | 2942 Coloma St.,Placerville | 530/642–2776 | fax 530/642–2109 | shafsky@directcon.net | 3 rooms | $90–$125 | AE, MC, V.

COLUMBIA

(Nearby towns also listed: Jamestown, Murphys, Sonora)

In 1854 Columbia came within two legislative votes of beating out Sacramento for state capital. Twenty years and $87 million worth of gold later, Columbia's population had nearly vanished. Today the extensively restored buildings and most of the town in the Sierra foothills are within a state historic park that looks like a Gold Rush settlement.

Information: Tuolomne County Chamber of Commerce | 222 S. Shepherd St., Sonora, 95370 | 209/532–4212 | www.tcchamber.com.

Attractions

★ **Columbia State Historic Park.** The 12-square block downtown park is partially restored to its Gold Rush days look. There's a schoolhouse, bank, newspaper building, barbershop, saloons, the Wells Fargo Express Co. building, Fallon Hotel, and City Hotel. The Masonic Temple has been reconstructed on its original site. See a play in the Fallon House theater, or enjoy stagecoach rides, horseback tours, gold panning, and gold-mine tours.| 22708 Broadway St.| 209/532–0150 | fax 209/532–5064 | www.sierra.parks.state.ca.us/cshp.htm | Free; theater $15 ($17 weekends), stagecoach $5, horseback tours $18–$30, gold panning $10, gold mine tour $10 | Daily, museum, stores 10–5, plays Thurs.–Sat. 8PM, Sun. 2PM, stagecoach and horseback rides 10–6.

Moaning Cavern. Miners discovered this cavern in 1851. It yielded no gold, but did hold prehistoric human remains. You can take a guided tour 165 ft down into the cavern along a 235-step spiral staircase that wraps around the perimeter of a room large enough to hold the Statue of Liberty. The more adventurous minded can rappel down (ropes and instruction provided). The caves are 13 mi north of Sonora off Hwy 4 east of Angels Camp. | 5350 Moaning Cave Rd. | 209/736–2708 | fax 209/736–0330 | www.longbarn.com/caverns.htm | $8.75 | Weekdays 10–5, weekends 9–5.

ON THE CALENDAR
NOV.: *Champagne Tasting and Brunch.* This three-course meal and champagne tasting event at the City Hotel is a fifteen-year tradition. | 209/532–1479, 800/532–1479 | www.cityhotel.com.

Dining
City Hotel Restaurant. French. Grilled medallions of venison with roquefort polenta and wine sauce, and roasted leek-crusted salmon with vodka cream and new potatoes are some examples of the seasonal dishes found at this elegant dining room with white table cloths and floor-to-ceiling red curtains.| 22768 Main St.| 209/532–1479 | fax 209/532–7027 | www.cityhotel.com/dining | $18–$35 | AE, D, MC, V.

Lodging
Blue Nile Inn. Hardwood floors, quilts, and wicker and brass furniture fill the rooms of this replica Victorian farmhouse bed and breakfast. Complimentary breakfast. Some in-room hot tubs, no room phones, TV in common areas. No pets. No smoking. | 11250 Pacific

St. | 209/532–8041 | innkeeper@blue-nile-inn.com | www.blue-nile-inn.com | 4 rooms | $105–$135 | AE, D, MC, V.

City Hotel. Some of the rooms in this downtown 1856 hotel overlook Main Street, and others face a second-floor parlor. The hotel has a sitting parlor, Victorian antiques, customized wall coverings, and lithographs. Shower baskets. No smoking. Restaurant, bar, complimentary Continental breakfast. | Main St. between State &Jackson Sts. | 209/532–1479 or 800/532–1479 | fax 209/532–7027 | www.cityhotel.com | 10 rooms | $95–$115 | AE, D, MC, V.

Fallon Hotel. The state restored this downtown 1857 hotel with a theater and ice cream parlor. All rooms have antiques and a private half-bath. There's a sitting parlor, wall coverings, and lithographs. You can see live theater productions and eat in the ice cream parlor. Restaurant, bar. Complimentary Continental breakfast. No smoking. | 11175 Washington St. | 209/532–1470 | fax 209/532–7027 | www.cityhotel.com | 14 rooms | $60–$115 | AE, D, MC, V.

CONCORD

MAP 3, D8

(Nearby towns also listed: Berkeley, Oakland, Vallejo, Walnut Creek)

In the early 1900s Concord was a community of orchards and open fields, where Japanese farmers worked ranches and harvested fruit and nuts. Jazz pianist Dave Brubeck, the son of a rodeo cowboy, was born here at the site of today's Concord Pavilion, where the annual Fujitsu Concord Jazz Festival attracts a roster of international artists. Concord is one of the fastest-growing communities east of San Francisco.

Information: **Contra Costa Convention and Visitors Bureau** | 1333 Willow Pass Rd., Suite 204, 94520 | 925/685–1184 | www.cccvb.vom.

Attractions

Waterworld USA. Part of the Six Flags chain of amusement parks, this popular water-themed complex includes such rides as the Honolulu hurricane, Cliff Hanger, Big Kahuna, Hurricane Waterslides, and more. Parking is $6 extra. | 1950 Waterworld Pkwy. | 925/609–1364 | fax 925/609–1360 | www.sixflags.com | $17–$24 | Sat.–Thurs. 10:30 –6, Fri. 10:30–8; closed in winter.

ON THE CALENDAR

SEPT.: *Fall Fest.* Held every Labor Day in Todos Santos Park, Fall Fest includes arts and crafts, live music, magic shows, face painting, commercial booths, food vendors, and wine and beer tasting. | 925/685–1181 | www.concordchamber.com.

Dining

Elephant Bar Restaurant. Eclectic. Palm trees, vines, rock formations and a small waterfall make a fitting backdrop to the varied cuisine served here, which includes fresh fish, steaks, pasta, salads, and a few in-house creations. Just off the 880 freeway. | 1225 Willow Pass Rd. | 925/671–0119 | fax 925/671–7757 | $10–$25 | AE, MC, V.

Rocco's Ristorante and Pizzeria. Italian. Standouts at this friendly family restaurant include hand tossed gourmet pizza, *ricci con pollo* (marinated chicken), and prawns di Savona. | 2909 Ygnacio Valley Rd. | 925/947–6105 | fax 925/947–6106 | Open daily | $10–15 | AE, D, DC, MC, V.

Wild Rose Restaurant. American. Right on Todos Santos Park, specialties here include prime rib, homemade soups, lobster bisque, and an excellent marinated pork dish. The Wild Rose is 1½ mi east of Rte. 680. | 2151 Salvio St. | 925/680–1300 | Closed Mon. | $20–$25 | AE, DC, MC, V.

Lodging

Best Western Heritage Inn. This two-story hotel has landscaped grounds and a large fountain. It is in a residential neighborhood. Complimentary Continental breakfast. In-room data ports, refrigerators, cable TV. Pool. Hot tub. Business services. | 4600 Clayton Rd. | 925/686–4466 | fax 925/825–0581 | www.bestwestern.com | 126 rooms | $65–$110 | AE, D, DC, MC, V.

Comfort Inn. This three-story hotel is 5 mi from Mount Diablo Park, and 2 mi from both Water World USA and downtown. Complimentary Continental breakfast. In-room data ports, kitchenettes, cable TV, in-room VCRs (and movies). Pool. Exercise equipment. Laundry facilities. Business services. | 1370 Monument Blvd. | 925/827–8998 | fax 925/798–3374 | www.comfortinn.com | 41 rooms | $74–$89 | AE, D, DC, MC, V.

Concord Holiday Inn. One block from Buchanan Fields Golf Course and from Rte. 680, this large hotel is in two buildings. Restaurant, bar. Some microwaves, some refrigerators. Pool, hot tub. Exercise equipment. | 1050 Burnett Ave. | 925/687–5500 | fax 925/363–5500 | 199 rooms | $129–$189 | AE, D, DC, MC, V.

El Monte Motor Inn. This two-story Spanish-style motel is about 1 mi from the 242 freeway. Comlimentary Continental breakfast. Pool. Spa. Laundry facilities. | 3555 Clayton Rd. | 925/682–1601 | fax 925/827–4756 | 43 rooms | $75–$85 | AE, D, DC, MC, V.

Hilton. There are restaurants across the street, and a shopping mall a few blocks away from this 11-story Hilton. Restaurant, bar (with entertainment). In-room data ports, some in-room hot tubs, cable TV. Pool. Exercise equipment. | 1970 Diamond Blvd. | 925/827–2000 | fax 925/671–0984 | www.concordhilton.com | 330 rooms, 4 suites | $89–$157, $375–$475 suites | AE, D, DC, MC, V.

Sheraton Hotel and Conference Center. This three-story complex is 1 mi from downtown and is accessible by taking the Burnett/Concord exit off of I–680. Weekly and monthly rates are available. Restaurant, bar (with entertainment). In-room data ports, refrigerators, cable TV, in-room VCRs. Pool. Hot tub. Putting green. Exercise equipment. Laundry facilities. Business services. Airport shuttle. | 45 John Glenn Dr. | 925/825–7700 | fax 925/674–9567 | www.sheraton.com | 324 rooms | $89–$145 | AE, D, DC, MC, V.

CORONA

MAP 4, J15

(Nearby towns also listed: Anaheim, Irvine, Mission Viejo, Ontario, Pomona, Riverside)

This residential and commercial region of Orange County, with more than 76,000 residents, is at the northern apex of the Santa Ana Mountain Range, the source of hot, easterly "devil winds" or "Santa Anas."

Information: Corona Chamber of Commerce | 904 E. 6th St., 92879 | 909/737–3350.

Attractions

Fender Museum and Educational Center. A prototype of Kurt Cobain's Jagstang, guitars used by Jimi Hendrix, and vintage lap steels that belonged to Leo Fender himself are just a few of the performing arts "artifacts" you can see here. Sponsored by the famous Fender Guitar company, which has a factory just down the street, this museum also provides free instrumental lessons for kids. | 365 N. Main St. | 909/735–2440 | fax 909/735–2576 | Free | Fri.-Sat 11–3, Sun. 11–5.

Glen Ivy Hot Springs. You can relax here in the hot springs surrounded by palm trees. Besides soaking in the springs, admission includes use of the steam room, sauna and the famous red clay mud baths of "Club Mud." For an addition fee you can have a variety of spa treatments. | 25000 Glen Ivy Rd. | 909/277–3529 | www.glenivy.com | $24–29 | Apr.–Oct., daily 9:30–6; Nov.–Mar. 9:30–5.

Prado Basin County Park. You can go fishing, horseback riding, camping, have a picnic, golf, shoot, and take your dog to the dog-training facility at this 2,000-acre park in the Chino Valley Basin. | 16700 Euclid Ave., Encino | 909/597–4260 | fax 909/393–8428 | www.co.san-bernardino.ca.us/parks | $5 per vehicle | Daily 7:30–dusk.

ON THE CALENDAR

OCT.: *Lemon Festival.* Corona was once the "Lemon Capital of the World". Though the trees are all but gone, a festival in their honor remains. Arts and crafts booths, live music, children's activities, and food vendors populate the grounds of the City Hall for a family-oriented fall weekend. | 909/737–3350.

Dining

Claim Jumper Restaurant. American. Western to the core, this kitschy eatery serves hickory beef back ribs, swordfish steak, and smoked salmon. Kids' menu. No smoking. | 380 McKinley St., at Rte. 91 and I–15 | 909/735–6567 | Reservations not accepted | $7–$26 | AE, D, DC, MC, V.

Mimi's Café. Contemporary. You can eat outside on the patio of this western-based chain restaurant. Choose from grilled beef liver, BBQ ribs, Benson's New York steak, or fillet of "soul." Kids' menu. No smoking. Breakfast menu. | 2230 Griffin Way | 909/734–2073 | $7–$12 | AE, MC, DC, V.

T.B. Scott's Seafood Landing. Seafood. A huge aquarium and a coastal village mural set the tone for house specials like Oysters Rockefeller, stuffed salmon, steamed littleneck clams, and swordfish. Kids' menu. No smoking. | 103 N. Lincoln Ave. | 909/340–3474 | Reservations essential | No lunch Sat. | $8–$19 | AE, MC, V.

Villa Amalfi Ristorante. Italian. Penne Bombay, brick-oven pizzas, and a seasonal cranberry-walnut cheesecake are some of the favorites at this dimly-lit spot. Try the chicken parmagiana and the Mud pie. No smoking. | 1237 W. 6th St. | 909/278–3393 | Reservations essential | $7–$40 | AE, DC, MC, V.

Lodging

Best Western Kings Inn. This 2-story motel, is 8 mi from Riverside and Glen Ivy Hot Spring. Complimentary Continental breakfast. Some refrigerators, cable TV. Pool. Hot tub. Business services. Free parking. | 1084 Pomona Rd., 92882 | 909/734–4241 | fax 909/279–5371 | www.bestwestern.com | 84 rooms | $54–$69 | AE, D, DC, MC, V.

Country Inns by Ayres–Corona West. The reception area has a log-cabin feel, while each large studio-suite has southwestern decor. Complimentary breakfast. In-room data ports, microwaves, refrigerators. Outdoor pool. Hot tub. Business services. | 1900 Frontage Rd. | 909/738–9113 | 114 studio-suites | $95 | AE, D, DC, MC, V.

Country Side Inn. Rooms here have an elegant marble entry, sofa sitting area, writing desk, armoire, four-poster beds. Complimentary breakfast. Refrigerators, cable TV. Exercise equipment. Pool. Hot tub. Laundry services. Business services. | 2260 Griffin Way; 91 Fwy. at McKinley | 909/734–2140 or 800/448–8810 | fax 909/734–4056 | www.country-suites.com | 102 rooms | $96 | AE, D, DC, MC, V.

Dynasty Suites. This two-story hotel of suites is 1 mi from the downtown civic center. Restaurant, complimentary Continental breakfast. Microwaves, refrigerators, some in-room hot tubs, cable TV, in-room VCRs (and movies) available. Pool. Hot tub. Business services. Some pets allowed (fee). | 1805 W. Sixth St. | 909/371–7185 or 800/842–7899 | fax 909/371–0401 | www.dynastysuites.com | 56 rooms | $59 | AE, D, DC, MC, V.

Super 8 Motel. Taking the Main St. exit off of I–91 will bring you to this motel which boasts comparatively affordable rates and no-frills accommodations. Air conditioning. | 304 Ramona Ave. | 909/738–0888 | www.super8.com | 36 rooms | $55 | AE, D, MC, V.

CORONA DEL MAR

(Nearby towns also listed: Costa Mesa, Irvine, Mission Viejo, Newport Beach, Santa Ana)

A small jewel on the Pacific Coast, this town has beaches that rival their majestic northern California counterparts. Like its neighbors to the north and south, this beachside village boasts tony stores and pricey restaurants. You can walk out into the bay on a rock jetty, wander around the tide pools, but if you want to snorkel or dive on the two offshore reefs, you'll have to rent gear elsewhere.

Information: Corona del Mar Chamber of Commerce | 2843 East Coast Hwy., Box 72, 92625-0072 | 949/673–4050 | www.cdmchamber.com.

Attractions
Big Corona Beach. This is a great place to romp in the surf, join a game of volleyball, or just stroll along the seashore with your shoes off. The bluff overlooking the beach is called Lookout Point, and is a favorite among locals for watching the sun set over Catalina Island. | Jasmine Ave. at Ocean Blvd. | 949/644–3047 | Parking fee $6.

ON THE CALENDAR
SEPT.: *Castles in the Sand.* Break out your plastic pail and shovel and your camera as intricate castles and fantastic creatures rise out of the sand. Over thirty entries, and hundreds of spectators, make this annual tradition, usually held on the first or second Sunday of the month, a sight to behold. | 949/729–4400 (the Newport Harbor chamber of commerce).

Dining
The Bungalow. Seafood. You can eat outside on the patio at this Craftsman-style restaurant known for its lobster with wild rice. Top dishes also include hazelnut-crusted chilean seabass, New York strip pepper steak, and rack of lamb. No smoking. | 2441 E. Coast Hwy. | 949/673–6585 | No lunch | $17–$25 | AE, MC, V.

C'est Si Bonne. French. Fresh, hearty pâté-and-cheese plates and interesting sandwiches at lunch are popular at this intimate café. No smoking. | 3444 E. Coast Hwy. | No dinner | $20 | AE, D, DC, MC, V.

Quiet Woman. Continental. This British pub is known for its traditional English dishes, and also for pasta, seafood, lamb, burgers, and mesquite-grilled black angus steak. Entertainment Wed.–Sat. No smoking. | 3224 E. Pacific Coast Hwy. | 949/640–7440 | No lunch Sat. & Sun. | $20–$26 | AE, MC, V.

CORONADO

(Nearby towns also listed: Chula Vista, San Diego, San Ysidro)

This narrow isthmus south of San Diego is one of southern California's prettiest beach resorts, popular with tourists as well as full-time residents. It's also home to a U.S. Naval Air Station and many hotels. The famous Hotel Del Coronado, recognizable to many from *Some Like it Hot* with Tony Curtis, Jack Lemmon and Marilyn Monroe, is here.

Information: Coronado Chamber of Commerce | 1224 10 St., Suite 103, 92118 | 619/435–9260 | www.coronadochamber.com.

Attractions

Coronado City Beach. The sand is white, and the beach is dotted with small sand dunes where the kids can play. There are fire rings, rest rooms, and lifeguards on duty May–September. There's free parking on Ocean Boulevard and side streets. | 900 Ocean Blvd. | 619/522–7380 | Free | Daily.

Silver Strand State Beach. You can see 10 mi across to the Point Loma bluffs from here, a breathtaking view with large naval vessels and cruise ships on San Diego Bay. You can go swimming, surf fishing, and clamming in the mild water. Pedestrian tunnels lead from the parking lot to the beach, with rest rooms, fire pits, picnic tables, showers, and concession stands. | 5000 State Hwy. 75 | 619/435–5184 | $4 per vehicle | 8AM–9PM.

ON THE CALENDAR

JUNE–SEPT.: *Concerts in the Park.* Free concerts in Spreckels Park are perfect for lawn chairs and picnic lunches. Locals and visitors alike soak in the sun and sea breeze, as a variety of local and rising musicians ply their trade. | 619/435–9260.

Dining

Azzura Point. Contemporary. You can see Coronado Bridge and San Diego from here. Menu specials are roasted black bass, lobster tails, red pepper salad, crab salad, salmon, scallops, and rack of lamb. Kids' menu. No smoking. | 4000 Coronado Bay Rd. | 619/424–4000 | No lunch | $55–$75 | AE, D, DC, MC, V.

Brigantine. Seafood. Swordfish, prime rib, and twin lobster tails are popular here. There's an outside lounge area. Kids' menu, early-bird suppers. No smoking. | 1333 Orange Ave. | 619/435–4166 | No lunch weekends | $14–$36 | AE, DC, MC, V.

Chez Loma. French. Lots of windows, soft lighting, and an upstairs Victorian parlor for coffee and dessert are some of the comforts here. Among the more elaborate dishes are carpaccio de filet mignon, New York steak au poivre, and herb-roasted double pork loin chop with a braised fennel and Dijon mustard sauce. Outdoor sidewalk dining. Sunday brunch. No smoking. | 1132 Loma Ave. | 619/435–0661 | No lunch | $17–$30 | AE, DC, MC, V.

L'Escale. Mediterranean. L'Escale overlooks San Diego skyline and bay, and its terrace is surrounded by ponds, flowers, and lush plants. Choose from grilled beef tenderloin, sautéed salmon, grilled rack of lamb, lobster and shellfish. Jazz Friday and Saturday Memorial Day–Labor Day. Breakfast. Kids' menu. No smoking. | 2000 2nd St. | 619/435–3000 | $16–$21 | AE, D, DC, MC, V.

Marius. French. One of San Diego's top restaurants, this refined establishment serves an impressive menu of regional dishes, from Parisian haute cuisine to Provencal country cooking, in an elegant dining room. | 2000 2nd St. | 619/435–3000 | Reservations essential on weekends | Closed Sun.–Mon. No lunch | $42–$52 | AE, D, DC, MC, V.

Mexican Village Restaurante. Mexican. With lots of tile, a skylight, and a fountain, this restaurant achieves the south-of-the-border look. But it's not all tacos and burritos. You can also try Caesar salad with cheese dressing and marinated grilled chicken, penne with tequila tomato cream sauce. Entertainment Thurs.–Sat. Kids' menu. No smoking. | 120 Orange Ave. | 619/435–1822 | Sunday brunch. No lunch or supper Sun. | $9–$16 | AE, D, DC, MC, V.

Peohe's. Contemporary. You can see San Diego Harbor and skyline while tasting halibut with bananas and macadamia nuts, and swordfish with sweet-and-sour fruit sauce and coconut. Kids' menu. Sunday brunch. No smoking. | 1201 1st St. | 619/437–4474 | No supper Sun. | $17–$39 | AE, D, DC, MC, V.

Primavera. Italian. The split-level restaurant has osso bucco, penne putanesca and other pasta, and chicken campagnola on the menu. No smoking. | 932 Orange Ave. | 619/435–0454 | No lunch weekends | $13–$33 | AE, D, DC, MC, V.

Prince of Wales. American. The silver-and-white grill at Hotel Del Coronado has towering windows overlooking the ocean. It's a perfect setting for seafood – try the roasted sterling salmon, flash-seared California spiny lobster and day- boat halibut Lemon grass broth or heavier fare such as venison trio loin chop and braised shank, and white corn polenta. Jazz piano nightly. No smoking. | 1500 Orange Ave. | 619/522–8818 | No lunch | $25–$29 | AE, D, DC, MC, V.

Rhinoceros Café and Grill. Seafood. This restaurant's modest interior is belied by its top quality dishes—local favorites include the filet mignon, and the lobster bisque, which is said to be the island's best. | 1166 Orange Ave. | 619/435–2121 | No lunch | $10.95–$20.95 | AE, D, DC, MC, V.

Lodging

Cherokee Lodge. This small inn, brought across the bay more than a century ago by barge, exudes elegance and charm with armoires, embroidered couches, polished headboards and beautiful woodwork. Cable TV, telephone. | 964 D Ave. | 877/743–6217 (toll–free) or 619/437–1967 | fax 619/437–1012 | www.cherokeelodge.com | 12 rooms | $110 | Complimentary Continental breakfast | AE, D, V, MC.

HOTEL DEL CORONADO

This beautiful, stately building is a must-see for anyone in the San Diego area. "The Del," as it's known, was made famous by its legions of celebrated guests, and its role in the 1959 movie *Some Like it Hot*. When Jack Lemmon and Tony Curtis head out of town posing as women in an all-girl band—with Marilyn Monroe as the band's singer and ukulele player—they hop a train south to Florida. Where they really end up is the Hotel Del Coronado. Set on 26 acres of Pacific Ocean beachfront, this Victorian jewel still charms and delights.

In the late 1800s, two businessmen from the Midwest, Elisha Babcock and H. L. Story, dreamed of building a resort hotel that would become the "talk of the Western world." They imported lumber and labor from San Francisco, had a mahogany bar built in Pennsylvania, then had the bar transported by ship (fully assembled) around the tip of South America. An electrical powerplant and a kiln to fire the bricks were built on site. Even back then, the hotel cost the astronomical sum of $1 million to construct and furnish.

In 1891 Benjamin Harrison became the first of many U.S. Presidents to stay at the Del. Charles Lindbergh was honored at the Del after his legendary trans-Atlantic flight in 1927. L. Frank Baum, the author of *The Wonderful Wizard of Oz*, is said to have based his vision of the Emerald City on the turret-design of the hotel. And many think that Edward (the then Prince of Wales) first met Wallis Spencer Simpson, the divorcee for whom he gave up the English throne, at the Del when he visited in 1920.

© Corbis

Coronado Inn. Nine blocks from the beach and two blocks from the bay, this small establishment looks more like a summer home than a hotel. Special touches include gas barbecue grills and a large poolside patio. Complimentary Continental breakfast. Refrigerators. Pool. Laundry facilities. | 266 Orange Ave. | 619/435–4121 | www.coronadoinn.com | 31 rooms | $110–$160 | AE, D, DC, MC, V.

★ **Coronado Island Marriott Resort.** From your patio or balcony you can overlook the 16-acre waterfront view of the San Diego Bay and see wildlife, waterfalls, and lush landscaping. There is a dock for guests arriving by water. Restaurants, bar (with entertainment), room service. Minibars, cable TV. 3 pools. Hot tub, spa. Tennis. Gym, water sports. Bicycles. Business services. Parking (fee). | 2000 2nd St. | 619/435–3000 or 800/543–4300 | fax 619/435–3032 | www.marriott.com | 265 rooms, 35 suites | $200–$275, $424 suites | AE, D, DC, MC, V.

El Cordova Hotel. Built as a countryside mansion in 1902, this 2-story Spanish-style building was converted into a hotel in 1930. You can walk to the beach from here. Restaurant, bar, picnic area. Some kitchenettes, cable TV. Pool. Business services. | 1351 Orange Ave. | 619/435–4131 or 800/229–2032 | fax 619/435–0632 | www.elcordovahotel.com | 40 rooms | $99–$329 | AE, D, DC, MC, V.

Glorietta Bay Inn. This harbor-side, Edwardian-style 2-story mansion, with five wings, was built in 1908 for sugar king John D. Spreckels. Some of the rooms have garden, ocean, or bay views. Complimentary Continental breakfast. In-room data ports, refrigerators, some kitchenettes, microwaves, cable TV. Pool. Hot tub. Laundry facilities. Business services. | 1630 Glorietta Blvd. | 619/435–3101 or 800/283–9383 | fax 619/435–6182 | www.gloriettabayinn.com | 100 rooms | $135–$225 | AE, D, DC, MC, V.

★ **Hotel Del Coronado.** "The Del" is an 1888 building with a rich history of guests such as Marilyn Monroe, Frank Sinatra, and, it's rumored, a resident ghost. A newer building was added in 1977. Dining rooms, bar (with entertainment), room service. In-room data ports, in-room safes. 2 pools. Beauty salon, hot tub, massage. Tennis. Gym. Business services. Parking (fee). | 1500 Orange Ave. | 619/435–6611 or 800/468–3533 | fax 619/522–8262 | www.hoteldel.com | 609 rooms, 91 suites | $205–$600 rooms, $650–$975 suites, $850–1000 apartment | AE, D, DC, MC, V.

La Avenida Inn. A 2-story motel 1 block from historic Hotel Del Coronado and 1½ blocks to the beaches. Restaurant, complimentary Continental breakfast. Cable TV. Pool. | 1315 Orange Ave. | 619/435–319 or 1800/437–0162 | fax 619/435–5024 | 29 rooms | $140–$185 | AE, DC, MC, V.

Loews Coronado Bay. You can dock your boat at the 80-slip marina here on the Silver Strand, 10 mi southwest of San Diego. All rooms have views of the bay, ocean, or marina. The lounge offers nightly entertainment. Its restaurant, Azzura Point, *above,* is known for its fresh seafood. 4 restaurants, bar (with entertainment), room service. In-room data ports, minibars, microwaves, cable TV. 3 pools. Beauty salon, hot tubs, massage. 5 tennis courts. Gym, beach, marina, water sports, boating, bicycles. Video games. Kids' programs. Laundry facilities. Business services. Some pets allowed. | 4000 Coronado Bay Rd. | 619/424–4000 or 800/235–6397 | fax 619/424–4400 | www.loewscoronadobay.com | 405 rooms, 33 suites | $209–$315 rooms, $300–$1,300, suites | AE, D, DC, MC, V.

Villa Capri. Look for the world-famous "Diving Lady" neon sign outside this hotel. The classic 1950s architecture is fitting for its frequent brushes with fame—ask innkeeper John Miller about the hotel's storied history. Microwaves, refrigerators, in-room VCRs. Pool. | 1417 Orange Ave. | 619/435–4137 | www.villacapribythesea.com | 14 rooms | $150–$300 | AE, D, DC, MC, V.

CORTE MADERA

(Nearby towns also listed: Sausalito, Tiburon)

Incorporated in 1916, Corte Madera is a small town of 8,300 residents nestled in the green Marin countryside. The city of 4 square mi extends from San Francisco Bay on the east side of U.S. 101 to Mt. Tamalpais on the west. This bedroom community, about 10 mi north of the Golden Gate Bridge, is within hiking, biking, and driving distance of some of the state's most beautiful areas. It's an easygoing, friendly suburban town with open space in every direction.

Information: **Corte Madera Chamber of Commerce** | 129 Town Center, 94925 | 415/924–0441 | chamber@www.cortemadera.org | www.cortemadera.org.

Attractions

Town Center and The Village. The Village has many of the major chain stores, including Nordstrom, Macy's, The Limited, and more. Across the highway, the Town Center features boutique and specialty shops. Both are outdoor malls, with plenty of pleasant strolling to be had. | U.S. 101 at Paradise Dr. | Daily around 9 AM–7 PM.

ON THE CALENDAR
JULY: *4th of July Parade.* A huge local event, up to 15,000 people head to the town center to see the floats and enjoy live music, food vendors, arts and crafts booths, and children's activities. Starts in downtown Larkspur and ends in the Corte Madera Town Park. | 415/924–0441 | www.cortemadera.org.

Dining

California Café. Contemporary. This café has a comfortable, spacious setting and is decorated with modern artwork. The menu is basic but solid; people come here for steaks, fish, and pasta. In nice weather, you can eat on the patio at a table covered with a green umbrella. Kids' menu. Sunday brunch. No smoking. | 1736 Redwood Hwy. | 415/924–2233 | Reservations essential | $20–$25 | AE, D, DC, MC, V.

Lodging

Best Western Corte Madera Inn. This is not your usual two-story chain motel. Rooms at this beautifully landscaped five-acre property, built in the 1960s, are furnished in a casual, California style, and the big, square pool is lovely. There's a free shuttle to the San Francisco ferry, and a pleasant shopping mall, with food courts and one good restaurant, is across the street. Restaurant, picnic area, complimentary Continental breakfast. In-room data ports, refrigerators, cable TV. Pool, wading pool. Hot tubs, massage. Exercise equipment. Playground. Laundry facilities. Business services. | 1815 Redwood Hwy. | 415/924–1502 | fax 415/924–5419 | www.bestwestern.com | 110 rooms, 6 suites | $110–$131, $155–$200 suites | AE, D, DC, MC, V.

Howard Johnson Express Inn. A smaller version of a Howard Johnson chain motel, the inn is next door to one restaurant and within two or three blocks of several others. Complimentary Continental breakfast. Microwaves, refrigerators. | 1595 Casa Buena Dr. | 415/924–3570 | fax 415/924–6153 | www.hojo.com | 18 rooms | $153–$150 | AE, D, DC, MC, V.

Lark Creek Inn. Contemporary. Chef Bradley Ogden put this Victorian house-turned-restaurant among the redwoods on the map for his innovative twists on American cuisine. The menu changes daily. Depending on the season, you might try the butter potato and spring onion soup, grilled Norwegian salmon, rosemary-braised lamb shank, or butterscotch pudding. There's open-air dining on creekside patio. Sunday brunch. No smoking. | 234 Magnolia Ave., Larkspur | 415/924–7766 | Reservations essential | No lunch Sat. | $15–$35 | AE, MC, V.

Marin Suites. This all-suite hotel has fully equipped kitchens and separate living rooms. The three-story building is in a residential area practically next door to a movie theater and close to restaurants and shopping malls. The furnishings are standard contemporary. Complimentary Continental breakfast. Cable TV. Pool, sauna. Exercise equipment. Laundry facilities. | 45 Tamal Vista Blvd. | 415/924–3608 or 800/362–3372 | fax 415/924–0761 | 128 suites | $119–$199 | AE, D, DC, MC, V.

COSTA MESA

MAP 9, I8

(Nearby towns also listed: Corona Del Mar, Huntington Beach, Irvine, Newport Beach)

The mid-19th century saw a flurry of development in this small community, but in 1889, a storm washed out the railroad and brought financial disaster. The area soon reverted to farming country. The economic situation was looking up, but then the Depression and a 1933 earthquake struck. However World War II brought thousands of people to the area for training at the Santa Ana Army Air Base. After the war ended, many soldiers returned with their families, setting in motion a population boom that continues today. The area is now a major commercial, industrial, and residential center with 96,400 residents. The town slogan, however, is, "The City of the Arts." It is now home to a regional symphony orchestra and the South Coast Repertory Theater. The 3,000-seat Segerstrom Hall inside the Orange County Performing Arts Center hosts symphony concerts, operas, ballets, and Broadway musicals.

Information: Costa Mesa Chamber of Commerce | 1700 Adams Ave., Suite 101, 92626 | 714/885–9090.

Attractions

★ **South Coast Plaza.** One of the first mega-malls, South Coast Plaza includes a merry-go-round, Macy's, Nordstroms, J. Crew, Guess, and many other department stores and specialty shops. | 2333 Bristol St. | 714/435–2100 | Daily.

ON THE CALENDAR
MAY: *Scottish Games.* Held Memorial Day weekend, this two-day festival was inspired by the customs, culture, and sports of British Isles. | 714/885–9090.
JULY: *Orange County Fair.* This large, traditional fair has rides, food, and agricultural exhibits. | 714/708–3247.
SEPT.: *Costa Mesa Pow Wow.* For three full days, you can enjoy the music, dancing and food of numerous Native American tribes, as well as cultural displays and children's activities. | 714/663–1102 | www.indiancenter.org.

Dining

★ **Bangkok IV.** Thai. Despite its shopping mall location and stark black and white decor, this restaurant holds its own as a serious eatery. Among the specialties are *pla dung* (steamed catfish with a chile-garlic-lemongrass sauce) and the *kai pudd keng* (ginger chicken with mushrooms and garlic). | 3333 Bear St., across from South Coast Plaza | 714/540–7661 | $8.95–$18.95 | AE, D, DC, MC, V.

★ **Diva.** Continental. Convenient to the Performing Arts Center, Diva offers dishes that combine unusual ingredients, artfully presented. The bistro-style dining room is quiet, with candles on the tables. The vegetable plate includes artichoke, steamed vegetables, and a mushroom ragu. The grilled veal chops with hazelnut butter are another favorite, as are prawns served over mashed potatoes. No smoking. | 600 Anton Blvd., Ste. 100 | 714/754-0600 | $19–$24 | AE, DC, MC, V.

El Torito Grill. Southwestern. This lively and upscale offshoot of the El Torito chain is great place for margaritas, and the guacamole couldn't be fresher—it's prepared tableside. Try the grilled fresh fish, enchiladas, and fajitas. Sunday brunch. No smoking. | 633 Anton Blvd. | 714/662-2672 | $8–$15 | AE, D, DC, MC, V.

Golden Truffle. Southwestern. This is innovative California cooking with French and Caribbean influences. The fashionable, yet casual restaurant serves dishes like "Red Hot" lobster taquitos, chipotle barbecue duck legs with potatoes Beaujolais, and braised lamb shank with noodles. There's also an extensive wine list. The covered patio has heaters. Open-air dining. Jazz Thurs. in summer. No smoking. | 1767 Newport Blvd. | 949/645-9858 | Closed Sun. & Mon. | $13–$19 | AE, MC, V.

Habana. Cuban. With rustic candelabras and murals, this industrial space blends an Old World flavor with a hip contemporary flair. The Cuban and other Caribbean specialities are as flavorful as the setting is cool. Try the ropa vieja (shredded beef) or the plantain-crusted chicken. Cuban music plays inside and out. You can dine on the small patio. Entertainment six nights a week. No smoking. | 2930 Bristol St. | 714/556-0176 | $12–$18 | AE, D, DC, MC, V.

★ **Memphis Soul Café.** American. Some say that the gumbo here rivals the best, that the turkey sandwich with pesto may be addictive and that the pork chops are works of art. The retro setting and the southern menu have made this one of the area's most worthwhile eateries—and it's one of the most affordable as well. Umbrellas shade the tables on the patio. Jazz Thursday. No smoking. | 2920 Bristol St. | 714/432-7685 | $17–$20 | AE, DC, MC, V.

Pinot Provence. French. With a mix of fresh California ingredients and traditional Provencal cooking, the menu boasts innovative fare such as braised oxtail ravioli with Swiss chard and grilled Portobello mushrooms in brown-butter sauce. Eighteenth century antiques adorn the main dining room. There is an outdoor patio. | 686 Anton Blvd. | 714/444-5900 | Reservations essential | $25–$38 | AE, D, DC, MC, V.

Trattoria Spiga. Italian. Don't let the mall setting fool you. This place is elegant in an understated way and has a regular crowd that enjoys its trattoria-style cooking. You can order *bucatini all'amatriciana* (hollow straw-shaped noodles sautéed with onions, Italian smoked bacon in a lightly spicy tomato sauce), thin-style crust pizza, or a simple *bruschetta al pomodoro*. In nice weather you can eat on the patio, styled after an Italian villa. No smoking. | 3333 Bear St. | 714/540-3365 | $11–$25 | AE, D, DC, MC, V.

Lodging

Best Western Newport Mesa Inn. Near the center of the Irvine corporate business community is this three-story building, accessible by taking the Del Mar exit off of the 55. Complimentary Continental breakfast. Refrigerators, some in-room hot tubs, cable TV. Pool. Fitness center. Hot tub, sauna. Laundry facilities. Business services. Some pets allowed. | 2642 Newport Blvd. | 949/650-3020 | fax 949/650-1220 | www.bestwestern.com | 97 rooms | $69–$149 | AE, D, DC, MC, V.

Costa Mesa Residence Inn by Marriott. More like an apartment complex than a hotel, accomodations here include furnished kitchens, sofas, grocery service, and some bi-level units. Barbecue pits are a nice touch, especially for families. Complimentary appetizers and drinks are served Mon.–Thurs. from 5–7. Complimentary Continental breakfast. Pool, hot tub. Exercise equipment. | 881 W. Baker St. | 714/241-8800 | fax 714/546-4308 | 65 studios, 55 penthouses (bi-level) | $149–$199 | AE, D, DC, MC, V.

Country Side Inn and Suites. This two-building inn, built in the mid-1980s, is on the border of Newport Beach and Costa Mesa. The Queen Anne-style rooms, with a vaguely European feel, are homey and inviting. You can mingle with other guests at the evening cocktail and hors d'oeuvres hour, or near the fountain in the courtyard. Restaurant, bar, complimentary breakfast. Microwaves, refrigerators, room service, cable TV. 2 pools. Hot tubs. Exercise equipment. Laundry facilities. Business services. Airport shuttle, parking (free). | 325 Bristol St. | 714/549–0300 or 800/322–9992 | fax 714/662–0828 | www.countrysuites.com | 290 rooms, 168 suites | $89–$112, $101–$144 suites | AE, D, DC, MC, V.

Cozy Inn. This two-story motor lodge with outside corridors overlooks a small pool. It is 1½ mi from Newport Beach, the Orange County Fairgrounds, and the Pacific Amphitheater. Some microwaves, refrigerators, cable TV. Pool. Business services. | 325 W. Bay St. | 949/650–2055 | fax 949/650–6281 | www.cozyinn.com | 29 rooms | $58 | AE, D, DC, MC, V.

Doubletree Hotel. Near John Wayne Airport, this modern, spacious 7-story hotel has a glittering atrium lobby with glass elevators. Rooms have a contemporary feel and a warm sage and yellow color-scheme. The hotel is next to the South Coast Plaza shopping center. 1 restaurant, bar (with entertainment), room service. In-room data ports, refrigerators, cable TV. Pool. Beauty salon, hot tub, massage. Exercise equipment. Business services. Airport shuttle. Some pets allowed. | 3050 Bristol St. | 714/540–7000 | fax 714/540–9176 | www.doubletreehotels.com | 484 rooms | $89–$179 | AE, D, DC, MC, V.

Holiday Inn–Costa Mesa. This 5-story chain property is 1½ mi from John Wayne Airport and one block from South Coast Plaza Retail Center, one of California's major shopping malls. Restaurant, bar, picnic area, room service. In-room data ports, cable TV. Pool, wading pool. Exercise equipment. Laundry facilities. Airport shuttle. | 3131 S. Bristol St. | 714/557–3000 | fax 714/957–8185 | www.holiday-inn.com | 229 rooms | $89–$120 | AE, D, DC, MC, V.

La Quinta Inn. Just 3 blocks from the I–405, this L-shaped chain hotel surrounds the central swimming pool. Complimentary Continental breakfast. Some microwaves, some refrigerators, cable TV. Pool. Exercise equipment. Airport shuttle. | 1515 S. Coast Dr. | 714/957–5841 | 160 rooms, 2 suites | $59–$69, $99 suites | AE, D, DC, MC, V.

Marriott Suites. This 11-story, all-suites hotel is in the heart of the business district, an ideal location for the business traveller. Restaurant, bar. In-room data ports, refrigerators, cable TV. Pool. Hot tub. Exercise equipment. Laundry facilities. Business services. Airport shuttle. | 500 Anton Blvd. | 714/957–1100 | fax 714/966–8495 | www.marriott.com | 253 suites | $109–$169 | AE, D, DC, MC, V.

Ramada Limited. In the business district, this simple 3-story hotel is one mi from Newport's attractive beaches and restaurants. Restaurant, complimentary Continental breakfast. Some microwaves, refrigerators, cable TV. Pool. Hot tub. Exercise equipment. Laundry facilities. Airport shuttle. Some pets allowed. | 1680 Superior Ave. | 949/645–2221 | fax 949/650–9125 | 140 rooms, 20 suites | $79–$109 rooms, $119–$169 suites | AE, D, DC, MC, V.

Travelodge Hacienda. A block from I–55, this hotel is just 1 mi from the beach. Mini-bars, microwaves, refrigerators. Pool, hot tub. Laundry facilities. | 1951 Newport Blvd. | 949/650–2999 | fax 949/650–2699 | www.travelodge.com | 53 rooms, 5 suites | $59–$85 | AE, D, DC, MC, V.

Vagabond Inn. The Costa Mesa branch of this western-based chain is has lots of windows and lots of plants make the interior cheery, and the rooms are spacious. Complimentary Continental breakfast. Microwaves, cable TV. Pool. Hot tub. Exercise equipment. Business services. Airport shuttle. Free parking. Some pets allowed (fee). | 3205 Harbor Blvd. | 714/557–8360 | fax 714/662–7596 | www.vagabondinn.com | 125 rooms | $63–$80 | AE, D, DC, MC, V.

Westin South Coast Plaza. This 16-story hotel is downtown, next to the South Coast Plaza Retail Center and Orange County Performing Arts Center. Restaurant, bar (with entertainment), room service. In-room data ports, minibars, cable TV. Pool. Tennis. Exercise equipment. Business services. Airport shuttle. Parking (fee). Some pets allowed. | 686 Anton Blvd. | 714/540–2500 | fax 714/662–6695 | www.westin.com | 390 rooms | $125–$275 | AE, D, DC, MC, V.

come out for the parade and street fair by day and the the fireworks over Lake Gregory by night. | 909/338–2706.

Dining
Cliffhanger Restaurant. American. Two miles outside of Crestline on the way to Lake Arrowhead, this restaurant is known for the prime rib and barbecue pork. | 25187 Rte. 18 | 909/338–3397 | fax 909/338–2482 | In winter, lunch only Thurs.–Sun., closed Mon. | $15–$25 | AE, D, MC, V.

Lodging
North Shore Inn. Ten rooms and a suite occupy this three-story Swiss chalet-styled inn. Every room has a private balcony overlooking Lake Gregory, and a few have stone fireplaces. Ask about special discounts to area restaurants, rentals and activities. | 24202 Lake Dr. | 909/338–5230 | www.thenorthshoreinn.com | 10 rooms, 1 suite with full kitchen | $50–85, $95–115 suite | AE, MC, V.

CULVER CITY

(Nearby towns also listed: Beverly Hills, Los Angeles, Marina del Ray, Venice, West Hollywood, Westwood Village)

This district is primarily recognized as a base for television and motion picture companies like Sony Studios, but it is also home to an ethnically mixed, middle class population of 38,800.

Information: **Culver City Chamber of Commerce** | 4249 Overland Ave., 90230 | 310/287–3850.

Attractions
Sony Pictures Studio. Once the MGM Studios of Scarlett O'Hara and Laurel and Hardy fame, today's Sony provides two-hour guided tours that include visits to soundstages, wardrobe shops, backdrops sets and more. When not in use, visitors can take the stage on the sets of such shows as Jeopardy or Family Law. You must be 12 years old to be admitted. | 10202 W. Washington Blvd. | 323/520–8687 | $20 | Tours at 9:30, 11, noon, and 3.

ON THE CALENDAR
DEC.: *Western Hemisphere Marathon.* Second only to Boston as the oldest marathon in the United States, the race starts and ends in Culver City, and includes the alternative divisions of in-line skating, bicycling and a 5K walk. | 310/287–3850 | www.culvercitychamber.com.

Dining
George Petrelli's Famous Steak House. American. Founded in 1931, this Culver City institution is famous for its prime rib, filet mignon and steaks. Busy, causual and family-oriented, they also serve seafood and Italian dishes. | 5615 Sepulveda Blvd. | 310/398–9777 | Sat. and Sun. no lunch | $18–$25 | AE, MC, V.

Lodging
Culver Hotel. Built in 1924 and designated an Historic Landmark, the Culver Hotel was owned briefly by John Wayne, and movie stars and cast members dating back to Laurel & Hardy have stayed here. Each room is furnished with French antiques that pre-date 1888 and each bathroom is marble tiled. Restaurant, bar, room service. In-room data ports, some in-room hot tubs, cable TV. | 940 Culver Blvd. | 310/838–7963 or 888/328–5837 | fax 310/815–9618 | www.culverhotel.com | 48 rooms, 2 suites | $129–$189 | AE, D, DC, MC, V.

Ramada Plaza Hotel. This 12-story, modern chain hotel is two mi north of the airport, in a residential area. Restaurant, bar. Some refrigerators, cable TV. Pool. Hot tub. Exercise equipment. Laundry services. Business services. Airport shuttle. | 6333 Bristol Pkwy. | 310/670–3200 | fax 310/641–8925 | ramada@earthlink.net | www.ramada.com | 265 rooms | $149 | AE, D, DC, MC, V.

CUPERTINO

MAP 6, E9

(Nearby towns also listed: Mountain View, San Jose, Sunnyvale)

During the 1776 expedition to found the presidio of St. Francis in San Francisco, Don Juan Bautista de Anza encamped in what is now Cupertino, and there his cartographer christened a nearby creek Arroyo San Joseph Copertino in honor of his patron from Copertino, Italy. It wasn't until 1904, though, that the name Cupertino was actually applied to the village. Many early European settlers and later industry leaders based their livelihoods on vineyards and grapes. The farmlands have been turned under, and turned over to high-tech. Apple Computers, along with Hewlett-Packard, figure prominently in this largely residential and commercial community.

Information: Cupertino Chamber of Commerce | 20455 Silverado Ave., 95014-4439 | 408/252–7054 | info@www.cupertino-chamber.org | www.cupertino-chamber.org.

Attractions

Flint Center for the Performing Arts. Many professional performing arts organizations use the Flint Center, which also hosts South Bay series performances by the San Jose Symphony, the San Francisco Symphony, and Broadway companies. Call for show times. | 21250 Stevens Creek Blvd. | 408/864–8820 | www.flintcenter.com.

ON THE CALENDAR
AUG.: *Art and Wine Festival.* You can enjoy live music, stroll amidst artists displaying their work, sample wines and food, and visit with local companies at the business expo in Memorial Park. | 406/252–7052.

Dining

Fontana's Italian Restaurant. Italian. There's a cozy fireplace and display kitchen in this Italian restaurant that's been around since 1985. The beige walls of the dining room are lined with murals, and there are lots of plants. Specialties include crab-stuffed scampi with roasted garlic, and angel-hair pasta with lobster, mushrooms, and green onions, in a light cream sauce. The restaurant is also known for a variety of fresh fish. Early-bird suppers. Beer and wine only. | 20840 Stevens Creek Blvd. | 408/725–0188 | No lunch Sun. | $11–$19 | AE, DC, MC, V.

Lodging

Courtyard by Marriott. The three-story hotel was built in the mid-1990s and caters to business travelers visiting Silicon Valley. Some rooms have views of the courtyard. Restaurant, bar. In-room data ports, refrigerators, cable TV. Pool. Exercise equipment. Laundry facilities. | 10605 Wolfe Rd. | 408/252–9100 | fax 408/252–0632 | www.marriott.com | 149 rooms, 12 suites | $99–$239 rooms, $139–$259 suites | AE, D, DC, MC, V.

Cupertino Inn. This luxurious, intimate hotel boasts an attractive central courtyard and nicely appointed rooms, some with fireplaces. In the business district, the four-story hotel was built in the mid-1990s. In-room data ports, refrigerators, cable TV, in-room VCRs. Pool. Laundry facilities. Business services. Airport shuttle. | 10889 N. De Anza Blvd. | 408/

996–7700 | fax 408/257–0578 | info@cupertinoinn.com | www.cupertinoinn.com | 125 rooms | $99–$214 | AE, D, DC, MC, V.

Hilton Garden Inn. In the heart of Silicon Valley, this 5-story, beige stucco Mediterranean-style contemporary hotel is 600 ft from I–280 and 7 mi from downtown San Jose. You can walk 4 blocks to the Valco Mall. The Great America theme park is 5 mi northeast in Santa Clara and Winchester Mystery house is 3 mi south. The restaurant serves a full American style breakfast. Restaurant, bar. Cable TV. Outdoor pool. Outdoor hot tub. Laundry service. Airport shuttle. | 10741 N. Wolfe Rd. | 408/777–8787 | fax 408/777–8040 | 165 rooms, 6 suites | $249 rooms, $329 suites | AE, D, DC, MC, V.

DANA POINT

(Nearby towns also listed: Laguna Beach, Mission Viejo, San Clemente, San Juan Capistrano)

This Orange County seaside town's claim to fame is its small-boat marina nestled in a dramatic natural harbor surrounded by towering bluffs. Inside Dana Point Harbor, Swim Beach has a fishing pier, barbecues, food stands, parking, rest rooms, and showers.

Information: Dana Point Chamber of Commerce | Box 12, 92629 | 949/496–1555 | www.danapoint-chamber.com.

Attractions
Doheny State Beach. This broad, sandy beach stretches for 1 mi, and is shielded from the highway by eucalyptus trees. It's good for beginning surfers and swimming, sunning, picnicking, and barbecueing. For smaller crowds, go next door to wide and sandy Capistrano Beach, which is less well known. | 25300 Dana Point Harbor Dr. | 949/496–6172 | fax 949/496–9469 | parks.ca.gov | $5 per vehicle | 6 AM–8PM.

Salt Creek Beach Park. More than a mile of long, sandy beach is at the foot of the scenic coastal bluffs overlooking the Pacific. The beach is longer than it initially appears. Bluffs to the north and south obscure several hundred yards of sandy beach. The beach is popular for swimming, surfing, and Boogie board riding. You can go surf fishing or explore tide pools at a rocky area toward the south end of the beach. Lifeguards are on duty from Memorial Day to Labor Day. | 34551 Puerto Pl | 949/661–7013 | www.oc.ca.gov/pfrd/hbp/salt-crek.htm | Free; parking $1 | 5AM–midnight.

ON THE CALENDAR
FEB.–MAR. *Festival of Whales.* Grey whales headed south to Mexico (or back north to Alaska) pass Dana Point from December to mid-April. At the height of the migration, this small community celebrates their passage with a whale-sized street fair, complete with educational displays, tours of the Oceanic Institute, whale-watching trips, children's activities, food vendors and live music. | 949/496–1555.

Dining
A Tavoli Ferrantelli. Italian. Roman columns and arches as well as hand-painted murals set the stage for your Italian meal. The specialties include Chilean sea bass, spaghetti tutto mare, and veal chop pienontese. You can dine on the patio, which has multiple waterfalls, a rose garden, and statues. No smoking. | 25001 Dana Point Harbor Dr. | 949/493–1401 | $12–$28 | AE, D, MC, V.

Dining Room. Contemporary. Located in the luxurious Ritz-Carlton Laguna Niguel resort, this restaurant serves Mediterranean cuisine in a dining room adorned with large mirrors and chandeliers. Dishes include fillet of turbot with wild mushrooms and foie gras crust and seared fillet of daurade with Szechuan pepper and confit onions in Cabernet bouillabaisse broth. A selection of seafood and salads is also on the menu. A five-course food and wine pairing is available. | 1 Ritz Carlton Dr., Dana Point | 949/240–2000 | Reservations essential | Jacket required | Closed Sun., Mon. No lunch | $75–$85 | AE, D, DC, MC, V.

Harbor Grill. Seafood. The dining area includes an outdoor patio with a harbor view. A local favorite, the Harbor Grill serves up mesquite-broiled, blackened, and grilled fresh seafood entrées that include marinated swordfish, grilled sea bass, and scallops with curry sauce. The open-view grill lets you watch the chef at work. No smoking. | 34499 Golden Lantern St. | 949/240–1416 | $12–$22 | AE, D, DC, MC, V.

Luciana's. Italian. The intimate dining room with fire places and French windows, friendly service, and carefully prepared Northern Italian dishes give Luciana's strong appeal. Try the seafood Luciana, shellfish, pasta in a light tomato sauce, and osso bucco. You can eat on the small patio in nice weather. No smoking. | 24312 Del Prado | 949/661–6500 | No lunch | $16–$30 | AE, DC, MC, V.

© Corbis

FUNK ART

An agricultural school in the Sacramento Valley was the last place a "serious" artist would go to work, and that was fine with longtime University of California at Davis instructor Robert Arneson (1930–1992). Described by San Francisco art critic Thomas Albright as "the type one might expect to find presiding over a keg of beer at a Future Farmers' Fourth of July picnic," Arneson tossed aside all the formal constraints of tradition and used clay, considered a lowly craft material, to fashion "neglected images": sculptural beer bottles, garish self-portrait heads, and even a toilet—an object of critical wrath when Arneson displayed it in his first group show at the Richmond Art Center. Although few realized it at the time, Arneson and his peers at UC Davis were at the forefront of a 1970s West Coast movement that would revolutionize the art world. It was brash, funny, and populist, and it would be known loosely as Funk Art.

One of Arneson's most famous pieces, *Alice Street,* mocks the standard suburban housing he occupied while teaching art at Davis in 1962. Following suit, other Bay Area artists took positions at Davis; over the years the campus was a hothouse for experimental work by William Wiley, Roy de Forest, Robert Hudson, Manuel Ner, and Bruce Nauman. In part, their distance from the commercial demands of sophisticated San Francisco collectors and the security of teaching jobs that paid the bills enabled these artists to go out on a creative limb. Even as they matured and became less funky and more part of the old guard, most never lost their sense of humor. A delightful aspect of the Davis campus are the "Eggheads" Arneson created for strategic locations. You'll spot these large, off-white oval heads as you thread your way among the buildings. One in front of the main administration building sports eyes in back of its head, keeping watch on the policymakers within; in front of the school of law, two Eggheads face each other, an eyeless head that sees no evil, and an earless one that purports to hear nothing.

Proud Mary's. Casual. On a terrace overlooking the fishing boats and pleasure craft in Dana Point Harbor, Proud Mary's boasts of the best burgers and sandwiches in southern Orange County, as well as steaks and chicken. Breakfast is served all day. | 34689 Golden Lantern St. | 949/493–5853 | No supper | $7–$16 | AE, D, MC, V.

Regatta Grill. Seafood. Walls of glass afford spectacular views of the Pacific, an inspiring vista for enjoying creative seafood preparations. Specialties include seared ahi with stir-fried vegetables and grilled swordfish. The furnishings are nautical in style, with lots of pictures of yachts and wooden replicas of ships. You can also be served on the large patio, which has heat lamps. No smoking. | 25135 Park Lantern | 949/661–5000 | Breakfast also available | $50–$65 | AE, D, DC, MC, V.

Lodging

Best Western Marina Inn. This large modern hotel overlooking the Dana Point Harbor is one mi from the Pacific Coast Highway. Suites have a separate living room, fireplace, and kitchen. Complimentary Continental breakfast. Pool. Exercise equipment. Laundry facilities. | 24800 Dana Point Harbor Dr. | 949/496–1203 or 800/255–6853 | 180 rooms, 8 suites | $99–$149 | AE, D, DC, MC, V.

★ **Blue Lantern Inn.** Perched above Dana Point Harbor, this gabled inn offers remarkable views of the Pacific and the coast as it stretches to the south. Each luxurious guest room is cheerfully and individually decorated, and contains a gas log fireplace. All rooms have Jacuzzis, fireplaces, and teddy bears. Room service. In-room hot tubs. Excerise equipment. Bicycles. | 34343 St. of the Blue Lantern | 949/661–1304 or 800/950–1236 | fax 949/496–1483 | 29 rooms, 3 suites | $150–$220 rooms, $275–$500 suites | AE, DC, MC, V.

Capistrano Seaside Inn. Across the Pacific Coast Highway from Capistrano Beach, this 1928, two-story inn offers small but cozy rooms at a good price for the location. Each room has a wood-burning fireplace and a balcony or small patio screened by shrubbery. Refrigerators, cable TV. | 34862 Pacific Coast Hwy., Capistrano Beach | 949/496–1399 or 800/252–3224 | 28 rooms | $99–$139 | AE, MC, V.

Dana Marina Inn. Not to be confused with the larger Best Western of the same name, this hotel is just a three minute drive from the harbor. | 34111 Pacific Coast Hwy. | 949/496–1300 | fax 949/661–7822 | 25 rooms | $66 | MC, V.

Dana Point Harbor Inn. This simple motel with outside corridors is an economical option in Dana Point. No smoking rooms. Pool. | 25325 Dana Point Harbor Dr. | 949/493–5001 | fax 949/661–6895 | 46 rooms | $59–$69 | AE, D, DC, MC, V.

Doubletree Guest Suites. French doors connect the bedrooms and living areas in the suites at this four-story all-suites hotel across from Doheny State Beach on the south side of town, where each suite includes a video game console. Restaurant, bar. In-room data ports, microwaves, refrigerators. Pool. Massage. Exercise equipment. Business services. Parking (fee). | 34402 Pacific Coast Hwy., Dana Point | 949/661–1100 | fax 949/489–0628 | www.doubletreehotels.com | 196 suites | $129–$149 | AE, D, DC, MC, V.

Holiday Inn Express Dana Point Edgewater. Most rooms have ocean views at this small chain property. Hot tub, sauna. | 34744 Pacific Coast Hwy. | 949/240–0150 | fax 949/240–4862 | 30 rooms | $59–$69 | AE, D, DC, MC, V.

Marriott Laguna Cliffs Resort. On a hill overlooking Doheny State Beach, this 1985 property has attractive, comfortable rooms and first-rate service in one of the area's most scenic locations. The bar and deck area afford great views of the ocean and Orange County. Some rooms in the four-story hotel have a patio or balcony. 2 pools. Hot tub, sauna. 2 tennis courts. Health club. | 25135 Park Lantern | 949/661–5000 or 800/533–9748 | fax 949/661–3688 | 346 rooms | $179–$219 | AE, D, DC, MC, V.

Quality Inn and Suites. A half block from Doheny State Beach, a marina, art galleries, shops, and restaurants, this is a standard 1980s, four-story hotel with California contemporary furnishings. Complimentary Continental breakfast. Some in-room hot tubs. Pool. | 34280 Pacific Coast Hwy. | 949/248–1000 | fax 949/661–3136 | 86 rooms | $75 | AE, D, DC, MC, V.

★ **Ritz-Carlton Laguna Niguel.** This Mediterranean-style resort set into a cliff overlooking Salt Creek Beach is easily the area's most luxurious hotel. The spacious rooms and suites have marble baths, and many have views of the ocean or the coastline and beach. The rooms are furnished with antiques and 19th-century paintings. 3 restaurants. 12 pools. Massage, beauty salon. 4 tennis courts, health club. | 1 Ritz-Carlton Dr., Dana Point | 949/240–2000 | 393 rooms, 150 suites | $365–$560 rooms, $1,050–$3,700 suites | AE, D, DC, MC, V.

DAVIS

MAP 3, D7

(Nearby towns also listed: Sacramento, Vacaville, Woodland)

Though originally and still a rich agricultural area, Davis doesn't feel like a cow town. It's home to the University of California at Davis, and the student crowd—an even mix of hippies, gen-x'ers, and greeks—hangs at the cafés and bookstores in the central business district, making the city feel a little more cosmopolitan. Davis is also known for its energy conservation programs and projects, including an entire solar village. In addition, it is a leading institution for wine education and has one of the top veterinary programs on the west coast.

Information: **Davis Chamber of Commerce** | 130 G St. #B, 95616-4630 | 530/756–5160 | information@www.davischamber.com | www.davischamber.com.

Attractions

The Artery. The work by Northern California craftspeople displayed at this artists' cooperative includes decorative and functional ceramics, glass, wood, jewelry, fiber arts, paintings, sculpture, drawings, and photography. | 207 G St. | 530/758–8330 | Mon.–Sat. 10–6, Sun. 12–5.

Davis Campus of the University of California. This university ranks among the top 25 research universities in the United States. You can take tours of the campus. | 1 Shields Ave. | 530/752–8111 or 530/752–8111 | www.ucdavis.edu | Daily. Tours depart from Buehler Alumni and Visitors Center Sat-Sun at 11:30 and 1:30. Weekdays by appointment.

ON THE CALENDAR

FEB.: *California Duck Days.* At this wildlife viewing festival, you'll find workshops on birdwatching, decoy carving, and wildlife photography; demonstrations on duck calling and trained bird dogs; and a banquet and raffle. | 530/758–1286 or 860/425–5001 | www.dcn.davis.ca.us/duckdays.

APR.: *Picnic Day.* U.C. Davis welcomes thousands for this annual open house and party. Festivities include a traditional parade, musical entertainment, dancing, departmental exhibits, sporting events, campus tours, and animal exhibitions, all on the campus. | 916/752–8030.

Dining

Café California. Contemporary. The locals who gather at this downtown Davis eatery favor such dishes as salad of prawns and baby greens with avocado-tarragon vinaigrette, Cajun-style prime rib with chile onion rings, and roast chicken with garlic mashed potatoes, served in a contemporary dining room set with white linens. | 808 2nd St. | 530/757–2766 | fax 530/758–5236 | $9–$18 | AE, MC, V.

Soga's. Contemporary. Watercolors by local artists hang on the walls of this elegant restaurant. The California-style menu features variations on salmon filet, swordfish, and veal, and also offers vegetable plates. You can eat at the long, covered patio in good

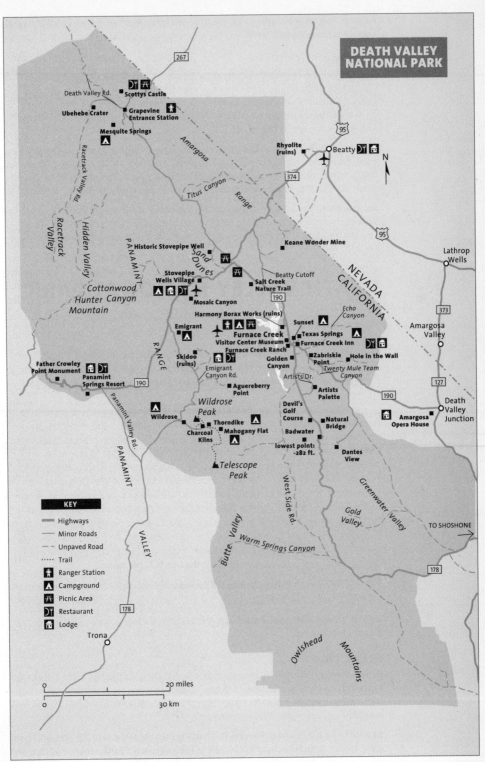

DEATH VALLEY NATIONAL PARK

267

Death Valley Rd.
Scottys Castle
Ubehebe Crater
Grapevine Entrance Station
Mesquite Springs

Amargosa

Racetrack Valley Rd.

95

Rhyolite (ruins)
Beatty

374

Racetrack Valley

Hidden Valley

Titus Canyon Range

N

Lathrop Wells

Keane Wonder Mine

95

NEVADA
CALIFORNIA

Cottonwood Hunter Canyon Mountain

PANAMINT

Sand Dunes

Historic Stovepipe Well
Stovepipe Wells Village
Mosaic Canyon

Beatty Cutoff

190

Salt Creek Nature Trail

Echo Canyon

Amargosa Valley

373

Harmony Borax Works (ruins)

Emigrant

Furnace Creek
Visitor Center Museum
Furnace Creek Ranch

Sunset
Texas Springs
Furnace Creek Inn

Hole in the Wall
Zabriskie Point
Twenty Mule Team Canyon

127

Father Crowley Point Monument
Panamint Springs Resort

RANGE

190

Skidoo (ruins)

Emigrant Canyon Rd.

Golden Canyon

Artists Dr.

Artists Palette

190

Death Valley Junction

Amargosa Opera House

Aguereberry Point

Wildrose Peak

Wildrose
Thorndike
Charcoal Kilns
Mahogany Flat

Devil's Golf Course

Badwater
lowest point: -282 ft.

Natural Bridge

Dantes View

Telescope Peak

West Side Rd.

Greenwater Valley

TO SHOSHONE

PANAMINT

Gold Valley

Butte Valley

Warm Springs Canyon

178

KEY

— Highways
— Minor Roads
--- Unpaved Road
···· Trail
Ranger Station
Campground
Picnic Area
Restaurant
Lodge

178

Trona

Owlshead Mountains

0   20 miles
0   30 km

weather. Full bar. No smoking. | 217 E St. | 530/757–1733 | Reservations essential | No lunch weekends | $24–$30 | AE, D, MC, V.

Lodging

Aggie Inn. Named for the University of California at Davis "Aggies," this hotel is less than 1 block from the campus. Some kitchenettes, some in-room hot tubs. Outdoor hot tub, sauna. Laundry service. | 245 First St. | 530/756–0352 | fax 530/753–5738 | aggieinn@stayanight.com | www.stayanight.com | 25 rooms, 9 suites | $83–$102 rooms, $127–$132 suites | AE, D, DC, MC, V.

Best Western University Lodge. This three-story lodge is a good place to stop if you have business at the university, which is one block away. Some kitchenettes, microwaves, refrigerators, cable TV. Spa. Exercise equipment. Some pets allowed. | 123 B St. | 530/756–7890 | fax 530/756–0245 | www.bestwestern.com | 53 rooms | $75–$99 | AE, D, DC, MC, V.

Hallmark Inn. Two buildings make up this inn, which is five blocks from the University of California campus. Next door is Louis' restaurant. Restaurant. Some refrigerators. Pool. Free parking. | 110 F St. | 800/753–0035 | www.hallmarkinn.com | 135 rooms | $89–$150 | AE, D, DC, MC, V.

DEATH VALLEY NATIONAL PARK

MAP 3, J9

(Nearby town also listed: Lone Pine)

Stretching over three million acres, an area larger than Connecticut, Death Valley is the largest national park in the lower 48 states. The park is named for the unfortunate emigrants who met their demise in 1849 searching for a short-cut to the Mother Lode Country.

One of the hottest places on Earth, Death Valley can vanquish the unprepared with its supercharged hot breath. Winters are mild, but summers are extremely hot and dry; temperatures commonly run above 120 degrees F. If you're coming in the summer, be forewarned: you'll need nine quarts of water each day, just to stay alive.

You can take in the blunt and evocative landscape while staying in the historic, four-star Furnace Creek Inn, or the more affordable Stove Pipe Wells Village or Furnace Creek Ranch (the latter two both run by the Park Service's concessionaire). Spectacular panoramas make Zabriskie Point and Dante's View two of the park's top attractions. A 4-wheel drive vehicle is recommended for backcountry travel; check at the Furnace Creek Visitor Center for road conditions, weather, and other conditions that will affect your visit. Because the terrain is rough and the area large, you should get directions or a map before venturing to the sights listed below.

Information: **Death Valley Chamber of Commerce** | 118 S. Rte. 127, Shoshone, CA 92384 | 760/852–4524 | fax 760/852–4592.

Death Valley National Park | Box 579, Death Valley, 92328 | 760/786–2331 | www.nps.gov/deva/.

Attractions

Artist's Drive. Artist's Drive is a scenic 9 mi route that skirts the foothills of the Black Mountains and provides colorful views of changing landscape. You can reach this one-way road by heading north off Badwater Road. | 760/786–2331 | www.nps.gov/deva | $10 per vehicle | Daily.

Badwater. At 282 ft below sea level, Badwater is the lowest point in the Western Hemisphere, even more notable for its contrast to Telescope Peak, the highest point in the park at 11,049 ft above sea level. From the west you can get here by taking I–78. | 760/786–2331 | www.nps.gov/deva | Free | Daily.

Charcoal Kilns. In 1877 George Hearst's Modock Consolidated Mining Company completed construction of the charcoal kilns in Wildrose Canyon to fuel nearby silver-lead smelters. The kilns closed in 1878 after the mines shut down. From the south you can get here by taking Rte. 178 from Ridgecrest. | 760/786–2331 | www.nps.gov/deva | Free | 8AM–6PM.

Dante's View. Dante's View marks the eastern boundary of the park, accessible by Rte. 190, and measures 5,475 ft. In the dry desert air you can see nearly 100 mi. | 760/786–2331 | www.nps.gov/deva | Free | Daily.

Devil's Golf Course. Wildly varied but barren terrain includes thousands of miniature salt pinnacles, carved into surreal shapes by the desert wind. From the east you can take Rte. 190 to get here. | 760/786–2345 or 800/528–6367 | www.nps.gov/deva | Free | Daily.

Furnace Creek Visitor Center. A helpful visitor center has exhibits, literature, and an 18-minute film about the park. From November to April, when the weather is more moderate, you can take one of the naturalist walks. You can rent horses at the Furnace Creek Ranch, next door. From the east, Rte. 190 will bring you to the Visitors Center. | 760/786–2331 | www.nps.gov/deva | Free | 8AM–6PM.

Golden Canyon. Five mi north of the entrance to Artist's Drive, Golden Canyon winds through striking carved rock formations. | 760/786–2331 | www.nps.gov/deva | Free | Daily.

Harmony Borax Works. Built in 1882 by W. T. Coleman, the Harmony Borax Mill was the first successful borax mining operation in Death Valley. The facility was moved after only 8 years to the town of Daggett, where train-access was better. Now long gone, among the ghostly remains are crumbling adobe walls, the old boiler and some of the vats. | Harmony Borax Works Rd. off Rte. 190 | 760/786–2331 | www.nps.gov/deva | Free | Daily.

Natural Bridge. This 50-ft arch was formed by cascading water that poked a hole in the rocks beneath it to create a curious, but natural, formation. To get here take Bad Water Rd. which is slightly east of the Furnace Creek Visitor's Center. | 760/786–2331 | www.nps.gov/deva | Free | Daily.

Sand Dunes at Mesquite Flat. You can explore these ever-changing creatures of the earth and wind with their steep rippled sides, sharp curving crests and beautiful sun-bleached hue. Be sure to bring plenty of water and avoid losing your way—it's easy to become disoriented here. This spot is 23 mi north of Furnace Creek. | Rte. 190 | 760/786–2331 | www.nps.gov/deva | Free.

DEATH VALLEY
NATIONAL PARK

INTRO
ATTRACTIONS
DINING
LODGING

PACKING IDEAS FOR HOT WEATHER

- ☐ Antifungal foot powder
- ☐ Bandanna
- ☐ Cooler
- ☐ Cotton clothing
- ☐ Day pack
- ☐ Film
- ☐ Hiking boots
- ☐ Insect repellent
- ☐ Rain jacket
- ☐ Sport sandals
- ☐ Sun hat
- ☐ Sunblock
- ☐ Synthetic ice
- ☐ Umbrella
- ☐ Water bottle

*Excerpted from *Fodor's: How to Pack: Experts Share Their Secrets*
© 1997, by Fodor's Travel Publications

Scotty's Castle. At the northern end of the park, this Moorish mansion was begun in 1924 and never completed. Death Valley Scotty (whose real name was Walter Scott) told many that he paid for the Castle with gold from his secret mine. In actuality, Chicago millionaire Albert Johnson paid for its construction. Once a hotel, the Castle hosted such famous folk as Bette Davis and Norman Rockwell. Visitors today can take a walk on the grounds or join costumed park rangers on a 1939 living history tour of the mansion, which contains handmade furniture and an enormous pipe organ. | 760/786–2331 | www.nps.gov/deva | Grounds, picnic area: free; Castle: $8 | Grounds: daily 7–6; Tours: daily 9–5.

Telescope Peak. At 11,049 ft above sea level, Telescope Peak is a remarkable sight. Even more remarkable is that the park also contains Badwater, which at 282 ft below sea level is the lowest point in the Western Hemisphere. From Ridgecrest head a mile past Wild Rose and look for signage. The road that takes you there is not recommended for passenger vehicles. | 760/786–2331 | www.nps.gov/deva | Free | Daily.

20-Mule-Team Canyon. Part of Death Valley named after famous 49-er travelers who were challenged by the harsh landscape of the Valley. At times along the loop road off Rte 190, the soft rock walls reach high on both sides, making it seem like you're on an amusement-park ride. | 760/786–2331 | www.nps.gov/deva | Free | Daily.

Ubehebe Crater. This craggy impression in the earth of debatable origin is 8 mi from Scotty's Castle. It is 500 ft deep in places and covers a diameter of ½ mi. | 760/786–2331 | www.nps.gov/deva | Free | Daily.

Zabriskie Point. Zabriskie Point provides views of eroded, contoured hills. Although it's only about 710 ft. high, it overlooks a striking badlands panorama. Film buffs may recognize it (or at least its name) from the film "Zabriskie Point." | 760/786–2331 | www.nps.gov/deva | Free | Daily.

ON THE CALENDAR

NOV.: *Shoshone Old West Days.* Just outside of Death Valley National Park, an annual festival here celebrates Wild West heritage with live music, arts and crafts, competitions and contests, children's activities and plenty of hot and hearty food. | 760/852–4524.

Dining

Inn Dining Room at the Furnace Creek Inn. Continental. You might want to dress up a little if you're having supper at this beautiful Mission-style establishment with stucco walls, fireplaces, beamed ceilings, and views of the Panamint Mountains. The seasonally changing main courses could include seared ahi tuna, Southwestern grill, and a boneless rack of lamb. Close out your meal with Indian River peaches, and don't forget the great wine list. Sunday brunch. No smoking. | Box 1, Death Valley National Park | 760/786–2361 | Reservations essential | Breakfast also available | $35–$45 | AE, D, DC, MC, V.

Panamint Springs Resort Restaurant. American. A simple California menu has some excellent options, including top-quality steak, homemade pasta, fresh salads and more. | Rte. 190, 31 mi west of Stove Pipe Wells. | 775/482–7690 | www.deathvalley.com/reserve/reserve.html | Reservations essential | $10–$25 | AE, D, MC, V.

Stove Pipe Village Restaurant. American. This hotel restaurant has a certain rustic elegance, with natural stone and a small waterfall inside the the large dining room. The menu covers all the basics, from steaks and pasta to seafood, for dinner. Breakfast and lunch are also served in this casual and family-oriented spot. | Rte. 190, Panamint Springs | 760/786–2387 | fax 760/786–2389 | Reservations not taken for groups under six | $10–$25 | AE, D, DC, MC, V.

Lodging

Furnace Creek Inn. Opened in 1927, this elegant four-story inn maintains a classic 1930s feel. Grounds include a spring-fed pool, palm gardens, and the Stargazers Deck. The guest rooms are bright and airy, and afternoon tea is served everyday. The closest town is Bahrump, a 45-minute drive away. Restaurant(see Inn Dining Room), bar (with entertainment), room service. Refrigerators. Pool. Massage (seasonal). 4 tennis courts. Exercise equipment. | Rte. 190 | 760/786–2345 | fax 760/786–2423 | www.furnacecreekresort.com | 68 rooms | $245–$260 | AE, D, DC, MC, V.

Furnace Creek Ranch. What was originally crew headquarters for a borax company is now the family-oriented, less expensive sister motel to the Furnace Creek Inn. Though it exudes a a sense of the rustic life, facilities are thoroughly modern. The rooms all have views of an 18-hole golf course, and some have balconies. The Borax museum is on the property where you can get a sense of mining and prospecting days as well as the history of Death Valley National Park. Restaurant. Some refrigerators, cable TV. Pool. Driving range, golf, tennis. Basketball. Playground. Laundry facilities. | Rte. 190 | 760/786–2345 or 800/528–6367 | fax 760/786–2423 | www.furnacecreekresort.com | 224 rooms | $99–$139 | AE, D, DC, MC, V.

Opera House Hotel. Just outside of Death Valley National Park and adjoining the theater is a 1920s-style adobe bungalow structure. A long row of rooms have murals on the walls, antique furniture and lamps topped with frilly velvet shades. | Rte. 127, Death Valley Junction | 760/852–4441 | 14 rooms | $45–$55 | MC, V.

Panamint Springs Resort. Located 10 mi inside the west entrance of Death Valley National Park, this low-key resort overlooks the sand dunes and peculiar geological formations of the Panamint Valley. Choose from standard rooms, two-bedroom cottages ($130), full 50-amp RV hook-ups ($20), and campsites ($10). Restaurant, bar. Shops. | Rte. 190, 48 mi east of Lone Pine | 775/482–7680 | fax 775/482–7682 | www.deathvalley.com/reserve/reserve.html | 15 rooms, 1 cabin, 12 rvs, 40 water only, 20 camps | $57–$65 | AE, D, MC, V.

Stove Pipe Wells Village. An aircraft landing strip is an unusual touch for an Old West-style motel, as is a heated mineral pool, but everything else here is pretty standard. There are, however, also some great panoramic views of mountains, the desert, and dunes. The property is 25 mi from Furnace Creek at the west end of Death Valley National Park. Restaurant, bar. No room phones. Pool. Some pets allowed (fee). | Rte. 190 | 760/786–2387 | fax 760/786–2389 | 82 rooms in 5 buildings | $64–$83 | AE, D, MC, V.

DEL MAR

MAP 4, J16

(Nearby towns also listed: La Jolla, Rancho Santa Fe)

This northern San Diego coastal town of 4,900, deemed the "Toast of the Coast," is best known for its race track, chic shopping strip, celebrity visitors, and wide beaches. Del Mar has become the headquarters for romantic hot-air-balloon excursions, and year-round rides can be arranged over Del Mar's rolling headlands, coastline, and reservoir-dotted valley.

Information: The Greater Del Mar Chamber of Commerce | 1104 Camino del Mar, Suite #1, 92014 | 858/793–5291 | info@delmarchamber.org | www.delmarchamber.org.

Attractions
Cardiff State Beach. Here the coastal bluffs drop away, creating a flat, sandy beach. The beach narrows at the south end, and you're never too far away from Old Rte. 101, but the view of whitecaps rushing toward the cliffs to the south compensates for the noise. You can swim and surf, plus there are gorgeous views and tidal pools. | U.S. 101, Encitas | 760/753–5091 | $4 per vehicle | Daily dawn to dusk.

Del Mar City Beach. The beach is long and picturesque, with grassy bluffs rising at either end. You'll find good swimming, surfing, and fishing. The south end of the beach is near an Amtrak station. | 17th St. and Coast Blvd. | 858/793–5291 | Free | Daily.

Moonlight Beach. This small beach takes its name from Encinitas' early days when residents held nighttime picnics on the sand. The beach still offers lots of soft, clean sand, along with excellent recreational facilities. You can swim, surf, and play volleyball and tennis. | Encinitas Blvd., west end | 858/793–5291 | Free | Daily.

San Elijo State Beach. A high bluff separates a 171-site campground from the beach below. The view from the heights is spectacular, and stairs are positioned along the long, narrow campground for beach access. The campground includes a bait shop, grocery store, rest rooms, and hot showers. Rental beach equipment available. | U.S. 101 in Cardiff | 760/753–5091 | $4 per vehicle | Daily dawn to dusk.

Swami's Beach. The wide, terraced reef extending out from the shore several hundred yards makes this narrow, sandy beach a great place for surfers and fisherman. The reef also attracts scuba divers and snorklers. Swimming is great at the southern end, away from the reef. To reach the beach, you must take a long, steep stairway down from the bluffs above. | U.S. 101, at border of Cardiff and Encinitas | 858/793–5291 | Free | Daily.

Torrey Pines State Beach. The coastline leading to Torrey Pines is as breathtaking as any in Southern California. The beach itself runs for nearly a mile between the Del Mar bluffs and the sandstone cliffs of the Torrey Pines State Preserve. You can swim, surf, scuba dive, and go clamming. | 120600 N. Torry Pines Rd., La Jolla | 835/755–2063 | $4 per vehicle | 8AM–dusk.

ON THE CALENDAR

JUNE AND JULY: *Del Mar Fair.* This pleasant family-oriented fair has food, rides, and displays. | 619/755–1161.

JULY–SEPT.: *Thoroughbred Races.* For six weeks every summer, the Del Mar Thoroughbred Club hosts close to 30 major stakes races, worth as much as $6 million. The signature event is the Pacific Classic, with a $1 million purse. The races were originally founded by Bing Crosby. | 858/793–5291.

Dining

Cilantros. Southwestern. Subtly spiced dishes are served here, where the furnishings are also Southwestern in style. Open-air dining. No smoking. | 3702 Via de la Valle | 858/259–8777 | $13–$23 | AE, DC, MC, V.

Dining Room. Contemporary. This skylit restaurant is known for California cuisine with an international flavor. The specialties include filet mignon, rack of lamb, and sea bass. You can eat on the patio, which has two small waterfalls. Early-bird suppers. No smoking. | 1540 Camino Del Mar. | 858/259–1515, ext. 460 | Breakfast also available | $12–$24 | AE, D, DC, MC, V.

Epazote. Southwestern. The menu changes seasonally at this offspring of Cilantros, serving good Southwestern-style cuisine. The happy-hour appetizers and drinks are a bargain. Specialties include sesame ahi tuna, lobster chimichangas, and fajitas. The large rock wall and open kitchen make for an interesting interior. Jazz Wed., Sunday brunch. No smoking. | 1555 Camino del Mar. | 858/259–9966 | $10–$22 | AE, DC, MC, V.

Jake's Del Mar. Continental. The open-beam ceilings provide a fresh and airy atmosphere at this basic waterfront grill. Each night the menu includes five kinds of fresh fish. On Friday and Saturday, the menu includes live Maine lobster. You can also get steaks and chicken. Sunday brunch. No smoking. | 1660 Coast Blvd. | 858/755–2002 | No lunch Mon. | $20–$32 | AE, D, MC, V.

Pacifica Del Mar. Contemporary. Known for spectacular views of the Pacific Ocean and fresh Pacific Rim coastal cuisine, this restaurant's signature dishes include Northwest smoked salmon jerky "Caesar" salad, Pacifica kim chee "shrimp" martini, and "Takoshimi" of peppered Hawaiian Ahi with chinese salsa, sushi rice and azuki beans. The Art Deco-style interior includes works by local and international artists. The outdoor dining area overlooks the Pacific. Early-bird suppers. No smoking. | 1555 Camino del Mar. | 858/792–0476 | $16–$26 | AE, D, DC, MC, V.

Pamplemousse Grille. Continental. One of North County's best restaurants, this grill offers French country dining with an emphasis on grilled meat and main-course salads. Specialties include Osso buco, mixed grill of seafood, salmon, and sea bass. The interior has murals of farm and family scenes. No smoking. | 514 Via de la Valle, Solano Beach | 858/792–9090 | No lunch Sat–Tues. | $21–$32 | AE, D, DC, MC, V.

Poseidon Restaurant. American. The patio dining area at this beachfront restaurant is as large as the indoor dining room and overlooks the ocean. The menu reflects the casual atmosphere. The Pojo burger, a half-pound patty topped with cheese, cooked onions, and mushrooms, is a house specialty. Try the fresh seafood entrées. Sunday brunch. No smoking. | 1670 Coast Blvd. | 858/755–9345 | $15–$30 | AE, D, DC, MC, V.

Shrimply Delicious, the Original Crabhouse. Seafood. Some of the Cajun-style seafood dishes are measured by the pound here. Try the Sons of the Beaches, which consists of four pounds of shrimp, Alaskan king crab, and blue crab, and the Luziana Tidal Wave, two and a half pounds of spiced crawfish. The interior is crabhouse casual. No smoking. | 559 First St., Encinitas | 760/944–9172 | No lunch weekdays | $10–$20 | AE, D, DC, MC, V.

Torrey Pines Café. Contemporary. The big, bright room with lots of windows and pictures of the lagoon makes a cheerful place for a meal. The restaurant overlooks the Torrey Pines State Park. Locals come for such dishes as the California seafood stew, mussels, and halibut. Outside, tables with umbrellas overlook the lagoon. No smoking. Sunday brunch. | 2334 Carmel Valley Rd. | 858/259–5878 | $12–$18 | AE, D, DC, MC, V.

Lodging

Best Western Stratford Inn. During racing season this equestrian-themed inn hosts horse owners and jockeys. Many rooms have ocean views and all are surrounded by six lushly landscapes acres. The two-story inn was built in the early 1950s. Restaurant, complimentary Continental breakfast. Some kitchenettes, some microwaves, refrigerators, cable TV. 2 pools. Hot tub. Laundry facilities. | 710 Camino del Mar | 858/755–1501 | fax 619/755–4704 | www.bestwestern.com | 95 rooms, 29 suites | $109–$149 rooms, $129–$189 suites | AE, D, DC, MC, V.

Clarion Carriage House Inn. Pleasing amenities include a free, in-room breakfast and afternoon tea and homemade cakes in the library. The inn is Victorian style and furnished accordingly, and overlooks a lush garden and a spa. Some rooms have patios. You can use the clubhouse for business meetings or cocktail parties. Complimentary Continental breakfast. Some kitchenettes, cable TV. Pool. Hot tub. Exercise equipment. Laundry facilities. Business services. | 720 Camino del Mar | 858/755–9765 or 800/451–4515 or 800/453–4411 | fax 619/792–8196 | www.delmarinn.com | 80 rooms | $150–$170 | AE, D, DC, MC, V.

Country Side Inn. Part of a California chain, this small two-story hotel is in a residential area that's one mi from the ocean. Built in 1985, it has comfortable rooms furnished in country French style. The lobby has a marble fireplace. Complimentary breakfast. In-room data ports, refrigerators, cable TV. Pool. Hot tub. Business services. | 1661 Villa Cardiff, Cardiff-by-the-Sea | 760/944–0427 or 800/322–9993 | fax 760/944–7708 | www.country-suites.com | 102 rooms | $98–$140 | AE, D, DC, MC, V.

Del Mar Motel. Just meters from the seashore, this spot feels more like a comfortable beach house than a standard motel. On the west and north sides of the complex, barbecue pits are available as are tables and chairs for picnicking. Outdoor showers let visitors rinse off after swimming. Refrigerators, cable TV. | 1702 Coast Blvd. | 858/755–1534 or 800/223–8449 | www.delmarmotelbythesea.com | 21 rooms | $120–$170 | AE, D, DC, MC, V.

Hilton Del Mar. This two-story Tudor-style hotel is four blocks away from the beach, and next to the Del Mar Racetrack and Fairgrounds. For those who want some exercise, an outdoor jogging track and eight tennis courts are next door. Restaurant, bar. In-room data ports, minibars, some microwaves, refrigerators, cable TV. Pool. Hot tubs. Business services. | 15575 Jimmy Durante Blvd. | 835/792–5200 | fax 835/792–9538 | www.hilton.com | 245 rooms | $119–$229 | AE, D, DC, MC, V.

L'Auberge Del Mar Resort and Spa. Built in the late 1980s to resemble a 1950s establishment, this three-story resort is situated in a colorful garden setting and decorated throughout with dark-wood antiques. Many of the spacious rooms have garden or coastal views. Restaurant, bar. Minibars, cable TV. 2 pools. Spa. 2 tennis courts. Gym. Business services. Parking (fee). | 1540 Camino del Mar | 835/259–1515 or 800/553–1336 | fax 619/755–4940 | www.destinationtravel.com | 120 rooms | $225–$385 | AE, D, DC, MC, V.

Les Artistes Inn of Del Mar. Every room is different in this two-story Spanish-style building designed by its owner. There's the Georgia O'Keefe room, the Art Deco room (a la French designer Erte), the Remington old-west room, and others. Some include special amenities, like a soaking tub in the Japan room, and ocean views. Complimentary Continental breakfast. Cable TV. | 944 Camino del Mar. | 858/794–7880 | www.lesartistesinn.com | 12 rooms | $85–$195 | AE, D, MC, V.

DESERT HOT SPRINGS

MAP 4, K15

(Nearby towns also listed: Joshua Tree National Park, Palm Springs, Yucca Valley)

Nine miles north of Palm Springs, and just southwest of Joshua Tree National Park, Desert Hot Springs is the land of 1,000 natural hot mineral pools and 40 spa resorts. It is neither as tony or as pricey as most of its neighbors.

Information: Desert Hot Springs Chamber of Commerce | 11711 West Dr., 92240 | 760/329–6403 | fax 760/329–2833 | dhschamber@ccinet.com | www.deserthotsprings.com.

Attractions
Mineral Water Spas. A fragment of the San Andres fault creates two aquifers, one hot and one cold. The cold water won the 1999 International Water Tasting contest; the hot water fills luxurious spas and pools in Desert Hot Springs' hotels. Almost all the hotels have spas for their guests, and many open their facilities to day-visitors, charging a small fee.

ON THE CALENDAR
DEC.: *Holiday Parade.* Celebrate Christmas, Kwaanza, Hanukkah, or just the "Holiday Spirit" at this annual community event. The competition for Best Float is friendly but fierce–the Women's Garden Club float is the one to beat. Parade starts at the top of Palm Dr. and ends in the K-Mart parking lot. | 760/329–6403.

Dining
Capri Italian Restaurant. American. It's either an Italian restaurant that serves great steaks, or it's a steak restaurant that serves great Italian food—in either case, choose between marinara and medium rare at this casual, family-oriented spot. | 12260 Palm Dr. | 760/329–6833 | fax 760/251–5125 | No lunch Sun. | $15–$25 | AE, DC, MC, V.

El Charro Restaurant. Mexican. You can quickly fill up on chile rellenos, enchiladas, and flautas at this small, family-run eatery. Mexican posters and crafts adorn the walls, and ranchero music plays in the background. | 13156 Palm Dr. | 760/251–0852 | Breakfast served daily | $7–$12 | No credit cards.

Palm Korea BBQ Restaurant. Korean. Straight from the grill, beef and pork ribs are the specialty here, though a variety of dishes will suit most tastes. | 13440 Palm Dr. | 760/329–2277 | $10–$15 | MC, V.

Lodging

Adobe Inn and Spa. More hacienda than hotel, this 1960s Adobe-style structure is nicely adorned with lustrous wood furniture, plant-filled courtyards and such amenities as full kitchens. Kitchenettes, microwaves, refrigerators, cable TV. Pool. Spa. | 66365 Seventh St. | 760/329–7292 | fax 760/329–4402 | www.adobespa.com | 10 rooms | $55–$75 | AE, D, DC, MC, V.

Desert Hot Springs Spa. Spacious rooms surround a palm tree-filled courtyard that contains eight natural hot mineral pools, one of which is Olympic sized. Although this is a traditional hotel, you can also rent a room for the day or, for a small fee, just enjoy the pool area. The two-story property was built in the late 1960s and is in the middle of the desert. Restaurant, bar (with entertainment). Cable TV. Pool. Beauty salon, massage,7 Jacuzzi mineral pools, sauna. Business services. | 10805 Palm Dr. | 760/329–6000 or 800/808–7727 | fax 760/329–6915 | info@dhsspa.com | www.dhsspa.com | 50 rooms,2 suites | $79–$119 rooms, $89–$139 suites | AE, D, DC, MC, V.

Las Primaveras Resort Health Spa. The resort rests on an acre of land, filled with flowers, rock formations and a small waterfall, but the real treats are the spa services that include facials, manicures, herbal body wraps, lymph drainage and eight different types of massage (including water massage). Spa services are available for an additional fee. Pool, hot tub, spa. | 66659 6th St. | 760/251–1677 or 800/400–1677 | fax 760/329–0220 | www.lasprimaveras.qpt.com | 9 rooms | $55–$115 | AE, D, MC, V.

Miracle Springs Hotel, Resort and Spa. This more upscale sister hotel to the Desert Hot Springs Spa is nestled in the foothills of Joshua Tree National Park and overlooks the scenic Palm Springs Valley. There are eight mineral pools, along with excellent spa service. Built in 1994, it's a 15-minute drive from downtown Palm Springs. Restaurant. Pool. Spa, sauna. | 10625 Palm Dr. | 760/251–6000 | fax 760/251–0460 | hotel@miraclesprings.com | www.miraclesprings.com | 110 rooms, 6 suites, 1 villa | $99–$139 rooms, $189–$499 suites, $599 villa | AE, D, DC, MC, V.

Two Bunch Palms Resort and Spa. This gated property is one of the most exclusive and romantic resorts in the desert. It's the spa of choice for celebrities who savor the 148° mineral waters, the laid-back atmosphere, and the privacy. Landscaped grounds contain secluded picnic areas, meditation benches, outdoor mud baths, and two mineral pools surrounded by palms. Accommodations range from hotel-style guest rooms to luxury villas with living rooms, kitchens, and private hot tubs. Bar, dining room, complimentary Continental breakfast. Some kitchenettes, refrigerators, some in-room hot tubs, cable TV, in-room VCRs. 2 pools, lake. Hot tub, massage, spa, sauna. Tennis. Bicycles. No kids allowed. Business services. | 67425 2 Bunch Palms Trail | 760/329–8791 or 800/472–4334 | fax 760/329–1317 | whiteowl@twobunchpalms.com | www.twobunchpalms.com | 45 varying accommodations | $295–$435 | Closed Aug. | AE, MC, V.

DUNSMUIR

MAP 3, D2

(Nearby town also listed: Mount Shasta)

The town's original name was Pusher, after the steam engines that used to push trains up the steep canyon. In 1886 a coal baron named Alexander Dunsmuir made a deal: rename the place after him, and he'd donate a handsome fountain. The railroad was central to the town's life, and still is—an Amtrak train station continues to serve Dunsmuir. The first tracks arrived in 1886; during the boom years of the mid-1920s nearly 2,000 men worked in the shops and train yards. Tourists arrived to spend the summer at the many resorts in the Dunsmuir vicinity.

By the 1950s, steam engines were on the wane, and so were the town's fortunes. I–5 was completed in 1961, bypassing Dunsmuir. All for the better; the little town's vintage character was preserved, and local merchants have pitched in to restore the turn-of-the-20th-century brick buildings to their old grace. The 1920s live on in a downtown that is on the National Registry of Historic Places, making it a good place to stroll, browse art galleries, and reflect on the good old days in one of the cafés.

Information: Dunsmuir Chamber of Commerce | Box 17, Dunsmuir 96025-0017 | 530/235–2177 | chamber@dunsmuir.com | www.dunsmuir.com.

Attractions

Castle Crags State Park. This park practically surrounds the town of Dunsmuir. The 225-million-year-old granite crags tower up to 6,000 ft above the Sacramento River. There are many hiking trails and picnic areas, and campsites with rest rooms and showers are nearby. Reservations recommended for the campsites in summer. | 20022 Castle Creek Rd. | 530/235–2684 or 800/444–7275 | $2 per vehicle | Daily 7:30 AM–10 PM.

Dunsmuir City Park. Babe Ruth played at the ballpark here, with Mount Shasta as backdrop. The park has tennis courts, picnic areas, a playground, hiking paths, and fishing spots. The 10-acre botanical gardens are under development, with many native plants. | Dunsmuir Ave. | 530/235–4740 | Free | Daily dawn to dusk.

Mossbrae Falls. This waterfall spills over a lush hillside into the Sacramento River. From I–5, take the Central Dunsmir exit onto Dunsmir Ave. Head north ¾ mi to Scarlett Way, and then follow Scarlett Way across a small bridge and to the right. Park by the railroad track and walk 1 mi to see the falls in the woods. | Scarlett Way | 530/235–2177 | Free | Daily dawn to dusk.

Hedge Creek Falls. A beautiful picnic area and gazebo afford breathtaking views of the falls just off Dunsmir Avenue at the North Dunsmir exit of I–5. You reach the falls by a five-minute walk. Wading is permitted. | Dunsmir Ave. | 530/235–2684 or 800/444–7275 | Free | Daily dawn to dusk.

ON THE CALENDAR

APR.: *Sacramento River Festival.* The opening of trout-fishing season is celebrated with a pancake breakfast served by firemen, and information booths on river ecology and the watershed. | 530/235–2177.
JUNE: *Dunsmuir Canyon Days.* A Fun Run on Saturday, a parade, a children's carnival, crafts and food booths, and a softball tournament downtown celebrate the city's culture. | 530/235–2177.
JUNE: *Tribute to the Trees.* The Palo Alto Chamber Orchestra performs in Dunsmuir City Park to benefit the Botanical Gardens. | 530/235–2177.
OCT.: *Fall Colors Rail Fair.* Photos, slides, and models of old trains accompany food and craft vendors at this downtown festival. | 530/235–2177.
DEC.: *Candles in the Canyon Holiday Celebration.* A Christmas concert, a tree-lighting ceremony, a parade through downtown, and a visit from Santa and Mrs. Claus are the highlights of this celebration. | 530/235–2177.

Dining

Cafe Maddalena. Italian. This café serves appetizing dishes with Mediterranean and Sardinian influences. White tablecloths add a bit of class to this casual, comfortable place. The mixed grill is among the most popular dishes. | 5801 Sacramento Ave. | 530/235–2725 | Reservations essential | Closed Mon.–Wed. No lunch | $10–$20 | AE, D, MC, V.

Cornerstone Bakery Cafe. American. A casual, homey place known for pasta, sandwiches, salads. | 57 Dunsmuir Ave. | 530/235–4677 | Breakfast also available. No supper Tues.–Thurs., Sun. | $5–$14 | AE, D, MC, V.

Gary's Pizza Factory. American. This is a sports-oriented eatery with big-screen TV and a game room. It's known for pizza, pasta, and sandwiches. | 5804 Dunsmuir Ave. | 530/235–4849 | $5–$15 | AE, D, MC, V.

House of Glass. American. The large dining room has floor-to-ceiling glass walls to take advantage of spectacular views of Mount Shasta. This 24-hour restaurant is known for home-style breakfasts and New York steaks; pasta dishes such as pesto pasta and fettuccini Alfredo are also popular. | 4221 Siskiyou Ave. | 530/235–0777 | Breakfast also available | $5–$15 | AE, D, MC, V.

Julianne's Victorian Shoppe. American. This old-fashioned soda shop is inside a charming giftshop. You can get ice cream, milkshakes, sodas, tea, and sandwiches. Formal afternoon tea is served Monday through Saturday at 2:30–4:30. | 5816 Dunsmuir Ave. | 530/235–2044 | Closed Sun. | $5–$15 | MC, V.

Lodging

Acorn Inn. Fishing and boating enthusiasts appreciate the proximity to the Upper Sacramento River, and Mount Shasta is only 5 mi away. The single-story motel surrounded by sprawling lawns and oaks is next door to the Ted Fay Fly Shop. Cable TV, no phones. Pool. | 4310 Dunsmuir Ave. | 530/235–4805 | fax 530/235–4805 | 15 rooms | $55 | MC, V.

Best Choice Inn. A tree-lined canyon is just outside this motel, which is home to the House of Glass restaurant. You can arrange to be picked up at the Amtrak Station or Mott Airport. Restaurant. Pool. | 4221 Siskiyou Ave. | 530/235–2021 | 30 rooms | $33–$55 | AE, D, MC, V.

Castle Rock Inn. The rooms in this rustic 1903 inn are paneled in original knotty pine. The two-story building is located across from the Dunsmuir Rail Cam, which displays videos of passing trains. You can hear live blues, jazz, and other entertainment here on weekends. Complimentary Continental breakfast. | 5829 Sacramento Ave. | 530/235–0100 | 8 rooms | $60 | AE, MC, V.

Cedar Lodge. This single-story lodge 6 mi away from Mount Shasta ski park is set on secluded, tree-shaded grounds near the Sacramento River. You'll find a large aviary with exotic birds on the premises. The lodge was built in the 1920s and has many wildlife photographs on the walls. Some rooms have wood-burning fireplaces or stoves. Picnic area. Some kitchenettes, cable TV, in-room VCRs. Some pets allowed (fee). | 4201 Dunsmuir Ave. | 530/235–4331 | fax 530/235–4000 | www.cedarlodgedunsmuir.com | 25 rooms | $40–$50 | AE, D, MC, V.

Dunsmuir Inn Bed and Breakfast. This homey, simply decorated inn is close to downtown. Three of the rooms are on the second floor, which also has a balcony over a quiet street. You'll find an ice cream parlor on the ground floor and three porches around the house. Picnic area, complimentary breakfast. Fishing. | 5423 Dunsmuir Ave. | 530/235–4543 | fax 530/235–4154 | www.dunsmuirinn.com | 5 rooms | $60–$70 | AE, D, MC, V.

Dunsmuir Travelodge. This attractive, modern motel has affordable accommodations in the downtown business loop, 1 block from the Upper Sacramento River and ¼ mi from I–5. It was built in the 1950s and has two floors. Cable TV. | 5400 Dunsmuir Ave. | 530/235–4395 | fax 530/235–0229 | www.travelodge.com | 18 rooms, 3 suites | $40–$75, $75–$85 suites | D, MC, V.

Oak Tree Inn. This quiet hotel with simply furnished rooms is owned and run by the Paganini family, whose motto is "Once a guest, always a friend." There are picnic areas and BBQ pits within the tree-lined plot. You can arrange to be picked up from the Amtrak station or Mott Airport. Picnic area. Cable TV. | 6604 Dunsmuir Ave. | 877/235–2884 or 530/235–2884 | fax 530/235–0208 | www.oaktreeinn.com | 20 rooms, 2 family suites | $48–$68, $72–$96 suites | AE, D, MC, V.

Railroad Park Resort. One of Dunsmuir's major attractions, this resort is a fitting tribute to the area's railroad legacy. You can stay in cabins or in restored antique cabooses that have been converted into wood-paneled guest rooms. The cabooses are loosely arranged in a semi-circle around a swimming pool and spa. The restaurant and lounge are in converted antique dining cars. On the grounds are a huge steam engine and a restored water tower from Dunsmuir's railroad days. Built in 1968, the resort is 1 mi north of Dunsmuir and within walking distance of the Sacramento River. RV hookups. Restaurant, bar, picnic area. Refrigerators, cable TV. Hot tubs. Laundry facilities. Some pets allowed (fee). | 100 Railroad Park Rd. | 530/235–4440 or 530/235–0430 (campground) | fax 530/235–4470 | rp@rrpark.com | www.rrpark.com | 27 rooms | $75–$80 | AE, D, MC, V.

Riverwalk Inn. This inn has charming bedrooms with dormer windows. The rooms are furnished with antiques and family heirlooms. There are gardens in the front yard from which you can view Mt. Shasta and a piano in the sitting room. Reservations essential. Picnic area, complimentary Continental breakfast. In-room VCRs. | 4300 Stagecoach Rd. | 530/235–4300 or 800/954–4300 | 4 rooms | $35–$65 | AE, D, MC, V.

EL CAJON

MAP 4, K17

(Nearby towns also listed: Pine Valley, San Diego)

El Cajon is nestled in a valley surrounded by hills, hence its name, which means "the box." This San Diego satellite of 89,000 residents is a growing residential and industrial community, with factories manufacturing electronic equipment and aircraft and missile parts. More pastoral pursuits here include grape and citrus growing. The highly diverse population is celebrated each year at the International Friendship Festival, hosting some eighty ethnic heritages with native songs, dancers, art, and food in a lively two-day event.

Information: **San Diego East County Chamber of Commerce** | 201 S. Magnolia Ave., 92020 | 619/440–6161.

Attractions

Heritage of the Americas Museum. This museum is dedicated to the natural and human history of the Americas, which it displays in a variety of forms, including meteorites, tribal tools, and jewelry. The museum overlooks the Quyamaca Community College campus and the surrounding area. | 12110 Quyamaca College Dr. W | 619/670–5194 | $3 | Tues.–Fri. noon–4, Sat. noon–5.

ON THE CALENDAR

SEPT.: *International Friendship Festival.* A Native American pow-wow, and 55 booths with foods and crafts, each representing a different country, highlight El Cajon's annual celebration of culture and diversity in the City Hall parking lot. New U.S. citizens are sworn in at the opening ceremony. | 619/440–6161.

Dining

Carrows Restaurant. American. This popular chain of restaurants serves up such standard American fare as omelettes, sandwiches, steak, shrimp, chicken, and salads. It's a casual, family-oriented place with something for everyone. You'll find it 1 block off of Route 67. | 368 Broadway | 619/477–4640 | Breakfast also available | $10–$15 | AE, D, DC, MC, V.

Echo's Restaurant. Continental. Part of the Singing Hills Resort, this restaurant is decorated with classic St. Andrews golf memorabilia and overlooks a lush garden courtyard. The menu includes choice steaks, prime rib, and fresh fish. Three of the most popular dishes are pancetta-wrapped filet mignon, grilled pork chops with honey cider sauce, and sea bass. No smoking. | 3007 Dehesa Rd. | 619/442–3425 | Reservations essential | No lunch. Sunday brunch | $11–$20 | AE, D, MC, V.

Red Oak Steakhouse. American. Prime rib and filet mignon are the specialties in this busy, family-friendly restaurant. Pasta and salad round out the hearty menu. It's in the Parkway Plaza, at the intersection of I–8 and Route 67. | 402 Fletcher Rd. | 619/442–0517 | $12–$25 | MC, V.

Lodging

Best Western Continental Inn. This modern, suburban motel is within easy driving distance of many championship golf courses. Complimentary Continental breakfast. Some kitchenettes, some minibars, microwaves, some refrigerators, cable TV. Pool. Hot tub. Exercise equipment. Laundry facilities. Business services. | 650 N. Mollison Ave. | 619/442–0601 | fax 619/442–0152 | www.bestwestern.com | 97 rooms, 12 suites | $89–$99, $89–$129 suites | AE, D, DC, MC, V.

Parkside Inn. Rooms at this hotel, a block off the I–8 freeway, are in a two-story structure; some overlook the pool and patio area. Cable TV. Pool. | 1274 Oakdale St. | 619/442–4330 | 32 rooms | $55–$70 | Continental breakfast in summer | AE, D, MC, V.

Plaza International Inn. This economical motel built in 1972 is in a residential area not far from two casinos, a golf course, and the Lindbergh Field Airport. In-room data ports, refrigerators, cable TV. Pool. Hot tub, sauna. Business services. | 683 N. Mollison Ave. | 619/442–0973 or 800/675–7105 | fax 619/593–0772 | www.k-online.com/~plazainternational | 59 rooms | $47 | AE, D, DC, MC, V.

Singing Hills Resort. Established in 1955, this resort, 3 mi from San Diego Airport, is on 425 acres. Many guest rooms have views of the mountains, the Dehesa Valley, and the three championship 18-hole golf courses on the premises. Restaurant, bar (with entertainment), dining room. Some microwaves, refrigerators. 2 pools. Hot tubs, massage. 3 18-hole golf courses, 3 putting greens, 11 tennis courts. Exercise equipment. Laundry facilities. Business services. | 3007 Dehesa Rd. | 619/442–3425 or 800/457–5568 | fax 619/442–9574 | tidbitts@connectnet.com | www.singinghills.com | 102 rooms | $103–$140 | AE, D, MC, V.

Travelodge. This hotel follows the standard chain model, with light landscaping around a modern, multi-story building. Palm trees and evergreens dot the grounds, which are just a block and a half south of I–8. Complimentary Continental breakfast. Refrigerators, microwaves, cable TV. Pool. | 471 N. Magnolia Ave. | 619/447–3999 | fax 619/447–8403 | www.travelodge.com | 47 rooms, 2 suites | $70–$110, $130–$170 suites | AE, D, DC, MC, V.

EL CENTRO

MAP 4, M17

(Nearby town also listed: Calexico)

Once a desert, modern irrigation efforts have turned this area into one of the most productive agricultural regions in the state. Today, more than 500,000 acres are under cultivation in Imperial County, yielding nearly $1 billion from beef cattle, alfalfa, and other crops. Predominantly Latino, El Centro (pop. 31,400) is also the winter home of the navy's death-defying Blue Angels aerobatic team.

Information: **El Centro Chamber of Commerce** | 1095 S. 4th St., 92243 | 760/352–3681 | generalinfo@elcentrochamber.com | www.elcentrochamber.com.

Attractions

Old Post Office Pavilion. This stately complex did once house the old post office, but now it's home to the El Centro Arts Council. Frequently changing exhibits include local and national artists in painting, sculpture, multimedia, and more. | 230 S. 5th St. | 760/337–1777 | Free | Weekdays 8–5.

ON THE CALENDAR

MAR.: *Midwinter Fair.* Brush up on your dart throwing and ring tossing at this midwinter fair. El Centro hosts eight days of carnival games, rides, and arts and crafts booths, plus hot dog and cotton candy stands. | 760/337–1777.

Dining

Barbara Worth Restaurant. Continental. This country club restaurant is garden-like, with large windows providing a view of the 9th green of the golf course, and the lake. The room has a Polynesian flavor, with bamboo chairs, and orchids on the tables. The restaurant is known for its Beef Wellington, the prime rib, and lamb chops. Open-air dining is available. Kids' menu. Sunday brunch. No smoking. | 2050 Country Club Dr., Holtville | 760/356–2806 | Breakfast also available | $18–$35 | AE, D, DC, MC, V.

Celia's. Mexican. The quesadillas and carne asada (grilled beef) are standouts at this classic south-of-the-border family-oriented restaurant with photographs of customers adorning the walls. The eatery is less than 1 mi from I–8. | 1530 W. Adams Ave. | 760/352–4570 | No lunch Mon.–Sat. | $8–$12 | No credit cards.

Scribbles. Steak. There are two dining areas here, and the red, green, and peach tablecloths and napkins complement the colorful abstract paintings on the walls, which recall the restaurant's name. At lunch, the menu is sandwiches and salads. In the evening, however, the menu is taken over by steak, shrimp, and chicken. Try the prime rib or the roasted chicken. Kids' menu. No smoking. | 2015 Cottonwood Circle | 760/352–9523 | Breakfast also available. No supper Sun. June–Aug. | $9–$16 | AE, D, DC, MC, V.

Lodging

Barbara Worth Golf Resort and Convention Center. This resort was named after the 1911 Harold Bell Wright book *The Winning of Barbara Worth,* about reclaiming the desert and turning it into farmland by diverting the Colorado River. Gary Cooper made his feature-film debut in the movie that was made of the novel in 1926. The basic, two-story buildings have outside entrances, and house simple rooms, some with plants. Golf is the main draw at this place. Restaurant, bar, room service. Some microwaves, refrigerators, cable TV. 2 pools. Hot tub. Driving range, 18-hole golf course, putting green. | 2050 Country Club Dr., Holtville | 760/356–2806 or 800/356–3806 | fax 760/356–4653 | www.bwresort.com | 103 rooms | $70 | AE, D, DC, MC, V.

Best Western John Jay Inn. One of two John Jay Best Westerns in the area (the other is in Calexico), this 3-story motel has interior entrances. Only 14 mi north of the U.S./Mexican border, it's also near NAF El Centro, home of the Blue Angels. Complimentary Continental breakfast. Pool. Hot tub, sauna. Exercise equipment. Laundry facilities. | 2352 S. 4th St. | 760/337–8677 | fax 760/337–8693 | www.bestwestern.com | 58 rooms | $50–$110 | AE, D, DC, MC, V.

Brunner's Inn and Suites. There are standard rooms, mini-suites (bedrooms with kitchenettes), and full suites (bedrooms with full-size kitchens)at this two-story, exterior-entrance motel 2 mi north of I–8 in the center of town. 2 restaurants, bar. Pool. Hot tub. Exercise equipment. Laundry facilities. | 215 Imperial Ave. | 760/352–6431 | 85 rooms, 12 mini-suites, 15 full suites | $55–$65, $70 suites | AE, D, DC, MC, V.

El Dorado Motel. This two-story motel, built in the 1970s, is within walking distance of a fast-food restaurant and a Mexican restaurant. Restaurant, complimentary Continental breakfast. Some kitchenettes, some refrigerators, cable TV. Pool. Airport shuttle. Some pets allowed. | 1464 Adams Ave. | 760/352–7333 | 72 rooms | $49 | AE, D, DC, MC, V.

Executive Inn. This small, two-story motel is in the downtown area, near to shopping and movie theaters. Some of the rooms have views of the pool. Restaurant, complimentary

Continental breakfast. Some kitchenettes, some microwaves, refrigerators, cable TV. Pool. Laundry facilities. Some pets allowed. | 725 State St. | 760/352–8500 | fax 760/352–1322 | 42 rooms | $30 | MC, V.

Ramada Inn. This two-story brick motel is in a residential neighborhood across from a medical center ¼ mi from I–8. Most of the basic rooms are accessed by interior corridors, and some rooms have pool views. It's only 11 mi from Mexicali. Restaurant, bar, room service. Cable TV. Pool. Hot tub. Gym. Laundry facilities. Airport shuttle. Some pets allowed. | 1455 Ocotillo Dr. | 760/352–5152 | fax 760/337–1567 | www.ramada.com | 147 rooms | $57–$70 | AE, D, DC, MC, V.

ELK

(Nearby towns also listed: Albion, Boonville, Little River, Mendocino, Point Arena)

Elk was originally called Greenwood, after four brothers who became successful by harvesting the coastal redwoods. But when Mendocino County opened a post office there, a dilemma was discovered: the brothers' dad had established a town in Eldorado County, and it too was named Greenwood. The Mendocino County post office then took the name Elk, and gradually the town adopted the name, too. The Greenwoods' legacy has almost vanished; the pier they used to export logs has crumbled, and the grand mansions of the logging barons have been renovated into bed-and-breakfast inns.

Elk is a sleepy, pleasant town largely undiscovered by tourists and city folk, most of whom drive by without stopping. And the hundred or so residents there today are happy to keep it that way. Most of the hills sheltering the town are part of a large private ranch, and while the town welcomes you, it's determined to prevent widespread development of its precious open space.

Information: Redwood Coast Chamber of Commerce | Box 338, Gualala 95445 | 707/884–1080 | info@redwoodcoastchamber.com | www.redwoodcoastchamber.com.

Attractions

Force Ten Ocean White Water Tours. Sign up for a two-hour kayaking tour with experienced guides. You launch at Greenwood Beach and glide through sea caves and kelp forests, viewing wildlife and panoramic views of the Mendocino coast along the way. | Box 167 | 707/877–3505 | $95 | Year-round, daily 8–4.

Horseback Riding. Take guided trail rides through the Elk Mountain area or along the beach. | Ross Ranch, 28300 Greenwood Rd. | 707/877–1834 | $45 for 2 hours on the trail; $55 for 2 hours on the beach | Year-round; reservations only.

ON THE CALENDAR

AUG.: *Great Day in Elk.* The entire village turns out for this late-summer celebration. There's a parade at noon, games and food all afternoon, and a dinner and dancing in the evening. | 707/877–3308.

Dining

Bridget Dolan's Irish Pub. Irish. This is a small, cozy, family pub with a kelly green interior and turn-of-the-20th-century decorations. You'll find Guinness on tap. Try the grilled halibut, rib-eye steak, fish and chips, corned beef and cabbage, clam chowder, or simply a burger. | 5910 Rte. 1S | 707/877–3422 | No lunch | $11–$15 | AE, MC, V.

Greenwood Pier Cafe. American. With garden views and art hung on pastel walls, this airy café is a wonderful place to spend a leisurely lunch. The service is relaxed and friendly, albeit slow during peak times. Simple, hearty fare is prepared from fresh, local, and organic ingredients (watch for huckleberries and mushrooms in season). Vegetarian selections include the popular ravioli. The menu changes daily but is known for chili, steaks, and seafood—ask about the catch of the day. Breakfast is also available. | 5928 Rte. 1S | 707/877–9997 | Closed Tues., Wed. | $10–$14 | AE, MC, V.

Lodging

Coast Guard Guest House. Built in 1901 as a Coast Guard life-saving station, this Cape Cod–style structure, now a B&B, is 15 mi south of Elk. The interior has the classic lines of the American Arts and Crafts period, when simple, uncluttered interiors were a rebellion against perceived Victorian excess. Some rooms have complete private bath. Complimentary breakfast. No room phones, no TV. Outdoor hot tub. | 695 Arena Cove, Point Arena | 707/882–2442 | fax 707/882–3233 | www.coastguardhouse.com | 5 rooms, 1 suite, 1 cottage | $115–$155 rooms, $155 suite, $175 cottage | MC, V.

★ **Elk Cove Inn.** This rural, four-story inn was built in 1883 as a private guest house for logging company executives. In 1968, it opened as an inn and was given an Arts-and-Crafts look. You can enjoy the half-acre botanical garden on the property. It overlooks about a mile of beachfront. Some rooms have fireplaces. Picnic area, complimentary breakfast. Refrigerators, no room phones, TV in common area. Hot tubs. Beach. Library. No kids under 12. Business services. No smoking. | 6300 Rte. 1S | 707/877–3321 | fax 707/877–1808 | www.elkcoveinn.com | 14 rooms | $148–$318 | AE, MC, V.

Elk Guest House. With over a mile of private beach access, you'll find seclusion as well as beautiful ocean views from every room in this guest house. One room has a fireplace and a feather bed beneath a skylight for stargazing. In the 60-acre gardens, you'll find a 200-ft waterfall, clear pools, and fern-filled grottos, and you can pick your own herbs, flowers, and vegetables. The guest house provides complimentary canoes and kayaks for paddling on the Navarro River. Some kitchenettes. Hot tub. Hiking. Beach. Pets allowed (fee). | 1900 Pacific Coast Hwy. | 707/877–3308 | www.elkguesthouse.com | 2 rooms, 2 cottages | $95 rooms, $195–$230 cottages.

Greenwood Pier Inn. On a rocky cliff 150 ft above sea level, these cottages guarantee spectacular ocean views. Each room is uniquely furnished with antiques, quilts, and original art. Some rooms have skylights, others have large spa tubs, fireplaces or wood-burning stoves. The lush garden is the source of the fresh flowers in every room, and there's an outdoor hot tub set on the cliff. Restaurant (*see* Greenwood Pier Cafe), complimentary breakfast. Refrigerators, no room phones, no TV. Hot tub. Some pets allowed. No smoking. | 5928 Rte. 1S | 707/877–9997 | fax 707/877–3439 | www.elkcoast.com or greenwoodpierinn.com | 13 cottages | $120–$235 | AE, MC, V.

Griffin House at Greenwood Cove. These snug Victorian cottages have private decks and wood-burning stoves. Serene, pale green and white interiors contribute to the country feel. Mendocino is 16 mi away. Restaurant, complimentary breakfast. No room phones, no TV. No smoking. | 5910 Rte. 1S | 707/877–3422 | fax 707/877–3439 | www.griffinn.com | 8 rooms | $95–$175 | AE, MC, V.

Harbor House Inn. This 1916 building has wood paneling, lofty ceilings, and even a grand piano. Rooms, each decorated in a unique and luxurious way, have garden and ocean views, wood-burning fireplaces, and four-poster or sleigh beds. Staying here affords you access to a private beach. Restaurant. No TV. | 5600 Rte. 1S | 800/720–7474 | fax 707/877–3452 | www.theharborhouseinn.com | 10 rooms | $195–$315 | MAP | MC, V.

Sandpiper House. This cozy, gray-shingled building (built in 1916) has coffered ceilings, redwood paneling, French antiques, and Oriental rugs. Rooms have garden and/or ocean views, and some rooms have fireplaces. You'll have access to a private beach. Dining room, complimentary Continental breakfast. Refrigerators, no TV. Massage. No kids under 12. | 5520 Rte. 1S | 707/877–3587 or 800/894–9016 | www.sandpiperhouse.com | 5 rooms | $135–$225 | MC, V.

EMERYVILLE

(Nearby towns also listed: Berkeley, Oakland, San Francisco)

The Ohlone people once camped here, at the mouth of Temescal Creek, living on the bounty of seafood available in the bay. The huge shell mounds they left behind weren't considered the trove of archaeological clues they are today; in 1876, an amusement park was built over one mound, which later was excavated and paved over as the freeway was widened.

The town is the result of settler Joseph Emery's refusal to pay Oakland taxes, as one story goes. Instead, he opted to incorporate his own parcel of land as a town. Another story recounts how the owners of a race track that was built near the border urged incorporation to avoid crackdowns by Oakland police. In any case, Emeryville had a reputations for rowdiness for many years. Bootleg operations, bars and gambling joints lined Park Avenue, and city government was so corrupt that future governor Earl Warren called it "the rottenest city on the Pacific Coast."

Today, it's the shopping-est city along the East Bay. To increase its tax base, Emeryville approved a number of shopping malls in the last decade, and it's become the land of warehouse-size consumerism. The most notable addition is IKEA, the ubiquitous home furnishings store. This blue-and-yellow landmark on Highway 880 reportedly turns over more inventory than any of the other outlets in the world.

Information: Emeryville Chamber of Commerce | 5858 Horton St., 94608 | 510/652–5223.

Attractions

Ikea. Believe it or not, this home furnishings store is one of the most popular destinations in northern California, with people lining up for hours just to spend money on assemble-it-yourself Swedish furniture. The building is a massive landmark at the side of I–80, at the Powell St. exit. | 4400 Shellmound St. | 510/420–4532 | Daily 10AM–9PM.

Kimball's East. This concert venue and supper club features top name jazz, R & B and soul bands and comedy acts. The semi-circular room has a seating area if you're coming just for the music, and comfortable booths and small tables if you decide to grab dinner as well. Dinner is served 6:30-9 pm.; two shows nightly, 8 and 10 pm. Off I–80, at the Powell St. exit, in Emeryville Public Market. | 5800 Shellmound Dr. | 510/658–2555 | Tickets, $18–$30; dinner $20–$30 | Daily.

Dining

Bucci's. Mediterranean. This brick building in former industrial area offers a warm, casual setting with exhibitions of paintings and drawings by local artists. Although the menu changes daily, Bucci's is known for east coast-style pizza, risotto prepared with seasonal vegetables and seafood, a generous antipasti plate. Simple dishes such as spaghetti and meatballs get raves from critics. A small patio is open during good weather. | 6121 Hollis St. | 510/547–4725 | fax 510/547–0780 | Closed Sun. No lunch Sat. | $13–$17 | MC, V.

Doug's Barbeque. American. This take-out joint sells the best Texas-style barbecue in the area. In addition to chicken, ribs, brisket and links, Doug's is also known for goat, turkey and lamb. Sides include beans, coleslaw, heavily-spiced peach cobbler, and sweet potato pie. No table service. The restaurant will take fax orders for large groups and parties. | 3600 San Pablo Ave. | 510/655–9048 | fax 510/655–1670 | Closed Sun. | $10–$11 | MC, V.

Townhouse Bar and Grill. Mediterranean. Once known as Emeryville's unofficial City Hall, this former speakeasy had two seats permanently at the bar for the mayor and the chief of police. Today, open-beam ceilings, fresh flowers and local art contribute to a cozy, rustic interior. The menu emphasizes fresh grilled meats and seafood, pasta. Specialties include garlic fries, cornmeal deep-fried calamari, cilantro chicken potstickers. | 5862 Doyle St. | 510/652–6151 | fax 510/652 0173 | Reservations recommended | Closed Sun. No lunch Mon. | $9–$18 | MC, V.

Lodging

Courtyard by Marriot. This brand new facility offers rooms geared for business travelers. The lobby has high ceilings and marble floors; suites have pale wood furnishings, wet bars, and many have sleeper sofas. The inn is less than 1 mi from I–80. Restaurant, bar, room service. Some refrigerators, some microwaves, in-room data ports, cable TV. Indoor pool. Hot tub. Exercise room. Business services. Laundry facilities. No pets. | 5555 Shellmound St. | 510/652–8777 | fax 510/652–8799 | www.courtyard.com | 297 rooms | $154–$264 | AE, D, DC, MC, V.

Holiday Inn San Francisco Bay Bridge. Right off I–80 (Powell St. exit) and near the Bay Bridge, this standard chain hotel boasts wonderful views–rooms face either the East Bay hills or the San Francisco bay. Suites have wet bars. Restaurant, bar. Cable TV. Hot tub. Gym. Business services. Meeting rooms. No pets. Free parking. | 1800 Powell St. | 510/658–9300 | fax 510/547–8166 | 279 rooms, 2 suites | $139–$169 rooms, $300–$350 suites | AE, D, DC, MC, V.

Woodfin Suite Hotel. This brand-new facility is geared toward corporate travelers planning long-term stays. All of the 1- or 2-bedroom suites have a sitting room, marble baths, and fully equipped kitchens. Décor is sleek, with an earthtone color scheme and laminated beech furnishings. Some suites have balconies. Complimentary Continental breakfast. Microwaves, refrigerators, in-room data ports, cable TV, in-room VCRs. Pool. Hot tub. Gym. Laundry facilities. Business services. | 5800 Shellmound St. | 510/601–5880 | fax 510/601–5833 | www.woodfinsuitehotels.com | 202 suites | $295–$395 suites | AE, D, DC, MC, V.

ENCINO

MAP 9, C2

(Nearby towns also listed: Sherman Oaks, Van Nuys, Woodland Hills)

This suburb of Los Angeles is a busy, thriving community (pop. 62,000) of homes and businesses on rolling hills at the foot of the Santa Monica Mountains. The main street is Ventura Blvd., which snakes across the entire San Fernando Valley. The Sepulveda Basin Recreation Area, an urban oasis, includes a rare natural remnant of the predominantly concrete-entombed Los Angeles River, as well as crisscrossing walking/cycling paths.

Information: **Encino Chamber of Commerce** | 4933 Balboa Blvd., 91316 | 818/789–4711 | fax 818/789–2485 | www.encinochamber.org.

Attractions

Encino Velodrome. Recreational bikers as well as professionals come to train on this banked, oval-shaped, outdoor track. On Wednesday nights, bicycles are provided to beginners who want to participate in an introductory training class. | 17301 Oxnard St. | 818/881–7441 | www.encinovelodrome.com | $5 | Tues.–Thurs. 5 PM–8 PM.

Lake Balboa. In 70-acre Beilenson Park, you can kayak or ride unmotorized boats in this man-made lake. There is also 1³/₁₀ mi walking path that follows the perimeter of the lake. | 6300 Balboa Blvd. | 818/756–9743 | Free | Daily, 8:30–sunset.

Los Encinos State Historic Park. Formerly a stagecoach stop, and a sheep and cattle ranch, this park now serves as a picnic ground. The park also contains a smithy and a spring-fed lake. | 16756 Moorpark St. | 818/784–4849 | Free | Wed.–Sun. 10–5; tours Wed.–Sun. 1–4.

SEPT./OCT.: *A Taste of Encino.* Local and out-of-town eateries entice you with samples, while such activities as boxing matches and square-dancing lessons make sure you never have a dull moment. There's also an auto show, live music, and an extensive children's area. | 818/789–4711.

Dining

Buca di Beppo. Italian. The menu at this restaurant includes hearty pastas, many made from scratch every day, and family-style dishes for three to five people. The ravioli and chicken cacciatore are house favorites. | 17500 Ventura Blvd. | 818/995–3288 | No lunch except Sun. | $15–$25 | AE, DC, MC, V.

Lodging

Tokyo Princess Inn. This two-story inn located in the heart of Encino was built in the 1960s. In keeping with its name, there are paintings from Japan and China in the lobby. Refrigerators, cable TV. Hot tub. | 17448 Ventura Blvd. | 818/788–3820 | fax 818/788–3818 | 26 rooms | $89–$119 | AE, MC, V.

ESCONDIDO

MAP 4, K16

(Nearby towns also listed: Carlsbad, Del Mar, Oceanside, Rancho Bernardo, Rancho Santa Fe)

The so-called Gateway to San Diego is a thriving, rapidly expanding residential and commercial city of more than 80,000 people and the center of a variety of attractions like North County Fair Mall, the largest mall in the county, and 20 golf courses—certainly not the 'Hidden Valley' its name suggests.

Information: **San Diego North Convention and Visitors Bureau** | 360 N. Escondido Blvd., 92025 | 760/745–4741 or 800/848–3336 | info@sandiegonorth.com | www.sandiegonorth.com.

Attractions

California Center for the Arts. The center hosts artistic and cultural events, from headliner musical acts such as Jewel to elementary and high school art exhibits. | 340 North Escondido Blvd. | 800/988–4253 | www.artcenter.org.

★ **San Diego Wild Animal Park.** This 1,800-acre wildlife preserve shows you herds of exotic animals as they might have appeared in their native Asia and Africa. More than 3,500 animals represent 260 species. You'll see giraffes, elephants, rhinos, and gazelles roaming freely through the huge enclosures that simulate the animals' natural habitats. The park also is an accredited botanical garden. Take the hour-long informative monorail ride before you walk through the aviaries, gardens, and exhibits. | 15500 San Pasqual Valley Rd. | 760/747–8702 or 760/480–0100 | www.sandiegozoo.com | Admission $22, parking $5 | Daily, 9–4.

Escondido Heritage Walk Museum. This museum has an 1888 Santa Fe train depot, a furnished 1890 Victorian house, other 19th-century buildings, as well as Escondido's first library, which is now the museum office. | 321 N. Broadway | 760/743–8207 | $3; special rate for children | Thurs.–Sat. 1–4.

Palomar Observatory. The observatory, located at the top of Mount Palomar, consists of four domes that house a variety of telescopes used for astronomical research. The telescopes measure the physical properties of stars, galaxies, and planets. It's an active research facility, so you can't look through the telescopes—and nighttime visits, when the important work is done, are not allowed. There is a visitors' gallery where you can see the famous Hale telescope. The Greenway Museum contains a photographic gallery of some of the observatory's sightings. Take Route 76 to County Road S6, a winding mountain road that ends at the observatory gate. | 760/742–2119 | Free | Daily 9–4.

San Pasqual Battlefield State Historic Park and Museum. The 50-acre park commemorates a battle of the Mexican War. On December 6, 1846, General Stephen Watts Kearny's American troops (with Kit Carson along as guide) battled Spanish-Californians under General Andres Pico. Kearny's force suffered greater losses but was not prevented from reaching San Diego, and the battle is considered an important step in the conquest of California. At the visitor center you can pick up a pamphlet that illustrates a nature trail showcasing native plants. | 15808 San Pasquel Valley Rd. | 760/489–0076 | Free | Weekends 10–5.

Welk Resort Center Theatre-Museum. Built by bandleader Lawrence Welk in the 1960s, this resort sprawls over 600 acres and has a theater, museum, conference center, two golf courses, an entertainment complex, shops, a restaurant, condominiums, and hotel accommodations. The 330-seat dinner theater is known for variety productions and Broadway-style musical comedy. The museum houses memorabilia from Welk's long life and musical career. Call ahead for the theatre's schedule. | 8860 Lawrence Welk Dr. | 760/749–3448 or 760/749–3000 | www.welkresort.com | Museum free | Museum: daily 9–5.

Wineries. San Diego's Mediterranean climate is particularly well-suited to grape-growing. There are several wineries in the area. | San Diego North Convention and Visitors Bureau | 760/745–4741 or 800/848–3336.

Deer Park. This park is composed of three buildings that include a car museum with the largest vintage collection of convertibles in the country (130 in all), 5 acres of vineyards, an orchard, a gazebo and a winery. | 29013 Champagne Blvd. | 760/749–1666 | $6; special rate for seniors; children 12 and under free | Museum daily 10–4; winery daily 10–5.

Ferrara Winery. One of several wineries that capitalizes on San Diego's climate, the 3 ¼ acres of Ferrara vineyards and winery have been family-owned and operated for 68 years. Tours are self-guided, tastings are free, and you can see the outside crushing process. | 1120 W. 15th Ave. | 760/745–7632 | Free | Daily 10–5.

Orfila Winery. Grape arbors and picnic areas overlook the San Pasqual Valley at this 30-acre vineyard with a 1-acre park, which includes a formal rose garden. | 13455 San Pasqual Rd. | 760/738–6500 | Free | Daily 10–5.

ON THE CALENDAR

SEPT.: *Grape Day Festival.* This festival at the end of the month celebrates the anniversary of California's admission to the United Sates and honors the area's vibrant grape industry by presenting live music, theatrical and dance performances, pony rides, a parade—and grapes. | 760/745–4741.

Dining

150 Grand Cafe. Eclectic. Airy and open, with fresh flowers on the tables, this elegant restaurant is known for its seasonal menu showcasing contemporary California-style dishes prepared with a European flair. Try the portobello Wellington or Australian lamb with mussels. Other popular dishes are excellent filet mignon and carmelized pork tenderloin. You can dine in an outdoor garden room if you choose. The restaurant is within walking distance of the California Center for the Arts. No smoking. | 150 W. Grand Ave. | 760/738–6868 | Closed Sun. | $14–$25 | AE, DC, MC, V.

Quails Inn. Steak. This two-tiered restaurant is built over a lake and has glass walls to take advantage of the view. The furnishings are contemporary, in pastel colors that do nothing to detract from the panoramic views. Favorites here are prime rib or a fresh seafood salad of shrimp, oysters, salmon, and calamari. Salad bar. Entertainment nightly. Kids' menu, earlybird suppers. No smoking. | 1035 La Bonita Dr., Lake San Marcos | 760/744–2445 | Sunday brunch | $12–$14 | AE, DC, MC, V.

Sirino's. Continental. Here's an excellent choice for dining before attending an event at the nearby California Center for the Arts. Try some steamed mussels followed by grilled salmon with roasted garlic, duck breast, rack of lamb, or one of the creative pizzas. All are accompanied by homemade bread. The wine list is serious, as are the desserts. A small patio on the sidewalk has seating for about 20 people. Beer and wine only. No smoking. | 113 W. Grand Ave. | 760/745–3835 | Reservations essential for supper | Closed Sun., Mon. No lunch Sat. | $14–$23 | AE, D, DC, MC, V.

Lodging

Castle Creek Inn Resort and Spa. Nestled between the San Diego Wild Animal Park and the Temecula wineries, this two-story inn was built in 1988. Full of well-tended plants and flowers, it reflects its scenic location in mountains. A championship golf course is nearby. Cable TV. Pool. Sauna, spa. | 29850 Circle R Way | 760/751–8800 or 800/253–5341 | fax 760/751–8787 | www.castlecreekinn.com | 30 rooms, 1 cottage | $109–$159, $450 cottage | AE, MC, V.

Comfort Inn. This three-story hotel in a commercial area is within walking distance of shops and restaurants and only 5 mi from the San Diego Wild Animal Park. Restaurant, complimentary Continental breakfast. In-room data ports, cable TV. Pool. Hot tub. Free parking. | 1290 W. Valley Parkway | 760/489–1010 | fax 760/489–7847 | www.comfortinn.com | 93 rooms | $79 | AE, D, DC, MC, V.

Parsonage Bed and Breakfast. This two-story wood-frame house 2 blocks from downtown was built in 1910, when it was the home of a local minister. Now its guest rooms have a turn-of-the-20th-century look, furnished with some Victorian antiques and new beds. One bathroom has a claw-foot tub. Dessert and beverages are served every evening. Complimentary breakfast. | 239 S. Maple St. | 760/741–9160 | 3 rooms (2 with shared bath) | $85–$95 | No credit cards.

Quails Inn. This two-story 1970s inn on a mile-long lake is surrounded by a lush garden of pine trees, palms, flowering hibiscus, bougainvillea, and avocado groves. Some rooms have lake views. Restaurant, room service. Cable TV. 2 pools. Hot tub. Gym, boating. Some pets allowed (fee). | 1025 La Bonita Dr., Lake San Marcos | 760/744–0120 or 800/447–6556 | fax 760/744–0748 | www.quailsinn.com | 140 rooms | $99–$149 | AE, D, DC, MC, V.

Sheridan Inn. The amenities available include golf, water sports, and a complimentary athletic club where you can train with workout equipment. Also available are an Olympic-size pool, tennis, racquetball, and a sauna. The rooms are decorated in a Southwestern theme. The inn is 3 mi from San Diego's largest enclosed shopping mall. Complimentary Continental breakfast. In-room data ports, some microwaves, some refrigerators, cable TV. Pool. Hot tub. | 1341 N. Escondido Blvd. | 760/743–8338 | fax 760/743–0840 | www.thesheridan.com | 55 rooms, 2 suites | $89, $165 suites | AE, D, DC, MC, V.

Welk Resort Center. Built by bandleader Lawrence Welk in the 1960s, this resort covers more than 600 acres of rugged, oak-studded hillside and includes a hotel, condominiums, recreation facilities, and an entertainment complex that presents Broadway-style musicals year-round. A museum displays Welk memorabilia, and the rooms, decorated with a Southwestern flair, have golf-course views. Bar, dining room. In-room data ports, some refrigerators, cable TV. 2 pools. Beauty salon, hot tub, massage. 3 18-hole golf courses, putting green, 3 tennis courts. Exercise equipment. Children's programs. Some pets allowed. | 8860 Lawrence Welk Dr. | 760/749–3000 or 800/932–9355 | fax 760/749–5263 | www.welkresort.com | 133 rooms | $109–$119 | AE, D, DC, MC, V.

Zosa Ranch and Garden Country Inns. This three-building stucco and Spanish tile B&B 1 mi west of I–15 has nine working fountains on its 22-acre grounds, with 7,000 guava trees, 500 avacado trees, and manicured flower gardens. Each guest room highlights a different flower found in the garden. Complimentary breakfast. Pool. Hot tub. Tennis court. | 9381 W. Lilac Rd. | 760/623–9093 | fax 760/723–3460 | www.zosagarden.com | 11 rooms, 2 suites, 1 cottage | $139–$175, $250 suites, $250 cottage | AE, D, MC, V.

EUREKA

MAP 3, B3

(Nearby towns also listed: Arcata, Trinidad)

While much of this city of 28,600 residents is filled with strip malls, motels, fast-food joints, and gas stations, it does have history. In 1850, trains filled with workers, food, and tools restocked their supplies in Eureka's port before heading to the mines, and the town was founded and named after a gold-miner's hearty exclamation. Humboldt Bay is named after German naturalist Alexander Humboldt, who explored the southern coast as far north as Santa Barbara, but never saw this particular bay. And while this former whaling and logging town may not be consistently attractive, it does boast the largest number of Victorian homes per capita of any city in the United States.

Information: **Eureka (Gtr.) Chamber of Commerce** | 2112 Broadway, 95501-2189 | 707/442–3738 | eurekacc@northcoast.com | www.eurekachamber.com.

Attractions

Sequoia Park and Zoo. You get a taste of nature, both native and exotic, in this 50-acre, redwood-filled zoo. The most famous resident is the third oldest chimpanzee in captivity. The zoo also has an aviary, municipal garden, and snackshop. | Glatt and W Sts. | 707/442–6552 | www.eurekawebs.com/zoo | $2 suggested donation | Tues.–Sun., 10–5 Oct.–Apr., 10–7 May–Sept.

ON THE CALENDAR

MAR.: *Dixieland Jazz Festival.* More than a decade old, this jazz festival draws thousands of music-lovers and popular acts from around the state and country. Entertainment sites range from theatres to tents to open-air stages. | 707/445–3378 or 707/442–3738 | www.eurekachamber.com.

KODAK'S TIPS FOR PHOTOGRAPHING WEATHER

Rainbows
- Find rainbows by facing away from the sun after a storm
- Use your auto-exposure mode
- With a SLR, use a polarizing filter to deepen colors

Fog and Mist
- Use bold shapes as focal points
- Add extra exposure manually or use exposure compensation
- Choose long lenses to heighten fog and mist effects

In the Rain
- Look for abstract designs in puddles and wet pavement
- Control rain-streaking with shutter speed
- Protect cameras with plastic bags or waterproof housings

Lightning
- Photograph from a safe location
- In daylight, expose for existing light
- At night, leave the shutter open during several flashes

From Kodak Guide to Shooting Great Travel Pictures © 2000 by Fodor's Travel Publications

Dining

Café Waterfront. Seafood. Best known for its bottomless oyster bar and clam chowder, this small eatery also serves fresh fish fillets, steak, and pasta. Glass windows overlook a bay and marina. | 102 F St. | 707/443–9190 | $13–$25 | MC, V.

Celestino's in Old Town. Italian. You can find vegetarian dishes (including vegan, on request) as well as seafood, specialty pastas, and made-to-order pizzas. Grilled eggplant rolls and fried calamari are popular appetizers, while grilled salmon and Gorgonzola with Dijon and tomato stands out among the entrées. | 421 3rd St. | 707/444–8995 | Closed Mon. No lunch | $18–$29 | AE, D, MC, V.

Ramone's at Harrison. Café. This is a casual bakery across from two large hospitals that serves light sandwiches and hot drinks as well as a variety of pastries and muffins. | 2223 Harrison Ave. | 707/442–6082 | No dinner | $5–$7 | No credit cards.

Restaurant 301. Contemporary. This elegant, candlelit restaurant uses vegetables and herbs grown in the adjacent hotel's greenhouse or at a nearby ranch. Known for fish fillet, halibut tempura, and Dungeness crab, as well as Oregon rabbit wrapped in apple-smoked bacon, salmon with shiitake and pinenut salad, or duck confit in puff pastry. The wine list is considered one of the finest in northern California. Vegetarian menu available. | 301 L St. | www.carterhouse.com | 707/444–8062 | No lunch | $16–$26 | MC, V.

★ **Samoa Cookhouse.** American. Loggers and miners have chosen to dine at this landmark for over a century. The giant restaurant serves up hearty family-style meals at long wooden tables. The menu is pre-set, and consists of soup or salad, an entrée like meatloaf, roast pork, or fried chicken, a side dish like scalloped potatoes or corn, and desert. | 79 Cookhouse La. | 707/442–1659 | $12 | AE, D, MC, V.

Sea Grill. Seafood. Located in a restored Victorian building (ca. 1870) and best known for grilled, poached, and deep-fried fish. Try salmon and halibut fillet, calamari, stuffed sole, Dungeness crab, baked oysters, or beer-battered prawns. There are also Harris Ranch steaks. Salad bar. No smoking. Kids' menu. | 316 E St. | 707/443–7187 | Closed Sun. and early–mid-Nov. | $9–$18 | D, DC, MC, V.

Lodging

Bayview Inn. Aptly named, this two-story, Victorian-style hotel has the best views in town. Each room has an exterior patio for taking in the bay, city, and surrounding landscape. Some in-room hot tubs. | 2844 Fairfield St. | 707/442–1673 | fax 707/268–8681 | www.bayview-motel.com | 17 rooms | $75–$150 | AE, D, MC, V.

Bell Cottage. Affiliated with the Carter House, this single-level turn-of-the-20th-century mansion is graced with European antiques, marbles floors, and a parlor with a fireplace and a marina view. Guests have unlimited use of a full kitchen, and two of the guest rooms have fireplaces. Dining room, complimentary breakfast. In-room hot tubs, cable TV, in-room VCRs. | 301 L St. | 707/444–8062 or 800/404–1390 | fax 707/444–8067 | reserve@carterhouse.com | www.carterhouse.com | 3 rooms | $125–$297 | AE, D, DC, MC, V.

Best Western Bayshore Inn. The lobby of this 3-story hotel is distinguished by a chandelier, a player-piano, gold-trimmed walls, and hand-made furniture. Marie Callender's shares the building and handles the room service. Rooms have exterior entrances. Complimentary Continental breakfast. Pool. Hot tub, sauna. Laundry service. Business services. | 3500 Broadway | 888/268–8005 | fax 707/268–8002 | www.bwbayshore.com | 81 rooms | $105–$155 | AE, D, DC, MC, V.

Best Western Humbolt Bay Inn. This two-story inn motel is in downtown Eureka, just 4 blocks from historic Old Town. It is nicely landscaped with fountains, trees, and flowers with rooms decorated with standard, modular furniture. Restaurant, room service. In-room data ports, some refrigerators, cable TV. Pool. Hot tub. Game room. Laundry facilities. Business services. | 232 W. 5th St. | 707/443–2234 | fax 707/443–3489 | www.bestwestern.com | 112 rooms | $100 | AE, D, DC, MC, V.

★ **Carter House.** The Carter House Victorians are an enclave of Victorian buildings run by the Carter family. The Carter House is a re-creation of an 1884 mansion built in San Francisco and destroyed in the famous earthquake and fire of 1906. After coming across the original plans in an antique shop, Mark and Christi Carter rebuilt the three-story Victorian in Eureka and opened it as a B&B in 1981. Pine furniture, antiques, and Oriental carpets decorate the attractive guest rooms and common areas. As a guest you have access to a full kitchen. The Carter Cottage, next-door to the Carter House, is a Victorian cottage decorated in contemporary Southwestern style. While you are staying there, a chef prepares your meals in the cottage's full kitchen. Complimentary breakfast. In-room data ports, cable TV, in-room VCRs (and movies). Massage. Business services. No kids under 10. No smoking. | 301 L St. | 707/444–8062 or 800/404–1390 | fax 707/444–8067 | reserve@carterhouse.com | www.carterhouse.com | 5 suites, 1 cottage | $125–$397 suites, $195–$297 cottage | Open year-round | AE, D, DC, MC, V.

Cornelius Daly Inn. In the heart of Eureka's historic area, this three-story mansion was built as a family home in 1905 by Cornelius Daly, a department store magnate. Completely restored, it serves today as a B&B. Four wood-burning fireplaces, Victorian gardens, ornate floral wallpaper, a third-floor ballroom, and antiques retain the building's originality. You'll be served complimentary refreshments in the afternoon. Picnic area, complimentary breakfast. In-room VCRs (and movies), no room phones. Laundry facilities. Business services. No smoking. | 1125 H St. | 707/445–3638 or 800/321–9656 | fax 707/444–3636 | dalyinn@humboldt1.com | www.dalyinn.com | 5 rooms (2 with shared bath), 2 suites | $85–$150, $150 suites | AE, D, MC, V.

★ **Elegant Victorian Mansion.** Victorian furnishings fill each room, and the innkeepers may even greet you in vintage clothing. Entertainment includes croquet, silent movies, old records on a wind-up Victrola, and free tours of downtown in a 1930 model A coup driven by the innkeeper, who will share his knowledge of the town history and architecture. Complimentary Continental breakfast. Sauna. Bicycles. Laundry service. | 1406 C St. | 707/444–3144 | fax 707/442–3295 | info@eureka-california.com | www.eureka-california.com | 3 rooms, 1 suite (2 shared baths) | $85–$215 | MC, V.

Eureka Inn. This large Tudor-style hotel was built in 1922 and named to the National Register of Historic Places in 1982. Its vast, high-ceilinged lobby with polished redwood beams, crystal chandeliers, and massive brick fireplace plays host to swing dances and a 22-ft Christmas tree. Past guests have included Winston Churchill, Robert F. Kennedy, J. D. Rockefeller, Cornelius Vanderbilt, Jr., Shirley Temple, Ronald Reagan, Bill Cosby, Steven Spielberg, and Mickey Mantle. 2 restaurants, 2 bars (1 with entertainment). Cable TV. Pool. Hot tub, saunas. Business services, airport shuttle. Some pets allowed. | 518 7th St. | 707/442–6441 or 800/862–4906 | fax 707/442–0637 | www.eurekainn.com | 95 rooms, 9 suites | $99–$145, $175–$289 suites | AE, D, DC, MC, V.

Eureka Red Lion Inn. This three-story inn, built in 1974, is located in downtown Eureka. Restaurant, bar (with entertainment), room service. In-room data ports, cable TV. Pool. Hot tub. Business services, airport shuttle, free parking. Some pets allowed. | 1929 4th St. | 707/445–0844 | fax 707/445–2752 | 178 rooms | $89–$109 | AE, D, DC, MC, V.

Eureka Travelodge. This two-story hotel was built in the early 1950s. Located in the center of downtown Eureka, it makes an economical option and is within walking distance of Old Town with its shops and restaurants. Complimentary Continental breakfast. Cable TV. Pool. Business services. Some pets allowed. | 4 4th St. | 707/443–6345 | fax 707/443–1486 | 46 rooms | $50–$74 | AE, D, DC, MC, V.

Gingerbread Mansion. Built at the turn of the 20th century, this grand Victorian mansion was first a doctor's private residence, then a hospital, then a rest home, and finally restored and turned into a B&B in 1983. The Queen Anne/Eastlake–style exterior is painted in warm peaches and yellows and surrounded by a colorful garden and topiary. The guest rooms, elegant and opulent, are furnished with period antiques, and some have clawfoot tubs and/or fireplaces. You can partake of complimentary afternoon high tea in the parlor. Dining room, complimentary breakfast. Business services. No smoking. | 400 Berding St., Ferndale | 707/786–4000 or 800/952–4136 | fax 707/786–4381 | innkeeper@gingerbread-mansion.com | gingerbread-mansion.com | 4 rooms, 7 suites | $150–$185, $240–$385 suites | AE, MC, V.

Hotel Carter. The Hotel Carter, right across the street, is another re-creation of a long-gone structure, in this case a turn-of-the-20th-century Eureka hostelry. It has three stories, an elegant lobby, and rooms featuring French country antiques and local artwork. Many of the rooms and suites have views of the marina, and some have fireplaces. Complimentary breakfast. In-room data ports, in-room hot tub, cable TV, in-room VCRs (and movies). Massage. Business services. No kids under 10. No smoking. | 301 L St. | 707/444–8062 or 800/404–1390 | fax 707/444–8067 | reserve@carterhouse.com | www.carterhouse.com | 14 rooms, 7 suites | $95–$187, $195–$297 suites | AE, D, DC, MC, V.

Old Town Bed and Breakfast. Built in 1871, this two-story B&B is located in the restored historic district. It is decorated with antiques, and some of the rooms have fireplaces. The garden is perfect for a relaxing moment—or why not just walk over and gaze out across the water? Complimentary breakfast. Some room phones. Hot tub. No kids under 10. Business services. No smoking. | 1521 3rd St. | 707/443–5235 or 800/331–5098 | fax 707/268–0231 | 6 rooms (2 with shared bath) | $75–$130 | AE, D, DC, MC, V.

Quality Inn Eureka. This 2-story motel with exterior corridors is in the heart of downtown Eureka, right off U.S. 101. If you want a quiet room, ask for one in the back of the building. Complimentary Continental breakfast. Cable TV. Pool, wading pool. Hot tub, sauna. Business services. Some pets allowed. | 1209 4th St. | 707/443–1601 or 800/772–1622 | fax 707/444–8365 | www.qualityinn.com | 60 rooms | $68–$150 | AE, D, DC, MC, V.

Weaver's Inn. This B&B is in a quiet residential area a few blocks from downtown Eureka and 1 mi east of the Old Town area. It occupies a stately Colonial Revival house built in 1883. Special touches include overstuffed canopied beds and a Japanese Contemplation Garden. Complimentary breakfast. No room phones, TV in common area. Pets allowed. | 1440 B St. | 707/443–8119 or 800/992–8119 | fax 707/443–7923 | www.humboldt1.com/~weavrinn/weaversinn | 3 rooms, 1 suite | $75–$110, $125 suite | AE, D, DC, MC, V.

FAIRFIELD

INTRO
ATTRACTIONS
DINING
LODGING

FAIRFIELD

MAP 3, D7

(Nearby towns also listed: Napa, Vacaville, Vallejo)

Located about 10 mi east of Napa and about 40 mi southwest of Sacramento, Fairfield has a population of approximately 78,000. This residential community, the seat of Solano County, is probably best known as the home of Travis Air Force Base, the town's largest employer, which drew many military families to the community. The Northay Medical Center, affiliated with the base, is Fairfield's second largest employer.

Information: **Fairfield-Suisun Chamber of Commerce** | 1111 Webster St., 94533-4841 | 707/425–4625 | fchamber@ffsc-chamber.com | www.ffsc-chamber.com.

Attractions

Budweiser Brewery Tours. You can taste complimentary samples of lager and ale and visit the cool beechwood aging cellar and the production floor, where high-speed machinery fills thousands of cans and bottles every minute. No kids under 5. | 3101 Busch Dr. | 707/429–7595 | www.budweisertours.com | Free | Mon.–Sat. 9–4.

Jelly Belly Factory. Various works of art that have been made out of jelly beans, including the Statue of Liberty and portraits of former presidents, are housed in this art gallery inside the Visitor Center. You can also take a tour of the factory and see exactly how jelly beans are made. | 2400 N. Watney Way | 707/428–2838 | www.jellybelly.com | Free | Daily 9–5.

The Thompson Candy Company Factory Store. Opened in 1999, this is Thompson's most modern facility. An enormous window overlooking the factory will give you a glimpse into the chocolate-manufacturing process. | 2445 S. Watney Way | 707/435–1140 | fax 707/435–1143 | www.thompsoncandy.com | Free | Weekdays 9–5.

ON THE CALENDAR

SEPT.: *Harbor Days Festival.* The rebirth of Old Town is celebrated with art and wine, a bathtub derby, crafts fair, carnival, music, and food. | 707/421–7309.

Dining

Fusilli. Italian. This bistro-style restaurant, which is a favorite with couples, has an open kitchen. It's best known for wood-oven baked pizza, but also serves steaks, veal, and pasta dishes. Beer and wine only. | 620 Jackson St. | 707/428–4211 | Closed Sun. | $9–$20 | AE, MC, V.

Old San Francisco Express Pasta Restaurant. American. Eleven railroad cars have been joined together to form two large dining areas; some cars form private dining rooms. The decor continues the railroad theme, with such artifacts as railroad lights. Speak up if you see an object that interests you—a lot of these antiques are for sale. There's plenty of pasta here, but also seafood and beef. In fact, the place is best known for steak and prime rib. Kids' menu. | 4560 Central Way | 707/864–6453 | Closed Mon. | $7–$17 | AE, MC, V.

Vineyards Grill. Continental. Baby back ribs, grilled chicken breast with Dijon mustard cream sauce, grilled salmon with lemon butter and dill, and slow-roasted prime rib are among the choices at this Holiday Inn restaurant. There is karaoke in the bar on Thursday, Friday, and Saturday evenings. | 1350 Holiday La. | 707/422–4111 | fax 707/422–2988 | $12–$20 | AE, D, DC, MC, V.

Lodging

Best Western Cordelia Inn. This two-story hotel with modern decor stands out for its location, which is quiet but also close to many interesting sites: Jelly Belly, the Thomkins chocolate factory, Budweiser tours, the Napa Valley wineries, and championship golf courses. Complimentary Continental breakfast. In-room data ports, microwaves. Pool. Spa. Laundry facilities. No smoking. | 4373 Central Pl. | 707/864–2029 or 800/422–7575 | fax 707/864–5834 | www.bestwestern.com | 60 rooms | $66–$80 | AE, D, DC, MC, V.

Hampton Inn. This three-story hotel, built in 1989, is ¼ mi from I–80, and is across the street from several fast-food restaurants. Complimentary Continental breakfast. In-room data ports, microwaves, some in-room hot tubs. Pool. Exercise equipment. Laundry facilities. Business services. No smoking. | 4441 Central Pl. | 707/864–1446 | fax 707/864–4288 | www.hampton-inn.com | 57 rooms | $89–$145 | AE, D, DC, MC, V.

Holiday Inn Select. Only 1 mi from the Solano Mall, this four-story hotel is 3 mi from downtown, and within 5 blocks of several chain restaurants. Geared towards business travelers, all of the rooms have work desks and computer hook-ups. Restaurant, bar. In-room data ports, microwaves. Pool, wading pool. Exercise equipment. Laundry facilities. Business services. No smoking. | 1350 Holiday La. | 707/422–4111 | fax 707/428–3452 | www.holiday-inn.com | 142 rooms | $109–$119 | AE, D, DC, MC, V.

Inns of America. At this contemporary chain motel adjacent to I–80, you'll be 5 mi from downtown Fairfield and 10 mi from Six Flags Marine World. In-room data ports, cable TV. Outdoor pool. Laundry facilities. Pets allowed. | 4376 Central Place, Suisun City | 707/864–1728 | fax 707/864–8226 | 101 rooms | $75–$130 | AE, MC, V.

FALLBROOK

(Nearby towns also listed: Carlsbad, Oceanside, Temecula)

Fallbrook is about 50 mi northeast of San Diego, and one of its nearest neighbors is the U.S. Marine Corps' sprawling Camp Pendleton. The Vital Reche family settled here in 1869, creating the area's first recorded permanent settlement. They named the new community Fall Brook after their former homestead in Pennsylvania. By the 1920s, olives had become a major crop for the town and remained so through World War II; eventually, avocados and flowers of all types came to dominate the local agricultural scene. The more than 40,000 residents are spread over 127 square mi, helping to maintain the region's peaceful, rural quality.

Information: Fallbrook Chamber of Commerce | 233 E. Mission Rd. #A, Fallbrook 92028 | 760/728–5845 | fax 760/728–4031 | fallbrook@primemail.com | www.fallbrookca.org.

Attractions

Fallbrook Art and Cultural Center. This spacious building with 20-ft ceilings and exposed beams serves as a gallery for local and regional art shows of watercolors, oils, glass sculpture, bronzework, ceramics, and even gourd art. You can also watch bronze casting and glass-blowing (call ahead for firing times). | 103 S. Main St. | 800/919–1159 or 760/728–1414 | fax 760/723–7618 | $3 suggested donation.

ON THE CALENDAR

APR.: *Fallbrook Avocado Festival.* Fallbrook is the undisputed Avocado Capital of the world, and this one-day festival celebrates the little green fruit that put the town on the map. Highlights include avocado pie, guacamole, and avocado decorating contests along with carnival rides, arts and crafts, kids' activities, bike races, and live music. | 760/728–5845 | www.fallbrookca.org.

Dining

Alexander's. Continental. Part of the Pala Mesa resort, this is one of the most popular restaurants in the area. The white-paneled dining room has a cathedral ceiling, and is lined with picture windows that overlook a golf course. Special dishes include stuffed chicken, portobello mushroom and seafood pasta, and baked halibut with artichoke hearts. Kids' menu, earlybird suppers. No smoking. | 2001 Old U.S. 395 | 760/728–5881 | Reservations essential | Breakfast also available, Sunday brunch | $12–$25 | AE, MC, V.

Le Bistro Restaurant. Continental. In summer, you can eat on the patio, or upstairs in the casual indoor dining room where rack of lamb, black pepper filet mignon, stroganoff, duck, and shrimp fill the menu. Earlybird suppers. Beer and wine only. No smoking. | 119 N. Main St. | 760/723–3559 | Closed Mon. No lunch Sun. | $11–$24 | AE, D, DC, MC, V.

Lodging

Best Western Franciscan Inn. This terra-cotta–topped motel is the nearest lodging to Camp Pendleton; the Naval Weapons Station is only 2 mi away. Complimentary Continental breakfast. In-room data ports, many kitchenettes, cable TV. Pool. Hot tub. | 1635 S. Mission Rd. | 760/728–6174 | fax 760/731–6404 | www.bestwestern.com | 51 rooms | $75–$80 | AE, D, DC, MC, V.

Fallbrook Country Inn. This simple hotel provides no-frills accommodations and service. Modern rooms occupy three inward-facing units, with a swimming pool in the center. Restaurant, complimentary Continental breakfast. Pool. | 1425 S. Mission Rd. | 760/728–1114 | dpatel@pinnaclehotelusa.com | www.pinnaclehotelusa.com | 28 rooms | $85–$95 | AE, D, MC, V.

Fallbrook Lodge. This two-story hotel with interior corridors was built in 1991 and is in a commercial area 1 mi from downtown. Complimentary Continental breakfast. Some kitchenettes, cable TV. | 1608 S. Mission Rd. | 760/723–1127 | fax 760/723–2917 | 36 rooms | $50 | AE, D, DC, MC, V.

La Estancia. This medium-size hotel with Spanish-style architecture and southwestern-style rooms is one block from I–15 across from a convenience store. Restaurant. Some kitchenettes, some microwaves, some refrigerators. Pool. Hot tub. | 3135 Old U.S. 395 | 760/723–2888 | 41 rooms, 8 suites | $69–$95 | Restaurant closed Mon.–Tues. | AE, MC, V.

Pala Mesa. In a secluded area of rolling foothills on the grounds of a former ranch, this two-story luxury resort, built in the 1970s, boasts a championship golf course. All guest rooms have golf course or foothills views, and many have wet bars and private terraces. Restaurant (*see* Alexander's), bar (with entertainment), dining room, room service. In-room data ports, cable TV. Pool. Hot tub, massage, spa. Driving range, 18-hole golf course, putting green, 4 tennis courts, jogging trail. Exercise equipment. Business services, airport shuttle. | 2001 Old U.S. 395 | 760/728–5881 or 800/722–4700 | fax 760/723–8292 | www.palamesa.com | 133 rooms | $135–$160 | AE, DC, MC, V.

FELTON

MAP 4, D9

(Nearby towns also listed: Aptos, Capitola, Santa Cruz)

Felton is nestled in the San Lorenzo Valley beneath the majestic redwood forests of the Santa Cruz Mountains, 9 mi from Santa Cruz. Originally a logging town, it is home of one of the last running steam trains, the Roaring Camp and Big Trees Narrow Gauge Railroad, and to one of the tallest covered bridges in the country (and the only one made of redwood). Now known as a resort and recreation area, Felton is known for its small-town charm—very, very small town, mind you.

Information: **San Lorenzo Valley Chamber of Commerce** | Box 67, 95018 | 831/335–2764.

Attractions

Henry Cowell Redwoods State Park. Henry Cowell Redwoods State Park features 15 mi of hiking and riding trails through a forest that looks much the same as it did 200 years ago when it was home to the Zayante Indians. The park shelters the Redwood Grove, with a self-guided nature path through Douglas fir, madrones, oaks and Ponderosa pines. There is a picnic area above the San Lorenzo River, where anglers fish for steelhead and salmon during the winter. Camping information is available at 800/444-7275. Hours vary with the season so call ahead. | 101 N. Big Trees Park Rd. | 831/335–4598 | www.cal-parks.ca.gov/DISTRICTS/santacruz/hcrsp418.htm | Free.

Roaring Camp & Big Trees Narrow Gauge Railroad. America's last steam-powered passenger railroad with year-round passenger train service, the RC&BTNGRR; traces its heritage back to 1857, when gold-miners, lumberjacks and other early pioneers trudged over the mountains of the American West in search of adventure. Hour-long excursion to Bear Mountain travels through giant redwoods and traverses a dizzying switchback route. Call ahead for schedule. | 1 Graham Hill Rd. | 831/335–4484 | fax 831/335–3509 | www.roaring-camp.com | $14.50.

Dining

Tyrolean Restaurant and Cottages. German. This quaint, wood-beamed Bavarian lodge surrounded by lush redwoods serves up authentic Bavarian and German cuisine, with specialties like *sauerbraten, weinerschnitzel* and *kaesspaetcle* (Bavarian noodles). There is outdoor dining on a spacious garden patio. Sunday brunch. Ben Lomond is 3 mi north east of Felton on Hwy. 9. | 9600 Hwy 9, Ben Lomond | 831/336–5188 | fax 831/336–8654 | www.tyrolean-inn.com/ | Reservations essential | Closed Mon. No lunch Tues. | $12–$19.95 | AE, MC, D, DC, V.

Lodging

Fern River Resort. These rustic cottages along the San Lorenzo River are across from the Henry Cowell State Park, 1 mi south of town, on Hwy 9. Some rooms have fireplaces and kitchens. Water sports, fishing. Playground. | 5250 Hwy. 9 | 831/335–4412 | fax 831/335–2418 | fernriver.com/cabins.html | 13 rooms | $48–$99 | AE, MC, V.

Inn at Felton Crest. This romantic bed and breakfast is situated on an acre in the Santa Cruz Mountains overlooking the San Lorenzo Valley. The new Victorian-style 2-story home has sitting and dining rooms and decks with inspiring redwood views. The luxurious rooms, each on a separate level for privacy, are simply but elegantly furnished. You get complimentary champagne with your stay. All rooms have fireplaces. Complimentary Continental breakfast. In-room hot tubs, cable TV, in-room VCRs. | 780 El Solyo Heights Dr. | 831/335–4011 or 800/474–4011 | fax 831/331–1859 | www.feltoncrestinn.com | 4 rooms | $375–$445 | AE, D, DC, MC, V.

FORT BRAGG

MAP 3, B5

(Nearby towns also listed: Albion, Little River, Mendocino)

The military outpost of Fort Bragg was built in 1857 to oversee the Pomo and Yuki people interned at the Mendocino Indian Reservation. The developing community collapsed however, after the fort was cited for "gross mismanagement" in 1867. Today, the huge Georgia Pacific lumber mill stands on the fort's old land, with seemingly endless stacks of "former forests" giving mute testimony to the dominance of the lumber industry here. Fort Bragg also has many important institutions (such as hospitals and government offices) which provide services that are absent from smaller towns on the coast, so it's a very important place to the entire region. The town is not yet a tourist mecca, though it might not be long before the quaintness of neighboring Mendocino creeps into much plainer Fort Bragg, bringing in the tourists and driving up the prices.

Information: Fort Bragg–Mendocino Coast Chamber | Box 1141, 95437-1141 | 707/961–6300 | chamber@mcn.org | www.mendocinocoast.com or www.fortbragg.com.

Attractions

California Western Railroad Skunk Train. Following the same coastal "Redwood Route" between Fort Bragg and Willits that it has since 1885, the Skunk Train crosses some 30 bridges and trestles and passes through two deep mountain tunnels. Originally a steam-powered logging line, the train's "Skunk" cars were inaugurated in 1925 and nicknamed for their gas engines, which prompted locals to say, "You can smell 'em before you can see 'em." | 100 W. Laurel St. | 707/964–6371 or 800/777–5865 | fax 707/964–6754 | www.skunk-train.com | $27–$47 | July–Nov., 9–2.

Mendocino Coast Botanical Gardens. Formal flower gardens, pine forests, 100 species of birds, and 80 species of mushrooms fill the lush grounds here, the only public garden in the continental states that is on the ocean. | 18220 N. Rte. 1 | 707/964–4352 | www.gardenbythesea.org | $6 | Mar.–Oct., daily 9–5, Nov.–Feb., daily 9–4.

ON THE CALENDAR

SEPT.: *Portuguese Festa.* The traditional festivities include a fish dinner, coronation of the queen, and a parade. | 707/964–4177.

Dining

Gardens Grill. Continental. The restaurant at the Mendocino Coast Botanical Gardens specializes in apple-wood grilled steak, seafood, and vegetarian dishes. You can view the gardens from the outdoor deck. Brunch is served on Sunday. | 18218 Rte. 1N | 707/964–7474 | No dinner Sun.–Wed. | $15–$30 | MC, V.

Headlands Coffee House. Café. Musicians perform most nights at this local meeting place and cultural center. Along with pastries, cheesecakes, and biscotti to go with your coffee, you can order lasagna, chicken enchiladas, panini, soups, stews, and sandwiches for lunch or dinner. Belgian waffles are breakfast favorites. | 120 E. Laurel St. | 707/964–1987 | Breakfast also available from 7 AM daily | $8–$12 | D, MC, V.

The Ivanhoe. Italian. In the oldest building in town, dating from 1875, this restaurant, which boasts an antique gun collection on the walls and serves hearty, old-fashioned fare, used to be a hotel. Fridays and Saturdays have prime rib and clam chowder specials. Try chicken cacciatore, gnocchi, or risotto. | 315 Main St. | 707/786–9000 | Closed Mon. No lunch | $8–$18 | MC, V.

The Restaurant. Contemporary. You can see the Skunk Train depot across the street, and the ocean from the window seats, at this two-room place with art on the walls for sale. Lemon prawns, razor clams, burgers and a pasta of the day are among the menu choices. A jazz brunch takes place on Sunday. | 418 N. Main St. | 707/964–9800 | Closed Wed. No lunch Mon., Tues., Sat. | $20–$24 | MC, V.

Samraat Restaurant. Indian. Traditional dishes such as tandoori, curry, and seafood are served to the sounds of recorded sitar music. | 546 S. Main St. | 707/964–0386 | $16–$25 | AE, DC, MC, V.

The Wharf. Continental. From the dining room you can enjoy views of fishing boats in the harbor, and there's plenty fresh seafood on the menu: Pacific red snapper, prawns, scallops, Dungeness crab. There's also prime rib. At lunch you can sit out on the patio under a big green umbrella. Kids' menu. Beer and wine only. | 780 N. Harbor Dr. | 707/964–4283 | $15–$23 | D, MC, V.

Lodging

Annies Jughandle Beach Bed and Breakfast Inn. If you stay at this 1880s Victorian farmhouse, you'll get a gourmet breakfast with Cajun flair, a guest room with a private bath and family antiques, perhaps a fireplace and a Jacuzzi, and expert advice on the area from the B&B's fun-loving owners. The large Redwood Room has an ocean view and a 20-ft vaulted ceiling. The Forest Room, the most affordable option, has a handmade four-poster bed. The romantic Enchanted Barn Room is a 600-ft loft that includes a giant skylight, private fireplace, and a private deck overlooking the forest. Complimentary breakfast. Refrigerators, cable TV. | 32980 Gibney La. | 707/964–1415 | fax 707/961–1473 | annies@jughandle.com | www.jughandle.com | 7 rooms, 3 suites | $119–$229, $189–$229 suites | AE, MC, V.

Cleone Gardens Inn. A homey inn situated on five acres of lawns, flowerbeds, firs, and redwoods. Some rooms have fireplaces, some have kitchens with dining areas, and there is one larger cottage near a pasture. The beach is 5 blocks away. Picnic area. Some kitchenettes, some refrigerators, cable TV, some room phones. Hot tub. Business services. | 24600 Rte. 1N | 707/964–2788 | www.cleonelodgeinn.com | 10 rooms, 1 cottage | $77–$145, $110 cottage | AE, D, MC, V.

Colonial Inn. Built as a private residence in 1912 and converted to a hotel in the 1940s, this inn 4 blocks east of Main St. in a residential neighborhood is recognized as an architectural jewel of the Arts and Crafts Movement. The rooms, individually furnished in styles compatible with the Craftsman tradition, contain original art; two have wood-burning fireplaces. Cable TV, in-room VCRs, no room phones. Pets allowed (fee). | 533 E. Fir St. | 707/ 964–1384 or 877/964–1384 | innkeeper@colonialinnfortbragg.com | www.colonialinn-fortbragg.com | 10 rooms | $80–$130 | No credit cards.

Grey Whale. Every guest room in this 1915 four-story B&B has a private bathroom and views of the garden, town, hills, or the ocean—which is 6 blocks away. Some rooms have fireplaces, and one has a double hot tub. There's a fireside lounge, a TV-VCR room, and a recreation area with a pool table. Restaurant, complimentary breakfast. TV in common area. Library. Business services. No smoking. | 615 N. Main St. | 707/964–0640 or 800/382–7244 | fax 707/964–4408 | stay@greywhaleinn.com | www.greywhaleinn.com | 14 rooms, 1 suite | $88–$165, $165 suite | AE, D, MC, V.

Harbor Lite Lodge. Located at the south end of Fort Bragg, the two-story lodge was built in the 1970s. Some of the guest rooms have wood-burning stoves, and most overlook the Noyo River and the fishing village. The beach is ¼ mi away, and the lodge is 2 mi from the Mendocino Coast Botanical Gardens. Refrigerators, cable TV. Sauna. | 120 N. Harbor Dr. | 707/964–0221 or 800/643–2700 | fax 707/964–8748 | stay@harborlitelodge.com | www.harborlitelodge.com | 79 rooms, 9 deluxe units | $64–$106, $120–$125 deluxe units | AE, D, DC, MC, V.

Noyo River Lodge. Built in 1868 by a lumber baron who was also one of the area's first settlers, this two-story lodge on a wooded bluff above the harbor overlooks the river, the fishing village, and the Noyo River Bridge. Many of the rooms have antiques and redwood-paneled walls. Picnic area, complimentary breakfast. Cable TV (in suites), no room phones. No smoking. | 500 Casa Del Noyo Dr. | 707/964–8045 or 800/628–1126 | fax 707/964–9366 | reinhart@mcn.org | www.mcn.org/a/noyoriver | 16 rooms, 8 suites | $115–$130, $155 suites | AE, MC, V.

Pine Beach Inn and Suites. Situated on 12 acres by the sea next to the Jughandle State Reserve, this complex is composed of two single-story buildings and one two-story building. The two-story has ocean views. There are boardwalk trails to a private beach and cove. Restaurant, bar. Cable TV. Tennis. Beach. | 16801 Rte. 1N | 707/964–5603 | fax 707/964–8381 | www.pinebeachinn.com | 50 rooms, 9 suites | $65–$165, $175 suites | AE, MC, V.

Surf and Sand Lodge. Located practically on the beach (about 150 ft away), this white two-story motel has unimpeded views of the ocean, and pathways lead you down to the rock-strewn shore. The six least expensive rooms don't have views, but the extra amenities (coffeemakers, hairdryers, and binoculars) make them somewhat nicer than standard motel rooms. The fancier of the second-story rooms have hot tubs and fireplaces. Built in 1997. Some kitchenettes, refrigerators, some in-room hot tubs, cable TV. Business services. | 1131 N. Main St. | 707/964–9383 or 800/964–0184 | fax 707/964–0314 | www.mcn.org/a/surf-sand | 30 rooms | $79–$175 | AE, D, DC, MC, V.

Tradewinds Lodge. A large, two-story, family-friendly property in the center of Fort Bragg's commercial area. Restaurant, bar. Some refrigerators, cable TV. Indoor pool. Hot tub. Laundry facilities. Business services. | 400 S. Main St. | 707/964–4761 or 800/524–2244 | fax 707/964–0372 | www.fortbragg.org/thome.html | 92 rooms, 9 suites | $45–$120, $85–$120 suites | AE, D, DC, MC, V.

Weller House Inn. Swedish, French, English, and Asian antiques and furnishings fill the guest rooms of this 1886 home. The baths have hand-painted tiles, and a third floor 900-square-ft ballroom, paneled in California redwood, serves as the breakfast room. | 524 Stewart St. | 707/964–4415 | fax 707/964–4198 | www.wellerhouse.com | 7 rooms | $120–$175 | AE, D, DC, MC, V.

FREMONT

MAP 3, D8

(Nearby towns also listed: Livermore, Palo Alto, Pleasanton)

Situated on the southeast side of the San Francisco Bay (the "Southeast Bay" as locals call it), Fremont is a city of over 203,600 people on 92 square mi, making it California's fifth largest city in area. The town was named for pioneer John Fremont, who was so enamored of a Spanish/native Ohlones–built mission that he bought the adjacent land. Fremont really took shape in 1956 with the incorporation of five southeastern communities and adjoining farmland. Today it is a bustling yet homey mix of both commercial and residential pursuits.

Information: **Fremont Chamber of Commerce** | 39488 Stevenson Pl., #100, 94539 | 510/795–2244 | info@sandiegonorth.com | www.fremontbusiness.com.

Attractions

Ardenwood Historic Farm. This living museum on 205-acres demonstrates the 1870–1920 period of American daily life. A working farm, you can tour the place on a horse-drawn wagon with one of the informative staff members, who are dressed in period costumes, and who give demonstrations of the daily chores that were necessary to running a turn-of-the-20th-century farm. You can also view the home of George Washington Patterson, the first owner of the farm. | Arden Wood Blvd. | 510/796–0663 | $5; special rate for children | Tues.–Sun. 10–4.

Coyote Hills Regional Park. This wildlife sanctuary covers 966 acres and contains 40 mi of hiking and cycling trails, a museum, a boardwalk atop a freshwater marsh, and a 2,400-year-old reconstructed Indian village. | 8000 Patterson Ranch Rd. | 510/795–9385 | $4 per vehicle | Daily 8 AM–dusk.

Don Edwards San Francisco Bay National Wildlife Refuge. The refuge includes 20,000 acres of protected land for migratory birds and endangered area wildlife. | 1 Marshlands Rd. | 510/792–0222 | www.r1.fws.gov/sfbnwr | Free | Daily 7 AM–dusk.

Fremont Central Park. You'll find room here for picnicking, bicycling, jogging, and lake sports. There's a 400-acre exercise course and even a waterfowl refuge. | 40000 Paseo Padre Pkwy. | 510/791–4340 | Free | Daily dawn–10 PM.

Mission San Jose Chapel and Museum. A 1797 reconstructed Catholic church with gold-leaf altar, chandeliers, and murals. The museum documents the history of the mission, its restoration, and the Ohlone Indians. | 43300 Mission Blvd. | 510/657–1797 | Donations accepted | Daily 10–5.

ON THE CALENDAR

JULY: *Fremont Festival of the Arts.* This two-day arts and crafts festival is the largest of its kind in California, attracting over 100,000 people annually. Hundreds of local artists and artisans set up booths all over downtown Fremont to sell their hand-crafted wares. | 510/795–2244.
AUG.: *Niles Antique Market.* Now in its 36th year, this crafts and antiques market hosts over 300 vendors and 50,000 people who come to enjoy the food and music on the last Sunday in August. | 510/742–9868.

Dining

Applebee's Neighborhood Bar and Grill. American. Ribs, chicken, steaks, and pasta are mainstays at this chain of oak-furnished brasseries; the New Orleans skillet of sautéed shrimp, chicken, and andouille sausage, and the oversized dinner salads are equally popular. | 39139 Farwell Dr. | 510/742–6400 | $8–$14 | AE, D, MC, V.

China Chili. Chinese. Beef, pork, chicken, seafood, vegetarian dishes, and specials such as lobster gai kew, honeyed pecan prawns, Hunan lamb, and imperial shrimp are served while a computer-programmed piano provides music at this traditional eastern restaurant, decked in Chinese art and sculpture. | 39116 State St. | 510/791–1688 | fax 510/791–5181 | $10–$19 | AE, D, DC, MC, V.

Spin A Yarn. Mediterranean. Basic fare has been given a Greek or Italian twist since 1905 in this restaurant and lounge. Specialties include pasta, three different cioppinos, breaded and sautéed veal Milanese, and rack of lamb. You can catch up on current sports events in the cocktail TV lounge. | 45915 Warm Springs Blvd. | 510/656–9141 | fax 510/656–9298 | www.Spin-a-Yarn-Restaurant.com | $12–$21 | AE, D, DC, MC, V.

Lodging

Best Western Garden Court Inn. Built in 1975, this three-story inn is situated on several acres of landscaped gardens in a suburban area. Restaurant, bar, complimentary Continental breakfast. Cable TV. Pool. Hot tub, sauna. Business services, free parking. Some pets allowed (fee). | 5400 Mowry Ave. | 510/792–4300 | fax 510/792–2643 | www.bestwestern.com | 122 rooms | $89–$149 | AE, D, DC, MC, V.

Courtyard by Marriott. This three-story hotel was built in 1987. Rooms are spacious and geared toward business travel, with sitting areas, work desks and two phone lines in each room. Only 2 mi from the Bayside Technology Park. Restaurant, bar. In-room data-ports, some refrigerators, cable TV. Indoor pool. Exercise equipment. Laundry facilities. Business services. | 47000 Lakeview Blvd. | 510/656–1800 | fax 510/656–2441 | 146 rooms, 12 suites | $159, $179 suites | AE, D, DC, MC, V.

Courtyard Suites Victorian Inn. Bare-bones 2-bedroom suites have a small area with a table and chairs, and are arranged around a courtyard with a fountain. The motel is 2 mi from Travis Air Force Base and various Fairfield wineries. Some in-room hot tubs. Laundry facilities. | 200 E. Tabor Ave. | 707/428–0340 or 800/953–1185 | fax 707/428–3274 | www.victorianinnfairfield.com | 20 rooms | $68–$110 | MC, V.

Hilton Newark–Fremont. A convenient place to stay if you're doing business in Silicon Valley or the East Bay. There are three buildings, two of them seven-story towers; many rooms have garden or pool views. Built in 1980, the hotel is in a residential area. The casual American restaurant is connected to a bar that has live music. Restaurant, bar (with entertainment). Some refrigerators, cable TV. Pool. Spa, sauna. Exercise equipment. Airport shuttle. | 39900 Balentine Dr., Newark | 510/490–8390 | fax 510/651–7828 | www.hilton.com | 316 rooms | $199–$349 | AE, D, DC, MC, V.

Lord Bradley's Inn. This B&B maintains its Victorian-style delicacy inside and out: an English rose garden out front, and period antiques in all the guest rooms. Ohlone College is next to the property, and several restaurants and cafés are within walking distance. Seasonal fruit, and freshed baked goods such as scones and muffins, are served every morning. Restaurant, complimentary Continental breakfast. No room phones. Laundry facilities. | 43344 Mission Blvd. | 510/490–0520 | fax 510/490–3015 | ladysusan@lordbradleysinn.com | www.lordbradleysinn.com | 8 rooms | $85–$135 | DC, MC, V.

Residence Inn by Marriott. This two-story building on the east side of Fremont is next to New Port Mall, 2 mi from the local BART station, and 10 mi from Great America Theme Park. Suite-style rooms have separate living and sleeping areas, work desks, and fully equipped kitchens, perfect for business travelers and families. The inn is also within 7 mi of eight major companies. Restaurant, picnic area, complimentary Continental breakfast. Kitchenettes, cable TV. Pool. Hot tub. Laundry facilities. Business services, airport shuttle. Some pets allowed (fee). | 5400 Farwell Pl. | 510/794–5900 | fax 510/793–6587 | 80 suites | $149–$169 suites | AE, D, DC, MC, V.

FRESNO

MAP 4, G10

(Nearby towns also listed: Madera, Selma)

Fresno, by far the largest town in this part of the valley, is surrounded by one million acres of San Joaquin Valley agricultural lands. Besides being grape, orange, and cotton country, Fresno (pop. 354,200) is also turkey territory. In fact, more gobblers are raised here than anywhere else in the U.S. A good way to get acquainted with the city's agricultural heritage is via the Blossom Trail, which winds its way through 63 mi of vineyards, orchards, and historically significant points. The optimum period is February–March when many fruit and nut trees bloom.

Information: **Fresno Convention and Visitors Bureau** | 848 M St., 93721 | 559/233–0836 or 800/788–0836 | info@sandiegonorth.com | www.fresnocvb.org.

Attractions

Chaffee Zoological Gardens. These landscaped gardens house reptiles, birds, and mammals in replicated natural habitats. | 894 W. Belmont Ave. | 559/498–2671 | www.chaffee-zoo.org | $6, parking $1 | Mar.–Oct., daily 9–5, Nov.–Feb., daily 10–4.

Fresno Art Museum. The work of national and international artists is displayed in eight galleries. There is also a theater and concert series. | 2233 N. 1st St. | 559/441–4220 | www.fresnoartmuseum.com/ | $4 | Tues.–Fri. 10–5, weekends 12–5. Closed Mon.

Fresno Metropolitan Museum of Art, History and Science. Temporary exhibits and permanent collections highlight Asian art, American and European still-life paintings, and regional history at this museum. | 1555 Van Ness Ave. | 559/441–1444 | www.fresnomet.org | $6 | Tues., Wed., Fri.–Sun. 11–5, Thurs. 11–8, closed Mon.

★ **Roeding Park.** This park has a carousel, a children's train ride, a Japanese-American war memorial, and recreational facilities such as tennis courts, horse shoe pits, playgrounds, and children's fishing ponds. Paddle boats can be rented to explore Lake Washington, a small lake in the park. | 890 E. Belmont St. | 559/498–4239 | $1 per vehicle | Daily.

Storyland and Playland. This children's fairytale theme park has mechanical rides, paddle boats, and electric motor boats. | 890 W. Belmont Ave. | 559/264–2235 | $3 | Mar.–Oct., daily 10–5; Nov.–Feb., weekends 11–5.

Wild Water Adventures. Waterslides, wading pools, and an aquatic playground are all yours all day with a day pass to this water park. Call ahead for hours from mid-June through Labor Day. | 11413 E. Shaw Ave. | 559/297–6500 or 559/299–9453 | www.wildwaterone.com | $20 | Memorial Day–mid-Jun., weekends 11–8; mid-Jun.–Labor Day, daily.

ON THE CALENDAR

FEB., MAR.: *Fresno County Blossom Trail.* This trail is full of fruit blossoms, vineyards, and historical points of interest. Maps for self-guided tours are available at the Visitor Center. | 559/495–4800.

APR.: *Clovis Rodeo.* Calf roping, a clown parade, and bull riding take place at the rodeo grounds in Clovis on Rodeo Drive, 10½ mi northeast of Fresno. | 559/299–8838.

MAY: *Swedish Festival.* The Swedish community holds this town-wide event to celebrate the food, culture, and influence of Swedes in America. There's an early morning pancake breakfast in Kingsburg City Park, a Swedish arts and crafts pavilion in Kingsburg Memorial Park, and a parade down Draper Street. | 559/897–1111 or 800/788–0836.

SEPT.: *Highland Gathering and Games.* The caber toss, hammer throw, and other Scottish games are held at Cooms Ranch, on Avenue 12 and Route 41. Highlands sword dancing, bagpipe band music, and traditional Scottish food complement the games. | 559/233–0836.

OCT.: *The Big Fresno Fair.* You can enjoy food, concerts, carnival rides, livestock shows, and vendors during this 10-day festival. Competitions include a fine art and photography category, a "Floriculture" contest, and a "Fur and Feathers" category, abounding with chickens and rabbits. | 559/650–3247.

Dining

Armenian Cuisine. Middle Eastern. Lamb, beef, and chicken kabobs served with pita bread, eggplant salad, and stuffed grape leaves are favorites of many local Armenians. This unassuming family-owned restaurant with booths and glass-topped tables is in a shopping mall near the center of town. | 742 W. Bullard | 559/435–4892 | Closed Sun. | $15–$20 | AE, DC, MC, V.

Bobby Salazar's. Mexican. Fajitas, carnitas, and combination plates of enchiladas, tacos, and chili rellenos are served quickly and efficiently—but patrons still have time to start off with margaritas and freshly made salsa. The restaurant, full of bright prints by Mexican artists such as Diego Rivera, is buzzing with the business crowd at lunch, and fills with families during the dinner hours. | 2839 N. Blackstone Ave. | 559/227–1686 | $7–$11 | AE, D, DC, MC, V.

Elbow Room. Continental. Prime beef, traditional favorites such as surf-and-turf, fresh grilled fish, and pasta dishes such as prawns pomodoro with olives, capers, tomato, and rosemary have made this a popular choice for locals since 1956. You can sit out underneath a large tree on the heated patio, open year-round, or, for more intimacy, grab one of the cushy leather booths in the dimly lit dining room. | Fig Garden Center, 731 W. San Jose | 559/227–1234 | $18–$35 | AE, MC, V.

Giulia's Italian Trattoria. Italian. Hearty and intensely flavored Abruzzi cuisine (from southern Italy's Adriatic coast) such as bruscetta, steamed mussels, and polenta with grilled sausage are served here by a sophisticated wait staff. The adjoining b.b.'s Oyster Bar & Grill serves seafood appetizers and sandwiches; many patrons have cocktails at b.b.'s before dining at Giulia's. | Winepress Shopping Center, 3050 W. Shaw Ave. | 559/276–3573 | Closed Sun. No lunch weekends | $25–$40 | AE, D, DC, MC, V.

The Landmark. Eclectic. Basque specialties such as seafood stew, halibut with clams, mussels, boiled eggs and asparagus, and pickled tongue share space with a full menu of American classics including fried chicken, prime rib, and hamburgers. You can eat in one of two separate dining rooms in this restored Carnation Dairy building. Live entertainment, usually a pianist, Wednesday through Saturday evenings. | 644 East Olive Ave. | 559/233–6505 | Closed Sundays June–Aug. | $13–$18 | D, MC, V.

Shanghai Chinese Cuisine. Chinese. The menu at this local favorite, which is in a busy commercial area near central Fresno, includes traditional seafood, chicken, pork, beef and vegetarian dishes, and seasonal house specialties such as orange chicken, hot black bean beef, and veggie stir-fry. You can also order take-out. | 4011 N. Blackstone Ave. | 559/221–0227 | $7–$12 | AE, D, MC, V.

Silver Dollar Hofbrau. American. Freshly carved platters of roast beef, turkey, ham, and pastrami, as well as sandwiches and late-night specials, are on this sports bar's menu, located on one of Fresno's main commercial strips. | 333 E. Shaw Ave. | 559/227–6000 | fax 93710 | $6–$10 | MC, V.

Lodging

Chateau Inn. This 2-story rock and wood motel is in a commercial area ½ mi from the Fresno Yosemite International Airport and 5 mi from downtown Fresno. Rooms have floral print bedspreads, and most of them have recliners. The diner next door gives you a 20 percent discount with your stay. Restaurants and shops are within walking distance. Some refrigerators, cable TV, in-room VCRs. Pool. Airport shuttle. | 5113 E. McKinley Ave. | 559/456–1418 or 800/445–2428 | fax 559/456–1418 ext. 200 | 78 rooms | $65–$71 | AE, D, DC, MC, V.

Doubletree of Fresno. Formerly the Hilton of Fresno, this hotel is 4 blocks west of the convention center and 7 mi west of the airport. All rooms have an ironing board, coffee maker, and alarm clocks. Of the three restaurants on the property, one serves a casual breakfast, and one offers the only rooftop lounge in Fresno, with a great view of the city. 3 restaurants, bar. In-room data ports, cable TV. Pool. Hot tub. Airport shuttle. Some pets allowed. | 1055 Van Ness Ave. | 559/485–9000 | fax 559/485–7666 | www.doubletreehotels.com | 192 rooms | $55–$79 | AE, D, DC, MC, V.

Holiday Inn Fresno–Airport. This atrium-style hotel is adjacent to Fresno Yosemite International Airport. Six restaurants are within 1 mi, and the Fresno business district is 4½ mi to the southwest. Rooms are spacious, and have large sofas, desks and king sized beds. Restaurant, lounge. Complimentary Continental breakfast. 2 pools (1 indoor). Fitness Room. Laundry service. Business services, airport shuttle. | 5090 E. Clinton Ave. | 559/252–3611 | fax 559/456–8243 | www.basshotels.com/holiday-inn | 210 rooms, 8 suites | $76–$95 | AE, D, DC, MC, V.

La Quinta Inn. A three-story chain motel 4 blocks east of the center of downtown, La Quinta has an outdoor heated pool. No-smoking rooms are available. An International House of Pancakes and an El Torrito Mexican restaurant are on either side of the hotel. Complimentary Continental breakfast. Some microwaves, some refrigerators. Outdoor pool. | 2926 Tulare St. | 559/442–1110 | www.laquinta.com | 130 rooms | $65–$70 | AE, D, DC, MC, V.

Piccadilly Inn West Shaw. Situated on 7½ attractively landscaped acres in a residential neighborhood, this hotel is 10 mi north of downtown Fresno and the convention center. Some of the modest rooms have fireplaces. Restaurant. Complimentary Continental breakfast. Pool. Hot tub, gym. Laundry facilities, laundry service. Business services. | 2305 W. Shaw Ave. | 559/226–3850 | fax 559/226–2448 | www.piccadillyinn.com | 194 rooms | $80–$130, suites $180–$230 | AE, D, DC, MC, V.

Piccadilly University Inn. This hotel is adjacent to California State University and is 8 mi from downtown Fresno. Several restaurants and shopping destinations are within walking distance. Restaurant, bar. Complimentary Continental breakfast. Some refrigerators. Pool. Hot tub. Laundry facilities. Airport shuttle. | 4961 N. Cedar Ave. | 559/224–4200 or 800/468–3587 (outside CA), 800/468–3522 (CA) | fax 559/227–2382 | www.piccadillyinn.com | 190 rooms | $80–$130 | AE, D, DC, MC, V.

Radisson Hotel and Conference Center. Eight stories high with an atrium and three-story waterfall, this brick hotel and conference center is 2 mi from the historic downtown Tower District. The spacious rooms have an elegant appearance, filled with dark wood furniture. The hotel is adjacent to Fresno's Convention center, and less than 10 mi to the airport, shopping and golf courses. Restaurant, Bar. In-room data ports, cable TV. Outdoor pool. Beauty salon, sauna. Shops, video games. Laundry service. Airport shuttle. Pets allowed. | 2233 Ventura | 559/268–1000 or 800/333–3333 | fax 559/441–2954 | www.radisson.com | 321 rooms | $79–$125 | AE, D, DC, MC, V.

Ramada Inn University. This two-story hotel in the center of Fresno's business district has been in service for thirty years. From this Ramada, it's a 90-minute drive to Yosemite, Kings Canyon, and Sequoia National Parks. Your stay here will include a complimentary daily newspaper. Restaurant, bar, room service. Cable TV. Outdoor pool. Outdoor hot tub. Airport shuttle. No smoking. | 324 E. Shaw Ave. | 559/224–4040 or 800/241–0756 | fax 559/222–4017 | www.ramada.com | 168 rooms | $76–$150 | AE, D, DC, MC, V.

San Joaquin Hotel. This all-suites hotel is in the residential "Fig Garden" neighborhood, in northwest Fresno 2 mi west of Route 41. You can choose one of seven types of suites, each with different furnishings, with one to three beds; some of the suites are custom designed by local interior decorators. Restaurant. In-room data ports, refrigerators, cable TV. Pool. Hot tub. Laundry facilities. Business services, airport shuttle. | 1309 W. Shaw Ave. | 559/225–1309 or 800/775–1309 | fax 559/225–6021 | www.sanjoaquinhotel.com | 68 suites | $89–$195 suites | AE, D, DC, MC, V.

Village Inn. This hotel is 1 mi from the Fresno Art Museum and 4 mi from the Fresno Yosemite International Airport. The restaurants and shops of Fresno are nearby. Restaurant, complimentary Continental breakfast. In-room data ports, cable TV. Pool. Hot tub. Business services. | 3110 N. Blackstone Ave. | 559/226–2110 | fax 559/226–0539 | 153 rooms | $46–$52 | AE, D, DC, MC, V.

FULLERTON

(Nearby towns also listed: Anaheim, Brea, Buena Park, La Habra)

The citrus crops and oil fields which once dominated have given way to a community of 114,100 mostly suburban residents 22 mi south of metro Los Angeles. It is an educational and cultural center in Orange county. Fullerton is home to Cal State Fullerton, the Western State College of Law, and Hope International University, and to the Muckenthaler Cultural Center.

Information: **Fullerton Chamber of Commerce** | 219 E. Commonwealth Ave., 92832-0529 | 714/871–3100 | chamber@fullerton.org | www.fullerton.org.

Attractions

Fullerton Arboretum. This 26-acre landscaped garden has a waterfall, streams, lakes, horticultural collections, and relics from the 1894 Victorian Heritage House which is on the grounds. | 1900 Associated Rd. | 714/278–3579 | Donations suggested | Daily 8–4:45.

Muckenthaler Cultural Center. This circa 1924 Italian Renaissance style building displays cultural exhibits and produces seasonal theater performances. | 1201 W. Malvern Ave. | 714/738–6595 | $2 | Tues.–Fri. 10–4, weekends 12–4.

ON THE CALENDAR

JAN. 1: *First Night Fullerton.* Fullerton celebrates the New Year with improvisational performances, comedy sketches, live carnival rides, children's activities, and fireworks. This event is part of a broader program to host alcohol-free New Year's Eve gatherings in communities across the nation. Admission is free. | 714/871–3100 or 714/871–6575 | www.ci.fullerton.ca.us.

Dining

Angelo's & Vinci's Cafe Ristorante. Italian. This boisterous café serves huge portions of Sicilian-style pizza and pasta. Its lively surroundings include giant knights in shining armor, tableaux of Italian street scenes, and puppets and a tightrope walker prancing overhead. | 550 N. Harbor Blvd. | 714/879–4022 | $15–$33 | AE, D, MC, V.

The Cellar. French. More than 1,200 vintage wines from 15 countries are available to complement such entrées as Dover sole with slivered almonds or veal chop with apples, walnuts, and Calvados. Fortunately, knowledgeable staff can help you choose just the right one. | 305 N. Harbor Blvd. | 714/525–5682 | Closed Sun.–Mon. No lunch | $29–$49 | AE, D, DC, MC, V.

Mulberry Street Ristorante. Italian. A favorite among North Orange County hipsters, this restaurant resembles a turn-of-the-20th-century eatery with grainy photos of old Mulberry haunts. All the pasta is homemade. The menu also includes chicken, veal, and several daily fish specials. | 114 W. Wilshire Ave. | 714/525–1056 | No lunch Sun. | $17–$31 | AE, D, DC, MC, V.

Lodging

Chase Suites. This hotel is on the east end of Fullerton. The five-story building, built in 1985, has shopping destinations and restaurants within walking distance. The campus of Cal State Fullerton is literally across the street. Restaurant, complimentary Continental breakfast. In-room data ports, refrigerators. In-room hot tubs, cable TV. Pool. Exercise equipment. Laundry facilities. Business services. | 2932 E. Nutwood Ave. | 714/579–7400 or 800/797–8583 (for reservations) | fax 714/528–7945 | www.woodfinsuitehotels.com | 97 suites | $124 suites, $224 penthouse suite | AE, D, DC, MC, V.

Heritage Inn. One mile from Route 57, this hotel has oversized rooms with queen-size beds and 6-ft bathtubs. Free passes are available to a fitness center across the street. Bar. | 333 E. Imperial Hwy. | 714/447–9200 | fax 714/773–0685 | 123 rooms | $55–$92 | AE, D, DC, MC, V.

Holiday Select Inn. This eight-story building just north of I–15, in nearby La Mirada, is an upscale version of a traditional Holiday Inn. Restaurant, bar. Pool. Hot tub, sauna. Gym. Laundry service. | 14299 Firestone Blvd., La Mirada | 714/739–8500 | fax 714/521–9642 | www.holiday-inn.com/lamiradaca | 392 rooms, 12 suites | $129 rooms, $165–$250 suites | AE, D, DC, MC, V.

Howard Johnson Express Inn. Disneyland, Knott's Berry Farm, Medieval Times, Movieland Wax Museum, and the Anaheim City Convention Center are all within a 4-mi radius of this motel. Disneyland vacation packages are available. Restaurant, complimentary Continental breakfast. Refrigerators, cable TV, in-room VCRs. Pool. Business services. | 1000 S. Euclid St. | 714/871–7200 | fax 714/871–3929 | www.hojo.net | 59 rooms | $49 | AE, D, DC, MC, V.

Marriott at California State University. This hotel is next to California State University Fullerton and 7 mi from Disneyland. Restaurants and the city's corporate center are within walking distance. All rooms are furnished with a work desk and the daily newspaper is complimentary. Restaurant, bar. In-room data ports, refrigerators, cable TV. Pool. Hot tub. Exercise equipment. Business services. Some pets allowed. | 2701 E. Nutwood Ave. | 714/738–7800 | fax 714/738–0288 | www.marriott.com/marriott/laxel | 224 rooms | $79–$125 | AE, D, DC, MC, V.

Radisson Fullerton. The Fullerton Arboretum and the Fullerton Municipal Airport are both within a mile of this hotel. The 50 shops of the Metrocenter shopping center are adjacent to the property. Disneyland is the main attraction just 3½ mi to the south. Restaurant, bar. Room service. Cable TV. Pool, wading pool. Exercise equipment. Laundry facilities. Business services, Disneyland shuttle. | 222 W. Houston Ave. | 714/992–1700 | fax 714/992–4843 | www.radisson.com | 289 rooms | $139 | AE, D, DC, MC, V.

Sheraton Four Points. Positioned in the business district, this hotel is close to some of the largest corporate headquarters in the country. Disneyland and Knott's Berry Farm are 5½ mi and 7 mi away, respectively. Restaurant, bar. Room service. Cable TV. Pool. Hot tub. Laundry facilities. Business services, Disneyland shuttle, free parking. | 1500 S. Raymond Ave. | 714/635–9000 | fax 714/520–5831 | www.sheraton.com | 223 rooms | $85–$129 | AE, D, DC, MC, V.

GARBERVILLE

MAP 3, B4

(Nearby towns also listed: Eureka, Fort Bragg)

Founded by J. E. Wood in 1862, the town was actually named for a store owner who came along 11 years later, Jacob Garber. Although the region owed its economy to the harvesting of the huge redwood forests, enough of the old growth is preserved to make it a living museum of natural beauty. Garberville is thought of as a portal to the acres of sheltered redwood wilderness; RV hookups outnumber motel rooms in this recreational haven, whose main industry is tourism. Plan to spend lazy afternoons cooling off in the Eel River, fishing, or relaxing at several outdoor music festivals during summer.

Information: **Garberville-Redway Area Chamber of Commerce** | Box 445, 95542-0445 | 707/923–2613 | www.garberville.org.

Attractions

Humboldt Redwoods State Park. This 31-mi trek, known as Avenue of the Giants, runs through redwoods along Eel River to a 51,000-acre park. Attractions along Avenue of the

Giants include 78-ft hollow Chimney Tree gutted by fire; the Shrine Drive-Thru Tree, the Eternal Tree House, a 20-ft room in a living redwood. The park is 9 mi north of Garberville. Camping permitted in the park; reservations are essential. | Avenue of the Giants, Weott | 707/946–2263 or 800/444–PARK (camping) | www.humboldtredwoods.org | $5 per vehicle | Daily dawn to dusk.

King Range National Conservation Area. You can hike on more than 20 separate trails—most of them quite vigorous—along the seabreak and coastal forests and mountains, 20 mi west of Garberville. | Shelter Cove Rd. | 707/825–2300 or 707/923–2513 | Free.

ON THE CALENDAR

JUNE: *Jazz on the Lake.* World-class jazz and blues is performed in the warm evening air at Benbow Lake, 2 mi south of Garberville. | 707/923–4599.

JUNE: *Redwood Run.* Live music and bar celebrations welcome hundreds of Harley-Davidson riders during their summer pilgrimage to Eel River, 10 mi south of Garberville. | 707/247–3424.

JULY, AUG.: *Reggae on the River.* Rastafarians and music lovers come out to see the largest outdoor reggae festival on the West Coast at French's Camp, next to Eel River, 10 mi south of Garberville. Ska, dub, and reggae bands come from all over the world to perform. | 707/923–4583.

Dining

Benbow Inn Restaurant. Contemporary. This wood-paneled restaurant is decorated in the Tudor tradition with a hint of contemporary California style. Original salmon, rack of lamb, and salads are on the menu. Every item has a little twist, perhaps a truffle vinaigrette sauce or an apricot and ginger glaze. The eatery is 26 mi southeast of Garberville alongside the Eel River. Reservations on weekend recommended. Kids' menu. No smoking. | 445 Lake Benbow Dr. | 707/923–2124 | Breakfast also available. Closed Jan.–Mar. No dinner Sun. | $16–$32 | AE, D, MC, V.

★ **Woodrose Café.** American. This restaurant serves traditional breakfast items on the weekends and healthy lunches every day. Dishes include chicken, pasta, and vegetarian specials. | 911 Redwood Dr. | 707/923–3191 | No dinner | $5–$9 | No credit cards.

Lodging

★ **Benbow Inn.** Tucked into woodlands and perched on cliffs overlooking the Eel River, this 1926 Tudor mansion designed by Albert Farr is a National Historic Landmark–it has hosted Eleanor Roosevelt, Herber Hoover and other highly regarded guests throughout the years. Cherrywood panelled halls lead from the lobby to the antique-filled rooms, some of which offer fine views of the Eel River. Videos of classic vintage movies are played nightly. The inn is 2 mi south of town. Restaurant (*see* Benbow Inn Restaurant), bar. Some refrigerators, no TV in some rooms, some in-room VCRs. Pool. 9-hole golf course, putting green. Beach, boating, bicycles. Business services, airport shuttle. | 445 Lake Benbow Dr. | 707/923–2124 or 800/355–3301 | fax 707/923–2897 | benbow@benbowinn.com | www.benbowinn.com | 55 rooms, 1 cottage | $115–$155, $305 cottage | Closed Jan.–Mar. | AE, D, MC, V.

Best Western Humbolt House. One block from U.S. 101, this medium-size hotel has three buildings arranged around a heated pool. Complimentary Continental breakfast. Pool. Hot tub. Laundry facilities. | 701 Redwood Dr. | 707/923–2771 | fax 707/923–4254 | www.bestwestern.com | 76 rooms, 10 suites | $89–$133 | AE, MC, V.

Humboldt Redwoods Inn. These simple accommodations are 9 mi south of the Humboldt Redwoods State Park in central Garberville. Restaurant. Cable TV. Pool. Business services. | 987 Redwood Dr. | 707/923–2451 | 22 rooms | $42–$62 | AE, D, DC, MC, V.

Miranda Gardens. Redwood paneling, antiques, outdoor campfire, stately trees, and cozy patios reward you for driving the 12 mi from Garberville. Some rooms have fireplaces and fully furnished kitchens. Pool. | 6766 Ave. of the Giants | 707/943–3011 | fax 707/943–3584 | www.mirandagardens.com | 16 rooms, 7 duplex cabins | $75–$185 | AE, D, MC, V.

Sherwood Forest. This one-story hotel is one of the few lodgings in central Garberville. The rustic setting, which includes 3 acres of pine and redwood trees, reflects the flavor of the town. Popular with tourists, the grounds also offer a flower garden and barbecue pits. Humbolt State Park is 10 mi to the north and Benbow Lake is 2 mi south. Restaurant, picnic area. Some refrigerators, cable TV. Pool. Hot tub. Fishing. Laundry facilities. Business services. Some pets allowed. | 814 Redwood Dr. | 707/923–2721 | fax 707/923–3677 | 32 rooms | $54–80 | AE, D, MC, V.

GARDEN GROVE

MAP 9, H7

(Nearby towns also listed: Anaheim, Cerritos, Orange, Santa Ana, Seal Beach)

Garden Grove was once mostly a farming community, now it is famous for the all-glass Crystal Cathedral of TV minister Dr. Robert H. Schuller. Garden Grove's next biggest claim to fame is its annual Strawberry Festival, which began in 1958. It is the second largest community-sponsored event in the Western U.S.—only the Rose Parade is bigger. Although mainly a bedroom community to Los Angeles, Garden Grove is the 4th largest city in Orange County, and, along with hosting a large residential community, has become a hub for tourism. The city has over 160 acres of parks and recreation areas, and the thriving historic Main Street shows off its original storefronts and light fixtures.

Information: **Garden Grove Chamber of Commerce** | 12866 Main St., Suite 102, 92840 | 714/638–7950 | fax 714/636–6672 | connie.margolin@gardengrovechamber.org | www.gardengrovechamber.org.

Attractions
Crystal Cathedral. The Crystal Cathedral was designed by Philip Johnson and is an all-glass sanctuary enclosed by 10,000 mirrored windows. It is the home of TV minister Dr. Robert H. Schuller's congregation. | 12141 Lewis St. | 714/971–4013 | Donations accepted | Mon.–Sat. 9–3:30.

Korean Business District. Nearly one-fifth of Garden Grove's population is Korean or Korean-American, giving rise to a vibrant Korean district. A stroll through this area reveals everything from acupuncture clinics and herbal shops to modern clothing stores and Korean BBQ. | Garden Grove Blvd., between Brookhurst and Magnolia Sts. | 714/638–7950 | Free.

ON THE CALENDAR
LATE MAY: *Garden Grove Strawberry Festival.* The World's Biggest Strawberry Short-cake serves up to 6,000 visitors on opening day (Friday) of the four-day festival. Other highlights are carnival rides, baby pageants, arts and crafts, food booths, and live music. | 714/638–7950 | www.gardengrovechamber.org.

Dining
Carolina's Italian Restaurant. Italian. Pictures and knickknacks lend an old-country flavor to this low-key restaurant. Gnocchi, lasagna, and manicotti are a few of the daily specials. | 12045 Chapman Ave. | 714/971–5551 | No lunch weekends | $8–$15 | AE, D, DC, MC, V.

La Fayette. French. Contemporary French cuisine is served beneath high ceilings and chandeliers. The Veal La Fayette is the house signature dish. Rack of lamb, filet mignon, and rabbit are other menu selections. Cocktail lounge. Live piano music Fri., Sat. No smoking. | 12532 Garden Grove Blvd. | 714/537–5011 | Closed Sun. | $16–$28 | AE, DC, MC, V.

Lodging

Best Western Plaza International Inn. This two-story inn is 6 mi from Disneyland and 5 mi from Knott's Berry Farm. It is also within walking distance of the city's business community and restaurants. Microwaves, some refrigerators, cable TV. Pool. Sauna. Business services. | 7912 Garden Grove Blvd. | 714/894–7568 | fax 714/894–6308 | www.bestwestern.com | 100 rooms | $48–$58 | AE, D, DC, MC, V.

Hampton Inn. One mile west of I–5, this seven-floor, family-oriented hotel is part of the Hilton chain. Complimentary Continental breakfast. Pool, wading pool. Hot tub. Exercise equipment. Laundry service. | 11747 Harbor Blvd. | 714/703–8800 | fax 714/703–8900 | 172 rooms, 36 suites | $89–$119 | AE, D, DC, MC, V.

GEYSERVILLE

(Nearby towns also listed: Healdsburg, Hopland)

Geyserville calls itself "the wine capital of Sonoma County." Its location in the Anderson Valley puts it at the center of California's lesser-known—and blessedly less-congested—viticultural territory. Compared to neighboring Napa, the wineries of the Anderson Valley are smaller and less touristy. The Anderson Valley takes pride in the low-pressure lifestyle.

Geyserville itself is a great place to unwind. In fact, there's nothing much to do except wake up in one of the bed-and-breakfast inns, eat a big breakfast, and take a bike or canoe ride along the Russian River. Who needs more?

Information: Geyserville Chamber of Commerce | Box 275, 95441-0275 | 707/857–3745 | www.geyservillecc.co.

Attractions

Chateau Souverain. This winery, 9 mi north of Healdsburg, has daily tastings and a restaurant which serves contemporary cuisine. | 400 Souverain Rd. | 707/433–8281 | www.chateausouverain.com | Free | Daily 10–5.

Lake Sonoma. The Army Corps of Engineers created this lake in the 1970s when they built the Warm Springs Dam at the northern end of the Dry Creek Valley. You'll find a visitor center, fish hatchery, and recreation areas with picnic tables, hiking trails, swimming, outdoor cooking facilities, and seasonal camping and boating rentals. | 3333 Skaggs Springs Rd. | 707/433–9483 | Daily.

ON THE CALENDAR

OCT.: *Fall Colors Event.* On the last Sunday in October, you can enjoy a car show, crafts, and booths for wine, food, and beer at this midtown Geyserville event. | 707/857–3745.

Dining

Santi Restaurant. Italian. An extensive menu of authentic dishes from northern Italy changes with the seasons and reflects the freshest ingredients available. The dining room is often lively with wine industry insiders who come for the wonderful *crespelle* (Italian crêpes) with bechamel sauce, risotto, osso bucco, and chicken grilled under a brick. The wine list includes an extensive selection of Italian imports. | 21047 Geyserville Ave. | 707/857–1790 | $15–$25 | AE, D, MC, V.

Lodging

Geyserville Inn. This lazy country inn is just off of U.S. 101. Over 70 wineries are within a 15-mi radius of the two-story lodge. Complimentary Continental breakfast. In-room data ports, no smoking. Pool. Hot tub. | 21714 Geyserville Ave. | 707/857–4343 | fax 707/857–4411 | www.sonic.net/~iav/welcome.html | 38 rooms | $97–$160 | AE, D, MC, V.

Hope–Merrill House. A late 1800s Victorian built entirely of redwood, this inn has maintained its original woodwork. The silk-screened wallpapers of designer Bruce Bradbury accent each unique guest room along with antique furnishings. The 357 vineries of Sonoma Valley are all within an hour drive of the inn. Complimentary breakfast. No in-room phones, no smoking. Pool. Hot tubs. | 21253 Geyserville Ave. | 707/857–3356 | fax 707/857–4673 | www.hope-inns.com | 12 rooms, 4 with shower only | $119–$215 | AE, MC, V.

GILROY

MAP 4, E9

(Nearby town also listed: Aptos)

Over the years, quite a few lofty titles have been attached to the town of Gilroy. In the 1860s, it was known as the hay and grain capital of California. In the 1870s Gilroy proclaimed itself to be the tobacco capital of the nation. Things then shifted to dairy and cheese, and later the town went through a stint as the Prune Capital in the 1920s.

With its roots deep in agriculture, this peaceful residential community is actually probably best known today for its annual Garlic Festival in July. However, there is some good shopping to be had all year round at one of the largest outlet malls in the nation as well as a quaint downtown area lined with boutiques and antique stores. The addition of major commerce hasn't kept this town from being designated as a "Tree City USA." It keeps it bucolic reputation intact with some beautiful open spaces, scenic wineries, and fine parks.

Information: **Gilroy Chamber of Commerce** | 7471 Monterey St., 95020-5823 | 408/842–6437 | chamber@gilroy.org | www.gilroy.org/.

Attractions
Outlet Stores. You can find giant discounts in over 150 name-brand outlet stores, including Nike, Versace, Polo, and more. | 408/842–3732 | www.primeretail.com | Free.

© Artville

STRANGE BUT TRUE

There are bison in San Francisco (Golden Gate Park, to be specific).
There are 400 buffalo on Catalina Island.
Jack London began writing *The Call of the Wild* in Oakland.
The *Queen Mary* is docked in Long Beach.
Selma, California, is the "raisin capital of the world."
You're safe from vampires in Gilroy; it produces 90% of the country's garlic.
The Winchester Mystery House in San Jose—a monument to paranoia— has more than 160 rooms and 10,000 windows.
According to geologists, more than 70 percent of California's gold lies undiscovered. So what are you waiting for?

Castle Island Getaway. Located on a private two acre plot one block from Cresent City's scenic Pebble Beach, rooms here look out to forest views from every window. Bicycles are available to guests for exploring the beach or nearby wildlife refuge. Wine and cheese are served upon your arrival. Complimentary breakfast. | 1830 Murphy Ave. | 707/465-5102 | www.castleislandgetaway.html | 2 rooms | $85–$110.

Curly Redwood Lodge. A single redwood tree produced the 57,000 ft of lumber used to build this lodge in 1957. The room furnishings make the most of that tree, with paneling, platform beds, and dressers built into the walls. The lodge is across the street from the harbor and close to the national and state parks. No smoking, cable TV. | 701 Redwood Hwy S | 707/464-2137 | fax 707/464-1655 | www.curlyredwoodlodge.com | 36 rooms, 3 suites | $37–$60, $68–$86 suites | AE, DC, MC, V.

Lighthouse Cove Bed & Breakfast. From its perch, 27 ft above the crashing breakers, this beauty grants spectacular views of the sunset, Battery Point lighthouse, breakwater, pier, whales, seals, birds and boats. Complimentary Continental breakfast. | 215 South 'A' St. | 707/465-6565 | www.moriah.com/cove | 1 suite | $115–$140 | Closed Nov.-Dec., and sometimes Jan. and Feb. | No credit cards.

Super 8. Three blocks south of Cresent City, these affordable accommodations overlook the city and the marina. The large rooms in the two-story hotel have modern furnishings. Restaurant. Cable TV. Business services. Some pets allowed. | 685 U.S. 101 S | 707/464-4111 | fax 707/465-8916 | www.super8.com | 49 rooms | $66–$75 | AE, D, MC, V.

CRESTLINE

MAP 4, J14

(Nearby towns also listed: Lake Arrowhead, Rancho Cucamonga, San Bernardino)

Quaint and leafy, and characterized by hilltop honkytonk cafés and antique shops, Crestline is a literal wide-spot on the 107 mi long Rim-of-the-World Drive, which is punctuated by elevations of 5,000 to 7,200 ft. Also known as Rte. 18, this ultrascenic route bisects the larger and adjacent mountain resorts Lake Arrowhead and Big Bear Lake.

Information: Crestline Chamber of Commerce | Box 926, 92325 | 909/338-2706.

Attractions

Lake Gregory Regional Park. You can fish from the shore, picnic, hike, swim, and boat on 150-acres lake at this park, nestled in the forests of the San Bernardino Mountains. | 24171 Lake Dr. | 909/338-2233 | fax 909/338-4590 | www.co.san-bernardino.ca.us/parks | $3 | Apr–Oct., daily dawn to dusk; swimming: Memorial Day–Labor, daily 10–5.

Silverwood Lake State Recreation Area. Silverwood lake was formed by the 249-ft Cedar Springs Dam. At 3,350 ft, it is the highest reservoir in the State Water Project. Within the park, you can hike, swim, and, in designated areas, boat, water ski, and fish. The lake has trout, large-mouth bass, catfish, and bluegill. There is a marina with a launching ramp, boat and equipment rentals, and a store. Three of the park's picnic areas can only be reached by boat. The lakes attracts waterfowl, raptors, and songbirds. Canadian geese and an occasional bald eagle can be seen in the area. | Off I–15 and Rte. 138, between Victorville and Crestline | 760/389-2281 or 760/389-2303 | cal-parks.ca.gov/districts/loslagos/slsra.htm | $6 per vehicle | 7am–dusk.

ON THE CALENDAR

JULY: Jamboree Days. By far Crestline's biggest annual event, Jamboree Days always starts Saturday morning on the 4th of July weekend. Thirty to forty thousand visitors

Redwood National and State Parks. Encompassing 105,516 acres along the northern Californian coast between Crescent City and Orick, this is a congregation of natural areas including Del Norte Coast, Jedediah Smith, and Prairie Creek Redwoods state parks. Found here are dense forests of coastal redwoods, marshland, beaches, rugged coastline, rivers, streams, prairies, beaches, and oak woodlands. More than 150 mi of trails provide access to the magnificent redwood groves and views of sea lion colonies and migrating whales. Birds inhabit bluffs, lagoons, and offshore rocks. The park staff provides free guided walks and other activities in summer. Camping is available. Some pets are allowed with restrictions. | Crescent City Information Center: 1111 2nd St., off U.S. 101 | 707/464-6101 | www.nps.gov/redw/index.htm | Free | Daily dawn to dusk.

Del Norte Coast Redwoods State Park. On 6,400 acres, this state park, 5 mi south of Crescent City, contains 15 memorial redwood groves. The growths extend down steep slopes almost to the ocean shore. For camping information call (800) 444-7275. | 707/464-6101 ext. 5101 | $5 per vehicle. Camping $16 May–Sept; $14 Oct.–Apr. | Daily dawn to dusk.

Jedediah Smith Redwoods State Park. This park is home to the Stout Memorial Grove. Swimming, fishing, hiking, picknicking, camping are popular activities. | Rte. 199, two mi from Hiouchi | 707/464-9533 | $5 per vehicle. Camping $16 May–Sept; $14 Oct.–Apr. | Daily dawn to dusk.

Prairie Creek Redwoods State Park. Fourteen thousand acres of spectacular redwoods and lush ferns make up this section, which is in Orick, 40 mi south of Cresent City. You can fish, hike, and picnic, and also camp and take part in the educational programs. To get here take the Rte. 101 exit off the Newton Drury Scenic Parkway. | 707/488-2171 or 800/444-7275 | $5 per vehicle. Camping $16 May–Sept; $14 Oct.–Apr. | Daily dawn to dusk.

ON THE CALENDAR

JULY: *Gasquet Raft Race.* Canoes, kayaks, rafts and innertubes bob down the scenic Smith River in this annual event that starts at the Horace Gasquet Bridge and ends 2½ mi later at Shady Bend Park. After the race, the community of Gasquet hosts a deep-pit BBQ. | 707/464-3174.

Dining

Apple Peddler. American. This busy chain-style eatery serves breakfast around the clock, plus burgers, steaks, and seasonal seafood. | 308 U.S. 101-S | 707/464-5630 | Open 24 hours | $10–$15 | D, MC, V.

Da Lucianna Restaurante. Italian. The two dining rooms, one done in red and the other in blue, have wall-hangings and sculptures by local artists. In addition to the usual Italian dishes, they serve some seafood—prawns, halibut, snapper, lobster, and salmon. Kids' menu. | 575 U.S. 101-S | 707/465-6566 | $10–$20 | AE, D, MC, V.

Harbor View Grotto. Seafood. Modest prices and views of the harbor, the ocean, and fishing boats set this place apart. It's known for prawns, oysters, scallops, lobster, prime rib, and rib eye. | 150 Starfish Way | 707/464-3815 | $11–$18 | MC, V.

Lodging

Best Value Hotel. A U-shaped driveway leads to this family resort with shingled siding, across the street from the fairgrounds and close to both the town and the beach. Rooms are done in a decorative theme. In-room data ports, some microwaves, refrigerators, cable TV, Hot tub, sauna. Business services. | 440 U.S. 101 N | 707/464-4141 or 800/323-7917 | fax 707/465-3274 | 61 rooms, 4 suites | $45–$65, $55–$70 suites | AE, D, DC, MC, V.

Best Western Northwoods Inn. You're across the street from the harbor at this two-story inn. The building was constructed in the early 1970s. Restaurant (*see* Northwood's Restaurant), bar, complimentary breakfast, room service. In-room data ports, some microwaves, refrigerators, cable TV, Hot tubs. Laundry facilities. Business services. | 655 U.S. 101 | 707/464-9771 | fax 707/464-9461 | www.bestwestern.com | 89 rooms | $69 | AE, D, DC, MC, V.

JULY: *Gilroy Garlic Festival.* For dozens of years now, the last full weekend in July has marked a celebration of the garlic clove in Gilroy, at Christmas Hill Park. There's a giant open-air kitchen, live gourmet demonstrations, food and drink booths, entertainment, and arts and crafts. | $10 | 408/842–1625 | www.gilroygarlicfestival.com.

Dining

Harvest Time. Contemporary. Many locals say this is Gilroy's best "garlic restaurant." Steaks, seafood, pasta, and salads show off that rich flavor in a 1925 former hotel with high, exposed-beam ceilings. | 7397 Monterey St. | 408/842–7600 | Breakfast available weekends | $15–$25 | AE, D, DC, MC, V.

Lodging

Forest Park Inn. This inn is adjacent to the over 150 outlet stores in Gilroy. You can choose between three different types of rooms and queen- or king-size beds for standard rooms. A golf course, winery, and an amusement park are all within a 10-mi radius. In-room data ports, refrigerators, some in-room hot tubs, cable TV. Hot tub, sauna. Tennis. Laundry facilities. Business services. No smoking. | 357 Leavesley Rd. | 408/848–5144 | fax 408/848–1138 | fpi@forestparkinn.co | www.forestparkinn.com | 123 rooms | $60–$62 | AE, D, DC, MC, V.

Hilton Garden Inn. Geared to Gilroy's fast-growing tourist industry, this modern hotel provides Internet access and shuttle service to area businesses. Restaurant. Pool. Hot tub. Exercise equipment. Business services. | 6070 Monterey Hwy. | 408/846–7600 | fax 408/846–7601 | www.gilroyhilton.com | 136 rooms | $110–$150 | AE, D, DC, MC, V.

Inn of Gilroy. This hotel is in a commercial area near the Gilroy business district. Most of the basic motel rooms have views of surroundings hills and forested areas. Several restaurants are within 4 blocks. Complimentary Continental breakfast. In-room data ports, refrigerators, no smoking, some in-rooms hot tubs. Pool. Laundry facilities. | 360 Leavesley Rd. | 408/848–1467 | fax 408/848–1424 | 42 rooms | $92–$108 | AE, D, DC, MC, V.

GLENDALE

MAP 9, E2

(Nearby towns also listed: Burbank, North Hollywood, Pasadena, Universal City, West Hollywood)

The first Spanish land grant in California, handed down in 1784 by King Charles, is now the east entrance to the San Fernando Valley, a largely middle-class residential area with a large downtown business district. At the foot of the Verdugo mountains, the community is almost 200,000 strong, and functions largely as a bedroom community to nearby Los Angeles. Glendale is reputed as being the third largest financial center in California, due largely to its enourmous retail and service industry. It's outskirt location also makes it a popular stop-over for tourists wanting to take in some of the attractions north of Los Angeles county.

Information: **Glendale Chamber of Commerce** | 200 S. Louise St., 91205 | 818/240–7870 | info@glendalechamber.com | www.glendalechamber.com.

Attractions

Brand Library and Art Galleries. This Moorish-style facility is now host to a music and art library and gallery as well as performance and studios. | 1601 W. Mountain St. | 818/548–2051 | Free | Tues., Thurs. 1–9, Wed. 1–6, Fri., Sat. 1–5.

Descanso Gardens. This 165-acre botanical garden includes the Rosarium, a showcase of 4,000 modern and antique roses, 100,000 camellia shrubs growing in a California live oak forest, and many other annuals and perennials. | 1418 Descanso Dr. | 818/952–4401 or 818/952–4400 | www.descanso.com/ | $5 | Daily 9–4:30.

ON THE CALENDAR

OCT.: *Days of Verdugo Festival and Parade.* Glendale was first settled by the Verdugo clan, and the city still celebrates its founding family more than a century later. Carnival rides, arts and crafts, live music, and over 50,000 visitors fill Verdugo Park during this three-day, family-oriented event. | 818/240–7870 | www.glendalechamber.com.

Dining

Cinnabar. Contemporary. This restaurant, in the early 1930s Art Deco Bekins Building, is known to a small, but informed clientele. At the vintage bar, you can order a Mai Tai, while the restaurant serves California-Chinese cuisine. The menu includes charbroiled ostrich tenderloin, spicy lemongrass bouillabaisse, and roasted halibut with kale and asparagus. No smoking. | 933 S. Brand Blvd. | 818/551–1155 | Closed Mon. No lunch Sat.–Fri. | $30–$50 | D, DC, MC, V.

Far Niente Ristorante. Italian. This eatery might seem to be always bustling with families, but the quality of the Northern Italian cuisine does not suffer. Homemade gnocchi, ravioli, other pastas, and ice cream make this a popular destination. Piano bar. No smoking. | 204½ N. Brand Blvd. | 818/242–3835 | No lunch | $14–$26 | AE, D, DC, MC, V.

Lodging

Best Western Golden Key. LA's financial center, Hollywood, golf courses, the city zoo, and a handful of museums are at your fingertips while staying at this hotel. If you're not up to doing business or sightseeing, you can enjoy something from the free movie library or shop at the 270-store Glendale Galleria, one block east of the hotel. Complimentary Continental breakfast. In-room data ports, microwaves, refrigerators, cable TV, in-room VCRs (and movies). Pool. Hot tub. Business services. | 123 W. Colorado St. | 818/247–0111 | fax 818/545–9393 | bwgoldenkey@worldnet.att.net | www.travelweb.com | 55 rooms | $99–$149 | AE, D, DC, MC, V.

Glendale Hilton Hotel. The stepped-pyramid roof makes it hard to miss this 19-story deluxe hotel, 2 blocks north of Route 134, which has many conveniences for business travelers. 2 restaurants, 3 bars. Pool. Hot tub, sauna. Health club. | 100 W. Glenoaks Blvd. | 818/956–5466 | fax 818/956–4590 | www.hilton.com | 350 rooms | $169–$229 | AE, D, DC, MC, V.

Homestead Village Guest Studios. These studios, 2 mi north of I–5 and Route 134, are designed to be a home away from home, with full kitchens, king-size beds, and large dining rooms. Passes are available to a nearby fitness center. Laundry service. | 1377 W. Glenoaks Blvd. | 888/782–9742 reservations, or 818/956–6665 | fax 818/956–6667 | www.stayhsd.com | 86 units | $94–$114, reduced prices for extended stays | AE, D, DC, MC, V.

Vagabond Inn. Rooms at this three-story hotel are equipped with work desks, ergonomic chairs, and other furnishings with business in mind. The hotel is in the commercial district, but there are also a number of tourist attractions nearby including Universal Studios, Dodger Stadium, and the Hollywood Rose Bowl. Restaurant, complimentary Continental breakfast. Some in-room data ports, some microwaves, refrigerators, cable TV. Pool. Some pets allowed (fee). | 120 W. Colorado St. | 818/240–1700 | fax 626/548–8428 | www.vagabondinn.com | 52 rooms | $89 | AE, D, DC, MC, V.

GLENDORA

(Nearby towns also listed: Arcadia, Claremont, Pomona, West Covina)

Tucked into the foothills of the San Gabriel Mountains, this town of 50,000 residents is about 27 mi from downtown Los Angeles. Founded in 1887, Glendora was officially incorporated as a city in 1911. Until the late 1950s, citrus farms and citrus-packing companies ruled the landscape and economy. Soon after, residential development and careful city planning took precedence over agriculture. However, there is still plenty of nature to be enjoyed here.

Glendora contains the largest growth of bougainvillea in the United States. Planted around the turn of the 20th century, the vines cover the lower portion of 25 90-ft palm trees, stretching for 1,200 ft on two avenues. Not only is Glendora a pretty town, but it's a safe one as well. The "Pride of the Foothills" has the reputation of having one of the lowest crime rates in the nation.

Information: Glendora Chamber of Commerce | 131 E. Foothill Blvd., 91741 | 626/963–4128 | info@glendora-chamber.org | www.glendora-chamber.org.

Attractions

The Village. Several blocks of boutiques are here for window shopping or stopping to buy. Shops have everything from kitchenware or intimate apparel to bicycles and classic cars. | Glen Ave., north of Foothill | 626/963–4128 | Free.

ON THE CALENDAR
OCT.: *Great Glendora Festival.* Over 10,000 people enjoy Glendora's largest annual event, with business booths, arts and crafts, live music, dance and theater performances, and a children's area. The festival is held on Glendora Ave., near The Village. Admission is free. | 626/963–4128.

Dining
Derby East. Steak. The original Derby opened its doors in 1938, and was styled as an after-race spot for visitors to nearby Santa Anita Park. Derby East was established in 1990, and has a similar look and feel to its sister restaurant; race track memorabilia and equipment appear throughout the dining room. Steak is the headliner, but some pasta, chicken, and lamb dishes have also joined the fray. Earlybird suppers. Entertainment. No smoking. | 545 W. Alosta Ave. | 626/914–2977 | No lunch weekends, Sunday brunch | $16–$40 | AE, D, DC, MC, V.

Lodging
Guest House Inn. This two-story building, in a commercial area, is only a five-minute walk from downtown. Complimentary breakfast. In-room modems, pets allowed, refrigerator, kitchenettes, cable TV. Pool. Hot tub, spa. Laundry service. | 606 W. Alosta | 626/963–9361 | fax 626/914–2037 | 38 rooms | $74 | AE, D, DC, MC, V.

Red Roof Inn. Two blocks from Route 210 in nearby San Dimas, this hotel provides basic accommodations and services at an affordable price. Some microwaves, some refrigerators. Pool. Hot tub. | 204 N. Village Ct | 909/599–2362 | fax 909/599–7903 | www.redroof.com | 134 rooms, 2 suites | $50–$70 | AE, MC, V.

GRASS VALLEY

(Nearby towns also listed: Marysville, Nevada City)

Though Grass Valley was truly incorporated in 1893 as a "gold rush town", its name predates the gold rush and refers to the pastoral grasslands where the earliest settlers let their cattle graze. After the whirlwind of the gold rush died down, mining and logging became the industries that sustained the town. Unlike many towns, where the gold was exhausted, a few gold mines still remain here.

Today about 9,500 people reside here, a third of whom are retired. Tourists generally come here to learn about Grass Valley's gold rush history, but the historic section, where Main and Mill streets meet, has many preserved Victorian homes as well. Some of these are still homes and some are museums.

In the foothills of the Sierra Nevadas, at 2,100 ft above sea level, Grass Valley is 60 mi northeast of Sacramento, and surrounded by lakes. There are four seasons in Grass Valley, with fabulous fall foliage, and you can even expect to see a dusting of snow a few times in winter.

Information: Grass Valley Chamber of Commerce | M248 Mill St., 95945 | 530/273–4667 | fax 530/272–5440 | info@gvncchamber.org | www.gvnchamber.org.

Attractions

★ **Empire Mine State Historic Park.** One of California's richest mines until the mid-1950s, the Empire Mine extracted gold from the Sierra foothills for almost half a century. Now you can visit the mine yard, owner's mansion, and mouth of the mine. The park also has 700 acres of forest and grasslands and many miles of hiking and biking trails. On weekend "living history" days, volunteer docents dress in period costume and re-create the turn-of-the-20th-century mining community that once thrived here. | 10791 Empire Dr. | 530/273–8522 | www.cal-parks.ca.gov | $1 | May–Oct.

ON THE CALENDAR

NOV.–DEC.: *Cornish Christmas.* On the four consecutive Fridays from Thanksgiving to late December, Grass Valley celebrates Christmas and the long Cornish heritage of this foothills town. Festivities include hay rides, roasted chestnuts, hot apple cider, and performances by the Cornish Choir. Held downtown, 5:30–9 PM. | 530/273–4667.

Dining

Arletta's. American. Part of the Holbrooke Hotel, Arletta's serves up a little history with every dish. James Garfield, Ulysses S. Grant, Mark Twain, and famous outlaw Black Bart all supped at this establishment. It's also the state's oldest working saloon. Specialties nowadays include mesquite-smoked prime rib and seared salmon. | 212 W. Main St. | 530/273–4667 | $15–$25 | AE, D, DC, MC, V.

Jack's Internet Cafe. American. Soups, salads, sandwiches, and snacks are served here along with access to high speed internet connections at $6.00 per hour. | 115 South Church St. | 530/477–surf | www.jackscafe.com | Breakfast also available | $3–$12 | No Credit Cards.

Tofanelli's. Eclectic. Homemade soups and dishes made with special attention to healthful eating are served here. Salads are popular, like the spinach salad and shrimp Louie salad. Another favorite is the Macho Tofu, a tofu dish served with Mexican spices and vegetables. You can eat out on the atrium patios. | 302 W. Main St. | 530/272–1468 | $15–$25 | MC, V.

Lodging

Holbrooke Hotel. Built in 1851, this Gold Rush-era hotel has been visited by such notables as Ulysses S. Grant and Mark Twain. Details like the original elevator have been preserved, giving the inn its distinctive 19th-century appeal. Rooms have exposed brick walls, private balconies, and antiques like brass beds and hardwood armoires, which conceal TVs and VCRs. On Sundays the hotel sponsers a wine tasting, in which a local winery is showcased. Restaurant, bar, complimentary Continental breakfast. Cable TV, in-room VCRs. Beauty salon. Library. No pets. | 212 W. Main St. | 530/273–1353 or 800/933–7077 | fax 530/273–0434 | www.holbrooke.com | 29 rooms | $75–$155 | AE, D, DC, MC, V.

GUALALA

(Nearby towns also listed: Boonville, Elk)

Gualala (pronounced two ways by locals: "wah-LA-la" and "gwah-LA-la) overlooks the ocean at the southern border of Mendocino County at the mouth of the Gualala River. Once the center for logging on the northern California coast, the town is now patronized by locals from up and down the coast—including a large contingent from the nearby Sea Ranch housing development—for its well-stocked grocery stores, video stores and cheap gasoline. This part of the coast is stunningly beautiful but the twisting and turning highway, shared by cars, RV's logging trucks and bicyclists, can be a stressful drive for those not used to it. Ocean-view motels along the Coast Highway are often used as convenient bases for fishing or canoeing trips up the river, and there are also several shops and art galleries worth exploring.

The origins of the town's name have been debated for more than 100 years. Some claim it's an old Indian word for "water coming down place," while others insist it's a Spanish rendering of Valhalla.

Information: Redwood Coast Chamber of Commerce | Box 338, 95445 | 707/884–1080 | info@redwoodcoastchamber.com | www.redwoodcoastchamber.com.

Attractions
Gualala Point Regional Park. You can watch birds along the surf, learn about local flora and fauna from the visitor center displays, eat your lunch at picnic tables, and stroll to the beach along a paved walkway. | Rte. 1 | 707/785–2377 | $3 | Daily.

Dining
Java Point. Café. With ocean sounds in the background, you can order a scone or muffin with your coffee or espresso or go for a fuller lunch of lasagna, a garlic chicken sandwich, or one of the homemade soups (a different one each day) or salads (garlic chicken is a favorite). You can top it all off with one of the desserts–they also change daily and include specialties made with seasonal fruits. | Seacliff Center, Rte. 1 | 707/884–9020 | $5–$10 | No dinner | No credit cards.

Old Milano Restaurant. Contemporary. Mendocino Hills Cabernet 1994, made from locally grown grapes, is a favorite at this restaurant in The Old Milano Hotel (also listed). The house wines—chardonnay, sauvignon blanc, and pinot noir—are also from a local vineyard. The menu changes daily, but you'll always find fresh salmon (sometimes with ginger-chile sauce); filet mignon served with fresh mashed potatoes, a black cherry and port wine reduction sauce, and a blue cheese/butter compound; fresh seasonal vegetables; and homemade soups and salads. Desserts also change daily but always include ice cream sundaes and chocolate oblivion torte with fresh raspberry sauce. Your dinner will be served at a candle-lit table with an ocean view. | 38300 Rte. 1 | 707/884–3256 | www.old-milanohotel.com/omres.html | $25–$40 | MC, V.

Lodging

Agate Cove Inn. Built in 1860 on a bluff above the Pacific, the farmhouse and cottages are set on two acres surrounded by 100-year-old cypress trees. Several apple trees in the turn-of-the-20th-century orchard still produce fruit, and a garden frames the front entry. All rooms have CD players; most have ocean views and fireplaces. The two farmhouse rooms have private outside entries. Complimentary tea, coffee, hot chocolate, and homemade biscotti are available all day. You'll find complimentary sherry in your room and the San Francisco Chronicle newspaper delivered to your door each morning. The giftshop showcases work by local artists. A concierge can help you plan your activities. GC, the resident poodle, may join you on your walks around the property. Cable TV, in-room VCRs. Massage. No pets. No kids under 12. No smoking. | 11201 N. Lansing St., Box 1150 | 800/527–3111 or 707/937–0551 | www.agatecove.com | 10 rooms | $159–$189 single cottages, $179–$269 duplex cottages, $119–$219 farmhouse rooms | AE, MC, V.

Breakers Inn. Custom designed in a Cape Cod style, you will see panoramic views of the Pacific through the guest room's beveled glass windows at this hotel. Private decks and fireplaces are in most rooms. Galleries, restaurants, a beach, and shops are within 1 mi in every direction. Restaurant, complimentary Continental breakfast. Some refrigerators, some in-room hot tubs, cable TV. No smoking. | 39300 S. Rte. 1 | 707/884–3200 or 800/273–2537 | fax 707/884–3400 | www.breakersinn.com | 23 rooms, 4 spa rooms | $125–$235 | AE, D, MC, V.

Gualala Country Inn. Situated on the Mendocino coastline, this inn affords views of the surf, the whales, and the breathtaking sunsets. Some rooms have wood-burning fireplaces and ocean views. The rooms each have their own country theme. Several beaches are within walking distance. Some pets allowed (fee). No smoking. | 47955 Center St. | 707/884–4343 or 800/564–4466 | fax 707/884–1018 | countryinn@gualala.com | www.gualala.com | 20 rooms | $89–$159 | AE, D, DC, MC, V.

Gualala Hotel. This hotel was restored in 1983 but retained its original furnishings since its inception in 1903. A yellow bannister and vintage bar welcomes you to this one-floor inn. Several beaches for whale-watching, fishing, and skin diving are within walking distance. Restaurant, bar, dining room. No room phones, TV in common area. Business services, airport shuttle. | 39301 South Coast Hwy. | 707/884–3441 | 19 rooms | $44–$75 | AE, D, MC, V.

North Coast Country Inn. Each country-style cottage has antiques, a private entrance off a porch or surrounding deck, a wood-burning fireplace, and a private bathroom. Shops, galleries, and restaurants as well as the Point Area Lighthouse are in Mendocino Village 4 mi away. Complimentary breakfast. Some kitchenettes, refrigerators. No TV. Hot tub. No kids under 12. | 34591 S. Rte. 1 | 707/884–4537 or 800/959–4537 | ncci@mcn.org | www.northcoastcountryinn.com | 6 rooms | $175–$195 | AE, MC, V.

★ **Old Milano Hotel.** One of the private cottages at this 1905 B&B inn is an authentic train car ("The Caboose"). Listed on the National Trust For Historic Preservation's List of Historic Hotels of America, the Old Milano is on a three-acre estate overlooking the Pacific Ocean—you'll have ocean views from the suite and the two newer cottages (added in 1997). It's all been redone in Victorian style with antiques in every room and in the four cottages—each of which has either a fireplace or a wood-burning stove. Two cottages have in-room hot tubs, one has a custom stained-glass window, and another has a reading loft. During dinner in the hotel's restaurant (also listed), a fire burns in a stone fireplace and candles light the tables. The restaurant also serves homemade breakfast, in your room if you wish. Some in-room hot tubs. Outdoor hot tub. | 38300 Rte. 1 | 707/884–3256 | coast@oldmilanohotel.com | www.oldmilanohotel.com/omres.html | 6 rooms (2 shared baths), 1 suite, 4 cottages | $115–$225 | MC, V.

St. Orres. This 42-acre complex is home to 12 rustic, yet modern cottages. The exterior of the main house/hotel has onion-domed towers; the interior has a spiral staircase constructed of rough-hewn timbers circling a finished tree trunk. Eight "Creekside Cottages" sit in a secluded area across from the St. Orres Creek. Restaurant, complimentary break-fast. Some in-room hot tubs, no room phones, no TV. Outdoor hot tub, sauna, spa. | 36601 Rte. 1S | 707/884–3303 | fax 707/884–1840 | www.saintorres.com | 11 cottages (all share 3 bathrooms) | $70–$85, $100–$225 cottages | MC, V.

Sea Ranch Lodge. Perched high on the edge of an oceanside cliff overlooking the Pacific sits a small complex of modern, wooden structures with sloping roofs. The oversized guest rooms are adorned with local artwork and ocean views, and some have fireplaces. Beaches and wineries are the key attractions in the area. You can even try your hand at kayaking here. Restaurant, bar. No air-conditioning, some in-room hot tubs. Some room phones. Driving range, 18-hole golf course, putting green. Hiking. Fishing, bicycles. Business ser-vices. | 60 Sea Walk Dr. | 707/785–2371 or 800/732–7262 | fax 707/785–2917 | www.sear-anchlodge.com | 20 rooms | $205–$395 | AE, MC, V.

Seacliff on the Bluff. At Seacliff you will awaken to the sounds and smell of the ocean, with views of the beach and surf, and from the bluff you can watch passing ships, fish-ing boats, and migrating whales. All rooms have ocean views and gas fireplaces. Seacliff is on Route 1 in central Gualala. Refrigerators, in-room hot tubs, cable TV. | 39140 South Rte. 1 | 800/400–5053 or 707/884–1213 | fax 707/884–1731 | information@seacliffmotel.com | www.seacliffmotel.com/default.html | 16 rooms | $125–$160 | MC, V.

Whale Watch Inn. This B&B contains five modern buildings and is set high on the edge of a bluff overlooking the Pacific. Rooms have a bath, a fireplace, and a private deck with an ocean view. On Saturday evenings, a spread of appetizers, wine, and champagne is laid out in the Whale Watch Room. Each room is furnished with a mix of modern and Victorian pieces. Complimentary breakfast, room service. Some kitchenettes, some in-room hot tubs, some refrigerators. No room phones. Business services. No kids. | 35100 Rte. 1 | 707/884–3667 or 800/942–5342 | fax 707/884–4815 | www.whale-watch.com | 18 rooms | $170–$270 | AE, MC, V.

GUERNEVILLE

MAP 3, C7

(Nearby towns also listed: Healdsburg, Jenner, Santa Rosa)

Guerneville's official history boasts of its role as a lumber town dedicated to sawing down what was then "the tallest forest on earth" (one of its trees was noted in the *Guiness Book of World Records*). In the 1970s, after the logging industry went bust and before the wine industry elevated property values, Guerneville became known as a hippie paradise. Housing was cheap and back-to-the-landers could revel in the natural beauty of the Russian River region. Since then, it's become almost a bedroom commu-nity to the burgeoning urban areas of Santa Rosa and San Francisco, and remains a popular vacation spot in the summer. Try visiting in spring or fall if you'd like a better glimpse of Guerneville's rural appeal.

Information: Russian River Region Visitors Bureau | 13250 River Rd., Guerneville 95448 | 800/253–8800 | www.russianriver.com.

Attractions

Armstrong Redwoods State Reserve. Shady, towering redwoods hint at the majestic forests that lured logging companies during the last century at this natural reserve. You can explore the hiking trails or have a picnic. | 1700 Armstrong Woods Rd. | 707/865–2391 or 707/824–7000 | www.mcn.org/1/rrparks/parks/armsr.htm | Free; $5 parking | Daily dawn to dusk.

Iron Horse Vineyards. Iron Horse makes sparkling and still wine for the White House. The 300-acres of rolling, vine-covered hills are named after a railroad station that originally sat on the property. Tours are available, but you should call in advance, as the schedule changes periodically. Tastings are held outdoors, weather permitting. | 9786 Ross Station Rd., Sebastopol | (707) 887–1507 | www.ironhorsevineyards.com | Free | Tours weekdays, 10 or 2; tastings daily, 10–3:30. Please call in advance.

Korbel Champagne Cellars. Korbel welcomes you to taste locally made sparkling wine and tour the operation. | 13250 River Rd. | 707/887–2294 | www.korbel.com | Free | Daily 9–5.

ON THE CALENDAR

JUNE: *Russian River Blues Festival.* Blues aficionados and some of the best bands in the region come to show their stuff at this riverside revival at the Russian River Resort grounds adjacent to Guerneville. Wine tasting is conducted and festival merchandise is available. | $35–$85 | 707/869–3940 | www.russianriverbluesfest.com.

JULY–AUG.: *Vineman Triathlons.* This series of triathlons and half-triathlons takes place on various weekends during July and August. Races are divided into several categories: men and women's, pro and amatuer, and by age group. Races begin on Johnson's Beach. | 707/528–1630 | www.vineman.com.

SEPT.: *Russian River Jazz Festival.* World-class jazz acts come to play at the beaches of the Russian River resort district. | 707/869–3940.

Dining

Applewood Inn. Contemporary. You can look out over the courtyard from your table as you dine on cuisine with French and Mediterranean overtones. The "Wine Country Fare" includes grilled pork tenderloin, roasted salmon, angus beef rib eye, and vegetable entrées. Beer and wine only. No smoking. | 13555 Rte. 116 | 707/869–9093 | Reservations essential | Closed Sun., Mon. | $19–$25 | AE, D, MC, V.

Blue Heron Restaurant. American. A turn-of-the-20th-century restored tavern in neighboring Duncan Mills, the Blue Heron's specialties include fish, chicken, and vegetarian dishes. On summer Sundays, barbecued oysters are served in the garden. | 25300 Steelhead Blvd., Duncans Mills | 707/865–9135.

Main Street Station Ristorante and Cabaret. Italian. Bob Jones of Jazz Now Magazine has praised the acoustic (no amplification) vocal and instrumental jazz you can listen to as you dine at Main Street Station. Specialties (apart from jazz) include pizza, pasta, lasagna, appetizers, salads, and sandwiches. | 16280 Main St. | 707/869–0501 | www.mainststation.com | pizza@mainststation.com | $8–$15 | AE, D, MC, V.

Lodging

Applewood Inn. The Mission Revival–style villas on the inn's six acres are surrounded by fruit trees and herb gardens. Rooms are furnished with French country antiques and some reproductions. You can explore the wine tasting country which encompasses the area or take the Sonoma Thunder-Balloon Safari Tour which leaves from 11 mi south of the inn. Restaurant, picnic area, complimentary breakfast. In-room data ports, some in-room hot tubs, cable TV. Pool. Hot tub. Library. Business services. No smoking. | 13555 Rte. 116 | 707/869–9093 | fax 707/869–9170 | stay@applewoodinn.com | www.applewoodinn.com | 16 rooms | $125–$250 | AE, D, MC, V.

Brookside Lodge and Motel. You'll have vineyard views and country privacy in these contemporary, cabin-like rooms surrounded by redwoods. Most of the rooms have fireplaces, and the pool is solar heated. You're free to use the barbecues and picnic tables scattered about the lawns. Smoking and no-smoking rooms are available. A block's walk will take you to Guerneville's antiques shops and restaurants. Some kitchenettes, some minibars, some in-room hot tubs, cable TV, in-room VCRs. Outdoor pool. Outdoor hot tub, sauna. | 14100 Brookside La. | 800/551–1881 or 707/869–1881 | fax 707/869–0714 | brookside@sonic.net | www.sonic.net/welcome | 33 rooms | $120 rooms, $280 suites | AE, MC, V.

Cazanoma Lodge. Two creeks border the guest cabins and lodge on this 147-acre property. Redwoods can be seen from the studio and one-bedroom units with wood-burning fireplaces. The lodge is 16 mi west of Guerneville. Complimentary Continental breakfast. Some kitchenettes, microwaves, refrigerators, some in-room hot tubs. Pond. | 1000 Kidd Creek Rd., Cazadero | 707/632–5255 or 888/699–8499 | fax 707/632–5256 | 6 rooms, 2 cabins | $83, $108–$118 cabins | MC, V.

Huckleberry Springs. This 56-acre property, 6 mi south of Guerneville, above the Russian River was designed to preserve the habitat of the area. Cottages have skylights and some wood burning stoves. You can hike, horseback ride, canoe, and kayak at Armstrong State Redwood Park which is 8 mi to the north. Picnic area, complimentary breakfast. No air-conditioning, refrigerators, no room phones. In-room VCRs. Pool. Hot tub. Business services. No kids allowed. No smoking. | 8105 Old Beedle Rd., Monte Rio | 707/865–2683 or 800/822–2683 | hucksprings@netdex.com | www.huckleberrysprings.com | 4 cottages | $155–$175 cottages | Closed mid-Dec.–Feb. | AE, MC, V.

Ridenhour Ranch House. Each guest room in this 1906 home is uniquely embellished with antiques, handmade quilts, and fresh flowers. There's a common living room with a brick fireplace. Guerneville is 3 mi to the east. Picnic area, complimentary breakfast. No smoking. Hot tub. Water sports. Library. Business services. | 12850 River Rd. | 707/887–1033 | fax 707/869–2967 | ridenhourinn@earthlink.net | www.ridenhourranchhouseinn.com | 6 rooms, 2 cottages | $105–$145, $150–$165 cottages | AE, MC, V.

Santa Nella. Santa Nella is nestled in a redwood forest 1/2 mi south of the Russian River and 1 mi north of Korbel Champagne Cellar (when the summer bridge is in). The main house of this late 1800s country Victorian B&B has a wraparound veranda, and all the rooms have fireplaces, private baths, English antiques, and down comforters. You can visit the inn's library or sit by the parlor woodstove with the resident cat and two dogs to enjoy the complimentary wine you'll receive when you check in. You'll be 2 mi from Guerneville's shops and restaurants and 1/2 hour east of the Pacific coast. Complimentary breakfast. TV in common area. No kids. No pets. No smoking. | 12130 Rte. 116 | 707/869–9488 | fax 707/869–0355 | www.santanella.com | 4 rooms | $120–$130, $25 for extra person in room | MC, V.

HALF MOON BAY

MAP 6, B8

(Nearby towns also listed: Burlingame, Menlo Park, Palo Alto, San Francisco, San Mateo)

Established in 1840 as "Spanishtown," this is the oldest town in San Mateo County. First came Spanish land grant holders; then Mexican and Chilean laborers arrived to work and eventually establish a town. The town was renamed Half Moon Bay in 1874 in honor of the huge half moon-shaped harbor on which the town sits. By the late 1800s, workers from Canada, China, Europe, and the Pacific Islands made the little town a bustling community of traders and farmers. Probably the most action took place during the Prohibition years, when the foggy coves provided excellent cover for rum-runners bringing in booze from Canada.

Today the town is a bustling tourist destination that retains its small-town qualities: there are only a few traffic lights, there are no chain restaurants or franchises, and most of the downtown businesses are housed in historic buildings from the 1910s. Primary industries include floriculture (ornamental plants), vegetables such as artichokes, brussel sprouts, and peas, fishing, and tourism.

Information: Half Moon Bay Chamber of Commerce | 501 Main Street, Half Moon Bay 94019 | 650/726–8380 | www.halfmoonbaychamber.org.

Attractions

Fitzgerald Marine Reserve. This reserve is one of the most diverse intertidal zones in California. Large tidepools are submerged and re-exposed twice each day with the rise and fall of the tides. At low tide, you can walk along the reefs, discovering the animals and plants living in this ever-changing habitat. Guided tours are also available. The reserve is located on Moss Beach, just west of Route 1. | California Ave. | 650/728–3584 | www.gladman.com/mb/fitzgerald.html | Free.

ON THE CALENDAR

OCT.: *Art and Pumpkin Festival.* Half Moon Bay is famous for its Great Pumpkin Weigh-Off. The heaviest pumpkin is crowned on Columbus Day and displayed as Gourd of Honor during the festival that follows. Past winners have topped half a ton! Activities include parades, pie eating contests, fun-runs, pumpkin carving, food booths, beer and wine tasting, and hundreds of arts and craft booths. | 650/726–8380 | www.halfmoonbaychamber.org.

Dining

Caddy's. Contemporary. This restaurant overlooks the Pacific ocean as well as Half Moon Bay Golf Links. The gourmet menu includes such items as wild mushroom and goat cheese omelets. | 2000 Fairway Dr. | 650/726–6384 | www.halfmoonbaygolf.com/caddy/caddy.html | No dinner | $12–$17 | AE, MC, V.

Miramar Restaurant. Seafood. This restaurant is just a few yards from the beach, and the views are breathtaking especially at sunset. Specialties include fresh seafood, steaks, and famous clam chowder. | 131 Mirada Rd. | 650/726–9053 | fax 650/726–5060 | www.miramarbeach.com/mirar | $15–$30 | AE, D, MC, V.

Moss Beach Distillery. Contemporary. Steaks and seafood on a very large outdoor patio with spectacular ocean views have made this restaurant a favorite among locals and tourists for almost a century. A resident "ghost" called The Blue Lady plays pranks on the patrons. Call ahead for the best tables. | Beach and Ocean St. | 650/728–5595 | www.mossbeachdistillery.com | $20–$55 | AE, D, DC, MC, V.

Pasta Moon. American. The pizza here has thin crust, unlike the usual doughy California-style. The kitchen in this small restaurant also turns out handmade pastas, crisp-skinned roast chicken, and other roasted meats. | 315 Main St. | 650/726–5125 | $12–$28 | MC, V.

San Benito House. Contemporary. Whether you want deli-style sandwiches on home-baked bread for a picnic by the sea, or a candlelight dinner of fresh fish or homemade pasta, you can find it at this intimate eatery tucked inside an old inn in the heart of Half Moon Bay. | 356 Main St. | 650/726–3425 | No lunch. Dinner only Mon.–Wed. | $12–$25 | MC, V.

Sushi Main Grill. Japanese. You can savor sushi specialties or innovative dishes such as sake-steamed clams and kelp salad while feasting your eyes on a mixture of Pacific Island art and Balinese woodwork. | 696 Mill St. | 650/726–6336 | www.sushimainst.com | $12–$18 | MC, V.

Two Fools. American. You don't have to be a fool to enjoy the big organic salads or old-fashioned meat loaf sandwiches. Locals drop in for lunch and dinner takeout, while tourists are drawn to the weekend brunch. | 408 Main St. | 650/712–1222 | No lunch weekends | $12–$28 | MC, V.

Lodging

Beach House. High on a bluff overlooking the Pacific Ocean and Pillar Point Harbor, the Beach House has private patios with views of the breakers. You stay in 500-square-ft bi-level loft suites with wood-burning fireplace, granite counters, wet bar, and stereo system. Conference facilities are available. Complimentary breakfast. Pool. Hot tub, spa. | 4100 N. Cabrillo Hwy. | 650/712–0220 | fax 650/712–0693 | www.beach-house.com | 54 units | $195–$365 | AE, D, DC, MC, V.

Costanoa Coastal Lodge. Named after the Native Americans who once lived here, this lodge plus camping area is next to five state parks and overlooks coastal hills and beaches. Accommodations include: luxury rooms in the lodge with oversize beds, semi-private patios, and full access to hot tub and spa; furnished cabins and tent bungalows with modern amenities but shared baths and spa access only; and several camping sites and RV hookups. You have easy access to over 30,000 acres of foot trails. Complimentary Continental breakfast. Hot tub, spa. | 2001 Rossi Rd. at Rte. 1, Pescadero | 650/879–1100 | fax 650/879–2275 | www.costanoa.com | 40 rooms, 12 cabins, RV and camping sites | $175–$240 lodge, $145 cabins, $40 camping | AE, D, DC, MC, V.

Cypress Inn. This three-story beachfront inn is 2 mi north of Half Moon Bay. Natural pine and wicker furnishings adorn each room. Miramar Beach is literally "ten steps away" as the proprietors are fond of saying. Complimentary breakfast. Refrigerators, cable TV. Massage. Business services. | 407 Mirada Rd. | 650/726–6002 or 800/83–BEACH | fax 650/712–0380 | www.cypressinn.com | 12 rooms, 1 suite | $200–$325, $325 suite | AE, D, MC, V.

Goose and Turrets. This hotel was built in 1906 in Montara, 8 mi north of Half Moon Bay. Antique shopping is a popular activity in the sleepy village. Complimentary breakfast. No smoking. | 835 George St., Montara | 650/728–5451 | fax 650/728–0141 | 5 rooms, (2 with shower only) | $110–$150 | AE, D, DC, MC, V.

Half Moon Bay Lodge. Built in 1976 on the southern edge of town, this inn overlooks the Half Moon Bay Golf Links designed by Arnold Palmer. You can choose from rooms with one king- or two queen-size beds topped with European-style duvetyns. Private balconies and terraces afford views of passing whales on the Pacific. Beaches, horseback riding, and the Purisma Creek Redwoods Open Space Reserve are all in close proximity. Complimentary Continental breakfast. No air-conditioning, refrigerators, cable TV. Pool. Spa. Dry sauna. Exercise equipment. Laundry facilities. Business services. | 2400 S Cabrillo Hwy. | 650/726–9000 or 800/368–2468 | fax 650/726–7951 | www.woodsidehotels.com | 81 rooms | $175–$235 | AE, D, DC, MC, V.

Harbor House. A stone's throw from the water, this small hotel provides excellent views and intimate accommodations. Rooms have pine, wicker, and teak furniture, private patios, and working fireplaces. Several restaurants are within easy walking distance. Complimentary breakfast. No air-conditioning, no room phones. Beach. Library. No kids under 12. No smoking. | 346 Princeton Ave. | 650/728–1572 | fax 650/728–8271 | www.harborhousebandb.com | 6 rooms, 1 suite | $145–$195 | AE, MC, V.

Holiday Inn Express. This hotel is in downtown Half Moon Bay. Tennis and golf facilities are 2 mi away. You can go deep sea fishing at Princeton Harbor (4 mi), or hike in the Purisma Redwoods (4 mi). Complimentary Continental breakfast. In-room data ports. Business services. Some pets allowed (fee). | 230 S. Cabrillo Hwy. | 650/726–3400 | fax 650/726–1256 | www.hiexpress.com/halfmoonbay | 52 rooms, 1 suite | $79–$149, $179 suite | AE, D, DC, MC, V.

Landis Shore. This luxurious inn has spacious rooms with fireplaces, private patios with ocean views, and wine and appetizers every evening. Miramar Beach is just out the back door. Conference facilities are available. Complimentary breakfast. In-room data ports, in-room hot tubs. | 211 Mirada Rd. | 650/726–6642 | fax 650/726–6644 | www.landisshores.com | 8 rooms | $275–$345 | AE, MC, V.

Mill Rose Inn. This two-story inn was built in the early 1900s in the Old Town district. Restaurants and shopping are within walking distance. Furnishings from Georgian antiques to European feather beds adorn each of the six unique theme rooms. Five blocks west on Kelly Drive, you can bicycle or hike along the 10 mi beach trail. Complimentary breakfast. In-room data ports, refrigerators, cable TV, in-room VCRs. Hot tub. Laundry facilities. Business services. | 615 Mill St. | 650/726–8750 or 800/900–7673 | fax 650/726–3031 | tb@millroseinn.com | www.millroseinn.com | 6 rooms, 2 suites (2 with shower only) | $180–$280, $270–$310 suites | AE, D, DC, MC, V.

Old Thyme Inn. This 1899 Queen Anne Victorian cottage has a English garden with over 80 varieties of herbs and flowers. Each room has its own motif; four-poster beds and antiques from the days of Louis XVI are typical. Nature trails, golf courses, wineries, and other attractions are nearby. Complimentary breakfast. In-room VCRs. Business services. No smoking. | 779 Main St. | 650/726–1616 | fax 650/726–6394 | www.oldthymeinn.com | 7 rooms | $100–$255 | AE, D, MC, V.

Ramada Limited. In a quiet area with views of the foothills, this hotel is within walking distance of downtown Half Moon Bay. Complimentary Continental breakfast. Microwaves, refrigerators, in-room hot tubs. | 3020 N. Cabrillo Hwy. | 650/726–9700 | www.ramada.com | 29 rooms | $65–$200 | AE, D, MC, V.

Ritz Carlton. Perched on a bluff overlooking the Pacific Ocean, this super-deluxe resort and spa was built in the tradition of late 19th century seaside lodges. It has spacious rooms, suites, and bungalows, and many amenities including valet dry cleaning. Restaurant. Hot tub, spa. 2 golf courses, 6 tennis courts. Gym. Baby-sitting, children's programs (2–12). Business services. | 1 Miramontes Point Rd. | 650/712–7000 | fax 650/712–7070 | www.ritzcarlton.com | 239 rooms, 22 suites | $265–$615 rooms, $465–$2000 | AE, D, DC, V, MC.

★ **Seal Cove Inn.** The entrance to this secluded country inn, 6 mi north of town at Moss Beach, is marked by a path of towering cypress trees; inside, understated elegance is found in the details. On foggy days you'll find a fire blazing in the common area, filled with country antiques, fine fabrics, and original artwork. Linens are turned down each night, and complimentary wine and soft drinks come with each of the individually decorated rooms, which are furnished with antiques. Views from all of the rooms are luscious, overlooking the distant coastline; all of the rooms have fireplaces and balconies or terraces. Families with children are welcome in the garden level rooms. Complimentary breakfast. Refrigerators, in-room VCRs. Beach. Laundry facilities. Business services. | 221 Cypress Ave., Moss Beach | 650/728–4114 or 800/995–9987 | fax 650/728–4116 | sealcove@coastside.net | www.sealcoveinn.com | 10 rooms, 2 suites | $200–$225, $280 suites | AE, D, MC, V.

HANFORD

MAP 4, G11

(Nearby towns also listed: Fresno, Selma, Visalia)

★ Hanford is named for 19th-century Southern Pacific Railroad paymaster James Madison Hanford who, although he never actually resided there, became a leading figure in the community. Hanford died in 1911 in Oakland. At one time this San Joaquin Valley city of 31,000 had one of the larger Chinese communities in the state. The Chinese had come to help build the railroads but stayed to develop the town, building a "city within a city" called China Alley to preserve their culture and to provide a Chinese community for their children. What remains of the original China Alley are a Taoist temple and a restaurant run by the heirs of the family who founded it in 1883. Today, many Hanford Chinese play an active part in the thriving business community as business owners and shop keepers.

Information: **Hanford Visitor's Agency** | 200 Sante Fe, Suite D, Hanford 93230 | 559/582–5024 or 800/722–1114 | www.visithanford.com.

Attractions

Hanford Carnegie Museum. Exhibits and literature at this museum chronicle the local history of Hanford and the surrounding area. | 109 E. 8th St. | 559/584–1367 | $2 | Tues.– Fri. 12–3, Sat. 12–4.

OCT.: *Renaissance Fair.* Knights and knaves and maidens gather in the Civic Center Park for two days of medieval revelry. You can enjoy jousting, sword fighting, wandering bards, theatre-in-the-round, and old-time food at this family-oriented festival. | 559/582–5024 | www.visithanford.com.

Dining
Imperial Dynasty. French. Despite its name and teak-and-porcelain Chinese look, Imperial Dynasty serves mainly French cuisine. Garlicky escargots are a popular hors d'oeuvre preceding such main dishes as veal sweetbreads or rack of lamb. The extensive wine list has many prized vintages. | China Alley, at corner of 7th and Green Sts. | 559/582–0196 | Closed Mon. No lunch | $18–$33 | AE, MC, V.

Lodging
Comfort Inn. Just 2 blocks from the freeway, this hotel is a three-story building with a swimming pool and hot tub on one side. Complimentary Continental breakfast. Pool. Spa. Gym. | 10 N. Irwin St. | 559/584–9300 | fax 559/584–0300 | www.comfortinn.com | 65 rooms | $60–$100 | AE, D, MC, V.

Irwin Street. At this B&B inn you'll find four tree-shaded, restored Victorian homes that have been converted into rooms and suites. Most accommodations contain four-poster beds, leaded-glass windows, and dark wood detailing; bathrooms have marble basins, brass fixtures, and old-fashioned tubs. Restaurant, complimentary Continental breakfast. Cable TV. Pool. Some pets allowed. | 522 N. Irwin St. | 559/583–8000 or 888/583–8080 | fax 559/583–8793 | 33 rooms in 4 buildings | $69–$125 | AE, D, DC, MC, V.

HAYWARD

MAP 6, E6

(Nearby towns also listed: Fremont, Palo Alto)

Known as the "heart of the Bay," this southern Alameda County of 130,000 is now a sedate East Bay community south of Oakland and prides itself on its cultural diversity.

Information: Hayward Chamber of Commerce | 22561 Main St., 94541 | 510/537–2424 | www.hayward.org.

Attractions
Japanese Gardens. Plants, rocks, and trees from the "Land of the Rising Sun" and California are permanent residents at this reserve. | 22373 N. Third St. | 510/881–6700 | Free | Daily 8:30–4.

The McConaghy Home and Carriage House. This restored 1886 house still has many of its original furnishings. | 18701 Hesperian Blvd. | 510/276–3010 | $3 | Thurs.–Sun. 1–4.

FEB.: *Battle of the Bands.* Shake, rattle, and roll to the beat at this premier music showcase. Since 1962, the event has brought together jazz, pop, and alternative musicians and vocalists for a giant jam session—one of the longest-running music festivals in the state. The "battle" usually lets loose the first Saturday of February at Chabot College Auditorium. | 510/317–2314.

Dining
Manzella's Seafood Loft. Seafood. Take in a sweeping view of the bay from this large (it seats 300), family-run restaurant. The eatery prides itself on fresh fish and shellfish,

delivered twice weekly. Specials include lobster tail, crab legs, or seafood stew. Don't want seafood? The restaurant also serves Irish stew and steak, as well as pasta, chicken, and veal dishes. Look for earlybird specials, weekdays. | 1275 W. Winton Ave. | 510/887–6040 | No lunch Sat. Closed Sun. | $10–$26 | AE, D, DC, MC, V.

Lodging

Best Western Inn of Hayward. A good choice if you're visiting California State University at Hayward, this three-story hotel is 2 mi away from campus. It's also convenient to restaurants, shopping, golf, tennis, and a local park, all within ½ mi. Complimentary Continental breakfast. In-room data ports, some kitchenettes, some refrigerators, some in-room hot tubs, cable TV. Pool. Hot tub, sauna. Exercise equipment. Laundry services. Business services, free parking. | 360 West A St. | 510/785–8700 | fax 510/782–0850 | www.bestwestern.com/innofhayward | 91 rooms | $93–$109 | AE, D, DC, MC, V.

Comfort Inn. This two-story hotel is close to the local subway, museums, and California State University. The commercial district is 1½ mi away in downtown. Restaurant, complimentary Continental breakfast. Some kitchenettes, refrigerators, some in-room hot tubs, cable TV. Sauna. Laundry facilities. Business services. | 24997 Mission Blvd. | 510/538–4466 | fax 510/581–8029 | www.comfortinn.com | 62 rooms | $75–$125 | AE, D, DC, MC, V.

Executive Inn. This three-story hotel is downtown among restaurants, shopping, and the business district. A golf course and a movie theater are nearby. Restaurant, complimentary Continental breakfast. Refrigerators, cable TV. Pool. Exercise equipment. Laundry facilities. Business services, airport shuttle, free parking. Some pets allowed. | 20777 Hesperian Blvd. | 510/732–6300 or 800/553–5083 | fax 510/783–2265 | 168 rooms | $95–$109 | AE, D, DC, MC, V.

HEALDSBURG

MAP 3, C6

(Nearby towns also listed: Calistoga, Geyserville, Guerneville)

Here's a typical California story: A widow with 11 children tries to make a living from a 48,000-acre ranch. Uprisings and skirmishes with local Indians drive her to take refuge at Sutter's Fort, whereupon a bunch of scraggly miners and ne'er-do-wells squat on her abandoned ranch. One of the interlopers has the nerve to establish a settlement on her land and names it after himself. That's exactly what happened to Josefa Fitch, and why the town of Healdsburg is named after the villain in this story, squatter Harmon Heald. Of course, once you see how close this tree-shaded rural burgh is to the Russian River, the vineyards and beautiful backcountry, it's easy to understand the scoundrel's greed.

Healdburg is a calm, quiet place you wish you could keep all to yourself. The town plaza has a bandshell where musicians still send melodies into the air. There are numerous antique shops to visit and dozens of nearby wineries where you can stop for a glass of local vintage. In summer, produce stands, laden with fruits and vegetables, waft a sweet perfume. Tourism has increased here in recent years due to the 60 wineries within a 15-mi radius, although it still remains a smaller community than Napa.

Information: Healdsburg Chamber of Commerce and Visitors Bureau | 217 Healdsburg Avenue, Healdsburg 95448 | 707/433–6935 | www.healdsburg.org.

Attractions

J. Shaw and Co. You can visit local vineyards and farms on individually tailored tours of the region. | 327 Burgundy Rd. | 707/433–1145 | fax 707/433–9620 | jesse@gourmetwine.com | Daily.

Healdsburg Area Wineries. More than 50 wineries in the area surrounding Healdsburg have tours and tastings.

Simi Winery. Giuseppe and Pietro Simi began growing grapes in Sonoma in 1876. Though the winery's operations are high-tech, these days, its tree-lined entrance avenue and stone buildings recall a more genteel era. Tours end with a sampling of the current vintage. | 16275 Healdsburg Ave. | 707/433–6981 or 800/746–4880 | www.simiwinery.com | Free | Tours daily at 11, 1, and 3.

Trowbridge Canoe Trips. This operator conducts canoe and kayaking trips up and down the Russian River. Some excursions end with a BBQ dinner. Shuttle service is available. | 13840 Old Redwood Hwy. | 707/433–7247 or 800/640–1386 | fax 707/433–6384 | www.trowbridgecanoe.com | $50 full day; half-day $40; 2-day $75 | Apr.–Oct. call to schedule.

Warm Springs Dam/Lake Sonoma. Warm Springs Dam, which forms the 381,000-acre Lake Sonoma, was built by the U.S. Army Corps of Engineers in 1983. Swimming, fishing, boating, hiking, and picnicking are popular activities. Call for the hours of the Visitor Center, which is open daily. | 333 Skaggs Springs Rd. | 707/433–9483 | Free.

ON THE CALENDAR

JUNE–AUG.: *Music on the Square.* Cajun, swing, blues, flamenco, jazz, and world music is performed free of charge, every Sunday, at the Healdsburg Avenue Square. | 707/433–3064 or 800/648–9922 (in CA).

JULY: *Healdsburg Harvest Century Bicycle Tour.* Riders can sign up for up to 60 mi jaunts through the Alexander, Russian River, and Dry Creek Valleys. Road and mountain bikes are OK. Rest stops, lunch provided. | 707/433–6935 or 800/648–9922 (in CA).

Dining

Bistro Ralph. Contemporary. Duck, lamb, chicken, calamari, and Caesar salad are served in a stark industrial setting. Dishes are influenced by the culinary traditions of France and California. Kids' menu. Beer and wine only. No smoking. | 109 Plaza St. | 707/433–1380 | $15–$25 | MC, V.

Catelli's the Rex. Italian. Mahogany details, mirrors, and linen tablecloths are the stage for dishes like veal piccata, seared in a white wine and garlic sauce and served with capers and lemon and the homemade snow crab ravioli in a saffron cream sauce. | 241 Healdsburg Ave. | 707/433–2340 | www.catellistherex.com | Closed Mon. No lunch weekends | $15–$25 | D, MC, V.

El Farolito. Mexican. Burritos, chili rellenos, grilled steak, tacos, and other Cal-Mex entrées make up the selections. Paintings with a Southwestern flavor adorn the walls, and flowers complement the tables. Kids' menu. Beer and wine only. | 128 Plaza St. | 707/433–2807 | Breakfast also available | $5–$15 | D, MC, V.

Giorgio's Restaurant. Italian. Housed in a 1910 farmhouse, this eatery still contains the original cupboards. There are three separate dining rooms as well as a covered patio that overlooks vineyards. Try the veal cutlet Parmesan or the pasta with pesto. | 25 Grant Ave. | 707/433–1106 | No lunch on weekends | $13–$15 | AE, D, MC, V.

Lotus Thai. Pan-Asian. Authentic Thai dishes include pad thai and tom kagai as well as a host of beef, chicken, pork, and vegetarian specialties. Statues and paintings reflect the culture of the owner's native land. Beer and wine only. No smoking. | 109A Plaza St. | 707/433–5282 | Closed Mon. | $15–$25 | AE, D, MC, V.

Madrona Manor. Contemporary/French. The dining rooms in this Victorian mansion overlook lush gardens. Smoked meats are prepared on the premises, and vegetables come from a nearby garden. The fillet of beef and the grilled yellow tail ahi headline the menu. Live music Fri., Sat. No smoking. | 1001 Westside Rd. | 707/433–4231 | www.sterba.com/healdsburg/madrona | No lunch | $40–$50 | MC, V.

Ravenous Cafe. Contemporary. Raven Theater patrons often come here to dine before and after shows. A decidedly Italian influence plays a role in the menu of beef, seafood, and pasta with scallops, prawns, mussels, cherry tomatoes, mushrooms, and white wine basil sauce. Dim lighting, leopard chairs, and mirrors give the dining room its appeal. Beer and wine only. No smoking. | 117 North St. | 707/431–1770 | Closed Mon., Tues. | $10–$16 | No credit cards.

Western Boot Steak House. Steak. American Longhorns, branding irons, and other cowboy tools attempt to recreate a cattle ranch motif of the Old West. The restaurant serves large portions of prime rib, New York Strips, and, of course, filet mignon. Ribs, chicken, and some seafood selections round out the menu. Kids' menu. Beer and wine only. | 9 Mitchell La. | 707/433–6362 | $15–$25 | AE, MC, V.

Lodging

Belle de Jour. This single-story property was built around 1873 on six acres. Cottages are appointed with fireplaces, queen-size beds, as well as European and American antiques. The wineries and state parks of Sonoma County are within a 20-mi radius. Picnic area, complimentary breakfast. In-room data ports, some refrigerators, in-room hot tubs. Business services. No smoking. | 16276 Healdsburg Ave. | 707/431–9777 | fax 707/431–7412 | www.belledejourinn.com | 5 cottages | $165–$275 cottages | AE, MC, V.

Best Western Dry Creek Inn. The rooms in this Spanish-style building have king- or double queen-size beds. Upon arrival, you'll find a welcoming bottle of local wine. The three-story inn is on the north side of town. Complimentary Continental breakfast. In-room data ports, refrigerators, cable TV. Pool. Hot tub. Exercise equipment. Laundry facilities. Business services. Some pets allowed (fee). | 198 Dry Creek Rd. | 707/433–0300 or 800/222–5784 | fax 707/433–1129 | www.drycreekinn.com | 103 rooms | $69–$149 | AE, D, DC, MC, V.

Calderwood Inn. From the swings on the covered porch, you can look out on a forested estate of redwood, cedar, and cypress trees as well as rose gardens, fountains, and ponds. Inside the Queen Anne B&B are silk-screened Victorian wall and ceiling papers and antiques and a fireplace in the common area. In the rooms are more antiques, including clawfoot tubs, and down comforters. Appetizers and sweets are served in the evenings, and you can borrow the inn's books, puzzles, and games. You'll be 3 blocks from the town square, which has antique shops, theaters, and restaurants. The Dry Creek wineries, the Russian River, and Lake Sonoma are a bicycle ride away. Complimentary breakfast. No TV in some rooms. | 25 West Grant St. | 800/600–5444 or 707/431–1110 | www.travelpick.com/ca/calderwood | 6 rooms | $110–$185 | No credit cards.

Camellia Inn. This two-story inn dates from 1869 and is 2 blocks from central Healdsburg. Oriental rugs and canopy beds accent the guest rooms. At night, guests gather in the double parlor by the marble fireplace. Dining room, complimentary breakfast and evening snacks. In-room data ports, no smoking, some in-room hot tubs. Pool. Business services. | 211 North St. | 707/433–8182 or 800/727–8182 | fax 707/433–8130 | www.camelliainn.com | info@camelliainn.com | 9 rooms, 1 suite | $139–$199, $159 suite | AE, MC, V.

Grape Leaf Inn. This restored 1900 Queen Anne Victorian inn has 65 wineries within a 10-mi radius. Samples of the Sonoma Valley vintages are tasted every night in the parlor. Guest rooms are named after wines and are furnished with 19th-century rural France in mind. Restaurant, picnic area, complimentary breakfast and afternoon snacks. Some in-room hot tubs, no room phones. No smoking. | 539 Johnson St. | 707/433–8140 | fax 707/433–3140 | suite@sonic.net | www.grapeleafinn.com | 7 rooms | $90–$145 | D, MC, V.

Haydon Street Inn. Dating from 1912, this two-story inn is in downtown Healdsburg. Each room has its own motif, and all are furnished with Victorian antiques and beds. The restaurants, boutiques, and curiosity shops of the town plaza are 3 blocks away. Restaurant, picnic area, complimentary breakfast. Some in-room hot tubs, no room phones, no TV in rooms, TV in sitting room. Business services. No smoking. | 321 Haydon St. | 707/433–5228 or 800/528–3703 | fax 707/433–6637 | www.haydon.com | 8 rooms | $110–$180 | D, MC, V.

Healdsburg Inn on the Plaza. This building houses an art gallery and shop; the inn is on the two floors above. Eclectic antique furnishings, artwork, stained glass, lace curtains, and fireplaces lend a classically elegant feel to the inn. You can participate in water sports at the Russian River or tour the Sonoma Valley wineries in the vicinity during your stay. Complimentary breakfast. In-room hot tubs, cable TV, in-room VCRs (and movies). No smoking. | 110 Matheson St. | 707/433–6991 or 800/431–8663 | fax 707/433–9513 | www.healdsburginn.com | 9 rooms, 1 suite | $235–$265, $285 suite | MC, V.

Honor Mansion. This mansion, on the northeast edge of Healdsburg, is surrounded by a white picket fence and shaded by magnolias. Fireplaces, antiques, feather beds with down comforters, and luxurious linens adorn the rooms. There's a garden with a waterfall and koi pond on the grounds. Restaurant, picnic area, complimentary breakfast. Minibars. No TV in some rooms, TV in parlor. Pool. No smoking. | 14891 Grove St. | 707/433–4277 or 800/554–4667 | fax 707/431–7173 | cathi@honormansion.com | www.honormansion.com | 5 rooms (2 with shower only), 3 suites, 1 cottage | $150–$250, $300 suites, $270 cottage | D, MC, V.

Madrona Manor. This three-story mansion is joined by a carriage house on an eight-acre wooded knoll on the west side of town. The wraparound porch affords views of the extensive gardens. Rooms have many authentic Victorian antiques. Restaurant, picnic area, complimentary breakfast. Pool. Business services. | 1001 Westside Rd. | 707/433–4231 or 800/258–4003 | fax 707/433–0703 | madronaman@aol.com | www.madronamanor.com | 21 rooms, 3 suites | $185–$360, $275–$380 suites | MC, V.

Raford House. On four acres overlooking lush vineyard, The Raford House is a Sonoma County Historical Landmark. Palm trees flank the Victorian house. | 10630 Wohler Rd. | 707/887–9573 or 800/887–9503 | fax 707/887–9597 | www.rafordhouse.com/rooms.html | 7 rooms | $110–$180 | AE, D, MC, V.

Villa Messina. The vineyards, rolling hills, and geysers of Sonoma County's Wine Country surround Villa Messina's high hilltop. Art and antiques fill the high-ceilinged rooms at this B&B, which has its own redwood forest and gardens where Messina grapevines grow. During the afternoon, complimentary cheese and crackers are served near the fireplace in the common room. All rooms have fireplaces and goosedown comforters. In-room hot tubs, cable TV, in-room VCRs. Outdoor pool. | 316 Burgundy Rd. | 707/433–6655 | fax 707/433–4515 | messina@sonic.net | www.villamessina.com/ | 5 rooms | $160–$310 | AE, D, DC, MC, V.

HEMET

MAP 4, K15

(Nearby towns also listed: Beaumont, Idyllwild)

Nestled in the San Jacinto Valley on Route 74, Hemet is surrounded by the hills east of Greater Los Angeles. The development of Hemet began in 1887 with the formation of the Lake Hemet Water Company and the Hemet Land Company by W. F. Whittier and E. L. Mayberry. Work on a masonry dam in the San Jacinto Mountains commenced in 1891, and the Hemet Dam was completed in 1895. The subsequent formation of Lake Hemet and the completion of a water distribution system to and through the valley made future development possible. Early in the 20th century and into the 1960s, Hemet was primarily an agricultural community. Now the town expands in the winter when retirees from colder climates take up residence in Hemet's numerous mobile home communities, spurring the development of associated senior citizens' community services.

Information: Hemet Chamber of Commerce | 395 E. Latham Ave., 92543 | 909/658–3211 or 800/334–9344 | mail@hemet-chamber.com | www.hemet-chamber.com.

Attractions

Lake Hemet Campgrounds. This serene campground in the San Bernardino Mountains is 1½ mi south of Hemet Dam by boat. There is a full campground with hook-ups and dry camping as well. Swimming is not allowed in the lake; boating and fishing are allowed year-round. | 56570 Rte. 74, #4, Mountain Center 92561 | 909/659–2680 | camping $13 per vehicle dry camping; $16.25 per vehicle with hook-ups | Daily.

Orange Empire Railway Museum. All aboard! This museum displays the largest collection of locomotives and rail cars in the Western U.S. Stare up at massive steam and diesel engines, and peer into freight and passenger cars. Also tour antiquated City of Los Angeles trolley cars, and check out other railway artifacts dating from as early as the 1870s. Ride a vintage freight train or streetcar, weekends and holidays. Picnic areas are scattered about the grounds. The museum is in Perris, 28 mi northwest from Hemet off I–215. | 2201 South A St., Perris | 909/657–2605 | www.oerm.mus.ca.us | Free except on special event days; train or trolley ride, $7 | Daily 9–5. Closed Thanksgiving and Christmas Day.

San Jacinto Valley Museum. The San Jacinto Valley Museum displays artifacts pertaining to the human and geologic history of the San Jacinto Valley and Hemet. | 181 E. Main St. | 909/654–4952 | Donations accepted | Daily 12–4, closed Mon.

ON THE CALENDAR

APR., MAY: *Ramona Pageant.* This pageant, inspired by the 1884 novel by Helen Hunt Jackson, began in 1923 and has run continuously out on Ramona Bowl Rd. with only a few exceptions during the Great Depression and World War II. The Pageant depicts a Native American love story. | 800/645–4465 or 909/658–3111.

MAY: *Hemet Motorcycle Show.* Easy riders take note: it's bikes, bikes, bikes at this lively event. Motorcycles are judged on more than a dozen categories, including the "People's Choice" award and "Best Paint." There's also live music, games, kids' activities, food and vendor booths, and a beer garden. This one-day event, usually held on a Sunday, takes place at Weston Park. | 909/765–3855.

OCT.: *Farmers Fair.* Delicious local produce and prepared foods abound at this outdoor fair in Perris. Farmers come from throughout the San Jacinto Valley and neighboring agricultural valleys to exhibit at 18700 Lake Perris Drive. | 909/657–4221.

Dining

Arturo's Grill. Mexican. Banners and bright paintings enliven this family-owned Mexican café. Settle down at the counter, or at a table or booth, for dishes celebrating the chef's native Guadalajara, such as *Campechano* mixer (a seafood cocktail of shrimp, abalone, and octopus). Other standouts include shrimp enchiladas in chili tomatillo sauce, and *carnitas* (flour tortillas) filled with pork. You'll also find well-prepared tacos, burritos, enchiladas, and chile rellenos. Top it off with creamy flan for dessert. Beer and wine are available. | 253 E. Stetson | 909/766–6658 | Closed Wed. | $5–$12 | MC, V.

Dattilo Ristorante. Italian. Green, white, and red furnishings, Roman murals, marble floors, and a large dining room combine to create this restaurant's hearty Italian presence. The menu ranges from pasta and chicken to seafood and steak. Try the veal or chicken scallopini, *gamberi aglio con fettucini* (shrimp with lemon butter and caper sauce served with pasta), or chicken Jerusalem (breast of chicken cooked with demiglace, cream, and mushrooms). Kids' menu. No smoking. | 2288 E. Florida Ave. | 909/658–4248 | Closed Mon. No lunch Sat. | $9–$15 | AE, DC, MC, V.

Marie Callender's. American. This dependable chain is known for its pies, but it also serves rib-sticking comfort food. Look for pot roast, meatloaf, country-fried steak, and turkey pot pies, along with burgers, sandwiches, soups, and salads. Don't forget to leave room for dessert: pies, baked fresh daily, include apple, cherry, peach, Boston cream, lemon meringue, and many, many others. One slice isn't enough? Whole pies are available. Kids' menu. | 3969 W. Florida Ave. | 909/925–7727 | fax 909/925–0278 | www.mcpies.com | Reservations not accepted | $4–$11; $5.95 whole pie | AE, D, DC, MC, V.

Lodging

Best Western Hemet Motor Inn. On the west side of Hemet, this two-story inn built in the early 1980s provides some unique activities, such as shuffleboard courts. Palm trees dot the grounds. Only 90 minutes from beaches, Disneyland, and mountain resorts, this inn flourishes in the San Jacinto Valley. Some kitchenettes, refrigerators, cable TV. Pool. Hot tub. Laundry facilities. Business services. Some pets allowed. | 2625 W. Florida Ave. | 909/925–6605 | fax 909/925–7095 | www.bestwestern.com | 68 rooms | $46–$58 | AE, D, DC, MC, V.

Pierson's Country Place. Whether you want to go Hollywood or settle into Old World luxury, this expansive, two-story lodging can suit your mood. Rooms in the 6,500-square-ft home have various themes and appointments to match. The Casting Couch Room harkens back to movie-making's heyday, the French Country Room has gracious European-style furnishings, and Oriental carpets warm the Mai Funn Room. The inn, with views of the San Jacinto Range, has three rooms with private balconies. All rooms have private, outside entrances. Evenings, warm yourself by the outdoor fireplace in the Southwest-style patio, also the site of champagne breakfast on weekends. Complimentary breakfast. No room phones, no TV in some rooms. Outdoor hot tub. No children under 14. No smoking. | 25185 Pierson Rd., Homeland | 909/926–4546 | fax 909/926–1456 | piersonscountryplace@linkline.com | www.linkline.com/personal/piersonscountryplace | 5 rooms | $100–$125 | MC, V.

Ramada Inn Hemet. Built in 1986, this two-story hotel sits in the center of town, with shopping, restaurants, and golf nearby. Complimentary Continental breakfast. In-room data ports, some kitchenettes, some refrigerators, cable TV. Pool. Hot tub, sauna. Laundry facilities, laundry service. Free parking. | 3885 W. Florida Ave. | 909/929–8900 or 888/298–2054 | fax 909/925–3716 | www.ramada.com | 99 rooms | $55–$90 | AE, D, DC, MC, V.

Super 8. Built in the early 1990s, the three-story configuration with interior corridors provides privacy and security. This motel is a thrifty choice for the budget-minded traveler. In a commercial district off Route 74, restaurants and shopping are within a few blocks, and golf packages are available. Complimentary Continental breakfast. Some microwaves, refrigerators, cable TV. Outdoor pool. Hot tub. Business services. | 3510 W. Florida Ave. | 909/658–2281 or 800/769–6346 | fax 909/925–6492 | www.super8.com | 60 rooms, 8 suites | $35–$55, $51–$61 suites | AE, D, DC, MC, V.

Travelodge. A basic two-story lodge hotel built in 1990 has exterior corridors and nothing fancy. However you have a few more amenities here than you normally would see at this price. Complimentary Continental breakfast. Refrigerators, cable TV. Pool. Hot tub. Laundry facilities. Some pets allowed. | 1201 W. Florida Ave. | 909/766–1902 | www.travelodge.com | 46 rooms | $45–$75 | AE, D, DC, MC, V.

HOLLISTER

MAP 4, E10

HOLLISTER

INTRO
ATTRACTIONS
DINING
LODGING

(Nearby towns also listed: Carmel, Carmel Valley, Monterey, Pacific Grove, Pebble Beach, Santa Nella, Watsonville)

Fifty-four miles south of San Jose, Hollister (pop. 19,200) originated when some locals bought 21,000 acres of land from Colonel William Welles Hollister and named the town after him. The Southern Pacific Railroad arrived in 1870 and contributed to growth of the town, as did its main industry: sheep wool. Today, you can explore several western clothing stores, pubs, and breweries downtown. Hollister plays host to a rodeo and state fair each year, and not too far away is the Justo Reservoir, popular with fishers and boaters.

Information: San Benito County Chamber of Commerce | 615c San Benito St., 95023 | 831/637–5315 | fax 831/637–1008 | www.sbccc.org | sbccc@hollonline.com.

Attractions

Pinnacles National Monument. Scramble around the shards of an ancient volcano in this 24,000-acre preserve, 32 mi south of Hollister. Explore eroded spires, crags, and caverns on the park's trail system, open to hikers only. It's not unusual to see rock climbers scaling some of the more dramatic formations. Also look for signs of mountain lions, coyotes, and other wildlife. There are two entrances; park headquarters and visitor center are on the east side. You'll have company if you visit in spring, when visitors throng to see spectacular wildflower displays. Summer temperatures soar (over 100° is not unusual). Autumn, when temperatures drop and crowds lessen, makes a great time to visit. | 5000 Rte. 146, Paicines | 831/389–4485 | www.nps.gov/pinn | $5 per vehicle (7-day pass); $2 walk-in (7-day pass) | Year-round.

ON THE CALENDAR

SEPT.: *San Benito County Fair.* Enjoy all the classic fun, with carnival rides, games, magic and puppet shows, music, monster truck pulls, livestock auction, and food booths. The four-day event fills the Bolado Park Fairgounds, which you'll find 8 mi south of Hollister on Route 25, beyond Tres Piños. | 831/628–3421 | www.sanbenitocountyfair.com.

Dining

Vault Restaurant. Continental. Why the name? This 1930s structure once housed a bank—as did the previous building on the site, built in 1873. Since 1998, dollars and cents have made way for filet mignon, apple-brandy–flavored chicken, beef Stroganoff, and other menu favorites. The upscale interior still highlights the building's Art Deco styling and its banking past: the original vault was preserved and stands in the back of the dining room by the bar. | 452 San Benito St. | 831/636–5216 | fax 831/636–4974 | www.thevaultrestaurant.com | $6–$17 | AE, MC, V.

Lodging

Best Western San Benito Inn. White picket-style fencing surrounds the ground floor rooms, and second floor rooms have an exterior corridor overlooking the pool. Along the scenic Route 156 toward San Luis Reservoir, this hotel is also only 1 mi north of town. Some no smoking rooms. Complimentary Continental breakfast. Cable TV. Pool. | 660 San Felipe Rd. | 831/637–9248 | fax 831/637–4584 | www.bestwestern.com | 42 rooms | $65 | D, DC, MC, V.

Casa de Fruta Garden Motel. You can visit the famous Casa de Fruta roadside down the road to buy local produce. This single-story motel in a commercial area on the county line of Hollister and Gilroy welcomes families and RVers, and the campground has shade trees and space along the creek. Pool. Playground. Laundry service. Business services. | 10031 Pacheco Pass Hwy. | 408/842–9316 | 14 rooms | $61–$70 | D, MC, V.

Cinderella Motel. See if you can spot the motel's namesake in its doll collection, on display in the lobby. The small, single-story lodging sits on the north side of town, about 2 blocks from downtown and 1 mi north of Route 25. Complimentary Continental breakfast. Refrigerators, cable TV. Pool. Pets allowed. | 110 San Felipe Rd. | 831/637–5761 | 20 rooms | $42–$85 | AE, D, DC, MC, V.

Ridgemark Guest Cottages. These single-story cottages were constructed in the early 70's in a rural area 2 mi southeast of downtown. Furnishings are upscale and modern with a touch of luxury. A golf course and tennis courts are available down the road. Restaurant. Some in-room hot tubs. | 3800 Airline Hwy. | 831/637–8151 | fax 831/636–3168 | 32 rooms | $85–$110 | AE, D, DC, MC, V.

HOLLYWOOD (L.A.)

(Nearby towns also listed: Burbank, Glendale, Los Angeles, San Fernando, Santa Monica, Thousand Oaks, Valencia)

A one-time religious retreat for early evangelicals such as Aimee Semple MacPherson (1890–1944), Hollywood became ground zero for the motion picture business in 1911 when the Nestor Company opened the first film studio in a tavern on the corner of Gower and Sunset. The magic of Hollywood really takes place, for the most part, on sound stages that are not even in Hollywood anymore. And if you want glitz, head for neighboring Beverly Hills. But Hollywood, though a little frayed at the edges, is still considered the entertainment capital of the world, and boasts several internationally known sights including the Hollywood Bowl Amphitheater, Hollywood Wax Museum, and Mann's Chinese Theatre. There's no charge to view the famous Hollywood sign, easily visible for miles (unless it's a smoggy day).

Information: Hollywood Chamber of Commerce | 7018 Hollywood Blvd., 90028 | 323/469–8311 | fax 323/469–2805 | www.hollywoodchamber.net.

Attractions

Celebrity Lingerie Hall of Fame. The world-famous Frederick's of Hollywood flagship store, opened in 1946, includes the Celebrity Lingerie Hall of Fame, displaying lingerie from Hollywood movie stars. | 6608 Hollywood Blvd. | 323/466–8506 | Mon.–Thurs. 10–9, Fri. 10–6, weekends 12–5.

Guinness World Record Museum. Where early movies once flickered, you can learn about record-breaking achievements in virtually every category. Taking over *The Hollywood*, the city's first movie house and now on the National Register of Historic Places, the museum lets you marvel at various feats through displays using computers, videos, sound, and life-like replicas. | 6764 Hollywood Blvd. | 323/463–6433 | $8.95 | Sun.–Thurs., 10 AM–midnight, Fri.–Sat., 10 AM–1 AM.

Hollywood and Vine. In the days of classic Hollywood, starlets came to this intersection in hopes of being "discovered." Today, Hollywood and Vine is where starlets listen to rock music when they are not waiting to be discovered. You can also begin a walking tour of gritty Los Angeles, including sights along Hollywood Boulevard such as the Walk of Fame and Mann's Chinese Theatre. | Free | Daily.

Hollywood Bowl. A natural outdoor amphitheater in the foothills above Hollywood, musicians love the acoustics and beautiful architecture of the stage built in 1922. The Los Angeles Philharmonic, Hollywood Bowl Orchestra, Mel Torme, and Ella Fitzgerald are a few of the spectacular stars to perform here. You can go for the music and perhaps to picnic at the symphony. The Hollywood Bowl Museum displays a multimedia look at the history of Hollywood Bowl. Call ahead for show schedule. | 2301 N. Highland Ave. | 323/850–2000 | Prices for shows vary | Daily 9–5.

Hollywood Entertainment Museum. Right across the street from the Hollywood Chamber of Commerce, this museum contains memorabilia, history, and artifacts from the industry and the town. | 7021 Hollywood Blvd. | 323/465–7900 | $8 | Thurs.–Tues. 10–6.

Hollywood Heritage Museum. Dedicated to preserving Hollywood's past, this museum's goals include taking an active role in issues involving the preservation of venerable buildings along the Hollywood Boulevard Commercial and Entertainment National Register District. | 2100 N. Highland Ave. | 323/874–2276 | www.hollywoodheritage.org | $5 | Weekends 11–4.

Hollywood Memorial Park Cemetery Mortuary. You can indulge your morbid tendencies and visit this landscaped cemetery, in which the likes of Douglas Fairbanks Sr. and Jr. lie interred. | 6000 Santa Monica Blvd. | 323/469–1181 | Free | Daily 7–7.

Hollywood Wax Museum. Over 220 life-size figures of people and sets complete the images presented here. Tableau subjects appear from politics, sports, religion, television, and motion pictures. You can get a chilly thrill in the Chamber of Horrors or visit the Last Supper for a more spiritual experience. | 6767 Hollywood Blvd. | 323/462–8860 | $10 | Daily Sun.–Thurs. 10 AM–12 AM, Fri., Sat. 10 AM–2 AM.

★ **Mann's Chinese Theater.** This ornate building hosts many celebrity-filled movie premieres, and indelibly preserves celebrities identities with concrete moldings of handprints, footprints, and other body parts on the front walk. You can compare handprints with Tom Cruise or noseprints with Jimmy Durante. Call for show times | 6925 Hollywood Blvd. | 323/464–8111 | Free; $9 for shows.

★ **Walk of Fame.** Bronze stars bearing the names of Hollywood's immortals line a 1-mi stretch of sidewalks in a gritty but historic section of Los Angeles from which Tinsel Town conquered the world, on Hollywood Boulevard between Gower and La Brea. It remains one of the area's most popular tourist destinations. The stars are a prestigious honor bestowed on film, television, and recording celebrities. The City of Los Angeles designated the Walk of Fame a Cultural/Historic Landmark in 1978. | 323/469–8311 | Free | Daily.

© Corbis

STAR WATCHING—THE HOLLYWOOD KIND

They're everywhere. And nowhere. And when you see one, pretend that you haven't. That's the star treatment in L.A. Tom Hanks driving next to you? Who cares? Meg Ryan on the escalator? Look the other way. It's just another sunny day in LA.

If, however, you think seeing a few of the glitterati would top off your trip to SoCal—and allow you to respond affirmatively to the question "Did you see any stars out there?"—then try a few tricks of the star-spotting trade:

Drive around the B's: Bel Air, Beverly Hills, and Brentwood. But not too slowly. You'll be tapped as a tourist by the local police force and asked to move on.

Make reservations. If a pricey dinner isn't in your budget, maybe you could splash out for a lush lunch. Spago is still a popular spot, as is Les Deux Cafes. Or simply cruise through West L.A.; you might get lucky in spots where there is valet service and luxury cars in sight.

Squeeze the fruit. The Farmers Market is a source of produce and produces star-spottings aplenty. Remember: even Julia Roberts has to eat.

Window shop. It may be cliché, but try Rodeo Drive. Or loiter with intent at one of the cafés along the way. If you don't see anyone famous, at least you'll be able to regale your friends with your tale of how much you overpaid for your coffee.

Become an audience member. Call the studios in advance and see if you can get into a taping of one of the sitcoms or game shows. Then you'll be guaranteed to have seen someone of at least minor renown.

* Give in and take a tour of one of the studios. Studios usually dredge up some up-and-coming celebrity, or dust off someone from a bygone era. But, hey, it's a name.

APR.: *Easter Sunrise Services.* The Hollywood Bowl holds traditional Easter Morning Christian religious services as the sun rises. | 213/480–3232.

JULY: *Celebrate July 4th at the Hollywood Bowl.* Join nearly 18,000 other revelers at this blow-out concert and fireworks display. Listen to the L.A. Philharmonic Orchestra serenade the country and its birthday with a patriotic medley of American pops and Sousa marches. Boxed cold meals are available, or bring your own picnic. | 323/850–2000.

NOV.: *Hollywood Christmas Parade.* This nighttime Christmas parade along Sunset Blvd. from Hollywood Blvd. and Orange Ave. to Vine St. traditionally brings out a large number of celebrities. | 323/469–8311 | www.hollywoodchristmas.com.

Dining

Alto Palato Trattoria. Italian. This eatery with a dramatic modern glass facade is friendly, casual, and easy on the wallet. There might be a lot of Italian places in the area like this, but Alto Palato has true goods and a strong crowd of locals. The wood-fired arugula and prosciutto pizza provides a great beginning taste, while their homemade chocolate gelati finishes with a chocolaty richness. Open-air dining accommodates cooler evenings with canopy and heaters. No smoking. | 755 N. La Cienega Blvd., Los Angeles | 310/657–9271 | No lunch Sun.–Thurs. | $15–$35 | AE, DC, MC, V.

Antonio's. Mexican. This seek-it-out spot with lively musical accompaniment serves the complex, lively, yet not spicy cooking of one of Mexico's most respected culinary regions, Oaxaca. The standouts include the red, yellow, and brown moles. But be sure to check out pizza-like clayudas topped with white cheese and *tasajo* (dried beef), *cecino* (chili-marinated pork), *chorizo* (sausage), or barbecued goat tacos. No smoking. | 7470 Melrose Ave. | 323/655–0480 | $20–$30 | AE, MC, V.

Ca' Brea. Northern Italian. Starters make the meal here, such as baked goat cheese wrapped in pancetta and served atop a giant mound of spinach. You can follow this with lamb chops and black-truffle with mustard sauce or the very popular osso buco. Daily specials include soup, salad, pasta, and fish dishes. Terra-cotta or mustard-colored walls combined with dark wood paneling and cozy booths give the lively main room a warm Venetian look, and the cozy loft is ideal if you seek privacy. Trees provide shade and green coolness on the patio. No smoking. | 346 S. La Brea Ave., Los Angeles | 323/938–2863 | Closed Sun. No lunch Sat. | $15–$22 | AE, D, DC, MC, V.

Campanile. Mediterranean. This restaurant, housed in a warren of converted offices once used by Charlie Chaplin, serves rustic dishes influenced by French, Mediterranean, and California cuisines. Expect an upscale, urban crowd, one that appreciates the outstanding wine list and varied menu. Grilled sardines with marinated fennel, cedar-smoked king salmon with horseradish, sea bass in butter sauce, prime rib with olive tapenade, and pork loin with sweet potatoes and turnip greens are some of the richly flavored choices. For a romantic night, try to sit on the enclosed candlelit patio with a glass roof. Brunch Sat.–Sun. | 624 S. La Brea Ave. | 323/938–1447 | Reservations essential | No dinner Sun. | $16–$40 | AE, D, DC, MC, V.

Chan Dara. Thai. If you're looking for a young and lively crowd, consider this Asian restaurant. Try any of the noodle dishes, especially those with crab and shrimp. Also tops on the menu are *satay* (skewered meat appetizers with peanut sauce), barbecued chicken, grilled catfish, and clams topped with basil and chili sauce. | 1511 N. Cahuenga Blvd. | 323/464–8585 | Reservations advised | No lunch weekends | $10–$23 | AE, D, DC, MC, V.

Chianti Ristorante and Cucina. Northern Italian. Established in 1938, Chianti has a long and illustrious history as the oldest Northern Italian restaurant in L.A, which includes hosting the wrap party for the cast and crew of *Gone with the Wind*. The interior includes two dining areas, a venerable walnut bar, and marble floors. Grigliata di carni, scaloppine al funghi are local specialties. Beer and wine only. No smoking. | 7383 Melrose Ave. | 323/653–8333 | No lunch (Ristorante); No lunch Sun. (Cucina) | $15–$35 | AE, DC, MC, V.

★ **Citrus.** Contemporary. Seated under of the large umbrellas in the landscaped interior patio, you can see Melrose Avenue on one side and a glass-walled kitchen on the other. Lunch begins on the light side, with starters such as artichoke terrine or ahi tuna carpaccio, followed by chicken ravioli with Parmesan sauce. Dinner at this Hollywood industry favorite can be crab cakes with tomato-mustard sauce or chicken in porcini crust. No smoking. | 6703 Melrose Ave. | 323/857–0034 | Reservations essential | No lunch Sat., Sun. | $17–$31 | AE, DC, MC, V.

Fenix. Contemporary. Creative contemporary American dishes like Alaskan cod with Yukon gold risotto, daikon sesame salad, and grilled Texas black antelope only touch the surface on this rising star. Art deco styling and a terrace mix well with the culinary excellence. Popular dishes include the *le course* tasting menu and filet mignon. No smoking. | 8358 Sunset Blvd. | 323/848–6677 | Breakfast also available, Sun. breakfast and brunch only | $22–$34 | AE, D, DC, MC, V.

L'angolo. Italian. This high style, contemporary eatery with exquisite marble floors and high white walls serves an equally contemporary menu. The sautéed shrimp with a Thai cucumber salad, saffron fettuccine with thyme, or sautéed veal medallion with artichoke mousse and crawfish sauce illustrate a sampling of the unique culinary delights. No smoking. | 6602 Melrose Ave. | 323/935–4922 | Closed Mon. | $21–$35 | AE, MC, V.

Le Petit Four. Contemporary. The many mirrors inside this bistro reflect the clientelle—famous and otherwise—while big white umbrellas shade the patio in nice weather. Great salads complement the entrées or stand alone as a meal. The penne pasta with lemon butter and Parmesan cheese, chicken ravioli, and Norwegian salmon with herb butter are popular. Top off your meal with a selection of homemade baked goods (chocolate pecan cake is a specialty) and ice cream. No smoking. | 8654 Sunset Blvd. | 310/652–3863 | Breakfast also available (weekends), Sunday brunch | $20–$32 | AE, D, DC, MC, V.

L'Orangerie. French. It might be the most expensive European restaurant in town, but there's good reason. L'Orangerie serves some of the finest food in Southern California. Although the poached lobster tail on asparagus risotto or seabass fillet skewered with fennel branches are specialties, you're bound to have an incredible meal even if you close your eyes and point to make your selection. A courtyard terrace and patio add to the elegance. No smoking. | 903 N. La Cienega Blvd. | 310/652–9770 | Reservations essential | Jacket required | Closed Mon. No lunch | $30–$48 | AE, D, DC, MC, V.

Musso and Frank Grill. Continental. Opened in 1919, this is LA's oldest eatery and seems it, but in a very good way. Notables such as Orson Welles used to slide into the red-leather booths under the wood-beamed ceilings for a martini or two. This isn't exactly the weight watchers menu (which changes daily), but the comfort fare has kept people coming back for years. No smoking. | 6667 Hollywood Blvd. | 323/467–7788 | Closed Sun., Mon. | $18–$28 | AE, D, DC, MC, V.

★ **Patina.** Contemporary. The exterior is so understated that it's easy to miss; the interior is a study in spare elegance. Generally considered one of the best restaurants in Los Angeles, some of its mainstays include a corn blini filled with fennel-marinated salmon and crème fraîche, and scallops wrapped in potato slices with brown-butter vinaigrette. A pre-set menu is also available. No smoking. | 5955 Melrose Ave. | 323/467–1108 | Reservations essential | Lunch Fri. only | $28–$34; pre-set menu: $30–$80 | AE, D, DC, MC, V.

Pinot Hollywood. French. One of a chain of glamorous bistros, this one near Paramount Studios. At lunch try poached salmon salad with tomato vinaigrette. Dinner favorites are fresh grilled sardines a la Provençal or parsnip gnocchi with lobster and veal shank and caramelized root vegetables. Outdoor deck. No smoking. | 1448 N. Gower St. | 323/461–8800 | Closed Sun. | $17–$27 | AE, D, DC, MC, V.

Sonora Café. Southwestern. While southwestern cuisine isn't as fashionable as it used to be in Los Angeles, Sonora Café keeps the tradition alive and well on the La Brea strip. The Sante Fe–style dining room with wooden beams, copper chandeliers, and American

Indian upholstery perfectly showcases a consistently strong menu that includes Texas barbecued pork chops, green corn tamales, blue-corn muffins, and potent margaritas. A small patio connected to the bar seats up to six tables. No smoking. | 180 S. La Brea Ave., Los Angeles | 323/857–1800 | No lunch weekends | $17–$27 | AE, D, MC, V.

Lodging

Best Western Hollywood Hills. In a residential area, two four-story buildings built in 1949 provide views of the Hollywood sign from a few of the rooms. Two miles from Universal Studios and 2 blocks from Mann's Chinese Theater and the Hollywood Walk of Fame, this choice is all about location. Restaurant, room service. Some kitchenettes, refrigerators, cable TV. Pool. Business services. Some pets allowed (fee). | 6141 Franklin Ave. | 323/464–5181 | fax 323/962–0536 | www.bestwestern.com | 86 rooms | $99–$130 | AE, D, DC, MC, V.

Clarion Hollywood Roosevelt. After opening in 1927, this hotel became a haven for actors and writers, including Clark Gable and Carol Lombard, and Ernest Hemingway and F. Scott Fitzgerald. In the heart of Hollywood, these two 12-story Spanish Colonial buildings provide local history and access to many restaurants and sights. Several cabana rooms surround the Olympic-size swimming pool and courtyard. Restaurant, 2 bars (with entertainment), room service. Some in-room data ports, minibars, microwaves. Pool. Hot tub, massage. Exercise equipment. Laundry service. Business services. | 7000 Hollywood Blvd. | 323/466–7000 | fax 323/462–8056 | reserve@hollywoodroosevelt.com | www.hollywoodroosevelt.com | 288 rooms, 47 suites | $159, $250 suites | AE, D, DC, MC, V.

Days Inn Hollywood. This two-story hotel keeps you close to the action, with the Wax Museum and Walk of Fame 3 blocks to the northeast. The nearest beach is 10 mi west. Inside, the lobby has wood accents and marble flooring, and the rooms are decorated in plain yet comfortable furnishings. A Continental breakfast is served in the lobby. Some rooms overlook the pool area. Complimentary Continental breakfast. Some kitchenettes. Some in-room hot tubs, cable TV. Pool. Laundry services. Business services, free parking. | 7023 Sunset Blvd. | 323/464–8344 or 800/346–7723 | fax 323/962–9748 | www.daysinn.com | 72 rooms | $100–$125 | AE, D, DC, MC, V.

Hollywood Orchid Suites Hotel. If you plan to visit Mann's Chinese Theatre, you might consider this three-story hotel; it's right behind the famed cinema. It's also adjacent to Hollywood Boulevard and the Walk of Fame. The hotel was built in 1960. Junior suites have kitchenettes; all other suites have completely outfitted kitchens, right down to the toasters. Some suites have balconies. Complimentary Continental breakfast. In-room data ports. Kitchenettes. Microwaves, refrigerators, cable TV. Pool. Laundry facilities. Business services, free parking. | 1753 North Orchid Ave. | 323/874–9678 or 800/537–3052 | fax 323/874–5246 | www.orchidsuites.com | 40 rooms | $59–$99 | AE, D, DC, MC, V.

HOPLAND

(Nearby towns also listed: Boonville, Clear Lake Area, Lake County, Ukiah)

Hopland is nestled along U.S. 101 and the Russian River, in the heart of Mendocino wine country. A lush valley, this part of California boasts magnificent sunsets, many state parks and recreation areas with hiking trails and golf couses, and vineyards galore. The town's name comes from the hops, a grain used to make beer, that were cultivated from 1860 on for brewing beer. Prunes, walnuts, grapes, and pears displaced hops as the dominant crops in the 1940s. Today wine grapes and Bartlett pears provide the main agricultural harvest in Hopland, which is blessed with rich alluvial soil and a benign climate. Downtown Hopland remains fairly quaint, with a small main street that features the Hopland Brewery, which has several tasting rooms along the same block. Other wineries and breweries offer daily tastings as well.

Information: Hopland–Sanel Valley Chamber of Commerce | Box 677, 95449-0677 | 707/744–1379 | hopps@hoplandchamber.org | www.hoplandchamber.org.

Attractions

Fetzer Vineyards. You can tour the vineyards and wineries, and taste wine in the landscaped gardens, on the 7 acres of this all-organic vineyard. The bustling vineyard is a popular spot for tourists. | 13601 Eastside Rd. | 800/846–8637 | www.fetzer.com | Free | Daily 9–4.

Mendocino Brewing Company. American. This building, over 100 years old, is one of the oldest structures in Hopland and houses the Hopland Brewery, California's first brewpub since prohibition. Substantial beers and the European attitude that beer is food prevail at this pub, which brews about 200,000 barrels a year. The menu includes burgers, burritos, nachos, quesadillas, chicken sandwiches, and wings plus a daily special such as seafood pasta with salmon and snapper. | 13351 U.S. 101S | 707/744–1361 | $2.95–$7.50 | MC, V.

HUNTINGTON BEACH

MAP 9, H8

(Nearby towns also listed: Costa Mesa, Newport Beach)

One of Orange County's largest cities (pop. 181,500), Huntington Beach proudly touts its 8½-mi stretch of continuous beach linked by a paved bike/skate/pedestrian path. Named for Henry E. Huntington who brought the railroad to this one-time seaside village, the Central Library, Cultural Center, and 320-seat Playhouse also bear his name. The large shopping pavilion on Main Street, a lively pier with fishing and restaurants, and waters filled with surfing beckon. Before hitting the waves you can research the local surf history at the International Surfing Museum.

Information: Huntington Beach Chamber of Commerce | 2100 Main St., Suite 200, 92648 | 714/536–8888 | www.hbchamber.org.

Attractions

★ **Bolsa Chica Interpretive Center.** Established in 1990, the non-profit organization Bolsa Chica Conservancy attempts to ensure the preservation, restoration, and enhancement of the Bolsa Chica Wetlands. The 185-acre center illustrates and presents the cause to save the Bolsa Chica Ecological Reserve, one of the rapidly disappearing large wetlands area that hosts egrets, plovers, and avocets. The 1½-mi loop trail provides you with a close-up view of the wetlands and the wildlife. | 3842 Warner Ave. | 714/846–1114 or 888/265–7248 | Free (donations accepted) | Tues.–Fri. 10–4, Sat. 9–12, Sun. 12–3.

Huntington Beach Mall. Specialty shops and chain stores, such as a large Barnes and Noble, draw visitors to this mall on the coast. The Old World Village, a Bavarian theme shopping mall, sits across the street. | 7777 Edinger Ave. | 714/897–2533 | Free | Weekdays 10–9, Sat. 10–7, Sun. 11–6.

International Surfing Museum. A local museum with every detail of surfing you ever wanted to know, this facility carries its own collection of surfing memorabilia as well as special exhibits. These range from surfboards and swimsuits used by surfing legends, such as Corky Carroll an early enthusiast and one of the first paid professional surfers, to event posters and medallions. Dedicated in May 1994, the Huntington Beach Surfing Walk of Fame places a granite stone for each inductee in the sidewalk extending from the corners of Pacific Coast Highway and Main Street. Call ahead for hours. | 411 Olive | 714/960–3483 | www.surfingmuseum.org | Donations accepted.

JULY: *Bluetorch Pro of Surfing.* Watch the world's best surfers catch a wave at this five-day surfing championship, the only world-class event held in the continental U.S. The world's top pros, both men and women, compete for a total of $150,000 in prize money. Music, vendor booths, and food can also be found at the event. | 949/215–8008 | www.bluetorch.com.

Dining

Alice's Breakfast in the Park. Café. Tranquility reigns at this brunch spot, nestled among Huntington Park's eucalyptus trees near Huntington Lake. The cozy wooden building is filled with flowers and antiques. Outside, kids love to feed the ducks from the patio. Don't miss Alice's outrageous cinnamon rolls, freshly baked breads, and homemade muffins. More substantial fare includes pancakes, omelettes, and burgers. Kids' menu. | 6622 Lakeview Dr. | 714/848–0690 | Reservations not accepted | No dinner. Breakfast also available | $4–$7 | No credit cards.

Market Broiler. Seafood. This popular mesquite grilled seafood restaurant known for such samplings as halibut and swordfish also serves up some strong steak, chicken, and pasta dishes. The casual Southern California aura can help you relax. No smoking. | 20111 Brookhurst St. | 714/963–7796 | $8–$18 | AE, D, MC, V.

Wahoo's Fish Taco. Mexican. Three Chinese brothers, Brazilian-born but later moving to Southern California, own this widespread chain. Frequent surfing trips to Mexico sparked the idea for healthy fast-food eateries specializing in tacos, burritos, quesadillas and other Mexican fare. But the menu also pays tribute to the brothers Asian heritage, with "Da Plate Lunch"–choice of teriyaki steak, char-broiled or blackened chicken or fish, or teriyaki vegetables served with ahi rice and black or Cajun white beans. Surf stickers cover the walls. Lines can be long at peak times. Kids' menu. | 120 Main St. | 714/536–2050 | www.wahoos.com | Reservations not accepted | $5–$7 | MC, V.

Lodging

Best Western Regency Inn. This three-story hotel, off I–405, is 1½ mi from the beach. There are a restaurant and bar adjacent to the hotel. Complimentary Continental breakfast. Some refrigerators. Some in-room hot tubs, cable TV. Pool. Barbershop, beauty shop. Outdoor hot tub. Laundry services. | 19360 Beach Blvd. | 714/962–4244 or 888/962–4244 | fax 714/963–4724 | www.bestwestern.com | 64 rooms, 2 suites | $69–$99, $120 suite | AE, D, DC, MC, V.

Comfort Suites. An open, airy lobby, comfortable, contemporary rooms with soft coastal colors, and its location 5 mi north of the beach make this all-suites hotel an appealing choice. Complimentary Continental breakfast. Refrigerators, cable TV. Outdoor pool. Hot tub. Exercise equipment. Laundry facilities. | 16301 Beach Blvd. | 714/841–1812 | fax 714/841–0214 | www.comfortinn.com | 100 suites | $89–$99 suites | AE, D, DC, MC, V.

Hilton Waterfront Beach Resort. Practically on the beach, all rooms have an ocean view. The 12-story Mediterranean-style resort hotel was built in the early 1990s in a residential area, minutes from the Pier and the beach. Although it would appear that this hotel is best suited for those on vacation, there are also many amenities geared toward the business traveler. This resort prides itself in being able to accommodate your needs for a special event or a simple weekend getaway. Restaurant, bar (with entertainment). In-room data ports, minibars, cable TV. Pool. Hot tub. Tennis. Basketball, health club, volleyball. Beach, bicycles. Kids' programs (ages 2–8). Business services, airport shuttle. | 21100 Pacific Coast Hwy. | 714/960–7873 | fax 714/960–3791 | www.waterfrontbeachresort.hilton.com | 266 rooms, 24 suites | $179–$324, $369–$579 suites | AE, D, DC, MC, V.

Hotel Huntington Beach. A luxurious home away from home, just off I–405 and next to the Huntington Beach shopping mall, this eight-story hotel is 5 mi from the beach and just down the street from Golden West College. Fresh flower arrangements, extensive amenities such as full-time room service and exercise facilities, and an attentive staff make for a pleasant stay. Rooms are fairly luxurious; the hotel caters mainly to a corporate clientelle. Restaurant, bar. Refrigerators, cable TV. Indoor pool. Hot tub. Exercise equipment, health club. Business services, airport shuttle, free parking. | 7667 Center Ave. | 714/891–0123 | fax 714/895–4591 | www.hbhotel.com | 224 rooms | $95–$130 | AE, D, DC, MC, V.

Quality Inn. Built along the coast-hugging Pacific Coast Highway, this three-story hotel gives you quick access to the beach. Some rooms have balconies with ocean views. If you've packed the running shoes, you'll appreciate the nearby jogging track. Complimentary Continental breakfast. Some microwaves. Some refrigerators. Some in-room hot tubs, cable TV. Outdoor hot tub. Laundry services. Business services, free parking. | 800 Pacific Coast Hwy. | 714/536–7500 or 800/228–5151 | fax 714/536–6846 | www.qualityinn.com | 50 rooms | $89–$189 | AE, D, DC, MC, V.

Ramada Limited Sunset Beach. Across the street from the Sunset beach, most rooms have private patios or balconies with ocean views. The two-story hotel is approximately 30 minutes from the International Airport and 3 mi from the Huntington Beach pier. Complimentary Continental breakfast. Refrigerators, cable TV. Hot tub. Exercise equipment. Business services. | 17205 Pacific Coast Hwy., Sunset Beach | 714/840–2431 | fax 310/592–4093 | www.ramada.com | 50 rooms | $119–$149 | AE, D, MC, V.

IDYLLWILD

MAP 4, K15

(Nearby towns also listed: Cathedral City, Hemet, Palm Desert, Palm Springs, Rancho Mirage)

Perched high in the San Jacinto Mountains between Hemet on one side of the mountains and Palm Springs on the other, this eclectic resort community is popular with hikers and rock climbers. There are two large-slab climbing areas with enough cracks and crevices to keep you occupied for days. The town was founded in 1890 by George and Sarah Hannahs, who built the first sawmill for the fledgling lumber community, and later established the tent resort of Camp Idylwilde (the spelling of the town name changed later). Today, Idyllwild is popular as the starting point for countless adventure-seekers exploring thousands of pristine acres of state parks and national forests. Galleries and pubs can keep you busy in town. Before you go, call the chamber of commerce for road conditions.

Information: **Idyllwild Chamber of Commerce** | 54295 Village Dr., 92549 | 909/659–3259 | www.idyllwild.org.

Attractions

Hay Dude Ranch. Clippety-clop through pines, meadows, and rocky hill tops for panoramic views of the valley and mountains. You can take one- or two-hour guided trail rides, as well as sunset rides and overnight pack trips. The ranch also runs horse-drawn carriage and trolley rides around town, starting at the totem pole, which stands on Village Center Dr. off Ridgeview Dr., in the heart of town. Call for prices and reservations. | McCall Park, Rte. 74 | 909/763–2473 | www.idyllwild.com | Daily 9:30–4.

Mt. San Jacinto State Park and San Bernardino National Forest. A wilderness area adds to the 13,522 acres of State Park land bordered by the San Bernardino National Forest, Palm Springs, and Idyllwild. You can participate in numerous popular outdoor activities in the park, such as hiking, backpacking, picnicking, camping, cross-country skiing, and bird watching. If you are more adventurous, take a rock climbing expedition up Tahquitz and Suicide Rocks. If you do venture into the wilderness areas, even just for the day, be sure to pick up a permit (no fee) at the State Park headquarters in town. | 25905 Rte. 243, at Pine Crest Ave. | 909/659–2607 | www.sanjac.statepark.org | $2 per vehicle | Daily 24 hours; Ranger's Station: 8–5.

Within the San Jacinto wilderness area, **Tahquitz and Suicide Rocks,** internationally known climbing area, were first explored for technical climbing in the 1950s. Access begins in the village of Humber Park where North Circle Drive from Idyllwild ends. Even if you don't want to attempt the more technical routes, it's worth the steep hike up to Lunch Rock (pack a lunch) to view the expansive and mountainous valley below and to watch climbers as they grunt up the rockface that stretches above you.

In the space of 6 horizontal mi, these stupendous mountains rise in a rocky escarpment from less than 1,100 ft to the summit of 10,804-ft San Jacinto Peak, providing some of the greatest vertical relief anywhere in the nation. Starting in Chino Canyon on the north edge Palm Springs, Tramway Road off Route 111, 3½ mi up the hill, the **aerial tram** takes you from the Valley Station to Mountain Station and the visitor center on the edge of the Wilderness at elevation 8,516 ft. | Tramway Rd., Palm Springs | 760/325–1391 or 888/515–TRAM | www.pstramway.com | $19.65 | Weekdays 10–8, weekends and holidays 8–8.

Riverside County Parks. There are seven county parks spread throughout the Idyllwild mountain area, including: Lawler Lodge Park, a youth group site; Pine Cove Park with 19 acres of controlled access; Idyllwild Park; Idyllwild Park Nature Center; Indian Relic Archaeological Site; McCall Memorial Park; and Hurkey Creek. Camping reservations are recommended during peak seasons. | 4600 Crestmore Rd., Riverside | 800/234–PARK | www.co.riverside.ca.us/riverside.asp | $2 | 8 AM–dusk.

With 202 acres, camping, equestrian trails, hiking/interpretive trails, picnic facilities, **Idyllwild Park** can keep you busy with outdoor activities. Only 1 mi north of town at the end of County Park Road, you can, if you're feeling energetic, walk into town. | County Park Rd. | 909/659–2656 | $2 | 8 AM–dusk.

On Route 243 1 mi north of town, the **Idyllwild Park Nature Center** has an interpretative facility that includes a museum, environmental education, and interpretive programs, exhibit and trails. | 55233 Hwy. 243 | 909/659–3850 | $2 | 8 AM–dusk.

On Pine Crest Avenue, 1 mi north of Idyllwild, the undeveloped **Indian Relic Archaeological Site** is worth a gander, just to see the progress on this archaeological dig. You can obtain more information at the Nature Center. | Pine Crest Ave. | 909/659–3850 | 8 AM–dusk.

Mountain fishing, camping, and picnicking along scenic **Hurkey Creek** provide beautiful views during all seasons. This park contains 59 acres and 91 developed campsites, including group camping. | 56375 Hwy. 74, Mountain Center | 909/659–2050 | $2 | 8 AM–dusk.

ON THE CALENDAR

AUG.: *Idyllwild Jazz in the Pines.* A worldwide collection of artists keep the music coming at this two-day event, held at the Idyllwild Arts Campus. You'll hear jazz, blues, gospel, Latin, fusion, and funk at three different venues. No pets. | 909/659–3774.

Dining

Gastrognome. American. Referred to by regulars as "The Gnome," the restaurant is nestled in the middle of a pine forest with a view of Tahquitz Peak. The rough hewn rustic cabin and large stone fireplace inside provide a perfect backdrop for such dishes as baby salmon brushed with garlic butter and hollandaise, rack of New Zealand lamb, and pecan pie made with Mary Alice's secret recipe. Seasonal patio dining has seating for about 50 people. No smoking. | 54381 Ridgeview | 909/659–5055 | Sunday brunch | $6–$40 | D, DC, MC, V.

Idyllwild Café. American. Red-and-white trim brightens the outside of this gingerbread-style café. It's cheerful inside, too, with polished wood, blue-and-white-checkered curtains, and a rack of coffee mugs bearing the names of the regular customers. Morning finds them enjoying hearty, Western-style breakfasts of biscuits and gravy, waffles, and eggs. When leaves start to fall outside, look for special pumpkin pancakes. For lunch, there are rib-eye steak sandwiches, burgers, and salads. Kids' menu. | 26600 Rte. 243 | 909/659–2210 | No dinner | $5–$7 | D, MC, V.

Jo'Ann's Restaurant. American. This casual spot in the middle of town has a wide-ranging menu of traditional American fare with a few international offerings tossed into the mix. Eat inside or, when weather permits, on the outside patio. Start the day with an omelette, French toast or other breakfast fare. For lunch, choose from assorted hot and cold sandwiches such as classic Reubens and tuna melts. Dinner features large portions of steaks and seafood, plus Irish stew and teriyaki chicken. Friday and Saturday are prime rib nights. | 25070 N. Village Center Dr. | 909/659–0295 | Closed Wed. | $6–$16 | AE, D, MC, V.

Vercollini's Italian Restaurant. Italian. Formerly the River Rock Cafe, tucked in a stand of pines just off the highway, this cozy, casual restaurant has a selection of pastas, small pizzas, and other local favorites such as Vercollini scampi and baked meat and cheese lasagna. Top it all off with homemade ice cream. Kids' menu. Beer and wine only. No smoking. | 26290 Rte. 243 | 909/659–5047 | Reservations not accepted | Closed Mon.–Wed. and early to mid-Dec.; No lunch | $18–$27 | D, MC, V.

Lodging

Cedar Street Inn. On a quiet street, this inn is actually two 1930s cottages and three cabins, all within walking distance of the village, hiking trails, and Strawberry Creek. Furnishings are a mix of English country and New England nautical-style pieces, with a few antiques. The cabins accommodate up to four guests each, and have a hot tub and kitchen. Two cabins also have fireplaces, as do all rooms in the cottages. One cabin has a private deck. Some kitchenettes, microwaves, refrigerators, some in-room hot tubs, cable TV. No smoking. | 25880 Cedar St. | 909/659–4789 | fax 909/659–1049 | www.cedarstreetinn.com | 8 cottage rooms, 3 cabins | $110–$125 cabins; $130 cottage | AE, MC, V.

Cedar View Cottage. This 1920s gingerbread-style cottage was once owned by Dwight Taylor, author of *Top Hat* and other Fred Astaire films. Built of knotty pine and tucked into a woodsy corner of town, this housekeeping cottage, rented as a single unit, has a make-yourself-comfortable appeal, with a stereo and CD collection, lots of books and videos, espresso maker, popcorn popper, a gas grill on the back deck, fresh flowers, and a chocolate on your pillow at the end of the day. Downstairs there's a living room, fireplace, full kitchen, dining nook, queen-size bed and full bath. Upstairs, stretch out in a loft with 2 twin beds and ½-bath. Cable TV, in-room VCRs. Pets allowed (fee). | 25165 Cedar St. | 909/659–3339 (info) or 909/659–2966 (reservations) | www.towncrier.com/inns/cedarview.html | 1 cottage | $110–$125 | AE, D, MC, V.

Fern Valley Inn. You can hibernate in one of these cottages under the pine trees. Each cottage contains western antiques and such surprises as hand-made quilts, rock fireplace, or cedar walls. In the residential area of Fern Valley, this inn is ½ mi from Idyllwild. Several cottages have a full kitchen including pots, pans, dishes, utensils and condiments. Some kitchenettes, microwaves, refrigerators, cable TV, in-room VCRs. Pool. No smoking. | 25240 Fern Valley Rd. | 909/659–2205 | fax 909/659–2630 | www.fernvalleyinn.com | 11 cottages | $80–$125 cottages | MC, V.

Fireside. Nestled within the San Jacinto Mountains 3 blocks from the village center, you can sit back and feed the squirrels, birds, and raccoons from your front porch. If you're lucky, you may even see a black squirrel. Each cottage has a distinctive personality and rustic design, a fireplace, and sitting room; several have private porches and kitchens. Picnic area. Some refrigerators, some kitchenettes, cable TV, in-room VCRs, no room phones. Some pets allowed. No smoking. | 54540 N. Circle Dr. | 909/659–2966 | www.idyll-wild.com/fireside.htm | 7 duplex cottages, 1 private | $60–$110 cottages | AE, D, MC, V.

Pine Cove Inn. On a three-acre, wooded lot, this B&B has an apartment for two, three A-frame chalets, and a 1930s lodge, which also has a common lounge area and dining room. Gas, electric, or woodburning fireplaces provide cozy warmth. All rooms have porches or decks where you can smell the pines, watch the wildlife, and gaze at the imposing visages of the surrounding mountains. If you're looking for a meal or shopping, the Idyllwild village center is 3 mi south. Dining room, picnic area, complimentary breakfast. Microwaves, refrigerators. No room phones, TV in sitting room. Business services. | 23481 Rte. 243 | 909/659–5033 | fax 909/659–5034 | www.idyllwild.com/pinecove.htm | 10 rooms (3 with shower only) in 4 buildings | $70–$100 | AE, MC, V.

Quiet Creek Inn. The scent of cedar wafts subtly through each of the five high-ceilinged cabins built in 1985 in a residential area just south of town. Strawberry Creek runs through the grounds with picnic tables and chairs creek side below your cabin. Picnic area. Kitchenettes, cable TV, no room phones. Business services. | 26345 Delano Dr. | 909/659–6110 or 800/450–6110 | www.quietcreekinn.com | 5 rooms, 5 suites | 10 rooms in 5 cabins | $80 rooms, $93 suites | MC, V.

Silver Pines Lodge and Creekside Cabins. Built in 1923 and an inn since the early 1950s, this rustic collection of free-standing cabins and rooms sits on 1½ acres of wooded pine forest overlooking Strawberry Creek, 2 blocks from the village. Overstuffed chairs in the 1,100-square-ft main lodge room invite you to set a spell. Most lodge rooms have fireplaces; some also have kitchens. Or, use the gas grill on the lodge's back deck. Several of the larger cabins work well for families, and all of the rooms have porches. Refrigerators, cable TV. No room phones. Pets allowed (fee). No smoking. | 25955 Cedar St. | 909/659–4335 | www.silverpinesidyllwild.com | 6 cabins; 11 rooms | $55–$130 cabins; $55–$90 rooms | AE, D, MC, V.

Strawberry Creek Inn. A large rambling home nestled in the mountains, Strawberry Creek runs along the edge of the property. Surrounded by pine and oak forest, a cedar shingled exterior leads to a glassed-in porch where you can enjoy breakfast and the wildlife. Each room in this 1941, two-story lodge, has a personal touch to make it unique. A library common area with a fireplace, outdoor decks, and hammocks are there for you to relax; soak up the sun in the summer or watch the snow fall in the winter. Complimentary breakfast (for rooms in Inn), some in-room VCRs, no TV in some rooms. No smoking. | 26370 Rte. 243 | 909/659–3202 or 800/262–8969 | www.strawberrycreekinn.com | 9 rooms, 1 cottage | $89–$115, $150 cottage | D, MC, V.

Woodland Park Manor. These 11 cottages sit on five acres of pine and cedar forest in the Fern Valley area of Idyllwild. All cottages have redwood construction with fireplaces and floor-to-ceiling windows overlooking a deck. Built in the 1950s, rooms are simple and cozy, with open beam ceilings and wood-paneled walls. The manor also has rental homes available. Picnic area. Some kitchenettes, in-room VCRs (and movies). Pool. Playground. | 55350 S. Circle Dr. | 909/659–2657 | fax 909/659–2988 | www.woodlandparkmanor.com | 11 cottages, 5 rental homes | $75–$165 | MC, V.

INDIAN WELLS

MAP 4, L15

(Nearby towns also listed: Cathedral City, Desert Hot Springs, Indio, Joshua Tree National Park, La Quinta, Palm Desert, Rancho Mirage)

East of Rancho Mirage in the Coachella Valley, Indian Wells began its current history late in the 1860s as a stop along the Bradshaw stage line. This access opened the site of old Native American Indian wells in the area to agricultural development. In 1917 Caleb Cook moved from Los Angeles into the vicinity of Indian Wells to become a successful date farmer. For the next forty years the fertile valley lured agricultural settlers to the area. In the 1950s, President Eisenhower golfed at Indian Wells; he was so impressed with that it became his winter residence. In 1960, the first Bob Hope Desert Classic was played at Indian Wells Country Club forever making Indian Wells synonymous with top-ranked golf. Tennis and golf courses developed rapidly, and the town incorporated in 1967.

Now an exclusive and meticulously maintained city, Indian Wells encompasses 14 square mi adjacent to Palm Desert on Route 111. By some measures, it's the wealthiest city in California, with some vacant lots fetching upwards of $1 million from the wealthy elite, including Lee Iacocca, Bill Gates, and John Elway, quarter-back for the Denver Broncos. No powerlines mar the desert skyline. Neither do school yards or gas stations. There's not even a pothole in sight. Scenery alternates between picturesque desert and lush manicured greenery.

Information: **Palm Desert Chamber of Commerce** | 73710 Fred Waring Dr., Suite 114, Palm Desert, 92260 | 760/346–6111 | info@pdcc.org | www.indianwells.org.

ON THE CALENDAR

MAR.: *Tennis Masters Series Indian Wells.* Top men and women pros serve, volley, and smash at this premier tennis event, held in a sparkling $77 million facility, completed in 2000; Indian Wells Tennis Garden includes three stadiums (the main one seating 16,000 spectators), 189 acres of gardens, 11 sunken tennis courts, and a halfdozen practice courts. | 800/999–1585 | www.masters-series.com.

Dining

Santa Rosa Grill. Mediterranean. Dine under the desert sky—or at least a mural of it—at this restaurant in the Hyatt Grand Champions Resort. Sit in the comfortable dining room beneath that ceiling-spanning painting and enjoy coconut shrimp, calamari steak, fresh sea bass or red snapper, steaks, veal, chicken, pasta, or one of many specialty pizzas. Outside on the terrace, take in the view of the golf course and surrounding San Jacinto Mountains. | 44-600 Indian Wells Lane | 760/674–4165 | $15–$25 | AE, D, DC, MC, V.

Sirocco. Mediterranean. This romantic room in the Renaissance Esmerelda Resort surrounds you with views of waterfalls, green fairways, and mountain vistas. Chefs prepare nightly specials such as ahi tuna served with fried polenta, roasted peppers and saffron-leek sauce, beef tenderloin with mushroom risotto, and veal tortellini. Fresh fish and shellfish are flown from across the country. | 44-400 Indian Wells La. | 760/773–4444 | No lunch | $18–$30 | AE, D, DC, MC, V.

Vicky's of Santa Fe. American. This casual restaurant, here since 1989, looks like a little piece of the Southwest, with adobe architecture, high ceilings, and warm desert-sunset colors. Original artwork lines the walls of the three dining rooms. The menu includes whole rotisserie chicken, New York strip steak and filet mignon (corn-fed Nebraska beef), veal chops, rack of New Zealand lamb, tiger shrimp, broiled halibut, and Norwegian salmon. After dinner, sink into a sofa by the fire in the softly lit piano bar (music begins at 6:30 nightly). | 45100 Club Dr. | 760/345–9770 | www.desert-resorts.com/vickyssf | No lunch | $16–$22 | DC, MC, V.

Lodging

Hyatt Grand Champions Resort. Expansive courtyards, sparkling fountains, formal gardens, and celebrated artwork can keep you occupied from the moment you cross the threshold, without even considering the golf course and tennis courts. The suites at this five-story Hyatt resort feature step-down parlors and a balcony or patio. There are also penthouse accommodations and garden villas. Built in 1988 on 35 acres at the foot of California's San Jacinto mountains, the grounds include impeccably landscaped lawns with pristine views overlooking the golf course and pools, as well as the San Jacinto Mountains. This versatile resort, a mecca for business and vacation travelers, is 10 mi southeast of the Living Desert, the Desert Museum, and the Oasis Water Park; Palm Desert Business Center is 10 mi to the west, and downtown Palm Springs is 20 mi to the northwest. Guests have privileges to the public golf course. Restaurant. Pool. Steam room. Golf, tennis. Playground. Laundry service. Business services. Some pets allowed. | 44-600 Indian Wells La. | 760/341–1000 | fax 760/568–2236 | www.grandchampions.hyatt.com/champ/ | 338 suites | $290–$375 | AE, D, DC, MC, V.

Indian Wells Resort Hotel. With virtually boundless views of the Santa Rosa Mountains—and overlooking the Indian Wells Country Club—this two-story hotel connects with nature at every turn. A light contemporary style dominates the rooms, evoking cool, elegant comfort, with pool or desert mountain views. Common areas have contemporary furnishings, and there is a pond with palm trees beneath a circular stairway. Some suites have marble baths. Restaurant, 2 bars. Pool. Beauty salon, massage. 3 golf courses, tennis. Gym, health club. Business services. | 76-661 Rte. 111 | 760/345–6466 | fax 760/772–5083 | info@indianwellsresort.com | www.indianwellsresort.com | 130 rooms, 25 suites | $129–$269 | AE, D, DC, MC, V.

Miramonte Resort. A retreat on 11 lush and landscaped acres at the base of the Santa Rosa Mountains in the heart of Indian Wells, Miramonte is a series of 12 two-story villas with plenty of outdoor lounging areas to relax and enjoy the warmth of the sun, or conduct business if you must. The Italianate design incorporates arches and columns, with stonework and wrought-iron touches. Each room has a private terrace and either a king-size bed or two queens, with marble baths and luxury bath products. Restaurant, room service. Pool. Spa. Gym. Laundry service. Business services. Some pets allowed. | 4500 Indian Wells La. | 760/341–2200 | fax 760/568–0541 | info@miramonteresort.com | www.miramonte-resort.com | 177 rooms, 45 suites | $239–$279 rooms; $299–$399 suites | AE, D, DC, MC, V.

Renaissance Esmeralda Resort. The spectacular lobby has faux marble floors, a fountain and a curved double stairway leading to a large and gracious leisure area. Rooms are light and airy, in cool, crisp colors with mediterrenean-style wood furniture. Noted as having one of the best resort pool facilities in the United States; one pool has a sandy beach entrance, another a 20-ft waterfall. Kid's programs are offered daily from 9AM–1PM for $30, and include lunch, a tour of the hotel, and a free T-shirt. 3 restaurants, bar (with entertainment). 3 pools, wading pool. Hot tub, sauna, steam room. 2 18-hole golf courses, tennis. Exercise equipment, gym, health club, volleyball. Baby-sitting, children's programs (ages 5–12). Laundry service. Business services, airport shuttle. | 44-400 Indian Wells La. | 760/773–4444 | fax 760/346–9308 | www.renaissancehotels.com/pspsr/ | 560 rooms | $240–$288 | AE, D, DC, MC, V.

Sands Hotel at Indian Wells. Wet or dry? You choose at this two-story hotel, as rooms overlook either the desert landscape or the pool. The hotel, 1 mi from about 10 golf courses and 2 mi from Palm Desert, is adjacent to The Nest Restaurant and Lounge, which is open for lunch and dinner. Or, do it yourself: barbecue pits are available in a guest picnic area. Studios sleep up to 4, 1-bedrooms sleep up to 6. Some rooms have Murphy beds. Picnic area. Some kitchenettes, some microwaves, refrigerators, cable TV. Pool. Hot tub. Putting green. Playground. Laundry facilities. Free parking. | 75-188 Rte. 111 | 760/346–8113 | fax 760/568–3698 | 48 rooms | $59–$159 | AE, DC, MC, V.

INDIO

MAP 4, L15

(Nearby towns also listed: Indian Wells, La Quinta, Palm Desert)

One hundred forty miles southeast of Los Angeles lies this largely agricultural town of 36,800. In 1886, C. P. Huntington, president of the Southern Pacific Railroad, took a trip to Algeria, bringing back a few date shoots he gave to a local farmer. Indio is now the largest producer of dates in the Western World, and its annual National Date Festival draws upwards of 275,000 people. Indio also hosts the Desert Circuit, the country's largest horse shoe jumping (hunter-jumper) show in which riders compete for more than $1 million in prize money.

Information: Indio Chamber of Commerce | 82-503 Rte. 111, 92201 | 760/347–0676 or 800/44–INDIO | fax 760/347–6069 | indiochmbr@aol.com | www.indiochamber.org.

Attractions

All American Canal. This historic canal brought water to the Indio region, enabling the rich agricultural development. Authorized for construction under the Boulder Canyon Project Act of 1928, the 80-mi-long All American Canal serves the Imperial and Coachella valleys in southern California and the Yuma Project in both California and Arizona. | 760/347–0676 or 800/44–INDIO | Free | Daily.

Coachella Valley Museum and Cultural Center. Learn about local history here, with displays on date farming and other agriculture, Cahuilla Indian artifacts, and assorted heirlooms donated by locals. | 82-616 Miles Ave. | 760/342–6651 | Free. Donations welcome | Oct.–May, Wed.–Sat. 10–4, Sun. 1–4; June and Sept., weekends only. Closed July–Aug.

Fantasy Springs Casino. The Cabazon Band of Mission Indians make the arid and sun-drenched Coachella Valley home. The tribe's casino provides jobs for more than 500 people. The casino began operations in 1988 and has grown over the years to a 95,000-square-ft gaming and entertainment venue. Voted the No. 1 casino in the Palm Springs desert resorts region between 1995 and 2000 by those who frequent resorts in the area, Fantasy Springs Casino attracts more than one million visitors annually. The Casino has numerous card games, machines, and off-track horsewagers, and there is live music Wednesday through Sunday evenings. Covered outdoor smoking patio. | 84-245 Indio Springs Dr. | 760/342–5000 | fax 760/347–7880 | www.fantasyspringsresort.com | Free | Daily 24 hours.

General George S. Patton Memorial Museum. The Patton Memorial Museum contains memorabilia from World War II and other eras of American military history. Displays include a relief map illustrating desert training camp sites, tanks and artillery, and a video which highlights Patton's life and career. East of Indio 24 mi, this is a site worth visiting if for nothing else but the scenic drive through the desert. | 2 Chiriaco Rd. | 760/227–3483 | $4 | Daily 9:30–4:30.

Salton Sea State Recreation Area. The Salton Sea is one of the world's largest inland bodies of saltwater, measuring 35 by 15 mi. Created in 1905 by the flooding Colorado River, the Sea is fairly shallow with an average depth of less than 20 ft. The climate surrounding the sea is typically extremely hot and dry in mid-summer and is best from October to June. You can hike, fish, swim, water-ski, and boat, though do watch out for your boat's propeller in these shallow waters. About 15 mi southeast of Indio. | 10025 State Park Rd., North Shore | 760/393–3052 or 393–3059 | www.cal-parks.ca.gov/DISTRICTS/colorado/salton-sea/sssra623.htm | $2 per vehicle | Daily 24 hours.

ON THE CALENDAR

FEB.: *Riverside County Fair and National Date Festival.* Livestock and agricultural exhibits, amusement rides, and food (specializing in date recipes) highlight this mid-winter festival Feb. 18–27 at Riverside Fairgrounds on Hwy. 111. | 760/863–8247.
FEB.: *Southwest Arts Festival.* Since 1987, this three-day festival, usually held the first weekend of the month on the festival grounds, highlights over 150 traditional and contemporary artists from all over the Southwest. | 760/347–0676 | www.swartfest.com.
DEC.: *Indio International Tamale Festival.* A celebration of Indio's cultural heritage with food, fun, and entertainment including cooking demonstrations in Old Town Indio. This once-small town festival now draws over 70,000 for a two-day weekend. The tamale contests are the highlight for sure; come hungry. | 760/347–0676 or 800/44–INDIO.

Dining

Ciro's Ristorante and Pizzeria. Italian. It's pizza, pizza, pizza at this casual eatery, family owned and run since 1966. Though you could order spaghetti or other pasta or perhaps a meatball sandwich, pizza reigns supreme, with toppings ranging from the traditional pepperoni, Italian sausage, and mushrooms, to jazzier offerings such as jalapeño and onions, smoked oysters, and pineapple with Canadian bacon. Eat in or take out. Kids' menu. | 81-

963 Hwy. 111 | 760/347–6503 | fax 760/347–8598 | Reservations not accepted | No lunch Sun. | $8–$13 | AE, D, MC, V.

Lodging

Best Western Date Tree. Surrounded by palm trees and cactus gardens, this two-story Best Western 2 mi north of downtown has adopted the unique landscape native to the area for its landscaping. It's less than 3 mi from virtually all of Indio's attractions. Suites with kitchenettes can accommodate you for an extended stay. Restaurant, picnic area, complimentary Continental breakfast. In-room data ports, refrigerators, cable TV. Pool. Hot tub. Exercise equipment. Video games. Playground. Laundry facilities. Business services. Some pets allowed. | 81-909 Indio Blvd. | 760/347–3421 or 800/292–5599 | fax 760/347–3421 | www.datetree.com | 119 rooms | $49–$109 | AE, D, DC, MC, V.

Quality Inn. Two blocks south of I–10 at the Monroe St. exit, this three-story inn received a facelift in 2000. Interior corridors and some handicap facilities make this hotel easily accessible. Free newspapers are a special morning treat along with your breakfast. Complimentary Continental breakfast. Some microwaves, refrigerators, cable TV. Pool. Hot tub. Business services. Pets allowed. | 43505 Monroe St. | 760/347–4044 | fax 760/347–1287 | www.comfortinn.com | 63 rooms | $49–$119 | AE, D, DC, MC, V.

Travelodge. Just off I–10 at the Washington St. exit, this dependable chain hotel consists of a two-story unit and is within 3 mi of golf courses and the Riverside Fairground, home to the annual Indio Date Festival. If you packed the racket, check out the on-site tennis court next to the pool. Cable TV. Pool, hot tub. Tennis court. Laundry service. Business services, free parking. Some pets allowed (fee). | 80651 Hwy. 111 | 760/342–0882 or 888/515–6375 | fax 760/342–7560 | www.travelodge.com | 50 | $39–$109 | AE, D, DC, MC, V.

INVERNESS

MAP 3, C7

(Nearby towns also listed: Bodega Bay, Petaluma, Point Reyes Station)

When Bay Area residents want to get away close to home, one of the favorite places to head to is Inverness. It's only an hour or so from the urban world, but provides a serenity usually reserved for the back country. It's also a good place to refuel and pick up supplies on the way to Pt. Reyes National Seashore. The Czech-style architecture—peaked roofs and compact buildings—is the result of a crew of Czech sailors who jumped ship and settled here in 1935 when their freighter ran aground.

A devastating fire in 1996 destroyed many homes and businesses around Inverness, and tourists stayed away. The area is back on its feet now, and you're advised to make dinner reservations for popular restaurants. To make impromptu visits easier, a coalition of hoteliers operates a telephone and website service, Point Reyes Lodging, that tells you where rooms are available for the upcoming weekend. Call 415/663–1872 or check www.ptreyes.com.

Information: Drakes Beach Information Center | Drakes Beach Rd., 94937 | 415/669–1250.

Attractions

Heart's Desire Beach. The water at this popular swimming beach is warmer than in less-protected parts of the Point Reyes area. Hiking trails, rest rooms, showers, and a picnic area with grills provide a comfortable site to spend the day. | Free.

Johnson's Oyster Company. Drive down the crunchy driveway littered with bleached-white shells at this bustling oyster farm, where workers harvest shellfish from adjacent Tomales Bay. Several sizes of oysters are for sale, shucked or not. The staff is happy to give you a deft demonstration of how to wield a shucking knife. | 17171 Sir Francis Drake Blvd. | 415/669–1149 | Closed Mon.

★ **Point Reyes National Seashore.** This seashore has all a wild shoreline can provide: windswept headlands, dunes, tide pools, and secluded beaches on 65,300 acres of protected park land. Inland rolling hills and freshwater lakes link together with more than 140 mi of hiking and horse trails, 35 of which are open to bicycles. There are four hike-in campgrounds. Educational areas include Kule Loklo, a replica of a Miwok Indian village; Pierce Ranch with self-guided tour of the former dairy ranch; Point Reyes Lighthouse; and Point Reyes Bird Observatory. You can spot harbor seals, sea lions, and migrating gray whales in season from observation points. Visit Bear Valley Visitor Center for information and camping permits. On weekends beginning in December and continuing through April, Sir Francis Drake Boulevard at Drake's Beach is closed to private vehicles; the Park provides an on-demand shuttle bus from Drake's Beach to the lighthouse and back, with an additional leg to Chimney Rock. | Sir Francis Drake Blvd. | 415/663–1092 | www.nps.gov/pore | Free; shuttle $3.50 per person | Daily dawn to dusk.

Samuel P. Taylor State Park. A 2,700-acre park with 60 campsites nestled among redwoods, this area has many wilderness activities ranging from a swimming hole to hilly hiking trails with occasional ocean views. If you're camping in the summer, make reservations well in advance; the sites fill rapidly between May and September. | Sir Francis Drake Blvd. | 415/488–9897 | www.parks.ca.gov/north/marin/sptsp233.htm | $5 per vehicle | Mar.–Oct., daily.

Tomales Bay State Park. Sheltered coves, surf-free beaches, tidal marshes, and Bishop pine forests occupy much of this 2,000-acre park north of Inverness on Point Pierce Road. A popular area for swimming, clamming, picnicking, and boating, you can best explore this area by sea-kayak or hiking. A short self-guided interpretive trail identifies native plants and provides some history for the area once home to the Miwok Indians. | 415/669–1140 | $2 per vehicle | Daily dawn to dusk.

ON THE CALENDAR

JULY: *Big Time Festival at Kule Loklo.* Following the Native American tradition of the annual gathering, this family-friendly event gives you a hands-on chance to try assorted Indian skills, such as basketry, and flint knapping—arrowhead making. Held at a reconstructed village site in the Point Reyes National Seashore, the event gives a glimpse into tribal life. Watch Native American dance groups perform, and peruse plenty of handmade crafts. To reach the event, usually held on a Saturday, walk ¼ mi along a gentle path starting at the park's Bear Valley Visitor Center. | 415/663–1092 | www.nps.gov/pore/home.htm.

Dining

Grey Whale. American. A casual café overlooking Tomales Bay where you can relax in the salt-scented air, or warm yourself inside on cooler days. They claim to serve the best vegetarian pizza in three counties, and other pizzas, hot and cold sandwiches, and salads complete the menu. There are high-chairs and toys for kids. Beer and wine only. | 12781 Sir Francis Drake Blvd. | 415/669–1244 | $8–$15 | MC, V.

Manka's Inverness Lodge Restaurant. American. Built as a hunting lodge in 1917, this became one of the first restaurants in the area. Candles in three wood-paneled dining rooms lend a romantic touch at dinner. Known for fresh-caught fish and wild game grilled in a fireplace. You can expect unique daily specials including local king salmon and rabbit. Kids' menu. Beer and wine only. | 30 Calendar Way | 415/669–1034 | Reservations essential | Closed Tues., Wed.; No lunch | $20–$30 | MC, V.

Lodging

Blackthorne Inn. Built in 1982 from salvaged railway station doors and timber from the San Francisco wharves, this Inn truly exudes rustic history, including mythical magic. The living room has a stone fireplace and stained-glass window, while the overall architecture resembles a tree house architecture. An expansive 3,500-square-ft partially shaded sundeck, gives you a secluded area up above the grounds and a firepole as a descent option to the ground. Complimentary Continental breakfast. Hot tub. Business services. No smoking. | 266 Vallejo Ave. | 415/663–8621 | www.blackthorneinn.com | 5 rooms (2 with shared bath) | $175–$300 | MC, V.

Hotel Inverness. With sweeping views of forested parklands, the redwood-shrouded Inverness Ridge, and peaceful Tomales Bay, this 1906 hotel makes a tranquil retreat. It's a quick leg-stretch to the tiny village's shops and restaurants. Rooms each have their own look, such as the lively chili-red hues of Room 3, or Room 4's Bentwood-style queen canopy bed made from willow trees. That room also has a private deck. Enjoy breakfast in your room, on the main deck, or in the pretty garden. Complimentary breakfast. No TV. No room phones. No smoking. | 25 Park Ave. | 415/669–7393 | fax 415/669–1702 | www.hotelinverness.com | 5 rooms | $135–$195 | MC, V.

Manka's Inverness Lodge. Built in 1917, the lodge is surrounded by 8,000 acres of Point Reyes National Seashore, which has biking and hiking trails, gentle bay beaches, and wildlife. Vintage fishing gear and local artifacts decorate the rustic wood beams and evoke a hunting lodge aura. Deep red and black plaids reflect the warmth of the fireplaces. Rooms have log framed beds and deep comfy reading chairs. Restaurant, complimentary breakfast. In-room data ports, some kitchenettes, refrigerators, cable TV, in-room VCRs. Some room phones. Hiking. Business services. Some pets allowed (fee). No smoking. | 30 Calendar Way | 415/669–1034 or 800/585–5634 | fax 415/669–1598 | www.mankas.com | 8 rooms (4 with shower only), 1 suite, 2 cabins | $215–$465 | MC, V.

Point Reyes Seashore Lodge. This elegant country inn encompasses two acres of beautifully landscaped gardens with many paths and ocean views. Fireplaces, decks, and whirlpools are available in some rooms. The attractive grounds make this lodge a popular venue for weddings, banquets, and conferences. Restaurant, complimentary Continental breakfast. Some refrigerators, some in-room hot tubs, cable TV (and movies), TV in common area. Business services. | 10021 Rte. 1 | 415/663–9000 or 800/404–5634 (in CA) | fax 415/663–9030 | www.pointreyesseashore.com | 21 rooms (7 with shower only), 3 suites | $125–$165, $205–$295 suites | AE, D, MC, V.

Sandy Cove. Balconies reach out from every room in this B&B on four acres at Point Reyes National Seashore. The Cape Cod style brings a touch of New England to the Pacific coast, with antique pine furniture and fireplaces or woodburning stoves in every room. You'll discover magnificent beaches and glorious wildflower-covered hills, quiet lagoons, hidden streams and meadows, enchanting woods and curious wildlife all from trails out of Sandy Cove. Breakfast, perhaps pumpkin-pecan pancakes and grilled pears, comes from the organic garden. Restaurant, picnic area, complimentary breakfast. In-room data ports, refrigerators. Beach. Business services. No smoking. | 12990 Sir Francis Drake Blvd. | 415/669–2683 | fax 415/669–7511 | innkeeper@sandycove.com | www.sandycove.com | 3 rooms (2 with shower only) | $200–$300 | AE, D, MC, V.

Ten Inverness Way. Antiques, handmade quilts, and fresh flowers abound in this turn-of-the-20th-century shingle house one block from Tomales Bay. In the rural and naturally scenic area, you can view Tomales Bay from the house's garden. Rooms are painted in warm tones and accented with wicker furniture and quilts. Warm-from-the-oven buttermilk spice coffeecake, cheese and basil scrambled eggs, and banana buttermilk buckwheat pancakes are examples of breakfast items served in the sunroom every morning. Dining room, complimentary breakfast. No room phones. Hot tub. Library. No smoking. | 10 Inverness Way | 415/669–1648 | fax 415/669–7403 | www.teninvernessway.com | 4 rooms | $145–$180 | MC, V.

IRVINE

MAP 4, I15

(Nearby towns also listed: Corona del Mar, Costa Mesa, Newport Beach, Santa Ana)

A mini-Dallas in southern California off I–405, this fast-growing residential and commercial center (pop. 111,300) took shape atop a Spanish land grant that subsequently became the Irvine Ranch. Today, it's a slightly surreal suburban vision of tree-lined streets, perfectly manicured lawns, and pristine parks. It has also been ranked as one of America's safest cities in several country-wide surveys. This bastion of impeccable city-planning proudly extols its excellent schools, a university, and lots of shopping.

Information: Irvine Chamber of Commerce | 17755 Sky Park E, Ste. 101, 92614 | 949/660–9112 | icc@irvinechamber.com | www.irvinechamber.com.

Attractions

Nascar Silicon Speedway. Shake, rattle, and even roll—or at least feel like you do—on these race cars mounted on full-motion platforms, part of the Irvine Spectrum entertainment complex. Simulated straightaways and S-curves are projected on a screen in front of your vehicle, making you feel like you're leading (or trailing) the pack of 29 other racers. Kids love this one (and so do their parents). | 71 Fortune Dr. | 949/753–8810 | $7.50/driver; $2.50/crew seat | Daily 11–11 (Fri. and Sat. until midnight).

University of California, Irvine. One of the more rapidly growing campuses of the University of California system. The University frequently hosts interesting speakers, exhibits, and artistic productions. The campus extends along a mesa with views of the ocean and many open fields and common areas. You can check their website for upcoming events. | 4500 Berkeley Pl | 949/824–5011 | www.uci.edu | Free | Daily.

ON THE CALENDAR

JAN. OR FEB.: *Chinese New Year Performances.* Over 300 students from the Irvine Chinese School perform at the Irvine Barclay Theater. Enjoy cultural folk dance, drama, a string orchestra, choirs, and kung-fu demonstrations. | 949/845–4646.

Dining

Chanteclair. French. The culinary artistry and extensive wine list of this six-room place take you abroad without leaving town. Sautéed foie gras, Dover sole, and herb-crusted rack of lamb are just a few of the selections you can enjoy on the covered patio or inside listening to the nightly pianist next to one of the five fireplaces. Smoking permitted on the patio. | 18912 MacArthur Blvd. | 949/752–8001 | $25–$35 | AE, D, DC, MC, V.

Chicago Joe's. Continental. Eat Canadian steaks and Hawaiian ahi in a California joint that's supposed to look like the Windy City in the late 19th century. Somehow with the careful preparation and presentation of the meals, they carry it off. Don't fill up on the homemade bread—the food that follows is too good, including the filet mignon and Louisiana chicken salad. Fresh fish possibilities change daily. Raw bar. Earlybird suppers. | 1818 N. Main St. | 949/261–5637 | No lunch Sun. | $17–$30 | AE, D, DC, MC, V.

McCormick and Schmick's. Continental. Though the menu changes daily, this bistro-style eatery always serves no less than 30 varieties of fresh seafood. If you don't want fish, there's a large selection of meats, poultry, salads, and pasta. British Columbian salmon and Alaskan halibut are seasonal specialties. There's also an on-site microbrewery. | 2000 Main St. | 949/756–0505 | No lunch weekends | $13–$34 | AE, D, DC, MC, V.

★ **Prego.** Italian. Reminiscent of a Tuscan villa, both dining rooms in this restaurant glow with soft lighting and golden walls. Try the spit-roasted meats and chicken, charcoal-grilled fresh fish, or pizzas from the oak-burning oven. There are also two attractive outdoor patios. | 18420 Von Karman Ave. | 949/553–1333 | No lunch weekends | $12–$24 | AE, DC, MC, V.

Lodging

Atrium Hotel. Next to John Wayne Airport, this 1981, three-story hotel in southwest Irvine has a touch of the exotic. There are trees both inside and outside, creating an attractive, warm, and very green appearance. Restaurant, bar (with entertainment), room service. In-room data ports, refrigerators, room service. Cable TV. Pool. Beauty salon. Exercise equipment. Shops. Laundry facilities. Business services, airport shuttle, parking fee. | 18700 MacArthur Blvd. | 949/833–2770 or 800/854–3012 | fax 949/757–1228 | info@atriumhotel.com | www.atriumhotel.com | 214 rooms | $79–$107 | AE, D, DC, MC, V.

Crowne Plaza. In the heart of Orange County's business center and a five-minute drive from John Wayne Airport, this 14-story luxury hotel built in 1986 caters to the business traveler. A multilingual staff can meet your needs in many languages. Within 2 mi of the hotel you can shop, play a set of tennis, or play a round of golf. Rooms are pleasantly furnished with light wood furniture and floral bedspreads, and you can enjoy a spot of sun on the deck. Restaurant, bar, room service. In-room data ports, cable TV. Indoor pool. Hot tub, sauna. Exercise equipment. Laundry facilities. Business services, airport shuttle, parking fee. | 17941 Von Karman Ave. | 949/863–1999 | fax 949/474–7236 | CP-irvine@bristolhotels.com | www.crowneplaza.com/irvineca | 335 rooms, 14 suites | $89–$169 | AE, D, DC, MC, V.

Doubletree Hotel Irvine–Spectrum. In the heart of Southern California's technology district and 10 mi east of the John Wayne Orange County Airport, this hotel makes a convenient choice if you want to be close to the action. It's a short walk to the Irvine Spectrum Center, a huge entertainment complex with a 21-screen movieplex (including IMAX), video arcade, restaurants, and shopping. Restaurant, bar (with entertainment). In-room data ports, cable TV. In-room video games. Pool. Hot tub. Exercise equipment. Laundry service. Business services, airport shuttle, free parking. | 90 Pacifica Ave. | 949/471–8888 | fax 949/471–8996 | www.doubletree.com | 252 rooms | $99–$149 | AE, D, DC, MC, V.

Embassy Suites–Orange County Airport. A sleek and unique facade greet you as you approach this all-suites hotel 1 mi from John Wayne Airport. Built in 1985, the 10-story hotel continues to maintain the suites' class and service. Restaurant, bar, complimentary breakfast. In-room data ports, refrigerators, cable TV. Indoor pool. Hot tub, massage. Exercise equipment. Video games. Business services, airport shuttle. | 2120 Main St. | 949/553–8332 | fax 949/261–5301 | www.embassy-suites.com | 293 suites | $109–$159 | AE, D, DC, MC, V.

Hilton Irvine/Orange County Airport. Built in 1972, this 10-story hotel hugs the perimeter of Orange County Airport at the John Wayne Airport exit of I–405. Try your hand at tennis (lighted for night play), or lounge by the palm-tree-fringed pool. Newport Beach, is 6 mi southwest. Restaurant, bar (with entertainment). In-room data ports. Some refrigerators, cable TV. Pool. Tennis court. Exercise equipment. Airport shuttle. | 18800 MacArthur Blvd. | 949/833–9999 | fax 949/833–3317 | www.hilton.com | 285 rooms, 4 suites | $79–$239, suites $395–$495 | AE, D, DC, MC, V.

Hyatt Regency. An L-shape configuration with 14 floors, this hotel is 1½ mi from John Wayne Airport off I–405. The contemporary lobby contains many native plants and a fountain. Palm trees frame the exterior. 2 restaurants, bars, room service. Cable TV. Pool. Hot tub. Tennis. Exercise equipment. Business services, airport shuttle. | 17900 Jamboree Rd. | 949/975–1234 | fax 949/852–1574 | www.hyatt.com | 536 rooms, 20 suites | $104–$225 | AE, D, DC, MC, V.

Marriott. Four blocks northeast of the John Wayne Airport, this 17-story hotel, with its many meeting rooms and business services, is geared toward the business traveler. For those on vacation, Newport Beach and Balboa Island, the Orange County Performing Arts Center, and shopping are all within a few miles. A beauty salon and spa are across the street. Both Disneyland and Long beach are within a half-hour's drive. 2 restaurants, bars (with entertainment). In-room data ports, refrigerators, microwaves, cable TV. Indoor-outdoor pool. Barbershop, beauty salon. Tennis. Exercise equipment, health club. Laundry facilities. Business services, airport shuttle, parking (fee). Some pets allowed. | 18000 Von Karman Ave. | 949/553–0100 | fax 949/261–7059 | www.marriott.com | 485 rooms, 10 suites | $189–$219 | AE, D, DC, MC, V.

JACKSON

MAP 3, F7

(Nearby towns also listed: Coloma, Murphys, Placerville, Rancho Codova)

Fifty miles southeast of Sacramento, in the rugged Gold Country at the base of the Sierra Nevada mountains, lies Jackson. A large share of the original 1848 mining settlement burned down in 1862, and most of the structures along Main Street are reproductions of the originals. The last mine closed in 1942, but several mine heads still stand at the town's north end, and one mine shaft is 6,000-ft deep. Most of the gold workers were Serbian or Italian, and they gave the town a European character which still exists today.

Information: **Amador County Chamber of Commerce** | 125 Peek St., 95683 | 209/223–0350 | info@amadorcountychamber.com | www.amadorcounty.com.

Attractions

Amador County Museum. A working scale model of the Kennedy Mine, a gold mine with the deepest vertical shaft in the United States wherein the disastrous fire of 1922 killed 48 miners, is the prize exhibit at the museum. Other artifacts and displays from Amador County's gold mining past illustrate the area's rugged and rough history. | 225 Church St. | 209/223–6386 | Donations accepted | Wed.–Sun. 10–4.

Daffodil Hill. Nearly a half-million yellow, creamy white, and pale orange blossoms spread across six acres at this family-owned ranch, growing daffodils for over 100 years. Walk the paths, then enjoy lunch at a picnic area overlooking the 300 varieties of bulbs. Bloom season is typically mid-March to mid-April. | Shake Ridge Rd. | 209/296–7048 | Free, donations welcome | Daily 10–5.

Indian Grinding Rock State Historic Park. A 135-acre park named for the Miwok Indians' use of the main geological feature of the area. The Miwok Indians chiseled into the huge bedrock slab over a thousand grinding "bowls" where they pulverized acorns and other seeds for food generation after generation. A re-created village and ceremonial round-house reside with the Park. The Chaw'se Regional Indian Museum documents the history of 10 Sierra Nevada Indian tribes. | 14881 Pine Grove-Volcano Rd., Pine Grove | 209/296–7488 | $2 per vehicle | Daily dawn to dusk.

The collection at the **Chaw'se Regional Indian Museum** includes Northern, Central and Southern Miwok, Maidu, Konkow, Monache, Nisenan, Tubatulabal, Washo, and Foothill Yokuts. Displays include examples of basketry, feather regalia, jewelry, arrowpoints, and other tools used over the centuries by the indigenous peoples. | 14881 Pine Grove-Volcano Rd., Pine Grove | 209/296–7488 | $2 per vehicle | Weekdays 11–3, weekends 10–4.

Sutter Gold Mining Co. An operational mine 9 mi east of Jackson on Route 88, this place provides you with a peek into the past and the rough life of a gold miner. Your fee includes an underground mining tour and gold panning in water troughs. | Box 1689, Sutter Creek | 888/818–7462 | info@suttergold.com | www.suttergold.com | $14.50 | Daily 10–6, call for holiday hours.

ON THE CALENDAR

SEPT.: *California Bluegrass and Cowboy Music Festival.* Get your yodel in gear and mosey on down to the Amador County Fairgrounds, where dozens of regional and national bluegrass bands and cowboy entertainers perform at this four-day event (which may be held every other year after 2001). There's also wine tasting, a craft fair, and a barbecue cooking contest. Many people camp on the festival site, and prizes are awarded to the best-dressed and funniest campsites. For kids, check out the youth music camp. | 503/261–9887 | www.greatmusicfestivals.com.

Dining

Imperial Hotel Restaurant. Contemporary. The snap of white linen and the sparkle of bevel-cut mirrors greet you at this elegant restaurant in the Imperial Hotel, 2 mi north of Sutter Creek and 6 mi south of Plymouth. Victorian paintings hang from exposed brick walls in the dining room, where you can peruse a menu that shifts with the seasons. Offerings might include roasted pork loin with apple-Gorgonzola stuffing, filet mignon, daily fish specials, and creative pasta dishes. In warmer months, there's outdoor dining on the stone patio. | 14292 Hwy. 49, Amador City | 209/267–9172 | www.imperialamador.com | Reservations essential | No lunch. No dinner Mon. or Tues. | $14–$26 | AE, D, MC, V.

Raging River Restaurant. Continental. The gold miners who used to work this rolling hill country back in the 1800s never ate like this. The restaurant, upstairs from the Jackson Rancheria Casino 3 mi east of Jackson, presents impressive buffets each Friday (seafood) and Saturday (carver's board) night. The rest of the week, look for filling pasta dishes (mushroom ravioli, fettuccini Alfredo with prawns), as well as lobster and other seafood, steak and chicken items, and baby back ribs. Kids' menu. | 12222 New York Ranch Rd. | 209/223–1677 or 800/822–9466 | www.jacksoncasino.com | Breakfast also available | $6–$16 | AE, D, DC, MC, V.

★ **Rosebud's Classic Café.** American. Art Deco touches and music from the 1930s and 1940s set the mood at this friendly and homey café. Among the classic American dishes served are hot roast beef, turkey, and meat loaf with mashed potatoes smothered in gravy. Char-broiled burgers, Philly cheese steak, homemade pies, and gourmet coffee drinks round out the lunch menu. In the morning, dig into omelettes, hotcakes, and other breakfast staples. | 26 Main St. | 209/223–1035 | No dinner. Breakfast available daily | $5–$10 | MC, V.

Teresa's Place. Italian. One mile away from downtown Jackson, with the Jackson Creek tumbling nearby and sheep grazing in the fields, the view may be bucolic but you aren't focusing on the view at this casual eatery. It's the hearty portions of family-style Italian food that you're after. Pasta and other Italian favorites have been served at this restaurant since 1921. The saloon-like room at the front can be loud. | 1235 Jackson Gate Rd. | 209/223–1786 | No lunch | $8–$15 | AE, D, MC, V.

Upstairs Restaurant and Streetside Bistro. International. This charming little eatery hosts some of the more imaginative cooking in the area under the direction of its chef, Layne McCollum. By day, you can lunch in the Streetside Bistro on pumpkin and portobello mushroom soup, pasta puttanesca, or other soups, sandwiches, and salads. At night the Upstairs Restaurant opens for somewhat fancier fare. Kids' menu. | 164 Main St. | 209/223–3342 | $13–$25 | D, MC, V.

Lodging

Best Western Amador Inn. This inn fits the town's old time style, and has gas fireplaces in some rooms. Opened in 1990, this two-story inn sits on the edge of the downtown commercial area, about three blocks from Main Street. Restaurant, bar. In-room data ports, some refrigerators, microwaves, cable TV. Pool. Business services. | 200 S. Rte. 49 | 209/223–0211 | fax 209/223–4836 | www.bestwestern.com | 118 rooms | $72–$76 | AE, D, DC, MC, V.

Court Street Inn Bed and Breakfast. This 1870 Victorian has a gracious porch out front, pressed tin ceilings and a polished redwood staircase inside. In the main house are antique-filled guest rooms on both floors, some with fireplace. There's also a second building, Vintage Court, with 14-ft ceilings and two guest rooms sharing a parlor and deck. A third option is Indian House, a two-bedroom cottage with 20-ft ceilings, large bath and a large screen TV/VCR and stereo. Kids' over 12 are permitted in the cottage. Complimentary breakfast. Some in-room VCRs. Hot tub. No smoking. | 215 Court St. | 209/223–0416 or 800/200–0416 | fax 209/223–5429 | www.courtstreetinn.com | 6 rooms, 1 cottage | $110–$150 rooms, $170–$220 cottage | AE, D, MC, V.

The Foxes. Formerly the Brinn House, this two-story inn was built during the 1857 Gold Rush. Each room has a different name and personality. Choose from the Victorian Suite, the Anniversary Room, the Honeymoon Suite, the Garden Room, the Fox Den, the Blue Room, or the Hideaway. The romantic upstairs Victorian suite has a private breakfast room, library, and fireplace, built-in music system, spacious bath with an old fashioned tub and separate shower. Sutter Creek, 8 mi northeast of Jackson, has 18 wineries and several gold mines where you can pan for gold, plus many antique shops. Complimentary breakfast. Some Cable TV, no room phones. No smoking. | 77 Main St., Sutter Creek | 209/267–5882 or 800/987–3344 | fax 209/267–0712 | www.foxesinn.com | 7 rooms | $135–$205 | D, MC, V.

Gate House Inn. Built in 1903, this B&B is surrounded by beautiful gardens. You can enjoy breakfast served in the original family dining room. Your room may have Victorian or Irish Pine furnishings, a fireplace, or overlook the colorful garden in spring and summer. The two-story house sits about 1/2 mi outside of downtown in a quiet residential area. Restaurant, complimentary breakfast and afternoon snacks. No room phones. Pool. Business services. No kids under 12. No smoking. | 1330 Jackson Gate Rd. | 209/223–3500 or 800/841–1072 | fax 209/223–1299 | info@gatehouseinn.com | www.gatehouseinn.com | 6 rooms; 2 cottages | $110–$185, $155–185 cottage | AE, D, MC, V.

Hanford House. On a quiet corner on the main street in downtown Sutter Creek, this ivy-covered redbrick inn awaits you. It's well-situated for travelers hoping to explore the town's historic Gold Rush buildings, local wineries, or the foothills surrounding the town. Room furnishings range from simple to sumptuous, with private baths, roof-top sun deck overlooking the hills, and a shaded patio. Your day here begins with the morning paper, tea, and coffee starting at 7:30. Breakfast is served between 8:30 and 9:30 in the parlor dining room. Restaurant, complimentary breakfast and afternoon snacks. In-room data ports. Business services. No smoking. | 61 Hanford St., Sutter Creek | 209/267–0747 or 800/871–5839 | fax 209/267–1825 | bobkat@hanfordhouse.com | www.hanfordhouse.com | 9 rooms | $99–$185 | D, MC, V.

Imperial Hotel. Built in 1879, this hotel overlooks Main St. in Amador City 10 mi southwest of Jackson. Some rooms have balconies overlooking the street scene; all have antique pine and other period furnishings. One room has a canopy bed. Restaurant, bar. Complimentary breakfast. No kids under 12. No smoking. | 14292 Hwy. 49, Amador City | 209/267–9172 or 800/242–5594 | www.imperialamador.com | 6 rooms | $80–$110 | AE, D, MC, V.

Jackson Holiday Lodge. One eighth of a mile from the historic Kennedy mines, 12 mi from local vineyards, and other town attractions, this motel 1/2 mi north of Jackson with simple rooms provides a quaint central home base from which to tour the area. Complimentary Continental breakfast. Some kitchenettes, cable TV. Pool. Some pets allowed. | 209/223–0486 | fax 209/223–2905 | kennedy.amadornet.net/travelers/lodging/holiday.html | 850 N. Rte. 49 | 36 rooms | $70–90 | AE, D, DC, MC, V.

Sutter Creek Inn. This 1859 house claims to be the first B&B in California. A grape arbor and shaded hammocks provide cool spots where you can while away an afternoon. You can end up in one of the four popular, romantic "swinging bed" rooms(the beds are suspended from the ceiling on chains, and can be stablized upon request) or a rustic room with brick walls and exposed beam ceiling. A wood-burning fireplace in your room will keep you snug, with a private patio for a breath of fresh air. In the center of Sutter Creek, you can take a short drive to the golf course, visit wineries, or explore the quaint shops in the area. Complimentary breakfast and afternoon snacks. No room phones, no TV in some rooms. Business services. No smoking. | 75 Main St., Sutter Creek | 209/267–5606 | fax 209/267–9287 | www.suttercreekinn.com | 17 rooms (15 with shower only) | $65–$175 | MC, V.

Wedgewood Inn. Landscaped grounds include a rose garden and fountain, with impressive views of Mt. Zion to the east. Antiques reflect the style of the mid-19th-century period. The rooms, in two Victorian-style three-story houses built in 1987, all have private baths and queen beds, and many have cozy fireplaces. All are stuffed with mementos of the family that owns the inn, and a Christian blessing is said at every breakfast. Picnic area, complimentary breakfast and afternoon snacks. No room phones. Hot tub. No smoking. | 11941 Narcissus Rd. | 209/296–4300 or 800/933–4393 | fax 209/296–4301 | www.wedgewoodinn.com | 6 rooms | $110–$175 | AE, D, MC, V.

Windrose Inn. Take a footbridge across pretty Jackson Creek to reach the front of this 1897 farmhouse, on an acre of informal gardens and shaded lawns in the Sierra Nevada foothills. Outside, swing in a hammock, stroll the rose garden, or sit on the brick terrace or wraparound porch. Inside, rooms are an eclectic mix. One room has a carved mahogany queen bed; others have wicker, oak, or brass furniture. The suite on the second floor has a hot tub, fireplace, complimentary champagne, and a queen sleigh bed. Enjoy complimentary wine and hors d'oeuvres every afternoon. Kids staying here should be good swimmers, as the creek, an open well, and a fishing pond are all on the premises. Complimentary breakfast. Some in-room hot tubs. No kids under 8. No smoking. | 1407 Jackson Gate Rd. | 209/223–3650 or 888/568–5250 | www.windroseinn.com | 4 rooms | $110–$165 | D, MC, V.

JAMESTOWN

MAP 3, F8

(Nearby towns also listed: Murphys, Sonora)

"Jimtown", as it was once called, might prompt a case of déjà vu if you saw the films *High Noon* or *Butch Cassidy and the Sundance Kid* because this town was the backdrop for those productions. Several structures here date back to the 1870s, and were constructed not long after the first Tuolumne County gold strike in 1848. The present population is approximately 3,500. Today Jamestown is a gateway to Yosemite and boasts five local theaters, fifteen restaurants with distinct menus, thirty galleries and a variety of boutiques and shops.

Information: Tuolumne County Chamber of Commerce | 222 S. Shepherd St., Sonora, 95370 | 209/532–4212 | info@tcchamber.com | www.tcchamber.com.

Attractions

Jimtown 1849 Gold Mining Camp. Living history museum complete with costumed prospectors with specialty tours available for an additional fee. | 18170 Main St. | 209/984–4653 | Free | Daily 9:30–5 | www.goldprospecting.com.

Railtown 1897 State Historic Park. The Sierra Railway Company began carrying freight and passengers through the gold-mining area in 1897. On the site of the Jamestown station, the park has interpretive center, station yard, and train facilities. Take a look at the huge roundhouse and its 60-ft turntable used for routing the giant vintage engines and railroad cars that are on display. When the weather warms, and in November, there are regular 40-minute weekend excursions on steam-powered trains through the Gold Country hills. The costumed staff are all former railroaders or railroad buffs. If anything looks familiar along the way, it's probably because the site has been used in more than 200 films and television productions, including *High Noon* and *Petticoat Junction*. It's at Reservoir Road, off Route 49 | 5th Ave. | 209/984–3953 | fax 209/984–4936 | parks.ca.gov/north/goldrush/r1897shp.htm | $2 | Daily 9:30–4:30. Train rides, Apr.–Oct., weekends 11–3; Nov., Sat. 11–3.

Dining

National Hotel Restaurant. Mediterranean. This wooden, two-story western hotel dates back to 1859 and reportedly plays host to a ghost who's expanded her visits to include the kitchen. The menu includes steak, seafood, chicken, and pasta dishes, in addition to more upscale fare such as Coquilles Vanderbilt (sherried scallops, bay shrimp, shallots and mushrooms in a sweet cream sauce). Kids' menu. Sun. brunch. Open air dining (seasonal). | Main St. | 209/984–3446 | $10–$17 | AE, D, DC, MC, V.

Lodging

1859 Historic National Hotel. Brass beds, patchwork quilts, and lace curtains fill the rooms of this country inn in Jamestown, 3 mi south of Sonora via Route 108. Some rooms have private baths (with modern but funky looking pull-chain toilets) and some share baths fitted out with, among other things, antique wash basins. The 19th-century saloon has the orginal redwood bar. Dining room, complimentary breakfast, room service. No room phones, no TV in some rooms. Pets allowed (fee). No kids under 10. | 75 Main St. | 209/984–3446, 800/894–3446 from CA or 800/446–1333, Ext. 286 | fax 209/984–5620 | info@national-hotel.com | www.national-hotel.com | 9 rooms | $80–$120 | AE, D, DC, MC, V.

Palm Hotel Bed and Breakfast. This hotel in a century-old country Victorian wood house has guest rooms with antiques and special amenities such as clawfoot tubs and twin corner sinks. Each room is uniquely appointed with details including stained glass windows, vaulted ceilings, arched windows and quilts on each bed. Complimentary breakfast. | 10382 Willow St. | 209/984–3429 | fax 209/984–4929 or 888/551–1851 | www.palmhotel.com/ | 8 rooms | $95–$155 | AE, MC, V.

Royal Hotel. This Victorian built during the Gold Rush is right in the middle of the Main Street shops and restaurants. Inside, carpeted floors and patterned wallpaper lend a homey touch. Rooms are dressed up with assorted antiques. The Sassy Judy, for example, has a skylight and twin brass beds, ideal for kids. The Patricia Room opens onto a porch with a bench swing. Planning a family reunion? Consider the 5 cottages. The Greenhouse #1 cottage has a pond and garden view. Ask innkeepers to arrange golf, dinner or theater evenings, and white-water rafting. Complimentary Continental breakfast. No room phones. No smoking. | 18239 Main St. | 209/984–5271 or 800/523–6722 | fax 209/984–1675 | www.aroyalhotel.com | 14 rooms, 5 cottages | $65–$95 rooms, $80–$110 cottages | MC, V.

JENNER

MAP 3, C7

(Nearby towns also listed: Bodega Bay, Guerneville, Santa Rosa)

About 170 people reside in the minuscule coastal town of Jenner, halfway between San Francisco and Seattle, whose main street consists of a few restaurants, a deli, and a gift shop. Once largely inhabited by Russian immigrants who have since abandoned the area, but the Russian heritage is preserved at the Fort Ross State Park.

Information: Monte Rio Chamber of Commerce | 20385 Hwy. 116, Monte Rio, 95462 | 707/865–1533.

Attractions

Fort Ross State Historic Park. Forest canyons, coastal grasslands, and precipitous ridges with ocean views fill the park. The San Andreas fault line runs along the base of the hills, and there are areas of protected second-growth redwoods, first logged by Russian settlers in the 19th century. The area was once inhabited by the Kashaya Pomo tribe. There is plenty of wildlife and some ocean access. Camp sites are available at Fort Ross Reef. | 19005 Coast Hwy. 1 | 707/847–3286 | $2 per car | Daily | parks.ca.gov/north/russian/frshp207.htm.

The restored and reconstructed **Historic Fort Ross** was the settlement of the Russian pioneers who came in 1812 to hunt sea otter and grow crops for Russian settlements in Alaska. The redwood chapel, barracks, and stockade were built using joinery typical of

Russian architecture of the period. The visitor center has displays, books, and a gift shop. | 19005 Coast Hwy. 1 | $2 per car | Daily 10–5.

ON THE CALENDAR
JULY: *Living History Days.* On the last Saturday of the month performers dress in period clothing and reenact the daily lives of the Russians in Fort Ross in the early 1800s. The performance takes place in the Fort Ross Historical State Park. | 19005 Hwy. 1 | 707/847–3286.

Dining

Salt Point Bar and Grill. American. Watercolor paintings decorate the dining room of this casual spot which overlooks the Pacific Ocean. Try the peppercorn steak or the scallop and prawn pasta. | 23255 Hwy. 1 | 707/847–3238 | Jan.–Apr.; breakfast also available Fri.–Mon., no lunch Tues.–Thurs.; Apr.–Thanksgiving, breakfast also available; Closed Thanks-giving–Christmas | $14–$21 | AE, D, MC, V.

Lodging

Fort Ross Lodge. 1 ½ mi north of Historic Fort Ross overlooking the ocean, many of the rooms—each individually furnished, some with antiques—in this lodge have ocean views, and all have fireplaces. Refrigerators, cable TV, VCRs. Some in-room hot tubs. Hot tub, sauna. No pets. | 20705 Hwy. 1 | 707/847–3333 | fax 707/847–3330 | www.fortross-lodge.com | 17 rooms, 5 suites | $60–$185, suites $185–$225 | AE, MC, V.

Jenner Inn. The innkeepers turned three large homes into B&B rooms and suites (some with fireplaces). Wildlife viewing is popular here: the inn is located where the Russian River runs into the sea. Sea lions, river otters, seals, and pelicans, osprey, and other seabirds are abundant. You can also choose a smaller cottage. Waterfront rooms have both estuary and ocean views, and creekside rooms have river views. Antiques and local art can be found throughout the guest rooms and the main lodge. The inn hosts three yoga classes each week. Complimentary American breakfast. Some kitchenettes, no TV, some room phones. Massage. | Hwy. 1, Box 69F | 800/732–2377 or 707/865–2377 | fax 707/865–0829 | innkeeper@jennerinn.com | www.jennerinn.com | 21 | $88–$238 rooms, $138–$258 cottages | AE, MC, V.

Salt Point Lodge. You can enjoy Sonoma ocean views from many of the guest rooms and from the solarium bar. Accomodations range from rooms with fireplaces and private decks to a family room with a set of bunk beds. Restaurant, bar. Some in-room hot tubs, some in-room VCRs, cable TV. Hot tub, sauna. Playground. | 23255 Coast Hwy. Rte. 1 | 707/847–3234 | lodging@saltpoint.com/ | www.saltpoint.com/ | 16 rooms in lodge | $60–$147 | D, MC, V.

Timber Cove Inn. This inn is perched on a rugged oceanfront cliff perfect for watching whales and sea birds. Extend your commune with nature by hiking the property's 26 acres of trails. The lobby has a cavernous stone fireplace and a vaulted wooden ceiling, and the huge win-dows in the dining area have picture-perfect views of the sea. Rooms overlook the ocean or the Japanese-style pond. Restaurant, picnic area, room service. Some in-room hot tubs, no room phones. | 21780 N. Coast Hwy./Rte. 1 | 707/847–3231 or 800/987–8319 (for reserva-tions) | fax 707/847–3704 | timbercoveinn.com/ | 50 rooms | $110–$390 | AE, MC, V.

JOSHUA TREE NATIONAL PARK

MAP 4, L15

(Nearby towns also listed: Desert Hot Springs, Indian Wells, Indio, La Quinta, Twentynine Palms)

★ As rugged as it is sublime, Joshua Tree National Park covers 1,238 square mi encircled by I–10 to the south, Rte. 62 to the north and east, and Rte. 177 to the west. Elevations here span 1,800- to 5,813-ft at Quail Mountain. An ever popular rock climbing locale, members of the Los Angeles Police Department's elite SWAT team polish their climbing and rope skills here. The Park nourishes a terrific variety of wildlife, resident and migratory birds, and Nelson's desert bighorn sheep. The park is named after the spiny, evergreen yucca plants, pollinated by moths, called Joshua Trees by the Mormons who thought their twisted, outstretched arms recalled the biblical figure beckoning to his followers. In good-natured competition, both Twenty-nine Palms and the small town of Joshua Tree vie for the claim, "Gateway to Joshua Tree."

Information: **Joshua Tree Chamber of Commerce** | 61325 29th St., Palm Highway Suite F, Box 600, Joshua Tree, 92252 | 760/366–3723 | fax 760/366–2573.

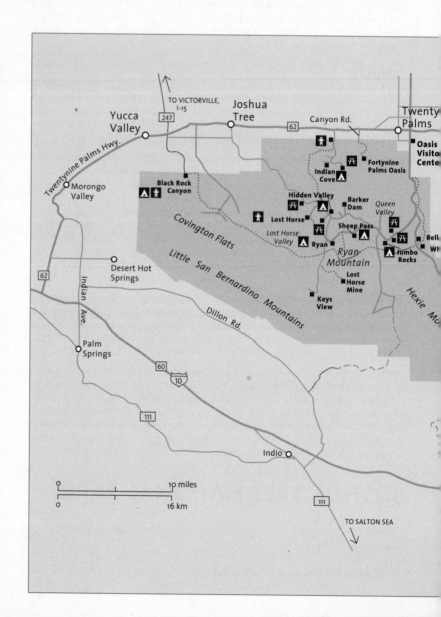

Attractions

Joshua Tree National Park. This park of 794,000 acres spans the transition between the Mojave and Colorado deserts of Southern California. Proclaimed a National Monument in 1936 and a Biosphere Reserve in 1984, Joshua Tree was designated a National Park in 1994. The area possesses a rich human history and a pristine natural environment. Two deserts whose characteristics are determined primarily by elevation come together at Joshua Tree National Park. Below 3,000 ft, the Colorado Desert encompasses the eastern part of the park and you can find natural gardens of creosote bush, ocotillo, and cholla cactus. On the western half you'll find the higher, moister, and slightly cooler Mojave Desert which is the special habitat of the Joshua tree, a spiney-leafed member of the yucca family. Some of the most interesting geologic displays, like granite monoliths, alluvial fans,

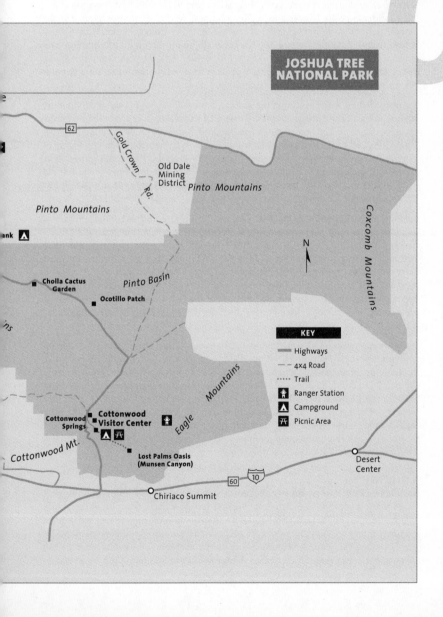

JOSHUA TREE
NATIONAL PARK

KEY

— Highways
--- 4x4 Road
····· Trail
Ranger Station
Campground
Picnic Area

and amazing twisted mountains found in California's deserts are in the Mojave. In addition, five fan palm oases dot the park, where water occurs naturally and wildlife abounds. | 74485 National Park Dr., Twentynine Palms | 760/367–5500 or 800/365–2267 | www.nps.gov/jotr/ | $10 per vehicle | Daily 24 hours; visitor center daily 8–5.

ON THE CALENDAR

MAR.–MAY: *Joshua Tree Wildflowers.* From mid-March through mid-May—depending on weather—carpets of wildflowers turn Joshua Tree National Park into a technicolor wonder. To find out what's in bloom and where to find it, call the park's Wildflower Hotline. | 760–767–4684.

Dining

Arturo's. Mexican. Piñatas, butterfly decorations, and light-catching mirrors make this an eye-catching place to grab a taco. The restaurant, next to a health food store at the intersection of Hwy. 62 and Sunset Rd. is especially noted for its combination burrito green, a burrito with moderately spicy beef-and-bean filling served juicy (melted cheese and natural juices), dry, or with ranchero sauce. All the traditional Mexican favorites—enchiladas, tostadas—are on the menu, too. Chicken tacos with guacamole are a popular choice. | 61695 Twentynine Palms Hwy. | 760/366–2719 | Closed Mon. | $6–$9 | AE, MC, V.

Country Kitchen. American. From the outside, this small café looks like a little red barn. Inside, pull up a chair at the counter or around a handful of tables to tuck into homestyle cooking, dished up here since the 60s. Breakfast favorites include biscuits with gravy, home fries, and stacks of steaming pancakes. At lunch, try homemade split pea soup or clam chowder, or order one of the hearty plate-lunch specials such as country-fried steak served with mashed potatoes and vegetables. Lighter fare includes crêpes, omelettes, and fruit smoothies (non-dairy available). | 61768 Twentynine Palms Hwy. | 760/366–8988 | Reservations not accepted | No dinner. Breakfast daily | $4–$5 | No credit cards.

Joshua Tree Park Center Café and Deli. Café. Buy a meal here, and part of the profits benefit Joshua Tree National Park Association. Stoke up on breakfast, then order a box lunch before heading into the park 5 mi southeast. The café creates some unusual and interesting sandwiches that are a far cry from tuna and PB&J, such as Nutty Chicken Salad (chicken, apples, celery, peanuts, pineapple juice, mayonnaise, and plain yogurt), or roast beef and cheddar with Ortega chile. Fresh soups and salads are also available, as are croissants, muffins, cakes, pies, cookies, and cheesecake. Wash it all down with a fruit smoothie or assorted coffee drinks. | 6554 Park Blvd. | 760/366–3622 | No dinner. Breakfast daily | $4–$6 | D, MC, V.

Palms Restaurant and Saloon. American. This saloon-style eatery makes a fun stop on your way to or from Joshua Tree National Park. Open since the early 50s, the 2,100-square-ft building, complete with patio and outdoor stage, has long been a favorite spot to dig into barbecued ribs, chicken, and other hearty fare. But the expansive menu has lighter options, too, such as quesadillas, burgers, and hot dogs. Friday and Saturday nights, look for special barbecue dinners and live entertainment. Call about guided tours of the nearby Dale District gold mines. The restaurant is 10 mi east of Twentynine Palms, just north of Hwy. 62. | 83131 Amboy Rd., Wonder Valley | 760/361–2810 | www.thegrid.net/denweb/palms/ | $3–$12 | No credit cards.

Lodging

Joshua Tree B&B. Housed in a 1930s hacienda-style building with a large swimming pool and a charming rose garden, all rooms here have private showers (no tubs), antiques and Old West memorabilia. Next to the Joshua Tree National Park. Dining room, picnic area, complimentary breakfast. In-room data ports, some microwaves, refrigerators, cable TV. Pool. Massage. Playground. Business services, airport shuttle. Some pets allowed. | 61259 Twentynine Palms Hwy., Joshua Tree | 760/366–1188 or 800/366–1444 | fax 760/366–

3805 | joshuatreeinn@thegrid.net | www.joshuatreeinn.com | 8 rooms, 2 suites, 4 cottages (with shower only) | $85–$275 | AE, D, DC, MC, V.

Mojave Rock Ranch Cabins. If peace, solitude, and stunning desert views are what you seek, try one of these cabins near Joshua Tree National Park. The cabins, sitting on 120 acres of Mojave Desert land, are about 6 mi north of Highway 62 and 10 mi from either the east park entrance in Twentynine Palms, or the west entrance in Joshua Tree. Which to choose? Rock Ranch cabin has two bedrooms and a sleeping porch, great for star-gazing. The Bungalow has a hand-built stone-and-iron fireplace, outdoor dining on a covered patio, mesquite, and desert willow trees, and a pond. The Homesteader has authentic knotty pine paneling, antiques, and down pillows and comforters. All cabins have full kitchens, hammocks, and "Cowboy Spas" (private, outdoor hot tubs). There is a corral for your horses and dogs as well. If you need something to do, peruse the inn's library, or check-out a complimentary video. Cable TV. Hot tubs. Pets allowed (fee). No smoking. | Box 552 | 760/366–8455 | fax 760/366–1996 | www.mojaverockranch.com | 4 cabins | $275–$325 | No credit cards.

Rosebud Ruby Star. Off the beaten path, each room at this extremely private spot is complete with a sunken desert library and a deck with futon couch and CD player. Some rooms glow orange-red, others cool sage greens in this B&B overlooking Joshua Tree National Park. The colors echo the shades of the surrounding desert, with owner's original artwork gracing the walls of the common rooms. Individual rooms have queen beds, private baths, and private entrances from a rear patio. Breakfast at your patio table, or in the main dining area. At night, keep an ear tuned for the eerie sound of coyotes yapping and by day keep a watchful eye for jack rabbits, bobcats and the endangered desert tortoise. Complimentary breakfast. No room phones, no TV. No smoking. | Box 1116, Joshua Tree | 760/366–4676 | sandy@rosebudrubystar.com | www.rosebudrubystar.com | 2 rooms | $140 | Closed July–Sept. | MC, V.

JULIAN

MAP 4, K16

(Nearby towns also listed: Borrego Springs, Escondido, Pine Valley)

This town at the northern edge of Cleveland National Forest was a very lucrative mining center in the late 19th century. More than $15 million worth of gold was extracted from these parts. Nowadays, Julian is better known for its spring wildflowers and autumn apple harvests. There are quite a few antiques stores here, as well as shops displaying and selling the work of the many artists who maintain hillside studios.

Information: Julian Chamber of Commerce | 2129 Main St., 92036 | 760/765–1857 | www.julianca.com.

Attractions

Eagle & High Peak Mine. Hour-long guided tours take you through one of Julian's original producing gold mines and tell tales of early residential life and industry. | Five blocks off of Main St. at the end of C St. | 760/765–0036 | $8; special rate for children | Daily 10–4.

Julian Pioneer Museum. History of the region and its inhabitants is illustrated in a late-1800s building, with American Indian artifacts, pioneer clothing and furnishings, and mounted indigenous animals. | 2811 Washington St. | 760/765–0227 | $2 | Apr.–Nov., Tues.–Sat. 10–4.

ON THE CALENDAR

SEPT.: *Julian Grape Stomp Fiesta.* Clean your feet and head 2 mi north of town to enjoy music, dancing, wine-tasting, food, and crafts. Oh yes, and two tons of grapes to crush, too. Festivities take place every second Saturday in Sept. at the Menghini Winery, 1150 Julian Orchards Dr. | 760/765–2072.

Dining

Julian Grille. American. Inside a turn of the century cottage, this restaurant has some vegetarian choices as well as chicken, burgers, and smoked pork chops served with applesauce. The apple pies are made by the Julian Pie Company across the street. Open-air patio dining. Kids' menu. Sun. breakfast. | 2224 Main St. | 760/765–0173 | No lunch Mon. | $14–$21 | AE, MC, V.

Pine Hills Lodge and Dinner Theater. Continental. With handsome furnishings shaped from logs and a fire crackling in the native-stone fireplace, this 1912 lodge on eight wooded acres casts a warm and welcoming glow. Entrées include broiled salmon, shrimp, steak, and pasta dishes, with lighter fare for lunch and brunch. On Fri. and Sat. nights, local performers take the stage for dinner theater shows, where an all-you-can-eat rib dinner is served. Earlybird dinners Sun.–Thurs. 4–6. Sunday brunch. | 2960 La Posada Way | 760/765–1100 | $11–$19 | AE, MC, V.

Romano's Dodge House. Italian. This restaurant serves both traditional and creative versions of Italian fare. Menu choices include zucchini frittata, spicy apple cider sausage, pork loin in cinnamon, garlic and whiskey sauce. For desert try the cappuccino ice cream. Open-air dining. | 2718 B St. | 760/765–1003 | $10–$17 | No credit cards.

Lodging

Apple Tree Inn. Three miles west of downtown Julian in a residential country area, this homey single-story inn is convenient for those wanting to explore local shops and galleries. Rooms are unpretentious, but do have phones and satellite TV. Pool. Some pets allowed. | 4360 Rte. 78 | 760/765–0222 | 16 rooms | $82–$87 | AE, D, MC, V.

Butterfield Bed and Breakfast. Built in the 1930s, this inn on a three-acre hilltop is cordial and romantic with knotty pine ceilings, and Laura Ashley accents. One room opens to a gazebo patio and another out to a garden. Some rooms have fireplaces. A horse drawn carriage can take you into Julian which is just 1 mi west of the property. Complimentary breakfast. Cable TV. Library. | 2284 Sunset Dr. | 760/765–2179 | fax 760/765–1229 | info@butterfieldbandb.com/ | www.butterfieldbandb.com/ | 5 rooms | $115–$175 | AE, MC, V.

Homestead Bed and Breakfast. This cozy B&B has king-size beds with heirloom furniture and quilts in each room. All rooms have full baths as well. A large common room has a two-story rock fireplace, a game table, and a view of the peaceful wooded countryside. Some kitchenettes, no smoking. | 4924 Rte. 79 | 760/765–1536 | homestead@abac.com | www.homesteadbandb.com | 4 rooms | $130–$150 | MC, V.

Julian Lodge. Built as a replica of a late 19th-century hotel, this B&B is one block off the main street, in the heart of town. Its comfortable rooms are furnished with antiques, all have private baths. Complimentary breakfast. | 2720 C St. | 760/765–1420 | 23 rooms | $72–$92 | AE, D, MC, V.

Julian White House. Take a wrong turn south? No, this really is a petite replica of an antebellum mansion, right down to the Greek Revival columns out front. Read a book in the rose garden, or take a spin on one of the complimentary bicycles to tour the surrounding countryside. The Southern theme continues inside, with assorted antiques and interesting collections on display. For example, the "French Quarter" has Mardi Gras feather masks and a Louis XVI bed. Breakfast is served on fine china in the candlelit dining room. Complimentary breakfast. Refrigerator available. Hot tubs. No kids. No smoking. | 3024 Blue Jay Dr. | 760/765–1764 or 800/948–4687 | fax 760/765–1764 | www.julian-whitehouse-bnb.com | 5 | $105–$175 | MC, V.

Orchard Hill Country Inn. This luxurious B&B overlooking the town and hillside is a welcome alternative to the more basic accommodations found in Julian. Reconstructed country cottages and a massive craftsman-style lodge are set on four acres of greenery, with hammocks and walking paths. The cottages, large enough for families, have private entrances, wicker furnishings, wet bars, whirlpool tubs and dual fireplaces. The rooms in the lodge are smaller, but have skylights, tasteful rustic furniture, and sweeping views of the mountains. A gold mine and shops are within walking distance. Complimentary breakfast. Some in-room hot tubs, in-room VCRs (and movies). Library. No pets. Business services. | 2505 Washington St. | 760/765-1700 | fax 760/765-0290 | www.orchardhill.com/ | 22 rooms | $185-$285 | AE, MC, V.

Wikiup Bed and Breakfast. You won't be lonely here, not with a llama, dogs, cats, a donkey, sheep, goats, and assorted birds keeping you company at this rustic lodge. The contemporary cedar-and-brick structure, less than a mile east of Julian, has a relaxed, family appeal, with play equipment and, of course, the critters roaming across three wooded acres. Inside, high open-beam ceilings with sky lights, cedar paneling, and modern Danish furnishings set the tone in the common areas. Guest rooms have an eclectic flair, with names such as "Rose's Secret" (Victorian florals and cedar hot tub), "Dreamcatcher" (rustic, four-poster bed and two terra-cotta fireplaces), and "Willow Warren" (queen-size bed crowned by a canopy of willow branches). Complimentary breakfast. Refrigerators, microwaves, in-room hot tubs. Outdoor hot tub. TV in common area. Library. Pets allowed. | 1645 Whispering Pines Dr. | 760/765-1890 or 800/526-2725 | fax 760/765-1515 | www.wikiupbnb.com | 4 | $155-$175 | MC, V.

JUNE LAKE

(Nearby towns also listed: Lee Vining, Mammoth Lakes, Yosemite National Park)

June Lake is an idyllic alpine spot atop 8,041-ft Deadman Summit on U.S. 395. The town's 600 full-time residents live surrounded by an impressive collection of world-class recreational areas: Inyo National Forest; the Ansel Adams Wilderness; the Devil's Postpile National Monument; and Yosemite. Stop at the kiosk on Route 158, off I-395, for information on the area.

Information: June Lake Loop Chamber of Commerce | Box 2, 93529 | 760/648-7584 | www.visitjunelake.com/chamber.

Attractions
Panum Craters. Twenty-one unusual volcanic cones of pumice and obsidian are among the natural wonders in the Inyo National Forest, just south of Mono Lake. | Inyo National Forest | 760/873-2400 | www.reserveusa.com | Free | Daily.

ON THE CALENDAR
APR.: *Opening Day Fishing Season.* Fishermen throughout the region look forward to this annual monster trout contest that kicks off the fishing season. | 760/648-7584.

Dining
Carson Peak Inn. American. At the base of Carson Peak in a wooded area, this place serves barbecue back ribs, seafood and steak. Kids' menu. Beer and wine. | Rte. 158 | 760/648-7575 | No lunch | $7-$35 | D, MC, V.

Lodging
Boulder Lodge. This old-fashioned lodge, directly on June Lake, is tailor-made for those on a trout-fishing vacation. Kitchenettes, cable TV. Pool. Hot tub, sauna. Tennis. Fishing. Video games. Playground. Business services. | 2282 Rte. 158 | 760/648-7533 or 800/458-6355 | 60 rooms in 11 buildings | $52-$300 | AE, D, MC, V.

Double Eagle Resort and Spa. These fully furnished, pine-paneled two-bedroom cabins have wood-burning stoves, fireplaces, overstuffed sofas and armchairs, and decks, and the spa's services are an unusual luxury in this forested location. Find the resort off

Highway 158, within 1 mi of skiing areas. Restaurant. Kitchenettes, microwaves, refrigerators, cable TV. Beauty salon, spa. Gym, health club. Fishing. Business services. Pets allowed. No smoking. | Spa Rt. 3 | 760/648–7004 | fax 760/648–7017 | www.double-eagle-resort.com | 13 cabins | $153–$288 | AE, D, DC, MC, V.

KERNVILLE

(Nearby towns also listed: Bakersfield, Tehachapi)

Kernville (pop. 1,700) is scattered along the Kern River at the north tip of Lake Isabella at Sequoia National Forest's southern edge. The river, which flows from Mount Whitney to Bakersfield, provides some of the most exciting white-water rafting in the state. In addition to being a center for rafting outfitters, Kernville has quaint lodgings, several restaurants, and antiques shops.

Information: Kernville Chamber of Commerce | 11447 Kernville Rd., 93238 | 760/376–2629 | fax 760/376–4371.

Attractions

Chuck Richards' Whitewater Inc. Whitewater day trip tours of the Kern River, overnight tours also available. | 6075 Isabella Blvd., Lake Isabella | 760/379–5950 or 800/624–5950 | www.chuckrichards.com | $15–$150 per day trip | May–Sept., daily, trips leave 8–10AM.

ON THE CALENDAR
OCT.: *Kernville Rod Run.* Since 1975, car enthusiasts with models built between 1933 and 1957 come to Kernville to show off their hot rods in Riverside Park and throughout town. Live musical entertainment punctuates the event. | 760/376–2629.
OCT.: *Kernville Stampede.* Bronco and bull riding, plus roping competitions and other rodeo events are held at the Johnny McNally Rodeo Arena. | 760/376–2629.
FEB.: *Whiskey Flat Days.* Reminiscent of Kernville's lively Gold Rush days, the town takes off work to eat, drink and listen to music downtown. | 760/376–2629.
JUNE: *Whitewater Wednesday.* Bring your swimsuit and old sneakers to this community fundraiser, and prepare to get wet during your one- or two-hour guided rafting trip down the rapids of the Kern River. Refreshments await you at the end of your run. | 760/376–2629.

Dining

Johnny McNally's Fairview Lodge. Steak. Overlooking the Kern River, this lodge serves up huge portions in Old West-style. Steaks can weigh up to 40 oz. Other menu items include poultry and fish and the Fairview specialty—steak and butterfly shrimp. Homemade desserts include cheesecake and mud pies. | Star Rte. 1 | 760/376–2430 | Closed mid-Dec.–mid-Feb. No supper weekdays in Nov.–Mar. No lunch | $9–$27 | MC, V.

Robin's River Restaurant. American. Popular with locals, this down-home restaurant on the Kern River serves hamburgers, fried chicken, biscuits and gravy, and meatloaf. Don't miss the freshly baked pastries and pies; the cranberry-apple cobbler is first-rate. | 13423 Sierra Way | 760/376–4663 | Breakfast also available | $7–$14 | DC, MC, V.

That's Italian Restaurant. Italian. Fresh fruit and vegetable murals on the walls of this place with high-backed antique chairs and Dean Martin in the background warm up the palate for Northern Italian dishes. The house specialties are fishermen's linguine—pasta with fresh mixed seafood—and braised lamb shanks in chianti sauce with garlic mashed potatoes. Outdoor patio dining in season. | 9 Big Blue Rd. | 760/376–6020 | No lunch weekdays | $8–$14 | AE, D, MC, V.

Lodging

Hi-Ho Resort Lodge. The Kern River runs just behind this lodge which is frequented by anglers; launches on Lake Isabella are only 10 minutes away. The property has simple accommodations and has fish-cleaning facilities on site. Downtown is just 1 mi away. Picnic area. Kitchenettes, cable TV, no room phones. Pool. Hot tub. Playground. Laundry facilities. | 11901 Sierra Way | 760/376–2671 | 8 cottages | $65–$125 cottages | AE, D, MC, V.

River View Lodge. Knotty-pine walls, compact rooms, and views of the Kern River make this small motel in the middle of town a great stopover. Complimentary Continental breakfast. Some microwaves, some refrigerators. | 2 Sirretta St. | 760/376–6019 | fax 760/376–3157 | 11 rooms | $55–$95 | AE, D, DC, MC, V.

Whispering Pines Lodge. This hotel overlooks the Kern River. Some rooms have fireplaces. Cottages include refrigerators, ranges, dishwashers, and gas barbecue grills on their decks overlooking the river. Golf, water-skiing, hiking trails, and river rafting are within a 15 minute drive. Kernville is less than ½ mi away. Picnic area, complimentary breakfast. Some kitchenettes, refrigerators, cable TV. Pool. No smoking. | 18 Nevada St. | 760/376–3733 | fax 760/376–6513 | 17 rooms in lodge | $99–$159 | www.kernvalley.com/whisperingpines | AE, DC, MC, V.

KING CITY

MAP 4, E11

(Nearby towns also listed: Big Sur, Cambria, Coalinga, Paso Robles, San Simeon)

This small agricultural town lies in the Salinas Valley and is named for Charles H. King who, in 1884, purchased 13,000 acres with the intention of planting wheat. King was thought a fool at the time, as the area was called "the great Salinas desert"; but he proved his naysayers wrong by producing bountiful crops, and enjoyed the last laugh when the town was named after him. King City's economic base remains agricultural and centers around the growing of broccoli, barley, and beans. The town is a good place to stay while exploring nearby Salinas and the Monterey Valley's wine region.

Information: **King City Chamber of Commerce** | 203 Broadway, 93930 | 831/385–3814 | www.kingcitychamber.com.

Attractions

Lake San Antonio. On this fresh-water lake, approximately 22 mi south of King City, you can fish and boat; you can also camp, hike, and bike along the shoreline. Full hookups. Boat and jet ski rental available. | 805/472–2311 | www.gonzales-ca.com/lakesan.html | $6 per vehicle | Daily.

Los Padres National Forest. This national forest has nearly 2 million acres of land in the coastal mountains of central California. From the Carmel Valley to the western edge of Los Angeles County (about a 220-mi stretch roughly following Hwy. 101), the forest provides the scenic backdrop for many towns in the region, including Big Sur, Ojai, and Santa Barbara. Much of the forest is remote and unroaded, providing endless prime back country exploring adventures. Many of its campgrounds and picnic areas, however, can be reached by vehicle. | 805/968–6644 | www.r5.fs.fed.us/lospadres/ | $5 | Daily.

Mission San Antonio de Padua. This was the third mission founded by Father Junípero Serra (in 1771); it was known as the Jewel of the Santa Lucias. The church was completed in 1813. A self-guided tour takes you through ruins of Indian homes, an orchard, a cemetery, and other original buildings. At the end of Mission Creek Rd. inside Fort Hunter-Liggett Military base. | 831/385–4478 | www.missionsanantoniopadua.com/ | Free, museum: donations are accepted | July–Aug., daily 8–6, after Labor Day 8–5.

San Lorenzo Park. In the Santa Lucia foothills along the Salinas River, this park has nature trails, two playgrounds, volleyball, and RV and tent camping. | 1160 Broadway, | 831/385–5964 | $3 per vehicle weekdays, $5 per vehicle weekends | Daily.

Monterey County Agricultural and Rural Life Museum. This museum in a barn in San Lorenzo County Park holds more than 20 exhibits tracing the evolution of agriculture in Monterey County. Beside the museum are a working blacksmith shop, a turn-of-the-20th-century school, and a restored farmhouse. An 1886 Southern Pacific train depot is also located within the park. Guided tours by appointment. | 1160 Broadway | 831/385–8020 | Museum Free. County Park vehicle fee Mon.–Fri. $3, weekends $5 | Museum Daily 10–4, Park dawn to dusk.

ON THE CALENDAR

MAY: *Salinas Valley Fair.* Rodeo, rope twirling, livestock, exhibits, carnival rides, and live country and pop music. | 625 Division St. | 831/385–3243 | www.salinasvalleyfair.com.

JUNE: *Mission San Antonio de Padua Fiesta.* An annual fiesta fundraiser at Fort Hunter-Liggett (at the end of Mission Creek Rd.) to raise money necessary for the upkeep of the Mission building and grounds. Arts, crafts, food booths, historical re-creations. 11 AM mass. | 408/385–4478.

Dining

Keefer's Restaurant. American. A casual family restaurant next to a motor lodge. Burgers and sandwiches, as well as prime rib and shrimp scampi, are on the menu. Salad bar. Kids' menu. | 611 Canal St. | 831/385–3543 | Breakfast also available | $15–$25 | AE, MC, V.

Lodging

Best Western/King City Inn. Built in 1985, this two-story Spanish-tiled hotel is next to Monterey County Park and one block from local businesses. Complimentary Continental breakfast. Microwaves, refrigerators, cable TV. | 1190 Broadway | 831/385–6733 | fax 831/385–0714 | 47 rooms | $79 | AE, D, DC, MC, V.

Courtesy Inn. This modern all-suites hotel is right off U.S. 101 at the Broadway exit next to a family restaurant and several fast food chains, and 1 mi from town. Rooms are decorated in cool tones of blue and mauve. Restaurant, complimentary Continental breakfast. In-room data ports, microwaves, refrigerators, some in-room hot tubs, cable TV, in-room VCRs (and movies). Pool. Hot tub. Laundry facilities. Business services. Some pets allowed. | 4 Broadway Circle | 831/385–4646 or 800/350–5616 | fax 831/385–6024 | 63 suites | $85–$175 suites | AE, D, DC, MC, V.

Keefer's Inn. You enter the second-story room of this simple two-story motor hotel across the freeway from the fairgrounds, off U.S. 101 at the Canal Street exit from the inside, and the ground floor rooms exit to parking. Restaurant (*see* Dining), complimentary Continental breakfast. Refrigerators, cable TV. Pool. Hot tub. Laundry facilities. Business services. | 615 Canal St. | 831/385–4843 | fax 831/385–1254 | 47 rooms | $53–$59 | AE, D, DC, MC, V.

LAGUNA BEACH

MAP 4, J15

(Nearby towns also listed: Dana Point, Irvine, Mission Viejo, San Clemente, San Juan Capistrano)

★ Part bohemian artist colony, part gay enclave, this Orange County resort town of 23,200 has a laid-back mix of artists, hippies, and counterculture dropouts, but also a much wealthier, more conservative component. Laguna Beach has managed to maintain a balance between luxury tourism and communal values. The country's largest housing project for AIDS patients, for example, is only blocks from the town's $200-a-night hotels. For day trips, there are scores of art galleries, plenty of arts and crafts and antiques shops, and a very active swimming/surfing beach.

Information: **Laguna Beach Visitors Bureau** | 252 Broadway, 92651 | 800/877–1115 or 949/497–9229 | www.lagunabeachinfo.org.

Attractions

Crystal Cove State Park. Biking and hiking trails are plentiful at this park 1½ mi north of town, but the main attraction is the 1,000-acre underwater park for scuba divers and snorkelers. | 8471 N. Pacific Coast Hwy. | 949/494–3539 | fax 949/494–6911 | $6 | 6 AM–sunset.

Laguna Playhouse. The Laguna Playhouse presents comedies, dramas, and musicals chosen from among the most exciting and acclaimed works in today's theatre. The Playhouse is also very involved in youth theatre, education, and development. September through June the Playhouse stages six adult and four youth-oriented productions. | 606 Laguna Canyon Rd. | 949/497–2787 | www.lagunaplayhouse.com | $16–$43 | Sept.–June, Tues.–Sun. Ticket hours 10–8.

ON THE CALENDAR

JUNE, AUG.: *Sawdust Festival.* In a eucalyptus grove, on Laguna Canyon Road, artisans construct booths in which you can throw a pot, paint, air brush, or print. A food court and live entertainment complement these activities. | 949/494–3030.

JULY, AUG.: *Festival of Arts.* Work by local artists and talented students is represented in this juried show. Demonstrations, workshops, and live performances complement the art. | 650 Laguna Canyon Rd. | 800/487–FEST.

JULY, AUG.: *Pageant of the Masters.* A tradition since 1933, classic works of art are brought to life through actors, lighting, and sets. | 800/487–FEST.

OCT.: *Laguna Beach Film Festival.* Filmmakers from around the world screen their work at this annual event that raises money for the prevention of child abuse. | 949/494–1313 | www.lagunafilmfestival.org.

Dining

Al a Carte. Café. Popular for gourmet takeout meals, this restaurant also has a small dining area. Menu items include salads, sandwiches, a weekend hors d'oeuvres bar, a selection of vegetarian entrées and great desserts. Try the boneless breast of chicken with pasta in tequila lime and cream sauce, or a cajun fried chicken sandwich. For dessert there's the lemon cake with fresh pineapple filling. Small patio for open-air dining. | 1915 S. Coast Hwy. | 949/497–4927 | $5–$12 | MC, V.

Beach House. Seafood. This cozy little beach house of a restaurant is right on the water, so you might get a faceful of spray at high-tide. It's seafood lovers paradise with a raw bar and entrées such as fresh Cajun mahimahi and lobster tails. If you don't want fish, though, there are still plenty of options, like prime rib and pastas. Kids' menu. No air-conditioning. | 619 Sleepy Hollow La. | 949/494–9707 | Breakfast also available | $18–$35 | AE, MC, V.

Cafe Zinc. Contemporary. Laguna Beach locals gather at the tiny counter and plant-filled patio of this vegetarian breakfast-and-lunch café. Oatmeal is sprinkled with berries, poached eggs are dusted with herbs, and the o.j. is fresh squeezed. For lunch, try a sampler plate, with various salads such as spicy Thai pasta, and asparagus salad with orange peel and capers; or one of the gourmet pizzas. Open air dining. | 350 Ocean Ave. | 949/494–6302 | No supper | $7–$10 | No credit cards.

Cedar Creek Inn. Continental. The interior has a hunting lodge look with its wood beam ceilings and stone fireplace. On the menu at this casual restaurant are burgers, pot roast, fresh fish, pasta, and hearty salads. Open-air patio dining with heating. Entertainment

Tues.–Sun. Kids' menu. Sun. brunch. | 384 Forest Ave. | 949/497–8696 | $19–$27 | AE, D, DC, MC, V.

The Cottage. Seafood. This 1917 Victorian-style cottage has several intimate dining areas with fireplaces. The menu includes dishes like chicken in pineapple and honey-mustard sauce and charbroiled lamb in rosemary Cabernet sauce. Open-air patio dining. Kids' menu. Beer and wine only. | 308 N. Coast Hwy. | 949/494–3023 | Breakfast also available | $8–$16 | AE, D, DC, MC, V.

Las Brisas. Seafood. The candle-lit cliffside dining room overlooks Laguna's scenic, craggy, coastline with the waves and tidal pools below. This romantic restaurant concentrates on seafood and fish dishes like bouillabaisse with a half-lobster tail, filete de calamari, and fish in a tomato saffron broth. Sun. brunch. | 361 Cliff Dr. | 949/497–5434 | Breakfast also available | $15–$30 | AE, D, DC, MC, V.

Mosun Sushi. Japanese. A restaurant and dance club in one, this establishment serves sushi and cooked entrées. A wide assortment of wines and sake fill out the menu. On Thursday, Friday, and Saturday nights the restaurant transforms into a dance club, where you will find DJs spinning hip-hop, top 40s hits, and techno. | 680 S. Coast Hwy. | 949/497–5646 | No lunch | $8–$24 | AE, D, MC, V.

Partners Bistro. Eclectic. French-influenced dishes and candlelight make this café an attractive dinner destination. Rack of lamb, salmon en papillote, and spinach en croûte are complemented by an excellent wine list. | 448 S. Coast Hwy. | 949/497–4441 | $16–$24 | AE, MC, V.

Royal Thai Cuisine. Thai. Wood paneling warms the dining room at this restaurant which serves authentic Thai dishes like Thai chicken flame and crying tiger prawns. | 1750 South Pacific Coast Hwy. | 949/494–8424 | $14–$21 | AE, D, MC, V.

Rumari. Italian. This friendly place, about a mile south of the town center, serves Italian food with a full selection of pastas, meats, and fresh grilled seafood. Open-air dining. | 1826 S. Coast Hwy. | 949/494–0400 | No lunch | $11–$24 | AE, D, DC, MC, V.

Lodging

Aliso Creek Inn. In a secluded area of Aliso Canyon, 2½ mi south of the downtown area, this all-suites property of townhouse-style buildings has flower-lined walkways and is within a couple hundred feet of the beach and a fishing pier. Restaurant, bar (with entertainment). Some in-room hot tubs, cable TV. Pool, wading pool. 9-hole golf course, putting green. Laundry facilities. Business services. | 31106 Coast Hwy. | 949/499–2271 or 800/223–3309 (CA) | fax 949/499–4601 | www.alisocreekinn.com | 62 suites | $146–$310 suites | AE, D, DC, MC, V.

Best Western Laguna Brisas Spa Hotel. All rooms at this hotel have in-room whirlpool tubs, and each is furnished with a bright tropical theme. There's also a sun deck where you can relax next to the pool. Complimentary Continental breakfast. Refrigerators, in-room hot tubs, cable TV. Pool. Hot tub, massage. Laundry facilities. Business services. | 1600 S. Coast Hwy. | 949/497–7272 | fax 949/497–830 | www.bestwestern.com | 65 rooms | $169–$299 | AE, D, DC, MC, V.

Best Western Laguna Reef Inn. On the inland side of Pacific Coast Hwy., this two-story hotel is 2½ mi south of many Laguna art galleries. Also within an hour's drive are the Rogers Gardens, Mission San Juan Capistrano, and Modjeska Bird Sanctuary. Some rooms are named and decorated for famous artists. Complimentary Continental breakfast. Some microwaves, refrigerators, cable TV, in-room VCRs (and movies). Pool. Hot tub, sauna. | 30806 S. Coast Hwy. | 949/499–2227 | fax 949/499–5575 | www.bestwestern.com | 43 rooms | $160–$219 | AE, D, DC, MC, V.

By the Sea Inn. Next to Heisler's Park Marine Life Sanctuary and only a few feet from the beach, this hotel has great ocean views and modern furnishings. Complimentary Continental breakfast. Some kitchenettes, cable TV. Sauna, spa, steam room. Laundry facilities.

| 475 N. Coast Hwy. | 949/497–6645 or 800/297–0007 | fax 949/497–9499 | www.bythe-seainn.com | 36 rooms | $99–$159 | AE, D, DC, MC, V.

Capri Laguna. This four-story complex built into a hillside on the beach has sundecks and a pool on the upper levels. Shops, restaurants, and art galleries are 1 mi north. Complimentary Continental breakfast. Some kitchenettes, refrigerators, cable TV. Outdoor pool. Sauna. Exercise equipment. | 1441 S. Coast Hwy. | 949/494–6533 or 800/225–4551 | fax 949/497–6962 | www.caprilaguna.com | 45 rooms | $75–$140 | AE, D, DC, MC, V.

Carriage House. Just two blocks from the beach and 1 mi south of downtown, this 1920s country-style inn is one of Laguna's architectural landmarks. Complimentary fresh fruit and wine, antique furniture, a garden courtyard, and large sitting rooms in the themed suites—Lilac Time has floral bedding, a brass bed, and French doors to the courtyard, Green Palms has white wicker furniture and netting over the bed—make the inn a local favorite. Complimentary breakfast. Pets allowed. | 1322 Catalina St. | 949/494–8945 | fax 949/494–6829 | crgehsebb@aol.com | www.carriagehouse.com | 6 suites | $125–$165 | AE, MC, V.

Casa Laguna Inn. Majestic queen palms, a colorful tropical garden, a deck with banana and avocado trees, and antique furnishings are among the charms of this B&B near Victoria and Moss Point beaches. Complimentary breakfast. Some kitchenettes, cable TV. Outdoor pool. Library. | 2510 S. Coast Hwy. | 949/494–2996 or 800/233–0449 | fax 949/494–5009 | 21 rooms, 4 suites, 1 cottage | $120–$170, suites $180, cottage $250 | AE, D, MC, V.

Courtyard by Marriott. This five-story hotel, just off I–5 at the Lake Forest Drive exit, is a 20-minute drive north of Laguna Beach. Restaurant, bar. In-room data ports, refrigerators, cable TV. Pool. Hot tub. Exercise equipment. Laundry facilities. Business services. | 23175 Avenida de la Carlota, Laguna Hills | 949/859–5500 | fax 949/454–2158 | www.marriott.com | 136 rooms | $119–$149 | AE, D, DC, MC, V.

★ **Eiler's Inn.** Guest rooms at this full-service B&B, in the center of town, are individually furnished with antiques and paintings by local artists. The sunny central courtyard has a bubbling fountain, and is a good place to relax. Check out the in-room traveler's journal where you can add your own travel prose. Complimentary Continental breakfast. No room phones. Business services. No smoking. | 741 S. Coast Hwy. | 949/494–3004 | fax 949/497–2215 | 12 rooms | $120–$195 | AE, D, MC, V.

Holiday Inn. Right off I–5, at the La Paz exit, in the heart of the Laguna hills, this four-story hotel sits 10 mi northeast of Laguna Beach and its attractions. Rooms are generously sized and have views of either the pool or mountains. Restaurant, bar (with entertainment), room service. In-room data ports, cable TV. Pool. Business services, airport shuttle. | 25205 La Paz Rd., Laguna Hills | 949/586–5000 | fax 949/581–7410 | www.hol-iday-inn.com/lagunahillca | 147 rooms | $129–$139 | AE, D, DC, MC, V.

Hotel Laguna. Opened in 1890, this is the oldest hotel in Laguna. It has manicured lawns, a private beach, and an ideal downtown location. Some rooms have canopy beds and good reproduction Victorian furnishings; others have whitewashed furniture with pastel bedspreads and curtains. Restaurant, bar (with entertainment), complimentary Continental breakfast. Cable TV. Beauty salon. Beach. Business services. | 425 S. Coast Hwy. | 949/494–1151 or 800/524–2927 (CA) | fax 949/497–2163 | hotellaguna@msn.com | www.men-bytes.com/hotellaguna | 65 rooms | $100–$195 | AE, D, DC, MC, V.

Inn at Laguna Beach. Terra-cotta tiles, exotic flowers throughout the grounds, and its location on a bluff overlooking the ocean, make this inn seem like it's on the Mediterranean. Most rooms have ocean views. Several art galleries, village shops, and restaurants are two or three blocks away. Restaurant, complimentary Continental breakfast. In-room data ports, minibars, refrigerators, cable TV, in-room VCRs (and movies). Pool. Hot tub, massage. Beach. Business services, free parking. | 211 N. Pacific Coast Hwy. | 949/497–9722 or 800/544–4479 | fax 949/497–9972 | www.innatlagunabeach.com | 70 rooms | $99–$529 | AE, D, DC, MC, V.

La Casa Del Camino. A popular choice for wedding receptions, this 1927 Mediterranean-style hotel with period furniture has been a filming location for movies, such as Evangeline and All Quiet on the Western Front, and a getaway for Hollywood stars, like Humphrey Bogart and Douglas Fairbanks. There is an oceanfront banquet room and a roof-top garden. Restaurant, complimentary Continental breakfast. Some in-room hot tubs, cable TV. Business services. | 1289 S. Coast Hwy. | 949/497–2446 | fax 949/494–5581 | www.casacamino.com | 39 rooms | $125–$165 | AE, D, DC, MC, V.

Laguna House. Just two blocks from the beach, this hotel has spacious and nicely furnished guest rooms. Picnic area. Kitchenettes, microwaves, cable TV, in-room VCRs (and movies). | 539 Catalina St. | 949/497–9061 or 800/248–7348 | 8 suites (2 with shower only) | $125–$185 suites (2–day minimum stay weekends) | AE, MC, V.

Laguna Riviera Beach Resort and Spa. At this oceanfront five-story hotel you'll find sun decks and terraces, and a glassed-in pool with a view of the outdoors. Individually decorated guest rooms are cool and airy, as well as generously sized. Restaurant, complimentary Continental breakfast. Some kitchenettes, cable TV. Indoor pool. Hot tub, sauna. | 825 S. Coast Hwy. | 949/494–1196 or 800/999–2089 | fax 949/494–8421 | www.laguna-riviera.com | 41 rooms | $85–$201 | AE, D, DC, MC, V.

Sea Cliff Motel. Just steps away from the beach, this two-story 1950s motor hotel, approximately 1 mi south of downtown, has modest rooms with ocean views and sun decks. Complimentary Continental breakfast. Some microwaves, refrigerators, cable TV. Outdoor pool. | 1661 S. Coast Hwy. | 949/494–9717 or 800/500–2164 | fax 949/497–1031 | www.sea-clifflaguna.com | 27 rooms | $79–$109 | AE, D, MC, V.

★ **Surf and Sand.** This hotel is right on the beach and all rooms are oceanfront with plantation shutters, bleached wood furnishings, and light colors. The suites have a spa bath and fireplace. The Laguna Art Museum is 1½ mi north of the property and Laguna Beach is 1 mi away. Restaurant, bar (with entertainment). In-room data ports, minibars, refrigerators, some in-room hot tubs, cable TV. Pool. Massage. Beach. Kids' programs (ages 5–17). Business services. | 1555 S. Coast Hwy. | 949/497–4477 or 800/524–8621 | fax 949/494–2897 | rvanness@jcresorts.com | www.jcresorts.com | 164 rooms in 3 buildings | $305–$400, $475–$1,000 (suites) | AE, D, DC, MC, V.

Vacation Village. With 300 ft of its own private beach, this hotel has stunning views of the ocean and Catalina Island. It's just two blocks from the center of town with plenty of shops, restaurants, and art galleries to explore. The casual tone makes this a good choice for families. Rooms are contemporary with light walls, red and black abstract patterned bedspreads, and dark carpeting; some have ocean views. Restaurant, bar. Kitchenettes, refrigerators, cable TV. 2 pools. Hot tub. Video games. Some pets allowed. Free parking. | 647 S. Coast Hwy. | 949/494–8566 or 800/843–6895 | fax 949/494–1386 | vvillage@earthlink.net | www.vacationvillage.com | 133 rooms, 70 suites in 5 buildings | $90–$204, $246–$324 suites | AE, D, DC, MC, V.

LA HABRA

MAP 9, I5

(Nearby towns also listed: Brea, Buena Park, Fullerton, Whittier)

La Habra is just inside the Orange County line, 20 mi southeast of Los Angeles. It was incorporated in 1925, and at that time citrus fruits, avocados, and walnuts dominated the local economy. Like many small California towns, the crops have given way to malls and homes, and La Habra is now a residential and commercial city of 52,300 residents.

Information: La Habra Beach Visitors Bureau | 321 E. La Habra Blvd., 90631 | 562/697–1704 | www.lahabrabiz.com.

Attractions

La Habra Children's Museum. Hands-on exhibits and many natural science displays make this one of Southern California's best children's museums. Check out the antique caboose outside. | 301 S. Euclid St. | 562/905–9793 | www.lhcm.org | $4 | Mon.–Sat. 10–5, Sun. 1–5.

ON THE CALENDAR

FEB.: *I Love La Habra Street Fair.* This fair held on La Habra Boulevard in front of City Hall includes food vendors, arts and crafts booths, live music, and a classic car show. | 562/905–9705 | Free.

Dining

Cat and the Custard Cup. Contemporary. The menu changes four times a year, but staples include some surprises such as tortilla-crusted prawns with cocktail sauce, and pork with Chinese mustard sauce. Desserts include a decadent tri-color chocolate mousse. Open-air dining is on the garden-like patio. | 800 E. Whittier Blvd. | 562/694–3812 | No lunch | $18–$25 | AE, DC, MC, V.

Lodging

Heritage Inn. These lodgings with an unusual rock-filled lobby are 8 mi from theme parks and 2 mi southeast of downtown La Habra. Beige no-frills rooms come with free passes to the World Gym. Complimentary Continental breakfast. In-room data ports, some microwaves, refrigerators, cable TV. Outdoor pool. Outdoor hot tub. Exercise equipment. Laundry facilities. Business services. | 333 E. Imperial Hwy., Fullerton | 714/447–9200 | fax 714//773–0685 | 113 rooms, 11 suites | $68 rooms, $92 suites | AE, D, DC, MC, V.

LA JOLLA

MAP 4, J17

(Nearby towns also listed: Del Mar, El Cajon, Encinitas, Rancho Sante Fe, San Diego)

Within the San Diego city limits but feeling more like its own hamlet, the cove-hugging village of La Jolla has long been known for its rugged coast, choice beaches, and sandstone cliffs etched and sculpted by endless wave action. Stay here if you want easy access to scuba, snorkeling, and surfing. It's also pretty affluent here and is home to the University of California at San Diego (UCSD), so there are lots of boutiques to shop in and interesting, fun places to eat.

Information: **La Jolla Town Council** | 7734 Herschel Ave., Suite F, 92037 | 858/454–1444.

Attractions

Children's Pool Beach. Point La Jolla, a rocky outcrop jutting north into the Pacific, separates Children's Pool Beach and La Jolla Beach. Children's beach is characterized by clear water, which makes snorkeling and scuba diving popular. Lifeguards year-round. | 900 Coast Blvd. | 858/454–1444 | Free | Daily.

Kellogg Park. This grassy park which stretches along Caminito del Oro between El Paseo Grande and Avenida de la Playa provides a panoramic, breezy view of the ocean. A popular site for family picnics and barbeques, it also has a children's playground. | Caminito del Oro between El Paseo Grande and Avenida de la Playa | 858/454–1444 | Free | Daily.

★ **Museum of Contemporary Art.** This museum is housed in a two-story building with a sculpture garden. The permanent collection includes conceptual and minimalist art, plus art by many California artists. The visiting exhibitions range from sculpture and prints to drawings and paintings. | 700 Prospect St. | 858/454–3541 | $4; special rates for students and seniors; free 1st Sun. and 3rd Tues. of each month | Daily 11–5; Thurs. 11–8; closed Wed.

Scripps Beach and Tidepools. This sandy beach is separated from La Jolla Shores only by the Scripps Pier. Here you will find numerous tide pools that offer a close-up view of marine life. You can look, but touching marine life is prohibited. Off-street and metered parking. | 7734 Herschel Ave., Suite F | 858/454–1444 | Free | Daily.

Stephen Birch Aquarium-Museum. The aquarium contains marine life from both the warm tropical seas of the Pacific Ocean and the cold northern waters. The Aquarium-Museum also has very good interactive exhibits and changing displays. During January and February, there are whale-watching boat rides and exhibits about migrating gray whales. | 2300 Expedition Way | 858/534–3474 | www.aquarium.ucsd.edu | $8.50, $3.00 per vehicle, special rates for students, seniors, and children | Daily 9–5.

University of California, San Diego. Striking architecture and wooded grounds grace this seaside campus of the University of California known especially for its scientific pursuits. | 9500 Gilman Dr. | 619/534–8273 | www.ucsd.edu | Free | Daily.

Wind 'n' Sea Beach. This narrow, rocky beach is considered one of Southern California's best for surfing. There isn't a great deal of sand, but it is popular for swimming. The smooth, rocky ledge that lines most of the beach makes for interesting exploration. There are no amenities, although lifeguards are stationed on the beach during the summer. Park along Neptune Street or in a small, unpaved lot at the end of Nautilus Street. | 858/454–1444 | Free | Daily.

ON THE CALENDAR
SEPT.: *La Jolla Art Festival.* Artists from around the country come to downtown La Jolla to sell their artwork at this festival sometimes held in the elementary school on Girard Ave. | 858/454–5718 | Free.

Dining
Bernini's. American. Half country kitchen, half modern art museum, Bernini's serves typical breakfast foods, as well as pasta, salads, and sandwiches. Browse through the well-stocked newsstand as you sip your coffee. The downtown La Jolla crowd metamorphoses as the day progresses—from businesspeople to escapees from the local high school to UCSD students. Try some oriental chicken salad or the pesto chicken pizza. Homemade breads. | 7550 Fay Ave. | 858/454–5013 | No dinner (breakfast and lunch only) | $11–$18 | MC, V.

Bird Rock Cafe. Seafood. Moderate prices and good food made this cottage-turned-restaurant into a local favorite. Creative dishes include locally harvested mussels in a savory Thai curry, grilled Atlantic salmon, and pasta with a red curry mussel sauce. Two patios for open-air dining. | 5656 La Jolla Blvd. | 858/551–4090 | www.birdrockcafe.com | No lunch | $15–$21 | AE, D, DC, MC, V.

Brockton Villa. Contemporary. This informal restaurant resides today in a restored 1894 beach cottage with vertical tongue-and-groove siding of pure heart redwood and a wrap-around veranda that overlooks La Jolla Cove and the ocean. The extensive menu includes dishes like pan seared filet mignon and herbed crab stuffed lobster tail. Take advantage of the fabulous daytime view by sitting on the outdoor veranda or patio. Sun. brunch. Beer and wine only. | 1235 Coast Blvd. | 858/454–7393 | $12–$23 | AE, D, MC, V.

Cafe Japengo. Pan-Asian. Framed by marble walls accented with leafy bamboo trees and unusual black-iron sculptures, this Pacific Rim restaurant serves Asian-inspired cuisine with many North and South American touches. There's a selection of grilled, wood-roasted, and wok-fried entrées, as well as very fresh sushi ordered from your table or at the sushi bar. | 8960 University Center La. | 619/450–3355 | No lunch weekends | $16–$29 | AE, D, DC, MC, V.

Crab Catcher. Seafood. Set high on a cliff with a spectacular ocean view, this restaurant serves fresh seafood and pastas in the dining room or on the outdoor patio. Have the catch of the day stuffed with crab or try the coconut shrimp tempura. Open-air dining. Kids' menu. Sun. brunch. | 1298 Prospect St. | 858/454–9587 | $16–$30 | AE, D, DC, MC, V.

Crescent Shores Grill. American. Between white-washed walls and expansive plate glass windows overlooking the ocean from the 11th floor, you can dine on such dishes as grilled pork chops with sweet potato hash, seafood gumbo, and bacon-wrapped Gulf shrimp in white-truffle oil. Open bistro kitchen. Jazz Fri., Sat. Earlybird suppers. Sun. brunch. | 7955 La Jolla Shores Dr. | 858/459–0541 | Breakfast also available | $14–$33 | AE, DC, MC, V.

Daily's Fit and Fresh. Contemporary. Established by a cardiac surgeon, this is the place for low-calorie and low-fat entrées. No dish, including the brownie sundae, exceeds 10 grams of fat. The majority of the menu is vegetarian, but there are some chicken and fish choices. Open-air dining. Kids' menu. | 8915 Towne Centre Dr. | 858/453–1112 | $5–$10 | MC, V.

French Pastry Shop. Continental. For over 20 years this casual restaurant has been selling their popular quiches, salads, pâtés, and desserts such as fruit tartes, cheesecakes, and chocolates. Their speciality is their many different homemade breads and pastries. Open-air patio dining. | 5550 La Jolla Blvd. | 858/454–9094 | www.frenchpastery.com | No supper Mon. | $7–$10 | MC, V.

★ **George's at the Cove.** Seafood. Choose between semi-formal indoor dining and more casual dining on the upper terrace with a sweeping view of the coast. The eclectic California cuisine emphasizes seafood such as sautéed Arctic char served on poached fennel, garlic roasted Mexican prawns, and Pacific red snapper. Meat dishes are available. Extensive wine list. Open-air dining. | 1250 Prospect Pl | 858/454–4244 | georgesatthecove.com | $25–$35 | AE, D, DC, MC, V.

Marine Room. Seafood. Gaze at the ocean at this seaside restaurant and you might see the grunion run. The contemporary menu includes such creative dishes as baked Alaskan halibut in a potato net served with artichokes, crawfish tails, chanterelle mushrooms, and candied onions in a mustard-seed Riesling sauce. Dancing. Entertainment Tues.–Sat., Sun. brunch. | 2000 Spindrift Dr. | 619/459–7222 | $20–$40 | AE, D, DC, MC, V.

Piatti Ristorante. Italian. The interior is light and airy, with pastel murals of overflowing plates of pasta gracing the walls. A wood burning oven turns out flavorful pizzas; creative pastas include wide saffron noodles with shrimp, fresh tomatoes, and arugula, and garlicky spaghetti served with clams in the shell. There's also a good rotisserie roast chicken and grilled rib-eye steak. A fountain splashes softly on the tree-shaded patio, where heat lamps allow diners to sit even on chilly evenings. Open-air dining. Sun. brunch. | 2182 Avenida de la Playa | 858/454–1589 | www.piattiristorante.com | $10–$14 | D, DC, MC, V.

Sammy's California Woodfired Pizza. Contemporary. This casual western-based chain serves generously portioned pastas, pizzas, salads, and entrées such as grilled pork chops, Norwegian salmon steak fillet, and rotisserie chicken. Open-air sidewalk dining is available. Kids' menu. | 702 Pearl St. | 619/456–5222 | $8–$20 | AE, DC, MC, V.

SamSon's. Delicatessen. Cozy up to the lunch counter or choose between two simple dining rooms with wood booths and brass at this New York–style deli. A full bakery, over 100 dishes on the menu, enormous portions, and excellent chicken soup are reason enough to visit. The lox plate for breakfast and the overstuffed corned-beef-and-slaw sandwich for lunch are especially good. Kids menu. | 8861 Villa La Jolla Dr. | 858/455–1462 | Breakfast also available | $13–$30 | AE, D, DC, MC, V.

Sante Ristorante. Italian. Your seating choices include two sidewalk terraces, a stunning courtyard, a handsome formal dining room, and a cozy bar with a fireplace. Savor truffles in the fall when they get heavy play here, or try the roasted salmon with black truffles, jumbo shrimp with artichokes and cherry tomatoes, or breast of duck with rosemary sauce. Everything is made fresh on the premises: pastas, sauces, sausages, breads, and desserts. Open-air dining. Pianist Thurs.–Sat. | 7811 Herschel Ave. | 858/454–1315 | www.san-teristorante.com | No lunch Sun. | $10–$26 | AE, D, DC, MC, V.

Top o' the Cove. Contemporary. This romantic turn-of-the-20th-century cottage has ocean views and serves fine contemporary cuisine including fresh salmon, swordfish, and abalone creations. Extensive wine list. Homemade pastries. Open-air dining. Pianist Thurs.–Sun. | 1216 Prospect Place | 858/454–7779 | 11:30 AM–2:30 PM, 5:30–10:30 PM; Sun. brunch 10:30 AM–3 PM | $30–$45 | AE, DC, MC, V.

Torreyana Grille. Continental. The dining room here is filled with original artwork and lush plants surrounding a large marble fountain. The contemporary menu includes fresh seafood, New York cut beef, chicken, Maine lobster, rack of lamb and filet mignon. Open-air terrace dining. A pianist plays live jazz every night Monday through Saturday and during brunch on Sundays. Kids' menu. Sun. brunch. | 10950 N. Torrey Pines Rd. | 858/450–4571 | Breakfast also available | $15–$26 | AE, D, DC, MC, V.

Trattoria Acqua. Italian. The central courtyard, ocean views, and charming frescos on walls provide a perfect backdrop for great Italian cuisine such as osso bucco, an array of pastas, and flavorful grilled meats and fishes. Try the aged black angus, New York steak, or baby lamb chops with herb bread crumbs, rosemary roasted new potatoes, garlic sautéed spinach and scampi al aglio. Open-air patio dining. Raw bar. Sun. brunch. | 1298 Prospect St. | 858/454–0709 | www.trattoriaacqua.com | No supper Sun. | $16–$30 | AE, MC, V.

Lodging

Andrea Villa Inn. This two-story hotel is a 15-minute walk uphill to the Scripps Institute of Oceanography. Shops, golf, and the beaches are slightly further west, 1.5 mi from the hotel. Units are roomy and comfortable, and if you get hooked, the inn has weekly and monthly rates. Complimentary Continental breakfast. Some kitchenettes, cable TV. Pool. Hot tub. Laundry facilities. Business services. Pets allowed. | 2402 Torrey Pines Rd. | 858/459–3311 or 800/411–2141 | fax 858/459–1320 | www.andreavilla.com/ | 49 rooms | $119–$165 | AE, D, DC, MC, V.

Bed and Breakfast Inn at La Jolla. Built in 1913, noted architect Irving Gill designed this beige stucco Cubist-style house. Attractive guest rooms have Laura Ashley fabrics and antiques, fireplaces, and ocean or garden views. The Museum of Contemporary Art is across the street and the beach is a block away. Complimentary Continental breakfast. Some refrigerators, no TV in some rooms, TV in common area. | 7753 Draper Ave. | 858/456–2066 or 800/582–2466 | fax 858/456–1510 | www.innlajolla.com | 15 rooms | $159–$379 | MC, V.

Best Western Inn by the Sea. All rooms of this five-story tourist and business hotel amidst boutiques and restaurants are appointed in beige and gold and have village or ocean views, many with private balconies. You can have your morning juice, coffee and pastries in the breakfast room by the pool. Restaurant, complimentary Continental breakfast. Some microwaves, refrigerators, cable TV. Outdoor pool. Spa. Health Club. Free parking. | 7830 Fay Ave. | 858/459–4461 or 800/526–4545 | fax 858/456–2578 | www.bestwestern.com/innbythesea | 132 rooms | $119–$179 | AE, D, DC, MC, V.

Cove Suites. Most accommodations at this all-suite property have balconies with ocean-front views of the Pacific. All rooms are uniquely appointed in soothing pastels borrowed from the palette of the beach. Refrigerators, cable TV. Pool. Hot tub, spa. Putting green. Laundry facilities. Business services, free parking. | 1155 Coast Blvd. | 858/459–2621 or 800/248–2683 | fax 858/454–3522 | www.lajollacove.com/ | 90 rooms | $130–$179 min-isuite (no ocean view), $165–$175 studio, $195–$279 mini-suites, $285–$369 full suites, $239–$349 2–bdrm suites (no ocean view), $259–$549 2–bdrm suites, $478–$698 4–bdrm suites | AE, D, DC, MC, V.

Embassy Suites. Sleek and modern, this all-suites hotel is 15 minutes away from down-town San Diego via freeway. There's a 12-story tropical atrium and central courtyard with landscaped koi ponds, and plenty of amenities for both the leisure and business traveler. University Town Center mall is across the street where you'll find a movie theatre and an indoor ice skating rink. Restaurant, bar, complimentary breakfast. In-room data ports, microwaves, refrigerators, cable TV. Indoor pool. Hot tub. Exercise equipment. Laundry facilities. Business services. | 4550 La Jolla Village Dr. | 858/453–0400 | fax 858/453–4226 | www.embassysuites | 335 suites | $175–$265 suites | AE, D, DC, MC, V.

Empress Hotel. Within two blocks of shops, restaurants, art galleries and the beach, this five-story upscale hotel offers extra touches such as terry robes, and pastries and coffee served on the sundeck each morning. Rooms are contemporary, rendered in purple and reddish hues. Some rooms have ocean views, kitchenettes and whirlpools. Restaurant, bar, complimentary Continental breakfast. Refrigerators, cable TV. Exercise equipment. Business services. | 7766 Fay Ave. | 858/454–3001 or 888/369–9900 (for reservations) | fax 858/454–6387 | www.empress-hotel.com | 73 rooms | $129–$199 | AE, D, DC, MC, V.

Grande Colonial. One block from the ocean, this elegant hotel, established in 1913, boasts mahogany woodwork and leaded-glass chandeliers. Rooms have breathtaking views and goose-down comforters and pillows on the beds. You can walk to the nearby shops, art galleries, and restaurants. Restaurant, complimentary Continental breakfast. Some kitchenettes, some microwaves, some refrigerators, cable TV. Pool. Beach. Laundry service. | 910 Prospect St. | 858/454–2181 | www.thegrandecolonial.com | 55 rooms, 20 suites | $159–$329, $209–$429 suites | AE, DC, MC, V.

Hotel La Jolla. A luxury boutique hotel 5 blocks from the beaches of La Jolla Shores and 1 mi north of art galleries, restaurants and specialty shops. Staff accompany you to the beach with beach chairs and umbrellas. Guest rooms have white plantation shutters, overstuffed chairs, floral fabrics, fresh seasonal flowers in the bathroom, private balconies, and either ocean or garden views. Restaurant, bar (with entertainment). Refrigerators, cable TV. Pool. Hot tub. Exercise equipment. Laundry facilities. Business services. | 7955 La Jolla Shores Dr. | 858/459–0261 or 800/666–0261 | fax 858/459–7649 | www.hotellajolla.com | 108 rooms | $159–$209 | AE, D, DC, MC, V.

★ **Hyatt Regency La Jolla at Aventine.** Built in 1989, this 16-story hotel east of downtown in a business and restaurant complex that encompasses 11 scenic acres of northern La Jolla was designed by noted architect Michael Graves who combined neoclassical, postmodern and Mediterranean elements. The hotel is in the heart of La Jolla's Golden Triangle, a commercial district framed by I–5, I–805 and Rte. 52. Guest rooms are spacious and have cherrywood furnishings. Restaurants on the hotel property have something for any palate, including casual American, Italian, Continental and Pan Asian fare. 5 restaurants, lounge, bar. In-room data ports, minibars, cable TV. Pool. Hot tub, massage. Tennis. Business services, parking (fee). | 3777 La Jolla Village Dr. | 858/552–1234 | fax 858/552–6066 | 419 rooms | $214–$325 | AE, D, DC, MC, V.

Inn at La Jolla. In a residential neighborhood 3 mi north of downtown La Jolla, the standard guest rooms have either one king-size or two double beds and have ocean pool, or parking lot views. Several chain restaurants are within two blocks of the motel and the beach is one block away. Complimentary Continental breakfast. Kitchenettes, some refrigerators, cable TV. Pool. Hot tub. Putting green. | 5440 La Jolla Blvd. | 858/454–6121 | fax 858/459–1377 | 84 rooms | $99–$109 | AE, D, DC, MC, V.

La Jolla Riviera Apartments. Across the street from the La Jolla Beach and Tennis Club, these quiet, fully furnished apartments have easy access to the beach and shops there. Kitchenettes, cable TV. Outdoor pool. Laundry facilities. | 2031 Paseo Dorado | 858/454–0437 | fax 858/454–0437 | 7 apartments | $120 | MC, V.

La Jolla Shores Inn. This small, economical hotel is centrally located between downtown La Jolla and Pacific Beach. Restaurant. Some kitchenettes, some refrigerators, cable TV. Pool. | 5390 La Jolla Blvd. | 858/454–0175 | fax 858/551–7520 | 43 rooms | $70–$79 | AE, D, DC, MC, V.

LA JOLLA

INTRO
ATTRACTIONS
DINING
LODGING

★ **La Jolla Torrey Pines Hilton.** Set on a bluff above La Jolla, this luxury hotel overlooks the sea. The Torrey Pines Golf course sits in the backyard of this hotel and provides an amazing view from most rooms. Amenities include complimentary butler service and free town-car service to downtown La Jolla and Del Mar. You'll feel pampered sleeping between Egyptian cotton linens and down comforters or just taking in views of the golf course or ocean while lounging on the oversized stuffed chair with your feet up on the ottoman. Ground floor rooms have patios, all other rooms have balconies. Restaurant, bar (with entertainment), room service. In-room data ports, in-room safes, minibars, cable TV. Pool. Hot tub. Tennis. Exercise equipment. Bicycles. Children's programs (summer; ages 5–12). Business services. | 10950 N. Torrey Pines Rd. | 858/558–1500 | fax 858/450–4584 | 400 rooms | $205–$280 | AE, DC, MC, V.

★ **La Valencia.** In the 1930s, this red tile and pink stucco hotel attracted film stars from Hollywood. Most guest rooms overlook Cove Beach and have a genteel European look with antique furnishings, richly colored rugs, grand bathrooms, and comfy plush robes. Studio apartments completed in 2000 are now available. The deluxe suite has a large wrap-around balcony and two fireplaces. Restaurant, bar (with entertainment), room service. Some kitchenettes, minibars, some refrigerators, cable TV. Pool. Hot tub. Exercise equipment. Business services. | 1132 Prospect St. | 858/454–0771 or 800/451–0772 | fax 858/456–3921 | www.lavalencia.com | 90 rooms, 10 suites, 15 villas | $250 rooms with garden view, $500 rooms w/ocean view, $550–$725 1 bdrm. villas, $950 1 bdrm. suites w/partial ocean view, $1,050 1 bdrm. suites w/full ocean view, $3,500 deluxe 1 bdrm. suite | AE, D, DC, MC, V.

Marriott. In the heart of La Jolla's Golden Triangle, a commercial district framed by I–5, I–805 and Rte. 52, this full-service 15-story hotel 3 mi east of downtown is geared toward the business traveler. A large shopping mall with movie theaters and an indoor ice rink are across the street. Restaurant, bar. In-room data ports, cable TV. Indoor-outdoor Pool. Hot tub. Gym. Video Games. Laundry facilities. Business services, parking (fee). Some pets allowed. | 4240 La Jolla Village Dr. | 858/587–1414 | fax 858/546–8518 | www.marriott.com | 360 rooms | $189–$268 | AE, D, DC, MC, V.

Prospect Park Inn. This European-style three-story inn has a prime location in La Jolla Village, it's just one block from the beach, and across the street from some of the area's best shops and restaurants. Many rooms have sweeping ocean views and private balconies. Complimentary Continental breakfast. In-room data ports, some kitchenettes, refrigerator, cable TV. Library. Business services. No pets. No smoking. | 1110 Prospect St. | 858/454–0133 or 800/433–1609 | fax 858/454–2056 | 20 rooms, 2 suites | $150–$200, $350–$400 suites | AE, D, DC, MC, V.

Radisson. Overlooking a tropical garden with a cascading waterfall and koi pond, rooms here are rendered in light sand colors with bright printed bedspreads. In-room extras include coffee/tea makers and video games. The University of California is across the street; La Jolla Cove's beaches and tide pools are 5½ mi west, and boutiques and shopping are 3 mi east of the hotel. Restaurant, bar (with entertainment), room service. In-room data ports, refrigerators, cable TV, in-room VCRs (and movies). Pool. Hot tub. Putting green. Exercise equipment. Business services, airport shuttle, free parking. | 3299 Holiday Court | 858/453–5500; 800/333–3333 reservations | fax 858/453–5550 | 251 rooms in 4 buildings | $169–$275 | AE, D, DC, MC, V.

Residence Inn by Marriott. If you want self-sufficiency for an extended stay this two-story hotel is a good bet. The large, comfortable suites have living rooms and full kitchens and some have fireplaces. Choose from a traditional suite, a penthouse suite, or a studio-style suite. Downtown is 4 mi away, beaches 3 mi. Complimentary Continental breakfast. In-room data ports, microwaves, refrigerators, cable TV. 2 pools. Hot tubs. Laundry facilities. Business services. Free parking. Some pets allowed. | 8901 Gilman Dr. | 858/587–1770 | fax 858/552–0387 | 288 suites | $179 suites | AE, D, DC, MC, V.

Scripps Inn. This modern inn is next door to the San Diego Museum of Contemporary Art and two blocks from La Jolla Village. All rooms are done in a Mediterranean style and contain king-size beds. Some have balconies and fireplaces. Complimentary Continental breakfast. Some kitchenettes, refrigerators, cable TV. Free parking. | 555 S. Coast Blvd. | 858/454–3391 | www.jcresorts.com/scripps-inn/scripps_inn.html | 13 rooms | $105–$220 | AE, D, DC, MC, V.

Sea Lodge. Mexican tile work, fountains, red-tile roofs, and palms lend a Spanish flavor to this low-lying compound on La Jolla Shores beach. Rooms have rattan furniture and floral-print bedspreads, and wooden balconies that overlook the sea and lush landscaping. Downtown just 2 mi away. Restaurant, bar, room service. In-room data ports, refrigerators, cable TV. Pool, wading pool. Hot tub, massage. Tennis. Exercise equipment. Laundry facilities. Business services, free parking. | 8110 Camino del Oro | 858/459–8271 or 800/237–5211 | fax 858/456–9346 | 128 rooms | $205–$479 | AE, D, DC, MC, V.

Shell Beach Apartment-Motel. These townhouse-style accommodations fill an entire block along the coastline. Many of the apartments with one, two, or three bedrooms have patios or decks with ocean views. Kitchenettes, cable TV. | 1155 Coast Blvd. | 858/459–4306 | www.lajollacove.com | 46 apartments | Studio $70–$199, 1 bdm. $110–$399, 1 bdm. with hot tub $450–$749, 2 bdm. $150–$329, 3 bdm. $450–$329 | AE, D, DC, MC, V.

Travelodge La Jolla Beach. This three-story motel with exterior corridors is one block from Wind 'n' Sea Beach and 1 mi from La Jolla Village. Non-smoking rooms available. Refrigerators, microwaves. In-room data ports, cable TV. Pool. Hot tub. Beauty salon. Laundry facilities. | 6750 La Jolla Blvd. | 858/454–0716 | fax 858/454–1075 | 44 rooms | $59–$99 rooms, $149–$259 suites | AE, D, DC, MC, V.

LAKE ARROWHEAD

MAP 4, J14

(Nearby towns also listed: Big Bear Lake, Crestline, Rancho Cucamonga, Redlands, San Bernadino)

This mile-high town was named in 1826 when the first European settler of the area, Father Francisco Dumetz, discovered a huge arrowhead in the foothills of the San Bernardino Mountains. Today the mystery of the giant enigmatic arrow shaped rock remains to be solved. In its early stages of settlement, around the 1850s, logging and cattle were the primary industries of the area. In 1979, a fire destroyed much of the town leaving only the post office and bank. Fortunately, Lake Arrowhead was almost completely reconstructed. Today, the industries that exist in Lake Arrowhead are exclusively aimed at tourists, such as resorts and restaurants. Most of the residents of the area commute to jobs, or live here part-time.

Information: Lake Arrowhead Chamber of Commerce | 28200 Hwy. 189, Suite F290, 92352 | 909/337–3715 | lachamber@js-net.com | www.lakearrowhead.net.

Attractions

Astronomy Village. Built in 1999, this facility run by the Mountain Skies Astronomical Society houses an observatory, science center, workshop space, and library. The society regularly hosts evening "star watches" that use an outdoor projection screen. | 2001 Observatory Way and Hwy. 18 | 909/336–1699 | fax 909/336–4497 | www.mountain-skies.org | $2 | Mon.–Sat. 10–4.

ON THE CALENDAR

OCT.: *Oktoberfest.* Locals converge on Lake Arrowhead Village Peninsula every weekend of the month for this popular event that includes German food, live music, and activities for kids. | 909/337–3715.

Dining

Papagayo's Mexican Restaurant. Mexican. This cozy, friendly eatery serves the best margaritas and the largest burritos on the mountain. Sample a variety of flautas or go with one of the many combo platters. | 26824 State Hwy. 189 | 909/337–9529 | $8–$18 | AE, MC, V.

Royal Oak Restaurant. Contemporary. This local institution serves seafood, pasta, and all types of meat dishes. Try the ground-sirloin peppersteak or the Chicken Sheba with eggplant, fresh mushrooms, shrimp, and a Madeira sauce. | 27187 State Hwy. 189 | No lunch Sept.–May | $14–$55 | AE, D, MC, V.

Lodging

Carriage House. Down comforters, afternoon refreshments, and lakeside views keep guests returning to this woodland retreat. Complimentary breakfast. Cable TV, in-room VCRs, no room phones. No kids under 12. No smoking. | 472 Emerald Dr. | 909/336–1400 | fax 909/336–6092 | www.lakearrowhead.com/carriagehouse/ | 3 rooms | $95–$135 | AE, MC, V.

Saddleback Inn. Constructed as the Raven Hotel in 1917, this Victorian inn later became a retreat for the Hollywood crowd. It sits at the entrance to Lake Arrowhead Village, surrounded by pines and a beautiful stone wall. Laura Ashley fabrics complement the country furnishings in rooms and cottages, many of which have fireplaces. Restaurant. Microwaves, refrigerators, cable TV, some in-room VCRs. Pool. Exercise equipment. Laundry facilities. Business services. Pets allowed in cottages. | 300 S. State Hwy. 173 | 909/336–3571 or 800/858–3334 | fax 909/336–6111 | www.saddlebackinn.com/ | 10 rooms in main bldg., 24 1–3 bdrm. cottages | $99–195 rooms, $165–$294 1 bdrm. cottages, $144–$294 2 bdrm. cottages, $165–$294 3 bdrm. cottages w/ 2 bathrooms, $317–$533 3 bdrm. cottages w/ 3 bathrooms | AE, D, DC, MC, V.

LAKE COUNTY

MAP 3, E1

(Nearby towns also listed: Clear Lake Area, Hopland, Ukiah)

Two incorporated towns, Clearlake and Lakeport, as well as 18 other smaller villages make up Lake County, which had a population of about 61,000 people. The first Spanish soldier set foot in Lake County around 1821, a date that marked the begin-

KODAK'S TIPS FOR USING LIGHTING

Daylight
- Use the changing color of daylight to establish mood
- Use light direction to enhance subjects' properties
- Match light quality to specific subjects

Dramatic Lighting
- Anticipate dramatic lighting events
- Explore before and after storms

Sunrise, Sunset, and Afterglow
- Include a simple foreground
- Exclude the sun when setting your exposure
- After sunset, wait for the afterglow to color the sky

From Kodak Guide to Shooting Great Travel Pictures © 2000 by Fodor's Travel Publications

ning of a period of strife and bloodshed between Mexicans, Native Americans, and Spaniards. Cattle operations gave the area early prosperity. Clear Lake, the largest freshwater lake in California, has over 100 mi of pristine shoreline crisscrossed with hiking trails. Aside from the endless natural beauty of the area, historical sites and homes are plentiful, as are art galleries, and wineries.

Information: **Clearlake Chamber of Commerce** | 4700 Golf Ave., Clearlake, 95422 | 800/525–3743 or 707/994–3600 | www.lakecounty.com.

Dining

Lamplighter. Steak. Steaks and seafood reign here, with the prime rib and sautéed shrimp heading the list of top menu picks. Large bay windows provide an impressive view of the lake. | 14165 Lakeshore Dr., Clearlake | 707/994–5855 | $8–$34 | AE, D, MC, V.

Mario's Lodge. Italian. Come for the Italian specialties, fish, and steak at this casual family restaurant in an old log cabin. Try the cannelloni stuffed with sausage, veal, and spinach or the veal scallopini. | 14825 Lakeshore Dr., Clearlake | 707/995–3645 | $7–$16 | D, MC, V.

Lodging

Anchorage Inn. This downtown motel has great views of the lake and its own pier and boat slips. Vacationers bring their own boats and rent the white no-frills rooms for the ease of boating; a few rooms have lake views. Picnic area. Some kitchenettes, cable TV. Outdoor pool, lake. Sauna, spa. Dock. Laundry facilities. | 950 N. Main St., Lakeport | 707/263–5417 | 34 rooms | $54 | AE, D, MC, V.

Arbor House Inn. This turn-of-the-20th-century inn with English gardens lies just north of downtown Lakeport and one block from Clear Lake. All rooms have private porches and in-room whirlpool baths. Wine and cheese are served each evening. Complimentary breakfast. Some microwaves, some refrigerators, cable TV. | 150 Clear Lake Ave., Lakeport | 707/263–6444 | www.arborhouseinn.net | 5 rooms | $79–$119 | AE, MC, V.

Mallard House. These quiet, homey guest units are in four houses scattered along the shore of Clear Lake. Boat-launching facilities are on the premises, and downtown is a few blocks away. Picnic area, complimentary Continental breakfast. Kitchenettes, cable TV. Spa. Dock, boating, fishing. No smoking. | 970 N. Main St., Lakeport | 707/262–1601 | fax 707/263–4764 | www.mallardhouse.com | 13 rooms | $59–$139 | AE, D, MC, V.

LAKE TAHOE AREA

MAP 3, G6

(Nearby towns also listed: South Lake Tahoe, Tahoe City, Tahoe Vista, Truckee)

Some believe "Tahoe" was the name of a brave and ancient Native American woman, or a Washoe Indian man who was condemned from his own tribe. Others historians claim the word means a squaw in the morning, and others assert it means nothing at all. The Spanish word, "tajo," describes a cut or a cleft, which may describe the canyon the lake possesses. Wherever the mysterious name came from, it didn't win without a fight. Lake Bonpland and Lake Bigler were two other names the area was known by until July 1945, when it was declared Lake Tahoe. The lake's history is rich; the Washoe Tribe were the first humans to live off the lake, and today there are still nearly 2,000 members of their tribe living in surrounding areas. During the late 1880s, Lake Tahoe was settled by Chinese immigrants.

Today the country's biggest Alpine lake serves as a unique getaway. Surprisingly, the high season is summer, although many skiers come in winter, thus the 12 ski resorts. Around 70% of the homes on the lake are second homes.

Information: **Resort Association** | 950 N. Lake Blvd. # 3, Tahoe City, 96145 | www.tahoefun.org or www.tahoeinfo.com.

Attractions

★ **Gatekeeper's Cabin Museum.** Housed in a log cabin, this museum and the surrounding 3½ acres are maintained by the Lake Tahoe Historical Society. Exhibits and artifacts trace Lake Tahoe's rich heritage from its Native American roots to the present. A highlight is the Steinbach Indian Basket Collection, representing the work of over 50 tribes. | 130 W. Lake Blvd., Tahoe City | 530/583–1762 | $2 | May 1–June 15, Wed.–Sun. 11–5; June 15–Oct. 15, daily 11–5.

ON THE CALENDAR

JULY: *Isuzu Celebrity Golf Championship.* You can watch more than 70 celebrities compete for cash prizes at the Edgewood Tahoe Golf Course, one of the top courses in the country. | 530/544–5050 | www.virtualtahoe.com.

Dining

Sprouts Natural Foods. Vegetarian. This small California kitchen uses organically grown produce for its sandwiches and veggie plates. Try the tempeh burgers or fruit smoothies. | 3123 Harrison Ave., S. Lake Tahoe | 530/541–6969 | $4–$8 | No credit cards.

Lodging

River Ranch Lodge. The site of this lodge was once that of the Deer Park Inn, a fashionable watering hole and resort from 1888 until the Great Depression of the 1930s when tourism came to a standstill. Today rooms in this 1950s lodge next to the Truckee River have warm down comforters on the beds and either lodgepole-pine or antique furniture. Many have balconies and riverfront views. Ask about ski and rafting packages. Restaurant, bar, complimentary Continental breakfast. In-room data ports, some kitchenettes, cable TV. No smoking. | Hwy. 89 and Alpine Meadows Rd. | 530/583–4264 or 800/535–9900 | 19 rooms | $85–$150 | AE, MC, V.

LANCASTER

MAP 4, I13

(Nearby town also listed: Palmdale)

Lancaster was founded in 1876, when the Southern Pacific Railroad was built alongside the developing community. Before that it was inhabited by the Native American tribes: Kawarisu, Kitanemuk, Serrano, Tataviam, and the Chemehuevi. Today ancestors of some of these tribes still live in the surrounding mountains.

Seventy miles northeast of Los Angeles, nearly 40% percent of the 123,402 residents make the commute "down below" to the greater L.A. area. The local industry is space shuttle building, making Lancaster the "Aerospace Capital" of the nation. Visit in spring and you'll witness the bloom of bright California poppies that cover the land around Lancaster for miles.

Information: **Lancaster Chamber of Commerce** | 554 W. Lancaster Blvd., 93534-2534 | 805/948–4518.

Attractions

Lancaster Museum/Art Gallery. Exhibits are constantly changing at this cultural facility. Past exhibits have included Mayan artifacts, Egyptian art, and civil war memorabilia. | 44801 N. Sierra Hwy. | 661/723–6255 | www.city.lancaster.ca.us/Museum.htm | Free | Tues.–Sat. 11–4, Sun. 1–4.

Lancaster Performing Arts Center. Since 1991, this center has hosted more than 400 dance performances, musical concerts and theatrical shows. Natalie Cole, Little Richard, and the Winnipeg Ballet are among the more notable acts that have graced the stage. | 750 W. Lancaster Blvd. | 661/723–5950 | www.lpac.org | $10–$60 | Box Office: weekdays 12–6, Sat. 12–4.

Western Hotel Museum. This 19th-century former hotel and its contents celebrate the history of the people of Antelope Valley. Historic photographs and artifacts such as household utensils and clothing are on display. | 557 West Lancaster Blvd. | 661/723–6260 | city.lancaster.ca.us/Parks/westernhotel.htm | Free | Fri.–Sat. 12–4.

Dining

Casa Roma. Italian. Green dominates the dining room and fresh flowers decorate each table at this casual spot. Try a veal dish, such as the veal Parmesan or picatta, or try the cioppino, which is a seafood soup with shellfish. | 320 W. Ave. J-2 | 661/942–2166 | $9–$16 | AE, D, MC, V.

Rocamar Mexican and Seafood Restaurant. Seafood. Arched windows and pictures of fish dress up this well-lit restaurant. Try the halibut del sol, grilled and served with a mushroom sauce, or the shrimp Rocamar (shrimp wrapped in bacon and served on a bed of rice). The traditional Mexican fare, especially the chicken fajitas and carne asada, is equally popular. Sun. brunch. Kids' menu. | 1020 E. Ave. K | 661/940–6304 | $8–$26 | AE, MC, V.

Village Grill. American. The dining area of this eatery is spruced up with numerous plants. Classic dishes like pot roast, prime rib, and corned beef with cabbage fill the menu. Kids' menu. | 44303 Sierra Hwy. | 661/942–7760 | Breakfast also available | $5–$9 | D, DC, MC, V.

Lodging

Desert Inn. Year after year, this 1950s hotel wins community awards for dining and lodging excellence. The well-kept parklike grounds are ½ mi from downtown and 15 mi from both the L.A. County and Yellowsprings raceways. 2 restaurants, bar, room service. In-room data ports, some kitchenettes, microwaves, refrigerators, some in-room hot tubs, cable TV. 2 outdoor pools, wading pool. Hot tub, massage, steam room. Exercise equipment. Racquetball. | 44219 N. Sierra Hwy. | 661/942–8401 or 800/942–8401 | fax 661/942–8950 | www.desert-inn.com | 144 rooms | $88–$118 | AE, D, DC, MC, V.

LA QUINTA

MAP 4, L15

LA QUINTA

INTRO
ATTRACTIONS
DINING
LODGING

(Nearby towns also listed: Cathedral City, Indian Wells, Indio, Palm Desert, Rancho Mirage, Temecula)

This near perfect desert spot in the Santa Rosa foothills in the center of Coachella Valley, is 30 minutes from Palm Springs and known for its world-class golf courses. Agriculture (specifically, the harvest of cotton and sugar cane, and cattle-raising) kept this town afloat in the early 19th century. Today though, with approximately 24,250 people, La Quinta is one of the fastest growing cities in California and continues to spread out as the open desert is developed. It rains about 15 to 20 days a year, making this area a sunny and popular spot to visit year-round.

Information: **La Quinta Chamber of Commerce** | 78371 Hwy. 11, 92253 | 760/564–3199 | laquintachamber@aol.com | www.laquintachamberofcommerce.com.

Attractions

Air Museum. Home to one of the largest collections of WWII aircraft in the world, this museum also displays military artifacts, original artwork, and rare combat photos. Be sure to stick around for the daily flight demonstrations. | 745 North Gene Autry Trail, Palm Springs | 760/778–6262 | www.air-museum.org | $6 | Daily 10–5.

Lake Cahuilla Regional Park. This 710-acre park, at the base of the Santa Rosa Mountains, 12 mi south of Indian Wells, offers camping, hiking, fishing, and boating (no gas-powered motors) in a lake fed by the Colorado River. April through October, there's also a swimming pool with shower facilities. | 58075 Jefferson St. | 760/564–4712 | $2, $12–$16 per day for a campsite | Daily.

ON THE CALENDAR

SEPT.: *La Quinta Chamber Mayor's Cup.* Over 400 golfers annually compete for prizes at the PGA West golf course. Register before noon to compete in the shotgun that begins around 1. | 760/564–3199 | $125.

Dining

La Quinta Cliffhouse. Contemporary. Sweeping mountain views at sunset and the early California ambience of a Western movie set draw patrons to this restaurant perched halfway up a hillside. The eclectic menu roams the globe: Caesar salad with grilled chicken, ahi tuna Szechwan style, and for dessert, Kimo's Hula Pie with house-made macadamia nut ice cream. The three indoor dining areas are decorated in earth tones and bare wood, with crockery on the walls. The 40-seat outdoor terrace features a waterfall. Kids menu. | 78-250 Hwy. 111, La Qunita | 760/360–5991 | www.hulapie.com | No lunch | $15–$30 | AE, D, DC, MC, V.

Lodging

★ **La Quinta Resort and Club.** Built in 1926, this vast luxury resort is brimming with Old World charm. Guest rooms are in tastefully decorated Spanish-style guest casitas arranged in groups around several dozen pools throughout the manicured grounds. Multiple gardens scent the air with flowers, and the state-of-the-art spa and fitness facility encompasses 23,000 square feet adjacent to the main resort complex. Be prepared to enjoy—and pay for—first-class service. 5 restaurants, bar, dining room, room service. In-room data ports, some kitchenettes, some microwaves, some refrigerators, some in-room hot tubs, cable TV, some in-room VCRs. 39 pools. Beauty salon, hot tub, massage, sauna, spa. Golf courses. Exercise equipment. Shops, video games. Laundry service. Business services. | 49-499 Eisenhower Dr. | 760/564–4111 | fax 760/564–5758 | www.laquintaresort.com | 740 rooms, 69 suites | rooms $340–$550, suites $850–$3,500 | AE, D, DC, MC, V.

LASSEN VOLCANIC NATIONAL PARK

MAP 3, E3

(Nearby towns also listed: Chester, Red Bluff, Redding, Susanville)

Fifty miles northeast of Red Bluff lies 106,000 acres of distinctive volcanic landscape now protected by the National Park Service. The volcanoes here, including shield volcanoes Prospect Peak and Mount Harkness, were active from 1914 to 1921. The area is now marked by fumaroles, mudpots, and lakes. The park is open year-round, but be aware that at least a light snow covers the ground from mid-October to early June. From July to September, days are sunny and warm, and nights are cool.

Information: **Lassen Volcanic National Park** | Box 100, Mineral, 96063 | 530/595–4444 | lavoinformation@nps.gov | www.nps.gov/lavo/home.htm.

Attractions

Lassen Peak. When this now-dormant plug dome volcano erupted in 1915, it spewed a huge mushroom cloud with debris 7 mi into the air. For a fabulous panoramic view of the area, hike the easy 2½ mi to the 10,457-ft summit. | Lassen Volcanic Park | 530/595–4444 | fax 530/595–3262 | www.nps.gov/lavo/index.htm | $10 per vehicle, $4 per walk-in | Daily.

ON THE CALENDAR

JAN.: *Snowshoe Days.* On Saturdays throughout the first three months of the year, rangers lead snowshoe hikes for the public. | 530/595–4444, ext. 5133 or 5132.

Dining

Lassen Chalet. American. Stock up on your camping provisions here. This grocery and the Manzanita Lake Camper Store are the only places to buy food in the park. | Lassen Park Rd. | 530/595–4444 | Oct.–May | No credit cards.

Lodging

Drakesbad Guest Ranch. This 100-year-old cabin at 5,700 ft provides the only lodging within the park itself. Kerosene lamps light most of the rustic rooms, while quilts, propane heating, and the natural hot springs help keep you warm on brisk evenings. Meals are included in the price of your stay and are served family- or buffet-style in the main dining room. The kitchen uses the freshest ingredients and lots of local produce to create healthful, hearty dishes. Complimentary breakfast. No air-conditioning, no room phones, no TV. Hiking, horseback riding, volleyball. Fishing. | Warner Valley | 530/529–9820 | www.drakesbad.com | 6 rooms (3 with shared bath) | $108–$153 | Closed early Oct.–early Jun | AE, MC, V.

LEE VINING

MAP 3, H8

(Nearby towns also listed: Bridgeport, June Lake, Yosemite National Park)

This one-street town was founded around 1880 and named after an early resident. On an ice age–formed lake terrace surrounded by the steep Sierra Nevadas, Lee Vining is a visually striking place to be. There are no chains in this semi-deserted place with a population of only 350, and it is mostly known as an eastern gateway to Yosemite National Park. Today, locals work in tourism or forestry.

Information: Lee Vining Chamber of Commerce and Mono Lake Committee | Hwy. 395 at 3rd St., 93541 | 760/647–6595 | arya@monolake.org | www.leevining.com.

Attractions

Mono Lake. If you're leaving Yosemite's eastern gateway, don't miss this unusual and fragile watershed area northeast of town. The heavily salted lake is an important stopover for migrating birds and is home to countless brine shrimp and the weirdly beautiful tufa—limestone formations—that grace its shoreline. | Off U.S. 395 | 760/647–6629 | www.monolake.org | Free | Daily.

ON THE CALENDAR

OCT.: *South Tufa Walk.* If you join one of these naturalist-guided walking tours, bring your binoculars for close-up views of Mono Lake's wildlife and calcified tufa towers. The tours depart from the South Tufa parking lot 5 mi east of Highway 395 on Highway 120 and last about 1½ hours. | 760/647–3044 | www.monolake.org/main/natact.htm | $3 | Weekends, 1 PM.

Dining

Nicely's. American. Plants and pictures of local attractions decorate this eatery that has been around since 1965. Try the blueberry pancakes and homemade sausages for breakfast. For lunch or dinner try the country-fried steak or the fiesta salad. Kids' menu. | Hwy. 395 and 4th St. | 760/647–6477 | Breakfast also available. Nov.–Apr. closed Tues.–Wed. | $9–$15 | MC, V.

Lodging

Tioga Lodge. Just 2½ mi north of Yosemite's eastern gateway, this 19th-century building has been by turns a store, a saloon, a tollbooth, and a boarding house. Now restored and expanded, it's a popular lodge that's less than 3 mi from local skiing and fishing. No room phones, no TV. | Hwy. 395 | 760/647–6423 or 888/647–6423 | fax 760/647–6074 | tioga-lodge@qnet.com | www.monolake.org/chamber/allmotels.htm | 16 rooms | $95–$105 | AE, MC, V.

LITTLE RIVER

MAP 3, B5

(Nearby towns also listed: Albion, Elk, Fort Bragg, Mendocino)

This tiny, unincorporated, coastal town, known for the surrounding pygmy forests and fern caverns, started out as a center for the lumber industry. The inns and hotels draw guests interested in stunning views of the Pacific Ocean, golf courses, parks, and the nearby redwood forests.

Information: **Fort Bragg/Mendocino Chamber of Commerce** | 332 N. Main St., PO Box 1141, Fort Bragg, 95437 | 707/961–6300 | www.mendocinocoast.com.

Attractions

Van Damme State Park. This state park is made up of 1,381 acres of beach and forested land. Highlights include the Pygmy Forest, where cypress and pine trees are abundant, and lush Fern Canyon. Ten miles of walking and biking trails traverse Fern Canyon. | Hwy. 1 | 707/937–5804 | www.parks.ca.gov/north/russian/mendo/vdsp142.htm | $2.50 | Daily dawn to dusk.

ON THE CALENDAR

DEC.: *Candlelight Inn Tours.* Inns throughout Little River are covered with holiday lights and decorations in celebration of the winter holidays. Drive between them and stop in for wine and cheese. | 800/726–2780.

Dining

Heritage House Restaurant. Contemporary. The windows which line this restaurant will afford you an excellent view of the Pacific Ocean. Try the grilled salmon filet or the oven-roasted chicken breast. You can dine under individual umbrellas on the outdoor deck. | 5200 Hwy. 1 | 707/937–5885 | Reservations essential | Breakfast also available. No lunch | $20–$25 | AE, MC, V.

Little River Inn Restaurant. Continental. You will have a view of either the garden or the ocean from this casual spot. Large watercolor paintings hang on the walls. Lamb brochette and the pork tenderloin are among the more popular entrées. | 7533 Hwy. 1 | 707/937–5942 | Reservations essential | Breakfast also available. No lunch | $20–$29 | AE, MC, V.

Stevenswood Restaurant. Mediterranean. The dining room of this elegant spot is candlelit and has big bay windows that overlook a sculpture garden. Try the pine nut-crusted salmon filet or the lamb osso bucco. | 8211 Hwy. 1 | 707/937–2810 | Reservations essential | No lunch | $24–$32 | AE, D, DC, MC, V.

Lodging

Andiron Lodge. Each of the cottages at this lodge has a private deck that faces the ocean. Van Damme State Park is 1 mi to the north. Some kitchenettes, some refrigerators, cable TV, some in-room VCRs, no room phones. Business services. Some pets. | 6051 Hwy. 1 | 707/937–1543 or 877/488–5332 | fax 707/937–1542 | reservations@andironlodge.com | www.andironlodge.com | 2 rooms, 5 cabins | $70, $150 cabins | MC, V.

Fools Rush Inn. Oak furniture fills all of the cottages that were built in the early 1990s. You will have a view of the ocean from your room and there is a restaurant two blocks away. Kitchenettes, microwaves, refrigerators, cable TV. No pets. | 7533 Hwy. 1 | 707/937–5339 | www.mendocino.org/foolsrushinn | 9 cottages | $59–$89 | No credit cards.

★ **Glendeven Inn.** Fields and trees surround this 1857 New England Federalist farmhouse. Rooms are furnished with contemporary art and antiques and most have fireplaces and ocean views. Complimentary breakfast. Some kitchenettes, some microwaves, some refrigerators. No room phones, no TV. Business services. No pets. | 8205 Hwy. 1 | 707/937–0083 | fax 707/937–6108 | innkeeper@glendeven.com | www.glendeven.com | 10 rooms, 1 house | $140–$225; $275 house | AE, D, MC, V.

Heritage House Inn. Most of the rooms at this inn are in cottages that are spread out over 37 acres of manicured lawns and overlook the Pacific Ocean. The old farmhouse which serves as the centerpiece of the inn was built in 1877, but did not become a lodging facility until 1949. Restaurant. Some minibars, some in-room hot tubs. No room phones, no TV. Business services. No pets. No smoking. | 5200 Hwy. 1 | 707/937–5885 or 800/235–5885 | fax 707/937–0318 | info@heritagehouseinn.com | www.heritagehouseinn.com | $137–$325, $285–$375 suites | AE, MC, V.

Inn at Schoolhouse Creek. The farmhouse which now serves as the guest services center was constructed in 1862 by one of Little River's founders and most of the surrounding cottages were built in the 1890s. The inn is on eight acres of landscaped grounds and the ocean is across the street. Complimentary breakfast. In-room data ports, some kitchenettes, some microwaves, some refrigerators, some in-room hot tubs, cable TV, in-room VCRs (and movies). Outdoor hot tub. Business services. Some pets. No smoking. | 7051 Hwy. 1 | 707/937–5525 | fax 707/937–2012 | www.schoolhousecreek.com | 4 rooms, 2 suites, 9 cottages | $115–$225, $205–$240 suites, $140–$200 cottages | AE, D, MC, V.

Little River Inn. Almost all of the rooms at this resort, which was built by a Maine lumberman in 1853, have ocean views. Some rooms also have fireplaces and private hot tubs out on a deck. Restaurant, bar, room service. Some in-room hot tubs, cable TV, in-room VCRs (and movies). Spa. 9-hole golf course, 2 tennis courts. Business services. No pets. No smoking. | 7751 Hwy. 1 | 707/937–5942 | fax 707/937–3944 | lri@mcn.org | www.littleriverinn.com | 67 rooms | $140–$285 | AE, MC, V.

Rachel's Inn. Most rooms at this oceanside inn are decorated with antiques and have fireplaces. The main house was constructed in the 1860s and has a brick patio. Complimentary breakfast. Cable TV, some in-room VCRs, no TV in some rooms. Business services. No pets. No smoking. | 8200 Hwy. 1 | 707/937–0088 or 800/347–9252 | fax 707/937–3620 | www.rachelsinn.com | 9 rooms, 2 cottages | $125–$225, $275 cottages | MC, V.

Seafoam Lodge. A forested hillside provides the background scenery for this lodge which is spread out over six acres of manicured lawns and pine trees. All rooms provide a panoramic view of the Pacific Ocean, which is across the street. Complimentary Continental breakfast. Some kitchenettes, refrigerators, cable TV, in-room VCRs (and movies). Hot tub. Pets allowed. | 6752 Hwy. 1 | 707/937–1827 | fax 707/937–0744 | info@seafoamlodge.com | www.seafoamlodge.com | 24 rooms in 8 buildings | $95–$175 | AE, D, MC, V.

Stevenswood Lodge. Distant ocean views and fireplaces are available in some of the rooms at this lodge built in 1988. You can stroll through two acres of landscaped gardens littered with sculptures or cross the street and jog along the bluffs that overlook the ocean. Restaurant, complimentary breakfast. Refrigerators, cable TV. Pool. Spa. Business ser-

LITTLE RIVER

INTRO
ATTRACTIONS
DINING
LODGING

vices. No pets. No smoking. | 8211 Hwy. 1 | 707/937–2810 or 800/421–2810 | fax 707/937–1237 | www.stevenswood.com | 10 rooms | $150–$250 | AE, D, DC, MC, V.

LIVERMORE

MAP 3, D8

(Nearby towns also listed: Fremont, Pleasanton)

Originally settled by Costonoan Indians, this suburban town of 73,000 people was incorporated in 1876 and was quickly turned into an agricultural area. A sprawling suburban community 40 mi east of San Francisco, Livermore is the oldest grape-growing district in the state; its historic wineries and fabulous restaurants draw many visitors here. In a seemingly odd juxtaposition with the vintners, the technological companies in the area are responsible for developing the hydrogen bomb in the 1950s and the Star Wars project in the '80s. Today they are conducting the leading research for energy from "clean fusion".

Information: Livermore Chamber of Commerce | 2157 First St., 94550 | 925/447–1606 | www.livermorechamber.org or www.ci.livermore.ca.us.

Dining

Casa Orozco. Mexican. This lively spot full of music and laughter has garnered a loyal following since it opened in 1985. The restaurant specializes in burritos, enchiladas, and pitchers of tasty margaritas. | 325 South L St. | 925/449–3045 | www.casaorozco.com | $6–$19 | AE, D, MC, V.

Lodging

Livermore Inn. This quiet, downtown budget motel is across the street from several restaurants and 3 mi from I–580. Refrigerators, cable TV. Outdoor pool. | 1421 1st St. | 925/447–3865 | 23 rooms | $65 | AE, D, MC, V.

Queen Anne Cottage on 8th. Behind the white picket fence are a Victorian home and cottage elegantly appointed with period furnishings and china. The lush garden hides a rock spa and gazebo, and each room is outfitted with one-of-a-kind antique pieces and designer linens. There are fourteen vineyards within a 3-mi radius. Complimentary breakfast. In-room VCRs, some room phones. Outdoor hot tub. No smoking. | 2516 8th St. | 925/606–7140 | fax 925/373–1737 | www.queenanneon8th.com | 2 rooms, one cottage | $135–$195, cottage $195–$225 | AE, D, DC, MC, V.

LODI

MAP 3, E7

(Nearby town also listed: Stockton)

Agriculture made Lodi's founding possible in the 1900s, and today agriculture remains central to the community's identity. Just south of Sacramento, and a bit north of Stockton, the western side has an abundance of waterways perfect for canoeing and swimming. Weather is tempered here which makes for a short mild winter and a long, rain-free summer. Lodi is ideal for outdoor recreation.

First inhabited by the Miwok Indians, the goldrush brought the first settlers from the east. The city was once the watermelon capital of the country, exemplifying the pride that is taken in the produce which is grown here. Today, it has become the "Wine Grape Capital," rightfully so as it produces more Zinfandel, Merlot, Cabernet Sauvignon, Chardonnay, and Sauvignon Blanc grapes than anywhere else in the state. If wine grapes don't excite you, maybe fields of asparagus, pumpkins, beans, almonds, safflower, sunflower, kiwis, melons, squash, peaches, and cherries will draw you to this land of plenty.

Information: Lodi Conference and Visitors Bureau | 35 S. School St., 95240 | 209/367–7840 | editor@visitlodi.com | www.visitlodi.com.

Attractions
Micke Grove Park And Zoo. This 65-acre county park off I–5 includes an amusement park, a zoo, a Japanese garden, picnic areas, and a historical museum with a collection of 94 tractors. | 11793 N. Micke Grove Rd. | 209/953–8840 | fax 209/331–2057 | www.mgzoo.com | zoo $1.50; parking $2 weekdays, $4 weekends | summer, Mon.–Fri. 10–5, weekends 10–7; winter, daily 10–5.

ON THE CALENDAR
MAY, OCT.: *Lodi Street Faire.* Arts and crafts, antiques, entertainment, and lots of food draw large crowds to downtown Lodi for this twice-yearly event. | 209/367–7840 | www.lodichamber.com/html/lodi_street_faire.html | Free.

Dining
Avenue Grill. American. This family-style grill with an open cooking pit is a best bet for burgers and steaks. | 506 W. Lodi Ave. | 209/333–8006 | $5–$9 | No credit cards.

Habanero Hots. Mexican. If your mouth can handle the heat the restaurant name promises, try the tamales. If you have a timid palate, stick with the gringo menu. | 1024 E. Victor Rd. | 209/369–3791 | $7–$13 | AE, D, MC, V.

Lodging
Inn at Locke House. This English country B&B 5 mi east of downtown was home to a pioneer family and is now on the National Register of Historic Places. Refreshments welcome you upon arrival, and rooms have antiques, fireplaces, and guest robes. In the oak-paneled parlor you'll find books, games, historical artifacts, and an old pump organ. Complimentary breakfast. No room phones, no TV in some rooms. Library. No smoking. | 19960 Elliott Rd. | 209/727–5715 | www.theinnatlockehouse.com | 4 rooms, 1 suite | $110 rooms, $155 suite | AE, D, DC, MC, V.

Lodi Comfort Inn. This Spanish-style downtown motel accented with palm trees has quiet rooms with contemporary furnishings. Doughnuts brought in from a chain bakery and coffee make up breakfast. Complimentary Continental breakfast. Refrigerators, cable TV. Outdoor pool. Hot tub. Baby-sitting. Laundry facilities, laundry service. | 118 N. Cherokee La. | 209/367–4848 | fax 209/367–4898 | www.lodichamber.com/comfortinn | 35 rooms | $55–$75 | AE, D, MC, V.

LOMPOC

MAP 4, F13

(Nearby towns also listed: Los Olivos, Santa Maria)

The area that now surrounds the town of Lompoc was settled over a thousand years ago by the Chumash Indians, who named it after their word meaning "little lake" or "lagoon". The town's natural attractions are the Lompoc Mountains and the Santa Ynez River. Today the town has a huge flower industry which is apparent simply by driving through the area in spring. In 1988, a mural project was started in an effort to draw more tourism. Some sixty murals are spread out throughout the town, with subjects ranging from historical tragedies to a depiction of Main Street a hundred years ago. The old town contains antiques shops and cafés that often showcase live entertainment. Many people in this family and retiree community commute to Santa Barbara, which is only a 40-minute drive.

Information: **Lompoc Chamber of Commerce** | 111 S. I St., 93436 | 805/736–4567 | chamber@lompoc.com | www.lompoc.com.

Attractions

Lompoc Museum. Housed in a former Carnegie Library built in 1910, this museum recounts the history of the Lompoc Valley and Santa Barbara County through exhibits, artifacts, films, and lectures. | 200 S. H St. | 805/736–3888 | Free | Tues.–Fri. 1–5, weekends 1–4.

ON THE CALENDAR

JULY: *4th of July.* Celebrate with music, food, and—of course—fireworks, on South H Street. | 805/736–456 | Free.

Lodging

1890 House. This two-story Queen Anne Victorian built by one of Lompoc's founding families is now completely restored to its former glory with an intriguing blend of turn-of-the-century antiques and California-modern touches. The overall effect is a refreshing departure from the usual lace-doilies-and-découpage theme found in most Victorian B & Bs. Afternoon high tea is available, and you can start the day with a fresh-baked fruit scone with jam and compote. Complimentary breakfast. TV in common area. Library. No smoking. | 122 W. Cypress St. | 805/736–9423 or 888/736–9422 | 2 rooms | $80–$120 | No credit cards.

LONE PINE

MAP 4, I10

(Nearby towns also listed: Death Valley National Park, Kings Canyon National Park, Sequoia National Park)

This rural, high-desert community was named after a single pine tree found at the bottom of the Lone Pine Canyon. Home to Mt. Whitney, the highest peak in the Continental U.S., at over 14,000 ft, hikers come from all over to climb the mountain as well as explore the surrounding area.

Information: **Lone Pine Chamber of Commerce** | 126 S. Main St., 93545 | 760/876–444 or 877/253–8981 | filming@lone-pine.com | www.lone-pine.com.

Attractions

Whitney Portal National Recreation Trail. This 4-mi hiking trail is one of the most well traveled in the Inyo National Forest, and for good reason. There are spectacular views of Mt. Whitney rising to the west, and the Alabama Hills, Owens Valley, and the Inyo/White Mountains to the east. | Whitney Portal Road, Inyo National Forest | 760/876–6200 | Free | Daily.

ON THE CALENDAR

MAR.: *Diaz Lake Trout Derby.* The first Saturday of the month, you can take a shot at the "big one" in this fully stocked lake at 3,700 ft above sea level and 3 mi south of Lone Pine. Prizes are awarded for all age groups. | 760/876–4444 | Free.

Lodging

Winnedumah Hotel. Built in 1927, this B&B with mahogany woodwork once hosted the Hollywood stars and film crews that shot early Westerns in the Alabama Hills. Today you can still enjoy the old-fashioned lobby, wisteria-covered patio, and the inviting guest rooms with vintage hand-painted furniture. Complimentary Continental breakfast. Cable TV, some room phones. Hiking, fishing. Business services. No smoking. | 211 N. Edwards, Independence | 760/878-2040 | fax 760/878-2833 | winnedumah@qnet.com | www.winnedumah.com | 20 rooms | $47-$70 | MC, V.

LONG BEACH

(Nearby towns also listed: Anaheim, Buena Park, Cerritos, Costa Mesa, Fullerton, Garden Grove, Huntington Beach, Irvine, Los Angeles, Manhattan Beach, Orange, Redondo Beach, Santa Ana, Seal Beach, Torrance)

Twenty-one miles south of downtown Los Angeles, Long Beach is a bustling city in its own right. The city gained popularity in the 19th century as a seaside resort, and has evolved into California's fifth largest locale. It has 450,000 residents and a harbor that is among the Pacific Rim's busiest. The stately Queen Mary stands permanently moored here and if you board one of the largest passenger liners ever to grace the seas you can enjoy shops, restaurants, and a 365-stateroom hotel. A socially diverse city, Long Beach has plenty to explore from landmark Art Deco buildings to artists' neighborhoods, and clusters of funky cafés, shops, and restaurants.

Information: Long Beach Area Convention and Visitors Bureau | One World Trade Center, 3rd floor, 90831-0300 | 562/436-3645 or 800/4LB-STAY | fax 562/435-5653 | www.golongbeach.org | staff@longbeachcvb.org.

Attractions

★ **Aquarium of the Pacific.** The Long Beach Aquarium of the Pacific has over 550 species in 17 major living habitats and 30 smaller exhibits where you learn about the Pacific Ocean's three regions: Southern California/Baja; the Tropical Pacific; and the Northern Pacific. | 100 Aquarium Way | 562/590-3100 | www.aquariumofpacific.org/ | $14.95 | 9-6 daily except December 25th and during the weekend of the Toyota Grand Prix of Long Beach (early April).

California State University, Long Beach. Large commuter campus within blocks of the water, part of the state educational system in California. | 1250 Bellflower Blvd. | 562/985-4111 or 562/985-5358 | www.csulb.edu | Free | Weekdays by appointment.

El Dorado East Regional Park and Nature Center. A welcome getaway from the industrial fast-pace of Long Beach, this 102-acre area has a wildlife sanctuary, natural plant areas, and nature trails. | 7550 E. Spring St. | 562/570-1745 | www.ci.long-beach.ca.us/park/dorado.htm | Free | Tues.-Fri. 10-4, weekdays 8:30-4; trails Tues.-Sun. 8-4.

General Phineas Banning Residence Museum. Specialty museum of the General Phineas Banning residence and surrounding region. Banning arrived in San Pedro, California, in 1851 from Philadelphia, and soon established himself as a prosperous businessman involved in the stagecoach and railroad business. He helped develop the bay, the town of Wilmington, and eventually had a family; his sons developed Santa Catalina Island. He also served as a California state senator. This museum is in his residence and has a collection of Victorian furnishings. | 401 E. M St. | 310/548-7777 | fax 310/548-2644 | www.banning.org | Donations accepted | Tues.-Thurs. 12:30-2:30, weekends 12:30-3:30.

Long Beach Convention and Entertainment Center. The Long Beach Convention and Entertainment Center facilities include the Long Beach arena and exhibition halls, the Terrace and Center theaters, ballroom and meeting rooms. | 300 E. Ocean Blvd. | 562/436-3636 or 562/436-3661 (box office) | fax 562/436-9491 | www.longbeachcc.com | Call for schedule.

Municipal Beach. Over 5 ½ mi of public beach winds along the waterfront on the west side of town, just off Ocean Blvd. | 562/570–3215 | Free | Daily.

Museum of Latin American Art. Housed in what was a silent-film studio in the 30s, this cultural center is the only place in the western United States to exclusively show contemporary art from Mexico, Central America, South America, and the Spanish-speaking Caribbean. | 628 Alamitos Ave. | 562/437–1689 | fax 562/437–7043 | www.molaa.com | $7 | Tues.–Sat. 11:30–7:30, Sun. noon–6.

★ *Queen Mary* Seaport. Both a hotel and living museum of a past way of life and travel, the Queen Mary is an historic luxury liner now permanently docked at Long Beach. The Queen Mary has a wedding chapel, restaurants, and salons for private parties. Planning for the ship began in 1926. Named the Queen Mary in 1934 by England's Queen Mary the ship went into service in 1936. She served as a troop ship during World War II, and then returned to private service until 1967 when she was permanently docked. | 1126 Queens Hwy. | 562/435–3511 | fax 562/437–4531 | www.queenmary.com | $17 | Mon.–Thurs. 10–6, Fri.–Sun. 10–9.

Queenway Bay. Next to downtown, this 300-acre oceanfront development includes the Long Beach Aquarium of the Pacific and Rainbow Harbor, home of the tall ships *Pilgrim of Newport, Californian,* and *American Pride,* as well as up to 50 commercial vessels with scheduled dinner cruises and various tours. A multi-level, 2,000-ft-long public esplanade surrounds the harbor, which is also within a landscaped park. The walk connects Shoreline Village to the Aquarium of the Pacific. There is also an IMAX theater. | Off Ocean Blvd. | 562/570–6684 | Admission varies by activity/event | Daily.

Queen's Wharf. You can catch a boat for a fishing trip here or learn more about the industry by watching the locals gut and scale. | 555 Pico Ave. | Free | Daily.

Rancho Los Alamitos. A former ranch headquarters with a 200-year-old adobe ranch house, Rancho Los Alamitos has six early 20th-century barns once used for the Shire horses that were raised here. From the Native Garden to the Rose Garden, there are eleven distinct garden areas reflecting the indoor/outdoor Southern California lifestyle. There is also a smithy (where blacksmiths made iron products). In its heyday Rancho Los Alamitos encompassed 28,500 acres. | 6400 Bixby Hill Rd. | 562/431–3541 | www.ci.long-beach.ca.us/park/rancho.htm | Free | Wed.–Sun. 1–5.

Rancho Los Cerritos. An early Monterey style adobe surrounded by four acres of gardens. The 1844 house was built as the center of a 27,000-acre cattle ranch. The house was remodeled in 1930s Monterey Colonial style, but has since been furnished in 1870s style to reflect its heyday as one of the largest sheep ranches in the area. | 4600 Virginia Rd. | 562/570–1755 | fax 562/570–1893 | www.ci.long-beach.ca.us/park/ranchlc.htm | Free | Wed.–Sun. 1–5; tours weekends 1–5 on the hour.

Shoreline Village. You'll be beside the ocean at this shopping area with specialty shops, a restored carousel, restaurants, and street performers. | 419 Shoreline Village Dr. | 562/435–2668 | www.golongbeach.org/AttIndex.htm | Free | Daily.

Sightseeing Cruises. Long Beach Harbor is one of the busiest shipping centers on the Pacific Coast. It is also a beautiful part of the coast, with views of Catalina Island, the South Bay, and oil tankers on the ocean. You can take a whale-watching tour. | Long Beach Area Convention and Visitors Bureau, One World Trade Center, 3rd floor, Long Beach | 562/436–3645 or 800/4LB–STAY | www.golongbeach.org/RecIndex.htm | Prices vary per cruise | Call for schedule.

Catalina Channel Express. The boat to Catalina Island leaves from Long Beach. You'll have a 55-minute ride across the Pacific, followed by time to explore the island, before catching the boat back to Long Beach. | 1045 Queen Highway N. | 310/519–7957 | fax 310/548–7389 | www.catalina.com | $38 round trip | Daily.

Catalina Island. Beaches, rocky areas, restaurants, and shops greet you at this resort community on an island just off the coast of Los Angeles. On Catalina you can enjoy hiking and water sports such as water-skiing, snorkeling, swimming, and diving. You'll have to take the Catalina Cruise from Golden Shore Blvd., or Catalina Channel Express from Long Beach to reach the island. | 562/436–3645 | www.catalina.com | Free | Daily.

ON THE CALENDAR

APR.: *Toyota Grand Prix.* Grand Prix race cars take to the streets of Long Beach for this three-day event. | 562/436–9953.

JUNE: *Beach Fest.* This annual beach party boasts 50 bands on five stages, as well as what may be the world's largest chili cook-off. | 949/376–6942.

AUG.: *Jazz Festival.* Local and national jazz musicians come together at the Rainbow Lagoon Park on Shoreline Dr. in this festival featuring music, dancing, food and drink held on the 2nd full weekend in August. | 562/424–0013.

SEPT.: *Long Beach Blues Festival.* Blues recording and performing artists perform at this music gathering at 1288 N. Bellflower Blvd. | 562/985–1686.

Dining

L'Opera. Italian. Considered by many a real find in downtown Long Beach, this Northern Italian restaurant serves in a former bank. Flavorful goose prosciutto is paired with fresh mozzarella and drizzled with olive oil and sun-dried tomatoes. The lobster-and-ricotta-stuffed mezzaluna pasta has loads of lobster flavor. Many desserts. | 101 Pine Ave. | 562/491–0066 | No lunch weekends | $17–$25 | AE, D, DC, MC, V.

The Madison. Steak. With its plush dining room, mahogany walls, crystal chandeliers, and restored 1923 Kimball piano, this steakhouse resembles a 1920s supper club. Try the dry aged steaks or chops for which it's well known. | 102 Pine Ave. | 562/628–8866 | $16–$48 | AE, MC, V.

Mariposa. Mexican. Traditional Mexican entrées, from tacos and burritos to Oaxacan mole and fresh seafood, are the order of the day here. Streetside patio dining and live salsa music Thursday through Saturday help make it a popular spot. | 110 Pine Ave. | 562/437–2119 | $8–$24 | MC, V.

Mum's. Contemporary. A pioneer in the redevelopment of downtown Long Beach, this swank, romantic restaurant has an outdoor patio with umbrellaed tables and a reputation for its eclectic California cuisine and sushi bar. On the menu are delectable options like chili sesame-crusted halibut with papaya-mango salsa sided with whipped potatoes, or rack of lamb with herb crust, roasted shallot demi-glaze sided with baby root veggies and smashed potatoes. After dinner, go upstairs and check out Cohiba, Mum's dancehall-pool club. Jazz Fri. and Sat. | 144 Pine Ave. | 562/437–7700 | www.mumsrestaurant.com | $14–$30 | AE, D, DC, MC, V.

Parker's Lighthouse. Seafood. This Long Beach landmark, built to look like a giant New England lighthouse, overlooks the Queen Mary and the marina. There are three different floors to dine on, including a circular bar at the top. Among the many selections, you'll find mesquite-grilled fresh fish, a seafood platter, and prime black Angus beef. You can watch the harbor from the outdoor patio on the first floor. The open-air dining area is casual with white plastic square tables that have umbrellas and iron chairs. Jazz Sun. | 435 Shoreline Dr., No. 1 | 562/432–6500 | $15–$34 | AE, D, DC, MC, V.

Viva. Latin American. Next to the entrance courtyard from the Museum of Latin American Art, Viva serves such dishes as Bolivian tamal de pollo, Salvadoran *enchilada da espinacca y ajo* (enchiladas with spinach and garlic), a traditional Mexican torta, or a sandwich of marinated beef, lettuce, and avocado. Sunday brunch. | 644 Alamitos Ave. | 562/435–4048 | $6–$9 | AE, D, DC, MC, V.

Yard House. Contemporary. Harbor views and a staggering selection of over 250 draft beers draw the crowds to this restaurant. You can savor American–Asian fusion dishes of meat or seafood al fresco on the waterfront patio or within the quieter confines of the Harbor Room. | 401 Shoreline Dr. | 562/628–0455 | $9–$29 | AE, DC, MC, V.

Lodging

Best Western Golden Sails Hotel. You'll have a private patio or balcony, overlook nicely landscaped grounds to step onto from your large room done in light earth tones and pastels. The hotel is next to a marina, and specialty shops, restaurants, and movie theaters are within 5 blocks. The hotel was built in the early 1960s and is a gray concrete building. It is 5 mi east of downtown. Restaurant, bar (with entertainment), room service. In-room data ports, refrigerators, some in-room hot tubs, cable TV. Pool. Hot tub. Exercise equipment. Laundry facilities. Business services, airport shuttle, free parking. | 6285 E. Pacific Coast Hwy. | 562/596–1631 | fax 562/594–0623 | www.bestwestern.com | 172 rooms | $129–$151 | AE, D, DC, MC, V.

Courtyard by Marriott. Designed by business travelers, Courtyard strives to provide conveniences that make business and pleasure travel easier. There are computers and printers available in a full business center, plus you'll get a newspaper in the morning, and have a work desk in your room. Only three blocks from Long Beach Convention and Entertainment Center, ¼ mi from beach, 1 mi from Catalina Island Cruise, Shoreline Village, World Trade Center and ARCO, 2 mi from Long Beach Naval shipyard, and 5 mi from California State University at Long Beach. This is a nine-story modern American concrete hotel, built in 1995. Restaurant. In-room data ports, room service. Cable TV. Pool. Hot tub. Exercise equipment. Laundry facilities. Business services. Parking (fee). | 500 E. 1st St. | 562/435–8511 | fax 562/435–1370 | www.courtyard.com | 216 rooms | $109–$129 | AE, D, DC, MC, V.

Dockside Boat and Bed. Enjoy a night on your own private yacht! This organization provides bed and breakfast aboard your pick of ships, including an authentic 50-ft Chinese junk and a 44-ft motor yacht. No skills are necessary; all the sailing is done for you. Complimentary Continental breakfast. Kitchenettes, some in-room VCRs. | Dock 5, Rainbow Harbor, 316 E. Shoreline Dr. | 562/436–3111 | fax 562/436–1181 | www.boatandbed.com | 4 boats | $220–$300 | AE, MC, V.

Guesthouse Hotel. You'll have complimentary shuttle service to sites within a 5-mi radius of this hotel with its western-theme restaurant and saloon. It is ¼ mi off the Pacific Coast Hwy. and across the street from a golf course. Built in 1985, the three, two-story buildings underwent changes in 1997. Now your room will have extras like a recliner and work table in it. Complimentary Continental breakfast. In-room data ports, some kitchenettes, some in-room hot tubs, cable TV. Pool. Laundry facilities. Business services, airport shuttle, free parking. | 5325 E. Pacific Coast Hwy. | 562/597–1341 or 800/990–9991 | fax 562/597–1664 | varreguin@guesthouselb.com | www.guesthouselb.com/home.html | 143 rooms | $73–$109 | AE, D, DC, MC, V.

Hilton. An upscale hotel providing extensive business support services, this 14-story marble hotel has an L-shape tower of guest rooms above two floors of public spaces, with balconies facing the city and harbor. It is downtown, just four blocks from the Long Beach Aquarium. Built in 1992, your room will have modern furniture. Restaurant, bar. In-room data ports, minibars, cable TV. Pool. Hot tub. Gym. Business services, airport shuttle, parking (fee). Some pets allowed. | Two World Trade Center | 562/983–3400 | fax 562/983–1200 | www.hilton.com | 393 rooms | $119–$189 | AE, D, DC, MC, V.

Hotel Queen Mary. Stay on board the legendary "Grey Ghost" 1930s oceanliner, withdrawn from the British registry in 1967. The floating museum still retains its luxurious Art Deco touches, and a shipwalk tour comes with your overnight stay. 4 restaurants, bar, room service. Spa. Exercise equipment. Shops. | 1126 Queens Hwy. | 562/435–3511 | fax 562/437–4531 | www.queenmary.com | 365 rooms | $105–$400 | AE, D, DC, MC, V.

Hyatt Regency. Across the street from the harbor, this 17-story hotel, built in 1983 with lots of green glass, is also a five block walk from the Aquarium of the Pacific. The Long Beach Convention and Entertainment Center is next door and Shoreline Village is across the street. You can take advantage of 6 mi of beach with walking, jogging, and bicycling paths. Extensive business services are available. Spacious rooms are furnished in a mix of contemporary and Early American styles, and in earth, purple, and red tones. Restaurant, bar. In-room data ports, some minibars, cable TV. Pool. Hot tub. Exercise equipment. Business services.Free parking. | 200 S. Pine Ave. | 562/491–1234 | fax 562/432–1972 | www.hyatt.com/ | 522 rooms, 19 suites | $195–$249, $400–$775 suites | AE, D, DC, MC, V.

Inn of Long Beach. This hotel provides nothing out-of-the-ordinary, but it's rate is one of the best you'll find in the L.A. area. You'll be able to see the hotel pool from most of the rooms in this late-1960s, two-story white stucco building. Two blocks north of Ocean Blvd. Complimentary Continental breakfast. In-room data ports, refrigerators, cable TV, in-room VCRs. Pool. Hot tub. Business services. Free parking.| 185 Atlantic Ave. | 562/435–3791 or 800/230–7500 | fax 562/436–7510 | 46 rooms | $69–$79 | AE, D, DC, MC, V.

Marriott. Built as an eight-story configuration lined with interior corridors, this hotel is right at the Long Beach Airport and 7 mi east of downtown. A big cream-colored lobby leads to rooms that have earth-tone pastel walls and carpets, with cheerful flowered bedspreads; 43 rooms are specifically designed for business travelers with work desks, halogen desk lamps, and ergonomic swivel chairs. Restaurants, bar. In-room data ports, cable TV. 2 pools (1 indoor). Hot tub, massage, sauna. Exercise equipment. Business services, airport shuttle, free parking. | 4700 Airport Plaza Dr. | 562/425–5210 | fax 562/425–2744 | www.marriotthotels.com | 311 rooms | $109–179 | AE, D, DC, MC, V.

Renaissance Long Beach. In the heart of the Long Beach financial district, this 12-story, black marble building, built in 1985, is across from the Long Beach Convention and Entertainment Center. Guest rooms are large, with a contemporary Southwestern flair and blond wood furniture. 2 restaurants, bar. In-room data ports, cable TV. Pool. Exercise equipment. Business services. Free parking. | 111 E. Ocean Blvd. | 562/437–5900 | fax 562/499–2509 | www.renaissancehotels.com | 374 rooms | $159–$215 | AE, D, DC, MC, V.

Seaport Marina Hotel. Overlooking the marina, this 14-acre resort with landscaped gardens has rooms with sitting areas and balconies. It's within 5 blocks of shops, restaurants, and recreation. Room service. Cable TV. Pool. Hot tub. Laundry service. Business services. | 6400 E. Pacific Coast Hwy. | 562/434–8451 | fax 562/596–6480 | www.seaportmarinahotel.com | 200 rooms | $85–$105 | AE, D, DC, MC, V.

Turret House. This 1906 Queen Anne home has been completely refurbished and decorated with period furniture, silver, and china—even a vintage player piano in the front parlor. Complimentary breakfast. No room phones, TV in common area. No kids. No smoking. | 556 Chestnut Ave. | 562/983–9812 or 888/488–7738 | fax 562/437–4082 | www.turrethouse.com | 5 rooms | $100–$140 | AE, D, MC, V.

Westcoast Long Beach. Wonderfully situated, this luxury Mediterranean-style stone and wood hotel is right on the waterfront and has both a city and bay view. The landscaped pool has a surrounding patio with palm trees and is right off the marina, 1/2 mi from the Queen Mary Seaport. Restaurant, bar. Cable TV. Pool. 2 tennis courts. Exercise equipment. Video games. Business services, airport shuttle. Parking (fee). | 700 Queensway Dr. | 562/435–7676 or 800/426–0670 | fax 562/437–0866 | infosales@westcoasthotesl.com | www.westcoasthotels.com | 195 rooms | $140–$150 | AE, D, DC, MC, V.

Westin Long Beach. This 16-story hotel made of concrete and glass is next to the Long Beach Convention and Entertainment Center and one block from the beach. Rooms have contemporary furnishings; many have ocean views. If you are traveling on business, you'll like the rooms with ergonomic chairs and in-room laser printer/fax/copiers. You can also take advantage of the hotel's limousine service. Restaurant, bar, room service. In-room data ports, cable TV. Pool. Hot tub. Exercise equipment. Business services.Free parking. Some pets allowed. | 333 E. Ocean Blvd. | 562/436–3000 | fax 562/436–9176 | www.westin.com | 460 rooms | $218–$236 | AE, D, DC, MC, V.

LOS ANGELES

(Nearby towns also listed: Beverly Hills, Burbank, Culver City, Glendale, Long Beach, North Hollywood, Studio City, Torrance, Venice, West Hollywood)

The sprawling metropolis of Los Angeles is impossible to classify. The Los Angeles area, which includes the entire county and surrounding areas, is populated by 16.3 million residents and is bounded to the north and south by bedroom communities that creep toward Santa Barbara and San Diego. To the west, a series of sleepy beach towns dapple the coast. To the east, movie studio lots and million-dollar homes reach toward the foothills.

Angelenos come from 140 countries and speak 96 different languages. This diversity dates back to the first settlers, who came to the area in 1781. The adventurous group of 44 came from the Mexican provinces of Sonora and Sinaloa and included Indians, blacks, mestizos, and Spaniards. Olvera Street marks the settlers' home and is the center of Los Angeles' Mexican-American heritage. The cultural diversity that is a long-standing tradition in Los Angeles has left its indelible mark on the city: A lively arts community features performance installations, graffiti art, and cultural commentary, and the entire city joins in cultural celebrations such as Cinco de Mayo and Chinese New Year.

This diversity, however, has caused Los Angeles its share of growing pains. As the 20th century wound down legal battles about bilingual education and bilingual street signs heated up ballots and courtrooms, and the city has yet to recover from the riots following the 1992 acquittal of the police officers accused of beating Rodney King. Since that time, the city has made large strides toward healing, prompted by disasters that served to unite neighbors, such as the 1994 Northridge earthquake and the 1996 Malibu wildfires.

The freeways are the best way to get around town, although if possible you should avoid them at rush hour. Locals will refer to travel time by minutes and to freeways by numbers: "It's 20 minutes on the 10 'til you get to the 210."

Information: **Los Angeles Convention and Visitors Bureau** | 633 W. 5th St., Ste. 6000, 90071 | 213/624–7300 or 800/228–2452 | fax 213/624–9746 | www.lacvb.com.

NEIGHBORHOODS

Chinatown. Although the Chinese communities in New York, San Francisco, and Vancouver are larger, this part of downtown opposite Union Station still represents a colorful slice of Southeast Asian life with its population of 15,000 Chinese and Southeast Asians and its savory market stocked with dried squid, shark's fin, various roots, and other exotic foods. Bordered by Yale, Bernard, Ord, and Alameda streets, it is focused on North Boradway, especially during Chinese New Year, when giant dragons snake down the street. At any time of year, drop into one of the local dim sum parlors for a savory brunch or lunch. For details you can contact the Chinese Chamber of Commerce. | 213/617–0396.

Fashion District. Few streets in LA are more entertaining than the blocks around Los Angeles and 7th streets, where retailers, wholesalers, and manufacturers sell clothing, fabric, textiles, and accessories. Hawkers try to coax you into shops and buy everything from kids' clothing to men's suits to discounted designer dresses and yard goods. A clutch of retail shops occupies Santee Alley; the heart of the district is CaliforniaMart 110 E. 9th Street (213/630–3600); normally its 1,200 showrooms are wholesale only, but several times a year it opens to the public for a sale. Sample sales are a regular event. The Downtown Property Owners Association can give you the scoop. | 213/488–1153.

Melrose Avenue. Between Highland and Fairfax this street is a cool area where you can spot celebrities, have a decent meal, shop for everything from second-hand novelties to high-priced antiques, or just hang out. You'll find art galleries, bookstores, day spas, and both vintage clothing and current fashions here. Be sure to visit nearby La Brea Avenue, between First and Sixth streets; it has a similar spirit.

★**Olvera Street.** Named for the 1877 county judge who owned a home at the street's end, this street is the birthplace of the City of Angels; it became a vibrant 1-block Mexican market place in 1930. Historic buildings line the street, including the Avila Adobe, built around 1818 by former mayor Francisco Avila and considered the oldest standing building in Los Angeles. A self-guided tour brochure describing the historic buildings is available at the Information Desk in the Plaza and at the El Pueblo Visitors Center in Sepulveda House, a former hotel and boardinghouse built in 1887. On weekends the restaurants are packed and there are usually strolling Mexican singers, mariachi bands, and other performers in the plaza. You can shop for Mexican handicrafts, puppets, leather goods, and other souvenirs; eat tacos or enchiladas at the outdoor cafés; or simply relax on one of the benches under the giant Moreton Bay fig tree. Across the street on the corner of Caesar Chavez and Alameda is the historic Union Station, used as a location in countless films, including *Blade Runner*. The area is especially colorful, lively, and crowded during the weekends around Cinco de Mayo (May 5), the annual Blessing of the Animals on the Saturday before Easter, and during Las Posadas (every night between December 16 and 24 during which Mary and Joseph's Christmas Eve search for lodging is commemorated).

MELROSE PLACE AND BEYOND

Do you have some money burning a hole in your wallet, or an afternoon you'd like to spend imagining what it would be like to have too much cash?

Stroll down the 2-mi stretch of Melrose that begins around Crescent Heights Boulevard and winds down around La Brea. Don't waste your time looking for an apartment building resembling the old home of Melrose Place characters Amanda, Billy, Allison, or Sydney—it's not here. But some tremendously interesting shops are. From designer fashions to used clothes and old movie posters, you'll find something that catches your eye.

If the weather doesn't suit you and you want some indoor strolling, go to the Beverly Center. This multilevel shopping mall includes major department stores and has virtually everything you'd ever want to see, plus a lot more.

Want to ogle an orange? Grab some greens? Pick up some potatoes? Then head to the Farmers Market. Founded in 1934 as a co-operative, the Farmers Market hosts more than 150 vendors daily. Pick up something or sit down and have a bite; you'll find the flavor you're craving here. And, of course, what shopping trip to L.A. would be complete without a visit to Rodeo Drive? The main stretch of conspicuous consumption hovers around three blocks in Beverly Hills, between Santa Monica and Wilshire Boulevards.

© Artville

TRANSPORTATION

Airports: There are several airports in the LA area. The major gateway is the country's third-largest airport, **Los Angeles International Airport,** also known as LAX (310/646–5252). Give yourself plenty of time before departure as LAX traffic is heavy.

Located 35 mi south of Los Angeles in Santa Ana is the **John Wayne Airport,** the Orange County airport (949/252–5006). You can see a 9-ft statue of the airport's namesake, the Duke, on the lower level of the Thomas F. Riley Terminal.

At the southern tip of Los Angeles County is **Long Beach Airport** (562/570–2600). **Airport Transportation:** There are several routes to and from the airport. The most direct is the San Diego Freeway (I–405), although it's congested. Other options include the I–105 to or from the east and La Cienega Boulevard to or from Hollywood and the mid-Wilshire area. Be forewarned: I–405 can be a parking lot, with travel times varying between $\frac{1}{2}$ hour and $1\frac{1}{2}$ hours from the airport to various points in the area, especially the San Fernando Valley). From the airport, take I–405 north to I–10 west

STAR WATCHING—THE CELESTIAL KIND

Who would think that through the smog you could see much of anything? Fortunately, someone less cynical did—and built a fabulous observatory to prove it.

If you want to explore one of the greatest planetariums on the West Coast, get thee to the Griffith Observatory and Planetarium in Los Angeles. Inside there are refracting telescopes, a Hall of Science with an astronomy museum, and a 600-seat theater where you can take in star shows and a Laserium light show. The nearly two million people who visit the observatory each year can't be wrong!

The 12-inch Zeiss refracting telescope is on the roof of the east dome. It's open to the public to view the moon and planets—free of charge. The solar telescopes are located in the west dome. While you can't get access to these telescopes, you can see what they are viewing from the main floor exhibit area, where the images are projected.

The Hall of Science includes a large collection of meteorites, one Mars rock, a $\frac{1}{5}$ scale model of the Hubble Space Telescope, Foucault Pendulum, spacecraft, and a lot more.

When you're finished exploring the universe, the rest of the park is up for grabs. In 1896 the repetitively named Griffith J. Griffith donated 3,000 acres to the city for a park. The city bought adjoining land so that Griffith Park itself is now on 4,100 acres and is the largest municipal park and urban wilderness area in the United States. Within the park are tennis courts, horse stables, a zoo, a collection of vintage locomotives, and the Greek Theater. From April to October there are concerts in the 1,600-seat theater. The Los Angeles Zoo—noted for its work breeding endangered species—is also in the Park. So you won't be at a loss for things to do or see.

There are four main entrances to Griffith Park: from the west, enter at Western Canyon Road, off Los Feliz Boulevard and Western Avenue; from the south, at Los Feliz Boulevard and Vermont Avenue; from the east, at Crystal Springs Drive near Los Feliz Boulevard and Riverside Drive; and from the north, at the Golden State Freeway (I–5) and Ventura freeway (Rte. 134).

to get to Santa Monica. Take I–405 north to I–10 east to West Los Angeles and Beverly Hills. The I–405 south to Orange County turns into I–5 South (San Diego Freeway); this takes you to Anaheim, Newport Beach (via I–55 south), Irvine, Laguna Beach, and points farther south, heading toward San Diego.

If you're not driving yourself, you have several other options including door-to-door shuttle van, local bus lines, light rail, and taxicabs. Throughout the airport you can use computers at Quick-Aid kiosks to get airport and transportation information. Costs and computer printouts are available for ground transportation; the operators themselves sell the tickets. Wait for buses and shuttles on the Lower/Arrival Level islands in front of each terminal under the appropriate sign. (Inbound buses, vans, trams, and the LAX shuttle arrive on the upper level.)

Taxis can be found on the lower level. You will be presented with a ticket stating typical fares to major destinations. Don't use anything but authorized taxis—those bearing an official seal on the vehicle. Request the flat fee option or travel with a company that offers set rates because, while the ride to downtown from LAX can take as little as 30 minutes, it can also take a couple of hours depending on the traffic.

Your least expensive option is the train-bus combo. A free shuttle bus ("Aviation Shuttle") connects LAX with the MTA's Metro Green Line Aviation Station. From there, you can take trains to 50 stations in the LA area, including various points in the San Fernando Valley. Trains run every 7 to 15 minutes depending on the time of day. Another free shuttle ("Parking Lot C") takes you to the LAX Transit Center, where you can catch the bus. MTA offers limited airport service to all areas of greater Los Angeles. Prices vary from $1.35 to $3.10; some routes require transfers. The best line to take to downtown is the direct express line 439, which costs $1.85 and takes 45 to 60 minutes. Los Angeles area city bus information is available in each terminal by telephone on the Information Display Board in the baggage claim area. Contact the MTA for details. | 213/626–4455 | www.mta.net.

SuperShuttle provides shared ride door-to-door service 24 hours a day between LAX and the surrounding area. The trip to or from your destination, in a seven-passenger van, costs between $16 (Santa Monica) and $45 (Newport Beach), $25 and $41 for trips to the valley (Glendale, Burbank, Van Nuys). At the airport, you can talk to a curbside representative outside baggage claim or use the SuperShuttle courtesy phone in the luggage area; the van should arrive within 15 minutes. | 310/782–6600, 323/775–6600, or 800/554–3146; 818/556–6600 for trips to the Valley | www.supershuttle.com.

Shuttle One offers door-to-door service for $12 per person from LAX to hotels in the Disneyland/Anaheim area, $35 to the San Fernando Valley. | 310/670–6666 or 800/400–7488.

Airport Coach has regular service between LAX and Anaheim hotels ($14) or the Hilton and the Sheraton in Pasadena ($12). | 714/938–8900 or 800/772–5299.

Inland Express offers van service to LAX, Ontario International Airport, and John Wayne Airport and the counties of eastern Los Angeles, San Bernardino, and Riverside. Reserve a couple of days ahead. | 909/626–6599, 888/938–4500.

Southern California Coach provides shuttle service to LAX, Ontario International Airport, John Wayne Airport, the Santa Monica Pier, and Orange County and the southern portion of L.A. County. To reserve, call 2 to 3 days in advance with a major credit card. | 714/978–6415.

FlyAway Service has transportation between LAX and the central San Fernando Valley for $3.50 ($6 round-trip). | 818/994–5554.

Rail: Union Station in Los Angeles is one of the grande dames of railroad stations. It is served by **Amtrak.** The Coast Starlight runs along the California coast between Seattle and Portland and from Oakland to San Francisco down to Los Angeles. The Sunset Limited goes to Los Angeles from Florida via New Orleans and Texas, and the Southwest Chief originates in Chicago and takes you through Albuquerque to Los Angeles. | 800 N. Alameda St. | Union Station 213/683–6979, Amtrak 800/872–724 | www.amtrakwest.com.

Bus: The city is served by **Greyhound Lines.** The terminal is at the corner of 7th Street and Alameda. Arrive in the daytime, if possible. | 1716 E 7th St. | 800/231–2222.

Intra-city Transport: Although it's easiest to get around by car, you do have other options.

You can get anywhere you need to go in downtown LA for 25 cents via **DASH** (Downtown Area Short Hop). The nine shuttle lines run weekdays every 5 to 12 minutes from about 5:50AM to 7PM, less frequently on weekends. | 213/808–2273.

MTA offers bus and rail service in LA County. The one-way fare is $1.35, $1.60 with a transfer. Buses require exact change. At some stations you can buy a weekly pass for $11. These passes expire on Saturday no matter what day you buy them—it is not a seven-day pass. All Metrolink stations have ticket vending machines (TVMs) from which you may purchase tickets and passes. TVMs accept cash, VISA, MasterCard, Novus, Discover, and ATM cards with the Explore, Interlink, or Maestro symbols. You must have a valid ticket before you board Metrolink. Metrolink uses the honor system, and tickets are not collected. You must show your ticket to the conductor or fare verifier on request. Passengers without a valid ticket are subject to citation and fine. | 213/626–4455 | www.mta.net.

Driving Around Town: Los Angeles is at the western terminus of I–10, a major east–west interstate highway that runs all the way east to Florida. I–15, angling down from Las Vegas, swings through the eastern communities around San Bernardino before

© Corbis

ON AND OFF THE FREEWAYS

Get used to it. In L.A., driving is almost as necessary as breathing. The city actually used to have a public transit system. Old-time Los Angelenos recall the charming trolley cars called the "Big Red Cars" that used to run through the town and cover 1,100 mi of track. In 1925 there was even a subway line from downtown to Hollywood. Beginning in the late 1930s, however, the Big Red Cars were phased out, with the last one shutting down in 1961.

Today L.A. is a web of freeways. Directions from any Point A to any other Point B usually require at least one merger on and off a numbered freeway—and plenty of courage. Locals treat the cement byways as a necessity of life, and as a visitor, so must you. Inhale, remember where you are going, and merge.

But driving in L.A. is not entirely hair-raising: some of L.A.'s best views are discovered in the car, so if you have a few hours on a clear afternoon, hop behind the wheel.

Pick up Sunset Boulevard in Hollywood and head west. Along the way you'll travel through West Hollywood, then wind through Beverly Hills, Bel Air, and Brentwood on the way out to the Pacific Coast Highway. It's a beautiful, winding road that takes you through some of the nicest parts of LaLaLand.

When you arrive at the end of Sunset, go north via the PCH (Pacific Coast Highway, also known as Route 1). Again, beautiful water views abound along the winding route up to Malibu. As evening comes on, either catch the sunset from the beach or head back east on Sunset to West L.A. and up to Mulholland Drive, named for William Mulholland, who brought water to the L.A. basin. You can reach Mulholland via canyon drives such as Coldwater Canyon or Laurel Canyon. At night this famous vista offers breathtaking vistas of L.A., a seemingly endless ribbon of lights.

heading on down to San Diego. I–5, which runs north and south through California, leads up to San Francisco and down to San Diego. These thoroughfares, along with a mix of local freeways, create a matrix of transportation routes that intersect at various points throughout the greater Los Angeles area. Traffic around Los Angeles is severe and at its worst weekdays during rush hour, which extends between 7AM and 9AM and then again from 3PM to 7PM. Freeways may be backed up at any time of day, though many reserve an express carpool lane for cars with more than one passenger. Rules about carpool lanes and metered entrances to freeways are strictly enforced. Meter costs range up to 25 cents for 15 minutes depending upon the area. However, note that parking rules are strictly enforced in Los Angeles and illegally parked cars are speedily ticketed and towed. Garages and parking lots cost about 25 cents to $2 per half hour or a few dollars to $25 per day; downtown and in Century City you may pay as much as $25 per hour on weekdays. Many restaurants offer $3–$5 valet parking.

WALKING TOUR

Begin a downtown LA tour by heading north on Broadway from 8th or 9th Street. Around 3rd Street, look for cheap parking at one of the small lots. At the southeast corner of Broadway and 3rd is the Victorian **Bradbury Building.** Across the street is the **Grand Central Market,** a maze of tantalizing stalls. Make your way through and come out onto Hill Street. Cross Hill Street and climb aboard **Angels Flight Railway,** a funicular that sweeps you up a steep incline to a courtyard called Watercourt, surrounded by bubbling, cascading fountains. From here, walk towards the glass pyramidal skylight topping the **Museum of Contemporary Art,** also known as MOCA, visible 1/2 block north on Grand Avenue. Now either retrace your steps to Watercourt for the Angels Flight descent to Hill Street, Grand Central Market, and your car; or walk 2 blocks south on Grand to 5th Street. There you'll find two more of downtown's treasures, the elaborate **Biltmore Hotel** and the 1926 **Central Library,** the third-largest public library in the country, with the tranquil MacGuire Gardens behind it. Across 5th Street are the **Bunker Hill Steps,** the city's monumental staircase. Back in your car, continue north on Broadway to 1st Street. A right turn takes you into **Little Tokyo** and the **Japanese American National Museum,** which explores Japanese-American culture and issues via changing exhibits. The **Geffen Contemporary** art museum, an arm of MOCA, is 1 block north on Central. If you're ready for a break, backtrack on Central to 2nd Street and head 2 blocks north to Los Angeles Street to get to the rooftop **Japanese Garden** at the New Otani Hotel. From Little Tokyo, turn left (north) from 1st onto Alameda. As you pass over the freeway, you'll come to **Union Station,** on the right. Park in the pay lot here, take a look, then cross Alameda to explore **Olvera Street,** where Los Angeles began. Back at Union Station, make a right onto Alameda and then immediately left on Cesar Chavez Avenue; follow it 3 blocks. At Broadway, turn right to **Chinatown,** the end of your tour.

Attractions

ART AND ARCHITECTURE

Broadway Plaza. The city's premier shopping district from 1909 to 1929, the area is dotted with beautiful landmarks like the Pantages Theater and the Fine Arts Building. 7th and 8th Sts. between Hope and Flower. | 750 W. 7th St. | 213/624–2891 | Free | Daily.

City Hall. A majestic city building that anchors downtown Los Angeles has been the location of many films. | The building is being retrofitted for earthquakes; tours will resume in 2003 | 200 N. Main St. | 213/485–2121 | www.cityofla.org | Free.

Los Angeles Mall. Designed to be used like a town square, with a fountain, sculpture, trees, and benches, this open space is bordered by City Hall, shops, and restaurants. | 201 N. LA St. | Free | 213/687–3050 | Daily.

Watts Towers. These famous towers were built by self-taught artist Simon Rodia over a 33-year period between 1921–1954 from steel, broken glass, shells, and pottery shards. Now they are a National Historic Landmark. | 1727 E. 107th St. | 213/847–4646 | Free | Gallery Tues.– Sat. 10–4, Sun. 12–4.

CULTURE, EDUCATION, AND HISTORY

CBS Television City. *Hollywood Squares,* and other shows often offer free tickets to a taping. | 7800 Beverly Blvd. | 323/575–2345 | studiotours.ourfamily.com | Free | Weekdays 9–5.

El Pueblo de Los Angeles Historic Monument. This 44-acre area is the oldest section of the city and reflects the diversity of the people who settled and developed Los Angeles. | 125 Paseo De La Plaza | 213/628–1274 | www.cityofla.org/elp/ | Free | Tours Wed.–Sat. 10–12.

Avila Adobe. An adobe house built in 1818 by rancher Don Francisco Avila has been restored to show daily life in 1840s California. | 10 E. Olvera St. | 213/628–1274 | Free | Apr.– Sept., daily 9–5; Oct.–Mar., daily 9–4.

Sepulveda House. This two-story Eastlake Victorian was built in 1887 for Eloisa Martinez de Sepulveda, who ran a boarding house here and rented out shops. | 622 N. Main St. | 213/628–1274 | www.cityofla.org/elp/sepul.htm | Free | Mon.–Sat. 10–3.

Greek Theatre. This natural outdoor amphitheater, beneath the trees in Griffith Park, seats more than 6,000 for summer performances. Call for a schedule of performances. | 2700 N. Vermont Ave. | 323/665–1927.

Lummis Home and Garden State Historical Monument. Author and historian Charles Lummis built Alisal by hand between 1896 and 1910 from granite boulders. It is surrounded by a desert garden. | 200 E. Ave. 43 | 213/222–0546 | fax 213/222–0771 | Free | Fri.–Sun. 12–4.

Music Center of Los Angeles County. The Music Center is home to the Los Angeles Philharmonic, the Music Center Opera, and the Master Chorale. The complex includes the Dorothy Chandler Pavilion, the Mark Taper Forum, the Ahmanson Theatre, and the future Walt Disney Concert Hall. Educational events for young performers are part of its program. Call for the center's schedule. | 135 N. Grand Ave. | 213/972–7211 or 213/972–8001 | www.musiccenter.org.

Old Plaza Firehouse. The firehouse was built in 1884 and houses antique firefighting equipment, historic photographs, and an original chemical wagon. | 134 Paseo de la Plaza | 213/628–1274 | Free | Tues.–Sun. 10–3.

★ **Olvera Street.** One of the oldest streets in the city was named after Agustin Olvera, Los Angeles' first judge. It's the center of LA's Mexican heritage, with sidewalk shops, stalls, restaurants, and frequent mariachi music. Exit Hollywood Freeway (U.S. 101) at Arcadia. | Olvera St. between Cesar Chavez and Alameda | 213/628–1274 | Free | Daily.

University of California, Los Angeles (UCLA). The cross-town rival of USC, UCLA is a well-regarded branch of the UC system, in the lively town of Westwood. The university is known for its film, drama, and medical schools. | 405 Hilgard Ave. | 310/825–8764 | www.ucla.edu | Free, parking $6 | Daily.

University of Southern California (USC). On a campus of brick buildings and tree-lined paths, this prestigious university is known for its film school and the Trojan marching band. | 3551 University Ave. | 213/740–2311 | www.usc.edu | Free | Daily.

Westwood Memorial Cemetery. Stars from Hollywood's past are buried here. | 1218 Glendon Ave. | 310/474–1579 | Free | Daily dawn to dusk.

MUSEUMS

★ **California Science Center.** A hands-on museum with exhibits relating to space, physics, the natural environment, and health. A space docking simulator is a virtual reality ride that mimics a condition of zero-gravity. In Digital Jam Session you can create music with a variety of instruments, then alter the sounds using computers. The Science Center also houses an IMAX theater with a five-story screen. | 700 State Dr. | 213/744–7400 | www.casciencectr.org | Free | Daily 10–5.

Fowler Museum of Cultural History. This UCLA museum celebrates the world's diverse cultures and visual arts, especially those of Africa, Asia, Oceania, Native America, and Latin America, through exhibitions, publications, and public programs. Enter the UCLA campus at Westwood Plaza on Sunset Blvd. | 310/825–4361 | fax 310/206–7007 | $5; free Thurs. and Sun. | Wed., Fri.–Sun. 12–5, Thurs. 12–8.

★ **The Getty Center.** The Getty Museum collections comprise seven areas of art: Greek and Roman antiquities, Medieval manuscripts, European paintings, sculpture, drawings and decorative arts, and photographs. The building architect was Richard Meier, and the landscape was designed to complement the building, adding color to the travertine surfaces and bringing warmth to the geometry. | 1200 Getty Center Dr. | 310/440–7300 | www.getty.edu/museum | Free, parking $5 | Tues., Wed. 11–7, Thurs., Fri. 11–9, weekends 2–10; parking reservations required.

Griffith Observatory and Planetarium. This lookout point in Griffith Park affords a sweeping view of Los Angeles, and the planetarium has star-gazing tours and laser shows. | 2800 E. Observatory Rd. | 323/664–1181, 323/664–1191 (recording), or 818/901–9405 | fax 323/663–4323 | www.griffithobservatory.org | Free; planetarium $4 | Mid-June–early Sept., daily 12:30–10; early Sept.–mid-June, Tues.–Fri. 2–10, weekends 12:30–10; under age 5 admitted only to 1:30 shows and special children's shows.

★ **Japanese American National Museum.** The permanent exhibit chronicles Japanese life in the U.S.; temporary exhibits highlight aspects of Japanese-American culture, such as internment camps. | 369 E. 1st St. | 213/625–0414 | $4 | Tues., Wed, Fri.–Sun. 10–5, Thurs. 10–8.

Los Angeles Children's Museum. This hands-on museum has a wide range of learning experiences for ages 2–10. Interactive exhibits include a recording studio and a video studio. | 310 N. Main St. | 213/687–8800 | fax 213/687–0319 | www.lacm.org | $5 | Tues.–Fri. 9–1, weekends 10–5; reservations required Tues.–Fri.

TOURS OF STUDIOS

So you wanna see a star? Then you've come to the right place. Tickets to tapings of television shows are free, but you'll need to call well in advance to get seats on the days you plan to be in town.

Audiences Unlimited (818/753–3483) handles tickets for a lot of shows as well as for some of the smaller studios. **CBS Television City** (213/852–2624) and **NBC Television** (818/840–3537) offer free tickets to tapings; the latter also offers a 70-min tour of the studios.

Warner Bros. Studios (818/954–1744) offers 2-hr tours that require a lot of walking, and **Universal Studios** (818/508–9600) has a whole theme park with the movies as its motif.

As the last major studio still located in Hollywood, **Paramount Studios** (213/956–5575) is a great place to see what a movie studio looks like. Two-hr tours leave from the pedestrian gate on Melrose.

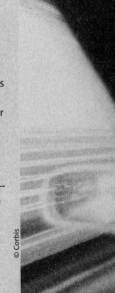

© Corbis

Los Angeles County Museum of Art. This vast museum of more than 150,000 works is housed in five buildings. It includes costumes, textiles, decorative arts, paintings, and sculpture from around the world. The museum also presents more than 30 exhibitions a year, with coordinated lectures, and films. | 5905 Wilshire Blvd. | 323/857–6000 | fax 323/857–6216 | www.lacma.org | $6 | Mon., Tues., Thurs. 12–8, Fri. 12–9, weekends 11–8.

★ **Museum of Contemporary Art (MOCA).** MOCA houses international works from the 1940s to the present. The building was designed by Arata Isozaki in 1982 and is itself a landmark. | 250 S. Grand Ave. | 213/626–6222 or 213/621–2766 | fax 213/620–8674 | www.moca.org | $6 | Tues., Wed., Fri.–Sun. 11–5, Thurs. 11–8.

★ **Museum of Tolerance.** The Simon Wiesenthal Center's Museum is a center for Holocaust remembrance and the defense of human rights. | 9786 W. Pico Blvd. | 310/553–8403 | www.wiesenthal.com | $8.50 | Nov.–Mar., Mon.–Thurs. 10–4, Fri. 10–3, Sun. 10:30–5; Apr.–Oct., Mon.–Thurs. 10–4, Fri. 10–3, Sun. 11–5.

★ **Natural History Museum of Los Angeles County.** Exhibits show life in the Southwest and California from 1540–1940 as well as pre-Columbian artifacts. The museum also has displays of mammals, birds, insects, and marine life in African and North American habitats, an underwater world, and a butterfly pavilion. | 900 Exposition Blvd. | 213/763–3466 | www.nhm.org | $8; free 1st Tues. of the month | Daily 10–5.

George C. Page Museum of La Brea Discoveries. On the site of the La Brea Tar Pits, where many important fossils have been found, the Museum displays reconstructed fossils of Ice-Age animals, ranging from birds of prey and saber-toothed cats to mammoths and dire wolves. You can watch the paleontological laboratory clean, identify, and catalog fossils. | 5901 Wilshire Blvd. | 323/934–7243 or 323/936–2230 | www.tarpits.org/ | $6; parking $5 | Daily 10–5.

Southwest Museum. The diversity of Native American cultures from South America to Alaska and from prehistoric times to the present is on display in exhibits of paintings, textiles, basketry, pottery, and decorative arts. | 234 Museum Dr. | 323/221–2163 | fax 323/224–8223 | www.southwestmuseum.org | $5 | Tues.–Sun. 10–5.

Travel Town Museum. A transportation museum with early railroad equipment and steam locomotives, period automobiles and wagons, and firefighting equipment used in LA from 1869 to 1940. A miniature train circles the area. | 5200 W. Zoo Dr. | 323/662–5874 | www.cityofla.org/RAP/grifmet/tt/index.htm | Free | Weekdays 10–4, weekends 10–5.

Wells Fargo History Museum. The history of the American West is told through the history of the Wells Fargo stagecoach and pony express services. | 333 S. Grand Ave. | 213/253–7166 or 213/253–7169 | fax 213/680–2269 | www.wellsfargohistory.com | Free | Weekdays 9–5.

PARKS, NATURAL AREAS, AND OUTDOOR RECREATION

Elysian Park. This large park hosts many organized sports, including indoor soccer, a girls' basketball league, NFL flag football, drill team competition, and an after-school kids' club. | 929 Academy Rd., Elysian Pk. | 323/226–1402 | Free | Daily.

Exposition Park. This park borders USC and contains the Natural History Museum. | 900 Exposition Blvd. | Free | Daily.

Griffith Park. The largest urban municipal park in the U.S. accommodates the Los Angeles Zoo, Travel Town Museum, and Griffith Observatory. You can take in sweeping views of the city from its heights. | 4730 Crystal Spring Dr. | 323/913–4688 or 323/485–5515 | www.laparkrangers.com | Free | Daily.

Los Angeles Zoo. Home to 1,200 animals representing 350 species, the zoo is in Griffith Park. | 5333 Zoo Dr. | 323/644–6400 | fax 323/662–9786 | www.lazoo.org | $8.25 | Daily 10–5.

Los Encinos State Historic Park. This park is all that remains of Rancho El Encino, a 4,500-acre sheep and cattle ranch that served as a stagecoach stop from 1845 to 1915. The park contains some period buildings and a spring-fed lake. | 16756 Moorpark St. | 818/784–4849 | cal-parks.ca.gov/DISTRICTS/angeles/leshp546.htm | Free | Wed.–Sun. 10–5; house tours Wed.–Sun. 1–4.

Mildred Mathias Botanical Garden. Approximately 5,000 species in 225 families from all over the world grow in this seven-acre garden on the campus of UCLA. Many plants are tropical and subtropical. | 707 S. Tiverton Ave. | 310/825–3620 | www.pisces.lifesci.ucla.edu/botgard | Free | Weekdays 8–5, weekends 8–4.

South Coast Botanic Garden. More than 150,000 plant species are represented here, with an emphasis on the arid climate of southern California. A children's garden depicts fairy tale themes. | 26300 Crenshaw Blvd. | 310/544–6815 | www.palosverdes.com/botanicgardens/ | $5 | Daily 9–5.

RELIGION AND SPIRITUALITY

Nuestra Señora La Reina de Los Angeles. The oldest church in the city dates back to 1822. Today it is also known as the Old Plaza Church and still serves an active parish. | 535 N. Main St. | 213/628–1274 | Free | Daily.

SHOPPING

Arco Plaza. The plaza's shopping area and restaurants make it a popular lunchtime spot for business people. | 505 S. Flower St. | 213/625–2132 | Free | Daily.

★ **Farmers Market.** This large market is housed in a permanent structure, near several movie studios. The breakfast counter has had its share of devotees, including James Dean. | 6333 W. 3rd St. | 323/933–9211 | fax 323/549–2145 | www.farmersmarketla.com/ | June–Sept., Mon.–Sat. 9–7, Sun. 10–6; Oct.–May, Mon.–Sat. 9–6:30, Sun. 10–5.

SIGHTSEEING TOURS

Guided Walking Tours. Take a free guided walking tour of Olvera Street and the historic El Pueblo de Los Angeles, where 27 old buildings have been restored. Start at the docent office next to Old Plaza Firehouse. | 622 N. Main St. | 213/628–1274 | Free | Tues.–Sat. 10–1.

SPORTS AND RECREATION

Amateur Athletic Foundation. Founded with 1984 Olympics funds, the AAF supports youth sports programs and has a large sports library and research center, as well as a collection of historic sports artifacts. | 2141 W. Adams Blvd. | 323/730–9600 | www.aafla.org | Free | Mon., Tues., Thurs., Fri. 10–5, Wed. 10–7.

Los Angeles Clippers. This National Basketball Association team plays at the Staples Center (11th at Figueroa) and is known for a very lively cheering section. Call for the team's schedule. | 1111 S. Figueroa St., Ste. 1100 | 213/745–0400 or 213/742–7500 | www.nba.com/clippers.

Los Angeles Dodgers. The Brooklyn Dodgers moved to Los Angeles in the 1950s and since then have become a very popular southern California National League team, particularly because of the much-loved Tommy Lasorda. Call for a schedule of games. | Dodger Stadium, 1000 Elysian Park Ave. | 323/224–1448 or 323/224–1400 | fax 323/224–2609 | www.dodgers.com.

Los Angeles Kings. National Hockey League games are a good opportunity for transplants from colder climates to wear their winter jackets. The Kings play at Staples Center, 11th at Figueroa Sts. Call for the team's schedule. | 3900 W. Manchester Blvd., Inglewood | 888/KINGS–LA or 310/419–3160 | www.lakings.com.

Los Angeles Lakers. The National Basketball Association Lakers games are a true LA sporting experience, complete with celebrity fans, players' wives, and the Laker Girls. Call for a schedule of games. | 3900 W. Manchester Blvd., Inglewood | 310/419–3182 or 310/419–3100 | www.nba.com/lakers.

Los Angeles Memorial Coliseum and Sports Arena. Built in stages beginning in 1923, the Coliseum played host to the 1932 and 1984 Summer Olympic Games and the first Super Bowl. It is a National Historic Landmark, a State Historical Landmark, and is on the National Register of Historic Places. Call for the schedule of events. | 3939 S. Figueroa St. | 213/748–6136 | www.lacoliseum.com.

OTHER POINTS OF INTEREST

Chinatown. The area is most impressive during holidays and procession days. Come on Saturday morning to shop and have lunch. The Chinese Chamber of Commerce sponsors a 10-hour walking tour of the area; call for details. Between Broadway and Hill St., near Rte. 110. | 213/617–0396 | www.lachinesechamber.org | Free | Daily.

Little Tokyo. The center of Los Angeles' Japanese-American community, Little Tokyo hosts the Nisei and Cherry Blossom festivals and is well-known for its shops and restaurants. Between Central and 3rd St. | Free | Daily.

San Antonio Winery. You can tour the vineyard and wine-making facility and taste the latest vintage. | 737 Lamar St. | 323/223–1401 | fax 323/221–7261 | www.sanantoniowinery.com | Free | Mon., Tues. 8–6, Wed.–Fri. 8–7, Sat. 9–7, Sun. 10–6.

ON THE CALENDAR

FEB.: *Chinese New Year.* Celebrate the Chinese New Year with a parade, fireworks, music, and food. In Chinatown's Central Plaza, 947 Broadway. | 213/617–0396.
MAY: *Cinco de Mayo Celebration.* Festive music, dancing, food, and drink celebrates Mexican independence at this event hosted by El Pueblo de Los Angeles, the center of the original Los Angeles and today's Mexican-American community. | 213/625–5045.
JUNE–SEPT.: *Greek Theatre.* Greek tragedies and comedies are presented at the hillside amphitheater in Griffith Park. | 2700 Vermont Canyon Rd. | 323/665–1927.
JULY: *Lotus Festival.* A two-day celebration of the cultures of Asia and the Pacific Islands with arts, music, dance, drama, martial arts, food, Dragon Boat Races, and orchid and tropical flower displays. In Echo Park. | 213/485–1310.
AUG.: *Nisei Week.* This celebration honors American-born children of Japanese parents, in Little Tokyo. | 213/687–7193.
SEPT.–JUNE: *Los Angeles Music Center Opera.* A respected, fledgling opera company presents new and classic works at Dorothy Chandler Pavilion. | 135 N. Grand Ave. | 213/972–8001 | www.laopera.org.

Dining

INEXPENSIVE

Cassell's. American. This downtown LA hamburger joint is popular with locals who like fast food. Food photography adorns the walls. No smoking. | 3266 W. 6th St. | 213/480–8668 | Closed Sun. No supper | $6–$10 | No credit cards.

Cheesecake Factory. American. Always a good standby, this eatery offers everything from big salads to lobster tail, in a friendly, casual setting. | 11647 San Vicente Blvd., Brentwood | 310/826–7111 | $10–25 | AE, DC, MC, V.

★ **El Cholo.** Mexican. LA's oldest Mexican restaurant is famous for its margaritas, nachos, guacamole, and green-corn tamales. The 1927 building has wooden booths and Mexican furnishings, You might have to wait for a table. No smoking. | 1121 W. Western Ave. | 323/734–2773 | $10–$20 | AE, DC, MC, V.

Hard Rock Cafe. American. You know what to expect at this international chain: rock 'n' roll memorabilia and rock 'n' roll noise. Try the chicken or beef fajitas, burgers, or the Ringo special (appetizer platter with spring rolls, onion rings, and chicken). In the Beverley

Center, 15 mi west of downtown. Kids' menu. No smoking. | 8600 Beverly Blvd. | 310/276–7605 | $10–$15 | AE, DC, MC, V.

Mongols BBQ. Mongolian. An unassuming red-and-white awning marks this cafeteria-style eatery, which is popular among students. A mix of Asian knick-knacks and statues welcome you. Meats, seafood, vegetables, or noodles are grilled Mongolian-style with spicy oils on large iron woks. No smoking. | 1064 Gayley Ave. | 310/824–3377 | $7–$12 | No credit cards.

★ **Phillipe the Original.** American. This turn-of-the-20th-century restaurant hasn't changed much over the years. Come for the hearty sandwiches and salads served at long, lacquered tables. Leave room for the baked apples, homemade cinnamon rolls, muffins, or donuts. Beer and wine only. No smoking. | 1001 N. Alameda St. | 213/628–3781 | Breakfast also available | $6–$10 | No credit cards.

MODERATE

Anna's. Italian. This old-fashioned, family-style restaurant is popular for basic, hearty Italian fare served in comfy red booths. Try the cannelloni (homemade crêpe stuffed with ground beef, cheese, and spinach) or linguini Soriento with shellfish. Separate bar area. No smoking. | 10929 W. Pico Blvd. | 310/474–0102 | No lunch weekends | $9–$30 | AE, D, DC, MC, V.

Ciao Trattoria. Italian. In the historic Fine Arts building, Ciao Trattoria has tall, arched ceilings, white linens, and wrought iron fixtures. Try the ravioli aragosta or the filet mignon. Free shuttle service to the LA Music Center. No smoking. | 815 W. 7th St. | 213/624–2244 | Dinner only weekends | $12–$20 | AE, DC, MC, V.

La Golondrina. Mexican. Using fresh ingredients and centuries-old recipes, the chefs create Mexican and early California dishes such as soft corn tortillas with snow crab and shrimp, topped with tomatillo sauce and avocado, or fresh whole tilapia fish marinated in lime juice and herbs. The blue, yellow, and orange interior is filled with Mexican art and artifacts. There's a dance floor and small outdoor dining patio. Mexican guitarist upon request. Kids' menu. No smoking. | 17 W. Olvera St. | 213/628–4349 | Breakfast also available weekends | $15–$25 | AE, DC, MC, V.

Les Freres Taix. French. Authentic country French food has kept people coming back since 1927, when the family first bought the place. Settle into a booth under the high tin ceiling and enjoy homemade soup, roast chicken, or trout almondine. Extensive wine list. Kids' menu. No smoking. | 1911 Sunset Blvd. | 213/484–1265 | $12–$20 | AE, D, DC, MC, V.

Patinette at MOCA. Contemporary. Much better than your average museum café, Patinette serves a nice selection of healthy California-French soups, salads, sandwiches, and light entrées in a minimalist setting. No smoking. | 250 S. Grand Ave. | 213/626–1178 | Closed Mon. | $10–$25 | AE, D, DC, MC, V.

Sisley Italian Kitchen. Italian. Portions are hearty in this small chain Mediterranean café in the Westside Pavilion, 10 mi west of downtown. You'll find osso bucco and cioppino (mixed seafood in broth), homemade ravioli, and eggplant pasta platter. No smoking. | 10800 W. Pico Blvd. | 310/446–3030 | $10–$21 | AE, MC, V.

Tam-O-Shanter. Continental. This restaurant with a Scottish theme has been drawing crowds since 1922. Try the prime rib or the roast duckling. Kids' menu. Sunday brunch. No smoking. | 2980 Los Feliz Blvd. | 323/664–0228 | $15–$25 | AE, D, DC, MC, V.

EXPENSIVE

Bernard's. Continental. Fresh seafood is one of the standouts in the grand Biltmore Hotel dining room. The cuisine might be contemporary, but the atmosphere is a nod to an earlier era of romance and elegance, with gilded, polished pillars, bountiful palms, and fresh flowers. Entertainment. No smoking. | 515 S. Olive St. | 213/612–1580 | No lunch. Closed Sun. | $17–$40 | AE, D, DC, MC, V.

★ **Cafe Pinot.** Contemporary. Overlooking the Maguire Gardens of the Central Library, you dine in a glass house with the lights of the city all around. This is a longtime favorite of critics and patrons alike; it's convenient for theater-goers. Open-air dining. No smoking. | 700 W. 5th St. | 213/239–6500 | Reservations essential | $20–$30 | AE, D, DC, MC, V.

La Cachette. French. Haute cuisine and elegant presentation are the hallmarks of this establishment. The romantic, pale interior is lavish with flowers. Try the roast rack of lamb with garlic Dijon mustard or the tuna tartare. No smoking. | 10506 Little Santa Monica Blvd. | 310/470–4992 | No lunch weekends | $18–$32 | AE, DC, MC, V.

Locanda Veneta. Italian. This cozy northern Italian trattoria has an open kitchen that cooks up flattened grilled chicken, veal chops, lobster ravioli with saffron sauce, and an unusual apple tart with polenta crust and caramel sauce. Some of the recipes have been handed down through generations. Beer and wine. No smoking. | 8638 W. 3rd St. | 310/274–1893 | Reservations essential | Closed Sun. | $20–$35 | AE, D, DC, MC, V.

Madeo. Italian. The dark, old-fashioned interior of wood, brass, and silk wall tapestries feels like Italy; maybe that's why so many natives eat here. The wood-burning oven turns out broiled Italian sea bass with sliced potatoes and tomatoes, veal chops sautéed in butter and sage with spinach, and risotto with artichokes or asparagus. No smoking. | 8897 Beverly Blvd. | 310/859–4903 | No lunch weekends | $20–$30 | AE, D, DC, MC, V.

Pangaea. Contemporary. The award-winning Pangaea in Le Meridien hotel in Beverly Hills serves Pacific Rim cuisine in an elegant setting. The large split-level dining room is done in lavender, blue, and warm yellow. Try the swordfish and eggplant Napoleon or the braised sea bass with asparagus. Sunday brunch. No smoking. | 465 S. La Cienega | 310/247–0400 | Breakfast also available | $15–$31 | AE, D, DC, MC, V.

Windows. Contemporary. Dining on the 32nd floor of the Transamerica Center means an unobstructed 360° view, perhaps the best in LA, from the Hollywood sign to San Pedro and, on a clear day, as far as Catalina Island. The full name of the place is Windows, Steaks, and Martinis, so you know what to order. No smoking. | 1150 S. Olive St. | 213/746–1554 | Closed Sun. No dinner Mon. | $18–$33 | AE, DC, MC, V.

VERY EXPENSIVE

★ **Bel-Air Hotel Dining Room.** Continental. Known to locals as one of the most beautiful and romantic restaurants in town, this intimate eatery in the Bel Air Hotel overlooks a garden with a flower-covered trellis and a stream with swans. Favorite dishes are cobb salad, tortilla soup, and chocolate soufflé. Pianist nightly. Kids' menu. Sunday brunch. No smoking. | 701 Stone Canyon Rd., Bel Air | 310/472–1211 | Reservations essential | Jacket required | Breakfast also available | $30–$60 | AE, DC, MC, V.

★ **Campanile.** Contemporary. One of LA's favorites for California cuisine. Dine on Manila clams, pork loin with sweet potatoes and turnip greens, prime rib, or rosemary-charred baby lamb, and some of the best desserts anywhere—try the apple puff pastry with spiced nuts and sabayon. The upstairs dining rooms have wingback leather chairs. The downstairs dining rooms have the original 1920s Mexican tile floors and gray stone walls. Sunday brunch. No smoking. | 624 S. La Brea Ave. | 323/938–1447 | Breakfast also available weekends | $25–$40 | AE, D, DC, MC, V.

Charisma Cafe. Contemporary. Near the Westin Hotel, Charisma has polished granite walls and large windows. Creative dishes are served on colorful unmatched china. Try crispy-skin whitefish with chanterelles and haricot vert, warm lamb salad with pinenut mint aioli, or grilled fillet of beef with sweet shallot and shiitake watercress ragout. Kids' menu. Salad bar. No smoking. | 5400 W. Century Blvd. | 310/216–5858 | Breakfast also available | $22–$43 | AE, D, DC, MC, V.

Checkers. Continental. Dine on grilled fish and meat in an elegant, quiet room with potted palms and low lighting. Try the mashi mashi (New Zealand scampi with pineapple).

This is the place to impress a date. Small outdoor patio. Sunday brunch. No smoking. | 535 S. Grand St. | 213/624–0000 | Reservations essential | Breakfast also available | $24–$35 | AE, D, DC, MC, V.

Delmonico's. Seafood. This San Francisco–style fish house is part of a local chain. Slip into a wooden booth and sample hearty portions of steamed clams and oysters, cracked crab, fish stews, and grilled seafood. | 9320 W. Pico Blvd., | 310/550–7737 | $25–$35 | AE, MC, V.

Four Oaks. Contemporary. Built in 1889 and set in a grove of trees, this bistro feels like an artist's canyon house. Dine by the fireplace or the fountain on a flowery patio. The seasonal menu might include risotto, sesame-seared filet of salmon, or roast quail with apricot and wild mushrooms. Sunday brunch. No smoking. | 2181 N. Beverly Glen | 310/470–2265 | Reservations essential | No lunch Sun., Mon. | $29–$34 | AE, MC, V.

Gardens. Contemporary. If you want to buck the casual trend and go for something a little more formal, try the luxurious Gardens in the Four Seasons Hotel. The dining room has a Florentine theme, with hand-painted frescoes on the walls. Try the lobster and Oregon morel mushroom potstickers and mustard-crusted rack of lamb. Garden patio. Kids' menu. Sunday brunch. No smoking. | 300 S. Doheny | 310/273–2222 | Breakfast also available | $31–$45 | AE, DC, MC, V.

Seoul Jung. Korean. The ethnic fare is pricey but excellent at this restaurant in the Omni Hotel. Try kal vi (boneless beef ribs) or bool go gi (slices of marinated rib eye). Every table has a built-in grill so you can cook your food bite by bite. No smoking. | 930 Wilshire Blvd. | 213/688–7880 | $25–$35 | AE, D, DC, MC, V.

Lodging

INEXPENSIVE

Best Western Eagle Rock Inn. Simple and low on frills, this three-story hotel is in the commercial and cultural district, 10 mi away from the Burbank Airport, with modern rooms. Restaurant, complimentary Continental breakfast. Microwaves, cable TV, in-room VCRs (and movies). Pool. Hot tub. Business services. | 2911 Colorado Blvd., Los Angeles | 323–256–7711 | fax 323/255–6750 | www.bestwestern.com | 50 rooms | $90–$120 | AE, D, DC, MC, V.

Best Western Mid-Wilshire Plaza. This three-story hotel is a few miles from downtown and Dodger Stadium. Rooms are standard. Indoor pool. Sauna. Gym. No pets allowed. | 603 S. New Hampshire Ave. | 213/385–4444 | fax 213/380–5413 | 89 rooms | $85 | AE, DC, MC, V.

Holiday Inn Downtown. This six-story hotel is downtown, in the financial district, near the Convention Center and Dodger Stadium. The building is set on sloping, landscaped grounds. Rooms have basic amenities. Restaurant, bar, room service. In-room data ports. Cable TV. Pool. Laundry facilities. Business services, parking (fee). | 750 Garland Ave. | 213/628–5242 | fax 213/628–1201 | 204 rooms | $89–$199 | AE, D, DC, MC, V.

Hotel Del Capri. A tropical aquarium embellishes the lobby of this hotel built in 1954 and now almost hidden by high-rises; vine-covered walls surround the hotel garden. Rooms have vases of fresh flowers on tables and nightstands, and an airy, pastel color theme. The hotel is 5 blocks from the UCLA campus. Complimentary Continental breakfast. Some kitchenettes, refrigerators, some in-room hot tubs, cable TV. Pool. Exercise equipment. Laundry facilities. Business services, free parking. Pets allowed. | 10587 Wilshire Blvd. | 310/474–3511 or 800/44–HOTEL | fax 310/470–9999 | www.hoteldelcapri.com | 80 rooms, 46 suites | $105, $130 suites | AE, DC, MC, V.

Hotel Figueroa. Constructed in the early 1920s, this hotel is charming and friendly. It's near the Staples Center arena and the University of Southern California. Restaurant, bar. In-room data ports. Cable TV. Pool. Laundry service. Free parking. | 939 Figueroa Blvd. | 213/627–8971 | fax 213/689–0305 | 285 rooms | $74–$145 | AE, MC, V.

MODERATE

Courtyard Marriott. This modern hotel is 6 mi east of downtown, close to LA International Airport, Marina del Rey, and the Hollywood Race Course. Its Art Deco style makes for pleasantly spare common areas. Guest rooms have well-designed, comfortable furniture. There is a garden courtyard. Restaurant, bar. In-room data ports. Cable TV. Exercise equipment. Video games. Laundry facilities. Business services, parking (fee). | 10320 W. Olympic Blvd. | 310/556–2777 | fax 310/203–0563 | www.courtyard.com | 134 rooms | $159–$179 | AE, D, DC, MC, V.

Doubletree. This high-rise hotel is between Beverly Hills and Westwood Village. Rooms are furnished with sleek, wood-and-metal tables, chairs, and dressers. There's a free shuttle to many area attractions. Restaurant, bar. In-room data ports, refrigerators, cable TV. Pool. Hot tub. Exercise equipment. Video games. Business services. | 10740 Wilshire Blvd., | 310/475–8711 | fax 310/475–5220 | www.doubletreehotels.com | 295 rooms | $195–$215 | AE, D, DC, MC, V.

Holiday Inn Brentwood-Bel Air. In prestigious Brentwood, this 17-story tower is near the Getty Center Museum and ½ mi from UCLA, at I–405 and Sunset Blvd. Rooms have bright, geometric-print bedspreads and private balconies, most with a view of the city. Restaurant, bar. In-room data ports. Cable TV. Pool. Hot tub. Exercise equipment. Video games. Laundry facilities. Business services, parking (fee). Some pets allowed. | 170 N. Church La. | 310/476–6411 | fax 310/472–1157 | hibelair@deltanet.com | 211 rooms | $139–$250 | AE, D, DC, MC, V.

Holiday Inn City Center. This nine-story downtown hotel is accessible from all major freeways, next to the Staples Center. Business travelers and conventioneers are frequent guests. Restaurant, bar. Cable TV. Pool. Exercise equipment. Laundry facilities. Business services, parking (fee). Some pets allowed. | 1020 S. Figueroa St. | 213/748–1291 | fax 213/748–6028 | 195 rooms | $119–$179 | AE, D, DC, MC, V.

Holiday Inn Express. A reasonably priced hotel with an inviting yellow and blue exterior, 2 mi from UCLA, ½ mi from Beverly Hills, adjacent to 20th Century-Fox Studios. Loft rooms are available. Complimentary Continental breakfast. Cable TV, in-room VCRs (and movies). | 10330 W. Olympic Blvd. | 310/553–1000 | fax 310/277–1633 | 47 rooms, 14 suites | $104–$169 | AE, D, DC, MC, V.

Hyatt Regency. A 24-story downtown hotel in the Broadway Plaza shopping area is near the Convention Center, the Music Center, and Dodgers Stadium. Every room has large windows with views of the city. Restaurant, bar, room service. In-room data ports, some minibars. Cable TV. Exercise equipment. Video games. Shops. Laundry service. Business services, parking (fee). | 711 S. Hope St. | 213/683–1234 | fax 213/629–3230 | www.hyatt.com | 485 rooms | $190–$225 | AE, D, DC, MC, V.

Oxford Palace. This full-service hotel has an elegant two-story lobby with a waterfall, pillars, and marble accents. Rooms provide welcome extras such as large easy chairs with ottomans. It's 6 mi west of downtown, 10 minutes from Hollywood. Restaurants, bar. Cable TV, in-room VCRs (and movies). Shops. Business services. | 745 S. Oxford Ave. | 213/389–8000 or 800/532–7887 | fax 213/389–8500 | www.oxfordhotel.com | 95 rooms | $175 | AE, DC, MC, V.

Radisson Wilshire Plaza. The lobby of this gleaming 12-story building, 3 mi west of downtown, has grand marble pillars. Guest rooms are simply furnished and most have a floor-to-ceiling window with a view of the Hollywood Hills. Restaurants, bar. In-room data ports, some refrigerators. Cable TV. Pool. Beauty salon. Exercise equipment. Business services, parking (fee). | 3515 Wilshire Blvd. | 213/381–7411 | fax 213/386–7379 | www.radisson.com | 385 rooms | $149–$199 | AE, D, DC, MC, V.

EXPENSIVE

Beverly Plaza. This mid-size five-story hotel is across from the Beverly Shopping Center, 10 mi west of downtown. The nicely furnished rooms have graceful armchairs and lamps.

Most of the clientele are business people. Restaurant, bar, room service. Cable TV. Pool. Hot tub. Exercise equipment. Parking (fee). | 8384 W. 3rd St. | 323/658–6600 or 800/624–6835 outside CA | fax 213/653–3464 | www.beverlyplazahotel.com | 98 rooms | $189–$259 | AE, DC, MC, V.

★ **Chateau Marmont.** This 1929 castle is a Hollywood landmark, the meeting place of legends like Jean Harlow and Clark Gable. Rooms, suites, and bungalows in beautifully maintained gardens have views of the city and the Hollywood Hills. It's 3 mi west of downtown. Restaurant, room service. In-room data ports, some kitchenettes. Cable TV, in-room VCRs. Pool. Gym. Laundry service. Business services, parking (fee). Some pets allowed. | 8221 Sunset Blvd. | 323/656–1010 | fax 323/655–5311 | chateaula@aol.com | 63 rooms | $220–$345 | AE, DC, MC, V.

★ **New Otani Hotel and Garden.** This large 21-story hotel in Little Tokyo has a striking lobby with a vaulted ceiling and skylight and a Japanese garden on the roof. Rooms are done in pale tones with simple, clean-lined furnishings; some have traditional shoji screens and tatami mats. Restaurants, bar. Cable TV. Beauty salon, spa. Shops. Business services, parking (fee). | 120 S. Los Angeles St. | 213/629–1200 or 800/273–2294 (in CA), 800/421–8795 | fax 213/622–0980 | www.newotani.com/ | 434 rooms | $180–$250 | AE, D, DC, MC, V.

Park Hyatt Los Angeles. This peach-colored pyramid-shape high-rise in the city's business and financial district has elegant rooms with scenic views. Some overlook 20th Century-Fox's back lot, 12 mi west of downtown. Restaurant, bar, room service. In-room data ports. Cable TV. Indoor pool, outdoor pool. Hot tub, massage. Exercise equipment. Business services, parking (fee). | 2151 Ave. of the Stars | 310/277–1234 | fax 310/785–9240 | www.hyatt.com | 367 rooms, 189 suites | $244–$424, $304–$850 suites | AE, D, DC, MC, V.

Summit Belair. Conveniently located just west of I–405 in Brentwood, this upscale hotel is on eight acres of landscaped hillside, with a view of the city. It's 1 mi from UCLA, 15 mi west of downtown. Restaurant, bar. In-room data ports. Cable TV. Pool. Tennis. Exercise equipment. Business services, airport shuttle, parking fee. | 11461 Sunset Blvd. | 310/476–6571 or 800/468–3541 for reservations | fax 310/471–6310 | 162 rooms | $225–$265 | AE, D, DC, MC, V.

W Los Angeles. This all-suite hotel is in a quiet, tree-lined neighborhood. Rooms have attached parlor areas for working, relaxing, or socializing. The Avenue of the Stars and the 20th Century Fox studios are 2 mi to the west. 3 restaurants, bar with entertainment. In-room data ports, refrigerators, room service, cable TV. 2 pools. Massage. Exercise equipment. Business services. Pets allowed. | 930 Hilgard Ave. | 310/208–8765 or 800/421–2317 | fax 310/824–0355 | 257 suites | $225–$650 suites | AE, D, DC, MC, V.

Westin Bonaventure. The largest hotel in Los Angeles, its five futuristic glass towers house 20 restaurants and a grand lobby with pools and glass elevators. It boasts five floors of boutiques and a revolving 35th-floor cocktail lounge. The pie-shape rooms have views of the city. *In The Line of Fire* and *True Lies* were filmed here. Restaurants, bars, room service. In-room data ports. Cable TV. Pool. Beauty salon. Business services. | 404 S. Figueroa St. | 213/624–1000 | fax 213/612–4797 | www.westin.com | 1,354 rooms | $150–$245 | AE, D, DC, MC, V.

Westin Century Plaza Hotel and Tower. On seven landscaped acres with tropical plants and reflecting pools, this 19-story high-rise is 10 mi west of downtown in Santa Monica. Rooms have ocean or city views. 2 restaurants, bar, room service. In-room data ports. Cable TV. Pool. Beauty salon, hot tub, massage. Exercise equipment. Laundry facilities. Business services, parking (fee). | 2025 Ave. of the Stars | 310/277–2000 or 800/228–3000 | fax 310/551–3355 | www.centuryplaza.com | 724 rooms | $199–$350 | AE, D, DC, MC, V.

★ **Wyndham Checkers Hotel.** This residential-style luxury hotel is one of this downtown neighborhood's few remaining historical buildings, built in 1923. It has a beautiful carved stone facade. Guest rooms have oversize beds, upholstered easy chairs, original artwork, and writing tables. The lobby is furnished with antiques and Oriental and contemporary art works. It's 4 blocks south of the Museum of Contemporary Art. Restaurant, bar, room service. In-room data ports. Cable TV. Pool. Hot tub, massage. Exercise equipment. Library. Business services, airport shuttle, parking (fee). | 535 S. Grand Ave. | 213/624–0000 | fax 213/626–9906 | 188 rooms | $279 | AE, D, DC, MC, V.

VERY EXPENSIVE

Hotel Bel-Air. This luxurious Mission-style hotel, set in 1½ acres of beautifully landscaped gardens with waterfalls, footbridges, and swans, is a favorite getaway for celebrities. It is 2 mi from the Getty Museum. Restaurant, bar, room service. In-room data ports, some kitchenettes. Cable TV, in-room VCRs (and movies). Pool. Massage. Exercise equipment. Business services, parking (fee). | 701 Stone Canyon Rd. | 310/472–1211 or 800/648–4097 (for reservations) | fax 310/476–5890 | www.hotelbelair.com | 92 rooms | $375–$485, suites $650–$2,500 | AE, DC, MC, V.

Hotel Sofitel. Reminiscent of a country chateau, this 10-story marble Mediterranean-style hotel is across from the Beverly Center and 10 mi west of downtown. Pierre Deux fabrics are used throughout. Restaurant, bar, room service. In-room data ports. Cable TV. Pool. Exercise equipment. Business services, parking (fee). | 8555 Beverly Blvd. | 310/278–5444 or 800/521–7772 | fax 310/657–2816 | sofitella@aol.com | 311 rooms | $300–$400 | AE, DC, MC, V.

★ **Mondrian.** Designer Phillippe Starck brings his trademark white, light elegance to this hotel. You can rub elbows with celebrities and movie execs, or relax in a teak chaise longue by the pool and relish the LA skyline. Most rooms have floor-to-ceiling glass walls with citywide views, 15 mi west of downtown. Restaurant, bar, room service. In-room data ports. Cable TV. Pool. Exercise equipment. Business services, parking (fee). | 8440 Sunset Blvd. | 323/650–8999 or 800/525–8029 (for reservations) | fax 323/650–5215 | www.mondrianhotel.com | 238 suites | $285–$345 | AE, D, DC, MC, V.

Regal Biltmore. Built in 1923 and known as downtown's neoclassical treasure trove, this 12-story Spanish/Italian Renaissance-style hotel is famed for its ballroom and lobby, fine dining, and service. It's a must-see for travelers who love beautiful old hotels. Bernard's restaurant is on site. 3 restaurants, 2 bars, room service. In-room data ports. Cable TV. Pool. Beauty salon, hot tub, massage. Gym. Business services, parking (fee). | 506 S. Grand Ave. | 213/624–1011 or 800/245–8673 | fax 213/612–1545 | www.thebiltmore.com | 683 rooms | $235–$315 | AE, D, DC, MC, V.

Sunset Marquis Hotel and Villas. Set on 3½ acres of tropical gardens, this Mediterranean-style oasis is less than 7 mi from the city center. Rooms are lavish, and a recording studio is on site. It's 6 mi from Universal Studios and 1 mi from the Beverly Center. Kids under 12 stay free. Restaurant, bar, room service. In-room data ports, some kitchenettes. Cable TV. Pools. Hot tub, massage. Exercise equipment. Business services. | 1200 N. Alta Loma Rd. | 310/657–1333 or 800/858–9758 for reservations | fax 310/652–5300 | 114 suites, 12 villas | $305–$1,200 | AE, D, DC, MC, V.

LOS ANGELES INTERNATIONAL AIRPORT AREA

Crowne Plaza LAX. Just over ½ mi east of the airport, this large 16-story chain hotel 13 mi west of downtown offers city or runway views from its rooms. Restaurant, bar. Cable TV. Pool. Hot tub. Exercise equipment. Video games. Laundry facilities. Business services, airport shuttle, parking fee. | 5985 W. Century Blvd. | 310/642–7500 | fax 310/417–3608 | www.crowneplaza.com | 615 rooms | $129–$169 | AE, D, DC, MC, V.

Furama Hotel. One mi north of LAX, 2.5 mi north of Marina del Rey, and 4 mi north of Venice Beach, the four buildings that comprise this hotel at the intersection of Manchester Blvd. are built around a garden patio. All rooms have views of the city, but those in three of the buildings have unique attributes: the Fountain Wing rooms look onto a fountain and courtyard built in the center of the building; Main Building rooms surround and have views of the pool and gardens, and elevated rooms in the 12-story Tower Wing provide

6 "I'm thirsty"'s, 9 "Are we there yet"'s, 3 "I don't feel good"'s,
1 car class upgrade.
At least something's going your way.

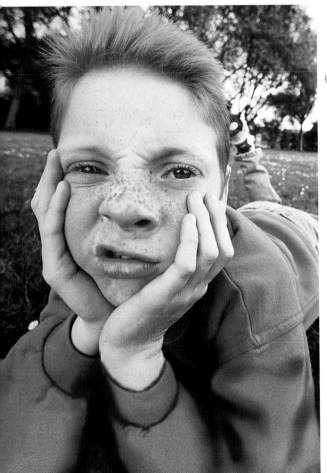

Hertz rents Fords and other fine cars. ® REG. U.S. PAT. OFF. © HERTZ SYSTEM INC.. 2000/005-00

Make your next road trip more comfortable with a free one-class upgrade from Hertz.

Let's face it, a long road trip isn't always sunshine and roses. But with Hertz, you get a free one car class upgrade to make things a little more bearable. You'll also choose from a variety of vehicles with child seats, Optional Protection Plans, 24-Hour Emergency Roadside Assistance, and the convenience of NeverLost,® the in-car navigation system that provides visual and audio prompts to give you turn-by-turn guidance to your destination. In a word: it's everything you need for your next road trip. Call your travel agent or Hertz at **1-800-654-2210** and mention PC# **906404** or check us out at **hertz.com** or AOL Keyword: **hertz**. Peace of mind. Another reason nobody does it exactly like Hertz.

Hertz
exactly.®

the best vantage point from which to view the city and airport skyline. Restaurant, bar. Cable TV. Pool. Beauty salon. Exercise equipment. Video games. Airport shuttle, parking (fee). | 8601 Lincoln Blvd. | 310/670–8111 or 800/225–8126 for reservations | fax 310/337–1883 | www.furama-hotels.com | 773 rooms, 55 suites | $99–$129 | AE, D, DC, MC, V.

Hilton and Towers Los Angeles Airport. This 5-story airport Hilton, 2 blocks north of the airport and 15 mi south of downtown, has a handsome lobby with a central staircase and chandelier and three gardens. Some rooms have bathrobes and lighted work desks. Restaurants, bar. In-room data ports. Cable TV. Pool. Hot tubs. Gym. Laundry facilities. Business services, airport shuttle, parking (fee). Some pets allowed. | 5711 W. Century Blvd. | 310/410–4000 | fax 310/410–6250 | 1,234 rooms | $188 | AE, D, DC, MC, V.

Los Angeles Airport Marriott. This large business hotel ½ mi east of the airport is 4 mi northeast of El Segundo Golf Course and 16 mi southwest of downtown. Some rooms are designed for business travelers. 2 restaurants, bar, room service. In-room data ports, some refrigerators. Cable TV. Pool. Beauty salon, hot tub. Exercise equipment. Shops, video games. Laundry facilities. Business services, airport shuttle, parking fee. Some pets allowed. | 5855 W. Century Blvd. | 310/641–5700 | fax 310/337–5358 | www.marriotthotels.com | 1,010 rooms | $155 | AE, D, DC, MC, V.

Quality Hotel Los Angeles Airport. Rooms of this 10-story hotel 1.5 mi east of the airport and 4 mi west of Manhattan Beach were renovated in 2000 and have whitewashed furniture and turquoise carpeting. Restaurant, bar. Cable TV. Pool. Exercise equipment. Video Games. Business services, airport shuttle, parking (fee). Some pets allowed. | 5249 W. Century Blvd. | 310/645–2200 | fax 310/641–8214 | 278 room | $110–$140 | AE, D, DC, MC, V.

Renaissance. This 11-story airport hotel has a grand lobby, with pillars, classical statues, and $14 million worth of artwork. Rooms are standard, furnished with easy chairs and work desks. It's 4 blocks east of the airport entrance and 18 mi southwest of downtown. Restaurants, bar, room service. In-room data ports. Cable TV. Pool. Hot tub, massage. Exercise equipment. Business services, airport shuttle, parking (fee). | 9620 Airport Blvd. | 310/337–2800 | fax 310/216–6681 | www.renaissancehotels.com | 561 rooms, 56 suites | $99–$198 | AE, D, DC, MC, V.

Sheraton Gateway. This 15-story structure is outfitted for business and time-challenged travelers. In addition to business services, there are a variety of stores including a cigar lounge, gift and sports shops, and boutiques; for those seeking recreation Santa Monica beach is just 5 mi away and the Westchester Golf Course is a mere 10 minute drive. Triple-paned windows block out noise from the airport runway, 1 block away. It's 15 mi southwest of downtown. 3 restaurants, bar, room service. In-room data ports. Cable TV. Pool. Hot tub. Exercise equipment. Video games. Business services, airport shuttle, parking (fee). | 6101 W. Century Blvd. | 310/642–1111 | fax 310/410–1267 | www.sheraton.com | 727 rooms | $119–$144 | AE, D, DC, MC, V.

Traveloge LAX. This two-story hotel is just 1 mi east of the airport, and 20 mi southwest of central downtown. Some rooms have private terraces, and a tropical garden surrounds the pool. Restaurant, bar, room service. Cable TV. Pool. Exercise equipment. Video games. Laundry facilities. Airport shuttle, free parking. Some pets allowed. | 5547 W. Century Blvd. | 310/649–4000 | fax 310/649–0311 | www.travelodgelax.com | 147 rooms | $74–$110 | AE, D, DC, MC, V.

★ **Westin L.A. Airport.** This 12-story hotel with floor-to-ceiling windows in the lobby is 4 blocks east of the airport, 4 mi west of Manhattan Beach and 15 mi southwest of central downtown. Some rooms have balconies and all have pool, garden or city views. Restaurant, bar, room service. In-room data ports, some minibars. Cable TV. Pool. Hot tub. Laundry facilities. Business services, airport shuttle, parking (fee). Some pets allowed. | 5400 W. Century Blvd. | 310/216–5858 | fax 310/645–8053 | www.westin.com | 720 rooms, 43 suites | $179 rooms, $229 suites | AE, D, DC, MC, V.

LOS GATOS

(Nearby towns also listed: Campbell, Cupertino, Menlo Park, San Jose, Saratoga, Sunnyvale)

Dozens of small California towns have names straight out of the journals of Spanish explorers—names that say worlds about the wild, open country of two centuries ago. Los Gatos is one of them. The name means "the cats," and it is assumed that it refers to the native mountain lions or bobcats spotted in the area. Other towns named for fauna include Tiburon, or Shark, and Las Pulgas, or The Fleas, in a valley where the conquistadors woke up scratching.

Los Gatos is a modest but fairly wealthy suburb in Silicon Valley between San Jose and Santa Cruz. It combines close proximity to urban amenities and expansive nature; the town boasts 19 parks, plus hiking trails along Los Gatos creek, and an open preserve where the Santa Cruz Mountains loom invitingly on the horizon. Los Gatos has 30,000 permanent residents.

Information: **Los Gatos Chamber of Commerce** | 333 N. Santa Cruz Ave., 95030 | 408/354–9300 | www.losgatosweb.com.

Attractions

Billy Jones Wildcat Railroad. In 1970 the city moved railroad buff Billy Jones's steam-engine railroad—originally built in his orchard—to Oak Meadow Park. A carousel was added in 1980. You can take a ride when weather permits. | 110 Blossom Hill Rd. | 408/395–RIDE | www.los-gatos.ca.us/los_gatos/businesses/toll_house/index.html | $1 | Labor Day–Nov. 1, 10:30–4:30 weekends; Nov. 1–March 15, 11–3 weekends; March 15–June 10:30–4:30 weekends; June–Labor Day 10:30–4:30 daily.

Los Gatos Forbes Mill History Museum. Changing exhibitions in this old mill include collections of memorabilia donated by local residents. | 75 Church St. | 408/395–7375 | lgmuseum@aol.com | www.accesscom.com/~hcscc/directinfo/forbes.htm | Donations accepted | Wed.–Sun. 12–4.

Los Gatos Museum. Art, science, and nature displays are the focus of this local museum. | 4 Tait Ave. | 408/354–2646 | Donations accepted | Wed.–Sun. 12–4.

Old Town. The shopping district has restored Spanish and Victorian buildings, topiary trees and gardens, and a public amphitheater. | 50 University Ave. | Free | Daily.

ON THE CALENDAR

MAY: *Children's Fantasy Faire.* Food, crafts, and game booths are part of this family-oriented event that takes place on the grounds of the Los Gatos High School. | 408/354–9300.

AUG.: *Fiesta de Artes.* Take part in two days of art and wine at this festival sponsored by the Kiwanis Club at 123 E. Main St. Wine tasting, food booths, crafts, art, entertainment. | 408/354–9300.

Dining

C.B. Hannegan's Restaurant. American. You can match Hannegan's beers, single-malt scotches, and local wines to a full menu that ranges from traditional pub food such as nachos, potato skins, fish and chips, and spicy chicken wings to fish tacos, soups, and a barbecue plate that mingles ribs, chicken, and sausages. Nightly dinner specials include corned beef and cabbage, roast turkey, and angel hair pasta with smoked salmon. You can also order hot and cold sandwiches and pizza. | 208 Bachman Ave., | 408/395–1233 | leprechaun@cbhannegans.com | $6.95–$22 | MC, V.

La Hacienda. Italian. Next to La Hacienda Inn, this restaurant has a country kind of mood, with a flickering fireplace, and a garden patio. The patio has tiled floors, wooden tables and chairs, and a screen roof. There are two dining rooms with champagne colored tablecloths, mint colored linen napkins, fireplaces, and chandeliers. The menu has Italian specialties and pasta. Entertainment Thur.–Sat. Kids' menu. | 18840 Saratoga-Los Gatos Rd. | 408/354–6669 | $20–$25 | AE, D, DC, MC, V.

Lindsey's at the Summit. Contemporary. You can always have fresh salmon at Lindsay's along with other seafood, New York steak, lamb shank, pork loin, prime rib on Sundays, and pasta specials. Roasted artichokes, roasted beets, grilled portobello mushrooms, squash puree, and roasted red potatoes are among Lindsey's vegetable choices. Desserts include homemade apple tarts, pineapple upside down cake, lemon pudding, and chocolate torte. Local California wines are poured. Outdoor dining. | 23123 Santa Cruz Hwy. | 408/353–5679 | $12–$26 | MC, V.

2wenty 9ine East Main Cafe. Italian. In the old brick building that houses the 29, you'll find a gallery devoted to local artists and an espresso bar along with dishes made from scratch every day. The menu includes pizzas such as the Thai version with spicy peanut sauce, Thai chicken, red onion, red bell peppers, and cilantro pesto; salads, of which the local favorite is a mandarin sesame chicken salad with almonds and sweet-and-sour dressing; calzones, including the local favorite Green Meanie, with spinach, pine-nut pesto, goat cheese red bell peppers and red pepper pesto; and sandwiches (meats are from local purveyors; vegetarian choices include roasted marinated eggplant, portobello mushroom, and avocado) on locally baked breads. Desserts include chocolate cake and carrot cake from the popular local bakery Icing on the Cake. Wine list. | 29 E. Main St. | 408/395–4889 | DC, MC, V.

Lodging

La Hacienda Inn. High ceilings, stone fireplaces, and big rooms make for a comfortable overnight stay. In a residential area, 12 mi south of San Jose, the Inn nestles among lots of trees and gardens. Built in 1968 but extensively redone in 1998, the wood building has a tiled roof. Complimentary Continental breakfast. In-room data ports, some kitchenettes, refrigerators, cable TV, in-room VCRs (and movies). Pool. Hot tub. Laundry facilities. Business services. | 18840 Saratoga-Los Gatos Rd. | 408/354–9230 | fax 408/354–7590 | www.lahaciendainn.com | 17 rooms, 3 suites | $120 rooms, $175 suites | AE, D, DC, MC, V.

Lodge at Villa Felice. Perched on a hill overlooking Lake Vasona, this concrete building with a stone blend built in 1985 has a Spanish influenced architecture. Your room will have a private balcony. The Standford Shopping Center is less than 3 mi away. Complimentary Continental breakfast, room service. Refrigerators, some in-room hot tubs, cable TV. Pool. Spa. Business services. | 15350 S. Winchester Blvd. | 408/395–6710 or 800/662–9229 | fax 408/354–1826 | www.gtesupersite.com/villafelice | 24 rooms, 9 suites | $140–$160 rooms, $170–$250 suites | AE, DC, MC, V.

Los Gatos Lodge. The lodge is in a serene example of California landscaping, with plenty of trees on eight acres. Floral patterns and dark, soothing colors predominate in the rooms. Studios with living room area are available. There's even a garden wedding chapel. In a residential area, 10 mi west of San Jose, the lodge has eight wooden buildings completed in 1958 that had extensive improvements made in 1999. Restaurant, bar (with entertainment), complimentary Continental breakfast. Some kitchenettes, cable TV. Pool. Hot tub. Putting green. Laundry facilities. Business services. Some pets allowed. No smoking. | 50 Saratoga Rd. | 408/354–3300 or 800/231–8676 | fax 408/354–5451 | www.losgatoslodge.com | 128 rooms | $135–$175 | AE, D, DC, MC, V.

Los Gatos Motor Inn. Family owned and in a quiet location, there's nothing fancy about this motel. In a commercial area, 8 mi south of San Jose, this concrete and wood building with a stucco finish was built in 1961. Complimentary Continental breakfast. Some refrigerators. Pool. Business services. | 55 Saratoga Rd. | 408/356–9191 or 800/642–7889 | fax 408/356–7502 | 60 rooms | $89–$130 | AE, DC, MC, V.

Toll House Hotel. Big rooms with lots of polished wood trim and deep colors suggest an English manor, though the wood and concrete building resembles a European boutique. Most of the rooms have private balconies. This hotel is at the old Santa Cruz Gap Turnpike Toll House in Los Gatos and 10 mi west of San Jose. Restaurant, bar, complimentary Continental breakfast, room service. In-room data ports, some refrigerators, cable TV. Business services. Video games. Airport shuttle. | 140 S. Santa Cruz Ave. | 408/395–7070 or 800/238–6111 (outside CA), 800/821–5518 (CA) | fax 408/395–3730 | www.los-gatos.ca.us/los_gatos/businesses/toll_house/index.html | 118 rooms | $182 | AE, D, DC, MC, V.

LOS OLIVOS

MAP 4, F13

(Nearby towns also listed: Lompoc, Santa Barbara, Santa Maria, Solvang)

The Victorian town of Los Olivos is tucked into the heart of Santa Barbara County's wine country. Numerous buildings in the modest downtown have been standing for over a century and are listed as Santa Barbara County landmarks. With a population of about 800 residents and 85 businesses, Los Olivos is a quiet but vibrant town known for its wineries, art galleries, and antiques stores.

Information: Los Olivos Business Organization | 2980 Grand Ave., 93441 | 805/688–1222 | www.losolivosca.com.

Attractions
Beckmen Vineyards. This family-owned operation specializes in Rhone-style wines. There are three gazebos overlooking the duck pond that can be reserved for picnics. | 2670 Ontiveros Rd. | 805/688–8664 | fax 805/688–9983 | www.beckmenvineyards.com | Free | Daily 11–5.

Firestone Vineyard. The Firestone family's winemaking tradition dates back to 1972, when father-and-son team Leonard and Brooks Firestone planted the first estate vineyard in Santa Barbara County. The vineyards are in the heart of Santa Ynez Valley. The Firestone Vineyard has a reputation for producing some of the region's finest Chardonnays, Rieslings and Bordeaux-style wines. You can take tours that explore the winemaking process from vine to bottle. Picnic facilities overlook Zaca Canyon and the towering Los Padres Mountains. | 5000 Zaca Station Rd. | 805/688–3940 | www.firestonevineyard.com/ | Free | Tasting room open daily 10–5 with tours at quarter past the hour until 3:15.

Zaca Mesa Winery. The Zaca Mesa vineyards are among the highest in Santa Barbara County and you can take a tour or sample at a tasting. Spanish settlers named the area "La Zaca Mesa," borrowing the word "Zaca" from the Chumash Indians—meaning "peaceful"—and adding their own "Mesa"—meaning "table." | 6905 Foxen Canyon Rd., | 805/688–3310 | www.zacamesa.com | Free | Daily 10–4; tours at 11:30 and 2:30.

ON THE CALENDAR
OCT.: *A Day in the Country.* This small-town celebration of the harvest is a downtown street fair held on the third Saturday of the month. It begins with a pancake breakfast at 8. There is a parade, crafts, an apple pie contest, food, wine tasting, stagecoach rides, and music from local artists. | 805/688–1222 | www.losolivosca.com.

Dining
Mattei's Tavern. American. A meat and potatoes kind of place, Mattei's Tavern is a restored 19th-century stagecoach stop that evokes the Old West. Enjoy steak and prime rib. Kids' menu. | 805/688–4820 | No lunch weekdays | $13–$23 | MC, V.

Vintage Room. Eclectic. Well-selected local wines complement such entrées as oven-roasted salmon, Peking Muscovy duck breast, and grilled lamb T-bone in a casually elegant dining room. The Vintage Room looks like a French country place with antique armoires in the dining area, but is in Fess Parker's Inn, so lots of tourists eat here as well as locals. Sun. brunch. Kids' menu. | 2860 Grand Ave. | 805/688–7788 | $12–$38 | AE, D, DC, MC, V.

Lodging

Ballard Inn. This romantic getaway amidst vineyards and orchards is 3 mi from Los Olivos in Ballard. There are no televisions or phones, but wine and hors d'oeuvres are served nightly in The Vintner's Room. Restaurant, bar, complimentary breakfast. No room phones, no TV. No pets. No kids under 12. No smoking. | 2436 Baseline Ave., Ballard | 805/688–7770 or 800/638–2466 | fax 805/688–9560 | www.ballardinn.com | 15 | $175–$265 | AE, MC, V.

Fess Parker's Wine Country Inn. If you're looking for luxury in the country within 5 mi or so from Santa Barbara's galleries, shops, and wineries, this inn fits the bill. A lobby with a fireplace and a handsome staircase lead to your room adorned in French country style. You can enjoy the wall garden and courtyard. Restaurant, bar, room service. Refrigerators. Pool. Hot tub, spa. Business services. | 2860 Grand Ave. | 805/688–7788 | fax 805/688–1942 | www.fessparker.com/ | 21 rooms | $175–$400 | AE, MC, V.

MADERA

MAP 4, F9

(Nearby towns also listed: Fresno, Hanford, Merced, Modesto, Oakhurst, Santa Nella, Visalia)

A former logging town, Madera is now a commercial and residential suburb of 36,665 residents situated between Fresno and Modesto. On May 10, 1993, mammoth bones were discovered at the Fairmead Disposal Site, and now there is an on-going paleontological dig there which has drawn dinosaur enthusiasts from far and wide. At press time, there were plans for a visitor's center, but an opening date was not yet confirmed.

Information: Madera Chamber of Commerce | 114 E. Yosemite Ave., 93638 | 559/673–3563 | madcofc@madnet.net | www.maderachamber.com.

Attractions

Cornfield Maze. You can wind through 2 ½ mi of twists and turns in this 7-acre uniquely shaped cornfield labyrinth—one year it was a bulldog—across from the Valley Children's Hospital each fall. All the proceeds are donated to the Make-a-Wish Foundation. | Ave. 10 and Hwy 41 | 559/674–2391 | $7 | Sept. 15–Nov., Wed.–Fri. 6–10, Sat. 10–10, Sun 1–10.

Ground Zero. An 8-ft. quarter pipe, two 5½ ft. high bowls, three take-off ramps, a concrete 'K' rail wall, and other skating delights fill this indoor skate park. Equipment for rent. Skate clinic Monday evening 6–10. | 1162 Noble St. | 559/662–1819 | $6 | Wed.–Fri. 3:30–10, Sat. 11–10, Sun. 1–8.

Pizza Farm. A different pizza ingredient—wheat, tomatoes, peppers, etc.—grows in each slice-shaped field at this circular farm, which is also home to chickens, ducks, cows, pigs, and other livestock. The 1-hour educational tour emphasizing the importance of farm products in our everyday lives begins in a classroom and continues on the fields. You can also have pizza for lunch after the tour. | 1850 West Cleveland Ave. | 559/675–3668 | $5.50 | Tours by appt. only.

ON THE CALENDAR

SEPT.: *Old Timers Day Parade.* The mayor comes out for this nostalgic celebration in downtown Madera, which also involves horses, boy scout troops, school bands, car clubs, and military displays. | 559/674–7081.

Dining

Fruit Basket. American. You'll find it casual in this coffee shop and adjoining dining room, both with a plain and unpretentious style, though there are white linen tablecloths. This restaurant has been in business since 1936 and lots of locals gather here. The split level dining room has wood floors and the walls are covered with both wood and wallpaper, in a pale green. Try northern halibut steak. Kids' menu. | 117 S. Gateway Dr. | 559/674–2805 | Breakfast also available | $6–$12 | AE, D, MC, V.

The Village. Chinese. This restaurant two blocks from downtown has the usual menu items like lemon chicken, sweet-and-sour pork, and Mongolian beef, as well as some of the best steaks in town. The restaurant is in a somewhat faceless commercial district, and the interior takes a backseat to the menu. | 319 N. Gateway Dr. | 559/674–6425 | Reservations not accepted | Closed Mon. | $5.95–$11.95 | No credit cards.

Lodging

Best Western Madera Valley Inn. In a commercial area just five blocks from the Madera County Museum, this five-story concrete structure was built in 1973. Local shopping and restaurants surround the motel, and it's about an hour's drive to Yosemite and 25 mi to the Fresno Convention Center. Restaurant, bar, room service. Cable TV. Pool. Gym. Airport shuttle. | 317 North G St. | 559/673–5164 | fax 559/661–8426 | www.bestwestern.com | 94 rooms | $68–$80 | AE, D, DC, MC, V.

Holiday Inn Express. This hotel 3 mi north of town has high ceilings and an L-shape pool. It is across the street from Farnesi's, an American restaurant. Restaurant, complimentary breakfast. Microwaves, refrigerators, cable TV, room phones. Pool. Hot tub. Exercise equipment. Laundry facilities, laundry service. No pets. | 2290 Marketplace Dr. | 559/661–7400 or 800/HOLIDAY | fax 559/673–4800 | www.holidayinnexpress.com | 53 rooms, 9 suites | $79, $99–$149 suites | AE, D, DC, MC, V.

Super 8 Motel. This modest, no-frills lodging is right across the street from the Madera Fairgrounds. It's also within a mile of shopping and movie theaters. Restaurant, complimentary Continental breakfast. Cable TV. Pool. Laundry facilities. Some pets allowed. | 1855 W. Cleveland Ave. | 559/661–1131 | fax 559/661–0224 | www.super8.com | 80 rooms | $46–$60 | AE, MC, V.

MALIBU

MAP 9, A4

(Nearby towns also listed: Beverly Hills, Burbank, Calabasas, Camarillo, Culver City, Glendale, Los Angeles, Manhattan Beach, Marina Del Rey, Oxnard, Pacific Palisades, Redondo Beach, Santa Monica, Thousand Oaks, Torrance)

Arguably one of the most fabled stretches of coast anywhere, Malibu draws as many people-watchers as it does beachgoers. Many famous entertainers, artists, and writers call the spectacular 27 mi of bluffs and blue-green coastline home. Nature keeps it all in perspective, however, with a calamitous brush fire or mud slide every so often.

Information: **Malibu Chamber of Commerce** | 23805 Stuart Ranch Road, Suite 100, 90265 | 310/456–9025 | info@malibu.org | www.malibu.org.

Attractions

Malibu Lagoon Museum and Adamson House. You can see exhibits on the pre-"Baywatch" era of the city at this 1920s residence with Moorish-Spanish–style elements. | 23200 Pacific Coast Hwy. | 310/456–1770 | Free | Wed.–Sat. 11–3, last tour at 2.

Pepperdine University. Private university right on the beach in Malibu. | 24255 Pacific Coast Hwy. | 310/456–4000 | www.pepperdine.edu | Free | Daily.

ON THE CALENDAR

JULY: *Malibu Arts Festival.* This annual, two-day celebration showcasing the beach and its artists originated in 1971. It has a food court, live music, photography, ceramics, henna tattoos, and artisans of all mediums. | 310/456–9025 | www.malibu.org.

Dining

Beau Rivage. Mediterranean. One of the few Malibu restaurants with a view of the beach and ocean, this romantic Mediterranean villa-style dining room has copper domes and lush landscaping. You can see the Pacific Ocean from each of the six dining areas. The main dining area has French doors, a wood beam ceiling, a fireplace, and large wood-framed windows. You can eat outside in the garden patio with its retractable roof. There are lots of hanging plants that blend with the red, white, and green colors on the patio. The menu ranges from roast duck breast served with a wild cherry sauce and portobello mushrooms served atop polenta with a lemon-ginger sauce, to pasta with shellfish, mussel soup, and filet mignon with a mushroom marsala sauce. Wine cellar. Pianist Mon.–Wed., guitarist weekends. | 26025 Pacific Coast Hwy. | 310/456–5733 | www.br-malibu.com | No lunch Mon.–Sat. | $15–$38 | AE, D, DC, MC, V.

Geoffrey's. Eclectic. Enjoy panoramic views of the ocean at this gazebo-style restaurant. It has open sides, and the dining room has a stone floor, padded wooden chairs, and hand-painted glass-top tables. There is also an uncovered patio with hand-painted glass-top tables and plastic chairs. You can order some fine California food here. Try the marinated sea bass with creamed leeks, curry oil, and crispy carrot; steamed two-pound Maine lobster with vegetable ribbons and Madeira butter, or fresh ahi with wasabi caviar and ginger vinaigrette. 1 mi south of Paradise Cove and 4 mi south of Pepperdine University. | 27400 Pacific Coast Hwy. | 310/457–1519 | $18–$44 | AE, MC, V.

★ **Granita.** Contemporary. Wolfgang Puck's famed Granita is a glamourous—some call it garish—fantasy world of handmade tiles embedded with seashells, brown-glass lighting fixtures, and etched-glass panels with wavy edges; its beachside location adds to the marine mood. It's designed to make you feel as if you are underwater. Take note of the blown glass sculptures in the dining area. The menu changes daily, but always has seafood, such as the potato gillete (smoked salmon), polenta crêpes with Maine lobster, and bigeye tuna with spicy miso glaze. There are also sautéed foie gras with spiced Asian pears, and roasted Cantonese duck with a pomegranate-plum glaze. You can eat on the patio beneath an awning and in a landscaped spot with terrazzo floor. One mile north of the Pier. Sun. brunch. | 23725 W. Malibu Rd. | 310/456–0488 | Reservations required weekends | Mondays | $24–$32 | D, DC, MC, V.

Il Sogno. Café. This café-restaurant's brick patio surrounded by wrought iron and hanging vines is the perfect place to enjoy Spanish paella or a grilled eggplant and feta sandwich for dinner. Or earlier in the day, you can order sandwiches, soups, and salads. Of course, you are more than welcome to sip some coffee and nibble a cherry tart or a slice of chocolate marble cake anytime. | 863 Swarthmore Ave. | 310/454–6522 | $5–$8 | MC, V.

Lodging

Casa Malibu Inn on the Beach. As its name suggests, this small California beach bungalow is right on the coast. You will have a choice of ocean view units or cozy rooms that have views of the gardens on the property. Some rooms have fireplaces. The hotel is less than ½ mi from the pier. Restaurant. No air-conditioning in some rooms, some kitchenettes, refrigerators. | 22752 Pacific Coast Hwy. | 310/456–2219 or 800/831–0858 | fax 310/456–5418 | www.casamalibu.com | 21 rooms | $99–$329 | AE, MC, V.

Malibu Beach Inn. This tile-roofed, California mission–style beachfront hotel is an excellent choice for a weekend (or longer) getaway. All rooms have fireplaces and hand-painted tile baths. Eat breakfast on the patio, browse through the gift shop's Native American crafts, or plan a day's activities aided by the inn's savvy staff. One of your stops might be the pier, which is right next door. Complimentary Continental breakfast, room service. In-room data ports, minibars, some in-room hot tubs, cable TV, in-room VCRs (and movies). Business services. | 22878 Pacific Coast Hwy. | 310/456–6444 or 800/462–5428 (U.S.), 800/255–1007 (CAN) | fax 310/456–1499 | www.malibubeachinn.com/ | 47 rooms | $219–$249 | AE, DC, MC, V.

Malibu Country Inn. Perched on a bluff overlooking Zuma Beach and 3 mi south of the pier, this Cape Cod–style hotel has three acres of manicured gardens. Established in 1947, the inn's exterior is charming, with roses climbing the walls around entryways and the 16 guest room doors. Once inside the rooms, you find it pleasant if not sumptuous, with wooden furniture and matching bedspreads and draperies. Some rooms have privately enclosed patios overlooking the garden and pool; suites have fireplaces and whirlpool tubs. Restaurant, complimentary Continental breakfast, room service. No air-conditioning, refrigerators, cable TV. Pool. Business services. | 6506 Westward Beach Rd. | 310/457–9622 or 800/386–6787 | fax 310/457–1349 | www.malibucountryinn.com | 16 rooms | $165–$250 | AE, DC, MC, V.

Malibu Riviera Motel. Sandwiched between Zuma Beach and Paradise Cove, this one-story, no-frills property is ¼ mi from the beach. Cable TV, room phones. Hot tub. No pets. | 28920 Pacific Coast Hwy. | 310/457–9503 | 13 | $90–$100 | AE, DC, MC, V.

Malibu Shores Motel. Most rooms at this motel across the street from Surfrider Beach have a view of the Pacific. Shopping, cafés, theaters, and nightclubs are within ½ mi. Continental breakfast. Room phones. Beach. | 23033 Pacific Coast Hwy. | 310/456–6559 or 877/malibu4 | fax 310/456–6549 | www.malibushores.com | $125–$170 | AE, D, MC, V.

MAMMOTH LAKES

MAP 3, H8

(Nearby towns also listed: Bishop, June Lake, Lee Vining, Yosemite National Forest)

Mammoth Lakes (pop. 5500) is one of California's leading year-round resort destinations. It's a high-country portal to Rainbow Falls and Red's Meadow, the 200,000-acre Mammoth Mountain ski/mountain bike park, five-star trout fishing, and home to four three-star lodges. There are alpine lakes, pine forests, horseback riding, and hiking.

Information: Mammoth Lakes Visitors Bureau | Box 48, 93546 | 800/367–6572 | mmthvisit@qnet.com | www.visitmammoth.com.

Attractions

Devils Postpile National Monument. The Devils Postpile National Monument is within 10 or so mi of Mammoth Lakes and surrounded by Inyo National Forest. The Monument lies in the eastern Sierra Nevada at 7,560 ft elevation and encompasses 800 acres. A sheer wall of symmetrical basaltic columns over 60 ft high, buffed into shape by glacial action, crowns the Monument. | Minaret Rd., | 760/934–2571 (Mammoth Mountain Inn) | www.nps.gov/depo/ | Free; Shuttle bus: $7.50; special rates for students, seniors, and children | June–mid-Sept. you must use shuttle bus to get to the monument. From mid-Sept.–Oct. you can drive and there is no bus, daily 7:30–5:30.

Mammoth Balloon Adventures. A tour over the Mammoth Lakes, Crowley Lake Basin, and the Bishop area takes an hour and a half. Brunch is available upon request. | 2593 W. Line St., Bishop | 760/937–UPUP | www.mammothballoonadventures.com | $165 per person | Sunrise flights only, reservations required.

Mammoth Mountain Ski Area. In the winter, Mammoth Mountain is a popular ski destination for Southern Californians because of its location, views, and runs. | 1 Minaret Rd. | 760/934–2571 or 760/934–6166 | www.mammoth-mtn.com | Nov.–June, daily.

Mammoth Visitor Center Ranger Station. Operated jointly by the Inyo National Forest and the town of Mammoth Lakes, at this visitor center you can learn about the historical and recreational aspects of this National Forest, and get information about lodging, restaurants, and local services in town. Lodging reservations can be made through special phones outside the center's front door | 2500 Main St. | 760/924–5500 | www.r5.fs.fed.us/inyo/vvc/mammoth/index.htm | Free | Daily 8–5.

Mammoth Lakes Pack Outfit. This small company organizes backpacking trips and sells rental outdoor gear. You can go on adventures ranging from 2 hours to a whole week. | Lake Mary Rd. | 760/934–2434 | Prices vary per expedition | June–Labor Day, daily 8–4.

McGee Creek Pack Station. If you're a backpacking enthusiast, this shop and guide station can fulfill your every need. | 760/935–4324 | Free | June–Labor Day, daily 8–5.

Red's Meadow Pack Station and Resort. A general store for outdoors people, you can also arrange horseback excursions and pack trips with these folks. | Red's Meadow Rd. | 760/934–2345 or 800/292–7758 | www.reds-meadow.com | Free | Mid-June–Sept., daily 7–7.

The Trout Fly. This fly-fishing-only shop has experienced, professional guides available with a reservation to lead tours or teach fly fishing. You can also rent waders, float tubes, and fins. | 26 Old Mammoth Rd. | 760/934–2517 | Prices vary per activity | Daily 7–7.

ON THE CALENDAR

JULY: *Mammoth Lakes Jazz Jubilee.* This festival founded in 1989 is hosted by the local group Temple of Folly Jazz Band and has 10 venues and several dance floors. Bands come from Tennessee, California, Nevada, and Florida. | 760/934–2478 | www.mammothjazz.org.

Dining

Berger's. American. Don't even think about coming to this bustling pine-paneled institution unless you're hungry. Berger's is known for, you guessed it, burgers. And they serve other generously sized sandwiches as well. Everything comes in big, even mountainous, portions. For dinner try the beef ribs or the buffalo stew. | 6118 Minaret Rd. | 760/934–6622 | Closed 1 week in May and June and 6 weeks in Oct. and Nov. (call ahead) | $5–$16 | MC, V.

Blondie's Kitchen and Waffle Shop. American. A good place to stoke up before a morning on the slopes or trails (it opens at 5:30 AM), this bright yellow, comic-strip–theme diner serves up Belgian waffles, pancakes, omelettes, and Dagwood "pig-out" plates. There's blue carpeting and either booths or glass top tables. | 3599 Main St. | 760/934–4048 | Breakfast also available. No supper | $4–$12 | AE, MC, V.

Giovanni's Pizza. Pizza. This family restaurant 2 mi south of town specializes in pizza pies and has a full Italian menu. | 437 Old Mammoth Rd. | 760/934–7563 | No lunch Sun. | $8–$29 | AE, MC, V.

Lakefront at Tamarack Lodge. Continental. This upscale restaurant is on the grounds of Tamarack Lodge and Resort. Chef Frederic Pierrel uses local ingredients in his French onion soup, filet mignon, veal, rack of lamb, ahi, walnut-crusted chicken breast, and peppered elk medallions, which are grilled medium-rare and served with a juniper and blueberry sauce. | Twin Lakes Rd. | 760/934–3534 | www.tamaracklodge.com | Reservations essential | $17–$25 | AE, MC, V.

Lodging

Econo Lodge Wildwood Inn. You will have mountain views from some of the rooms at this downtown beige two-story wood hotel. Horseback riding, hiking, and fishing are within 5 mi. Complimentary Continental breakfast. No air-conditioning, some refrigerators, cable TV. Pool. Hot tub. Some pets allowed. | 3626 Main St. | 760/934–6855 or 800/845–8764 | fax 760/934–8208 | www.econolodge.com | 32 rooms | $59–$119 | AE, D, DC, MC, V.

Mammoth Mountain Inn. The inn 5 mi west of downtown is less than a mile of Mammoth Mountain Ski Area, and the hotel staff here will keep you informed of the snow and weather conditions over breakfast. Accommodations at this three-story rustic Alpine hotel are mostly standard rooms (some of which are pretty small) with bleached pine furnishings. Some rooms have a sitting area with a table and two chairs. Some have sleeping lofts. One- and two-bedroom condominiums and suites are also available. Restaurant, bar, picnic area, room service. Some kitchenettes, cable TV. Hot tubs. Hiking, horseback riding. Bicycles. Cross-country skiing, downhill skiing. Video games. Baby-sitting, kids' programs from ages 3–10, playground. Laundry facilities. Business services, airport shuttle. | 1 Minaret Rd. | 760/934–2581 or 800/228–4947 | fax 760/934–0701 | inn@mammoth-mountain.com | www.mammothmountain.com | 213 rooms | $115–$210 | AE, MC, V.

Quality Inn at Mammoth Lake. You can catch the shuttle to Mammoth Mountain Ski Area across the street from this motel, or if you prefer, you can drive the 5 mi distance to the ski runs. Shopping and restaurants abound in the immediate area. This wood building, constructed in 1990, is also handy for hiking, biking, and boating on the lake. Complimentary Continental breakfast. No air-conditioning, cable TV. Hot tub. Business services. | 3537 Main St./Rte. 203. | 760/934–5114 or 800/626–1900 | fax 760/934–5165 | www.qualityinn.com | 61 rooms | $89–129 | AE, D, DC, MC, V.

Shilo Inn. With a rock exterior, this all mini-suites hotel has a fireplace in the lobby. An ice-skating rink is 1½ blocks away. Complimentary Continental breakfast. Refrigerators, cable TV. Indoor pool. Exercise equipment. Laundry facilities. Business services, airport shuttle. Some pets allowed. | 2963 Main St./Rte. 203 | 760/934–4500 | fax 760/934–7594 | www.shiloinn.com/California/mammoth_lakes.html | 70 rooms | $115–$150 | AE, D, DC, MC, V.

Snow Goose Inn. When you stay at this country-style downtown inn, you can choose from rooms in a main lodge or suites in a detached outer building. The individually styled rooms and suites are furnished with log, canopy, or brass beds, antique pieces, and quilts; a snow goose motif is shown throughout. During the winter, a free shuttle bus to the ski area has a pickup spot ½ block away. For summer travelers, the east entrance of Yosemite National Park is under an hour's drive away. Complimentary full breakfast. No air-conditioning, some kitchenettes, some in-room hot tubs, cable TV. Library. Business services. | 57 Forest Trail | 760/934–2660 or 800/874–7368 (CA) | fax 760/934–5655 | frmve-gas@aol.com | www.snowgoose-inn.com | 19 rooms, 4 suites | $108–$128 rooms; $208 suites | AE, D, MC, V.

Swiss Chalet Motel. Just off Main Street, this small, family-run motel has views of Sherwin Mountain Range and is minutes from hiking and skiing trails. There is parking in front of each room, and some rooms have balconies. No air-conditioning, some microwaves, refrigerators, cable TV, room phones. Hot tub, sauna. No pets. | 3776 Viewpoint Rd. | 760/934–2403 or 800/937–9477 | fax 760/934–2403 | www.mammoth-swisschalet.com | 21 | $65–$120 | AE, DC, MC, V.

Tamarack Lodge and Resort. This lodge and cabin complex on Twin Lakes has 25 mi of cross-country skiing trails and a staff of trained instructors, as well as boat and canoe rentals in the summer. Rooms are cleaned by a maid service, but cabins are do-it-yourself. Restaurant, picnic area. Kitchenettes, no TV. Lake. Boating. Cross-country skiing. Shops. No pets. | Twin Lakes Rd. | 760/934–2442 or 800/237–6879 | www.tamarack-lodge.com | 10 rooms, 25 cabins | $80–$180, $115–$325 cabins | AE, MC, V.

MANHATTAN BEACH

(Nearby towns also listed: Anaheim, Beverly Hills, Brea, Culver City, Fullerton, Garden Grove, Huntington Beach, Long Beach, Los Angeles, Malibu, Marina del Rey, Orange, Redondo Beach, Santa Ana, Santa Monica, Seal Beach, Torrance)

Between industrial/commercial El Segundo and Redondo Beach lies this quiet, though increasingly upscale beach town of 40,000. Once a funky surf haven, Manhattan Beach appears ready for its close-up. Currently, it's home to many Los Angeles Kings and other professional athletes.

Information: **Manhattan Beach Chamber of Commerce** | 425 15th St., 90266 | 310/545–5313 | mbchamberk@aol.com | www.mbchamber.net.

Attractions

Manhattan Village Shopping Center. This Mediterranean-style mall is 2 mi south of the airport and across from the Manhattan Beach pier. Stores include B Dalton, Bath & Body Works, Foot Locker, Great Earth Vitamins, Mrs. Fields Cookies, Pacific Theatres, Sees Candies, and Wolf Camera. | 3200 Sepulveda Blvd. | 310/546–5558 | Free | Weekdays 10–9, Sat. 10–8, Sun. 11–7.

ON THE CALENDAR

SEPT.: *Manhattan Beach Arts Festival.* The town becomes a gallery during this annual, one-day event. Craft items like mosaics, Lithuanian Easter eggs, sandcastles, and origami are on display, and dancers, musicians, storytellers, and clowns perform in the street festival. | 310/802–5416 or 310/376–9511 | www.ci.manhattan-beach.ca.us.

Dining

Beaches. Contemporary. This three-story oceanfront property with two bars was formerly known as Sunset's and serves grilled fish and chicken dishes. Brunch is available on Saturday and Sunday, and the restaurant becomes a nightclub on weekend evenings. | 117 Manhattan Beach Blvd. | 310/545–2523 | Breakfast also available | $8–$20 | AE, D, MC, V.

Good Stuff. American. This busy but laid-back restaurant has a view of the beach from both the upstairs and downstairs. Blackened mahi salad is the most popular dish, but

you can also have a burger or pasta. | 1300 Highland Ave. | 310/545–4775 | $5–$13 | AE, D, DC, MC, V.

Manhattan Bar and Grill. Continental. Every kind of meat is served in every way imaginable at this restaurant 1 mi from downtown, and all entrées come with soup or salad, and pasta or vegetable. There's nightly entertainment at the piano bar. | 1019 Manhattan Beach Blvd. | 310/546–4545 | Closed Sun. No lunch Sat. | $9–$19 | AE, D, MC, V.

Michi Restaurant and Bar. Pan-Asian. Sea bass cigars, like egg rolls, are popular at this downtown restaurant where the bar has over 50 different martinis. There is live entertainment Monday through Wednesday. | 903 Manhattan Ave. | 310/376–0613 | Closed Sun. No lunch Sat., Mon. | AE, D, DC, MC, V.

Lodging

★ **Barnabey's.** In Manhattan Beach, 2 mi from the airport, this inn offers a welcome respite from the frantic pace of downtown LA. Victorian-style rooms are furnished with antiques and towel warmers; some have canopied beds, crystal chandeliers, and balconies overlooking the courtyard. Complimentary transportation to the beach and local shopping. Restaurant, bar. In-room data ports, cable TV. Pool. Video games. Airport shuttle, parking (fee). | 3501 Sepulveda Blvd., | 310/545–8466 or 800/552–5285 (in U.S.) | fax 310/545–8621 | www.barnabeys-hotel.com | 120 rooms | $135–$144 | AE, D, DC, MC, V.

Comfort Inn. Less than 2 mi from Manhattan Beach and Hermosa Beach and in a residential area, this Spanish-style wood building has a stucco finish and dates to 1988. Complimentary Continental breakfast. Some in-room hot tubs, cable TV. Pool. Hot tub, sauna. Laundry service. Airport shuttle. | 850 N. Sepulveda Blvd. | 310/318–1020 | fax 310/376–3545 | www.comfortinn.com | $89–$99 | AE, D, DC, MC, V.

Doubletree Club. This seven-story hotel is 2 mi from the airport in a business park in quiet El Segundo, near golf, shopping, restaurants, and beaches. Restaurant, bar, complimentary breakfast. In-room data ports, cable TV. Pool. Hot tub. Exercise equipment. Business services, airport shuttle. | 1985 E. Grand Ave., El Segundo | 310/322–0999 | fax 310/322–4758 | www.doubletree.com | 215 rooms | $126 | AE, D, DC, MC, V.

El Camino Motel. This no-frills motel is 1 mi east of the beach and less than ½ mi from two movie theaters. Cable TV, room phones. Pets allowed. | 3301 N. Sepulveda Blvd. | 310/546–5464 | 18 rooms | $60 | MC, V.

Embassy Suites. This Spanish Mission-style all-suites hotel has a sun deck, lobby atrium, and made-to-order breakfasts. It's near the beach, 16 mi west of downtown LA. Restaurant, bar, complimentary breakfast. In-room data ports, cable TV. Indoor pool. Hot tub. Exercise equipment. Business services, airport shuttle, parking (fee). Some pets allowed. | 1440 E. Imperial Ave., El Segundo | 310/640–3600 | fax 310/322–0954 | www.embassy-suites.com | 350 suites | $159–$174 suites | AE, D, DC, MC, V.

Hampton Inn. This basic, reliable chain hotel, 1 mi from LAX, is all about convenient location. Rooms have standard decor, with table and chairs for working or dining. Complimentary Continental breakfast. In-room data ports, cable TV. Airport shuttle, free parking. | 10300 La Cienega Blvd., Inglewood | 310/337–1000 | fax 310/645–6925 | www.hampton-inn.com | 148 rooms | $95–$159 | AE, D, DC, MC, V.

Holiday Inn Express. In a residential area, 1 mi west of Manhattan Pier, this three-story wood building with a stucco finish has some rooms with fireplaces. Some in-room hot tubs. Pool. Hot tub, sauna. Laundry service. Airport shuttle. | 900 N Sepulveda Blvd. | 310/318–6132 | fax 310/372–9134 | www.hiexpress.com | 44 rooms | $105–$110 | AE, D, DC, MC, V.

Manhattan Beach Marriott. You can unwind at the hotel's par-3 executive golf course and have a view of it from your room as well. This seven-story, creme-colored building, built in 1985, caters to business travellers. There are a full business center, use of PCs and printers, and complimentary scheduled shuttle service to the Manhattan Beach pier, which is 1 mi away. 2 restaurants, bar. Cable TV. Pool. Gym. Golf course. Laundry service. Business services, airport shuttle. | 1400 Parkview Ave. | 310/546–7511 | fax 310/546–7520 | www.marriott.com | 385 rooms, 12 suites | rooms $185–$200, suites $240–$500 | AE, D, DC, MC, V.

Residence Inn by Marriott. All-suites hotel with studio (one-bedroom) and split-level penthouse suites (two-bedroom/two-bath), all with fully equipped kitchens, though you get breakfast and dinner as part of your stay. In a residential area 1 mi from Manhattan Beach pier. The hotel, built in 1985, has 22 two-story French-style wood buildings. There is a courtyard on the lush landscaped property. Complimentary Continental breakfast. In-room data ports, kitchenettes, refrigerators, cable TV, in-room VCRs. Pool. Exercise equipment, gym. Hot tub. Some pets allowed. Laundry service. Business services. | 1700 N. Sepulveda Blvd. | 310/546–7627 | fax 310/545–1327 | www.residenceinn.com/laxmh | 176 suites | $185–$195 | AE, D, DC, MC, V.

Sea View Inn at the Beach. You will be two blocks from the beach at this small hotel. It has four Mediterranean-style stucco buildings; the main one dates back to 1960. Many rooms have views of the beach and ocean. There are plantation shutters and balconies. Pool. Bicycles. | 3400 Highland Ave. | 310/545–1504 | fax 310/545–4052 | www.seaview-inn.com | 29 rooms, 10 suites | $95–$130, $150–$215 suites | AE, MC, V.

Seahorse Inn. This two-story motel is 2½ mi from downtown and surrounded by a number of fast-food restaurants. Cable TV, phones. No pets. | 233 N. Sepulveda Blvd. | 310/376–7951 or 800/233–8057 | fax 310/376–6721 | 33 | $59–$79 | AE, MC, V.

MARINA DEL REY

MAP 9, C4

(Nearby towns also listed: Beverly Hills, Culver City, Long Beach, Malibu, Manhattan Beach, Pasadena, Redondo Beach, Santa Monica, Venice)

Tourist-friendly and kick-back, the Marina (pop. 67,000) is colored by two distinct shades. On the north end you'll find lively bars, vibrant coffee houses, small nightclubs, and restaurants that reverberate into the night. At the other end stands kitschy Fisherman's Village, a replication of a New England port brimming with trinket shops and restaurants. Whale-watching tours, deep-sea fishing excursions, sea kayaks, and jet-skis are all available here.

Information: Marina del Rey Chamber of Commerce | 9800 S. Sepulveda Blvd., Suite 214, Westchester, 90045-5227 | 310/645–5151 | rich@laxmdrchamber.com | www.wlaxmdrchamber.com.

Attractions

Del Rey Sportfishing and Whale Watch. Charter boats for up to 75 people are available for fishing yellow tail, barracuda, and halibut, and seasonal whale watches scout grey whales. They can be seen in their natural habitat with seals, sea lions, and dolphins. | Dock 52, Fiji Way | 310/822–3625 or 310/372–3712 | www.delmarsportfishing.com | $15 | Daily 6:30–5.

Fisherman's Village. Quaint shopping and dining in a village design. The Fisherman's Village is just a few yards off the bike path and walkway by the marina. | 13755 Fiji Way | 310/822–6866 | Free | Daily.

ON THE CALENDAR
SEPT.: *California Coastal Cleanup Day.* Students, professionals, divers, surfers, tourists, and beach lovers lend a hand to this annual, one-day effort to clean the beach. There are special parking rates for volunteers, and all supplies are provided. | 310/453–0395 or 800/HEALBAY | www.healthebay.org.

Dining

Cafe Del Rey. Contemporary. A lively-yet-sophisticated place to enjoy a beautiful harbor view from the long sweep of windows and a menu that's strong on Pacific Rim cuisine. Enjoy grilled aged Angus rib-eye steak or pan-fried seafood in an airy, modern café. In the lounge you can sit at long tables or on the sofa. There's even a fireplace for chilly days. Good wine selection. Sun. brunch. | 4451 Admiralty Way | 310/823–6395 | www.calcafe.com | $21–$40 | AE, D, DC, MC, V.

Dining Room. Mediterranean. It's definitely Victorian in this formal, well-lit, and romantic dining room that has a view of the marina. There are Victorian drapes, dark wood walls adorned with paintings, and chandeliers in the dining room. Both locals and out-of-towners like this restaurant for romantic dining. Try the sea bass with tomatoes and eggplant, grilled salmon with saffron sauce, lamp chops, or herb-roasted chicken. | 4375 Admiralty Way | 310/823–1700 | $28–$55 | AE, D, DC, MC, V.

Shanghai Reds. Continental. This waterfront restaurant has views of the marina, and a heated patio is available for outdoor seating. The fresh fish creations change weekly, but swordfish and salmon are always available. | 13813 Fiji Way | 310/823–4522 | Reservations essential | $16–$34 | AE, D, DC, MC, V.

Yankee Doodles. American. This boisterous sports bar for the 21-and-older crowd has pool tables, foosball, video games, big screen TVs, and greasy appetizers. Beer is served by the pitcher. | 300 Washington Blvd. | 310/574–6868 | $6–$18 | AE, MC, V.

Lodging

Courtyard by Marriott. In a commercial area, three blocks east of the Marina del Rey beach and 1½ mi east of Venice Beach, this is a five-story peach building built in 1977. Ideal for business travellers with fax, copier and even secretarial services. Restaurant, bar, room service. In-room data ports, cable TV. Pool. Hot tub. Exercise equipment. Business services. | 13480 Maxella Ave. | 310/822–8555 | fax 310/823–2996 | cymdr@aol.com | www.courtyard.com/laxcm | 276 rooms | $125–$189 | AE, D, DC, MC, V.

Foghorn Harbor Inn. Comfortable beachfront accommodations nestled amidst the palms. In a residential area, 4 mi from LAX and 12 mi northeast of downtown, the two-story inn was built in 1965. The building has a wood paneled exterior. Restaurant, complimentary Continental breakfast. Refrigerators, cable TV, in-room VCRs (and movies). Beach. Airport shuttle. | 4140 Via Marina | 310/823–4626 or 800/423–4940 (outside CA), 800/624–7351 (CA) | fax 310/578–1964 | www.foghornhotel.com | 23 rooms | $129–$159 | AE, D, DC, MC, V.

Holiday Inn Express. Surrounded by palm trees, this hotel is ½ mi from the Venice boardwalk. Complimentary Continental breakfast. In-room data ports, in-room safes, some microwaves, some refrigerators, cable TV, room phones. Pool. Spa. | 737 Washington Blvd. | 310/821–4455 or 800/821–8277 | fax 310/821–8098 | www.holidayinnmarinadelrey.com | 32 rooms, 36 suites | $102–$114, $116–$129 suites | AE, D, DC, MC, V.

★ **Marina Beach Marriott.** This Marriott overlooks Marina del Rey and the Pacific Ocean, and grounds include a garden patio with a gazebo. Rooms have views of the marina, ocean, and mountains. This 11-story hotel, built in 1985, is 16 mi west of downtown L.A. Restaurant, bar (with entertainment). In-room data ports, refrigerators, cable TV. Pool. Exercise equipment. Business services. Parking (fee). | 4100 Admiralty Way | 310/301–3000 | fax 310/448–4870 | www.marriotthotels.com | 370 rooms | $189–$255, $235–$700 suites | AE, D, DC, MC, V.

Marina del Rey Hotel. In the heart of the world's largest man-made, small-craft harbor, this hotel is also just 10 minutes from LAX. Grounds include lush, tropical gardens. All rooms have a view of the marina and each has a private balcony. The three-story, wood and plaster building in a Y-shape, dates from 1985. Restaurant, bar. In-room data ports, room service. Cable TV. Pool. Boating. Business services, airport shuttle. | 13534 Bali Way | 310/301–1000; 800/862–7462 (CA) | fax 310/301–8167 | www.marinadelreyhotel.com | 157 rooms | $230–$320 | AE, DC, MC, V.

Marina International Hotel and Bungalows. This locally owned establishment 2 mi from downtown opened in 1962. It is steps from a public beach, and all rooms have private balconies or patios overlooking a central courtyard. Restaurant, bar, room service. Cable TV, room phones. Pool. Hot tub. Beach. Airport shuttle. | 4200 Admiralty Way | 310/301–2000 | fax 310/301–6687 | www.marinaintlhotel.com | 110 rooms, 24 bungalows | $120–$140, $160 bungalows | AE, D, DC, MC, V.

★ **Ritz-Carlton, Marina del Rey.** If sumptuous is what you want, this is the place with rooms that have French doors opening to balconies overlooking the Pacific Ocean. Rooms have marble baths, a fully stocked mini refreshment bar, goosedown and non-allergenic foam pillows, plush terry or lightweight bathrobes, and multi-line telephones. You can even have in-room yoga lessons. You have a choice of fancy lounges and dining rooms, and are right on the marina and only six blocks from Venice Beach. Restaurant, bar (with entertainment), dining room, room service. In-room data ports, minibars, refrigerators, cable TV. Pool. Hot tub, massage, spa, sauna. 2 tennis courts. Basketball. Gym. Bicycles. Shops. Video games. Parking (fee). Business services. | 4375 Admiralty Way | 310/823–1700 | fax 310/823–2403 | www.ritzcarlton.com | 306 rooms | $169–$575 | AE, D, DC, MC, V.

MARYSVILLE

MAP 3, E6

(Nearby towns also listed: Grass Valley, Nevada City)

When Marysville was incorporated in 1851, it called itself the "Gateway to the Gold Fields" of northern California. Indeed, the surrounding mines shipped more than $10 million worth of nuggets back east in 1857 alone. The town took its official name from Ms. Mary Murphy, wife of one of the area's original farmsteaders and one of the few survivors of the famously unlucky Donner Party.

Along with the 49ers seeking fortune and glory came several thousand Chinese immigrants who left their homeland to toil underground alongside the American miners. Both Marysville and neighboring Yuba City celebrate their Asian influences—Marysville's Chinese New Year celebration is among the most elaborate in the nation.

Marysville sits on the shores of Ellis Lake between the courses of the Feather, Yuba, and Sacramento rivers. The Sierra Nevada foothills rise to the east, making the town popular among nature enthusiasts who come to boat, fish, hike, and camp in the surrounding wilderness. The nearby Beale Air Force Base contributes to the town's economic base, along with a healthy tourist trade.

Information: **Yuba-Sutter Chamber of Commerce** | 429 10th St., Yuba City, 95901 | 530/743–6501 | chamber@yuba.net.

Attractions

Ellis Lake. In 1924, The Women's Improvement Club of Marysville commissioned the designer of San Francisco's Golden Gate Park to transform this former swamp into the city's centerpiece. It has ducks, paddle boats, a fountain, picnic areas, and it's the site of Independence Day fireworks. | Bounded by Ninth St., B St., 14th St., and D St. | 530/743–6501 | www.syix.com | Free | Daily.

Mary Aaron Memorial Museum. Built in 1855 and occupied by the Aaron family from 1874–1935, this Gothic Revival home now houses a museum devoted to preserving the history of the area. Old photographs, period clothing, and a display illustrating the experiences of early Chinese immigrants are just a few of the things to see here. | 704 D. St. | 530/743–1004 | Free | Thurs.–Sat. 1–4 or by appointment.

Historic D Street. Many of Marysville's original brick and wooden buildings can still be seen south of D Street's 700 block. You can get a self-guided walking tour map at the Mary

Aaron museum and set out to appreciate the street's turn-of-the-20th century architecture. | D Street, | 530/743–1004 | Free.

Bok Kai Temple. The only one of its kind in the United States, this temple was founded by Chinese immigrants in the mid-1800s. The orginal temple structure burned to the ground and was rebuilt in 1880. Today the temple, with its green-tiled roof and dragon-shaped cornices, is still a place of worship and functions as the focal point of Marysville's Chinese New Year festival. | Corner of D and First Sts. | 530/743–6501 | Free | Tours by appointment only.

ON THE CALENDAR

SEPT.: *California Prune Festival.* This annual festival hosts 30,000 visitors who taste a variety of foods made with prunes, including pasta, yogurt, milkshakes, wine, cake, chili, and ice cream. There's also a 10K run, performances by a Dixieland band, and a petting zoo. | 530/671–3100 | www.prunefestival.org.

MAR.: *Bok Kai Festival and Parade.* For over a century, this colorful festival has been ringing in the Chinese New Year in downtown Marysville. There is food, music, and a 15K run, and the festival culminates with a parade down historic D street to Chinatown, complete with glittering dragon dancers, gongs, and fireworks at the end. | 530/743–7309.

Dining

The Refuge. Eclectic. This friendly, neighborhood restaurant 3 mi west of Marysville in Yuba City blends Italian, French, and Mexican flavors with a generous helping of garlic. Seafood pastas, calamari, and rib-eye steaks are popular. | 1501 Butte House Rd., Yuba City | 530/673–7620 | No lunch weekends | $14–$34 | AE, MC, V.

Lodging

Amerihost Inn Marysville. This modest motel off Highway 70 is 1 mi from downtown and 12 mi west of Beale Air Force Base. Complimentary Continental breakfast. Some microwaves, some refrigerators, some in-room hot tubs, cable TV, room phones. Pool. Hot tub. Laundry service. Business services. Pets allowed (fee). | 1111 N. Beale St. | 530/742–2700 | www.amerihost.com | 50 rooms, 12 suites | $69–$99, $99–$139 suites | AE, D, DC, MC, V.

Best Western Bonanza Inn. In a commercial area, this two-story wood building built in 1974, is next to a steak house and three blocks from a movie theater. Restaurant, bar. Some refrigerators, in-room hot tubs, cable TV. Video games. Pool. Hot tub. | 1001 Clark Ave., Yuba City | 530/674–8824 | fax 530/674–0563 | 125 rooms | $68 | AE, D, DC, MC, V.

Villager Lodge. Within 4 blocks of the Greyhound bus terminal, this 1939 lodge has four blue and lavender buildings. Complimentary Continental breakfast. Some kitchenettes, refrigerators, microwaves, cable TV. Some pets allowed (fee). | 545 Colusa Ave., Yuba City | 530/671–1151 or 800/593–4666 | 39 rooms | $65 | AE, D, MC, V.

MENDOCINO

MAP 3, B5

(Nearby towns also listed: Albion, Boonville, Elk, Fort Bragg, Gualala, Little River, Ukiah)

★ Mendocino (pop. 1100) has an interesting beginning: in 1852 a German immigrant, William Kasten, washed up on its shore, the only survivor of a shipwreck (not surprising, given the treacherous-looking rocks just offshore). He soon realized that he was better off selling lumber from the ample redwood forests than charging off after elusive gold, so he settled down and built Mendocino into a logging center.

To the New England settlers who arrived to work the logging industry in the mid-19th century, this craggy, weatherbeaten coast must have resembled home. They built the New England–style houses (one of them made famous as Angela Lansbury's abode in the TV series *Murder, She Wrote*) and contributed a certain reticent air that, despite its reputation as a tourist destination, pervades the town to this day.

In the 1960s, long after high demand for lumber faded, the town was a retreat for artists and back-to-nature pioneers running from city life, and Mendocino still wears some of that unpretentious charm. However, it's also become a favorite spot for Californians looking for a relaxing weekend jaunt to a place that's secluded yet full of things such as sophisticated (some call it fancy) food and romantic B&Bs.

Information: **Fort Bragg–Mendocino Coast Chamber of Commerce** | 332 N. Main St., Box 1141, Fort Bragg, 95437 | 707–961–6300 | chamber@mcn.org | www.mendocinocoast.com.

Attractions

Jughandle State Reserve. Five miles of nature trails explore coastal and forest environments. The Ecological Staircase trail leads to a pygmy forest of trees that are over 100 years old but only a few feet tall. | 15700 Rte. 1N, Fort Bragg | 707/937–5804 | Free | Daily dawn to dusk.

Kelley House Museum and Library. Restored residence of William Henry Kelley, a Gold Rush pioneer who arrived in 1852 and bought out the holdings of shipwrecked William Kasten, Mendocino founder. The residence is now used as a research center, museum, and popular wedding spot. | 45007 Albion St. | 707/937–5791 | kelleyhs@mcn.org | www.homestead.com/kellyhousemuseum | $2 | Sept.–May, Fri.–Sun. 1–4; June–Aug., daily 1–4.

Mendocino Art Center. There are two galleries as well as studios for ceramics, textiles, jewelry, sculpture, scattered among landscaped grounds. The center hosts community theater productions and has arts and crafts fairs in summer and at Thanksgiving. | 45200 Little Lake St. | 707/937–5818 or 800/653–3328 | www.mendocinoartcenter.org | Free; special rates for exhibits and classes | Daily, call for class and exhibit schedules.

Mendocino Headlands State Park. This 347-acre day-use park surrounds Mendocino village. The visitor center has exhibits on local history. You can also hike and explore the beach. | Headrow Dr. and Main St., off Hwy. 1 | 707/937–5804 | Free | Daily dawn to dusk.

Russian Gulch State Park. The craggy wilderness at this 1,162-acre state park with 7,630 ft of ocean frontage is characteristic of the north coast. You can explore heavily forested Russian Gulch Creek Canyon, a headland that includes the Devil's Punch Bowl (a large, collapsed sea cave with churning water), and a beach where you can swim, skin dive, and check out tidal pools. Inland, there is a 36-ft high waterfall. Hikers enjoy miles of hiking trails. The park also has a paved 3-mi bicycle trail, hiking trails, group campsites, and showers. Two miles north of Mendocino. | Hwy. 1 | 707/937–5804 | $2 per vehicle | Apr.–Nov., daily dawn to dusk.

ON THE CALENDAR

JAN.: *Mendocino Wine and Crab Days.* The first annual Wine and Crab Days Festival was held in the last week of January 2000. Events include winemaker dinners, crab cruises, and historical reenactments. | www.mendocinoalliance.com/mccrab.htm.

MAR.: *Whale Festival.* The celebration coincides with the spring-time, homeward migrations of the California gray whale. | 707/961–6300.

SEPT.: *Mendocino County Fair and Apple Show.* Called "the best little fair in California," a parade, livestock, rodeo, sheepdog trials, and other traditional events are featured at the Mendocino Fairgrounds. | 9 AM–midnight | 707/895–2336.

APR.–DEC.: *Mendocino Galleries.* Galleries hold artist receptions and openings on the second Saturday of each month through the season. Pick up your gallery guide at Mendocino Art Center and other locations around town. | 707/937–5818.

JUNE: *Mendocino Coastal Garden Tour and Lunch.* Visit the extensive gardens between Little River and Fort Bragg, and pick up some samples at the specimen plant sale before having a catered lunch. The event benefits the Mendocino Art Center. | 707/937–5818 or 800/653–3328.

JULY: *Mendocino Music Festival.* Orchestral and chamber music, jazz, opera, and big band concerts are part of this festival in a tent on Mendocino headlands. | 707/937–4041.

DEC.: *Mendocino Christmas Festival.* The town celebrates the holidays with special events, tours of local inns, and musical performances. | 707/937–4041.

Dining

★ **Café Beaujolais.** French. A renowned restaurant established in 1972 by Margaret Fox, Café Beaujolais is in a Victorian farmhouse surrounded by gardens that are a part of Sweet Water Gardens. It has an intimate air with Victorian wallpaper, wood beam ceilings, wood floors, and white linen tablecloths. There is an enclosed atrium where you can eat in the summer. Fresh French-inspired food with organic local ingredients are the specialty here. Try braised asparagus, roasted free-range chicken, duck, or lamb loin in herb crust with white beans, accompanied by homemade bread. Beer and wine served. | 961 Ukiah St. | 707/937–5614 | $18–$26 | MC, V.

Hill House Inn and Restaurant. Contemporary. From your table with an ocean view, you can start with seafood cake appetizers and then move on to warm quail salad or the house salad of mixed greens with fuji apples and blue cheese in balsamic dressing. Soups include a seafood chowder with lobster, crab, and fresh seasonal fish. The signature vegetarian dish is baked polenta served over a marinated portobello mushroom with a sweet onion and pepper medley sauce. Another favorite entrée is rack of lamb in a blueberry cabernet reduction sauce. Desserts include blueberry pudding made with locally grown berries and served with whiskey sauce—and always something chocolate. Ocean views from all tables. Sunday brunch includes complimentary champagne. | In the Hill House Inn (also listed) | 800/422–0554 | Breakfast also available. No lunch. Dinner Thurs., Fri., Sat. in restaurant; dinner daily in upstairs lounge | $25–$40 | AE, D, MC.

MacCallum House Restaurant/Grey Whale Bar and Café. Contemporary. This delightful house with lacy trim and an expansive porch was built in 1882 as a wedding gift to Daisy MacCallum from her father. It has three dining rooms; the two main ones have some of MacCallum's original antique furniture. Menu choices include tequila-cured salmon quesadilla, pan-seared duck breast, carmelized scallops with basmati rice, or peach napoleon. | 45020 Albion St. | 707/937–5763 | No lunch | $11–$24 | MC, V.

Mendocino Hotel Restaurant. Continental. Turn-of-the-20th-century furnishings, such as antique mirrors and paintings, establish an elegant air in the dining room. You can order oysters on the half shell, French onion soup, or grilled seafood. | 45080 Main St. | 707/937–0676 or 800/548–0513 | $14–$26 | MC, V.

955 Ukiah Street. Contemporary. The daily menu includes brandy prawns and a seafood menagerie, as well as steaks, roast duck, and pasta dishes such as giant ravioli with spinach and red chard and duck-filled cannelloni. | 955 Ukiah St., | 707/937–1955 | No lunch. Closed Tues. | $16–$22 | MC, V.

Paterson's Pub. Irish. The Reuben is the signature sandwich; other favorites are traditional Irish corned beef and Swiss and sauerkraut on grilled rye with Thousand Island dressing. | 10485 Lansing St., | 707/937–4782 | $11–$15.

The Ravens. Vegetarian. Named for the raven pair who moved to the site before the owners broke ground for the dining room in 1995, The Ravens serves vegetarian and vegan food. The signature dish is sea palm strudel: whole-wheat phyllo dough layered with caramelized julienned carrots, red onions, and sea palm and finished with two sauces—wasabi and Ume plum sauce—with Asian greens and shiitake mushrooms on the side. The menu always always includes baked tofu, usually nut encrusted and served with garden greens (from the restaurant's own organic gardens) and pistachio and locally harvested, garlic-stuffed morelles as well as a portobello mushroom burger and two pizzas, one topped with fresh local veggies. You can always order freshly made soups and salads, For dessert, there's vegan chocolate torte—"you won't believe it's vegan," according to the executive chef—and chocolate brûlée. The organic and nonorganic wines are from from France, America, Italy, Australia, and other spots around the world. | In the Stanford Inn (also listed) | 800/331–8884 or 707/937–5615 | $15–$22 | AE, D, DC, MC, V.

Lodging

Agate Cove Inn. In a residential area, 1 mi south of the Russian Gulch State Park and situated on a bluff, this inn was built in 1860 and sits on a half acre garden. Your room will have an ocean view. Complimentary full breakfast. No air-conditioning, in-room VCRs. | 11201 N. Lansing | 707/937–0551 or 800/527–3111 | fax 707/937–0550 | www.agatecove.com | 10 rooms | $109–$269 | AE, MC, V.

Blackberry Inn. Each single-story unit here has a false front, creating the image of a frontier town. There are a bank, a saloon, Belle's Palace, and "offices" for doctors and sheriffs. Most rooms have ocean views and fireplaces. It is in a residential area 2 mi north of Russian Gulch State Park and makes you think you are in a Hollywood movie set. Complimentary Continental breakfast. No air-conditioning, some kitchenettes, some refrigerators, in-room hot tubs, cable TV, some room phones. | 44951 Larkin Rd. | 707/937–5281 or 800/950–7806 | www.innaccess.com/bbi | $95–$145, $175 cottage | MC, V.

Cypress Cove at Mendocino. On a cliff at the edge of the Pacific, this contemporary B&B gives you an ocean view across the cove to the village of Mendocino, about a mile south. Each of the suites has a private deck and entrance, wood-burning fireplace, and an entertainment center that includes CD and tape players. You'll find complimentary brandy, chocolate, and flowers in your room. Deer and birds fill the surrounding forest, and you can watch whales and seals from the cliff. Kitchenettes, in-room hot tubs, cable TV, in-room VCRs. No smoking. | 800/942–6300 | www.cypresscove.com | 2 rooms | $190–$225 | MC, V.

Headlands Inn. Built in 1868, this redwood and cedar Victorian house has an English garden and ocean views. Rooms are furnished with antiques, and many have fireplaces or woodburning stoves. In a Mendocino residential area, it is one block from the shopping district. Complimentary breakfast. No air-conditioning. No room phones, no TV in some rooms. No smoking. | Corner of Albion and Howard Street | 707/937–4431 or 800/354–4431 | fax 707/937–1442 | innkeeper@headlandsinn.com | www.headlandsinn.com | 7 rooms, 1 cottage | rooms $110–$195, cottage $149–$169 | AE, D, MC, V.

Hill House. Angela Lansbury spent a lot of time here since *Murder She Wrote* was filmed here for eight years. The country-style wood house, constructed in 1978, is in a residential area across the street from St. Anthony's Catholic Church and 2 mi north of Russian Gulch State Park. Like Angela, you can enjoy the sitting garden on the premises. Dining room, bar, picnic area. Complimentary Continental breakfast. No air-conditioning, cable TV. Library. Business services. | 10701 Palette Dr. | 707/937–0554 or 800/422–0554 (in Northern CA only) | fax 707/937–1123 | www.hillhouseinn.com | 44 rooms, 4 suites | $165–$195, $225–$300 suites | AE, D, MC, V.

Joshua Grindle. Built in 1879 by a local banker, this Victorian farmhouse sits on a two-acre knoll overlooking the town and the ocean. There is a New England country mood and an English-style garden. Two other buildings on the property, the Watertower (an upper room with windows on all four sides) and the Cottage, hold five additional rooms. Furnishings throughout are simple but comfortable American antiques: Salem rockers, wing chairs, steamer-trunk tables, painted pine beds, and a pump organ. In a residential area, three blocks from the shopping district and ¼ mi north of the Mendocino Headlands State Park. Complimentary full breakfast. No air-conditioning, in-room data ports. No smoking. | 44800 Little Lake Rd. | 707/937–4143 or 800/474–6353 | stay@joshgrin.com | www.joshgrin.com | 10 rooms | $140–$215 | MC, V.

McElroy's Cottage Inn. Gardens surround the house, water tower, and cottage that make up this early 1900s Craftsmen Period inn, which faces the ocean at the east end of the village of Mendocino. A ½ mi walk west will bring you to the other end of town. The beach is about three blocks away (down the cliffside via a staircase with safety railings); the headlands, where you can do some whale watching, are three blocks west. Two rooms have ocean views and two, garden views; all rooms have radios, games, books and puzzles, and flannel sheets and quilts on the beds. Breakfast includes homemade breads. Kids are welcome. Complimentary Continental breakfast. Some pets allowed. | 998 Main St. | 707/937–1734 | 4 rooms | $85–$125 | MC, V.

Mendocino Hotel. Stained-glass lamps, Frederic Remington paintings, polished wood and Persian carpets lend a swank 19th-century feeling to this 1875 building overlooking the bay. The location is top-notch, too, since it's across the street from the Mendocino Headlands State Park. Guest rooms are filled with antiques, and some have wood-burning fireplaces and private balconies or patios. The hotel has two restaurants; the Garden Room—a casual breakfast and lunch nook with lots of greenery—and the Victorian Room—an elegant, candlelit dinner place. Dining room, 2 restaurants, 2 bars, room service. Cable TV, no TV in some rooms. Business services. | 45080 Main St. | 707/937–0511 or 800/548–0513 | fax 707/937–0513 | www.mendocinohotel.com | 51 rooms, including 14 with shared bath; 6 suites | $95–$205, $275 suites | AE, MC, V.

Mendocino Seaside Cottage. Quirky elements reflect the owner's taste for whimsy. Rooms are individually furnished. The wooden exterior of the building belies the marble interior; the cottage was built in 1997. You will have an ocean view, fireplace, and whirlpool tub. Some rooms have fireplaces and telescopes, so you can spot whales and other wildlife. Mendocino Headlands State Park is across the street. It's four blocks to the heart of the village's shopping area, and 3 mi north of the Point Cabrillo Lighthouse. No air-conditioning, microwaves, refrigerators, some kitchenettes, some minibars, some in-room hot tubs, cable TV, in-room VCRs. Some pets allowed. | 10940 Lansing Street | 707/485–0239 or 800/94–HEART | fax 707/485–9746 | romance@romancebythesea.com | www.romancebythesea.com | 4 rooms | $157–$301 | No credit cards.

Packard House. A Carpenter's Gothic B&B built in 1878, the Packard is in the midst of Mendocino Village's shops and restaurants and across the street from the Art Center. The four rooms, all of which have fireplaces and CD players, are in period style, with a mix of antique and contemporary pieces. You can choose from rooms with views of the ocean, village, or garden courtyard and original watertower. A two-block walk south takes you to the entrance of Headlands State Park. Complimentary wine, cheese, and crudités are served in the afternoons. Some in-room hot tubs, cable TV, in-room VCRs (and movies). | 45170 Little Lake St. | 888/453–2677 or 707/937–2677 | fax 707/937–1323 | www.packardhouse.com | 4 rooms, 1 suite | $165–$210, suite $145–$165 | D, DC, MC, V.

★ **Stanford Inn by the Sea.** Extensive renovations that were underway in the fall of 2000 made this former motel-style lodge, located at the mouth of Big River, into a charming country inn. Big ocean-view rooms and 10 acres of landscaped property are two reasons to stay here; there is a certified organic farm on the property as well. It is 1 mi southeast of Mendocino Headlands State Park in a residential area. Complimentary full breakfast. No air-conditioning, in-room data ports, some kitchenettes, refrigerators, cable TV, in-room VCRs (and movies). Indoor pool. Hot tub, sauna. Exercise equipment. Boating, bicycles. Business services, airport shuttle. Some pets allowed. No smoking. | 44850 Comptche Rd. | 707/937–5615 or 800/331–8884 | fax 707/937–0305 | www.stanfordinn.com | 41 rooms | $242–$410 | AE, D, DC, MC, V.

Stevenswood Lodge. You can enjoy a wooded glen accented by sculptures at this contemporary Scandinavian wood, cedar, and oak lodge built in 1988. Van Damme State Park adjoins the property, which is 2 mi north of Mendocino Village. Restaurant, complimentary breakfast. Hot tub. | 8211 Hwy. 1, Little River | 707/937–2810 or 800/421–2810 | fax 707/

937–1327 | info@stevenswood.com | www.stevenswood.com | 1 room, 9 suites | $125–$150, $150–$250 suites | AE, D, DC, MC, V.

★ **Whitegate Inn.** With a white-picket fence, a latticework gazebo, and a romantic garden, the Whitegate is picture-book Victorian. The wooden house with large bay windows, built in 1883, has 19th-century French and Victorian antiques, including the owner's collection of Civil War memorabilia. Three rooms have ocean views. It is one block west of Mendocino Headlands State Park. Complimentary full breakfast. No air-conditioning. | 499 Howard St. | 707/937–4892 or 800/531–7282 | www.whitegateinn.com | 7 rooms | $119–$229 | AE, D, DC, MC, V.

MENLO PARK

MAP 6, D8

(Nearby towns also listed: Mountain View, Palo Alto)

Once a sleepy suburb of San Francisco, Menlo Park (pop. 30,000) and its neighbor Palo Alto mark the northern reaches of the Silicon Valley boom. A wealthy bedroom community, Menlo Park offers sought-after real estate and easy access to neighboring SV towns. Drive around town and you'll notice all the dot-com advertising.

Information: Menlo Park Chamber of Commerce, | 1100 Merrill St., 94025 | 650/325–2818 | mpchamber@worldnet.att.net | www.mpchamber.com.

Attractions

Allied Arts Guild. Artisans practice their craft here in an early 19th century Spanish settlement. | 75 Arbor Rd. | 650/325–3259 | www.finofino.com/AlliedArtsGuild.html | Free | Mon.–Sat. 10–5.

Flood Park. This 21-acre retreat at the edge of town is known for large native oak and bay trees. There are baseball and softball fields, tennis, petanque, and volleyball courts, a playground, and picnic areas. | 215 Bay Rd. | 650/363–4022 | www.eparks.net | Free | Daily, 8AM to sunset.

Sunset Publishing Corporation. Sunset Magazine publishers have cultivated a garden with more than 300 varieties of annuals, perennials, ground cover, vines, and shrubs. | 80 Willow Rd. | 650/321–3600 | www.sunset.com | Free | Weekdays 9–4:30.

ON THE CALENDAR
JULY: *Connoisseur's Marketplace.* This annual weekend event, sponsored by the Menlo Park Chamber of Commerce, features more than 250 artists, a demo tent with local and celebrity chefs, a "kid zone", and a free concert Saturday night. | 650/325–2818 | www.mpchamber.com.

Dining

Fontana's Italian Restaurant. Italian. Fresh fish specials and homemade pastas are served in this dining room filled with Mediterranean beach photos, light brown carpets, light peach walls and white tablecloths. The open-air kitchen cooks up cappellini astice (angel hair pasta with lobster, mushrooms, and green onion in a light seafood cream sauce) and pollo girarrosto (rotisserie chicken with linguini). There's also outside dining on the patio. No smoking. | 1850 El Camino Real | 650/321–0610 | No lunch weekends | $12–$21 | AE, DC, MC, V.

Lodging

Menlo Park Inn. This 1961 two-story Colonial-style concrete building is in a residential area, 3 blocks north of the Chamber of Commerce. In-room data ports, refrigerators, cable TV, in-room VCRs. Business services. | 1315 El Camino Real | 650/326–7530 or 800/327–1315 | fax 650/328–7539 | 30 rooms | $95–$150 | AE, D, DC, MC, V.

Red Cottage Inn. This two-story motel off I–280 is 4 blocks north of antique stores and coffee shops, and less than 2 mi north of Stanford University and the Stanford Shopping Mall. All rooms are non-smoking, but each has a private patio. Complimentary Continental breakfast. In-room data ports, some kitchenettes, microwaves, refrigerators, cable TV, some in-room VCRs. Pool. No pets. No smoking. | 1704 El Camino Real | 650/326–9010 | fax 650/326–4002 | 27 rooms | $100–$145 | AE, D, DC, MC, V.

Stanford Park. This Cape Cod-style wooden building with a shingle finish and white trim was built in 1985. Rooms are furnished in French Provincial style. The hotel is in a commercial area, 1 block north of the Stanford Shopping Center and 2 mi north of Stanford University. Restaurant, bar, room service. In-room data ports, minibars, some refrigerators, cable TV. Pool. Hot tub. Exercise equipment. Business services. | 100 El Camino Real | 650/322–1234 or 800/368–2468 | fax 650/322–0975 | www.woodsidehotels.com | 163 rooms | $265–$375 | AE, D, DC, MC, V.

MERCED

MAP 3, F9

(Nearby towns also listed: Madera, Modesto, Oakhurst, Santa Nella)

This largely agricultural town of 65,000 stands along the western approach to Yosemite National Park via the scenic, all-season Route 140, or via Route 99 and Route 41 from Mariposa County. Yosemite is the main reason people come through here, so you won't find many tourist attractions in town. You can find many reasonably priced motels, though.

Information: **Merced Conference and Visitors Bureau.** | 690 W. 16th St., 95340 | 209/384–7092 or 800/446–5353 | mercedvb@yosemite-gateway.org | www.yosemite-gateway.org.

Attractions

Castle Air Museum. This small museum is devoted to the history and design of flying machines. | 5050 Santa Fe Rd. | 209/723–2178 | fax 209/723–0323 | www.elite.net/castle-air/ | $5 | Daily 9–5.

Grassland Wetlands. The Central Valley was once home to four million acres of wetlands, and much of the remaining five percent is in Merced County. The area is home to 550 species of plants, animals, and birds. You can hike through the wetlands on foot paths. Guided tours of the Grasslands Environmental Education Center are arranged by appointment. | Rte. 140 and Rte. 59 | 209/826–5188 | www.yosemite-gateway.org/attractions.htm | Free | Daily dawn to dusk.

Lake Yosemite Park. Roughly 5 ½ mi northeast of town, this 855-acred natural park has a 450-acre reservoir popular with anglers and wildlife enthusiasts. No camping. | 5714 N. Lake Rd. | 209/385–7426 | $4 per car | Daily 7:30AM–11PM.

Merced County Courthouse Museum. The Old County Courthouse, built in 1875, is now devoted to the history of the Merced area. The museum's exterior resembles the state capitol, which was also executed in Italian Renaissance style. | 21st and N St. | 209/723–2401 | www.mercedmuseum.org/ | Free | Wed.–Sun. 1–4.

Merced Multicultural Arts Center. This arts center is devoted to exploring and celebrating different cultures and art media. | 645 W. Main St. | 209/388–1090 | fax 209/388–1106 | www.arts.merced.ca.us/ | Weekdays 9–5, Sat. 10–2, also by appointment.

MAY–OCT.: *Farmer's Market.* Main Street becomes a pedestrian's paradise when it closes to traffic from 6 to 9 Thursday evenings. There's music, produce, and educational booths. | 209/383–6908.

JUNE: *West Coast Antique Fly-in.* Dozens of old planes buzz into Merced County over the course of the day, and pilots and spectators gather for food and music. | 209/384–3333.

JULY: *Merced County Fair.* The Merced County Fair welcomes locals from the surrounding rural communities. Highlights include livestock exhibits, food booths, and entertainment. | 209/384–3333.

NOV.: *Central California Band Review.* This is a one-day event, with a downtown parade and musical competitions. | 209/383–6908.

Dining

★ **DeAngelo's.** Italian. One of the most popular restaurants in Merced, DeAngelo's has two dining rooms and two banquet rooms. Each of the dining rooms has dark red booths and white linen tables set on deep red carpet. The chef specializes in fresh fish and seafood dishes using fresh, locally grown produce. The menu includes the "Trip around Italy" combo plate with ravioli, veal scaloppine, and shrimp scampi, or the cannelloni Lombardi (pasta filled with chicken and artichoke in a sherry cream sauce). And the delicious, crusty bread, from the Golden Sheath in Watsonville, is a meal in itself. No smoking. | 350 W. Main St. | 209/383–3020 | Closed Sun. in Jan.–late Nov. | $14–$25 | AE, D, DC, MC, V.

Main Street Cafe. Cafe. This bright downtown café dishes up soups, pizza, salads, sandwiches, pastries, ice cream, and espresso in upstairs and downstairs dining rooms. Both areas have bare wood tables; the downstairs room has a tiled floor and the upstairs is carpeted and has large surrounding windows. Sandwiches (like the chicken breast with pesto mayonnaise on Francesi bread) are served with side salads. | 460 W. Main St. | 209/725–1702 | No dinner | $4–$8 | AE, MC, V.

Lodging

Best Western Sequoia Inn. A pink two-story building with exterior corridors, built in 1964, the inn is in a residential area 1 mi from downtown. Room service. Pool. Pets allowed. | 1213 V St. | 209/723–3711 | fax 209/722–8551 | www.bestwestern.com | 98 rooms | $64–$74 | AE, D, DC, MC, V.

Merced Days Inn. This one-story motel is ½ mi from the Wild Life Museum and 80 mi from Yosemite National Park. Restaurant, bar, complimentary Continental breakfast. In-room data ports, microwaves, refrigerators, cable TV, in-room VCRs. Pool. Spa. Tennis. Laundry service. Pets allowed. | 1199 Motel Dr. | 209/722–2726 or 800/544–8313 | fax 209/722–7083 | www.daysinnmerced.com | 24 rooms, 1 suite | $68–$78, $98–$150 suite | AE, D, DC, MC, V.

MILL VALLEY

MAP 6, A3

(Nearby towns also listed: San Francisco, Sausalito, Tiburon)

Mill Valley (population 13,000) is a sleepy, affluent town nestled amid California redwoods on the eastern flank of Mt. Tamalpais, just north of San Francisco in Marin County. It's a good place to catch the flavor of Marin County life before you explore the coast, nearby parks, forests, and windswept beaches.

Information: Mill Valley Chamber of Commerce | 85 Throckmorton Ave., 94942 | 415/388–9700 | www.millvalley.org.

MILL VALLEY

INTRO
ATTRACTIONS
DINING
LODGING

Attractions

Marin Headlands. Consisting of several small but steep bluffs overlooking San Francisco Bay and the Pacific Ocean, this undeveloped 1,000 acres is part of the Golden Gate National Recreation Area, and runs from Sausalito to Tennessee Valley. During World War II, it served as the first line of protection of the Bay Area against invasion; you can still see remnants of the old Army bunkers. In the 1960s, portions of the headlands were rescued from development after the Nature Conservancy got behind local rescue efforts. Point Bonita lighthouse is stunningly sited, accessible via a ½-mi trail that runs through a tunnel and across wild moorlands. To reach the headlands from the Marin County side of the Golden Gate Bridge, exit the freeway at Alexander Avenue, turn left and go under the freeway, turn right onto Conzelman Road. About ⅓ mi farther you can find picnic tables and a view of ships. The Marin Headlands Visitor Center is in the historic Fort Barry Chapel, at the intersection of Field and Bunker Roads. The Visitor Center is approximately 3 mi from either entrance to the Marin Headlands. It's best to explore on foot; the farther north you go, the fewer people you see. | 415/331–1540 | Daily; visitor center 9–4:30; lighthouse Sat.–Mon. 12:30PM–3:30PM.

Muir Woods National Monument. One of the San Francisco Bay Area's last uncut stands of old-growth redwood was growing here in 1905 when Congressman William Kent and his wife, Elizabeth Thacher Kent, bought some 295 acres for $45,000 and donated the land to the government. Today this preserve about 12 mi northwest of San Francisco encompasses 560 acres and is part of the Golden Gate National Recreation Area. Some of the oldest redwoods on earth grow here (some more than 300 ft high, 15 ft around, and over 2,000 years old), along with Douglas fir, maple, tanbark oak, and bay laurel trees. Trails take you into the woods and to the semi-circular cove where you'll find striking Muir Beach, a quiet strip of sand littered with oddly shaped pieces of driftwood and punctuated with tidal pools; the views are dramatic. You can also hike in the Olema Valley, along wooded ridges and across grassy fields. Trails from Redwood Canyon connect with trails in Mt. Tamalpais State Park. Sandy Stinson Beach stretches beneath steep hills rising to Mount Tamalpais. To get there drive north on U.S. 101 to the Route 1 exit, then follow signs to the Panoramic Highway. | Muir Woods Rd. | 415/388–2595, 415/388–7059 | www.visitmuirwoods.com/forest.htm, www.nps.gov/muwo/home.htm | $2 | Daily 8–sunset.

Stinson Beach. Surfers brave the chilly waters and sunbathers soak up the natural beauty on this 3½-mi sweep of white sand, which curves across the mouth of Bolinas Bay and Bolinas Lagoon 6 mi north of Stinson Beach. The strand is immensely popular and life guards are on duty daily. A 51-acre park adjoins the beach. The adjacent town of the same name got its start in 1906, when earthquake refugees sought a safe haven; it's loaded with weather-beaten wooden houses and neighborly general stores, and there are surf shops where you can rent sea kayaks for scenic paddles. The incredible drive to get here from Muir Beach takes you past towering cliffs and jagged granite peaks. Call for a weather report before you pack your sun gear, because it's often dramatically different from that of San Francisco or inland. To get there, cross Golden Gate Bridge, take U.S. 101 north 3 mi to the Rte. 1 Stinson Beach exit | Daily | 415/868–0942, 415/868–1922 weather | www.stinsonbeachonline.com.

Mt. Tamalpais State Park. Mount Tam, as locals call it, has a long summit that dominates this park, rising about 2,600 ft from the ocean to its highest peak to the east and offering dazzling California vistas. On a clear day, it's possible to see snow-capped Sierra Nevada to the east, and Mount Diablo, Mount Hamilton, and other coastal mountains to the north and south. The name comes from the Spanish, who called the southern Miwok Indians Tamales, perhaps for their favorite food item. The 6,200-acre park is crisscrossed by 50 mi of hiking trails (which in turn connect with 200 mi on adjacent public lands); it's a favorite destination for San Francisco outdoors lovers. Every spring since 1913, a natural-stone amphitheater in the park has hosted performances of the Mountain Play. It's 13 mi north of the city via Route 1. | 801 Panoramic Hwy. | 415/388–2070 | www.mtia.net, www.cal-parks.ca.gov/north/marin/mtsp239.htm | $2 day fee | Daily 7AM–sunset.

There are 16 first-come-first-served camping sites at the park's **Pantoll Campground** with tables, grills, food lockers, and tent space. Toilets, drinking water, and telephones are nearby. | Camping $15 weekdays, $16 Fri.–Sat.

ON THE CALENDAR
SEPT.: *Mill Valley Fall Arts Festival.* At the foot of Mt. Tamalpais, this 2-day arts festival rests quietly in the shadow of thousands of redwoods. | 415/381–0525 | www.mvfaf.org | $5.

Dining
Buckeye Roadhouse. Barbecue. Have a drink in the bar while you wait for a table in the crowded, lodge-style dining room beneath numerous mounted moose and deer heads. Portions are large, and the smoky, spicy, pork sandwich and fries are popular. It's 1 ½ mi from the town center. | 15 Shoreline Hwy. | 415/331–2600 | $10–$28 | AE, MC, V.

Lucinda's Mexican Food To Go. Mexican. This take-out restaurant known for its "zookie burrito" is off U.S. 101 about 1 ½ mi from the center of town. Vegetarian fare is the specialty, though meat options are also available. | 930 Redwood Hwy. | 415/388–0754 | Closed weekends | $4–$12 | No credit cards.

Stinson Beach Grill. Contemporary. Seafood is the specialty at this restaurant one block from Stinson Beach, though it also serves pasta, sandwiches, and southwestern fare. Try jambalaya or the oyster sampler. Enjoy sunset jazz on an outdoor deck warmed by heat lamps and decorated with trees and flowers. There's homemade key lime pie and bread pudding for dessert. | 3465 Rte. 1, Stinson Beach | 415/868–2002 | $10–$30 | AE, MC, V.

Lodging
Acqua Hotel. This quietly elegant hotel 3 mi from downtown is on the waterfront, and rooms have private balconies with views of the San Francisco Bay and Mt. Tamalpais. There's tea every afternoon. Dining room, complimentary Continental breakfast, room service. In-room data ports, minibars, cable TV. Health club. Laundry service. Business services. No pets. No smoking. | 555 Redwood Hwy. | 415/380–0400 or 888/662–9555 | fax 415/380–9696 | www.acquahotel.com | 50 rooms | $155–$175 | AE, D, DC, MC, V.

Casa Del Mar Inn. Extensive landscaping and white stucco set a Mediterranean mood at this 1991 B&B in a residential area. A hiking trail from Mt. Tamalpais is right behind the property. Restaurant, complimentary Continental breakfast. No air-conditioning, some refrigerators, no room phones. No smoking. | 37 Belvedere, Stinson Beach | 415/868–2124 or 800/552–2124 | fax 415/868–2305 | inn@stinsonbeach.com | www.stinsonbeach.com | 6 rooms (4 with shower only) | $160–$270 | AE, MC, V.

Holiday Inn Express. Completely surrounded by the Golden Recreation Area, this Spanish-style stucco building is 3 mi west of downtown and 7 mi west of the Mt. Tamalpais State Park. Complimentary Continental breakfast. In-room data ports, cable TV, some in-room VCRs. Pool, wading pool. Video games. Business services. Free parking. | 160 Shoreline Hwy. | 415/332–5700 | fax 415/331–1859 | jperry9945@aol.com | www.hiexmv.com | 100 rooms | $110–$150 | AE, D, DC, MC, V.

Mill Valley Inn. This charming European-style stucco hostelry, built in 1994, looks like something out of Italy. A creek runs through the property, which has a grove of redwood trees and a sun terrace. Original art by North Bay craftspeople hangs on the guest room walls; some rooms also have fireplaces. In-room data ports, cable TV. Laundry facilities. Business services. No smoking. | 165 Throckmorton Ave. | 415/389–6608 or 800/595–2100 | fax 415/389–5051 | www.millvalleyinn.com | 25 rooms, 2 cottages | $160–$240 | AE, MC, V.

Mountain Home. This redwood building on the road to Mt. Tamalpais, built in 1912, has a cathedral ceiling and bay windows. All rooms have views of Mt. Tamalpais or San Francisco Bay. Restaurant, dining room, complimentary breakfast. No air-conditioning. Business services. | 810 Panoramic Hwy. | 415/381–9000 | fax 415/381–3615 | www.mtnhome-inn.com | 10 rooms | $159–$289 | AE, MC, V.

Tam Valley Bed and Breakfast. This private, one-room cottage has been in operation since 1995 and can house three. It has a queen-size bed, a sofa that folds out to a double bed, a separate bath, and a garden patio. Continental breakfast. Microwave, refrigerator, cable TV. No smoking. | 508 Shasta Way | 415/383–8716 | fax 415/383–0139 | 1 room | $135 | AE, DC, MC, V.

MISSION VIEJO

MAP 4, J15

(Nearby towns also listed: Corona del Mar, Dana Point, Irvine, Laguna Beach, San Clemente)

Mission Viejo is a sleepy south Orange County suburb (pop. 98,464) just north of I–5. Like many Orange County communities, it's characterized by a sea of red-tile roofed tract houses in expensive cookie-cutter subdivisions.

Information: **South Orange County Regional Chambers of Commerce** | 23166 Los Alisos #246, 92691 | 949/830–1100 | www.socchambers.com.

Attractions

Lake Mission Viejo. Boating and swimming are for members only, but you can walk, jog, or skate on the smooth, surrounding path. The lake is manmade and spans 124.6 acres on the outskirts of town. | 22555 Olympiad Rd. | 949/770–1313 | www.lakemissionviejo.org | Free | Daily 8–dusk.

ON THE CALENDAR

DEC.: *Four Corners.* Beginning the weekend after Thanksgiving, the holidays are celebrated with emblems of the season on all corners of the square. Santa Claus is at one corner, a nativity is across the street, and a huge Christmas tree looms over a Hannukah display. | 949/830–7066 | www.ci.mission-viejo.ca.us.

Dining

Mission Viejo Stuft Pizza and Brewing Company. Pizza. Locals flock to this restaurant across the street from Alicia Park, which has "stuft" pizza, pastas including chicken porcini and shrimp tequila, and homemade beer. There's plenty of action with two big-screen TVs and 29 little ones, all tuned to different games. Drink the California Gold, made on the premises. | 23641 Via Linda | 949/458–7883 | $5–$15 | AE, MC, V.

Lodging

Country Suites by Ayres. All rooms are European-style boutique suites at this motel in the center of town. Each room has a ceiling fan and a writing desk. Complimentary breakfast. No air conditioning, in-room data ports, cable TV. Pool. Spa. Exercise equipment. Laundry facilities. No pets. No smoking. | 28941 Los Alivos Blvd. | 949/455–2545 or 800/329–0227 | fax 949/455–9885 | www.countrysuites.com | 107 rooms | $85–$99 | AE, D, DC, MC, V.

Fairfield Inn by Marriott. On attractively landscaped 3 acres, this five-story Southwestern-style building with stucco finish was built in 1986. Off I–5 in a commercial area, it's next to two gas stations. Pool. Hot tub. Laundry service. Business services. | 26328 Oso Pkwy. | 949/582–7100 | fax 949/582–3287 | 147 rooms | $82–$100 | AE, D, DC, MC, V.

MODESTO

(Nearby towns also listed: Merced, Oakdale, Stockton)

Modesto (pop. 189,000) is a gateway to Yosemite. This frontier town, deep in the heart of fruit orchard country, was founded in 1870 to serve the Central Pacific Railroad. It was originally named Ralston, after a banking baron, but legend has it that he modestly declined the offer—thus "Modesto." "Star Wars" creator George Lucas immortalized Modesto with a nostalgic love letter to his hometown called "American Graffiti." The tree-lined city is also well known as the site of the annual Modesto Invitational Track Meet and Relays.

Information: **Modesto Convention and Visitors Bureau.** | 1114 J St., Box 844, 95353 | 209/571–6480 or 800/266–4282 | mcvb@modestocvb.org | www.modestocvb.org.

Attractions

John Thurman Stadium. Cheer on the Modesto A's, an affiliate of the Oakland A's, at the oldest professional sports franchise in the western United States. | 501 Neece Dr. | 209/572–HITS or 209/529–7122 | www.modestoatheletics.com | $4–$7 | Apr.–Aug.

McHenry Mansion. A wheat farmer and banker built the 1883 McHenry Mansion, sole surviving original Victorian home. The Italianate-style mansion has been decorated to reflect Modesto life in the late 19th century. Oaks, elms, magnolias, redwoods, and palms shade the grounds. | 15th and I Sts. | 209/577–5341 | Free | Sun.–Thurs. 1–4, Fri. noon–3.

McHenry Museum. This museum is actually a jumbled repository of early Modesto and Stanislaus County memorabilia, including re-creations of an old-time barbershop, a doctor's office, a blacksmith's shop, and a general store—the latter stocked with goods from hair crimpers to corsets. | 1402 I St. | 209/577–5366 | Free | Tues.–Sun. noon–4.

ON THE CALENDAR

JUNE: *American Graffiti Classic Car Show.* George Lucas, eat your heart out. Many of these babies are in mint condition. There are usually more than 450 vehicles for sale or display here. | 888/746–9763.

OCT.: *International Festival.* This food-fest features eats from across the nation and around the globe. | 209/558–8628.

OCT.: *Riverbank Cheese and Wine Exposition.* The autumnal outdoors serves as a backdrop for this fair, with cheese and wine from Central California agricultural regions. | 209/869–4541.

Dining

Dewz. Contemporary. The food is the most important interior decoration at this 20-table restaurant ½ mi from the center of town. "California Fresh Cuisine" is defined here as rack of lamb, prime rib, chicken, and vegetarian selections. | 1101 I St. | 209/549–1101 | Breakfast also available | $11–$24 | AE, MC, V.

Hazel's Elegant Dining. Continental. This restaurant has served Modesto since 1985. Your seven-course dinner centers around a choice of more than 40 entrées, including veal, rack of lamb, Australian lobster, and duck à l'orange. The two front rooms seat more than 100, while low ceilings live up to the town's "modest" reputation. | 431 12th St. | 209/578–3463 | www.hazelsmodesto.com | Reservations essential | No lunch Sat., closed Sun.–Mon. | $17–$44 | AE, MC, V.

Lodging

Courtyard by Marriott Modesto. Surrounded by 5 acres of landscaped grounds, this 1980 hotel is made of brick with a stucco finish. It's within walking distance of several popular chain restaurants and only 3 mi from downtown. Restaurant, room service. Some refrigerators, cable TV. Pool. Hot tub. | 1720 Sisk Rd. | 209/577–3825 | fax 209/577–1717 | www.mariott.com | 126 rooms | $129–$199 | AE, D, DC, MC, V.

Doubletree Hotel Modesto. This 14-story luxury hotel 4 blocks south of downtown is just off Rte. 99 and less than 1 mi from St. Stans Brewery and factory outlet stores. There's an espresso cart in the lobby. 2 Restaurants, 1 bar [with entertainment], room service. In-room data ports, some refrigerators, cable TV, some in-room VCRs. Pool. Beauty salon, hot tub, spa, sauna. Exercise equipment. Shops. Laundry service. Business services, airport shuttle, free parking. Pets allowed. | 1150 9th St. | 209/526–6000 | fax 209/526–6096 | www.hilton.com | 258 rooms, 6 suites | $114–$158, $160–$250 suites | AE, D, DC, MC, V.

Holiday Inn. This two-story light brown concrete building, built in 1975, has an enclosed pool and carefully landscaped public areas. Downtown is 3 mi north. Restaurant, bar [with entertainment], room service. Cable TV. 2 pools (1 indoor). Exercise equipment. Video games. Playground. Laundry facilities. | 1612 Sisk Rd. | 209/521–1612 | fax 209/527–5074 | 186 rooms | $95–$105 | AE, D, DC, MC, V.

Vagabond Inn. This is a 1974 stucco building with a Spanish tiled roof, 2 mi north of downtown. A garden is on the property. Restaurant, complimentary Continental breakfast. Cable TV. Pool. Business services. | 1525 McHenry Ave. | 209/521–6340 | fax 209/575–2015 | 99 rooms | $75–$84 | AE, D, DC, MC, V.

Vineyard View Bed and Breakfast. The owners here invite you to their quiet, country home filled with patchwork quilts. The inn sits on a bluff 4 mi west of town and overlooks 72 acres of vineyard. Complimentary breakfast. Room phones, TV in common area. Pets allowed. No smoking. | 2839 Michigan Ave. | 209/523–9009 | 3 rooms (with shared bath) | $70–$80 | AE, D, MC, V.

MOJAVE NATIONAL PRESERVE

MAP 4, M13

(Nearby town also listed: Needles)

The Desert Preservation Act created the 1.4 million acre Mojave National Preserve in the heart of the Mojave Desert. Given the protected desert climate, more than 300 species of animals are found throughout the preserve.

There are no restaurants in the Mojave National Preserve. You can get water at the campsite listed below, but park rangers strongly recommend that all travelers carry at least one gallon of water per person, per day into the preserve. There are limited general supply stores throughout the preserve.

Information: **Mojave National Preserve** | 72157 Baker Blvd., Baker, 92309 | 760/733–4040 | www.nps.gov/moja.

Lodging

Mojave National Preserve Campgrounds. There are no motel accommodations available within the preserve. Camping is permitted for backpackers throughout the preserve, and there are three developed compounds for camping. Sites in these compounds are on a first-come first-served basis. Campsites include a picnic table and a fire ring. | Black Canyon Rd., 5.2 mi south of the Hole-in-the-Wall Ranger's Station, on the east side of Black Canyon Road | 760/733–4040 | www.desertusa.com/mnp/mnp_camp.html | $20.

MONTEREY

(Nearby towns also listed: Carmel, Carmel Valley, Hollister, Pacific Grove, Pebble Beach)

Monterey (population 32,000) occupies a distinctive position in California history. During the Spanish and Mexican periods from 1542 through 1846 Monterey was the military and ecclesiastical capital of Alta California. First claimed for Spain by Juan Rodrigues Cabrillo, Monterey was the site of the first presidio in California and served as home and administrative headquarters for Father Junipero Serra as he oversaw the founding of the California missions.

Later several Mexican governors called Monterey home as did writers and artists such as Robert Louis Stevenson, Jack London, Henry Miller, and photographer Ansel Adams. By mid-1840s Monterey had evolved into a Yankee-dominated bustling fishing port with a whaling industry that flourished until the early 1880s. While Monterey still belonged to Mexico, Commodore John Sloat raised the Stars and Stripes over the Custom House and claimed the city of Monterey. California became a state in 1850, after gold was discovered. Monterey served as the first capital.

By the 1880s, tourism had replaced whaling as a major industry in the area, with the opening of the elegant Del Monte Hotel; the golf course added to the resort in 1897 was the first west of the Mississippi.

Without the whales to hunt, fishermen began harvesting the sardines, which schooled in the bay. "Cannery Row" as it became known, was then lined with sardine-processing plants – and with the human drama captured by writer John Steinbeck, who called the area "a poem, a stink, a grating noise, a quality of light, a tone, a habit, a nostalgia, a dream." The sardines disappeared mysteriously in the 1940s. The canning sheds are gone, but memories remain. The working waterfront has been largely replaced by tourist shops and eateries. In recent years, retail development has caused many arguments between developers and environmentalists. For a glimpse of the stakes in this battle, take a walk (or rent a bike) along the 18-mi trail that leads past the wharf and some of the most scenic points along the state's coast.

Information: Monterey Peninsula Visitors and Convention Bureau | 380 Alvarado St., 93942 | 408/649–1770 | www.monterey.com.

Attractions

Dennis the Menace Playground. Since it opened in 1956, cartoonist Hank Ketchum has worked on three renovations of this colorful locale for running, climbing, and generally making mischief. There's a lake with paddle boats and a retired Southern Pacific steam locomotive. | Pearl St. | 831/646–3866 | Free | Daily 10AM to dusk.

Fisherman's Wharf. Once the hub of an active fishing industry, the wharf has evolved into a tourist stop filled with restaurants and souvenir shops. It's an inviting destination for an afternoon's meandering, especially for families, and the place to charter a boat or join a whale-watching tour. On Delmonte St. behind Custom House Plaza. | www.montereywharf.com | Free | Daily.

La Mirada. This 19th-century home is filled with Asian and European antiques. | 720 Via Mirada | 831/372–3689 | www.mtryart.org | $5 | Wed.–Sat. 11–5, Sun. 1–4.

Maritime Museum of Monterey and Stanton Center Museum. A ship's bell, scrimshaw, ship models, sextons, and other articles from whaling and sailing ships illustrate the impact of Spanish explorers, the U.S. Navy, and the fishing trade in Monterey's past. | #5 Custom House Plaza | 831/373–2469 | $5 | Tues.–Sun. 11–5.

★ **Monterey Bay Aquarium.** This has become one of the major attractions along the California coast. Interactive exhibits and special habitats offer a look at unusual species, including the phosphorescent lanternfish, pink mushroom coral, green-eyed catsharks, and ratfish; you'll also see a three-story kelp forest and many types of fish and sea mammals. In the "Mysteries of the Deep" exhibit, you learn about a massive underwater gorge, 2 mi deep and as large as the Grand Canyon, just off the Monterey Coast. In the Aquarium's theater, you can see live video from a robot submarine exploring the canyon. | 886 Cannery Row | 831/648–4888 | www.mbayaq.org | $15.95 | Memorial Day–Labor Day, daily 9:30–6; Labor Day–Memorial Day, daily 10–6.

Monterey Museum of Art. Works by Ansel Adams, Edward Weston, and other Californians stand out in this fine collection of largely contemporary art. The museum also displays folk art from around the world. Changing exhibitions. | 559 Pacific St. and 720 Via Mirada | 831/372–5477 or 831/372–3689 | www.montereyart.org | $3 | Wed.–Sat. 11–5, Sun. 1–4.

Monterey State Beach. High dunes back this narrow, sandy beach. It's unsafe for swimming, but great for long walks and jogging. | 2211 Garden Rd. | 831/384–7695 | www.mbay.net/~nbeaches | Free | Daily 9 to sunset.

★ **Monterey State Historic Park.** This 7-acre park includes most of Monterey's historic sites. The Visitor Center is at 5 Custom House Plaza; pick up a guide to the 2-mi Path of History or see a film about the city's past. Admission includes entrance to several restored buildings, each a mini-museum. | #20 Custom House Plaza | 831/649–7118 | www.mbay.net | $5 | Memorial Day–Labor Day, daily 10–5; Labor Day–Memorial Day, daily 10–4.

Casa Soberanes is a well-preserved house built in 1842, filled with period antiques. | 336 Pacific St. | 831/649–7118 | www.mbay.net | $5; free with park admission | Tours Mon.–Sun. 10–4.

Back in 1849, California's first state Constitution was drafted in the building that now houses the **Colton Hall Museum.** Today, the museum mounts exhibits of artifacts and memorabilia tracing Monterey's history. A jail built in 1854 is next door. | Pacific St. at Jefferson | 831/646–5640 | www.mbay.net | Free | Daily 10–noon and 1–5.

The **Cooper-Molera House** is the restored home of a Yankee captain who married into the family of General Mariano Vallejo, a California rancher who owned great chunks of the territory. The estate includes several other adobe buildings and a period garden. Tours are given throughout the day; call ahead for specific tour times. | 525 Polk St. | 831/649–7111 | www.mbay.net | $5; free with park admission | Daily 10–4.

The **Custom House and Garden** is the oldest government building in California. Inside there's a display of trade goods from the 1840s. | 925 Front St. | 831/649–7118 | www.mbay.net | Free | June–Aug., daily 10–5; Sept.–May, daily 10–4.

Combining Mexican Colonial and New England architectural features, the two-story **Larkin House** served as the American Consulate from 1843 to 1846. Antiques—many brought from New Hampshire by the Larkin family—fill the rooms. Tours are offered periodically throughout the day; call ahead for specific tour times. | 510 Calle Principal | 831/649–7118 | www.mbay.net | $5; free with park admission.

Formerly a hotel and saloon, the **Pacific House** displays Gold Rush relics, historical photographs, a costume gallery, and Native American artifacts. | Custom House Plaza | 831/649–7118 | www.mbay.net | Free | Daily 10–5.

My Museum (Monterey County Youth Museum). A kids-oriented museum with changing exhibits, it encourages children to explore theater, sound, and science via a "Creation Station," communication station, and more. | 601 Wave St. | 831/649–6444 | www.mymuseum.org | $5.50 | Mon., Tues., Thurs.–Sat. 10–5, Sun. noon–5.

"Path of History" Tour. This is a 2-mi self-guided tour leading from the Stanton Center at Custom House Plaza to downtown historic sites. You can start with a 14-min film shown three times an hour at the State Park History Theatre, then pick up a map and follow the round gold tiles set in the sidewalk to points of interest. | 831/649–7118 | Free | Daily 10–4.

Robert Louis Stevenson House. In the fall of 1879, the author of *Treasure Island* stayed briefly in a small room in this old French hotel. It's furnished with antiques donated by the family estate. | 530 Houston St. | 831/757–8085 | $5 | Tours daily 10–4.

ON THE CALENDAR
APR.: *Adobe Tour.* Once a year, historic adobe homes open to the public for a tour sponsored by the Monterey History and Art Association. | 831/372–2608.
APR.: *Monterey Wine Festival.* "America's Original Wine Festival" celebrates the small yet fine vineyards of the surrounding region. Tastings, lectures, and dinners are held at restaurants, vineyards, and places of interest, such as the Monterey Bay Aquarium. | 831/656–WINE or 800/656–4282.
AUG.: *Monterey Historic Automobile Races.* Restored classic cars—Bugattis, Ferraris, Rolls Royces— are shown off on a grand concourse, then race, sometimes at sedate speeds. | 831/372–1000.
SEPT.: *Monterey Jazz Festival.* The longest-running jazz festival in the world has hosted the legends of blues, bebop, swing, and acid jazz. In addition to the main stage, there's continuous music on four other stages, as well as film screenings, panel discussions, and a noted high-school band competition. | Monterey Fairgrounds | 925/275–9255 or 800/373–3366 (outside CA) | www.montereyjazzfestival.org.

Dining

Abalonetti Seafood Trattoria. Seafood. This relaxed Italian trattoria offers views of the harbor and a menu full of the fruits of the sea, including squid in many forms: deep-fried, sautéed, in pasta sauce, and antipasto. There's an exhibition kitchen where you can watch the chefs at work. Open-air dining is available. | 57 Fisherman's Wharf | 831/373–1851 | $10–$20 | AE, D, DC, MC, V.

Billy Quon's. Pan-Asian. Blond wood, exposed light-rigging, and plenty of windows make the inside of Billy's look like a cross between a dining room and a dojo. There's a martini bar along one side of the main dining area that serves a number of creative interpretations of the classic beverage. The menu here is creative as well, offering appetizers like "sand dabs"—chunks of boneless, panko-crusted chicken sided with wasabi aioli and tartar sauces—and dinner entrées like Pacific rim salmon and fire-seared rotisserie duck. For dessert, try the arctic mini hot fudge sundaes, served in a red-laquered wok full of smoking dry ice. | 1 Harris Ct. at Ryan Beach | 831/647–0390 | $9–$20 | AE, D, MC, V.

Cafe Abrego. California. This downtown café, known for steaks, seafood, pasta, and sweet potato fries, is surrounded by gardens, fountains, and a fully-stocked koi pond. In the dining area, a yellow and blue color scheme and cathedral ceiling add to the French country feeling. You can eat outside on the adjacent tiled patio. Live jazz. Sunday brunch, early-bird suppers. | 565 Abrego St. | 831/375–3750 | $10–$25 | AE, DC, MC, V.

Casa Cafe and Bar. American. Casa Cafe, whose chef, David Tyler, was named 1998 Chef of the Year in Monterey Bay, serves traditional American food. Lunches include burgers and fries, soups, and sandwiches. Dinners range from prime rib or fish and chips, to delicacies such as coconut prawns or filet mingon. | 700 Munra Ave. | 831/375–2411 | fax 831/375–1365 | No lunch weekends | $10–$20 | AE, D, MC, V.

Cafe Fina. Italian. Just a mile north of downtown, this small, friendly restaurant on the wharf has views of the bay. The dining room has white linen tablecloths and a white and beige color scheme. Consider ordering the pasta fina (baby shrimp with pasta) or the fresh Monterey Bay mesquite salmon. No smoking. | 47 Fisherman's Wharf | 831/372–5200 | $15–$25 | AE, D, DC, MC, V.

Chart House. Seafood. The Chart House offers hearty fare and a bay view. The dining room has a dark wood interior with wood tables and booths. The halibut macadamia and the prime rib are menu standouts, and there's a large salad bar. It's in a commercial area opposite Cannery Row, 4 mi west of downtown. | 444 Cannery Row | 831/372–3362 | No lunch | $15–$30 | AE, D, DC, MC, V.

Cibo. Italian. Downtown, right across from Fisherman's Wharf, Cibo has two dining areas, both furnished with maroon carpets, red terra cotta walls adorned with antique paintings, vases and sculptures, white linen tablecloths, and wooden chairs. The Sicilian recipes, including lasagna Scalone with sausage, vegetables and halibut, are prepared with locally grown produce. Entertainment nightly from 9PM. | 301 Alvarado St. | 831/649–8151 | No lunch | $13–$23 | AE, DC, MC, V.

Domenico's. Seafood. This seafood house overlooks the harbor, less than ½ mi from downtown. Built in 1950, it has a nautical theme— blue and white tables, gray and white tiled floor and wire mesh fish on the walls. You can choose booth or table seating. On the menu: mesquite-grilled meats, fish and shellfish, all prepared Italian style. Kids' menu. | 50 Fisherman's Wharf | 831/372–3655 | $18–$60 | AE, D, DC, MC, V.

Duck Club. Contemporary. In the Mediterranean-style Monterey Plaza Hotel, this Monterey institution is a clubby, wood-panelled restaurant with white linen tablecloths and big windows with views of Monterey Bay. The menu is full of dishes made from fresh local ingredients. Try the wood-roasted duck or the sugarcane-cured scallops. Pianist Fri., Sat. Kids' menu. No smoking. | 400 Cannery Row | 831/646–1706 | Breakfast also available. No lunch | $20–$30 | AE, MC, V.

Fresh Cream. French. All five of the oak-trimmed dining rooms here are wallpapered in sea-foam green or dove-gray and have superb harbor views. Dark green carpeting, accented by light gray linen tablecloths, complete the elegant style, reminiscent of the French seaside. The menu changes weekly, but the rack of lamb or the Grand Marnier soufflé are worth trying. You can eat outside in summer. The restaurant is across the harbor from Fisherman's Wharf and 3 blocks north of downtown. | 99 Pacific St. | 831/375–9798 | Reservations essential | No lunch | $26–$36 | AE, D, DC, MC, V.

Montrio. Mediterranean. In this bistro housed in a high-ceilinged former firehouse, brick and wrought iron keep company with wooden chairs and white linen tablecloths and locals mix with tourists. Try the grilled Portobello mushroom with polenta or rotisserie chicken with garlic mashed potatoes. Kids' menu. No smoking. Downtown, next to the Monterey Marriott, 1 mi south of the Aquarium. | 414 Calle Principal | 831/648–8880 | $10–$20 | AE, D, MC, V.

Paradiso Trattoria. Mediterranean. With its large bay windows and ocean views, peach linen tablecloths and ceramics-decorated walls, this is a cheerful, casual spot. You can sample the pizza prepared in the gas-burning pizza oven, the raw bar, or the crab rissotto or fresh lobster. It's downtown across from a shopping mall, next to the Spindrift Inn. | 654 Cannery Row | 831/375–4155 | www.eatfree.com/paradiso/barlg.htm | $10–50 | AE, D, MC, V.

Rappa's. Italian. This casual restaurant has glass windows offering a panoramic view of the water. Vintage photos add a sense of place. Try the cioppino or the home-made ravioli. Downtown, 1 mi east of Cannery Row. | 101 Fisherman's Wharf | 831/372–7562 | fax 831/372–1932 | $10–$20 | AE, D, DC, MC, V.

Sandbar and Grill. Seafood. Sweeping views of the bay distinguish this casual small restaurant, on the water, less than 1 mi west of downtown, where at one table, you can also see the waterfront. Inside, there's blue everywhere, and pictures of Broadway plays hang on the walls. The Sandbar is primarily known for pasta, steak, and ribs. There's a pianist in the bar Friday and Saturday. Sunday brunch. | 9 Fisherman's Wharf, #2 | 831/373–2818 | $10–$20 | AE, D, DC, MC, V.

Sardine Factory. Seafood. One of Monterey's best known restaurants, the Sardine Factory is often packed with tourists. There are four dining rooms, each with a distinct mood and theme. The Captain's room is done in early 19th-century style with gilt wallpaper, scrollwork, and lots of fringed velveteen. Menu items range from prime cuts of beef to the freshest of seafood, but the restaurant's signature offering is abalone bisque, which has been served at two Presidential inauguration dinners. | 701 Wave St. | 831/373–3775 | www.sardinefactory.com/~sardine2 | No lunch | $15–$25 | AE, D, DC, MC, V.

Sly McFly's. American. Sly McFly's serves American food in a jazz and blues club atmosphere. Live entertainment changes weekly, and was voted Best Blues Club 2000 by Coast Magazine. Sly's has a happy hour and a full menu, with items such as prime rib, salads, and grilled salmon. | 700-A Cannery Row | 831/649–8050 | fax 831/372–0321 | www.restauranteur.com/slymcflys/ | Daily, 11AM–2AM | $15–$20 | M, V.

★ **Stokes Adobe.** Mediterranean. The kitchen in this 1833 adobe building serves contemporary cuisine from Italy and Spain. The five separate dining rooms all have old California furnishings, white tablecloths and tile floors. You can eat by the fire or on a terrace. Try the T-bone lamb or lavender-infused pork chops. No smoking. Downtown behind the Monterey Library, 1½ mi south of the Aquarium. | 500 Hartnell St. | 831/373–1110 | $12–$25 | AE, MC, V.

Tarpy's Roadhouse. American. In lush gardens with a pond and trailing ivy, this is the spot where an unfortunate local, Mr. Tarpy, was hanged for the murder of a neighbor in the late 1870s. The stone building has four dining areas; one with a fireplace and full of white linen and large windows. Gourmet meatloaf and lobster tails highlight the menu. Open-air dining available in the courtyard. Sunday brunch. Near Monterey Airport, 1½ mi east of downtown. | 2999 Monterey-Salinas Rte. 68 | 831/647–1444 | www.tarpys.com | $7–$32 | AE, D, MC, V.

★ **Whaling Station.** Seafood. This casual, lively restaurant with multi-colored tiled floors, European vintage posters, and white linen tablecloths recalls a manor in Tuscany. Mesquite scents the air and both prime steak and seafood are on the menu. Kids' menu. No smoking. | 763 Wave St. | 831/373–3778 | No lunch | $20–$30 | AE, D, DC, MC, V.

Lodging

Bay Park. In this 1917 hotel among the trees on Carmel Hill, rooms have bay views, a light beige and ivory color scheme, and plump chairs that make things cozy. It's 1 mi north of Pebble Beach. Restaurant, bar [with entertainment], room service. Refrigerators, cable TV. Pool. Hot tub. Business services. Pets allowed (fee). | 1425 Munras Ave. | 831/649–1020 or 800/338–3564 | fax 831/373–4258 | baypark@montereybay.com | 80 rooms | $105–$200 | AE, D, DC, MC, V.

Best Western Monterey Inn. A garden accents this stucco 1984 chain hotel with spacious rooms; a few have ocean views. One-half mile west of Fisherman's Wharf. No air-conditioning. Refrigerators. Cable TV. Pool. Hot tub. No smoking. | 825 Abrego St. | 831/373–5345 or 800/528–1234 | fax 831/373–3246 | 80 rooms | $119–$219 | AE, D, DC, MC, V.

Best Western Victorian Inn. All rooms have Victorian furnishings and gas fireplaces in two Victorian-style buildings (one dates from 1907, the other went up in 1986). A courtyard and garden are on the property. It's near Cannery Row, 2 blocks from the bay, 5 blocks east of the Monterey Bay Aquarium. Complimentary Continental breakfast. Refrigerators, cable TV, in-room VCRs (and movies). Hot tub. Business services. Pets allowed (fee). | 487 Foam St. | 831/373–8000 or 800/232–4141 | fax 831/373–4815 | 68 rooms | $249–$500 | AE, D, DC, MC, V.

Cannery Row Inn. This stucco motel built in 1984 is in a commercial area 4 blocks from Fisherman's Wharf and within easy walking distance to the aquarium. Complimentary Continental breakfast. No air-conditioning, refrigerators, some in-room hot tubs, cable TV. Hot tub. Business services. | 200 Foam St. | 831/649–8580 or 800/876–8580 | fax 831/649–2566 | 32 rooms | $109–$399 | AE, D, MC, V.

Casa Munras Garden Hotel. Casa Munras, in Old Monterey, was built around the original estate of Don Estaban Munras. The hotel complex has 11 buildings on 4½ acres, surrounded by gardens. Restaurant, bar. Cable TV. Pool. Laundry service. | 700 Munras Ave. | 800/222–2446, in CA; 800/222–2558, outside CA | fax 831/375–1365 | infor@casamunras-hotel.com | 166 rooms | $129–$189 | AE, D, DC, MC, V.

Colton Inn. Spacious rooms, tile floors, and Mission-style furnishings set the tone in this wood-and-stucco hotel in a commercial area 2 mi from downtown and other attractions. Fisherman's Wharf is 1/4 mi south. No air-conditioning, some kitchenettes, refrigerators, microwaves, some in-room hot tubs, cable TV, in-room VCRs. Sauna. Business services. | 707 Pacific | 831/649–6500 or 800/848–7007 | fax 831/373–6987 | 50 rooms | $110–$310, $209–$329 suites | AE, D, MC, V.

Comfort Inn. This Comfort Inn is 2 mi from the beach, 3 mi from Fisherman's Wharf, and is surrounded by serene flower gardens. Complimentary Continental breakfast. In-room data ports, cable TV. Pool. Beach. | 1252 Munras Ave. | 831/372–2908 | fax 831/372–7608 | 36 rooms | $59–$94 | AE, D, DC, V.

Cypress Gardens Inn. The modern facade of this 1962 stucco building belies its old-fashioned interiors, done up with floral wallpaper, brass beds, and dark wood furniture. On landscaped grounds in a commercial area 1/2 mi south of downtown. Complimentary Continental breakfast. No air-conditioning, some kitchenettes, refrigerators, cable TV. Pool. Hot tub. Business services. Pets allowed. No smoking. | 1150 Munras Ave. | 831/373–2761 | 46 rooms, 1 suite | $99–$199, $269 suite | AE, D, MC, V.

Cypress Tree Inn. Tucked away on a quiet street 1 1/2 mi east of downtown, this 2-acre property built in 1974 consists of five stucco buildings. The gardens are a bonus, and there are fireplaces in suites. No air-conditioning, some kitchenettes, refrigerators, some in-room hot tubs, cable TV. Hot tub, sauna. Laundry facilities. Business services. | 2227 N. Fremont St. | 831/372–7586 | info@cypresstreeinn.com | www.cypresstreeinn.com | 55 rooms, 12 suites, 6 cottages | $68–$149, $140–$229 suites, $59–$139 cottages | AE, D, DC, MC, V.

Doubletree. If you leave this seven-story downtown hotel through the back door, you'll stumble right onto the Maritime Museum. Also nearby are Fisherman's Wharf and downtown Monterey's restaurants and nightspots. 2 restaurants, bar. No air-conditioning, cable TV. Pool. Hot tub. Video games. Business services, parking (fee). | 2 Portola Plaza | 831/649–4511 | fax 831/372–0620 | www.doubletreemonterey.com | 375 rooms, 10 suites | $165–$245 | AE, D, DC, MC, V.

El Adobe Inn. This stucco-faced building is between the Delmonte Shopping Center and downtown. Complimentary Continental breakfast. No air-conditioning, cable TV. Hot tub. Business services. Pets allowed. | 936 Munras Ave. | 831/372–5409 or 800/433–4732 | fax 831/375–7236 | www.montereyrooms.com | 26 rooms | $99–$169 | AE, D, MC, V.

Embassy Suites. This Mediterranean-style 1995 pink concrete building has a 12-story atrium. It's in a commercial area 3 mi south of downtown, 2 blocks from the beach and the aquarium. Restaurant, bar, complimentary breakfast. Microwaves, refrigerators, cable TV. Indoor pool. Hot tub, sauna. Video games. | 1441 Canyon Del Rey, Seaside | 831/393–1115 | fax 831/393–1113 | 225 suites | $189–$289 suites | AE, D, DC, MC, V.

Holiday Inn Express. This wood and concrete hotel built in 1987 is decorated to look like a country inn. It's downtown, one block from the bay and 3 blocks north of the Aquarium. Complimentary Continental breakfast. No air-conditioning, cable TV. Hot tub. Business services. | 443 Wave St. | 831/372–1800 or 800/HOLIDAY | fax 831/372–1969 | 43 rooms | $169–$299 | AE, D, DC, MC, V.

Hotel Pacific. In this Spanish-style adobe built in 1985 rooms are decorated with original artwork and antiques. There's a fireplace in the lobby and fountains in the gardens outside. It's downtown 1 mi from the Monterey Aquarium. Complimentary Continental breakfast. Refrigerators, cable TV, in-room VCRs (and movies). Business services. | 300 Pacific St. | 831/373–5700 or 800/554–5542 | fax 831/373–6921 | www.hotelpacific.com | 105 suites | $209–$469 suites | AE, D, DC, MC, V.

Hyatt Regency–Monterey Resort and Conference Center. On 23 landscaped acres in a residential area 2 mi east of downtown, this resort was designed in the early 1950s as a retreat for working executives. There are 10 buildings. Some suites have fireplaces, and many overlook the golf course. Restaurant, bar. No air-conditioning, microwaves, cable TV. 3 Pools. Beauty salon, hot tub. 18-hole golf course, putting green, 6 tennis courts. Exercise equipment, bicycles. Video games. Business services. | 1 Golf Course Dr. | 831/372–1234 or 800/824–2196 | fax 831/375–3960 | hyattmon@oldshift.com | www.montereyhyatt.com | 555 rooms, 20 suites | $175–$235, $250–$355 suites | AE, D, DC, MC, V.

Jabberwock. In a residential area 4 blocks from Cannery Row, this Craftsman-style brick B&B was built in 1911. There's a waterfall in the 1/2-acre garden, and some rooms have an ocean view. Complimentary breakfast. No air-conditioning, some in-room hot tubs, no room phones. Library. Business services. | 598 Laine St. | 831/372–4777 or 888/428–7253 | fax 831/655–2946 | www.jabberwockinn.com | 7 rooms (2 with shared bath) | $115–$225 | MC, V.

Mariposa Inn. These European-style wooden split-level townhouses built in 1982 have a stucco finish. Rooms are arranged around a large swimming pool. It's across from the Delmonte Shopping Mall, 2 mi south of downtown, Cannery Row, and the Wharf. Complimentary Continental breakfast. No air-conditioning, some refrigerators, some in-room hot tubs, cable TV. Pool. Hot tub. Business services. | 1386 Munras Ave. | 831/649–1414 or 800/824–2295 | fax 831/649–5308 | 30 rooms, 20 suites in 12 buildings | $109–$179, $129–$229 suites | AE, D, DC, MC, V.

Marriott. A 10-story pink concrete building built in 1983, this is in the heart of downtown Monterey, right across the street from Fisherman's Wharf and about 1 mi from the aquarium. 2 restaurants. Cable TV. Pool. Beauty salon. Exercise equipment. Business services. | 350 Calle Principal | 831/649–4234 | fax 831/372–2968 | www.marriott.com | 341 rooms, 22 suites | $209–$279, $300–$1000 suites | AE, D, DC, MC, V.

Merritt House Inn. One of the buildings in this California-style adobe inn dates back to 1830; most rooms were added in 1976. Each has a fireplace and hand-painted brass beds, and there's a private garden to stroll through. The inn is in a commercial area, 2 blocks east of downtown. Complimentary Continental breakfast. Refrigerators, cable TV. Business services. No smoking. | 386 Pacific St. | 831/646–9686 or 800/541–5599 | fax 831/646–5392 | www.merritthouse.com | 22 rooms, 3 suites | $155–$187, $179–$259 suites | AE, D, DC, MC, V.

Monterey Bay Inn. There are close-up views of the bay from most rooms in this 1985 concrete property. Three units have gas fireplaces. The hotel is across from San Carlo's Beach and Park, 1 mi west of downtown in a commercial area. Complimentary Continental breakfast. No air-conditioning, minibars, cable TV, in-room VCRs (and movies). Hot tubs. Exercise equipment. Business services. | 242 Cannery Row | 831/373–6242 or 800/424–6242 | fax 831/373–7603 | www.montereybayinn.com | 47 rooms | $199–$339 | AE, D, DC, MC, V.

Monterey Hilton. This hotel is in a beautiful garden setting and each guest room has a private patio with a view of the pool or hillside. It's 1 mi from downtown and Fisherman's Wharf, and only 3 mi from Cannery Row and the Monterey Bay Aquarium. Pebble Beach is just minutes away. Restaurant, room service. In-room data ports, cable TV. Pool. Hot tub. Putting green, tennis. Exercise room. Laundry service. | 1000 Aguajito Rd. | 831/373–6141 | fax 831/655–8606 | www.hilton.com/hotels | 204 rooms | $79–$279 | AE, D, DC, MC, V.

Monterey Hotel. The four-story facade of this 1904 building is a Victorian fantasy, complete with arched windows and decorative details. Rooms are decorated with Victorian furniture and antiques. It's 1 1/2 mi from downtown, 1 mi from the Monterey Bay Aquarium. Complimentary Continental breakfast. No air-conditioning, some refrigerators, cable TV. | 406 Alvarado St. | 831/375–3184 or 800/727–0960 | fax 831/373–2899 | www.montereyhotel.com | 45 rooms, 6 suites | $160–$189, $219–$299 suites | AE, D, DC, MC, V.

★ **Monterey Plaza Hotel.** This grand, five-story Mediterranean-style hotel is on the waterfront near Cannery Row. Rooms are large, and many have balconies jutting over the bay. Rooms have deep wood paneling and marble. You can get massages, facials, or aromatherapy treatments at the rooftop spa. The hotel is 2 mi west of downtown. Restaurant, bar. Minibars, some in-room hot tubs, cable TV. Hot tub, massage, spa. Exercise equipment, boating, bicycles. Business services. No smoking. | 400 Cannery Row | 831/646–1700 or 800/631–1339 (outside CA), 800/334–3999 (CA) | fax 831/646–0285 | www.woodsidehotels.com | 291 rooms, 10 suites | $205–$420, $460–$660 1–bedroom suites, $660–$960 2–bedroom suites, $520–$1900 penthouse suites, $2800 presidential penthouse suite | AE, D, DC, MC, V.

★ **Old Monterey Inn.** This English-style stucco inn was built in 1929. The property, in a residential area ²/₃ mi southeast of downtown, includes a ¹/₂-acre garden complete with hammock. Complimentary breakfast. No air-conditioning, some in-room VCRs. Business services. No smoking. | 500 Martin St. | 831/375–8284 or 800/350–2344 | fax 831/375–6730 | www.oldmontereyinn.com | 8 rooms, 1 suite, 1 cottage | $220–$390, $330 suite, $390 cottage | MC, V.

Otter Inn. This converted cannery dates from the late 1960s and is just 2 mi west of downtown and one block from Cannery Row. Rooms have an ocean view; some have fireplaces. Complimentary Continental breakfast. No air-conditioning, refrigerators, some in-room hot tubs, cable TV. Hot tub. Business services. | 571 Wave St. | 831/375–2299 or 800/385–2299 | fax 831/375–2352 | 33 rooms | $99–$309 | AE, D, MC, V.

Quality Inn. Spacious rooms are decorated like a country inn with wood paneling and fireplaces in some. This hotel, in the heart of the Monterey Peninsula, is surrounded by colorful flower gardens. Beaches and a picnic area are within walking distance. Complimentary Continental breakfast. In-room data ports, some refrigerators, cable TV. Pool. Outdoor hot tub. Laundry service. | 1058 Munras Ave. | 831/372–3381 | www.montereyqualityinn.com | 50 rooms | $84–$114 | AE, D, DC, V.

Sand Dollar Inn. This 1960s hotel in the heart of downtown, not far from the Bay and Laguna Grande Lake, has three stucco buildings. Some rooms have gas or wood-burning fireplaces, balconies, or patios. Complimentary Continental breakfast. Some refrigerators, cable TV. Pool. Hot tub. Laundry facilities. Business services. | 755 Abrego St. | 831/372–7551 or 800/982–1986 | fax 831/372–0916 | www.sanddollarinn.com | 63 rooms | $99–$139 | AE, DC, MC, V.

★ **Spindrift Inn.** This small hotel on Cannery Row is a Louisiana Mardi Gras-style wooden building, dating back to 1927 but rebuilt in 1985. Rooms have fireplaces and elegant furnishings. Located 2 mi northwest of downtown, and 1 ¹/₂ blocks from the Monterey Bay Aquarium. Complimentary Continental breakfast. No air-conditioning, refrigerators, cable TV, in-rooms VCRs (and movies). Parking (fee). | 652 Cannery Row | 831/646–8900 or 800/841–1879 | fax 831/646–5342 | www.innsofmonterey.com | 42 rooms | $229–$399 | AE, D, DC, MC, V.

Sunbay Suites Resort. SunBay, within walking distance of scenic coastal trails and 5 mi from downtown, is on two 18-hole championship, PGA Tour Qualifying courses, Bayonet and Black Horse, and overlooks the Monterey Bay. Suites are available in one-bedroom, two-bedroom, and studio size. Kitchenettes, cable TV. Pool. Hot tub, sauna. Golf courses, 2 tennis courts. Basketball, exercise room, volleyball. Business services. | 5200 Coe Ave., Seaside | 831/394–0136 | fax 831/394–0221 | www.sunbaysuites.com | 53 rooms | $129–$169 | AE, MC, V.

Travelodge Downtown. This hotel is in the heart of Old Town Monterey, 4 blocks from Monterey Beach and 6 blocks from Fisherman's Wharf. There are more than 20 restaurants within 3 blocks. In-room data ports, some refrigerators, cable TV. Pool. Business services. | 675 Munras Ave. | 831/373–1876 | fax 831/373–8693 | www.montereytravelodge.com | 51 rooms | $71–$169 | AE, D, MC, V.

Way Station Inn and Suites. This hostelry on four forest-ringed acres is across from the airport, 4 mi northeast of downtown and 3 mi from Cannery Row and the Bay. In the five tan-colored wooden buildings, some rooms have gas fireplaces. Complimentary Continental breakfast. No air-conditioning, cable TV. | 1200 Olmsted Rd. | 831/372–2945 or 800/858–0822 | fax 831/375–6267 | 46 rooms | $89–$200 | AE, D, DC, MC, V.

MORRO BAY

(Nearby towns also listed: Atascadero, Cambria, Paso Robles, Pismo Beach, San Simeon)

If you drive south on Route 1 through Big Sur, you can spend hours looking through the windshield at incredible vistas of ocean, rock, and meadow. Just before the road turns inland away from the ocean, you'll catch a glimpse of the majestic Hearst Castle at San Simeon.

Just past Leffingwell's Landing State Beach, civilization peeks warily from behind the pine forests. First you reach the artists' colony of Cambria; then an unmistakable monument to industry – the puffing towers of an electric power plant looming from the water. A huge mound of rock rises nearby, as if in challenge. Those two landmarks let you know you've arrived in Morro Bay, populated by 9,927 permanent residents.

To the right of the access road to Morro Rock, a dirt track leads to two parking lots with beach access. The first ends in a windy, kelp-strewn strip of sand. Keep going and you'll reach a sheltered nook of rolling sand dunes and waves ideal for body surfing. When you reach the town of Morro Bay, you'll see that it is centered around a cozy downtown filled with antique and rummage shops. Every small town has its teen hangout; here, it's Morro Bay Mud Fudge, a tiny candy store with a few outdoor tables. Skaters in grungewear gather here before heading to the ramps at the miniature skate/bike park near the beach.

Information: **Morro Bay Chamber of Commerce** | 880 Main St., 93442 | 805/772–4467 or 800/231–0592 | www.morrobay.org.

Attractions

Morro Bay Aquarium. Tanks of fish and other marine life offer glimpses of underwater Morro Bay; a marine rehabilitation center is also at the site. | 595 Embarcadero | 805/772–7647 | www.morrobay.com/morrobayaquarium | $2 | Weekdays 9:30–6, weekends 9:30–6:30.

Morro Bay State Park. A seaside park with 3,500 acres of evergreen groves, woodlands and grasslands. | State Park Rd. | 805/772–7434 | Free | Daily.

Interactive displays and dioramas at the **Museum of Natural History** show the geology, animals, and marine life of the central coast. A historical exhibit has artifacts from local Chumash Indian culture. Audiovisual presentations, nature walks, and lectures are also available, and you can take a trail from the hilltop museum to a scenic view spot. | Morro Bay State Park Rd. | 805/772–2694 | $2 | Daily 10–5.

Paradise Island Fun Park. This park is an indoor arcade with virtual-reality games, miniature golf course, and a snack bar. | 231 Atascadero Rd. | 805/771–8760 | Free | Mon.–Thurs. 11–10, Fri. 11–midnight, Sat. 10–midnight, Sun. 10–9.

Sub-Sea Tours. A semi-submersible vessel provides a peek at giant kelp forests, eels, schools of fish, and other marine life. | 699 Embarcadero, #8 | 805/772–9463 | $12.50 | Daily 9–5.

Tiger's Folly II Harbor Cruises. Take a 1-hour narrated tour of the bay, the great blue heron rookery, and Morro Rock aboard a stern-wheeler riverboat. Reservations are required for the Sunday Champagne brunch cruise, and departure times vary on weekdays, so be sure to call ahead for specifics. | 1205 Embarcadero | 805/772–2257 or 805/772–2255 | $10 | Weekends at 12:30, 1:45, and 3PM.

ON THE CALENDAR

OCT.: *Morro Bay Harbor Festival.* Seafood and wine tastings, a sand sculpture contest, entertainment, ship tours, exhibits, and a chance to see inside the Duke Energy Plant at the Morro Bay waterfront, here at the foot of the Embarcadero. | 800/366–6143.

Dining

Dorn's Original Breaker's Cafe. American. Dorn's has a garden room especially for breakfast and lunch, and a newly built patio overlooking the bay for dinner. Specialties include lobster tail and salmon pasta. | 801 Market St. | 805/772–4415 | fax 805/772–4695 | www.morrobay.com/Dorn's/ | $11–$25 | MC, V.

Galley. Seafood. This established restaurant is in a wooden building on pilings over the water, with a great view of Morro Bay and Morro Rock. There are large windows all around the dining area. White linen tablecloths, decorative wine bottles, and paintings depicting the Morro Bay area set the stage for fresh seafood, much of it from the waters surrounding the town. Kids' menu. Beer and wine only. No smoking. | 899 Embarcadero | 805/772–2806 | Closed late-Nov.–late-Dec. | $5–$40 | AE, D, MC, V.

Lolo's Mexican Restaurant. Mexican. The salsa at this restaruant is so popular that it's sold at local grocery stores. Try the traditional Tex-Mex foods, such as tacos and enchiladas, along with contemporary pastas and salads, in the restaurant or on the patio. | 2848 N. Main St. | 805/772–5686 | www.lolos.com/ | Daily, 9–9 | $6–$11.

Margie's Diner. American. Margie's has traditional American favorites such as steak, BBQ chicken, and meatloaf in a fun and upbeat setting. | 1698 N. Main St. | 805/772–2510 | $9–$13 | Daily, 6:30 AM–9 PM | MC, V.

Otter Rock Cafe. Seafood. Watch sea otters, pelicans, and sea lions frolic in the water below this restaurant overlooking the bay. Enjoy steak and seafood on the patio and local live entertainment on Thursday evenings. | 885 Embarcadero | 805/772–1420 | $11–$16 | 7 AM–9PM | MC, V.

Papa Julio's. Mexican. Fresh, flavorful Mexican fast food comes from the kitchen of this tiny black-and-white tiled café. You can eat inside or outside on the sidewalk or get your food to go. Try the combination plates, vegetable enchilada, or the authentic pozole—a pork stew not often found on restaurant menus. | 430 Morro Bay Blvd. | 805/772–4091 | $3–$7 | No credit cards.

Rock Espresso Bar. Café. The Rock serves coffees, espressos, pastries, and juices, and is one block west of the intersection of Main Street and Morro Bay Boulevard. | 275 Morro Bay Blvd. | 805/772–3411 | dbowers@aol.com | $2–$5.

Rose's Landing. American. Right on the Embarcadero, this fish restaurant has two levels, both with bay views. Upstairs, the dining room has light gray walls and white tablecloths, while the downstairs lounge is a bit more casual. Everything on the menu is made with fresh ingredients. Entertainment Wed.–Sun. nights in summer. Kids' menu, early-bird suppers. | 725 Embarcadero | 805/772–4441 | No lunch weekends | $15–$25 | AE, D, DC, MC, V.

Windows on the Water. Contemporary. This restaurant is on the second floor of a seafront building. Inside, everything is creamy yellow and white, and there's a view of the water and Morro Rock. The kitchen produces some creative interpretations of stand-bys like salmon steak and grilled chicken. Sunday brunch. | 699 Embarcadero, #7 | 805/772–0677 | Fri.–Sat. dinner only | $14–$26 | AE, D, MC, V.

Lodging

Ascot Inn. One block from the ocean, this all-suite, Cape Cod-style motel built in 1980 is 1½ blocks from the Embarcadero. Complimentary Continental breakfast. No air-conditioning, in-room data ports, some refrigerators, cable TV. | 845 Morro Ave. | 805/772–4437 or 800/887–6454 | fax 805/772–8860 | www.ascotinn.com | 25 rooms | $73–$173 | AE, D, DC, MC, V.

Ascot Suites. The Tudor-style facade of this downtown property 1 mi west of Morro Rock gives way inside to floral patterns, reproductions of antiques, and four-poster beds. Some rooms have fireplaces. Complimentary Continental breakfast. Air-conditioning, some in-room hot tubs, cable TV, in-room VCRs (and movies). Hot tub. Gym. | 260 Morro Bay Blvd. | 805/772–4437 or 800/887–6454 | fax 805/772–8860 | www.ascotinn.com | 32 rooms | $163–$295 | AE, D, DC, MC, V.

Bay View Lodge. This two-story tan brick building with a stucco finish was built in 1975. Some rooms overlook the water and have gas fireplaces. It's in a commercial area one block from the Bay. No air-conditioning, refrigerators, cable TV, in-room VCRs (and movies). Hot tub. Laundry facilities. | 225 Harbor St. | 805/772–2771 or 800/742–8439 | 22 rooms | $80–$105 | AE, MC, V.

Best Western El Rancho. This 1960s southwestern-style hotel just north of town consists of two stucco-faced buildings with bay views in some rooms. Restaurant. Refrigerators, cable TV, in-room VCRs (and movies). Pool. Laundry facilities. Business services. Pets allowed (fee). | 2460 Main St. | 805/772–2212 | fax 805/772–2212 | 27 rooms | $59–$99 | AE, D, DC, MC, V.

Best Western San Marcos Inn. A Spanish-style tiled fountain and tropical plants decorate the lobby of this motor inn 1½ blocks from downtown. The three-story stucco structure, built in 1974, has great views of Morro Rock from many rooms. Complimentary Continental breakfast. No air-conditioning, refrigerators, cable TV. Hot tub. Business services. No smoking. | 250 Pacific St. | 805/772–2248 | fax 805/772–6844 | 32 rooms | $89–$169 | AE, D, DC, MC, V.

Blue Sail Inn. This small fishing-village-style motel is on a bluff overlooking the bay, and many rooms have views; seven have fireplaces. No air-conditioning, in-room data ports, refrigerators, cable TV. Hot tub. Business services. No smoking. | 851 Market Ave. | 805/772–2766 or 888/337–0707 | fax 805/772–8406 | www.bluesailinn.com | 48 rooms | $75–$145 | AE, D, DC, MC, V.

Breakers. Right downtown, this three-story wooden motel is within walking distance of the stairway in the bluff leading to shops, restaurants, and the water. The property is lush and landscaped, and some rooms have wood-burning fireplaces. Refrigerators, cable TV. Pool. Hot tub. Business services. | 780 Market St. | 805/772–7317 or 800/932–8899 | fax 805/772–4771 | www.morrobay.com/breakersmotel/ | 25 rooms | $95–$120 | AE, D, DC, MC, V.

Cabrillo Motel. Rooms at this motor lodge-type motel are simple, but many have a fireplace. Two room suites are also available. Kitchenettes. | 890 Morro Avenue | 805/772–4435 or 800/222–9915 | info@cabrillomotel.com | www.cabrillomotel.com | 50 rooms | $68–$90 | MC, V.

Days Inn Harbor House. In this two-story wooden building, some rooms have ocean views and some have wood-burning fireplaces. It's downtown, 3 blocks from the Embarcadero. Complimentary Continental breakfast. No air-conditioning, in-room data ports, refrigerators, cable TV. Hot tub. Business services. Pets allowed (fee). | 1095 Main St. | 805/772–2711 or 800/247–5076 | fax 805/772–2711 | thrturk@aol.com | www.daysinn.com | 46 rooms, 1 suite | $69–$145, $125–$199 suite | AE, D, DC, MC, V.

MORRO BAY

INTRO
ATTRACTIONS
DINING
LODGING

El Morro Masterpiece Motel. Formerly known as El Morro Lodge, the El Morro Masterpiece has Spanish-Moorish architecture and framed prints from 16th-century masters on the walls. Most rooms have balconies, Jacuzzis, or fireplaces. The motel is a 5-min stroll to the waterfront, restaurants, shops, and galleries. Complimentary Continental breakfast. In-room data ports, refrigerators, cable TV. Exercise room. No smoking. | 1206 Main St. | 800/527–6782 or 805/772–5633 | info@masterpiecemotels.com | www.masterpiece-motels.com | 27 rooms | $68–$100 | AE, D, MC, V.

Embarcadero Inn. This cozy inn is right on the waterfront. All rooms face the bay and most rooms have fireplaces and/or balconies. Complimentary Continental breakfast. Refrigerators, cable TV, in-room VCRs. | 456 Embarcadero | 800/292–7625 or 805/772–2700 | www.morrobay.com/Embarcaderoinn/ | 32 rooms | $95–$190 | MC, V.

Inn at Morro Bay. A ½ mi from downtown Morro Bay, this secluded blue-gray two-story wood building has lush shaded gardens and a courtyard. Rooms are decorated in a romantic French country style, some with gas fireplaces and bay views. A golf course and a heron rookery are next door. Restaurant, bar [with entertainment]. No air-conditioning, some refrigerators, some in-room hot tubs, cable TV. Pool. Massage. Bicycles. Business services. | 60 State Park Rd. | 805/772–5651 or 800/321–9566 | fax 805/772–4779 | www.innatmorrobay.com | 98 rooms | $129–$429 | AE, D, DC, MC, V.

Keystone Inn. This motel has excellent views of the bay and Morro Rock. It's within walking distance of the restaurants in town, and the Embarcadero. All of the rooms were refurbished in 1999. They consist of freshly painted off-white walls, modern wooden furniture, an aqua color theme with curtains and bed spreads. Refrigerators, cable TV. No smoking. | 540 Main St. | 805/772–7503 or 888/900–3629 | fax 805/772–2953 | www.keystoneinn.com | 30 rooms | $65–$125 | MC, V.

La Serena Inn. This hostelry in downtown is done in California-Spanish style, with a tiled roof and adobe-colored stucco exterior. Restaurant, complimentary Continental breakfast. In-room data ports, cable TV. Sauna. Business services. | 990 Morro Ave. | 805/772–5665 or 800/248–1511 | fax 805/772–1044 | www.laserinainn.com | 37 rooms, 5 suites | $85–$125, $135–$175 suites | AE, D, DC, MC, V.

Marina Street Inn. This bed and breakfast has only four units, but each is a suite with a patio or balcony. The Bordeaux Room has tiger oak furnishings and antiques, the Garden Room features a canopy willow bed and gardening motif, the Dockside Room is filled with nautical antiques, and the Rambling Rose Room has warm reds and greens with a four-poster bed and English writing desk. The living room has a fireplace and wine and cheese are served daily. Complimentary breakfast. Cable TV, In-room data ports. No pets. No smoking. | 305 Marina St. | 888/683–9389 or 805/772–4016 | fax 805/772–8667 | www.marinastreetinn.com | 4 rooms | $99–$140 | AE, MC, V.

Travelodge Sunset. You can watch the sunset from this chain hotel one block from the harbor and 2 blocks from downtown. A sundeck is attached to the wood structure, constructed in 1980. Complimentary Continental breakfast. No air-conditioning, in-room data ports. | 1080 Market Ave. | 805/772–1259 or 800/863–6205 | fax 805/772–8967 | 31 rooms | $110–$159 | AE, D, DC, MC, V.

Twin Dolphin. This modest, stucco-sided motel was built in 1987 and occupies a strip of other hotels right downtown, one block east of the Aquarium. Restaurant, complimentary Continental breakfast. Cable TV. Hot tub. | 590 Morro Ave. | 805/772–4483 | twindolphinmotel@aol.com | 31 rooms | $85–$105 | D, MC, V.

The Villager. In a commercial area, this wood-framed, Southwestern-style building was built in 1973. It's 2½ blocks from the bay. Cable TV. Hot tub. Pets allowed (fee). | 1098 Main St. | 805/772–1235 | fax 805/772–1236 | www.villager-morrobay.com | 22 rooms | $119–$129 | AE, D, DC, MC, V.

MOUNTAIN VIEW

(Nearby towns also listed: Menlo Park, Palo Alto, Sunnyvale)

Surrounded by influential neighbor cities like Fremont, San Jose, and Palo Alto, Mountain View (pop. 75,000) suffers from a bit of an inferiority complex. But it stands tall as a homey, mostly residential community once known as "The Valley of Heart's Delight." Now primarily an industrial city, it's home to high-tech companies such as Sun Microsystems, U.S. Robotics, and Microsoft. A large concert venue, Shoreline Amphitheatre, hosts big-name entertainment.

Information: **Mountain View Chamber of Commerce** | 580 Castro St, 94041 | 650/968–8378 | www.mountainviewchambermv.org.

Attractions

Shoreline Amphitheatre. An open amphitheater and tented pavilion provides the setting for international touring acts and cultural festivals. | 1 Amphitheatre Pkwy. | 650/967–4040 | fax 650/967–4994 | www.shoreline-amp.com.

Shoreline Park. Bicycle and walking paths wind through a marine bird sanctuary here. You can picnic here, too. | 2600 N. Shoreline Blvd. | 650/903–6331 | Free | Daily dawn–dusk.

ON THE CALENDAR

SEPT.: *Art and Wine Festival*. This festive conglomeration of crafts and fine arts booths, world cuisine, and premium wines and microbrews takes place the weekend after Labor Day on Castro Street downtown. | 650/968–8378.

Dining

Chez T.J. French. This restaurant is in one of the most historic homes of Old Mountain View (circa 1894). Specialties include pecan crusted chicken, sweet mustard glazed salmon, and roasted monkfish with Yukon Gold potato puree. | 938 Villa St. | 650/964–7466 | Reservations essential | Closed Sun., Mon. No lunch | $42–$65 | AE, D, DC, MC, V.

Fibber Magee's. Irish. Kelly green paint and Irish flags out front will let you know you're here; interior hallmarks include soccer on the big-screen TV, frequent live Irish bands, and pints of domestic and imported beer. You can eat burgers, bangers, and fish and chips in the dining room of bare wood tables and chairs, a few booths, and painted wood walls. | 223 Castro St. | 650/964–9151 | $5–$25 | AE, MC, V.

Passage to India. Indian. Seating is in both booths and at tables here, and saucy curries, flatbread, and piquant masalas are among the traditional Northern Indian fare served at this family restaurant. | 110 W. El Camino, between Castro and Shoreline | 650/964–5532 | fax 650/964–1456 | www.passagetoindia.net | Closed 3–5 PM | $14–$20 | AE, D, MC, V.

Lodging

Best Western Mountain View Inn. This hotel of marble, polished rock, and wood sits on a wooded lot 2 mi north of downtown. Ideal for the business traveler, the hotel has comfortable, simple rooms in a commercial area near many restaurants. Restaurant, complimentary Continental breakfast. In-room data ports, refrigerators, some in-room hot tubs. Pool. Exercise equipment. Laundry facilities. Business services, free parking. | 2300 El Camino Real W | 650/962–9912 or 800/528–1234 | fax 650/962–9011 | 72 rooms, 2 suites | $99–$159, $199–$250 suites | AE, D, DC, MC, V.

Comfort Inn. The bay is less than 5 mi from this suburban motel, which occupies a strip of like facilities in a largely commercial area of Mountain View. Microwaves, refrigerators, cable TV. Pool. Hot tub. | 1561 El Camino Real | 650/967–7888 | fax 650/967–3579 | 44 rooms | $109–$159 | AE, D, DC, MC, V.

County Inn. This two-story hostelry is near the shore, less than 1 mi from downtown. Motel-style rooms are comfortable, with basic furnishings. Complimentary Continental breakfast. In-room data ports, minibars, refrigerators, cable TV, in-room VCRs (and movies). Pool. Exercise equipment. Laundry facilities. Business services, free parking. | 850 Leong Dr. | 650/961–1131 or 800/828–1132 | fax 650/965–9099 | 53 rooms | $89–$169 | Closed Dec. 24–Jan. 2 | AE, D, DC, MC, V.

Crestview Hotel. Popular among Silicon Valley dot-com business people, this two-story wooden building with oyster-grey siding looks more like a big house than a corporate hotel. Rooms have wood furnishings, and some have private whirlpool tubs. Microwaves, refrigerators, cable TV, in-room VCRs (and movies). Hot tub. | 901 E. El Camino Real | 650/966–8848 | fax 650/966–8884 | 58 rooms, 9 suites | $189–$249 | AE, DC, MC, V.

Holiday Inn Express. This two-story western-style building is two stoplights from downtown. Restaurant, complimentary Continental breakfast. Some kitchenettes, refrigerators, cable TV, in-room VCRs (and movies). Pool. Hot tub. Exercise equipment. Laundry facilities. | 93 West El Camino Real | 650/967–6957 or 800/445–7774 | fax 650/967–4834 | www.hitowncenter.com | 58 rooms, 5 suites | $159, $200–$299 suites | AE, D, DC, MC, V.

Residence Inn by Marriott. Business travelers are the primary clients of this particular Marriott, which has one- and two-bedroom suites. The grounds of the contemporary stucco building are landscaped, with three courtyards. The hotel is 1 mi from downtown. Complimentary Continental breakfast. Kitchenettes, refrigerators, cable TV. Pool. Hot tub. Laundry facilities. Business services, free parking. Pets allowed (fee). | 1854 W. El Camino Real | 650/940–1300 | fax 650/969–4997 | www.residence.com | 112 suites | $149–$329 | AE, D, DC, MC, V.

MT. SHASTA

MAP 3, D2

(Nearby towns also listed: Dunsmuir, Yreka)

"When I first caught sight of Mount Shasta over the braided folds of the Sacramento Valley," wrote John Muir, "my blood turned to wine, and I have not been weary since." This contemporary reaction has been echoed for centuries. Native Wintu, Shasta, Pit River, Karuk, Okwanuchu, and Modoc Indians thought that the dramatic, snow-topped lava cone of Mt. Shasta was a tribute to the power of the Great Creator. Rounding the bend on I–5 into the town of Mt. Shasta (pop. 3,490), you're confronted with the dormant volcano's majestic presence. It rises 10,000 ft from the valley floor, filling the horizon from almost every vantage point. The volcano slopes, snow-covered in winter, flower-filled in spring, make an attractive playground.

The town has long been the site of vision quests, meditation retreats, and Harmonic Convergence theories. Galleries in town are filled with metaphysical accessories and angel adornments, and restaurants go by names like The Light of Love and Heart Rock Cafe.

Information: Mount Shasta Chamber of Commerce and Visitor's Bureau | 300 Pine St., 96067 | 800/926–4865 | www.mtshastachamber.com.

Attractions

The Art Center Gallery and Angel Boutique. Angel lovers will be in heaven: this store's host of angel collectibles includes porcelain angels, angel bumper stickers, angel books, and angel cards. You'll also find art supplies, posters, and crystal jewelry. | 315 Chestnut St. | 530/926–2297 | Free | Daily 9–5:15.

Crystal Wings Bookstore. This is a good source for spiritual and metaphysical books, drums, incense, candles, local herbs, and seminars. | 226 N. Mt. Shasta Blvd. | 530/926–3041 | www.crystalwings.com | Free | Daily 10–5:30.

Lake Siskiyou. This manmade lake has boating, fishing, swimming, camping, and hiking trails. | 4239 W. A. Barr Rd. | 888/926–2618 | www.lakesis.com | Free | Apr.–Oct., Daily dawn–dusk.

There are 250 acres of pine trees surrounding a beach and marina at **Lake Siskiyou Camp Resort,** along with tent and RV sites, and 20 cabins with lofts, decks, and views of the lake. You can fish, rent canoes, kayaks, pedal boats, and rafts. | 4239 W. A. Barr Rd. | 530/926–2618 or 888/926–2618 | www.lakesis.com | $1 | Apr.–Oct., daily; marina daily.

Mt. Shasta. Dominating the landscape, this dormant volcano was holy ground for native peoples. The mountain, snow-capped year-round, has hiking, camping, skiing, and mountaineering. Bunny Flats, at 7,000 ft, is a popular place for snowshoeing and sledding (rent tubes north of Mt. Shasta). Bring adequate food and clothing; there are no facilities besides restrooms. | Ranger office, 204 West Alma | 530/926–4511 | www.avalanche.org | Free | Oct.–Mar., weekdays; Apr.–Sept., daily.

Mt Shasta Ski Park. This 425-acre resort offers snowboarding, downhill and cross-country skiing in winter, and mountain biking and hiking in summer on 27 trails. | 4500 Ski Park Hwy., McCloud | 530/926–8610 or 800/754–7427 | Daily 10–4.

Mt. Shasta Hatchery. Three to five million trout are hatched a year here at the state's oldest fish hatchery. The fish replenish California lakes and streams. You can feed fish in open ponds. | 3 N. Old Stage Rd. | 530/926–2215 | Free | Daily 7–dusk.

Next door to the hatchery is the **Sisson Museum,** where you can view exhibits tracing the history of climbing on Mt. Shasta, local geography, and other regional topics. | 1 N. Old Stage Rd. | 530/926–5508 | Free | Mar.–Dec., daily 1–4; June–Sept., daily 10–4.

ON THE CALENDAR

SEPT.: *Montague Rotary Balloon Faire.* This nonprofit festival attracts hot-air balloon lovers from all over the country. | info@montague-balloon-fair.com | www.montague-balloon-fair.com.

Dining

Avalon Square Heart Rock Cafe. American. This popular coffeehouse serves an unusual combination of sandwiches, Mexican dishes, pasta, salads, and espresso drinks. You can dine in the garden patio, with a mountain view. | 401 N. Mt. Shasta Blvd. | 530/926–4998 | $3–$12 | No credit cards.

Lily's. Contemporary. Modern American cuisine with Asian touches is served at this white clapboard house with a picket fence. There are two patios and the rooms inside have paintings of Mt. Shasta. Good options: grilled fish with basil, chicken teriyaki, delicate sautéed vegetables, soups, homemade pasta, and cheesecake. Sunday brunch. | 1013 S. Mt. Shasta Blvd. | 530/926–3372 | Breakfast also available | $15–$25 | AE, D, MC, V.

Michael's. Italian. Mt. Shasta and Main Street are in view as you savor steaks, chicken, seafood, and Italian specialties at this small restauraunt in the middle of town. | 313 N. Mt. Shasta Blvd. | 530/926–5288 | Closed Sun.–Mon. | $15–$25 | D, MC, V.

Piemont. Italian. This local favorite has been serving pastas, ravioli, meatballs, and other Italian dishes since the 1950s. There are two dining areas and a lounge with a fireplace. Old photos line the walls. | 1200 S. Mt Shasta Blvd. | 530/926–2402 | Closed Tues. Jan.–Feb. Closed Mon. No lunch | $15–$25 | D, MC, V.

Lodging

Best Western Tree House Motor Inn. This chain motel has landscaped grounds, views of Mt. Shasta, pleasant rooms, and a spacious lobby with a large fireplace. It's near skiing and bike trails. The three wooden buildings, built in 1974, are 3 mi from downtown. Restaurant, bar. Cable TV. Indoor pool. Business services. Pets allowed. | 111 Morgan Way | 530/926–3101 or 800/545–7164 | fax 530/926–3542 | www.bestwestern.com | 98 rooms | $79–$149 | AE, D, DC, MC, V.

Carriage House Lodging. Surrounded by trees and a short drive to Lake Siskiyou, this rustic log house gives the impression of being very remote and private. You can rent just one room and share the common areas with fellow travelers, or rent the entire house. All linens are included, and the full kitchen is stocked with everything but food. There's a huge wraparound deck outside, and a fireplace and vast plate-glass picture windows inside. No air conditioning, microwave, cable TV, in-room VCR. Lake. Hot tub. | 700 N. Old Stage Rd. | 530/926–0296 | fishasta@inreach.com | 3 rooms | $85–$150 | MC, V.

Finlandia. Choose from regular or deluxe rooms, some with lake or mountain views, at this 1969 European-style wood building with a stucco finish. The motel is 3 mi west of Lake Siskiyou. Picnic area. No air-conditioning in some rooms, some kitchenettes, cable TV. Sauna. Business services. Pets allowed. | 1612 S. Mt Shasta Blvd. | 530/926–5596 | finlandia@snowcrest.net | 22 rooms | $34–$75 | AE, D, DC, MC, V.

McCloud Hotel. This restored 1916 inn has an inviting peaked-roof exterior with porches. The homey interior has a guest lounge lined with books, and a fireplace. The landscaped property includes an outdoor garden room. Dining room, complimentary breakfast. Some in-room hot tubs, no room phones, TV in common area. No pets. No smoking. | 408 Main St., McCoud | 530/964–2822 or 800/964–2823 | fax 530/964–2844 | 13 rooms, 5 suites | $98–$177, $162–$177 suites | AE, D, DC, MC, V.

Mt. Shasta Ranch. This two-story ranch-style bed and breakfast was originally built as a thoroughbred horse ranch in the early 1920s. Today, it has rooms furnished with period antiques and large bathtubs, a huge native-stone fireplace in the living room, and an expansive veranda out back for relaxing and taking in the views. Some guest rooms share baths, and most have fabulous views of Mt. Shasta. Complimentary breakfast. No room phones, no TV in some rooms. Hot tub. | 1008 W. A. Barr Rd. | 530/926–3870 | alpinere@snowcrest.net | 11 rooms, 1 cottage | $40–$125 | AE, D, MC, V.

Mount Shasta Resort. "It's always tee time on the mountain," is this resort's slogan. There's more to the resort than just golf, however. The facility has a private beach on Lake Siskiyou for swimming, sunbathing, and fishing. All guest accomodations are in mini-chalets, some with lake views and all are surrounded by tall pine forest. The entire resort sprawls beneath the shadow of Mt. Shasta. Restaurant, bar. No air-conditioning, kitchenettes, refrigerators, cable TV. Lake. 18-hole golf course. Beach, boating, fishing. Laundry service. Business services. No pets. No smoking. | 1000 Siskiyou Lake Blvd. | 530/926–3030 | fax 530/926–0333 | msresort@inreach.com | 65 chalets | $82–$179 | AE, D, DC, MC, V.

O'Brien Mountain Inn. Fresh flowers, champagne, and candles are part of this romantic B&B. Four rooms have musical themes, with a CD library. The Classical Room has an iron tulip bed and clawfoot tub; the Folk Room has an antique wood bed and handcrafted furnishing; the Jazz Room and World Beat rooms have Murphy beds. The inn sits on 47 acres of landscaped property on Shasta Lake, 47 mi south of Mt. Shasta. The inn has three buildings and a spa house. Complimentary full breakfast. Cable TV. Pool. Hot tub. Library. | 18026 O'Brien Inlet Rd., O'Brien | 530/238–8026 or 888/799–8026 | fax 530/238–2027 | www.obrienmtn.com | 5 rooms | $100–$225 | AE, D, DC, MC, V.

Swiss Holiday Lodge. This two-story southwestern-style wood building has quiet, affordable rooms overlooking Mt. Shasta. The lodge is 1 ½ mi from downtown. Picnic area, complimentary Continental breakfast. Some kitchenettes, cable TV. Pool. Hot tub. Pets allowed. | 2400 S. Mt. Shasta Blvd. | 530/926–3446 | fax 530/926–3091 | 21 rooms, 1 suite | $46–$54, $95 suite | AE, D, DC, MC, V.

MURPHYS

(Nearby towns also listed: Jackson, Sonora)

One of the most charming of the Gold Country towns, Murphys (population 1,500), straddles scenic Rte. 4, about 10 mi east of Gold Country main drag, Rte. 49. The town is rich in Gold Rush-era history, a storied gathering place for the rich and famous of the day. Among the guests who have signed the register at Murphy's HIstoric Hotel and Lodge are Ulysses S. Grant and Horatio Alger. Today several excellent wineries operate out of Murphys, Main Street supports an array of boutiques, and historic lodgings offer hospitality.

Information: **Calaveras County Visitors Bureau** | 1211 S. Main St., Angels Camp, 95222 | 209/736–0049 | visitcalaveras.org.

Attractions

Calaveras Big Trees State Park. In this park, 15 mi northeast of Murphys off Route 4, trails take you past hundreds of magnificent giant sequoia redwood trees, some almost 3,000 years old, 90 ft around at the base, and 250 ft tall. Blooming dogwoods in spring are breathtaking. The park's paths range from a 200-yard trail to 1- and 5-mi loops through the groves. There are campgrounds and picnic areas, plus swimming and fishing in the Stanislaus River in summer, snowshoeing and cross-country skiing in winter. | 1170 E. Rte. 4, Arnold | 209/795–2334 | fax 209/795–7306 | www.bigtrees.org | $2 per car, $12 per night campsites | Daily.

Mercer Caverns. A little over a mile north of town is Mercer Caverns, with 10 different caves, including one of the largest arrays of rare white crystal. | 1665 Sheep Ranch Rd. | 209/728–2101 | www.mercercaverns.com/ | $8 | Memorial Day–Sept., Sun.–Thurs. 9–6, Fri.–Sat. 9–8; Oct.–Memorial Day, Sun.–Thurs. 10–4:30, Fri., Sat. 10–6.

ON THE CALENDAR

OCT. *Calaveras Grape Stomp and Goldrush Street Faire.* This light-hearted annual event, organized by local vintners, encourages you to take off your shoes and squish around in a vat of ripe grapes, all for fun and charity. The faire has grape-stomping contests, wine tastings, belly dancing, live music, and lots of food. | 209/736–6722 or 800/225–3764 ext.25.

Dining

Murphy's Grill. Contemporary. This family owned and operated eatery puts an emphasis on grilled cuisine, served with innovative sauces and side dishes. Fresh and creatively prepared dishes occupy the menu, which changes every three months, along with a well balanced wine list that includes some local wineries. Outdoor seating is available on a patio with views of Main St., while inside a long bar with pleated copper, Italian tile, and art work by local artists completes the summary. | 380 Main St. | 209/728–8800 | fax 209/728–0304 | Closed Wed. | $15–$25 | AE, DC, MC, V.

Lodging

★ **Dunbar House 1880.** Surrounded by a rose garden and white picket fence and decorated with French antiques and hand-crocheted items, this 1880 two-story wood inn is a step back in time. A horse-drawn carriage frequently pulls up to the inn to transport you around town. Water fountains and birdhouses abound in the garden along with many private sitting areas. Complimentary breakfast. Cable TV, in-room VCRs, room phones. No pets. No smoking. | 271 Jones St. | 209/728–2897 | fax 209/728–1451 | 5 rooms | $135–$195 | AE, MC, V.

....

Murphy's Historic Hotel and Lodge. These two western-style wood buildings, dating back to 1856, are one block from the Malvadino winery. The rooms in the Main Building are furnished with authentic period antiques and have been occupied by such notables as Mark Twain, Black Bart, and Ulysses S. Grant. Have a drink in the old fashioned saloon on the first floor. The rooms in the adjacent building have more modern furnishings. Restaurant. Cable TV, room phones. | 457 Main St. | 209/728–3444 | fax 209/728–1590 | www.murphyshotel.com | 29 rooms | $70–$80 | AE, D, DC, MC, V.

....

Redbud Inn. Each of the 12 rooms at this cedar-shingled bed and breakfast is furnished with antiques and heirlooms. Some rooms have double-sided glass fireplaces. Several area wineries are within easy driving distance, and the inn hosts complimentary wine tastings daily. Complimentary breakfast. Cable TV. | 402 Main St. | 209/728–8533 or 877/4–REDBUD (473–3283) | fax 209/728–8132 | innkeeper@redbudinn.com | 11 rooms | $95–$195 | MC, V.

NAPA

MAP 3, D7

(Nearby towns also listed: Fairfield, Rutherford/St. Helena, Sonoma, Vacaville, Yountville)

The largest city in the Napa Valley, Napa (population 120,000) is both the county seat and the commercial hub of one of the richest wine growing and producing regions in the world. The city itself is urban, suburban, busy and commercial. But it's surrounded by some of California's most scenic agricultural lands. Just a short drive out of Napa in any direction you can find yourself on an unpaved country lane that meanders through rows and rows of vineyards, all carefully labeled with the name of the grape variety being grown. If you look around, you'll see an embrace of softly rolling hills the color of spun gold most of the year and dotted with dark green ancient oak trees.

The Napa Valley, which lures 5 million visitors annually, has been called "Disneyland for adults." True. You'll find nearly 250 wineries in the valley, a collection of romantic bed and breakfast inns, numerous very expensive restaurants purveying cutting edge cuisine, and a selection of adult-oriented tour options ranging from a slow ride on an excursion train to a bird's-eye view from the gondola of a hot air balloon.

Grapes have been grown and wine has been made in the Napa Valley for more than a century, excluding a brief period during Prohibition. But the industry began to take off in the years following World War II, when the winemakers began producing better and better products and wineries such as Beringer, Krug and Louis Martini began welcoming visitors for tours and tastings as a way to call attention to themselves and sell wine.

If this is your first visit to Napa Valley you'll want to get the overview of the winemaking process from one of these big operations; they have knowledgeable guides. And if you really want to learn about wine, plan your trip for the off-season (December through March) to avoid crowds on the tours and in the tasting rooms.

Napa Valley is long and narrow. The main highway is Rte. 29 which runs the entire 30 mi length of the valley from Napa in the south to Calistoga at the northern end. Wineries and vineyards front the highway most of the way. Use extra caution when driving the highway since most of the other drivers will have stopped at a tasting room or two.

Information: **The Napa Valley Conference and Visitors Bureau** | 1310 Napa Town Center, 94559 | 707/226–7459 | www.napavalley.com.

Attractions

Di Rosa Preserve. More than a thousand pieces by 675 artists fill two galleries and a century-old converted stone winery. Outside are sculptures, pepper gardens, meadows, and the shores of a 35-acre lake. Two-and-a-half-hour tours show much of the collection. | 5200 Carneros Hwy. (Rtes. 12 and 121) | 707/226–5991 | www.dirosapreserve.org | $10 | reservations required; Tues.–Fri. 9:25 and 12:55, Sat. 9:25 and 10:25.

Hot Air Balloon Rides. Several companies offer balloon rides over the Napa Valley. Passengers ride in a gondola with the pilot, suspended beneath rainbow-hued balloons. Some packages have brunch or lunch on the ground after the hour-long flight. Professional Balloon Pilots Association has referrals. | 5200 Carneros Hwy. (Rtes. 12 and 121) | 707/944–8793 | $175–$185.

If you dream of floating high in the air above some of the most beautiful scenery in the nation, consider a **Balloons Above the Valley** tour. Balloons lift off at sunrise for one-hour tours of the Napa Valley wine country. A champagne brunch after your aerial excursion celebrates your return to the ground. Reservations are essential. | 5091 Solano Ave. | 707/253–2222 or 800/464–6824 | info@balloonrides.com | www.balloonrides.com.

Napa Valley Expo Center. This center has 31,000 sq ft of showroom space. The Napa County Fair is held here annually and a host of other events year-round. | 575 3rd St. | 707/253–4900 | fax 707/253–4943 | nvexpo@aol.com | Mon–Fri 9–5, sales office.

Napa Valley Wine Train. A series of restored 1915 Pullman cars, including a dining car, makes daily round trips alongside the vineyards between the city of Napa and the far side of St. Helena. You can catch the train by driving south to downtown Napa via Highway 29, about a 15-min drive. Besides lunch, dinner, and brunch excursions, the train also has evenings of murder mysteries and kids' nights. | 1275 McKinstry St. | 707/253–2111 or 800/427–4124 | fax 707/253–9264 | www.winetrain.com | $69–$76 | Daily.

Wineries. Napa Valley is home to more than 240 wineries, a few of which produce some of the best wine in the world. Most of the wineries are open to the public for tastings, purchases, tours, or picnicking. Innkeepers and concierges can make arrangements for visits to small, boutique wineries that are off the beaten path and not normally open; if you visit one of these wineries expect to purchase wine there.

Well known for its vintages of Pinot Noir and Chardonnay, the 38-acre **Bouchaine Vineyards** estate is 2 mi south of downtown Napa. | 1075 Buchli Station Rd. | 707/252–9065 | info@bouchaine.com | www.bouchaine.com | Free | Daily 10–4.

The **Carneros Creek Winery** was founded in 1972 and is famous for its Pinot Noir. A stock of rare older wines is for sale. | 1285 Dealy Ln | 707/253–WINE | www.carneros-creek.com | $2.50 | Daily 10–5.

The sloping mountainside walls at the **Artesa** winery are covered with live native grasses. You can admire the view from the visitor center and terrace, or visit the adjacent art gallery and museum. An elevated walkway affords a bird's-eye tour of the winery operation. | 1345 Henry Rd. | 707/224–1668 | Free; tasting $4–$6 | Daily 10–5.

The grand hilltop chateau of **Domaine Carneros by Taittinger** makes this one of the most aesthetically pleasing wineries in the region. Champagne is the producer's speciality beverage. | 1240 Duhig Rd. | 707/257–0101 | www.domaine.com | Free, wine is sold by the glass | Daily 10:30–6.

★ The ivy-covered **Hess Collection Winery** also houses a collection of contemporary art and has self-guided tours. | 4411 Redwood Rd. | 707/255–1144 | www.hesscollection.com | Free; tasting $3 | Daily 10–4.

Varieties of Pinot Grigio, Merlot, and Sangiovese are produced at the **Luna Vineyards** Tuscan villa, which calls to mind the hills of central Italy. | 2921 Silverado Trail | 707/255–5862 | www.lunavineyards.com | $3 | Daily 10–5.

Pine Ridge Winery. In the Stags Leap district you'll find the **Pine Ridge Winery,** where you can linger over a picnic lunch beneath the pine trees after your tour. The winery's barrel-aging caves run for ½ mi. | 5901 Silverado Trail | 707/252–9777 or 800/575–9777 | www.pineridgewinery.com | Free; tasting $5–$15 | Daily 11–5.

Wine is converted to brandy at **RMS Brandy Distillery,** the oldest alambic brandy distillery in the United States. The French-style building resembles those found in Cognac. You can tour the Still House with its French-built copper stills, and view the 4,000 casks aging in the Barrel House. | 1250 Cuttings Wharf Rd. | 707/253–9055 | www.rmsbrandy.com | Free | Daily 10–5.

Cool-climate Chardonnay and hillside Cabernet Sauvignon and Merlot are the primary products at the **William Hill Winery.** Tours and tastings are by appointment only. | 1761 Atlas Peak Rd. | 707/224–4477 | fax 707/224–4484 | www.williamhillwinery.com | Free | Daily 10–4:30.

ON THE CALENDAR

FEB.–MAR.: *Napa Valley Mustard Festival.* You can celebrate the blooming of the mustard plant with wine auctions, special "mustard menu" dinners, cooking demonstrations, arts and crafts, kids' activities, and sporting events. | 707/938–1133 | www.mustardfestival.org.

MAR.: *Sutter Home Annual Napa Valley Marathon* This 26-mi race from along Silverado Trail from Calistoga to Napa starts at the Napa Valley Marriott. | 707/255–2609.

MAY–OCT.: *Farmer's Market.* Tuesday morning shopping is best among the piles of produce, flowers, baked goods, and other goodies trucked in from surrounding small farms and sold on Texas and Madison streets. An outdoor café sells coffee and snacks. | 707/252–7142.

SEPT.: *Wine Festival and Crafts Fair.* Celebrate the harvest with a traditional grape crushing. You can taste a variety of wines and foods, and shop for crafts. | 707/257–0322.

NOV.: *Autumn Wine Tasting and Festival.* Held annually in early November at the Christian Brothers Monastery and Retreat, 15 Mount Veeder winemakers avail their beverages to the public. Reservations essential. | 707/965–3735.

Dining

Bistro Don Giovanni. Continental. This bistro 8 mi from downtown specializes in French and Italian. An outdoor terrace with mountain and valley views creates a Mediterranean mood. The surrounding garden has fig trees and herb beds. Risotto dishes change daily. | 4110 St. Helena Rte. 29 | 707/224–3300 | $16–$24 | AE, D, DC, MC, V.

Chanterelle Restaurant. Contemporary. You can see the adjacent Wine Train Depot from your vibrant gold and red chair while you dine at this restaurant. Lunch includes gourmet pastas and innovative dishes such as the dungeness crab sandwich. Calimari steak, baked Chilean sea bass, and filet of venison are but some of the dinner selections. Wine list. Cocktail lounge. Sunday brunch. | 804 1st St. | 707/253–7300 | No breakfast | $12.50–$21.50 | AE, DC, MC, V.

French Laundry. Continental. This elegant spot is housed in a two-story stone house that served as a a French steam laundry in the early 1900s. Sirloin of young rabbit wrapped in applewood smoked bacon and red-wine braised prime beef short ribs are among the numerous American dishes with a distinct French flair that are prepared by renowned chef Thomas Keller. The menu changes daily. | 6540 Washington St., Yountville | 707/944–2380 | Reservations essential | Jackets required | No lunch Mon.–Thurs. | $80–$105 prix-fixe | AE, MC, V.

Geezer's Grill and Bar. American. More than 250 microbrews and imported beers are here, plus a selection of wines. Salads, soups, appetizers, pasta, sandwiches, and steaks round out the tavern-style menu. | 829 Main St. | 707/224–4322 | www.geezers.com | Closed Sun. No breakfast | $5–$16 | AE, D, MC, V.

Jonesy's Famous Steak House. Steak. Watch planes landing and taking off at this restaurant beside Napa County Airport. The restaurant is known for its steaks, which are hand-carved on premises. The menu also includes chicken, seafood, and salads. Artwork from Napa Valley artists adorn the walls, and there are sculptures and colored candles throughout the dining room. Kids' menu. | 2044 Airport Rd. | 707/255–2003 | Closed Mon. | $7–$22 | AE, D, DC, MC, V.

Mustards Grill. American. Surrounded by vineyards, this casual spot serves American cuisine with global influences. Try the marinated Mongolian pork chops, baby back ribs, or the slow-smoked barbecue pork sandwich. | 7399 St. Helena Hwy., | 707/944–2424 | Reservations essential | $9–$19 | D, DC, MC, V.

Pearl. Contemporary. Beneath the high ceilings of this bistro is vibrantly colored artwork and a well-lit, hip dining area. You can start with oysters, and move on to the entrées of fish and pasta specials, thick pork chops, strip steaks, or poultry. Patio dining. Wine and microbrews available. | 1339 Pearl St., Suite #104 | 707/224–9161 | fax 707/224–1552 | Closed Sun. and Mon. | MC, V.

Piccolino's Cafe. Italian. Earthy walls adorned with mirrors, flatware, wooden tables and chairs, and hanging vines attempt to recreate a café of the Italian Old Country in the dining room. Pizettes, pasta, salads, and focaccia bread sandwiches are served in individual portions; lasagne and spaghetti dinners can be ordered family style for up to five people. Live jazz on the weekends. Wine list. No smoking. | 1385 Napa Town Center | 707/251–0100 | www.piccolinoscafe.com | No breakfast | $6–$16 | AE, MC, V.

Royal Oak. Seafood. The 1870 home of General John Miller, this is one of two restaurants at the Silverado Country Club. The dining room overlooks huge oak trees, the golf course, and mountains. High-back chairs, an open kitchen, and high beam ceilings create visual texture inside as well. Besides fresh fish, try grilled pheasant sausage, and the many steaks. Casual attire. | 1600 Atlas Peak Rd. | 707/257–0200, ext. 5363 | www.silveradoresort.com | No lunch | $25–$32 | AE, D, DC, MC, V.

Rutherford Grill. American. Paintings by various American artists and wood furnishings decorate the dining room of this casual eatery. Try the baby-back ribs or the rotisserie chicken. Outdoor dining is available under umbrella-covered tables. | 1180 Rutherford Rd., Rutherford | 707/963–1792 | Reservations not accepted | $9–$25 | AE, MC, V.

Tra Vigne. Italian. Italian dishes with Tuscan influences and American items fill the menu at this restaurant which is dressed up with large wine-related paintings, including one that shows a top hat overflowing with wine. Try the ravioli stuffed with sweet and sour squash or the pan-seared New York strip. | 1050 Charter Oak Ave., St. Helena | 707/963–4444 | Reservations essential | $13–$28 | D, DC, MC, V.

Vintners Court. Contemporary. Overlooking the Silverado Country Club golf course, this seafoam green dining room has elegant wood panelling, high ceilings, white plantation shutters, and an exquisite, 13-ft-wide chandelier. The restaurant is known for its extensive wine list, and dishes like seared ahi tuna, ancho-roasted chicken, hoisin-glazed pork tenderloin. There is live piano music. | 1600 Atlas Peak Rd. | 707/257–0200 | www.silveradoresort.com | Jacket required | Closed Mon.–Tues. No lunch | $20–$30 | AE, D, DC, MC, V.

Lodging

Beazley House. Two Victorian wood houses built in 1902 are the site of Napa's first B&B, which is ideal for couples seeking a romantic getaway downtown. The carriage house behind the main mansion has six rooms with fireplaces. Afternoon tea is served in the guest living room. Extensive gardens include a 200-year-old oak tree. Dining room, complimentary breakfast, some in-room hot tubs. Library. Business services. Pets allowed. No smoking. | 1910 1st St. | 707/257–1649 or 800/559–1649 | fax 707/257–1518 | www.beazleyhouse.com | 11 rooms | $125–$275 | AE, MC, V.

Best Western Elm House Inn. Three old elms shelter this chateau-style three-story wood motel, which has sound-insulated rooms with pine furnishings, rosy fabrics, and vanities. A few rooms have wood-burning fireplaces. The motel is 2 mi from downtown Napa. Complimentary Continental breakfast. Refrigerators, cable TV. Hot tub. | 800 California Blvd. | 707/255–1831 | fax 707/255–8609 | 17 rooms | $149–$189 | AE, D, DC, MC, V.

Candlelight Inn. The green grounds and peaked roofs of this 1929 English Tudor building flanking Napa Creek give it a fairy-tale charm. To continue the fantasy, suites have marble fireplaces. Complimentary breakfast. In-room data ports, cable TV. Some in-room hot tubs. Pool. No pets. No kids under 14. No smoking. | 1045 Easum Dr. | 707/257–3717 | fax 707/257–3762 | www.candlelightinn.com | 10 suites | $135–$255 | AE, D, MC, V.

Carlyle Inn. Some of the extras you'll receive at this contemporary four-story hotel include wine, cheese, bathrobes, and hair dryers. Complimentary Continental breakfast. Cable TV. Gym. | 1119 S. Robertson Blvd. | 310/275–4445 | 32 rooms | $95–$105 | AE, D, MC, V.

Chablis Inn. This Victorian-style two-story hotel 2 mi south of downtown was built in 1982. Affordable rates and spacious rooms make it popular with business travelers. Complimentary Continental breakfast. Some kitchenettes, refrigerators, cable TV. Pool. Hot tub. Business services. | 3360 Solano Ave. | 707/257–1944 or 800/443–3490 | fax 707/226–6862 | 34 rooms | $90–$155 | AE, D, DC, MC, V.

The Chateau. Slate-colored shingles top a country-style motel. Large rooms have separate dressing areas and sitting areas. Convenient to area wineries and hot-air balloon rides, this is a stucco building 4 mi from downtown. Couples, families, and senior citizens frequent this hotel. Restaurant. Some refrigerators, cable TV. Pool. Hot tub. Business services. | 4195 Solano Ave. | 707/253–9300 or 800/253–6272 | fax 707/253–0906 | 115 rooms, 5 suites | $140, $195–$240 suites | AE, D, DC, MC, V.

Country Garden. Enter through a landscape of mature trees and flower beds to reach the inn, formerly an 1860 coach house on the Silverado Trail. Brick and stone paths wind through the riverside property, leading to a lily pond. Picnic area, complimentary breakfast. Some in-room hot tubs, no room phones. No smoking. | 1815 Silverado Trail | 707/255–1197 | fax 707/255–3112 | www.countrygardeninn.com | 10 rooms | $155–$235 | AE, MC, V.

Embassy Suites Napa Valley. This modern two-story Mediterranean-style wood building has lush landscaping and gardens, an outdoor mill pond, and an indoor atrium with dining. The hotel, 1 mi west of downtown, offers one- and two-bedroom suites. Restaurant, bar [with entertainment], complimentary breakfast, room service. In-room data ports, refrigerators, cable TV. Outdoor pool, indoor pool. Hot tub, sauna. Bicycles. Business services. | 1075 California Blvd. | 707/253–9540 or 800/EMBASSY | fax 707/253–9202 | www.embassynapa.com | 205 suites | $234–$284 | AE, D, DC, MC, V.

John Muir Inn. This contemporary three-story wood and stucco hotel has attractive landscaping, and offers standard and deluxe rooms. It's 5 mi from downtown. Complimentary Continental breakfast. In-room data ports, some kitchenettes, some refrigerators, cable TV. Pool. Hot tub. Business services. | 1998 Trower Ave. | 707/257–7220 or 800/522–8999 | fax 707/258–0943 | www.johnmuirnapa.com | 59 rooms | $85–$190 | AE, D, DC, MC, V.

La Residence Country Inn. This French barn and mansion sits on two acres of property, and has fountains and two ponds. Large rooms and suites have French doors opening to verandas or patios, and are beautifully furnished with antiques. Some minibars, some microwaves, no TV in rooms. Pool. Hot tub. Business services. No pets. No smoking. | 4066 St. Helena Rte. 29 | 707/253–0337 or 800/253–9203 | fax 707/253–0382 | www.laresidence.com | 20 rooms | $200–$350 | AE, D, DC, MC, V.

Laurel Street Inn. One of the two rooms here has a Tuscan-style shower for two and the other boasts a double, hydro-therapy massage bath and shower combo. Floral prints and Victorian antiques adorn the bedrooms. There's wine in the afternoon and port or sherry in the evening. Restaurants, golf courses, and, of course, wineries are all a short distance away. Complimentary breakfast. No room phones. No TV. | 1737 Laurel St. | 888/724–4700 | www.thelaurelstreetinn.com | 2 rooms | $159–$199 | AE, MC, V.

Marriott Napa Valley. This 1980 Mediterranean-style building is 5 mi from downtown. It's convenient primarily to business travelers. Restaurant, bar, room service. In-room data ports, cable TV. Pool. Hot tub. Business services. | 3425 Solano Ave. | 707/253–7433 or

800/228–9290 | fax 707/258–1320 | www.marriott.com | 191 rooms | $229–$269 | AE, D, DC, MC, V.

Napa Valley Lodge. A poolside champagne breakfast awaits you at this hotel. The concierge can arrange balloon excursions and wine tastings as well as trips to nearby restaurants and shops. Each spacious room affords an excellent view of Napa Valley. Complimentary Continental breakfast. Refrigerators, cable TV. Outdoor pool. Hot tub, sauna. Golf priviledges. Gym. Library. | 2230 Madison St. | 707/944–2468 or 800/368–2468 | fax 707/944–9362 | www.woodsidehotels.com/napa | 55 rooms | $282–$593 | AE, D, DC, MC, V.

Napa Valley Spanish Villa. Each room in this Mediterranean-style villa has a king-size bed with a handcarved Spanish headboard and reproduction Tiffany lamps. The villa's patio overlooks an ornate European fountain, canopied swing, and abundant rose gardens. Complimentary Continental breakfast. Library. No children. No pets. No smoking. | 474 Glass Mountain Rd. | 707/963–7483 | fax 707/967–9401 | www.napavalleyspanishvilla.com | 3 rooms | $155–$215 | MC, V.

Old World Inn. This 1906 three-story wooden Victorian inn is bright and comfortable. Painted antiques complement the color scheme of the rooms, most of which contain fireplaces. The house is just a 10-min walk from downtown. Dining room, complimentary breakfast. No TV in soom rooms. Some in-room hot tubs. No pets. No smoking. | 1301 Jefferson St. | 707/257–0112 or 800/966–6624 | fax 707/257–0118 | www.oldworldinn.com | 8 rooms | $140–$240 | AE, D, MC, V.

Silverado Country Club and Resort. This luxurious resort 5 mi north of downtown offers hotel rooms to three-bedroom cottages with fireplaces. A southern-style mansion here dates back to 1870. The resort encompasses 1,200 acres. 2 restaurants (see Vintners Court, Royal Oak), bar [with entertainment]. In-room data ports, some kitchenettes, minibars, refrigerators, cable TV. 8 pools. Hot tub. Driving range, 2 18-hole golf courses, putting greens, 20 tennis courts. Laundry facilities. Business services, airport shuttle. | 1600 Atlas Peak Rd. | 707/257–0200 or 800/532–0500 | fax 707/257–5400 | www.silveradoresort.com | 280 suites | $165–$535 | AE, D, DC, MC, V.

Stahlecker House. This 1947 country-style B&B is on an acre of manicured lawns, shade trees, and flower gardens. Rooms have canopy beds, fireplaces, and antique furnishings. Breakfast is served in a dining room overlooking the garden. Dining room, complimentary breakfast. In-room data ports. No room phones. Some in-room hot tubs. Spa. No pets. | 1042 Easum Dr. | 707/257–1588 or 800/799–1588 | fax 707/224–7429 | www.stahleckerhouse.com | 4 rooms | $139–$269 | AE, D, DC, MC, V.

Travelodge Napa Valley. This motel in Old Town Napa is an affordable way to stay in Napa's commercial district. The three-story 1963 motel is close to restaurants, galleries, and shops. Restaurant. In-room data ports, some in-room hot tubs, in-room VCRs (and movies). Pool. | 853 Coombs St. | 707/226–1871 | fax 707/226–1707 | www.travelodge.com | 45 rooms | $99–$209 | AE, D, DC, MC, V.

NEEDLES

MAP 4, N13

(Nearby town also listed: Mojave National Preserve)

This small, low-desert town of 5,200 was named for the abrupt, jagged demeanor of nearby mountains. From June through September the town sizzles in the 90s to the low 120s. The East Mojave National Scenic Area offers a variety of desert scenes and wildlife, and, for some relief from the summer heat, the Colorado River has some fine boating and fishing possibilities. You can see a brief glimpse of the town in the classic film "Grapes of Wrath"—it's the site of a one-lane wooden bridge over the Colorado River. Needles lies 107 mi south of Las Vegas and 144 mi east of Barstow.

Information: **Needles Chamber of Commerce** | 100 G St., Box 705, 92363 | 760/326–2050 | fax 760/326–2194.

Attractions

Moabi Regional Park. You can camp, fish, boat, swim, and waterski at this park on the banks of the Colorado River, 11 mi southeast of Needles. | Mark Moabi Rd. | 760/326–3831 | fax 760/326–3272 | www.co.san-bernardino.ca.us/parks | $6 per vehicle | Daily.

Providence Mountains State Recreation Area. This family recreation area, 16 mi north of town off I–40 on Essex Road has caves and camping. | 760/928–2586 | www.cal-parksmojave.com/providence | Free; caverns $6 | Daily.

Havasu National Wildlife Refuge. The refuge is made up of gorge, marsh, and wilderness extending 24 mi along the Colorado River. It protects many endangered species. | I–40 and Arizona State Rte. 95 intersect the refuge at many points. Main entrance, 317 Mesquite Ave. | 760/326–3853 | www.coloradoriverinfo.com/lakehavasucity/havasurefuge | Free | Daily.

Dining

Hungry Bear. American. This restaurant 2 mi west of downtown has a Route 66 theme. The large menu here includes steaks (porterhouse and filet mignon), swordfish, halibut, sandwiches, and pasta. | 1906 W. Needles Hwy. | 760/326–2988 | Breakfast also available | $7–$14 | AE, D, DC, MC, V.

Lucy's Mexican Restaurant. Mexican. This is a family-owned restaurant that serves green chili burritos and chile rellenos. | 811 Front St. | 760/326–4461 | Closed Mon.–Wed. | $5–$7.25 | No credit cards.

Mudshark Pizza and Pasta. American. A busy restaurant, it has pizzas and pastas. | 819 West Broadway | 760/326–9191 | $5–$16 | MC, V.

Lodging

Best Western Colorado River Inn. This 2-story rural stucco motel built in 1993 is 1½ mi west of downtown. Restaurant. Refrigerators, microwaves. Sauna. Indoor pool. Pets allowed. | 2371 W. Broadway | 760/326–4552 | fax 760/326–4562 | www.bestwestern.com | 63 rooms | $60–$70 | AE, D, DC, MC, V.

Best Western Royal Inn. This 1990 wood and stucco 2-story motel is 1½ mi northwest of downtown. In-room data ports, cable TV. Pool. Hot tub, spa. Laundry facilities. Pets allowed (fee). | 1111 Pashard St. | 760/326–5660 | fax 760/326–4002 | www.bestwestern.com | 60 rooms | $60–$70 | AE, D, DC, MC, V.

Days Inn. Rooms surround a courtyard pool at this 2-story motel built in 1985, just off I–40 at the J street exit, 25 mi northwest of Lake Havasu. Complimentary Continental breakfast. In-room data ports, some microwaves, some refrigerators, cable TV. Pool. Pets allowed. | 1215 Hospitality Lane | 760/326–5836 | fax 760/326–4444 | www.daysinn.com | 121 rooms | $90–$119 | AE, D, MC, V.

Red Roof Inn. This is a three-story southwestern style stucco building built in 1991. On one side of the hotel are mountains and on the other is I–40. It's ¼ mi from downtown and ideal for families and business travelers. Pool. Laundry service. Business services. | 1195 3rd St. Hill | 760/326–4900 | fax 760/326–4980 | 117 rooms | $45–$50 | AE, D, DC, MC, V.

River Valley Motor Lodge. One mile east of downtown, this motel, built in 1978, is a very affordable option. Cable TV. Refrigerators. Pool. Pets allowed. | 1707 W. Broadway | 760/326–3839 | fax 760/326–3881 | 26 rooms | $23–$29 | AE, D, DC, MC, V.

Super 8 Motel of Needles. This two-story peach motel on the edge of Needles off I–40 is near golf and fishing. It offers standard rooms, with basic amenities. Cable TV. Pool. Laundry services. Pets allowed. | 1102 E. Broadway | 760/326–4501 or 800/800–8000 | fax 760/326–2054 | 30 rooms | $50–$60 | AE, D, DC, MC, V.

NEVADA CITY

(Nearby towns also listed: Grass Valley, Marysville, Oroville)

Nevada City (population 2,900) is one of the most delightful and most complete of the Gold Rush-era towns. Set in a gorge of Deer Creek, it's ringed by forested hillsides, where two of the most productive mines yielded half the gold that came out of the Gold Rush. The well-preserved downtown district is a national historic landmark. Now the iron-shuttered brick buildings that line the narrow downtown steets contain antiques shops, galleries, a winery, bookstores, and boutiques. Horse-drawn carriages and gas-powered street lights add to the romance.

Today the gold in Nevada City is found in the colors of its maple and liquid-amber trees in autumn, California's answer to New England fall foliage. Other treasures include the Gold Rush-era downtown and miles of hiking trails and historic sites.

Information: Nevada City Chamber of Commerce | 132 Main St, 95959 | 530/265–2692 | www.ncgold.com/ncchamber.

Attractions

Firehouse Museum. This museum in old Firehouse No. 1 includes pioneer relics, Indian artifacts, and a Chinese altar. | 214 Main St. | 530/265–5468 | Free | Jan.–mid-Apr., weekends 11–4; mid-Apr.–Dec., daily 11–4.

The Foothill Theatre Company. This professional theater company stages a season of musicals, classics, historical plays, and entertainment for kids. | 401 Broad St. | 530/265–8587 | Mar.–Dec.

Malakoff Diggings State Historic Park. This mine site remains a symbol of greed's effect on the landscape. Entire sides of the mountain were washed away by intense hydraulic operations in the last days of the Gold Rush. The park has reconstructed mining buildings as well as several lakes, hiking trails, campgrounds, and a museum. | 23579 N. Bloomfield Rd. | 530/265–2740 or 800/444–7275 | $2 per vehicle | Daily dawn–dusk.

Miners Foundry Cultural Center. Built of native stone in 1856 to support the metalworking enterprise, the center now serves as a performing arts facility with more than 200 annual events. | 325 Spring St. | 530/265–5040 | Daily 9–5.

The Teddy Bear Castle Museum. This 1855 castle features about 2,000 teddy bears collected from artists, collectors, and manufacturers. | 203 South Pine St. | 530/265–5804 | fax 530/478–0728 | www.teddybearcastle.com | Free | Sat. and Sun., 11–3 | Closed Dec. 21–Mar. 15.

ON THE CALENDAR

APR.: *International Teddy Bear Convention.* Buy, sell, or swap all manner of teddy bears and toy animals at the Miners Foundry Cultural Center. Teddy bears admitted free. | 530/265–5804.

JUNE: *Nevada City Classic Bicycle Tour.* Bike races wind through downtown on Father's Day weekend. | 530/265–2692.

SEPT.: *Constitution Day.* This weekend event includes Civil War re-enactments and a parade. | 530/265–2692.

OCT., NOV.: *Fall Color Spectacular.* Pick up a map at the Chamber of Commerce to follow a self-guided viewing tour of brilliant-hued trees. | 530/265–2692.

DEC.: *Victorian Christmas.* On the weekends leading to Christmas, downtown is closed to traffic and filled with street vendors in 19th-century costume selling hot cider and roasted chestnuts. | 530/265–2692.

Dining

Country Rose Cafe. French. Historic photographs of the building that the restaurant is housed in and small white lights decorate the dining area of this small restaurant in which you can see into the kitchen. Try the poulet escoffier, a boneless chicken breast in a mushroom sauce or the sauteed salmon filet. | 300 Commercial St. | 530/265–6248 | Reservations essential on weekends | $15–$37 | AE, DC, MC, V.

Friar Tuck's. Swiss. Fondue is the specialty at this spot with three separate dining rooms. It is housed in an 1850s building and the Pine St. dining room overlooks Nevada City's historic district. Try the roast duck. | 111 N. Pine St. | 530/265–9093 | No lunch | $17–$21 | AE, MC, V.

Off Broad Street. Inside a small theater, this dessert café serves cakes, pies, and ice cream along with live entertainment. Shows are $16-$18, and performance times vary, so be sure to call ahead. | 305 Commercial St. | 530/265–8686 | obs@foothill.net | $2–10 | No credit cards.

Lodging

Deer Creek Inn. Some rooms in this Queen Anne Victorian home have claw-foot bathtubs and private patios that overlook landscaped grounds and Deer Creek. The grounds are highlighted by a 100-ft cherry and various other trees. Complimentary breakfast. No TV in some rooms. No pets. No kids under 12. No smoking. | 116 Nevada St. | 530/265–0363 or 800/655–0363 | fax 530/265–0980 | deercreek@gv.net | www.deercreekinn.com | 5 rooms | $120–$165 | AE, MC, V.

Emma Nevada House. This Victorian inn, the childhood home of 19th-century opera star Emma Nevada, offers romantic decor in individually furnished rooms with names like Empress Chamber, Mignon's Boudoir, and Emma's Hideaway. The 1856 wooden inn also has sitting rooms, porches, and a creekside garden. Complimentary full breakfast. Some in-room hot tubs, no TV in some rooms, TV in common area. No room phones. No pets. No children under 10. No smoking. | 528 Broad St. | 530/265–4415 or 800/916–EMMA | fax 530/265–4416 | www.nevadacityinns.com | 6 rooms | $105–$160 | AE, D, DC, MC, V.

Flumes's End. Built in 1860, this Victorian B&B sits on three acres of landscaped property. There's a lovely footbridge and alongside the house, a historic flume. Picnic area, complimentary breakfast. No TV in rooms, TV in common area. No smoking. | 317 S. Pine St. | 530/265–9665 or 800/991–8118 | 6 rooms | $95–$150 | MC, V.

Grandmere's Inn. This 1856 two-story Victorian B&B is in the downtown historic district. Spacious rooms have four-poster beds and antiques. The grounds have formal gardens. Complimentary breakfast. No TV in rooms. No smoking. | 449 Broad St. | 530/265–4660 | fax 530/265–4416 | www.nevadacityinns.com | 6 rooms | $110–$175 | AE, MC, V.

Northern Queen Inn. On 34 acres of landscaped property, this 1972 two-story inn is a mile from downtown. Most rooms at this bright, creek-side inn are typical motel units, but there are eight two-story chalets and eight rustic cottages with kitchenettes and gas log fireplaces in a secluded, wooded area. You can ride on the hotel's narrow-gauge railroad, which offers excursions through Maidu Indian homelands and a Chinese cemetery from Gold Rush days. Restaurant, picnic area. Refrigerators, cable TV. Pool. Hot tub. | 400 Railroad Ave. | 530/265–5824 | fax 530/265–3720 | 70 rooms, 8 cottages, 8 chalets | $65–$70, $85 cottages, $100 chalets | AE, D, MC, V.

Outside Inn. This is a 1940s motel in a residential area, 2 blocks from downtown Nevada City. Rooms are individually appointed, many with knotty pine paneling and hardwood floors. Some kitchenettes, some refrigerators. Cable TV. Pool. | 575 E. Broad St. |

530/265–2233 | fax 530/265–2236 | manager@outsideinn.com | www.outsideinn.com | 11 rooms | $60–$125 | AE, MC, V.

★ **Red Castle.** This 1860 red brick, four-story Gothic Revival mansion sits on 1½ acres of wooded hillside overlooking the city. Complimentary breakfast. No TV. Pond. Library. No room phones. No kids under 12. No smoking. No Pets. | 109 Prospect St. | 530/265–5135 | www.historiclodgings.com | 7 rooms | $110–$145 | MC, V.

NEWPORT BEACH

(Nearby towns also listed: Corona del Mar, Costa Mesa, Huntington Beach, Irvine)

Newport (pop. 73,000) has two personalities: a casual beachy side which has drawn visitors for a century and an all-business side with high rise office buildings and expensive business hotels. Between these two are waterfront homes of some of southern California's wealthiest residents.

The summer beach crowd gravitates to Balboa Peninsula, Balboa Island, Bay Shores and Lower and Upper Newport Bay. Those wearing suits and ties will be more comfortable around the high-rise office buildings near John Wayne/Orange County Airport and Newport Center.

Newport Beach boasts a major shopping center which draws visitors from all over the region, Fashion Island in Newport Center. For the purposes of finding your way around, these are interchangeable.

Information: **Newport Harbor Area Chamber of Commerce** | 1470 Jamboree Rd., 92660 | 949/729–4400 | www.newportbeach.com.

Attractions

Orange County Museum of Art. This museum showcases the history of California art from mid 19th-century art to the present with permanent collections of paintings, sculptures, and mixed-media works. | 850 San Clemente Dr. | 949/759–1122 | fax 949/759–5623 | www.ocma.net | $5 | Tues.–Sun. 11–5.

Sherman Library and Gardens. The cultural center has a tea garden and a touch-and-smell garden. The gardens display tropical and subtropical flora. | 2647 E. Pacific Coast Hwy. | 949/673–2261 | fax 949/675–5458 | $3 | Daily 10:30–4.

ON THE CALENDAR
SEPT.: *Taste of Newport.* This three-day festival features entertainment and food on Newport Center Drive. | 949/729–4400.
DEC.: *Christmas Boat Parade.* Festively decorated boats parade in celebration of the holidays at Newport Harbor. | 949/729–4400.

Dining

Amelia's on Balboa Island. Italian. Amelia's, one of Orange County's restaurant pioneers, has been serving great Italian food since 1961. Try the linguine with fresh bay scallops and five varieties of lasagna, in addition to five or more fresh fish dishes. | 311 Marine Ave., Balboa Island | 949/673–6580 | No lunch Mon.–Thur | $14–$30 | AE, D, DC, MC, V.

★ **Aubergine.** French. This tiny husband-and-wife-run restaurant (he mans the kitchen and she handles the dining room) have set new standards for fine cuisine in Orange County. You can choose between vegetarian 10-course or non-vegetarian five-course prix-fixe menus. Try the rack of rabbit and glazed baby carrots, slow-braised pork belly with poached white aspargus and cream of morel mushrooms, and kabocha squash agnolotti with fresh truffles and browned butter. | 508 29th St. | 949/723–4150 | Closed Sun. and Mon. | $65–$90 | AE, MC, V.

Crab Cooker. Seafood. In business for almost half a century, this immensely popular eatery serves tasty seafood on paper plates and has the best clam chowder for miles around. Dinner entrées range from skewered scallops with bacon to cracked crab. You can sit down in the restaurant or get your food to go from the adjoining market. There's always a wait during dinner hours. | 2200 Newport Blvd. | 949/673–0100 | Reservations not accepted | $12–$26 | AE, MC, V.

★ **El Torito Grill.** Southwestern. This restaurant in Fashion Island serves Southwestern and Mexican specialities, including a great tortilla soup and *carne asada* (grilled beef). Freshly baked tortillas with salsa are complimentary. The bar serves hand-shaken margaritas and 80 brands of tequila. An open-air patio with wrought iron tables seats 75. | 951 Newport Center Dr. | 949/640–2875 | $15–$20 | AE, D, DC, MC, V.

Koto. Japanese. This Japanese tea house has a sushi counter and two dining areas decorated with Japanese dolls. You can dine on the floor in a traditional manner while being served by staff dressed in traditional kimonos. An outdoor patio overlooks landscaped gardens and a koi pond. | 4300 Von Karman Ave. | 949/752–7151 | $20–$30 | AE, D, DC, MC, V.

Marrakesh. Moroccan. At this restaurant you can sit on pillows and low couches in a tent-like interior and enjoy Moroccan-style multi-course dinners of chicken, vegetables, and fish. There is nightly belly dancing. | 1976 Newport Blvd. | 949/645–8384 | No lunch | $17–$23 | AE, D, DC, MC, V.

Newport Beach Brewing Co. American. The largest outdoor patio in Newport Beach makes this Cannery Village brewery a great place to eat while people-watching. Hardwood floors, two separate bars, and a refreshing absence of the usual pub paraphernalia make for comfortable dining. The restaurant is known for its barbequed chicken pizza, and its Chinese chicken salad. | 2920 Newport Blvd. | 949/675–8449 | $12–$20 | AE, D, DC, MC, V.

Oysters. Seafood. This decidedly hip yet surprisingly convivial seafood restaurant, complete with a bustling bar and live jazz, caters to a late night crowd. The eclectic menu includes fire-roasted artichokes to excellent ahi dishes. | 2515 Pacific Coast Hwy. | 949/675–7411 | No lunch | $8–$20 | AE, DC, MC, V.

Pavilion. Contemporary. You can sit outdoors on a patio overlooking the garden (with white lights on every tree), or opt for the ambient, candlit interior, decorated with fine linens, flowers, and works by local artists. The seasonally rotating menu at this restaurant in the Four Seasons hotel might include roasted butternut squash and pumpkin ravioli with madeira wine sauce, or pepper-crusted lamb with a port wine reduction. | 690 Newport Center Dr. | 949/760–4920 | Breakfast also available | $20–$32 | AE, D, DC, MC, V.

P. F. Chang's China Bistro. Chinese. The tasty Cal-Chinese food at this trendy chain restaurant includes Mongolian spicy beef and Chang's chicken, stir-fried in a sweet-and-spicy Szechuan sauce. Almost every table has an ocean view, but many diners are too busy people-watching to notice. Food can also be ordered at the lively bar. | 1145 Newport Center Dr. | 949/759–9007 | $8–$15 | AE, D, DC, MC, V.

The Ritz. Continental. Indeed, this is one of the ritziest restaurants in southern California, complete with black-leather booths and polished-brass trim. Try the "carousel" appetizer—cured gravlax, prawns, dungeness crab legs, Maine lobster tails, goose liver paté, fillet of smoked trout, Parma prosciutto, filet mignon tartare, and marinated herring, all served on a lazy susan. | 880 Newport Center Dr. | 949/720–1800 | $19–$32 | AE, DC, MC, V.

21 Oceanfront. Seafood. A long wood bar, brass fixtures, burgundy carpeting, and black leather booths create an Old World atmosphere at this oceanfront restaurant. Sample fresh ahi sashimi from Hawaii, blue point oysters, and Maryland blue crab cakes. Entrée selections include Norwegian salmon, and pink Baja abalone. There's live piano music Thursday through Sunday. | 2100 W. Oceanfront | 949/673–2100 | Reservations essential | Jacket required | No lunch | $25–$75 | AE, D, DC, MC, V.

Lodging

Balboa Bay Club. You have beach access at this hotel on 15 acres of bay-front property. Restaurant, bar. In-room data ports. Pool. Exercise equipment. Dock. | 1221 West Coast Highway | 949/645–5000 | fax 949/645–3727 | www.balboabayclub.com | 106 rooms, 15 suites | $185–$575 | AE, D, DC, MC, V.

Best Western Bay Shores Inn. This hotel ½ block from the beach has a sun deck and offers ocean and bay views from some of its rooms. It's 4 mi south of Fashion Island. Complimentary Continental breakfast. In-room data ports, cable TV, some refrigerators, in-room VCRs (and movies). Laundry facilities. Business services. No pets. | 1800 W. Balboa Blvd. | 949/675–3463 | fax 949/675–4977 | 25 rooms | $149–$189 | AE, D, DC, MC, V.

Doryman's. This 1900 Victorian hotel is right on the beach, across the street from a pier. It has a sun deck, and is ideal for couples. Complimentary Continental breakfast. In-room data ports, cable TV. Business services. No pets. | 2102 W. Ocean Front | 949/675–7300 | 10 rooms, 4 suites | $175–$325 | AE, MC, V.

★ **Four Seasons Hotel.** This 20-story contemporary marble-and-stucco building has tropically landscaped grounds and caters to couples, families, and business travelers. It's across the street from Fashion Island. Restaurants, bar [with entertainment], room service. In-room data ports, refrigerators, cable TV. Pool. Beauty salon, spa, hot tub, massage. Tennis. Gym, bicycles. Business services, airport shuttle. Pets allowed. | 690 Newport Center Dr. | 949/759–0808 or 800/332–3442 | fax 949/759–0568 | www.fourseasons.com | 285 rooms, 92 suites | $340–$465, $400–$3900 suites | AE, D, DC, MC, V.

Hyatt Newporter. These three three-story Spanish-style stucco buildings are ideal for families. The hotel is on 26 acres of tropical landscaped property; across the street is the Fashion Island Shopping Center. Bar [with entertainment], dining room, room service. In-room data ports, cable TV. Refrigerators. 3 pools. 3 spas. 9-hole golf course. Exercise equipment, bicycles. Baby-sitting. Laundry facilities, laundry services. Business services, airport shuttle. Pets allowed. | 1107 Jamboree Rd. | 949/729–1234 | fax 949/644–1552 | www.hyatt-newporter.com | 405 rooms, 11 suites | $190–$275, $350 suites | AE, D, DC, MC, V.

Little Inn by the Bay. This inn is on the beach, 2 blocks from the boardwalk. Complimentary Continental breakfast. In-room data ports. | 2627 Newport Blvd. | 949/673–8800 | 18 rooms | $80–$229.

Marriott Hotel and Tennis Club. Tennis enthusiasts will enjoy their stay at this 1975 contemporary 16-story hotel across the street from Fashion Island and 2 mi from the beach. Restaurant, bar, room service. In-room data ports, cable TV. 2 pools. Hot tub. 8 tennis courts. Gym. Laundry facilities. Business services. Pets allowed. | 900 Newport Center Dr. | 949/640–4000 | fax 949/640–5055 | 570 rooms | $250–$305 | AE, D, DC, MC, V.

Marriott Suites. This nine-story, C-shaped hotel overlooks Newport Beach. One bedroom suites are available; each has a private balcony. The hotel is 8 mi from the beach and 2 mi from Fashion Island. There's a garden area with gazebo on the property. Restaurant, bar. In-room data ports, refrigerators, cable TV. Pool. Hot tub. Exercise equipment. Business services, airport shuttle. | 500 Bayview Circle | 949/854–4500 | fax 949/854–3937 | www.marriott.com | 250 suites | $179–$199 suites | AE, D, DC, MC, V.

Newport Channel Inn. There's a roof deck for sunbathing and beach towels are provided at this hotel across the street from the beach. | 3060 West Coast Highway | 949/642–3030 | www.newportbeach-cvb.com/channelinn.html | 30 rooms | $59–$155 | AE, D, DC, MC, V.

Portofino Beach Hotel. This two-story hotel, built in 1965, is across the street from the beach. The hotel is ideal for couples and families. Dining room, complimentary Continental breakfast. In-room data ports, some in-room hot tubs, cable TV, in-room VCR's. Library. Business services. No pets. | 2306 W. Ocean Front | 949/673–7030 or 800/571–8749 | www.portofinobeachhotel.com | fax 949/723–4370 | 15 rooms | $159–$399 | AE, D, DC, MC, V.

Radisson Hotel. This 7-story hotel, just south of John Wayne County Airport, has beautifully landscaped grounds with a tropical theme and sits 6 mi from the beach. Restaurant, bar, room service. In-room data ports. Pool. Hot tub. Tennis courts. Exercise equipment. Shops. Airport shuttle. No pets. | 4545 MacArthur Blvd. | 949/833–0570 | fax 949/838–0187 | www.ci.newport-beach.ca.us | 335 rooms | $109–$500 | AE, D, DC, MC, V.

Sutton Place. This 1985 Mediterranean-style, 10-story concrete-and-marble hotel is 4 mi east of the beach. Rooms are decorated in soft pastels Restaurant, bar [with entertainment], room service. In-room data ports, minibars, cable TV. Pool. Hot tub, massage. Tennis. Exercise equipment. Business services. | 4500 MacArthur Blvd. | 949/476–2001 or 800/243–4141 | fax 949/476–0153 | www.travelweb.com/sutton.html | 435 rooms | $185–$215 | AE, D, DC, MC, V.

NORTH HOLLYWOOD

MAP 9, D2

(Nearby towns also listed: Burbank, Glendale, Studio City, Universal City)

North Hollywood is bounded by the Hollywood Freeway, or the 170, to the east, and is south of the Burbank Airport. The NoHo Arts District is evolving into a theater center and the NoHo Arts Festival is a popular spring event.

Information: **Universal City–North Hollywood Chamber of Commerce,** | 11335 Magnolia Blvd., Suite 2D, 91601 | 818/508–5155 | www.noho.org.

Dining

Ca' Cafedel Sol. Italian. Showbiz types and locals are drawn to this Venetian-style establishment in search of such classics as sautéed fresh rock shrimp in a spicy garlic-tomato sauce; citrus-marinated chicken wings braised with Italian bacon, rosemary, and sage; and linguini with scallops and Manila clams. Save room for a giant hunk of Italian-style cheesecake covered with marinated strawberries. You can dine by the fireplace, on the patio, or in one of three rooms amidst antique wood hutches and copper moldings. Sunday brunch. No smoking. | 4100 Cahuenga Blvd. | 818/985–4669 | Reservations essential | No lunch Sat. | $18–$31 | AE, DC, MC, V.

Lodging

Best Western Mikado. This branch of the Best Western chain is named for one of Gilbert and Sullivan's light operas. In a residential area 3 mi west of Universal Studios, the hotel is 15 mi north of downtown LA. Restaurant, bar, complimentary breakfast. Room service, cable TV. Pool. Hot tub. Business services. | 12600 Riverside Dr. | 818/763–9141 | fax 818/752–1045 | www.bestwestern.com | 58 rooms | $109–$119 | AE, D, DC, MC, V.

Holiday Inn–Beverly Garland. The seven landscaped acres surrounding these twin towers are 1 mi west of Universal Studios and 11 mi northwest of downtown LA. Each room has a private balcony. Restaurant, bar. Room service, cable TV. Pool, wading pool. Tennis. Business services, free parking. | 4222 Vineland Ave. | 818/980–8000 | fax 818/766–5230 | www.beverlygarland.com | 255 rooms | $129–$169 | AE, D, DC, MC, V.

OAKDALE

(Nearby towns also listed: Modesto, Sonora, Stockton)

This town of 15,000 along Stanislaus River east of Modesto has its roots in gold and the railroad, but today is known as the "Cowboy Capital of the World" because of the number of Professional Rodeo Association cowboys who have lived here. This probably has something to do with the fact that the Oakdale Rodeo was the first outdoor rodeo in the western United States. The town is also famous for its Hershey chocolate plant, and in May you can indulge at the Oakdale Chocolate Festival.

Information: Oakdale Visitors' Bureau | 590 N. Yosemite Ave., 95361 | 209/847–2244 | info@yosemite-gateway.net | www.yosemite-gateway.net.

Attractions

Hershey Chocolate USA. This museum chronicles the history of the Hershey Company and illustrates the chocolate-making process. | 1400 S. Yosemite Ave. | 209/848–5100 | fax 209/847–2622 | www.hersheys.com | Free | Weekdays 9:30–3.

Oakdale Cowboy Museum. Displays the sights, sounds and smells of the Wild West. Exhibits emphasize the history of the land and the people, and their future in modern day society. You will find saddles, buckles, ranching implements and memorabilia from pioneer ranching families, as well as rodeo stars Ted Nuce, Jerold Camarillo, Ace Berry and many more Oakdale greats on display. | 355 F St. #1 | 209/847–7049 | www.yosemite-gateway.net/cowboy.html | Free | Weekdays 11–3.

Woodward Reservoir. This 3,767 acres of land and 2,900-acre reservoir have beautiful views as well as good duck hunting by permit, Picnic shelter, fishing, boating, swimming, water skiing. | 14528 26 Mile Rd. | 209/847–3304 | Free | Daily.

ON THE CALENDAR

APR.: *PRCA Rodeo.* This large rodeo draws crowds to the Oakdale Saddle Club Arena. | 209/847–2244.
MAY: *Chocolate Festival.* Bring your appetite. | 3rd weekend in May | 209/847–2244.
SEPT.: *California Dally Team Roping Championships.* This roping competition lures off-season rodeo fans. | 209/847–2244.

Lodging

Ramada Inn. This two-story contemporary stucco hostelry is in a commercial area ½ mi from downtown Oakdale and 10 mi from the Hershey Factory and Visitor Center. Restaurant, bar. Cable TV. Pool. Hot tub. | 825 East F St. | 209/847–8181 | fax 209/847–9546 | www.ramada.com | 70 rooms | $83 | AE, D, DC, MC, V.

OAKHURST

(Nearby towns also listed: June Lake, Lee Vining, Mammoth Lakes, Merced, Yosemite National Park)

This town of 14,000 sits at the western edge of Yosemite, and is a good place to find reasonable prices for gas before you enter the park. Most people pass through Oakhurst to stock up at the local shops on their way to Bass Lake.

Information: Yosemite-Sierra Visitors Bureau | 40637 Rte. 41, 93644 | 559/683–4636 | ysvb@sierranet.net | www.yosemite-sierra.org.

Attractions

Fresno Flats Historical Park. This typical 19th-century community includes a collection of wagons and stagecoaches, a schoolhouse, and a logging facility. | Rd. 427 and Rd. 418 | 559/683–6570 | Free | Daily; tours: Apr.–Nov., Wed.–Sun. by appointment.

Yosemite Mountain–Sugar Pine Railroad. This 4-mi, narrow-gauge, steam-powered railroad excursion, riding the rails near Yosemite National Park's south gate, lets you chug into history. Travel back to a time when powerful locomotives once hauled massive log trains through the Sierra. There's also a moonlight special, with dinner and entertainment. | 56001 Rte. 41, Fish Camp | 559/683–7273 | www.ymsprr.com | $7.50–$33.50 | Mar.–Oct., daily.

Dining

Erna's Elderberry House. Contemporary. This popular restaurant, in a residential area ½ mi from the center of Oakhurst, is an expression of the owner's passion for beauty, charm, and impeccable service. Ruby-red walls and dark beams accent the dining room's high ceilings, and arched windows reflect the glow of many candles. Locals, celebrities, and tourists flock here as much for the surroundings as for the elegantly paced six-course, prix-fixe dinner and superb wines in rhythm with the seasons. A terrace overlooks the Sierra. Servers recite the menu, which changes daily. Sunday brunch. No smoking. | 48688 Victoria La. | 559/683–6800 | Daily dinner only, Sunday brunch | $75 per person (six-course prix fixe) | AE, D, MC, V.

Lodging

Best Western Yosemite Gateway Inn. This rustic building on six landscaped acres has a unique brick and rock lobby with a fireplace and baby grand piano. It's in a commercial area 15 mi from the south gate of Yosemite and 1 mi from downtown Oakhurst. Restaurant, bar, picnic area. Some kitchenettes, some refrigerators, cable TV. Indoor pool. Hot tub, sauna. Laundry facilities. | 40530 Rte. 41 | 559/683–2378 or 800/545–5462 | fax 559/683–3813 | www.bestwestern.com | 118 rooms | $96 | AE, D, DC, MC, V.

★ **Château du Sureau.** This hostelry has two buildings: one, a two-story wood and tile structure reminiscent of a French château, and the other, the Villa Sureau, which evokes a Parisian manor house. Both are 16 mi south of the southern entrance of Yosemite, about 1 mi from downtown Oakhurst. Also located here is Erna's Elderberry House restaurant described above. Restaurant, complimentary breakfast. Pool. No smoking. | 48688 Victoria La. | 559/683–6860 | fax 559/683–0800 | www.chateausureau.com | 10 rooms | $325–$510 | AE, MC, V.

The Homestead. Built in 1992 on 160 acres of forest, this bed and breakfast has four cottages, all with fireplaces and full kitchens. The Homestead is in Awahnee, about 3 mi west of Oakhurst and 13 mi south of Yosemite. Complimentary Continental breakfast. Kitchenettes, cable TV, no room phones. | 41110 Road 600, Ahwahnee | 559/683–0495 | fax 559/683–8165 | homesteadcottages@sierratel.com | www.homesteadcottages.com | 5 cottages | $125–$209 | AE, D, MC, V.

Pines Resort. You can stay in the lodge with lake views or in an A-frame chalet at this resort on Bass Lake, 14 mi from the southern entrance to Yosemite National Park. Restaurant, bar [with entertainment], complimentary Continental breakfast, room service.

Refrigerators, some in-room hot tubs, cable TV, in-room VCRs (and movies). Pool. Hot tub. Tennis. Laundry facilities. Business services. | 54432 Road 432, Bass Lake | 559/642–3121 or 800/350–7463 | fax 559/642–3902 | www.basslake.com | 20 suites, 84 chalets | $249–$399 suites | AE, D, DC, MC, V.

Shilo Inn. This contemporary hostelry is surrounded by shops and restaurants, and is 15 mi from Yosemite National Park. Complimentary Continental breakfast. Microwaves, refrigerators, cable TV, in-room movies. Pool. Exercise equipment. Laundry facilities. | 40644 Rte. 41 | 559/683–3555 | fax 559/683–3386 | www.shiloinns.com | 80 rooms | $129 | AE, D, DC, MC, V.

OAKLAND

MAP 3, D8

(Nearby towns also listed: Berkeley, Concord Fremont, Palo Alto, San Francisco)

You may have heard the famous comment by writer Gertrude Stein about her hometown: "There's no there there." Stein was actually referring to her razed childhood house, but her sorrowful observation has often been misconstrued as an anti-Oakland dig. It's true that misguided redevelopment and damage from the 1989 earthquake decimated a once-lively downtown, leaving hollow shells of department stores, restaurants, and nightclubs. The fact that it was once rated one of the most crime-ridden cities in the country hasn't helped Oakland's image, either.

But much has changed since then, and you will find many rewarding surprises. Colorful mayor (and former Califonia Governor) Jerry Brown was elected in 1998 and pledged to revitalize the neglected downtown. Already, the restored Victorians are becoming a center for art galleries and cozy eateries, and the plazas of Jack London Square are busy every weekend with farmer's markets and seasonal events.

Of course, some neighborhoods always have thrived. Patrons crowd Chinatown's produce stands and restaurants and joggers fill the path around tranquil Lake Merritt. Above, the preserved open space in the Oakland hills presents grand views of the bay, underscoring the city's latest civic adage: "It's a great day in Oakland!"

Information: **Oakland Chamber of Commerce** | 475 14th St., 94612 | 510/874–4800 | www.oaklandchamber.com.

Attractions

Camron-Stanford House. Stately columns, arched windows and a widow's walk grace the last Victorian left on the shores of Lake Merritt. Built in 1876, it was for many years a small public museum. In the 1970s, its collection was incorporated into that of the Oakland Musuem a few blocks away. The house is open for tours. | 1418 Lakeside Drive | 510/444–1876 | $4 | Wed. 11–4, Sun. 1–5.

Chabot Space and Science Center. You can explore the universe in the planetarium, or see a space-related film on the 70-ft screen at the Megadome Theater at this complex. | 10000 Skyland Blvd. | 510/336–7300 | fax 510/336–7491 | www.chabotspace.org | $8 | Tue.–Sat. 10–5, Sun. noon–5; planetarium and theater also Fri. and Sat. 7PM–9PM.

Dunsmuir House and Gardens. This grand, century-old mansion was built by Alexander White Dunsmuir (the same coal baron who established the town of Dunsmuir) for his wife, Josephine. Theirs was a star-crossed romance. She was married to one of his associates, whom she divorced to live in sin with Dunsmuir for 20 years—he was afraid that if he married a divorcee, he'd lose his inheritance. When they finally married, Alexander fell ill and died during their honeymoon. It's said Josephine's unhappy ghost walks the corridors of her restored home. Perhaps she enjoys the Family Sundays, Scottish Highland Games, December Holiday Faire, concerts and festivities that enliven the estate year long. Event schedules vary, so be sure to call ahead for specific times. | 2960 Peralta Oaks Ct | 510/615–5555 | www.dunsmuir.org | Free.

East Bay Regional Park District. Fifty-four parks in the EBRPD system sprawl across Alameda and Contra Costa counties. In Oakland, the parks preserve redwood forests, hilltop open space, wildfowl habitat, manmade lakes and miles of trails. Contact the main office for a map and schedules of seasonal programs. | 2950 Peralta Oaks Ct | 510/635–0135 or 510/526–PARK (24–hour information) | www.ebparks.org | Free | Daily.

At **Anthony Chabot Regional Park and Lake Chabot** you'll find 47,000 acres of grassland and forests of oak and bay trees. There are also picnic areas, camping sites, a rifle range, archery, an equestrian center, a golf course and Lake Chabot, constructed as one of Oakland's first managed water supplies. | 17500 Lake Chabot Rd., Castro Valley | 510/652–CAMP | www.ebparks.org | Free | Daily 7–10.

Great blue herons stalk **Martin Luther King, Jr., Regional Shoreline,** a strip of marsh and mudflats between the Oakland Airport and I–880. There's also a small beach for soaking up sun, picnic tables, and a boat launch ramp. | www.ebparks.org | Free | Daily.

Shady trails and picnic spots dot **Redwood Regional Park,** a vestige of the redwood forests that fueled the northern California logging boom. You can go for a peaceful horseback ride through the park. Roberts Recreation Area in the park has a pool and kids' playground. | 7867 Redwood Rd. | 510/562–PARK | www.ebparks.org | $3 per vehicle | Daily 5AM–10PM; for vehicles Nov.–Mar., daily 8–6; Apr.–Oct., daily 8–10.

Ebony Museum. The museum contains collection of African and African-American artifacts: masks, musical instruments, dolls, and some oddities. | 1034 14th St. | 510/763–0745510/763–0141 | Free | Tues.– Sat., 11–6; Sun. noon–6.

Heinold's First and Last Chance Saloon. Step down to a dim watering hole with lots of character—and a lot of paraphernalia on the walls. The story is that the original owner, Johnny Heinold, befriended young Jack London, underwrote his first sailboat, and urged him to continue his education. London referred to the saloon in his novels, several of which are set in Oakland and northern California. It's next to a public parking lot at Jack London Square. | 56 Jack London Sq. | 510/839–6761 | www.firstand lastchance.com | Free | Daily noon–midnight.

Jack London Square. Along the Oakland estuary, part of the Port of Oakland, you'll find a complex of office buildings, shops, and restaurants. The area has undergone extensive development, which has revitalized the waterfront. Today it's a pleasant place to stroll, grab a bite to eat, see a movie, catch the ferry to San Francisco, and, on weekends, to enjoy seasonal entertainment—everything from farmers markets to the annual fall Dragon Boat races. The square's name salutes one of California's best-known authors, who spent part of his wild youth selling newspapers and hanging around on the docks at the turn of the 20th century. Nearby is a replica of a Klondike cabin, of the sort London probably occupied as a gold seeker in Alaska (the inspiration for such stories as "White Fang.") There's also a small collection of books and artifacts at the Jack London Museum in the collection of shops called Jack London Village. Follow the wolf tracks embedded in walkways around the square to find diamond-shaped markers listing historic facts about the area. As you come off any of the freeways, look for the Sail Boat sign to direct you to Jack London Square on Broadway. Jack London Square has an AMTRAK station one block from the center of the Square on Alice Street and the Embarcadero. | 510/814–6000 | www.jack-londonsquare.com | Free | Daily.

Joaquin Miller Park. This city park has redwood groves, picnic sites, and hiking trails. | 3954 Sanbourn Dr. | 510/238–3187 | Free | Daily.

Woodminster Amphitheater. Musicals are performed here every summer. | 3300 Joaquin Miller Rd. | 510/531–9597 | July–Sept.

Lake Merritt. This natural salt-water lake in the middle of downtown was designated as a wildlife sanctuary in 1872. It's a regular wintering stop for migrating wild ducks and geese; in spring, fluffy chicks hatch and people turn out to feed them. In addition to a shoreline path popular with walkers and joggers, there are several attractions in surrounding Lakeside Park, including Children's Fairyland, supposedly the inspiration for Disneyland. | 568 Bellevue Ave. | 510/444–3807 | $2 parking | Daily.

Children's Fairyland, a 10-acre kiddie park, is a marvel of retro kitsch. Enter through a giant shoe (home of the Old Lady and her many children) and explore 1950s-era concrete dioramas of nursery tales. Rides, puppet shows, refreshment stands, picnic areas round out the experience. | 699 Bellevue Ave. | 510/452–2259 | $5 | Nov.–Mar., Fri.–Sun. 10–4; Apr.–mid-June and Sept.–Oct. Wed.–Sun. 10–4; mid-June–Aug., weekdays 10–4, weekends 10–5.

Gondola Servizio. Take a 55-minute tour of the lake in an authentic Italian gondola as the gondolier serenades you with Venetian love songs. Package deals include an antipasto lunch and the "Pomessi Sposi" wedding package with rowers in 17th-century costumes. | Lake Merritt Boathouse at 568 Bellevue Ave. | 510/663–6603 | fax 510/238–7199 | www.oaklandsports.org/boating/gondola | $45 | Daily.

EUCALYPTUS TREES

They tower throughout the Oakland-Berkeley hills, these odd monuments to one man's folly. Blue gum eucalyptus trees have made themselves so at home and have spread so rapidly, that many people believe they're native to California. (Unless, of course, you're from Australia, in which case you experience a weird sense of displacement on seeing the familiar columnar trunks, peeling red bark, and gray-green foliage in a landscape of oak, manzanita, and redwoods.)

Eucalyptus are here to stay, thanks to an early 20th-century entrepreneur named Frank Havens, founder of the Mahogany Eucalyptus and Land Company. As the original redwood forests in the Oakland hills were razed, Havens came up with a scheme to renew the lumber industry and get rich quick—or so he thought. He'd heard that eucalyptus trees were a valuable source of building material in Australia and was convinced, as he explained to thousands of investors, that eucalyptus was "the most valuable tree on the face of the globe," capable of growing several inches a day. In 1911 Havens began a full-scale planting operation, keeping up to 200 men a day busy tending saplings along 14 mi of hills between north Berkeley and the site of today's Redwood Park in Oakland. In 1913 he harvested his first trees.

That's when he learned that the species of eucalyptus he'd imported was the worst possible candidate for lumber. The wood warped terribly, was partial to rot, and difficult to mill. Havens abandoned his enterprise and his angry investors, and disappeared into history. The trees grew on unhindered. They're a potential nuisance—their oily leaves were blamed for feeding the 1991 Oakland hills fire that consumed hundreds of homes—but the East Bay wouldn't feel the same without them.

© Artville

The **Lakeside Park Garden Center** presents seasonal flower shows, lectures, and classes. Step outside to see the trail and show gardens, filled with dahlias, palms, fuschias, Japanese and Polynesian specimens, and cacti. | 666 Bellevue Ave. | 510/238–3208 | Free | Daily.

Kids enjoy the small displays of flora and fauna at the **Rotary Nature Center.** There's also a beehive where you can watch the drones in action. | 552 Bellevue Ave. | 510/238–3739 | www.lakemerritt.com | Free | Daily 10–5.

Museum of Children's Art. Stop in for hands-on art activities. There's a gallery of kids' art and lots of paint, clay, and other materials for making whatever you want. | 560 2nd St. | 510/465–8770 | Free | Tues.–Sat. 10–5, Sun. noon–5.

Oakland Asian Cultural Center. This center is the largest in the United States devoted to Asian-American cultural arts. The venue hosts concerts (such as premieres by the renowned Asian-American Jazz Orchestra), art exhibits, classes in Chinese opera, martial arts and folk dance, and cultural programs. It's in the Pacific Renaissance Plaza, a shopping mall reminiscent of those in Hong Kong. | 388 9th St., Ste. 290 | 510/208–6080 | fax 510/208–6084 | www.asianculture.org | Free | Tues.–Fri. 10–5, weekends, 9–5.

Oakland Ballet Company. Started in 1965, this troupe performs year-round at the Paramount Theater. The season culminates with their rendition of the Nutcracker Suite. Event schedules vary from season to season, so call ahead for specifics. | 1428 Alice St. | 510/452–9288 | fax 510/452–9557 | www.oaklandballet.org.

Oakland Coliseum. The stadium is home base for the Oakland Athletics National League baseball team, the National Basketball Association's Golden State Warriors, and the National Football League's Oakland Raiders. Concerts, trade shows, and other events are also held here year-round. | 7000 Coliseum Way | 510/569–2121.

★ **Oakland Museum of California.** The premier museum of California culture celebrated its 30th anniversary in 2000. The inviting concrete structure encompasses terraces, a grassy courtyard, and a café. Galleries show permanent and changing exhibitions celebrating California's art, history, and natural sciences. Permanent exhibits include a simulated "Walk across California," with dioramas depicting biotic zones from ocean to mountains in the Gallery of Natural Sciences; a collection of artifacts from pre-colonial times to the present in the Cowell Hall of California History; and a collection of art dating from the early 19th century in the Gallery of California Art. | 1000 Oak St. | 510/238–3514 or 510/238–2200 | www.museumca.org | $6; free 2nd Sun. of the month | Wed., Thurs., Sat. 10–5; 1st Fri. of month 10–9, all other Fri. 10–5.

Oakland Museum Sculpture Court at City Center. A serene court in the American President Lines corporate building in downtown is the scene for changing exhibits of contemporary sculpture, organized by the museum's chief curator of art. | 1111 Broadway, at 12th St. | 510/238–3401 | Free | Mon.–Sat. 8–6.

Oakland Zoo in Knowland Park. An exhibit, "California 1820," is devoted to the theme of regional extinction and has species native to California prior to the Gold Rush. You'll find grizzly bears, jaguars, gray wolves, bald eagles, and great horned owls in their habitats of canyon, grassland, chaparral, and oak woodland. You can also expect lions, elephants, seals, aviary and other zoological mainstays, plus an aerial tram and picnic areas. | 9777 Golf Links Rd. | 510/632–9525 | fax 510/635–5719 | www.oaklandzoo.org | $6.50; parking car or van $3 | Daily 10–4.

★ **Paramount Theatre.** This beautifully restored Art Deco movie theater is a center for touring performances and the home of Oakland East Bay Symphony. | 2025 Broadway | 510/465–6400 | www.paramounttheatre.com | Jan.–May.

USS *Potomac*. Two-hour cruises go out from mid-March through mid-November on Franklin D. Roosevelt's restored presidential yacht, docked at Jack London Square. Year-round guided dockside tours are available. | 540 Water St. | 510/839–8256 or 510/839–7533 | www.usspotomac.org | Cruise $30, tour $3.

Walking Tours. The Oakland Heritage Alliance conducts a number of unusual city tours. Among them: a tour of Mountain View Cemetery, where many historical figures are buried, and a Black Panther Legacy Tour that visits significant sites in the history of the 1960s movement. | 510/763–9218 | Mon.–Thurs., 11–4.

Yoshi's. The real draw at this Japanese restaurant is the intimate, semicircular jewel of a jazz club that books international headliners. The sightlines are good from every seat. A monthly calendar has world-class jazz, blues, and Latin jazz artists such as McCoy Tyner, Phil Woods, Eddie Palmieri—the roster is extremely diverse and satisfying. Although freight and passenger trains regularly chug by on the tracks just outside, soundproofed walls keep noise to a minimum. The menu has sushi, Japanese snacks, sake, and draft beer. Sunday afternoon family programs present renowned jazz artists in abbreviated concerts at a reduced cover charge. | 510 Embarcadero | 510/238–9200 | www.yoshis.com | Shows daily 8PM and 10PM.

ON THE CALENDAR

JULY–SEPT.: *Woodminster Summer Amphitheater.* Musicals fill the stage here through the summer. | 510/531–9597.

JULY: *Community Dance Day.* You can take sample classes in samba, jazz, hip hop, African, and other dance forms for a flat fee, all day long, at the Citicentre Dance Theater, a lively community arts center. | 510/451–1230.

JULY: *The Oakland Scottish Games.* Sheepdog herding, bagpipe bands, athletic competitions, and wearing o' the tartans characterize this annual celebration of Scots culture at Dunsmuir House and Gardens. | 510/615–5555.

JULY: *Pacific Fine Arts Festival.* Montclair Village, a tony shopping district in the Oakland hills, hosts a sidewalk art festival with food, entertainment, arts and crafts. | 510/339–1000.

AUG.: *The Eddie Moore Jazz Festival.* Organized in 1990 by friends of the late San Francisco drummer, the festival now has a real presence in town. A roster of headliners pay tribute to the late jazzman in the week-long celebration at Yoshi's Japanese restaurant. | 510 Embarcadero | 510/238–3234.

AUG.: *International Dragon Boat Festival.* The ancient sport of dragon boat racing brings teams from Europe, Asia, Australia, and the United States to the Oakland estuary at Jack London Square. Festivities begin with a Buddhist blessing. Rowers on boats with dragon heads at the bow pull to the beat of a drum. There's food, music, and crafts booths. | 510/452–4272.

Dining

Bay Wolf. Mediterranean. Long at the forefront of California's creative cuisine, this restaurant in a converted Victorian home serves its own take on duck, grilled meats, and pasta; ravioli with goat cheese is a specialty. It's 3 mi east of downtown. In nice weather, you can eat out front on the verandah. No smoking. | 3853 Piedmont Ave. | 510/655–6004 | www.baywolf.com | No lunch weekends | $15–$20 | MC, V.

Chef Paul's. Eclectic. In this elegant Victorian, you'll find fresh flowers on the white- and pink-draped tables and fresh scallops, seafood crêpes, and salmon on the menu. You can order à la carte or prix fixe; there's a tasting menu and a vegetarian menu. Umbrella'd tables are outside. No smoking. | 4179 Piedmont Ave. | 510/547–2175 | Closed Mon. No lunch | $14–$20 | AE, D, MC, V.

El Torito. Mexican. Spanish murals and high ceilings dominate the scene at this family-style eatery downtown near the waterfront. It's known for its huge margaritas and combo platters. Try the shredded beef, fajitas, or fish taco. There are 16 umbrella'd tables outdoors. Kids' menu. Sunday brunch. | 67 Jack London Sq | 510/835–9260 | $7–$15 | AE, D, DC, MC, V.

Everett and Jones. Barbecue. Locals chow down at this area chain of barbeque joints, established in 1974. Coca-Cola machines and record players dating from the 1950s set the stage for hot links, pork and beef ribs, and chicken, which you can get piled on a plate or as sandwiches with sides of potato salad, lemon cake, or sweet potato pie. Lots of people leave with a jar of the famous, sweet, smoky red sauce in hand. It's in Jack London Square, 1½ mi from downtown. | 126 Broadway | 510/663–2350 | $10–$20 | MC, V.

Jack's Bistro. Mediterranean. Near Jack London Square on the waterfront, this eatery with murals on the walls and bare poplar-wood tables and chairs has a view of Oakland estuary. The menu has pasta, pizza, and rotisserie chicken in generous portions; try the vegetarian frittata. There's a piano bar and a patio with marble-top tables. There's a business crowd at lunch; people come to celebrate special occasions in the evening. Sunday brunch. Pianist; musicians Fri.–Sat. No smoking. | 1 Broadway | 510/444–7171 | Breakfast also available | $8–$20 | AE, D, DC, MC, V.

Le Cheval. Vietnamese. A giant horse sculpture stands at the door of this light, airy restaurant in a commercial area next to Chinatown. Large windows allow for people-watching; murals on peach-colored walls, white linen tablecloths, and ceiling fans are an atmospheric backdrop for beautifully prepared lemongrass soup, orange beef, fresh seafood, and noodles. | 1007 Clay St. | 510/763–8957 | No lunch Sun. | $6–$20 | AE, D, DC, MC, V.

Oliveto. Italian. Mellow, rosy plaster walls, tile floors, and polished copper counters suggest an Italian retreat. On the ground floor a café serves espresso drinks, pastries, pizza, and salads. Upstairs, you can order from an imaginative changing menu of Italian and regional specialties. The pasta is homemade and there are grilled portobello mushrooms, roast meats, and menus created around seasonal produce. Four gray stone tables are set on a small covered patio for al fresco dining. No smoking. | 5655 College Ave. | 510/547–5356 | $19–$25 | AE, MC, V.

Quinn's Lighthouse. Contemporary. Model boats hang from the ceilings and the walls of this spare, woody place inside a harbor lighthouse; on top is a widow's walk and the original tower that housed the lighthouse lens, and the dining room is all butcher block, with brass touches. A deck outdoors overlooks Oakland estuary. Try the Gilroy burger, served on a garlic sourdough bun, the seafood curry-topped linguine, the paella, or the brandy cream pepper steak. Kids' menu, early-bird suppers. Sunday brunch. | 51 Embarcadero Cove | 510/536–2050 | www.quinnslighthouse.com | $6–$15 | MC, V.

Scott's Seafood Grill and Bar. Seafood. Fresh fish on ice greets you at the front counter of this white-tablecloth restaurant with green slate floor. You can have your halibut with wild rice or the three-fish mixed grill either inside or outside on the mosaic-topped concrete tables on the water-view patio. Pianist Tues.–Sat.; jazz trio Sunday brunch | 2 Broadway | 510/444–3456 | $15–$25 | AE, D, DC, MC, V.

Silver Dragon. Chinese. This café in the heart of Chinatown was a small place when it opened in 1962; today it includes two large dining rooms on three floors and is known for its banquets and its retro Hong Kong glitter. | 835 Webster St. | 510/893–3748 | $8–$15 | AE, MC, V.

Soizic. French. The artist-owners have transformed this nondescript cinderblock warehouse building into a warm, studio-like environment hung with original paintings and set with an eclectic assortment of old tables and chairs. Rib-eye steak served with pistachio and mustard sauce or lamb served in Madeira sauce with grilled shiitake mushrooms and watercress are the dishes to try. It can get hectic on weekends. No smoking. | 300 Broadway | 510/251–8100 | Closed Mon. No lunch weekends | $30–$40 | MC, V.

Lodging

Bates House. Lake Merritt, the centerpiece of Oakland, is a block away from this bed and breakfast built in 1907. Rooms have mahogany and brass furnishings with floral prints adorning the walls. Grand Lake, Lakeside Park, shops, and restaurants are all within 500 ft. Dining room, complimentary Continental breakfast. No room phones, no TV. | 399 Bellevue Ave. | 510/893–3881 | fax 510/893–9401 | reservations@bateshouse.com | www.bateshouse.com | 4 rooms | $85–$130 | AE, D, MC, V.

Best Western Inn at the Square. This contemporary three-story hostelry is in Jack London Square, close to the ferry, shopping, and restaurants. Most rooms on the first floor face an open courtyard. Restaurant, complimentary Continental breakfast. In-room data ports, room service, cable TV. Pool. Sauna. Exercise equipment. Business services. | 233 Broadway | 510/452–4565 or 800/633–5973 | fax 510/452–4634 | www.innatthesquare.com | 102 rooms | $120–$180 | AE, D, DC, MC, V.

Clarion Suites Lake Merritt. Echoing the 1930s, this six-story Art Deco hostelry is by Lake Merritt and most guest rooms have water views. A popular spot for visiting musicians, the lounge has live jazz on Thursday nights. Restaurant, bar, complimentary Continental breakfast. In-room data ports, kitchenettes, minibars, microwaves, refrigerators, cable TV. Business services. Pets allowed (fee). | 1800 Madison | 510/832–2300 or 800/933–4683 | fax 510/832–7150 | 51 rooms, 38 suites | $259, $189–$259 suites | AE, D, DC, MC, V.

Coral Reef. This Mediterranean-style wood and stucco hostelry is 5 mi from Jack London Square on Alameda, the small island in the bay beside Oakland. Complimentary Continental breakfast. Kitchenettes, microwaves, cable TV. Pool. Laundry facilities. Business services. | 400 Park St., Alameda | 510/521–2330 or 800/533–2330 | fax 510/521–4707 | 93 rooms, 36 rooms, 53 suites | $96, $106–$127 suites | AE, D, DC, MC, V.

Dockside Boat and Bed. Spend the night on a yacht moored on Oakland's waterfront, lulled by gently lapping waves. Choose from motor or sailing yachts from 35 ft and larger; some have classic teak fittings and others are sleek and modern. All boats have staterooms, living rooms, baths, and galley. Many have great views of the bay. You can charter some and actually leave the marina. Complimentary Continental breakfast. Microwaves, refrigerators, in-room VCRs. No smoking. | 419 Water St. | 510/444–5858 or 800/436–2574 | fax 510/444–0420 | boatandbed@aol.com | www.boatandbed.com | 10 boats | $140–$340 boats | AE, DC, MC, V.

Executive Inn at Embarcadero Cove. The rooms on the south side of this hotel overlook the Oakland Estuary. Shops and restaurants are at Jack London Square 1 ½ mi to the east. Outdoor pool. Hot tub. Gym. Laundry services. Business services, airport shuttle, free parking. | 1755 Embarcadero East | 510/536–6633 | 145 rooms | $95–$100 | AE, D, DC, MC, V.

Garratt Mansion. Built in 1890, this four-story bed-and-breakfast is on the Gold Coast of Alameda, surrounded by other restored Victorians, 4 blocks from the San Francisco Bay and 6 mi from Jack London Square. A fountain anchors the courtyard, and rooms are large and comfortable. Dining room, complimentary breakfast. Some room phones. No smoking. | 900 Union St., Alameda | 510/521–4779 | fax 510/521–6796 | garrattm@pacbell.net | www.garrattmansion.com | 7 rooms (2 with shared bath) | $95–$160 | AE, MC, V.

Hampton Inn Airport. This three-story brick chain hotel is in a commercial area right on Route 880, 5 mi from downtown Oakland. Restaurant, complimentary Continental breakfast. Cable TV. Pool. Hot tub. Business services. Free parking. | 8465 Enterprise Way | 510/632–8900 or 800/HAMPTON | fax 510/632–4713 | 152 rooms | $99–$119 | AE, D, DC, MC, V.

Hilton Airport. Five three-story buildings sit on 10 acres at this chain hotel with a large conference facility. The Oakland Coliseum is 2 mi north. 2 restaurants, bar [with entertainment], room service. In-room data ports, cable TV. Pool. Exercise equipment. Business services, airport shuttle. | 1 Hegenberger Rd. | 510/635–5000 | fax 510/729–0491 | www.hilton.com | 363 rooms | $165–$215 | AE, D, DC, MC, V.

Holiday Inn–Airport. This chain hotel, a six-story tower and a two-story courtyard building, is in a commercial area off Route 880 ½ mi south of the Oakland Coliseum. Many guest rooms overlook a garden plaza. Restaurant, bar. In-room data ports, cable TV. Pool.

Exercise equipment. Laundry facilities. Business services, airport shuttle. | 500 Hegenberger Rd. | 510/562–5311 or 800/HOLIDAY | fax 510/636–1539 | www.holidayinnoakland.com | 293 rooms | $129–$149 | AE, D, DC, MC, V.

Jack London Inn. This hotel is among the bistros and boutiques of Jack London Square. Chinatown, the Convention Center, and downtown Oakland are only blocks away. Restaurant, complimentary Continental breakfast. In-room data ports, some kitchenettes, cable TV. | 444 Embarcadero West | 800/549–8780 or 510/444–2032 | fax 510/834–3074 | info@jack-londoninn.com | www.jacklondoninn.com | 110 rooms | $115 | AE, DC, D, MC, V.

Marina Village Inn. Most rooms have waterfront views in this Cape Cod hostelry on the island of Alameda, just across Oakland estuary from Jack London Square. It's between two yacht clubs; water taxis shuttle you to the Square and ferries leave from here for San Francisco. The shoreline jogging trails are nearby. By spring 2001, 36 suites will be available, some with fireplaces and hot tubs. Complimentary Continental breakfast. In-room data ports, microwaves, refrigerators, cable TV. Pool. Business services. | 1151 Pacific Marina, Alameda | 510/523–9450 or 800/345–0304 | fax 510/523–6315 | marinavillageinn@aol.com | 51 rooms | $102–$155 | AE, D, DC, MC, V.

Marriott City Center. This 21-story tower built in 1981 next to the Convention Center affords views of the central city. It's 3 blocks from Chinatown and 10 blocks from the Oakland Museum. The lounge attracts employees from nearby city hall and government buildings on Fridays. 2 restaurants, bar. In-room data ports, some refrigerators, cable TV. Pool. Hot tub. Exercise equipment. Business services, airport shuttle. | 1001 Broadway | 510/451–4000 or 800/228–9290 | fax 510/835–3466 | www.marriott.com | 478 rooms, 15 suites | $154–$169, $350 1–bedroom suites, $650 2–bedroom suites | AE, D, DC, MC, V.

Washington Inn. This 1915 brick Victorian with modern rooms is across from the Convention Center downtown. Rooms have a vanity area with pedestal sinks and polished wood furniture. Restaurant, bar, complimentary breakfast. In-room data ports, cable TV. Business services. | 495 10th St. | 510/452–1776 or 800/477–1775 | fax 510/452–4436 | 47 rooms, 8 suites | $158, $178–$250 suites | AE, D, DC, MC, V.

Waterfront Plaza. Two nautical-style buildings connected by a covered ramp make up this hostelry on the water in Jack London Square. Rooms have either city or water views. You can dock your boat in one of two slips. The hotel is also a 5 min. walk from the Amtrak station. Restaurant, bar, room service. In-room data ports, minibars, cable TV, in-room VCRs. Pool. Exercise equipment. Business services, parking (fee). | 10 Washington St. | 510/836–3800 or 800/729–3638 | fax 510/832–5695 | wfp@ix.netcom.com | www.waterfront-plaza.com | 144 rooms, 27 suites | $180–$225, $220–$375 suites | AE, D, DC, MC, V.

OCEANSIDE

MAP 4, J16

(Nearby towns also listed: Carlsbad, Del Mar, Escondido, Rancho Bernardo, Rancho Santa Fe)

Oceanside (pop. 165,000) is poised at the fulcrum of the San Luis Rey Valley. Its best feature is its 3½-mi beach, with year-round recreation on the water—swimming, boating, fishing and whale-watching. It owes its prominence to the presence of Camp Pendleton, the enormous U.S. Marine base north of town.

Information: Oceanside Chamber of Commerce | 928 N. Coast Hwy., 92054 | 800/350–7873 | info@oceansidechamber.com | www.oceansidechamber.com.

Attractions

Oceanside Museum of Art. Exhibits here range from landscape paintings to eclectic furnishings. | 704 Pier View Way | 760/721–2787 | $5 | Tues.–Sat. 10–4, Sun. 1–4.

Antique Gas and Steam Engine Museum. Steam as a power source is the focus of this museum where you can see steam engines and exhibits relating to the use of steam on the railroads. | 2040 N. Santa Fe Ave., Vista | 760/941–1791 | fax 760/941–0690 | www.agsem.com | $3 | Daily 10–4.

California Surf Museum. This museum documents the history of surfing. | 223 N. Coast Hwy. | 760/721–6876 | fax 760/721–6876 | www.surfmuseum.org | Free | Thur.–Mon 10–4.

Mission San Luis Rey de Francia. This is the 18th and largest of the California missions. It was established in 1798 by Father Fermin de Lasuen and named after Louis IX. The double-dome construction made by Native Americans is unusual, and there are lofty beamed ceilings and hand carved doors with signatures. Arched windows greet visitors as they enter the Mission church. The original baptismal font, made of hand-hammered copper, is on display in the Church baptistry. The Mission Church reredos and altar combine Classical and Baroque styles typical of the California missions. The Mission museum has artifacts relating to mission life. | 4050 Mission Ave. | 760/757–3651 | www.sanluisrey.org | $3 | Daily 10–4:30.

Oceanside Harbor and Marina. Walkways take you through this area, a launching point for boats, fishing excursions, and whale-watching trips. | 1540 Harbor Dr. N | 760/435–4000 | Free | Daily 8–4.

ON THE CALENDAR

AUG.: *Oceanside Longboard Surfing Contest.* Hang ten—or at least watch somebody else do it—at this exciting three-day event, where top-rated surfers challenge the Pacific's not-so-pacific breakers. Polynesian dancers keep things lively on the beach. Also tour vendor booths for surfer gear and information. | 760/434–0987.

Dining

Bay Cannery. Seafood. Small fishing and pleasure boats head out to sea outside this seafood eatery decorated with stained glass and seafood paraphernalia on Oceanside Harbor. Tables are outside on front and back patios as well as inside. The chowders, halibut, steamed clams, and Caesar salad get high marks. Sunday brunch. No smoking. | 1325 Harbor Dr. | 760/722–3474 | $9–$35 | AE, D, MC, V.

Jolly Roger. American. Locals and tourists alike gather at this casual eatery with views of Oceanside Harbor. Teriyaki steak is one of the best bets on the menu, and there's fresh seafood and prime rib. Seating is in leather-lined booths as well as laminate-topped tables. Live music and comedy. Thurs., Fri. and Sat. karaoke. No smoking. | 1900 Harbor Dr. N | 760/722–1831 | Breakfast also available | $13–$19 | AE, D, MC, V.

101 Cafe. American. This local favorite, which started out as a modest diner in 1928, is now a bustling eatery over three times the size with seating at tables and at stools at the bar. Look for all the diner staples, including chicken-fried steak, roast beef, and breakfast food all day long. | 631 S. Coast Hwy. | 760/722–5220 | Breakfast also available | $6–$9 | No credit cards.

Lodging

Best Western Marty's Valley Inn. Set 2 mi east of downtown and 3 mi east of the beach, in the San Luis Rey area. Restaurant, bar, complimentary Continental breakfast. Cable TV. Pool. Spa. Exercise equipment. Business services. | 3240 Mission Ave. | 760/757–7700 | fax 760/439–3311 | bwmartys@inetworld.net | www.bwmartys.com | 110 rooms | $85–$105 | AE, D, DC, MC, V.

Best Western Oceanside Inn. It's a ³/₄-mi trip to the beach from here. Complimentary Continental breakfast. Som refrigerators, cable TV. Pool. Hot tub, sauna. Laundry facilities. Business services, free parking. | 1680 Oceanside Blvd. | 760/722–1821 | fax 760/967–8969 | 80 rooms | $89–$129 | AE, D, DC, MC, V.

Days Inn El Camino. Two two-story buildings make up this reasonably priced motel in a commercial area 2 mi east of the beach and 2½ mi east of downtown. Complimentary Continental breakfast. Cable TV. Pool. 18-hole golf course, tennis. | 3170 Vista Way | 760/757–2200 or 800/458–6064 | 44 rooms | $79–$99 | AE, D, DC, MC, V.

Motel Nine. The Pacific is 4 blocks west of this two-story hostelry. Complimentary Continental breakfast. Some kitchenettes, microwaves, refrigerators, some in-room hot tubs, cable TV, in-room VCRs. Laundry facilities. Business services. No pets. | 822 N. Coast Hwy. | 760/722–1887 | fax 760/757–1861 | motel9@motelnine.com | www.motelnine.com | 45 rooms | $70–$80 | AE, D, MC, V.

Ramada Limited Oceanside. This four-story chain hotel is 1½ mi from the beach and entrance to Oceanside Harbor west of I–5. Complimentary Continental breakfast. In-room data ports, some microwaves, refrigerators, cable TV. Laundry facilities. Pets allowed. | 1440 Mission Ave. | 760/967–4100 | fax 760/439–5546 | ramada@ramada-oceanside.com | www.ramada-oceanside.com | 67 rooms | $69–$99 | AE, D, DC, MC, V.

OJAI

MAP 4, H14

(Nearby towns also listed: Camarillo, Oxnard, Santa Barbara, Simi Valley, Ventura)

Ojai (pronounced "Oh, hi") is scenic, artsy, low-key, and small, with a fairly affluent population of 8,200. It is located in a beautiful valley, surrounded by orange groves and a mountain backdrop. There are plenty of art galleries, interesting boutiques, and restaurants. It's bordered by acres of the Los Padres National Forest.

Information: Ojai Valley Chamber of Commerce and Visitors Bureau | 150 W. Ojai Ave., 93023 | 805/646–8126 | info@the-ojai.org | www.the-ojai.org.

Attractions

Lake Casitas Recreation Area. There's good fishing in this lake in a valley formed by high mountains and you can row or motor across the reservoir, cast a line, pitch a tent, or enjoy a picnic. No swimming. | 11311 Santa Ana Rd., Ventura | 805/649–2233 or 805/649–1122 (reservations) | www.ojai.org/casitas.htm | $6.50 per vehicle; $11.50 per boat; $1 per pet | Daily.
Casitas Pass. This visually striking byway loops through mountains passes, alongside lakes, and affords a sweeping view of the coastline. From Ventura, head north on U.S. 101 to Carpenteria, then head west on Route 150 to Lake Casitas Recreation Area. From here, return south to the coast via Route 33. | 805/649–2233 | Free | Daily.

Ojai Center for the Arts. Ojai has long been known as an artists' colony, and the Center for the Arts has exhibitions of California artists and theatre productions. | 113 S. Montgomery St. | 805/646–0117 or 805/649–9443 | Tues.–Sun. 12–4.

Ojai Valley Historical Society and Museum. This museum documents the history of Ojai Valley as an artists' colony and retreat. | 130 W. Ojai Ave. | 805/640–1390 | fax 805/640–1342 | ojaivalleymuseum.com | $2 | Wed.–Fri. 1–4, weekends 10–4.

ON THE CALENDAR
MAY: *Ojai Festivals.* This is one of the longest running and most respected music festivals in southern California featuring big name conductors and musicians. | 805/646–2094.
AUG.: *Ojai Shakespeare Festival.* The outdoor Shakespeare Festival is presented by a local company. It takes place at the Libbey Bowl in Libbey Park. | 805/646–9455.
SEPT.: *Bowlful of Blues.* This festival spotlights regional blues musicians and singers, Southern cuisine, and arts and crafts booths. Buy tickets in advance or at the door. |

Lake Casitas Olympic Event Site, Rte. 150 and Santa Ana Rd. | 805/646–7230 |
www.bowlfulofblues.com.

OCT.: *Ojai Studio Artists Tour.* Artists of Ojai display their work in their studios at
this event. | 805/646–8126.

Dining

L'Auberge. French. Tasty made-to-order meals are served on Belgian lace-covered tables
at this 1905 country mansion. When the weather's fine, those in the know reserve a table
on the patio so they can accompany their rack of lamb with a glorious sunset behind the
mountains. Sunday brunch. Beer and wine only. No smoking. | 314 El Paseo St. | 805/646–
2288 | No lunch weekdays | $17–$25 | AE, MC, V.

Ranch House. Contemporary. Lush foliage and streams border the redwood decks at this
white-tablecloth restaurant. Appetizers include rich pâtés and main dishes run to offerings such as baked chicken stuffed with wilted spinach, wild mushrooms, goat cheese,
toasted walnuts, and thyme, poached salmon, and grilled pork with blue cheese and ver-
mouth sauce. This kitchen makes its own bread. Kids' menu. Sunday brunch. No smok-
ing. | 102 Besant Rd. | 805/646–2360 | www.theranchhouse.com | Closed Mon., no lunch
Tues. | $20–$26 | AE, D, DC, MC, V.

Suzanne's Cuisine. Contemporary. Settle down in this cozy European-style dining room
for peppered filet mignon, sauerkraut-trimmed salmon in dill beurre blanc, and other
interesting offerings. Or relax in the garden-view courtyard. | 502 W. Ojai Ave. | 805/640–
1961 | Closed Tues. Also closed first 2 weeks in Jan. | $12–$28 | MC, V.

Lodging

Best Western Casa Ojai. Surrounded by mountains, this southwestern-style building is
1 mi east of downtown Complimentary Continental breakfast. In-room data ports, some
refrigerators, cable TV. Pool. Hot tub. Business services. Pets allowed. | 1302 E. Ojai Ave. |
805/646–8175 | fax 805/640–8247 | www.bestwestern.com | 45 rooms | $119–$199 | AE, D,
DC, MC, V.

Blue Iguana Inn. Local artists run this 1930s Mission-style hotel, with arched entrances
and terra cotta-tiled roofs. The fountain in the inn's central courtyard is iguana-shaped,
and Mexican-style domed ceilings, sandblasted wood beams, murals, and works by local
painters and artisans fill the rooms. All rooms have private outdoor patios. In-room data
ports, some kitchenettes, microwaves, refrigerators, cable TV. Outdoor pool. Outdoor hot
tub. Business services. Pets allowed. | 11794 N. Ventura Ave. | 805/646–5277 | fax 805/646–
8078 | innkeeper@blueiguanainn.com | www.blueiguanainn.com | 4 rooms, 7 suites |
$95–$125, $129–$189 suites | AE, D, DC, MC, V.

Oaks at Ojai. This well-known spa keeps you moving through assorted exercises and
fitness classes. Dining room, complimentary Continental breakfast. Cable TV. Outdoor
pool. Beauty salon, indoor hot tub, massage, sauna, spa. Exercise equipment. Laundry
facilities. Business services. No pets. | 122 E. Ojai Ave. | 805/646–5573 or 800/753–6257 |
fax 805/640–1504 | www.oaksspa.com | 46 rooms | $680–$1080 (2–day minimum) | AP
| AE, D, MC, V.

★ **Ojai Valley Inn.** These four Spanish terra-cotta style stucco buildings, built in 1923, have
a view of the Topa Topa mountains, the courtyard, or the Ojai Valley Inn Golf Course. The
property has 220 landscaped acres. 2 Restaurants, bar, room service. In-room data ports,
minibars, refrigerators, cable TV. 3 pools. Beauty salon, hot tubs, spa. Driving range, 18-
hole golf course, putting green, tennis. Gym, hiking, horseback riding, bicycles. Kids' pro-
grams, playground. Business services. | 905 Country Club Rd. | 805/646–5511 or 800/422–
6524 | fax 805/646–7969 | www.ojairesort.com | 209 rooms | $255–$450, $390–$450 suites
| AE, D, DC, MC, V.

ONTARIO

MAP 4, J15

(Nearby towns also listed: Claremont, Pomona, Rancho Cucamonga)

Once the heart of southern California's citrus and wine grape-growing industry, this Inland Empire city is now home to manufacturing and commerce. It has a population of 150,000. It's the home of Los Angeles' second international airport.

Information: **Ontario Convention and Visitors Authority** | 2000 Convention Center Way, 91764 | 800/455-5755 or 909/937-3000 | info@ontariocva.org | www.ontariocvb.com.

Attractions

Scandia Amusement Park. Extremely popular with kids, this attraction has all the usual suspects—roller coasters, race cars, bumper boats—plus two Scandinavian-theme miniature golf courses. | 1155 Wanamaker Ave. | 909/390-3092 | www.scandiafun.com | $1–$6.50; $18 for all-access pass | Sun.–Thurs. 10 AM–11PM, Fri.–Sat. 10AM–1 AM.

California Speedway. Professional racing takes place regularly. | 9300 Cherry Ave., Fontana | 888/849-7223 | fax 909/429-5199 | www.california.com | May–Oct.

Cucamonga-Guasti Regional Park. This 150-acre park is ½ mi north of the Ontario Convention Center. | 800 N. Archibald Ave. | 909/481-4205 | fax 909/481-4202 | www.co.san-bernardino.ca.us/parks | $5 per vehicle | Daily 7–7.

Graber Olive House. The Mediterranean climate makes Ontario a good location for growing olives. Here, the staff explains the history of the 100-year-old company, and in fall you can watch the harveted olives being graded, cured, and canned. | 315 E. 4th St. | 909/983-1761 or 800/996-5483 | fax 909/984-2180 | www.graberolives.com | Free | Mon.–Sat. 9–5:30, Sun. 9:30–6.

Museum of History and Art, Ontario. This museum occupies Ontario's former city hall, a Spanish-Mediterranean building completed in 1937. The permanent collection is devoted to documenting Ontario's agricultural past, industrial heritage, and aviation history. There are also changing art exhibitions. | 225 S. Euclid Ave. | 909/983-3198 | fax 909/983-8978 | Free | Wed.–Sun. 12–4.

Ontario Mills Mall. The largest outlet mall in Southern California has a mix of outlet stores, including some high-end outlets such as Saks Fifth Avenue. | 1 Mill Circle | 909/484-8300 or 888-LA-MILLS | www.ontariomills.com | Free | Mon.–Sat. 10–9:30, Sun. 10–8:30.

Planes of Fame Air Museum. Founded by Ed Maloney, the Air Museum Planes of Fame was one of the first air museums in the United States. The collection is unique because it spans from the early gliders to modern jets. Many aircraft in the collection are capable of flying and are flown regularly. | 7000 Merrill Ave., Chino | 909/597-3722 | fax 909/597-4755 | www.planesoffame.org | $8.95 | Daily 9–5.

Prado Regional Park. Here's a rural getaway on more than 2,000 acres in the Chino Valley Basin on the borders of Orange and Los Angeles counties. You can fish, go horseback riding or camping, have a picnic, or play golf. | 16700 S. Euclid Ave., Chino | 909/597-4260 | fax 909/393-8428 | www.co.san-bernardino.ca.us/parks | $5 per vehicle; fishing $5 | Daily 7:30–8.

ON THE CALENDAR

DEC.: *Christmas on Euclid.* More than 300 booths display crafts in downtown Ontario during this holiday fair. A business expo and classic car show coincide with the event. | 909/984-2458.

Dining

Black Angus Restaurant. Steak. Country-western music plays in the background and pictures of cowboys adorn the walls at this casual spot. There's prime rib, filet mignon, and seafood. Kids' menu. | 3640 Porsche Way | 909/944–6882 | $12–$24 | AE, D, DC, MC, V.

Dave & Busters. American. With virtual reality arcade games, billiards, and shuffleboard tables, this spot is part attraction, part restaurant. Go for the barbecued ribs or have a California wrap sandwich (bacon, lettuce, and tomato rolled inside a flour tortilla). Kids have fun here, too, and their own menu. | 4821 Ontario Mills Circle | 909/987–1557 | $7–$21 | AE, D, DC, MC, V.

Grinder Haven. American. Family-run since the 1950s, this deli builds a bevy of hot and cold sandwiches. Top honors go to the towering barbecued beef and pastrami. All seating is outside on a covered patio overlooking the busy street. | 724 W. Holt Blvd. | 909/984–1470 | $5–$6 | No credit cards.

Tokyo Tokyo Fine Japanese Restaurant. Japanese. Do your socks have holes in them? Put on a new pair before you come to this traditional Japanese restaurant, where everyone sheds shoes at the door and you sit on the floor at low tables. Menu highlights include live lobster and crab (you pick which one you want) and luscious Kobe beef. There's also a sushi bar. Kids' menu. | 990 Ontario Mills Dr. | 909/983–4966 | Reservations essential | No lunch on weekends. Closed Mon. | $9–$19 | AE, D, DC, MC, V.

Vince's Spaghetti. Italian. This casual spot has been dishing up spaghetti and mostaccioli with its celebrated meat sauce since 1945. The home-country's flag gets a nod from the green-and-red color scheme, and there are family pictures. Kids' menu. | 1206 W. Holt Blvd. | 909/986–7074 | Reservations not accepted | No lunch on weekends. Closed Wed. | $5–$8 | AE, D, MC, V.

Yangtze Restaurant. Chinese. A trio of cooking styles meet at this family-owned restaurant. You'll find Cantonese, Mandarin, and American dishes such as chicken chow mein, cashew nut chicken, and kung pao shrimp. Kids' menu. | 126 N. Euclid Ave. | 909/986–8941 | $7–$14 | AE, MC, V.

Zendejas Mexican Restaurant. Mexican. This casual eatery serves traditional south-of-the-border fare in a pleasant setting dressed up with Mexican landscape paintings. Try carne asada con camarones (roast beef with shrimp) or the enchiladas. Kids' menu. | 2411 S. Vineyard Ave. | 909/947–1400 | $6–$18 | AE, D, DC, MC, V.

Lodging

Best Western Airport. This stucco hostelry is in a residential area 3 mi west of Ontario Mills Mall and just 2 blocks north of the airport. Complimentary Continental breakfast. Refrigerators, cable TV. Pool. Hot tub. Laundry facilities. Airport shuttle. Pets allowed. | 209 N. Vineyard Ave. | 909/937–6800 | fax 909/937–6815 | www.bestwestern.com | 150 rooms | $72 | AE, D, DC, MC, V.

Country Side Suites. You can enjoy views of the San Gabriel mountains from most of the rooms at this French country-style motel. The Ontario Convention Center is next door and downtown is 1 mi west. Restaurant, complimentary breakfast. Microwaves, cable TV. Pool. Hot tub. Exercise equipment. Laundry facilities. Business services, airport shuttle, free parking. | 204 N. Vineyard Ave. | 909/937–9700 or 800/248–4661 | fax 909/937–4227 | www.countrysideinn.com | 106 suites | $185–$195 | AE, D, DC, MC, V.

Country Suites by Ayres. Several beautiful rooms overlook a landscaped courtyard in this three-story, European-style motel 2½ mi east of downtown and 4 mi east of Ontario Mills Mall. Restaurant, complimentary breakfast, room service. Microwaves, refrigerators, some in-room hot tubs, cable TV. Pool. Hot tub, massage. Exercise equipment. Laundry facilities. Business services, airport shuttle. | 1945 E. Holt Blvd. | 909/390–7778 or 800/248–4661 (for reservations) | fax 909/937–9718 | www.countrysuites.com | 167 rooms | $195–$205 | AE, D, DC, MC, V.

Doubletree. On weekday nights business travelers account for much of the clientele at this three-story stucco chain hotel. This hostelry is in a commercial area just off I-10, 3 mi west of downtown and 5 mi east of Ontario Mills Mall. 3 restaurants, bar [with entertainment], room service. In-room data ports, cable TV. Pool. Hot tub. Exercise equipment. Business services, airport shuttle, free parking. | 222 N. Vineyard Ave. | 909/983–0909 | fax 909/983–8851 | www.doubletreehotels.com | 340 rooms | $79–$159 | AE, D, DC, MC, V.

Fairfield Inn by Marriott. At this three-story stucco hostelry you're 2 mi west of the Ontario Mills Mall and 5 mi east of downtown. Complimentary Continental breakfast. In-room data ports, cable TV. Pool. Laundry service. Business service. No pets. | 3201 Centre Lake Dr., | 909/390–9855 | fax 909/390–9835 | www.marriott.com | 117 rooms | $64 | AE,D,DC,MC,V.

Motel 6. This reasonably priced chain hostelry is close to fast-food restaurants and 2 mi from Ontario International Airport. Cable TV. Outdoor pool. Pets allowed (fee). | 1560 E. 4th St. | 909/984–2424 | fax 909/984–7326 | www.motel6.com | 69 rooms | $56 | AE, D, DC, MC, V.

Quality Inn Ontario Airport. The airport is $3\frac{1}{2}$ mi from this two-story hotel. Complimentary Continental breakfast. Some in-room data ports, cable TV. Outdoor pool. Outdoor hot tub. Laundry facilities. Business services, airport shuttle. No pets. | 1655 E. 4th St. | 909/986–8898 | fax 909/986–1377 | www.qualityinn.com | 80 rooms | $50–$65 | AE, D, DC, MC, V.

Sheraton Ontario Airport. This six-story hotel is 2 mi west of Ontario Mills Mall and 2 mi west of the airport. Restaurant, bar. In-room data ports, cable TV. Pool. Hot tub. Exercise equipment. Business services, airport shuttle. | 429 N. Vineyard Ave. | 909/937–8000 | fax 909/397–8020 | www.sheraton.com/ontario | 170 rooms | $133–$150 | AE, D, DC, MC, V.

ORANGE

MAP 9, I7

(Nearby towns also listed: Anaheim, Santa Ana)

Its seed was planted in 1869. That's when two lawyers unearthed their vision of a city (now 127,000) that would rise from 1,300 acres they received as vouchsafe from a client. The picturesque town then developed around a circular plaza at Chapman Avenue and Glassell Street, which is now known as the heart of Old Towne Orange. The area is a worthy stop for antique shoppers and vintage architecture fans.

Information: **Orange Chamber of Commerce and Visitor Bureau** | 531 E. Chapman Ave. Ste. A, 92866 | 714/538–3581 | info@orangechamber.org | www.orangechamber.org.

Attractions

Orange County Zoo. Inside Irvine Regional Park, this zoo sprawls over 8 acres, with the focus on animals native to the southwestern United States. Check out the black bear, mountain lion, and bald eagle. | 1 Irvine Park Rd. | 714/633–2022 | fax 714/633–8493 | $1 | Daily 10–3:30.

Tucker Wildlife Sanctuary. The Tucker Wildlife Sanctuary is known for its hummingbirds and native plants. The 12-acre site is crisscrossed by nature trails, and an observation porch and plaques provide ample opportunity to observe and identify. A nature center displays several small native animals, both live and mounted. | 29322 Modjeska Canyon Rd. | 714/649–2760 | fax 714/649–2760 | Donations accepted | Daily 9–4.

ON THE CALENDAR

SEPT.: *Orange International Street Fair.* A tradition since 1910 (and attracting a staggering quarter-million visitors), this event celebrates the diversity of Orange. Enjoy international offerings in music, food, and arts and crafts during the Labor Day weekend. | 714/532–6260.

Dining

Citrus City Grill. Contemporary. Innovative cuisine and striking decor that combines historic and modern elements characterize one of the best restaurants in the county. The citrus theme plays out in the art on the walls, old packing labels, and accents throughout the restaurant. Don't miss the ahi poke salad (tuna on wonton strips), or Chilean sea bass with an oyster-lemongrass teriyaki sauce served with couscous. The elegantly lit half-moon bar is a lively spot for martini aficionados. No smoking. | 122 N. Glassell St. | 714/639–9600 | Closed Sun. | $8–$16 | AE, DC, MC, V.

P.J.'s Abbey. American. Locals like to walk from their bungalows in historic Old Towne to this former abbey to enjoy American favorites such as pork tenderloin in cherry-walnut sauce with garlic-mashed potatoes. The Victorian-era building features vaulted ceilings and stained glass throughout. Entertainment Fri., Sat. No smoking. | 182 S. Orange St. | 714/771–8556 | $15–$20 | AE, MC, V.

Yen Ching. Chinese. Regulars have been coming here for more than 20 years for Yen Ching's Mandarin and Szechwan fare in a Chinese atmosphere marked by hanging pink lanterns. Beer and wine only. No smoking. | 574 S. Glassell St. | 714/997–3300 | $10–$12 | AE, D, MC, V.

Lodging

Days Inn Orange. This three-story lodging makes a good choice if you're visiting Chapman University, 1½ mi northeast, and nearby amusement parks—Disneyland is 5 mi northwest, Knotts Berry Farm 12 mi northwest. For shopping, there's Main Place Mall 5 blocks south. Complimentary Continental breakfast. Refrigerators, cable TV. Outdoor hot tub, spa. Business services. No pets. | 279 S. Main St. | 714/771–6704 or 800/544–8313 | fax 714/771–5522 | www.daysinn.com | 30 rooms | $64–$74 | AE, D, DC, MC, V.

Doubletree-Anaheim/Orange County. This hotel is a 20-story tower 5 mi north of downtown. The property has a manmade lagoon, and a wide range of fitness activities. There's a shuttle to Disneyland from here. 2 Restaurants, bar. In-room data ports, some refrigerators, cable TV. Pool. Hot tub. Tennis. Exercise equipment. Business services, parking (fee). | 100 The City Dr. | 714/634–4500 | fax 714/978–2370 | anaheimdtree@earthlink.com | www.doubletreehotels.com | 454 rooms | $139, $215–$615 suites | AE, D, DC, MC, V.

Hawthorn Suites. This modern boutique-style stone-and-wood property is 3 mi west of downtown and a 5-min walk from shopping at the Block At Orange. Restaurant, complimentary breakfast. In-room data ports, microwaves, refrigerators, cable TV, in-room VCRs (and movies). Pool. Hot tub. Video games. Laundry facilities. Business services, free parking. | 720 The City Dr. S. | 714/740–2700 or 800/278–4837 | fax 714/971–1692 | reservations@hawthornoc.com | www.hawthornoc.com | 123 suites | $150–$214 suites | AE, D, DC, MC, V.

Hilton Suites. An atrium hotel ½ mi south of Anaheim Stadium and 2 mi west of downtown, the 1989 10-story property caters to business travelers. Restaurant, bar, complimentary breakfast. In-room data ports, microwaves, refrigerators, cable TV, in-room VCRs (and movies). Exercise equipment. Indoor pool. Hot tub. Business services. | 400 N. State College Blvd. | 714/938–1111 | fax 714/938–0930 | www.hilton.com | 230 suites | $150–$200 suites | AE, D, DC, MC, V.

Howard Johnson Express Inn. Walk to assorted restaurants and shops from this two-story chain offering. The lodging is 4 mi west of Disneyland, 10 mi north of John Wayne Airport. In-room data ports, microwaves, refrigerators, cable TV. Outdoor pool. Business services. No pets. | 1930 E. Katella Ave. | 714/639–1121 or 800/406–1411 | fax 714/639–3264 | www.hojo.com | 30 rooms | $79–$89 | AE, D, DC, MC, V.

Residence Inn by Marriott. Three mi west of downtown near Anaheim Stadium, this 1988 property is 2 blocks from the Block At Orange shopping district. Landscaped walkways encourage leisurely strolling on the grounds. Picnic area, complimentary Continental breakfast. Kitchenettes, microwaves, cable TV. Pool. Hot tub. Basketball, volleyball. Laundry facilities. Business services, airport shuttle. Pets allowed. | 3101 W. Chapman Ave. | 714/978–7700 | fax 714/978–6257 | 104 rooms | $92–$114 | AE, D, DC, MC, V.

OROVILLE

MAP 3, E5

(Nearby towns also listed: Chico, Nevada City)

On the Feather River near the base of Oroville Dam, Oroville was the site of a major strike during the Gold Rush, when John Bidwell discovered gold here in 1848 and thousands flocked to the area to seek their fortune. When the gold played out, miners and others planted citrus, nut and olive orchards and set up cattle ranches. A few old-timers remember spectacular journeys on the California Zephyr train through the scenic Feather River Canyon on its way from Oakland to Chicago. The scenic train rides ended in 1968 when the dam was completed and the lake filled.

Now Lake Oroville, at 770 ft, the highest earth-filled dam in the nation, draws visitors for swimming, boating, fishing, waterskiing, and houseboating. There are 167 mi of shoreline, a marina, visitor center, and camping areas along its scenic shore.

Information: Oroville Area Chamber of Commerce | 1789 Montgomery St., 95965 | 530/538–2542 or 800/655–4653 | oroville-city.com.

Attractions

Butte Country Pioneer Museum. Get a glimpse of California's past at this museum, built in 1932 as a replica of a 49-er's cabin. Don't miss the extensive arrowhead collection, the Native American baskets, or the preserved "invitation" card for an 1884 hanging. | 2332 Montgomery St. | 530/538–2529 | $2 | Fri.–Sun. Noon–4.

Chinese Temple. This is an 1863 temple decorated with furnishings donated by the Emperor of China. The grounds have three temples devoted to Buddhism, Taoism, and Confucianism, plus a courtyard garden and a collection of costumes, tapestries, and puppets. | 1500 Broderick St. | 530/538–2496 or 530/538–2497 | $2 | Thurs.–Mon. 11–4:30, Tues., Wed. 1–4.

Feather Falls. Visitors can take a long and rewarding hike to the overlook of this waterfall, which, at 640-ft high, is one of the tallest in the United States. The trailhead is on Lumpkin Road 10 mi east of Oroville. | 530/534–6500 | www.r5.fs.fed.us/plumas/scenic/ffalls/ffallsa.htm | Free | Daily.

Feather River Fish Hatchery. The Feather River Fish Hatchery releases more than 10 million salmon and steelhead fingerlings each year. The hatchery is most interesting during spawning season, from early October to mid-November. | 5 Table Mountain Blvd. | 530/538–2222 | Free | Daily 8AM to dusk.

Historic Judge C. F. Lott House. This 19th-century house features Victorian furnishings and decor. | 1067 Montgomery St. | 530/538–2497 | $2 | Feb.–mid-Dec., Sun., Mon., Fri. 12–4.

Oroville Dam and Reservoir. At one time Oroville hosted a large hydraulic mining operation. The town was later deserted by the miners but the striking dam and peaceful reservoir remain. Follow Canyon Drive east of Oroville. | 530/538–2219 | fax 530/589–4938 | $3 per vehicle | Daily.

Lake Oroville State Recreation Area. Here's a family area for leisure activities. | 400 Glen Dr. | 530/538–2200 or 800/444–7275 | losravc@norcal.parks.state.ca.us | $3 per vehicle | Daily.

Visitor Center and Overlook. The Visitor Center neighbors the dam and reservoir and documents the mining, wildlife, and water project history of the region. | 917 Kelly Ridge Rd. | 530/538–2219 | losravc@norcal.parks.state.ca.us/Lake%20Oro.htm | Free | Daily 9–5.

ON THE CALENDAR

SEPT.: *Salmon Festival.* Marking the start of the salmon run, when the fish begin their journey to spawning grounds up the Feather River, this festival aims to educate and entertain. The 1-day event at the Feather River Nature Center and Fish Hatchery includes nature tours, kayak demonstrations, and arts and crafts booths. | 530/538–2542.

MAR.: *Old Time Fiddlers' Contest.* This is a musical event with food and drink in the old mining town. | 1200 Meyers St. | Last weekend in Mar. | 530/538–2542 or 530/589–4844.

MAY: *Bidwell Bar Days.* A long-standing Oroville tradition, it runs from the first Saturday of May | 530/538–2219.

MAY: *Dam Days.* The Oroville area has several fish hatcheries and dams. Dam Days celebrate the industry with festive and educational activities, and runs first Sat. of May–Mother's Day. | 530/534–7690.

Dining

Depot. American. This 1907 rail depot has been transformed into a casual restaurant with high-back wooden booths and an open-air dining area. The walls hold pictures of old trains that served Oroville, and a glass-enclosed observation area allows you to watch modern-day rail traffic. The fare is mainstream American—seafood, prime rib, sandwiches and such. Salad bar, early-bird suppers. Karaoke Fri. No smoking. | 2191 High St. | 530/534–9101 | $15–$35 | AE, D, MC, V.

Gold City Grill. American. Something's fishy at this casual eatery—namely the decor. The dining room is trimmed with fishing lures and fishing scenes on the wallpaper. You'd think fish would be the biggest draw on the menu, but no, it's the BBQ ribs and deep-fried prawns. You can eat outdoors on a covered patio overlooking the street. Kid's menu. | 935 Oro Dam Blvd. | 530/533–9332 | Breakfast also available | $7–$14 | MC, V.

Kwong's Palace. Chinese. Traditional Chinese artwork dresses up this casual eatery. Favorites include the kung pao chicken and the chicken chow mein. Kids' menu. | 245 Table Mountain Blvd. | 530/533–2960 | Closed Sun. | $5–$11 | AE, MC, V.

Lodging

Best Inn and Suites. Near the Oroville Dam boating and fishing area, the hotel is near two casinos. Built in 1989 in a largely residential area, the property caters to business travelers. Complimentary Continental breakfast. In-room data ports, refrigerators, cable TV. Pool. Hot tub. Exercise equipment. Laundry facilities. Business services. Pets allowed (fee). | 1470 Feather River Blvd. | 530/533–9673 | fax 530/533–5862 | 54 rooms, 8 suites | $66–$89, $80–$130 suites | AE, D, DC, MC, V.

Lake Oroville Bed and Breakfast. This 1990 inn reflects French Provincial style with covered porches. Most of the rooms have a view of the lake. Picnic area, complimentary breakfast. Some in-room hot tubs, in-room VCRs. Hiking. Business services. Pets allowed. No smoking. | 240 Sunday Dr., Berry Creek | 530/589–0700 or 800/455–5253 (for reservations) | fax 530/589–4761 | lakeinn@cncnet.com | www.lakeoroville.com | 6 rooms | $75–$145 | AE, D, MC, V.

Motel 6. This two-story motel has the usual amenities of this dependable chain, with the added bonus of being within walking distance to Feather River. You can try your hand at fishing, or just relax and watch life float by. The Feather River Casino is 5 mi south. Restaurant. Cable TV. Laundry facilities. Business services. Pets allowed. | 505 Montgomery St. | 530/532–9400 | fax 530/534–7653 | www.motel6.com | 102 rooms | $51–$61 | AE, D, DC, MC, V.

Travelodge. This one-story motel, built in 1960, sits squarely in the middle of town, with plenty of restaurants within walking distance. Oroville Dam is 8 mi north. Picnic area. Complimentary breakfast. Microwaves, refrigerators, cable TV. Outdoor pool. Laundry services. Business services. Pets allowed. | 580 Oro Dam Blvd. | 530/533–7070 | fax 530/532–0402 | www.travelodge.com | 70 rooms | $55–$65 | AE, D, DC, MC, V.

Villa Court Inn. Comfortable rooms at reasonable prices are the slate at this small 1984 motel. A restaurant is nearby. Cable TV. Pool. | 1527 Feather River Blvd. | 530/533–3930 | 20 rooms | $52–$62 | AE, DC, MC, V.

OXNARD

MAP 4, H14

(Nearby towns also listed: Camarillo, Channel Islands National Park, Ojai, Port Hueneme, Thousand Oaks, Ventura)

Oxnard has a reputation as a quiet agricultural burg, (a broccoli and lettuce capital) but lately it's promoting its charms as an undiscovered beach town. The Channel Islands attract fishermen and boaters, and 7 mi of little-trammeled beaches are heaven for folks who just want to feel sand between their toes. Boasting a busy harbor and un-busy beaches, this community of 142,000 offers a myriad of water and outdoor activities, ranging from quiet beachcombing to sailboard surfing.

Information: **Oxnard Convention and Visitors Bureau** | 200 W. 7th St., 93030-7154 | 805/385–7545 or 800/2–OXNARD | oxtour@west.net | www.oxnardtourism.com.

Attractions

Heritage Square. Take a stroll along this city block to see more than a dozen late 19th-century homes and other structures, many trimmed with manicured gardens and courtyards. Some of the buildings were brought here from outlying ranchlands. Docent-led tours take you inside to see the equally gracious interiors. | 715 South A St., | 805/483–7960 | www.ci.oxnard.ca.us/heritagesquare.html | $2 | Guided tours Sat. 10–2.

Carnegie Art Museum. Housed in a 1906 neoclassical building, the permanent collection focuses on contemporary California painters. There are changing exhibits of work by Ventura County artists as well as photography and decorative arts. | 424 South C St. | 805/385–8157 | www.vcnet.com/carnart | $3 | Thurs.–Sat. 10–5, Sun. 1–5.

Channel Islands Harbor. More than 2,500 boats are moored at this classic seaside harbor in Southern California style; it also serves as the site for concerts, boat shows, fireworks displays, arts festivals, and other events year-round. You can rent bikes, paddleboats, or even an electric boat. The Visitor Center will help you get oriented. | County of Ventura, Channel Islands Harbor; 3900 Pelican Way, | 805/985–4852 | www.oxnardtourism.com/ciharbor.html | Free | Daily.

Ventura County Gull Wings Children's Museum. Kids will enjoy exploring fantasy worlds in the hands-on exhibits of this ocean-inspired kids' museum. Possibilities include a stage complete with costumes and videotape equipment, a puppet theater, a roomful of optical illusions, and a computer room. | 418 W. 4th St. | 805/483–3005 | $3.50 | Tues.–Sun. 10–5.

Ventura County Maritime Museum. Everything you ever wanted to know about shipping, whaling, and maritime history in the Channel Islands and along the California coast is found here in permanent and changing exhibits. | 2731 S. Victoria Ave. | 805/984–6260 | fax 805/984–5970 | By donation | Daily 11–5.

ON THE CALENDAR

JULY: *Salsa Festival.* This weekend event celebrates everything salsa—music, food, and fun. Dance the day away as salsa bands heat things up. Get even more heat from salsa taste-testing and food vendors. | Plaza Park, 5th and B Sts. | 805/289–4875.

APR.: *Point Mugu Airshow.* Oxnard's expansive vistas offer a clear view of the airshow's aerial events at the Naval Air Station. | 805/989–8786 or 805/684–0155.

MAY: *California Strawberry Festival.* Celebrate Oxnard's heritage as a fruit-producing region with food, music, fine arts and crafts, entertainment and, as always, strawberries prepared more ways than you could imagine. Shortcake is just the beginning. The event takes place at College Park Meadow Grounds. | 888/288–9242 or 805/385–7545.

OCT.: *Dia de los Muertos Celebration.* Mexico's Day of the Dead is observed with colorful altars, masks and a procession at the Inlakech Cultural Arts Center. | 805/385–7545.

Dining

Capistrano's. Mediterranean. The four dining areas here include a room with indoor courtyard and fountain, and a Polynesian-style room filled with bamboo, flowers, and plants. The color scheme is burgundy and cream, and some booths have ocean views. Try the Asian shrimp "tower" (wonton pastry with jumbo shrimp, fresh vegetables, and baby greens), crabcake stew, ruby rare ahi tuna with Cajun spices, rice and exotic salsa, or filet mignon with smoked and roasted shiitake mushrooms in madeira sauce. It's ½ mi from the main harbor. Entertainment Fri., Sat. Sunday brunch. No smoking. | 2101 Mandalay Beach Rd. | 805/984–2500 | $8–$22 | AE, D, DC, MC, V.

Port Royal. American. With its setting on the Channel Islands Marina, you practically dine on the water. Sit in front of the fireplace to partake of steak, fresh seafood, or pasta. Kids' menu. Sunday champagne brunch. No smoking. | 3900 Bluefin Circle | 805/382–7678 | $15–$25 | MC, V.

Sal's Mexican Food. You'll hear lots of Spanish in this friendly spot 1 mi south of downtown, where Oxnard's Mexican-American community gathers for authentic south-of-the-border fare. The red-splashed decor is casual but cheery. Try the carne asada or one of the large combination plates. No smoking. | 21450 S. Oxnard Blvd. | 805/483–9015 | $8–$13 | AE, D, MC, V.

Lodging

Best Western Oxnard Inn. This chain offers lots of services, making it an easy stop for families or business travelers. If you're not in the mood for a dip in the pool, consider a jaunt to Point Hueneme Beach, 4 mi northwest. Complimentary Continental breakfast. In-room data ports, some microwaves, some refrigerators, some in-room hot tubs, cable TV. Outdoor pool. Outdoor hot tub, spa. Exercise equipment. Laundry facilities. Business services. Pets allowed. | 1156 S. Oxnard Blvd. | 805/483–9581 or 800/469–6273 | fax 805/483–4072 | www.bestwestern.com | 99 rooms, 3 suites | $79–$89, $169 suites | AE, D, DC, MC, V.

Casa Sirena Resort. This modest motor inn is 6 mi from downtown on the Channel Islands Harbor, with views of the marina from many rooms. The four Spanish-style wood buildings were constructed in 1962. The grounds are landscaped and a park is next to the property. Restaurant, bar, room service. No air-conditioning in some rooms, in-room data ports, some kitchenettes, refrigerators, cable TV. Pool. Beauty salon, hot tub. Putting green. Tennis. Exercise equipment. Video games. Playground. Business services, airport shuttle, free parking. | 3605 Peninsula Rd. | 805/985–6311 or 800/228–6026 | fax 805/985–4329 | www.casasirenahotel.com | 261 rooms, 12 suites | $99–$148, $168 suites | AE, D, DC, MC, V.

Mandalay Beach Resort. On a 7½-acre beach property, this 1980s Embassy Suites complex 6 mi west of downtown has small waterfalls and greenery between the nine buildings on the landscaped grounds. Two-bedroom suites are available. Restaurant, bar, complimentary breakfast. In-room data ports, refrigerators, some in-room hot tubs, cable TV. Pool. Hot tub. Tennis. Bicycles. Kids' programs. Business services, airport shuttle, parking (fee). | 2101 Mandalay Beach Rd. | 805/984–2500 | fax 805/984–8339 | 250 suites | $214–$344 suites | AE, D, DC, MC, V.

Radisson Hotel. This hotel is a six-story 1979 building with expansive grounds and a variety of resort-type amenities. Five miles west of downtown, it has a landscaped courtyard, tennis courts and a pool complex. Restaurant, bar [with entertainment]. Refrigerators, cable TV. Pool. Beauty salon, hot tub. Tennis. Business services, airport shuttle, free parking. | 600 Esplanade Dr. | 805/485–9666 | fax 805/485–2061 | www.radisson.com | 163 rooms, 2 suites | $99, $159 suites | AE, D, DC, MC, V.

Residence Inn by Marriott. On 15 acres that include a gazebo, this hotel has an expansive lobby with tile floors, cherrywood interior and a fireplace. Some of the spacious, comfortably furnished rooms have wood-burning fireplaces. The complex is next to the River Ridge Golf Course, 4 mi east of downtown. Complimentary breakfast. In-room data ports, kitchenettes, cable TV. 2 Pools. Hot tubs. Tennis. Exercise equipment. Laundry facilities. Business services, airport shuttle. | 2101 W. Vineyard Ave. | 805/278–2200 or 800/333–3333 | fax 805/983–4470 | www.residenceinn.com | 252 suites | $115–$150 suites | AE, D, DC, MC, V.

Vagabond Inn Oxnard. Less than 2 mi from the Carnegie Cultural Arts Center, this is next door to a 24-hour eatery. Complimentary Continental breakfast. In-room data ports, some refrigerators, cable TV. Outdoor pool. Business services. Pets allowed (fee). | 1245 N. Oxnard Blvd. | 805/983–0251 or 800/522–1555 | fax 805/988–9638 | www.vagabondinns.com | 69 rooms | $59–$69 | AE, D, DC, MC, V.

PACIFIC GROVE

MAP 4, D10

(Nearby towns also listed: Carmel, Carmel Valley, Monterey, Pebble Beach)

The village of Pacific Grove (pop. 17,400) is right next door to Monterey and shares its amenities, enjoying year-round pleasant weather and ocean breezes. On a small point at the southernmost end of Monterey Bay, it kicks off the ultra-scenic Seventeen Mile Drive to Carmel along the coast. En route such spots as Seal Rock, Cypress Point and Lone Cypress captivate sightseers. The town was established as a Methodist retreat, and an aura of serenity pervades the cottage-lined streets. It's now home to a large number of retirees who have relocated for the peace and proximity to quiet walks and golf courses. The residential areas have numerous Craftsman-style bungalows, and Victorian mansions perch above the seashore drive. Also known as "Butterfly Town," it's a wintering spot for monarch butterflies. Beginning in October, thousands of butterflies fill the trees like living leaves—quite a sight.

Information: Pacific Grove Chamber of Commerce | 584 Central Ave., 93950 | 831/373–3304 or 800/656–6650 | chamber@pacificgrove.org | www.pacificgrove.org.

Attractions

Pacific Grove Art Center. Tour four galleries showcasing paintings, sculptures, and other works by local, regional, and international artists. | 580 Lighthouse Ave. | 831/375–2208 | www.pgartcenter.org | Free | Wed.–Sat. 12–5; Sun. 1–4.

★ **Asilomar State Beach and Conference Center.** On the Monterey Peninsula, Asilomar (which means "a refuge by the sea") boasts amazing views of coastal nature, water, and sand dunes. Originally a YMCA campsite in 1913, the grounds are now operated by the state. The conference center is famous as a retreat for corporate groups and negotiators. Most of the 105 secluded, natural acres remain undisturbed; the retreat complex has dining halls, meeting facilities, and guest rooms. The nearby beach and tidal pool area is accessible by boardwalk. There's also a heated pool and a social hall with a piano and billiards. | 800

Asilomar Blvd. | 831/372–4076 or 831/372–8016 | cal-parks.ca.gov/districts/monterey/asilo-mar.htm | Free | Daily.

Ocean View Boulevard. The main shopping street of this much-used walk skirting the ocean includes 125 factory-direct and specialty stores inside the American Tin Cannery retail center at 125 Ocean View. | Ocean View Blvd. | Free | Daily.

Pacific Grove Museum of Natural History. This museum is devoted to the natural attractions of this region. You can view an extensive collection of rocks and minerals, 400 mounted birds, and a butterfly collection. Kids enjoy the Touch Gallery. There are also rotating exhibits. | 165 Forest Ave. | 831/648–3116 or 831/648–3119 | www.pgmuseum.org | Free | Tues.–Sun. 10–5.

★ **Point Pinos Lighthouse.** This spot at Asilomar Beach also has a small museum with exhibits on lighting and foghorn operations, as well as memorabilia from the U.S. Coast Guard. It's at the corner of Lighthouse Avenue and Asilomar. | 831/646–8540 or 831/648–3116, ext. 13 | www.pgmuseum.org | Free | Jan. 2–late-Nov., Thurs.–Sun. 1–4.

ON THE CALENDAR

APR.: *Good Old Days.* This retro-themed small town festival celebrates bygone times with a Victorian fashion show, parade, arts and crafts booths, firefighters' muster, and dancing in the streets. | 831/373–3304.

APR.: *Wildflower Show.* More than 600 types of native Monterey County wildflowers are arranged in systematic order at this curated educational show. It's very popular with plant collectors and photographers. | 831/648–3116 or 831/373–3304.

JULY: *Feast of Lanterns.* This annual community festival culminates in a night of spectacular fireworks. | 831/372–7625.

OCT.: *Butterfly Parade.* Thousands of monarch butterflies return to their winter home in the Ridge Road pine trees every October. Costumed elementary school kids march through downtown Pacific Grove to welcome them, and the parade is followed by the Butterfly Bazaar. | 831/646–6540.

OCT.: *Pacific Grove Historic Home Tour.* Visit—and learn about—an array of Victorian homes, B&B's, and churches selected each year for this tour. Hostesses decked out in Victorian-era garb provide historic high points and architectural details as you tour each locale. | 831/373–3304 | $12.

NOV.: *Marching Band Festival.* About 30 high school, college, and amateur marching bands come together to talk music and take part in a competition of marching and field displays. The event takes place on the Pacific Grove High School campus. | 1st Sat. in Nov. | 831/646–6595 or 831/646–6590.

DEC.: *Christmas at the Inns.* Take a self-guided tour of well-preserved Victorian bed-and-breakfast inns, dressed up for the holidays. There's entertainment and refreshments. Admission is $12, including a map. | Pacific Grove Chamber of Commerce, 584 Central Ave. | 831/373–3304 or 800/656–6650.

Dining

Fandango. Contemporary. With its stone walls, fireplaces, window seats, and overhead lanterns with skirted shades, Fandango has the earthy feel of a southern Spanish farmhouse. Complementing the ambience are the robust flavors of the cuisine, which ranges from southern France, Italy, Spain, and Greece to North Africa, from paella and cannelloni to couscous. You can eat outside on a small patio with seven tables. No smoking. | 223 17th St. | 831/372–3456 | $10–$20 | AE, D, DC, MC, V.

Fishwife. Caribbean. Fresh fish with a Latin accent makes this colorful spot a favorite of locals for lunch or a casual dinner. The blue-green interior features an aquarium in the lounge, and a large stained-glass window depicting an underwater scene. Most popular are the "fisherman bowls," with scallops, shrimp and lobster, or sautéed calamari steaks. Fishwife is right in front of the Asilomar Center grounds and just one block from the beach.

Kids' menu. Sunday brunch. Beer and wine only. No smoking | 1996½ Sunset Dr. | 831/375–7107 | Closed Tues. | $12–$18 | AE, D, MC, V.

★ **Old Bath House.** Continental. Romantic atmosphere permeates this former Victorian bathhouse overlooking Lover's Point. Rouge-colored tablecloths and dark cherry-wood paneling enhance the sense of intimacy. Regional dishes are based on local seafood and produce such as salmon and Monterey Bay prawns. The wine list has 360 different vintages. The restaurant has a less expensive menu for late-afternoon diners. Early-bird supper. Kids' menu. No smoking. | 620 Ocean View Blvd. | 831/375–5195 | www.oldbathhouse.com | No lunch | $20–$30 | AE, D, DC, MC, V.

Passion Fish. Seafood. Try imaginative local twists on classic Latin dishes such as roast duck or local halibut, served with a variety of imaginative sauces. The casual, tropical atmosphere is accented by carved crocodiles and toucans, South American artwork and artifacts form the decor. Wines are an exceptional value here. It's in central Pacific Grove a mile from the Monterey Bay Aquarium. No smoking. | 701 Lighthouse Ave. | 831/655–3311 | Closed Tues. No lunch | $15–$25 | AE, D, MC, V.

Peppers Mexicali Cafe. Mexican. This cheerful white-walled restaurant serves fresh seafood and traditional dishes from Mexico and Latin America. Pine furniture and artwork of chile peppers bolsters the Latin theme. The red and green salsas are excellent. Beer and wine only. No smoking. | 170 Forest Ave. | 831/373–6892 | Closed Tues. No lunch Sun. | $7–$14 | AE, D, DC, MC, V.

The Tinnery. American. This family-oriented restaurant has an enviable location with a view of Lovers Point. Each of the four dining areas has a view of the ocean, and pictures of the old cannery line the walls. The menu has pancakes and omelettes for breakfast, burgers and sandwiches for lunch. Broiled salmon with hollandaise sauce, mesquite-grilled meats and fish-and-chips are dinner highlights. Open-air dining is available on an uncovered 50-seat patio. Entertainment Fri.–Sat. Kids' menu. No smoking. | 631 Ocean View Blvd. | 831/646–1040 | Breakfast also available | $15–$30 | AE, D, DC, MC, V.

Toasties Cafe. American. Three-egg omelettes, burritos, pancakes, waffles, French toast, and other breakfast items are served at this crowded café until 3PM. The lunch selections include burgers and other sandwiches. Toasties also serves dinner—fish and chips, seafood pasta—but its daytime meals are the best bets. No smoking. | 702 Lighthouse Ave. | 831/373–7543 | Breakfast also available. No supper Sun., Mon. | $8–$12 | AE, MC, V.

Lodging

Asilomar Conference Center. The state-owned facility caters to large conferences, but individual rooms can be booked by single travelers and families when they're available. The rooms are in rustic buildings between the beach and redwood forest. Most rooms lack radios or other amenities, but are perfect for a peaceful retreat. The center is a former YMCA retreat built in 1913 on 105 acres, still mostly natural. You can eat in the dining room with conference attendees, at a separate table. The menu is set by the chef, but the food has a reputation for being fresh and delicious. It's 2 mi west of downtown. Dining room, complimentary breakfast. No air conditioning, some kitchenettes, some room phones, no TV in some rooms. No smoking. | 800 Asilomar Blvd. | 831/372–8016 | fax 831/372–7227 | www.asilomarcenter.com | 314 rooms in 28 buildings, 1 guesthouse | $78–$100, $133 guesthouse | AE, MC, V.

Best Western. This chain motel is 3 blocks from the beach and a mile west of downtown Pacific Grove. Complimentary Continental breakfast. Some refrigerators, cable TV. Pool. Hot tub, sauna. Business services. | 1111 Lighthouse Ave. | 831/646–8885 | fax 831/646–5976 | 49 rooms, 5 suites | $160–$500, $400–$650 suites | AE, D, DC, MC, V.

★ **Centrella Inn.** The Centrella Inn, in operation since 1889, is a designated National Historic Landmark in the heart of the Monterey Peninsula. Choose from private cottages with claw-foot tubs, fireplaces, and wetbars, attic suites, or Victorian guest rooms. Complimentary breakfast. Some refrigerators, some in-room VCRs, no TV in some rooms. | 612 Central Ave. | 831/372–3372 | fax 831/372–2036 | www.centrellainn.com/ | 17 rooms | $154–$269 | AE, D, MC, V.

Days Inn Suites. This well-appointed motel is in a quiet forest 3 blocks from the Asilomar Conference Center. The 1975 wood-sided building has some larger rooms with gas fireplaces. Complimentary Continental breakfast. No air-conditioning, some kitchenettes, microwaves, refrigerators, cable TV, in-room VCRs (and movies). | 660 Dennett Ave. | 831/373–8777 | fax 831/373–2698 | 30 suites | $159–$225 suites | AE, D, DC, MC, V.

Deer Haven Inn. This small inn has one and two-bedroom suites close to the beaches, about a mile west of downtown Pacific Grove in a residential area. The building dates to 1970. Complimentary Continental breakfast. No air-conditioning, microwaves, cable TV. Hot tub, sauna. No smoking. | 740 Crocker Ave. | 831/373–1114 or 800/525–3373 | fax 408/655–5048 | 22 suites | $179–$239 suites | AE, D, MC, V.

Gatehouse. John Steinbeck visited here; there's even a room named after the local author. One block from the beach and 3 blocks from the Monterey Bay Aquarium, this 1884 Victorian is one of the oldest homes in Pacific Grove, and the decor reflects the period. The Turkish Room has a Persian rug, brass headboard, and a camel-saddle chair. The Steinbeck Room features a fireplace; some rooms have clawfoot tubs or wood-burning stoves. Complimentary full breakfast. No air-conditioning. Business services. No smoking. | 225 Central Ave. | 831/649–8436 or 800/753–1881 | fax 831/648–8044 | www.sueandlewinss.com | 9 rooms | $125–$195 | AE, D, MC, V.

Gosby House. J. E. Gosby, a cobbler from Nova Scotia, built some of the town's first rooming houses, including this turreted 1888 gem with a stained-glass bay window and gingerbread adornments on the front porch. Rooms have antique furnishings; some have private patio entrances. Two private rooms in the carriage house have fireplaces. There's a small garden and courtyard on the property, in downtown Pacific Grove 4 blocks from the ocean. Complimentary breakfast. No air conditioning, some in-room hot tubs. Bicycles. Business services. | 643 Lighthouse Ave. | 831/375–1287 or 800/527–8828 | fax 831/655–9621 | www.foursisters.com | 22 rooms (two with shared bath), 2 rooms in guesthouse | $100–$170 | AE, DC, MC, V.

Grand View Inn. Built in 1910 and completely restored since, the inn has hardwood floors, private marble tile baths, and antique furnishings. The grounds feature a fountain garden. The inn is in a residential area across from the beach, 2 blocks from downtown. Complimentary breakfast. No air conditioning, no room phones. No kids under 12. | 557 Ocean View Blvd. | 831/372–4341 | www.pginns.com | 10 rooms | $165–$285 | MC, V.

★ **Green Gables.** Bay windows deserve their name in this 1888 Queen Anne-style mansion, with many of them, in almost every room, overlooking Monterey Bay. Guest rooms in this green-and-white gabled house have intricately detailed woodwork, window seats, built-ins, stained glass, and clawfoot tubs. The Chapel Room resembles a church, with its vaulted ceiling and pew-like window seat. Carriage house rooms have more privacy and modern amenities. Some rooms have fireplaces. The inn is across from the bay shore, a 5-min walk from downtown Pacific Grove. Complimentary breakfast. No air-conditioning, no TV in some rooms. Bicycles. Business services. | 104 5th St. | 831/375–2095 or 800/722–1774 | fax 831/375–5437 | www.foursisters.com | 6 rooms in main house (4 with shared bath), 5 rooms in guesthouse | $120–$240 | AE, DC, MC, V.

Inn at 17-Mile Drive. All the rooms in this 1920s Craftsman treat you with a view of Monterey Bay or the inn's lush gardens. Furnishings aim to complement the region's wildlife—painted flowers on Oriental screens in one room are a nod to Monarch butterflies, which winter in nearby eucalyptus groves; deep sea blues in another room honor the sea otter, which thrives in local waters. Fireplaces keep things toasty in some rooms. A few rooms can work for families. Dining room, complimentary breakfast. Cable TV. Outdoor hot tub. Library. Business services. No pets. No smoking. | 213 17-Mile Dr. | 831/642–9514 or 800/526–5666 | fax 831/642–9546 | 213@innat17.com | www.innat17.com | 14 rooms | $135–$240 | AE, MC, V.

Larchwood Inn. Rooms here are apartment-type units, one- and two-bedroom suites as well as individual rooms. Most rooms at this cozy inn, 2 blocks from the ocean and 1 mi from downtown, have gas fireplaces. There's a communal sauna. Complimentary Continental breakfast. No air conditioning, cable TV. Hot tub, sauna. Business services. | 740 Crocker Ave. | 831/373–7784 or 800/525–3373 | fax 831/655–5048 | www.montereyinns.com/larchwood | 27 rooms | $99–$149, $119–$179 suites | AE, D, MC, V.

Lighthouse Lodge and Suites. Really two lodgings in one, with economical, motel-style rooms in a building on one side of the street, a roomier, all-suite facility on the other. The Pacific Ocean is one block away and there are a number of eateries within walking distance. Complimentary breakfast. Microwaves, refrigerators, some in-room hot tubs, cable TV. Outdoor pool. Outdoor hot tub. Business services. Pets allowed (fee). | 1150 and 1249 Lighthouse Ave. | 831/655–2111 or 800/858–1249 | fax 831/655–4922 | www.lhls.com | 68 rooms, 31 suites | $149–$171, $219–$288 suites | AE, D, DC, MC, V.

★ **Martine Inn.** First built as a Victorian home and later redesigned, this 1899 stucco property has an extensive collection of American antiques, including a bedroom suite that once belonged to costume designer Edith Head, and an enviable collection of classic cars. There are two solarium sitting rooms, and a guest parlor with a baby grand piano that automatically plays during hors d'oeuvres hour. Some rooms have fireplaces and/or stunning views of Monterey Bay. The inn is just 4 blocks from the Monterey Bay Aquarium. Complimentary breakfast. Refrigerators. Hot tub. Library. Business services. | 255 Ocean View Blvd. | 831/373–3388 or 800/852–5588 | fax 831/373–3896 | www.martineinn.com | 23 rooms | $165–$300 | AE, D, MC, V.

Old St. Angela Inn. Once a convent but now a B&B, this richly shingled, 1910 Craftsman-style home invites you to relax only 100 yards from Monterey Bay. Rooms, some with water views, are decorated in period antiques. Don't miss afternoon tea and cookies in the garden, or—if the fog rolls in—in the glass solarium. The inn is close to area shops and sites, including the Monterey Bay Aquarium. A few rooms can accommodate kids. Dining room, complimentary breakfast. Some in-room hot tubs, no TV. Spa. Business services. No pets. No smoking. | 321 Central Ave. | 831/372–3246 or 800/748–6306 | fax 831/372–8560 | lew@sue-andlewinns.com | www.sueandlewinns.com | 9 rooms | $110–$195 | D, MC, V.

Pacific Grove Inn. You can walk to the beach from this 1904 late-Victorian house overlooking Monterey Bay. Most rooms in this National Historic Landmark have gas fireplaces. It's 3 blocks from downtown Pacific Grove. Complimentary Continental breakfast. Refrigerators, cable TV. No smoking. | 581 Pine Ave. | 831/375–2825 or 800/732–2825 | 16 rooms in two buildings | $122–$142 | AE, D, DC, MC, V.

Rosedale Inn. Each of the six redwood cottages that make up this 1989 inn have two or more suites or rooms. Ceiling fans give off a breeze in summer and fireplaces keep you warm when it gets chilly in this peaceful setting surrounded by the bay. The ocean is only 2 blocks away, downtown is 2 mi east. Complimentary Continental breakfast. No air-conditioning, kitchenettes, microwaves, refrigerators, in-room hot tubs, cable TV, in-room VCRs (and movies). No smoking. | 775 Asilomar Blvd. | 831/655–1000 or 800/822–5606 | fax 831/655–0691 | www.rosedaleinn.com | 19 suites in 6 buildings | $135–$225 suites | AE, D, DC, MC, V.

Seven Gables. This Victorian-style inn is actually a collection of five clapboard buildings with breathtaking views of the ocean. It's next door to the Grand View Inn and is connected to it by a garden path with a goldfish pond. Fountains, gardens, and statues cover the grounds. Inside, the bed and breakfast is decorated with Victorian-style antiques and collectibles, gold-leaf-trim mirrors, a Tiffany window, Oriental rugs, and marble statues. All rooms have queen-size beds, some with partial canopies. Complimentary breakfast. No air conditioning, some refrigerators, no room phones. No kids under 12. No smoking. | 555 Ocean View Blvd. | 831/372–4341 | www.pginns.com | 14 rooms in five buildings | $165–$375 | MC, V.

Sunset Motel. In a quiet residential neighborhood, this two-story lodging has features not often found in a motel, including vaulted ceilings and fireplaces in some rooms. It's a quick walk to nearby restaurants. Lovely Asilomar Beach is only a few blocks west. Complimentary Continental breakfast. Some refrigerators, some in-room hot tubs, cable TV. Outdoor hot tub. Business services. No pets. No smoking. | 133 Asilomar Blvd. | 831/375–3936 | fax 831/375–7573 | sunset@montereyinns.com/sunset | www.montereyinns.com | 21 rooms | $99–$169 | AE, D, DC, MC, V.

Terrace Oaks Inn. Head one way out the door of this inn and you're at the ocean. Take a walk in the other direction and you're surrounded by the shops, restaurants, and coffee bars of Pacific Grove. And, there's also a golf course within walking distance (if you don't mind carrying your clubs). The one-story lodging, built in the 1950s, got spruced up in the '90s. Complimentary Continental breakfast. Some in-room hot tubs, cable TV. Business services. No pets. No smoking. | 1095 Lighthouse Ave. | 831/373–4382 | fax 831/647–2178 | terraceoaks@montereyinns.com | www.montereyinns.com/terraceoaks | 12 rooms | $109–$179 | AE, D, MC, V.

PACIFIC PALISADES

MAP 9, B3

PACIFIC PALISADES

INTRO
ATTRACTIONS
DINING
LODGING

(Nearby towns also listed: Los Angeles, Malibu, Santa Monica, Venice, Westwood)

A lodestar for SUV-piloting soccer moms, this handsome residential realm is tucked between Santa Monica and Malibu, flanked by the lush Santa Monica Mountains and sandy Pacific beaches. The upscale town of 23,000 has quite its share of shops, restaurants, and offices, but manages to maintain a small-village feel.

Information: Pacific Palisades Chamber of Commerce, | 15330 Antioch St., 90272 | 310/459–7963 | www.pp90272.com.

Attractions

Self-Realization Fellowship Lake Shrine. A bird refuge, Gandhi World Peace Memorial, and a sunken garden are here on 10 acres of attractions, representing the five major religions of the world. | 17190 Sunset Blvd. | 310/454–4114 | fax 310/459–7461 | www.yogananda-srf.org | Free | Tues.–Sat. 9–4:30, Sun. 12:30–4:30.

Will Rogers State Historic Park. Perched on steep bluffs overlooking the beaches below, the park has hiking trails, picnic facilities, polo games on the weekends, and tours of the humorist's home. The view and the air are breathtaking. | 1501 Will Rogers State Park Rd., | 310/454–8212 | www.parks.ca.gov | $3 per vehicle | Daily 8–sunset; tours daily 10:30–4:30.

ON THE CALENDAR
MAY: *Pacific Palisades Autoshow.* Start your engines and check out more than 300 vehicles and related displays at this one-day event, which takes over the village area along Sunset Blvd. | 310/459–7963.

Dining

Atrio Cucina. Italian. Food, food, and more food—that's what adorns the walls in pictures and paintings at this Northern Italian eatery. That said, there's a good chance you won't leave hungry if try one of the local favorites, such as linguine seafood, grilled salmon, or chicken cannelloni (served with a mushroom herb sauce). Kids' menu. | 1032 Swarthmore Ave. | 310/459–9423 | $7–$12 | AE, D, MC, V.

Lodging

Pacific Palisades Bed & Breakfast. This no-frills B&B is the only place you'll find lodging directly in Pacific Palisades. Both rooms, 1 with full bath, are rented as a single unit, even if you only need 1 room. The village and restaurants are 1 ½ mi away. Picnic area. Complimentary Continental breakfast. No room phones, TV in common area. No pets. No smoking. | 541 Muskingum Ave. | 310/454–5893 | 2 rooms | $75 | No credit cards.

PALM DESERT

MAP 4, K15

(Nearby towns also listed: Cathedral City, Indian Wells, Indio, La Quinta, Palm Springs, Rancho Mirage)

This resort haven of 36,300 is the second largest of Palm Springs' satellite communities and sits at the base of the striking Santa Rosa Mountains range. Within the Palm Springs/Desert Resorts area you'll find abundant exclusive shopping, 80 championship golf courses, and 50 luxury hotels and resorts.

Information: **Palm Desert Visitor Information Center** | 72990 Rte. 111, 92260 | 800/873–2428 | info@palm-desert.org | www.palm-desert.org.

Attractions

Jude E. Poynter Golf Museum. Opened in 1990, this museum has dozens of golf-related artifacts, such as a rare, wicker golf bag from Hong Kong, and a 1926 reproduction of "Calamity Jane," the prized putter used by champion Bobby Jones. | 73450 Fred Waring Dr. | 760/341–2491 | Free | Daily, 7AM–10PM.

★ **The Living Desert Wildlife and Botanical Park.** This sprawling desert park has bighorn sheep, mountain lions, Mexican wolves, and birds of prey. The living desert also features live animal shows, hiking trails, and tram tours. | 47-900 S. Portola Ave. | 760/346–5694 | www.palm-springs.com | $6.50 | mid-June–Aug., daily 8–1:30; Sept.–mid-June, daily 9–4:30.

Palms to Pines Highway. This picturesque drive along Route 74, south of Palm Desert, has many different views of the California desert landscape. | Free | Daily.

ON THE CALENDAR

JAN.: *Bob Hope Chrysler Classic.* This is the famed golf tournament named after the area's biggest golf enthusiast. | 760/346–8184.

APR.: *Agua Caliente Indian Heritage Festival.* This spring event on S. Palm Canyon Dr. celebrates the culture and history of the Agua Caliente tribe. Top draw are the spirited dance performances, along with arts and crafts displays. Kids love the pony rides and face painting. | 760/325–5673.

Dining

Augusta. Contemporary. Artwork fills this showplace, one of the region's most talked-about eateries. Two popular items on the eclectic menu are spit-roasted duck with a cilantro sauce and Chilean sea bass marinated in sake. No smoking. | 73-951 El Paseo | 760/779–9200 | Reservations essential | Closed Aug. No lunch Sun. | $40–$60 | AE, DC, MC, V.

Cafe des Beaux Arts. French. The café brings a little bit of Paris to the desert, with sidewalk dining, colorful flower boxes, and a bistro menu of French and California favorites like a hefty bouillabaisse, broiled portobello mushroom with grilled chicken and artichoke heart served with sherry sauce, and rabbit dijonnaise. Leisurely dining is encouraged, and the menu prices are prix fixe. No smoking. | 73-640 El Paseo | 760/346–0669 | Closed July–mid Sept. | $26–$30 | AE, DC, MC, V.

★ **Cuistot.** Contemporary. French trained chefs take a worldly approach at this restaurant, tucked into the back of an El Paseo courtyard. The atrium building has lots of glass. Signature dishes rotate seasonally, but could include grilled shrimp with spinach linguine, oven-roasted young duck in black currant sauce, and rack of lamb with rosemary. No smoking. | 73-111 El Paseo | 760/340–1000 | Closed Mon. and Aug. | $20–$40 | AE, DC, MC, V.

Daily Grill. American. A combination upscale coffee shop and bar, the Daily Grill serves good salads (the niçoise is particularly tasty), a fine gazpacho, zesty pasta dishes, and various blue-plate specials like chicken pot pie. In a downtown shopping district, the restaurant's sidewalk terrace with eight marble-top tables invites people-watching. The black-and-white decor includes photographic prints on the walls. Sunday brunch is a regular party. No smoking. | 73-061 El Paseo | 760/779–9911 | $7–$19 | AE, D, DC, MC, V.

Jillian's. Continental. The husband tends the kitchen and the wife runs the business at this fancy yet casual restaurant. Antiques and framed art decorate the three dining rooms, and the nighttime sky provides the ambience in the center courtyard. Try the monumental appetizer called tower of crab (layers of crab, tomatoes, avocados, and brioche), and the entrées such as salmon baked in parchment, fettuccini with lobster and rack of lamb. Desserts are the popular Hawaiian cheesecake with macadamia nut crust. Men might feel more comfortable wearing jackets. Pianist, vocalist. No smoking. | 74-155 El Paseo | 760/776–8242 | Reservations essential | Closed mid-June–Sept. No lunch | $30–$46 | AE, DC, MC, V.

Loscanda Toscana. Italian. Celebrities and celebrity-watchers patronize this Tuscan-style restaurant that's known for excellent service, many antipasto choices, and fine soups. Veal, chicken, and fish all receive snazzy preparations. Homemade pasta, baked goods. No smoking. | 72-695 Rte. 111, next to Von's | 760/776–7500 | Reservations essential | Closed Aug. No lunch | $25–$45 | AE, D, DC, MC, V.

Mayo's. Italian. The Art Deco dining room has textured stucco walls, mirrors and celebrity photos. There's even a private room dedicated to Hollywood's famed Rat Pack. The menu has an updated version of Continental cuisine: pasta, Lake Superior whitefish, New York steak, osso bucco. You can eat outside on a nine-table patio. Free valet parking. Entertainment nightly. No smoking. | 73-990 El Paseo | 760/346–2284 | Reservations essential | Summer, Thur., Fri. and Sat. | No lunch | $16–$30 | AE, D, DC, MC, V.

McGowan's Irish Inn. Irish. Home-style comfort foods—meatloaf, chicken and dumplings, corned beef and cabbage, lamb shanks, liver and onions, and beef stew—get the full Irish treatment at this restaurant with a full bar and brick-lined interior. The portions are beyond generous. Open-air dining is available in a small fenced-off sidewalk space. It's one block from the El Paseo shopping district. No smoking. | 73-340 Rte. 111 | 760/346–6032 | Closed Sun. June–Sept. | $16–$28 | MC, V.

Palomino Euro Bistro. Mediterranean. One of the desert's longtime favorites is known for grilled and roasted entrées. Huge reproductions of famous French Impressionist paintings cover the walls of this bustling bistro. Open-air dining is available on a small patio with eight wrought-iron tables. Kids' menu. No smoking. | 73-101 Rte. 111 | 760/773–9091 | No lunch | $14–$27 | AE, D, DC, MC, V.

Ristorante Mamma Gina. Italian. The greatest hits of Florence and Tuscany appear on the menu at this festive, upscale restaurant. The three dining rooms have high ceilings, carpeted floors, and rustic decor. The appetizers and salads are superb, but save room for pasta dishes or smartly crafted chicken, veal, and fish dishes. The wine selection favors Italian and California vintages. Known for pasta and veal. It's in the heart of the Palm Desert shopping district. No smoking. | 73-705 El Paseo | 760/568–9898 | No lunch Sun. | $15–$33 | AE, DC, MC, V.

Lodging

Comfort Suites of Palm Desert. Built in 2000, this all-suite hotel of the familiar chain is off I–10 at the Washington Street exit. A good bet if you're a golfer, the lodging has several courses within a 5-mi radius. There's also a restaurant within walking distance, so you can work up an appetite, or work off that dessert. Complimentary Continental breakfast. In-room data ports, in-room safes, microwaves, refrigerators, some in-room hot tubs, cable

TV. Outdoor pool. Outdoor hot tub. Gym. Laundry facilities. Business services. Pets allowed (fee). | 39585 Washington St. | 760/360–3337 or 800/517–4000 | fax 760/360–5496 | www.palmdesertcomfort.com | 72 suites | $95–$145 | AE, D, DC, MC, V.

Deep Canyon Inn. Completely remodeled in 1999, this inn has a small pond and water-fall. The 1965 three-story stucco building is in a residential area a bit more than a mile from the El Paseo shopping area. Complimentary Continental breakfast. Some kitchenettes, refrigerators, cable TV. Pool. Hot tub. Business services. Pets allowed. | 74470 Abronia Trail | 760/346–8061 or 800/253–0004 (for reservations) | fax 760/341–9120 | innkper@aol.com | www.inn-adc.com | 32 rooms | $119–$219 | AE, D, MC, V.

Desert Patch Inn. The ubiquitous palm trees sway and exotic flowers scent the air of this one-story inn. Pottery and pastel hues give the rooms a Southwestern look; all have views of the landscaped grounds. The El Paseo area (fine shops, restaurants) is one block away. Complimentary Continental breakfast. Some kitchenettes, some microwaves, refrigerators, cable TV, in-room VCRs. Outdoor pool. Outdoor hot tub. Business services. Pets allowed. No smoking. | 73785 Shadow Mountain Dr. | 760/346–9161 or 800/350–9758 | fax 760/776–9661 | desertpatch@earthlink.net | www.desertpatch.com | 11 rooms, 3 suites | $59–$89, $104 suites | AE, D, MC, V.

Embassy Suites. Offers excellent accommodations. Second and third floor suites have balconies at this hotel which is less than a mile east of El Paseo shopping. Restaurant, bar, complimentary breakfast, room service. In-room data ports, refrigerators, cable TV. Pool. Hot tub. Putting green, tennis. Exercise equipment. Video games. Business services. | 74-700 Rte. 111 | 760/340–6600 | fax 760/340–9519 | www.embassy-suites.com | 198 suites | $249–$279 suites | AE, D, DC, MC, V.

Fairfield Inn by Marriott. One block from the Palm Desert Mall, this 1987 three-story building was remodeled in 1999. Complimentary Continental breakfast. Some refrigerators, cable TV. Pool. Hot tub. Gym. Putting green. Business services, airport shuttle. | 72-322 Rte. 111 | 760/341–9100 | fax 760/773–3515 | www.marriott.com | 113 rooms, 6 suites | $104–$124, $189–$219 suites | AE, D, DC, MC, V.

Holiday Inn Express. This 1985 three-story stucco property is in a residential area, 2 blocks from El Paseo shops. Restaurant, picnic area, complimentary Continental breakfast. In-room data ports, some refrigerators, cable TV. Pool. Hot tub. Tennis. Exercise equipment. Laundry facilities. Business services, free parking. | 74675 Rte. 111 | 760/340–4303 | fax 760/340–3723 | www.hiexpress.com/palmdesertca | 129 rooms | $89–$159, $129–$199 suites | AE, D, DC, MC, V.

International Lodge. Built in 1970, each room in this two-story brick building has a private balcony. The grounds feature a fountain and garden, and it's just 2 blocks to shopping at El Paseo. Kitchenettes, microwaves, cable TV, some in-room VCRs. 2 pools. Hot tub. Laundry facilities. Business services. | 74-380 El Camino | 760/346–6161 or 800/874–9338 | fax 760/568–0563 | www.internationallodge.net | 52 rooms (50 with shower only) | $115 | AE, D, MC, V.

Marriott's Desert Springs Resort and Spa. This resort is a sprawling 423-acre property with a manmade lake and large beach. The rooms are in a 1987 eight-story tower; the grounds are extensively landscaped. It's 2 mi east of El Paseo. Bar, dining room. In-room data ports, cable TV. 5 pools. Beauty salon, hot tub, spa. Driving range, 36-hole golf course, putting green, 20 tennis courts. Gym. Kids' programs. Business services, parking (fee). | 74855 Country Club Dr. | 760/341–2211 or 800/331–3112 | fax 760/341–1872 | www.marriott.com/marriott/ctdca | 884 rooms | $370–$470, $300–$700 suites | AE, D, DC, MC, V.

Residence Inn of Palm Desert. This all-suite option, built in 1999, aims to have a low-key, neighborhood feel, with lodgings (studios and two bedroom suites) spread out among several two-story buildings. All rooms have views of the Santa Rosa Mountains or the adjacent Desert Willow Golf Resort. The Children's Discovery Museum of the Desert is 6 mi away and there are a number of restaurants within a short drive. Complimentary Continental breakfast. In-room data ports, in-room safes, kitchenettes, microwaves, refrigerators, cable TV, in-room VCRs (and movies). Outdoor pool. Outdoor hot tub. 1 tennis court. Gym. Laundry facilities, laundry service. Business services. Pets allowed (fee). | 38305 Cook St. | 760/776–0050 | fax 760/776–1806 | www.residenceinn.com | 130 suites | $159–$259 | AE, D, DC, MC, V.

Shadow Mountain Resort and Racquet Club. One of the desert's classic tennis resorts, this 4-acre property has a 1946 stucco building and extensive landscaping with a small creek. It's in a residential area ½ mi northwest of downtown. In-room data ports, cable TV. 4 pools. Hot tub, massage. 16 tennis courts. Exercise equipment, bicycles. Kids' programs. Laundry facilities. Business services. | 45750 San Luis Rey | 760/346–6123 or 800/472–3713 | fax 760/346–6518 | www.shadow-mountain.com | 125 suites | $160–$282, $252–$572 suites | AE, DC, MC, V.

Tres Palmas. A 1993 Spanish-style stucco building, this small B&B is decorated with Navajo rugs and other Native American artwork. Complimentary Continental breakfast. Cable TV, no room phones. Pool. No kids under 10. No smoking. | 73135 Tumbleweed La. | 760/773–9858 or 800/770–9858 (for reservations) | fax 760/776–9159 | www.innformation.com/ca/tres-palmas | 4 rooms | $120–$185 | AE, MC, V.

Vacation Inn. Reasonable rates will appeal to sports lovers at this 1986 Southwestern-style property. It's 2 mi east of downtown. Complimentary Continental breakfast. Refrigerators, cable TV. Pool. Hot tub. Putting green, tennis. Business services, airport shuttle. | 74-715 Rte. 111. | 760/340–4441 or 800/231–8675 | fax 760/773–9413 | www.vacationinn.com | 150 rooms | $160 | AE, D, DC, MC, V.

PALM SPRINGS

INTRO
ATTRACTIONS
DINING
LODGING

PALM SPRINGS

MAP 4, K15

(Nearby towns also listed: Cathedral City, Desert Hot Springs, Hemet, Indio, La Quinta, Palm Desert, Rancho Mirage)

Palm Springs (pop.42,900) lies at the heart of a fast-growing desert community that now includes six distinct cities. Situated in the Coachella Valley and surrounded by 8,000-ft-high mountains, this oasis is home to 95 golf courses, 600 tennis courts and 30,000 swimming pools. There are museums, world-class spas, shopping, art galleries, botanical parks, wildlife viewing, casinos, and hot air ballooning. Until recently the Palm Springs area has been a winter/spring resort luring visitors from cold climates to spend a few days or weeks in the sun, golfing, swimming, playing tennis or simply enjoying beautiful desert scenery. Within the last decade, however, the desert has become a year-round playground drawing many summer visitors who want to experience first-hand the 100-degree plus scorching heat.

Celebrities have vactioned in the desert since the 1920s, when the first resort opened in La Quinta. Although the names and faces have changed in the intervening years, the glamour remains. Today you can cruise along Bob Hope or Frank Sinatra drive, or you might run into former President Gerald Ford strolling along Palm Canyon Drive. Tiger Woods might even be staying at your hotel.

While it wasn't always so, shopping here is first rate, particularly along El Paseo in Palm Desert and at the many consignment and antiques shops scattered throughout the Coachella Valley. The same could be said for dining. You can now enjoy a delicious meal and first-class service at fine restaurants, some of which star celebrity chefs.

Expect your visit to be casual and relaxed. But heed the advice to newcomers. The desert can be dangerous. Wear sunscreen, cover up, wear a broad brimmed hat, and drink lots of water. Don't venture out alone; and avoid dirt roads unless you have four-wheel-drive.

Information: **Palm Springs Desert Resorts Convention and Visitors Authority** | 69-930 Rte. 111, Suite 201, Rancho Mirage, 92270 | 760/770–9000 or 800/967–3767 | info@palm-desert.org | www.desert-resorts.com.

Attractions

Indian Canyons. Palm, Murray, and Andreas Canyons hold the ancestral home of the Agua Caliente band of the Cahuilla people. Explore remnants of their ancient life, including rock art, mortars ground into the bedrock, pictographs, and shelters built atop high cliff walls. Hiking trails lace the canyons, which are home to bighorn sheep and wild ponies. Join rangers for free interpretive walks daily. | 38-500 S. Palm Canyon Dr. | 760/325–5673 | www.indian-canyons.com | $6 | Daily 8–5.

Moorten's Botanical Garden. These 2 acres of lush grounds serve as a bird sanctuary for native species, including cactus wrens, hummingbirds, and blue birds. Check out thousands of informational displays on the plant species in the garden, which have been gathered from around the world. | 1701 S. Palm Canyon Dr. | 760/327–6555 | $2.50 | Mon.–Sat. 9–4:30, Sun. 10–4.

Oasis Waterpark. Water, water everywhere. That's the theme of this family fun park, with flume rides, pools, and other ways to get wet. | 1500 Gene Autry Tr | 760/325–7873 or 760/327–0499 | $19.95 | Mar.–Labor Day, daily 11–6:30; Labor Day–Oct., weekends 11–5.

★ **Palm Springs Aerial Tramway.** Feel like you're flying on this spectacular ride, with jaw-dropping, 360-degree views of the San Jacinto Range and desert beyond. The 80-passenger, enclosed tram climbs more than a vertical mile in 15 minutes from Valley Station (elev. 2,643 ft) to Mountain Station (elev. 8,516 ft). Both stops have picnic areas and observation decks. The tram is at the base of the mountains north of Palm Springs, on Tramway Rd., 3½ mi north of Route 111. | 1 Tramway Rd. | 760/325–1391 or 888/515–8726 | www.pstramway.com | $19.65 | Mid-August–July, weekdays 10–9, weekends 8–9:45.

Palm Springs Air Museum. Ready to take flight—that's the caliber of the vintage, WWII military aircraft carefully restored and displayed here. Other highlights include period photographs and video documentaries. | 745 N. Gene Autry Tr. | 760/778–6262 | www.air-museum.org | $7.50 | Daily 10–5.

★ **Palm Springs Desert Museum.** This cultural center presents exhibits on natural sciences and the performing arts. There's an emphasis on natural history of the surrounding Coachella Valley, as well as contemporary and Western art. The Annenberg Theater, which presents dance, music, and drama performances, is also on site. | 101 Museum Dr. | 760/325–7186 or 760/325–0189 | www.psmuseum.org | $7.50; free 1st Fri. of month | Tues.–Sat. 10–5, Sun. 12–5.

Tahquitz Creek Palm Springs Golf Resort. One of Palm Springs' two municipal golf courses, this resort ranks as one of the most popular golf destinations in the area. Designed by Ted Robinson, the architect behind some of the desert's best resort courses, Tahquitz offers challenges for both the average and experienced golfer. The Traditions Grill is open daily until 2PM. The Legends Course, which is slightly smaller than the main resort course, has no water. | 1885 Golf Club Dr. | 760/328–1005 or 760/328–1956 | fax 760/324–8122 | www.palm-springs.com/golf/tahquitz.html | Resort course: Mon.–Thurs. $80, Fri.–Sun. $90; Legends course: Mon.–Thurs. $70, Fri.–Sun. $60 | May–Oct. 5:45AM–6PM; Nov.–Apr. 6:10AM–5:30PM.

Village Green Heritage Center. This center has two 19th-century pioneer homes and is administered by the Palm Springs Historical Society. The McCallum Adobe, built in 1884 by John McCallum, the first permanent white settler, has an extensive collection of photographs, paintings, clothing, tools, books, and Indian ware from the earliest days of Palm Springs. Miss Cornelia's "Little House," built by the city's first hotel proprietor in 1893, is furnished with antiques donated by local residents. | 221 S. Palm Canyon Dr. | 760/323–8297 | fax 760/320–2561 | www.palmsprings.com/history | $1 | Mid-Oct.–Memorial Day, Thurs.–Sat. 10–4, Wed., Sun. 12–3.

ON THE CALENDAR

JAN., AUG.: *Palm Springs International Film Festivals.* Hunker down with the popcorn and watch the latest offerings in international films from more than 50 countries at these entertaining, and expanding, film festivals. The winter festival showcases full-length features; the summer festival screens short films. Events at area theaters include special premieres, seminars, and panel discussions. | 760/322–2930 | www.psfilmfest.org.

Dining

Agua Bar and Grill. Eclectic. This casual spot, in the Spa Hotel & Casino, serves a vast selection of dishes—from Mediterranean salads to chicken-fried buffalo steaks. Enjoy your meal in the plant-filled dining room, or outside in a pleasant garden. | 901 E. Tahquitz Canyon Way | 760/778–1515 | Reservations essential | Breakfast also available | $8–$30 | AE, D, MC, V.

Blue Coyote. Tex-Mex. Sit under blue umbrellas in a flower-filled patio at this casual restaurant, 1 block north of the Hyatt Hotel. Munch on the usual Tex-Mex offerings—burritos, tacos, fajitas—or try something different, like Yucatan lamb. Dining rooms are dressed up with lush tropical plants and Southwestern furnishings. Two busy cantinas serve margaritas to a young crowd. | 445 N. Palm Canyon Dr. | 760/327–1196 | $10–$27 | AE, DC, MC, V.

Cafe Jasmin. Mediterranean. Try a plateful of healthy, homemade food while gazing at the mountains from the sunny patio of this cozy café. Consider the popular chicken noodle and potato soups, or perhaps a Mediterranean salad. | 125 E. Tahquitz Canyon Way | 760/320–7535 | Breakfast also available | $6–$11 | No credit cards.

Cedar Creek Inn. American. This restaurant has three light-filled dining rooms. Look for poached salmon or sautéed halibut in Vera Cruz sauce, and a salad of romaine, watercress, bay shrimp, tomato, mushrooms, walnuts, and hearts of palm. The restaurant also has a small patio with a bubbling fountain for outside dining. Entertainment Wed.–Sun. | 1555 S. Palm Canyon Dr. | 760/325–7300 | $12–$20 | AE, D, DC, MC, V.

EARTHQUAKES

The tremors keep rolling in this part of the world. In fact, there are tremors in California every week. Really. Some newspapers even have an Earthquake Watch section next to the weather report. It's a part of life in California.

Some natives claim that they can smell an earthquake coming. The more cynical among Californians trust their dogs, who, it is said, start to bark for what seems like no reason right before a big one hits.

Because earthquakes are common Californians know just what to do in case a Big One hits: They know to get under a desk or table to protect themselves from falling objects, or stand in a doorjamb. They keep away from bookshelves. They avoid windows, which may shatter, and large objects, such as mirrors, which may fall off the wall. They have a battery-operated portable radio available, as well as some bottled water. Sometimes they even keep a pair of shoes under the bed in case they have to get out in the middle of the night.

Your California tour will probably not include an actual earthquake experience, but if you want more information, you can call the **Earthquake Preparedness** hotline at 818/908–2671. You never know.

© Artville

Delhi Palace. Indian. This restaurant has a sophisticated air, with paintings of the Taj Mahal decorating the walls. Try the house special, tandoori chicken, or assorted curries with lamb, seafood, or vegetables. | 1422 N. Palm Canyon Dr. | 760/325–3411 | Reservations essential | $8–$13 | AE, D, DC, MC, V.

Doug Arango's. Italian. Colorado corn-fed lamb with brandy sauce and other northern Italian preparations fill the menu in this ceramic-tiled dining room 15 mi east of town. | 73-520 El Paseo | 760/341–4120 | fax 760/341–5690 | $12–$30 | AE, D, DC, MC, V.

Edgardo's Cafe Veracruz. Mexican. If you're hankering for the traditional dishes of Mexico, the ones without the rice and beans on the side, head to this lively restaurant. The menu highlights the owner's own collection of family recipes from the Mayan region of Las Huatecas on Mexico's east coast, including desert cactus soup, a traditional dish with beans, squash, fresh corn, and prickly pear cactus, and Veracruz gulf red-snapper, wrapped in banana leaves and sautéed in garlic. Sunday brunch has a special zing, with chilaquiles, a traditional Mexican breakfast dish of chicken, sour cream, and cheese on a corn tortilla baked and topped with eggs. | 494 N. Palm Canyon Dr. | 760/320–3558 | Reservations essential | $11–$29 | AE, D, DC, MC, V.

Europa. Continental. Candlelight, white linen on the tables, and fine art on the walls set the mood for this European-style restaurant. Sit by the fireplace inside, or outside on the moonlit patio for rack of lamb and salmon specials. The restaurant is about ½ mi north of downtown. Sunday brunch. | 1620 Indian Trail | 760/327–2314 | Closed Mon. No lunch | $17–$34 | AE, D, MC, V.

Flower Drum Restaurant. Chinese. A stream filled with live koi fish, slicing across the dining room floor, makes for an entertaining evening here. Try the kung pao chicken or the Mongolian beef. Chinese dancers entertain on Fri. and Sat. nights. | 424 S. Indian Canyon Dr. | 760/323–3020 | $9–$13 | AE, MC, V.

Johannes. Eclectic. Although a relative newcomer on the Palm Springs dining scene (it opened in 1999), this restaurant has already become one of the most popular restaurants in the area. European, Asian, Middle Eastern, and Californian cooking styles meet in this elegant spot. Try the exotic coconut broth or the duck breast with brazed onions and caramelized apples. Outdoors on the covered patio, take in the view of the San Jacinto Mountains. Inside, watch chefs prepare your meal in the open kitchen. | 196 S. Indian Canyon Dr., | 760/778–0017 | Reservations essential | Closed Sun.–Mon. | $24–$42 | AE, DC, MC, V.

Las Casuelas Terraza. Mexican. Palm Springs locals have enjoyed the cool, adobe-walled setting of Las Casuelas since 1958, but the dishes served are hardly dated. Instead, the accent is on Mexican fare with a lighter touch—less salt, less fat. Try the house specialty, camarones diablos, large shrimp wrapped in crisp bacon, served atop rice and garnished with lemon, tomatoes, and parsley. Or sit at the antique bar and sip a fine tequila, and take note of the wall mural depicting old Mexico. The downtown restaurant, across from the Palm Springs Historical Society, has three dining rooms with simple wooden tables and leather booths. Outside, sit on the patio beneath a large palapa (cone-shaped covering), or at umbrella-topped tables or covered booths. Guitar and singing nightly. Kids' menu. | 222 S. Palm Canyon Dr. | 760/325–2794 | $7–$18 | AE, D, DC, MC, V.

Le Vallauris. Mediterranean. The setting in this stately home-turned-restaurant is fit for a king. Seating, linen tablecloths trimmed in colorful fringe, tapestries and paintings on the walls evoke the time of French finery, but the menu has a distinctly contemporary air. Look for grilled veal chop with porcini ravioli and grilled halibut with sun-dried-tomato crust drizzled with lemon sauce. There's also outdoor dining on a tree-lined patio or a large gazebo. A pianist entertains nightly at this popular downtown restaurant, across from Desert Fashion Plaza. Sunday brunch. | 385 W. Tahquitz Canyon Way | 760/325–5059 | www.levallauris.com | $25–$34 | AE, D, DC, MC, V.

LG's Prime Steakhouse. Steak. Whether you sit on the shaded patio or inside the window-lined dining room, you can't miss the restaurant's sweeping view of Palm Canyon. LG's specializes in steak, but you'll also find many seafood offerings. | 255 S. Palm Canyon Dr. | 760/416–1779 | Reservations essential | No lunch | $22–$40 | AE, D, DC, MC, V.

Lyons English Grille. English. Be a knight for a night, or just dine like one, at this entertaining theme restaurant. Servers in costumes harkening back to Merry Olde England bring platefuls of traditional country fare, such as slabs of prime rib and fresh popovers, or steak-and-kidney pie. All recipes, including the rich trifle for dessert, are gleaned from family recipes collected by the Lancastershire-born proprietors. In the dimly lit dining room, colorful coats of arms in leaded glass, Medieval banners, gleaming copper pots and polished suits of armor keep you wondering when King Arthur might pop in for a pint. Expect good service; much of the staff has worked here since the restaurant's opening some 20 years ago. Early-bird suppers. | 233 E. Palm Canyon Dr. | 760/327–1551 | No lunch | $16–$30 | AE, DC, MC, V.

Melvyn's at the Ingleside. Continental. This designated historical landmark, built in 1925, was first a private home, then an inn, now an upscale restaurant popular with the rich-and-famous set, and anyone else looking for a special meal. Run by Palm Springs legend Mel Haber since 1975, the restaurant, 4 blocks south of Desert Fashion Plaza, has four dining rooms with antique oak furniture, fine paintings, sparkling white linens, and an 1895 carved oak and mahogany bar. Try fresh grilled whitefish with mango and sweet basil sauce, chicken Charlene (sautéed chicken topped with jumbo shrimp, avocado, and a sauvignon blanc sauce), and veal Ingleside (veal cutlet and avocado hollandaise sauce served with fettucini). Pianist and vocalist nightly. Sunday brunch. | 200 Ramon Rd. | 760/325–2323 | www.inglesideinn.com | Reservations essential | Jacket required | $19–$27 | AE, D, DC, MC, V.

Nicolino's Italian Kitchen. Italian. Monet and Van Gogh prints mingle with pictures of Venice and Milan on the walls of this casual eatery. You can also relax outdoors on the covered patio. Popular dishes include lasagne and chicken portofino with a garlic white wine sauce. Kids' menu. | 440 S. El Cielo Rd. #14 | 760/322–5579 | Closed Sun. | $8–$13 | AE, D, DC, MC, V.

Otani Garden Restaurant. Japanese. Sushi, tempura, and teppan (grilled) specialities are served in a serene garden setting, open for 11 years. You sit outside at plastic tables and chairs at this restaurant, 1 mi east of downtown and across from the convention center. Locals turn out for the Sunday brunch buffet, including tempura, stir-fried entrées, salads, sushi, and for dessert, green tea ice cream. | 266 Avenida Caballeros | 760/327–6700 | No lunch Sat. | $8–$30 | AE, D, MC, V.

★ **Palmie.** French. The humble location of this unobtrusive restaurant, tucked into the back of a shopping arcade, doesn't begin to hint at the caliber of food served inside. Simply framed Toulouse-Lautrec and other Gallic posters surround you inside, but you'll probably spend more time looking at—and enjoying—the food, with choices of two-cheese soufflé, roasted duck breast served with pear slices in red wine, and fish stew in a butter-cream broth. | 276 N. Palm Canyon Dr. | 760/320–3375 | Closed Sun. and Aug.–mid-Sept. No lunch | $26–$44 | AE, DC, MC, V.

Rock Garden Cafe. Eclectic. Jagged rocks on the walls may not seem like typical decor for a restaurant, but this eatery aims for an unusual look and lively air. Locals and tourists flock to this café to order from a large and inexpensive menu, with large portions of seafood, ribs, Greek dishes, and burgers, plus homemade breads and pastries. Eat indoors or outside in the mist garden with a bubbling brook. The restaurant is in a commercial area 2 mi south of downtown. Pianist Wed.–Sun. Kids' menu, early-bird suppers. | 777 S. Palm Canyon Dr. | 760/327–8840 | Breakfast also available | $8–$18 | AE, D, DC, MC, V.

St. James at the Vineyard. Contemporary. This is the local hot spot for cocktails and dining. Set in the back of a courtyard amid all the action on Palm Canyon Drive, this is a place to be seen. Dining is either inside in a multihued room sporting a collection of African masks or outside in the courtyard next to a bubbling fountain. Menu mainstays include salmon osso bucco, beef curries, and Burmese bouillabaisse. | 265 S. Palm Canyon Dr. | 760/320–8041 | No lunch | $18–$34 | AE, D, DC, MC, V.

Lodging

Ballantines Movie Colony Hotel. Originally opened as the San Jacinto Hotel in 1937, this stucco lodging in the heart of Palm Springs became a favorite hideaway for celebrities including Marilyn Monroe and Gloria Swanson. Refurbished in the Bauhaus style, it still affords fine mountain views. Added are lush gardens, swimming pool and hot tub. Rooms are decorated in the style of the '50s with fabrics and furnishings of the period. Clothing is optional in this adults-only retreat. Complimentary Continental breakfast. Some kitchenettes, microwaves, refrigerators. Pool. Spa. No kids allowed. | 1420 N. Indian Canyon Dr. | 760/320–1178 or 800/780–3464 | fax 760/320–5308 | ballantines@palmsprings.com | www.palm-springs.com/ballantines | 14 rooms | $69–$89 | AE, D, MC, V.

Bee Charmer Inn. This Southwestern-style inn with red-tile roof and terra-cotta tile floors caters exclusively to lesbians. Spacious rooms surround a pool and tropical courtyard, all done in soothing earth tones. Complimentary breakfast. Some minibars, microwaves, refrigerators, some in-room hot tubs, cable TV, some in-room VCRs. Outdoor pool. Massage. No kids under 18. No pets. | 1600 E. Palm Canyon Dr. | 760/778–5883 or 888/321–5699 | fax 760/416–2200 | www.beecharmer.com | 13 rooms | $105–$130 | AE, D, MC, V.

Best Western–Las Brisas. This three-story 1989 stucco building in a commercial area one block east of downtown, has a Spanish-style courtyard with a gazebo and fountains. Bar, complimentary breakfast. Refrigerators, cable TV. Pool. Hot tub. Laundry facilities. Business services. | 222 S. Indian Canyon Dr. | 760/325–4372 or 800/346–5714 | fax 760/320–1371 | lbrisas@ix.netcom.com | www.lasbrisashotel.com | 90 rooms | $129–$169 | AE, D, DC, MC, V.

Best Western–Palm Springs. They aren't the Alps, but the mountains south of town are enough to inspire the Swiss chalet-styling of this 3-story hotel, built in 1986. The lodging is 1 mi south of downtown. Restaurant, complimentary Continental breakfast. In-room data ports, some microwaves, refrigerators, cable TV. Pool. Hot tub. Business services. | 1633 S. Palm Canyon Dr. | 760/325–9177 | 72 rooms | $149 | AE, D, DC, MC, V.

Casa Cody. Founded in the 1920s, this B&B in the San Jacinto Mountains captures the look and feel of the Southwest. Take off the evening chill with your own fireplace. The acclaimed Palm Springs Desert Museum is a short walk. Dining room, complimentary Continental breakfast. In-room data ports, some kitchenettes, some microwaves, some refrigerators, cable TV, some in-room VCRs. 2 outdoor pools. Outdoor hot tub. Business services. Pets allowed. | 175 S. Cahuilla Rd. | 760/320–9346 or 800/231–2639 | fax 760/325–8610 | 14 rooms, 8 suites, 1 house | $79–$149, $159–$189 suites, $249–$349 house | AE, D, DC, MC, V.

Courtyard by Marriott. Striking landscaping of pebble-size rocks on 2 acres draws attention to this chain lodging. The hotel, built in 1988, is a Southwestern-style, 3-story building topped by deep red Spanish roof tiles. It sits next to the Palm Springs Convention Center 1 mi west of downtown. In-room data ports, microwaves, cable TV. Pool. Exercise equipment. Laundry facilities. Business services, airport shuttle. | 1300 Tahquitz Canyon Way | 760/322–6100 | fax 760/322–6091 | www.marriott.com | 149 rooms | $129–$169 | AE, D, DC, MC, V.

Coyote Inn. Don't be surprised if you get dive-bombed by a hummingbird in the flower-filled courtyard of this sheltered, Spanish Mission-style inn. The peaceful courtyard makes a pleasant retreat from the bustling shops, restaurants, and museums of downtown, 4 blocks away. Kitchenettes, microwaves, refrigerators, cable TV, in-room VCRs. Outdoor pool. Outdoor hot tub. Laundry facilities. Pets allowed. No kids under 14. | 234 S. Patencio Rd. | 760/327–0304 or 888/334–0633 | fax 760/327–4304 | info@gardeninns.com | www.coyoteinn.gardeninns.com | 5 rooms, 2 suites | $109–$139, $159–$189 suites | AE, MC, V.

East Canyon Hotel. Catering exclusively to gay men, this lodging trims its spacious rooms in muted browns. Spa services include facials, assorted treatments, and body wraps. Complimentary breakfast. In-room data ports, minibars, some refrigerators, cable TV, in-room VCRs. Outdoor pool. Outdoor hot tub, spa, massage. Laundry services. Business services. No pets. No kids under 18. No smoking. | 288 E. Camino Monte Vista | 760/320–0599 or 877/

324–6835 | fax 760/320–0599 | info@eastcanyonhotel.com | www.eastcanyonhotel.com | 15 suites | $195–$395 | AE, D, DC, MC, V.

El Rancho Lodge. This comfortable, reasonably priced, family-oriented hotel is in a residential area on Route 111, 2 mi southwest of downtown. Built in 1953, the wooden lodge has a Southwestern air. Complimentary Continental breakfast. Some kitchenettes, some microwaves, refrigerators, cable TV. Pool. Hot tub. Laundry facilities. | 1330 E. Palm Canyon Dr. | 760/327–1339 | 19 rooms, 5 suites | $70–$80, $131 suites | AE, MC, V.

Hampton Inn. This dependable chain lodging, 1 mi west of downtown, has a Spanish-style building, opened in 1988. Complimentary Continental breakfast. In-room data ports, some microwaves, refrigerators, cable TV. Pool. Hot tub. Business services. | 2000 N. Palm Canyon Dr. | 760/320–0555 | fax 760/320–2261 | www.hampton-inn.com | 96 rooms | $89–$129 | AE, D, DC, MC, V.

Harlow Club Hotel. This secluded resort, designed for gay men, has hacienda-style lodgings, complete with bougainvillea cascading from the rooftop. Lush gardens and a landscaped pool finish the scene. Complimentary Continental breakfast. Cable TV, in-room VCRs (and movies). Outdoor pool. Outdoor hot tub. Gym. Laundry facilities. Business services. No pets. No kids under 17. | 175 E. El Alameda | 760/323–3977 or 888/547–7881 | fax 760/320–1218 | harlowhotel@webtv.net | www.harlowhotel.com | 14 rooms, 1 suite | $135–$220, $235 suites | MAP | AE, D, DC, MC, V.

Hilton. Catering to the upscale crowd, this full-service 3-story hotel sits in the heart of downtown across the street from the action of the Spa Casino. Restaurant. In-room data ports, refrigerators, cable TV. Pool. Hot tubs 6 tennis courts. Exercise equipment. Kids' programs. Business services, airport shuttle. Pets allowed. | 400 E. Tahquitz Canyon Way | 760/320–6868 | fax 760/320–2126 | pshilton@aol.com | www.palmsprings.hilton.com | 260 rooms | $159–$235 | AE, D, DC, MC, V.

Howard Johnson Resort. If you want a dependable chain close to the aerial tramway and water park, consider this 2-story lodging, 2 mi west of downtown. The 1960 hotel aims for the look of a desert oasis, with lushly landscaped grounds, including a waterfall. Restaurant, bar. Cable TV. Pool. Hot tub. Laundry facilities. Business services. | 701 E. Palm Canyon Dr. | 760/320–2700 or 800/854–4345 | fax 760/320–1591 | www.howardjohnson.net | 205 rooms | $79–$109 | AE, D, DC, MC, V.

Hyatt Regency Suites Palm Springs. This strikingly asymmetrical lobby here holds an enormous metal sculpture hung from the ceiling. The six-story hotel has one-, two- and three-bedroom suites with views of the city, or the golf course and mountains beyond. The downtown lodging, built in 1987, has shops and restaurants nearby. Restaurant, bar [with entertainment], refrigerators, cable TV. Pool. Hot tub, massage. Business services, airport shuttle. | 285 N. Palm Canyon Dr. | 760/322–9000 | fax 760/325–6009 | www.hyatt.com | 192 suites | $230–$475 suites | AE, D, DC, MC, V.

Ingleside Inn. Settle into a Queen Anne-style chair, or swing open the French doors and relax on your own private terrace. You can do either at this graceful lodging, built in 1925. There's also a pretty courtyard on the grounds. Rooms are in the original Spanish Colonial-style building, built in 1925 and in newer villas around the perimeter of the property. It's a block west of Palm Canyon Dr. Restaurant (Melvyns), bar [with entertainment], complimentary Continental breakfast, room service. Some microwaves, refrigerators, in-room hot tubs, cable TV. Pool. Hot tub. Business services. | 200 W. Ramon Rd. | 760/325–0046 or 800/772–6655 | fax 760/325–0710 | ingleside@earthlink.net | www.inglesideinn.com | 30 rooms, 12 suites, 2 villas | $95–$160, $205–$375 suites, $145–$265 villas | AE, D, DC, MC, V.

Ken Irwin's La Mancha Resort Village. With 20 acres of landscaped property surrounded by forest, this collection of Mediterranean-style hotel suites and 1-,2-, and 3-bedroom villas, built in 1976, is a secluded choice ½ mi east of downtown. Bar, dining room, room service. In-room data ports, some kitchenettes, some in-room hot tubs, cable TV. Pool. Hot tub. Putting green, tennis. Exercise equipment, bicycles. Laundry facilities. Business services, airport shuttle. | 444 Avenida Caballeros | 760/323–1773 or 800/255–1773 | fax 760/323–5928 | reservations@la-mancha.com | www.la-mancha.com | 13 suites, 53 villas | $195–$225 suites, $250–$895 villas | AE, D, DC, MC, V.

Korakia Pensione. This Moorish-style villa with keyhole entrance, built in the 1920s by Scottish artist Gordon Couts, has long hosted artists visiting Palm Springs. The tradition continues now that it's a bed and breakfast. Rooms come in various configuration and are furnished with antiques, Oriental rugs, and handmade beds; some have fireplaces. Located in an old residential section of Palm Springs, where many celebrities have made their homes. Restaurant, picnic area, complimentary Continental breakfast. Some kitchenettes, refrigerators. Pool. Business services. | 257 S. Patencio Rd. | 760/864–6411 | fax 760/864–6423 | 20 rooms (6 with shower only) | $110–$160 | No credit cards.

La Siesta Villas Condominium Resort. These fully outfitted rental units are an attractive choice for couples looking for a pampered getaway. All but one of the units are individually owned—and decorated—but all have fireplaces, private patios, and spas. You can also enjoy the shared garden. Movie stars sometimes retreat to this complex, built in 1937 and ½ mi north of downtown. Restaurant. Microwaves, refrigerators, cable TV, in-room VCRs. Pool. Hot tub. Business services. No kids allowed. | 247 W. Stevens Rd. | 760/325–2269 | fax 760/778–6533 | www.palmsprings.com/Hotels/LaSiestaVillas | 19 condominiums | $110–$265 apartments (2–night minimum) | AE, MC, V.

L'Horizon. Landscaped grounds comprise 2½ acres and house 7 buildings at this resort in an exclusive residential section of Palm Springs. Originally the winter home of Jack Wrather, a Hollywood producer, the estate was designed for great privacy. Each suite, furnished in pastels to compliment the beauty of the surrounding desert, has an awe-inspiring view of Mt. San Jacinto. Picnic area, complimentary Continental breakfast. Some kitchenettes, cable TV. Pool. Hot tub. Business services. No smoking. | 1050 E. Palm Canyon Dr. | 760/323–1858 or 800/377–7855 (for reservations) | fax 760/327–2933 | 22 rooms (19 with shower only), 7 suites in 7 buildings | $115–$140, $255 suites | AE, D, DC, MC, V.

★ **Merv Griffin's Resort Hotel and Givenchy Spa.** This spa aims to capture the ambience of the Givenchy spa in Versailles, France, right down to the manicured rose gardens and Empire-style decor. Private patios with mountain or garden views enhance most rooms. Pamper yourself with an array of spa services—from traditional facials to marine mud wraps and aromatherapy. The 4,200-sq-ft, four-bedroom Grand Suite has a grand piano in the living room. 2 restaurants, room service. Some minibars, cable TV, some in-room VCRs. 2 outdoor pools. Outdoor hot tub, barber shop, beauty salon, spa. 6 tennis courts. Gym. Laundry services. Business services. Pets allowed. | 4200 E. Palm Canyon Dr., | 760/770–5000 or 800/276–5000 | fax 760/324–6104 | info@merv.com | www.merv.com/hotel/givenchyspa/default.asp | 103 rooms, villas, and suites | $290–$350, $400 suite, $600–$1,150 villa, $4,000 Grand Suite | AE, D, DC, MC, V.

Motel 6. This economical chain is a three-story building opened in 1990, is in the heart of downtown, and close to shops and restaurants. Cable TV. Pool. Laundry facilities. Business services. Pets allowed. | 660 S. Palm Canyon Dr. | 760/327–4200 or 800/466–7356 | fax 760/320–9827 | www.motel6.com | 148 rooms (shower only) | $51–$57 | AE, D, DC, MC, V.

Orchid Tree. Old mixes with new in this collection of five buildings on 7 acres. The oldest one, which has always been a lodging facility, dates back to 1915, the newest to 1950; rooms in all of the buildings range in style— Queen Anne, southwestern, Spanish bungalow, 1950s American— and are individually decorated. All have been refurbished to create a comfortable, desert garden retreat for couples and families. The lodging is one block west of Palm Canyon Dr. Some microwaves, cable TV. 3 pools. Hot tub. Business services. | 261 S. Belardo Rd. | 760/325–2791 or 800/733–3435 | fax 760/325–3855 | www.orchidtree.com | 40 rooms | $120–$280 | AE, D, MC, V.

Palm Springs Marquis. This Southwestern-style, 3-story stucco building, built in 1984, is in downtown, near shops, restaurants, and the Plaza Theater and Cinema Arts theaters.

Luxury rooms are decked in pastel colors and prints that reflect the desert surroundings, and all have private balconies. Restaurant, bar [with entertainment], room service. In-room data ports, cable TV. 1 pool, wading pool. Hot tub, massage. Tennis. Exercise equipment. Business services, parking (fee). | 150 S. Indian Canyon Dr. | 760/322–2121 | fax 760/322–4365 | www.psmarquis.com | 166 rooms | $250–$270 | AE, D, DC, MC, V.

Place in the Sun. The oldest, and one of the most charming, lodgings in Palm Springs, this collection of 1948 bungalows has gardens, gazebos, and a putting green for the kids (or the kids at heart). The all-suite lodgings have cathedral ceilings and private patios. It's ½ mi southeast to both the downtown area and the shopping district. Restaurant. Kitchenettes, microwaves, refrigerators, cable TV. Pool. Laundry facilities. Pets allowed (fee). | 754 San Lorenzo Rd. | 760/325–0254 or 800/779–2254 | fax 760/237–9303 | www.palmsprings.com/placeinthesun | placeinthesun@yahoo.com | 16 bungalows | $79–$139 | AE, MC, V.

Quality Inn. Surrounded by 7 acres of landscaped gardens and backing up to its own private park, this lodging is an appealing, economical escape for families and couples. The hotel, 1½ mi southeast of downtown, has two-story stucco buildings. Restaurant. In-room data ports, some refrigerators, cable TV. Pool, wading Pool. Hot tub. Laundry facilities. Business services. | 1269 E. Palm Canyon Dr. | 760/323–2775 | fax 760/416–1014 | www.qualityinn.com | 145 rooms, 8 suites | $79–$139, $125–$169 suites | AE, D, DC, MC, V.

Ramada Resort. This 3-story hotel, built in 1980, has rooms with handmade wood furniture from Mexico. Rooms also have a private patio or balcony, with views of the mountains or the hotel's enormous pool. It's in a quiet area 2 mi south of the Palm Canyon Dr. shopping/entertainment district. Restaurant, bar [with entertainment]. In-room data ports, refrigerators. Pool. Hot tubs. Exercise equipment. Laundry facilities. Free airport shuttle. Pets allowed. | 1800 E. Palm Canyon Dr. | 760/323–1711 or 800/245–6907 (outside CA), 800/245–6904 (in CA) | fax 760/322–1075 | www.ramada.com | 254 rooms | $89–$119, $99–$109 suites | AE, D, DC, MC, V.

Riviera Resort and Racquet Club. Another Palm Springs classic, this large complex, built in 1958 consists of eight wooden buildings on 23 acres of landscaped grounds. The resort is 2 mi north of downtown. Restaurant, bar [with entertainment], room service. In-room data ports, refrigerators, cable TV. 2 pools. Hot tubs, massage. Tennis. Exercise equipment. Airport shuttle. Pets allowed. | 1600 N. Indian Canyon Dr. | 760/327–8311 or 800/444–8311 | fax 760/327–4323 | psriviera.com | 477 rooms | $219 | AE, D, DC, MC, V.

Sakura Japanese-Style Bed & Breakfast. Japanese artwork, sliding *shoji* doors, antique kimonos, and the sounds of the *koto* and bamboo flute capture the feeling of Japan in this unusual B&B. Unwind with a stroll through the elegant garden, or try a Japanese-style massage. Complimentary Continental breakfast. Refrigerators, cable TV, in-room VCRs. Outdoor pool. Outdoor hot tub. Massage. Laundry facilities. No pets. No smoking. | 1677 North Via Miraleste | 760/327–0705 or 800/200–0705 | fax 760/327–6847 | sakura@travelbase.com | www.travelbase.com/destinations/palm-springs/sakura | 3 rooms | $80–$90 | No credit cards.

Shilo Inn. This desert-style lodging, built in 1984 and 1 mi south of downtown, is ideal for families— one of the pools is a shallow water pool for kids, and all of the larger than average rooms have seperate seating areas. Complimentary Continental breakfast. Refrigerators, cable TV. 2 pools, 2 hot tubs. Laundry facilities. Business services, airport shuttle. | 1875 N. Palm Canyon Dr. | 760/320–7676 | fax 760/416–1014 | www.shiloinns.com | 124 rooms | $119–$149 | AE, D, DC, MC, V.

Spa Hotel and Casino Resort Mineral Springs. Natural springs, thought to have healing powers, bubble up on the property of this resort. The 5-story hotel was built in 1963 and sits on Native American property; owned by the Agua Caliente Indians, it is the oldest casino in Palm Springs. 1 block east of Palm Canyon Dr. Restaurant, bar. Refrigerators, room service. Cable TV. 3 pools. Beauty salon, hot tub. Exercise equipment. Business services, airport shuttle. | 100 N. Indian Canyon Dr. | 760/325–1461 or 800/854–1279 | fax 760/325–3344 | www.aguacaliente.org | 230 rooms | $119–$239 | AE, D, DC, MC, V.

Sundance Villas. Wooden villas dot the resort's 3½ landscaped acres, 1½ mi north of downtown. Each of the villas has a private pool and patio. Couples and families especially enjoy this get-away. Restaurant. Kitchenettes, microwaves, cable TV, in-room VCRs. Pool. Hot tub. Tennis. Business services. | 303 W. Cabrillo Rd. | 760/325–3888 or 800/455–3888 | fax 760/323–3029 | sundanceps@aol.com | www.palmsprings.com | 19 villas | $250–$495 villas | AE, D, DC, MC, V.

Super 8. Reasonable rates, a casual atmosphere, and an easy walk to many restaurants make this lodging (this one with Southwestern styling) a good choice for families on a budget. The motel, built in 1980, sits in a mixed commercial and residential area, 1 mi north of downtown. Complimentary Continental breakfast. Refrigerators, cable TV. Pool. Hot tub. Laundry facilities. Business services. | 1900 N. Palm Canyon Dr. | 760/322–3757 or 800/800–8000 | fax 760/323–5290 | www.super8.com | 61 rooms | $75 | AE, D, DC, MC, V.

Travelodge. This cluster of two-story buildings, with Southwestern styling, attracts couples and families. The lodging is 1½ mi south of downtown. Some microwaves, refrigerators, cable TV. Pool. Hot tub. Laundry facilities. Business services. | 333 E. Palm Canyon Dr. | 760/327–1211 or 800/578–7878 | fax 760/320–4672 | plpsts@aol.com | www.travelodge.com | 157 rooms | $99–$125 | AE, D, DC, MC, V.

Vagabond Inn. The mood here is low-key and relaxed, for both vacationers and business travelers. The lodging, 2½ mi south of downtown, has rooms in a three-story structure, built in 1962. Pool. Hot tub, sauna. Business services. | 1699 S. Palm Canyon Dr. | 760/325–7211 | fax 760/322–9269 | www.vagabondinn.com | 120 rooms | $64–$96 | AE, D, DC, MC, V.

Villa Royale. This Spanish-style stucco complex of buildings ¾-mi south of downtown, was built as apartments in 1947. Today, its individually decorated rooms and suites carry various European themes; French, Swiss, English, Spanish. Many have sitting areas and kitchens. Gardens here are particularly colorful with bougainvillea cascading from rooftops, huge potted planters, and rose gardens. Bar, dining room. Some refrigerators, room service, cable TV. 2 pools. Hot tub. No kids allowed. Business services. | 1620 Indian Trail | 760/327–2314 or 800/245–2314 (outside CA) | fax 760/322–3794 | www.villaroyale.com | 31 rooms, 19 suites | $125–$175, $230–$275 suites | AE, DC, MC, V.

★ **The Willows.** Privacy is the key at this luxury B&B, a Mediterranean villa built in the 1920s. At the time it was the grandest mansion in the desert. Current owners have brought it back to its original condition. Rooms, named for famous guests such as Albert Einstein and Marion Davies are beautifully decorated with antique furnishings, oriental rugs, and hardwood floors. A 50-ft waterfall tumbles into a pond just outside the dining room. And guests are invited to stroll to the top of the hill above the inn for a bird's-eye view from one of the highest residential points in Palm Springs. Restaurant, complimentary breakfast. In-room data ports, refrigerators. Pool. Hot tub. Business services. No smoking. | 412 W. Tahquitz Canyon Way | 760/320–0771 | fax 760/320–0780 | innkeeper@thewillowspalmsprings.com | www.thewillowspalmsprings.com | 8 rooms | $275–$525 | AE, D, DC, MC, V.

Wyndham. This large, all-service lodging, located adjacent to the Palm Springs Convention Center, caters to business travelers. The five-story, Mediterranean-style building went up in 1987. Restaurant, bar. In-room data ports, cable TV. Pool, wading pool. Beauty salon, hot tub. Exercise equipment. Business services, airport shuttle. | 888 E. Tahquitz Canyon Way | 760/322–6000 | fax 760/322–5351 | www.wyndham.com | 410 rooms, 158 suites | $189, $358 suites | AE, D, DC, MC, V.

PALMDALE

(Nearby towns also listed: Lancaster, Valencia, Victorville)

This fast-growing bedroom community of nearly 123,000 along Route 14 boasts proximity to great hiking, cross-country skiing, mountain biking, and horseback riding at Angeles National Forest, which extends south and west of here.

Information: Palmdale Chamber of Commerce | 38260 10th St. East, 93550 | 661/273–3232 | www.chamber.palmdale.ca.us.

Attractions

Blackbird Airpark. Learn the Air Force's secrets, or at least get a chance to peer at one of them, at this small airpark, part of Edwards Air Force Base. On display is a D-21 drone aircraft, which the military once kept cloaked in secrecy. All the planes, including a Lockheed SR-71A and an A-12, belong to the Blackbird class—sleek, black aircraft that look straight out of Top Gun. | 3620 E. Ave. P | 661/943–2022 | www.edwards.af.mil/museum/docs_html/blackbird_airpark.html | Free | Fri.–Sun. 10–5.

ON THE CALENDAR

OCT.: *Fall Festival.* Choose from works by regional and national artists at this huge weekend arts and crafts fair at McAdam Park. Live musical entertainment adds some energy, with performers ranging from local kids to big-name artists. | 661/267–5611.

Dining

Apple Annie's. American. In the Lake Los Angeles Area, this home-style eatery has a sizable menu that includes chicken, seafood, and beef dishes, as well as sandwiches. Kids' menu. No smoking. | 16943 E. Avenue P | 661/264–2169 | Reservations not accepted | Closed Mon., Tues. No lunch | $12–$27 | AE, D, DC, MC, V.

Don Juan Mexican Seafood. Seafood. This casual spot, decorated with pictures of old-time Mexico, serves up seafood dishes with a Mexican flavor. Try the camarones Don Juan, shrimp wrapped in bacon, or the halibut del sol, a filet topped with mushrooms and garlic. Kids' menu. | 38350 30th St. E., | 661/947–7166 | $6–$25 | D, MC, V.

Lodging

Palmdale Days Inn. If you're a fast-paced fan heading for the LA County Raceway, this two-story motel is a convenient choice—it's 3 mi from the track. Built in the mid-1970s and updated in 1996, the lodging has a restaurant open 24 hours. Restaurant. Complimentary Continental breakfast. In-room data ports, some microwaves, some refrigerators, cable TV. Outdoor pool. Outdoor hot tub. Business services. No pets. | 130 E. Palmdale Blvd. | 661/273–1400 or 800/544–8313 | fax 661/272–9473 | www.daysinn.com | 100 rooms | $53–$69 | AE, D, DC, MC, V.

Ramada Inn. This 1974 stone and stucco property is just 5 min from Lockheed Corporation's main production facilities. The hotel caters to business travelers. Restaurant, bar, room service. Some refrigerators, cable TV. Pool. Hot tub. Laundry facilities. Business services. | 300 W. Palmdale Blvd. | 661/273–1200 | fax 661/947–9593 | www.ramada.com | 135 rooms | $72 | AE, D, DC, MC, V.

PALO ALTO

MAP 3, D8

(Nearby towns also listed: Cupertino, Fremont, Livermore, Pleasanton, Sunnyvale)

Palo Alto (population 60,000) is known mainly as the location of Stanford University, one of the nation's finest and most beautiful. It's a lively, but expensive, university community with upscale lodgings, fine dining, and shopping areas packed with chic boutiques. Long before railroad baron and Governor Leland Stanford dedicated the university in 1891, the area served as a waystation for early travelers and explorers. The name refers to a landmark redwood tree used by the travelers.

Information: **Palo Alto Chamber of Commerce** | 325 Forest Ave., 94301-2525 | 650/324–3121 | info@paloaltochamber.com.

Attractions

Hewlett-Packard Garage. This garage was home to William Hewlett and David Packard's creative endeavors into the computer age. | 367 Addison Ave. | 650/324–3121 | Free.

Stanford University. Originally the property was former California governor Leland Stanford's farm for breeding horses. For all its stature as one of the nation's leading universities, Stanford is still known as "The Farm." Free one-hour walking tours leave daily at 11 and 3:15 from the Visitor Information Center (650/723–2560 or 650/723–2053) in front of Memorial Hall on Serra Street, opposite Hoover Tower.

★   After a 10-year closure for structural repairs necessitated by the 1989 earthquake, the Stanford Museum, now named the **Iris and B. Gerald Cantor Center for Visual Arts,** is bigger and better than ever. Works span the centuries as well as the globe, from pre-Columbian to modern, including the world's largest collection of Rodin sculptures outside Paris. | Lomita Dr. and Museum Way, off Palm Dr. | 650/723–4177 | Free | Wed.–Sun. 11–5, Thurs. until 8.

For a look at some less-traditional art, seek out the inconspicuous **Papua New Guinea Sculpture Garden,** tucked into a small, heavily wooded plot of land. The garden is filled with tall, ornately carved wooden poles, drums, and carved stones–all created on location by 10 artists from Papua New Guinea who spent six months here in 1994. | Santa Teresa St. and Lomita Dr. | Free | Daily.

ON THE CALENDAR

MAY: *Annual May Fete Parade.* Northern California's oldest kids' parade bans all motorized vehicles and commercial or political material. Instead, downtown Palo Alto is filled with marching bands, decorated floats, and hundreds of kids in costume. | 650/329–2121.

Dining

Blue Chalk Cafe. Southern. A historic landmark building houses this restaurant. You can climb the curving central staircase to dine on the second floor with fireplaces and Southern folk art on the walls. Southern-inspired dishes include Carolina fritters, crawfish, shrimp, and rice dishes. | 630 Ramona St. | 650/326–1020 | fax 650/326–1022 | No lunch Sat. | $11–$17 | AE, MC, V.

Duck Club Restaurant. Contemporary. Stanford Park Hotel is home to this restaurant, which serves dishes like roast muscovy duck breast with champagne stewed peaches. Also popular is the charbroiled veal porterhouse steak with truffle butter and grilled asparagus. Stark white tablecloths accent the simple and austere surroundings. | 100 El Camino Real | 650/322–1234 | $17–$30 | AE, DC, D, MC, V.

Elbe. German. Chef Carl Peschlow fuses traditional German dishes with California cuisine to create dishes such as the Straburger Schweinelendchen (herb-roasted pork tenderloin in spiced pear sauce). Wines from California, Germany, and France complement the dishes. | 117 University Ave. | 650/321–3319 | No breakfast | $9–$14 | D, MC, V.

★ **Evvia.** An innovative Greek menu and a stunning interior ensure that Evvia always packs in a crowd. Though the menu is written out in Greek (with English translations), there's an unmistakable California influence in such dishes as *lahanika pilafi* (risotto with butternut squash, mint, and leeks). | 420 Emerson St. | 650/326–0983 | Reservations essential | $15.95–$32.95 | AE, DC, MC, V | No lunch weekends.

Fanny and Alexander. Contemporary. You can sit on the patio and enjoy the live music and dancing at this restaurant. The European and Asian fusion cuisine includes spicy shrimp and shellfish cioppino stew, a hearty Burgundy concoction filled with clams, tomatoes, mussels and shrimp. | 412 Emerson St. | 650/326–7183 | Closed Sun. and Mon. | $12–$18 | AE, DC, MC, V.

Fish Market. Seafood. At The Fish Market, you can buy dozens of varieties of fresh seafood to go at the retail market, or sit in the dining room for a meal. Catches of the day are grilled over a mesquite wood fire; soups, like clam chowder, are prepared daily. The wine list includes Muscadet, the restaurant's own label. | 3150 El Camino Real | 650/493–9188 | fax 650/493–4738 | $10–$25 | AE, D, DC, MC, V.

Spago. Silicon Valley's best and brightest have made a hit out of Wolfgang Puck's splashy, dashing Spago. The fare is inventive Californian, the service flawless. Dinner might include barbecued free-range squab with herbed risotto and caramelized fennel or tamarind-glazed rack of lamb. | 265 Lytton Ave. | 650/833–1000 | Reservations essential | $21–$36 | AE, D, DC, MC, V | No lunch weekends.

★ **Zibibbo.** This lively restaurant's eclectic menu includes selections from an oak-fired oven, rotisserie, grill, and oyster bar. Service is family-style, with large platters placed in the center of the table—all the better to taste just a bite of the skillet-roasted mussels, Swiss chard tart with goat cheese and currants, leg of lamb with chickpea-tomato tagine, and more. | 430 Kipling St. | 650/328–6722 | $14.50–$22.95 | AE, MC, V.

Lodging

Cardinal Hotel. Built in 1924, this hotel has remained a downtown fixture for decades. Some rooms have a shared bath and antique fixtures while others are furnished in a modern style. Stanford University is 3 blocks away and the town's restaurants, galleries, and boutiques are within walking distance. In-room data ports, some refrigerators, some microwaves. Cable TV. Laundry service. Business services. | 235 Hamilton Ave. | 650/323–5101 | fax 650/325–6086 | mail@cardinalhotel.com | www.cardinalhotel.com | 60 rooms, 2 suites | $80–$155, $190–$225 suites | AE, DC, D, MC, V.

★ **Cowper Inn.** Built in 1896, this restored home has a piano and fireplace in the parlor and antiques in the guest rooms. Relax in a wicker rocker on one of the lodging's two decks overlooking the garden. The shops and restaurants downtown are 2 blocks north; Stanford University is 1 ½ mi west of the inn. Complimentary Continental breakfast. No air-conditioning in some rooms, some kitchenettes, cable TV. Business services. No smoking. | 705 Cowper St. | 650/327–4475 | fax 650/329–1703 | www.cowperinn.com | 14 rooms (2 with shared bath) | $70–$140 | AE, MC, V.

Creekside Inn. Sit under the oaks on 3½ landscaped acres, including a meandering creek, at this hotel. The lodging, built in 1955 is in the heart of Silicon Valley, 5 mi south of downtown and 1 mi from Stanford University. | 136 rooms. Restaurant, bar. In-room data ports, some kitchenettes, refrigerators, cable TV. Pool. Exercise equipment. Business services. No smoking. | 3400 El Camino Real | 650/493–2411 or 800/492–7335 | fax 650/493–6787 | AE, D, DC, MC, V.

Dinah's Garden Hotel. Tropical lagoons and landscaped gardens capture the look of a lush oasis at this lodging. Rooms, with private patios facing the lagoon or pools, are in three buildings on 5 acres. The tranquil setting, and the proximity to three international airports (San Francisco, Oakland, and San Jose) make it a good choice for business travelers. The hotel is 2 mi north of downtown. Restaurant, room service. Refrigerators, cable TV. 2 pools. Exercise equipment. Laundry facilities. Business services. | 4261 El Camino Real | 650/493–2844 or 800/227–8220 | fax 650/856–4713 | www.dinahshotel.com | 98 rooms, 50 suites | $230–$295, $215–$650 suites | AE, D, DC, MC, V.

★ **Garden Court.** In the heart of Palo Alto, this small luxury hotel aims for the upscale, with soft pastels, French doors, and custom-designed furniture gracing the Mediterranean style building and guest rooms. Private balconies overlook the hotel's flower garden; some rooms have fireplaces. The lodging, 1 mi east of Stanford University, is within walking distance of restaurants and shops. Restaurant, bar, room service. In-room data ports, some in-room hot tubs, cable TV, in-room VCRs (and movies). Exercise equipment, bicycles. Business services. | 520 Cowper St. | 650/322–9000 or 800/824–9028 | fax 650/324–3609 | www.garden-court.com | 62 rooms, 13 suites | $280–$325, $325–$500 suites | AE, D, DC, MC, V.

Hyatt Rickeys. Families and couples enjoy this resort-style hotel in the heart of Silicon Valley. The lodging's 16 acres have gardens, fountains, and a gazebo. The Mediterranean-style complex is 2 mi south of downtown. Restaurant, bar. In-room data ports, cable TV. Pool. Putting green. Exercise equipment. Business services. Pets allowed (fee). | 4219 El Camino Real | 650/493–8000 | fax 650/424–0836 | 336 rooms, 14 suites | $204–$300, $350–$375 suites | AE, D, DC, MC, V.

Sheraton Palo Alto. At the entrance to Stanford University—a convenient option for visiting families or business travelers—this hotel has a resort-like setting, with flower gardens, ponds, fountains, and a pool. The four-story Mediterranean-style stucco building has guest rooms that overlook a water garden and the pool. Downtown shops and restaurants are one block east. Restaurant, bar, room service. Some kitchenettes, in-room hot tubs, cable TV. Pool. Exercise equipment. Laundry facilities. Business services. | 625 El Camino Real | 650/328–2800 | fax 650/327–7362 | www.sheraton.com | 346 rooms | $229–$299 | AE, D, DC, MC, V.

Stanford Park. Oil paintings, antiques, tapestries, and a forest-green color cover the common areas and guest rooms of this hotel. The Stanford Shopping center is ½ mi to the north and the university is 1 mi south. Restaurant, bar. In-room data ports, minibars. Pool. Gym. Laundry service. Business services. | 100 El Camino Real | 650/322–1234 | 163 rooms | $270 | AE, DC, D, MC, V.

Stanford Terrace Inn. Across the street from apartments for its namesake university, this lodging is a good choice for visiting families. The Mediterranean-style, 3-story building has larger than average guest rooms that overlook a central courtyard with a deck, garden, and pool. The hotel is 2 mi south of downtown. Restaurant, complimentary Continental breakfast. Some kitchenettes, refrigerators, cable TV. Pool. Laundry facilities. Business services. | 531 Stanford Ave. | 650/857–0333 or 800/729–0332 | fax 650/857–0343 | 80 rooms | $160–$260 | AE, D, DC, MC, V.

Townhouse Inn. This inn is 2 mi south of Stanford University, 5 mi south of town, and has easy access to U.S. 101 and I–280. The townhouse-style lodgings have Mediterranean stucco styling. You can relax outdoors on the serene and beautifully landscaped patio. Restaurant, complimentary Continental breakfast. Some kitchenettes, refrigerators, cable TV, in-room VCRs. Hot tub. Exercise equipment. | 4164 El Camino Real | 650/493–4492 or 800/458–8696 | fax 650/493–3418 | www.townhouseinn.com | 37 rooms (15 with shower only), 7 suites | $79–$153, $136–$163 suites | AE, DC, MC, V.

Victorian on Lytton. This inn, a block away from downtown Palo Alto, is a former apartment building that was gutted and resurected as a hotel. Rooms are large and airy and some have canopy beds. The Barbie Hall of Fame is 3 blocks away and Stanford University is 1½ mi south. Complimentary Continental breakfast. In-room data ports, cable TV. Business services. | 555 Lytton Ave. | 650/322–8555 | 10 rooms | $165–$230 | AE, MC, V.

PASADENA

(Nearby towns also listed: Burbank, Glendale, Los Angeles, San Marino)

Millions of television viewers visit Pasadena (pop. 143,874) each New Years Day, when they tune in for the annual Tournament of Roses parade and football game. Each year the sun shines brightly as the flower-decked floats, bands and equestrian units proceed down Colorado Boulevard. It's a display of wealth and beauty, conceived more than a century ago by members of America's richest families. These are the Wrigleys (chewing gum), Gambles (Proctor and Gamble), Bissells (carpet sweepers) and Pillsburys (flour), all of whom built mansions in Pasadena in the 1880s and 1890s. Their legacy survives to this day in a display of old money in the stately mansions with manicured gardens, museums housing some of the world's most treasured art, and the Rose Parade.

But Pasadena has another side. It's young, hip, and hot. Old Pasadena, a lively, multicultural shopping/dining/entertainment district reclaimed from the slums of the west end of Colorado Boulevard, draws crowds nightly and on weekends from the entire Los Angeles area.

Hard to imagine with all its opulence, Pasadena has its high tech side as well. It's home to California Institute of Technology, renowned for having the most Nobel Laureates of any academic institution in the United States, and the Jet Propulsion Laboratory, the research, development and flight center operated for NASA.

Information: Pasadena Convention and Visitors Bureau | 171 S. Los Robles Ave., 91101 | 626/795–9311 | cvb@pasadenacal.net | www.pasadenacal.com.

Attractions

Angeles National Forest. The Angeles National Forest comprises Pasadena's backyard, filling thousands of mountain acres with chaparra and pine forests which rise more than 10,000 ft to the east. There are hiking trails, picnic areas, campsites. | 701 N. Santa Anita Ave. | 626/574–5200 | www.r5.fs.fed.us/angeles | Free, parking $5 | Daily.

Crystal Lake Recreation Area. This reservoir, 23 mi east of town, is a popular weekend destination for waterskiing, fishing, and picnickers. | 9877 Crystal Lake Rd., Azusa | 626/910–2848 | www.reserveusa.com | $5 | Daily 6 AM–10PM.

★ **Gamble House.** This house is a perfectly preserved illustration of the Arts and Crafts or Craftsman style of architecture and decor, currently staging a comeback. Designed by the renowned sibling architects Charles and Henry Greene, the 1908 former private home is a woodworker's dream, with hand-shaped beams and sculptured details. Take note of the striking stained-glass panels. Original, period furnishings grace the rooms. The house is managed by the University of Southern California School of Architecture, and staffed by knowledgeable docents. | 4 Westmoreland Pl | 626/793–3334 | gamblehouse.usc.edu/ | $8 | Thurs.–Sun. noon–3.

★ **Norton Simon Museum of Art.** This museum holds one of the world's finest collections, richest in its Rembrandts, Goyas, Picassos and Degas. As you walk through the galleries, you'll spot the originals of many paintings and sculptures you studied in art history. Renovations completed in 1999 have added a sculpture garden displaying bronzes by Rodin. | 411 W. Colorado Blvd. | 626/449–6840 | fax 626/796–4978 | www.nortonsimon.org | $6 | Wed.–Mon. noon–6.

Pacific Asia Museum. Inside, take in displays on the art, culture, and history of Asia and the Pacific Islands. Outside, tour the landscaped grounds, including a koi pond and a recreated Chinese Imperial Palace garden. | 46 N. Los Robles Ave. | 626/449–2742 | $5 | Wed.–Sun. 10–5.

Pasadena Historical Museum. This museum, research library and archives complex opened in 1924 for the purpose of preserving and presenting documents and exhibits on local history and culture. The compond includes the Finnish Folk Art Museum, and the Fenyes Mansion, a 1905 Beaux Arts-style house with the original furnishings. Both facilities are open for touring. | 470 W. Walnut St. | 626/577–1660 | fax 626/577–1662 | $4 | Thurs.–Sun. 1–4.

Rose Bowl. One of college football's hallowed grounds, this stadium is the site of the annual New Years Day Rose Bowl. But things happen here even when the pigskin is put away—the second Sunday of each month finds the Rose Bowl Flea Market in full swing, with more than a million items for sale. | 1001 Rose Bowl Dr. | 626/577–3100 | fax 626/405–0992 | www.ci.pasadena.ca.us/rosebowl.asp | Stadium tour $2; flea market $6, or $10–$15 for early admission | stadium tour Mon.–Fri.9–4.

ON THE CALENDAR

JAN.: *Tournament of Roses.* Watch flower-covered floats cruise by in this spectacular parade. People begin to nab prime spots long before the January 1 procession fills the streets; the floats are also on display after the parade. Up-close looks also let you appreciate the incredible attention to detail: as is stipulated in the parade rules, all surfaces must be decorated with hand-applied natural plant materials, including millions of petals, pods, leaves, and seeds. | 626/449–4100 or 626/449–7673 | www.tournamentofroses.com.

Dining

All India Cafe. Indian. Old Pasadena may be the last place you'd expect to find an authentic Indian restaurant, but authentic this is. Ingredients are fresh, and flavors are bold without depending on overpowering spices. Crisp rice wafers jazzed up with chutney, lime, and cilantro are a nice way to start a meal; follow this with the bhel puri, a savory puffed-rice-and-potatoes dish. In addition to meat curries and tikkas, there are many vegetarian selections. Red linen napkins contrast with white tablecloths and complement the red-tile floor in this downtown restaurant. | 39 Fair Oaks Ave. | 626/440–0309 | $16–$20 | AE, D, DC, MC, V.

Bistro 45. French. A stylish and sophisticated offering, this restaurant blends rustic French cooking—cassoulet, bouillabaisse, caramelized apple tarts—with modern California hybrids, like seared ahi tuna with black and white sesame crust. Add a superb wine list and smart service, and you've got a place that can make almost anyone happy. The downtown restaurant attracts a regular crowd of locals to the romantic Art-Deco interior and the tree-shaded terrace. | 45 S. Mentor Ave. | 626/795–2478 | www.bistro45.com | Closed Mon. | $16–$27 | AE, DC, MC, V.

Burger Continental. Continental. Part bar, part restaurant, and part belly-dancing venue, Burger Continental is popular with almost everyone in Pasadena. Besides inexpensive pitchers of beer, you'll find an excellent selection of Middle Eastern/Greek dishes. A standout is the chicken Corinthian, baked in phyllo dough with spinach and feta cheese. Beef and chicken kabobs are also popular. Most nights, a quartet of Greek musicians entertains diners on the outdoor patio. Inside, belly dancers perform in the dining room Thurs.–Sun. night. The restaurant is 12 mi north of downtown. Sunday buffet. | 535 S. Lake Ave. | 626/792–6634 | $16–$24 | AE, MC, V.

Mi Piace. Italian. People flock to this restaurant-heavy part of town and especially to this restaurant for its reasonably priced traditional basic Southern Italian dishes. The waits are long on weekends, so plan ahead and make reservations. Open-air dining. | 25 E. Colorado Blvd. | 626/795–3131 | $8–$20 | AE, DC, MC, V.

Parkway Grill. Contemporary. The setting of this well-respected restaurant is all-American brick walls, wood floors, a carved-wood bar, lots of greenery, and a khaki-clad waitstaff. The always-interesting dishes range from Italian to Mexican to Chinese: in one sitting you might have Dungeness crab tostadas, then Chinese-style roasted crispy duck—and s'mores for dessert. | 510 S. Arroyo Pkwy. | 626/795–1001 | Reservations essential | $12–$30 | AE, DC, MC, V.

Raymond Restaurant. American. An early 1900s Craftsman-style bungalow is the setting for this romantic spot. Try the roast duckling or the sauteed chicken in a cream sauce. Weekend brunch. | 1250 S. Fair Oaks Ave. | 626/441–3136 | Closed Mon. | $24–$47 | AE, D, DC, MC, V.

Saladang. Thai. Southern California is rife with Thai restaurants, but few stand out from the crowd as much as this smart yet casual bistro with vaulted ceilings set off by exposed purple air ducts and orange-and-black-striped tablecloths. Although it's a bit off the beaten track—1½ mi south of downtown—it's worth the trek, with reasonably priced offerings including spinach and duck salad, seafood soup, rice noodles with basil and bean sprouts, and beef panang, (beef in a coconut curry sauce). The prix-fixe lunches are a great value. | 363 S. Fair Oaks Ave. | 626/793–8123 | $7–$20 | AE, DC, MC, V.

★ **Shiro.** Continental. Look for trend-setting dishes in this popular, Asian-influenced bistro. White tablecloths and mustard-yellow walls create a vibrant setting for the fresh and exciting offerings, as far ranging as Chinese ravioli filled with shrimp mousse, or calamari-basil-tomato soup. And that's for starters. Sizzling whole catfish with soy-citrus-ponzu sauce is a signature dish. Other worthy options are duck with orange sauce, lobster and scallops with saffron sauce, and herb-mustard chicken. For dessert, try the warm lemon pudding. The restaurant is about 2 mi south of Pasadena. | 1505 Mission St., South Pasadena | 626/799–4774 | Closed Mon. and early–late Sept. No lunch | $20–$30 | AE, MC, V.

Twin Palms. Contemporary. Huge swaths of sail cloth stretch across a 470-seat outdoor eating area at this gigantic restaurant. Another 400 guests can sit in the richly hued formal dining area, actually a converted warehouse divided into two rooms, with hardwood floors, dramatic high-back wooden chairs, and an enormous wine rack running the length of the space. On warm evenings, there's an infectious air of bonhomie, influenced by two large bars and live music. The extensive Mediterranean/Pacific Rim/Gulf of Mexico menu also keeps spirits high. Seafood linguini, sea bass togarashi (with soy-citrus ponzu sauce), Yucatan chicken, and juicy meats flame-cooked over a huge rotisserie are all standouts at this setting. The restaurant is in Old Pasadena. Entertainment Wed.–Sun. night. Sunday brunch. | 101 W. Green St. | 626/577–2567 | $8–$20 | AE, D, DC, MC, V.

Xiomara. Contemporary. Voted in 1998 as one of the Top 10 Restaurants in LA by L.A. *Magazine,* this Old Pasadena restaurant casts a romantic glow. The Asian-Cuban menu includes Chilean sea bass and mashed potatoes flavored with roasted chiles, crispy salmon, pepper steak, and country cassoulet. Dining areas are usually bustling with regulars, who sit at crisp linen-covered tables. An antique Chinese dresser is a standout decoration against the restaurant's 100-year-old brick walls. Two tables are tucked into a tiny outdoor eating area on the sidewalk. | 69 N. Raymond Ave. | 626/796–2520 | No lunch weekends | $18–$30 | AE, D, DC, MC, V.

★ **Yujean Kang's Gourmet Chinese Cuisine.** Chinese. Forget any and all preconceived notions of what Chinese food should look and taste like—you won't find any of the familiar, cornstarch-gravied staples here. Instead, Kang's gives Chinese cooking a creative twist—one that's proved extremely popular with locals, especially at dinner. Try tender slices of veal on a bed of enoki mushrooms, topped with a tangle of quick-fried shoestring yams, or sea bass with kumquats and passion-fruit sauce. As for dessert, say goodbye to lychee nuts, and opt for poached plums or watermelon ice under a mantle of white chocolate. Expect excellent service in a contemporary Asian setting, with white tablecloths and Chinese paintings and wood furniture. In Old Pasadena. | 67 N. Raymond Ave. | 626/585–0855 | $7–$18 | AE, D, DC, MC, V.

Lodging

Artists' Inn Bed and Breakfast. Take your complimentary afternoon tea into the rose garden at this peaceful lodging, an 1895 Victorian farmhouse converted into an ideal escape for couples. Each of the theme rooms reflects the style of a famous painter: the Gauguin suite has drapes with Polynesian prints; the Van Gogh room recalls the room immortalized by the maestro's painting from Arles. The B&B is in a quiet residential area 2 mi north of Old Pasadena. Complimentary breakfast. Some in-room hot tubs. No kids under 9. | 1038 Magnolia St., S. Pasadena | 626/799–5668 or 888/799–5668 | fax 626/799–3678 | artists@artistsinns.com | www.artistsinns.com | 9 rooms | $140–$205 | AE, MC, V.

Best Western Colorado Inn. This motel's east Pasadena location in a busy commercial area right off the I–210 freeway, makes it a convenient headquarters for visiting east San Gabriel Valley attractions such as Santa Anita race track, the Huntington Library, and the L. A. County Arboretum. Complimentary Continental breakfast. Refrigerators, cable TV. Pool. Hot tub. Laundry facilities. Business services. | 2156 E. Colorado Blvd. | 626/793–9339 | fax 626/568–2731 | www.bestwestern.com | 77 rooms | $59–$200 | AE, D, DC, MC, V.

Comfort Inn. This chain offering at the eastern end of Pasadena is an option for business travelers using the Pasadena Center. It's a three-story Mediterranean style building. Complimentary Continental breakfast. In-room data ports, microwaves, refrigerators, cable TV, in-room VCRs (and movies). Pool. Hot tub, sauna. Laundry facilities. Business services. | 2462 E. Colorado Blvd. | 626/405–0811 | fax 626/796–0966 | thnpchen@hotmail.com | www.city-cent.com/comfort | 50 rooms | $67–$82 | AE, D, DC, MC, V.

Doubletree Hotel. Next to City Hall and 4 blocks north of Old Pasadena, this 12-story hotel has European styling, especially in the resplendent lobby with cathedral ceilings, marble details, chandeliers, and plants. Restaurant, bars [with entertainment], room service. Cable TV. Pool. Hot tub. Gym. Business services, airport shuttle, parking (fee). | 191 N. Los Robles Ave. | 626/792–2727 | fax 626/792–3755 | www.doubletreepasadena.com | 350 rooms | $199–$359 | AE, D, DC, MC, V.

Hilton. This hotel, 2 blocks from the shops and restaurants of Old Pasadena and Pasadena Center complex, makes a good choice for vacationing couples as well as business travelers. The 14-story building has a lovely lobby decorated with Portuguese marble, skylights and a fireplace. Rooms are spacious and well-equipped for business travelers. Those on the upper floors have mountain views. Restaurant, bar. Cable TV. Pool. Beauty salon, hot tub. Exercise equipment. Business services. Parking (fee). | 168 S. Los Robles Ave. | 626/577–1000 | fax 626/584–3148 | www.hilton.com/hotels/pasphhh/index.html | 291 rooms | $144–$229 | AE, D, DC, MC, V.

Old Pasadena Courtyard by Marriot. This Marriot, in the heart of historic Pasadena, is surrounded by shops, restaurants, and galleries. The Rose Bowl is 5 mi away and Universal Studios is 10 mi west. Room service. In-room data ports, cable TV. Outdoor pool. Gym. Laundry facilities, laundry service. Business services, parking (fee). | 180 N. Fair Oaks Ave. | 626/403–7600 | fax 626/403–7700 | www.mariott.com | 304 rooms, 10 suites | $139–$179, $189 suites | AE, CB, DC, D, MC, V.

★ **Ritz-Carlton Huntington.** A mansion among mansions, this legendary hotel is situated on 23 acres of old gardens in a quiet residential area 2 mi south of Colorado Boulevard. It's shaded by centuries-old oak trees, boasts California's first Olympic-sized swimming pool, and has a tranquil Japanese garden. Although the hotel dates back to 1906, it suffered extensive damage in a 1987 earthquake necessiting a total reconstruction; local pressure forced the builders to "put it back exactly the way it was." Rooms have been updated and lavishly appointed with marble, thick carpeting and original art on the walls. The Huntington Library and Cal Tech are 2 mi northeast of the hotel. Restaurants, bar [with entertainment], room service. Cable TV. Pool. Beauty salon, spa, hot tub, massage. Tennis. Gym, bicycles. Kids' programs. Business services. Parking (fee). | 1401 S. Oak Knoll Ave. | 626/568–3900 | fax 626/568–3700 | www.ritz-carlton.com | 387 rooms, 8 cottages | $235–$310, $395–$595 cottages | AE, D, DC, MC, V.

Saga Motor Hotel. Watch the floats cruise by your window at this 1957 motel, a three-story stucco building right on the parade route. The lodging, surrounded by attractive gardens, is across the street from Pasadena City College. Complimentary Continental breakfast. Cable TV. Pool. Business services. | 1633 E. Colorado Blvd. | 626/795–0431 or 800/793–7242 | fax 626/792–0559 | www.sagamotorhotel.com | 70 rooms | $65–$82 | AE, D, DC, MC, V.

PASO ROBLES

4, F12

(Nearby towns also listed: Atascadero, Cambria, Morro Bay, San Simeon)

When Spanish explorers first visited this gently rolling, tree-dotted countryside in 1776, they named it *paso de robles*, or "oak-lined pass." The rolling hillsides remained in Spanish (later Mexican) hands until the Americans took control in mid-1800s. Today, you can still see that Spanish heritage in a local museum, Mission San Miguel Arcángel, and several others in the surrounding areas.

Paso Robles (pop. 22,000) has been connected with several famous names over the years. The town of Paso Robles was officially formed in the late 19th century by a group of settlers who included Drury James, uncle of the notorious Jesse James. Buildings from those early West days still stand downtown. The area's mild climate lured acclaimed Polish pianist Ignace Paderewski, who came to cure neuritis in his hands in 1913, and remained to purchase two ranches and introduce zinfandel grapes to the region. Finally, Paso Robles has a connection with actor James Dean, whose starring movie *East of Eden* was set in the area; Dean was killed in a head-on collision on Route 46, at Chalone, 25 mi east of town.

The first wine grapes were grown at Mission San Miguel Arcángel, which continues to this day. By now, however, the area has emerged into a well-respected wine-producing region with more than 30 operating wineries and 135 vineyards. Many wineries, known for their zinfandels, merlots, and chardonnays are open for tasting and touring.

Information: Paso Robles Chamber of Commerce | 1225 Park St., 93446 | 805/238–0506 or 800/406–4040 | pasorobleschamber.com | Weekdays 8:30–5, Sat. 10–4.

Attractions

Antique Doll Museum. This museum has a collection of about 800 antique dolls, the oldest dating to 1540 said to have belonged to Edward VI (son of England's Henry VIII and the fictionalized royal in Mark Twain's *The Prince and the Pauper*. Gifts, collectibles, and doll supplies are available here. | 88 Wellsona Rd. | 805/238–2740 | $3 | Tues.–Sat. 11–5, Sun. 2–5.

El Paso de Robles Area Pioneer Museum. You can see Native American handicrafts, farm and ranching equipment, furniture, clothing, and other artifacts that illustrate life in Paso Robles in the mid-1800s. | 2010 Riverside Ave. | 805/239–4556 | Free | Thurs.–Sun. 1–4.

Lake Nacimiento Resort. Take your pick of outdoor activities at this reservoir. There's waterskiing, boating, fishing (large-mouth, small-mouth, and white bass, perch, catfish), hiking on more than 165 mi of shoreline trails, lake and pool swimming, and camping. The 5,000-acre resort, 25 mi northwest of Paso Robles, has 345 campsites (including RV hookups), a store, showers, barbecue grills, laundry facilities, and a marina with power boats for rent. Some pets allowed. Advance reservations essential. | 10625 Lake Nacimiento Dr. | 805/238–3256 or 800/323–3839 | www.tcsn.net/nacimientoresort | $7–$10 day use, $4 dogs, $22–$24 camping | Daily.

Lake San Antonio Recreation Area. This Monterey County-owned lake and surrounding 10,000 acres of rolling hills northwest of town has 2,300 campsites, RV hookups, restrooms, barbecue grills, picnic sites, a playground, and hiking trails. The reservoir offers fishing, swimming, waterskiing, windsurfing and a full service marina. | 2610 San Antonio Rd. | 805/472–2311 | $6 per vehicle day use, camping $16–$20 per night.

Mission San Miguel Arcángel. Founded in 1797, one of a chain of 21 missions marking the path of Spanish padres as they traveled up the California coast, this structure has been minimally restored—an intentional effort to leave the interior murals and hand-hewn beams

PASO ROBLES

INTRO
ATTRACTIONS
DINING
LODGING

in their original state. A self-guided tour with map is available. | 775 Mission St. | 805/467–3256 | Donations accepted | Daily 9:30–4:15.

Paso Robles Farmers Market on the Square. Pick up fresh produce, breads, and other goods garnered from surrounding farms. Also, there's entertainment, barbecue, and arts and crafts on 12th Street next to City Park. | Free | Fri. 5:30PM–8PM.

Wineries. The 35 wineries in and around Paso Robles are often family-run operations, which tend to have an intimate appeal, with low-key tasting rooms, room to relax and time to chat. A free, self-guided map, available from the Chamber of Commerce, helps you find assorted wineries. | 805/238–0506 or 800/406–4040.

ON THE CALENDAR

MAR.: *Paderewski Festival.* This weekend of piano concerts, tours, wine-tastings, and exhibits celebrates Paso Robles' famous Polish pianist-turned-winemaker, noted for bringing zinfandel grapes to the area in the early 1900s. The event fills downtown Paso Robles. | 805/238–0506 or 800/406–4040.

MAY: *West Coast Kustoms Car Show.* With no small nod to James Dean's nearby crash site (in Chalone, 25 mi east), this high-octane event brings lovers of pre-1970 cars to City Park for a night of cruising, a '50s dance, food vendors, and hundreds of buffed and polished classic cars. | 805/238–0506 or 800/406–4040.

MAY: *Wine Festival.* Area wineries host a tribute to the vineyards with tastings, tours, and special events. | 805/238–0506 or 800/406–4040.

AUG.: *Annual Basil Festival.* Sycamore Farms hosts a salute to the leafy herb with tastings of basil-enhanced foods, live music, horse-and-buggy rides, and face painting. | 805/238–5288 or 800/576–5288.

AUG.: *California Mid-State Fair.* Dubbed the "Biggest Little Fair Anywhere," this two-week event attracts top-name entertainment, a rodeo, agricultural exhibits, and a carnival. | 805/239–0655 | www.midstatefair.com.

Dining

Bistro Laurent. French. Try the chef's tasting menu, which changes weekly, or specialties like gratin with curry and fennel, Burgundy-style seafood fricassee, and veal cheeks in tomato and rosemary with penne to keep things interesting. You can dine shoulder-to-shoulder inside the exposed brick bistro or retreat to the outside patio to savor the warm chocolate tart with vanilla sauce. | 1202 Pine St. | 805/226–8191 | fax 805/227–4128 | Reservations highly recommended | Closed Sun. No lunch | $13–$19 | MC, V.

Busi's on the Park. Contemporary. You can enjoy a pre-dinner drink in the inviting 1870s walnut-paneled bar—the oldest barroom in San Luis Obispo County—then move to the spacious patio and lawn tables for alfresco dining. Signature dishes include an 18-ounce rib-eye stuffed with gorgonzola cheese and shiitake mushrooms in a glace de viande, noisettes of Colorado lamb with a sundried cherry reduction, and seared sea scallops in saffron beure blanc. | 1122 Pine St. | 805/238–1390 | fax 895/238–7407 | www.busis.net | Reservations necessary Fri.–Sun. nights | Closed Sun. No lunch | $15–$25 | AE, DC, MC, V.

F. McLintock's. Barbecue. In downtown north of City Park, this chain eatery specializes in oak-pit barbequed steaks, ribs, seafood, and chicken in a casual setting. The dining room has a Western theme, with cowboy brands, boots, hats, and trophy heads on the walls. Locals voted the kids' menu the best in the county. | 1234 Park St. | 805/238–2233 | $6–$25 | AE, MC, V.

Villa Creek. Contemporary. Chef/owner Cris Cherry adds a Mexican flair to the menu with items like baked butternut squash enchilada with sautéed onions, garlic, corn in tomatillo salsa, and charbroiled boneless breast of duck served with jalapeño jelly, mushroom sauté, and roasted poblano mashed potatoes. The California Mission-inspired setting has a soaring 18-ft ceiling, exposed beams, handmade furniture, and Oaxacan tapestries. | 1144 Pine St. | 805/238–3000 | fax 805/238–5439 | www.villacreek.com | Reservations necessary Fri.–Sun. | No lunch | $9–$25 | AE, D, MC, V.

Lodging

Adelaide Inn. Standard rooms at reasonable rates and attractively landscaped grounds make this Western-style motel a good choice for budget travelers. The lodging is 1 mi north of downtown. Picnic area. In-room data ports, refrigerators, cable TV. Pool. Hot tub. Sauna. Putting green. Playground. Laundry facilities. Business services. | 1215 Ysabel Ave. | 805/238–2770 or 800/549–7276 | fax 805/238–3497 | www.adelaideinn.com | 67 rooms | $45–$77 | AE, D, DC, MC, V.

Arbor Inn. Surrounded by vineyards and owned by the Treana Winery, the B&B is on 7 acres, and has a skylit, sunny, English country-style interior. Each room has a fireplace and balcony. Breakfasts such as Eggs Benedict or brioche French toast can be served in your room. Complimentary breakfast. Some in-room hot tubs, room phones. Library. Laundry service. No smoking. | 2130 Arbor Road | 805/227–4673 | fax 805/227–1112 | www.cabbi.com | 7 rooms, 2 suites | $165–$185, $215–$255 suites | MC, V.

Best Western Black Oak. This two-story motel is in a commercial area 1 mi north of downtown. The lodging is a good choice for families, with a grassy picnic area and playground. Restaurant. In-room data ports, refrigerators, cable TV. Pool. Hot tub, sauna. Laundry facilities. Business services. | 1135 24th St. | 805/238–4740 or 800/528–1234 | fax 805/238–0726 | 110 rooms | $61–$79 | AE, D, DC, MC, V.

Gillie Archer Inn. Look for classic Craftsman styling—custom woodwork, handsome built-in cabinetry, original arts-and-crafts fixtures—at this B&B, built as a private home in 1917. Furnishings are simple and eclectic; some rooms have tile floors, and one has a fireplace. The inn, especially suitable for couples, sits in a quiet residential area 3 blocks west of downtown. Don't miss the stained-glass details in the garden gazebo. Dining room, complimentary breakfast. In-room VCRs. No kids under 12. | 1433 Oak St. | 805/238–0879 | fax 805/238–2516 | gillie@tcsn.net | 5 rooms (2 with shared bath) | $85–$125 | AE, D, MC, V.

Just Inn. Dense vineyards surround this B&B, built in 1992 to resemble a French country inn. Take in the view from the formal gardens. Or settle into an enormous bed, with fine linens and a decadent number of pillows, in one of the antique-filled suites and listen to the logs crackle in your private fireplace. Arrange in advance to enjoy a multi-course meal prepared by the inn's chef ($100/couple, wine extra). The inn is 17 mi west of town, via Vineyard Drive. Dining room, complimentary breakfast. In-room hot tubs, some in-room VCRs. Massage. Bicycles. No kids under 12. | 11680 Chimney Rock Rd. | 805/238–6932 or 800/726–0049 | fax 805/237–4109 | www.justinwine.com | 3 suites | $230–$280 suites | AE, D, MC, V.

Melody Ranch. This simple, one-story ranch-style motel is an economical choice, especially for families, in the north end of town. Picnic area. Cable TV. Pool. | 939 Spring St. | 805/238–3911 or 800/909–3911 | 19 rooms | $56 | AE, D, DC, MC, V.

Paso Robles Inn. In the heart of Paso Robles, this 1890 Mission-style inn was completely modernized in 1999. Its unique "spa rooms," which come with private patios, have hot tubs that tap directly into the town's underground thermal hot springs. Many rooms have fireplaces. Restaurant. In-room data ports, some microwaves, some refrigerators, some in-room hot tubs, cable TV. Outdoor pool. Hot tub. Gym. Baby-sitting. Laundry service. Business services. | 1103 Spring St. | 805/238–2660 or 800/676–1713 | fax 805/238–4707 | pri@thegrid.net | www.pasoroblesinn.com | 70 rooms, 30 spa rooms | $95–135, $140–$215 spa rooms | AE, D, DC, MC, V.

Summit Creek Ranch. You will experience a great sense of space at this Mission-style adobe, beginning inside with the 15-ft cathedral timbered ceilings. From the living room, there are 60-mi panoramic views of the Salinas Valley. Each guest room has its own deck and is furnished with Mexican and Mission furniture and Oriental rugs. Hummingbirds, soaring hawks and eagles, and deer make frequent appearances. Complimentary breakfast. | 6350 Peachy Canyon Rd. | 805/237–1870 | fax 805/237–1870 | info@summitcreekranch.com | www.summitcreekranch.com | 3 rooms | $95–$110 | MC, V.

Vineyard Cottage. This spacious, stucco cottage with Mediterranean styling and red-tile roof, has views of the surrounding hills and wine country. The cottage, built in 1990 adjacent to the owners' home, is 10 mi west of town and has a private deck overlooking the vineyards. Complimentary Continental breakfast. Pool. Tennis. | 7840 Vineyard Dr. | 805/239–4678 | fax 805/238–6355 | mswan338@aol.com | 1 cottage | $225 | MC, V.

PEBBLE BEACH

MAP 4, D10

(Nearby towns also listed: Carmel, Carmel Valley, Monterey, Pacific Grove)

The 4,800 acres that comprise the Pebble Beach (pop 5,000) area of the Monterey Peninsula are among the most photographed in the world. The Lone Cypress, a single Monterey pine perched on a golf course green and surrounded on three sides by ocean, is the visual icon for this ultra-wealthy community. Trophy homes hug the hillsides near famous 17-Mile Drive, which meanders among rare Monterey pine forests and above frothy sea views; you must pay a fee at the gates to enter. The unincorporated area is also famous for the AT&T Pebble Beach National Pro-Am Golf Tournament.

People come to Pebble Beach to play golf at some of the finest courses in the world. There is no commercial area amid all this natural wildness. But there are two legendary resorts plus a recently opened small resort inn. Visitors not staying at the luxury resorts can experience a bit of Pebble Beach by exploring the 17-Mile Drive, dining at one of the resort restaurants or playing a round of golf where world champions play.

Information: The Pebble Beach Company | 17-Mile Dr., 93953 | 831/624–3811 | www.pebblebeach.com.

Attractions

Pebble Beach Golf Links. This course is home to the Pebble Beach Invitational and AT&T Pro-Am tournaments. Call one day ahead to request a reservation. | 1700 17-Mile Dr. | 831/624–3811 | www.pebblebeach.com | $350 | Daily 6:20 AM–3:20 PM.

★ **17-Mile Drive.** One of the most scenic drives anywhere, these two winding lanes roll past vistas of crashing surf, sea lions, and the thick pines of the 5,000-acre Del Monte Forest. Landmarks along the way include Bird Rock, Seal Rock, and the Lone Cypress. The drive is accessed off Rte. 1. | 831/649–8500 | $7.50 per vehicle.

ON THE CALENDAR

JAN., FEB.: *AT&T Pebble Beach National Pro-Amateur Golf Championship.* Celebrities and golf pros compete on three of the world's most challenging and scenic courses. | 800/541–9091.

MAR.: *Pebble Beach Spring Horse Show.* Five days of hunter-jumper competitions attract riders from throughout the state to the Pebble Beach Equestrian Center. | 831/624–2756.

Dining

Club XIX. Contemporary. Club XIX is the French country-styled restaurant at the Lodge at Pebble Beach. The cherrywood dining room and enclosed, heated terrace overlook the ocean and golf course. Top dishes include the Chilean seabass and lobster risotto. | 17-Mile Dr. | 831/624–3811 | Jacket required | $26–$35 | AE, D, DC, MC, V.

Peppoli. Italian. This casual restaurant overlooking the ocean and the Spanish Bay Golf Course is known for Tuscan-influenced fresh seafood and pasta, such as the grilled swordfish and the pasta with artichokes in a marinara sauce. | 2700 17-Mile Dr. | 831/647–7500 | No lunch | $25–$50 | AE, D, DC, MC, V.

Roy's. Eclectic. At this restaurant at the Inn at Spanish Bay, dine in an outdoor patio lit by firepits and a gas fireplace each night. The large windows in the dining room show views of the Pacific Ocean. There's an open kitchen, an open pizza bar, and an espresso bar. | 2700 17-Mile Dr. | 831/647–7423 | Breakfast also available | $16–$30 | AE, D, DC, MC, V.

Stillwater Grill. Seafood. Stunning views of Carmel Bay and its location on the 18th green at the Pebble Beach Golf Links give this grill a relaxed atmosphere. Try the raw bar selections or one of the uncomplicated and fresh grilled seafood dishes. Breakfast and lunch are also served. | 1700 17-Mile Dr. | 831/624–3811 | www.pebble-beach.com | Reservations recommended | Resort casual | Breakfast also available | $10–$23 | AE, DC, MC, V.

Lodging

★ **Casa Palmero.** A sister resort to the Lodge at Pebble Beach and the Inn at Spanish Bay, this Mediterranean–style villa is adjacent to the first tee of the Pebble Beach Golf Links. Opened in late 1999, Casa Palmero has luxury suites—some with outdoor hot tubs, private courtyards, and fireplaces—and prides itself on providing individual attention through its personal valet service. 4 restaurants. Complimentary breakfast. In-room data ports, some in-room hot tubs, cable TV, in-room VCRs. Outdoor pool. Spa. 18-hole golf course, 8 tennis courts. Library. Baby-sitting. Laundry service. Business services, airport shuttle. | 1518 Cypress Dr. | 800/654–8598 | www.pebble-beach.com | 24 rooms | $550–$1750 | AE, DC, MC, V.

★ **Inn and Links at Spanish Bay.** This four-story hotel, 3 mi from Fisherman's Wharf and 4 mi south of Pacific Grove, is amid tall Monterey pines overlooking the Pacific Ocean. The links are a rugged Scottish-style. All rooms have a bay or forest view and a gas-burning fireplace. 2 restaurants, bar, picnic area, room service. In-room data ports, cable TV. Video games. Pool. Hot tub, massage. 4 18-hole golf courses, putting green, tennis. Gym, hiking, horseback riding, beach, bicycles. Laundry facilities. Business services, airport shuttle. | 2700 17-Mile Dr. | 831/647–7500 or 800/654–9300 | fax 831/644–7955 | www.pebble-beach.com | 252 rooms, 17 suites | $375–$525, $675–$2165 suites | AE, D, DC, MC, V.

★ **Lodge at Pebble Beach.** This 1919 lodge is surrounded by four golf courses. Luxurious rooms are in the main and 11 adjacent buildings. They have fireplaces, and balconies or patios with wonderful views. Guests have privileges at the Inn at Spanish Bay. Nature trails lead to ocean vistas, an ancient Indian village, and S. F. B Morse Botanical Reserve. 4 restaurants, bar. In-room data ports, microwaves, cable TV. Pool, wading pool. Beauty salon, hot tub, massage. 2 driving ranges, 4 18-hole golf courses, putting green, tennis. Gym, horseback riding, beach. Shops, video games. Kids' programs. Business services, airport shuttle. Pets allowed. | 2790 17-Mile Dr. | 831/624–3811 or 800/654–9300 | fax 831/625–8598 | www.pebble-beach.com | 151 rooms, 10 suites | $450–$600, $1100–$2125 suites | AE, D, DC, MC, V.

PETALUMA

MAP 3, C7

(Nearby towns also listed: Inverness, Napa, Rutherford/St. Helena, Sonoma, Yountville)

Petaluma's historic downtown will make you feel as if you're in the middle of a 19th-century movie set. (It's actually a favorite with filmmakers, who have used it as a backdrop in scenes from *American Graffiti* and *Peggy Sue Got Married*, among others.) The main street, Petaluma Blvd., is flanked by majestic Victorian buildings, a real point of pride for the little town, which is slowly transforming from a dairy-and-egg capital to a day-trip destination for Bay Area dwellers.

The name Petaluma (pop. 52,000) is derived from a Coastal Miwok phrase meaning "little hills behind the river." Its roots are in the Gold Rush: established in 1858, the

PETALUMA

INTRO
ATTRACTIONS
DINING
LODGING

town was a main supplier of game and produce for the boom towns of San Francisco and Oakland. It claims a list of quirky honors—home to the world's first and only chicken pharmacy; the hometown of actors Lloyd Bridges and Winona Ryder; and the birthplace of the World's Wristwrestling Championship.

Information: **Petaluma Chamber of Commerce** | 799 Baywood Dr., 94954 | 707/762–2785 | www.petaluma.org.

Attractions

Cinnabar Performing Arts Theater. This refurbished schoolhouse is home to several performing arts groups, including the Cinnabar Opera Theater, Quicksilver II Theater Company, Ann Woodhead Dance Company, and the Cinnabar Young Repertory Theater Company. | 3333 Petaluma Blvd. N | 707/763–8920.

Garden Valley Ranch. This 9-acre ranch is covered with 8,000 rose bushes, which you can visit, along with a 1-acre fragrance garden, a test garden, and a nursery. | 498 Pepper Rd. | 707/795-0919 | www.gardenvalley.com | $4 | Wed.–Sun. 10–4.

Marin French Cheese Company. This 1865 cheese-making operation produces the Rouge et Noir label, one of the oldest in the state. There's a deli and picnic area on site. | 7500 Red Hill Rd. | 707/762–6001 | Free | Daily 10–5.

Petaluma Adobe State Historic Park. Once the headquarters for General Mario Vallejo's landholdings, the adobe building is restored to look as it did in 1840, with animals, farm tools, candle-making, and weaving on display. | 3325 Adobe Rd. | 707/762–4871 | $1 | Daily 10–5.

Petaluma Historical Museum and Library. Andrew Carnegie's bequest paid for this striking building in 1904. It boasts the largest free-standing leaded glass dome in northern California, and houses a permanent collection of historical artifacts, as well as the Carnegie Library. On weekends costumed docents lead guided tours and history walks. | 20 4th St. | 707/778–4398 | Free | Wed.–Sat., Mon. 10–4, Sun. 12–3.

Petaluma Village Factory Outlets. You can shop at 50 outlet stores—including Ann Taylor, Brooks Brothers, Levi's, Book Warehouse, and the Rocky Mountain Chocolate Factory. | 2200 Petaluma Blvd. N | 707/778–9300 | Free | Mon.–Sat. 10–8, Sun. 10–6.

Petaluma River Walk. This scenic walk follows the waterfront from the Balshaw footbridge to the Golden Eagle Center at D Street. | 707/769–0429 or 877/273–8258 | Free.

ON THE CALENDAR

APR.: *Butter and Egg Days Parade.* Petaluma's poultry and dairy past inspires a parade of dairy trucks decorated as floats, papier-mâché cows, and marching bands. | 707/763–0931.
JUNE: *Sonoma-Marin Fair.* Livestock exhibitions, flower shows, a carnival, and an Ugly Dog contest highlight the fair at the Petaluma Fairgrounds. | 707/763–0931.
OCT.: *World Wrist Wrestling Championships.* Strong-armed competitors come from as far as Russia, Africa, and Australia to compete at the Mystic Theatre. | 707/778–1430 or 707/766–9999.

Dining

Buona Sera. Italian. This restaurant in a turn-of-the-century building is known for Gorgonzola-crusted duckling and sesame-coated Hawaiian ahi, in addition to pasta. | 148 Kentucky St. | 707/763–3333 | No lunch | $14–$23 | AE, MC, V.

De Schmire. Contemporary. You can watch chefs prepare an eclectic mix of European, California, and Pacific rim cuisine through an open kitchen. Try the chicken curry or the rack of lamb. | 304 Bodega Ave. | 707/762–1901 | No lunch | $15–$25 | AE, MC, V.

Marvin's. American. This cute, tiny restaurant has a dairy theme and a narrow patio with a few tables set among flowerpots. Try the omelettes, home-baked pies, milkshakes, burgers, fries, or pancakes. | 317 Petaluma Blvd. N | 707/765-2371 | Breakfast also available | $9–$15 | AE, MC, V.

McNear's. Barbecue. This saloon next to the Mystic Theatre Music Hall has a patio and a game room with pool tables, shuffleboard, darts. It's known for a casual environment good for steaks, fish and chips, Memphis-style smoked pork, and microbrews. | 23 Petaluma Blvd. | 707/765-2121 | Breakfast also available | $5–$15 | AE, MC, V.

Lodging

Best Western. A floral theme, deep colors, and dark-toned antique reproductions decorate the spacious rooms of this two-story motel just off U.S. 101, across from the Washington Square Shopping Center, 2 mi east of downtown. Restaurant. In-room data ports, some refrigerators, cable TV. Pool. Laundry facilities. Business services. | 200 S. McDowell Blvd. | 707/763-0994 or 800/297-3846 | fax 707/778-3111 | 70 rooms, 5 suites | $84–$102, $112–$120 suites | AE, D, DC, MC, V.

Cavanagh Inn. Two former homes, one built in 1902, the other in 1912, make up Petaluma's first B&B. The formal Victorian building has redwood paneling and antiques. The Craftsman cottage has a mural on the upstairs landing that echoes the garden theme. Proprietor Jeanne Farris prepares a great gourmet breakfast. Complimentary breakfast. No air-conditioning, no room phones, no TV. No smoking. | 10 Keller St. | 707/765-4657 or 888/765-4658 | fax 707/769-0466 | www.cavanaghinn.com | 7 rooms | $75–$130 | AE, MC, V.

Chileno Valley Ranch Bed & Breakfast. This 1880s Victorian Italianate home, which was fully restored in 1997, sits amid 600 acres of ranchland, 10 mi west of Petaluma. Eleven-foot ceilings, original woodwork, and antique appointments throughout the home evoke a bygone era. Complimentary breakfast. In-room data ports, some room phones, no TV. Hiking, bicycling. | 5105 Chileno Valley Ranch Rd. | 707/765-3936 or 877/280-6664 | fax 707/765-3936 | www.chilenobnb.com | 4 rooms, 1 cottage | $135–$155 room, $135 cottage | AE, MC, V.

Quality Inn. Seven Cape Cod-style buildings are clustered around grounds landscaped with fruit trees and redwoods. Rooms have warm wood accents and an earth-tone color scheme. Complimentary Continental breakfast. Refrigerators, some in-room hot tubs, cable TV. Pool. Hot tub, sauna. Laundry facilities. Business services. | 5100 Montero Way | 707/664-1155 or 800/221-2222 | fax 707/664-8566 | 110 rooms, 4 suites | $124–$152, $175 suites | AE, D, DC, MC, V.

PINE VALLEY

MAP 4, K17

(Nearby towns also listed: El Cajon, Julian, Rancho Bernardo, San Diego)

Pine Valley (pop. 15,000) is a small community in the Laguna Mountains east of San Diego, off I-8 14 mi east at an altitude of 4,055 ft. The town sits on the edge of the Cleveland National Forest, making it a headquarters for a trek into the wilderness.

Information: **San Diego East Visitor's Bureau** | 5005 Willows Rd., Suite 208, 91901 | 619/445-0180 | www.visitsandiegoeast.com.

Attractions

Cuyamaca Rancho State Park. You can explore 25,000 scenic acres with sweeping poplar and oak rimmed meadows and waterfalls; there are hiking and nature tails, equestrian trails, horse camprgrounds, and relics of an 1870s gold rush. There's a nice picnic area among remnants of the Stonewall Mine, a photo display in a replica of a miner's house explains what took place here in the 1890s. The park has sweeping desert viewpoints, beautiful fall color, and winter snow. | 12551 Rte. 79, Descanso | 760/765–0755 | www.cuyamaca.statepark.org | $5 parking fee | Dawn-dusk.

Mount Laguna. This is a small mountain community at the summit of the Sunrise National Scenic Highway /Laguna Mountain Rd. As the road climbs into the mountains of the Cleveland National Forest oak woodlands become pine forests framing dramatic desert views to the east. Mount Laguna is the highest peak in these mountains. There are campgrounds, hiking trails, an information center, store and small primitive lodging at the town of Mount Laguna. | Cleveland National Forest, 3348 Alpine Blvd, Alpine | 858/673–6180 | www.r5.fs.fed.us/cleveland | $5 per vehicle.

ON THE CALENDAR
JULY: *Pine Valley Days.* This annual three-day fair has rodeo-style events, arts and crafts booths, an evening pit barbeque and dance, and a parade. | 619/473–9845 | www.pinevalleycalifornia.com.

Dining
Pine Valley House. American. The weekend prime rib special, surf and turf platter, and Sunday brunch draw locals who come for the hearty meals. Kids' menu. | 28841 Old Rte. 80 | 619/473–8708 | Closed Tues. | $11.95–$38 | AE, D, DC, MC, V.

Lodging
Victoria Rock Bed and Breakfast. This Mediterranean-style house, located 13 mi northwest of Pine Valley, is at an elevation of 2,300 ft and has stunning sunset views of the Pacific Ocean. When you head to the 3-acre backyard, you're in a registered National Wildlife Federation natural habitat, home to 100 hummingbirds, many rabbits, and an occasional mountain lion. Each room has a wood burning fireplace, deck, and private outside entrance. Complimentary breakfast. Some in-room hot tubs. Steam room. Exercise equipment. No smoking. | 2952 Victoria Dr., Alpine | 619/659–5967 | fax 619/445–6277 | info@victoria-rock-bb.com | www.victoria-rock-bb.com | 4 rooms | $100–$110 | MC, V.

PISMO BEACH

MAP 4, F13

(Nearby towns also listed: Atascadero, Morro Bay, Santa Maria)

At one time Pismo Beach (pop. 9,000) was the Clam Capital of the World—as many as 45,000 clams a day were harvested from these shores. Eroded by overzealous human harvesting, as well as hungry sea otters, the clams are mostly gone. But you can now admire the town's Monterey pine groves, where monarch butterflies winter. Balmy weather and cooperative waves are a nice setting for horseback riding, fishing, and surfing. Those pictures you've seen of off-road vehicles skimming the sand probably were taken in Pismo Beach, one of the few places where cars are allowed on portions of the beach. The town is 12 mi south of San Luis Obispo.

Information: **Pismo Beach Chamber of Commerce** | 581 Dolliver St., 93449 | 805/773–4382 | www.pismochamber.com.

Attractions
Lopez Recreational Area. Camping, fishing, waterskiing, and sailing are popular activities here. The swimming area has a water slide. | 6800 Lopez Dr., Arroyo Grande | 805/788–2381 | $5 per vehicle | Daily.

Monarch Butterfly Grove. From late October through February, thousands of migrating butterflies spend the winter in these groves of pine and eucalyptus. | Pismo State Beach,

North Beach entrance | 805/489–1869 | Nov.–Feb., daily; lectures offered Fri.–Sun. 11 and 2.

Oceano Dunes State Vehicular Recreation Area. Rent an all-terrain vehicle, ride horses, picnic, camp, or take a guided nature walk at this dune site where driving on the beach is allowed. | North 1 Pier Ave., Oceano City | 805/473–7220 | www.oceanodunes.com | Free.

Wineries of the Edna Valley and Arroyo Grande Valley. Eighteen wineries are within 8 mi of Pismo Beach; call Edna Valley and Arroyo Grande Valley Vintners Association for information on tastings and tours. | 805/541–5868.

Prime Outlets. Located along Route 101 in Pismo Beach, this outlet center has 35 brand-name stores. | 333 Five Cities Dr. | 805/773–4661 | fax 805/773–4686 | www.primeretail.com | Mon.–Sat. 10–8, Sun. 11–6.

ON THE CALENDAR

JAN.: *Monarch Butterfly Tours.* Take guided tours of the "butterfly trees" at Pismo State Beach. | 805/773–4382.

SEPT.: *Western Days.* You can mosey on down for a weekend filled with country and western line dancing, two-stepping, and live music. | 800/443–7778 or 805/773–4382 | www.pismochamber.com.

OCT.: *Clam Festival.* Re-live the old days when Pismo Beach was the Clam Capital, with food and music at this fest. | 805/773–4382.

Dining

Brad's Restaurant. Barbecue. Since 1955, the outdoor exhibition barbecue pit here has attracted diners who come to feast on the tri-tip beef sandwich and the fresh barbecued fish. The fish and chips is renowned in Pismo and the mud pie is homemade. | 209 Pomeroy St. | 805/773–6165 | www.bradsrestaurant.com | Reservations not accepted | Closed Dec. | $8–$18 | D, MC, V.

Cracked Crab. Seafood. Order one of the "bucket entrées" and get a bucket of shellfish dumped on your table, along with spicy sausage, potatoes, and corn-on-the-cob. A mallet and a bib make the job easier. There's a daily menu of fresh fish, and paper and crayons for kids. | 751 Price St. | 805/773–2722 | www.crackedcrab.com | $6–$48 | AE, D, MC, V.

F. McLintock's. Steak. The family restaurant has an ocean view from a block away. Popular dishes include steak with two lobster tails, and filet mignon with shrimp. | 750 Mattie Rd., Shell Beach | 805/773–1892 | Reservations not accepted | No lunch | $12–$35 | AE, D, MC, V.

Giuseppe's Cucina Italiana. Italian. You will find a boisterous atmosphere here, complete with strolling accordion players. Cioppino, mesquite-grilled seafood, and the wood-fired San Paolo pizza with homemade chicken sausage are popular. | 891 Price St. | 805/773–2870 | www.pismobeach.com/giuseppe's | Reservations not accepted | No lunch weekends | $11–$23 | AE, D, MC, V.

Rosa's. Italian. This cozy family-run trattoria a block from the beach is known for daily seafood specials, homemade ravioli and canneloni, steamed clams, and its freshly baked bread. | 491 Price St. | 805/773–0551 | No lunch weekends | $9–$20 | AE, D, DC, MC, V.

Shore Cliff. Seafood. With probably the best seafood and clam chowder in town, this restaurant also has spectacular cliff-top views. Sunday champagne brunch offers many buffet items. | 2555 Price St. | 805/773–4671 | www.shorecliff.com | Breakfast also available | $14–$30 | AE, D, DC, MC, V.

Splash Cafe. Seafood. Locals rave about the clam chowder that comes in its own sourdough bread bowl. Fish and chips are also available. Only 4 blocks from the ocean, the restaurant's beach theme is evident in the bright murals and pictures of surfers that adorn the walls. | 197 Pomeroy St. | 805/773–4653 | www.splashcafe.com | Reservations not accepted | $5–$9 | MC, V.

Lodging

Best Western Shelter Cove Lodge. Located on a 3-acre cliff park, this hotel's bright and airy rooms all have scenic ocean views. Restaurant, complimentary Continental breakfast. Refrigerators, cable TV. Outdoor pool. Hot tub. Tennis. Beach, fishing. Laundry facilities. Business services. | 2651 Price St. | 805/773–3511 | fax 805/773–3511 | www.bestwesterncalifornia.com | 52 rooms | $158–$228 | AE, D, DC, MC, V.

Best Western Shore Cliff Lodge. A stairway leads to the beach from this hotel's high bluff on four acres of park-like grounds. Rooms have ocean views. Exit at Oak Park Road off U.S. 101. Restaurant, bar, complimentary Continental breakfast. Some refrigerators, cable TV. Pool. Hot tub, sauna. Laundry facilities. Business services. | 850 Oak Park Rd., Arroyo Grande | 805/481–7398 | fax 805/481–4859 | 99 rooms | $99–$139 | AE, D, DC, MC, V.

Cliffs at Shell Beach. This spectacular location means most rooms have wonderful ocean views. There's beach access. The rooms are spacious and nicely furnished; white terra cotta tiles and palm trees surround the property. Restaurant, bar [with entertainment]. Some refrigerators, some in-room hot tubs, cable TV. Pool. Hot tub. Gym. Laundry facilities. Business services, airport shuttle. | 2757 Shell Beach Rd. | 805/773–5000 or 800/826–5838 | fax 805/773–0764 | 165 rooms, 27 suites | $186–$476 | AE, D, DC, MC, V.

Cottage Inn by the Sea. This hotel, built in 1998 on the waterfront, has Tudor architecture and landscaped grounds. Rooms have ocean views and fireplaces. The grounds include a large flower garden with a fountain. Complimentary Continental breakfast. Microwaves, refrigerators, cable TV. Pool. Business services. | 2351 Price St. | 805/773–4617 or 888/440–8400 | fax 805/773–8336 | www.cottage-inn.com | 80 rooms | $129–$189 | AE, D, DC, MC, V.

Edgewater Inn and Suites. Family-run for 25 years, this hotel has no-frills rooms and is across the street from the beach. Complimentary Continental breakfast. Some kitchenettes, some refrigerators, cable TV. Outdoor pool. Hot tub. Beach. Business services. | 280 Wadsworth Ave. | 805/773–4811 or 800/634–5858 | fax 805/773–5121 | info@edgewater-inn.com | www.edgewater-inn.com | 73 rooms, 20 suites | $69–$99, $99–139 suites | AE, D, DC, MC, V.

Kaleidoscope Inn. Sunny guest rooms are furnished with period antiques, stained-glass windows, and redwood details at this 1887 Victorian farmhouse B&B, located 10 mi from Pismo Beach. You can relax in the oak rockers on the wraparound front porch or play croquet and bocce in the 1-acre backyard. Breakfasts are made from scratch daily and homemade fudge arrives with the evening turn-down service. Complimentary breakfast. Some in-room hot tubs. No smoking. | 130 E. Dana St., Nipomo | 805/929–5444 | fax 805/929–5440 | kaleidoscopeinn@hotmail.com | www.kaleidoscopeinn.com | 3 rooms | $95–$110 | MC, V.

Kon Tiki Inn. Built in 1974, this three-story hotel is on 10½ acres of landscaped grounds. All rooms have an ocean view and suites have fireplaces. Restaurant, bar [with entertainment]. In-room data ports, refrigerators, cable TV. Pool. Hot tubs, massage. Tennis. Gym, racquetball. Laundry facilities. Business services. | 1621 Price St. | 805/773–4833 or 800/566–8454 | fax 805/773–6541 | www.kontikiinn.com | 86 rooms | $94–$104 | AE, D, MC, V.

Oxford Suites Resort. This hotel, 1 mi from the beach, has a tree-shaded courtyard and a rose garden. Complimentary breakfast. Microwaves, refrigerators, cable TV, in-room VCRs (and movies). Pool, wading pool. Hot tub. Laundry facilities. Business services. Pets allowed (fee). | 651 Five Cities Dr. | 805/773–3773 or 800/982–7848 | fax 805/773–5177 | www.oxfordsuites.com | 133 suites | $69–$129 suites | AE, D, DC, MC, V.

Sandcastle Inn. This three-story building lines the beach, with patios and balconies providing great views. Some rooms have fireplaces. There's whale watching nearby. Exit at Price Street off U.S 101. Complimentary Continental breakfast. Refrigerators, cable TV. Beach. Business services. | 100 Stimson Ave. | 805/773–2422 or 800/822–6606 | fax 805/773–0771 | www.sandcastleinn.com | 75 rooms | $129–$199 | AE, D, DC, MC, V.

Sea Crest Resort Motel. Billed as "a bit of Hawaii on the California coast," this family-oriented motel has ocean views from some rooms. Two-bedroom family suites are available.

There's shuffle board and a glass-enclosed sun deck. Restaurant, picnic area. Refrigerators, cable TV. Pool. Hot tubs. Laundry facilities. Business services. | 2241 Price St. | 805/773–4608 or 800/782–8400 | fax 805/773–4525 | 142 rooms, 16 suites | $79–109, $125–$175 suites | AE, D, DC, MC, V | www.sea-crest.com.

Sea Gypsy. This large motel is 3 blocks from the pier. Parlor units can be connected to additional rooms to make one-bedroom suites. Some rooms have ocean views with balconies. Some kitchenettes, microwaves, refrigerators, cable TV. Pool. Hot tub. Laundry facilities. Business services. | 1020 Cypress St. | 805/773–1801 or 800/592–5923 | fax 805/773–9286 | www.pismobeach.com/seagypsy | 77 rooms | $70–$120 | AE, D, MC, V.

Sea Venture Hotel. This two-story beachfront hotel has rooms with gas fireplaces, and many have ocean views. Most room balconies have a private hot tub. Restaurant, bar, complimentary Continental breakfast, room service. In-room data ports, minibars, refrigerators, some in-room hot tubs, cable TV, in-room VCRs (and movies). Pool. Massage. Beach. Business services. No smoking. | 100 Ocean View Ave. | 805/773–4994 or 800/662–5545 | fax 805/773–0924 | www.seaventure.com | 51 rooms | $139–$349 | AE, D, DC, MC, V.

Spyglass Inn. Landscaped grounds with palm trees overlook the ocean at this hotel on a bluff. Rooms have a nautical theme. There are ocean views from the outdoor pool and from a heated ocean view deck. Restaurant, bar. Refrigerators, cable TV. Pool. Hot tub. Business services. Pets allowed (fee). | 2705 Spyglass Dr. | 805/773–4855 or 800/824–2612 | fax 805/773–5298 | www.spyglassinn.com | 82 rooms | $79–$199 | AE, D, DC, MC, V.

Whaler's Inn. The rooms here are furnished with contemporary light wood pieces and many of them have stunning ocean views. Perched on a cliff, it's a cut above the standard beach hotels in the area. Some kitchenettes, some microwaves, some refrigerators, some in-room hot tubs, cable TV. Outdoor pool. Hot tub. Beach. Laundry facilities. | 2411 Price St. | 805/773–2411 or 800/245–2411 | fax 805/773–1508 | www.pismo.com | 95 rooms, 2 suites | $89–$145, $235–$250 suites | AE, D, DC, MC, V.

PLACERVILLE

MAP 3, F6

(Nearby towns also listed: Coloma, Rancho Cordova)

Shotgun racks and 4x4s characterize this Mother Lode town west of Lake Tahoe along U.S. 50. In other words, the spirit here hasn't changed much since the Gold Rush days. Formerly Old Dry Diggin's, this boomtown saw so much new fast money and crime that outlaws were hung in pairs. The practice led to the settlement being renamed "Hangtown." John Studebaker toiled here as a wheelwright until he had the bankroll to open his Studebaker motorworks. Today, Placerville (pop. 8,400) is a more peaceful town, and lumbering and agriculture have taken over bank-robbing as the town's economic base.

Information: El Dorado County Chamber of Commerce | 542 Main St., 95667 | 530/621–5885 | www.eldoradocounty.or.

Attractions

Apple Hill Growers. If you go 5 mi east of Route 49 and take the Camino exit from U.S. 50, you'll find these roadside stands that sell fresh produce from more than 50 family farms in this area. During fall harvest season (September through December), members of the Apple Hill Growers Association open their orchards and vineyards for apple and berry picking, picnicking, and wine and cider tasting. Many sell baked items and picnic food. The orchards and vineyards keep irregular hours mid-November–late August, so call ahead if you plan to visit then. | Main office: Larson Dr., 5 mi east of Placerville off U.S. 50 | 530/644–7692 | www.applehill.com | Free | Labor Day–mid.-Nov., daily 9–5.

El Dorado County Historical Museum. The museum has exhibits on local history, mining, logging, and ranching, plus displays devoted to Native American history. | 104 Placerville Dr. | 530/621–5865 | www.caohwy.com/y/yeldhimu.htm | Free | Wed.–Sat. 10–4, Sun. noon–4.

El Dorado National Forest. The forest covers 676,780 acres of the Sierra Nevada and is bordered by Mother Lode Country and Lake Tahoe. El Dorado is particularly popular for spring and summer sports, but it's a draw for snowmobiling, and downhill and cross-country skiing. Parts of the Pacific Crest National Scenic Trail pass through Eldorado. | 100 Forni Rd. | 530/622–5061 | fax 530/621–5297 | www.r5.fs.fed.us/eldorado | Free | Daily.

★ **Gold Bug Mine.** This is the only municipally owned mine in the U.S. The mine, just east of the Mother Lode vein, has a replica of a stamp mill, which crushes gold-bearing quartz. You can picnic here. | Rte. 50 at Bedford Ave. | 530/642–5232 (reservations) or 530/642–5238 | www.caohwy.com/h/hanggbpm.htm | Mid-Mar.–Apr., weekends noon–4; Apr.–Oct., daily 10–4; Nov., weekdays 10–4, weekends noon–4.

ON THE CALENDAR

JUNE: *El Dorado County Fair.* Enjoy a traditional country fair complete with pie-eating, livestock exhibits, and family entertainment. | 800/457–6279.

JUNE: *Wagon Train Week.* This historical fest celebrates the days when Placerville was called Old Dry Diggin's and was a bustling center of commercial and criminal activity. | 800/457–6279.

OCT.: *Annual Hangtown Jazz Jubilee.* California jazz bands transform historic Main Street into a live stage where good music and food are plentiful the second weekend of October. | 916/853–8555 | www.convmgmt.com/hangtown.

Dining

Cafe Luna. Contemporary. Tucked into the back of the Creekside Place shopping complex is this small restaurant with outdoor tables overlooking a creek. Entrées, which rotate weekly, might include grilled chicken breast with blueberry and pasilla salsa, pasta pomodoro served with or without sautéed prawns, and plank steak with ginger garlic marinade. | 451 Main St. | 530/642–8669 | Closed Sun. No dinner Mon.–Tues. | $23–$39 | AE, D, MC, V.

Lil' Mama D. Carlo's Italian Kitchen. Italian. This comfortable restaurant has a friendly staff and serves large portions of pasta, chicken, and some vegetarian dishes, heavy on the garlic, with lots of tomato. Try anything served in the signature carciofini (artichoke) sauce. | 482 Main St. | 530/626–1612 | Closed Mon.–Tues. No lunch | $12–$22 | MC, V.

Lodging

Best Western Placerville Inn. This three-story hotel 1 mi west of downtown was built in 1988. There's a flower garden in front of the building. Rooms are standard. Cable TV. Pool. Hot tub. Business services. | 6850 Greenleaf Dr. | 530/622–9100 | fax 530/622–9376 | www.bestwestern.com | 105 rooms | $80–$89 | AE, D, DC, MC, V.

Seasons Bed and Breakfast. Built in 1859, this historic home has been transformed into a lovely and relaxing oasis. Decorated with many antiques in an eclectic manner, the main house, two garden cottages, and the wonderful gardens are filled with original artwork. Complimentary breakfast. | 2934 Bedford Ave. | 530/626–4420 | www.theseasons.net | 3 rooms, 1 suite | $115–$125, $135 suite | MC, V.

PLEASANTON

MAP 3, D8

(Nearby towns also listed: Fremont, Livermore)

Discovering Pleasanton's downtown is like biting into the middle of a jelly doughnut. From I–580, Pleasanton (64,000) appears to be a bland wall of concrete shopping malls and business parks. But take the Hopyard Road exit, follow the main drag a couple of miles and you'll encounter a sweet surprise: a Main Street largely untouched since the middle of the 19th century. Pleasanton was settled in the 1850s by Mexican families with Spanish land grants. Alisal, as it was called back then, was known as "the most desperate town in the West"; one of the main routes to the gold fields led through town. Cowboys, farm hands, and miners on the way to the Mother Lode stopped by to stock up on supplies and raise a ruckus in the saloons. Renamed Pleasanton after a Civil War general, it was home to the nation's oldest horse-racing track and was used as the backdrop for the movie *Rebecca of Sunnybrook Farm*.

Modern cowboys still stop at Christensen's Tack Room on Main Street for boots and bridles. At Dean's Café, settle into a retro leatherette booth and eat like a farm hand from a list of 300 omelettes. The Pleasanton Hotel is a restaurant now, but the knotted plank sidewalk in front is a reminder of its Gold Rush-era heyday. Sip espresso at a sidewalk cafés or browse the many antique shops tucked into Victorian buildings.

Information: Pleasanton Chamber of Commerce | 777 Peters Ave., 94566 | 925/846–5858 | www.pleasanton.org.

Attractions

Alameda County Fairgrounds. The fairgrounds are home to the annual county fair and other events throughout the year: auto shows, home and garden fairs, and concerts. The grounds are on the site of one of the oldest racetracks in America, built by Don Augustin Bernal in 1858. | 4501 Pleasanton Ave. | 925/426–7600.

Rapids Waterslide at Shadow Cliffs. Shadow Cliffs Regional Recreation Area, part of the East Bay Regional Parks system, is a former quarry where you can now swim, go boating, picnic, and fish. The water slide has four flumes. | 2500 Stanley Blvd. | 925/846–4900 or 510/562–PARK | $14, parking $4 | June–Aug., daily 10:30–5:30; Sept.–May, weekends 10:30–5:30.

ON THE CALENDAR

MAY–OCT.: *First Wednesday Street Party.* Main Street is closed to auto traffic the first Wednesday of these sunny months for a big public party. Expect live music, food booths, crafts, and temporary beer gardens. Monthly themes include a Cinco de Mayo fiesta in May, Hot Rod Heaven in August, with more than 3,000 custom cars and street rods on display, and Oktoberfest. | 925/484–2199.

JUNE: *Heritage Days.* A beard-growing contest and a baking competition hearken back to old days in town. There's also live music on two stages, arts and crafts vendors, and three beer-and-wine gardens. | 925/426–7600.

JUNE, JULY: *Alameda County Fair.* Rides, an arcade, home and garden displays, livestock shows, a petting zoo, and food booths are all part of the fair fun. | 925/426–7600.

Dining

Casa Madrid. Spanish. Polished wood, white curtains and white tablecloths give a crisp look to this cozy restaurant known for tapas, paella, seafood, and grilled meats. There's live flamenco guitar music Wednesday nights. | 436 Main St. | 925/484–3877 | $10–$19 | AE, D, DC, MC, V.

Claude and Dominique's Bistro. French. This small, inviting bistro has a changing menu that emphasizes fresh seafood—see the sidewalk board for daily offerings. The restaurant, half a block from Main Street, is known for grilled seafood and beef, smoked Norwegian salmon, rabbit, and quail. | 210 Rose Ave. | 925/462–0100 | No lunch | $20–$30 | AE, D, DC, MC, V.

Dean's Cafe. American. The leatherette booths and brown faux-wood paneling haven't changed since the 1950s. The menu is probably very similar, too: omelettes in every variation imaginable (more than 300 are served), hearty farm breakfasts, burgers, and milkshakes. | 620 Main St. | 925/846–4222 | Breakfast also available | No dinner Sun. Closed Mon.–Tues. | $5–$8 | AE, D, DC, MC, V.

Pleasanton Hotel. Contemporary. The wooden sidewalk in front of this restaurant dates to the town's frontier days. House specialties are rack of lamb and five-spice roasted pork tenderloin. You can dine indoors or on an outdoor patio under the shade of a magnolia tree. The Fireside Room and Lounge has live blues and swing music Thursday through Sunday. | 620 Main St. | 925/846–8106 | $12–$24 | AE, D, DC, MC, V.

Stacey's Cafe. Contemporary. Whimsical murals and wrought iron decorate this fun, casual restaurant co-owned by "Dilbert" creator Scott Adams—the party responsible for the humorous menu. There are pasta specials and fresh seafood, including grilled salmon, but the garlic mashed potatoes are particularly memorable. All desserts are homemade. | 310 Main St. | 925/461–3113 | $16–24 | AE, D, DC, MC, V.

Lodging

Courtyard by Marriott. This 1987 well-maintained hotel has a landscaped courtyard, a 3-story building, and some rooms with balconies. It's 4 mi north of downtown with easy access off the highway. Bar. Some refrigerators, cable TV. Pool. Hot tub. Exercise equipment. Laundry facilities. Business services. | 5059 Hopyard Rd. | 925/463–1414 | fax 925/463–0113 | www.marriot.com | 145 rooms, 14 suites | $69–$169 | AE, D, DC, MC, V.

Crowne Plaza Hotel. You'll find reasonably priced rooms at this 6-story hotel 5 mi northwest of downtown. Restaurant, bar. In-room data ports, some refrigerators, cable TV. Pool. Hot tub. Exercise equipment. Laundry facilities. Business services. Pets allowed (fee). | 11950 Dublin Canyon Rd. | 925/847–6000 | fax 925/463–2585 | 244 rooms | $70–$135 | AE, D, DC, MC, V.

Evergreen Inn. This elegant wood-sided B&B is surrounded by oak trees, making it a secluded hideaway. Rooms are individually decorated. You can relax in a hot tub on the wooden deck, which overlooks a waterfall. There are hiking trails on the grounds. Complimentary breakfast. Refrigerators, some in-room hot tubs, cable TV. Hot tub. No smoking. | 9104 Longview Dr. | 925/426–0901 | fax 925/426–9568 | www.evergreen-inn.com | 5 rooms | $135–$225 | AE, MC, V.

Four Points Hotel Pleasanton. At the Hacienda Business Park, 1 mi east of where I–580 intersects I–680, the hotel's 10-acre property contains waterfalls, lagoons, and fountains. Convenient for business travelers. Restaurant, bar, room service. In-room data ports, cable TV. Outdoor pool. Hot tub. Gym. | 5115 Hopyard Rd. | 925/460–8800 | www.fourpoints.com | 214 rooms | $89–$109 | AE, D, DC, MC, V.

Hilton Pleasanton at the Club. Spacious guest rooms and suites cater to business travelers. Restaurant, bar. In-room data ports, some refrigerators, cable TV. Pool. Beauty salon. Tennis. Gym. Business services. Pets allowed. | 7050 Johnson Dr. | 925/463–8000 | fax 925/463–3801 | 290 rooms, 4 suites | $169–$179, $400–$600 suites | AE, D, DC, MC, V.

Plum Tree Inn. This 1906 Victorian B&B offers comfortable rooms, floral wallpaper, four-poster beds, handmade quilts, and reproduction antiques. One suite has French doors opening to a private veranda. There's also a garden terrace, and trees surrounding the property. The inn is one block west of Main St. Dining room, complimentary breakfast. Cable TV. No kids under 16. No smoking. | 262 W. Angela St. | 925/426–9588 | fax 925/417–8737 | www.plumtreeinn.com | 6 suites | $125–145 | AE, MC, V.

Sierra Suites Pleasanton. This hotel is 7 mi from Los Positas Golf Course and 13 mi from Oakland International Airport. The Rapids Waterslides are 2 mi north. In-room data ports, kitchenettes, microwaves, cable TV. Outdoor pool. Gym. Laundry facilities. | 4555 Chabot Dr. | 925/730–0000 | www.sierrasuites.com | 113 rooms | $70–$180 | AE, DC, D, MC, V.

Wyndham Garden Hotel Pleasanton. Across from Stoneridge Mall, this chain hotel has landscaped grounds with a flower garden 3 mi east of downtown. Bar. In-room data ports, some refrigerators, cable TV. Pool. Exercise equipment. Business services. | 5990 Stoneridge Mall Rd. | 925/463–3330 | fax 925/463–3315 | 171 rooms, 2 suites | $69–$139 | AE, D, DC, MC, V.

POINT REYES STATION

(Nearby town also listed: Inverness)

Point Reyes is just an hour north of San Francisco, and its shoreline and outposts seem worlds away from urban stress. Drive through a coastal forest to emerge on rolling dunes veiled in wisps of fog. Between the juncture of hills, the ocean rolls out before you like a shimmering carpet. Here, at Point Reyes National Seashore, you'll find plenty of hiking trails and memorable vistas. You may spy elk, rabbits, and an occasional bobcat. On sunny summer days, traffic to the beaches can back up on the narrow roads, filling the air with smog and impatience, but most of the year unpredictable weather keeps crowds away. If you plan to picnic on Point Reyes—even in summer—be prepared to bundle up, carry a warm drink in a thermos, and a Hibachi to huddle over when the sea breeze kicks up with a piercing chill.

Information: West Marin Chamber of Commerce | Box 1045, 94956 | 415/663–9232 | www.pointreyes.org.

Attractions

Point Reyes National Seashore. Bordering the northern portion of the Golden Gate National Recreation Area, Point Reyes is a great place for birdwatching, hiking, and driving through rugged, rolling grasslands. There are broad white secluded beaches from which you can watch towering breakers crash on shore during winter storms. | Sir Francis Drake Blvd. | 415/663–1092 | Free | Daily dawn–dusk.

Named for explorer Sir Francis Drake, who may have anchored here in 1579, **Drake's Beach** is a semi-sheltered spot that's good for sunbathing, surfing, and swimming in cold water.

Running for miles along the southern coast of Point Reyes Peninsula, **Limantour Beach** is framed by Limantour Spit, at the entrance to Drakes Estero. The spit is a large estuary habitat for hundreds of species of migrating birds. Hiking trails lead through dunes and coastal marshes. From the beach, you can see the chalky cliffs of Drakes Beach, and to the northwest, Chimney Rock.

McClure's Beach is a beautiful beach at the end of a steep ½-mi trail; there are rocky bluffs at each end. Be careful of cliff edges, which can crumble. Swimming is prohibited. Nearby is the trailhead for the 5-mi hike to Tomales Point, through Tule Elk Refuge.

The visitor center at **Point Reyes Lighthouse** offers exhibits on the region's flora, fauna, geography, and the stories of the many ships that have wrecked in the turbulent ocean below. You may be able to see migrating gray whales from atop the 300-step staircase. Open daily dawn–dusk; visitors center Thurs.–Mon. 10–4:30

You can walk for miles along this broad, sandy **South Beach** which runs along the peninsula's northwest coast. It's a good spot for solitude and long walks. It affords one of the best winter storm-watching beaches in California.

ON THE CALENDAR

SEPT.: *Annual Sand Sculpture Contest.* You can watch or, better yet, you can join in this Labor Day weekend event at Drake's Beach where contestants create masterpieces in sand. | 415/669–1534 or 415/669–1250 | www.nps.gov/pore/current.

Dining

Olema Farmhouse Restaurant and Bar. Continental. Housing a restaurant since 1890 (and here since 1845), this building holds lots of memories and mementos from the surrounding West Marin countryside. Check out the vast collection of antique bottles through-out the restaurant, and take note of the glass divider in the front dining room, hand-carved to depict a scene of what the room—and life—was like a century ago. Outside, sit on the broad deck overlooking rural Route 1. On the menu, consider the local Tomales Bay oys-ters, raw on the half-shell, barbecued, or in oyster stew. Or, try San Francisco-style ciop-pino, a seafood stew with crab, shrimp, clams, mussels, and fresh fish in an herb-tomato broth. Pasta and meat dishes are also available. The restaurant also serves a selection of regional microbrewed beer. | 10005 Rte. 1, Olema | 415/663–1264 | www.olemafarmhouse.com | Breakfast available on weekends | $13–$19 | AE, D, DC, MC, V.

Rancho Nicasio. American. On 4 acres of rolling, grassy hills, this restaurant has dark wood walls adorned with trophy animal heads. Prime rib, steaks, and rack of lamb are popular here. Live music weekends. Sunday brunch. | 1 Old Rancheria Rd., Nicasio. | 415/662–2219 | Closed Mon., Tues. Oct.–Apr. | $12–$22 | AE, MC, V.

Station House Café. Continental. This popular family restaurant is known for fresh fish, steak, pasta, and the locally harvested mussels. There's live music on weekends, and open-air dining in the garden. | 11180 Main St. | 415/663–1515 | Breakfast also available | $11–20 | D, MC, V.

Lodging

English Oak. Built in 1919 as a private home, this house and cottage, an inn since 1984, is at the corner of Bear Valley Road and Route 1 in Olema. The house's three rooms, with names like "Scottish Heather" and "English Rose," reflect the area's lush hills and meadows, with relaxed country touches throughout. Look for hand-embroidery and chintz, and scattered antiques. The cottage has Mayan blankets on the queen bed and double futon, and an African print and Moroccan mirror on the walls. The cottage, with a full kitchen, is a good choice for families. Complimentary breakfast. No room phones, no TV in some rooms. No smok-ing. | 88 Bear Valley Rd. Olema | 415/663–1777 | www.anenglishoak.com | 3 rooms, 1 cottage | $90–$120, $120–$160 cottage | MC, V.

Point Reyes Country Inn. Less than 1 mi from the equestrian trailhead, this southwestern-style inn on 4 acres of rolling pastures caters to horse enthusiasts. Rooms have decks or balconies above a garden. There are two beachfront cottages, and a loft above the two stu-dio aparments which can be rented together as a suite. Complimentary breakfast, dining room. No room phones, no TV. | 12050 Rte. 1. | 415/663–9696 | fax 415/663–8888 | www.ptreyescountryinn.com | 6 rooms, 2 apartments, 2 cottages | $125–$160, $95–$120 apart-ments, $185–$195 cottages.

Point Reyes Seashore Lodge. This lodge, built in 1988, has spacious, comfortable rooms with pine-board paneling. There's a billiard parlor with an antique pool table, conference rooms, and English gardens on the grounds. Many of the rooms have fireplaces, and all have views of the gardens or Inverness Ridge. You can walk to Olema shops and cafés from here, but the beach is 5 mi. Complimentary Continental breakfast. Some in-room hot tubs. TV in common area. Library. No pets. No smoking. | 10021 Rte. 1, Olema | 415/663–9000 | fax 415/663–9030 | 17 rooms, 3 suites, 2 cottages | $125–$165, $205–$215 suites, $295 cot-tages.

Ridgetop Inn and Cottages. The inn's main house and cottages are on 2 acres overlook-ing rolling farmland and Point Reyes National Seashore. The six rooms in the main house overlook the bucolic valley or the garden; some have an outdoor seating area. Or, grab a good book and relax by the fire in the house's common room. On bright sunny days, enjoy breakfast in the patio garden. Ridgetop Cottage has a private deck, a loft with queen bed, kitchenette, fireplace, and private bath. Olema Cottage has one bedroom, full kitchen, and a living room with a fireplace. Complimentary breakfast. No smoking. | 9876 Sir Francis Drake Blvd., Olema | 415/663–1500 | fax 415/663–8308 | www.ridgetopinn.com | 6 rooms, 2 cottages | $75–$145, $110–$150 cottages.

POMONA

(Nearby towns also listed: Ontario, Pasadena, Rancho Cucamonga)

Pomona (pop. 149,000) is home to the handsome campus of Cal State Polytechnic University. Cereal magnate W. K. Kellogg donated a section of his ranch, now known as the Kellogg Arabian Horse Center, to the campus, to further the breeding of Arabians. Pomona is also the home of the Los Angeles County Fair, one public area in southern California where you can see redwood trees.

Information: **Pomona Chamber of Commerce** | 485 N. Garey Ave., 91767 | 909/622–1256 | www.pomonachamber.org.

Attractions

Adobe de Palomares. This 13-room house built in 1854 was the home of Don Ygnacio Palomares, who owned much of the land that is now eastern Los Angeles County. By 1934, the site was in ruins, but the City of Pomona restored it to its original grandeur. You can also visit the gardens and blacksmith shop. | 491 E. Arrow Hwy. | 909/623–2198 | www.osb.net/pomona | $2 | Sun. 2–5 or by appointment.

California State Polytechnic University, Pomona. This university, known for its science and agriculture programs, is on beautifully landscaped grounds. | 3801 W. Temple Ave. | 909/869–7659 | fax 909/869–4848 | www.csupomona.edu | Free.

The **Kellogg Arabian Horse Center** is a breeding facility and showcase for Arabian horses. There are horse shows October to June on the first Sunday of the month. | 3801 W. Temple Ave. | 909/869–2224 | fax 909/869–4856 | Free | Weekdays 9–4.

ON THE CALENDAR

SEPT., OCT.: *Los Angeles County Fair.* Billed by promoters as the largest county fair in America, this huge event features quality entertainment, quarter horse racing, livestock exhibits and judging, floral displays, home arts, a gigantic midway and food. | 909/623–3111.

Dining

D'Antonio's. Italian. Enjoy fresh pasta, pizza, and chicken dishes in this comfortable, home-style restaurant, or get it to go. An outdoor patio helps you forget you're in a mall. There are 15 different pastas offered (many with fresh seafood). Try the fettuccini Caruso (chicken with cream sauce and a touch of marinara served over pasta) or the veal Nantua (veal and shrimp served scampi-style). | 808 N. Diamond Bar Blvd. | 909/860–3663 | $9–$25 | AE, D, DC, MC, V.

Lodging

Sheraton Suites Fairplex. This hotel ½ mi east of Pomona has landscaped grounds with rose bushes. It's directly adjacent to the LA County Fairgrounds. Restaurant. In-room data ports, minibars, microwaves, refrigerators, cable TV. Pool. Exercise equipment. Laundry facilities. Business services. Pets allowed. | 601 W. McKinley Ave. | 909/622–2220 | fax 909/622–3577 | 247 rooms | $189 | AE, D, DC, MC, V.

Shilo Hilltop Suites Pomona. This hotel has rooms with balconies or patios in each room to enjoy mountain views from this hilltop perch. Restaurant, bar, room service. In-room data ports, microwaves, refrigerators, cable TV. Pool. Exercise equipment. Laundry facilities. Business services, airport shuttle. | 3101 Temple Ave. | 909/598–7666 | fax 909/598–5654 | 129 rooms | $95–$175 | AE, D, DC, MC, V.

Shilo Hotel–Pomona. This hotel, across the street from the Shilo Hilltop Suites Pomona *(see above)*, also has mountain views, but is slightly more affordable. It has a new fitness center with a spa. Restaurant, room service. In-room data ports, microwaves, refrigerators, cable TV. Pool. Exercise equipment. Laundry facilities. Business services, airport shuttle. Pets allowed. | 3200 Temple Ave. | 909/598–0073 | fax 909/594–5862 | 160 rooms | $72–$114 | AE, D, DC, MC, V.

PORTERVILLE

MAP 4, H11

(Nearby towns also listed: Kernville, Three Rivers, Visalia)

This residential and agricultural town of 55,000 is one of the gateways to the southern Sierra Nevada mountains, Kings Canyon and Sequoia National Parks. Lying at the base of the mountains, it's surrounded by the miles and miles of fields and fruit orchards of the Central Valley. It was originally a stop on the stagecoach line to Los Angeles.

Information: **Porterville Chamber of Commerce** | 36 W. Cleveland Ave., 93257 | 559/784–7502 | www.ocsnet.net/porterville.

Attractions
Porterville Historical Museum. Learn about the early days of Porterville in this museum housed in a 1913 Southern Pacific passenger station. You can see vintage recreations of a dentist's office, a drug store, and an attorney's office, and china, furniture, and Native American Indian artifacts. | 257 N. D St. | 559/784–2053 | fax 559/784–4009 | $1 | Thurs.–Sat. 10–4.

ON THE CALENDAR
APR.: *Porterville Iris Festival.* This 1-day festival on Main Street celebrates Porterville's official flower, with iris garden tours, craft and food booths, and live entertainment. | 559/784–7502 | www.irisfestival.porterville.com.

Dining
Cookie Jar Cafe. American. This small restaurant near the courthouse serves up hearty breakfast and lunch dishes like biscuits and gravy, huevos rancheros, and ½ pound hamburgers. | 234 N. Main St. | 559/781–1107 | Reservations not accepted | Closed Sunday. No dinner | $4–$7 | No credit cards.

Lodging
Best Western Porterville Inn. Rooms at this hotel have views of the rosebush courtyard, or the mountains. Restaurant, complimentary breakfast, room service. In-room data ports, refrigerators, cable TV. Pool. Hot tub. Exercise equipment. Laundry facilities. Business services. Pets allowed. | 350 W. Montgomery Ave. | 559/781–7411 | fax 559/781–8910 | www.bestwestern.com | 116 rooms | $70 | AE, D, DC, MC, V.

Springville Inn. If you head northeast 17 mi from town, into the foothills of the Sierra Nevadas you'll find this inn that captures the feeling of the Old West, as it did when the first guests arrived in 1911. The guest rooms, some of which have mountain views, are furnished in a country style with antiques, pine wood, and handmade quilts. Restaurant, complimentary Continental breakfast. Cable TV, room phones. Golf privileges. Laundry service. Business services. | 35634 Rte. 190, Springville | 800/484–3466 | fax 559/539–7502 | info@springvilleinn.com | www.springvilleinn.com | 8 rooms, 2 suites | $85–$105, $165–$185 suites | AE, D, MC, V.

PORT HUENEME

(Nearby towns also listed: Camarillo, Oxnard, Simi Valley, Thousand Oaks)

Port Hueneme (pronounced "why-nee-mee") is a quiet beachtown of 22,000 along Ventura County's Gold Coast. The town was founded by entrepreneur Thomas Bard in 1865 as an outlet for export of crops produced by the surrounding ranches. Not far away, the Oxnard brothers were busy growing beets for their American Beet Sugar Company; their enterprise was the nucleus of nearby Oxnard incorporating as a town in 1903. The two cities share a symbiotic relationship to this day, the smaller city of Port Hueneme being almost an appendage to the coastal Oxnard.

Information: Port Hueneme Chamber of Commerce | 220 N. Market St., 93041 | 805/488–2023 | www.huenemechamber.com.

Attractions

CEC/Seabee Museum. This warehouse-size collection of naval memorabilia includes uniforms, photos, relics, and weaponry from the construction work done by the Seabees in World War II, and the Korean and Vietnam wars. This group built the landing strips, airports, housing, roads and facilities the troops used while fighting the wars. | 4111 San Pedro St. | 805/982–5163 or 805/982–5167 | www.cbcph.navy.mil/museum | Free | Mon.–Sat. 9–4, Sun. 12:30–4:30.

Port Hueneme Historical Museum. The museum houses an array of Port Hueneme-related items, including 19th-century photos of the town, Chumash Indian artifacts, and a collection of 1,500 salt and pepper sets. | 220 W. Market St. | 805/488–2023 | fax 805/488–6993 | www.huenemechamber.com | Free | Mon.–Fri. 9–4.

ON THE CALENDAR

OCT.: *Port Hueneme Harbor Days.* You can enjoy live entertainment, pony rides, kite demonstrations, food booths, an arts and crafts festival, and a parade at this annual event. | 805/487–4470 | www.harbordays.org.

Dining

Uncle Herb's Restaurant and Pancake House. American. Family-run for 34 years, breakfast, lunch, and dinner are served all day. Fresh strawberry-filled pancakes are popular, as is southern fried chicken. Ask for the giant hot cinnamon roll as a side dish. Kids' menu. No smoking. | 5141 S. Saviers Rd., Oxnard | 805/488–5515 | Closed Mon. | $6.95–$14.25 | AE, D, MC, V.

Lodging

Casa Via Mar Inn and Tennis Club. This cozy two-story Spanish-style hotel 1 ½ mi east of the beaches offers reasonable rates. Upper level rooms have balconies, lower level rooms have patios. Flowers surround the building. Complimentary breakfast. Kitchenettes, in-room VCRs (with movies). Pool. Hot Tub. 6 tennis courts. Business services. | 377 W. Channel Islands Blvd. | 805/984–6222 | fax 805/984–9490 | 74 rooms | $67–$78 | AE, D, DC, MC, V.

Channel Islands Inn and Suites. This hacienda-style hotel located 1 mi east of Port Hueneme has spacious, modern rooms accented with reproduction Shaker and Mission wood furniture. Complimentary breakfast. In-room data ports, minibars, microwaves, refrigerators, cable TV, in-room VCRs. Outdoor pool. Hot tub. Gym. Video games. Laundry facilities. | 1001 E. Channel Islands Blvd., Oxnard | 805/487–7755 or 800/344–5998 | fax 805/486–1374 | info@channelislandsinn.com | www.channelislandsinn.com | 92 rooms | $89 | AE, D, DC, MC, V.

Country Inn at Port Hueneme. Over-size rooms at this three-story motel near the ocean have wood paneling and nautical artwork. The inn is one block from the beach, and ½ mi east of downtown. Complimentary breakfast. In-room data ports, some kitchenettes, refrigerators, cable TV. Pool. Hot tub. Laundry facilities. Business services. | 350 E. Hueneme Rd. | 805/986–5353 or 800/447–3529 | fax 805/986–4399 | 135 rooms | $119–$169 | AE, D, DC, MC, V.

QUINCY

(Nearby towns also listed: Chester, Chico)

This town was a center for mining and logging in the 1850s. Today, the community of 5,000 in the High Sierras is a popular starting point for visits to the Lassen National Park and Forest. Quincy is also the county seat of Plumas County, and site of California's oldest county fair.

Information: Plumas County Visitors Bureau | Box 4120, Rte. 70, 95971 | 800/326–2247 | www.plumas.ca.us.

Attractions

Plumas County Museum. Exhibits display the history of the area since the 1850s. Highlights include Maidu Indian artifacts, as well as railroad, logging and mining exhibits. A neighboring Victorian house is furnished with museum pieces. | 500 Jackson St. | 530/283–6320 | fax 530/283–6080 | $1 | May–Sept. weekdays 8–5, weekends 10–4; Oct., daily 8–5; Nov.–Apr., weekdays 8–5.

Bucks Lake Recreation Area. Bucks Lake, 17 mi southwest of Quincy, at an elevation of 5,200 ft, has a broad range of outdoor, year-round recreation options. Its 17 mi of shoreline attract anglers and water sports enthusiasts in summer. Hiking and horseback riding are also popular. The winter snow brings snowmobilers and cross-country skiers who take advantage of the unplowed access roads. | Bucks Lake Road | 800/326–2247 | fax 530/283–5465 | www.plumas.ca.us | Free | Dusk–dawn.

Plumas National Forest. This 1,162,863-acre forest stretches from the Cascade Mountains in the north to Sierra Nevada in the south. Come here for spectacular natural scenery and gold country history. You can also hike, canoe, and go tubing and white-water rafting. Quincy is in the heart of the National Forest land; Rtes. 70 and 89, which transverse Quincy, offer many access points into the forest. | 159 Lawrence St. | 530/283–2050 | fax 530/283–4156 | www.r5.fs.fed.us/plumas | Free | Office open weekdays 8–4:30.

ON THE CALENDAR

AUG.: *Plumas County Fair.* This old-fashioned county fair has livestock showings, baking contests, a carnival, and more. | 530/283–6272.

OCT.: *Mountain Harvest Festival.* The lawn of the Plumas County Courthouse in downtown Quincy is the site for this festival, featuring a pumpkin carving contest, demonstrations of apple pressing and blacksmith work, and winetasting. The festival usually takes place the second Saturday of the month. | 530/283–3402 or 800/326–2247 | www.plumasarts.com.

Dining

Moon's. Italian. Locals are wild about the daily specials in this restored 1930 restaurant. It sports a verdant outdoor garden patio. Dishes include Tuscan pasta, and, for dessert, the homemade chocolate Kahlua pie. | 497 Lawrence St. | 530/283–0765 | Closed Mon. No lunch | $6–$21 | AE, D, MC, V.

Sweet Lorraine's Good Food Good Feelings. Contemporary. Hearty fare such as Cajun meatloaf with roasted garlic mashed potatoes and almond-crusted chicken is served upstairs in the intimate, candlelit dining room or in the more casual downstairs bar and dining area, where local artwork (some of it for sale) is displayed on the walls. | 384 Main St. | 530/283–5300 | Reservations recommended Fri.–Sun. | Closed Sun. | $9–$20 | MC, V.

Lodging

Feather Bed. When you see the goose weathervane atop the gable, you know you have found this 1893 Queen Anne Victorian B&B. Furnished with Victorian period pieces, the five guest rooms in the main house have iron beds and clawfoot tubs. There are two private guest cottages, both with fireplaces and outside decks. Fresh berries, herbs, and vegetables from the backyard gardens are used to create the hearty breakfasts, with fruit smoothies and frittatas as staple menu items. Homemade fudge and cookies are always available during the day. Complimentary breakfast. Room phones. Cable TV. Bicycles. Airport shuttle. | 542 Jackson St. | 800/696–8624 | fax 530/283–0167 | info@featherbed-inn.com | www.featherbed-inn.com | 5 rooms, 1 guest house, 1 cottage | $85–$136 | AE, D, DC, MC, V.

Lariat Lodge. This small, quiet, hotel was built in the 1970s out of cinder blocks. It's 2 mi west of downtown, near Plumas National Forest. Complimentary Continental breakfast. Some refrigerators, cable TV. Pool. | 2370 E. Main St. | 530/283–1000 or 800/999–7199 | fax 530/283–2154 | 20 rooms | $44–$75 | AE, D, MC, V.

Ranchito. Rustic Spanish Style. Exposed log rafters make up the exterior of this motel 1 ½ mi east of downtown. The quiet, 2½-acre grounds are mainly wooded, with a brook running through it. Picnic area. Some kitchenettes, cable TV. | 2020 E. Main St. | 530/283–2265 | fax 530/283–2316 | 34 rooms | $51 | AE, D, MC, V.

RANCHO BERNARDO

MAP 4, K16

(Nearby towns also listed: Del Mar, Escondido, Rancho Santa Fe)

This suburb of 55,000, within the city limits of San Diego, lies alongside I–15 about 25 mi north of the city. It's primarily a bedroom community centering around the famous Rancho Bernardo Inn Resort. In recent years, however, businesses such as Sony and IBM have opened facilities in the area.

Information: **Rancho Bernardo Chamber of Commerce** | 11650 Iberia Place, Suite 220, San Diego, 92128 | 858/487–1767 | www.ranchobernardochamber.com.

Attractions

Bernardo Winery. Experience San Diego's oldest operating winery, founded in 1889. There's a wine tasting room, wine sales, and a collection of boutiques and shops on the grounds. The winery also makes and sells cold pressed olive oil. | 13330 Paseo Del Verano Norte | 858/487–1866 | fax 858/673–5376 | www.bernardowinery.com | Free | Daily, 9–5.

ON THE CALENDAR

OCT.: *Arts and Crafts Fair.* The Bernardo Winery hosts this annual event, which includes crafts from native California artisans, food, and wine tasting. | 858/487–1866 | www.bernardowinery.com.

Dining

Anthony's Fish Grotto. Seafood. This small chain of casual, family-friendly restaurants is popular for its quality and good-size portions. The house specialties are the Alaskan halibut with an orange mint glaze, shrimp scampi with linguine and a basil cherry sauce, and the fresh grilled or broiled shark. | 11666 Avena Pl | 858/451–2070 | $8–$20 | AE, D, DC, MC, V.

Cafe Luna. Italian. The setting is low-key and intimate in this candlelit café with exposed brick. The house specialty is tournedos gorgonzola—two petit filets mignon, pan-seared with a cabernet demi-glace and topped with mushroom caps and gorgonzola. Pastas and desserts are homemade daily. | 11040 Rancho Carmel Dr. | 858/673–0077 | Reservations highly recommended | Closed Sun. | $10–$22 | AE, D, DC, MC, V.

Carver's. Steak. Dried-leaf and bark arrangements adorn the entrance to this upscale restaurant whose walls and tables are made of finished wood. House specialties here include prime rib and filet mignon. Seafood and chicken are also available. | 11940 Bernardo Plaza Dr. | 858/485–1262 | Reservations recommended | $17–$38 | AE, D, DC, MC, V.

El Bizcocho. French. This elegant restaurant in the Rancho Bernardo Inn, next door to the golf course, is considered one of San Diego's finest for classical and contemporary French cuisine and outstanding service. Dishes such as the table-side carved roast duckling for two or the medallions of veal loin in morel sauce are the main attractions. The five-course chef's tasting menu carefully pairs daily specialties with wines from around the world. Pianist nightly. | 17550 Bernardo Oaks Dr. | 858/675–8500 | fax 858/675–8443 | Reservations essential | Jacket required | Brunch also available Sunday. No lunch | $14–$20, $58 tasting menu | AE, D, DC, MC, V.

French Market Grill. Contemporary. This grill is in a mall, but has a stylish dark-wood dining room, and an outdoor patio with tropical plants and live music Tuesdays. The fare is seasonal, but often includes variations on lamb shank and bouillabaisse. | Ralph's Shopping Center, 15717 Bernardo Heights Pkwy. | 858/485–8055 | $15–$21 | AE, D, DC, MC, V.

Lodging

Doubletree Golf Resort. This three-story California-style resort is surrounded by 130 hilly green acres of golf course, 17 mi from downtown San Diego. All rooms have a patio or balcony. The resort offers many recreational activities on the well-landscaped grounds. Restaurant. Bar. In-room data ports, cable TV. 2 pools. Health club. 5 tennis courts, 18-hole golf course. Laundry facilities. Business services. | 14455 Penasquitos Dr. | 858/672–9100 | fax 858/672–9187 | 174 rooms | $119–$162 | AE, D, DC, MC, V.

Four Points by Sheraton Rancho Bernardo. The spacious rooms here attract both business travelers and families. Restaurant, complimentary breakfast. In-room data ports, cable TV. Outdoor pool. Hot tub. Gym. Laundry service. Business services. | 11611 Bernardo Plaza Ct. | 858/485–9250 | fax 858/451–7948 | www.fourpoints.com | 209 rooms | $109–$179 | AE, DC, MC, V.

Holiday Inn Rancho Bernardo. A two-story and a three-story building have comfortable and reasonably priced accommodations. The outdoor pool area has a nicely furnished patio. The hotel is off I–15 at the Bernardo Center Dr. exit. Restaurant, bar, complimentary breakfast. In-room data ports, cable TV. Pool. Exercise equipment. Video games. Laundry facilities. Business services. | 17065 W. Bernardo Dr. | 858/485–6530 | fax 858/485–7819 | 179 rooms | $99–$139 | AE, D, DC, MC, V.

La Quinta Inn. This attractive and reasonably priced four-story chain motel is in a suburban area near shopping. Complimentary Continental Breakfast. Cable TV. Pool. Video games. Pets allowed. | 10185 Paseo Montril | 858/484–8800 | fax 858/538–0476 | 120 rooms | $75–$85 | AE, D, DC, MC, V.

Radisson Suite Hotel. Its proximity to the commercial district makes this three-story hotel 20 min north of San Diego a favorite of business travelers. Restaurant, bar, complimentary Continental breakfast, room service. In-room data ports, minibars, cable TV. Pool. Exercise equipment. Laundry facilities. Business services. Pets allowed. | 11520 W. Bernardo Ct. | 858/451–6600 | fax 858/592–0253 | 181 suites | $109–$129 | AE, D, DC, MC, V.

Ramada Limited Poway. This hotel, 8 mi south of Rancho Bernardo, is 1½ mi east of I–15 at the Poway Rd. exit and is 10 mi from many northern San Diego attractions. Complimentary Continental breakfast. Some in-room hot tubs, cable TV. Outdoor pool. Hot tub. Laundry service. Business services. | 12448 Poway Rd., Poway | 858/748–7311 | fax 858/679–2717 | www.ramada.com | 47 rooms | $79–$89 | AE, D, DC, MC, V.

Rancho Bernardo Inn. In the foothills of North County, 25 mi north of the San Diego airport, this Mission-style golf and tennis resort offers an ambience rich with tradition—elegant, but not pretentious. Details like Spanish fountains, arched doorways, and, in the lobby, ongoing jigsaw puzzles by the fireplace create a welcoming feel. The spacious rooms have earth tones, large bouquets of fresh flowers, plush easy chairs, and spanish-tile bathrooms. 2 restaurants, bars, complimentary breakfast, room service. In-room data ports, in-room safes, cable TV. 2 pools. Hot tub, massage. Driving range, 3 18-hole golf courses, 1 27-hole golf course, putting green, tennis. Gym, volleyball, bicycles. Kids' programs. Business services, airport shuttle. | 17550 Bernardo Oaks Dr. | 858/487–1611 or 800/542–6096 | fax 858/675–8501 | www.jcresorts.com | 232 rooms, 53 suites | $299, $319–$1100 suties | AE, D, DC, MC, V.

Rancho Bernardo Travelodge. This simple motel is centered in a corporate area, and offers affordable rates. Microwaves, refrigerators, cable TV. Pool. Pets allowed. | 16929 W. Bernardo Dr. | 858/487–0445 | fax 858/673–2062 | www.travelodge.com | 49 rooms | $60–$135 | AE, D, DC, MC, V.

Residence Inn Carmel Mountain Ranch. At this all-suite chain hotel, the spacious rooms resemble modern apartments. Restaurant, complimentary Continental breakfast. In-room data ports, kitchenettes, refrigerators, cable TV, in-room VCRs. Outdoor pool. Gym. Babysitting. Laundry facilities, laundry service. Business services. | 11002 Rancho Carmel Dr. | 858/673–1900 | fax 858/673–1913 | www.residenceinn.com | 124 suites | $169–$239 suites | AE, D, DC, MC, V.

RANCHO CORDOVA

MAP 3, E7

(Nearby towns also listed: Davis, Sacramento)

Rancho Cordova is an eastern satellite town of Sacramento with a population of 93,461. The town, served by busy Folsom Boulevard, clings to the south side of the American River. Many hostelries here cater to the region's legion of corporate headquarters and regional offices and to people visiting nearby Mather Field Air Force Base.

Information: Rancho Cordova Chamber of Commerce | 3328 Mather Field Rd., 95670 | 916/361–8700 | www.ranchocordova.org.

Dining

Brookfield's. American. All the beef served at this coffee shop is Black Angus. The popular ranchhouse burger and the chicken-fried steak can be finished off with a hot fudge brownie sundae. You can eat outside on the patio or inside. Kids' menu. Beer and wine only. No smoking. | 11135 Folsom Blvd. | 916/638–2046 | Breakfast also available | $6.50–$9.95 | AE, D, DC, MC, V.

Slocum House. Contemporary. Originally a private residence, this stately home has been converted into a restaurant. You can choose to dine indoors or outside on the patio on a hilltop of flowers and ancient maple trees. The most popular dishes are king salmon, live Maine lobster, grilled filet mignon and the homemade chocolate mint cake. Sunday brunch. No smoking. | 7992 California Ave., Fair Oaks | 916/961–7211 | Closed Mon. | $19.95–$39.95 | AE, D, DC, MC, V.

Lodging

Best Inn and Suites. Built in the 1980s, this hotel is 12 mi east of Sacramento, and a ½ mi from Mather Field Air Force Base. At U.S. 50, exit at Mather Field. Complimentary Continental breakfast. Some refrigerators, cable TV. Pool. Hot tub. Laundry facilities. Free parking. Pets allowed (fee). | 3240 Mather Field Rd. | 916/363–3344 | fax 916/362–0903 | 95 rooms, 15 suites | rooms $69–$89, suites $89–$129 | AE, D, DC, MC, V.

Best Western Heritage Inn. This three-story hotel, 10 mi east of Sacramento, is close to restaurants and shopping. Restaurant, bar, complimentary breakfast, room service. Some refrigerators, in-room hot tubs, cable TV. Pool. | 11269 Point East Dr. | 916/635–4040 | fax 916/635–7198 | www.bestwestern.com | 125 rooms | $89 | AE, D, DC, MC, V.

Courtyard by Marriott. Built in 1988, this three-story hotel is 8 mi north of downtown Rancho Cordova. Restaurant, bar. Some refrigerators, cable TV. Pool. Exercise equipment. Laundry facilities. No pets. | 10683 White Rock Rd. | 916/638–3800 | fax 916/638–6776 | www.marriot.com | 144 rooms | $69–$119 | AE, D, DC, MC, V.

Days Inn. Cream colored Spanish-style stucco highlights the facade of this three-story hotel. The property, 2 mi east from a downtown shopping center, is off highway 50. Complimentary Continental breakfast. Cable TV. Pool. Laundry Facilities. | 10800 Olson Dr. | 916/638–2500 or 800/329–7466 | fax 916/638–2672 | www.daysinn.com | 158 rooms, 42 suites | $59, $62 suites | AE, D, DC, MC, V.

Hallmark Inn. This three-story hotel complex is close to many Rancho Cordova and Folsom corporations including Bank of America, Intel, and Kemper Insurance. One or two bedroom suites are available with a choice of queen or king-sized beds. Bar, complimentary breakfast. Some kitchenettes, some microwaves, some refrigerators, some in-room hot tubs, cable TV. Outdoor pool. Spa. Exercise equipment. Laundry facilities, laundry service. | 11260 Point East Dr. | 916/638–4141 | fax 916/638–4287 | www.hallmarksuites.com | 127 suites | $119–$165 | AE, D, DC, MC, V.

Inns of America. Surrounded by commercial Rancho Cordova, this Spanish-style stucco hotel was built in 1988 at Route 50 off Hazel Avenue. Aerojet is adjacent to the property; Folsom Lake is 2 mi south. Complimentary Continental breakfast. Cable TV. Pool. Pets allowed. | 12249 Folsom Blvd. | 916/351–1213 | fax 916/351–1817 | www.innsofamerica.com | 124 rooms | $70 | AE, MC, V.

Sheraton. Built in 1986 off the Sunrise Road exit of Route 50, this structure towers 11 stories over the surrounding suburban area. Restaurant, bar. In-room data ports, cable TV. Outdoor pool. Hot tub. Exercise equipment. Business services. No pets. | 11211 Point East Dr. | 916/638–1100 | fax 916/638–5803 | www.sheraton.com | 245 rooms, 17 suites | $89–$179 rooms, $205–$325 suites | AE, D, DC, MC, V.

RANCHO CUCAMONGA

MAP 4, J14

(Nearby towns also listed: Arcadia, Corona, Glendale, Los Angeles, Pasadena, Riverside)

"Sandy Place" was the original name the Serrano and Gabrielino Indians hung on the Inland Empire locale of Rancho Cucamonga, 37 mi east of downtown Los Angeles. This industrial, commercial, and residential development with a population of 125,585 displaced what was largely an agrarian settlement.

Information: **Rancho Cucamonga City Hall.** | 10500 Civic Center Drive, 91730 | 909/477–2700 | www.ci.rancho-cucamonga.ca.us.

Attractions

Casa de Rancho Cucamonga (Rains House). In 1839 Tabrucio Tapia was granted 13,000 acres of land by the Mexican governor of California. He started the Cucamonga Ranch and this is the landmark house from Cucamonga's days as a ranching community. | 8810 Hemlock St. | 909/989–4970 | Free | Wed.–Sat 10–5, Sun. 1–5.

OCT.: *Grape Harvest Festival.* These events celebrate the local wine-making tradition and grape harvest with pie-eating contests, arts and crafts, games, grape stomps, live music, food, and beer and wine tastings. Held at the Rancho Cucamonga Epicenter on Rochester Avenue, admission is $3 and parking is $2. | 909/984–2458 | www.ranchochamber.org/fest.

Dining

Magic Lamp Inn. Continental. Built in 1955, the restaurant and lounge has dark cherry wood paneling and hurricane lamps, and a fireplace. You can dine outside. Try the pink trout served with roasted red pepper, prime rib, or porterhouse steak. The wine cellar has more than 300 different vintages. Lunch buffet (Tue.–Fri.). Live entertainment Wed.–Sat. Kids' menu, early-bird suppers. No smoking. | 8189 E. Foothill Blvd. | 909/981–8659 | Closed Mon. | $10–$24 | AE, DC, MC, V.

Sycamore Inn. Continental. Established in 1921, the restaurant has Sycamore trees, a mammoth fireplace, and English gas lamps that give off a soft glow. The menu is highlighted by steak dishes, roast rib, hazelnut crusted Atlantic salmon, and "Mammy Hanna's" original fried chicken recipe with mashed potatoes and corn fritters. The inn has more than 600 varieties of wine which are stored in three temperature-controlled wine cellars. No smoking. | 8318 Foothill Blvd. | 909/982–1104 | No breakfast. No lunch | $15.95–$39.95 | AE, D, DC, MC, V.

Lodging

Best Western Heritage Inn. This six-story hotel is across the street from a shopping center and 1 mi west of the Rancho Cucamonga Epicenter. From Route 16 take the Foothill exit; from I–10, Haven. Restaurant, complimentary Continental breakfast. Refrigerators, cable TV. Pool. Hot tub. Exercise equipment. Business services, free parking. | 8179 Spruce Ave. | 909/466–1111 or 800/682–7829 | fax 909/466–3876 | sales4bwhi@aol.com | www.bestwestern.com | 116 rooms | $74–$109 | AE, D, DC, MC, V.

RANCHO MIRAGE

MAP 4, K15

(Nearby towns also listed: Desert Hot Springs, Palm Desert, Palm Springs)

Sophisticated and exclusive, this residential golf community labels itself the "Playground of Presidents." But heads of state weren't the only ones to hang out in this desert community: "Old Blue Eyes" himself, Frank Sinatra, was known to frequent the town. Today, the main drag is named after him. Unfortunately for visitors, much of the town's most spectacular scenery is hidden behind the walls of the gated estates and country clubs. But there's still an air of luxury and opulence, even outside the private enclaves. Though many of the rich and famous call the town home, some come only for a brief stay–at the Betty Ford Center, world-renowned for its alcohol and drug addiction programs.

Information:Chamber of Commerce | Cucamonga City Hall, 42-464 Rancho Mirage La., 92270 | 760/568–9351 | info@ranchomirage.org | www.ranchomirage.org.

Attractions

Children's Discovery Museum. This hands-on museum is an activities center specially designed to inspire and promote intellectual curiosity and self-expression through inventive and interactive exhibits. Activities include painting a car, dressing up in grown-ups' clothes, and a fix-it area complete with tools. | 71701 Gerald Ford Dr. | 760/321–0602 | $5 | Tues.–Sat. 10–5, Sunday noon–5.

ON THE CALENDAR

MAR.: *30th Annual Nabisco Championship.* This annual women's golf tournament is held at the Mission Hills Country Club and is a part of the National LPGA (Ladies Professional Golfing Association) Tour. Tournament and Clubhouse Badge admission packages are offered at varying prices. | 34600 Mission Hills Dr. | Tournament $20–$30, Clubhouse badge $60–$70 | 760/324–9400.

Dining

Kobe Japanese Steak House. Japanese. At this local favorite 6 mi east of downtown, wooden tables surround open grills where chefs slice, dice, set the food flying, and dish out stir-fried meats, seafood, and vegetables as soon as they're cooked. The mood is that of a gracious country inn, with paintings and antiques from Japan. Fri.–Sat. Kid's menu, early-bird suppers. | 69-838 Hwy. 111 | 760/324–1717 | No lunch | $20–$25 | AE, DC, MC, V.

Las Casuelas Nuevas. Mexican. Hundreds of artifacts from Guadalajara lend a festive charm to the dining room of this casual restaurant with a leafy patio. Seafood fajitas and crab enchiladas join the standard Mexican menu of tacos, enchiladas, and tamales. Margaritas in every color of the rainbow are also available. Sunday brunch. Guitarist and harpist Mon.–Thur., mariachi music on weekends. No smoking. | 70-050 Rte. 111 | 760/328–8844 | $9–$18 | AE, D, MC, V.

Shame on the Moon. Contemporary. The kitchen at this small bistro turns out fare like roasted salmon with horseradish crust, bourbon-glazed calf's liver with mushroom-and-shallot compote and apple-smoked bacon, roast duck with ginger-port sauce and dried fruit. No smoking. | 69-950 Frank Sinatra Dr. | 760/324–5515 | Reservations essential | No lunch | $27–$36 | AE, D, DC, MC, V.

Lodging

★ **Marriott's Rancho Las Palmas Resort.** At this 240-acre lodging complex built in 1979, two-story red tile-roof haciendas are scattered around a golf course landscaped with lakes and gardens. At 600 square ft, guest rooms are unusually large; oak balconies and archways embellish the buildings. The pool has a 100-ft water slide, and there's a Starbucks on the premises, along with the Cabrillo restaurant. Exit Route 111 at Bob Hope Drive. 2 restaurants, bar, room service. In-room data ports, some refrigerators, room service, cable TV. 2 outdoor pools, wading pool. Spa. Beauty salon, hot tub. Driving range, 27-hole golf course, putting green, tennis. Health club, bicycles. Kids' programs, playground. Laundry facilities. Business services. No pets. | 41000 Bob Hope Dr., | 760/568–2727 | fax 760/568–5845 | rlp-bus@earthlink.com | www.marriott.com/marriott/pspca | 450 rooms | $320–$370 rooms, $500–$800 suites | AE, D, DC, MC, V.

★ **Ritz-Carlton, Rancho Mirage.** Luxe is the operative word at this three-building resort in the foothills of the Santa Rosa mountains, built in 1988. Surroundings are elegant: gleaming polished brass and marble, original art, plush carpeting. Rooms are expansive and have king-size beds with designer sheets and quilts as well as balconies with French doors and sweeping views; the baths are all marble. The spa has more than 30 rejuvenating treatments. 3 restaurants, bar with entertainment, room service. In-room data ports, minibars, some in-room hot tubs, cable TV. Outdoor pool. Hair salon, hot tub, massage, spa. 2 golf courses, golf privileges, 10 tennis courts. Health club, hiking, volleyball. Kids' programs (ages 5–12). Business services. | 68900 Frank Sinatra Dr. | 760/321–8282 | fax 760/321–6928 | www.ritzcarlton.com | 240 rooms, 19 suites | $260–$325 rooms, $375–$525 suites, $2,500 for presidential suite | AE, D, DC, MC, V.

Westin Mission Hills. Lush gardens and meandering streams characterize the grounds of this 360-acre Spanish-Moorish golf resort. Rooms and suites are housed in 16 two-story pavilions that surround patios and fountains; guest quarters have terra-cotta tile floors and private patios or balconies, and fine linens cover the king-size beds. There are 10 championship golf courses within 3 mi and two on the property. 2 restaurants, bar (with entertainment), room service. In-room data ports, minibars, cable TV. 3 pools. Hair salon, hot tub, massage. 2 18-hole golf courses, 6 putting greens, 7 tennis courts. Basketball, gym, volleyball, bicycles. Video games. Kids' programs, playground. Laundry services. Business services. Some pets allowed. | 71333 Dinah Shore Dr. | 760/328–5955 | fax 760/321–2955 | www.westin.com | 512 rooms, 41 suites | $289–$309 rooms, $300–$1,100 suites | AE, D, DC, MC, V.

RANCHO SANTA FE

MAP 4, J16

(Nearby towns also listed: Escondido, Oceanside, San Diego)

Just outside the San Diego city limits, you'll find this town of 12,962 in the middle of horse country. It's common to spot families riding the many trails that crisscross the hillsides. Rancho Sante Fe Country Club golf course, considered by many to be one of the best courses in Southern California, is here; it's only open to members of the community and guests of the golf course inn.

Information: Solana Beach Chamber of Commerce | 103 N. Cedros Ave., 92075 | 858/ 350–6006.

Attractions
Cedros Design District. This block of upscale shops is one of the region's hippest enclaves of galleries, stores, and interior designer showrooms. | 444 S. Cedros | 858/755–0444 | Free | Daily.

ON THE CALENDAR
JUNE: *Siesta del Sol.* This 2-day celebration the first weekend of June marks the beginning of summer. Festivities take place at Fletcher's Cove Beach and include an arts and crafts fair, live music, a food court, and children's games such as train rides and spin art. | Santa Fe Dr. at Fletcher's Cove Beach | 858/755–4775.

Dining
Delicias. Contemporary. This restaurant has a main dining room furnished with European-style tapestries, dominated by a Lalique crystal table in the center of the room. You can choose to eat in the outdoor courtyard with working fireplace. Entrees range from seared ahi tuna, to filet mignon and crispy duck, to wood-fired pizzas. | 6106 Paseo Delicias | 858/ 756–8000 | No lunch | $13.50–$34 | AE, D, DC, MC, V.

★ **Mille Fleurs.** French. You can opt to eat in the elegantly barren candlelit dining room, or outside on the patio to view the fountain at this bistro. The menu changes, but dinner may start off with an appetizer such as crispy sautéed sweetbread salad, followed by a broiled sea bass with green herb crust or an oven-roasted breast of duck. Pianist Tues.–Sat. No smoking. | 6009 Paseo Delicias | 858/756–3085 | Reservations essential | $28–$34 | AE, DC, MC, V.

★ **Rancho Valencia Resort.** Contemporary. The dinner menu here changes seasonally and includes dishes such as duck breast with Asian plum sauce, and crispy ahi tuna roll with spinach, nori and ginger sauce. You can dine in the enclosed courtyard with fountains and a working fireplace, or inside by candlelight with a view of the tennis courts. Classical guitarist Fri., Sat. Kids' menu. Sunday brunch. No smoking. | 5921 Valencia Circle | 858/759–6216 | Breakfast also available | $24–$59 | AE, DC, MC, V.

Lodging
Inn at Rancho Santa Fe. Built in 1923, this 20-acre property's center is the main lodge, an adobe-style building with one floor and a domed roof. The cottages are made of wood and stucco and have outdoor patios. Landscaped grounds with eucalyptus trees and pines

surround the area. The San Diego Wild Animal Park is 12 mi to the southwest and seven golf courses are within 3 mi. (Guests here have priviledges at the Rancho Santa Fe Country Club golf course.) Restaurant, bar, room service. Some refrigerators, some in-room hot tubs, cable TV. Heated pool. Massage. Tennis. Exercise equipment. Business services. Pets allowed. | 5951 Linea del Cielo | 858/756–1131 or 800/654–2928 | fax 858/759–1604 | www.theinnatranchosantafe.com | 89 rooms, 21 cottages | $110–220 rooms, $350–$650 cottages | AE, DC, MC, V.

Morgan Run Resort and Club. In the rolling hills of Rancho Santa Fe, this resort is primarily a golf and tennis recreation facility, which is a stop along the Celebrity Players Tour. The lush grounds are filled with palm trees and colorful vegetation. Del Mar Racetrack and the Pacific Ocean are both 3 mi away. Downtown is 3 mi west. Restaurant, bar, room service. Some refrigerators, cable TV. Pool. Massage. Driving range, 27-hole golf course, putting green, 11 tennis courts. Exercise equipment. Baby-sitting. Laundry service. | 5690 Cancha de Golf | 858/756–2471 or 800/378–4653 | fax 858/756–3013 | www.morganrun.com | 83 rooms, 7 suites | $249 rooms, $339 suites | AE, MC, V.

Rancho Valencia. The views of the valley below from this resort's elevated location are incredible. You can stay in a duplex suite with whitewashed beams, cathedral ceilings, stucco walls, and private terraces. European massages, beauty treatments, and aromatherapy are offered at the sleek spa. The Farm at Rancho Santa Fe Golf Course is across the street and two wineries are 9 mi to the northeast. Restaurant, bar, picnic area, room service. In-room data ports, refrigerators, cable TV, in-room VCRs. Pool. Massage, sauna, spa. Golf privileges, 17 tennis courts. Exercise equipment, hiking. Laundry facilities. Business services. Pets allowed ($75 fee). | 5921 Valencia Cir | 858/756–1123 or 800/548–3664 | fax 858/756–0165 | www.ranchovalencia.com | 43 suites | $425–$695 suites | AE, DC, MC, V.

RED BLUFF

MAP 3, D4

(Nearby towns also listed: Lassen Volcanic National Park, Redding)

Named for its vibrant cliffs and sand, Red Bluff was a town built on mining and ranching. It began to flourish as a shipping center in 1850, providing steamer service on the Sacramento River to San Francisco. The town maintains a mix of Old West toughness and late 1800s gentility: restored Victorians line the streets west of Main Street, while the downtown looks like a stage set for a Western movie. This small, working class city of 13,000 makes a good place to stock up before heading east into sparsely settled country.

Information: **Red Bluff Chamber of Commerce** | 100 Main St., 96080 | 530/527–6220.

Attractions

City River Park. This park runs along the shore of the Sacramento River. There are boat ramps, horseshoe pits, picnic areas, and a swimming pool (fee) in the park. Concerts are held at the outdoor bandstand and there are two playgrounds for kids. | 119 Sycamore St. | 530/527–8177 | fax 530/527–4957 | www.ci.red-bluff.ca.us | Free | Daily 6 AM–11 PM.

Kelly-Griggs House Museum. This Victorian-era home is filled with period artifacts and local antiques. Photos and costumes are on display in several of the rooms. | 311 Washington St. | 530/527–1129 | Free | Thurs.–Sun. 1–4; other times by appointment.

Mt. Lassen Volcanic National Park. *(See* separate town listings.)

William B. Ide Adobe State Historic Park. This 1850 adobe home is a memorial to the President of the California Republic. Ide served as president for 24 days until the start of the Mexican-American War. | 21659 Adobe Rd. | 530/529–8599 | Free, parking $2 | Daily 8 to dusk.

Dining

Snack Box. American. Corny pictures and knickknacks, all rural and many depicting cattle and sheep, decorate the renovated Victorian cottage that holds the Snack Box. Soups, omelets, country-fried steaks, grilled cheese sandwiches, and burgers are available. No smoking. | 257 Main St. | 530/529–0227 | Breakfast also available. No dinner | $4–$8 | MC, V.

Lodging

Best Western Grand Manor Inn. This hotel is at the junction of I–5 and Route 36. Complimentary Continental breakfast. Refrigerators, cable TV. Pool. Hot tub. Exercise Room. Laundry facilities. | 90 Sale Ln | 530/529–7060 | fax 530/529–7077 | 67 rooms | $68–$96 | AE, D, DC, MC, V.

Lamplighter Lodge. This motel is in downtown Red Bluff less than ½ mi west of I–5. Restaurant, complimentary Continental breakfast. In-room data ports, cable TV. Pool. Business services. | 210 S. Main St. | 530/527–1150 | fax 530/527–5878 | 50 rooms | $44–$48 | AE, D, DC, MC, V.

REDDING

MAP 3, D3

REDDING

INTRO
ATTRACTIONS
DINING
LODGING

(Nearby town also listed: Red Bluff)

Situated on I–5, Redding is the largest city in the extreme northern portion of California, with a population of 80,000. With its close proximity to Shasta-Trinity National Forest and Whiskeytown/Shasta-Trinity National Recreation Area, Redding makes a good place to get your provisions before heading into the surrounding wilderness.

Information: **Redding Convention and Visitors Bureau.** | 777 Auditorium Dr., 96001 | 800/874–7562 or 530/225–4100 | cnvb@ci.redding.ca.us | www.ci.redding.ca.us/cnvb/cnvb-home.htm.

Attractions

Lake Redding-Caldwell Park. This park runs along the Sacramento River and has fishing, boating, and swimming facilities as well as picnic areas. | 1250 Park View Ave. | 530/225–4095 | fax 530/225–4585 | www.ci.redding.ca.us | Free | Daily dawn to dusk.

Lake Shasta Caverns. You'll get an eyeful of geological formations on the one-hour guided tour of these spacious caverns. The journey begins with a catamaran ride across Lake Shasta. Take I–5 to the Shasta Caverns Road exit. | 530/238–2341 or 800/795–CAVE | $15 | Daily 9–4.

Redding Museum of Art and History. Contemporary art exhibits, historical county artifacts, and ethnic arts and crafts form the collection of this museum. There's a Turtle Arboretum near the bayside walking trail. The Carters House has live animals and the Forest House has butterflies and snakes on exhibit. Paul Bunyan's Forest Camp features logging and ecology exhibits. | 56 Quartz Hill Rd. | 530/243–8801 or 530/243–8850 | www.turtlebay.org | $5 | Oct.–May, Tues.–Sun. 10–5, Jun.–Sept. daily 10–5.

Shasta State Historic Park. This park, 3 mi west of Redding, is on the site of a town that once was home to 2,500 people during the famed Gold Rush. The old courthouse is now a museum, while other buildings in the town have been restored to their original look. | 15312 Rte. 299 W, Old Shasta | 530/243–8194 | $1 | Daily 10–5.

Shasta-Trinity National Forests. With more than 2 million acres of richly wooded mountains in north-central California, Shasta-Trinity is the home of Mt. Shasta, Castle Crags, the Trinity Alps, and Whiskeytown-Shasta-Trinity National Recreation Area. The area is full of hiking trails, camping and backpacking opportunities, and other outdoor activities. | Mt.

Shasta Ranger Station, 204 W. Alma, Mt. Shasta | 530/926–4511 | www.r5.fs.fed.us/shasta-trinity/ | Free | Daily dawn to dusk.

Whiskeytown-Shasta-Trinity National Recreation Area, Whiskeytown Unit. This 42,500-acre natural area is centered around four reservoirs. Hiking, mountain biking, fishing, and other outdoor activities can keep you busy in this rugged, pine-and-oak wilderness. Lakes have picnic areas, lawns for grass sports, marinas, swimming areas, boat rentals and launch ramps. History buffs should check out the Power House Historic District, at Whiskeytown Lake, with preserved buildings from the Gold Rush era (gold-panning trips can be arranged; check with the ranger district). | Superintendent, Whiskeytown/Shasta-Trinity NRA, Box 188, Whiskeytown | 530/242–3400 or 530/246–1225 | www.nps.gov/whis/ | $5 | Daily.

Waterworks Park. This water-oriented amusement park has rides and activities including the Flash Flood, three flumes, and a kids' pool with slides. | 151 N. Boulder Dr. | 530/246–9550 | fax 530/246–9554 | www.waterworkspark.com | $13.95 | Memorial Day–Labor Day, daily 10–8.

Shasta Dam and Power Plant. Visitors can tour the dam and power plant, learn about water usage in California on an informative tour, and check out the dramatic spillway. Tours usually on the hour, 9–4. | Bureau of Reclamation, Northern California Area Office, 16349 Shasta Dam Blvd., Shasta Lake City | 530/275–4463 | Free | Daily 8–5.

ON THE CALENDAR

APR.: *Kool April Nites.* This week-long classic car show, which typically draws over 2,000 vintage vehicles from the '50s through the '70s, fills the Redding Convention Center grounds with polished chrome and poodle skirts. Vendors, food booths, and rock-and-roll. | 530/225–4100 or 800/874–7562.

MAY: *Redding Rodeo.* This high-energy rodeo, held at the Rodeo Grounds (on Auditorium Drive behind the Redding Convention Center) kicks up its heels with bull-riding, calf-roping, clowns, and other classic rodeo events. Kids love the sheep-riding and pig races. Food booths and merchandise vendors. | 530/225–4100 or 800/874–7562.

Dining

Buz's Crab. Seafood. This combination restaurant and seafood market has a low-key, family atmosphere, with red vinyl booths and larger-than-life aquatic murals on the walls. Kids' menu. | 2159 East St. | 530/243–2120 | fax 530/243–4310 | www.snowcrest.net/buzscrab/index.html | fish@buzscrab.com | $8–$10 | MC, V.

Hatchcover. Continental. Dark wood paneling and views of the Sacramento River combine to create a nautical theme here. The menu emphasizes seafood, but you can also get steaks, combination plates, and pasta. The appetizer menu is extensive, and there's an outside deck for open-air dining. No smoking. | 202 Hemsted Dr. | 530/223–5606 | No lunch weekends | $8–$28 | AE, D, MC, V.

Kennett Diamond Brewery and Restaurant. American. This popular microbrewery serves traditional fare, but the chef is a graduate of the Culinary Institute of America, so it's better than average. The pizza is cooked in a wood-burning oven and there's live music on Fri. and Sat. nights. The brewery has won several awards for its beer. | 1600 California St. | 530/242–6477 | www.kennett-diamond.com/ | $8–$10 | AE, MC, V.

Peter Chu's Mandarin Cuisine. Chinese. Along with a selection of traditional Mandarin dishes, this upscale Asian restaurant features Szechwan and Hunan style cuisine as well. The dining room is elegant and has views of Mt. Shasta and Mt. Lassen. | 6751 Airport Rd. | 530/222–1364 | $10–$22 | AE, MC, V.

Lodging

Best Western Hilltop Inn. Built in 1974, this downtown hotel affords panoramic views of Mount Lassen. I–5 at Cypress exit. Restaurant, bar. In-room data ports, cable TV. Pool, wading pool. Hot tub. Laundry facilities. Business services, free parking. | 2300 Hilltop Dr. | 530/221–6100 | fax 530/221–2867 | www.bestwestern.com | 115 rooms | $99–$119 | AE, D, DC, MC, V.

Best Western Hospitality House. Built in 1970, this two-story structure is 1½ mi north of downtown. Restaurant, complimentary Continental breakfast. Cable TV. Pool. Laundry facilities. Business services. | 532 N. Market St. | 530/241–6464 | fax 530/244–1998 | 61 rooms, 1 suite | $69–$79 | AE, D, DC, MC, V.

La Quinta Inn. The rooms of this white three-story hotel face a garden of flowers and trees in the courtyard. It's in central Redding's commercial district among a host of restaurants and shops. Complimentary Continental breakfast. In-room data ports, cable TV. Pool. Hot tub. Laundry facilities. Business services, free parking. Pets allowed. | 2180 Hilltop Dr. | 530/221–8200 | fax 530/223–4727 | 141 rooms | $69–$76 | AE, D, DC, MC, V.

Red Lion Hotel. The restaurants and businesses of central Redding are within walking distance of this two-story hotel. Restaurant, bar (with entertainment), complimentary breakfast, room service. In-room data ports, cable TV. Pool, wading pool. Hot tub. Business services, airport shuttle, free parking. Pets allowed. | 1830 Hilltop Dr. | 530/221–8700 | fax 530/221–0324 | www.redlion.com | 192 rooms | $84–$114 | AE, D, DC, MC, V.

River Inn. This hotel is across from the Redding Convention Center and a ½ mi west of the I–5 and Route 299 junction. You can borrow a fishing pole from the hotel to fish in the nearby lake. Restaurant, bar, picnic area. Refrigerators, some in-room hot tubs, cable TV. Pool. Hot tub, sauna. Business services. Pets allowed (fee $6). | 1835 Park Marina Dr. | 530/241–9500 or 800/995–4341 | fax 530/241–5345 | www.reddingriverinn.com | 79 rooms | $46–$80 | AE, D, DC, MC, V.

REDLANDS

MAP 4, K14

(Nearby towns also listed: Riverside, San Bernardino)

Named for the rich tone of the local soil, this one-time citrus dynamo is better known today for the University of Redlands, which stretches over 130 acres on the city's northeast side. The "Inland Empire" city of 67,000 is largely residential—with special care taken on its collection of restored Victorians.

Information: Redlands Chamber of Commerce | 1 E. Redlands Blvd., 92373 | 909/793–2546 | www.redlandschamber.org.

Attractions

Asistencia Mission de San Gabriel. You can see where vows were pledged, the guards kept watch, even where the fathers ate their daily bread here. Besides the restored wedding chapel, gatehouse, and dining room, this settlement, part of the second wave of missions, also has a museum in the buildings that were part of the Lugo ranch in the 1840s. | 26930 Barton Rd. | 909/793–5402 | $1 | Wed.–Sat. 10–5, Sun. 1–5.

Kimberly Crest House and Gardens. The original owners built Kimberly Crest House to sit on the hill where they could overlook the formal Mediterranean gardens. Inside the 1897 structure, furnishings all date to the late 19th and early 20th centuries. | 1325 Prospect Dr. | 909/792–2111 | fax 909/798–1716 | www.kimberlycrest.com | $5 | Sept.–July, Thurs.–Sun. 1–4.

Lincoln Memorial Shrine. Dedicated to Abraham Lincoln, this shrine has books and memorabilia related to the 16th President and to the Civil War—including articles associated with Confederate General Robert E. Lee and Union General Ulysses S. Grant. The Heritage Room, housed in a separate library on the grounds, houses historical reference materials for California and the Redlands area. | 125 W. Vine St. | 909/798–7636; Heritage Room, 909/798–7632 | Free | Tues.–Sat. 1–5.

Pharaoh's Lost Kingdom. At this Egyptian-themed amusement park, you'll find a long-boat swing, miniature golf, and bumper boats all year, plus a waterpark open in summer. | 1100 California St. | 909/335–PARK | Free; rides, $1–$5; waterpark, $14.95 | Weekdays 10–10, weekends 10–midnight; waterpark: May–Sept., daily 10–9, Sept.–Oct., daily 11–6.

San Bernardino County Museum. This regional museum has exhibits in both culture and natural history, along with a hands-on Discovery Hall, extensive research collections, and public programs for adults and kids. | 2024 Orange Tree La. | 909/307–2669 or 888/BIRD–EGG | fax 909/307–0539 | www.co.san-bernardino.ca.us/museum | $4 | Tues.–Sun. 9–5.

Dining

Joe Greensleeves. American. A replica of a ship coming out of the wall and wine corks suspended from the ceiling decorate this downtown restaurant off Route 10E. Specials are fresh fish, wild boar, and elk, all cooked on an orangewood grill. The alligator sausage is very popular. If you're not that adventurous, try the salmon with white cream sauce or the filet mignon with a sauce of sautéed mushrooms or champagne and capers. The crème brûlée and flourless chocolate cake are favorites among the homemade desserts. Outside, there's a tree-surrounded dining patio, and the wine cellar boasts 500 bottles. No smoking. | 220 N. Orange St. | 909/792–6969 | Closed Mon. | $15–$28 | AE, D, DC, MC, V.

Lodging

Best Western Sandman. If you're planning a big family day at Pharaoh's Lost Kingdom, 2 mi away, you might want to plan an early-evening dinner at the motel's picnic area. The two-story structure, built in 1986, has lots of trees around the property. Complimentary Continental breakfast. Some refrigerators, cable TV. Pool. Hot tub. Business services. | 1120 W. Colton Ave. | 909/793–2001 | fax 909/792–7612 | www.bestwestern.com | 65 rooms, 1 suite | $44–$67, $87 suite | AE, D, DC, MC, V.

REDONDO BEACH

MAP 9, D6

(Nearby towns also listed: Long Beach, Los Angeles, Manhattan Beach, Marina del Rey)

Redondo Beach is a vibrant middle-class community of 65,000, much of it packed along a heavily developed shoreline. Along the wide, sandy beach, you'll find shops, restaurants, excursion boats, an amusement park, and an artificial reef for good fishing and snorkeling. In summer, the pier rocks with assorted bands and jazz concerts.

Information: **Redondo Beach Visitors Bureau** | 200 N. Pacific Coast Hwy., 90277 | 310/374–2171 or 800/282–0333 | uvisitrb@southbay.com | www.visitredondo.com.

Attractions

Galleria at South Bay. This large mall off the Artisa exit of I–405 is filled with popular stores, including the larger Nordstrom and Robinsons-May as well as many specialty shops. | 1815 Hawthorne St. | 310/371–7546 | www.southbaygalleria.com | Free | Mon.–Fri. 10–9, Sat. 10–8, Sun 10–7.

Dining

Chez Melange. Contemporary. This California brasserie tucked into the Palos Verdes Inn has an eclectic menu: You can choose from oysters on the half shell to Shanghai noodles to filet mignon soft tacos. Save room for the decadent desserts. Raw bar. Daily brunch. No smoking. | 1716 S. Pacific Coast Hwy. | 310/540–1222 | Breakfast available | $11–$24 | AE, DC, MC, V.

Lodging

Best Western Sunrise at Redondo Beach Marina. Next door to the marina, this three-story sand-colored hotel has many bay windows to let you view sea and marina at sunrise and sunset. Rental bikes are available if you'd like to pedal to the beach. Complimentary Continental breakfast. In-room data ports, refrigerators, cable TV. Pool. Hot tub. Business services, free parking. | 400 N. Harbor Dr. | 310/376–0746 | fax 310/376–7384 | www. bestwestern-sunrise.com | 111 rooms | $109–$119 | AE, D, DC, MC, V.

Crowne Plaza–Redondo Beach Marina and Hotel. About 7 mi south of the LA airport, this five-story hotel directly across from King Harbor Marina is only a short walk from the beach. Or, if you're in the mood to shop, the hotel has a complimentary shuttle to several malls. Restaurant, room service. In-room data ports, refrigerators, cable TV. Pool. Spa. Tennis. Exercise equipment. Laundry facilities. Business services. | 300 N. Harbor Dr. | 310/318–8888 or 800/334–7384 | fax 310/376–1930 | www.hermosawave.net/crowneplaza | 339 rooms, 4 suites | $189–$199 | AE, D, DC, MC, V.

Hotel Hermosa. Locals may tell you that Old High Spot Point used to be the site of a roller skate drive-in theater. Since 1991, this three-story pink stucco motel has been here, with an outdoor deck looking to the sea and an award-winning Japanese bonsai garden on the grounds. Complimentary Continental breakfast. In-room data ports, refrigerators, cable TV. Pool. Exercise Equipment. Laundry facilities. Business services. | 2515 Pacific Coast Hwy., Hermosa Beach | 310/318–6000 or 800/331–9979 | fax 310/318–6936 | www.hotelhermosa.com | 80 rooms, 8 suites | $79, $139–$350 suites | AE, D, DC, MC, V.

Palos Verdes Inn. About three blocks from the beach, this four-story inn has been a Riverside destination since the 1970s. Rooms on the ocean side have private balconies open to the full panorama of the ocean. Restaurant, bar, room service. In-room data ports, some refrigerators, cable TV. Pool. Hot tub. Business services. | 1700 S. Pacific Coast Hwy. | 310/316–4211 or 800/421–9241 | fax 310/316–4863 | pvi1700s@aol.com | 110 rooms | $96–$106 | AE, D, DC, MC, V.

Portofino Hotel and Yacht Club. From the bay, its night-lighted roof looks almost trapezoidal. Inside the hotel adjacent to the marina, the lobby is a sunny double-height space with multi-paned windows around the fireplace. Each room has a private balcony open to the ocean views and a two-line speaker phone if you need to work while you're here. Restaurant, bar (with entertainment), room service. In-room data ports, refrigerators, cable TV. Pool. Hot tub. Exercise equipment. Business services. | 260 Portofino Way | 310/379–8481 or 800/468–4292 | fax 310/372–7329 | www.noblehousehotels.com | 163 rooms, 2 suites | $229–$335, $449 suites | AE, D, DC, MC, V.

Redondo Pier Lodge. This modest lodging, built in the late 1980s, is two blocks from the beach but has its own pool and hot tub if you'd rather avoid the sand-and-surf bunch. Complimentary Continental breakfast. Refrigerators, cable TV. Pool. Hot tub. | 206 S. Pacific Coast Hwy. | 310/318–1811 | fax 310/379–0190 | 37 rooms, 2 suites | $63–79, $95 suites | AE, D, DC, MC, V.

RIVERSIDE

MAP 4, J15

(Nearby towns also listed: Ontario, Redlands, San Bernardino)

At first, it was just a patch of orange groves against a backdrop of towering mountains. But a town sprouted there, too, and by 1895, Riverside had become Southern California's metro center—and, at the time, the nation's wealthiest city per capita. Many of the Victorian mansions of that day still stand, now flanked by museums and restaurants along palm-lined avenues in this city of 226,505. Remaining citrus groves continue to thrive, and in Low Park, you can see one of the parent trees that started it all.

Information: **Riverside Visitor Center.** | 3660 Mission Inn Ave., 92501 | 909/684–4636 | riversidecb@linkline.com | www.riverside-chamber.com.

Attractions

California Museum of Photography. An off-campus department of the University of California at Riverside, the downtown museum has a collection ranging from hand-colored Japanese prints of the 19th century to images produced with the latest in digital and laser technology. | 3824 Main St. | 909/784–3686 or 909/787–4787 | www.cmp.ucr.edu | $2, free Wed. | Tues.–Sun. 11–5.

Castle Amusement Park. You'll find many options for play at this park at the La Sierra-Riverside exit off Freeway 91, including a three-story arcade, four 18-hole miniature golf courses, and more than 35 rides. | 3500 Polk St. | 909/785–3000 | www.castlepark.com | Free; parking, $5 | Park, weekdays 10–10; rides, Fri.–Sat. 10–10, Sun. 10–9.

Heritage House. The upper-middle-class orange growers of the 1890s lived well, and you can see the furnishings that shaped their lifestyles, including many original items in this restored Queen Anne mansion. | 8193 Magnolia Ave. | 909/689–1333 or 909/826–5273 | fax 909/369–4970 | www.ci.riverside.ca.us/museum | Free | July 4–Labor Day, Sun. noon–3:30; Labor Day–July 4, Thurs.–Fri. noon–3, Sun. noon–3:30.

Mount Rubidoux Memorial Park. Two hiking trails and a staircase lead up the mountain off 9th Street from the Market Street exit of Route 60. At the top, you'll find a 360-degree view of the city, desert, and faraway peaks. | 4706 Mt. Rubidoux | 909/715–3440 | fax 909/715–3477 | Free | Daily dawn to dusk.

Orange Empire Railway Museum. From the late 1870s through the 1960s, the rails helped shape the growth of the West. At this 64-acre collection near the Riverside exit off Route 60, you can see more than 200 steam, electric, and diesel locomotives, passenger and freight cars, and streetcars. On weekends, you can ride some of the trains. | 2201 South A St. | 909/657–2605 | Free | Daily 9–5.

Parent Washington Navel Orange Tree, Low Park. One of two trees brought from Brazil in 1873, this is the surviving parent tree of the naval orange industry in California. It's still thriving and producing fruit. | 7101 Magnolia St. | 909/715–3440 | Free | Daily.

Riverside Art Museum. The permanent collection has prints from masters like Chagall and Piranesi, plus oils and other paintings by California artists, with an emphasis on landscapes. | 3425 Mission Inn Ave. | 909/684–7111 | fax 909/684–7332 | $2 | www.riversideartmuseum.com | Mon.–Sat. 10–4 | Closed last 2 weeks in Aug.

Riverside Municipal Museum. Behind the arched colonnade of the white Riverside Municipal Museum, you'll find a center for learning about the natural and the cultural history of the area, plus exhibits such as a silk quilt that interweaves locally meaningful symbols like poppies, branches, and berries from a pepper tree, and, of course, the orange. | 3720 Orange St. | 909/782–5273 | Free | Tues.–Fri. 9–5, Sat. 10–5, Sun. 11–5, Mon. 9–1.

University of California at Riverside Wide swaths of green lawn and trim walkways separate the various buildings on the spacious Riverside campus of the University of California. The botanic gardens showcase more than 3,500 species of plants from around the world on 39 acres with 4 mi of scenic trails. | 900 University Ave. | 909/787–1012 | www.ucr.edu | Free; gardens parking, $5 | Daily; gardens, 8–5.

ON THE CALENDAR

MAR. OR APR.: *Easter Sunrise Pilgrimage.* Following in the tradition of religious pilgrims the world over, this annual ceremony includes a procession to the Father Serra Cross and the World Peace Tower in the hillside Mt. Rubidoux Memorial Park. | 909/687–5746.

Dining

Ciao Bella. Italian. Overshadowed by the surrounding glass-walled office buildings, the main dining room here has an open kitchen and skylights, although meals are also served in the bottle-bedecked wine cellar. Outside, there's a hint of Rome in the large tree-shaded patio with fountains. The regular menu includes pasta, pizzas from a wood-fired oven, as well as such specials as veal sausage with polenta, a carpaccio antipasto platter, and linguine topped with sautéed shrimp, calamari, and porcini mushrooms. Favored desserts are homemade bread pudding, tiramisu, and crème brûlée. Jazz Friday and Saturday. No smoking. | 1630 Spruce St. | 909/781–8840 | Closed Sun. | $12–$35 | AE, D, MC, V.

Gérard's. French. This restaurant with bay windows looking out to Magnolia Street is somewhat sparce and country French, brightened throughout with original watercolors of Riverside. The menu has bouillabaisse and rack of lamb, plus a pepper steak flamed right at the table. Popular specials have included the marinated and grilled king salmon and the NY angus prime steak with carmelized onions. Beer and wine only. No smoking. | 9814 Magnolia Ave. | 909/687–4882 | Closed Mon.; no lunch | $15–$23 | AE, D, DC, MC, V.

Market Broiler. Seafood. When you walk into this setting of a tropical fish aquarium and stuffed fish, you know what you're here for—and a couple of mesquite grills behind plate glass, right in the middle of the restaurant, let you know how to expect most selections to be cooked. The restaurants in this small California chain have more than a dozen daily fish specials, along with a variety of pasta, steak, and chicken dishes. Kids' menu. No smoking. | 3525 Merrill St. | 909/276–9007 | $7–$34.95 | AE, D, MC, V.

Lodging

Comfort Inn. This is a warm, friendly hotel popular with families visiting students at University of California at Riverside. Off highway 60 at University exit, a mile north of downtown. Complimentary Continental breakfast. Some microwaves, cable TV. Pool. Business services, airport shuttle. Free parking. | 1590 University Ave. | 909/683–6000 | fax 909/782–8052 | www.choicehotels.com | 115 rooms | $58–$65 | AE, D, DC, MC, V.

Courtyard by Marriott. This six-story hotel off the University exit of Route 60 caters primarily to business travelers, although if you're a leisure traveler who's taken the hike up Mount Rubidoux, there's a pool and hot tub for relaxing before dinner. Restaurant. In-room data ports, cable TV. Pool. Hot tub. Exercise equipment. Business services. | 1510 University Ave. | 909/276–1200 or 800/321–2211 | fax 909/787–6783 | www.marriot.com | 163 rooms | $79–$95 | AE, D, DC, MC, V.

Dynasty Suites. Only ½ mi from the UC Riverside, this two-story suites hotel built in 1990 is about 14 mi from Ontario International Airport and 41 mi from Lake Arrowhead. The guest rooms use a lot of dark woods in kitchenettes and furnishings, and all suites have sofabeds and two-line speaker phones. Complimentary Continental breakfast. In-room data ports, kitchenettes, cable TV. Pool. Business services, free parking. No pets. | 3735 Iowa Ave. | 909/369–8200 or 800/842–7899 | fax 909/341–6486 | info@dynastysuites.com | www.dynasty-suites.com | 34 rooms | $59 | AE, D, DC, MC, V.

Holiday Inn Select–Riverside Convention Center. Adjacent to the convention center, this 12-story, sand-colored hotel built in 1987 also has the 120 shops and restaurants of the Antique Pedestrian Shopping Mall just beyond its site. The hotel has a free shuttle to places within 5 mi, although you'll have to drive if you want to shop at the Ontario Mills Outlet Mall, 15 mi away. Restaurant, bar, room service. Microwaves, cable TV. Pool. Hot tub. Exercise equipment. Business services, airport shuttle, free parking. | 3400 Market St. | 909/784–8000 | fax 909/369–7127 | rsmit@sunstonehotels.com | www.basshotels.com/holiday-inn | 292 rooms, 23 suites | $109–$236 | AE, D, DC, MC, V.

Mission Inn. In the heart of downtown, next door to the Riverside Antique Museum, this historic hotel built in 1902 has hosted U.S. Presidents Taft, Eisenhower, and Theodore Roosevelt. Film queen Bette Davis was twice married in one of its two chapels; a room displaying the wings of famous aviators include those of the lost flyer Amelia Earhart, the first woman to fly the Atlantic. About $7 million worth of European statues are scattered around the property, which takes up a whole city block, as well as a beautiful courtyard and a rose-garlanded gazebo. You'll find many antiques inside the Spanish Mission-style hotel. Restaurants, bars (with entertainment). In-room data ports, cable TV. Pool. Hot tub, massage. Exercise equipment. Business services, airport shuttle. | 3649 Mission Inn Ave. | 909/784–0300 or 800/843–7755 | fax 909/683–1342 | www.missioninn.com | 237 rooms (15 with shower only), 3 suites | $119–$230, $275–$900 suites | AE, D, DC, MC, V.

ROSEVILLE

MAP 3, E6

(Nearby towns also listed: Fair Oaks, Sacramento)

This community of 74,000 is only 18 mi northeast of Sacramento. There are plenty of outdoor activities in the area, including hiking in the Sierra foothills, skiing in the High Sierra, and exploring nearby lakes and rivers.

Information: **Roseville Chamber of Commerce** | 650 Douglas Blvd., 95678 | 916/783–8136 | www.rosevillechamber.com.

Attractions

Folsom Premium Factory Outlets. People from all around come to this factory outlet mall off the Folsom Boulevard exit of Route 50, where you can shop till you drop at more than 70 stores. | 13000 Folsom Blvd. | 916/985–0312 | www.premiumfactoryoutlets.com | Free | Mon.–Sat. 10–9, Sun. 10–6.

Carnegie Museum. The highlight here is an extensive model railroad collection, as well as a hodgepodge of historical memorabilia from the area's past. The museum is housed in the former Carnegie Library, built in 1912 with local brick, terra cotta, and granite. This library, like many others built during the early part of the century, was funded in part by financier Andrew Carnegie, hence the name. | 557 Lincoln St. | 916/773–3003 | Free | Daily noon–5.

Maidu Regional Park. This 152-acre park has plenty to keep you busy—a large sheltered picnic area, softball diamonds, a skate track for hockey and roller-blading, a walking and bike path, a large turf area, and play equipment. | 1550 Maidu Dr. | 916/774–5242 | Daily dawn to dusk.

At the **Maidu Indian Interpretive Center and Historic Site,** exhibits tell about life dating back as far as 8,000 B.C. Look for finely woven baskets, ancient stone artifacts, and contemporary artwork by Native Americans. Hands-on exhibits keep kids interested. Tours of the 30-acre site, which once supported a major village, are offered Saturdays at 10. | 1960 Johnson Ranch Dr. | 916/772–4242 | $4 | Tues.–Sat. 9–4.

Lodging

Heritage Inn. Like a small rise on the landscape, this gray-stone structure sits neatly among its landscaping of little evergreens, 14 mi from sightseeing in Old Sacramento. All rooms have either sunken tubs or whirlpools, and king rooms also have refrigerators. Restaurant. Some refrigerators, some in-room hot tubs. Pool. Laundry facilitites. Business services, free parking. | 204 Harding Blvd. | 916/782–4466 | http://bestlodging.com/sites/4147/index.shtml | 101 rooms | $65–$79 | AE, CB, D, DC, MC, V.

Hilton Garden Inn. Off the Eureka Road exit of I-80 and 35 mi east of the Sacramento Airport, this three-story hotel is within 10 mi of several high-tech firms. Rooms have a work desk and two phones, each with two lines, as well as data ports. It's 6 mi from a shopping mall, and—if you're in the mood for a day trip—75 mi east to Lake Tahoe and 75 mi north to Napa Valley. Restaurant. In-room data ports, microwaves, refrigerators, cable TV. Pool. Hot tub. Exercise equipment. Business services. | 1957 Taylor Rd. | 916/773–7171 | fax 916/773–7138 | 131 rooms | $79–$114 | AE, D, DC, MC, V.

RUTHERFORD/ST. HELENA

(Nearby towns also listed: Calistoga, Santa Rosa, Yountville)

In and around this pair of charming towns you can discover inviting inns, restaurants with the perfect recipe for relaxation and ivy-covered wineries. Mumm Napa Valley, bottlers of bubblies, and regal Beringer Vineyards, established in 1883, are both here. At Niebaum-Coppola Estate, film director and vintner Francis Ford Coppola and his wife, Eleanor, bottle an acclaimed wine. The region's worldwide popularity, the booming local economy, and the proximity to San Francisco mean that rooms here go for premium prices virtually year-round. Most hostelries require that you commit to a two-night stay, particularly on weekends.

Information: Chamber of Commerce | 1010A Main St., Box 124, St. Helena, 94574 | 707/963–4456 | www.sthelena.com.

RUTHERFORD/
ST. HELENA

INTRO
ATTRACTIONS
DINING
LODGING

Attractions

Lake Berryessa. Made by damming Putah Creek, with 165 mi of shoreline, this is one of northern California's largest manmade lakes. Anglers go for rainbow trout, bass, catfish, crappie, and bluegill. A 2,000-acre wildlife area flanks the lake's eastern fringes. A marina, camping, and hiking trails through the park's rugged hills are in the park. | Bureau of Reclamation Field Office: 5520 Knoxville Rd., Napa | 707/966–2111 | www.ncbf.com/beryessa.html | Free | Daily.

Robert Louis Stevenson Museum (Silverado Museum). The great and far-wandering Scottish author is memorialized in this, said to be the largest of five museums devoted to his life and work. While short on manuscripts, this one-room shrine sheds light on the years after he moved to the Napa Valley for health reasons and wound up writing most of *The Silverado Squatters* while ensconced with his wife in a nearby mountain cabin in what is now Robert Louis Stevenson State Park. | 1490 Library La. | 707/963–3757 | rlsnhs@calicom.net | By donation | Tues.–Sun. noon–4.

Wineries. Demand for wines from the bucolic Napa Valley is growing so fast that locals aren't above ripping up their flower beds to make room for tidy rows of grape vines. While these local opportunists will have to wait a few years to get their young vines to produce, you won't have to wait that long to benefit from the valley's already prodigious bounty. Dozens of well-rooted, award-winning wineries, many offering free tours and tastings, surround Rutherford and St. Helena.

Beaulieu Vineyard, founded in 1900 by Georges de Latour, makes (among other wines) a cabernet that's a benchmark for Napa Valley reds. | 1960 S. St. Helena Hwy. | 707/963–2411 | Free | Tours daily 11–4, last tour starts at 4; tasting room daily 10:30–4:30.

At handsome **Beringer Vineyards,** the oldest continuously operating winery in Napa Valley, you can tour century-old wine caves. Tastings are in the Rhine House mansion, filled with antiques and lit by stained-glass windows. | 2000 Main St. | 707/963–4812 or 707/963–7115 | Free; tastings free on weekdays, $3 on weekends | Nov.–Mar., daily 9:30–4; Apr.–Oct., daily 9:30–5; tours daily every 30 minutes.

Charles Krug Winery shows the share-and-share-alike history of the region: Count Haraszthy of Hungary, who started nearby Buena Vista Winery in the mid-1800s, loaned Krug a small press here in 1861. Today, more sophisticated equipment squeezes the juice at this winery, now owned by the Peter Mondavi family. It's a California Historical Landmark. | 2800 Main St. | 707/963–5057 | $3 | Daily 10:30–5; tours 11:30, 1:30, and 3:30; tasting room 10:30–5:30.

Two labels are available for tasting and buying at **Franciscan Vineyards,** Mt. Veder and Franciscan. | 1178 Galleron Rd. | 707/963–7111 | Free; $4–$7 for tastings | Daily 10–5; tours by appointment.

At **Louis M. Martini Winery** take a tour, sip wines at a complimentary tasting, or take your bread, cheese, and just-bought bottle to picnic facilities on the grounds. | 254 S. St. Helena Hwy. | 707/963–2736 or 800/321–9463 | Free | Daily 10–4:30.

Merryvale Vineyards was the first winery built in the Napa Valley after Prohibition. You can tour the operation and cask room, and attend wine-tasting seminars on weekends. | 1000 Main St. | 707/963–7777 or 707/963–2225 | Free | Daily 10–5:30.

Formal gardens and fountains greet you at the gates of vine-cloaked **Niebaum-Coppola Estate Winery.** Formerly the Inglenook Wine estate, established in 1879, it is now run by director Francis Ford Coppola. The massive stone château houses a museum on the region's wine industry, a few mementos from Coppola's films, and his five Oscars. | 1991 Rte. 29, Rutherford | 707/968–1100 | Free | 10–5 daily; estate tours 10:30 and 2:30.

Take the informative tour at **Robert Mondavi Winery** then stroll through the quiet gardens surrounding the main buildings and tasting room. Special jazz and other musical performances are presented in summer, outside on (usually) warm Napa evenings. The winery is 1 mi south of Rutherford. | Rte. 29 (St. Helena Hwy.), Oakville | 888/RMONDAVI | Free | Nov.–Apr., daily 9:30–4:30; May–Oct., 9–5.

The rustic buildings of **Mumm Napa Valley,** off the Silverado Trail 10 mi east of St. Helena, are tucked at the base of the Mayacamas Mountains. Learn how this winery uses the *méthode traditionelle* to produce its lauded sparkling wines. | 8445 Silverado Trail, Rutherford | 707/942–3434 or 800/MUM–NAPA | Free | Daily 10–5; tours hourly, 10–3.

ON THE CALENDAR

FEB.: *Savor St. Helena.* This event lets you sample wine and food by local chefs while enjoying live music. | 707/942–9783.

MAY: *Opening of the Farmers Market.* Shop for organic produce, jams, baked goods, and other items brought in by local farmers. | Fridays | 707/252–6222.

Dining

★ **Auberge du Soleil.** Contemporary. It's hard to pick the winner here—the view or the food. The restaurant, set on a terraced hillside studded with olive trees, has outdoor dining on a patio, or inside with handcrafted tiles, stucco walls, fireplaces, and fresh flowers. For breakfast (popular with guests staying at the adjacent inn, *see* Lodging), try poached truffled eggs or the Valrhona chocolate waffle; for lunch there's Zinfandel-flavored barbecued shrimp. At dinner, look for oak barrel-roasted salmon or coriander-crusted ostrich. | 180 Rutherford Hill Rd. | 707/967–3111 | $65 | AE, D, MC, V.

Brava Terrace. Contemporary. There's a full bar here, skylights, a terrace where you can eat while overlooking a shady brook with redwood trees, and a heated deck with views of the valley and Howell Mountain. Try the wild mushroom tortellini or the medallions of lamb. No smoking. | 3010 N. St. Helena Hwy. | 707/963–9300 | Reservations essential | Closed Wed. in Nov.–Apr. and last 2 wks of Jan. | $25–$35 | AE, D, DC, MC, V.

Restaurant at Meadowood. French. Enjoy fine French cuisine here, overlooking emerald green lawns and the golf course, trimmed by dark green redwood trees. A fun way to eat is at the bar, where you can sip exceptional local wines by the glass and order from a tastings menu. Or, eat more formally, either in the handsome dining room or outside, on a flower-decked courtyard or on the deck. Try the pork tenderloin or rack of lamb. Sunday brunch. | 900 Meadowood La. | 707/963–3646 | Jacket required | No lunch | $80 | AE, D, DC, MC, V.

Terra. French. With soft lighting bouncing off handhewn wood beams and fieldstone walls, it's hard to believe this restaurant's two dining rooms once housed a chicken hatchery. Today, chicken isn't even on the menu. What is served are dishes highlighting seasonal ingredients and intense seasoning. Try sake-marinated Chilean sea bass in shiso (Japanese chrysanthemum leaf) broth, spaghettini with a ragout of tripe and white beans, or salmon with basmati rice and Thai red curry sauce. Desserts range from classic tiramisu to goat-cheese cheesecake. The restaurant is one block east of St. Helena's main drag. Beer and wine only. No smoking. | 1345 Railroad Ave. | 707/963–8931 | Reservations essential | Closed Tues. No lunch | $18–$27 | CB, DC, MC, V.

★ **Tra Vigne.** Italian. If you're having one meal in town, this stunning, high-ceilinged restaurant might be the place. A large bar and an open kitchen redolent of garlic suit the earthy cuisine: hearty pastas, chewy breads, all manner of seafood. The complex includes a courtyard (best place to eat on autumn afternoons) and a cantinetta, site of Napa's only wine bar. No smoking. | 1050 Charter Oak Ave. | 707/963–4444 | $30 | D, DC, MC, V.

Wine Spectator Greystone Restaurant. Mediterranean. This 100-year-old stone building, former home of Christian Brothers Winery, resembles a medieval castle. Inside, sit in the splendor lent by wrought-iron chandeliers and a stone fireplace embellished with iron animal heads. Eat on the terrace, with views of the vineyard. The tapas menu has paella and grilled seafood. No smoking. | 2555 Main St. | 707/967–1010 | Reservations essential | Jacket required | Closed first 2 weeks of Jan. and Tues., Wed. in Dec.–Mar. | $35–$55 | AE, DC, MC, V.

Lodging

★ **Auberge du Soleil.** The inn, surrounded by lush landscaping, is on the side of Rutherford Hill. Each room has a terrace overlooking the hill and vine-cloaked valleys. Restaurant (*see* Dining), bar, dining room, room service. In-room data ports, refrigerators, cable TV, in-room VCRs (and movies). Pool. Beauty salon, massage. Tennis. Exercise equipment. Bicycles. Business services, free parking. | 180 Rutherford Hill Rd., Rutherford | 707/963–1211 or 800/348–5406 | fax 707/963–8764 | www.aubergedusoleil.com | 50 rooms, 2 cottages | $300–$400, $1,500–$2,500 cottages | AE, D, DC, MC, V.

Adagio Inn. This 19th-century inn sits on a quiet, residential street in downtown St. Helena. All rooms have queen-size beds and period furniture. Complimentary breakfast. Some in-room hot tubs, in-room VCRs. Library. Business services. | 1417 Kearney St. | 707/963–2238 or 800/959–4505 | fax 707/963–5598 | www.chestelson.com | 4 rooms | $159–$259 | DC, MC, V.

El Bonita. This family-run, two-story motel on Route 29 in downtown St. Helena has rooms with terraces or balconies. Picnic area, complimentary Continental breakfast. Some kitchenettes, microwaves, refrigerators, some in-room hot tubs, cable TV. Pool. Hot tub, sauna. Business services. Pets allowed (fee). | 195 Main St. | 707/963–3216 or 800/541–3284 | fax 707/963–8838 | www.elbonita.com | 41 rooms in 3 buildings | $85–$199 | AE, D, DC, MC, V.

Harvest Inn. An English Tudor-style inn, this lodging has rooms in the main building and cottages, some with elaborate brick fireplaces and antiques. Complimentary Continental breakfast. In-room data ports, refrigerators, cable TV. 2 pools. Hot tubs. Business services. Pets allowed, (fee). | 1 Main St. | 707/963–9463 or 800/950–8466 | fax 707/963–4402 | www.harvestinn.com | 54 rooms | $229–$649 | AE, D, DC, MC, V.

Hotel St. Helena. Walk to shops, wine-tasting rooms, and restaurants from this downtown inn. The lobby has a sitting room with fireplace. Complimentary Continental breakfast. No TV in some rooms. Business services. No smoking. | 1309 Main St. | 707/963–4388 | fax 707/963–5402 | www.hotelsthelena.com | 18 rooms (14 with shared baths) | $130–$275 | AE, D, DC, MC, V.

Inn at Southbridge. It's a pleasant stroll across a stone bridge to downtown St. Helena from this inn, which has vaulted ceilings and fireplaces. French doors open to private balconies with views of the courtyard, hills, and town. Restaurant, complimentary Continental breakfast, room service. Refrigerators, cable TV, in-room VCRs (and movies). Pool. Business services. | 1020 Main St. | 707/967–9400 or 800/520–6800 | fax 707/967–9486 | www.placestostay.com | 21 rooms | $205–$490 | AE, D, DC, MC, V.

Meadowood Napa Valley. This gorgeous resort will make you feel as if you're staying at your own country resort. It has a Craftsman-style, three-story main lodge with restaurants and conference facilities. Scattered about the 200-acre complex laced with hiking trails are elegant cottages, some with French doors opening onto private patios, fireplaces, and down comforters. Restaurant, bar, room service. Refrigerators, cable TV. 2 pools. Hot tub, spa. 9-hole golf course, putting green, 7 tennis courts. Gym, hiking. Bicycles. Business services. | 900 Meadowood La. | 707/963–3646 or 800/458–8080 | fax 707/963–3532 | www.meadowood.com | 38 rooms, 47 suites | $435–$570, $475–$625 small suites, $655–$785 large suites | AE, D, DC, MC, V.

Oliver House. Relax in front of the parlor's large stone fireplace in this Swiss-style chalet on 4 acres of landscaped grounds, including an orchard, and an abundance of oak trees. Complimentary breakfast. Business services. No smoking. | 2970 Silverado Trail N | 707/963–4089 or 800/682–7888 | fax 707/963–5566 | 4 rooms | $135–$305 | AE, MC, V.

Rancho Caymus. The buildings here have red-tile roofs, stucco walls, and stained-glass windows, and surround a courtyard with a fountain. Restaurant, complimentary Continental breakfast. Some kitchenettes, refrigerators, some in-room hot tubs. Business services. | 1140 Rutherford Rd., Rutherford | 707/963–1777 or 800/845–1777 | fax 707/963–5387 | www.ranchocaymus.com | 31 suites | $145–$295 suites | AE, MC, V.

Vineyard Country Inn. The all-suite inn has exposed-beam ceilings and tile floors in the common rooms, and wood-burning fireplaces and balconies with vineyard views in some suites. Complimentary breakfast. Refrigerators, cable TV. Pool. Hot tub. Business services. | 201 Main St. | 707/963–1000 | fax 707/963–1794 | 21 suites | $150–$220 suites | AE, DC, MC, V.

White Sulphur Springs Spa Retreat. Established in 1852, this 330-acre property has two inns and nine cottages surrounded by a redwood and madrone forest. Half of the rooms have private baths. Picnic area, complimentary Continental breakfast. No air-conditioning in some rooms, some kitchenettes, no room phones. Hot tub, massage. Hiking. Bicycles. Business services. | 3100 White Sulphur Springs Rd. | 707/963–8588 or 800/593–8873 | fax 707/963–2890 | www.whitesulphursprings.com | 28 rooms, 9 cottages | $115–$135, $155–$175 small cottages, $185–$205 large cottages | MC, V.

★ **Wine Country Inn.** Handmade quilts cover the beds in this inn. Some rooms have fireplaces. Complimentary breakfast. Some refrigerators, some in-room hot tubs. Pool. Hot tub. | 1152 Lodi La. | 707/963–7077 | fax 707/963–9018 | countryinn@aol.com | 24 rooms | $140–$258 | MC, V.

SACRAMENTO

MAP 3, D6

(Nearby towns also listed: Davis, Fair Oaks, Rancho Cordova, Roseville)

Bounded by the Sacramento and American rivers and shaded by thousands of trees, California's capital is peaceful and seems almost rural. But it's a center of art, music, and theater, and has several fine museums. Take your pick: you can observe politicians at work or admire pickled peaches at the state fair.

Historic Old Sacramento, a string of 19th-century buildings bordering the Sacramento River, has been turned into a pleasant collection of shops and restaurants. Downtown boasts a pretty mall stretching to the ornate, domed capitol building. Sutter's Fort, in the heart of downtown, is a reminder of the city's founder, John Augustus Sutter. It was at his sawmill, about 30 mi east of the this fort, that gold was discovered in the state in 1848—sparking the infamous California Gold Rush.

Many stately Victorians of various styles and ornateness dot the town, reminders of the city's past as a wealthy center of commerce during the state's early years.

Be sure to spend some time in Old Sacramento. Once the western terminus of the Transcontinental Railroad and the short-lived Pony Express, this national landmark and state historic park encompasses 28 acres along the Sacramento River waterfront and more than 100 restored Gold Rush-era buildings. You'll find a marketplace, new public docks, excursion cruises, museums, and some of Sacramento's best restaurants. The historic Delta King, a paddlewheeler that once traveled between San Francisco and Sacramento, is permanently moored here and has a hotel and restaurant.

An interesting up-and-coming neighborhood is Del Paso, just across the American River from Sacramento proper. Until recently a decaying street of auto-repair shops, it's become a haven for small, edgy art galleries, artists' studios, and antique and rummage shops. A few good restaurants have opened too. Several times a month, the businesses here stay open late for a neighborhood walk and sometimes an impromptu street festival.

On Sacramento's outskirts, ranch homes and shopping malls reflect the growth during the 1960s from sleepy cow town to a city complete with suburban sprawl. If the place seems quiet on weekends, it's because residents have fled to the great outdoors. Sacramento is nearly equidistant to the Sierras, the San Francisco Bay area, and the Napa Valley.

Information: Sacramento Convention & Visitors Bureau | 1303 J St., Ste. 600, 95814 | 916/264–7777 | www.sacramentocvb.org.

TRANSPORTATION INFORMATION

Airports: Sacramento International Airport, 12 mi northwest of downtown off I–5, is served by Alaska, America West, American, Delta, Northwest, Southwest, and United airlines. | 6900 Airport Blvd. | 916/874–0700. **Amtrak** serves Sacramento from its station at | 401 I St. | 916/444–7094 or 800/872–7245. **Bus Lines: Greyhound** serves Sacramento from its depot at | 7th and L Sts. | 800/231–2222. **Intra-city Transit: Sacramento Regional Transit** operates buses and light-rail vehicles around Sacramento. Most buses run from 6 AM to 10 PM, most trains from 5 AM to midnight. | 1400 29th St. or 818 K St. | 916/321–2877. **Driving Around Town:** Less heavily populated than other major cities in the state, Sacramento is generally easy to get around by car. Rush hour lasts from 7:30 to 8:30 in the morning and from 5 to about 5:45 in the afternoon. Downtown streets are lettered and numbered in a grid. Watch out for one-way streets. Downtown, there are many metered spots; they cost 25 cents per 20 minutes. Garages are all over town; they cost $1.25 for the first hour and 75 cents per additional hour.

Attractions

ART AND ARCHITECTURE

Governor's Mansion State Historic Park. Built in 1877 as a private home, the mansion housed 13 of California's governors from 1903 to 1967. | 1526 H St. | 916/323–3047 | $1 | Daily 10–4, tours on the hour.

La Raza/Galeria Posada. The art and life of Chicano/Latino and Native peoples are celebrated at this nonprofit cultural center, which has a bookstore and fine arts gallery. | 704 O St. | 916/446–5133 | Free | Tues.–Sat. 11–5.

★ **State Capitol.** Originally built in 1874, this elegant building is sited on a park-like mall with more than 400 plant varieties, a rose garden, and many memorials. With its Roman Corinthian architecture, the building was modeled after the nation's Capitol. Take a few moments to visit the magnificent interior, extensively restored in the late 1970s and early '80s. On the ground floor, you'll see dioramas dedicated to each of the state's 58 counties. The central rotunda is truly stunning: the ornate carved ceiling is painted in a blue-and-rose color scheme touched with gold. Note the balustrades as you climb the stairs, adorned with the carved heads of grizzly bears, the state symbol (and, ironically, now extinct in California). | 1315 10th St. | 916/324–0333 | Free | Daily 9–4, tours on the hour.

BEACHES, PARKS, AND NATURAL SIGHTS

Effie Yeaw Nature Center. Walking trails traverse this 77-acre preserve, which also has exhibits on area birds and wildlife. | Ancil Hoffman Park, 6700 Tarshes Dr. | 916/489–4918 | www.effieyeaw.org | Free, parking $4 | Nov.–Feb., daily 9:30–4; Mar.–Oct., daily 9–5.

CULTURE, EDUCATION, AND HISTORY

California State University, Sacramento. From September through May, you can take in a play produced by the university's award-winning theater department. | 6000 J St. | 916/278–6604 | Daily.

Historic City Cemetery. Many notable figures from California's early history are buried at this cemetery created in 1849, among them John Augustus Sutter (who owned the mill where gold was discovered in 1848, sparking the California Gold Rush), Edwin and Margaret Crocker (of Crocker Bank fame), and Mark Hopkins (of the illustrious hotel in San Francisco). | 1000 Broadway | 916/264–5621 | fax 916/554–7508 | Free | Daily 7–5; tours Sat. at 10.

Old Sacramento Historic District With wooden sidewalks, cobblestone streets, and horse-drawn carriages, this 28-acre district (now filled with shops and eateries) along the Sacramento River captures the look of the city's early life. The public market on Front Street has more than 100 shops and restaurants. | From I Street to Neasham Circle between Front and Second streets; visitor information at 1101 Second St. | 916/442–7644 | fax 916/264–7286 | www.oldsacramento.com | Free | Daily; public market Tues.–Sun.

CALIFORNIA TRIVIA

Amaze your friends with your California trivia:

The state flower is the Antelope Valley California Poppy.
California's coastline is 1,264 mi long.
There are 1,400 places to camp in Tahoe National Forest.
There are almost 10,000 acres of coastal water set aside as state parks.
Mavericks Beach, south of San Francisco in San Mateo County, hosts the Mavericks monster surfing competition.
There are more than 500 wineries in California. Napa Valley alone has more than 240.
Lake Tahoe is almost 1,650 ft deep.
The nation's largest state park is in California. Anza-Borrego Desert State Park has more than 600,000 acres.
California has 420 public beaches.
The nation's first freeway, the Arroya Seco Parkway, opened in 1940, linking Hollywood and Pasadena.
The sound barrier was first broken in California. Chuck Yeager did it at Edwards Air Force base.
There are 263 state parks in California, covering 1.4 million acres.
The Federal Bureau of Land Management oversees 14.5 million acres of land in California.

At the **Artists' Collaborative Gallery,** more than 40 members of a regional artists' cooperative display their works at the gallery. You can see glass, jewelry, paintings, photographs, weaving, and woodwork. | 1007 2nd St. | 916/444–3764 | Free | Daily 10–5.

At the **California State Railroad Museum,** you can take a real steam-train excursion on weekends here. Exhibits in this enormous warehouse-size building take you inside old passenger and freight cars, trace the history of trains, and tell the story of building the transcontinental railroad. | 2nd and I Sts. | 916/445–6645 | $3 | Daily 10–5.

Central Pacific Passenger Depot is a reconstructed train station; it takes you back to life at the depot circa 1876. | 930 Front St. | 916/445–6645 | Free with admission to California State Railroad Museum | Daily 10–5.

Hastings Building was once the western terminus for the Pony Express, the building now houses the Wells Fargo History Museum, with exhibits on stagecoaches, mining, and gold. Tours available. | 1002 2nd St. | 916/440–4263 | Free | Daily 10–5.

Old Eagle Theatre is a reconstruction of California's first public theater which was originally built in 1849. Docents here tell you all about Sacramento history. | 925 Front St. | 916/323–6343 | Free | Tues.–Fri. 10–5.

Riverboat Cruises. Sightseeing cruises along the Sacramento River are given on Victorian paddlewheelers *Spirit of Sacramento* and *Matthew McKinley.* You can take a brunch, lunch, dinner, happy-hour, or sunset cruise. | 110 L St. | 916/552–2933 or 800/433–0263 | www.oldsacriverboat.com | Prices vary | Daily 10–5.

Sacramento Ballet. This professional dance company brings classical and contemporary ballet to the area. | 1631 K St. | 916/264–5181 (ticket sales) or 916/552–5800 (office) | fax 916/552–5815 | Call for schedule.

Sacramento Community Center Theater. Sacramento's largest theater is home to the opera, ballet, and other performing arts. The exhibit hall hosts trade shows and other events. | 1302 L St. | 916/264–5181 | Call for schedule.

★ **Sutter's Fort State Historic Park.** Established by John Augustus Sutter in 1839, this now-restored settlement gives you a glimpse of life in early Sacramento, with its blacksmith shop, bakery, jail, and living quarters. Self-guided audio tours available. | 2701 L St. | 916/445–4422 | $3 | Daily 10–5.

★ **California State Indian Museum.** Exhibits here explore Native American life, culture, art, and crafts. | 2816 K St. | 916/324–0971 | $3 | Daily 9–5.

MUSEUMS

California Military Museum. Veterans lead tours at this museum tracing the state's military history. | 1119 2nd St. | 916/442–2883 | www.militarymuseum.org | $3 | Tues.–Sun. 10–4.

Crate/Artist Contemporary Gallery. Art of all kinds—paintings, prints, sculpture, ceramics, jewelry, wood, and glass—is displayed here in the Hyatt Regency Plaza. | 1200 K Street Mall, No. 9 | 916/446–3694 | fax 916/441–4136 | Free | Tues.–Sat. 11–4.

★ **Crocker Art Museum.** This museum is set in an 1873 building designed by Sacramento pioneers Edwin and Margaret Crocker. Its collections include early California paintings, European art, and contemporary northern California arts and crafts. | 216 O St. | 916/264–5423 | $4.50 | Tues., Wed., Fri. and weekends 10–5, Thurs. 10–9.

Discovery Museum. This kids-oriented museum, housed in a replica of the 1854 City Hall and Waterworks building, has interactive exhibits that combine history, science, and technology to examine how everyday life in the area has changed over time. | 101 I St. | 916/264–7057 | $5 | June–Aug., daily 10–5; Sept.–May, Tues.–Fri. noon–5, weekends 10–5.

Challenger Learning Center, with its hands-on exhibits, is an adjunct to the Discovery Museum. It also has a wildlife gallery, a nature trail, and a planetarium. | 3615 Auburn Blvd. | 916/575–3941 | $5 | June–Aug., daily 10–5; Sept.–May, Tues.–Fri. noon–5, weekends 10–5.

★ **Golden State Museum.** Audio tours and interactive exhibits teach you about California's culture, history, and politics. Documents, murals, photographs, holograms, and films enhance the experience. | 1020 O St. | 916/653–7524 | fax 916/653–7134 | $6.50 | Tues.–Sat. 10–5, Sun. noon–5.

Leland Stanford Museum. The former governor, senator, and railroad baron once lived in this 1856 mansion. When renovations are complete, it will operate as a museum as well as a site for official state receptions. | 802 N St. | 916/324–0575 | Free | Tours Tues. and Thurs. 12:15, Sat. 12:15 and 1:30.

McClellan Aviation Museum. Thirty-three military aircraft fill this museum, including a 1943 L-2M Grasshopper, an F-4C Phantom II, and a Flying Boxcar. Learn about Air Force history on guided tours and at lectures. | 3204 Palm Ave. | 916/643–3192 | Free | Mon.–Sat. 9–3, Sun. noon–3.

Towe Auto Museum. A 1931 Chrysler and 1960 Lotus are among more than 150 vintage automobiles displayed here. If you're curious about those cars or the bullet-proof Cadillac limousine once used by the U.S. State Department, you'll find docents around to enlighten you. | 2200 Front St. | 916/442–6802 | $6 | Daily 10–6.

Wells Fargo History Museum. The histories of Wells Fargo and Sacramento intertwine at this museum, where exhibits include an original, fully restored Concord stagecoach, a functioning telegraph, and treasure boxes. | 400 Capitol Mall | 916/440–4161 | Free | Weekdays 9–5.

KODAK'S TIPS FOR PHOTOGRAPHING PEOPLE

Friends' Faces
· Pose subjects informally to keep the mood relaxed
· Try to work in shady areas to avoid squints
· Let kids pick their own poses

Strangers' Faces
· In crowds, work from a distance with a telephoto lens
· Try posing cooperative subjects
· Stick with gentle lighting—it's most flattering to faces

Group Portraits
· Keep the mood informal
· Use soft, diffuse lighting
· Try using a panoramic camera

People at Work
· Capture destination-specific occupations
· Use tools for props
· Avoid flash if possible

Sports
· Fill the frame with action
· Include identifying background
· Use fast shutter speeds to stop action

Silly Pictures
· Look for or create light-hearted situations
· Don't be inhibited
· Try a funny prop

Parades and Ceremonies
· Stake out a shooting spot early
· Show distinctive costumes
· Isolate crowd reactions
· Be flexible: content first, technique second

From *Kodak Guide to Shooting Great Travel Pictures* © 2000 by Fodor's Travel Publications

RELIGION AND SPIRITUALITY

Cathedral of the Blessed Sacrament. Built in 1889 with a Parisian design, the cathedral has Austrian stained glass. | 1017 11th St. | 916/444–3071 | Free | Daily 9–4.

St. Paul's Episcopal Church. The city's oldest congregation is housed in this church, which has Tiffany stained-glass windows and a rare Johnson Tracker organ. | 1430 J St. | 916/446–2620 | Free | Wed.–Fri. 10–4:30; services Wed., Thurs., and Sun.

SHOPPING

Antique Plaza. California's largest antiques mall has 300 dealers. A second showroom in Rocklin has 150 dealers. | 11395 Folsom Blvd. | 916/852–8517 | www.antiqueplazaonline.com | Free | Daily 10–6.

Arden Fair. There's a carousel for the kids along with 165 specialty shops, department stores, and numerous restaurants at this mall, Sacramento's largest. | 1689 Arden Way | 916/920–1167 | Free | Mon.–Sat. 10–9, Sun. 10–6.

Westfield Shoppingtown, Downtown Plaza. At this shopping complex you'll find movie theaters and a branch of the Hard Rock Cafe, along with the usual specialty shops, department stores, and restaurants. | 547 L St. | 916/442–4000 | Mon.–Sat. 10–9, Sun. 11–6.

SPORTS AND RECREATION

American River Parkway. As the river winds its way through Sacramento, the adjacent parklands offer trails for bicycling, walking, jogging, and horseback riding. There's also fishing, rafting, or picnicking. To get here, take I–80W to the Discovery Park exit, or I–5 to the Richards Boulevard exit, or Route 50 to the South Lake Tahoe exit. | 916/875–6961 | Free | Daily.

ARCO Arena. Home of the NBA's Sacramento Kings and the WNBA's Sacramento Monarchs, the arena is also a venue for concerts and other entertainment. I–5, exit Del Paso. | 1 Sports Parkway | 916/928–0000 or 928–6900 (box office) | Call for schedule.

Jedediah Smith Memorial Bicycle Trail. On this 23-mi scenic trail from Old Sacramento's Discovery Park to Beals Point at Folsom, you can go biking, fishing, horseback riding, picnicking, and bird-watching. | Discovery Park, end of Richards Blvd. off I–5 | 916/264–7777 | www.sacramentocvb.org/visitors | Free | Daily.

SIGHTSEEING TOURS/TOUR COMPANIES

American River Raft Rentals. You can rent a raft for up to 12 people and enjoy a self-guided float down the American River here (must have valid driver's license or military ID to rent). I–5 to Route 50 east, exit at Sunrise. | 11257 South Bridge | 916/635–6400 | fax 916/635–4524 | www.raftrentals.com | $32, shuttle service $2 | Apr.–Oct.

Sacramento Gray Line Sightseeing Tours. The tours take you to the State Capitol, Old Sacramento, and other city highlights in comfortable, air-conditioned buses. Regional day trips are also available. | 2600 North Ave. | 916/927–2877 or 800/356–9838 | Daily.

OTHER POINTS OF INTEREST

Blue Diamond Growers Visitors Center. Almond-growing in the Sacramento Valley is the focus of the video presentation, displays and tastings at this center. | 1701 C St. | 916/446–8439 | Free | Weekdays 10–5, Sat. 10–4.

Cal Expo. This is the home of the California State Fair in fall and many other events throughout the year. | 1600 Exposition Blvd. | 916/263–FAIR | www.bigfun.org. Call for schedule.

Old Chinatown. Also known as Sacramento "Yee Fow," this area was populated by Chinese immigrants during the Gold Rush. At 3rd and 5th streets bounded by I and J streets, take I–5, exit J Street. | 916/448–6465 | fax 916/448–8969 | Free | Daily.

ON THE CALENDAR

MAR.: *Ishi Day.* The last member of the Yahi tribe is remembered at this event held the second Saturday of March at the California State Indian Museum. | 2618 K St. | 916/324–0971.

MAY: *Sacramento Jazz Jubilee.* This Memorial Day weekend celebration, sponsored by the city's Traditional Jazz Society, includes a New Orleans-style jazz funeral reenactment through the Old City Cemetery. Other highlights are jam sessions, dances, and concerts by vocalists, soloists, and big bands. | 916/372–5277.

MAY: *Viva Cinco de Mayo Celebrations.* The Mexican holiday is marked at Cal Expo with mariachi bands, cultural exhibitions, crafts, and food. | 1600 Exposition Blvd. | 916/263–3000.

MAY: *Waterfront Artfest.* Some 100 regional artists display and sell their work during this festival. | 916/443–6223.

JUNE: *Crawdad Festival.* Billed as the world's largest crawdad festival, this event features Cajun food, a crawdad cook-off, a parade, races, a carnival, live music, and dancing in the streets. | 916/777–5880.

JUNE: *Railfair.* This 10-day extravaganza brings steam locomotives, exhibits on railroading, historic reenactments, music, and entertainment to Old Sacramento. | 916/322–8485.

JUNE: *Sacramento Heritage Festival.* More than 100 local musical acts, representing blues, jazz, gospel, reggae, hip hop, and zydeco are showcased at this weekend festival at Camp Pollock. | 916/481–2583.

AUG., SEPT.: *California State Fair.* Livestock shows and a rodeo are two of the activities you'll find at the fair. | 916/263–FAIR.

DEC.: *Gold Christmas at Discovery Museum.* The museum is decked out in Victorian finery for the season. There are vintage toys and special exhibits, too. | 916/264–7057.

WALKING TOURS

A Capitol Tour

A walk through the "City of Trees" should include the **Capitol grounds,** practically a botanic garden in the middle of Sacramento. Start at 12th and L streets to walk along the palm-lined mall. On your right, you'll see **a monument to Father Junipero Serra,** founder of the chain of Early California missions that, in the words of the Native Sons and Native Daughters of the Golden West, "brought civilization to our land."

Walk through the grove of orange trees and clipped hedges toward the east corner of the grounds. On your right is a curved path leading through the **rose garden.** To the left is the sleek black obelisk of the **Veterans Memorial.** Work your way back to the center of the mall on one of the diagonal paths. You'll pass an incense cedar, a Southern magnolia, and an Irish yew; you'll know which is which because nearly every tree has a small green botanical label in front of it (there are more than 450 plant varieties in the mall). As you pass the Montezuma cypress on your right, enjoy a **trout pond** set in a pretty glade of Japanese and silver maples. The **bronze statue** in the center is dedicated to veterans of the Spanish war. Nearby is a **reproduction of the Liberty Bell.**

The Capitol Mall is a gallery of memorials, and the most evocative of them lies just behind the trout pond: the **Memorial Grove,** shady trees planted as saplings in 1897 by the Ladies of the Grand Army of the Republic in memory of Union soldiers who fought in the Civil War. You're now just steps away from the **Capitol Building,** constructed between 1861 and 1874.

Paintings of California governors hang on each level. Most are typically realistic oil renderings of stern gentlemen in dark suits, with the exception of Jerry Brown's portrait. Brown's term in the mid-1970s was symbolic of a particularly Californian, baby-boomer mentality. He refused to live in the governor's mansion, waved away the limo and drove his own car to work. He raised a ruckus by dating pop singer Linda Ronstadt and proposed the then-crazy idea of launching a communications satellite, earning him the moniker "Governor Moonbeam." He commissioned Sacramento painter Don Bacardy to create his official portrait. The result is an expressionist work that captures a rather doleful legislator in slashes of bright pink. It's on the third floor and definitely worth the trip. While you're there, you might also catch the Assembly in session.

To arrange a guided tour, stop at the California State Capitol Museum. You can choose from several one-hour tours for groups of 10 or more; tour guides impart the Capitol's history, provide a glimpse of the legislative process, or tell the stories behind the trees and shrubs on the grounds.

A TOUR OF THE NEIGHBORHOODS

This walk will take you past Sacramento's historic public and private architecture. Start at the **Capitol Mall** at 13th Street. Walk north to J Street and turn right two blocks to K Street. Here you'll find the **Sacramento Memorial Auditorium,** opened in 1927 in a wave of post-World War I patriotism to honor fallen soldiers. Its "Mediterranean Revival"-style is a mixture of stately columns and muscular brick. Closed for 10 years over concerns about earthquake safety, it reopened and is now home to many musical and theatrical productions.

Turn left on J Street and continue to the **Governor's Mansion** at the corner of H Street. This 15-room, Second Empire-style home, built in 1878, was the governors' residence until 1967, when then-governor Ronald Reagan built a ranch-style home in the suburbs. It's said the mansion was one of California's first homes with an indoor bathroom. Tours are given daily 10–5. Take a left along H Street for a look at several other buildings: at 1329 H St. is **an 1880 Italianate,** and at 1301 H St. is **an 1896 Queen Anne.**

Continue to 12th Street, where the area known as **Alkali Flat** begins. This is the city's oldest intact residential district, home to Sacramento's merchants, judges, and other movers and shakers. It's full of lovely Victorians rich with turned spindles, scrollwork, tall windows, and other decoration. At 900 H St., at the corner of 9th, look for the large **1885 Italianate** built for pioneer merchant Llewellyn Williams. Walk up 9th Street to F Street and turn right to see **a block of Gothic and Italianate structures. 1024 F St.** was an early governor's mansion, built in 1869. On 11th Street, turn left to view **a row of matching Queen Anne cottages.** Note the "Delta basements"—because the Sacramento River (and the surrounding Sacramento Delta) was prone to flooding, people built homes over a high first floor.

Head back the way you came, returning to H Street, and walk east to the **Boulevard Park neighborhood** at 21st Street. The Union Park Race Course once held pony races here to entertain the wealthy, who began moving in during the 1860s. Most of the homes you see today were built after the race track was relocated in 1904. In addition to Victorians, you'll see Craftsman homes and "Cube" houses with their simple, modern designs and open floor plans. You'll find examples of **Cube houses** on 21st Street at Nos. 608–630. At **2131 H St.** is a home combining **Colonial Revival and Craftsman styles,** with a carved lion head over the porch. When your feet get weary, head over to the **restaurants** on J Street between 22nd and 19th, or to K and 24th, where you'll find a cold beer at Paris Cafe or a burger at Rick's Dessert Diner.

Dining

INEXPENSIVE

Ernesto's. Mexican. Seafood platters are what this restaurant near downtown is known for, but its menu includes classic south-of-the-border dishes prepared in innovative ways. You can eat at outdoor tables on the sidewalk. | 1901 16th St. | 916/441–5850 | $6–$11 | AE, D, MC, V.

Park Plaza Cafe. Russian. You can get borscht, cabbage rolls, pirogi, and chicken Kiev at this small, simply-furnished café across from Cesar Chavez Park. It also serves omelets, sandwiches, and salads. | 924 J St. | 916/448–2925 | Breakfast also available. Closed Sun. | $5–$22 | MC, V.

Rick's Dessert Diner. American. If you have a sweet tooth, you'll love this diner, which only serves desserts. More than 500 of them, all homemade, are on the menu, and there's an espresso bar. An outdoor patio seats 60. | 2322 K St. | 916/444–0969 | $4–$5 | No credit cards.

MODERATE

Cafe Vinoteca. Mediterranean. This pleasant bistro is airy, with tile floors and Old World decor. Try veal Marsala and penne puttanesca, and don't miss the tiramisu. There's a full espresso bar, a brunch menu, and outdoor seating. | 3535 Fair Oaks Blvd. | 916/487–1331 | Breakfast also available | $8–$18 | AE, MC, V.

California Fat's. Chinese. This bustling restaurant in Old Sacramento is known for stir-fried seafood dishes and meats roasted in a wood-fired oven. | 1015 Front St. | 916/441–7966 | $12–$24 | AE, MC, V.

Chanterelle. Contemporary. With white-linen tablecloths and candles, this restaurant in the Sterling Hotel serves up romance with its menu of French food prepared with a California twist. You can eat outdoors on an enclosed patio. | 1300 H St. | 916/448–1300 | fax 916/448–8066 | No lunch | $15–$25 | AE, MC, V.

Chateau. Contemporary. This supper club features live music and dancing. It's known for steaks, seafood, and salads. There's also an adjoining catering service. | 26-27 Town and Country Place | 916/977–1877 | fax 916/977–1881 | 12–$20 | AE, DC, MC, V.

★ **City Treasure.** A curved wall of windows shows off the warm interior of this restaurant to its fashionable midtown neighbors. Burnished copper tables and lamps, grapevine-pattern booths and banquettes, and locally produced artwork create a delightful setting. The eclectic menu changes seasonally. Smoked salmon croutons, jambalaya, grilled salmon, and braised lamb shanks are among the past offerings. The triple-layer chocolate cake is a must for dessert. From the list of more than 200 California wines, you can choose one of almost 50 by the glass, or have a trio—a sampler of three 3-ounce pours. | 1730 L St. | 916/447–7380 | $14.50–$21.50 | AE, D, DC, MC, V | No lunch Sat.

Frank Fat's. Chinese. The house specialty at this restaurant, a meeting place for California politicians since 1939, is honey-walnut prawns, but it serves all manner of Peking, Szechuan, Cantonese and Shanghai dishes. Try the homemade banana-cream pie. | 806 L St. | 916/442–7092. or | fax 916/442–7092 | Reservations essential | $13.50–$28 | AE, MC, V.

Kyoto Restaurant. Japanese. This spacious restaurant also has an intimate tatami room (up to four guests are seated on the floor, which is covered with smooth, woven-grass mats). The extensive menu features sushi, teriyaki, sukiyaki, tempura, and combination dinners. | 1001 6th St. | 916/448–3570 | Closed Sun. No lunch Sat. | $8–$18 | AE, MC, V.

Lemon Grass. Vietnamese. Dine on this country's delicately flavored cuisine. There's outdoor dining in a brick-walled patio with many trees. | 601 Munroe St. | 916/486–4891 | No lunch weekends | $10–$22 | AE, DC, MC, V.

Marrakech. Moroccan. If you come on Friday or Saturday night, you'll get to see a belly dancer perform. The food is served by costumed waiters. | 1833 Fulton Ave. | 916/486–1944 | Closed Monday. No lunch | $18.50 | AE, MC, V.

Ristorante Piatti. Italian. Daily fish specials are served at this 250-seat restaurant with outdoor tables on a brick patio with a waterfall. One of the house specialties is a saffron pasta in a sauce of tomato, arugula, white wine, garlic, and grilled prawns. No smoking. | 571 Pavilions Lane | 916/649–8885 | $13–$26 | AE, DC, MC, V.

Rusty Duck. Seafood. Its name might suggest otherwise, but this is a true fresh-fish house. There are early-bird specials, and outdoor dining on a patio. Kids' menu. | 500 Bercut Dr. | 916/441–1191 | $15–$40 | AE, D, DC, MC, V.

Scott's Seafood. Seafood. Steaks are served along with the fish and oysters at this lively eatery with white tablecloths and friendly service. | 545 Munroe St. | 916/489–1822 | Reservations essential | $10–$32 | AE, D, DC, MC, V.

Tapa the World Restaurant. Spanish. Known for its tapas, this cozy restaurant also serves mussels and paella. Some nights there's live guitar music, and on the fourth Saturday of the month flamenco dancers perform. Outdoor dining is on a sidewalk courtyard. | 2115 J St. | 916/442–4353 | $8–$20 | AE, MC, V.

EXPENSIVE

Enotria Cafe and Wine Bar. Mediterranean. This relaxed, intimate restaurant has wine tastings on Tuesday nights and Cigar Night on the third Wednesday of the month. You can eat outdoors on a patio facing a garden where the restaurant grows some of its own fresh herbs. Menu choices include seafood, grilled meats, steaks, and pasta. | 1431 Del Paso Way | 916/922–6792 | fax 916/922–6794 | Closed Sun. No lunch Sat. | $17–$25 | AE, D, MC, V. **Firehouse.** Contemporary. Housed in a mid-19th century building that once was an actual fire station, this restaurant has traded in the fireman's paraphernalia for elegant period decor. Its most popular meal is steak Diane followed by tiramisu. | 1112 2nd St. | 916/442–4772 | Closed Sun. No lunch Sat., no supper Mon. | $17–$42 | AE, MC, V.

Pilothouse. Contemporary. This restaurant operates aboard the *Delta King* riverboat. It's known for fresh fish, grilled meats, and pasta dishes. Kids' menu. Sunday brunch. No smoking. | 1000 Front St. | 916/441–4440 | $17–$35 | AE, D, DC, MC, V.

Silva's Sheldon Inn. Contemporary. This restaurant, set in a 19th-century building, is known for fresh fish, steak, and Portuguese bean soup. It has outdoor seating on a flower-decked patio. Kids' menu. No smoking. | 9000 Grant Line Rd., Elk Grove | 916/686–8330 | Closed week of Jan. 1, week of July 4, and Mondays. No lunch | $18–$30 | MC, V.

Lodging

INEXPENSIVE

Best Western Expo Inn. This two-story hotel next to Cal Expo and 3 mi from downtown has two-room executive suites with sitting areas, ceiling fans, and computer work areas. Complimentary Continental breakfast. Some kitchenettes, some microwaves, some refrigerators, cable TV. Pool. Spa. Business services, airport shuttle, free parking. Pets allowed (fee). | 1413 Howe Ave. | 916/922–9833 or 800/643–4422 | fax 916/922–3384 | 127 rooms, 20 suites | $65, $90–$120 suites | AE, D, DC, MC, V.

Best Western Harbor Inn. Guest rooms at this hotel have balconies and views of downtown Sacramento, just ½ mi away. Complimentary Continental breakfast. Some refrigerators, in-room hot tubs, cable TV. Pool. Hot tubs. Business services, airport shuttle, free parking. Pets allowed (fee). | 1250 Halyard Dr., West Sacramento | 916/371–2100 or 800/371–2101 | fax 916/373–1507 | 138 rooms, 19 suites | $79, $89 suites | AE, D, DC, MC, V.

Best Western John Jay Inn. This inn, built in 1995, has a Colonial exterior and well-appointed rooms. It's 10 mi southeast of downtown, near the airport. Complimentary Continental breakfast. Microwaves, refrigerators, cable TV. Pool. Sauna, spa. Exercise equipment. Laundry facilities. Business services, free parking. No smoking. | 15 Massie Court | 916/689–4425 | fax 916/689–8045 | 50 rooms, 8 suites | $75–$85, $110 suites | AE, D, DC, MC, V.

Best Western Sandman Motel. From this two-story hotel, you have easy access to 27 mi of biking and jogging trails along the American and Sacramento rivers, and Old Sacramento is 10 min away. Rooms are comfortable but basic. I–5, exit Richards Boulevard. Complimentary Continental breakfast. Refrigerators, cable TV. Pool. Airport shuttle. | 236 Jibboom St. | 916/443–6515 | fax 916/443–8346 | 116 rooms | $103 | AE, D, DC, MC, V.

Best Western Sutter House. Basic rooms open onto a courtyard with a pool at this three-story hotel adjacent to the Capitol, shopping, and downtown. I–5, exit J Street. Restaurant, complimentary Continental breakfast. Cable TV. No smoking. | 1100 H St. | 916/441–1314 | fax 916/441–5961 | 98 rooms | $99–$156 | AE, D, DC, MC, V.

Candlewood Suites Sacramento. Housekeeping is performed once a week in this hotel, which stresses privacy and security. Half of the rooms are studios; the other half are 1-bedroom suites. There are video and CD libraries. Kitchenettes, cable TV, in-room VCRs. | 555 Howe Ave. | 916/646–1212 | fax 916/646–1216 | 60 studios, 66 suites | studios $69–$94, suites $89–$115 | AE, DC, V.

Days Inn Discovery Park. A comfortable atmosphere pervades this hotel set on tree-shaded grounds. I–5, exit Richards Boulevard. Complimentary Continental breakfast. Some refrigerators, cable TV. Pool. Hot tub. Free parking. No pets. | 350 Bercut Dr. | 916/442–6971 | fax 916/444–2809 | 100 rooms | $69–$99 | AE, D, DC, MC, V.

Governors Inn. Complimentary afternoon sherry is served at this deluxe three-story hotel 1 mi north of downtown, near the airport and the Sacramento River. An entrance to Discovery Park is on the property. Rooms are equipped with desks and work areas, and they all have balconies. I–5, exit Richards Boulevard. Complimentary Continental breakfast. Cable TV. Pool. Spa. Exercise Room. Airport shuttle. No smoking. | 210 Richards Blvd. | 916/448–7224 or 800/999–6689 | fax 916/448–7382 | 134 rooms (showers only) | $89–$99 | AE, D, DC, MC, V.

Holiday Inn–Capitol Plaza. This 16-story hotel is near Old Sacramento and the Downtown Plaza Mall. Take the J Street exit off I–5. Restaurant, bar, room service. Some refrigerators, cable TV. Pool. Sauna. Business services. | 300 J St. | 916/446–0100 | fax 916/446–0117 | www.holidayinn.com | 364 rooms | $95–$157 | AE, D, DC, MC, V.

La Quinta. This three-story hotel is near Old Sacramento, the Capitol, and the Arco Arena. I–5, exit Richards Boulevard. Complimentary Continental breakfast. In-room data ports, cable TV. Pool. Exercise equipment. Laundry facilities. Business services, airport shuttle. Pets allowed. | 200 Jibboom St. | 916/448–8100 | fax 916/447–3621 | 165 rooms | $69–$135 | AE, D, DC, MC, V.

La Quinta. This three-story hotel 8 mi west of downtown sits on attractive, landscaped grounds. At business I–80, take Madison Avenue exit. Complimentary Continental breakfast. In-room data ports, cable TV. Pool. Laundry facilities. Business services. Pets allowed. | 4604 Madison Ave. | 916/348–0900 | fax 916/331–7160 | 127 rooms | $65–$82 | AE, D, DC, MC, V.

On the Bluffs. At this bed and breakfast, you can borrow one of the house bicycles and take off for a ride on the miles of nearby trails. You can relax afterward on the inn's deck overlooking the American River. Pool. Spa. Bicycles. | 9735 Mira Del Rio Dr. | 916/363–9933 or 916/363–3412 | otbluffs@aol.com | 3 rooms | $90 | AE, V.

Red Lion Sacramento Inn. This large hotel near Arden Fair shopping and cinema has spacious grounds. Restaurant, bar (with entertainment), room service. Refrigerators, in-room hot tubs, cable TV. 3 pools, wading pool. Putting green. Exercise equipment. Laundry facilities. Airport shuttle. Pets allowed (fee). | 1401 Arden Way | 916/922–8041 or 800/733–5466 | fax 916/922–0386 | 376 rooms | $95–$119 | AE, D, DC, MC, V.

Sacramento International Hostel. A far cry from the stereotypical hostel, this one in the palatial landmark 1885 Williams mansion has a grand mahogany staircase, an atrium decked with stained glass, frescoed ceilings, and carved and tiled fireplaces. Accommodations are dormitory-style, but there are bedrooms for singles, couples, families, and groups. You may bunk with other same-sex guests and the bathrooms and kitchen are shared. You must be out and about every day between 10 in the morning and 5 in the afternoon. Other amenities are few—but there's internet access. Laundry facilities. No room phones. | 900 H St. | 916/443–1691 | fax 916/443–4763 | www.hiayh.org/ushostel/pnwreg/sacram.htm | 70 beds, 5 private rooms | $13–$18 | MC, V.

The Savoyard. Devotees of Gilbert and Sullivan will feel at home in this bed and breakfast: the rooms are named after their musicals. In the Mikado room, with a Japanese wedding dress on the wall, you can sleep in an eastern brass bed. Flowers grow high and full in the garden, which is part of the three blocks known as "Azalea Row." Complimentary Continental breakfast. No pets. | 3322 H St. | 916/442–6709 or 800/7–SAVOYARD | www.savoyard.com | 4 rooms | $120 | AE, D, DC, MC, V.

Vagabond Inn. This three-story hotel is near downtown and Cal Expo. Take Business I–80 to Rte. 99 north. Complimentary Continental breakfast. Cable TV. Pool. Spa. Free parking. Pets allowed (fee). | 1319 30th St. | 916/454–4400 | fax 916/736–2812 | 83 rooms | $65–$85 | AE, D, DC, MC, V.

Vagabond Inn. This three-story hotel is eight blocks from the Capitol, near the Chinese Cultural Center and Old Sacramento. I–5, exit J Street. Restaurant, complimentary Continental breakfast. Some refrigerators, cable TV. Pool. Airport shuttle, free parking. Pets allowed (fee). | 909 3rd St. | 916/446–1481 or 800/522–1555 | fax 916/448–0364 | 108 rooms | $86–$98 | AE, D, DC, MC, V.

MODERATE

Abigail's Bed and Breakfast. Trees shade this 1912 Colonial Revival mansion near the Capitol. Its living room and parlor flank a grand staircase, and some rooms have four-poster or canopy feather beds. One room has a hot tub. Complimentary Continental breakfast. | 2120 G St. | 916/441–5007 | 4 rooms | $189 | AE, D, DC, MC, V.

Amber House. Three Craftsman mansions built in 1905 and 1913 make up this hotel, near the Capitol and convention center. Each mansion has a different decor: Colonial Revival, Craftsman, and Mediterranean. Complimentary breakfast, room service. In-room data ports, some in-room hot tubs, cable TV, in-room VCRs. Bicycles. Library. Business services. No smoking. | 1315 22nd St. | 916/444–8085 or 800/755–6526 | fax 916/552–6529 | 14 rooms in 3 buildings | $139–$269 | AE, D, DC, MC, V.

Clarion. Ivy covers the two buildings of this hotel, which takes up an entire city block just across the street from the Governor's Mansion, near the Convention Center and the Capitol. Restaurant, bar, room service. In-room data ports, some refrigerators, cable TV. Pool. Business services, airport shuttle, free parking. Pets allowed. No smoking. | 700 16th St. | 916/444–8000 | fax 916/442–8129 | 238 rooms | $114–$139 | AE, D, DC, MC, V.

Courtyard by Marriott. This Marriot was designed for business travelers: it offers work stations, voicemail and fax services, and a free copy of USA Today every morning. Restaurant, bar, room service. In-room data ports, cable TV. Outdoor pool. Laundry facilities. Business services, free parking. | 2101 River Plaza Dr. | 916/922–1120 | fax 916/922–1872 | 139 rooms, 12 suites | rooms $124, suites $139 | AE, D, DC, MC, V.

Delta King. This old riverboat, now permanently moored on Old Sacramento's waterfront, once transported passengers between Sacramento and San Francisco. Its main staircase, stained-glass windows, mahogany paneling, and brass fittings are impressive. Restaurant, bar, complimentary Continental breakfast. | 1000 Front St. | 916/444–5464 | 43 rooms, 1 Captains' Quarters | $119–$184, Captains' Quarters, $400 | AE, D, DC, MC, V.

Doubletree. Redwoods adorn the grounds of this hotel, and you can admire them from the paths that run through the 22-acre property. Two restaurants, bar, complimentary breakfast, room service. In-room data ports, some refrigerators, some in-room hot tubs. Pool. Exercise equipment. Business services, airport shuttle, free parking. Pets allowed. | 2001 Point West Way | 916/929–8855 or 800/222–2733 | fax 916/924–4913 | 448 rooms in 6 buildings | $149–$159 | AE, D, DC, MC, V.

Hartley House Bed and Breakfast Inn. This inn is a beautifully restored 1906 Colonial Revival mansion that's quiet, elegant, and European in its atmosphere. Complimentary breakfast. In-room data ports. No pets. No smoking. | 700 22nd St. | 916/447–7829 or 800/831–5806 |

fax 916/447–1820 | www.hartleyhouse.com | 5 rooms (showers only) | $139–$190 | AE, D, DC, MC, V.

Hawthorn Suites. This comfortable all-suite hotel is within walking distance of downtown. On I–5, take Richards Boulevard exit. Restaurant, complimentary breakfast. In-room data ports, kitchenettes, microwaves, refrigerators, cable TV, in-room VCRs. Pool. Hot tub. Exercise equipment. Laundry facilities. Business services, airport shuttle. | 321 Bercut Dr. | 916/441–1444 or 800/767–1777 | fax 916/444–2347 | 272 rooms in 6 buildings | $109–$159 | AE, D, DC, MC, V.

Radisson. There's a lake on the grounds of this two-story hotel, 2 mi west of downtown. There are picnic tables and a courtyard on the grounds. Restaurant, bar (with entertainment), room service. In-room data ports, some refrigerators, cable TV. Pool, lake. Exercise equipment, boating, bicycles. Business services, free parking. Pets allowed (fee). | 500 Leisure Lane | 916/922–2020 or 800/333–3333 | fax 916/649–9463 | sales@radisson.com | www.radisson.com/sacramentoca | 307 rooms | $129–$169 | AE, D, DC, MC, V.

Vizcaya. This 1899 mansion in town is surrounded by landscaped grounds. Complimentary breakfast. Some in-room hot tubs, cable TV. Business services. No smoking. | 2019 21st St. | 916/455–5243 or 800/456–2019 | fax 916/455–6102 | 9 rooms | $139–$249 | AE, DC, MC, V.

EXPENSIVE

Hilton Inn–Sacramento Arden West. A newly remodeled 12th floor sits atop this upscale hotel that's 4 mi east of downtown near Cal Expo, the Capitol, and Old Sacramento. Restaurant, bar. In-room data ports, refrigerators, some in-room hot tubs, cable TV. Pool. Exercise equipment. Business services. No smoking. | 2200 Harvard St. | 916/922–4700 or 800/344–4321 | fax 916/922–8418 | 331 rooms, 3 suites | $79–$169, $300–$500 1–bedroom suites, $500–$650 2–bedroom suites | AE, D, DC, MC, V.

Hyatt Regency. This 15-story hotel is near the Capitol and the convention center. Restaurants. In-room data ports, minibars, cable TV. Pool, wading pool. Hot tub. Exercise equipment. Business services, airport shuttle. No smoking. | 1209 L St. | 916/443–1234 or 800/233–1234 | fax 916/321–6699 | 500 rooms | $209–$255 | AE, D, DC, MC, V.

Sterling Hotel. Built in 1896, this Victorian hotel two blocks from the convention center and Capitol has generous porches, a turret, and gables. Room are upscale, with Italian-marble bathrooms. I–5, exit J Street. Dining room, room service. In-room data ports, some refrigerators, in-room hot tubs, cable TV. Business services. No Pets. No smoking. | 1300 H St. | 916/448–1300 or 800/365–7660 | fax 916/448–8066 | 17 rooms | $169–$350 | AE, DC, MC, V.

SAN BERNARDINO

MAP 4, J14

(Nearby towns also listed: Redlands, Riverside)

An urban hub of the Inland Empire, 'Berdoo, as the locals call it, was settled by group of Latter Day Saints in the 1850s. Today, its 185,000 residents show an interesting mix of Spanish and Mormon cultures. The surrounding county, which bears the same name, is the largest in the United States and stretches to the Arizona border. The area is a gateway to the resort and sports areas of the San Bernardino Mountains and still maintains a very prominent citrus industry.

Information: San Bernardino Convention and Visitors Bureau | 201 North E. St., Suite 103, 92401 | 909/889–3980 | getinfo@san-bernardino.org | www.san-bernardino.org.

Attractions

Glen Helen Regional Park. Since prehistoric times, these 1,340 acres in the rolling hills at the mouth of Cajon Pass have introduced people to the region known as Southern California. Now, you can attend concerts in the 65,000-seat Blockbuster Pavilion amphitheater as well as camp, hike, swim at a lagoon with a pair of 350-ft water slides, fish, and picnic here. | 2555 Glen Helen Pky | 909/880–2522 | fax 909/880–2659; Pavilion, 909/880–6500 or 909/886–8742 | www.co.san-bernardino.ca.us/parks | $2 per person, or $5 per vehicle | Daily.

Mountain High Ski Area. The 8,200-ft-high mountain is divided into an east ski area with a vertical drop of 1,600 ft and a west section with a vertical drop of 1,000 ft. Both areas have lodges and other base facilities. The 12 lifts, including two high-speed quads, will take you to any of 47 trails set on 220 acres. Parking areas, about 30 mi from San Bernardino, have shuttles to take you to the lodges. | 24510 Rte. 2, Wrightwood | 760/249–5808; 888/754–7878 for snow report | fax 760/249–3155 | www.mthigh.com | Prices vary | Nov.–Apr., weekdays, lifts 8:30 AM–10 PM, lodges 8 AM–10 PM; weekends, lifts 8–10, lodges 7:30–10.

Rim of the World Highway. On the National Register of Historic Places, this scenic route begins at Mormon Rocks on Route 138 just west of I–15 and ends at Mill Creek. Along the way, you'll go through desert, foothill, and mountain terrain, and pass the Big Bear Dam. You can buy brochures at ranger stations for self-guided tours; for example, the Big Bear Ranger District site on Route 138 has directions for a 10-mi excursion along the "gold fever trail" with stops at Two Gun Bill's Saloon and the Hangman Tree. | 909/383–5588 or 800/280–CAMP | www.r5.fs.fed.us/sanbernardino/ | Free | Daily.

San Bernardino National Forest. The 660,000 acres of the San Bernardino National Forest have the highest mountains in Southern California and the San Jacinto and San Giogonio wilderness areas, as well as year-round sports resort centers at Big Bear Lake, Lake Arrowhead, and Idyllwild. You'll find a visitor center at Barton Flats, on Route 138 at milepost marker 26.84. | 909/383–5588 or 800/280–CAMP | www.r5.fs.fed.us/sanbernardino | $5 | Daily.

ON THE CALENDAR

MAY: *National Orange Show.* In homage to the all-important orange crop, San Bernardino celebrates with an annual Memorial Day weekend festival that includes carnival rides, entertainment, and other events, at the National Orange Show grounds. | 689 South E St. | 909/888–6788.

APR.–JUNE: *Renaissance Faire.* At this rollicking fantasy re-creation of 15th- and 16th-century England in Glen Helen Regional Park, you can watch as costumed performers joust, juggle, and perform in other light-hearted theatrical presentations, and you'll find plenty of traditional foods, too. | 2555 Glen Helen Pky | 800/52–FAIRE.

Lodging

Hilton. About halfway between LA and Palm Springs, this seven-story brick hotel has its own view of the Arrowhead Mountains, often snow-crested beyond the palm trees. Within a mile, you'll find 25 restaurants, with the San Manuel Casino in Highland about 7 mi away and the San Bernardino Museum 2 mi away. Restaurant, bar. Some refrigerators, some in-room hot tubs, cable TV. Pool. Hot tub. Exercise equipment. Business services. | 285 E. Hospitality Ln. | 909/889–0133 | fax 909/381–4299 | www.sanbernardino-hilton.com | 250 rooms | $150 | AE, D, DC, MC, V.

La Quinta. You'll find more than a dozen restaurants in the area around this turquoise-and-brown structure with the red tile roof. Built in 1983, the three-story motel is 3 mi from San Bernardino International Airport and 3 mi south of downtown. Complimentary Continental breakfast. Cable TV. Pool. Business services. Pets allowed. | 205 E. Hospitality Ln. | 909/888–7571 | fax 909/884–3864 | www.laquinta.com | 153 rooms | $65 | AE, D, DC, MC, V.

Leisure Inn and Suites. A modest lodging alternative a half-block from the 5th Street exit of I–215, this motel is also two blocks from Carousel Mall and 1 mi from the National Orange Show grounds. Complimentary Continental breakfast. Some microwaves, refrigerators. Pool. Hot tub. Free parking. | 777 W. 6th St. | 909/889–3561 | fax 909/884–7127 | 57 rooms | $33–$45 | AE, CB, D, DC, MC, V.

Radisson Hotel and Convention Center. A pale-toned tower rising next to the city's convention center, this 12-story hotel has an elevated walkway to the 107 shops and stores of Carousel Mall across the street. About 3 mi from beach access, the upper floors offer panoramic views of city and mountains, and you can work on your tan inside the hotel at the Oasis Sundeck by the hot tub. Restaurant, bar. Some refrigerators, cable TV. Hot tub. Exercise equipment. Business services, airport shuttle, free parking. | 295 N. E St. | 909/381–6181 | fax 909/381–5288 | www.radisson.com | 231 rooms | $140 | AE, D, DC, MC, V.

SAN CLEMENTE

MAP 4, J16

(Nearby towns also listed: Dana Point, San Juan Capistrano)

San Clemente made headlines in the 1970s as the site of Richard Nixon's California White House. Today this seaside town, a funky hillside village of 50,000, looks a lot like the California of beach blanket bingo movies with its crowd of dudes, surfers, and blondes in bikinis. It is also one of the friendliest spots on the Orange County coast. Since it's near Camp Pendleton, fatigue-dressed Marines join the mix every weekend. Tiny bungalows keep company with multimillion-dollar mansions and thrift stores with surf shops, and you'll find the usual boutique suspects and a real range of restaurants.

Information: **San Clemente Chamber of Commerce** | 1100 N. El Camino Real, 92672 | 949/492–1131 | info@scchamber.com | www.scchamber.com.

Attractions

Municipal Pier and Beach. If you just want to relax, join the anglers and your fellow tourists hanging out at the pier for people-watching on the palm-fringed beach. | 611 Avenida Victoria | Free | Daily.

San Clemente State Beach. Hiking down the steep paved trail to this mile-long beach, below a campground on a high bluff, is fairly easy, but coming back up may make you feel like you're doing a hard stint on a Stairmaster. Still, you are less likely to run into crowds at this beach than at some others. Surfers hang out at the north end; there's also scuba diving and body surfing. Lifeguards are on duty from Memorial Day to Labor Day; there's a pay lot for parking on the landscaped bluff above, where you'll also find picnic tables and hiking trails. Access is via I–5 (Basilone Rd.). The park entrance is reached via the Avenida Calafia exit. | Avenida Califia | 949/492–3156, 800/444–7275 for camping reservations | $2 parking | Daily dawn–10PM.

ON THE CALENDAR

AUG.: *San Clemente Fiesta.* The spirited party goes on all day on Avenue Del Mar, with three stages for continuous music, nonprofit food and game booths, contests and exhibits, and a 5K run. | 949/492–1131.

Lodging

Holiday Inn. You'll find some ocean views from the balconies of this three-story Mediterranean-style motel built in the early '90s with new furnishings in 2000. On a small hill two blocks from the ocean, it's 29 mi from John Wayne Airport, 4 mi from San Juan Capistrano Mission, and 30 mi from Disneyland. Restaurant, bar, room service. In-room data ports, refrigerators, cable TV. Pool. Business services, free parking. Pets allowed (fee). | 111 S. Ave. de Estrella | 949/361–3000 or 800/469–1161 | fax 949/361–2472 | holidaysc@aol.com | www.holiday-inn.com | 72 rooms, 20 suites | $139–$149 | AE, D, DC, MC, V.

Travelodge San Clemente Beach. Three blocks from the beach at the Magdelina Avenue exit of I–5, this three-story hotel's balcony set-backs lend a faintly Aztec look to the white structure. Rooms look out to the ocean or to greenery of the golf course next door, and some rooms have private hot tubs. It's about 2 mi from the pier and a mile from the north gate of Camp Pendleton. Complimentary Continental breakfast. Refrigerators, cable TV. | 2441 S. El Camino Real | 949/498–5954 or 800/843–1706 or 888/515–6375 | fax 949/498–6657 | www.travelodge.com | 19 rooms | $89–$189 | AE, D, DC, MC, V.

SAN DIEGO

(Nearby towns also listed: Carlsbad, Chula Vista, Coronado, Del Mar, El Cajon, Escondido, La Jolla, Oceanside, San Ysidro)

As the seventh-largest U.S. city, with a population of 1.3 million, sunny San Diego is a giant, sprawling metropolis, but it successfully maintains a laid-back, small-town feel. Its bay-front location, sandy beaches, temperate climate, and unusually clean streets add credence to its self-proclaimed label as "America's finest city."

A long, rich Hispanic heritage continues to shape San Diego. In 1542, Portuguese explorer João Rodrigues Cabrilho sailed into the bay, claiming the land for Spain and christening it San Miguel, a name that would change 60 years later to San Diego. The end of the 18th century witnessed construction of both the Presidio—the initial outpost of the Spanish government in Alta ("upper") California—and the first of Father Junipero Serra's 21 California missions, built in what's now Mission Valley. Only later, well into the 1800s, did the first American pioneers begin to trickle into the area. Today, San Diego's enduring Hispanic presence is evident everywhere, from Barrio Logan's Chicano Park to Old Town to the Centro Cultural de la Raza, and the city maintains close ties with Tijuana, 20 mi to the south.

Tourism is a booming industry for San Diego, but an even greater source of local revenue is the military. In 1908, after Theodore Roosevelt's Great White Fleet stopped in San Diego on a world tour, plans were made to build a destroyer base at the port. Now the city harbors the largest naval fleet in the continental U.S. and is home to many active and retired military personnel.

San Diego also boasts the nation's largest cultural park west of the Mississippi. Just north of downtown, manicured Balboa Park is the hub of San Diego's cultural activity. The park's extravagant Spanish Colonial buildings constructed for the 1915 Panama-California Exposition now house world-class museums and theaters. You can spend days in the park, especially if you visit the acclaimed zoo or take advantage of the recreation options that include golf and lawn bowling.

While you can explore the downtown's Gaslamp Quarter and shops on foot, you're best off seeing the city's score of neighborhoods by car. One of the best known is La Jolla, the cloistered community of boutiques and million-dollar homes perched on sandy hillsides along the coastline. Less known are the many other diverse neighborhoods that fan out from downtown, including hip, gay Hillcrest with its classy shops and restaurants; North Park with its vintage Craftsman bungalows; and fun, funky Ocean Beach with its impressive fishing pier, antiques shops, and beach just for dogs.

No longer insular and slow-paced, this handsome and economically vibrant city continues to grow by more than 50,000 people each year. Luckily, the extensive network of canyons that cuts through the city has reined in the unchecked building that created the megalopolis of Los Angeles 120 mi to the north.

Information: **San Diego Convention and Visitors Bureau** | 401 B St., 92101 | 619/232–3101 or 619/236–1212 | sdinfo@sandiego.org | www.sandiego.org.

NEIGHBORHOODS

Embarcadero. San Diego's original dockside, just west of downtown, is a clean and beautiful area to explore. Although it never developed as a major commercial port, you can use your imagination with the help of the old ships moored at the Maritime Museum, the Seaport Village, and the San Diego Convention Center, whose design was supposedly inspired by an ocean liner. There's a public fishing pier and an open-air amphitheater in the Embarcadero Marina Park where free concerts are held in summer.

Old Town. Set 2½ mi northwest of downtown, this was the site of the first civilian Spanish settlement in California. A plaza was built here in the 1820s and within 10 years it was surrounded by huts and whitewashed villas. It was the center of San Diego until 1872, when the current downtown area proved more favorable. Now a State Historic Park, Old Town has endured archaeological work, restoration of its few surviving original buildings, and the reconstruction of ruined buildings. The shady plaza is a good place for a stroll. You should also see the 1820s Casa de Carrillo, the oldest house in San Diego, just north of Old Town—but be prepared, it's now the pro shop for a golf course.

TRANSPORTATION

Airports: If you fly into San Diego you will probably arrive at the **San Diego International Airport** at Lindbergh Field, 3 mi northwest of downtown. There is both on-site and off-site parking. On-site parking facilities are available at all terminals and have an easy automated parking payment system. Rates range from 50 cents for 30 minutes to $12 for 24 hours. Major car rental agencies have desks at the airport. If you plan on driving to Mexico, make sure your rental agreement allows this. Taxies departing from the airport have regulated fares. All companies charge the same (about $2 for the first mile and $1.25 for each additional mile).

Rail: The Santa Fe Depot, one of the Spanish Colonial-style structures built during the 1915 exposition, is the center of train services to and from the city. **Amtrak** runs the San Diegan, which makes the three-hour trip to Los Angeles several times daily, with some trains continuing to Santa Barbara. During the morning and evening rush hours **Coaster** commuter trains run between Oceanside and San Diego, stopping in Del Mar, Solana Beach, Encinitas, and Carlsbad. | 1050 Kettner Blvd. | Depot 619/239–9021, Amtrak 800/762–7245, commuter lines 800/262–7837. **Bus:** Buses operated by **Greyhound** make the trip to and from San Diego and Los Angeles several times a day; there are also buses south to the Mexican border and east to Phoenix, Tucson, and El Paso. | 120 W. Broadway | 619/239–8082 or 800/231–2222.

Intra-city Transport: San Diego County's network of bus and rail routes covers most of the metropolitan area from Oceanside in the north to the Mexican border at San Ysidro and east to the Anza Borrego desert. **San Diego Transit** (619/233–3004) runs buses that connect with the San Diego Trolley light rail system and serve the San Diego Zoo, Balboa Park, Lindbergh Field, Mission Beach, Pacific Beach, La Jolla, and regional shopping centers. The bright orange San Diego Trolley's Blue and Orange lines serve downtown, Mission Valley, Old Town, South Bay, the U.S. border, and East County. Look for bus connection information at each station and bike lockers at most. The **San Diego–Coronado Ferry** (619/234–4111) makes hourly trips between Coronado and the Broadway Pier, on the extreme western edge of downtown. There are great cycle routes in Pacific Beach, Mission Beach, Mission Bay, and Coronado. MTS buses on some routes have a bike rack, and bikes can be transported without extra charge.

Taxis: Fares vary among companies along other routes. There are taxi stands at shopping centers and hotels; at other locations you need to call ahead to reserve taxis: **Silver**

Cabs (619/280–5555), **Coronado Cabs** (619/435–6211), **Orange Cab** (619/291–3333), **Yellow Cab** (619/234–6161), **Red Top Cab** (619/531–1111).

Driving Around Town: A car is a must for San Diego, with its extensive freeways, and it's useful for visiting Baja California (though the San Diego Trolley serves the Tijuana border). In downtown, streets are on a grid divided largely in alphabetical and numerical order. Numbered avenues and streets run north–south, and named and lettered streets run east–west in alphabetical order. North of Ash, streets continue as Beech, Cedar, Date, and so on. South of Ash you find A Street followed by B Street, and so on, interspersed with an occasional named street. I–5, which extends from Canada to the Mexican border, bisects San Diego. I–8 provides access from Yuma, Arizona, and points east. Drivers coming from Nevada and the mountain regions beyond can get to San Diego on I–15. Traffic is quite heavy during rush hour. Steer clear of I–5 and I–15 between I–805 and Escondido during the rush. Highways, although generally in good condition, can be hazardous when it's rainy—slow down and watch for accidents. Listen to radio traffic reports for information on the lines waiting to cross the border to Mexico. Speed limits are 35 mph on city streets and 65 mph on freeways unless a sign indicates otherwise. Parking at meters costs $1 per hour; enforcement is from 8AM to 6PM except Sunday. Be extra careful around rush hour, when certain street parking areas become tow-away zones. In the evenings and during events, it can be difficult to find parking spaces downtown. There are many lots downtown where fees range from $3 to $35 per day. Old Town has large lots off the Transit Center. as well. In La Jolla and Coronado, parking is more of a challenge. You will need to use expensive by-the-hour parking lots unless Lady Luck hands you a spot on the street. There are free parking lots in Balboa Park, Cabrillo National Monument, and Mission Bay, and though it may seem like you have to park a hundred miles from your destination, you should always find a space. Balboa Park, the 1,200-acre home to many of San Diego's museums and the zoo, can be a difficult place to park. If you're driving in via the Laurel Street Bridge, the first parking area you come to as you head toward Pan American Plaza is off the Prado to the right. You can get back to your car using the free trams, daily every 8 to 10 min between 9:30 and 4, from the large lot on the east side of the park at Presidents Way.

SAN DIEGO

INTRO
ATTRACTIONS
DINING
LODGING

THE GHOST IN SAN DIEGO

There's a ghost in San Diego. Or so say the people of Heritage Park. The Old Sherman-Gilbert House in Old Town San Diego is haunted. If you want to check it out, you won't need to have *X-Files* stars Fox Mulder and Dana Scully along. Just your nerves.

The people who work at the inn the 1887 Eastlake-style structure tell of things getting moved around in the night, aromas of old-fashioned perfume, and creaking sounds coming from nowhere in particular.

According to the locals, it's Bess Gilbert who's doing the haunting. Bess was a well-to-do socialite who entertained some of the famous people of her day; Anna Pavlova danced here and Artur Rubinstein played piano here, and Harold Bauer, Percy Grainger, Fritz Kreisler, Yehudi Menuhin, Mme. Modjeska, Ernestine Schumann-Heink, and Paderewski were guests. Bess lived in the house with her sister (whom she outlived) and, as in virtually all ghost stories, died in the house, in 1965. The theory is that Bess was so attached to the house that when it was moved to Heritage Park after her death, she came along for the ride and never left.

© Artville

WALKING TOUR

Balboa Park is a great place for a walk. Enter via Cabrillo Bridge through the west gate. Park south of the **Alcazar Garden,** your starting point. Just north across El Prado is the landmark California Building, now home to the **San Diego Museum of Man.** Look up to see busts and statues of heroes of the early days of the state. Next door is the **Simon Edison Centre for the Performing Arts,** which adjoins the sculpture garden of the **San Diego Museum of Art,** built to resemble Spain's 17th-century University of Salamanca. Walk east and you will come to the **Timken Museum of Art,** the **Botanical Building,** and the **Casa del Prado,** which houses the San Diego Floral Association. At the end of the row is the **San Diego Natural History Museum.** Go one block north to see the **Spanish Village Art Center.** Continuing north you will reach a carousel and a miniature railroad and the entrance to the **San Diego Zoo.** Return to the Natural History Museum and cross the Plaza de Balboa (its fountain is a popular meeting spot). You're now at the **Reuben H. Fleet Science Center.** Heading west you will pass the Casa de Balboa, home of the **San Diego Historical Society** and **San Diego Model Railroad Museum** and **Museum of Photographic Arts.** Next door is the House of Hospitality, where you will find the Balboa Park Visitor's Center. Across the Plaza de Panama is the **Mingei International Museum of Folk Art** and the **San Diego Art Institute** in the House of Charm. Your starting point, the Alcazar Garden, is west of the building.

Attractions

ART AND ARCHITECTURE

Centro Cultural de La Raza. You can't miss the bright murals of this Balboa Park museum housed in a former water cistern. Here you can view changing exhibits of contemporary Chicano, Mexican, and Native American art and attend theater, music, and dance performances. | 2125 Park Blvd. | 619/235–6135 | www.sddt.com/features/balboapark/museums/centro.html | Free | Wed.–Sun. 12–5.

SOUTH OF THE BORDER

If you're in San Diego, you may well be interested in a day in Mexico or at least Tijuana, as the international border is only 15 mi away. No longer is "TJ" the sleepy town of movies and images. The population of its metropolitan area now numbers two million people. It is the foreign city most visited by Americans.

If you're crossing the border and you're American, you'll need your driver's license as evidence of residency. If you're not an American citizen, bring your passport. You may not need it to get into Mexico, but you'll need it to get back into the United States.

The favorite activity of Tijuana visitors is shopping. If you decide to join them, make Avenida Revolucion your first stop. Here stalls and hawkers sell trinkets and touristy items and shops sell good leather goods, jewelry, and folk art.

U.S. dollars are welcome; take smaller denominations to avoid any exchange problems.

© Artville

CULTURE, EDUCATION, AND HISTORY

★ **Cabrillo National Monument.** The 144-acre Point Loma reserve that honors Juan Rodriguez Cabrillo's 1542 exploration of the Pacific Coast is the most-visited U.S. national monument. The lookout point was a critical defense point during WWI and WWII and is still a great place to scan for the gray-whale migration in late winter. As a bonus, the tidepools on the beach are great fun for kids, and views of the city and the harbor from the historical 1854 lighthouse can't be beat. | 1800 Cabrillo Memorial Dr. | 619/557–54500 | www.nps.gov/cabr/ | $5 per car | Daily 9–5:15.

Gaslamp Quarter. This 16-block historical district between 4th and 6th Avenues from Broadway to K Street contains most of the city's Victorian commercial buildings from the late 1800s. With San Diego's gold-rush and real-estate boom in the 1870s, the downtown's commercial district gradually moved north of Market Street, and many of the buildings south of Market became rundown, creating a red-light district known as the Stingaree. In 1887 the district was home to 120 bordellos and 71 bars. Ever since the so-called Gaslamp Quarter was placed on the National Register of Historic Places in 1980, many Victorians have been restored and the tattoo parlors and peep shows have largely been replaced by upscale restaurants, shops, galleries, and professional buildings. | 619/233–5227 or 619/233–4691 | Free | Daily.

You can visit the oldest surviving structure from "New Town" San Diego, the **William Heath Davis House.** One of the founders of New Town, William Davis never lived in the 1850 saltbox, which was later moved to its present site. The Gaslamp Historical Society hosts tours of the house and the greater Gaslamp District. | 410 Island Ave. | 619/233–4692 | $3 | Tues.–Fri. 11–3, weekends 11–4.

Photos and exhibits at the **Gaslamp Museum of Historic San Diego** tell stories of the city's colorful past, including Wyatt Earp's days as a gambling-hall operator. Hours vary, so call ahead. | 413 Market St. | 619/237–1492 | Free.

Marston House. This 1905 house on the National Register of Historic Places is a prime example of the Arts and Crafts period. Stickley and Roycroft furniture, Tiffany lamps, and Native American baskets grace the interior, and a formal English garden complements the landscaped 5-acre lot at the northwest tip of Balboa Park. | 3525 7th Ave. | 619/298–3142 | $5 | Fri.–Sun. 10-4.

Old Globe Theater. Built in 1935, this Tony Award–winning theater with three stages is one of the top professional theaters in the country. The Globe presents at least 12 main-stage productions a year, ranging from Shakespearean drama to musicals to contemporary plays. | El Prado east of Cabrillo Bridge | 619/239–2255 | www.oldglobe.org | Tues.–Sun.

★ **Old Town State Historic Park.** The six blocks around San Diego's original Spanish pueblo are the heart of Old Town. You can see seven original buildings from the mid 1800s and many more historical reconstructions. The museums, the shops in Bazaar del Mundo, and the lovely plaza make this a great place for a *paseo* (stroll). A free walking tour of Old Town begins at 11 and 2 at the Robinson Rose House. | Bordered by Congress, Juan, Taylor, and Twiggs Sts. | 619/220–5422 | fax 619/220–5421 | www.cal-parks.ca.gov/districts/sandiego/ | Free | Daily.

The 1827 adobe **Casa de Estudillo** was built by a former commander of the Presidio. You can get a glimpse of his family's 19th-century life in the period-furnished rooms. | 4001 Mason St. | 619/220–5426 | Free | Daily 10–5.

The seven Victorian buildings in 8-acre **Heritage Park** were rescued from demolition, moved to the present site, and restored to show off their architectural charm. Among them is California's first synagogue. | Heritage Park Row | 858/565–3600.

One of the two visitors centers is at the **Seeley Stable Museum,** which was one end of the San Diego-Los Angeles stage line in the mid 1800s and now stores covered wagons, stagecoaches, and Western memorabilia. | 2630 Calhoun St. | 619/220–5422 | Free | Daily 10–5.

Only two buildings in California have been recognized by the U.S. government as being haunted, and the creaky **Whaley House** is one of them. Over the years, the 1886 brick structure has served as a granary, store, courthouse, school, and theater. Today it displays antiques, historical photos, and a doll collection. | 2482 San Diego Ave. | 619/298–2482 | $4 | Daily 10–5.

San Diego Opera. The city's respected opera company generally stages five major productions each year—works by Wagner, Verdi, Mozart, and Carlisle Floyd, among others—and offers lectures to prep you for the operas ahead of time. At least two bonus recitals by international artists are scheduled, too. | Civic Theatre, 3rd Ave. and B St. | 619/232–7636.

San Diego State University. With 28,000 undergraduate and graduate students, SDSU is one of the largest universities in the west. Founded in 1897 to train grade-school teachers, it's now a teaching and research university, with $90 million in annually funded research programs. It's also home to the Aztec athletic teams, the Gwynn baseball stadium, and the 12,000-seat Cox Arena. | 5500 Campanile Dr. | 619/594–5200 | Free | Daily.

San Diego Symphony. Since 1998, the city's resurrected symphony has been flourishing under energetic artistic director Jung-Ho Pak. The diverse seasonal programs offer something for everyone, from the popular outdoor Summer Pops series to concerts for connoisseurs, families, and kids. | 750 B St. | 619/235–0804 | fax 619/231–3848 | www.sandiegosymphony.com.

University of San Diego. Founded in 1949, this 180-acre campus with its landmark Immaculata church began its mission as the San Diego College for Women. The current university remains Catholic by charter but now welcomes both sexes of any denomination for undergraduate and graduate studies. Schools for law, nursing, and education are among the academic programs offered at the Spanish-style complex overlooking Mission Bay. | 5998 Alcalá Pk. | 619/260–4600 | www.acusd.edu | Free | Daily.

Villa Montezuma. Built in 1887 for musician and spiritualist Jesse Shepard, this ornate Victorian mansion with an arabesque dome, gargoyles, period furnishings, and stained-glass windows now hosts community events such as Victorian-style teas, musicals, and poetry readings. Tours hourly. | 1925 K St. | 619/239–2211 | www.sandiegohistory.org | $5 | Fri.–Sun., 10–4:30.

MUSEUMS

Children's Museum/Museo de los Niños. This terrific kids' museum downtown includes lots of hands-on exhibits and art activities such as mural making, improvisational theater, and "Build a Piece of San Diego." | 200 W. Island Ave. | 619/233–5437 | $6 | Tues.–Sat. 10–4.

Maritime Museum. Climb aboard three historical ships at the downtown harbor: the 1863 barque *Star of India,* the oldest operational square-rigged ship in the world; the 1898 ferryboat *Berkeley,* one of the best examples of a triple-expansion steam engine; and the 1904 steam yacht *Medea,* which served in two world wars and under six national flags. | 1306 N. Harbor Dr. | 619/234–9153 | fax 619/234–8345 | www.sdmaritime.com | $6 | Daily 9–8.

★ **Mingei International Museum.** *Mingei* is a coined word meaning "art of the people." This Balboa Park museum hosts excellent changing exhibits of international folk art and traditional crafts in its spacious, open display areas on two floors. | 1439 El Prado | 619/239–0003 | fax 619/239–0605 | www.mingei.org | $5 | Tues.–Sun. 10–4.

★ **Museum of Contemporary Art.** This downtown annex of the city's modern art museum is on a tiny slice of land wedged between the downtown trolley terminus and the train station, so there's always a dynamic background hum of rumbling trains. Permanent and temporary exhibitions showcase conceptual, minimalist, and California art. The first Sunday of each month there's a family craft project and free admission. | 1001 Kettner Blvd. | 619/234–1001 | www.mcasandiego.org | $2 | summer, Thurs.–Tues. 11–5; fall–spring, Tues.–Sat. 10–5, Sun. noon–5.

Museum of Man. Balboa Park's anthropology museum inside the 200-ft-high California Tower displays artifacts and exhibits about the origins of humankind. You can visit the Children's Discovery Center, see Peruvian mummies, or watch demonstrations of weaving and tortilla making. | 1350 El Prado | 619/239–2001 | fax 619/239–2749 | www.museumofman.org | $6 | Daily 10–4:30.

Museum of Photographic Arts. One of the top photography venues worldwide, this museum in Casa del Balboa reopened in 2000 after an expansion that added a state-of-the-art theater and film program to its existing photography archive and exhibition space. | 1649 El Prado | 619/238–7559 | fax 619/238–8777 | www.mopa.org | $6 | Daily 10–5.

Natural History Museum. At the east end of Balboa Park, this museum is dedicated to the flora, fauna, and geology of San Diego and Baja California. There's an allosaurus skeleton, a seismograph, and a re-created mine shaft, among many other exhibits. | 1788 El Prado | 619/232–3821 | fax 619/232–0248 | www.sdnhm.org | $6 | Daily 9:30–5:30.

★ **Reuben H. Fleet Science Center.** Experience surfing a 30-ft wave or free-falling through the air when you watch the IMAX dome screen in this Balboa Park museum, then visit the five galleries with more than 50 hands-on science exhibits, or take the SciTours simulator ride. | 1875 El Prado | 619/238–1233 | www.rhfleet.org | Admission $6.50, IMAX, $9 | Fall–spring, Sun.–Thurs. 9:30–5, Fri.–Sat. 9:30–9; summer daily 9:30–9.

San Diego Aerospace Museum. This museum dedicated to aviation history is at the south end of Balboa Park. The International Aerospace Hall of Fame is here, as well as more than 65 aircraft, including an A-4 Skyhawk jet, a Spitfire XVI, and a replica of Lindbergh's *Spirit of St. Louis*. | 2001 Pan American Plaza | 619/234–8291 | www.aerospacemuseum.org | $8 | fall–spring, daily 10–4:30; summer, daily 10–5:30.

San Diego Automotive Museum. The history of the automobile is the subject of this Balboa Park museum, with rare photos, an active restoration display, and more than 80 vehicles, from horseless carriages to motorcycles. | 2080 Pan American Plaza | 619/231–2886 | www.sdautomuseum.org | $7 | Sept.–May, daily 10–4:30; June–Aug. 10–5:30.

San Diego Hall of Champions Sports Museum. At this 70,000-sq-ft museum in Balboa Park, you'll find sports from archery to yachting represented in interactive displays, memorabilia, and work by sports artists. Check out the Breitbard Hall of Fame, too. | 2131 Pan American Plaza | 619/234–2544 | fax 619/234–4543 | www.sandiegosports.org | $4 | Daily 10–4:30.

San Diego Historical Society Museum. Permanent and changing exhibits about San Diego show off the society's collection of 2 million photographs, huge research archives, and artifacts such as costumes, art, jewelry, and tools. Find the museum in Balboa Park's Casa de Balboa. | 1649 El Prado | 619/232–6203 | www.sandiegohistory.org | $5 | Tues.–Sun. 10–4:30.

San Diego Model Railroad Museum. The wonderland of miniature tracks and working toy trains—the largest operating display in the U.S.—make this Balboa Park museum a delight for all ages. It has four giant-scale model railroads of the Southwest. | Casa de Balboa | 619/696–0199 | $4 | Tues.–Fri. 10–4, weekends 11–5.

San Diego Museum of Art. Balboa Park's largest art museum houses an eclectic but highly regarded collection that includes works from Asia, European Old Masters, and 20th-century painting and sculpture. Even if the traveling exhibitions aren't to your taste, try not to miss the permanent collection here. | 1450 El Prado | 619/232–7931 | www.sdmart.org | $8 | Tues.–Sun. 10–4:30.

Serra Museum. Built in 1929 on the site of the original 1769 Spanish settlement that overlooks Old Town, this museum houses a collection of artifacts from San Diego's early days, including housewares, clothing, and military equipment. | 2727 Presidio Dr. | 619/297–3258 | www.sandiegohistory.org | $5 | Fri.–Sun. 10–4:30.

Timken Museum of Art. One of the jewels of Balboa Park, this modest 1960s building houses a collection of Russian icons and European and American masterworks. Among the treasures are paintings by Copley, Rubens, and Rembrandt, as well as Buonaccorso's 1387 illu- minated panel painting "Madonna and Child." | 1500 El Prado | 619/239–5548 | www.gort.ucsd.edu/sj/timken/ | Free | Oct.–Aug., Tues.–Sat 10–4:30, Sun. 1:30–4:30.

Veterans Memorial Center. Formerly part of the naval hospital, this Balboa Park museum now displays military artifacts, documents, and memorabilia from all branches of the armed forces, some material dating back to the Civil War. The paintings of Richard DeRossett are a highlight. The center also has social services for active and retired military personnel. | 2115 Park Blvd. | 619/239–2300 | www.sdvmc.org | Free | Daily 10–4.

PARKS, NATURAL AREAS, AND OUTDOOR RECREATION

Balboa Park. A dizzying array of recreational and cultural options await you within the 1,200-acre park developed for the 1915 exposition that celebrated the opening of the Panama Canal. The core of the park contains 15 museums (many housed in reconstructed or original 1915–1916 Spanish Colonial buildings), diverse botanical gardens, the San Diego Zoo, and amusements such as the carousel and nearby miniature train ride. The park's outskirts, including Morley Field, offer recreation from disc golf to tennis—there's even a velodrome. If you first visit the House of Hospitality (1549 El Prado), you can pick up a vis- itors' guide and map for the tram that runs throughout the park. You can also park within the grounds and explore on foot. A weekly pass to the park's museums is available. | Bounded by Upas St. on the north, 6th Ave. on the west, A St. on the south, and 27th St. on the east | 619/239–0512 | www.balboapark.org | Grounds free | Daily.

You have your choice of 9 or 18 holes at the 1927 **Balboa Park Municipal Golf Course,** which was artfully designed with the natural contours of its canyon terrain in mind. The 1st and 17th tees offer great views of the city, the harbor, and the Coronado Bridge. | 2600 Golf Course Drive | 619/235–1184 | $17–$32 | Daily.

The beautiful wood-lath structure west of the art museum is the 1915 **Botanical Build- ing,** with more than 2,000 tropical and flowering plants. | El Prado | 619/239–0512 | Free | Fri.–Tues. 10–4.

More than 30 national groups, from Philippine to Polish, maintain the clustered cot- tages that make up the **House of Pacific Relations.** On Sundays the cottages offer ethnic arts, crafts, dance, music, or food to promote international relations. | Presidents Way and Pan American Rd. E | 619/234–0739 | Free | Sun. 1–5.

Next to the organ pavilion, the tranquil **Japanese Friendship Garden** with tea pavil- ion, koi pond, bonsai collection, and 60-ft wisteria arbor grew out of San Diego's ties with its Japanese sister city Yokohama. | 2215 Pan American Rd. E | 619/232–2721 | Tues.– Sun. 10–4.

Besides the golf course, year-round **recreation areas** within the park include an archery range, disc golf course, a velodrome, a swimming pool, a baseball field, tennis courts, a lawn- bowling court, a play area for disabled kids, and a recreation center for the visually impaired. | 619/239–0512 or 619/692–4919.

More than 300 glassblowers, jewelers, sculptors, woodcarvers, and painters demonstrate their skills and sell their work in the 37 studio-galleries of the **Spanish Village Arts Center.** The courtyard was built in 1935 for the California-Pacific International Exposition and used as naval barracks during WWII. | 1770 Village Pl | 619/233–9050 | Free | Daily 11–4.

Take a seat in the 2,000-seat **Spreckels Organ Pavilion** and listen to Robert Plimpton play the magnificent 1914 Spreckels Organ, the world's largest outdoor pipe organ, with 4,518 pipes ranging in size from ¼ inch to 32 ft. | 2211 Pan American Rd. E | 619/702–8138 | Free | Concerts Sept.–June, Sun. at 2; July–Aug., Sun. at 2, Mon. at 7:30.

Chicano Park. The center of the Mexican-American barrio, this park with its many vibrant murals continues to be a symbol of community spirit and activism. | Logan Ave. and Crosby St. | 619/691–1044 | Free | Daily.

Crystal Pier. Take in the ocean breeze as you stroll along this peaceful pier, a popular spot for parents and their youngsters. The pier juts into the water from the foot of Garnet Avenue in Pacific Beach. | Free | Daily.

Embarcadero. Seafood restaurants and sea vessels of every kind line the piers along San Diego's famous waterfront walkway—a great place to get some exercise and fresh air. | N. Harbor Dr. bordered by Ash St. and B St. Pier | 619/232–3101 or 619/236–1212 | Free | Daily.

Mission Bay Park. In 1945 the mud flats of Mission Bay were dredged and transformed into this well-groomed 4,600-acre park with picnic areas, campgrounds, playgrounds, and boat launches. You can walk or rollerblade around the park's 27-mi perimeter, sail or water-ski on the bay, ride America's oldest wooden roller coaster in Belmont Park, walk on the beach, or watch for some of the 100 species of birds in the Kendall-Frost Marsh Reserve. Take the Mission Bay Drive exit off of I-5. | Bordered by Mission Blvd., W. Mission Bay Dr., Sea World Dr., and E. Mission Bay Dr. | 619/276–8200 | fax 619/276–6041 | www.infosandiego.com | Free | Park Grounds, daily; visitors center, Mon.–Sat. 9–5, Sun. 9:30–4:30.

Mission Trails Regional Park. Eight miles northeast of downtown is this 5,800-acre reserve, one of the largest urban parks in America and formerly the home of the Kumeyaay tribe. Forty miles of hiking trails, the historical Old Mission Dam, and views from Cowles Mountain—the highest point within the city—are worth the trip. | Mission Gorge Rd. | 619/668–3275 | www.mtrp.org | Free | Daily 9–5.

Pacific Beach Boardwalk. One of San Diego's most popular hangouts, this concrete promenade along the beach is a great place to walk, rollerblade, bicycle, or just see and be seen. | Pacific Beach Dr. | 619/276–8200 | Free | Daily.

Presidio Park. This park on the hill above Old Town marks the site of the city's first mission and military fortress. | Presido Dr. and Taylor St. | 619/692–4918 | Free | Daily.

★ **San Diego Zoo.** One of the largest and best zoos in the world, this 100-acre preserve is home to more than 800 species of animals, including rare giant pandas, Komodo dragons, and Andean condors. Take the aerial tramway to get an overview of Gorilla Tropics, the aviaries, Tiger River, Polar Bear Plunge, and the many other zoo enclosures. Graceful hippos? You'll believe it when you see them in action underwater. Parking is free. | 2920 Zoo Dr. | 619/234–3153 | www.sandiegozoo.org | $16 | late June–early Sept., daily 7:30 AM–9 PM; early Sept.–late June, daily 9–4.

Sea World. Spread over 166 tropically landscaped bay-front acres in Mission Bay, this is one of the world's largest and most famous marine-life amusement parks. The many attractions include Shamu the killer whale, the penguin encounter with 400 Antarctic penguins in a sub-freezing environment, the shark tank with underwater viewing tunnel, live animal shows, and the Shipwreck Rapids adventure ride. | Sea World Dr. | 619/226–3901 | www.seaworld.com | Admission $40, parking $6 | Daily 10–dusk.

RELIGION AND SPIRITUALITY

Mission San Diego de Alcala. This "mother" of the 21 California missions was established by Franciscan friar Junipero Serra in 1769 on Presidio Hill. Five years later, it was moved to the present site. The church now standing, the fifth to be built here, was constructed in 1931 with a 46-ft-high, five-bell campanario, the mission's most distinctive feature. Ask about the schedule for Sunday mass, delivered in English and Spanish. | 10818 San Diego Mission Rd. | 619/281–8449 | $3 | Daily 9–5.

SHOPPING

Bazaar del Mundo. At the heart of Old Town Historic Park, this courtyard of shops and lush gardens has plenty of shops with international merchandise, especially excellent crafts from south of the border. Restaurants and live mariachi music help make this a pleasant destination. | Old Town | 619/296–3161 | www.bazaardelmundo.com | Free | Daily, 10–9.

★ **Horton Plaza.** It's easy to get lost in this five-level, brightly colored mall with a myriad of architectural shapes and odd angles. There are 140 upscale shops, restaurants, theaters, and a multilingual visitors center spread over 11½ acres. If you simply have to mall-shop, this is the place. | Between Broadway and G Sts., 1st and 4th Aves | 619/238–1596 | Free, validated parking | Mon.–Sat. 10–9, Sun. 11–7.

Kobey's Swap Meet. You never know what you'll find at this huge flea market in the Sports Arena parking lot. Vendors sell new and used merchandise, everything from fresh produce to jewelry to folk art and rare books. | 3500 Sports Arena Blvd. | 619/226–0650 | $1 | Thurs.–Sun. 7–3.

Ocean Beach Antique District. Browse to your heart's content through the antiques shops that line Newport Avenue, Ocean Beach's main drag. One emporium has 18,000 square ft of collectible treasures. | Newport Ave. | Free | Daily, 10–6.

★ **Seaport Village.** Popular with tourists, this 14-acre complex stretches from the harbor to the hotel towers and convention center. A wooden boardwalk runs along the bay and 4 mi of winding pathways lead to 75 specialty shops, restaurants, an 1890s carousel, and an 8-acre park. | 849 W. Harbor Dr. | 619/235–4014 | www.spvillage.com | Free | June–Aug., daily 10–10; Sept.–May, daily 10–9.

SIGHTSEEING TOURS

Gaslamp Walking Tours. No reservations are needed for the 2-hr guided walking tours hosted by the Gaslamp Historical Society. You can choose the traditional tour offered Saturdays at 11 or the "Spirits, Spies, and Scandals" excursion held on weekends at 1. | 410 Island Ave. | 619/233–4692 | $8.

Ghosts and Gravestones Tour. This 2-hr "frightseeing" tour departs at night from the cruise ship terminal and takes you through downtown and Old Town while relating stories about the city's darker side, including the mysterious Villa Montezuma. Reservations essential. | Harbor Dr. | $28 | Wed.–Sat. 7 PM.

Gray Line Bus Tours. This company offers air-conditioned bus tours of the San Diego, Tijuana, Ensenada, Seaport Village, Legoland, and the San Diego Zoo. | 1775 Hancock St. | 619/491–0011 or 800/331–5077 | www.coachusa.com.

Little Italy Tour. Here's your chance to take a guided walking tour through the historical Italian section of town, with garden, bakery, and church stops along the way. An Italian lunch is included. Reservations essential. | 1704 India St. | 760/736–1138 | $20 | Sat. noon–3.

Naval Ship Tour. Tour a ship that's part of the largest naval fleet in the continental U.S. | 32nd St. and Harbor Dr. | 619/556–7356 | Free | Weekends 1–4.

San Diego–Coronado Ferry. The ferry runs on the hour from the San Diego dock at the foot of Broadway to the Ferry Landing Marketplace in Coronado and returns from Coronado on the half-hour. | 1050 N. Harbor Dr. | 619/234–4111 | $2 | Sun.–Thurs. 9–9, Fri.–Sat. 9 AM–10 PM.

San Diego Harbor Excursion. Take a 1- or 2-hr tour of the harbor and see up close the Coronado Bridge, the naval fleet, and one of the nicest cityscapes around. Buy your ticket half an hour in advance. | 1050 N. Harbor Dr. | 619/234–4111 or 800/442–7847 | $13–$18 | Daily 1-hr. tours at 10, 11:15, 12:45, 4:15, and 5:30; daily 2-hr tours at 9:45, 12:30, and 2.

San Diego Scenic Tours. Full- and half-day narrated tours take you to La Jolla Cove, the Gaslamp Quarter, Tijuana, and other destinations. Tours begin at hotels throughout San Diego. | 858/273–8687 | Full-day tour $50, ½-day tour $25 | Daily 8:30 and 2.

Old Town Trolley Tours of San Diego. These narrated trolley tours follow a 30-mi loop with eight stops, including Horton Plaza, Old Town, Seaport Village, Coronado, and the San Diego Zoo. You can get off and on at your leisure. | 619/298–8687 | fax 619/298–3404 | www.sandiegoattraction.com/sandiegotrolleytour.html | $24 | Daily.

Whale-Watching Trips. Orion Charters, Inc., offers 3- to 4-hr tours on one of two sailboats: an award-winning 64-ft yacht built of teak and mahogany in 1934, or a 32-ft sloop that accommodates up to six passengers per trip. These charters provide a pleasant afternoon on the water, even if the whales don't show. | 1380 Harbor Island Dr. | 619/574–7504 | fax 619/226–0575 | www.orionsailing.com | $55 | Dec.–Mar., daily 8:30 AM, 1 PM.

SPECTATOR SPORTS

San Diego Chargers. An AFC team in the National Football League, the Chargers play their home games at Qualcomm Stadium in Mission Valley. Ticket prices and game times vary, so call ahead for information and reservations. | 9449 Friars Rd. | 619/525–8282 or 619/280–2121 | www.chargers.com.

San Diego Gulls. San Diego's hockey team, one of nine teams in the West Coast Hockey League, plays about 70 games between October and April. All home games are held at the Sports Arena. | 3500 Sports Arena Blvd. | 619/224–4625 | fax 619/224–3010.

San Diego Padres. This National League baseball team currently shares Qualcomm Stadium with the Chargers, but a baseball stadium of its own is in the works. | 9449 Friars Rd. | 619/283–4494 or 619/881–6500 | www.padres.com.

San Diego Sockers. In 2001 the resurrected 10-time-champion Sockers rejoined the World Soccer Indoor League, which regularly hosts soccer teams from countries such as England and the Netherlands. | 3500 Sports Arena Blvd. | 877/410–4625 or 858/836–4625.

ON THE CALENDAR

APR.: *Chicano Park Days.* Held the third weekend in April, this festival has food, entertainment, and a great vintage car show. | Chicano Park | 619/691–1044.

JULY: *Over-the-Line World Championships.* More than 1,000 three-person teams from around the world compete in San Diego's original sport, over-the-line, a softball-type game played on sand. For two weekends, Mission Bay is a crowded flesh-fest and party that raises money for civic causes. It's free to watch, but the rules are "no bottles, babies, or bowsers" (dogs). | Fiesta Island | 619/688–0817 | www.ombac.org | Free.

SEPT., OCT.: *Cabrillo Festival.* This festival with costumed participants re-creates the discovery of San Diego Bay by Juan Rodriguez Cabrillo. It's staged at the beautiful Cabrillo National Monument, overlooking the harbor. | 619/557–5450.

DEC.: *Christmas Light Boat Parade.* Boats bedecked with lights and other seasonal decorations cruise the harbor for one of San Diego's most popular holiday traditions. | 619/232–3101.

DEC.: *Christmas on the Prado.* Adults and kids alike eagerly await San Diego's largest free community event, held the first two weekend nights of the month. The extravaganza includes choirs, bagpipes, international food, free admission to Balboa Park's museums, the lighting of the gigantic live Christmas tree, Santa, and the beloved Santa Lucia parade of costumed Swedish kids. Don't forget the hot spiced cider and wine, too. | Balboa Park | 619/232–3101.

Dining

INEXPENSIVE

Aesop's Tables. Greek. Stucco walls and a warming fireplace create a homey atmosphere here despite the shopping-center location in University City. Try the avgolemono (lemon-egg soup), the saganaki (flaming cheese), or the kotopita dijon (chicken breast sautéed in cream and dijon and wrapped with feta cheese in pita bread). Open-air dining on the patio in front. | 8650 Genesee Ave. | 858/455–1535 | No lunch Sun. | $6–$13 | AE, D, DC, MC, V.

Berta's Latin American Restaurant. Latin. This unassuming restaurant is a nice alternative to Old Town's Mexican restaurants. Enjoy Chilean wine and Latin food in the simple dining room or on the garden patio. Try the Peruvian chicken or the Brazilian seafood vatapa—shrimp, scallops, and fish served in a sauce flavored with ginger, coconut, and chili. | 3928 Twiggs St. | 619/295–2343 | Closed Mon. | $7–$13 | AE, MC, V.

Chilango's Mexico City Grill. Mexican. This tiny, cheerful storefront in Hillcrest offers burritos, tortas (sandwiches), and daily specials that might include pork adobada or chicken in mole poblano (a traditional chili and chocolate sauce). Consider either takeout or an off-hours visit, as the restaurant's 10 inside tables and eight sidewalk tables quickly overflow in the evening. | 142 University Ave. | 619/294–8646 | Breakfast also available | $4–$7 | No credit cards.

Corvette Diner Bar and Grill. American. Bop to the tunes of a live DJ in this fun Hillcrest diner crammed with '50s memorabilia and a sparkling full-size Corvette as the centerpiece. | 3946 5th Ave. | 619/542–1476 | $5–$10 | AE, D, DC, MC, V.

Crest Cafe. American. Usually jammed to the gills, this Hillcrest institution has a small Art Deco dining room that displays local photography and serves up American favorites such as pancakes, burgers, and onion rings. Try the barbecue ranchero or mango grilled-chicken salads. | 425 Robinson Ave. | 619/295–2510 | Breakfast also available | $5–$16 | AE, D, DC, MC, V.

D. Z. Akin's. Delicatessens. You'll see why this New York–style deli with adjoining gourmet shop and bakery keeps winning local awards. Fast service, a crock of kosher pickles on every table, and generous portions keep the regulars coming back for the blintzes, eggs scrambled with lox and onions, and fresh chopped liver and pastrami triple-decker sandwiches. Find the deli off I–8 close to La Mesa. | 6930 Alvarado Rd. | 619/265–0218 | Breakfast also available | $7–$15 | MC, V.

Filippi's Pizza Grotto. Italian. This no-frills, family-owned pizzeria in the heart of Little Italy has been serving up huge plates of hearty pasta to locals since 1950. You line up in the deli, to get a table in one of the five dining areas with chianti bottles hanging from the rafters. Try the pizza with homemade sausage or the shrimp Filippi over linguine. | 1747 India St. | 619/232–5094 | $4–$15 | AE, MC, V.

Hob Nob Hill. American. This midtown comfort-food restaurant still has the same ownership and management it had in 1944. Its dark wooden booths and patterned carpets are from a different era, but the home cooking served here is a bargain—and better than Mom ever made. Try the oat-raisin French toast, the fried chicken, or the corned beef. Kids' menu. | 2271 1st Ave. | 619/239–8176 | Breakfast also available | $6–$10 | AE, D, DC, MC, V.

Jimmy Carter's Cafe. Eclectic. Not the former president but a San Diego native owns this midtown corner café with picture windows and simple wooden booths and tables. Businesspeople, families, gay couples, and senior citizens alike patronize Jimmy's for the down-home fare that includes tasty chicken enchiladas, burgers, steaks, Thai salad, and a fiery Indian vindaloo. | 3172 5th Ave. | 619/295–2070 | Breakfast also available | $6–$12 | AE, MC, V.

Karl Strauss' Brewery and Grill. American. Past the brick entrance to this former downtown factory, the first thing you'll notice are the stainless-steel fermenting vats for the micro-brewed ales, stouts, and lagers. At least 10 home brews are available daily to complement the pub food, which includes pesto turkey sandwiches, fish and chips, and grilled sausages. Tours available on weekends. | 1157 Columbia St. | 619/234–2739 | $6–$15 | AE, MC, V.

Nati's. Mexican. This neighborhood favorite has been serving chiles rellenos, marinated steak, and sour-cream enchiladas to the surfers and bohemians of Ocean Beach since the '60s. Choose your dining area: the garden patio with cast-iron chairs or the brightly painted indoor room adorned with mariachi hats and instruments. | 1852 Bacon St. | 619/224–3369 | $5–$8 | MC, V.

Old Town Mexican Cafe and Cantina. Mexican. You can watch the women patting out handmade tortillas at this lively Old Town restaurant. The location, decibel level, and excellent margaritas draw tourists and locals alike to the booths in the festively painted dining room for plates of pork carnitas, carne asada, and roasted chicken. Open-air dining on the garden patio. Kids' menu. | 2489 San Diego Ave. | 619/297–4330 | www.oldtownmexcafe.com | Breakfast also available | $6–$20 | AE, D, MC, V.

Point Loma Seafoods. Seafood. Grab a number and wait in line to order freshly made New England clam chowder, seafood salads, sushi, or fat fish sandwiches on sourdough bread. Then enjoy your food and the harbor scene at your waterfront table, either inside the simple covered porch area or outside on the patio. | 2805 Emerson St. | 619/223–1109 | $5–$15 | No credit cards.

Saffron. Thai. Choose among the many Thai and Vietnamese noodle dishes and soups at this small Mission Hills eatery, or sample the special spit-roasted chicken with a choice of sauces. Dramatic glass sculptures and hanging red lamps enliven the otherwise plain dining area. If you're headed to the beach, order a to-go picnic at the busy take-out counter next door. Open-air dining on the patio. | 3737 India St. | 619/574–7737 | Closed Sun. | $5–$10 | AE, MC, V.

Vegetarian Zone. Vegetarian. Set back behind shrubbery and a peaceful patio, this spot between downtown and Hillcrest has just a few tables and booths surrounded by lots of plants. Indian, Italian, and Greek dishes are prepared with no preservatives, meat, or refined sugar. Try the spinach-mushroom lasagna or the layered tofu supreme with mushrooms and a ginger-basil sauce. | 2949 5th Ave. | 619/298–7302 | www.vegetarianzone.com | $9–$12 | MC, V.

MODERATE

Anthony's Fish Grotto. Seafood. The 18-seat diner founded in 1946 by Mama Ghio and her sons has expanded into four large family-friendly restaurants. The busy original harborside eatery overlooks the water and is always crowded, but rather than go next door to the fast "fishette," wait your turn for Mama's Old World recipes, the grilled shrimp with honey mustard glaze, or the halibut with orange, mint, and basil butter. | 1360 N. Harbor Dr. | 619/232–5103 | $11–$36 | AE, D, DC, MC, V.

Athens Market. Greek. This cheerful spot with three dining rooms has catered to the downtown business crowd and the small Greek community since 1964. You can make a meal of appetizers such as taramosalata (fish-roe dip), hummus, and stuffed grape leaves or order entrées such as roast leg of lamb or the Greek pasta with garlic, onion, and cheese. On weekend evenings, stick around for the belly dancers. | 109 W. F St. | 619/234–1955 | No lunch weekends | $10–$20 | AE, D, DC, MC, V.

Bayou Bar and Grill. Cajun/Creole. Ceiling fans, jazz posters, and light pink walls help set the mood for spicy Cajun and Creole specialties that include gumbo, seafood étouffée, and Mardi Gras pasta with crawfish and shrimp. Don't pass on the rich praline cheesecake or the bread pudding. Outdoor sidewalk seating allows you to keep track of the downtown foot traffic. | 329 Market St. | 619/696–8747 | $12–$19 | AE, D, DC, MC, V.

Bella Luna. Italian. Paintings of "beautiful moons" adorn the walls of this cozy but elegant Italian restaurant with attentive service to match. For a starter, try the sautéed baby artichokes or the fresh salmon carpaccio, followed by brightly flavored corkscrew pasta with tomatoes and herbs, the daily risotto, or the black linguine with shrimp. | 748 5th Ave. | 619/239–3222 | $10–$24 | AE, DC, MC, V.

Busalacchi's. Italian. You can enjoy Sicilian fare such as calamari steak parmigiana or the ravioli alla Nonna (ravioli stuffed with shrimp, lobster, and ricotta in a cream sauce) at this family-owned Old World restaurant in Hillcrest. For seating, choose either the formal dining room with white linen and chandeliers, the casual downstairs trattoria with potted plants and cast iron, or the sidewalk patio. | 3683 5th Ave. | 619/298–0119 | $14–$20 | AE, D, DC, MC, V.

Cafe Pacifica. Seafood. Exposed wooden beams, twinkling lights, and murals welcome you to this Old Town café known for its fresh seafood. Treat yourself to the café's signature tequila cocktail, the Pomerita, then opt for the griddle-fried mustard catfish, the seared ahi tuna, or the grilled fish served with your choice of shiitaki-ginger sauce, wasabi viniagrette, or papaya salsa. | 2414 San Diego Ave. | 619/291–6666 | www.cafepacifica.com | No lunch | $13–$23 | AE, D, DC, MC, V.

★ **California Cuisine.** Contemporary. Whether you sit on the lush garden patio with a gurgling fountain or in the minimalist dining "gallery" with colorful paintings and recessed lighting, you'll receive attentive service and artfully presented food. Entrée specials might include grilled ostrich fillet, Atlantic salmon with grapefruit butter sauce, or pistachio-crusted New Zealand lamb loin. Save room for a baked dessert or a sorbet. | 1027 University Ave. | 619/543–0790 | Closed Mon. | $8–$21 | AE, D, MC, V.

Casa de Bandini. Mexican. Expect to wait at this lively historical restaurant in Old Town patronized by locals and tourists alike. The restored 1829 adobe with festively painted walls and ironwork fixtures also has seating inside or on the lush patio with palms. Order a frosty margarita, then choose the pollo asado, shredded-beef burrito, or the kitchen's San Germán, a shrimp dish served inside a pineapple half. | 2660 Calhoun St. | 619/297–8211 | Breakfast also available | $6–$16 | AE, D, DC, MC, V.

Chateau Orleans. Cajun/Creole. This restaurant in a residential area 1 mi north of Pacific Grove looks, tastes, and sounds like a bit of New Orleans. The three intimate indoor dining rooms have mauve walls, maroon chairs, and New Orleans artwork on the walls. There's also an outdoor patio. Try shrimp and tasso pasta, St. Charles chops (pork loin chops wrapped in bacon and grilled with the house ginger barbecue sauce), or Mardi Gras jambalaya with shrimp, crawfish, chicken, sausage, and scallops. Blues and jazz Thurs.–Sat. Kids' menu. Beer and wine only. No smoking. | 926 Turquoise St., Pacific Beach | 858/488–6744 | www.chateauorleans.com | Closed Sun. No lunch | $12–$22 | AE, DC, MC, V.

Croce's. Contemporary. Ingrid Croce's hip corner spot, a tribute to her late husband, was one of the first restaurants to entice diners back downtown. Most come to sip drinks and listen to jazz, which is a nightly thing, but the meals in the dark-paneled dining room with black-and-white checkered floors is quite good, especially the seafood and pork tenderloin. Outdoor sidewalk seating lets you people-watch. | 802 5th Ave. | 619/233–4355 | www.croces.com | $8–$18 | AE, D, DC, MC, V.

Dakota. American. You can see the handsome carved ceiling from both levels of this Gaslamp Quarter restaurant known for its Southwestern flair with meat. Try the blackened rib-eye, the grilled beef tenderloin, or the grilled swordfish with white bean ragout in cilantro oil. Open-air dining on the sidewalk patio. Pianist Wed.–Sat. | 901 5th Ave. | 619/234–5554 | Reservations essential | No lunch weekends | $13–$25 | AE, D, DC, MC, V.

Dick's Last Resort. American. This warehouse-style space in the Gaslamp District has sawdust on the floor, picnic tables, the city's largest outdoor patio, an Animal House bar scene, and buckets-and-bibs dining. Order yourself a pail of ribs, king crabs, or chicken legs, or try to win your meal with a quarter and some luck at the "lobster machine." | 345 4th Ave. | 619/231–9100 | $5–$20 | AE, D, DC, MC, V.

Fio's. Italian. Glitzy young singles mingle with businessmen at this lively Gaslamp Quarter restaurant whose lofty, brick-and-wood dining room looks onto the street scene. Of the contemporary northern Italian dishes served here, best bets are the pizzas baked in a wood-fire oven, the pumpkin-stuffed ravioli, and the black linguine with seafood. Outdoor sidewalk seating available. | 801 5th Ave. | 619/234–3467 | $11–$18 | AE, D, DC, MC, V.

Green Flash. Mexican. A hip, local crowd gathers here for drinks, along with a great view of the ocean and setting sun to see if they can catch the phenomenon for which the place is named, a flash of green seen at sunset just as the sun disappears. The outdoor deck has 10 small tables. Indoors, the tables are unadorned oak and the wood walls hold kitschy nautical art such as plastic fish. The menu is mainstream California Mexican—enchiladas, tacos, burgers—and the place can get boisterous as the night goes on and the drink bills mount. Kids' menu, early-bird suppers. Sun. brunch. No smoking. | 701 Thomas Ave., Pacific Beach | 858/270–7715 | Breakfast also available | $18 | AE, D, DC, MC, V.

Jack and Giulio's. Italian. This family-owned trattoria offers seating on the large brick patio in front, on the side balcony, or indoors in the burgundy booths. The owners take pride in their scampi, minestrone soup, homemade pastas, and filet mignon with cognac sauce. Kids' menu. | 2391 San Diego Ave. | 619/294–2074 | www.jackandgiulios.com | $8–$19 | AE, D, DC MC, V.

Jasmine. Chinese. North of downtown in Kearny Mesa, Hong Kong-style Cantonese dishes are served in this enormous dining room full of tables set with white tablecloths and pink napkins. Fans swear by the spring rolls, the roast pork, the clams, and the fresh-from-the-tank lobster. Most popular is the dim sum service, with more than 50 dishes served from the roving silver carts every day from 10 to 3. | 4609 Convoy St. | 858/268–0888 | fax 858/268–7729 | $8–$19 | AE, MC, V.

La Vache and Co. French. The interior of this friendly bistro in Hillcrest resembles a French country farmhouse, with wooden tables, straw chairs, and lots of natural light. Order the rack of lamb or the fisherman's casserole, a traditional recipe from the south of France much like bouillabaisse. Open-air dining amid foliage and fountains on the patio. | 420 Robinson St. | 619/295–0214 | $11–$20 | AE, D, DC, MC, V.

Lamont Street Grill. American. You can't miss the theme of this casual Pacific Beach eatery—ocean scenes hang next to displays of miniature lighthouses. That watery motif echoes on the menu, too, with plenty of seafood dishes, such as the popular halibut filet. Turfside offerings include chicken dijon over pasta. You can eat indoors among the lighthouses, or outside on a small, uncovered patio. | 4445 Lamont St., Pacific Beach | 858/270–3060 | Reservations essential | No lunch | $14–$20 | AE, D, MC, V.

Montana's American Grill. Contemporary. One of Hillcrest's most popular restaurants, this trendy spot has a sleek interior with recessed lighting, dark wood paneling, and local artwork on the walls. Start with the duck cakes, then try the jalapeño linguine with grilled chicken or the blackened fillet with a red-wine and mustard sauce. Note the exemplary selection of West Coast wines and microbrews. | 1421 University Ave. | 619/297–0722 | www.montanasgrill.com | No lunch weekends | $9–$27 | AE, DC, MC, V.

Nick's at the Beach. Seafood. This laid-back restaurant in Pacific Beach offers two dining areas: the quieter downstairs room with aquatic artwork on the tan walls, or the upstairs sports bar with pool tables, jukebox, and an outdoor deck with an ocean view. The mussels in a cilantro-tomatillo broth make a good starter, and the salmon glazed with a peppery rum sauce or any of the seafood pastas are entrées sure to please. Kids' menu. | 809 Thomas Ave. | 858/270–1730 | $4–$15 | AE, D, DC, MC, V.

Osteria Panevino. Italian. If you're in a social mood, check out this popular, unpretentious downtown trattoria. Dine amidst old wine barrels and ceramic tile—and the elbows of fellow diners—on northern Italian fare such as fried calamari, lamb chops, pizza from a wood-burning oven, and lobster ravioli in saffron sauce. | 722 5th Ave. | 619/595–7959 | fax 619/232–4445 | Reservations essential | $9–$18 | AE, D, DC, MC, V.

Panda Inn. Chinese. High atop Horton Plaza, this classy dining room serves Mandarin and Szechuan dishes in an elegant room with large Mandarin vases, flower arrangements, and floor-to-ceiling windows commanding views of downtown. The menu includes honey walnut shrimp, Peking duck, spicy bean curd, and Panda beef. | 506 Horton Plaza | 619/233–7800 | $10–$18 | AE, D, DC, MC, V.

Salvatore's. Italian. Well-heeled locals, conventioneers, families, and business brokers alike enjoy this old-fashioned downtown restaurant with carved wood furnishings and original paintings on the walls. Try any of the homemade pastas with rich, creamy sauces, the filet mignon topped with duck paté and truffle sauce, or the veal with Madeira and tart cherries, then treat yourself to the tiramisu. | 70 Front St. | 619/544–1865 | No lunch | $6–$25 | AE, DC, MC, V.

San Diego Pier Cafe. Seafood. To dine alfresco on a pier with the waves crashing below is what draws most customers to this Seaport Village restaurant with a 19th-century design. While the fish and chips are the crowd-pleasers, the fried calamari, fish tacos, and seafood specials are also excellent. Sample the salmon Coronado, grilled and served over basil guacamole in a white wine sauce. Kids' menu. | 885 W. Harbor Dr. | 619/239–3968 | Breakfast also available | $10–$19 | AE, D, MC, V.

★ **Sushi Ota.** Japanese. Believe it or not, this small, unassuming eatery wedged into a Mission Bay mini-mall has some of San Diego's best sushi. If you can get a spot at the sushi bar, sample the sea urchin, scallop, or surf clam sushi, and the soft-shell crab roll. More than 30 appetizers are offered, as well as combination dinners. | 4529 Mission Bay Dr. | 858/270–5670 | No lunch weekends | $9–$22 | AE, D, MC, V.

Taka. Japanese. For good value, head to this minimalist dining room with bamboo, rice-paper screens, and a sushi bar staffed by 17 people. All the fish here is extremely fresh, and the sushi chefs are expert and no-nonsense. If sushi isn't your thing, try the soft-shell crabs or the spicy Oriental pancakes for an appetizer and the excellent seafood linguine or the filet mignon Maxim for an entrée. | 555 5th Ave. | 619/338–0555 | No lunch | $10–$25 | AE, MC, V.

Tom Ham's Lighthouse. Continental. Established in 1971, this well-known San Diego landmark actually has a working lighthouse, known as beacon #9, within its structure. If you go, you'll have panoramic views of San Diego Bay and the city skyline. The regulars order the jumbo stuffed shrimp wrapped in bacon, the grilled northern salmon topped with crab and hollandaise, and surf-and-turf combinations. Karaoke Wed.–Sat. Kids' menu | 2150 Harbor Island Dr. | 619/291–9110 | Reservations essential | $10–$28 | AE, D, DC, MC, V.

EXPENSIVE

★ **Anthony's Star of the Sea Room.** Seafood. The top of the line of Anthony's fleet of seafood restaurants, this dining room has floor-to-ceiling windows and outdoor seating on the water, which ensures that everyone has an excellent view of sunsets and cruise ships. The fine, seasonally changing menu may offer such favorites as wok-fried frogs' legs with Asian spices or sauté of Gulf prawns. Jackets and ties are not required, but are encouraged. | 1360 North Harbor Dr. | 619/232–7408 | www.starofthesea.com | No lunch | $19–$38 | AE, D, DC, MC, V.

★ **Belgian Lion.** Belgian. This dining room in the heart of Ocean Beach has lace curtains, candlelight, and a mom-and-pop attentiveness to service. One of the favorite dishes here is the cassoulet, a rich, hearty stew of white beans, sausage, and duck. Other dishes include oven-seared scallops and sea bass au vert, braised in white wine with spinach and sorrel. An impressive selection of carefully chosen wines complements the food. | 2265 Bacon St. | 619/223–2700 | www.belgianlion.com | Reservations essential | Closed Sun.–Wed. No lunch | $12–$26 | AE, D, DC, MC, V.

Blue Point Coastal Cuisine. Seafood. High ceilings, gleaming woodwork, and expansive windows give this seafood establishment the atmosphere of a 1940s supper club. The cuisine here is Pacific Rim, incorporating Asian and south-of-the-border flavors. Go for the griddle-fried crab cakes or spicy Baja clam chowder, followed by the miso-marinated sea bass or the sesame-crusted salmon with sake butter. Great wine list and raw bar. Sidewalk seating also available. | 565 5th Ave. | 619/233–6623 | No lunch | $17–$28 | AE, D, DC, MC, V.

★ **Dobson's.** Contemporary. Built for the Spreckels Theater in 1911, this brass-and-wood downtown bistro attracts politicos at lunchtime and theatergoers at night. The house salad is enhanced with fennel, and the mussel bisque comes topped with a crown of puff pastry. Excellent, predominantly Californina wine list. | 956 Broadway Cir. | 619/231–6771 | $17–$26 | AE, DC, MC, V.

Harbor House. Seafood. This refined wood-and-glass dining room is a fine choice for a special evening out. Gaze at the harbor while you relish cioppino, smoked mahi mahi, or pan-seared bay scallops. If you're in the mood for a more relaxed evening, pop upstairs to the oyster bar and pub and try the Maryland crab cakes or pepper seared ahi salad. Raw bar. An outdoor deck offers umbrella tables with panoramic views. Kids' menu. | 831 W. Harbor Dr. | 619/232–1141 | $20–$25 | AE, D, MC, V.

Laurel. French. One of the darlings of San Diego's dining scene, this acclaimed midtown restaurant uses the best fresh ingredients in its subtle, earthy French dishes such as chicken roasted in a clay pot with haricots verts, duck confit with portobello mushrooms and seasonal greens, or the lightly smoked trout with warm potato salad. The wine list is renowned. Nightly jazz and the simple elegance of the dining room that pairs chandeliers and marble with simple pine tables makes this a delightful spot. | 505 Laurel St. | 619/239–2222 | No lunch | $16–$26 | AE, D, DC, MC, V.

Le Fontainebleau. Continental. The lobby of the downtown Westgate Hotel reproduces a room at Versailles. The restaurant inside is only a tad more subdued, with a mere three chandeliers, a pink-and-green color scheme, and antique French furnishings. From the Continental menu, choose the wild-mushroom ravioli with French herb butter, whole Maine lobster au gratin, or the filet mignon with baby vegetables and black truffle sauce. On Fridays, check out the prix-fixe "seafood soirée." | 1055 2nd Ave. | 619/238–1818 or 619/557–3655 | www.westgatehotel.com | No lunch Sat. No dinner Sun. | $17–$28 | AE, D, DC, MC, V.

★ **Rainwater's.** Continental. The luxurious teak, brass, and leather booths have transformed the former Sante Fe train depot into a handsome, warm dining area. Try the prime porterhouse steak for two, the sea bass baked in an herb crust served over creamy mashed potatoes and crispy leeks, or the free-range veal chop sautéed with fresh herbs. Open-air dining on the terrace with views of Coronado and San Diego Bay. | 1202 Kettner Blvd. | 619/233–5757 | No lunch weekends | $21–$33 | AE, DC, MC, V.

Thee Bungalow. French. This favorite local spot, an architectural landmark in Ocean Beach, boasts one of San Diego's best wine lists. Inside, under exposed wood beams and chandeliers, you can choose from French dishes such as savory roast duck with a black-cherry or a green-peppercorn sauce, and baked sea bass and lobster served on a bed of carmelized onions, fennels and crabmeat. Save room for the Grand Marnier soufflé. | 4996 W. Point Loma Blvd. | 619/224–2884 | www.theebungalow.com | Reservations essential | No lunch | $18–$25 | AE, D, DC, MC, V.

Top of the Market. Seafood. Right on the bay above its more casual sister restaurant, the Fish Market, this downtown dining room with its teak wood and bay windows offers a refined, clubby setting and serves some of the freshest fish and lobster around. Enjoy great views of the harbor. Raw bar. Kids' menu. | 750 N. Harbor Dr. | 619/234–4867 | $14–$40 | AE, D, DC, MC, V.

Winesellar and Brasserie. Contemporary. This elegant upstairs restaurant in Sorrento Valley is one of San Diego's top restaurants. With a taupe, gray, and black color scheme, large upholstered chairs, and diffuse lighting, it's a dramatic stage for the French-influenced dishes such as roasted Hawaiian Opaka-Paka in a shellfish bouillon with saffron, leeks, and fingerling potatoes or pan-roasted veal loin with artichokes, chanterelles, and sweet-onion and potato crêpe. The phenomenal wine selection has earned a Wine Spectator Grand Award every year since 1989. | 9550 Waples St. | 858/450–9557 | www.winesellar.com/brasserie | Reservations essential | No lunch | $19–$32 | AE, D, DC, MC, V.

VERY EXPENSIVE

Bertrand at Mister A's. Contemporary. Although Italian chandeliers, expressionist paintings, and recessed lighting set the mood at this 12th-floor midtown restaurant, it's the amazing bay and city views through the glass walls that steal the show. The kitchen prepares fusion dishes and updated Continental classics. Try the miso-glazed sea bass, the lobster "fish and chips," or the beef Wellington with foie gras. No smoking. | 2550 5th Ave. | 619/239–1377 | No lunch weekends | $24–$40 | AE, D, DC, MC, V.

Sally's on the Bay. Seafood. The panoramic views of the bay at this chic downtown spot are outstanding. The dining room's black marble tables and bar, modern art, and plexiglass accents complement the stylish Mediterranean- and French-influenced dishes here: seafood paella, swordfish with potato crust and gazpacho sauce, and baked chicken breast stuffed with black truffles. The Maryland seared crab cakes are the best in town. | 1 Market Pl. | 619/687–6080 | $20–$37 | AE, D, DC, MC, V.

Lodging

INEXPENSIVE

Balboa Park Inn. Built in 1915, this inn has four Spanish Colonial-style buildings set around a courtyard with Spanish tiles and a sun terrace. The rooms and most of the suites are individually decorated, from dark reds and brass to California airy. There are the "specialty suites," for example, the "Tara," a tribute to Scarlett O'Hara, or the "Greystoke," with its Tarzan-inspired jungle/safari decor and papier-mâché taxidermy. Some of the rooms have fireplaces and/or Jacuzzis. The San Diego Zoo is two blocks north. Complimentary Continental breakfast. Some microwaves, some refrigerators, some in-room hot tubs, cable TV. Laundry facilities. | 3402 Park Blvd. | 619/298–0823 or 800/938–8181 | fax 619/294–8070 | www.balboaparkinn.com | 9 rooms, 17 suites | $89–$99, $119–$149 suites, $149–$199 specialty suites | AE, D, DC, MC, V.

Bay Club Hotel and Marina. This two-story, boutique style hotel has a Polynesian theme, with tropical plants, bamboo, and torches. Rooms are decorated in earth tones with bamboo furniture, each with private patio or balcony and views of the harbor or bay. It's 3 mi southwest of Lindbergh Airport and 5 mi south of Sea World, and there's a marina with boat rentals. Restaurant, bar, complimentary breakfast, room service. In-room data ports, refrigerators, cable TV. Outdoor pool. Hot tub. Exercise equipment, boating. Business services, airport shuttle. | 2131 Shelter Island Dr. | 619/224–8888 or 800/672–0800 | fax 619/225–1604 | www.bayclubhotel.com | 100 rooms, 5 suites | $149–$189, $209–$289 suites | AE, D, DC, MC, V.

Best Western Bayside Inn. This 12-story tower has rooms with balconies and is three blocks from San Diego Bay, and within walking distance of San Diego Trolley, Convention Center, and Seaport Village. Complimentary Continental breakfast. In-room data ports, cable TV. Outdoor pool. Hot tub. Business services, airport shuttle. | 555 W. Ash St. | 619/233–7500 | fax 619/239–8060 | www.bestwestern.com | 122 rooms | $129 | AE, D, DC, MC, V.

Best Western Hacienda Hotel. One block from Old Town, this two- story hacienda-style hotel has Spanish tiles, a landscaped courtyard, and Sante Fe furnishings in the lobby and rooms. Rooms are spacious and well appointed, many with balcony views of city, Old Town, and the bay. Its central location, three blocks from the trolley station, 3 mi north of the airport, and 2 mi south of Balboa Park and Sea World, makes it a good choice for vacationing families. 2 restaurants, bar, room service. In-room data ports, microwaves, refrigerators, cable TV, in-room VCRs (and movies). Outdoor pool. Hot tub. Exercise equipment. Video Games. Laundry facilities. Business services, airport shuttle. | 4041 Harney St. | 619/298–4707 | fax 619/298–4771 | www.bestwestern.com | 169 suites | $125–$145 suites | AE, D, DC, MC, V.

Best Western Island Palms Hotel and Marina. Nautical-themed rooms, 100-ft palm trees and lush foliage, and harbor/bay views are the highlights of this waterfront hotel. A 10-min walk from the beach, it has a waterside restaurant, a jogging trail along the bay, and 188 boat slips. The concierge can create custom sightseeing tours for area attractions. The hotel is 2 mi from Sea World and 10 mi from the zoo and downtown. Restaurant, bar. In-room data ports, refrigerators, some kitchenettes, microwaves, cable TV. Outdoor pool. Hot tub. Exercise equipment. Laundry facilities. Business services, airport shuttle. | 2051 Shelter Island Dr. | 619/222–0561 | fax 619/222–9760 | res@islandpalms.com | www.islandpalms.com | 97 rooms, 29 suites | $129–$149, $179–$269 suites | AE, D, DC, MC, V.

Best Western Seven Seas Lodge. Wrapped around a central courtyard with a pool, playground, and Ping-Pong tables, in touristy Mission Bay, this is an inexpensive choice for families who want to be close to the attractions. It's 5 mi southeast of Sea World and 5 mi north of the zoo. Restaurant, bar. In-room data ports, refrigerators, room service, cable TV. Pool. Hot tub. Playground. Laundry facilities. Airport shuttle. | 411 Hotel Cir. S | 619/291–1300 | fax 619/291–6933 | www.bestwestern.com | 307 rooms | $129 | AE, D, DC, MC, V.

Days Inn Hotel Circle–Sea World. The largest Days Inn in California, this sprawling three-story motel has a Spanish tiled roof and a separate hotel-style "Sunset Wing" with deluxe rooms. The Superior and Deluxe rooms offer a good deal of space, overlook the landscaped pool terrace, and are much quieter than the standard rooms. Decor ranges from "corporate executive," with dark woods, brass, and beige, to standard dark peaches and greens. It's 5 mi from Sea World and the zoo. Restaurant. Some kitchenettes, refrigerators, cable TV. Outdoor pool. Hot tub. Barbershop, beauty salon. Laundry facilities. Business services, airport shuttle. | 543 Hotel Cir. S | 619/297–8800 | fax 619/298–6029 | www.bartell-hotels.com | 329 rooms | $99–$129, $149 suites | AE, D, DC, MC, V.

Doubletree Carmel Highland Golf and Tennis Resort. Set back in the rolling green hills surrounding San Diego, 18 mi from downtown, this resort offers grand vistas and lots of exercise and sporting possibilities. The rooms are decorated in beiges and blues and overlook the golf fairways, hills, and the bay beyond. Dining room, bar, room service. In-room data ports, cable TV. 2 pools. Beauty salon, hot tub. 18-hole golf course, putting green, 5 tennis courts. Gym. Business services. Kids' programs. Pets allowed (fee). | 14455 Penasquitos Dr. | 858/672–9100 | fax 858/672–9187 | carmel@highland.doubletreehotels.com | www.highland.doubletreehotels.com | 166 rooms, 6 suites | $139–$179, $250–$350 suites | AE, D, DC, MC, V.

Elsbree House. Built in 1990, this replica of a 19th-century New England house features English country decor, a small garden courtyard, and is only a half block away from the beach. Each room has a private entrance, a constant supply of fresh cut flowers, and extra large closets. There are more than 200 antiques dealers and many restaurants within five blocks of the hotel, and it's 5 mi from Sea World and 15 mi from the zoo. Complimentary Continental breakfast. No air-conditioning, no room phones, TV in common area. No smoking. | 5054 Narragansett Ave. | 619/226–4133 | fax 619/223–4133 | ktelsbree@juno.com | www.oceanbeach-online.com/elsbree | 6 rooms, 1 apartment (4-day minimum stay) | $110–$125, apartment rates vary | MC, V.

Golden West Hotel. This is one of the cheapest hotels in the city, and it's clean and well kept. Most rooms share a bath, but there are tiny, closet-like bathrooms in some doubles. No TV in some rooms. Laundry facilities. | 720 4th Ave. | 619/233–7594 | 234 rooms | $29 | No credit cards.

Good Nite Inn. This two-story motel is set around a central courtyard with a pool, and makes up in price and location what it lacks in charm. The no-frills rooms are small. It's 8 mi northeast of downtown, and within walking distance of shops, movie theaters, and restaurants. Microwaves, cable TV. Pool. Laundry facilities. Pets allowed. | 4545 Waring Rd. | 619/286–7000 or 800/648–3466 | fax 619/286–8403 | www.good-nite.com | 94 rooms | $65 | AE, D, DC, MC, V.

Hampton Inn. Within a 10–15 min drive from major attractions, this five-story 1980s-style concrete and glass hotel has free local transportation. It attracts business people with its business and concierge services, and its executive floor with larger rooms. Its location, within 5 mi of Balboa Park, Old Town, and Sea World, makes it a viable family option as well. Named Hampton Inn's "Hotel of the Decade" for its service and amenities. Complimentary Continental breakfast. In-room data ports, refrigerators, cable TV. Pool. Laundry facilities. Business services. | 5434 Kearny Mesa Rd. | 858/292–1482 | fax 858/292–4410 | www.hampton-inn.com | 150 rooms | $105–$135 | AE, D, DC, MC, V.

Hanalei Hotel. This is a tropical-themed eight-story hotel with lush gardens in Mission Bay, within 5 mi of Sea World, the Zoo, and Lindbergh Airport. Rooms are decorated in subtle beiges and creams with tropical flourishes, and each room has a private balcony or patio. 2 restaurants, bar, room service. In-room data ports, some refrigerators, cable TV. Outdoor pool. Hot tub. Excercise equipment. Video Games. Laundry facilities. Business services. Pets allowed (fee). | 2270 Hotel Cir. N | 619/297–1101 or 800/882–0858 | fax 619/297–6049 | www.hanaleihotel.com | 402 rooms, 14 suites | $129–$149, $250–$350 suites | AE, D, DC, MC, V.

Handlery Hotel and Resort. This sprawling complex has columns, Spanish tiles, and lots of glass. For kids, there are two playgrounds and large landscaped grounds, and for adults there's a 27-hole golf course, the Riverwalk, adjoining the hotel, and the shopping and entertainment of Mission Valley. Rooms are spacious, decorated in a contemporary style, with light woods and bold colors. Within 5 mi of Sea World and the zoo, and about 10 mi north of San Diego Airport. Restaurant, bars. In-room data ports, room service. Cable TV. 3 pools. Barbershop, beauty salon, hot tub, massage. Tennis. Gym. Laundry facilities. Business services. | 950 Hotel Cir. N | 619/298–0511 or 800/676–6567 | fax 619/298–9793 | sales@handlery.com | www.handlery.com | 212 rooms, 5 suites | $129–$149, $175–$225 suites | AE, D, DC, MC, V.

★ **Heritage Park Inn.** This Victorian inn has two houses, an authentic 1889 Queen Anne with turrets, stained-glass windows, and a wraparound porch, and a replica addition with two rooms and a suite. A full breakfast is served in the formal dining room and, outside, you can lounge in the private Victorian garden. The rooms are small, furnished with period pieces and have great light, especially the room with the turret window. Views are of the garden and, across the street, of Old Town and the trolley stop. Complimentary breakfast. No air-conditioning, in-room data ports, some in-room VCRs (and movies). Airport shuttle. No smoking. | 2470 Heritage Park Row | 619/299–6832 or 800/995–2470 | fax 619/299–9465 | innkeeper@heritageparkinn.com | www.heritageparkinn.com | 11 rooms (6 with shower only), 1 suite | $100–$200, $250 suite | AE, D, DC, MC, V.

HI-AYH Hostel. In the Gaslamp Quarter, this youth hostel has modern furnishings, bike rentals, trips to Tijuana, and movie nights. Singles are available but be prepared to share a room. No room phones, TV in common area. Laundry facilities. | 521 Market St. | 619/525–1531 or 800/909–4776 | 75 rooms | $18–$35 | No credit cards.

Hilton Harbor Island. Across the street from the San Diego Harbor, this nine-story "coastal contemporary" tower has a unique three-sided design, which allows the furnished balcony of each room a water view. The lobby and rooms are spacious and modern. It's 2 mi northwest of downtown and within 1 mi of Lindbergh Airport. Restaurant, bar. In-room data ports, some refrigerators, cable TV. Outdoor pool. Hot tub. Exercise equipment. Video Games. Laundry services. Business services, airport shuttle. | 1960 Harbor Island Dr. | 619/291–6700 | fax 619/293–0694 | www.hilton.com | 190 rooms, 19 suites | $149–$179, $199–$249 suites | AE, D, DC, MC, V.

Hilton Mission Valley. Directly facing I–8, the hotel has soundproof rooms, and the lush greenery and rolling hills at the back will help you forget the closeness of the highway. There's a business center with leather executive chairs and a helpful concierge, making it an attractive spot for business travelers. Rooms are decorated in a bright, contemporary style. Restaurant, bar. In-room data ports, refrigerators, cable TV. Pool. Hot tub. Exercise equipment. Laundry services. Business Services. Pets allowed (fee). | 901 Camino del Rio S | 619/543–9000 | fax 619/543–9358 | www.hilton.com | 341 rooms, 9 suites | $189–$209, $250–$450 suites | AE, D, DC, MC, V.

Holiday Inn Bayside. This hotel has three buildings: two five-story contemporary hotel structures, and a landscaped two-story motel, all across the street from the harbor. It offers views of the waterfront and the boats, and is only 1.5 mi west of Lindbergh airport and 4 mi from downtown. Rooms are done in pastel colors, mainly pinks, purples, and peaches. In the courtyard, outdoor billiard tables, Ping-Pong, and a putting green will keep the kids entertained. The hotel has free bike rentals and can arrange sport fishing charters at the marina. Restaurant, bar. In-room data ports, refrigerators, cable TV. Outdoor pool. Putting green. Exercise equipment. Laundry services. Business services, airport shuttle. | 4875 N. Harbor Dr. | 619/224–3621 | fax 619/224–3629 | hisales@hollinnbayside.com | www.bartell-hotels.com/holinnbayside | 227 rooms, 10 suites | $109–$139, $159–$179 suites | AE, D, DC, MC, V.

Holiday Inn Mission Valley/Stadium. This four-story hotel has executive services for business travelers and is close to downtown. Rooms are spacious with rose colored floral window dressings, light-wood furniture, and dark green carpeting. It's 10 mi northeast of the San Diego Airport, with Old Town, Sea World, and the zoo within 8 mi. Restaurant, bar, room service. Refrigerators, cable TV. Outdoor pool. Hot tub. Exercise equipment. Laundry services. Business services. | 3805 Murphy Canyon Rd. | 858/277–1199 | fax 858/277–3442 | www.holiday-inn.com | 174 rooms, 19 suites | $110–$139, $159 suites | AE, D, DC, MC, V.

Holiday Inn Rancho Bernardo. Each room in this two-story motel has a private balcony or patio that overlooks the landscaped pool area. The furnishings are in dark woods, with earth tones, and rooms have window dressings and bedspreads in subdued patterns. It's 15 mi from downtown and the San Diego Airport. Complimentary breakfast. In-room data ports, some kitchenettes, some refrigerators, in-room hot tubs, cable TV. Outdoor pool. Hot tub. Exercise equipment. Video Games. Laundry facilities. Business services. | 17065 W. Bernardo Dr. | 858/485–6530 | fax 858/485–7819 | www.holiday-inn.com | 180 rooms, 3 suites | $139, $189 suites | AE, D, DC, MC, V.

Horton Grand. The hotel is a recreation of two 19th-century Victorian hotels that once stood here. Its history is linked with the Gaslamp district's colorful past (former guests include President Benjamin Harrison, George Raft, Joe Lewis, Babe Ruth, and Wyatt Earp) and supposedly Room 309 is home to one of the city's most famous ghosts. Following original plans, each room has been individually decorated, furnished with antique poster beds, hand-carved armoires, gas fireplaces, and lace curtains; some have bay windows with views of the street life below. The historic trolley tour stops here and restaurants and shopping opportunities abound. Restaurant, bar. In-room data ports, some refrigerators, cable TV. Business services, airport shuttle, parking (fee). | 311 Island Ave. | 619/544–1886 or 800/542–1886 | fax 619/544–0058 | www.hortongrand.com | 108 rooms, 24 suites | $189, $259 suites | AE, DC, MC, V.

J Street Inn. This concrete-and-glass structure is a full rental complex, with furnished rooms at daily, weekly, and monthly rates. Rooms are small but clean, with a spartan charm. In a neighborhood of pricey, high-rise condos, this is an excellent budget option, two blocks from the Gaslamp district and less than 2 mi from the San Diego Airport. Microwaves, refrigerators, cable TV. Exercise equipment. Parking (fee). | 222 J St. | 619/696–6922 | fax 619/696–1295 | 221 rooms | $45–$55 | AE, D, DC, MC, V.

La Pensione. This European-style hotel north of downtown in Little Italy offers spacious modern rooms. Extended-stay available. Kitchenettes, no TV in some rooms. Laundry facilities. | 1700 India St. | 619/236–8000 or 800/232–4683 | 81 rooms | $68 | AE, D, MC, V.

La Quinta Penasquitos. This four-story hotel has whitewashed walls, Spanish tiles, and semi-tropical landscaping. Its rooms are bright and airy in green and floral prints. It's 10 mi from the San Diego Wild Animal Preserve and 25 mi from Lindbergh Airport. Complimentary Continental breakfast. In-room data ports, cable TV. Outdoor pool. Pets allowed. | 10185 Paseo Montril | 858/484–8800 | fax 858/538–0476 | www.laquinta.com | 112 rooms, 8 suites | $86, $115 suites | AE, D, DC, MC, V.

Ocean Beach Motel. Home to many surfers in summer, this motel is across from the beach and municipal pier. Some of the older-designed rooms have ocean views, and studios as well as rooms for extended stays are available. Some kitchenettes, cable TV. Laundry facilities. | 5080 Newport Ave. | 619/223–7191 | 60 rooms | $50–$60 | AE, D, MC, V.

Ocean Villa Motel. Just 2 mi from Mission Bay and a block from Ocean Beach, this simple motel offers mainly peace and quiet. Some kitchenettes, cable TV. Outdoor pool. Laundry facilities. | 5142 W. Point Loma Blvd. | 619/224–3418 or 800/759–0012 | fax 619/224–9612 | 53 rooms | $49–$55 | D, MC, V.

Old Town Inn. This central inn has three separate structures: a three-story building with deluxe rooms and two one-story budget and economy wings. Even the deluxe rooms are small, but the location, across the street from Old Town and the trolley stop, can't be beat. It's 2 mi north of the San Diego Airport. Complimentary Continental breakfast. No air-conditioning in some rooms, in-room data ports, cable TV. Outdoor pool. Laundry facilities. Pets allowed (fee). | 4444 Pacific Hwy. | 619/260–8024 or 800/643–3025 | fax 619/296–0524 | 84 rooms (41 with shower only) | $65–$115 | AE, D, DC, MC, V.

Pacific View Motel. This place survives as the cheapest motel on the water in Pacific Beach. Don't expect much beyond a private bath. Kitchenettes, no room phones, no TV in some rooms. | 610 Emrald St. | 619/483–6117 | 26 rooms | $57–$65 | AE, D, MC, V.

Park Manor Suites. This 1926 Italian Renaissance hotel at the west side of Balboa Park has homey, spacious suites, most with antique furnishings, dining areas, and books for bed-time reading. A historical site with Old World charm, the manor was a popular stopover for the Hollywood set during the '20s and '30s. Rooftop sundeck and patio. Restaurant, complimentary Continental breakfast. Kitchenettes, refrigerators, cable TV. Business services. No pets. | 525 Spruce St. | 619/291–0999 or 800/874–2649 | fax 619/291–8844 | www.parkmanorsuites.com | 80 suites | $89–$129 | AE, D, DC, MC, V.

Pickwick Hotel. The rooms at this hotel, just above the Greyhound bus station, are clean and cheap. Ask for one of the remodeled rooms on the 6th or 7th floor. No TV in some rooms. Laundry facilities. | 132 W. Broadway | 619/234–9200 | fax 619/544–9879 | 248 rooms | $37–$40 | AE, D, MC, V.

Quality Resort. This is a two-story motel set around a central courtyard with over 20 acres of tropically landscaped grounds. Rooms are spacious and light, with plum accents and flower arrangements. About 5 mi east of Sea World, 6 mi northwest of the zoo, and 8 mi north of the San Diego Airport, the motel has a free shuttle to Old Town. Restaurant, bar, room service. Some microwaves, cable TV. Outdoor pool. Beauty salon, massage. Tennis. Health club. Video Games. Laundry facilities. | 875 Hotel Cir. S | 619/298–8282 or 800/362–7871 | fax 619/295–5610 | qualrst@adnc.com | www.qualityresort.com | 197 rooms, 5 suites | $99–$129, $159 suites | AE, D, DC, MC, V.

Quality Suites. A four-story low-rise with outside hallways, Spanish roof tiles, and court-yard fountains, the suites here offer plenty of room, light, and pastel color schemes. It's 10 mi from the beaches, and 16 mi northeast of downtown. Complimentary Continental breakfast. In-room data ports, microwaves, cable TV, in-room VCRs. Outdoor pool. Business services. | 9880 Mira Mesa Blvd. | 858/530–2000 | www.qualityinn.com | 132 suites | $109–$189 suites | AE, D, DC, MC, V.

Radisson. Seven miles north of downtown and a 10-min walk to the beach, this 13-story modern tower has easy access to I–8 and comfortable accomodations with special amenities for business travelers. Rooms have full desks, fuchsia and plum color schemes, and views of Mission Valley. The top two floors are "executive level," with complimentary cocktails and hors d'oeuvres, balconies, and spacious rooms. Restaurant, bar. In-room data ports, cable TV. Outdoor pool. Hot tub. Exercise equipment. Laundry service. Business services, airport shuttle. Pets allowed (fee). | 1433 Camino del Rio S | 619/260–0111 | fax 619/497–0853 | sand@radisson.com | www.radisson.com | 248 rooms, 12 suites | $129, $209 suites | AE, D, DC, MC, V.

Radisson Suite. This three-story Spanish-style hotel has suites overlooking the landscaped central courtyard, with fountains and vine-covered walkways. The lobby has an arched entry-way with Italian marble, and plants and flowers. The suites are studio-style, with semi-separate bedrooms in dark Spanish patterns with fresh cut flowers and overstuffed couches, and many suites have faxes. It's 10 mi north of the airport and a 15-min drive to the city's attractions. Plus, there are four wineries, the Wild Animal Park, and 15 golf courses within 5 mi. Restaurant, bar, complimentary breakfast. In-room data ports, microwaves, cable TV, in-room VCRs (and movies). Pool. Hot tub. Exercise equipment. Laundry facilities. Business services. Pets allowed. | 11520 W. Bernardo Ct. | 858/451–6600 | fax 858/592–0253 | www.radisson.com | 181 suites | $129 | AE, D, DC, MC, V.

★ **Ramada Limited.** A multi-million dollar makeover in 1999 transformed this Old Town hotel into a "European B&B." From the dark wood, ornamental moldings, and fireplace in the lobby to the dense foliage and gurgling fountain in the central courtyard, this hotel blends into its historic neighborhood. All rooms are one-bedroom junior suites that face inward onto the courtyard, and have the same dark woods and rich colors as the lobby. It's 5 mi north of the airport, within 8 mi of all major attractions, and across the street from the trolley. Complimentary Continental breakfast. In-room data ports, microwaves, refrigerators, cable TV. Outdoor pool. Hot tub. Laundry facilities. Business services, airport shuttle. | 3900 Old Town Ave. | 619/299–7400 or 800/451–9846 | fax 619/299–1619 | www.ramada. com | 125 rooms | $129 | AE, D, DC, MC, V.

Ramada Plaza Sea World Area. This hotel, with its whitewashed walls and Hacienda style, is 10 min from SeaWorld and the San Diego Zoo in Mission Valley. In 1999 it was Ramada's "Hotel of the Year." Spacious rooms, a central location, and friendly service make this a good choice for families. Restaurant, bar. In-room data ports, room service, cable TV. Pool. Hot tub. Exercise equipment. Video Games. Laundry facilities. Business services, airport shuttle. | 2151 Hotel Cir. S | 619/291–6500 | fax 619/294–7531 | www.ramada.com | 182 rooms | $110–$145 | AE, D, DC, MC, V.

Rodeway Inn Zoo/Downtown. This four-story, Southwest-style hotel has arches over the balconies and outdoor, glass-enclosed elevators. Rooms are large, with a neutral beige, mauve, and blue color scheme, and have original silkscreen artwork of boats and beaches. The Convention Center, San Diego Zoo, Balboa Park/Museums, Seaport Village, and San Diego Airport are within 2 mi. Complimentary Continental breakfast. In-room data ports, refrigerators, cable TV. Laundry facilities. Business services. | 833 Ash St. | 619/239–2285 | fax 619/235–6951 | rodeway@flash.net | www.rodewayinn.com | 45 rooms | $69–$139 | AE, D, DC, MC, V.

Sands of La Jolla. Halfway between Windansea Beach and Tourmaline Surf Park you'll find this roadside motel, which has ocean views and some of La Jolla's lowest rates, available even cheaper by the week. Complimentary Continental breakfast. Some kitchenettes, refrigerators, cable TV. Outdoor pool. | 5417 La Jolla | 619/459–3336 | fax 619/454–0922 | 40 rooms | $45–$68 | AE, D, MC, V.

Town and Country. Set on 32 acres of lush landscape in Mission Valley, this hotel is a San Diego landmark. It's a mixture of high-rise towers and country-style bungalows. The lobby has massive crystal chandeliers, vaulted ceilings, and a royal blue and white color scheme. Rooms are spacious, many with French doors and white tiles. Adjacent to the hotel is the 27-hole golf course, Riverwalk; an on-site trolley takes you to the Gaslamp District, Old Town, and Qualcomm stadium. 5 restaurants, 4 bars (with entertainment). In-room data ports, refrigerators, cable TV. 4 pools. Hot tub. Driving range. Business services. | 500 Hotel Cir. N | 619/291–7131 or 800/854–2608 | fax 619/291–3584 | consales@towncountry.com | www.town-country.com | 964 rooms | $129–$169, $250 bungalows and suites | AE, D, DC, MC, V.

Travelodge. In a quiet retirement community 15 min from the ocean, this two-story, no frills, 70s-style motel is close to shopping and restaurants. The rooms are small but clean. It's also close to the San Diego Wild Animal Park and several golf courses. Complimentary Continental breakfast. In-room data ports, microwaves, cable TV. Outdoor pool. | 16929 W. Bernardo Dr. | 619/487–0445 | fax 619/673–2062 | www.travelodge.com | 49 rooms | $79 | AE, D, DC, MC, V.

Travelodge Mission Valley. This motel is off the interstate. A two-story motel with central courtyard and pool, it has standard but comfortable rooms. It's near a movie theater and several restaurants, 3 mi north of downtown and 2 mi east of Sea World. Restaurant. In-room data ports, cable TV. Pool. Business services. | 1201 Hotel Cir. S | 619/297–2271 | fax 619/542–1510 | www.travelodge.com | 101 rooms, 1 suite | $99, $119 suite | AE, D, DC, MC, V.

Vagabond Inn. Built in 1959 and renovated in 1993, this motel has the standard, landscaped central courtyard design. The white and baby-blue color scheme and ranch-style design with slanted roofs evoke yesteryear, but its inexpensive rates and good location make it a choice for today's budget traveler. About 3 mi north of downtown and 6 mi east of Sea World. Complimentary Continental breakfast. In-room data ports, cable TV. 2 pools. Hot tub. Business services. Pets allowed (fee). | 625 Hotel Cir. S | 619/297–1691 | fax 619/692–9009 | www.vagabondinn.com | 88 rooms | $87 | AE, D, DC, MC, V.

Westin–Horton Plaza. This 16-story contemporary Hacienda tower with dramatic columns and arches has a startling lighted blue obelisk in front of it, but its marble and brass interior is more understated. Rooms are spacious, decorated in blue and coral pastels, with down bedding and lots of space. You can take advantage of the shopping in adjacent Horton Plaza Mall. It's 2.5 mi north of the San Diego Airport, and the Gaslamp District, Convention Center, and Old Town are each less than 1 mi away. 2 restaurants, bar (with entertainment), room service. In-room data ports, refrigerators, cable TV. Pool. Hot tub. Tennis. Gym. Laundry Services. Business services.| 910 Broadway Cir.| 619/239–2200 | fax 619/239–0509 | www.westin.com | 436 rooms, 14 suites | $149–$179, $299 suites | AE, D, DC, MC, V.

MODERATE

★ **Catamaran Resort Hotel.** Eight Polynesian-style buildings, including a 13-story tower, are the heart of this late-1950s resort on the beach, 12 mi south of downtown. The 8 acres of grounds are lavishly landscaped, and all rooms have a view of the bay or the ocean. Restaurant, bar (with entertainment). In-room data ports, some kitchenettes, some refrigeratorsble TV. Pool. Hot tub. Exercise equipment, boating. Parking (fee).| 3999 Mission Blvd., Pacific Beach | 858/488–1081 | www.catamaranresort.com | 313 rooms | $140–$450 | AE, D, DC, MC, V.

★ **Clarion Hotel Bay View.** Next to the Gaslamp District overlooking the water, this modern, 22-story hotel offers incredible views of the San Diego Bay and skyline. The health club is on the rooftop and the rooms are good-sized rooms, painted in pastel hues, decorated with Impressionist-style art work and potted plants. It's 3.5 mi west of the airport and 1 block from the Trolley stop. Restaurant, bar (with entertainment), room service. In-room data ports, microwaves, cable TV, in-room VCRs. Massage. Exercise equipment. Video games. Laundry service. Business services. | 660 K St. | 619/696–0234 | fax 619/231–8199 | www.clarionbayview.com | 312 rooms, 48 suites | $189, $214 suites | AE, D, DC, MC, V.

Comfort Inn and Suites-Zoo/Sea World Area. This four-story hotel, built in 1994, is 3 mi north of downtown, amidst a sea of restaurants and shopping options. Ideal for family vacationers, it has good-sized rooms with contemporary furnishings and plenty of light, and is adjacent to a small park. The Mission Bay Park and Sea World are a quick 15 min drive away. Complimentary Continental breakfast. In-room data ports, some refrigerators, in-room hot tubs, cable TV. Outdoor pool. Hot tub. Exercise equipment. Video Games. Laundry facilities. Business services, airport shuttle. | 2485 Hotel Circle Pl. | 619/291–7700 | fax 619/297–6179 | www.comfortinn.com | 170 rooms, 30 suites | $109–$159, $129–$189 suites | AE, D, DC, MC, V.

Dana Inn and Marina. Half a mile from the beach, this two-story motel-style inn is surrounded by lush tropical landscaping, with bike trails and a private marina. From the blue and white trim to the lobby aquarium, anchors, teak wood, and Polynesian pool bar, the theme is definitely nautical. All the rooms have exposed rafters and pastel color schemes, and the 2nd-floor rooms have higher ceilings and good views of the bay. It's 5 mi north of the airport and downtown, and a real bargain for waterside rooms. Restaurant, bar, room service. Cable TV. Pool. Hot tub. Tennis. Laundry facilities. Business services, airport shuttle. | 1710 W. Mission Bay Dr. | 619/222–6440 or 800/445–3339 | fax 619/222–5916 | www.danainn.com | 196 rooms | $129–$159 | AE, D, DC, MC, V.

Doubletree Mission Valley. An 11-story modern tower on beautifully landscaped grounds, the hotel has light-filled public areas with Italian marble and extravagant flower arrangements. Rooms are spacious, decorated in earth tones and brass fittings, with marble bathrooms. It's close to Route 163, I–8, and a San Diego Trolley station, with stops at the Gaslamp District and the convention center, is within walking distance. It's also near Fashion Valley Shopping Center and next door to Hazard Center with its seven-screen movie theater and major restaurants, and within 5 mi of San Diego airport, Old Town, and Balboa Park. Restaurant, bar (with entertainment). In-room data ports, cable TV. 2 pools. Hot tub. Tennis. Exercise equipment. Laundry Services. Business servicesm, airport shuttle. Pets allowed. | 7450 Hazard Center Dr.| 619/297–5466 | fax 619/297–5499 | dbltreemv@aol.com | www.doubletreehotels.com | 284 rooms, 16 suites | $149–$169, $295–$495 suites | AE, D, DC, MC, V.

Embassy Suites San Diego Bay–Downtown. This hotel is across the street from the convention center, and a short walk from San Diego Bay, the Embarcadero, and Seaport Village. Suites have a contemporary decor and are spacious. Views from rooms facing the harbor are spectacular, and each suite has a door opening onto a 12-story atrium with trees, fountains, and a turtle pond. The spacious suites and central location make this is a good choice for families. Restaurant, bar, complimentary breakfast. In-room data ports, microwaves, refrigerators, cable TV. Indoor pool. Beauty salon, hot tub. Tennis. Exercise equipment. Kids' programs. Laundry facilities. Business services, airport shuttle. | 601 Pacific Hwy. | 619/ 239–2400 | fax 619/239–1520 | es_sdb@ix.netcom.com | www.embassy-suites.com | 337 suites | $219–$239 suites | AE, D, DC, MC, V.

Hilton Beach and Tennis Resort. An eight-floor Hacienda-style highrise surrounded by 18 acres of bi-level villas, lush tropical flowers, and a private beach on Mission Bay, rooms here are large and bright, with Polynesian accents, and private balconies or patios. Referred to as "Hawaii on the Mainland," this sprawling resort has so many activities that it would attract guests even without its excellent location. The hotel is 8 mi from Lindbergh Airport, 3 mi from Sea World, and 4 mi from downtown. 2 restaurants, 2 bars (with entertainment). In-room data ports, refrigerators, cable TV. Pool, wading pool. Hot tub, massage, spa. Putting green, tennis. Health club, beach, dock, boating. Kids' programs, playground. Laundry facilities. Business services, airport shuttle. Pets allowed (fee). | 1775 E. Mission Bay Dr. | 858/276–4010 | fax 858/275–8944 | contact@hiltonsandiego.com | www.hiltonsandiego.com | 357 rooms | $155–$195; $229 and up for suites and bungalows | AE, D, DC, MC, V.

Holiday Inn on the Bay. This 14-story, triple-towered Holiday Inn is located on the Embarcadero and overlooks San Diego Bay. It has an outside glass-enclosed elevator. Rooms are spacious and comfortable with furnished balconies, and many have excellent bay views. The cruise ship terminal is across the street and both of San Diego's airports and the Amtrak station are within 6 mi. Restaurant, bar, room service. In-room data ports, refrigerators, cable TV. Pool. Exercise equipment. Laundry service. Business services, airport shuttle. Pets allowed (fee). | 1355 N. Harbor Dr. | 619/232–3861 | fax 619/232–4924 | www.holiday-inn.com | 600 rooms, 17 suites | $159–$199, $229 suites | AE, D, DC, MC, V.

Humphrey's Half Moon Inn and Suites. This long-time favorite has a bi-level, beachhouse-style building nearly covered with by palm trees and gardens. Rooms have earthy tones and pastel florals, with potted tropical plants, oversized windows, balconies (viewing either the bay or the marina), and some have kitchens. Summer concerts by the water, the jazz lounge, and a harbor-front seafood restaurant attract lots of locals. With Ping-Pong tables and croquet courts set amidst the foliage, extraordinary sunset views, and lots of space there's something to please everyone in the family. It's 6 mi northwest of downtown and 2 mi north of Lindbergh Airport. Restaurant, bar (with entertainment), room service. In-room data ports, some kitchenettes, refrigerators, cable TV. Pool. Hot tub. Bicycles. Laundry facilities. Business services, airport shuttle. | 2303 Shelter Island Dr. | 619/224–3411 or 800/542–7400 | fax 619/224–3478 | www.halfmooninn.com | 128 rooms, 54 suites | $179, $239–$259 suites | AE, D, DC, MC, V.

Hyatt Islandia. In Mission Bay Park, 2 mi west of Sea World and 5 mi northwest of downtown, this hotel has rooms in low-rise, lanai-style units and in a high-rise unit. Some rooms overlook the hotel's gardens and koi fish pond while others have bay views. There's whale watching in season (Dec.–Mar.) and it's an easy 15 min walk to the beach. The hotel is famous for its lavish Sunday brunch. Restaurant, bar (with entertainment). In-room data ports, some refrigerators, cable TV. Pool. Hot tub. Exercise equipment, boating, fishing, bicycles. Kids' programs. Business services. | 1441 Quivira Rd. | 619/224–1234 | fax 619/224–0348 | www.hyatt.com | 407 rooms, 14 suites | $210–$285, $285–$335 suites | AE, D, DC, MC, V.

★ **Hyatt Regency.** Built in 1992, next to Seaport Village, this 40-floor high-rise hotel combines ornate old-world elegance with a light-and-bright California style. The Regency-style rooms have poster beds, rich red and sage green color schemes, antique replicas, and plants. All the guest rooms have water views. It's 3 mi northwest of San Diego airport. Business travelers and tourists are attracted to its location, a 5-min walk to downtown and the convention center. There's a trolley stop across the street. Restaurants, bar, room service. In-room data ports, some refrigerators, cable TV. Pool. Hot tub, massage. 4 tennis courts. Exercise equipment. Baby-sitting. Laundry service. Business Services. | One Market Pl. | 619/232–1234 | fax 619/233–6464 | www.hyatt.com | 820 rooms, 55 suites | $250–$280, $500–$950 suites | AE, D, DC, MC, V.

Ocean Park Inn. This medium-size inn 8 mi south of downtown is right on the beach. All the rooms in the 1990 building have balconies or patios. 73 rooms, complimentary Continental breakfast. Microwaves, refrigeratorsble TV. Pool. Hot tub. Business services. Free parking. | 710 Grand Ave., Pacific Beach | 858/483–5858 or 800/231–7735 | fax 619/274–0823 | www.theoceanparkinn.com | $149–$224 | AE, D, DC, MC, V.

Paradise Point Resort. This single-story, lanai bungalow–style resort opened in 1962 occupies a private island about 1 mi from Sea World and 7 mi northeast of downtown. All rooms are done comfortable and beachy (but with marble bathrooms) and have patios that look out to the private beach, the lagoon, or one of the pools. Pathways wind through the lush grounds, inhabited by friendly ducks and landscaped with more than 600 different kinds of tropical plants. If you're interested, ask about jet ski, sailboat, and kayak rentals. Restaurants, bars (with entertainment), room service. In-room data ports, some refrigerators, cable TV. 5 pools, wading pool. Sauna. Putting green, tennis. Gym, beach, boating, bicycles. Video games. Kids' programs. Laundry facilities. Business services. Pets allowed. | 1404 W. Vacation Rd. | 858/274–4630 or 800/344–2626 | fax 858/581–5929 | reservations@paradise-point.com | www.paradisepoint.com | 462 rooms, 153 suites | $195–$350 rooms, $360–$550 suites | AE, D, MC, V.

San Diego Marriott Mission Valley. This 17-floor high-rise sits in the middle of the San Diego River valley near Qualcomm Stadium and the Rio Vista Plaza shopping center, minutes from the Mission Valley and Fashion Valley malls. The San Diego Trolley stops across the street. The hotel is well equipped for business travelers—the front desk provides 24-hour fax and photocopy services—but the Marriott also caters to vacationers by providing comfortable rooms (with individual balconies), a friendly staff, and free transportation to the malls. | 350 rooms, 5 suites. Restaurant, sports bar, in-room data ports, minibars, room service, pool, outdoor hot tub, sauna, tennis court, exercise room, health club, shops, nightclub, coin laundry, concierge, business services, airport shuttle, free parking. | 8757 Rio San Diego Dr., 92108 | 619/692–3800; 800/228–9290 for central reservations | fax 619/692–0769 | $129–$199 | AE, D, DC, MC, V.

Surf and Sand Motel. With the beach a half-block away, this Pacific Beach hostelry is well named. You have a variety of accommodation options here, including a house that sleeps eight. Restaurants are within walking distance. Some kitchenettes, refrigerators, some in-room hot tubs, cable TV, some in-room VCRs. Outdoor pool. Business services. No pets. | 4666 Mission Blvd., Pacific Beach | 858/483–7420 | fax 858/483–8143 | 27 rooms, 2 cottages, 1 house | $89–$129, $179–$210 cottages, $229–$300 house | AE, D, MC, V.

EXPENSIVE

Marriott Hotel and Marina. Built in 1988, this luxurious hotel sits on the bay in downtown San Diego, adjoining the convention center and Seaport Village. Two 25-story glass towers house the spacious, elegant rooms, all of which open onto spectacular views of the private marina. A variety of water sports are offered, and you can walk to shopping and entertainment. It's 2 mi north of the Lindbergh Airport. Restaurant, bar (with entertainment), room service. In-room data ports, refrigerators, some in-room hot tubs, cable TV. Pool. Beauty salon, hot tub. 6 tennis courts. Basketball, gym, boating. Video Games. Laundry services. Business services. Pets allowed. | 333 W. Harbor Dr. | 619/234–1500 | fax 619/234–8678 | www.sdmarriott.com | 1,302 rooms, 52 suites | $245–$270, $450+ suites | AE, D, DC, MC, V.

U.S. Grant. This classic hotel was built in 1910 by the grandson of Ulysses S. Grant; Franklin D. Roosevelt and Charles Lindbergh have stayed here. Declared a National Historic Site and fully restored in the early 1990's, the lobby, with marble pillars, tapestries, and crystal chandeliers, and the rooms, with high ceilings, ornamental moldings, and Queen Anne–style furnishings, are a transporting experience. An English high tea is served in the lobby every afternoon. In downtown and close to Old Town, it's a great match of luxury and convenience. Restaurant, bar (with entertainment). Cable TV. Massage. Gym. Laundry services. Business services, airport shuttle. Pets allowed. | 326 Broadway | 619/232–3121 or 800/237–5029 | fax 619/232–3626 | www.grandheritage.com | 280 rooms, 60 suites | $165–$245, $275–$1500 suites | AE, D, DC, MC, V.

Westgate Hotel. The lobby here looks like nothing less than the ante-room at Versailles, with Baccarat chandeliers and 18th-century antiques. Guestrooms are individually decorated with details in Italian marble and bath fixtures with gold overlays. If you want a room with a view, ask for one above the 7th floor. Afternoon tea is served in the lobby and the in-house restaurant, "Le Fontainebleau," is one of the city's best. The hotel is across the street from the Horton Plaza and two blocks from the Gaslamp District. It's 2 mi north of the San Diego Airport. 2 Restaurants, bar (with entertainment), room service. In-room data ports, cable TV. Exercise equipment. Laundry service. Business services, airport shuttle. | 1055 Second Ave. | 619/238–1818 or 800/221–3802 | fax 619/557–3737 | www.littleamerica.com | 213 rooms, 10 suites | $229–$289, $440–$1500 suites | AE, D, DC, MC, V.

Wyndham Emerald Plaza. This 25-story tower has a hexagonal shape that allows each room great views of the bay and city. Within walking distance of the water, government offices, and shopping, this hotel attracts both businesspeople and vacationers. The modern, minimalist design includes a lobby with escalators and glass elevators, and medium-size rooms in neutral colors with marble bathrooms and pale wood furnishings. Many upper floor rooms have panoramic views. There is a good health club. Restaurant, bar (with entertainment), room service. In-room data ports, cable TV. Pool. Hot tub, massage. Gym. Laundry services. Business services, airport shuttle. | 400 W. Broadway | 619/239–4500 | fax 619/239–3274 | www.wyndham.com | 416 rooms, 20 suites | $309–$389, $500–$700 suites | AE, D, DC, MC, V.

VERY EXPENSIVE

Marriott Suites–Downtown. All accommodations are suites in this hotel with a lobby on the 12th floor of the modern Symphony Towers, above Symphony Hall. It's near Balboa Park and the financial district, within walking distance of restaurants, shopping, and the beach, and 3 mi south of Lindbergh Airport. There are some good views of downtown, but no harbor views. Restaurant, bar. In-room data ports, refrigerators, cable TV. Indoor pool. Hot tub. Exercise equipment. Baby-sitting. Laundry service. Business services. Pets allowed (fee). | 701 A St. | 619/696–9800 | fax 619/696–1555 | www.marriott.com | 264 suites | $250–$310 suites | AE, D, DC, MC, V.

Pacific Terrace Inn. All rooms at this 1986 Mediterranean-style stucco beach hotel have either a private patio or balcony. It's on the water in a residential neighborhood 5 min from the Pacific Beach shopping area, 10 mi north of downtown. Restaurant, complimentary Continental breakfast. In-room data ports, some kitchenettes, refrigerators, cable TV. Video games. Pool. Hot tub. Business services. Parking (fee). | 610 Diamond St., Pacific Beach | 858/581–3500 or 800/344–3370 | fax 858/274–3341 | www.pacificterrace.com | 73 rooms | rooms $245–$365, suites $365–695 | AE, D, DC, MC, V.

Sheraton Marina. The San Diego airport is about 1 mi from this hotel in a pair of 11- and 12-story towers. The expansive waterside grounds are landscaped with winding paths, tropical plants, and two lagoon-style pools. Rooms have hardwood furniture, large windows, and amazing views of the bay and downtown. Don't be surprised by the name stickers on the chests of fellow guests—the hotel has some of the most comprehensive convention and meeting facilities in the city. Restaurant, bar, room service. In-room data ports, cable TV. 2 pools, 2 wading pools. Hot tub, massage. Tennis. Gym, volleyball, dock, boating, bicycles. Laundry service. Business services, airport shuttle, parking (fee). | 1380 Harbor Island Dr. | 619/291–2900 | fax 619/692–2337 | www.sheraton.com/sandiegomarina | 995 rooms, 50 suites | $115–$265, $335–$,1000 suites | AE, D, DC, MC, V.

SAN FERNANDO

MAP 4, I14

(Nearby towns also listed: Burbank, North Hollywood, Sherman Oaks, Studio City)

Father Juan Crespi was first to record the region's history in 1769, when 5,000 people lived in the area. By the early 1800s a settlement had blossomed where the Native Americans raised and traded crops, olives, wine, and livestock. After a brief gold rush in the 1840s, when a nearby canyon yielded a few nuggets, San Fernando became the valley's first organized community, thus earning the title "First City of the Valley." Property prices skyrocketed from $10 per lot to $150 with the arrival of the railroad in 1876. More recently, this suburban enclave north of Los Angeles became the first city in the nation to declare March 31st as a legal holiday in honor of labor leader Cesar Chavez. Shopping malls prevail around town, but you can still see mementos from the past at Mission San Fernando Rey de España. Local businesses produce commodities ranging from electronic components to hand-rolled tortillas.

Information: **San Fernando Valley Chamber of Commerce** | 519 S. Brand Blvd., 91340 | 818/361–1184 | www.sanfernando.com. **City of San Fernando** | 117 Macneil St., 91340 | 818/898–1200 | www.ci.san-fernando.ca.us/.

Attractions

Mission San Fernando Rey de España. Established in 1797, this was eventually one of the largest of the 21 California missions. Skilled Native American blacksmiths turned out tools like cattle brands and scissors as well as plows, hinges, and the like. Many a traveler was also welcomed; the friars were famous for their meals of corn mush with meat and vegetables. In the now-rebuilt structure you see the gardens, workrooms, living quarters, church, and monastery. The Archival Center preserves and interprets California's Catholic heritage with historic documents, records, and artifacts. It's about 1.5 mi from the Chamber of Commerce office. | 15151 San Fernando Mission Blvd., Mission Hills | 818/361–0186 | $4 | Daily 9–4:30.

ON THE CALENDAR
JULY: *July 4th Fireworks.* Thousands come to Recreation park for the patriotic musical pyrotechnics, which cap a day of entertainment, ethnic food, games, and other activities. | 818/898–1290.

SAN FRANCISCO

MAP 3, C8

(Nearby towns also listed: Berkeley, Burlingame, Concord, Corte Madera, Emeryville, Fremont, Half Moon Bay, Hayward, Menlo Park, Mill Valley, Oakland, Palo Alto, Pleasanton, San Mateo, San Rafael, Sausalito, Tiburon, Walnut Creek)

San Francisco has long attracted seekers of fortune, spiritual peace, and personal freedom. Few places have held such continuous allure to so many for so long. The first inhabitants, the Ohlone and other Native Americans, found rich stores of natural resources here. Next came Spanish missionaries and explorers who named its harbor the Golden Gate. Between 1849 and 1851, more than 200,000 people from around the world migrated to San Francisco, many enduring great hardships to seek their fortunes in the Gold Rush. Despite their almost universal failure, many of these adventurers, like so many wanderers after them, made their homes here. From those early days to now, the city has been known for its free spirit and lack of convention. That explains its attraction to the beatniks, hippies, and members of the gay and lesbian community. The late

Herb Caen, a beloved *San Francisco Chronicle* columnist, called the city Baghdad by the Bay in recognition of the city's permissive nature.

But it's always been more than that—there's a sense of optimism and possibility here. It's a city where people can not only reinvent themselves but in the process often bring dramatic change to the larger society. That sense of possibility is reflected in the fact that, for more than 40 years, San Francisco has been not only a center of political, social, and environmental activism but also for groundbreaking art, music, dance, and theater.

Perhaps its energy comes from the stunning natural beauty of the city and the surrounding Bay Area. Or, perhaps, it is because it has for so long been home to so many ethnic groups—Mexican, Chinese, Russian, Anglo, Italian, Japanese, African American, and on and on. Each has contributed to the region in a way that's simultaneously become a celebration of cultural diversity and a symbol of cultural collaboration.

San Francisco has long been a mecca for entrepreneurs. Unlike the railroad barons of the late 1800s, today's movers and shakers work in the high-tech and film industries. The city's economy is booming. With that has come a harsh increase in housing costs. Yet in the midst of the dot-com boom, residents are trying hard to protect the city's gemlike ethnic neighborhoods from gentrification and maintain their independent lifestyles. As a result of all this, there are few places where you can hear the languages, savor the food, and enjoy the music of so many different nationalities as you can in San Francisco.

A cultural center has emerged at and around the Yerba Buena complex on Mission Street between Third and Fourth streets. Within walking distance, you'll find six acres of gardens, the landmark San Francisco Museum of Modern Art and the Yerba Buena Center for the Arts, where cutting-edge music is often performed. The center includes the glitzy Metreon shopping complex, complete with interactive playstations, an IMAX theater and dozens of restaurants, galleries, and art spaces. Nearby SOMA (for SOuth of MArket Street), a once-industrial area, now houses software-design and high-tech development firms alongside live/work flats for artists.

Despite the notoriously steep hills, one of the best ways to explore the city is on foot—parking is a headache in most neighborhoods. Some of the best areas for walking include the Civic Center with its stunning, refurbished City Hall; North Beach with its Italian restaurants and X-rated shows; the Mission District, where dozens of walls are covered with brightly painted murals; Chinatown with its Asian architecture, shops filled with herbs and exotic vegetables, and its panoply of restaurants; and the Castro, the center of gay life in San Francisco. For an unforgettable outdoor experience, you can't beat an afternoon in vast Golden Gate Park. Besides acres of gardens and hiking trails, you can also find children's playgrounds, museums, and a planetarium in this lovely island of green. San Francisco also has a well-deserved reputation as a food-lovers' town. Chefs have star status and business, politics, and social life often revolve around the latest hot restaurant. For tips and ratings, check out the "pink pages," the pull-out calendar and events section of the Sunday San Francisco Chronicle. Locals say you can spend a year eating three meals a day at a different restaurant in San Francisco and still not try them all. In part that's because new restaurants are being created every day. What you will find is a formidable range of good restaurants in every range representing nearly every ethnic cuisine. And because so many San Franciscans are health-conscious, you can also find dozens of eateries specializing in vegetarian fare. It's no wonder that so many people, just like Tony Bennett, have left their hearts in this city by the bay.

NEIGHBORHOODS

Castro District. You know you're in the world's most famous gay neighborhood when you pass the huge rainbow flag on Market Street before it intersects with Castro

Street. The eponymous area is home to upscale restaurants, the Names Project workshop commemorating those who have died from AIDS, Cliff's Variety, an eclectic hardware store stuffed with accoutrements for the home, and the Spanish-Gothic Castro Theater, built in 1924. It's a great neighborhood for eating and people-watching. The Café Fiore at 2298 Castro Street is a favorite meeting place for gays. A Different Light Bookstore at number 489 Castro Street hosts numerous readings and has a terrific selection of books exploring gender issues. The city's best Halloween celebration occurs here with lots of cross-dressing and some of the most innovative costumes you're likely to see. In the fall, it's also the site of an annual street fair.

Chinatown. San Francisco's Chinatown has the largest Chinese population outside Asia. Its maze of narrow streets is packed beneath the skyscrapers of the Financial District. Besides being home to more than 130,000 residents and dozens of restaurants, you'll find streets and back alleys crammed with herb shops, garment sweatshops, temples, and food stores with live chickens, exotic greens, and sea creatures not found in the chain stores. Take a stroll down one of the many narrow alleys to find a hodgepodge of businesses and residences. The best approach is through the Chinese Gateway Arch on Grant Street. It's topped with dragons and Fu dogs of the sort that traditionally guard Chinese temples. Busy, aromatic Grant Street is lined with attractive shops like Canton Bazaar, selling porcelain, antiques, embroidery, and cloisonné. Trinket shops are everywhere, and the wares run the gamut from cheap souvenirs to beautiful silk pajamas and dresses, China tea sets, and hand-painted paper umbrellas. The Bank of America building on the southeast corner of Sacramento Street and Grant Avenue

© Artville

THE PACIFIC COAST LEAGUE

For 55 years, the players of the Pacific Coast League were the West Coast's home-run hitters. In the world of baseball before 1958, the league, formed in 1903 of semi-pro clubs from Portland to Los Angeles, was the only game this side of the Rockies. Back then, you could bankroll a day at the ballpark for less than a dollar; you'd sit in the bleachers or the "Booze Cage" at Seals Stadium in San Francisco, where, before Prohibition, you had a choice of a free shot or a sandwich with your ticket. You'd scream yourself hoarse rooting for the home team, wrapping your lips around nicknames like "Fuzzy" Hufft, "Kewpie Dick," and "Dummy" Taylor. And in the off-season, the players went home to your neighborhood, where they held jobs driving a dairy truck or delivering the mail.

A lot of big names got their start playing at Seals or the Oaks Ball Park in Emeryville: Casey Stengel was the Oaks' manager; Billy Martin was a rookie named Alfred Manuel Pasano; the DiMaggio brothers played for the Seals and the "Splendid Splinter;" and Ted Williams was fresh out of Hoover High when he signed with the San Diego Padres in 1936. The days of the Pacific Coast League were numbered, however, as the Dodgers and the Giants moved West and the advent of televised games kept spectators away.

is built in a traditional Chinese architectural style with more than 60 dragons on the front doors and encircling columns. The Eastern Bakery at 720 Grant is a favorite spot to take a break over mooncakes or almond cookies and tea. Nearby, you can find the Wok Shop stuffed with utensils for Chinese-style cooking and Chinese cookbooks. The Chinese Historical Society of America Museum at 650 Commercial Street is worth a stop to view a small but interesting collection that tells the story of Chinese immigration in America. You might also want to wander into some of the acupuncture or herb shops filled with an amazing array of ginseng roots and other herbs. Waverly Place is called the "Street of Painted Balconies" because of its colorful architectural details. Most buildings are private homes, centers for Chinese associations, or temples. You can visit the Tin How Temple at 125 Waverly Place on the fourth floor. It's dedicated to the Queen of the Heavens and the Goddess of the Seven Seas and has intricately carved wooden statues and Chinese lanterns hanging from the ceiling. On Stockton Street, the Chinese Six Company is headquarters to a Chinese secret society founded in 1862. The Golden Gate Fortune Cookie Company at 56 Ross Alley is a small shop in which two or three people cut up strips of paper, cook pancake-like cookies on circular, revolving presses, then fold the cookies into their signature triangular shape with a fortune inside.

Financial District. The Wall Street of the West is bordered by the Embarcadero and Market, Third, Kearny, and Washington streets. The Transamerica Pyramid, a San Francisco landmark, is here, in the Jackson Square area. Built in 1972, it's 853 ft high, 220 ft of which is a spire that holds the ventilation and heating equipment. The pyramid's base of isosceles tetrahedrons offers protection from earthquake damage. The financial district is built on what was once mud flats during the time of the Gold Rush. Five years after the first gold strike, Montgomery Street was becoming a commercial district. Today, it's lined with imposing buildings of glass, stone, and marble. It includes the Embarcadero Center, which houses the Gap, Banana Republic, and other stores, the Wells Fargo History Museum, the Hallidie Building, the Park Hyatt Hotel, and the Sheraton Palace Hotel, sophisticated restaurants like the Atrium and Splendido, as well as Belden Place, an alley filled with top-shelf restaurants that serve food outside under umbrella-topped tables. You can stroll along Market Street, where there are high-priced designer shops, small cafés, antiques stores, and the Federal Reserve Bank Building.

Fisherman's Wharf. The fishing fleet does unload hauls in the mornings here. But fishing is minimal here now, and tourist haunts predominate. Nonetheless, it's still beautiful on the wharf, especially on a clear evening, when lights shine on the waterfront. The National Maritime Museum, shaped like a ship—complete with portholes—displays the history of sailing, whaling, and fishing in the Bay Area. At the Hyde Street Pier, you can tour several historic ships. The Cannery on Jefferson Street, a former peach-packing plant, is now a shopping and entertainment complex. The highlight of the waterfront is Pier 39, a two-level shopping extravaganza in a former cargo pier, where street musicians and resident sea lions provide the entertainment. The wharf is the most northern point of the San Francisco peninsula, and thus has spectacular views of Alcatraz, the bay, and the Golden Gate Bridge. This is where you catch the ferry to Alcatraz or the Blue & Gold Fleet's sightseeing boats. Some of the more popular restaurants include Moose's, where the cuisine is Italian–Mediterranean, and A. Sabella, on the 3rd floor of 2766 Taylor Street, which has been serving pasta and local seafood for 80 years.

Haight-Ashbury. Haight Street, the hippie haven of the 1960s and 1970s, is as lively and totally unconventional as ever. The street urchins who beg money from passersby outside the Ben & Jerry's ice cream shop still espouse peace but high-priced designer clothing shops are shoehorned in among the smoke shops, second-hand clothing, and music stores. The Haight-Ashbury neighborhood has seen other changes as well. The

Victorian houses surrounding these two famous streets cost a million dollars these days, and many of the old hang-outs are gone. But the Red Vic, as the Red Victorian Bed and Breakfast Inn and Movie Theater at 1665 Haight Street is known, still rents rooms that haven't changed much from the paisley days. Grateful Dead fans still make a pilgrimage to the house at 710 Ashbury Street where Jerry Garcia once lived. And Amoeba Records still sells oldies and current hits at remarkably low prices. There's often a guest artist performing there in the late afternoon or evening.

Japantown. Loosely bordered by Octavia, Geary, Fillmore, and Pine streets, Nihon-machi—Japantown—is compact but otherwise nothing like Chinatown. It has a few Asian buildings, having shrunk to just 6 blocks during World War II, when Japanese Americans were forced to live in internment camps; the neighborhood never expressed Japanese culture to the degree that other ethnic neighborhoods have. Still, it's interesting for an afternoon stroll. Highlights include the Konko Church of San Francisco, a religion founded in 1858 to promote a belief in the law of universal behavior, at 1909

SOURDOUGH BREAD

Californians can be passionate about underrepresented flora and fauna. They'll defy chain saws to protect old-growth redwoods, or halt housing developments to protect endangered tarweed, but few stop to consider the one organism that's actually earned worldwide admiration for the San Francisco Bay Area's microenvironment. It's called Lactobacillus sanfrancisco, a microscopic plant form that's responsible for the tangy character of our famous export—sourdough bread.

Bread made from sourdough starters is a lot older than San Francisco. Generations of bakers have mixed a "sponge" of flour, water, and sugar, then left it out, uncovered, so that airborne bacteria could ferment the stuff into a living, bubbling batch of leavening. The starter could be kept alive indefinitely, and portions of it, passed from one generation to the next, were transported in the wagons of Gold Rush pioneers.

The original idea was not to produce sour-tasting bread; bakers went to great lengths to coddle their sponge so it wouldn't sour. Either the '49ers were preoccupied with hunting gold, or the bacterial strains of the Bay were too persistent; in any case, the sourdough bread produced in early San Francisco had a distinct, savory pucker that proved irresistible. Not only are sourdough loaves a popular souvenir today, Lactobacillus sanfrancisco cultures are laboratory-grown, freeze-dried, and sent to bakeries around the world to replicate the flavor of our homey sourdough.

The freeze-dried stuff may be responsible for the proliferation of those ubiquitous loaves hardening in airport gift shops. If you're looking for the real thing, visit one of northern California's artisan bakeries, which have revived Old World methods of handcrafting rustic loaves. Pull apart the chewy crust of a good baguette or a loaf of Pugliese from Semifreddi's, Acme Bread, or Artisan Bakers, and you'll be rewarded with a dense, fragrant middle, perhaps scented with rosemary or studded with olives. The flavor should be so satisfying you can eat it plain, or with just a dab of fruity California olive oil.

© Artville

Paris, France.

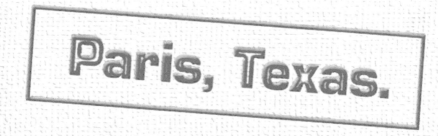

Paris, Texas.

When it Comes to Getting Cash at an ATM,

Same Thing.

Whether you're in Yosemite or Yemen, using your Visa® card or ATM card with the PLUS symbol is the easiest and most convenient way to get cash. Even if your bank is in Minneapolis and you're in Miami, Visa/PLUS ATMs make getting cash so easy, you'll feel right at home. After all, Visa/PLUS ATMs are open 24 hours a day, 7 days a week, rain or shine. And if you need help finding one of Visa's 627,000 ATMs in 127 countries worldwide, visit **visa.com/pd/atm**. We'll make finding an ATM as easy as finding the Eiffel Tower, the Pyramids or even the Grand Canyon.

It's Everywhere You Want To Be®

Find America *with a Compass*

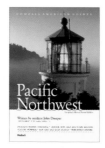
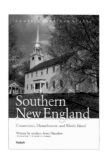

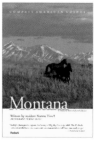

Written by local authors and illustrated throughout
with images from regional photographers, Compass
American Guides reveal the character and culture of
America's most spectacular destinations. Covering
more than 35 states and regions across the country,
Compass guides are perfect for residents who want to
explore their own backyards, and for visitors seeking
an insider's perspective on all there is to see and do.

Fodor's Compass American Guides

At bookstores everywhere.

Bush Street, and Soto Zen Mission Sokoji, a modern Japanese temple at 1691 Laguna St. The Mission is open to the public, but visitors are advised to call in advance (415/346–7540 or 415/567–7686).

Mission District. Once home to the Ohlone Indians, the area was named after the Mission Dolores, which was founded in 1776 by Spanish missionaries. It's been the home of many waves of immigrants since. The Mission Dolores was built with Native American labor and is the oldest building in San Francisco. Its walls are 3 ft thick. The ceiling was painted in vegetable dyes with Native American themes, and its beams were attached by leather thongs. The statues, altars, and mission facade were transported here by mules from Mexico. The property also contains a basilica, a museum, and a cemetery. The neighborhood is still multi-ethnic, but Latinos dominate the population. There are beautiful Victorian homes, restaurants that serve Latin food from a dozen nations, ethnic shops, wonderful nightclubs here that play Latin and world music, and several dozen colorful murals on walls, garage doors, and schools. Balmy Alley is lined with beautiful, bright murals, many of them political or religious. A group of graffiti artists calling themselves PLACA—the word used for the graffiti artist's tag name—joined together to protect existing mural art and create new work in the late 1970s and 1980s. Over the next few years, they painted 27 murals. You can pick up a map of the murals at the Precita Eyes Cultural Center at 348 Precita Avenue. As you're walking around, stop in at one of the numerous Latino bakeries, especially along 24th Street, the heart of the Latino shopping area. At 200 and 210 San Jose Avenue, you can view two Italianate homes with ornate woodwork; there's a handsome Victorian at 1286 Guerrero. After dark, head for El Rio, whose bar and dance room surround a large outdoor lounge ringed with tropical trees and Christmas lights.

Nob Hill. Dubbed "Snob Hill" by locals, the citadel of the city's wealthy founders rises 338 ft above sea level, bounded by Pine, Pacific, Stockton, and Polk streets and proudly topped by Grace Cathedral. The church has stunning stained-glass windows and religious frescoes and indoor and outdoor mazes. The Powell Street cable car line stops in front of the cathedral. The rococo Fairmont Hotel, the Top o' the Mark at the Mark Hopkins Inter-Continental Hotel, and the Masonic Auditorium are all here. The Stanford Court Hotel incorporates one of the walls of the original mansion built by former California governor Leland Stanford, who founded Stanford University. The Nob Hill Café is a nice place for a rest; it's often crowded but that's because the individual pizzas and the coffee are so inexpensive and good.

North Beach. Blessed with some of the best weather in San Francisco, this area is known as an Italian neighborhood, but Italians were actually one of the last immigrant group to live here. Before they began arriving in the late-1800s, Chileans, Irish, and Latin Americans had settled here. Now, it's shrinking as Chinatown expands. Still, there's a remnant of San Francisco's Bohemian face here, a leftover from the 1950s when Jack Kerouac, Allen Ginsberg, and Lawrence Ferlinghetti hung out in coffee shops, penning stream-of-consciousness prose and beat poetry. Sometimes, you can run into Ferlinghetti at his City Lights Bookstore, in a 1907 building at 261 Columbus Avenue. It's a wonderful place to spend an afternoon, pawing through the stacks of paperback and hardcover books stuffed into tall book shelves. One room is still dedicated to the Beats. Jack Kerouac Street is next door. Columbus Avenue slices diagonally through North Beach. It's lined with Italian cafés and restaurants, grocery stores, and pastry shops. Mario's Bohemian Cigar Store at 566 Columbus Avenue is a favorite stop for one of the best cups of espresso and focaccia sandwiches in town. When it's damp outside, it's wonderfully warm and steamy inside. Mario's overlooks Washington Square, one of the city's oldest parks. Older Chinese people often practice their tai-chi here. The nearby Sts. Peter and Paul Church is the religious center of the neighborhood. Called the Church of the Fishermen, it's the setting for the start of a procession to bless the fishing fleet every October. The Stinking Rose at 325 Columbus Avenue is a garlic-lovers' heaven. Other favorite eateries include the Caffè Trieste and the Gold Spike. North Beach also has a fair share of striptease cabarets, including the Finocchio Club, with transvestite shows. At Pearl's and several other clubs in North Beach, you can hear some of the best jazz in the country.

Telegraph Hill. Telegraph Hill rises sharply from the streets of North Beach and is named for the semaphore that was installed in 1850 atop its peak to alert city residents that ships had arrived at the Embarcadero. You can climb to the summit where the gray concrete Coit Tower sits atop the hill. It's named for Lillie Hitchcock Coit, who envisioned it as a monument to San Francisco's firefighters. Completed in 1937, the 210-ft-tall tower is decorated inside with wonderful WPA murals created by about 30 local artists and influenced by Mexican muralist Diego Rivera. The murals depict aspects of the Great Depression in northern California and have a distinctive socialist flavor. You can take an elevator to the top for a 360-degree view of the city. Several of America's most innovative writers lived in the surrounding neighborhood. The late Kenneth Patchen, a poet who was among the first to incorporate the rhythm of jazz into his poetry, lived at 377 Green Street. Richard Brautigan, author of *Trout Fishing in America*, lived at 1425 Kearny Street. Armistead Maupin, one of the nation's most famous gay writers, lived at 60-62 Alta Street, and many of his books include elements from the neighborhood. Two sets of steps—the Greenwich Steps and the Filbert Steps—wend through flower gardens past Victorian cottages. To relax, head for the Fog City Diner, a city landmark at 1300 Battery Street.

Twin Peaks. For a breathtaking view of the city, follow Market Street uphill to a neighborhood of vertiginous hills and winding streets.

Union Square. There's a concentration of performing arts in this neighborhood, the city's Theater District, but it's also home to a wonderful array of shops. The square is surrounded by Macy's, Saks Fifth Avenue, Louis Vuitton, and other large stores and chic designer outlets, not to mention Gump's, an upscale department store at 135 Post Street that specializes in San Francisco porcelains, Asian art, and museum-quality items as well as the unusual (exemplified by its paperweight collection). The Curran Theater (1922) and Geary Theater (1909) host many top-shelf performances. You'll probably want to stroll down Maiden Lane, once a center for debauchery. At 140 Maiden Lane, the Circle Gallery is the only building in San Francisco designed by Frank Lloyd Wright. It's thought to be the precursor to the Guggenheim Museum, with its spiral design. Union Square itself got its name from supporters of the Union side of the Civil War who regularly met here. Flower children in the late 1960s used the square as a gathering place. It was here also that the Sisters of Perpetual Indulgence, a small group of gay men who occasionally go out in public dressed like nuns, launched their 1987 protest of the visit of Pope John Paul II by demanding the canonization of Harvey Milk, a gay city supervisor who had been assassinated. These days, the park is far less political. When the weather's nice, and on weekends, people stroll around looking at local artists' work on display.

Attractions

ART AND ARCHITECTURE

★ **Coit Tower.** Among San Francisco's most distinctive skyline sights, the 210-ft-tall Coit Tower stands as a monument to the city's volunteer firefighters. During the gold rush, Lillie Hitchcock Coit (known as Miss Lil) was said to have deserted a wedding party and chased down the street after her favorite engine, Knickerbocker Number 5, while clad in her bridesmaid finery. She was soon made an honorary member of the Knickerbocker Company, and after that always signed her name as "Lillie Coit 5" in honor of her favorite fire engine. Lillie died in 1929 at the age of 86, leaving the city $125,000 to "expend in an appropriate manner . . . to the beauty of San Francisco." | Telegraph Hill Blvd., at Greenwich St. or Lombard St. | 415/362–0808 | $3.75 | Daily.

Haas-Lilienthal House. This is the only historically furnished Queen Anne Victorian in San Francisco that's open to the public. Built in 1886, it was home to a Bavarian trader, William Haas, and his family for more than 80 years. You can take a 1-hr, docent-led tour, and, because the Foundation for San Francisco's Architectural Heritage has its headquarters here, you can also get information about other architecturally significant buildings and architectural walking tours. | 2007 Franklin St. | 415/441–3004 | www.sfheritage.com | $5 | Wed. noon–3:15; Sun. 11–4.

Jackson Square. You can explore one of the last remnants of Gold Rush San Francisco in this neighborhood of low brick buildings bounded by the Financial District and North Beach. Once known as the Barbary Coast because of its slums and houses of ill repute, the neighborhood is now primarily given over to antiques and designer clothing shops. Many have columns made of old ship's masts and other salvage from Gold Rush clippers. Side streets like Gold Alley and Assay Alley retain their original names. The neighborhood incorporates Washington, Jackson, and Pacific streets from Montgomery to Battery St.

Mission Dolores. This is the oldest building in the city, part of the string of Spanish missions founded by Padre Junipero Serra. The small chapel next to the church was built in 1782 with Native American labor and is decorated with geometric Ohlone Indian motifs. Its 3-ft-thick adobe walls and sequoia beams, attached by leather thongs, helped it survive the 1906 earthquake, although the 1989 earthquake did considerable damage. The façade, hand-carved altars, and statues were brought here on mule from Mexico. There's a lovely small garden outside, a small museum, and a cemetery. | 3321 16th St. | 415/621–8203 | Donations accepted | Daily.

★ **The Palace of Fine Arts.** Bernard Maybeck designed this rococo fantasy as a temporary structure for the 1915 Panama-Pacific International Exposition in 1915 but it was never dismantled. San Franciscans so loved the building that it was permanently reconstructed in concrete between 1964 and 1975. You can stroll through the beautiful grounds, which are complete with a reflecting pool that's popular with tourists and wedding photographers. The adjacent buildings house a theater and the Exploratorium, a hands-on science museum. | 3601 Lyon St. | 415/563–6504.

KODAK'S TIPS FOR NIGHT PHOTOGRAPHY

Lights at Night
- Move in close on neon signs
- Capture lights from unusual vantage points

Fireworks
- Shoot individual bursts using a handheld camera
- Capture several explosions with a time exposure
- Include an interesting foreground

Fill-In Flash
- Set the fill-in light a stop darker than the ambient light

Around the Campfire
- Keep flames out of the frame when reading the meter
- For portraits, take spot readings of faces
- Use a tripod, or rest your camera on something solid

Using Flash
- Stay within the recommended distance range
- Buy a flash with the red-eye reduction mode

From *Kodak Guide to Shooting Great Travel Pictures* © 2000 by Fodor's Travel Publications

Precita Eyes Mural Arts Center. You can get an overview of the more than 100 murals in the Mission plus a map for a self-guided tour, postcards, books, and classes here. The center also leads walking tours of the Mission murals. | 348 Precita Ave. | 415/285–2287 | Free; tours $5 | Daily; tours Sat. 1:30.

CULTURE, EDUCATION, AND HISTORY

★ **Alcatraz Island.** One of the most famous prisons in history, the Rock was home to such notorious convicts as Al Capone, Machine Gun Kelly, and Robert Stroud, the Birdman of Alcatraz. Today the entire island is part of the immense Golden Gate National Recreation Area, and rangers provide tours of the rusting cells and echoing cafeteria. The setting is stunning. This is also the site of the first lighthouse on the West Coast as well as a Native American political protest and occupation from 1969 to 1971. It's accessible via Red and White Ferry from Pier 41 at Fisherman's Wharf; bring a jacket because it's often brisk on the way out to and on the island. Departures are every 30 min from 9:30–4:45. Reservations essential. | 415/705–5555 | Info:www.nps.gov/alcatraz/;Tickets:www.telesails.com | $12.25.

Aquatic Park. The park includes a curving pier for fishing, bocce ball courts, sweeping grassy lawns for lounging or flipping a Frisbee, a small beach for wading and watching the sunset, as well as the San Francisco National Maritime Museum and the San Francisco National Historical Park, the only national park with a fleet of floating vessels that can be seen from the grounds at Historic Hyde Street Pier. | Beach St. at Polk St. | 415/556–3002 | Daily, dawn to dusk.

Civic Center Plaza. The tree-lined United Nations Plaza and a broad esplanade lead to City Hall on Polk St. Bounded by Larkin, Grove, and Polk streets, and Van Ness Ave., the plaza also includes the glamorous new public library. The neighborhood is a mix of characters, from influential politicians to down-and-outers. Check out the local farmer's market every Wed. and Sun. in the plaza, which at all other times is a popular gathering spot for the city's homeless. There's an underground garage and conference center here as well.

Beautifully refurbished in 1999, **San Francisco City Hall** is one of the most dramatic government buildings in the country. Built in 1916, it has a gilded dome topped with a lantern. A staircase made of pink marble from Tennessee leads from the mayor's office into a lobby decorated in Neo-Classical style. | 415/554–4000.

There's often a dance, concert, or festivity at the **Bill Graham Civic Auditorium,** named for the city's rock-and-roll impresario who was killed in a helicopter accident in 1991. | 99 Grove St. | 415/974–4060.

The nearby **Brooks Hall** has 90,000 square ft of mostly underground convention space and is a popular location for trade shows. | 99 Grove St. | 415/974–4060.

The history of art in San Francisco is captured in the extensive collection of books, photographs, and articles at the **Performing Arts Library and Museum.** | 401 Van Ness Ave., Rm. 402 | 415/255–4800.

Since 1932, ballet and opera have been performed at the sumptuous **War Memorial/Opera House,** a beautiful structure with an Art Deco chandelier, vaulted ceiling, and two balconies. It is the home of the San Francisco Ballet Company, America's oldest dance company. The United Nations charter was signed here June 26, 1945. | 301 Van Ness Ave. and Grove St. | 415/864–3330 | www.sfopera.com&www.sfballet.com.

The sleek **Louise M. Davies Symphony Hall** with its thin, curved-glass façade reopened in 1992. It's home to the San Francisco Symphony as well as a program of classical and popular music year-round. Guided tours run 10–2, Mon–Fri. | 201 Van Ness Ave. and Grove St. | 415/864–6000 | www.sfsymphony.org.

The glossy **San Francisco Public Library** opened in 1996. Admittedly a bit confusing to use, you have to drop down a floor to access elevators to upper floors, but the interior is so visually stunning with its brilliant, five-story central shaft, which floods the space with natural light, and its special collection of books and artifacts that the unusual design seems irrelevant. It includes centers for gay and lesbian, African-American, and Asian history, a café, art gallery, and rooftop garden. | 100 Larkin St. | www.sfpl.lib.ca.us | 415/557–4400 | Daily.

Across from City Hall, you'll find **The Federal and State Buildings,** a complex that houses federal and state government offices.

Hyde Street Pier Historic Ships. Here you can climb aboard restored historic ships berthed on the bay like the Balclutha, a three-masted square-rigger built in Scotland in 1883. | Hyde St. | 415/556–3002 | $4 | Daily 10–5.

You can take a self-guided audio tour of the **USS *Pampanito,*** a WWII submarine that saw action in the Pacific. | Pier 45, Fisherman's Wharf | 415/775–1943 | $7 | Daily.

National Maritime Museum. This Art Deco building resembling a luxury liner complete with portholes was once a casino. Artist Hilaire Hiler painted the hallways with frescoes of underwater life. The collection includes ornately carved and painted figureheads from old ships, model ships, paintings, photos, and displays tracing the maritime history of the West Coast, including the lifestyles of sailors and their families. You can also view Navy ships and the Preussen, the largest sailing vessel ever built. | Polk St. | 415/556–3002 | Free | Daily 10–5.

MUSEUMS

African-American Historical and Cultural Society. This museum, art gallery, and history center strives to offer accurate accounts of the culture and history of African Americans. Exhibits include Civil War photographs and artifacts and oral history from the Civil Rights movement. The museum is at the Fort Mason Center. | Laguna St. and Marina Blvd., Bldg. C | 415/441–0640 | Donations | Wed.–Sun.

★ **Asian Art Museum.** This is the largest museum in the West devoted to Asian art. Changing exhibits of paintings, prints, textiles, and crafts illustrate the cultural history of more than 40 Asian countries. One entrance fee allows access to M. H. de Young Memorial Museum in the same building. The Asian Art Museum will move to a new downtown location adjacent to city hall at Larkin and McAllister streets in 2002. | 75 Tea Garden Dr., Golden Gate Park | 415/668–8921 | www.asianart.org | $7; first Wed. of the month, free | Tues.–Sun. 9:30–5, closed Mon.

★ **Cable Car Barn and Museum.** You can learn about the history of San Francisco's cable cars and the underground cables that pull the cars along the tracks. Displays include the original cars designed by Andrew S. Hallidie in 1873. | 1201 Mason St. | 415/474–1887 | cablecarmuseum.com | Free | Daily.

★ **California Academy of Sciences.** Located in Golden Gate Park, the oldest science museum in the West includes Morrison Planetarium, the Natural History Museum, and the Steinhart Aquarium. You can view sharks and alligators, enjoy a touch tank designed for hands-on exploration by kids, or watch a laser light show. A permanent exhibit lets visitors experience a simulated earthquake. One admission lets you into all three sites. | Music Concourse Dr. | 415/750–7145 | www.calacademy.org | $8.50 | Summer 9–6; Winter 10–5.

Watch an educational—and thoroughly entertaining—sky show in California's largest indoor space. Built in 1952, **Morrison Planetarium** was the first planetarium in the US. | Music Concourse Dr. | 415/750–7145.

In the south wing of the **Museum of Natural Science,** the Wattis Hall of Man traces mankind's evolution from prehistory to now. The African Hall displays dioramas of African fauna and the Earth and Space Hall show our planet's relationship to the solar system. In the Discovery room, kids can take part in hands-on exhibits that change periodically. | Music Concourse Dr. | 415/750–7145 | Summer 9–6; Winter 10–5.

At the **Steinhart Aquarium,** you can view the most diverse collection of sea life in the world, with more than 24,000 species of fish plus an array of amphibians, reptiles, marine mammals, and penguins. At the dizzying Fish Roundabout, you can find yourself surrounded by a doughnut-shaped, 100,000-gallon tank filled with sharks, rays, and other sea life. You can pick up and inspect live sea urchins, sea cucumbers, and sea stars at the Touch Tidepool. | Music Concourse Dr. | 415/750–7141 | Summer 9–6; Winter 10–5.

California Palace of the Legion of Honor. Spectacularly situated on cliffs overlooking the ocean, the Golden Gate Bridge, and the Marin Headlands, this landmark building is a fine repository of European art. A pyramidal glass skylight in the entrance court illuminates the lower level galleries, which exhibit prints and drawings; English and European porcelain; and ancient Assyrian, Greek, Roman, and Egyptian art. The 20-plus galleries on the upper level are devoted to the permanent collection of European art from the 14th century to the present day. The noteworthy Rodin collection includes two galleries devoted to the master and a third with works by Rodin and other 19th-century sculptors. An original cast of Rodin's *The Thinker* welcomes you as you walk through the courtyard. The Legion Café, on the lower level, has a garden terrace and a view of the Golden Gate Bridge. North of the museum (across Camino del Mar) is George Segal's *The Holocaust,* a sculpture that evokes life in concentration camps during World War II. | 34th Ave. at Clement St. | 415/863–3330 for 24–hr information | $8 ($2 off with Muni transfer), good also for same-day admission to Asian Art and M. H. de Young museums; free 2nd Wed. of month | Tues.–Sun. 9:30–5.

Cartoon Art Museum. From animation to political cartoons, this museum is dedicated to the preservation of original cartoon art. You can take a tour or class. A children's gallery often has great activities revolving around different cartoon themes and characters. On Thurs., you can pay what you wish. | 814 Mission St. | 415/227–8666 | www.cartoonart.org | $5 | Tues.–Fri. 11–5; Sat. 10–5, Sun. 1–5, closed Mon.

★ **Exploratorium.** Dr. Frank Oppenheimer, the brother of nuclear scientist J. Robert Oppenheimer, founded this museum in 1969 to promote an understanding of technology and the interdependent nature of art and science. Oppenheimer believed that people learned best by doing, making this one of the coolest places to take kids. But people of all ages enjoy operative machines like an oscilloscope with a microscope that turns sound into visual shapes. In all, the museum, which is behind the Palace of Fine Arts, has more than 650 interactive exhibits exploring scientific phenomena, mathematics, animal behavior, experimental art and music, and human perception, all utilizing the very latest technology. The special Tactile Gallery, where you crawl through a sensory maze, requires reservations by calling 415/561–0362. | 3601 Lyon St. | 415/561–7337 | www.exploratorium.com | $9; the first Wed. of the month is free | Summer 10–6, Wed. 10–9; Winter Tues.–Sun. 10–5, Wed. 10–9.

Friends of Photography at the Ansel Adams Center. This five-gallery center supports the advancement of creative photography with original Ansel Adams prints and revolving exhibits displaying a wide variety of photography from historical photographs to contemporary. | 655 Mission St. | 415/495–7000 | www.friendsofphotography.org | $5 | Daily, 11–5; first Thurs., of month, 11–8.

M.H. De Young Memorial Museum. With 22 galleries, this museum in Golden Gate Park has one of the most extensive collections of American art from the 17th century to the present. Collection includes work by John Singer Sargent, Mary Cassatt, Paul Revere, and James McNeill Whistler and more contemporary artists such as Georgia O'Keeffe and Grant Wood. Collections include Asian tribal rugs, African and British art, as well as an extensive crafts collection. A changing exhibition highlights the work of contemporary California artists. | 75 Tea Garden Dr. | 415/750–3600 | www.thinker.org/deyoung | $7 | Wed.–Sun. 9:30–5, closed Mon.–Tues.

Jewish Museum of San Francisco. Rotating exhibits and historical artifacts focus on Jewish tradition and culture. You can take a class in Judaism or attend special cultural, educational, and social programs. | 121 Stewart St. | 415/591–8800 | fax 415/591–8815 | www.jmsf.org | $4 | Mon-Thurs., Sunday.

The Mexican Museum. This small museum in the Fort Mason Center explores Mexican art from pre-Conquest times to the present through its exhibits of art and artifacts. | Laguna St. and Marina Blvd., Bldg. D | 415/441–0404 or 415/441–0445 | $4 | Wed.–Sun. 11–5, closed Mon.–Tues.

Museo Italo-Americano. This small museum in the Fort Mason Center celebrates the history, culture, and contemporary art of Italian Americans as well as the important role Italian Americans have played in San Francisco's history. | Laguna St. and Marina Blvd., Bldg. C | 415/673–2200 | $3 | Wed.–Sun. noon–5, closed Mon.–Tues.

Randall Museum. This small, kid-oriented science museum shows live animals in their natural environments, including see-through beehives, birdhouses, and snake pits. You can bring the kids to craft lessons and story hour on the weekends. | 199 Museum Way | 415/554–9600 | www.randallmuseum.org | Donations | Tues.–Sat. 10–5, closed Sun.–Mon.

Museum of Craft and Folk Art. You can view contemporary crafts, American folk art, and ethnic art from around the world on two floors of a pocket-size exhibition space in the Fort Mason Center. | Laguna St. and Marina Blvd., Bldg. A | 415/775–0990 | $3 | Tues–Sat 11–5, closed Sun.–Mon.

Presidio Army Museum. You can learn more about the Presidio's role as a military base here. Part of the Golden Gate National Recreation Area, the museum also has exhibits showing the city's growth and the 1915 Panama-Pacific Exposition. | Lincoln Blvd. | 415/561–3319 | Wed.–Sat. 10–5, closed Sun.–Tues.

★ **San Francisco Museum of Modern Art.** For the first 60 years of SFMOMA's existence, it was in the Beaux Arts War Memorial Veterans Building, located in San Francisco's Civic Center. In 1995, it moved into a striking geometric building in the city's developing cultural neighborhood south of Market St. With its angular brick walls and a striped oculus skylight, it is the second-largest single structure in the U.S. devoted to modern art. Here, you can see the West Coast's most comprehensive collection of 20th-century painting, sculpture, photography, and installation art. Galleries and open spaces are flooded with natural light coming from skylights. It also has a 280-seat theater; a library housing more than 85,000 books, catalogues, and periodicals; two large workshop/studio spaces; the Museum Store and Caffè Museo. Admission is free on the first Tuesday of every month. Admission is half-price Thursday 6–9 PM. | 151 Third St. | 415/357–4000 | www.sfmoma.org | $9 | Daily 10–5:45, Thurs. 10–8:45, closed Wed.

Treasure Island Museum. Housed in a 1937 Art Deco building left over from the Golden Gate International exposition, this museum houses photography, paintings, and ship and aircraft models detailing the history of the Sea Service, Treasure Island, and Yerba Buena Island. You get there by driving 2 mi east on the Oakland Bay Bridge and taking the Treasure Island exit. | Bldg. #1 | 415/705–1000 | Free | Daily.

Wells Fargo Bank History Museum. Artifacts trace the history of the Wells Fargo coach line and banking enterprise on two levels of the bank's headquarters. | 420 Montgomery St. | 415/396–2619 | www.wellsfargo.com | Free | Mon.–Fri. 9–5, closed weekends.

PARKS, NATURAL AREAS, AND OUTDOOR RECREATION

Cliff House. San Francisco families used to come to this resort off the Great Highway for day trips. Built in 1863, the building later became known as a hang-out for crime bosses and their molls. A schooner loaded with dynamite crashed into the rocks and blew a wing off the building in the late 1800s; the restored building burned a few years later. Adolph Sutro rebuilt it in 1895 but it burned within a year. The fifth building opened in 1909. | 1090 Point Lobos Ave. | 415/386–3330.

The 40-mi-long **Ocean Beach** stretches to the south of the Cliff House. Bathing is not allowed because of dangerous waves and currents but it's still very popular with San Franciscans who wade, jog, and fly kites here. | Great Hwy. | Daily 6–10, summer 6–7, winter 8–5.

Near the Cliff House, you can look down on the three-acre **Sutro Baths,** a spa built in 1896 by Adolph Sutro to resemble the baths of imperial Rome. There were six saltwater swimming pools heated to different temperatures beneath a sparkling glass roof. Fire destroyed the building in 1966. All that remains are algae-filled puddles frequented by shore birds. | Daily.

From the Cliff House, you can peer through binoculars to the **Seal Rocks at Cliff House** where sea lions frolic on rocks 400 ft offshore. | 1090 Point Lobos | Daily.

You can learn about activities at the Cliff House and other sites that are overseen by the Golden Gate National Recreation Center at the **Cliff House Visitors Center** | Daily, 10–5.

While you're at the Cliff House, you can pop into the tiny **Musée Mecanique,** which has a large and odd collection of antique mechanical amusement machines. | 1090 Point Lobos | 415/386–1170 | Daily.

When the weather permits, you can see the **Camera Obscura,** a replica of Leonardo da Vinci's invention. The camera is trained on Seal Rocks and Ocean Beach and the received image is magnified on a giant parabolic screen. | 1090 Point Lobos | Daily.

Ferry Building. Built in 1898, this was the gateway to and from the city when there were neither bridges nor freeways into or out of the city. Its strategic placement at the end of Market Street at the Embarcadero became more apparent with the destruction of the Embarcadero Freeway in the earthquake of 1989. Today, you can catch ferries to Sausalito and the East Bay. | Pier 1.

Fisherman's Wharf. This gaudy, touristy stretch along the bay is filled with souvenir shops, restaurant and street performers. It's a good place for a walk to get a feel for the sea industry that once characterized the city or to try some clam chowder served in a sourdough bread bowl. Don't miss the historic boats and the Maritime Museum at the west end of this busy strip. | Embarcadero at Taylor St.

You can see the weird and wonderful at **Ripley's Believe It or Not Museum** on Fisherman's Wharf. It displays the collection of Robert Ripley, who wrote the well known-syndicated column. | 175 Jefferson St., at Fisherman's Wharf | 415/771–6188 | www.ripleysf.com | Summer Sun.–Thurs. 9–11, Weekends 9–12, Winter Sun.–Thurs. 10–10, Weekends 10–12.

★ **The Golden Gate Bridge.** For a brisk and invigorating outing, you can walk across this stunning, orange-painted marvel of architecture. Its span of more than 4,200 ft was the longest in the world until 1959, when New York's Verrazano-Narrows bypassed it. It cost $35 million and opened on May 28, 1937, with President Roosevelt giving the telegraphed cue. Built to sway up to 27 ft to withstand winds of more than 100 mph coming off the bay, this San Francisco icon is 260 ft high at mid-span and carries traffic to the Marin County shore. Designed for cars and walkers, you'll find wide sidewalks. The round-trip walk is 1.2 mi and takes about an hour. Bring a jacket no matter what month it is. | 415/921–5858.

Under the southern end of Golden Gate Bridge, **Fort Point National Historic Site** was built between 1853 and 1861 to guard the bay from attacks at sea. Part of the far-flung Golden Gate National Recreation Area, the site has a museum with old swords, guns, cannons, uniforms, and historic photographs. You can walk around the four-tiered brick and granite fortress built between 1853 and 1861 and see concrete bunkers used during WWII. Civil War cannon loading and firing demonstrations are held daily. | Long Ave. at Marine Dr. | 415/556–1693 | Free | Daily.

A scenic bayshore walk stretches 3 mi along the **Golden Gate Promenade,** beginning at Fort Point and ending at Aquatic Park. It's a popular place to jog, rollerblade, or ride a bike.

Golden Gate National Recreation Area. Extending far beyond San Francisco, south to San Mateo county and north to encompass the Marin Headlands, Muir Woods National Monument, Mt. Tamalpais, and Pt. Reyes National Seashore, the GGNRA also includes much of the city's shoreline. Comprised of far-flung locations, it is simultaneously the largest urban national park in the country and one of the largest natural parks, encompassing beaches, museums, forts, cultural centers, an Army base, and an island. It's 74,000 acres in all, nearly 2½ times the size of San Francisco. The GGNRA also includes Alcatraz, Fort Funston, Fort Mason, and Fort Point National Historic Site. In the city, it also includes Ocean, Baker, and China beaches and the immense Presidio of San Francisco, a former military base. | Fort Mason, Building 201 | 415/556–0560 | www.nps.gov/goga.

Although swimming is dangerous at this 1-mi-long stretch of sand, local sun-wor-shippers—some in the nude—flock to **Baker Beach** when the weather allows. It has pic-nic benches, barbecue facilities, and rest rooms. Dogs on leashes are allowed. The beach has gorgeous views of the Marin Headlands and Golden Gate Bridge. Fishing, especially for striped bass, is excellent. The main entrance is at the SW corner of Gibson Rd. at Lin-coln Blvd. | Free | Summer 6–10 daily, Winter 6 –7.

You can swim at **China Beach,** nestled into a cove at the end of Seacliff Ave. It's shel-tered and often sunny. It was named for the Chinese fishers who used to camp here. No dogs are allowed. There are public rest rooms. | Free | Daily, summer 6–10; winter: 6–7.

For thousands of years, the Ohlone lived off the natural bounty of the region. In 1776, Spanish soldiers and missionaries arrived, beginning 218 years of military use of the area just south of the Golden Gate. **The Presidio** was a military post for Spain from 1776 to 1822, Mexico from 1822 to 1848, and the United States from 1848 to 1994. Today, the former mil-itary base in the northwest section of the city between Richardson Ave. and Lombard St. is being converted into housing and public-access land. Besides its military museum, coastal defense fortifications, and national cemetery, you can explore a saltwater marsh, forests, beaches, native plant habitats, coastal bluffs, and miles of hiking and biking trails with some of the most spectacular vistas in the world. You can also see how this former mil-itary base is being turned into housing for students, professors, and professionals. George Lucas is building a film studio here. Now part of the Golden Gate National Recreation Area, the Presidio's 500 buildings are managed by the Presidio Trust, a newly founded public-private governmental agency. The National Park Services manages the coastal resources. | Building 102, Montgomery St. | 415/561–4323 | www.nps.gov/prsf | Visitor's Cen-ter: Daily 9–5.

Golden Gate Park. John McLaren created this 3-mi-long park on sand dunes in 1887. It's a horticultural masterpiece with more than 10,000 varieties of plants from all corners of the world arranged in thematic gardens, with properly evocative names such as the fra-grance garden, the Biblical garden, the Shakespeare garden, and the succulent garden. Of these, the Japanese Tea Garden is probably the most famous. You'll also find recreational fields for baseball, bocce, soccer, horseshoe throwing, fly-casting, horseback riding, ten-nis, golf, and picnicking. The Kennedy Drive entrance closes on Sundays to accommodate skaters. You can also find lakes, outdoor theater in the Shakespeare Grove in summer, sev-eral museums, and a planetarium. Free walking tours are offered; call 415/263-0991 for information. The 1,017-acre park is bounded by Lincoln Avenue, Stanyan and Fulton Streets, and the Great Highway. | 415/831–2700 | Daily 10–6 | Free.

You can spend a splendid afternoon strolling through the 55-acre **Strybing Arboretum.** The public garden has about 7,000 plants, many in bloom year-round. The Fragrance Garden is designed for people with visual impairments. There's a small but healthy redwood grove. Docents lead free walks daily at 1:30 PM and also at 10:30 AM weekends. | 9th Ave. at Lincoln Way | 415/661–1316 | Donations | Daily 10–6.

You can watch boating enthusiasts maneuver model motor and sailboats on **Spreck-els Lake.** This sweet, small lake by the 36th Street entrance is also a good spot for bird-watch-ing, especially in fall when migratory fowl stop by. | At Kennedy Dr. | Daily.

You can rent a paddleboat or cross the bridge to climb Strawberry Hill, an artificial island in **Stow Lake.** This is the largest lake in the park and the only place to rent bicycles, row-boats, paddleboats, and motorboats. You can picnic on the island, which reaches 400 ft for a fine view. | Stow Lake Dr. | 415/752–0347 | Daily.

One of the first public playgrounds built in an American park, **Mary Connolly Children's Playground** has colorful climbing structures, swings, slides, and a restored carousel housed in a turn-of-the-century Greek temple. The 62 animals along with chariots and a turning tub (a spinning metal disc close to the ground with railings to hang on to while one per-son sets it in motion) were made in New York around 1912. Music comes from a 60-year-old organ. | Near King Dr. at 3rd Ave. | Daily.

Once nearly hunted to extinction, these stoic wooly giants are now paddocked and pet-ted at the **Buffalo Paddock.** The shaggy animals that roam this 35-acre enclosure are

American bison, some of which were brought here from the wild in 1984 to breed with an original herd that had become genetically weak due to inbreeding. | Near John F. Kennedy Dr. | Daily.

★ John McLaren had all but two structures torn down after the California Midwinter International Exposition of 1894, the Music Concourse and the **Japanese Tea Garden.** The Hagiwara family took charge of the garden and teahouse in 1895. Makato Hagiwara is credited with creating the fortune cookie here—now a staple of Chinese restaurants. The Hagiwaras maintained the garden and teahouse until World War II when they were sent to internment camps along with 110,000 other Japanese Americans. Today, the gardens are a blend of bridges, footpaths, shrines, pools, gates, flowers, and trees, all presented in Asian understatement. There's the Shinto Pagoda, a five-tiered wooden shrine; the Wishing Bridge, also called the Moon Bridge, casts a circular reflection on the pool below. The gardens are spectacular in spring. The teahouse is a sophisticated pavilion where you can relax and enjoy tea and cookies. It's between JFK and Martin Luther King Jr. drives. | 415/752–1171 | $2.50 | Daily.

A great way to see the park is on horseback. At the **Golden Gate Riding Academy,** you can ride your horse slowly—no cantering or trotting—along guided trails. Make sure to reserve your steeds at least two weeks ahead of time. Kids eight and up can also enjoy the riding. | 415/668–7360 | 36th Ave. at John F. Kennedy Dr.

Soccer and rugby clubs practice at **Golden Gate Park Polo Fields,** adjacent to the Riding Stables and south of John F. Kennedy Drive. | 415/751–8987 | Daily.

San Francisco–Oakland Bay Bridge. The bridge linking San Francisco and the East Bay runs through Treasure Island, an artificial landmass created from bay-bottom mud for the 1939 Golden Gate International Exposition. The bridge is the busiest in the nation, carrying more than 270,000 vehicles a day. The best viewing spot is from the Embarcadero. | Daily.

San Francisco Zoo. Updated habitats house 1,000 mammals and birds. You can visit the Primate Discovery Center, Gorilla World, an Australian Walk-About, and an antique carousel or watch the big cats chow down on chunks of beef Tues.–Sun. at 2 PM. | Sloat Blvd. at 45th Ave. | 415/753–7080 | www.sfzoo.com | $9 | Daily 10–5.

Sigmund Stern Memorial Grove. You can stroll through this lovely grove of eucalyptus trees at any time but it's a most lovely setting for summer concerts held in a grassy bowl. | Sloat Blvd at 19th Ave. | 415/252–6252 | Free | Daily.

★ **Yerba Buena Gardens.** The centerpiece of the SoMa redevelopment area is the two blocks that encompass the Center for the Arts, Metreon, Moscone Center, and the Rooftop@Yerba Buena Gardens. A circular walkway lined with benches and sculptures surrounds the East Garden, a large patch of green amid this visually stunning complex. The waterfall memorial to Martin Luther King Jr. is the focal point of the East Garden. Powerful streams of water surge over large, jagged stone columns, mirroring the enduring force of King's words that are carved on the stone walls. | Between 3rd, 4th, Mission, and Folsom Sts. | Sunrise–10 PM.

Rooftop@Yerba Buena Gardens. Fun is the order of the day among these brightly colored concrete and corrugated-metal buildings atop Moscone Convention Center South. A historic Looff carousel ($1 per ride) twirls from Wednesday to Sunday between noon and 6. South of the carousel is Zeum (415/777–2800,), a high-tech interactive arts and technology center ($7 adults, $5 children ages 5–18) geared to children ages 8 and over. Zeum is open in summer Wednesday to Sunday between 11 and 5, and in winter on weekends and school holidays from 11 to 5. Also part of the rooftop complex are gardens, an ice-skating rink, and a bowling alley. | 4th St. between Howard and Folsom Sts.

RELIGION AND SPIRITUALITY

Grace Cathedral. This Episcopal church in a gorgeous Gothic structure atop Nob Hill has a carillon, a ¼-mi spiral labyrinth, and an Interfaith AIDS Chapel. The city's history, with religious overtones, is painted on the church walls. Music concerts are held here throughout the year. | 1100 California St. | 415/749–6300 | www.gracecom.org | Daily 7–6.

★ **Tin How Temple.** Day Ju, one of the first three Chinese to arrive in San Francisco, dedicated this temple to the Queen of the Heavens and the Goddess of the Seven Seas in 1852. Climb three flights of stairs—on the second floor is a mah-jongg parlor whose patrons hope the spirits above will favor them. In the temple's entryway, elderly ladies can often be seen preparing "money" to be burned as offerings to various Buddhist gods or as funds for ancestors to use in the afterlife. Red-and-gold lanterns adorn the ceiling—the larger the lamp the larger its donor's contribution to the temple—and the smell of incense is usually thick. Oranges and other offerings rest on altars to various gods. | 125 Waverly Pl | no phone | Donations accepted | Daily.

SHOPPING

★ **City Lights Bookstore.** The hangout of Beat-era writers—Allen Ginsberg and Lawrence Ferlinghetti among them—remains a vital part of San Francisco's literary scene. Still leftist at heart, in 1999 the store unveiled a replica of a revolutionary mural destroyed in Chiapas, Mexico, by military forces. | 261 Columbus Ave. | 415/362–8193.

Cow Hollow. This lively neighborhood of designer clothing boutiques, antiques and shops, bakeries, and restaurants is becoming increasingly popular. On weekend nights, the intersection of Greenwich and Filmore beckons the bar hoppers and singles. Parking is at a premium. You can enjoy more relaxed browsing if you park at a lot along Van Ness and stroll. The neighborhood is bounded by Broadway, Lyon, and Lombard Streets, and Van Ness Avenue.

The Cannery. Once a peach cannery, this ivy-coated brick complex houses three levels of shops and restaurants. There's usually live entertainment in the courtyard. | 2801 Leavenworth St., at Beach St. | 415/771–3112 | www.thecannery.com.

The Embarcadero Center. This L-shaped complex between Sacramento and Clay Streets includes four office towers and two hotels. You can walk along overhead catwalks and staircases to traverse three blocks of shopping towers filled with jewelry shops, restaurants, and chain clothing shops like The Gap, Banana Republic, and Ann Taylor. It's next to the Hyatt Regency in the heart of downtown, directly across from Ferry Plaza. Daytime parking can be extremely expensive. Try a few blocks south of Market Street. | 415/772–0550 | Daily.

Ft. Mason Center. Once a World War II barracks, the bayside complex is home to many nonprofit arts organizations, the Cowell Theater, the Mexican Museum, Museo Italo-Americano, the African Art Museum, specialty shops, and Greens restaurant. Exhibit halls hold seasonal offerings such as the Celebration of Craftwomen gift show. | Marina Blvd. and Buchanon St. | 415/441–5706 | Daily 9–5:30.

Ghirardelli Square. The former chocolate factory built by Domenico Ghirardelli on the site of a Civil War–era woolen mill and overlooking the bay now has a charming courtyard, indoor and outdoor restaurants, shops, and, naturally, one of the most delicious sweet shops in town. | 900 North Point St. | 415/775–5500 | www.ghirardellisq.com.

Japan Center. A concrete Peace Pagoda marks this shopping center in the heart of Japantown. You can shop for pearls, electronics, and Japanese antiques and take your pick of restaurants. The National Japanese American Historical Society is here. | 1625 Post St. | 415/ 922–6776 | Daily.

Market Street. Many small businesses from antiques and plant shops to big department stores are strung along Market Street from Ferry Plaza to Castro Street. The best shopping is at San Francisco Shopping Centre, a nine-story mall housing the world's largest Nordstrom and 90 other retailers. Market Street between 16th and Castro Streets has many quirky boutiques in the Castro, the lively heart of the city's gay enclave. Not far from Castro and Market, you can spend an hour or two in Cliff's Variety, which may be the only hardware store in the world where you can pick up a bolt of spangly fabric and a feather boa as well as a garden hose and some fresh fuses.

Metreon. Sony's entertainment-shopping center at Yerba Buena Gardens is a mix of high-tech retailing and Disneyland. Restaurants and shops surround an IMAX movie theater and a state-of-the-art arcade called the "Airtight Garage" with virtual reality simulators. Kids can play at two interactive attractions—Where the Wild Things Are and How Things Work. | 101 4th St. | 415/537–3400 | www.metreon.com | $6.

Pier 39. Formerly an unloading dock, this pier 2 blocks east of Fisherman's Wharf is the northernmost point of the San Francisco peninsula. It was turned into a shopping complex in 1978. Today, this colorful tourist attraction and entertainment center has a playground, carousel, strolling entertainers, shops, and restaurants. The old Eagle Cafe is a touch of old San Francisco authenticity. Parking across the street. | 415/981–7437 | www.pier39.com | Daily.

SPORTS

San Francisco Giants. Whether or not you're a baseball fan, the new Pacific Bell Park on the edge of the South Beach waterfront may turn you into a convert. With views of the San Francisco skyline, the San Francisco–Oakland Bay Bridge, and the bay, the waterfront park is adjacent to the Cal-Trains train station. Both old-fashioned and newfangled, Pac-Bell Park is the first privately financed pro ballpark built since Dodger Stadium in 1963. Its drab exterior hides the exhilarating, stylish jewel inside. It feels like a mix of traditional baseball park, family theme park, and commercial success story. Fans in boats bobbing beyond right field net homerun balls while palm trees sway behind the scoreboard. To the west, a 107-ft wall rises in a jumble of color which, on closer inspection, is actually fans perched on the steep concrete decks. While the players compete on the beautiful green diamond, children can run the bases of Little Giants Park or make autograph rubbings from the raised player signatures that line an interactive play area's walls. Located in the stadium's Promenade level, the Fan Lot has four slides that are actually inside an 80-ft Coca-Cola bottle. When a Giant hits a home runs, a light and sound show erupts. All in all, this park is a home-run for San Francisco. | 319 3rd and Townsend Sts. | 415/468–3700 or 800/SFGIANT; Box office 415/656–4900 | www.sfgiants.com.

San Francisco 49ers. Though this NFL team is jockeying for a spot next to the new Pac Bell Stadium, the 49ers continue to play at less-than-hospitable 3Com Park, which loyal fans continue to call Candlestick or, more simply, "The 'Stick." The 60,000-seat park was built on a rocky promontory in 1957 and is one of the coldest, windiest, foggiest parks in the major leagues, due to its location on the San Francisco Bay. | Jamestown Ave. at Harney Way | 415/468–2249 | www.49ers.com.

SIGHTSEEING TOURS

Gray Line Bus Tours. You can choose from a full, half-day, or evening tour of the city and outlying areas such as the Monterey Peninsula and the wine country. | 350 8th St. | 415/558–9400 or 800/826–0202 | graylinesanfrancisco.com.

San Francisco Bay Cruises. | 415/394–8900 or 415/788–8866 | fax 415/788–8866.

You can take a 1-hr cruise beneath the Golden Gate Bridge, narrated in six languages, on the **Red and White Fleet.** Also available are land/water tours of Monterey and the wine country. Catch it at Pier 43 at Fisherman's Wharf. | 415/447–0597 | www.redandwhite-fleet.com | $16 | Daily.

You can choose from among several 1¼-hour cruises to Alcatraz and Angel Islands, around the Bay and Golden Gate Bridges with the **Blue & Gold Fleet.** Here, too, you can catch the ferry to Sausalito, Tiburon, Vallejo, and Oakland. The ferries leaves from Pier 41 at Marine Terminal. | 415/773–1188 | www.blueandgoldfleet.com | $11–52 | Daily.

On the **Hornblower Dining Yachts** you can eat and be entertained aboard yachts outfitted with white tablecloths and fine china. Choose among dinner-dance cruise, lunch, or Champagne brunch. The flagship is the 183-ft, 1,000-passenger *California Hornblower*. | Pier 33 | 415/394–8900, ext. 7 or 415/788–8866, ext. 7 | www.hornblower.com/sanfrancisco | $55–$81.

OTHER POINTS OF INTEREST

Cow Palace. Built for livestock shows, the cavernous building is used for everything from rock concerts to rodeos and gargantuan flea markets. | 2000 Geneva Ave., 1 mi west off Bayshore Blvd. | 415/469–6000 or 415/469–6065 | www.cowpalace.com.

★ **Lombard Street.** The block-long "Crookedest Street in the World" makes eight switchbacks down the east face of Russian Hill between Hyde and Leavenworth streets. Join the line of cars waiting to drive down the steep hill, or walk down the steps on either side of Lombard. You'll take in super views of North Beach and Coit Tower whether you walk or drive. | Lombard St. between Hyde and Leavenworth Sts.

ON THE CALENDAR

JAN.–FEB.: *Chinese New Year.* Traditional dancing dragons, extravagantly decorated floats, and marching bands cavort through Chinatown while firecrackers explode. | 415/982–3000.

MAR.: *St. Patrick's Day Parade.* This large, exuberant parade starts at 5th and Market streets and ends up at the Embarcadero. | 415/661–2700.

APR.: *Cherry Blossom Festival.* Japantown celebrates spring with an annual parade complete with a flower show, martial arts exhibitions, and craft displays. | 415/563–2313.

MAY: *Carnaval.* The Lenten celebration moved to Memorial Day weekend when the weather is better. The San Francisco version is untraditional in other ways. Everyone from Aztec dancers to clowns to naked beauties gets into the spirit in a long, colorful parade down Mission Street, ending at Harrison Street for live music and food. | 415/826–1401 | www.meca.bigstep.com.

JUNE–AUG.: *Make-A-Circus.* In summer, acrobats, clowns, and high-energy performers put on a show, then train children from the audience in simple circus skills like tumbling, juggling, and stilt-walking. Kids are invited to join the show's second half. There's also face painting, food booths, and live music. It opens in Golden Gate Park, then travels to parks around the bay. | 415/242–1414 | www.makeacircus.com.

JUNE: *The San Francisco Ethnic Dance Festival.* A showcase of dance from around the world runs over three weekends. Groups perform all sort of ethnic moves from Thai court dances to folk dances from Veracruz. | Palace of Fine Arts Theater | 415/392–4400 | www.worldartswest.org.

JUNE: *San Francisco Lesbian/Gay/Bisexual/Transgender Pride Celebration Parade.* The annual celebration of rainbow culture is the biggest gay-pride event in the West. There's music, floats, and annual appearances by Dykes on Bikes, buffed guys in leather, and the parent-support group P-FLAG. | 415/469–6005.

JUNE–AUG.: *Stern Grove Midsummer Music Festival.* You can eat a picnic meal. Listen to pop, jazz, and classical music and dance in a beautiful outdoor setting every Sunday afternoon in the summer. | 415/252–6252.

JULY: *Jewish Film Festival.* You can see a medley of Jewish films plus attend related symposia, lectures, and special events. | 415/621–0556 | www.sfjff.com.

AUG.: *Afro Solo Festival.* Through theater, dance, music, and poetry, the African-American experience is celebrated all over the city in this week-long festival. | 415/771–2376 | www.afrosolo.org.

SEPT.: *San Francisco Opera in the Park.* You can sit on the lawn and listen to free opera in Golden Gate Park. There's also a free lunch series called "Brown Bag Opera" held throughout the Bay Area in July and August. | 415/864–3330 | www.sfopera.com.

SEPT.–JULY: *San Francisco Symphony Orchestra.* You can listen to a free symphony concert on summer evenings in Golden Gate Park. | 415/864–6000 | www.sfsymphony.com.

SEPT.: *Stoli à la Carte, à la Park.* This gastronomic charity event in Golden Gate Park brings together chefs from more than 400 of the city's restaurants. It's considered the largest food and wine tasting in the country. | Sharon Meadow | 415/478–2277 | $9.

OCT.: *Grand National Rodeo, Horse and Stock Show.* Sometimes, it feels like you're in a foreign country rather than America's West when you're in San Francisco but not at this annual celebration of the rodeo. You can watch competitions in roping, riding, and other exhibition tricks. Winners qualify for the National Rodeo Finals. More than 80,000 people attend each year, in part because of the great country-style food and country music acts. | 415/469–6005 | www.cowpalace.com.

OCT.: *Halloween In the Castro.* This strictly unofficial romp is the city's version of Mardi Gras. The impromptu event began in the Castro neighborhood in the 1980s as an evening of cross-dressing and outrageous costumes. You're apt to see a few naked or nearly naked people. Although the Castro is the nation's most gay-friendly neighborhood and there's lots of men in drag on Halloween, you'll find a full gamut of costumed zaniness. It's not the place for the agoraphobic as the crowds tend to follow marching bands and costumed performers. In 1998, crowds got so large the city tried to move the event to a paid celebration at Civic Center. Although the Civic Center event continues, the unsanctioned Castro Street event retained its draw. It's a late-night party and it's next to impossible to get either in or out of the Castro by car or cab. Prepare to walk to the outskirts of the district for a cab or MUNI. | Castro St. at Market | 415/469–6005.

OCT.: *Open Studio.* Throughout October, more than 700 artists open their studios to the public. You can grab a map and check out an eclectic range of work, meet the artists, view the process, and, if something strikes your fancy, buy it. It's also a neat way to explore parts of the city you might not otherwise be exposed to. | 415/861–9838.

OCT.–NOV.: *San Francisco Jazz Festival.* Local players and international heavyweights fill the air with jazz at numerous venues throughout the city. The jazz comes in all its forms—classic and modern, swing, salsa, rhythm and blues, and world music. The festival is considered one of the best in the country, probably because jazz is alive and well in San Francisco. | 415/788–7353 | www.sfjazz.org.

DEC.: *San Francisco Ballet.* You can celebrate the holiday season at the local annual performance of the *Nutcracker.* Tickets go fast so order early. | 415/703–9400 | www.sfballet.com.

WALKING TOURS

Waterfront Walk

Begin at Embarcadero Center at the foot of Market St. (the easiest way to get there is on BART; get off at the Embarcadero stop). If you face the Ferry Building, you'll see the Hyatt Regency Hotel and the three-block-long Embarcadero Shopping Center on your left. The second-floor lobby of the Hyatt Regency is worth a detour. A monument to late-'70s opulence, its towering abstract sculpture, pod-like elevators, and Babylonian atrium were featured in the Mel Brooks movie *High Anxiety.* Shoppers will appreciate the Embarcadero Center's complex of shops and eateries. When you're ready to continue, walk east to Embarcadero Plaza and find Embarcadero Four. Here you can find the controversial Vaillencourt Fountain. This crumbling mass of bent, hollow tubes is an example of brute design that you'll either love or hate. The best way to experience it is to walk beneath its crashing waterfalls. Step carefully on the concrete pads or climb the outside stairs to upper-level catwalks for a view of this remarkable sculpture. Proceed north through the grassy field to Drumm St. Walk along Drumm past the Golden Gateway Tennis and Swim Club on the right. You may see horse-drawn carts and pedi-cabs winding through the Financial District traffic. At the end of the block, take a left-hand jog and follow the sheltered concrete footpath past 2 Jackson St. You'll emerge onto Embarcadero and a fine view of the Bay Bridge as it descends into Treasure Island. Sailboats and ferries dot the water on sunny days. Turn left and walk one block. If you're here on a Saturday between 8 am and 1:30 pm, you'll find the bustling Ferry Plaza Farmers Market, the best in the city. Organic farmers from all over northern California bring seasonal produce, honey, eggs, gourmet sausage, fresh flowers, and other wares. You can purchase just-pressed olive oil or order a steaming plate of eggs cooked to order at the Hayes St. Grill booth. Continue along one more long block until you're opposite Pier 19. Look down to find one of a trail of brass plaques embedded in the sidewalk to mark historical sites. This one tells of the 40 or so Gold

Rush–era ships entombed beneath your feet. About 40 yards farther on, find the stairs leading to a grassy oasis with a waterfall and chunky granite sculpture. Walk through this pocket park and cross Battery St. to Levi's Plaza. This is the corporate home of the jeans manufacturer founded by an enterprising pioneer who figured out a way to make sturdy pants for gold miners. If you're tired or have limited mobility, stop here or continue down the Embarcadero toward Pier 39 and Fisherman's Wharf, the third most-visited attraction in America. Otherwise, walk west cross the plaza, following the green sign indicating "Stairs to Coit Tower." You're about to make a grueling climb up the Filbert St. steps, which cling to the side of Telegraph Hill and lead to the famous Marchand Gardens. Years ago, when Telegraph Hill was a working-class neighborhood and artists' colony, Grace Marchand began planting a strip back yard and the vacant lot next to her home. Today it's a lovely jungle of camellias, tree ferns, and climbing roses. When you stop on one of the very few wooden staircases still maintained by the city to catch your breath, be sure to enjoy the incredible view of the bay. At the top of the path is the Art Deco building in which Humphrey Bogart met Lauren Bacall in the film noir classic *Dark Passage*. If you cross the street and continue up the stairs, you'll reach Coit Tower with its stunning Depression-era murals documenting not only California's idyllic beauty, but also its urban hazards. Images of Dust Bowl immigrants and a man being mugged on a downtown street indicate that times haven't changed much. When you look at San Francisco from the top of Coit Tower, however, all you can see is its sparkling jewel of hilltop houses surrounded by tourmaline waters. If you take the steps down, stop halfway at The Shadow's Restaurant, which occupies a 1920s grocery store, or Julius Castle restaurant, mentioned frequently in Dashiell Hammett's detective novels.

Mission District Walk

The Mission District evolved on the site of a Native American village called Alta-Mo. In 1772, the Spanish became the first foreigners to arrive in this neighborhood. The Mission Dolores was their first creation here. Over the years, the neighborhood has been home to many different ethnic groups—Germans, Italians, and Irish among them—but, although it remains multi-ethnic, today it's primarily a Latin enclave. The area can be rough at night but a daytime walk will take you by some of the most dramatic mural art in the world and restaurants with inexpensive and tasty food from Puerto Rico, Mexico, and Cuba to Trinidad and El Salvador. You can take Muni J–Church to Cesar Chavez (Army) St. or simply start at the corner of Cesar Chavez and Dolores streets. This walk will take 3 to 4 hours, not counting time for shopping. Walk one block to 26th St. and go right to Fairoaks St. Turn left to 464 and 435 Fairoaks St. where you'll find two homes designed in the late 1880s by John Coop in the San Francisco stick style. Each has ornate, carved friezes (decorative bands of flowers, ribbons, or letters) and wooden eyelet scalloping over doors and windows, and original ironwork over the doors. Walk to 25th St., turn right on Guerrero to 1286 Guerrero, a Queen Anne–style Victorian built around 1890. Go right at the corner of 23rd St. to San Jose Ave. Turn right again to see two Italianate homes at 210 and 200. Continue down San Jose. Turn left on 25th to Mission St. On your left is the Mission Cultural Center, decorated with a mural painted by Carlos Loarca that depicts early Native American and Mexican culture. Like many of the district's missions, however, the mural was a collaborative affair with two other painters helping out. Stop into the center for information on community activities and ongoing events. From Mission St., go right on 26th St. to Harrison. Go left on Harrison to Garfield Sq. where there are several murals. Follow Harrison back to 25th St. and look for Balmy Alley, where there's what's considered the largest number of murals per square ft anywhere in the world. Garages, houses, and fences are covered with murals from amateur to gifted, many of them political in nature. At the end of Balmy Alley, at 24th St., go left into the heart of the Latino shopping district. You can stop into one of the Latino bakeries or bookstores. At the corner of South Van Ness

Ave. and 24th, there's a mural called *Carnaval*, painted in 1893 by Daniel Galvez. Continue down 24th St. back to Mission St., turn right to 22nd St. Go left again at Valencia Street. Turn right to 1009 Valencia where the mural *Old Wives Tales* is painted on a women's bookstore that opened more than 30 years ago. From here, proceed back to Mission St. to 19th. Go left and follow it to Dolores St. where you'll find Mission Dolores Park and the Mission Dolores. The latter is worth the walk. Its ceiling and beams were painted with vegetable dyes in a design used by the Costanoan Indians, one of the tribes who lived in the Bay at the time of the first Spanish explorers. Mules brought the façade, hand-carved altars, and statues here from Mexico. The site includes a museum, cemetery, and basilica.

Dining

INEXPENSIVE

Biscuits and Blues. Southern. Reminiscent of a New Orleans supper club, with colored novena candles, red shutters on the wall, and a checkered dance floor, this first-class jazz and blues club attracts top-name entertainers. It's one of the only places in San Francisco where you can hear zydeco. The biscuits are excellent while the mix of Cajun classics and soul food is almost as good as the music. | 401 Mason St. | 415/292–2583 | Daily 5–1 | $8–$11 | AE, DC, MC, V.

Brainwash Café Laundromat. American. You can sip a beer and munch a burger at the L-shaped counter while doing your laundry in this very cool, very casual South of Market icon. Decked out in kitschy '50s corporate logos, it's a good place to see local bands and mingle with the hipsters. The food is cheap and tasty. You can fill up on the "wash day blues," a big stack of blueberry pancakes, hearty soups and salads, the nine beers on tap, and the homemade brownies. You won't want to miss the "Readers" and "Writers" bathrooms with interesting graffiti. | 1122 Folsom St. | 415/255–4866 | www.brain-wash.com | Sun–Thurs. 7:30–midnight, Fri.–Sat. 7:30–1 | $5–$8 | MC, V.

Cafe Marimba. Mexican. The restaurant is painted inside and out in a montage of lime-green, purple, red, and yellow. With its 10-ft-tall, papier-mâché diablo, and an eclectic array of folk art, it's a friendly, casual place for munching guacamole and sipping a margarita. The menu offers authentic regional Mexican food, not just run-of-the-mill burritos and tacos. Some unusual entrées include grilled swordfish tacos with mango sauce, chicken tamales steamed in banana leaves, Veracruz-style fresh fish, and the sampler of various Oaxacan mole sauces. | 2317 Chestnut St. | 415/776–1506 | Tues.–Thurs. 11:30–10, Mon. 5:30–10, Fri.–Sat. 5:30–11, Sat.–Sun. 10:30–2 | $8–$15 | AE, MC, V.

Delancey Street. Eclectic. A project of the non-profit self-help center of the same name, the restaurant wins acclaim in its own right. Look beyond the '80s-style pastel color scheme to views of the bay or choose the waterfront dining patio. The service is extremely friendly; the menu reflects cuisine from around the world. You can find matzo ball soup, Szechuan noodles, and a high tea from 3–5. Try the imaginative pasta dishes, fresh salads, and homemade desserts. | 600 Embarcadero | 415/512–5148 or 415/512–5179 | Tues.–Fri. 11–11, weekend 10–11, closed Mon. | $9–$13 | AE, DC, MC, V.

Dottie's True Blue Cafe. American. This old-fashioned coffee shop near Union Square has updated American breakfast standards all day. You can choose from a wide range of omelets like the massive Southwestern with andouille sausage. | 522 Jones St. | 415/885–2767 | Daily 7:30–2 | $4–$8 | D, MC, V.

Eagle Cafe. American. If you're looking for some authenticity at Pier 39, this is it. The Eagle was a fisherman's café scheduled to be razed when the developers thought differently and saved it. With its distressed rail-car siding, Formica tables, and sea-faring memorabilia as intact as they ever were, the café has simple, filling food. The clam chowder can't be beat. You can eat a burger on its outdoor dining deck with a view of the Golden Gate Bridge and Alcatraz. | Pier 39, #201 | 415/433–3689 | Daily 7:30 AM–10 PM | $8–$15 | MC, V.

El Toreador. Mexican. Piñatas hang from the ceiling and sombreros decorate the walls in this funky, hand-painted eatery that draws a young, fun-loving crowd. You can try the flautas el toreador or the massive enchilada with chile verde. They serve beer, wine, and excellent margaritas only. | 50 W. Portal | 415/566–8104 | Tues.–Thurs. 11–9, Fri.–Sat. 11–10, Sun. 3–9, closed Mon. | $8–$15 | AE, MC, V.

Eliza's. Chinese. Asia meets California here. Large local crowds flock for Hunan and Mandarin specialties, artfully presented on pastel dishes that match the dining room's potted orchids and colorful modern artwork. You can get a sunflower and celery salad with satay beef or the meatless mu-shu pancakes. | 1457 18th St. | 415/648–9999 | Mon.–Fri. 11–3, 5–10, Sat. 11–10, Sun. noon–10 | $8–$15 | MC, V.

Fino. Italian. When the sun is setting, large arched windows give the mahogany bar, glazed beige walls, and marble fireplace a heavenly glow. At night, when the candles are lit, the place becomes more intimate and romantic. A crowd of middle-aged couples and young professionals come for the seafood contadina, pasta carbonara, or the many thin crust, gourmet pizzas. | 624 Post St. | 415/928–2080 | Daily 5:30–10 | $7–$13 | AE, DC, MC, V.

Ghirardelli Chocolate Manufactory. American. The fragrance of melted chocolate leads to this ice cream parlor in a former chocolate factory built in the late 1890s. You can watch vats of chocolate being processed, then order the "World Famous Hot Fudge Sundae" for a closer inspection. Parking. | 900 North Point St. | 415/771–4903 | Daily 10–midnight | $8–$20 per box | MC, V.

Golden Dragon. Chinese. Crowds pack into its huge, ornate dining room, painted red and black with hand-carved dragon columns. One of Chinatown's best-known restaurants, it specializes in Cantonese food, Hong Kong–style, like Peking duck, dim sum, and banquet dinners. You can only order beer and wine. | 816 Washington St. | 415/398–3920 | Daily 8–midnight | $7–$12 | AE, DC, MC, V.

Hunan. Chinese. The warehouse-style space with long communal tables is a bit noisy has some of the most flavorful, spicy Hunan dishes in the city. You can select smoked duck or an incendiary kung pow chicken. | 924 Sansome St. | 415/956–7727 | Daily, 11:30–9:30 | $8–$14 | AE, D, DC, MC, V.

Isobune. Japanese. You can choose a plate of sushi from a little wooden boat that floats past your place at the sushi bar or take a table and order from the menu. While the boats draw a constant crowd, the sushi is only of average quality. | 1737 Post St. | 415/563–1030 | Daily, 11:30–10 | $8–$14 | MC, V.

Just Desserts. Café. This modern café plays alternative music, sells local art, and serves coffee and world-famous cheesecake on an outdoor garden patio. The black bottom cupcakes, oatmeal cookies, and fudge cakes are pretty irresistible as well. | 3 Embarcadero Center | 415/421–1609 | Weekdays 7–6, Sat. 9–5, closed Sun. | $2–$10 | MC, V.

Khan Toke Thai House. Thai. This traditional Thai dining room is a no-shoe affair with sunken tables, authentic Thai statues in carved teak, tapestries, and an outdoor herb garden. For an appetizer, you can try the yam pla muk, a tangy squid salad, and then the faultless pad thai or deep-fried pompano. | 5937 Geary Blvd. | 415/668–6654 | Daily 5–10:30 | $8–$14 | MC, V.

La Bodega. Spanish. In this eccentric, neon-colored bungalow in North Beach, you can eat yummy tapas and paellas, accompanied by pitchers of sangria at family-style tables. Some evenings a flamenco guitarist wanders in, kicking up the energy until the wee hours of the night. Inexpensive and a lot of fun, it's become a staple of the North Beach scene. | 1337 Grant Ave. | 415/433–0439 | Daily 5–midnight | $8–$12 | AE, D, MC, V.

Lhasa Moon. Tibetan. San Francisco's only Tibetan restaurant has a simple dining room with painted pillars, traditional musical instruments, and pictures of Tibetan salt flats on its green and cream walls. Try the MoMo, dough-filled with beef, chicken, or vegetables, or pasta stews with lamb, chicken, and spinach. A small shop in the front sells cookbooks, dresses, and incense. | 2420 Lombard St. | 415/674–9898 | Tues.–Sun. 5–10, closed Mon. | $9–$11 | AE, MC, V.

Mo's Gourmet Hamburgers. American. At this '50s diner with booths, soda counter, and portraits of the Three Stooges smiling down like patron saints, the burgers garner high praise, and they're not just all beef. You can get excellent venison, buffalo, turkey, and salmon varieties as well. Thick milk shakes, cheese fries, kebabs, and rotisserie chicken round out the menu. | 1322 Grant Ave. | 415/788–3779 | Sun.–Thurs. 11:30–10:30. Fri.– Sat. 11:30–11:30 | $6–$12 | MC, V.

O'Reilly's. Irish. This San Francisco institution is packed on St. Paddy's Day. But, as the *San Francisco Chronicle* once noted, any day here feels as if you're "smack in the middle of the Emerald Isle" with its cobblestone floor and antique Celtic, glass-back bar. The menu is full of hearty Irish staples like corned beef and cabbage, kidney pie, and the vegetarian colcannon. There's live Irish music Tues.–Thurs. and outdoor, sidewalk seating for a slightly less raucous time. | 622 Green St. | 415/989–6222 | Mon.–Fri. 11AM–2AM; Sat.–Sun. 10AM–2AM | $9–$13 | MC, V.

Pat Poag. Thai. You can order specialties like smoked tofu with shiitake mushrooms and snap peas or mixed vegetables with chicken in peanut sauce. | 2415 Clement St. | 415/379–9726 | $9–$13 | Daily 5–10 | MC, V.

Pot Sticker. Chinese. Painted screens, crystal chandeliers, and potted plants create an upscale atmosphere at this Chinese favorite. Its location on Chinatown's picturesque "street of the painted balconies" is a great excuse for a walk to the restaurant, as parking is difficult anywhere in Chinatown. The menu has Hunan, Mandarin, and Szechuan dishes, with a full lunch selection of dim sum, an excellent glazed prawn entrée, and the specialty pot-sticker dumplings. There's a downstairs dance club, 120, for an after-dinner drink and karaoke session. | 150 Waverly Pl. | 415/397–9985 | Daily, 10:30–10 | $7–$12 | AE, D, MC, V.

Puccini and Pinetti. Italian. This casual neighborhood spot has an American-style bar, Art Deco murals, yellow walls, modest wood tables, and a checkered floor but it's the wood-burning oven that brings people back. They churn out roasted prawns, smoked chicken, pizzas, and fresh fish. The devil's food cake has a sinful reputation. Weekly events, such as local bands on Tues. and celebrity bartenders on Thurs., draw a fun, friendly crowd. | 129 Ellis St. | 415/392–5500 or 800/669–7777 | Mon.–Thurs. 11:30–10, Fri.–Sat. 11:30–11, Sun. 5–10 | $5–$14 | AE, D, DC, MC, V.

Quetzal. Continental. In a former warehouse loft, split in the middle by 150 ft of continuous glass, this casual café has state-of-the-art electronics with your cappuccino: a primo audio system, video screens, and Web access from individual terminals. It has house-roasted coffee and cocoa, espresso drinks, pastries, sandwiches, beer, and wine. | 1234 Polk St. | 415/673–4181 | Mon.–Sat. 6AM–11, Sun. 7AM–11PM | $6–$10 | AE, D, DC, MC, V.

Ristorante Ideale. Italian. Simple Italian mosaics, large windows, wine racks, and white linen separate this space from its more touristy neighbors. With excellent homemade pastas such as the spaghetti carbonara and oven-baked specialties like the rack of lamb with artichokes, this restaurant is a high-quality, low-price favorite. | 1309 Grant Ave. | 415/391–4129 | Mon.–Thurs. 5:30–10:30. Fri.–Sat. 5:30–11, Sun. 5–10, closed Mon. | $10–$15 | D, MC, V.

Ryumon. Chinese. Large fish tanks, oriental-style painted wood screens, and the squeak of silver dim sum carts characterize this lunchtime favorite. You can create a varied and filling meal by choosing from more than 100 types of dim sum, which are assorted small servings of steamed dumplings and different vegetable, chicken, and fish concoctions. If you so desire, however, you can order a meal from the menu. | 646 Washington St. | 415/982–3308 | Daily, 10:30–10 | $8–$14 | AE, D, MC, V.

Saji Japanese Cuisine. Japanese. Neighborhood locals squeeze up to this favorite sushi bar, featuring three chefs preparing some of the freshest, most reasonably priced sushi in town.

The back room is much more peaceful. You can order sushi, teriyaki salmon, tempura prawns or yosenabe, which is chicken and seafood served simmering in a clay pot. Tea is served in an antique tea pot and the room is inviting with rice paper curtains over each window. | 3232 Scott St. | 415/931–0563 | Mon.–Thurs. 5:30–10:30, Fri.–Sat. 5:30–midnight, Sun. 5:30–10 | $7–$14 | AE, D, DC, MC, V.

Sears Fine Foods. American. This retro coffee shop, complete with big booths and a soda counter, is an unassuming but popular San Francisco institution, famous for high-calorie breakfasts. The plates seem to buckle under the piles of sizzling bacon, pancakes, eggs, and sausages. They also serve good burgers, grilled chicken sandwiches, and soups. | 439 Powell St. | 415/986–1160 | $6–$12 | No credit cards.

Titanic Cafe. American. At this popular breakfast spot with its casual Art Deco interior and large windows, you can choose from a large selection of omelets with a side of applewood-smoked bacon. | 817 Sutter | 415/928–8870 | No dinner. Open daily 7AM–2PM | $5–$12 | AE, DC, MC, V.

★ **Ton Kiang.** Chinese. The lightly seasoned Hakka cuisine of southern China, rarely found in this country, was introduced to San Francisco at this restaurant, with such regional specialties as salt-baked chicken, braised stuffed bean curd, delicate fish and beef balls, and casseroles of meat and seafood cooked in clay pots. Don't overlook the seafood offerings here—salt-and-pepper squid or shrimp, braised catfish, or stir-fried crab, for example. The dim sum is arguably the finest in the city; especially noteworthy are the dumplings stuffed with shark's fin. | 5821 Geary Blvd. | 415/387–8273 | $8.50–$19 | MC, V.

Trio Cafe. Eclectic. This European sandwich café with sidewalk seating is perfect for watching the famous Filmore Street scene. The breakfast is especially good, with poached eggs and homemade buttermilk waffles. | 1870 Filmore St. | 415/563–2248 | Closed Mon. No dinner | $6–$12 | No credit cards.

MODERATE

Ace Wasabi's Rock & Roll Sushi. Japanese. One local weekly calls it the Hard Rock Cafe of excellent sushi. It has dramatic lighting, exposed brick, a tiled ceiling, and abstract scales and sea life tattooed on the walls. With the largest selection of sake in San Francisco, an adventurous drink list, and a DJ, it can get crowded and loud, but the scene is fun and the food is outstanding. You can try the three-amigo roll, the flying kamikaze roll, or the tamari and honey-glazed salmon. | 3339 Steiner St. | 415/567–4903 | www.acewasabis.com | Mon–Thurs. 5:30–10:30, Fri.–Sat. 5–11, Sun. 5–10 | $10–$16 | AE, DC, MC, V.

Alain Rondelli. French. Though the dark woods, mirrors, and requisite brass fixtures may give the impression of an average bistro, the food and refined atmosphere elevate this place to a more sophisticated level. You can try the foie gras with black mission figs, roasted pear with roquefort, champagne vinegar, and black pepper, or the sautéed halibut with asparagus and citrus sauce. | 126 Clement St. | 415/387–0408 | Reservations essential | Tues.–Thurs. 5:30–10, Fri.–Sat. 5:30–10:30, closed Mon. | $14–$17 | MC, V.

Albona. Eastern European. The only Istrian (now part of Croatia) restaurant in Northern California, this family operation mixes northern Italian flavors with traditional Adriatic recipes in a small, candlelit space. You can try the pan-fried gnocchi in a cumin sirloin sauce or the braised rabbit with juniper berries and brown sugar. | 545 Francisco St. | 415/441–1040 | Tues.–Sat. 5–10, closed Sun.–Mon. | $13–$19 | AE, D, DC, MC, V.

Alegria's Foods from Spain. Spanish. With its dark-oak accents, dried flowers, and white walls covered by family photos and hand-painted plates, this place is reminiscent of an Iberian home. With more than 20 tapas, you can easily make an entire meal from these appetizer-sized dishes. Local favorites include poached octopus with potatoes and olive oil, and Spanish cheese flambéed with brandy. There's also a full menu of entrées including delicious paellas. | 2018 Lombard St. | 415/929–8888 | Daily 5:30–10 | $15–$18 | AE, DC, MC, V.

Annabelle's. American. The restaurant of the Mosser Victorian Hotel of Art and Music, this classic bistro is housed in a high-ceiling, former bank with a long wooden and brass bar, hanging fans and a glass divider running down the length of the restaurant. Although decked with French bistro posters on the walls, it primarily serves American staples like rotisserie chicken, New York sirloin, and grilled salmon. | 68 Fourth St. | 415/777–1200 | Daily 7–10:30 | $9–$19 | AE, DC, MC, V.

Antica Trattoria. Italian. On Russian hill, this sparse dining room with its simple dark-wood floors, cream-color walls and large windows serves sophisticated food. The menu changes with the chef's tendency to experiment with in-season produce, but noteworthy dishes have included the monkfish wrapped in pancetta with potatoes and wild mushrooms, and the grilled pork tenderloin atop a gorgonzola polenta. | 2400 Polk St. | 415/928–5797 | Tues.–Sun. 5:30–9:30, Fri.–Sat. 5:30–10:30, closed Mon. | $11–$20 | DC, MC, V.

Baker Street Bistro. French. Large windows allow natural light to flood this classic bistro with hardwood floors, mirrors, and banquettes. It's almost always busy, but many say it's worth the wait (and the lack of elbow space) to eat this well for this little. The goat cheese salad is a good starter, and you can try the signature dish, the blanquette de veau (creamy veal-stew). The four-course, prix-fixe dinner at $14.50 is a nearly unheard-of deal. There's also a brunch Sat.–Sun. | 2953 Baker St. | 415/931–1475 | Mon.–Fri. 11–2, 5:30–10:30, Sat.–Sun. 10–2, 5–9:30 | $9–$14 | AE, MC, V.

Balboa Cafe. Continental. Opened in the 1930s, this place attracts a boisterous young crowd who now hang their designer coats on hooks originally designed for derbies. However, the waiters, rushing through the high-ceiling space in old-fashioned white coats, do match the surroundings. Once you make it past the bar and into the dining room in back, the clientele mellows and you can find a place filled with faithful, neighborhood locals. The menu offers slightly modernized versions of old favorites like New York sirloin and double-cut pork chops. | 3199 Filmore St. | 415/921–3944 | Daily, 11–10, Sunday brunch 10:30–4 | $12–$20 | AE, DC, MC, V.

Basta Pasta. Italian. Open since 1978, this three-story restaurant has a rooftop-garden dining area, an elegant main room with skylights, muted colors, and panoramic views. Downstairs there's a trattatoria with a bar, wood-burning oven and Art Deco wall sconces. The pizzas and homemade pastas are excellent and the entrées, like lamb chops with balsamic vinegar and caramelized onions or veal and prawns in butter sauce, are filling, tasty, and very well prepared. | 1268 Grant St. | 415/434–2248 | Wed.–Sun. 4–12, closed Mon.–Tues. | $13–$18 | AE, D, DC, MC, V.

Betelnut Pejiu Wu. Pan-Asian. On warm evenings the floor-to-ceiling windows open up onto Union Square in this red, purple, and gold, Shanghai-style eatery. The menu takes inspiration from different Pan-Asian cuisines with monthly specialties inspired by the food of different Asian countries. You can find entrées such as Shanghai noodle soups, wok-seared Mongolian beef, and Thai green-curry chicken, complemented with an extremely extensive selection of Asian beers, sake, and original cocktails. Arrive early; it gets crowded quickly. There's limited seating at the sidewalk patio out front, ideal for people-watching. | 2030 Union St. | 415/929–8855 | Reservations essential | Sun.–Thurs. 11:30–11, Fri.–Sat. 11:30– midnight | $11–$19 | D, DC, MC, V.

★ **B44.** European. Tiny Belden Place is a restaurant gold mine, with a cluster of wonderful European eateries. This Spanish addition, with its spare, modern decor, abstract poster art, and open kitchen, draws locals who love the menu of authentic Catalan tapas and paellas. Among the superb small plates are white anchovies with pears and Idiazábal cheese; sherry-scented fish cheeks with garlic, parsley, and chili; warm octopus with tiny potatoes; and blood sausage with white beans and *aioli*. The paellas bring together such inviting combinations as chicken, rabbit, and mushrooms or monkfish, squid, shrimp, mussels, and clams. | 44 Belden Pl | 415/986–6287 | $15–$19 | AE, MC, V | Closed Sun. No Lunch Sat.

Black Cat. Eclectic. Look for the animated neon cat outside and don't be surprised if you're greeted at the door by a 6-ft-tall maître d' in fishnet stockings and a blue feather boa. The Black Cat is a campy theme restaurant in what used to be a café in the days of the Beats. The philosophy behind the menu is to offer the best cuisines San Francisco has to offer, not fusing them, but "celebrating" their independent diversity, you dig? This leads to foie gras terrine listed beside Hong Kong chow mein and steamed salmon wrapped in fig leaves. You can try the oyster bar or watch as lobster, prawns, and crab are fished out of a tank and cooked on the spot. A downstairs jazz and blues bar has live music every week. | 501 Broadway | 415/981–2233 | $8–$26 | Daily 5:30–1 | AE, MC, V.

Bonta Ristorante. Italian. This little, 30-seat trattoria is made intimate and romantic by its hand-painted floral walls, fresh-cut flowers, and colorful artwork. You can order grilled tiger prawns wrapped in pancetta or ravioli stuffed with sea bass, ricotta and spinach in tomato cream sauce, or, for that matter, any of the homemade pastas and desserts. Getting a table might be difficult, but for a romantic night for two it's worth the call ahead. | 2223 Union St. | 415/929–0407 | $12–$18 | www.bontaristorante.com | Reservations essential | Tues.–Thurs. 5:30–10:30, Fri.–Sat. 5:30–11, Sun. 5–10, closed Mon. | MC, V.

Cafe Bastille. French. This bistro on Belden Place, a street often compared to the French Quarter for its Continental restaurants and sidewalk cafés, has a zinc bar, mounted fish, tin ceiling, and large windows. You can choose from traditional Parisian dishes like mussels with French fries, eggplant and feta cheese terrine with aioli, or the roasted salmon served on polenta. | 22 Belden Pl. | 415/986–5673 | Mon.–Sat. 11–11, closed Sun. | $12–$15 | AE, DC, MC, V.

Cafe Pescatore. Italian. Adjoining the Tuscan Hotel, two blocks south of Fisherman's Wharf, the dining room has carved wooden boats and painted fish. Floor-to-ceiling windows open for semi-alfresco dining. There's a sidewalk patio for tourist watching and a gallery kitchen with a wood-fired oven. You can try yummy gourmet pizzas or the hearty, old-world calzone primavera. | 2455 Mason St. | 415/561–1111 | Mon.–Thurs. 7 AM–10 PM; Fri.–Sat. 7 AM–11 PM, Sun. 7–5 | $10–$16 | AE, D, DC, MC, V.

Cafe Riggio. Italian. Opened in 1979, this bustling, unpretentious eatery has hand-painted ceramic plates on the wall, high ceilings with track lighting, and a loyal, local clientele. Longtime favorites include the homemade rock shrimp ravioli and the grilled swordfish with a ragout of lentils. | 4112 Geary Blvd. | 415/221–2114 | www.caferiggio.com | Mon.–Thurs. 5–10, Fri.–Sat. 5–11; Sun. 4:30–10 | $10–$17 | MC, V.

Cha Cha Cha. Cuban. No reservations and good, cheap food equal long lines at this fun, Caribbean-style restaurant decorated with Santeria altars, potted palm trees, and large bay windows. Though the Haight St. waitstaff is quick to refill the excellent sangrias, the spicy entrées, like Cajun shrimp in a cream sauce and fried platanos maderas with black beans and sour cream, may take some time to reach your table. | 1801 Haight St. | 415/386–5758 | Sun.–Thurs. 11:30–4, 5–11; Fri.–Sat. 11:30–4, 5–11:30 | $11–$14 | MC, V.

Chic's Seafood. Located on Pier 39 and originally designed to look like a turn-of-the-century San Franciscan bistro, this is one of the most tasteful of the tourist restaurants with window tables overlooking the Golden Gate Bridge and Alcatraz. You can sample the city's historic dishes like roast crabs in the shell, grilled king salmon with a fruit salsa fresca, and cioppino with Dungeness crab and fish—it's like bouillabaisse, but with a thick tomato broth. | Pier 39 | 415/421–2442 | Daily 9–11 | $12–$24 | AE, D, DC, MC, V.

Coconut Grove Supper Club. Continental. This intimate supper club has wood-sided booths arranged around a central stage, where jazz and swing singers hold court; the decor suggests a tropical fantasy from a 1940s film. Try the whole Thai snapper, and wild mushroom bread pudding. | 1415 Van Ness Ave. | 415/776–1616 | Reservations | Jacket | 5:30–11 PM; Fri., Sat. til 2 AM | Closed Sun., Mon. | $12–$20 | AE, D, DC, MC, V.

David's Restaurant/Delicatessen. Contemporary. Another late-night stop for theatergoers or anyone with a hearty appetite, David's serves New York–style Jewish home cooking in a traditional diner atmosphere, with a long deli counter, checkered tiles, and booths. The bakery makes more than 100 homemade European pastries and fresh bread used for its monster sandwiches. You can try matzo ball soup, borscht, corned beef, blintzes, or European pastries. | 474 Geary St. | 415/276–5950 | Mon.–Fri. 7 AM–midnight, Sat.–Sun. 8 AM–midnight | $9–$20 | AE, MC, V.

★ **Delfina.** Italian. Although noisy and outfitted with benches and chairs that ensure neighborhood chiropractors a sure supply of new clients, Delfina is always hopping. Indeed, within several months of opening in 1999, success forced chef-owner Craig Stoll to take over a neighboring storefront to accommodate the throngs. The loyal crowd comes for the simple, yet exquisite Italian fare: grilled sardines, bitter greens tossed with walnuts and pancetta, halibut riding atop olives and braised fennel, and a wonderful tart made with puckery but sweet Meyer lemons. | 3621 18th St. | 415/552–4055 | $12–$18.25 | MC, V | No lunch.

Dot. Contemporary. Aside from tasty-and-interesting food, this hip, arty restaurant's main claim to fame is the 50-ft-long wall hanging screen-printed with a single water drop that hangs in the main dining area. Dot's lounge stays open until midnight during the week and until 1 AM Fridays and Saturdays. Popular menu fixtures include the steak tartare, grilled beef tenderloin, and fresh fish-and-chips. | 1611 Post St. | 415/922–7788 | $11–$22 | AE, D, DC, MC, V.

Empress of China. Chinese. This San Francisco fixture in Chinatown, opened in the mid-'60s, is gradually fading from elegance to kitsch with a gilded palatial decor that has begun to show its age. Nonetheless, the six-floor garden pavilion, with a 50-ton octagonal work of art built without a single nail, is still breathtaking. You can order glazed walnut prawns, Manchurian beef, or from one of the still fabulous fixed-priced menus at $19–$36 per person. | 838 Grant Ave. | 415/434–1345 | Daily 11:30–3, 5–11 | $12–$18 | AE, DC, MC, V.

Enrico's Sidewalk Cafe. Contemporary. Jazz musicians jam 7 nights a week on a raised dais in the center of the restaurant. This local favorite has simple chandeliers, a glass front wall, and a semi-enclosed sidewalk patio with views of busy Broadway. The food is fresh and light, with excellent salmon bruschetta, grilled salmon with cream frâiche and caviar, and a tangy ceviche. | 504 Broadway | 415/982–6223 | Reservations essential | Sun.–Thurs. noon–11, Fri.–Sat. noon to midnight | $13–$20 | AE, DC, MC, V.

Fattoush. Middle Eastern. This Noe Valley restaurant has a handsome, simple dining room with stone inlays, wood trim, white tablecloths and an ornate chandelier. The food is consistently good, with Middle Eastern spices offset by cool yogurt and mint. You can try the braised shank with grilled cauliflower or the lamb kebab on saffron rice. The garden patio in the back draws a constant crowd for the Sunday brunch where traditional Lebanese fare is served along with pancakes and omelets. | 1361 Church St. | 415/641–0678 | Daily 10:30–3:30, 5:30–10 | $10–$16 | AE, D, MC, V.

Faz. Mediterranean. The pale wood partitions and ocher-and-plum color scheme in this sleek, simple dining room can make you forget it's essentially in a mall. You can try the pizzas; the Mediterranean sampler with dolmades, hummus, tabbouleh, baba ghanouj, tomatoes, pepperoncini, and olives; or the fettuccine Marco Polo with jumbo prawns and a light curry sauce. A downtown business crowd packs in for lunch and fill the exterior tables in the outdoor mall walkway. | 161 Sutter St. | 415/362–0404 | Mon.–Fri. 11:30–3, 5–10, closed Sat.–Sun. | $9–$16 | AE, DC, MC, V.

Fior d'Italia. Italian. Open since 1886, this casual trattoria claims to be America's oldest Italian restaurant. The food is rich and the sauces heavy, with long-time regulars extolling the gnocchi, calamari, and osso buco. You can eat in a room with Roman murals and exposed white ceiling beams, in the Pantaleoni Room with its gilded mirrors, painted tiles, and arched ceiling supports or in the Tony Bennett room. | 601 Union St. | 415/986–1886 | Daily, 11:30–10:30 | $10–$23 | AE, D, DC, MC, V.

Fly Trap. Continental. Despite the unappetizing name, the restaurant wins kudos for its traditional San Francisco fare. The vine-laced courtyard entrance and the dining room, with dark woods, brass, and faded photographs, hark back to the 1898 restaurant for which the Fly Trap was named. The Hangtown Fry is a mix of fried oysters, bacon, and eggs. You can also have chicken Jerusalem or Dungeness crab cake. The other dishes consist of sturdy, turn-of-the-century fare like grilled meats and simply prepared fresh seafood. There's jazz on Sunday. | 606 Folsom St. | 415/243–0580 | Mon.–Fri. 11:30–10, Fri. 11:30–10:30, Sat.–Sun. 5:30–10:30 | $13–$18 | AE, MC, V.

Fog City Diner. American. Shiny metal siding and neon make it easy to find this fashionable diner on the Embarcadero. Inside it's outfitted with booths and an oyster bar. Though burgers and omelets are well represented, it specializes in San Franciscan favorites such as cioppino, a tomato stew with Dungeness crab and mussels, and horseradish rib-eye steak. Though the crowd is mostly tourists, locals will concede that the food, especially that cioppino, is quite good, if a bit pricey. | 1300 Battery St. | 415/982–2000 | Sun.–Thurs. 11:30–11, Fri.–Sat. 11:30–midnight | $13–$26 | D, DC, MC, V.

42 Degrees. Mediterranean. Behind the Esprit Outlet store, this minimalist, industrial-chic hot spot softens its edge at night with table linens and candlelight. With live jazz and a happening bar scene downstairs and a more subdued dining in the upstairs plush booths, you can see why this is a popular Potrero Hill hangout especially Wed.–Sat. when there's live entertainment. You can try risotto with fava beans, crimini mushrooms and pancetta, or the grilled king salmon with spring onions. | 235 16th St. | 415/777–5558 | fax 415/777–2938 | Reservations essential on weekends | Wed.–Sun. 6–9, closed Mon.–Tues. | $12–$20 | MC, V.

Fountain Court. Chinese. Though the over-lit, bland interior may look like every other Chinese restaurant, the food is considered to be among the best in the city. Using only fresh ingredients and eschewing MSG, the traditional dishes, especially the dim sum at lunch, are delicious. You can try the caramelized eggplant, the Lion's Head (steamed pork meatballs on a bed of greens), or the sautéed eel topped with black mushrooms and garlic oil. | 354 Clement St. | 415/668–1100 | Daily 11–3, 5–10. $13–$25 | AE, D, DC, MC, V.

★ **Fringale.** Contemporary. This cheerfully noisy and homey Basque-style bistro has earthtoned walls and furnishings and tropical flower arrangements. The frisée salad with warm bacon dressing and the Maine crab salad with mangos and red peppers make excellent light dinners. You can also find duck confit with lentils, tender rack of lamb, and homemade desserts. | 570 4th St. | 415/543–0573 | Mon.–Fri. 11:30–3, 5:30–10:30, Sat. 11:30–5:30, closed Sun. | $13–$21 | AE, MC, V.

Gabbianos. Italian. This bi-level tourist magnet at the end of a pier has a wonderful, outdoor patio area with umbrella tables, potted greenery, and panoramic views of the bay. While the large windows in the otherwise unremarkable second-level dining room has 180-degree views, the food, with the exception of a good paella, is not up to the caliber the prices would suggest. All the same, it's a good spot for watching the sunset with drinks and top-quality oysters. | 1 Ferry Plaza | 415/391–8403 | Mon.–Sat. 11–10, Sunday brunch 10:30–2 PM | $12–$23 | AE, D, DC, MC, V.

Golden Turtle. Vietnamese. With its elaborate carved-wood paneling, evocative nature murals, and romantic lighting, this is a lovely place to relax over imperial rolls, stuffed with pork, prawn, and crab, lemongrass chicken, or a wonderful concoction called bird's nest, a combination of seafood in an onion ginger sauce and served in a golden potato basket. You can order beer and wine only. | 2211 Van Ness Ave. | 415/441–4419 | Tues.–Sun. 5–11:30, closed Mon. | $10–$19 | AE, DC, MC, V.

Grand Café. French. The dining room of the Hotel Monaco is a perfect spot for an after-theater snack. You can settle into a warmly lit, fully restored turn-of-the-century ballroom and check out the Art Deco chandeliers and Art Nouveau murals and sculptures. The tables and bar in front are a good place for people-watching over polenta soufflé, New

Zealand venison, or grilled escolar with saffron risotto. | 415/292–0100 or 800/214–4220 | Mon.–Thurs. 7–10:30, Fri.–Sun. 7–11, Sunday brunch 9–2 | $15–$21 | AE, D, DC, MC, V.

Greens. Vegetarian. You don't have to be a vegetarian to enjoy the meatless menu at Green's, which revolutionized veggie fare. On the water at Fort Mason Center, a wall full of windows looks out on rugged piers and the bay. On Mondays the full-service restaurant closes, but you can pick up sandwiches, soup, and beverages at the counter to eat at the tables. The rest of the week, the place is packed. Past items on the ever-changing menu include braised fennel, onion tart, spinach and goat cheese salad, and a medley of creative soups. A prix-fixe dinner is served on Saturdays for $40 per person. You can get beer and wine only. | Building A at Fort Mason | 415/771–6222 | www.greensrestaurant.com | Reservations essential | Tues.–Fri. 11:30–2, 5:30–9:30, Mon. 5:30–9:30, Sat. 11:30–2:30, 6–9:30, Sunday brunch 10–2 | $14–$20 | D, MC, V.

Hayes Street Grill. American. One of the earliest restaurants to take up the banner of the fresh-food revolution, this place has simple, flavorful food prepared in a lively gallery kitchen. A block from the Opera House and Symphony Hall, its walls are hung with photo portraits of opera and symphony stars. It's known for fresh-grilled fish, innovative salads and sautéed soft-shell crab. | 320 Hayes St. | 415/863–5545 | Mon.–Thurs. 11:30–2, 5–9, Fri. 11:30–2, 5–10:30, Sat. 5:30–10:30, Sun. 5–8:30 | $13–$25 | AE, D, DC, MC, V.

Helmand. Afghan. Brass chandeliers, small table lanterns, and a desert-toned color scheme create an intimate dining room. Authentic recipes are served with in-house-prepared flat breads and yogurts. The house specialty is marinated beef dumplings filled with sautéed onions and beef. | 430 Broadway | 415/362–0641 | Mon.–Thurs. 5:30–10, Fri.–Sat. 5:30–11 | $12–$18 | AE, MC, V.

Hong Kong Flower Lounge. Chinese. A glitzy, gold-, green-, and red-gilded dining room showcases perfectly prepared Hong Kong specialties. You can pick from one of the chef's specials on the stand-up menu on each table or just pick out a fish from one of the many tanks. Meals include crispy-skinned roast chicken, Peking duck, succulent crystal scallops in shrimp sauce, and an excellent selection of dim sum. | 5322 Geary Blvd. | 415/668–8998 | Mon.–Fri. 11–2:30, 5–9:30, Sat.–Sun. 2:30–9:30 | $12–$24 | AE, DC, MC, V.

I Fratelli. Italian. Open since 1979, this simple trattoria has a gallery kitchen, blue-checkered tablecloths, and a wine rack running the length of the dining room. Its popularity comes from its inexpensive, excellent northern Italian fare. You can start with any of the excellent salads and an order of bruschetta, then try the salmon capellini or the sautéed medallions of veal with prosciutto. | 1896 Hyde St. | 415/474–8603 | Daily 5:30–10 | $11–$17 | AE, MC, V.

Il Fornaio Cucina Italiana. Italian. Part of a San Francisco chain of Italian bakeries and restaurants, it has a screened patio that looks onto a landscaped plaza and waterfall. Inside, high ceilings, polished marble and mahogany counters, and high ceilings that hint of Rome. You can choose from seasonal pasta dishes like pumpkin-stuffed ravioli, the antipasti, or the rotisserie chicken with rosemary. You can also order sandwiches, salads, and home-baked breads to go. | 1265 Battery St. | 415/986–0100 | Mon.–Fri. 7–11, weekends, 8–11 | $13–$18 | AE, DC.

Infusion. Contemporary. Plank-wood walls, sleek suspended lights, rock and roll and baseball artwork hang on exposed brick in this casual, contemporary place. Within two blocks of the new baseball stadium and named after a large selection of vodkas infused with fruit and herbal flavors, it has a bevy of boisterous, young urban professionals often in attendance. It's especially busy when local bands hit the stage Thurs.–Sat. The ambitious menu is a little hit-and-miss, but the mussel appetizer and the blackened mahi mahi, jerk chicken, and pan-fried soft-shell crab entrées are excellent. | 555 Second St. | 415/543–2282 | Mon.–Fri. 11:30–2, Sat.–Sun. 5–2 | $15–$20 | AE, DC, MC, V.

Jasmine House. Vietnamese. This simple, elegant dining room with white linen and wall sconces serves Vietnamese food with a French influence. The nightly dinner special is excellent and is a steal at only $9. The curry chicken and the Vietnamese roast crab are also good. | 2301 Clement St. | 415/668–3382 | Tues.–Thurs. 11–10, Mon. 5–10, Fri.–Sat. 5–11 | $7–$18 | MC, V.

Julie's Supper Club. Eclectic. The 1950s meet the Jeffersons at this popular SOMA meeting place that has lots of neon, comfortable booths, and a martini menu. Late nights, you'll often find a swing band at work. You can order beer-battered catfish, roast pork chops, or seared salmon on a bed of soba noodles. | 1123 Folsom St. | 415/861–0707 or 415/861–5518 | Mon.–Thurs. 5–10:30, Fri.–Sat. 5–11:30. Closed Sun. | $11–$19 | AE, MC, V.

Kabuto Sushi. Japanese. This restaurant is known for the freshest, most expertly prepared sushi in the city. In an austere white and wood dining room with rice paper blinds and a black lacquered sushi bar, the inventive chef constantly changes the selections, cultivating an obsessively loyal clientele. There's a $50 prix fixe or a huge selection of individual nigiri and sushi rolls, vegetarian choices, and Japanese hot dishes. | 5116 Geary Blvd. | 415/752–5652 | Tues.–Sat. 5:30–11 PM, closed Sun.–Mon. | $12–$20 | MC, V.

Katia's. Russian. Moscow with a definite Californian flair, this soothing space features peach walls, bent-wood chairs, white linen, and tinted sliding windows that are open on warm days. The lighter-than-usual Russian dishes include beef stroganoff and the excellent shashlik, strips of lamb in garlic, onion, and lemon. | 600 5th Ave. | 415/668–9292 | Tues.–Thurs. 11:30–2:30, 5–9; Fri.–Sat. 11:30–2:30, 5–10, Sun. 5–10, closed Mon. | $12–$17 | AE, D, DC, MC, V.

Kuleto's. Italian. With its vaulted ceilings and gorgeous Italian marble floors, this theater-district favorite is like a temple to the gods of northern Italian cuisine. Upon walking in, the subtle aroma of dried herbs, prosciutto, and garlic wafts into the air from behind the bar. You can try saffron risotto or roast duck with grappa-soaked cherries and polenta. | 221 Powell St. | 415/397–7720 | Reservations essential | Mon.–Fri. 7–10:30 11:30–11, Sat.–Sun. 8–10:30, 11:30–11 | $9–$18 | AE, D, DC, MC, V.

La Vie. Vietnamese. This simple unpretentious dining room has fresh roses at each table and Vietnamese instruments on the walls. Jovial waiters serve dishes like flaming beef, prawn entrées, and roasted crab. | 5830 Geary Blvd. | 415/668–8080 | Sun.–Thurs. 11–10, Fri.–Sat. 11–10:30 | $11–$16 | MC, V.

Laghi. Italian. Huge windows, an open kitchen and large antique tapestries surround the deep booths and white linen-covered tables. A loyal local clientele returns for the risotto specials, Western veal chops, and grilled Chilean sea bass. | 2101 Sutter | 415/931–3774 | $11–$22 | MC, V.

Little Garden Seafood. Chinese. Located just beyond the boundaries of Chinatown, this place has pleasant lighting and silk wall hangings. Its extensive menu includes unusual, authentic dishes. You can try sliced pork, mustard green and salted-egg soup, fried squab, spicy eggplant, lamb with bean curd clay pot, scallops with vegetables, or steamed oysters with black bean sauce. | 750 Vallejo St. | 415/788–2328 | Daily 11–9:30 | $10–$18 | MC, V.

Lolli's Castagnola. Seafood. Serving fresh, simple seafood since 1916, this two-tiered spot thrives on the throngs of tourists who visit Fisherman's Wharf. There's wrap-around outdoor seating on the second level and panoramic views from both dining rooms downstairs. The food is of good quality with no surprises. You can get bouillabaisse, fish and chips, and calamari. | 286 Jefferson St. | 415/776–5015 | Sun.–Thurs. 9–10, Fri.–Sat. 9–11 | $14–$23 | AE, D, DC, MC, V.

★ **Lulu.** Mediterranean. Tables are arranged in a large, open dining room that was formerly a 1910 warehouse. Voices echo under the vaulted ceilings. Food is roasted in two open wood ovens, giving everything a distinctive smoky flavor. Family-style dishes are served in hand-painted earthenware. It has a full oyster bar, extensive antipasto selections, wood oven-baked gnocchi, nightly rotisserie specials, and a whole black bass prepared in an oak-fired oven. | 816 Folsom St. | 415/495–5775 | www.restaurantlulu.com | Sun.–Thurs. 11:30–2:30, 5:30–10:30, Fri.–Sat. 11:30–2:30, 5:30–11:30 | $11–$22 | AE, DC, MC, V.

MacArthur Park. American. The woodwork, brick, and polished surfaces make this an inviting spot for a drink or leisurely meal. A Financial District hangout, there's often a crowd of businessmen sipping the home-brewed "Big Rib" wheat beer, but the traditional fare and large portions draw families as well. It's known for cobb salad, smoky ribs, and steaks but you can also select from many fresh fish dinners. | 607 Front St. | 415/398–5700 | 11:30–3:30, 5–10; Fri.–Sun. 11:30–3:30, 5–11; Sun. 4:30–10 | $12–$25 | AE, DC, MC, V.

Magic Flute Garden Restaurante. Italian. The restaurant is housed in a turn-of-the-century 1912 Victorian building that was completely restored with Tuscan decor and original artwork. Owned by the LaCavera family since 1981, the restaurant has been voted most romantic, best place to kiss, and Number 1 brunch house in the Bay Area by the *San Francisco Chronicle* (July). Popular dishes include the grilled veal chop, fruit/seafood pasta, and braised lamb shank. Enjoy dining in one of the two dining rooms or in the heated outdoor dining area on Italian white marble tables surrounded by a garden with classical music in the background. | 3673 Sacramento Ave. | 415/922–1225 | Mon–Fri. 11AM–2:30PM; Sat., Sun. from 10AM–2:30PM; Wed–Sat 5:30–10pm. Closed Dec. 25 | $10–$23 | AE, MC, V.

Mandarin. Chinese. This spacious restaurant in the 19th-century Ghirardelli Chocolate building has oriental antiques, silk scrolls with beautiful calligraphy, an intricately tiled floor, and an outstanding view of the bay. The upscale menu spotlights some hard-to-come-by delicacies, like traditional Peking duck and shark fin soup. You can also try the five-spiced prawns, beggar's chicken, or tangerine chicken. | 900 North Point St. | 415/673–8812 | www.themandarin.com | Daily 11:30–11 | $10–$18 | AE, D, DC, MC, V.

Marrakech Moroccan. Moroccan. A regal interior, carpeted walls, and plush couches have made this an exotic favorite for more than 25 years. It has an à la carte menu, but for a truly unique experience you can choose one of five prix-fixe, five-course meals for the table. You can be pampered, served fresh fruit, and entertained by belly dancers throughout the meal. | 419 O'Farrell St. | 415/776–6717 | Daily 6–10 | $12–$16; $24–$29 prix-fixe | AE, D, DC, MC, V.

Matterhorn Swiss. Swiss. This all-wood fondue spot resembles an up-scale Alpine ski lodge. You can dip everything from prawns to pork to fruit to beef. Besides fondue, you can order somewhat heavy Swiss and German entrées such as sliced veal and potatoes, and wild sturgeon wrapped in pancetta. | 2323 Van Ness | 415/885–6116 | Tues.–Sun. 5–10, closed Mon. | $11–$24 | AE, D, DC, MC, V.

Millennium. Vegetarian. In the Abigail hotel near the Civic Center, this is one of hippest and best vegetarian restaurants in the city. The area is benefiting from an ongoing facelift that includes the new Asian Art Museum. The interior has large bay windows overlooking a European garden, simple white walls, black and white–checkered tiles, and blue glass everywhere. The complex dishes are, seriously, good enough to convert meat-eaters. You can try the Asian-style vegetable Napoleon, vegetables and tofu in a sesame sauce over a bed of jasmine rice with coconut lime sauce, or a plantain tart with crisp whole-wheat tortilla and creamy cilantro tofu and mango salsa. | 246 McAllister St. | 415/487–9800 | www.millenniumrestaurant.com | Daily 5–9:30 | $12–$18 | AE, DC, MC, V.

Palio d'Asti. Italian. "An outpost of Italian culture," according to one restaurant critic and well regarded for its Piedmontese and Tuscan specialties, this large industrial-chic space has medieval-style banners hanging from a vaulted ceiling, curved walls, and a gallery kitchen. It's a popular lunch spot for downtown business types, but it really comes alive at night with an excellent menu supplemented by a very extensive selection of Italian and Californian wines by the glass. Favorites include the rosemary half chicken with bread salad, soft-shell crabs, and linguine with fresh clams. | 640 Sacramento St. | 415/395–9800 | www.paliodasti.com | 11:30AM–2:30AM, closed Sat.–Sun. | $14–$24 | AE, D, DC, MC, V.

Pane e Vino. Italian. Terra-cotta floors, fireplaces, and exposed beams adorn the two dining rooms of this rustic Tuscan eatery. Popular dishes include grilled striped bass and osso buco, served with homemade breads. | 3011 Steiner St. | 415/346–2111 | Sun.–Mon. 11:30–2:30, 5–10; Fri.–Sat. 11:30–2:30, 5–10:30 | $9–$20 | AE, DC, MC, V.

Pastis. French. This industrial-style bistro, designed with exposed ceiling beams, brick, simple white-linen tables, and copious wood accents, attracts a young crowd of downtown designers and Financial District workers. The menu is stocked full of bistro classics such as mussels, seared foie gras, steak and frites, and an excellent filet of salmon provençale. For dessert, you can try a warm banana and chocolate pannequet. | 1015 Battery St. | 415/391–2555 | 11:30–3, 5:30–10:30, closed Sun. | $12–$20 | AE, MC, V.

Perry's Downtown. American. A satellite location of the original sports bar, eatery, and watering hole, this bi-level café is decked out with sports memorabilia and video monitors. It's known for lobster platters, burgers, and nightly blue-plate specials. | 185 Sutter St. | 415/989–6895 | 11–9:30, closed Sun. | $10–$18 | AE, D, DC, MC, V.

Plouf. French. This seafood bistro is austere and modern yet warmed up by fireplaces, a social bar scene, and a friendly, loyal crowd. It has European-style sidewalk tables on Belden Place, an alley lined with restaurants. Fish and chips, day-boat scallops, mussels and oysters, and seafood pastas, like the crab ravioli, are the popular house specialties. The bar's masterfully-blended cocktails attract a global, cosmopolitan crowd. | 40 Belden Pl. | 415/986–6491 | Mon.–Fri. 11:30–2:30, 5:30–10; Sat. 5:30–10, closed Sun. | $14–$23 | AE, DC, MC, V.

Plumpjack Cafe. Contemporary. Named after Shakespeare's Falstaff, this café is playfully regal with metal and plaster curtains highlighted by gold, pewter, and bronze accents. Owned and operated by the Plumpjack Vineyards, it has an extensive and inexpensive list of California wines. You can find a grilled pork tenderloin with blackberry reduction or pan-roasted salmon on a bed of short ribs. | 3127 Filmore St. | 415/563-4755 | www.plumpjack.com/pjcafe | Reservations essential, dinner | Mon.–Fri. 11:30–2, 5:30–10, Sat. 5:30–10, closed Sun. | $13–$24 | AE, D, DC, MC, V.

Prego Ristorante. Italian. One of the first authentic trattorias in the city, it's settled into its role as a hip, neighborhood standard. Pastas are homemade and the meats are spit roasted in the gallery kitchen. The gourmet pizzas are among the best in the city. | 2000 Union St. | 415/563-3305 | Daily, 11:30–midnight | $10–$20 | AE, DC, MC, V.

Rocco's Seafood Grill. Seafood. This traditional San Francisco–style seafood restaurant has a massive, half-circle wooden oyster bar that dominates the mirror-lined dining room. A raised dining area with candlelight and plush booths separates the tables from the crowds at the bar. Try the Dungeness crab and rock shrimp salad, the cioppino, or the calamari steak piccata. | 2080 Van Ness Ave. | 415/567–7600, 415/567–7606 | Sun.–Thurs. 5–10, Fri.–Sat. 5–11 | $10–$20 | AE, D, DC, MC, V.

★ **Rose Pistola.** Italian. This popular North Beach restaurant has a warm glow that beckons passersby on Columbus Ave. Its long dining room has a minimalist style with mahogany wood accents and black-and-white jazz photos from the '50s. You can get whole roasted char, filet served tableside, or fried cream with brandied cherries, all served from the bustling, open kitchen, or stop by for late-night snacks. There's a late-night menu and frequent entertainment. | 532 Columbus Ave. | 415/399–0499 | Reservations essential | $10–$26 | AE, MC, V.

Rumpus. Contemporary. This unpretentious, white-walled restaurant is located in an alley off Union Square. You can eat inside in the multi-leveled dining room, or outside at a bistro table on the sidewalk when the weather is fine. The menu at Rumpus is an ever-changing homage to California cuisine, sometimes featuring options like pan-roasted chicken breast sided with smashed herb potatoes and assorted fresh veggies, or sautéed calf's liver with pearl onions. No smoking. | 1 Tillman Pl. | 415/421–2300 | Mon.–Thurs. 11:30–2:30, 5:30–10PM, Fri.–Sat. 11:30–2:30, 5:30–11, Sun. 5:30–11 | $12–$18 | AE, DC, MC, V.

Sam's Grill. Seafood. A former saloon built in 1867, this seafood restaurant still has the original private booths. It's popular with the Financial District crowd who appreciate the white linen tablecloths and traditional San Francisco fare like the Hangtown fry, cioppino, and charbroiled seafood. There's also an outdoor seating area with canvas umbrellas along a quiet, side alley. | 374 Bush St. | 415/421–0594 | Mon.–Fri. 11–9, closed Sat.–Sun. | $12–$21 | AE, DC, MC, V.

Scala's Bistro. Italian. Located in the Sir Francis Drake Hotel, this warm and welcoming spot has a gold bas-relief ceiling, lead pane windows, and Craftsman-style chandeliers. The food is primarily northern Italian with French accents and an emphasis on fresh pasta, fish, and daily specials. You can try porcini tagliatelle or the seared salmon filet with buttermilk mashed potatoes. | 432 Powell St. | 415/395–8555 | Reservations essential on weekends | Sun.–Thurs. 7–10:30, 11:30–midnight, Fri.–Sat. 8–midnight | $12–$18 | AE, D, DC, MC, V.

Schroeder's. German. The oldest and largest German restaurant in California, this bier-haus has European murals and frequent live polka music. The menu offers wiener schnitzel, roast calf's liver, grilled chicken, and fish specials. There are 18 German beers on tap. | 240 Front St. | 415/421–4778 | Mon.–Thurs. 11–9, Fri.–Sat. 11–9:30, closed Sun. | $8–$16 | AE, D, DC, MC, V.

Slanted Door. Vietnamese. This very popular and hip Asian bistro has a sleek two-tiered dining area with high ceilings, green tables, and velvet booths. The menu changes weekly, but recurring favorites include green papaya salad, Vietnamese crêpes, and seafood curries cooked in a clay pot. | 584 Valencia | 415/861–8032 | Sun.–Sat. 11:30–3, 5:30–10 | $10–$20 | MC, V.

Splendido. Italian. This pretty spot has a glass-enclosed terrace with Italian tile, potted plants, and views of the bay and city. Although tucked into the second floor of the Embarcadero Center, it's far from a mall restaurant. Indeed, for many, it's a destination in and of itself. At lunch, you can get excellent Italian sandwiches. For dinner, you can try the baked saffron gnocchi with Maine lobster, strip loin bruschetta, and mesquite-grilled rib-eye steak. | 4 Embarcadero Center | 415/986–3222 | Daily, 11:30–2:30, 5:30–10 | $14–$21 | AE, D, DC, MC, V.

Tadich Grill. Seafood. Opened in 1849, this venerable restaurant is older than the state of California. You'll probably have to wait for a table but it's worth it. You can pick from house favorites like the scrumptious crab and prawn casserole, seafood cioppino, or the petrale sole filet. | 240 California St. | 415/391–1849 | No reservations | Mon.–Fri. 11–9:30, Sat. 11–11:30, closed Sun. | $10–$20 | MC, V.

Universal Cafe. Contemporary. A young, hip crowd swears by the complex salads and grilled flat breads served in this rather industrial-looking space with minimal decorations besides black-and-white photos of San Francisco. Daily specials could include a pan-seared filet mignon or the tender grilled and peppered ahi tuna. | 2814 19th St. | 415/821–4608 | Reservations essential | Tues.–Fri. 7:30–10, Sat.–Sun. 9–9:30, closed Mon. | $10–$20 | AE, DC, MC, V.

Waterfront Restaurant & Cafe. Contemporary. This waterfront spot has a downstairs café with its 100-seat outdoor patio and inside exposed beams and glass walls where you can get crab cakes, wood oven-baked pizzas, and house-smoked salmon sandwiches. Upstairs, in a modern dining room, with black rattan chairs and Asian antiques, you can find a more refined menu with fusion preparations of fresh seafood like porcini mushroom roasted monkfish and linguine with smoked salmon. | Pier 7 | 415/391–2696 | Daily 11:30–10:30, Sunday brunch 10–3 | $8–$26 | AE, D, DC, MC, V.

Yank Sing. Chinese. The oldest Chinese restaurant in the city, established in 1848, it has three large formal dining rooms with potted plants, large windows, and a constant bustling crowd. It's famous for dim sum, served from tableside carts. These small portions include pork bao, foil-wrapped chicken, sweet rice in banana leaves, and various filled dumplings. You can also get Mandarin and Cantonese specialties like stuffed crab and wok-fried chili prawns. | 427 Battery St. | 415/781–1111 | www.yanksing.com | Mon.–Fri. 11–3, Sat.–Sun. 10–4 | $12–$18 | AE, DC, MC, V.

Zarzuela. Spanish. You can sample an extensive menu of tapas, zarzuela, a seafood stew, or a hearty oxtail stew in this homey and rustic dining room with hand-painted ceramic plates, murals of bull fighters, and Spanish-tile floors. | 2000 Hyde St. | 415/346–0800 | Tues.–Sat. 12:30–10:30, closed Sun.–Mon. | $9–$15 | MC, V.

EXPENSIVE

Acquerello. Italian. You can dine by the warm glow of lights in small sconces that illuminate wooden ceiling beams and watercolors on the white stucco walls. Its northern Italian dishes have a California flare, with a menu that changes seasonally. Past highlights have included the lemon buscatini with crab in garlic sauce, roast squab, and the marinated and grilled quail with fresh oranges and sage. There's an extensive wine and beer list. | 1722 Sacramento St. | 415/567–5432 | Reservations essential | Daily 5:30–10:30, closed Sun.–Mon. | $15–$25 | AE, D, DC, MC, V.

Anjou. French. This cozy bistro with arcing lamps and plush banquettes draws a large, mixed crowd from the neighboring Union Square theater, and business districts. You can start with the warm eggplant salad and then try the seafood cassoulet, a San Francisco specialty with lobster, monkfish, and lingo beans in a crayfish sauce. | 44 Campton Pl. | 415/392–5373 | Reservations essential | Tues.–Sat. 11:30–2:30, 5:30–10, closed Sun.–Mon. | $15–$28 | AE, D, DC, MC, V.

Bizou. French. With a name that means "little kiss," this sweet little bistro is housed in a 1906 building with flower boxes in the windows, vintage light fixtures, and a long oak bar. Contemporary French and Italian dishes, like the beef cheeks with parsnip chips and the salt cod ravioli, coexist with San Francisco staples such as the Dungeness crab salad. | 598 Fourth St. | 415/543–2222 | Sun.–Thurs. 11:30–2:30, 5:30–10; Fri. 11:30–2:30, 5:30–10:30; Sat. 5:30–10:30 | $17–$26 | AE, MC, V.

Bobby Rubino's. American. Though a nationwide chain, this Fisherman's Wharf location is made special by its large windows with sweeping views of the bay, Tiffany lamps, and roomy comfortable booths. Tourists flock here for sturdy, consistent entrées like the barbecued baby-back ribs, New York sirloin, and grilled salmon. | 245 Jefferson St. | 415/673–2266 | Daily 11:30–11 | $22–$25 | AE, D, DC, MC, V.

Café Kati. Pan-Asian. Cave drawings in the bistro-like front room and a back wall emblazoned with a huge golden kirin (a mythological creature from Japan) make for curious surroundings. You can ponder the décor over delicious miso-glazed sea bass or the dragon roll, tempura prawn wrapped in salmon and avocado. Fresh seafood and unorthodox recipes draw an eclectic crowd. | 1963 Sutter St. | 415/775–7313 | Reservations essential | Tues.–Sun. 5:30–10, closed Mon. | $20–$30 | MC, V.

Cafe Tiramisu. Italian. A little trattoria located on Belden Place in the Financial District, with excellent sidewalk dining, large windows, and stylized murals of Roman ruins inside, and cavernous, candlelit dining in the wine cellar. The menu changes daily and always emphasizes northern Italian cuisine. You can start with any of the excellent antipasti, and then try the spinach and cheese ravioli with truffle oil or the roasted rack of lamb with cabernet sauce. | 28 Belden Pl. | 415/421–7044 | Mon.–Sat. 11:30–2:30, 5–10, Sun. 5–10 | $15–$23 | AE, DC, MC, V.

Cliff House. American. While the current, modern design of this San Francisco institution doesn't do justice to its previous, Victorian incarnations, its location atop the cliffs and overlooking seal rocks continues to draw tourists and locals alike. There is an upstairs, light and airy dining room with Art Deco chandeliers that serves more than 20 types of omelets, a light lunch menu, and candlelit seafood dining after 5, as well as a downstairs "Seafood and Beverage Company." This warm, golden-lit space is decorated with Art Nouveau inlays, sumptuous wooden details, and beveled glass. The most coveted tables are at windows that overlook the waves crashing below. Downstairs there's a sports bar and cocktail lounge as well as the Musée Mecanique, a turn of the century arcade. On Sunday, it's a great spot for a relaxing champagne brunch. | 1090 Pt. Lobos | 415/666–4025 | Daily 11–11 | $16–$25 | AE, DC, MC, V.

Cypress Club. Contemporary. This brasserie, opened in 1990, has a whimsical 1940s-style design with copper archways, lush velvet booths, and cartoonish, bulging Deco columns. The popular menu highlights American and continental classics with contemporary touches. The braised veal cheeks are the standout appetizer, and, for an entrée, the seared Pacific king salmon with avocado relish or the wood-roasted beef rib-eye with cabernet reduction are both complex, masterfully prepared dishes. | 500 Jackson St. | 415/296–8555 | Reservations essential | $21–$30 | AE, DC, MC, V.

Dalla Torre Ristorante e Bar. Italian. This Mediterranean-style two-story villa near Coit Tower has views of the bay and Alcatraz from both dining rooms. Its Italian tiles, earth tones, vaulted ceilings and oversized windows create a romantic setting for its imaginative dishes. You can try veal carpaccio, pear and Gorgonzola salad, almond-stuffed quail with black olive risotto, or braised veal shank. | 1349 Montgomery St. | 415/296–1111 or 800/733–6218 | Wed.–Sun. 5–10 | $18–$29 | AE, DC, MC, V.

Eos. Asian. Expertly composed Asian and Californian fusion dishes are the highlight of this two-tiered, minimalist space. Exposed metal beams, brick, dramatic lighting, and one of the city's best wine bars draw a mix of hipsters and those who have read the reviews. The adventurous menu includes a Peking duck sautéed in blackberry sage tea and blackened catfish atop a bed of lemongrass risotto. | 901 Cole St. | 415/566–3063 | Mon.–Fri. 5:30–11, Sat.–Sun. 5–11 | $16–$26 | AE.

Firefly. Contemporary. Hidden in a cluster of homes west of the 24th Street shopping area, this small restaurant has two intimate dining rooms and a delightful collection of modern art and internationally eclectic statues and tchotkes. The menu shares this global attention to detail, combining Asian, South American, and Mediterranean flavors effortlessly. It's most famous for bouillabaisse, thick with monkfish, prawns, and scallops, and shrimp and scallop pot stickers. You can order wine and beer only. | 4288 24th St. | 415/821–7652 | Sun.–Thurs. 5:30–9:30, Fri.–Sat. 5:30–10 | $15–$25 | AE, MC, V.

Franciscan. American. The dining room is designed around the view, with three tiers of brown leather banquettes facing the Golden Gate Bridge and Alcatraz. Unlike many of the Fisherman's Wharf restaurants, this one does not dumb down for the tourists. You can pick from crab Louie, cioppino, seafood scampi, New York steak, or raw oysters. Kids' menu. | Pier 43| 415/362–7733 | Sun.–Thurs. 11–10, Fri.–Sat. 11–10:30 | $16–$25 | AE, DC, MC, V.

Frascati. Italian. This restaurant's modernized, Italian country décor has a mix of floor and balcony seating, tile floors, modern art, and a semi-open gallery kitchen. It's a perfect fit to the ambitious menu in which American and Mediterranean influences are fused in dishes such as baked polenta cakes in porcini mushroom broth with crumpled blue cheese, Andalusian seafood paella, and an excellent bouillabaisse. | 1901 Hyde St. | 415/928–1406 | Tues.–Thurs. 5:30–10, Fri.–Sat. 5:30–10:30, closed Mon. | $17–$22 | MC, V.

Garden Court. French. In the Palace Hotel, its formal turn-of-the-century lobby has a beautiful stained-glass dome, crystal chandeliers, marble columns, and vaulted ceilings. It's known for impeccable Old World service and an afternoon formal Wed.–Fri. 2–4:30 tea complete with china and the best silver. Specialties include crab bisque, rack of lamb, and pepper salmon. There's a sumptuous Sun. brunch and entertainment Fri. nights. | 2 New Montgomery St. | 415/546–5011 | Daily 6:30–10:30, 11:30–2, Tues–Sat 6–10 | $17–$28 | AE, D, DC, MC, V.

Gaylord India. Indian. One of the first Indian restaurants to cater to Western tastes when it opened 20 years ago, this upscale Indian eatery is decorated with potted palms and Chippendale-style chairs. It has large windows overlooking the bay and Marin Headlands. You can try the rack of lamb, spiced and cooked in a tandoori oven, or the chicken tikka masala. | 900 North Point St. | 415/771–8822 | www.gaylords.com | 11:45–1:45, 5–10:45, Sunday brunch noon–2:45 | $17–$28 | AE, D, DC, MC, V.

Hama Ko. Japanese. This tiny place dominated by the polished wood of a sushi bar has rice screens, museum-quality tea sets, and an authentic Japanese atmosphere. You can order an expensive ($75/person), but memorable, kaiseki meal of fresh seasonal seafood such as tuna belly, scallops, Dungeness crab, and shrimp. | 108B Carl St. | 415/753–6808 | Daily, 5–10 | $15–$26 | AE, MC, V.

★ **Hawthorne Lane.** Contemporary. Located on a small lane just south of Market St., its minimal, industrial interior has brick walls, club lamps, and fine prints on the walls. A hip, stylish crowd gathers here for fusion food influenced by Pacific Rim and traditional Mediterranean cuisine. You can choose Dungeness crab and sweet pea soup, tempura lobster salad, or miso-glazed cod. It also has a more casual café in the front with the same menu but a better chance of grabbing a table. | 22 Hawthorne St. | 415/777–9779 | Reservations essential | Sun.–Thurs. 11:30–2, 5:30–10, Fri.–Sat. 11:30–2, 5:30– 10:30 | $20–$30 | D, DC, MC, V.

House. Contemporary. Sister restaurant to the popular The House, Chef Larry Tse's Asian-fusion restaurant has a stark, artful interior with stone floors and sculptural lighting fixtures. You can have rack of lamb with Korean marinade, grilled sea bass, and delicate tempura. | 1269 9th Ave. | 415/682–3898 | Mon.–Thurs. 5:30–10, Fri.–Sat. 4:30–10, Sun. 4–10 | $16–$20 | AE, MC, V.

The House. Contemporary. This hip, local favorite has Pacific Rim–influenced dishes in a minimalist dining room with slate floors, pale wood and Expressionist art. Unlike many fusion menus, this one doesn't try to impress or intimidate with bizarre combinations. Instead, the simple dishes let Eastern and Western flavors achieve a harmonious balance. You can try grilled sea bass with ginger soy or veal chop with shiitake mushroom and oyster sauce. | 1230 Grant Ave. | 415/986–8612 | Tues.–Fri. 11:30–3, 5:30–10; Sat. 5:30–10., closed Sun.–Mon. | $15–$24 | AE, MC, V.

House of Prime Rib. American. This traditional steakhouse serves no-nonsense meat-and-potatoes fare in a lantern-lit room with mahogany-framed curved murals and deep booths. You can choose from four carving styles for the aged beef roasts. The prix-fixe menu includes the cut of your choice, chopped salad, baked potato laden with sour cream, Yorkshire pudding, and pecan or apple pie. Kids' menu. | 1906 Van Ness Ave. | 415/885–4605 | Mon.–Thurs. 5:30–10, Fri.– Sat. 4:30–10, Sun. 4–10 | $19–$26 | AE, MC, V.

★ **Jardiniere.** Continental. Designed by restaurateur Pat Kuleto, it has mottled mauve walls, plush velvet drapes and a gold-domed ceiling as dramatic as any of the surrounding theaters. For pre-show dining, there's a three-course "staccato" menu and the waiters will do all they can to get you there on time. There's dining on the mezzanine with live jazz nightly, perfect for a post-show dessert or nightcap. It's known for squab, sweetbreads, foie gras, short ribs, and seared sea scallops. | 300 Grove St. | 415/861–5555 | $20–$30 | Daily 5–12 | AE, DC, MC, V.

Kokkari. Greek. This place feels like a Greek villa, with its huge fireplace hung with cooking vessels, and cast-iron chandeliers. You can sit at the 20-ft communal table or one of the smaller tables along the wall, each with white linen and an oil lamp, and snack on the excellent homemade pita with melitzanosalata (eggplant salad). The menu offers upscale renditions of Greek favorites like octopus salad, moussaka, braised lamb shank scented with cinnamon and served over orzo, and, for dessert, the yogurt sorbet. | 200 Jackson St. | 415/981–0983 | Daily, 5–11 | $17–$30 | AE, DC, MC, V.

M. Point. Japanese. In the Hotel Milano, this Japanese/American eatery's happening bar scene takes place surrounded by a mural showing an abstract, panoramic view of the city that stretches the full length of the dining room. You can order fresh sashimi and creative rolls at the curved marble sushi bar, or sit at one of the tables and try the excellent selection of Western dishes such as porterhouse steak, roasted pork loin, and grilled fish. You can also get an American breakfast. | 55 5th St. | 415/543–7600 | Mon.–Sat. 7–10:30, 11:30–2:30, 5–10; Sunday brunch 9–2 | $19–$25 | AE, D, DC, MC, V.

McCormick & Kuleto's. Seafood. This upscale eatery was designed by San Francisco legend, Pat Kuleto, who put as much attention to detail in the food as in the exquisite building.

You can choose from more than 50 fresh specialties daily, including Dungeness crab cakes and ahi tuna seared with five types of pepper. A winding, wave-like walkway runs through the elegant dining room, preventing the staff from bustling between the tables. Oversized windows overlook the bay and shell-shaped sconces illuminate the dark wood walls. | 900 North Point St. | 415/929–1730 | www.mccormickandkuletos.com | Mon.–Sat. 11:30–11, Sun. 11:30–10:30 | $16–$25 | AE, D, DC, MC, V.

Mecca. Contemporary. At this 1940s-themed supper club, industrial influences such as exposed piping and zinc-topped cement columns contrast with leather and velvet furnishings to create a very distinctive and unusual interior. You can try barbecued oysters, oven-roasted sea bass with oyster sauce, or the Jamaican jerk pork chops. There's jazz Sun.–Thurs. | 2029 Market St. | 415/621–7000 | Reservations essential | Sun.–Wed. 6–11, Thurs.–Sat. 6–midnight | $16–$29 | AE, DC, MC, V.

Meeting House. American. Wood paneling and Shaker furnishings set the mood at this informal 40-seat restaurant that serves contemporary versions of old American dishes. Specialties include grilled pork chops with buttermilk mashed potatoes and the pan-seared scallops with sweet corn chowder. Desserts such as the strawberry shortcake are above average. | 1701 Octavia St. | 415/922–6733 | Wed.–Sun. 5:30–9:30, closed Mon.–Tues. | $21–$27 | AE, MC, V.

Mifune. Japanese. This popular noodle house in the Japantown Center has a display case in front that displays Tokyo-style replicas of the dishes served inside. It has a stark red and black dining room with wooden booths and small tables. It has chewy homemade soba noodles and more than 30 combinations of noodles, meat, and garnishes. | 1737 Post St. | 415/922–0337 | Daily 11:30–10 | $18–$30 | AE, MC, V.

Moose's. American. This watering hole for politicos and stockbrokers has views of Washington Square Park through its blue-tinted French windows. Past the happening bar scene and large bronze moose, it opens up into a spacious dining room, accented with terrazzo tiles and ceramics, and book-ended by a lively gallery kitchen. The menu has contemporary updates on American classics like grilled pork loin chop with rosemary polenta and braised greens, or the roasted Alaskan halibut with lemon-basil fettuccini in a lemon-caper-olive sauce. In addition, the moose burger is quite popular. Jazz piano duos and trios perform nightly. | 1652 Stockton St. | 415/989–7800 | Tues.–Thurs. 11:30–2:30, 5:30–10; Mon. 5:30–10; Fri.–Sat. 5:30–11, Sunday brunch 9:30–2:30 | $20–$30 | AE, DC, MC, V.

Morton's of Chicago. American. This dimly lit steakhouse with mahogany paneling, armchairs, and old photos of famous clientele has prime aged beef prepared unpretentiously in 14- to 24-oz cuts, along with chicken and seafood. | 400 Post St. | 415/986–5830 | www.mooses.com | Mon.–Sat. 5–11, Sun. 5–10 | $20–$30 | AE, DC, MC, V.

Murray's. Contemporary. Hidden away in the back of the Canterbury Hotel, this fantastic Deco space is covered by a 25-ft, arched greenhouse ceiling with views of a landscaped garden. Harlequin floors, 20-ft potted palms, and other tropical plants surround high-backed booths. The menu, focusing on seafood, manages to hold its own to the surroundings, with intriguing Pan-Asian touches and artful presentation. You can start with an innovative salad and then try the dry-aged filet mignon with ginger mashed potatoes and lobster jus or pan-seared mahi mahi crusted with garlic and sesame seeds. | 740 Sutter St. | 415/474–6478 | Wed.–Fri. 5:30–10, weekends 5:30–10:30, closed Mon.–Tues. | $18–$30 | AE, D, DC, MC, V.

Nob Hill. Contermporary. You can eat in a romantic garden atrium under a domed ceiling in the elegant Mark Hopkins Inter-Continental Hotel at the top of Nob Hill. The menu has Pan-Asian–influenced fare such as grilled hake with mushroom polenta, lamb tenderloins, or grilled sea scallops with papaya and avocado. A pianist plays nightly. | 1 Nob Hill | 415/392–3434 | Daily, 11:30–11 | $18–$21 | AE, D, DC, MC, V.

North Beach. Italian. The restaurant describes itself as "Old Word service with New World cooking." It lives up to the billing with Florentine tiles, skylights, an inlaid wood bar, potted palms, and consistently excellent meals. You can choose specialties like home-cured proscuitto, cannelloni antipasto, and veal scaloppine. *Wine Spectator* magazine put North Beach's wine list in America's top 100. | 1512 Stockton St. | 415/392–1700 | Daily, 11:30AM–1AM | $15–$23 | AE, D, DC, MC, V.

North India. Indian. Ignore the bland, '80s-style interior and focus on the men behind the glass-walled kitchen. The tandoori oven back there is capable of producing some intense flavors and is mainly responsible for its reputation as one of San Francisco's best. Try the tandoori murgh, roasted chicken marinated in yogurt with Indian spices, or any of the chicken, seafood, or meat curries. Kids' menu. | 3131 Webster St. | 415/931–1556 | 11:30–2:30, 5–10:30, Sat.–Sun. 5–10 | $18–$24 | AE, D, DC, MC, V.

Oritalia. Contemporary. With an open kitchen, velvet curtains, moody lighting, and modern art on the walls, it seems like a scene from out of the late '80s. Indeed, back then, it was one of the first restaurants to kick off the fusion craze. While the hype seems to have died down a bit, they're still making some of the most successful East meets West creations. You can sample grilled flatiron steak with shiitake mashed potatoes or shallot-crusted ahi tuna. | 1915 Filmore | 415/782–8122 | Sun.–Thurs. 5–10, Fri.–Sat. 5–11 | $18–$27 | AE, DC, MC, V.

Park Grill. Contemporary. This restaurant in the Park Hyatt hotel is known for business breakfasts and weekend brunches. It has a central dais with a raised flower display and a large visible wine cellar. It has beautiful lace, wood-trim, and Italian granite floors. Though it has the starched feel of a hotel restaurant, the grilled fare can be quite good, particularly the wild Pacific salmon with wilted spinach, cucumbers, and tomatoes, and the thyme-and-peppered beef tenderloin with fava bean and sweet corn succotash. | 333 Battery St. | 415/296–2933 | 6:30–9:30, Saturday and Sunday brunch 10–2:30 | $16–$21 | AE, D, DC, MC, V.

PJ's Oyster Bed. Cajun. This is a piece of Louisiana territory in the city, complete with thumping zydeco music and orders of spicy prawns or crawfish piled onto your newspaper-covered table, still steaming. The Mardi Gras atmosphere extends from the clamorous oyster bar to the cooks firing the grill. You can try oysters Rockefeller, gumbo, and a special Cajun-Creole menu Tues., Wed., Fri. | 737 Irving St. | 415/566–7775 | Reservations essential evenings | Daily, 11:30–10 | $18–$30 | AE, MC, V.

Postrio. Contemporary. Celebrity chef Wolfgang Puck's San Francisco outpost is a refined tri-level dining room with gallery quality art and ceramics, hand-crafted wall sconces, and hanging luminescent orbs. The diverse Asian, Californian, and Mediterranean menu lives up to the hype behind the name. Puck's specialties include crab-stuffed artichoke, lemon-glazed quail wrapped in bacon, Chinese-style duck, and chocolate soufflé cake. | 415/776–7825 | Reservations essential | Mon–Fri. 7–10, 11:30–2, 5:30–10; Sat.–Sun. 5:30–10, Sunday brunch 9–2 | $18–$32 | AE, DC, MC, V.

Red Herring. Seafood. In the Hotel Griffon, the restaurant's airy dining room resembles a film noir setting with dark-red booths and natural brick and saffron walls. The witty menu, "full of lures and bait," has lobster cone, a semolina cone filled with lobster, mango, and caviar, or, more traditionally, crisp whole snapper with shiitake mushrooms. | 155 Stewart St. | 415/495–6500 | $17–$30 | AE, D, DC, MC, V.

Scoma's. Seafood. Dark woods, simple iron chandeliers and a series of small dining rooms look the same as they have for 30 years. While the crowds are mostly tourists and the dishes rather standard, the portions are huge, the fish is straight off the boat, and the panoramic views are amazing. You can try lunch or dinner specialties like cioppino and seafood salad or the raw bar specials of the day. | Pier 47 | 415/771–4383 | www.scomas.com | No reservations | Sun.–Thurs. 11:30AM–10:30, Fri.–Sat. 11:30–11 | $15–$25 | AE, D, DC, MC, V.

Swiss Louis. Italian. At this Fisherman's Wharf institution, you can get decent versions of San Francisco and Italian classics. With its Italian murals and spectacular views, it's a popular tourist attraction but perhaps a bit too pricey. | Pier 39 | 415/421–2913 | Daily, 11:30–10, Saturday and Sunday brunch 10:30–4 | $18–$25 | AE, D, DC, MC, V.

Yabbies. Seafood. This neighborhood favorite, nestled on a mostly residential street, has a modern dining room with white-washed brick, vibrant murals, and a textured-glass oyster and wine bar specializing in such items as crispy seared snapper and ahi tuna with soba noodles. The owners manage the place in a way that makes customers feel at home. | 2237 Polk St. | 415/474–4088 | Sun.–Thurs. 6–10, Fri.–Sat. to 10:30 | $18–$20 | MC, V.

Yoshida-Ya. Japanese. In a casual downstairs dining room you can choose from dozens of items at the long sushi bar. Upstairs, you'll find private, floor-level tatami tables with thatched ceilings. Combination dinners include skewers, sashimi, dumplings, and shabu shabu, a beef and vegetable soup. | 2909 Webster St. | 415/346–3431 | Sun.–Thurs. 11:30–2, 5–10:30; Fri.–Sat. 5–11 | $16–$25 | AE, D, DC, MC, V.

Zax. Mediterranean. This upscale urban bistro has high ceilings, recessed lighting, cityscape photographs, and a stylish, boisterous clientele. You can try the goat cheese soufflé atop an apple fennel salad, peppered filet, or grilled local salmon with a sweet corn and pea sauté. | 2330 Taylor St. | 415/563–6266 | Tues.–Sat. 5:30–10, closed Sun.–Mon. | $17–$22 | MC, V.

Zingari Ristorante. Italian. This romantic, cozy restaurant in the Theater District has three-course signature dinners that emphasize fresh seafood and vegetables. The candlelit interior is full of Venetian marble and Florentine murals. It's a refined setting for Tuscan specialties like veal loin stuffed with truffles and fontina, marinated lamb chop, and grilled eggplant and baby squash. There's live gypsy and jazz music on Wed. and Sat. | 501 Post St. | 415/885–8850 | Reservations essential | Sun.–Thurs. 6:30–10:30, 5:30–10:30; Fri.–Sat. 5:30–11 | $15–$24 | AE, D, DC, MC, V.

★ **Zuni Cafe.** Italian. After two decades in business, it's become the standard by which other restaurants are measured. In an airy dining room with towering cacti, you can choose from daily specials inspired by northern Italian and Provençal cuisine. The simple, perfectly composed favorites include braised oxtails, salt cod, lobster ravioli, and some of the city's best homemade desserts. Also, at lunch and after 10PM, it serves one of the city's most acclaimed burgers. The place's patio dining on the busy street outside and the handsome copper bar inside feel very Continental. | 1658 Market St. | 415/552–2522 | Tues.–Sat. 11:30–midnight, Sun. 11:30–11, Sunday brunch 11–3, closed Mon. | $15–$24 | AE, MC, V.

VERY EXPENSIVE

A. Sabella's. Italian. The Sabella family hail from one of the original families to serve fresh seafood at Fisherman's Wharf. A 1,000-gallon tank holds crab, abalone, and lobster for your meal. You can overlook the wharf and Golden Gate Bridge through the floor-to-ceiling arched bay windows in the third-story, peach and aquamarine dining room. Besides the incredible views, there's also live piano music weeknights and dinner theater Fri.–Sat. evenings. The house specialties include bouillabaisse, mesquite-grilled sea bass, and petrale sole with bay shrimp in a brown butter and toasted capers sauce. | 2766 Taylor St. | 415/771–6775 | Reservations essential on weekends | 11–10:30, Sat. 11–11 | $25–$54 | www.asabella.com | AE, D, DC, MC, V.

★ **Aqua.** Seafood. Soothing earthtones, extravagant flower displays, and seasonal slip covers set the stage for some of the best, most innovative seafood preparations in town. Standout appetizers are the artfully presented caviar parfait and the ahi tuna tartar, while entrées include the miso-marinated sea bass or the decadent 1½-pound steamed Maine lobster pot pie. If you're having trouble deciding, you can try the five-course tasting menu. Although expensive, the food, romantic atmosphere, and service might make it worth the splurge. | 252 California St. | 415/956–9662 | Reservations essential | Mon.–Fri. 11:30–2:15, 5:30–10:30, Sat. 5:30–10:30, closed Sun. | $28–$42 | AE, DC, MC, V.

Big 4. Contemporary. Named after the big four San Francisco railroad tycoons of the 19th century and designed after a turn-of-the-century men's club, with rich cherry-wood paneling, beveled glass, and forest green banquettes. Future monopolists and tycoons start with the Dungeness crab cakes, a must, and then order the whiskey-marinated buffalo or the slightly lighter pan-seared sole with pine nut and garlic crust. | 415/771–1140 | fax 415/ 474–6227 | www.big4restaurant.com | Mon–Fri. 7–10 AM, 11:30–3, 5:30–10:30; Sat.–Sun. 7– 11 AM, 5:30–10:30 | $25–$35 | AE, D, DC, MC, V.

Bix. American. In an alley north of the Trans-American pyramid, this bi-level Art Deco sup-per club feels like a 1930s cabaret. It has an elaborate gold and green mural behind the bar and great views from the mezzanine tables. An upscale, young clientele packs the place for the nightly jazz shows. You can eat the yellowfin tuna carpaccio appetizer or, for an entrée, the grilled rib-eye steak with sautéed spinach, bone-marrow custard, and pommes frites, or the classic grilled filet mignon with béarnaise sauce. | 56 Gold St. | 415/433–6300 | www.bixrestaurant.com | Reservations essential | Mon.–Fri. 11:30–11, Fri. 11:30 AM–midnight, Sat. 5:30–midnight; Sun. 6–10 | $22–$32 | AE, D, DC, MC, V.

Boulevard. Contemporary. Chef Nancy Oakey, a local legend, resides over the kitchen of this top-rated restaurant. The dining room is inspired by contemporary art. It has mosaic tiles, a domed brick ceiling, and bay views. The food is astoundingly inventive, made with fresh seasonal ingredients. Past highlights have been the corn-fed filet mignon and the roasted scallops served on a warm salad of haricots verts, corn, and yellow tomato with pumpkin vinaigrette. | 1 Mission St. | 415/543–6084 | Reservations essential | Sun.–Wed. 11:30–2:15, 5:30–10; Thurs.–Sat. 11:30–2:15, 5:30–10:30 | $25–$32 | AE, D, DC, MC, V.

Campton Place. Continental. In the past 20 years, many of San Francisco's finest chefs got their start in this four-star dining destination. Subtle country French dishes with Basque influences are served in a formal dining room, done in baby blues and yellows with a cen-tral, crystal chandelier. Rarefied and romantic, it draws an older, wealthy crowd who come for dishes like the poached chicken stuffed with foie gras and the whole, roasted sweet-breads with a Napa Valley reduction. For true gastronomes, there's a six-course tasting menu and a wine list with more than 1,000 selections. Come on Sunday for brunch or, dur-ing the week, in the early evening, 6–7:30, for the $35, three-course tasting menu. | 415/ 955–5555 | Mon.–Fri. 8–10 AM, 11:30–2, 6–10; Fri. 8–10 AM, 11:30–2, 6–10:30; Sat. 8–11 AM, noon– 2, 5:30–10:30; Sun. 8–2, 6–9:30 | $29–$36 | AE, DC, MC, V.

Carnelian Room. Contemporary. Located on the top floor of the BankAmerica building, this elegant, corporate-style clubhouse with 10 private dining suites specializes in the newest in California cuisine. Its popularity with the Young Turks means it sometimes vibrates with deal-making. Dining rooms have panoramic views, antiques, heavy fabrics, and generally expensive-looking accoutrements. You can get fresh seafood and great steaks here. There's an impressive Sunday brunch. | 555 California St. | 415/433–7500 | Jacket | Mon.–Sat. 6–10, Sun. 10–2 | $20–$40 | AE, D, DC, MC, V.

Charles Nob Hill. Contemporary. This small, intimate Art Deco restaurant with rare wood panels inset in shining black varnish, silk panels, and dramatic light serves Californian dishes with a strong Gaelic influence, like the exceptional skate wing with caramelized turnips and a chive broth. Other strong dishes include the duck breast au poivre and the jondory (a light, white fish) with sunchoke au gratin. | 1250 Jones St. | 415/771–5400 | Tues.–Thurs. 5:30–10, Fri–Sat. 5:30–10:30, Sun. 5:30–9:30, closed Mon. | $28–$38 | AE, MC, V.

Compass Rose. Seafood. Towering fluted columns, eclectic European and Asian antiques, and a formally dressed clientele contribute to this restaurant's great reputation. It's a good place for dinner before the show or a drink after the show. A $21 afternoon tea, featuring a gorgeous tray of tea sandwiches, scones, berries and cream, and petit fours, is served daily 3–5. There's also an hors d'oeuvres menu with caviar and Dungeness crab cakes. Frozen vodka, champagne, and cocktails are served nightly from 5, accompanied by live jazz music and dancing. | 335 Powell St. | 415/774–0167 | $25–$55 | AE, DC, MC, V.

★ **Dining Room at the Ritz Carlton.** French. Exactly what you'd expect from the Ritz, you can experience this regal setting with its rich brocade, crystal chandeliers, and live harp music while an army of tuxedoed waiters fuss over you. You can start with the crayfish bisque and then try the fillet of roast Maine lobster or risotto with roast squab and butternut squash. An extensive wine list and three- or five-course tasting menus round out this portrait of opulence. A kids' menu is available for the youngsters who haven't yet developed a taste for foie gras. | 600 Stockton St. | 415/733–6198 | Reservations essential | 6–9:30, closed Sun. | $25–$43 | AE, D, DC, MC, V.

★ **Farallon.** Seafood. This dramatic restaurant, named for the islands just offshore, has glass chandeliers in the shape of sea urchins, octopus bar stools, and faux kelp columns; all of which are much more artful and tastefully created than they might sound. Hard to believe, but the menu is just as adventurous as the decor. If you're adventurous, you can get a lobster tart, roast Atlantic monkfish with wild mushroom duxelle, or the striped bass with lobster and oyster mushrooms in a tomato fondue. | 450 Post St. | 415/956–6969 | Reservations essential | Mon.–Sat. 5:30–11, Sun. 5–11 | $24–$34 | AE, MC, V.

★ **Fifth Floor.** Contemporary. San Franciscans began fighting for tables at this topflight hotel dining room within days of its opening in 1999. And chef George Morrone's elegant, sophisticated, visually stunning plates are the reason why. The 75-seat room is done in dark wood and zebra-striped carpeting, and such exquisite dishes as seared tuna with foie gras and medallions of beef and lamb in a pastry crust with a trio of vegetables purees are served. There's even ice cream made to order—yes, the machine churns out a creamy, cool, rich serving for one. | Palomar Hotel, 12 4th St. | 415/348–1555 | Reservations essential | $28–$44 | AE, DC, MC, V | Closed Sun. No lunch.

Fleur de Lys. French. Opened in 1970, this regal dining room has towering floral displays, mirrored walls, and rich red and gold fabric hanging, Bedouin tent–like, from the ceiling. You can expect sterling service and changing selections on the five-course tasting menus. Highlights have included pepper-crusted Hawaiian swordfish loin with truffle mushroom duxelle, or the marinated venison chop with a cabernet and black lentil sauce. | 777 Sutter St. | 415/673–7779 | Reservations essential | Jacket | Mon.–Thurs. 6–10, Fri.–Sat. 5:30–10:30 | $30–$38 | AE, DC, MC, V.

Fournou's Ovens. Mediterranean. Located in Renaissance Stanford Court hotel, it has greenhouse windows, 18th-century French Provincial artwork, a wood-burning oven, and such a profusion of flowers that you almost forget you're in a hotel restaurant. The seasonal menu includes an excellent rack of lamb and rack of veal. The Californian influence can be seen in dishes like citrus-ginger duck with a jicama and pecan salad in a blackberry and port dressing. The varied menu makes it a favorite for formal, family celebrations and holiday dinners. | 415/989–1910 | 905 California St. | Jackets at dinner | Mon.–Thurs. 6:30–2:30, 5:30–10, Fri.–Sat. 6:30–2:30, 5:30–10:30, Sunday brunch 10 AM–2:30 | $24–$32 | AE, D, DC, MC, V.

★ **Gary Danko.** French. In 2000, this place was the new addition to the fine dining scene. It's intimate, and warmly minimalist in the dining room with its exposed brick walls, recessed lighting, extravagant bouquets, and artwork from well-known contemporary artists. A showcase for the eponymous chef, the menu changes nightly, giving the diner the choice only between a three-course and a five-course tasting menu. Recurring highlights are the roast lobster with chanterelle mushrooms, tomato, and tarragon and the Moroccan-spiced squab with orange-cumin carrots. | 804 North Point St. | 415/775–2060 | fax 415/775–1805 | www.garydanko.com | Reservations essential | Tues.–Sun. 5:30–10:30, closed Mon. | $51 or $70 | MC, V.

Harbor Village. Chinese. Located at the Embarcadero Center, this Cantonese favorite with a window-lined atrium overlooking the Justin Herman Plaza packs a capacity crowd into communal banquet tables, a small ivy-enclosed patio, and three private dining rooms. It's known for Hong Kong–style seafood and weekend dim sum "brunches" or you can try minced squab with lettuce cups or shrimp and chive dumplings. There are several prix-fixe menus to choose from; prices start at $40 per person. | 4 Embarcadero Center | 415/781–8833 | Mon.–Fri. 11–2:30, 5:30–9:30 | $40–$80 | AE, D, DC, MC, V.

★ **Harris'.** American. One look at the glass display case, with prime USDA beef hanging like museum artifacts, and you know these people take their meat very seriously. The plush, spacious dining room, with its potted palms, dark-wood paneling, murals of Midwestern marsh land, and deep booths is reminiscent of a Kansas City men's club. Although known for its perfect cuts of thick aged steaks, prime rib, and huge T-bones, you can also get fresh seafood and Maine lobsters. | 2100 Van Ness Ave. | 415/673–1888 | www.harrisrestaurant.com | Sun.–Thurs. 5:30–9:30, Fri.–Sat. 5:30–10 | $20–$35 | AE, D, DC, MC, V.

Julius Castle. Italian. Known as one of the most romantic dining spots in San Francisco, this historical landmark has a breathtaking view of the entire Bay area. The food is pricey but you'll see plenty of locals celebrating anniversaries and birthdays. Try the standout ahi tuna carpaccio and the muscovy duck. | 1541 Montgomery St. | 415/362–3042 | 5–10 | $24–$34 | AE, D, DC, MC, V.

★ **La Folie.** French. An intimate, whimsical dining room with subtle clouds painted onto the sky-blue walls. A favorite of San Francisco's most critical diners, the artfully presented Cal-French food uses seasonal, mostly local ingredients, matched with an expertly compiled wine list. The menu changes seasonally, with past highlights including slow roasted Atlantic salmon. | 2316 Polk St. | 415/776–5577 | Reservations essential | Jacket required | Mon.–Sat. 6–11 | $30–$43 | AE, DI, DC, MC, V.

Masa's. French. One of the city's most exclusive restaurants, it has red Italian silk walls, modern art, and romantic lighting. It has two prix-fixe menus, a five-course tasting menu and the menu du jour, giving you the ability to choose between two or three dishes for each of the four courses. You can expect artistically prepared foie gras, truffles, and the fine-quality poultry, fish, and meats. It's closed two weeks in January and one in July. | 648 Bush St. | 415/989–7154 | Reservations essential | Jackets required | Tues.–Sat. 6–9:30, closed Sun.–Mon. | $75 or $80 | AE, D, DC, MC, V.

Pacific. Contemporary. On the third floor of the Pan-Pacific Hotel, past a densely landscaped atrium bar, it's one of San Francisco's best-kept secrets. The romantic dining room has brass, marble, and richly colored upholstery. The menu shines with ambitious seafood entrées like crudité of scallops, ahi tuna, kampachi, crawfish gnocchi, and roast lobster on sweet corn risotto. | 500 Post St. | 415/929–2087 | Sun.–Thurs. 5:30–9:30, weekends 5:30–10 | $22–$36 | AE, D, DC, MC, V.

Rubicon. Contemporary. The West Coast flagship of restaurateur Drew Nieporent is a large loft-like space with dark woods and oversized windows. The restaurant emphasizes California winemaking and fresh local ingredients prepared with French influences. You can try muscovy duck breast with baby turnips, seared red snapper with beurre blanc sauce, or the ever-changing pan-roasted chicken. | 558 Sacramento St. | 415/434–4100 | Mon.–Sat. 11:30–2, 5–10:30, closed Sun. | $25–$35 | AE, MC, V.

Ruth's Chris Steak House. American. This small, upscale chain eatery has thick, aged prime beef with all the trimmings, served in a traditional club room. The place is warm and cozy with lots of wood and brass and comfy booths. In addition to steak, try Maine lobster, fresh vegetable dishes, and homemade desserts. | 1601 Van Ness Ave. | 415/673–0557 | Mon.–Sat. 5–10:30, Sun. 4:30–9:30 | $25–$50 | AE, D, MC, V.

Silks. Contemporary. Located in the Mandarin Oriental Hotel, this formal dining room has vaulted ceilings, Japanese screens, exotic flower arrangements, and light-wood paneling. The intricate dishes, artfully presented on delicate china, include a lobster apple Napoleon, poached salmon with shiitake and fig, and beef tenderloin with foie gras. The desserts are uniformly excellent and there's an extensive, if extremely expensive, wine list. | 222 Sansome St. | 415/986–2020 | Daily 6:30–10, 11:30–2, 6–10 | $22–$33 | AE, D, DC, MC, V.

Tommy Toy's. Chinese. Exceptional French-influenced Chinese dishes are served in a room filled with Asian furnishings and orchids. Often, what passes for fusion amounts to Western chefs spicing up their standards with Eastern touches. Here, the tables are turned. You can get veal charred in a wok with Szechuan sauce, vanilla prawns with fresh melon, or a seafood bisque served in a coconut shell. | 655 Montgomery St. | 415/397–4888 | www.tom-mytoys.com | Reservations essential | Jacket | Mon.–Fri. 11:30–3, 6–10; Sat.–Sun. 6–10 | $20–$28; $49 tasting menu | AE, D, DC, MC, V.

Lodging

INEXPENSIVE

Adelaide Inn. The bedspreads at this quiet retreat may not match the drapes or carpets and the floors may creak, but the rooms are sunny, clean, and cheap. Tucked away in an alley, the funky European-style pension hosts many guests from Germany, France, and Italy, making it fun to chat over complimentary coffee and rolls downstairs in the mornings. Baths are shared. Complimentary breakfast. Some refrigerators. | 5 Isadora Duncan Ct. | 415/441–2474 | 18 rooms | $58 | AE, MC, V.

Andrews Hotel. Two blocks from Union Square, this small, homey inn has rooms with lace curtains and bouquets of fresh flowers. Restaurant, complimentary Continental breakfast. No air conditioning, in-room data ports, cable TV. Business services, parking (fee). | 624 Post St. | 415/563–6877 or 800 800/926–3739 | fax 415/928–6919 | www.andrewshotel.com | 42 rooms, 6 suites | $92 rooms, $142–$162 suites | AE, DC, MC, V.

Atherton. This six-floor townhouse was built in 1927 and retains its old San Francisco charm with an Italian marble lobby with vaulted ceilings and etched glass. Rooms are small, but share the same attention to period detail with crown moldings and antique furniture. It's less than a mile from the Opera House, Union Square, and two blocks from a cable car stop. Restaurant, bar, complimentary breakfast, room service. No air conditioning, in-room data ports, in-room safes, cable TV. Laundry service. Business services, airport shuttle, parking (fee). | 685 Ellis St. | 415/474–5720; 800/474–5720 | fax 415/474–8256 | www.hotelatherton.com | 75 rooms | $109–$129 | AE, D, DC, MC, V.

Bayside Thriftlodge. This rustic two-story, California-style motel with white and blue trim, Spanish tile roof, and flower accent beds is low-cost but clean. It's a 2-minute drive to Cow Palace and Candlestick Park. The deluxe rooms have a fold-up bed that allows the room to accommodate five, as well as patio or balcony views of the San Francisco Bay. Other rooms overlook a central pool courtyard. Restaurant. No air conditioning, cable TV. Indoor-outdoor pool. Sauna. Laundry service. Business services, free parking. | 2011 Bayshore Blvd. | 415/467–8811 or 800/525–9055 (exc. California), 800/468–1021 (California) | fax 415/468–3097 | www.travellodge.com | 103 rooms, 27 with shower only | $70–$93 | AE, DC, MC, V.

Bel-Aire TraveLodge. A block away from Lombard Street, this white and blue L-shaped motel has rooms with blond-wood furniture, beige walls, blue carpeting, and pastel leaf-pattern bedspreads. Bathrooms have showers only and there is a mirrored vanity table in each room. Rooms have coffeemakers. Local calls are free. Cable TV. | 3201 Steiner St. | 415/921–5162 | $100 | AE, D, DC, MC, V.

Best Western Civic Center. Built in the '50s, this small, no-frills, bi-level motel is five blocks from Civic Center and downtown. Deluxe rooms have foldout couches. There's a coffee shop. No air conditioning, in-room data ports, refrigerators, cable TV. Pool. Laundry service. Business services, free parking. | 364 9th St. | 415/621–2826 | www.bestwestern.com | fax 415/621–0833 | 57 rooms | $100–$115 | AE, D, DC, MC, V.

Best Western Miyako Inn. Located in the heart of Japantown, this seven-story, contemporary hotel is within ½ mi of Chinatown and Fisherman's Wharf. About half the rooms have steam baths, and most have patios and balconies. Restaurant, bar, room service. In-room data ports, cable TV. Beauty shop, saunas. Laundry service. Business services, parking (fee). | 1800 Sutter St. | 415/921–4000 | fax 415/923–1064 | www.bestwestern.com | miyakoin@ix.net-com.com | 123 rooms; 2 suites | $99–$129 rooms, $199 suites | AE, D, DC, MC, V.

Buena Vista Motor Inn. This modest, three-story, pink hotel in the Marina District is ½ mi walk to Fisherman's Wharf, public transportation, and Golden Gate Park. In-room data ports, cable TV. Free parking. | 1599 Lombard St. | 415/923–9600 or 800/835–4980 | www.buenavistamotorinn.com | fax 415/441–4775 | 49 rooms; 1 suite | $119–$129 rooms, $139 suite | AE, D, DC, MC, V.

Chelsea Motor Inn. Built in the '80s, this four-story, Victorian-style motor inn in the Marina District close to Fisherman's Wharf and Chinatown has light and airy rooms with bay windows, marble bathrooms, and a surprising amount of space. In-room data ports, cable TV. Free parking. | 2095 Lombard St. | 415/563–5600 | fax 415/567–6475 | 60 rooms | $98–$106 | AE, DC, MC, V.

Columbus Motor Inn. This squat, three-story brick building is clean and near shops, North Beach restaurants, and Fisherman's Wharf. Cable TV. Business services, free parking. | 1075 Columbus Ave. | 415/885–1492 | fax 415/928–2174 | 39 rooms; 6 suites | $114 rooms, $124–$259 suites | AE, DC, MC, V.

Coventry Motor Inn. A four-story Victorian, built in 1986, with red-trimmed bay windows and floral wallpaper. In the Marina District, it's 11 blocks to Fisherman's Wharf and about seven blocks to Golden Gate Park. Cable TV. Free parking. | 1901 Lombard St. | 415/567–1200 | fax 415/921–8745 | 69 rooms | $98–$106 | AE, DC, MC, V.

Cow Hollow Motor Inn. A three-story, brown-brick hotel built in 1985 in the Marina district, it's six blocks from the Golden Gate Bridge. Rooms have bay windows, antique replica furniture, and floral prints. Suites have fireplaces, some kitchenettes, and are spacious enough for a family. Restaurant. In-room data ports, cable TV. Free parking. | 2190 Lombard St. | 415/921–5800 | fax 415/922–8515 | 117 rooms, 12 suites | $108 rooms, $195–$245 suites | AE, DC, MC, V.

Essex. You'll find this reasonably priced hotel that openly caters to a gay clientele in a rougher but not scary stretch of Ellis Street close to downtown, the Civic Center, and Union Square. The slightly worn lobby is cozy, with marble floors, fresh-cut flowers, ornate molding, and antique furniture and rugs. Rooms are small, with the same quaint details and some shared baths. No air conditioning, cable TV. No parking. | 684 Ellis St. | 415/474–4664 or 800/453–7739 or 800/443–7739 (California) | fax 415/441–1800 | 100 rooms, 6 suites | $79–$99 rooms, $119 suites | AE, MC, V.

★ **Grant Plaza.** Its convenient, Chinatown location, clean no-frills rooms, and low rates make this a popular choice for travelers. It's within walking distance of Union Square, North Beach, and cable car transportation, and surrounded by dozens of good, affordable restaurants. In-room data ports, cable TV. Parking (fee). | 465 Grant St. | 415/434–3883 or 800/472–6899 | fax 415/434–3886 | grantplaza@worldnet.att.net | www.grantplaza.com | 72 rooms | $79–$109 | AE, DC, MC, V.

★ **Hotel Del Sol.** You can feel like you're in a beach house in this funky hotel with plantation shutters, tropical-stripe bedspreads, and rattan chairs. Windows face boldly striped patios, citrus trees, a heated swimming pool, and a hammock under towering palm trees. A room called "The Sandbox" features bunk beds, child-friendly furnishings, toys, and games. There are even free kites for kids. In-room data ports. Pool. Sauna. Laundry service. Free parking. | 3100 Webster St. | 415/921–5520 | 57 rooms | $120 | AE, D, DC, MC, V.

Howard Johnson. Two blocks from the wharf and adjacent to the Anchorage Shopping Center, this four-story structure has bay windows and an alternating color scheme that blends in with the surrounding rows of houses. In-room data ports, cable TV, laundry service. Business services, parking (fee). | 580 Beach St. | 415/775–3800 | fax 415/441–7307 | www.hojo.com | 122 rooms; 6 suites | $109–$159 | AE, D, DC, MC, V.

Lombard Motor Inn. This '70s-style, four-story concrete hotel within 10 blocks of Fisherman's Wharf and Union Square has clean, no-frills rooms in a safe neighborhood at a budget price. Rooms on the street side can be noisy, but some have partial bay views. Cable TV.

Free parking. | 1475 Lombard St. | 415/441–6000 or 800/835–3639 | fax 415/441–4291 | 48 rooms | $92–$116 | AE, DC, MC, V.

Marina Inn. This restored 1928 San Francisco Victorian "painted lady" near Union Square, the Wharf, and the financial district is a nice respite from the crowds of tourists. Rooms are country-style with four-poster beds and chocolates on the pillows. Restaurant, complimentary Continental breakfast. Refrigerators in some rooms, cable TV. Beauty salon. Business services, parking(fee). | 3110 Octavia St. | 415/928–1000 or 800/274–1420 | fax 415/928–5909 | www.marinainn.com | 40 rooms | $80–$125 | AE, MC, V.

Monarch Hotel. This six-story brick building has a marble lobby with wooden accents. Rooms are simple with white walls, blue curtains, and bright, patterned bedspreads. In San Francisco's performing arts district, two blocks from the cable car, Union Square, and Fisherman's Wharf, this hotel is budget-priced but has valet service. Restaurant. No air conditioning, in-room data ports, in-room safes, refrigerators, cable TV. Video games. Laundry service. Business services, parking (fee). | 1015 Geary St. | 415/673–5232 or 800/777–3210 | fax 415/885–2802 | www.themonarchhotel.com | 101 rooms | $74–$139 | AE, D, DC, MC, V.

Royal Pacific. A top-rated AAA Motor Inn, this five-story, '60s-style motel with white and blue trim may look a little dated, but the rooms, in pastel blues and greens, are bright and airy. The location is central, within three blocks of Chinatown and Washington Square Park. Some microwaves, some refrigerators, Cable TV. Sauna. Laundry service. Free parking. | 661 Broadway | 415/781–6661 or 800/545–5574 | fax 415/781–6688 | www.citysearch.com/sfo/royalpacific | 70 rooms; 4 suites | $89 rooms, $115–$125 suites | AE, DC, MC, V.

★ **San Remo.** Originally built to house maritime workers after the 1906 earthquake, this Victorian hotel in a quiet part of North Beach has budget accommodations with shared baths. The place is chock-full of period artifacts from brass beds to pedestal sinks and pull-chain toilets. The hotel has a rooftop penthouse with its own private bath and garden. The penthouse is quite popular; reservations are often needed months in advance. The hotel is just five blocks from Fisherman's Wharf. Bar. No room phones. Laundry service. Parking (fee). | 2237 Mason St. | 415/776–8688 or 800/352–7366 | fax 415/776–2811 | www.sanremo-hotel.com | 62 rooms, all with shared baths, 1 penthouse | $60–$85 rooms, $150 penthouse | AE, DC, MC, V.

Shannon Court. The elaborate wrought-iron and glass entrance into the marble-tiled lobby of the Shannon Court evokes the old world charm of turn-of-the-century San Francisco. Two of the luxury suites on the 16th floor have rooftop terraces with city views. Complimentary morning coffee and afternoon tea and cookies are served in the lobby area. Restaurant, bar. Refrigerators. Laundry service. | 550 Geary St. | 415/775–5000 | 172 rooms | $130 | AE, D, DC, MC, V.

MODERATE

Abigail. Although the neighborhood is a little rough, the nearby Main Library, Civic Center, and in-house vegetarian restaurant called Millennium make this a unique lodging choice. Steam radiators, twig wreaths, down comforters, and antiques gives this former B&B a distinctive atmosphere, drawing a mix of younger couples and European tourists. Restaurant, complimentary Continental breakfast. Some refrigerators, some microwaves, cable TV. Laundry service. Business services, parking (fee). | 246 Ellis St. | 415/861–9728 | fax 415/861–5848 | abigailhotel@worldnet.att.net | www.sftrips.com | 60 rooms, 6 with shower only; 1 suite | $139 rooms, $300 suite | AE, D, DC, MC, V.

Alamo Square Inn. Located on a hilltop park, this Victorian "painted lady" B&B has spectacular views of the city. It is actually two separate town houses, both with oak floors and paneling, and a charming lobby with a fireplace and skylight. Some rooms have fireplaces; all have vases filled with fresh-cut flowers and antique furnishings. Complimentary breakfast and afternoon wine, picnic area. No air conditioning, in-room data ports, some TVs. Laundry service. No smoking. | 719 Scott St. | 415/922–2055 or 800/345–9888 | fax 415/931–1304 | wcorn@alamoinn.com | www.alamoinn.com | 14 rooms | $85–$295 | AE, MC, V.

Albion House. The living room of this charming B&B in a 1907 Edwardian building has red-painted wood floors and paneling, a marble fireplace, and a grand piano. Meals are served in a dining hall with 20-ft vaulted ceilings. Rooms have armoires, tapestries, stained-glass lamps, and local modern art. It's near Market Street, City Hall, and the Hayes Valley shopping area. Complimentary breakfast and afternoon snacks. In-room data ports, cable TV. | 135 Gough St. | 415/621–0896 | www.subtleties.com | 9 rooms | $145–$185 | AE, D, DC, MC, V.

Amsterdam. When the fog rolls away, you can enjoy breakfast on the sunny garden patio of this inn just two blocks from Nob Hill. Built in 1906, it lives up to its claim of simple European charm. It has Louis XVI chairs and an antique radio in the lobby, hand-crafted furniture, and marble-topped dressers in the rooms. Complimentary Continental breakfast. In-room data ports, cable TV. Parking (fee). | 749 Taylor St. | 415/673–3277 or 800/637–3444 | fax 415/673–0453 | www.amsterdamhotel.com | 34 rooms | $109–$119 | AE, MC, V.

Bed and Breakfast Inn. Hidden in an alleyway, this ivy-covered Victorian has English country-style rooms full of antiques, plants, and floral paintings. The Mayfair, a suite above the main house, comes complete with a living room, kitchenette, and spiral staircase leading to a sleeping loft. The Garden Suite has a country kitchen, whirlpool bath, and room for four guests. Complimentary Continental breakfast. Some kitchenettes. Some in-room hot tubs. | 4 Charlton Ct. | 415/921–9784 | 10 rooms (5 with private bath), 2 suites | $90–$175 rooms, $280–$380 suites | No credit cards.

Best Western Americania. This three-story, attractive Mediterranean-style hotel surrounds a nicely landscaped, red-tiled courtyard and pool. Muted contemporary colors, modern furniture, and flower arrangements highlight the ample-size rooms. Restaurant, bar, room service. No air conditioning. In-room data ports, refrigerators, cable TV. Outdoor pool. Exercise equipment. Laundry service. | 121 Seventh St. | 415/626–0200 | fax 415/626–3974 | www.bestwestern.com | 143 rooms, 24 suites | $99–$159 rooms, $179–$265 suites | AE, D, DC, MC, V.

Bijou. This reasonably priced boutique hotel two blocks from Union Square is a must for cinephiles. In the updated, Deco-Noir lobby there's a mini-theater that screens films shot in San Francisco. Each of the small rooms is named and decorated after one of these films, with framed black-and-white still shots. The "Vertigo" room is almost always booked. Complimentary Continental breakfast. Cable TV. Laundry service. Parking (fee). | 111 Mason St. | 415/771–1200 or 800/771–1022 | fax 415/346–3196 | www.sftrips/hotels/bijou.html | 65 rooms | $159–$169 | AE, D, DC, MC, V.

Britton. Built in 1918, this five-story, budget-priced, boutique hotel within walking distance of Union Square, the Mosconi Convention Center, and cable car stops is a San Francisco historical landmark. Cozy rooms have floral wallpaper, plantation shutters, and cast-iron beds. There's a wine reception in the Colonial lobby every evening. Restaurant. In-room data ports, cable TV. Laundry service. | 112 7th St. | 415/621–7001 or 800/444–5819 | fax 415/626–3974 | www.renesonhotels.com | 74 rooms; 5 suites | $120–$169 rooms, $209 suites | AE, D, DC, MC, V.

Carlton. Built in 1928, this hotel gets high marks from loyal, repeat customers for its personalized service and attention. In the afternoon, you can relax with other guests at the fireside tea and wine social. Rooms are bright, with large windows, flowers, subtle contemporary colors, and photos of San Francisco. You can walk to Union Square or grab the free shuttle that goes to the Financial District. Restaurant, complimentary Continental breakfast. No air conditioning, refrigerators, in-room data ports, in-room safes, cable TV. Airport shuttle. | 1075 Sutter St. | 415/673–0242 or 800/227–4496 | fax 415/673–4904 | carlton@carltonhotel.com | www.carltonhotel.com | 165 rooms; 1 suite | $165–$180 rooms, $250 suite | AE, D, DC, MC, V.

Chancellor Hotel. Built for the 1915 Panama Pacific International Exposition, it was the tallest building in San Francisco when it opened. Floor-to-ceiling windows in the lobby overlook cable cars on Powell Street en route to nearby Union Square or Fisherman's Wharf. The

Edwardian-style rooms have high ceilings and peach and green color schemes. Restaurant, bar, room service. Laundry service. | 433 Powell St. | 415/362–2004 | 135 rooms | $145 | AE, D, DC, MC, V.

Clarion Bedford Hotel. Art Nouveau arches flank the bright yellow lobby of this handsome 1929 building. Avant-garde film posters from Russia in the 1920s adorn the walls. The light and airy rooms are decorated in yellow and peach with white furniture, canopied beds, and vibrant floral bedspreads. There is an evening wine reception in the lobby. Restaurant, bar, room service. In-room data ports, Laundry service. | 761 Post St. | 415/673–6040 | www.hotelbedford.com | 137 rooms, 7 suites | $130–$179 rooms, $179–$199 suites | AE, D, DC, MC, V.

Comfort Inn–By The Bay. This 11-story hotel, built in the '70s, features simple, no-frills rooms, some of which have excellent bay views. It's a six-block walk to Fisherman's Wharf. A cable car stop is two blocks away. Complimentary Continental breakfast. In-room data ports, cable TV. Laundry service. Business services, parking (fee). | 2775 Van Ness Ave. | 415/928–5000 or 800/228–5150 | fax 415/441–3990 | www.hotelchoice.com | 136 rooms, 2 suites | $125–$170 rooms, $239 suites | AE, D, DC, MC, V.

Commodore International. Popular with artists, filmmakers, and other trendsetters for its innovative decor, the hotel has a lobby that's reminiscent of an ocean liner. Next to the lobby, the Titanic Cafe has goldfish bowls and bathysphere-inspired lights. The Art Deco diner serves California cuisine alongside truck stop food. You can also relax and listen to jazz in Commodore's Red Room with its red velvet cushions and red Venetian tile. Rooms are exceptionally spacious, with modern, stylish furniture. The helpful concierge can arrange a tour or direct you to Union Square, Chinatown, and the Theater District, all within walking distance. Restaurant, bar (entertainment). In-room data ports, some refrigerators, cable TV. Laundry service. Business services, parking (fee). | 825 Sutter St. | 415/923–6800 or 800/338–6848 | commodorehotel@worldnet.att.net | www.sftrips.com/hotels/commodore.html | 113 rooms, 1 suite | $149–$169 rooms, $199 suite | AE, D, DC, MC, V.

Days Inn. Built in the late '80s, this simple, two-story, Ocean Beach motel is in a good neighborhood within walking distance of the beach and 4 mi from downtown. Rooms are average size, clean with Californian color schemes. Complimentary Continental breakfast. In-room data ports, some refrigerators, some microwaves, cable TV. Free parking. | 2600 Sloat Blvd. | 415/665–9000 | fax 415/665–5440 | daysinnsf@aol.com | www.daysinn.com | 30 rooms; 3 suites | $110–$140 rooms, $160 suites | AE, D, DC, MC, V.

Francisco Bay. You can almost feel like you're staying in an English country inn in this three-story motel separated from the street traffic by a flower garden. Rooms have flower boxes and bright cheery furnishings. In the Marina District, it's a quick seven-block walk south to Fisherman's Wharf. Complimentary Continental breakfast. In-room data ports, some microwaves, some refrigerators, cable TV. Free parking. | 1501 Lombard St. | 415/474–3030 or 800/410–7007 | fax 415/567–7082 | www.citysearch.com/sfo/franciscobay | 39 rooms | $125–$165 | AE, D, DC, MC, V.

Hotel Beresford. In the heart of San Francisco, this seven-story hotel, built in 1913, has Victorian furniture and an authentic English tavern off the lobby. Each floor is unique, with different floral wallpapers, crown moldings and faux antiques. It's a short walk to shops, theaters, Chinatown, and the Financial District, two blocks to Union Square and cable cars to Telegraph Hill, Fisherman's Wharf, and Pier 39. Restaurant, bar, complimentary Continental breakfast. No air conditioning, in-room data ports, refrigerators, cable TV. Business services, parking (fee). Some pets allowed. | 635 Sutter St. | 415/673–9900 or 800/533–6533 | fax 415/474–0449 | beresfordsfo@delphi.com | www.beresford.com | 114 rooms | $135 | AE, D, DC, MC, V.

Hotel Beresford Arms. Near its sister hotel, the Beresford Hotel, this place has kitchens and large rooms. The lobby has a worn, regal atmosphere with columns, crown moldings, lush red carpeting, and crystal chandeliers. It's three blocks from Union Square and the cable cars. Complimentary Continental breakfast. No air conditioning, in-room data ports, refrigerators, cable TV, in-room VCR (and movies). Some hot tubs. Some pets allowed. | 701 Post St. | 415/673–2600 or 800/533–6533 | fax 415/533–5349 | beresfordsfo@delphi.com | www.beresford.com | 86 rooms, 40 kitchenettes, 13 suites | $139 rooms, $160 kitchenettes, $195 suites | AE, D, DC, MC, V.

Hotel Bohème. In the middle of historic North Beach, this bay-window Victorian is full of nostalgic reminders of the past. Decorations, including lamps made from sheet music and black-and-white photos, recall the '50s and '60s and the colorful past of the Beat generation. Rooms have iron beds, armoires, bistro tables, and framed cubist prints. You can walk out your door into this popular Italian neighborhood with its vibrant dining and nightlife scene. In-room dataports, cable TV. No smoking. | 444 Columbus Ave. | 415/433–9111 | fax 415/362–6292 | ba@hotelboheme.com | www.hotelboheme.com | 16 rooms | $149–$179 | AE, D, DC, MC, V.

★ **Hotel Del Sol.** Once a typical '50s-style motor court, the Hotel Del Sol has been converted into an anything-but-typical artistic statement playfully celebrating California's vibrant (some might say wacky) culture. The sunny courtyard and yellow-and-blue three-story building are candy for the eyes. Rooms face boldly striped patios, citrus trees, and a hammock and heated swimming pool under towering palm trees. Even the carports have striped dividing drapes. Rooms evoke a beach house feeling with plantation shutters, tropical-stripe bedspreads, and rattan chairs. Some rooms have brick fireplaces, and suites for families with small children are outfitted with bunk beds, child-friendly furnishings, a kitchenette, and games. There are even free kites for kids. In-room data ports, in-room safes, no-smoking rooms, pool, sauna, laundry service, concierge, free parking. | 3100 Webster St., | 415/921–5520 or 877/433–5765 | fax 415/931–4137 | 47 rooms, 10 suites | $135–$410 | AE, D, DC, MC, V.

★ **Inn at the Opera.** Behind the Opera House, the inn has a sumptuous silk and damask lobby with antique chairs, French screens, and oriental rugs. Built in the 30s for visiting opera stars, the rooms have half-canopy beds, changing screens, and antique furnishings good enough for demanding divas. It's across the street from the Museum of Modern Art, and four blocks from Union Square. Restaurant, bar (pianist), complimentary breakfast. No air conditioning, in-room data ports, microwaves, refrigerators, cable TV. Laundry service. Baby-sitting. Business services, parking (fee). | 333 Fulton St. | 415/863–8400 or 800/325–2708 (exc. California) or 800/423–9610 (California) | fax 415/861–0821 | 30 rooms, 18 suites | $155–$185 rooms, $225–$255 suites | AE, D, DC, MC, V.

Inn San Francisco. You can take in the panoramic view of the city or relax in the library or an English garden at this 1872 Victorian mansion in the Mission District. Rooms have Victorian antiques and feather beds; some have private hot tubs and fireplaces. Public transportation is a few blocks away. Complimentary breakfast. No air conditioning, in-room data ports, refrigerators, cable TV. Hot tub. Laundry service. Parking (fee). Pets allowed (fee). | 943 S. Van Ness Ave. | 415/641–0188 or 800/359–0913 | fax 415/641–1701 | www.innsf.com | 21 rooms, 2 with shared bath | $85–$235 | AE, D, DC, MC, V.

Jackson Court. Built in 1900, this three-story brownstone mansion in Pacific Heights has comfortable, luxurious rooms. The clientele would just as soon keep the bed and breakfast a well-kept secret but it's too late for that. Homey rooms have antiques and private baths. The hotel is just two blocks to public transportation. Complimentary breakfast and afternoon tea. No air conditioning, in-room data ports, cable TV. Laundry service. Business services. Pets allowed (fee). No smoking. | 2198 Jackson St. | 415/929–7670 | fax 415/929–1405 | www.sftrips.com | 10 rooms, shower only | $150–$215 | AE, MC, V.

Juliana. While it retains a historic 1903 flavor, this hotel's distinctly European-style lobby is elegant yet intimate, centering on a cozy fireplace, the scene of nightly wine receptions. Rooms are an eclectic mix of yellows, mellow blues, and floral patterns. Although two blocks from Union Square, it's a world away from the bustling crowds. You can get a shuttle to the Financial District. In-room data ports, refrigerators, cable TV. Laundry service. Business services, parking (fee). | 590 Bush St. | 415/392–2540 or 800/328–3880 | fax 415/391–8447 |

sales@julianahotel.com | www.julianahotel.com | 90 rooms, 16 suites | $169–$199 rooms, $209–$259 suites | AE, D, DC, MC, V.

King George. This old-world hotel one block from Union Square opened in 1914 and still feels like an English inn. Rooms are simple and rustic with off-white walls and forest green and burgundy furnishings. Complimentary Continental breakfast and afternoon tea, room service. No air conditioning, in-room data ports, cable TV. Laundry service. Business services, parking (fee). | 334 Mason St. | 415/781–5050 or 800 800/288–6005 | fax 415/391–6976 | www.kinggeorge.com | 142 rooms, 1 suite | $140–$174 rooms, $225 suite | AE, D, DC, MC, V.

Maxwell. This 1908 hotel with Art Deco flair in the heart of the Theatre District and one block from Union Square has tiled fireplaces and dark-wood furnishings in both the lobby and rooms. It has two penthouses. Restaurant, bar (jazz), room service. In-room data-ports, in-room safes, cable TV. Video games. Laundry service. Business services. Parking (fee). | 386 Geary St. | 415/986–2000 or 888/574–6299 | fax 415/397–2447 | www.maxwellhotel.com | 153 rooms, 31 suites | $160–$180 rooms, $215–$750 suites | AE, D, DC, MC, V.

Monticello Inn. Built in 1906, this 18th-century, Colonial-style hotel is modeled after its namesake. It has Chippendale furnishings, an extensive Federal-period library, and soothing Colonial decor. Lest you forget what coast you're on, Union Square, the Theatre District, and the Powell Street cable car line are only three blocks away. Restaurant, complimentary Continental breakfast. In-room data ports, cable TV. Parking (fee). | 127 Ellis St. | 415/392–8800 or 800/669–7777 | fax 415/398–2650 | www.monticelloinn.com | 91 rooms, 33 suites | $179 rooms, $209–$249 suites | AE, D, DC, MC, V.

Nob Hill Motel. Located in the upscale Pacific Heights neighborhood, this 1950s wooden motel with landscape grounds seems more like a mom-and-pop operation. The rooms are large with lavender walls, dark-wood furniture, plants, and flowers. It's a great walking neighborhood. Fisherman's Wharf and Chinatown are about 20 min away by foot. There's also a cable car station two blocks away for transportation to downtown, Union Square, and the Civic Center. Complimentary Continental breakfast. In-room data ports, refrigerators, some microwaves, cable TV. Free parking. | 1630 Pacific Ave. | 415/775–8160 or 800/343–6900 | fax 415/673–8842 | sfmotelaol.com | www.citysearch.com/sfo/nobhillmotel | 27 rooms, 2 suites | $145 rooms, $160–$250 suites | AE, D, DC, MC, V.

Pacific Heights Inn. Built in 1955, this brick-and-wood, bi-level motel is two blocks from Union Square. Most of the simple rooms have showers only. Photos of San Francisco landmarks hang on the walls. Restaurant, complimentary Continental breakfast. No air conditioning, in-room data ports, some refrigerators, some microwaves, cable TV. Some hot tubs. Business services. | 1555 Union St. | 415/776–3310 or 800/523–1801 | fax 415/776–8176 | 23 rooms, 17 kitchenettes | $125–$150 rooms, $275 kitchenettes | AE, D, DC, MC, V.

Petite Auberge. You can relax on Nob Hill in this small hotel with French doors and a collection of French art. In the afternoon, you can relax with complimentary hors d'oeuvres and wine served by a crackling fire in the cozy lobby. Rooms have inviting beds with thick comforters, carved armoires, and a fireplace. The inn is within two blocks of the cable car line to Union Square and Fisherman's Wharf. Complimentary breakfast and afternoon hors d'oeuvres and wine. No air conditioning, in-room data ports, cable TV. Parking (fee). | 863 Bush St. | 415/928–6000 | fax 415/775–5717 | www.foursisters.com | 26 rooms, 1 suite | $145–$180 rooms, $245 suite | AE, DC, MC, V.

Phoenix. On the fringe of the seedy Tenderloin, this retro-'50s spot boasts a list of celebrity guests such as members of REM and Pearl Jam. Rooms have local art, bright color schemes, and bamboo furniture. There's also a happening scene by the courtyard pool and sculpture garden. Very hip, it's usually booked weeks or months in advance. Complimentary Continental breakfast, restaurant, bar. No air conditioning, some refrigerators. Cable TV (free movies). Pool. Laundry service. Business services, free parking. | 601 Eddy St. | 415/776–1380 or 800/248–9466 | fax 415/885–3109 | www.sftrips.com/hotels/phoenix.html | 42 rooms; 2 suites | $145–$150 | AE, D, DC, MC, V.

Queen Anne. The building was one of the first major structures in the historic Western Addition of 1899. It was a girls' finishing school, then a dinner club. The hotel has been restored to reflect its turn-of-the-century grace and elegance with stained glass, Victorian paintings, antiques, and hand-carved beds. Tea is served in the afternoon. It's six blocks to the cable car, one block from the bus to Union Square, and there's a free shuttle to the Financial District. Complimentary Continental breakfast. No air conditioning, in-room data ports, refrigerators, cable TV. Laundry service. Business services, parking (fee). | 1590 Sutter St. | 415/441-2828 or 800/227-3970 | fax 415/775-5212 | www.queenanne.com | 48 rooms, 8 suites | $129-$175 rooms, $199-$295 suites | AE, D, DC, MC, V.

Ramada Limited. This three-story white, blue, and teal hotel is within walking distance of Union Square, the Mosconi Convention Center, and the main cable car station. Built in the '70s but remodeled in 1997, the lobby is warm and welcoming with gray marble and flower arrangements. The rooms are small but clean, and the suites are large enough for small families. Complimentary Continental breakfast. In-room data ports, some refrigerators, cable TV. Laundry service. Business services, free parking. | 247 7th St. | 415/861-6469 | fax 415/626-4041 | www.ramada.com | 62 rooms, 18 with shower only; 6 suites | $159 rooms, $229-$499 suites | AE, D, DC, MC, V.

Sheehan. This 1909 redbrick building near the Theater District has a bright, welcoming lobby with high ceilings and spacious rooms. It's one block from Union Square and cable car stops. Complimentary Continental breakfast. Indoor pool. No air conditioning cable TV. Beauty salon. Exercise equipment. Parking (fee). | 620 Sutter St. | 415/775-6500 or 800/848-1529 | fax 415/775-3271 | www.sheehanhotel.com | 65 rooms, 3 with shared bath | $85-$189 | AE, D, DC, MC, V.

Stanyan Park. This three-story Victorian hotel across from Golden Gate Park in the funky Haight/Ashbury district has Victorian furnishings and an old-fashioned elevator. Rooms have red or yellow walls and down mattresses. Suites have full kitchens, fireplaces, and poster beds. Snacks are served every afternoon in a common room filled with fresh flowers. Complimentary Continental breakfast. No air conditioning. In-room data ports, some refrigerators, cable TV. | 750 Stanyan St. | 415/751-1000 | fax 415/668-5454 | info@stanyan-park.com | www.stanyanpark.com | 36 rooms, 6 suites | $115-$170 rooms, $249-$299 suites | AE, D, DC, MC, V.

Vagabond Inn–Midtown. Built in 1972, this five-floor motel wraps around a central pool courtyard. It's 12 blocks from Fisherman's Wharf and one block away from mass transit, making it a good choice for families wanting easy access to the city. Some rooms have views of the bay. Complimentary Continental breakfast. No air conditioning, in-room data ports, some kitchenettes, some refrigerators, cable TV. Pool. Parking (fee). | 2550 Van Ness Ave. | 415/776-7500 | fax 415/776-5689 | www.vagabondinn.com | 122 rooms; 10 suites | $139 rooms, $159-$179 suites | AE, D, DC, MC, V.

Victorian Inn On The Park. An historic landmark, this 1897 Queen Anne Victorian across from Golden Gate Park has an open octagonal turret and 19th-century wood block designs on the walls. Rooms have antique furnishings and fixtures. The inn is about 2 mi from downtown. Complimentary Continental breakfast. No air conditioning, in-room data ports, TV in common area. Parking(fee). | 301 Lyon St. | 415/931-1830 or 800/435-1967 | fax 415/931-1830 | vicinn@aol.com | www.citysearch.com/sfo/victorianinn | 12 rooms | $139-$179 | AE, D, DC, MC, V.

Villa Florence. Built in 1916, this seven-story Italian-styled luxury hotel in Union Square has arched entryways, Florentine murals, and marble columns. Rooms have high molded ceilings with a floral wooden headboard, European country-inn style furnishings, and white shutters. The downtown location is convenient to theaters and shopping. Restaurant, bar. In-room data ports, refrigerators, cable TV. Video games. Laundry service. Business services, parking (fee). | 225 Powell St. | 415/397-7700 or 800/553-4411 | fax 415/397-1006 | www.villaflorence.com | 180 rooms, 36 suites | $179-$199 rooms, $199-$249 suites | AE, D, DC, MC, V.

Vintage Court. This 1912, Colonial-style, eight-story hotel has a sunken lobby complete with fireplace and overstuffed couches where you can spend an evening tasting wines from Napa as a guest vintner describes each wine's attributes. The in-house restaurant, Masas, is one of San Francisco's most exclusive. Although one street up Nob Hill and two blocks from Union Square, it's separated from the noise and crowds of nearby Market Street. You can take a free shuttle to the Financial District. No air conditioning in some rooms, in-room data ports, refrigerators, cable TV. Laundry service. Business services. No smoking. | 650 Bush St. | 415/392–4666 or 800/853–1750 | fax 415/433–4065 | www.vintage-court.com | 106 rooms, 1 suite | $149–$234 rooms, $300 suite | AE, D, DC, MC, V.

Warwick Regis. This Theatre District hotel two blocks from Union Square has a Louis XIV court–style lobby with arched doors, chandeliers, a silver leaded dome, and velvet upholstered couches and chairs. Rooms have four-poster or canopy beds, intricate wooden headboards and Italian marble bathrooms. Restaurants, bar, room service. In-room data ports, refrigerators, cable TV. Baby-sitting. Laundry service. Business services, parking (fee). | 490 Geary St. | 415/928–7900 or 800/827–3447 | fax 415/441–8788 | www.warwickregis.com | 80 rooms, 16 suites | $149–$199 rooms, $200–$249 suites | AE, D, DC, MC, V.

Washington Square Inn. You can relax over complimentary wine and snacks in the afternoon in this small boutique inn. The place is decorated with English and French country furniture and antiques. It has a private garden patio and views of Washington Square. Some of the city's best restaurants are minutes away in North Beach. Fisherman's Wharf, cable car stops and Union Square are all within 1 mi. Complimentary Continental breakfast. No air conditioning, in-room data ports, cable TV. Laundry service. Parking (fee). No smoking. | 1660 Stockton St. | 415/981–4220 or 800/388–0220 | fax 415/397–7242 | www.wsisf.com | 13 rooms, 2 suites | $135–$210 rooms, $235 suites | AE, D, DC, MC, V.

Wharf Inn. With its brown wood construction, this four-story, 1960s motel place fits in with the surrounding wharf buildings. Rooms are of decent size with primary colors, light woods, and matching window dressing and comforters. There's an excellent two-bedroom penthouse with a full terrace overlooking the bay. It's close to the wharf and one block to the cable car. No air conditioning, in-room data ports, cable TV. Business services, free parking. | 2601 Mason St. | 415/673–7411 or 800/548–9918 | fax 415/776–2181 | www.wharfinn.com | 50 rooms; 1 suite | $149–$169 rooms, $375 suite | AE, D, DC, MC, V.

White Swan. Neighbor and sister-inn to Petite Auberge, this London-style townhouse B&B, built in 1915, was formerly a boarding house. It has Edwardian-style furnishings, dark-wood panels, and brass fixtures in the lobby while rooms are furnished in a light, country style. There's a delightful English garden out back, and the free breakfast is one of the best in the city. At the base of Nob Hill, it's a three-block walk to Union Square and a block from the cable car stop. Complimentary breakfast. Microwaves, cable TV. Laundry service. No smoking. | 845 Bush St. | 415/775–1755 | fax 415/775–5717 | www.foursisters.com | 23 rooms, 3 suites | $175–$190 rooms, $210–$250 suites | AE, DC, MC, V.

York. Built in 1922 and featured in Alfred Hitchcock's *Vertigo*, this hotel has a vaulted Neo-Classical lobby with Corinthian columns and early 20th-century furnishings. Internationally acclaimed acts perform in the hotel's plush cabaret. Just two blocks from Union Square, it's decorated in earth tones and dark green carpeting, with large windows and fresh flowers in each room. Complimentary Continental breakfast. In-room data ports, some refrigerators, cable TV. Exercise equipment. Laundry service. Business services, parking (fee). | 940 Sutter St. | 415/885–6800 or 800/808–9675 | fax 415/885–2115 | 96 rooms | $134–$220 | AE, DC, MC, V.

EXPENSIVE

★ **Archbishop's Mansion.** Built in 1904, this hotel is extravagantly romantic. Its chandelier, used in *Gone with the Wind*, hangs above a 1904 Bechstein piano once owned by Noel Coward. The lobby also has a redwood fireplace, Corinthian columns, and a sweeping staircase. Rooms were named and styled after characters in famous operas; some have fireplaces.

Complimentary Continental breakfast and afternoon wine. Cable TV, in-room VCR (and movies). Free parking. | 1000 Fulton St. | 415/563–7872 or 800/543–5820 | fax 415/885–3193 | www.sftrips.com/hotels/arch_mansion.html | 15 rooms | $195–$425 | AE, DC, MC, V.

Best Western Canterbury. Not your normal Best Western, the structure was built in 1928 and now functions as a boutique hotel featuring 1920s English antiques, suits of armor, and Corinthian columns. The lobby mural, painted by the renowned artist Jo Mora, depicts 14 pilgrims described in *The Canterbury Tales*. In addition, each room has a copy of Chaucer's book beside the silk floral bedspreads in a small desk with drawers; rooms also have floor lamps, marble bathrooms, and floral arrangements. Restaurant, bar, room service. In-room data ports, some refrigerators, cable TV. Exercise equipment. Laundry service. Business services, parking (fee). | 750 Sutter St. | 415/474–6464 | fax 415/474–5856 | reservations@canterbury-hotel.com | www.canterbury-hotel.com | 241 rooms, 12 suites | $150–$250 rooms, $395 suites | AE, D, DC, MC, V.

The Donatello. This small 15-story, European-style hotel has a gorgeous lobby with travertine marble, Venetian glass, and European antiques. Rooms feel roomier than they actually are because of the 10-ft. ceilings and over-size windows. Some rooms open onto a lushly landscaped terrace. It's in the heart of the Theater District. Restaurant, bar, room service. In-room data ports, cable TV (and movies). Exercise equipment. Baby-sitting. Laundry service. Business services, parking (fee). | 501 Post St. | 415/441–7100 or 800/227–3184 | fax 415/885–8842 | sfdntlo@aol.com | www.travelweb.com | 94 rooms | $225–$270 | AE, D, DC, MC, V.

★ **Galleria Park.** This nine-story building was built in 1913. Original details have been retained, including a glazed crystal skylight, marble stairways, and ironwork. You can relax in the lobby in front of the fireplace, especially at the evening wine reception. On the edge of the financial district and two blocks from Union Square, it caters to the business traveler with fax machines in every room, large desks, and 24-hr business and audio/visual center. 2 Restaurants. Refrigerators, in-room data ports, cable TV. Exercise equipment. Laundry service. Business services, parking (fee). | 191 Sutter St. | 415/781–3060 or 800/792–9639 | fax 415/433–4409 | sales@galleriapark.com | www.galleriapark.com | 162 rooms, 15 suites | $220–$250 rooms, $280–$450 suites | AE, D, DC, MC, V.

Handlery Union Square. A lovely swimming pool connects the eight-story club building with the main tower. Rooms are 450 square ft and luxurious. Amenities include plush robes, turn-down service, and complimentary morning newspaper. Union Square is half block away. Restaurant, bar, room service. In-room data ports, refrigerators, cable TV. Pool. Beauty salon. Parking (fee). | 351 Geary St. | 415/781–7800 or 800/843–4343 | fax 415/781–0269 | hushres@handlery.com | www.handlery.com | 363 rooms, 14 suites | $174–$210 rooms, $200–$265 suites | AE, D, DC, MC, V.

★ **Harbor Court.** Built in 1907, and once owned by the YMCA—the old facade is still visible from the back of the hotel—this eight-story hotel has an excellent health club. Rooms have dramatic views of San Francisco Bay and the Bay Bridge, as well as canopied beds, bronze fixtures, and tapestry-like window dressing. You can take a free shuttle to the Financial District. Restaurant, bar (entertainment). In-room data ports, in-room safes, refrigerators, cable TV. Health club. Video games. Laundry service. Business services, parking (fee). | 165 Steuart St. | 415/882–1300 or 800/346–0555 | fax 415/882–1313 | www.harborcourthotel.com | 130 rooms, 1 suite | $209–$249 rooms, $395 suite | AE, D, DC, MC, V.

Holiday Inn–Fisherman's Wharf. Completely renovated in 1993, this five-story, late-'50s, concrete and brick hotel is within walking distance of Fisherman's Wharf and both cable car lines. Rooms are reasonably spacious, with balconies and patios that overlook the Cannery and the bay. It's a good choice for families. Restaurants, bar, and room service. In-room data ports. Cable TV. Outdoor pool. Exercise facility. Laundry facility. Business service, parking (fee). Pets allowed (fee). | 1300 Columbus Ave. | 415/771–9000 | fax 415/771–7006 | www.hiwharf.com | 577 rooms, 7 suites | $190–$212 rooms, $350–$525 suites | AE, D, DC, MC, V.

Holiday Inn Select–Union Square. One block from Union Square, this centrally located hotel rises 30 stories, allowing great views of downtown and the bay. The lobby has a Mediterranean flair, with Italian marble and mixed wood inlays. Rooms are spacious with large desks and earth-tone color schemes. You can catch a free shuttle to the Financial District. Restaurant, bar. In-room data ports, some refrigerators, cable TV,. Exercise equipment. Laundry service. Business services, parking (fee). Pets allowed (fee). | 480 Sutter St. | 415/398–8900 | fax 415/989–8823 | www.basshotels.com/crowneplaza | 350 rooms, 51 suites | $199–$279 rooms, $329–$779 suites | AE, D, DC, MC, V.

Hotel Diva. Near Curran Theater, it has futuristic Asian Deco décor, angular sofas, black lacquer furniture, and dramatic, sculpted light fixtures. Rooms are ultra-modern with sculpted steel headboards, taupe beds, cobalt blue carpet, and high-tech entertainment systems. Not for the conservative, the hotel is quickly becoming a hip, international destination. Restaurant, complimentary Continental breakfast, room service. In-room data ports, in-room safes, refrigerators, cable TV, in-room VCR (and movies). Exercise equipment. Laundry service. Business services, parking (fee). | 440 Geary St. | 415/885–0200 or 800/553–1900 | fax 415/346–6613 | www.hoteldiva.com | 71 rooms, 40 suites | $140–$270 rooms, $219–$319 suites | AE, D, DC, MC, V.

Hotel Majestic. From the etched glass and tapestries to the luxurious wood furniture, this 1902 Edwardian building looks and feels like old San Francisco. Rooms have French and English antiques and four-poster canopy beds. Some have fireplaces and unobstructed city views. Away from the crowds, it features a superlative romantic restaurant and is a short stroll from Japantown and public transportation. A social hour is held every evening with light snacks and there's a brunch Sunday morning. Restaurant, bar, room service. Refrigerators in some rooms, cable TV. Laundry service. Parking (fee). | 1500 Sutter St. | 415/441–1100 or 800/869–8966 | fax 415/673–7331 | 51 rooms, 7 suites | $159–$269 rooms, $450 suites | AE, D, DC, MC, V.

★ **Hotel Rex.** Literary and artistic creativity are celebrated at the stylish Hotel Rex, where thousands of books, largely antiquarian, line the 1920s-style lobby. Original artwork adorns the walls, and the proprietors even host book readings and round-table discussions in the common areas, which are decorated in warm, rich tones. Upstairs, quotations from works by California writers are painted on the terra-cotta–color walls near the elevator landings. Good-size rooms have writing desks and lamps with whimsically hand-painted shades. Restored period furnishings upholstered in deep, rich hues evoke the spirit of 1920s salon society, but rooms also have modern amenities such as voice mail and CD players. Bar, lobby lounge, in-room data ports, minibars, no smoking rooms, room service, dry cleaning, laundry service, concierge, parking (fee). | 562 Sutter St., | 415/433–4434 or 800/433–4434 | fax 415/433–3695 | 92 rooms, 2 suites | $215–$255 | AE, D, DC, MC, V.

Hotel Triton. The lobby has whimsical curved gold chairs, purple ottomans, and a large mural of the god Triton. At night, it's the scene of wine reception and tarot card readings. Walls in the small-but-cheery guest rooms are adorned with work by local artists and craftspeople. The hotel regularly hosts bigwigs in the fashion, entertainment, music, and film industries. It's across the street from Chinatown's "Dragon Gates" and three blocks from Union Square. Restaurant, bar, complimentary snacks. In-room data ports, cable TV. Exercise equipment. Laundry service. Business services, parking (fee). Some pets allowed (fee). | 342 Grant Ave. | 415/394–0500 or 800/433–6611 | fax 415/394–0555 | sales@hotel-tritonsf.com | www.hotel-tritonsf.com | 134 rooms, 6 suites | $209–$239 rooms, $339 suites | AE, D, DC, MC, V.

Hotel Union Square. Housed in a 1913 building with a garden patio, this sophisticated, yet casual lodging has modern, European furniture, hanging hand-blown lanterns, large windows, and original artwork depicting San Francisco's most celebrated scenes. Bar, complimentary Continental breakfast. In-room data ports, refrigerators, cable TV. Video games. Laundry service. Business services, airport shuttle, parking (fee). | 114 Powell St. | 415/397–3000 or 800/553–1900 | fax 415/399–1874 | www.hotelunionsquare.com | 129 rooms, 2 suites | $189–$200 rooms, $365 suites | AE, D, DC, MC, V.

Inn at Union Square. Centrally located in Union Square, this elegant inn has a fireplace lobby at the end of each of its six floors. Rooms are decorated in sage, cream, and gold with a desk, overstuffed chairs, and fresh flowers. The inn prides itself on customized service, offering fine wine and hors d'oeuvres in the afternoon. The Howell suite has a fireplace, bar, hot tub, and sauna. Bar, complimentary breakfast, room service. No air conditioning, in-room data ports, cable TV. Laundry service. Business services, parking (fee). No smoking. | 440 Post St. | 415/397–3510 or 800/288–4346 | fax 415/989–0529 | www.union-square.com | 23 rooms, 7 suites | $195–$245 rooms, $245–$350 suites | AE, D, DC, MC, V.

Nob Hill Lambourne. This small boutique hotel caters to health-conscious travelers with full-spa treatments, subdued lighting, hardwood floors, and accommodations that look more like well-designed apartments than hotel rooms. It's three blocks to Union Square and the Financial District. Complimentary Continental breakfast. No air conditioning, in-room data ports, microwaves, cable TV, in-room VCRs and movies). Spa. Exercise equipment. Laundry service. Business services, parking (fee). No smoking. | 725 Pine St. | 415/433–2287; 800/274–8466 | fax 415/433–097 | www.nobhilllambourne.com | 14 kitchenettes, 6 suites | $220 kitchenettes, $360 suites | AE, D, DC, MC, V.

★ **Radisson Hotel at Fisherman's Wharf.** In 1999, Radisson built a new, four-story, contemporary complex with a central, landscaped pool courtyard on the grounds of a former TraveLodge. It's the only truly bayfront lodging in the wharf. The rooms, in soft pastels and light woods, have individual balconies, about half of which have incredible bay views. Because of its prime location, a block from the cable car and near the Convention Center and Wharf attractions, it draws an even mix of families and business people. 3 restaurants, room service. In-room data ports, some refrigerators, cable TV. Outdoor pool. Exercise equipment. Laundry service. Business service, parking (fee). | 250 Beach St. | 415/392–6700 | www.radisson.com | 342 rooms; 12 suites | $219–$279 rooms, $329–$399 suites | AE, D, DC, MC, V.

Radisson Miyako Hotel. This hotel in Japantown has Japanese art in the lobby and a choice of Western- or Eastern-style rooms. The latter have tatami mats on the floor. The Japanese garden has koi fish and you can have a shiatsu massage in your room. The Embarcadero waterfront is four blocks away and the cable car to Union Square and Fisherman's Wharf is two blocks away. Restaurant, bar, room service. In-room data ports, refrigerator, saunas in suites, cable TV. Exercise equipment. Laundry service. Business services, parking (fee). | 1625 Post St. | 415/922–3200 | fax 415/921–0417 | www.miyakahotel.com | 218 rooms, 16 suites | $189–$209 rooms, $279–$299 suites | AE, D, DC, MC, V.

Sir Francis Drake. Doormen in Beefeater costumes greet visitors at this Union Square institution, built in 1928. The regal lobby has chandeliers, gilded ceilings, Italian marble floors, and wrought-iron fixtures. Rooms have Victorian furnishings and high ceilings with ornate molding. Cable cars stop right outside. Restaurant, bar. In-room data ports, refrigerators, cable TV. Exercise equipment. Laundry service. Business services. parking (fee). | 450 Powell St. | 415/392–7755 or 800/227–5480 | fax 415/391–8719 | www.sirfrancisdrake.com | 412 rooms, 5 suites | $235–$245 rooms, $500–$700 suites | AE, D, DC, MC, V.

Tuscan Inn at Fisherman's Wharf. One of the nicest hotels on Fisherman's Wharf, this four-story, brick-and-wood hotel, built in the 1980s, has a lobby that feels like a clubroom with fireplace and nightly wine reception. Rooms have country furnishings, fresh flowers, and mirrored walls and there's a free shuttle to the Financial District. Restaurant, bar, room service. In-room data ports, refrigerators, cable TV. Laundry service. Business services. Parking (fee). Pets allowed (fee). | 425 North Point St. | 415/561–1100 or 800/648–4626 | fax 415/561–1199 | www.tuscaninn.com | 221 rooms, 12 suites | $230–$278 rooms, $308 and up for suites | AE, D, DC, MC, V.

Westin St. Francis. A Union Square landmark, this massive 32-story hotel, built in 1904, has exterior glass elevators and an exquisite, rosewood-panel, gilded, and thoroughly ornate lobby. Rooms range from simple hardwood furnishings and baby-blue hues to club-like accommodations with chandeliers, French antique desks, and overstuffed chairs. 2 restaurants, bar (with entertainment), room service. In-room data ports, microwaves, refrigerators, cable TV. Beauty salon. Exercise equipment. Laundry service. Business services, parking (fee). Some pets allowed. | 335 Powell St. | 415/397–7000 or 800/228–3000 | fax 415/774–0124 | www.westin.com | 1,192 rooms, 84 suites | $195–$315 rooms, $450–$2,000 suites | AE, D, DC, MC, V.

VERY EXPENSIVE

Argent Hotel. A deluxe hotel adjacent to the San Francisco Museum of Modern Art, one block from the Convention Center and within walking distance of Union Square shopping, its lobby has Italian marble inlays, gallery-quality paintings, a fireplace, and a gold-leaf dome. Rooms have floor-to-ceiling windows, stylish furnishings, and subdued earth tones. Upper rooms have views of the bay. Restaurant, bar room service. Refrigerators, in-room data ports, cable TV. Sauna. Exercise equipment. Tennis. Babysitting. Laundry service. Business services, parking (fee). | 50 3rd St. | 415/974–6400 or 800/ANA–HOTE | fax 415/543–8268 | www.argenthotel.com | 651 rooms; 26 suites | $269–$309 rooms, $459–$700 suites | AE, D, DC, MC, V.

★ **Campton Place.** This 18-floor luxury hotel showcases a unique European/Asian design scheme. The lobby has a carved Buddha statue, Japanese screens, and French furniture from the Chippendale and Louis XVI periods. Rooms have minimal Japanese furniture, fresh-cut flowers, and subtle, natural color schemes. There's also a landscaped rooftop patio with views of Union Square half a block away. Restaurant, bar, room service. In-room data ports, cable TV (and movies). Some pets allowed (fee). | 340 Stockton St. | 415/781–5555 or 800/235–4300 | fax 415/955–5536 | reserve@campton.com | www.camptonplace.com | 110 rooms; 9 suites | $295 –$415 rooms, $520 and up for suites | AE, DC, MC, V.

The Clift. Built for the 1915 Panama-Pacific Exposition, this elegant hotel towers over the Theater District, two blocks away. The opulent lobby has hand-carved balustrades, crystal chandeliers, and arched redwood ceilings and columns. Rooms have high ceilings, decorative moldings, carved woodwork, and marble bathrooms. You can have a cocktail in the dramatic Art Deco Redwood Room lounge. Restaurant, bar (entertainment), room service. In-room data ports, refrigerators, cable TV. Exercise equipment. Laundry service. Business services, parking (fee). Some pets allowed. | 495 Geary St. | 415/775–4700 | fax 415/441–4621 | 301 rooms; 25 suites | $285–$385 rooms, $440 and up for suites | AE, D, DC, MC, V.

★ **Fairmont Hotel & Tower.** Rising from the rubble of the 1906 quake, this hotel once served as a home for San Francisco's displaced elite. It's actually two buildings, the original classical structure and a modern tower built in the '80s with panoramic views of downtown. The lobby includes an elegant, French-inspired entry with arched ceilings, mosaics, and faux marble columns. Rooms in the older building are smaller but have more character. Some suites have private patios, and most overlook the landscaped, fountain terrace. There's a shuttle to the Financial District. 4 restaurants, 2 bars (jazz piano), room service. In-room data ports, in-room safes, refrigerators, cable TV, in-room VCR (and movies). Spa. Exercise equipment. Laundry service. Business services, parking (fee). | 950 Mason St. | 415/772–5000 | fax 415/781–4027 | www.fairmont.com | 528 rooms; 62 suites | $269–$339 rooms, $470 and up for suites | AE, D, DC, MC, V.

Grand Hyatt San Francisco. Built in 1973, this luxury hotel towers over Union Square and has a rooftop restaurant with incredible views. Renovated in 1997, the spacious rooms have modern furnishings and earth-tone color schemes. It's popular with conventioneers and business travelers because of its proximity to the Civic Center and downtown. Restaurant, bar (entertainment). In-room data ports, refrigerators, cable TV. Beauty salon. Exercise equipment. Laundry service. Business services. | 345 Stockton St. | 415/398–1234 | fax 415/392–2536 | www.hyatt.com | 687 rooms, 33 suites | $310–410 rooms, $475 and up for suites | AE, D, DC, MC, V.

Hilton and Towers. This sprawling complex in Union Square has a marble lobby with sculpted lions, chandeliers, a map-pattern carpet, and large globes. Rooms are spacious but bland with off-white walls and brass fixtures. 5 restaurants, 2 bars, room service. In-room data ports, cable TV (with movies). Pool. Beauty salon. Exercise equipment. Video games. Laundry service. Business services, parking (fee). | 333 O'Farrell St. | 415/771–1400 | fax 415/771–6807 | www.hilton.com/hotels | 1,741 rooms, 150 suites | $250–$350 rooms, $350–$1250 suites | AE, D, DC, MC, V.

Hilton Plaza at Fisherman's Wharf. Formerly a Ramada, this luxury hotel re-opened as a Hilton in 1999. From the fireplace, Italian marble and in-laid woods in the lobby to the largest rooms of any hotel on the waterfront, this four-story, glass-and-concrete tower now has the most deluxe accommodations in the wharf. It's within two blocks of a cable car stop and close to downtown and the Mosconi Convention Center. Restaurant, bar, room service. In-room data ports, some refrigerators, cable TV. Exercise equipment. Laundry service. Business services, parking (fee). | 590 Bay St. | www.hilton.com | 415/885–4700 | fax 415/771–8945 | 220 rooms; 12 suites | $259–$290 rooms, $350–$450 suites | AE, D, DC, MC, V.

★ **Hotel Palomar.** Famous "boutique hotel" trailblazer Bill Kimpton (Hotel Monaco) transformed the top five floors of the green-tiled and turreted 1908 Pacific Place Building into an urbane and luxurious oasis above the busiest part of the city. Guests enter under a glass-and-steel fan-shape canopy into a spare, modern lobby with a harlequin-pattern wooden floor and stylish gunmetal and brass registration desk. Rooms have muted leopard-pattern carpeting, walls covered in raffia weave, and bold navy and cream striped drapes. The look is from the '40s, but the cordless phones, CD players, and all-in-one faxing/copying/printing machines are definitely modern. Aveda products are provided in the sparkling baths, where a "tub menu" (consisting of items from aromatherapy infusions to cigars and brandy) tempts adventurous bathers. Restaurant, bar, lobby lounge, in-room data ports, minibars, no-smoking floor, room service, exercise room, dry cleaning, laundry service, concierge, business services, meeting rooms, parking (fee). | 12 4th St., | 415/348–1111 or 877/294–9711 | fax 415/348–0302 | 182 rooms, 16 suites | $295–$315 | AE, D, DC, MC, V.

Huntington Hotel. Atop Nob Hill, this family-owned and -operated hotel overlooking Huntington Park and the Grace Cathedral is gracious and formal. Spacious rooms are individually decorated with meticulous attention to detail. You can have tea or sherry upon arrival. The cable car stops outside for easy access to Union Square and Fisherman's Wharf. Restaurant, bar, room service. In-room data ports, cable TV. Spa. Exercise equipment. Laundry service. Business services, parking (fee). | 1075 California St. | 415/474–5400 or 800/227–4683 (except California), 800/652–1539 (California) | fax 415/474–6227 | www.huntingtonhotel.com | 100 rooms, 40 suites | $275–$420 rooms $450–$800 suites | AE, D, DC, MC, V.

Hyatt at Fisherman's Wharf. This four-story, brick Victorian structure is within walking distance of Ghirardelli Square, The Cannery, Pier 39, and docks for Alcatraz and bay cruises. Its Italian marble lobby has dark-wood accents and crystal chandeliers. Rooms are spacious with redwood furnishings and potted plants. Try to get a room off the street; it's a noisy neighborhood. Cable car transportation is four blocks away and you can get a free shuttle to the Financial District. Restaurant, bar, room service. In-room data ports, cable TV. Pool. Hot tub. Exercise equipment. Laundry service. Business services, parking (fee). | 555 North Point St. | 415/563–1234 | fax 415/749–6122 | www.hyatt.com | 306 rooms, 7 suites | $265–$295 rooms, $325–$350 suites | AE, D, DC, MC, V.

★ **Hyatt Regency.** Built in 1973, this 17-story contemporary hotel next to Embarcadero has a huge atrium with dramatic glass elevators. They're the ones that freaked out Mel Brooks in the movie *High Anxiety*. Rooms have sweeping views of the bay or the city. At the end of the California Street cable car line, it's also close enough to walk to downtown. Restaurant, 2 bars (entertainment), room service. In-room data ports, some refrigerators, cable TV. Exercise equipment. Laundry service. Business services, parking (fee). | 5 Embarcadero Center | 415/788–1234 | fax 415/398–2567 | www.hyatt.com | 760 rooms, 45 suites | $210–$325 rooms, $360–$475 suites | AE, D, DC, MC, V.

Kensington Park. On the corner of Union Square, this hotel was built in 1920 in a distinctive Spanish Gothic style. The cathedral-like lobby has a crystal chandelier and baby grand piano. Rooms are filled with Queen Anne furnishings, mahogany desks, and armoires, and the bathrooms have lots of brass and marble. The in-house restaurant, "Farallon," with its underwater decor, is a city favorite. It's in a prime location for shopping, restaurants, and theater, with a cable car stop only two blocks away. Restaurant, bar, complimentary Continental breakfast and afternoon snacks. In-room data ports, some refrigerators, cable TV. Exercise equipment. Laundry service. Business service, parking(fee). | 450 Post St. | 415/788–6400 or 800/553–1900 | fax 415/399–9484 | www.kensingtonparkhotel.com | 86 rooms, 1 suite | $269–$289 rooms, $575 suite | AE, D, DC, MC, V.

★ **Mandarin Oriental.** Occupying the top 13 floors of two glass and steel towers connected by a sky bridge, this Financial District hotel has panoramic views of the city and the bay. With its deluxe suites that seem perched in the sky, and upscale restaurant, it's popular with Asian dignitaries and heads of industry, especially the dot-comers. Restaurant, bar (entertainment), room service. In-room data ports, in-room safes, refrigerators, cable TV. Exercise equipment. Laundry service. Business services, parking (fee). | 222 Sansome St. | 415/885–0999 or 800/622–0404 | fax 415/433–0289 | mandarinsfo@mosfo.com | www.mandarin-oriental.com | 154 rooms, 4 suites | $455–$610 rooms, $1,300–$3,000 suites | AE, D, DC, MC, V.

Mark Hopkins Inter-Continental. With its blend of French château and Spanish Renaissance architecture, this luxurious and romantic hotel has been a city landmark since 1926. Everything about this hotel is aesthetically pleasing from the vaulted ceilings and Art Nouveau chandeliers in the lobby to the glass-walled Top of the Mark bar. A streetcar right outside provides transportation, and it is within walking distance of the wharf. There's also a shuttle to the Financial District. Restaurant, bars. Refrigerators, cable TV. Exercise equipment. Parking (fee). | 1 Nob Hill | 415/392–3434 or 800/327–0200 | fax 415/421–3302 | 390 rooms, 54 suites | $380–$460 rooms, $610–$3,000 suites | AE, D, DC, MC, V.

Marriott. Locals call this towering Modern-Deco building the Jukebox. Its five-story open interior atrium has skylights and a top-floor restaurant with panoramic views. The lobby is filled with marble, chandeliers, sculptures, and modern art. It's a 10-min walk to the Financial District and Union Square and a block from the Mosconi Convention Center and Yerba Buena Center. It's considered the ultimate convention hotel. Restaurant, bar, room service. In-room data ports, refrigerator, cable TV. Indoor pool. Health club. Laundry service. Business services, airport shuttle, parking (fee). | 55 4th St. | 415/896–1600 | fax 415/896–6175 | www.marriott.com/sfodt | 1,500 rooms, 133 suites | $259–$399 rooms, $400–$2800 suites | AE, DC, MC, V.

Marriott Fisherman's Wharf. This four-story modern concrete hotel is two blocks from Fisherman's Wharf and cable cars. Rooms are somewhat generic but spacious and you can catch a free shuttle to the Financial District. Restaurant, bar, mini-bars in some rooms. In-room data ports, cable TV. Exercise equipment. Laundry service. Business services, parking (fee). Pets allowed (fee). | 1250 Columbus Ave. | 415/775–7555 | fax 415/474–2099 | www.marriott.com | 285 rooms; 16 suites | $269 rooms, $349 and up for suites | AE, D, DC, MC, V.

★ **Monaco.** You can take part in the wine and cheese reception held each evening in this four-star, four-diamond property's sumptuous lobby or dine in its dramatic French restaurant. Rooms have canopy beds and bamboo writing desks. You can take a free shuttle to the Financial District. Restaurant, bar, room service. In-room data ports. Video games. Exercise facility. Cable TV. Spa. Laundry service. Business services, parking (fee). Pets allowed (fee). | 501 Geary St. | 415/292–0100 or 800800/214–4220 | fax 415/292–0111 | www.monaco-sf.com | 201 rooms, 34 suites | $239–$299 rooms, $329–$429 suites | AE, D, DC, MC, V.

Pan Pacific. This contemporary tower blends Asian and American elements in a 17-story glass and brass atrium with fountain sculptures. Asian simplicity predominates in the rooms too, with muted colors, granite desks, and arched windows. It's two blocks from Union Square. Restaurant, bar, room service. In-room data ports, in-room safes, cable TV. Some saunas. Exercise equipment. Laundry service. Business services, parking (fee). Some pets allowed (fee). | 500 Post St. | 415/771–8600 or 800/533–6465 | fax 415/398–0267 | www.panpac.com | 330 rooms | $325–$425 | AE, D, DC, MC, V.

Park Hyatt. This 24-floor contemporary tower in the center of the Financial District connects to the Federal Building. The lobby has extravagant flower arrangements, in-laid wood accents and a library. Neo-Classical rooms have black granite bathrooms. Some have balconies with bay views. Restaurant, bar (entertainment), afternoon snacks, room service. Cable TV (and movies). Exercise equipment. Laundry service. Business services. Some pets allowed. | 333 Battery St. | 415/392–1234 | fax 415/421–2433 | 360 rooms, 37 suites | $445–$520 rooms, $520–$545 suites | AE, D, DC, MC, V.

★ **Prescott Hotel.** The lobby of this Edwardian-style hotel on Union Square has a brick hearth, Italian marble, stained glass, and watercolor paintings. You can relax fireside in the evening with complimentary coffee or wine. Deluxe rooms have cherry-wood furnishings. Club-level rooms have a private concierge service, complimentary breakfast, and cocktails. Through a partnership with Wolfgang Puck's Postrio, the extremely popular and always-booked restaurant within the hotel, you can reserve a table or order room service. Restaurant, bar, room service. In-room data ports, refrigerators, cable TV. Exercise equipment. Video games. Laundry service. Business services, parking (fee). | 545 Post St. | 415/563–0303 or 800/283–7322 | fax 415/563–6831 | www.prescotthotel.com | 164 rooms, 7 suites | $265 rooms, $255–$280 suites | AE, D, DC, MC, V.

Renaissance Parc Fifty-Five. This 32-floor hotel, geared toward convention and business travelers and two blocks from Union Square, has a grand lobby with granite statues and modern crystal chandeliers. Rooms have bay windows, some with excellent views of the city. Restaurants, bar, room service. In-room data ports, in-room safes, cable TV. Sauna. Exercise equipment. Laundry service. Business services, parking (fee). | 55 Cyril Magnin St. | 415/392–8000 | fax 415/392–4734. www.renaissancehotel.com/sfosr | 1,008 rooms, 18 suites | $269–$459 rooms, $550–$1,800 suites | AE, D, DC, MC, V.

Renaissance Stanford Court. This 1912 luxury hotel on Nob Hill was built on the property where railroad baron, governor, and university founder Leland Stanford made his home before the 1906 earthquake. Its interior courtyard has a glass dome, French antiques, and Baccarat chandeliers. Rooms have mahogany desks and carved chairs as well as views of the city and bay. You can catch a free shuttle to the Financial District. Restaurant, bars, room service. In-room data ports, cable TV. Exercise equipment. Laundry service. Business services, parking(fee). | 905 California St. | 415/989–3500 or 800/227–4736 | fax 415/391–0513 | www.renaissancehotels.com | 402 rooms, 18 suites | $359–$489 rooms, $675–$875 suites | AE, D, DC, MC, V.

★ **Ritz-Carlton, San Francisco.** This columned neo-Classical landmark built in 1909 has a polished marble lobby with museum-quality art and a classical sculpture garden at the rear. Rooms have Victorian furniture, marble bathrooms, sumptuous Egyptian sheets, and down duvets. In the club rooms, you can relax over complimentary breakfast, tea, or evening cordials. It's near the Financial District, Union Square, and Chinatown. Restaurants, bar (with entertainment), room service. In-room data ports, cable TV. Indoor pool. Hot tub, spa. Laundry service. Business services, parking (fee). | 600 Stockton St. | 415/296–7465 | fax 415/296–8559 | 336 rooms, 44 suites | $379–$459 rooms, $490–$590 suites | AE, D, DC, MC, V.

Sheraton At Fisherman's Wharf. This four-story contemporary hotel has the best location in Fisherman's Wharf, one block from the bay and pier. It has a nautical lobby with rich wood, running lights, and rich hues of red and blue. The rooms are modern, painted in a California contemporary style, with teals and peaches, modern wood furniture, and great views. Restaurant, bar, room service. In-room data ports, cable TV. Outdoor pool. Exercise equipment. Laundry service. Business service, parking (fee). | 2500 Mason St. | 415/362–5500 | fax 415/956–5275 | www.sheratonatthewharf.com | 518 rooms; 6 suites | $250–$280 rooms, $600 and up for suites | AE, D, DC, MC, V.

SAN FRANCISCO

INTRO
ATTRACTIONS
DINING
LODGING

Sheraton Palace Hotel. At the time of its construction in 1875 it was the largest luxury hotel in the world. Enrico Caruso, Woodrow Wilson, and Amelia Earhart stayed here. It's also famous for its Garden Court restaurant with marble columns and stained-glass ceiling. The lobby has vaulted ceilings, copious gilding, and original crystal chandeliers. Spacious rooms have antique poster beds and large windows. Restaurant, bar (with entertainment), room service. In-room data ports, refrigerators, cable TV (with movies). Indoor pool. Hot tub. Laundry service. Business services. | 637 Market St. | 415/392–8600 | fax 415/543–0671 | www.sheraton.com | 553 rooms, 34 suites | $440–$500 rooms, $675–$925 suites | AE, D, DC, MC, V.

★ **Sherman House.** This exclusive 1876 Victorian mansion in Pacific Heights is next to the "most crooked street in the world." Rooms have authentic period antiques and rugs, canopied beds, black granite bathrooms, and marble fireplaces. Some rooms with private gardens and rooftop decks. There is also a ½ acre English garden and gazebo. The inn is a block from public transportation. Dining room, room service. In-room data ports, cable TV, in-room VCR (and movies). Hot tub in most rooms. Parking (fee). | 2160 Green St. | 415/563–3600 or 800/424–5777 | fax 415/563–1882 | www.theshermanhouse.com | 8 rooms, 6 suites | $485–$545 rooms, $775–$1200 suites | AE, DC, MC, V.

Suites at Fisherman's Wharf. While the three-story concrete tower doesn't look like much on the outside, inside this waterfront lodging you'll find charming touches like French doors and a manually operated elevator. Its spacious rooms are good for families and it's one block away from Ghirardelli Square and the water. No air conditioning. In-room data ports, kitchenettes, microwaves, cable TV. Laundry service. Parking (fee). No smoking. | 2655 Hyde St. | 415/771–0200 or 800/227–3608 | fax 415/346–8058 | 24 kitchen suites | $279–$379 suites | AE, D, DC, MC, V.

SAN GABRIEL

MAP 9, G3

(Nearby towns also listed: Los Angeles, Pasadena)

Marking the 18th-century crossroads between trade and wagon routes from Old Mexico and a pioneer trail from the east, the Mission San Gabriel Arcangel grew up here, and eventually spawned this town. Today, San Gabriel, with 37,000 residents, has shed its largely agricultural roots and become a major bedroom community for Los Angeles, 11 mi east.

Information: **San Gabriel Chamber of Commerce** | 620 W. Santa Anita St., 91776 | 626/576–2525 | fax 626/289–2901.

Attractions

Mission San Gabriel Arcangel. Amidst the freeways and the train tracks, slip into the past here, where padres and Native Americans once tended huge herds of livestock. Note the 1771 mission's church tower, toppled by an earthquake in 1812 but later restored, and walk through the quiet gardens and graveyard. | 428 S. Mission Dr. | 626/457–3035 | $4 | Daily 9–1 and 2–8.

Dining

Pizza Place California. Italian. Look for the usual Italian suspects here—pastas, pizzas, salads—as well as seafood and meat specialties. Three-cheese baked penne is a favorite. The restaurant gets its styling from the region's Mission heritage, with stucco walls surrounding comfortable booths and tables. Outdoor dining is on an enclosed patio. Beer and wine only. | 303 S. Mission Dr. | 626/570–9655 | $9–$17 | MC, V.

Lodging

New Century Inn. This two-story motel, at Las Tunas Drive and Walnut Grove Avenue, is a 15-min drive east of downtown LA. Room access is via outside corridors. Complimentary breakfast. Outdoor pool. Laundry facilities. | 1114 E. Las Tunas Dr. | 626/285–0921 | fax 626/285–8391 | www.newcenturyinn.com | 42 rooms | $58–$60 | AE, MC, D, V.

SAN JOSE

MAP 3, D9

(Nearby towns also listed: Campbell, Cupertino, Los Gatos, Saratoga, Sunnyvale)

In 1777 San Jose was the place where crops grew and cattle fattened before being sent to soldiers stationed at the presidios in San Francisco and Monterey. The farms grew into a thriving town, and, in 1850, San Jose became the state's first capital city. Today, major technology-based companies have set up shop here, and San Jose is rightfully known as the "Capital of Silicon Valley." The city's architecture is a mix of modern and mission-style buildings and 19th-century Victorians.

Information: San Jose Convention and Visitors Bureau | 333 E. San Carlos St., Ste. 1000, 95110 | 408/977–0900 or 800/847–4875 | www.sanjose.org.

SAN JOSE

INTRO
ATTRACTIONS
DINING
LODGING

Attractions

Alum Rock Park. Mineral springs, designated trails, and the Youth Science Institute all make worthy stops in this 730-acre foothill park. Dogs are not permitted. | 16240 Alum Rock Ave. | 408/259–5477 | Free, parking $3 per car Memorial Day–Labor Day and weekends | Daily 8 to dusk.

You'll find a host of kid-friendly exhibits focusing on the natural sciences in the **Youth Science Institute,** part of Alum Rock Park. | 16260 Alum Rock Ave. | 408/258–4322 | 50 cents | Tues.–Sat. noon–4:30.

Children's Discovery Museum. In an angular purple building surrounded by Guadalupe Park, across the creek from the convention center, this museum has changing interactive exhibits and programs in science, humanities, and arts. | 180 Woz Way | 408/298–5437 | $6 | Tues.–Sat. 10–5, Sun. noon–5.

Kelley Park. A family park and zoo, a Japanese garden, a historical museum, a train ride, and picnic areas make up this 156-acre park, 4 mi south of downtown. | 1300 Senter Rd. | 408/277–4192 | Free, parking $4 in spring and summer and holidays | Daily 8 to dusk.

The family-oriented **Happy Hollow Park and Zoo** has a playground, riverboat replica, tree house, rides, and a zoo. | 1300 Senter Rd. | 408/277–4193 | $4.50 | Daily 10–5.

Korakuen Garden in Okayama, Japan, was the model for the two-level, 6½-acre **Japanese Friendship Garden,** with its bridges, lanterns, and waterfall. In spring, look for elegant cherry blossoms. Free guided tours are available. | 1500 Senter Rd. | 408/277–4192 | Free | Daily 10–dusk. Twenty-eight structures, including a Chinese temple, a printing press shop, and a trolley showcase the diverse history and culture of San Jose and the Santa Clara Valley at the **San Jose Historical Museum.** | 1650 Senter Rd. | 408/287–2290 | $6 | Tues.–Fri. 9–5, weekends noon–5.

Lick Observatory. On the 4,209-ft summit of Mt. Hamilton, the 1888 observatory, part of the University of California at Santa Cruz, perches high above Santa Clara Valley. The observatory offers guided tours of the Great Lick Refractor and you can also view the Shane Reflector from the Visitor's Gallery. For six weekends during the summer, the observatory allows limited telescope viewings. Locals love to head here when occasional snow shuts down the roadway; call ahead if winter weather looms. | Mt. Hamilton | 408/274–5061 | Free | Weekdays 12:30–5, weekends 10:00–4:30.

MACLA San Jose Center for Latino Arts. You can see exhibits, many with social or political themes, by Chicano and Latino artists. The gift shop sells collectibles and objects made by local artists. | 510 S. 1st St. | 408/998–2783 | www.artelatino.org | Free | Wed.-Sat. noon–7.

Mexican Heritage Plaza. In the Alum Rock neighborhood, this cultural center has a 500-seat theater, art gallery, classrooms, and office space for community arts groups. It all surrounds a landscaped Mexican-style plaza. | 1700 Alum Rock Ave. | 800/MHC–VIVA | Free | Daily.

Municipal Rose Garden. The gardens here have more than 5,000 plants, with 186 varieties of roses. Colors peak in May and June, but blooms scent the air all summer. | 1650 Emory St. | 408/277–5422 | Free | Daily dawn to dusk.

San Jose Sharks. See this National Hockey League (NHL) team at the 17,483-seat San Jose Arena, known to area fans as "the Shark Tank." | 525 W. Santa Clara St. | 408/287–7070 | www.sj-sharks.com | $17 and up | Sept.–Apr.

Overfelt Gardens. Walk along the arboreal trail and wildflower path, visit the fragrance garden, and relax by three small lakes. The 5-acre Chinese Cultural Garden has statues, memorials, and displays. | 408/251–3323 | Free | Daily 10 to dusk.

KODAK'S TIPS FOR PHOTOGRAPHING THE CITY

Streets
· Take a bus or walking tour to get acclimated
· Explore markets, streets, and parks
· Travel light so you can shoot quickly

City Vistas
· Find high vantage points to reveal city views
· Shoot early or late in the day, for best light
· At twilight, use fast films and bracket exposures

Formal Gardens
· Exploit high angles to show garden design
· Use wide-angle lenses to exaggerate depth and distance
· Arrive early to beat crowds

Landmarks and Monuments
· Review postcard racks for traditional views
· Seek out distant or unusual views
· Look for interesting vignettes or details

Museums
· Call in advance regarding photo restrictions
· Match film to light source when color is critical
· Bring several lenses or a zoom

Houses of Worship
· Shoot exteriors from nearby with a wide-angle lens
· Move away and include surroundings
· Switch to a very fast film indoors

Stained-Glass Windows
· Bright indirect sunlight yields saturated colors
· Expose for the glass not the surroundings
· Switch off flash to avoid glare

Architectural Details
· Move close to isolate details
· For distant vignettes, use a telephoto lens
· Use side light to accent form and texture

In the Marketplace
· Get up early to catch peak activity
· Search out colorful displays and colorful characters
· Don't scrimp on film

Stage Shows and Events
· Never use flash
· Shoot with fast (ISO 400 to 1000) film
· Use telephoto lenses
· Focus manually if necessary

From Kodak Guide to Shooting Great Travel Pictures © 2000 by Fodor's Travel Publications

Peralta Adobe and Fallon House. The 1797 Peralta Adobe, the last remaining structure from El Pueblo de San Jose de Guadalupe, has antiques and an *horno* (outside oven). The 1855 Fallon House is a Victorian mansion with 15 rooms and served then as the home to San Jose's seventh mayor, Thomas Fallon. | 175 W. St. John St. | 408/993–8182 | $6 | Tues.–Fri. 11–4, weekends noon–5; tours Tues.–Sun. 12:15–3:30.

Raging Waters. This 18-acre waterpark has slides, a 350,000-gallon Buccaneer Bay wave pool, and Pirate's Cove. | 2333 S. White Rd. | 408/654–5450 | www.rwsplash.com | $21.99 | June 11–Aug. 29, Mon.–Thurs. 10–6, Fri.–Sun. 10–7; May 22–June 6, Sept. 4–Sept. 19, weekends only 10–7.

Rosicrucian Park. Established in 1927, this 5-acre park with an Egyptian Museum and planetarium is North American headquarters of the Rosicrucian Order. | 1342 Naglee Ave. | 408/947–3600 | www.rosicrucian.org | $7 | Late June–Aug., Tues., Wed. and Fri.–Sun., 10–5; Thurs. 10–8, closed Mon.; Sept.–late June, daily 10–5.

★ See the West Coast's largest exhibit of mummies, sculptures, jewelry, and other objects from ancient Egyptian life, including a replica of an Egyptian rock tomb at the **Egyptian Museum** at the corner of Park and Naglee. Look, too, for Babylonian, Sumerian, and Assyrian artifacts. | 1342 Naglee Ave. | 408/947–3636 | www.rosicrucian.org | $7 | Late June–Aug., Tues., Wed. 10–5 and Fri.–Sun., 10–5, Thurs. 10–8, closed Mon.; Sept.–late June, daily 10–5.

San Jose Museum of Art. Built in 1892 by local architect Willoughby Edbrooke, this museum shows contemporary art exhibits, with text panels in several languages. | 110 S. Market St. | 408/294–2787 | $6 | Tues, Wed., Fri.–Sun. 10–5, Thurs. 10–8.

San Jose Museum of Quilts and Textiles. See changing exhibits of historical, traditional, and contemporary art quilts. | 110 Paseo de San Antonio | 408/971–0323 | www.sjquiltmuseum.org | $4 | Tues., Wed., Fri.–Sun 10–4, Thurs. 10–8.

The Tech Museum of Innovation. Tour four galleries with 300 exhibits on high-tech, communication, the human body, and exploration. There's also the Hackworth IMAX Dome Theater. | 145 W. San Carlos St. | 408/279–7150 | www.thetech.org | $8 (free 3rd Thurs. of month) | Memorial Day–Labor Day, Fri.–Wed. 10–6, Thurs. 10–9; Labor Day–Memorial Day, Tues.–Sun. 10–5.

Winchester Mystery House. Where to turn? It's anyone's guess in this bizarre Victorian mansion, built by the eccentric heiress to the Winchester Arms fortune. Her delusions of evil spirits drove her to build secret passages, 40 staircases, 2,000 doors, 10,000 windows, and innumerable false closets filling 160 rooms warmed by 47 fireplaces. | 525 S. Winchester Blvd. | 408/247–2101 | $13.95 | Jan., Feb., Nov., Dec., daily 9:30–4; Mar., Labor Day–Oct., daily 9–5; Apr.–mid-June, Sun.–Thurs. 9–5, Fri., Sat. 9–8; mid-June–Labor Day, daily 9–8.

Wineries. While much of the San Jose region's once-extensive agricultural fields have disappeared under dot.com headquarters and sprawling subdivisions, vestiges of the once booming produce businesses remain. A few wineries still produce vintages here, and offer tours.

At **Mirassou Winery,** get a glimpse of the area's former life as a major agricultural area at this family-run business, operating since 1854. Take a tour and sample vintages. | 3000 Aborn Rd. | 408/274–4000 or 408/274–4001 | www.mirassou.com | Free | Mon.–Sat. noon–5, Sun. noon–4.

J. Lohr Winery, built in 1974 on a former Falstaff Brewery site, gives tastings of wines from red- and white-wine grapes growing in Monterey County and nearby Paso Robles. | 1000 Lenzen Ave. | 408/288–5057 | www.jlohr.com | Free | Daily 10–5; tours, daily 11 and 2; tastings daily 10–5.

ON THE CALENDAR
JULY: *Mariachi Festival.* Mariachi music, folklorico dancing, food, arts and crafts, celebrate Mexican cultural heritage at this lively event, held in the Performing Arts Center

and at Guadalupe River Park. There's an evening of concerts on the second Sunday of the month. | 408/292–5197.

JULY: *Obon Festival.* The annual Japanese-American outdoor celebration held the weekend after Independence Day honors the deceased with hundreds of costumed dancers, Taiko drummers, games, crafts, and food. | 640 N. 5th St. | 408/293–9292.

JULY: *San Jose America Festival.* This 2-day Fourth of July celebration has music, dance, food, and folk crafts from many cultures, kids' games, and fireworks. | Guadalupe River Park | 408/298–6861.

AUG.: *San Jose Jazz Festival.* Be blue, be bee-bop, be jazzy at this 3-day festival. You'll also find arts and crafts and food stands on the second weekend in August at Plaza de Cesar Chavez Park. | 408/288–7557.

JULY–AUG.: *Santa Clara County Fair.* Live entertainment, game booths, educational and agricultural exhibits, carnival rides, and food booths make up this local fair at Santa Clara County Fairgrounds. | 408/494–FAIR.

SEPT.: *Tapestry in Talent's Festival of the Arts.* Labor Day weekend brings four stages of world music, jazz, country music, and rock 'n roll. There are also arts and crafts, international foods, and hands-on art activities. | 408/293–9728.

Dining

★ **Emile's.** French. White tablecloths, fresh flowers, crystal, and a sculpture unexpectedly gracing the ceiling create a dramatic setting here. Try house-cured gravlax, rack of lamb, or Grand Marnier soufflé. No smoking. | 545 S. 2nd St. | 408/289–1960 | www.emiles.com | Closed Sun., Mon. No lunch | $27–$35 | AE, DC, MC, V.

Fung Lum. Chinese. This family-run restaurant is a Bay Area staple, and has been here since the 1950s. You can eat in the main dining room or in one of the smaller rooms. Try the house specialties, which include salt-and-pepper crab or honey-walnut prawn in cream sauce. Sunday brunch. No smoking. | 1815 S. Bascom Ave. | 408/377–6956 | $12–$15 | AE, DC, MC, V.

Lou's Village. Seafood. The walls of the large dining room are lined with photos of musicians, singers, and other celebrities who have played here since 1946, back when Lou's was a nightclub. Eat at a booth or table, and try the Pacific salmon fillet or Maine lobster special. Kids' menu. No smoking. | 1465 W. San Carlos St. | 408/293–4570 | www.lousvillage.com | No lunch weekends | $17–$33 | AE, DC, MC, V.

Original Joe's. Italian. A corner restaurant with large windows, booths, and a counter, the menu here has more than 150 rib-sticking dishes. Try the veal parmesan, chicken piccata, and the rib steak. Kids' menu. | 301 S. 1st St. | 408/292–7030 | $12–$25 | AE, D, DC, MC, V.

Pea Soup Andersen's. American. Established in 1924, this is the first restaurant of this California chain, specializing in—you guessed it—split pea soup. Look for the windmill out front. Inside, the dining room seats 200. Try the signature soup, plus sandwiches and salads. Kids' menu. Sunday brunch. No smoking. | 12411 Rte. 33 S, Santa Nella | 209/826–1685 | Breakfast also available | $11–$17 | AE, D, DC, MC, V.

★ **71 Saint Peter.** Mediterranean. This could easily be the best restaurant in San Jose. Each dish is prepared with care, from the seafood linguine, a mix of clams, shrimp, and scallops in a basil tomato broth, to the roasted duck prepared in a raspberry–black pepper demiglace. | 71 N. San Pedro St. | 408/971–8523 | fax 408/938–3440 | $12.50–$23 | AE, D, DC, MC, V | Closed Sun. No lunch Sat.

Teske's Germania Restaurant. German. Buffalo, elk, moose, and boar heads stare down at you from the walls of the two Victorian-style dining rooms. Look for game specialties here—wild venison and boar—as well as Bavarian and Schwäbisch dishes. Lawyers and jurors from the nearby courthouse come here at lunch and there's a diverse crowd at night. The outdoor beer garden, with bubbling fountain, seats 100 and has live music and dancing in summer. | 255 N. 1st St. | 408/292–0291 | Closed Mon., Sunday. No lunch weekends | $15–$28 | AE, DC, MC, V.

Lodging

Best Western Gateway Inn. This two-story hotel is 15 min north of downtown and 1 mi from San Jose International Airport. Complimentary Continental breakfast. In-room data ports, microwaves, refrigerators, cable TV. Pool. Hot tub, sauna. Laundry service. Business services, airport shuttle. | 2585 Seaboard Ave. | 408/435–8800 | fax 408/435–8879 | www.bestwestern.com | 147 rooms | $89–$129 | AE, D, DC, MC, V.

Briar Rose Bed and Breakfast Inn. This 1875 inn is surrounded by a ½-acre of gardens, including a fountain. Rooms have antiques and feather mattresses. Complimentary breakfast. Pond. No smoking. | 897 E. Jackson St. | 408/279–5999 | www.briar-rose.com | 6 rooms | $110–$150 | AE, DC, MC, V.

Comfort Inn Airport South. This hotel is 1 mi north of the airport, 3 mi west of downtown. Complimentary Continental breakfast. In-room data ports, microwaves, refrigerators, cable TV, in-room VCRs. Pool. Business services. | 2118 Alameda | 408/243–2400 | fax 408/243–5478 | www.comfortinn.com | 40 rooms | $110–$150 | AE, D, DC, MC, V.

Courtyard by Marriott. Gardens surround the pool in this three-story hotel, aimed at business travelers heading for nearby computer corporations. Restaurant. In-room data ports, microwaves, some refrigerators, cable TV. Pool, hot tub. Gym. Laundry service. Business services. No smoking. | 10605 N. Wolfe Rd. | 408/252–9100 | fax 408/252–0632 | www.marriott.com | 149 rooms | $119–$249 | AE, D, DC, MC, V.

Crowne Plaza San Jose–Downtown. This 12-story hotel is downtown, 3 mi north of San Jose International Airport. Restaurant, room service. In-room data ports, cable TV. Gym. Business services, free parking. | 282 Almaden Blvd. | 408/998–0400 | fax 408/289–9081 | www.crowneplaza.com | 239 rooms | $109–$219 | AE, D, DC, MC, V.

Crowne Plaza San Jose/Silicon Valley. The 12-story hotel is at the junction of Route 237 and I–880, 7 mi from downtown San Jose and 5 mi from the San Jose Airport. There's an hors d'oeuvres and wine reception every Tuesday evening. Restaurant. In-room data ports, some refrigerators, cable TV. Pool. Sauna. Gym. Laundry service. Business services, free airport shuttle. | 777 Bellew Dr., Milpitas | 408/321–9500 | fax 408/321–7443 | www.crowneplaza.com | 285 rooms, 20 suites | $85–$189 | AE, D, DC, MC, V.

Doubletree. This multi-level hotel with two high-rise towers is downtown, ½-mi from the San Jose Airport, and a 45-min drive from San Francisco Airport. Restaurant. In-room data ports, refrigerators, cable TV. Pool. Hot tub, sauna. Gym. Business services, airport shuttle. Pets allowed. | 2050 Gateway Pl. | 408/453–4000 | fax 408/437–2898 | www.doubletree.com | 505 rooms, 10 suites | $89–$275 | AE, D, DC, MC, V.

★ **Fairmont San Jose.** Linked to the famous San Francisco hotel of the same name, this local landmark notches up the definition of luxury: rooms have down pillows and comforters, and oversize bath towels are changed not once but twice a day. Restaurant. In-room data ports, refrigerators, cable TV. Pool. Massage. Gym. Laundry service. Business services, parking (fee). | 170 S. Market St. | 408/998–1900 or 800/527–4727 | fax 408/287–1648 | www.fairmont.com | 541 rooms, 28 suites | $109–$259, $400–$500 1–bedroom suites, $1,300–$1,800 2–bedroom suites | AE, D, DC, MC, V.

Holiday Inn South San Jose. This three-floor, Mission-style hotel is 10 mi south of downtown and San Jose International airport. Restaurant. In-room data ports, cable TV. Pool. Gym. Laundry service. Business services, airport shuttle. | 399 Silicon Valley Blvd. | 408/972–7800 | fax 408/972–0157 | www.holiday-inn.com | 210 rooms | $79–$119 | AE, D, DC, MC, V.

Hotel de Anza. The penthouse of this 10-story Art Deco–style hotel, built in 1931, has a fireplace and two balconies. Rooms are decorated with contemporary art and some offer views of the downtown skyline. Restaurant, complimentary breakfast. In-room data ports, some in-room hot tubs, cable TV. Gym. Laundry service. Business services, airport shuttle, parking (fee). | 233 W. Santa Clara St. at Guadalupe Expressway | 408/286–1000 or 800/843–

3700 | fax 408/286–0500 | www.hoteldeanza.com | 101 rooms, 1 luxury suite | $170–$220 rooms, $950 suite | AE, DC, MC, V.

Hyatt Sainte Claire. This 1926 hotel is across from the convention center, 3 mi east of the airport. Restaurants. In-room data ports, room service, some in-room hot tubs, cable TV. Laundry service. Business services, airport shuttle, parking (fee). | 302 S. Market St. | 408/885–1234 or 800/223–1234 | fax 408/977–0403 | www.hyatt.com | 170 rooms, 17 suites | $255–$290, $375–$795 suites | AE, D, DC, MC, V.

Hyatt San Jose. The large hotel is on 17 acres of lush landscaping with a gazebo and pavilion. Restaurant. In-room data ports, some refrigerators. Pool. Gym. Laundry service. Business services, airport shuttle. | 1740 N. 1st St. | 408/993–1234 or 800/233–1234 | fax 408/453–0259 | www.hyattsanjose.com | 519 rooms | $259–$279 | AE, D, DC, MC, V.

Pruneyard Inn. Some of the rooms in this two-story, white-exterior inn with a circular drive have fireplaces. In-room data ports, some kitchenettes, microwaves, refrigerators, cable TV, in-room VCRs. Pool. Gym. Laundry service. Bicycles. Business services, airport shuttle. | 1995 S. Bascom Ave. | 408/559–4300 or 800/559–4344 | fax 408/559–9919 | pruneyardinn.com | 118 rooms, 2 suites | $99–$149, $265 suites | AE, D, DC, MC, V.

Radisson Plaza. An upscale hotel with circular drive, the lodging is 1½ mi east of the airport. Restaurant. In-room data ports, refrigerators, cable TV. Pool. Gym. Business services, airport shuttle, free parking. | 1471 N. 4th St. | 408/452–0200 or 800/333–3333 | fax 408/437–8819 | www.radisson.com | 185 rooms | $79–$179 | AE, D, DC, MC, V.

Residence Inn by Marriott. The apartment-style suites in this two-story hotel have living rooms and dining areas, and some have fireplaces. In-room data ports, kitchenettes, microwaves, refrigerators, cable TV. Pool. Bicycles. Laundry service. Business services, airport shuttle. Pets allowed. | 2761 S. Bascom Ave. | 408/559–1551 | fax 408/371–9808 | residenceinn.com | 80 suites | $79–$135 suites | AE, D, DC, MC, V.

Sheraton. The hotel has a landscaped pool and courtyard, and some suites have balconies. Restaurant. In-room data ports, refrigerators, Pool. Gym. Laundry facilities. Business services, airport shuttle. No smoking. | 1801 Barber La. | 408/943–0600 | fax 408/943–0484 | www.sheraton.com | 229 rooms, 24 suites | $99–$185, $209 suites | AE, D, DC, MC, V.

Summerfield Suites. This all-suite hotel with red-tile roof is off I–880 at U.S. 101, and 1 mi south of San Jose International Airport. Picnic area, complimentary Continental breakfast. Kitchenettes, cable TV, in-room VCRs. Pool. Hot tub. Gym. Laundry service. Business services, airport shuttle, free parking. Pets allowed (fee). | 1602 Crane Ct. | 408/436–1600 or 800/833–4353 | fax 408/436–1075 | www.summerfieldsuites.com | 114 suites | $99–$299 | AE, D, DC, MC, V.

The Wyndham. The front of this nine-story, downtown hotel sports jaunty red awnings over some street windows. Restaurant. Some refrigerators, cable TV. Pool. Exercise equipment. Laundry service. Business services, airport shuttle. | 1350 N. 1st St. | 408/453–6200 or 800/538–6818 | fax 408/437–9558 | www.wyndham.com | 355 rooms, 3 suites | $79–$229 rooms, $350 suites | AE, D, DC, MC, V.

SAN JUAN CAPISTRANO

MAP 4, J15

(Nearby towns also listed: Dana Point, Laguna Beach, Mission Viejo, San Clemente)

You can see the rolling hills, the Santa Ana range, and the Pacific Ocean here in one of southern California's historical districts, with several adobe structures. The main mission was built under the supervision of Father Junipero Serra. Today, it is the beacon for thousands of swallows that arrive in mid-March after a 6,000-mi flight from their wintering grounds.

Information: San Juan Capistrano Chamber of Commerce | 31781 Camino Capistrano, Franciscan Plaza, Ste. 306, 92693-1878 | 949/493–4700 | www.sanjuanchamber.com.

Attractions

Mission San Juan Capistrano. Founded by Father Junipero Serra in 1776, the mission originally had three churches, one still intact, at this museum showcasing the area history. | 949/234–1300 | $6 | Daily 8:30–5.

Dining

★ **Cedar Creek Inn.** Contemporary. Eat here on an outdoor patio with a roaring fireplace. Try ahi burgers, rack of lamb, and herb-crusted halibut. Kids' menu. No smoking. | 26860 Ortega Hwy. | 949/240–2229 | $28–$38 | AE, MC, V.

El Adobe de Capistrano. Tex-Mex. The front of this restaurant was built in 1797 as the town jail. The house specials are steaks, chicken, and some Mexican dishes. Sunday brunch. No smoking. | 31891 Camino Capistrano | 949/493–1163 | $16–$30 | AE, D, DC, MC, V.

★ **L'Hirondelle.** French. Dine in site of the mission from this restaurant's patio. Specialties include poulet Marie Antoinette (chicken in sherry cream sauce), and roast duck with orange, cherry, and green peppercorn sauce. Early-bird suppers. Sunday brunch. Beer and wine only. No smoking. | 31631 Camino Capistrano | 949/661–0425 | www.sjc.net/dining/L'Hirondelle/index.html | Closed Mon. | $12–$18 | AE, MC, V.

Ramos House Cafe. American. This outdoor café serves breakfast and lunch on a cobblestone patio. Dinner, served only during a full moon, is an elaborate, five-course meal. No smoking. | 31752 Los Rios St. | 949/443–1342 | Closed Mon. | $17–$26 | AE, D, DC, MC, V.

Lodging

Best Western Capistrano Inn. This two-story hotel overlooks Capistrano Valley, and is ¼-mi east of Mission San Juan Capistrano. Complimentary breakfast. In-room data ports, cable TV. Pool. Hot tub. Business services. Pets allowed. | 27174 Ortega Hwy. | 949/493–5661 | fax 949/661–8293 | www.bestwestern.com | 108 rooms | $79–$99 | AE, D, DC, MC, V.

SAN MARINO

MAP 9, G3

(Nearby towns also listed: Arcadia, San Gabriel)

This community of 13,000 lies north of San Gabriel and east of Pasadena. Originally part of the Mexican Land Grant of 1830, San Marino's first mayor was general George S. Patton, Sr.

Information: San Marino Chamber of Commerce, | 2304 Huntington Dr., Suite 202, 91108 | 626/286–1022 | www.smnet.org/comm_group/smcofc.

Attractions

El Molino Viejo. A former grist mill for the 1816 Mission San Gabriel, the mill was built by Native Americans, as directed by the padres. There's a working model of the mill, changing exhibits, and photographs. | 1120 Old Mill Rd. | 626/449–5458 | Free | Tues.–Sun. 1–4.

Huntington Library, Art Collections, and Botanical Gardens. This highly respected museum houses many treasures, including a Gutenberg bible, Ellesmere's manuscript of Chaucer's *Cantebury Tales,* and original manuscripts by William Shakespeare. The sweeping art collection spans two centuries (1730s–1930s), including paintings, furniture, and other works. Take the time to stroll through the 150 acres of beautiful gardens. | 1151 Oxford Rd. | 626/405–2141 or 626/405–2100 | $8.50 | Memorial Day–Labor Day, Tues.–Sun. 10:30–4:30; Labor Day–Memorial Day, Tues.–Fri. noon–4:30, weekends 10:30–4:30.

Dining

Colonial Kitchen. American. There's plenty to keep your eyes popping at this restaurant—decorations include a juke box, a big brass eagle, photos of Elvis, plus Hummel and Ladro figurines. The menu focuses on hearty fare, like Swiss steak, Southern-fried chicken, filet of trout, and carrot cake. Kids' menu. No smoking. | 1110 Huntington Dr. | 626/289–2449 | Breakfast also available | $14–$21 | D, MC, V.

SAN MATEO

MAP 6, C7

(Nearby towns also listed: Half Moon Bay, Hayward)

This San Francisco suburb, named for St. Matthew by the de Anza expedition when it passed through in 1776, hardly resembles the ranch land it once was. The first town lots were sold once the railroad came through in 1864. Long known for a hoof-pounding racetrack, San Mateo now has museums showcasing the environment and aviation, as well as theater and opera houses.

Information: San Mateo County Convention and Visitors Bureau | 111 Anza Blvd., Suite 410, Burlingame, 94010 | 650/348–7600 or 800/288–4748 | www.smccvb.com.

Attractions

Bay Meadows Racecourse. Opened in 1934, this is the longest continually operating horse-racing track in California. It's also where the daily-double, all-enclosed starting gate, and use of the photo-finish camera originated. | 2600 S. Delaware St. | 650/574–7223 | www.baymeadows.com | $3 | Call for hrs.

Coyote Point Museum. Interactive, kid-friendly exhibits teach about the San Francisco Bay shoreline habitat, why it's important, and what lives there. Exhibits include dioramas and mini-habitats, and a working beehive. Special programs are offered regularly. Picnicking is permitted; nature hikes, too. | 1651 Coyote Point Dr. | 650/342–7755 | http://www.coyoteptmuseum.org/ | $3 | Tues.–Sat. 10–5, Sun. noon–5.

Filoli. The TV series *Dynasty* used this spectacular 43-room Victorian mansion and its surrounding 654-acre estate as the setting for its fictional homestead. It's that grand. The facility, 15 mi south of San Mateo off I–280, focuses on horticulture, with flower shows, pruning demonstrations, and special classes scheduled almost daily. Holiday decorations inside and out are spectacular. You're welcome to stroll the 16 acres of formal gardens, then have a cup of Earl Grey or English Breakfast tea and a sweet in the mansion's Quail's Nest Cafe. Horse shows are also on the Filoli calendar. To get here from San Mateo, take the Edgewood Road exit off I–280, go west ¼ mi, then north on Cañada Road and continue 1¼ mi. | 86 Cañada Rd., Woodside | 650/364–2880 | www.filoli.org | $10 | Mid-Feb.–Oct., Tues.–Sat. 10–3 (last admission at 2); reservations required for guided tours.

Japanese Garden. The garden, designed by Nagao Sakurai, chief landscape architect at Tokyo's Imperial Palace, has koi ponds, waterfalls, pagoda, teahouse, and curving pathways through labelled species. It's in Central Park, on El Camino between 5th and 9th Avenues. | 650/522–7040 | Free | Weekdays 10–4, weekends 11–4.

Lacy Park. Bring your dog (on a leash less than 5-ft long or you'll be fined) to this 30-acre park with two walking loops, a 60-year-old rose arbor, six tennis courts, and a picnic area. | 1485 Virginia Rd. | www.smnet.org | Free weekdays, fee weekends for nonresidents | Closed Thanksgiving, Christmas Eve and Day, New Year's Eve and Day.

Woodside Store Historic Site. This living history museum, 20 mi south of San Mateo off I–280, was built in the 19th century by one of the area's early residents, Dr. Robert Tripp. The building housed one of the first country stores on the San Francisco Peninsula. | 3300 Tripp Rd., Woodside | 650/851–7615 | Free | Tues., Thurs. 10–4, weekends noon–4.

JULY: *Festa Italiana.* This month-long celebration has a softball tournament, winemaking contest, and street fairs. | 650/312–0730.
AUG.: *San Mateo County Fair and Floral Fiesta.* See garden exhibits, a home show, demonstrations, taste Mexican specialties, and watch live entertainment. | 415/574–FAIR.

Dining

Buffalo Grill. Contemporary. Terrazzo tiles, cherrywood, and marble embellish the inside of this restaurant. The menu has buffalo carpaccio with olive relish, grilled ahi tuna with eggplant and white beans, and maple-cured pork chops with spoon bread. No smoking. | 66 31st Ave. | 650/358–8777 | $20–$30 | MC, V.

Tapenade Mediterranean Grill. Mediterranean. Richly polished wood and tinted plaster walls fill the dining room of this grill in the Marriott San Mateo. The menu has dishes influenced by Provence and North Africa. No smoking. | 1770 S. Amphlett Blvd. | 650/653–6000 | $20–$30 | MC, V.

Lodging

Holiday Inn Express. The four-story hotel is 4 mi north of San Francisco International Airport. Complimentary Continental breakfast. In-room data ports, some refrigerators, cable TV. Laundry facilities. Business services, airport shuttle, free parking. | 350 N. Bayshore Blvd. | 650/344–6376 | fax 650/343–7108 | www.holiday-inn.com | 111 rooms, 4 suites | $100, $130 suites | AE, D, DC, MC, V.

Marriott San Mateo. This six-floor, white stucco building with a red-tile roof curves around this lodging's landscaped parking lot and grounds. The hotel, at the intersection of U.S. 101 and Route 92, is 7 mi south of San Francisco International Airport. Restaurant, bar, room service. Some refrigerators, cable TV. Pool. Exercise equipment. Laundry facilities, laundry service. Airport shuttle. Pets allowed (fee). | 1770 S. Amphlett Blvd. | 650/573–7661 or 800/ 843–6664 (outside CA), 800/238–6339 (CA) | fax 650/573–0533 | www.marriott.com | 316 rooms | $105–$145 | AE, MC, V.

Villa Hotel–Airport South. Restaurants, shopping, and entertainment are within 4 mi of this hotel, 8 mi south of San Francisco's airport. Restaurant, bar (with entertainment), room service. Some refrigerators, cable TV. Pool. Beauty salon. Exercise equipment. Business services, airport shuttle. Pets allowed. | 4000 S. El Camino Real | 650/341–0966 | fax 650/573–0164 | www.villahotel.com | 285 rooms | $89–$119 | AE, D, DC, MC, V.

SAN PEDRO

MAP 9, E7

(Nearby towns also listed: Long Beach, Redondo Beach, Seal Beach, Torrance)

This gritty industrial and residential harbor town of 71,000 contains one of the nation's largest deepwater ports, so many a cruise departs from here. Scores of boats of all sizes and shapes line the waterfront; away from the water, it's full of tidy, 1920s-era white clapboard homes. Sizable Greek and Yugoslavian communities lend a strong Mediterranean and Eastern European flavor. San Pedro was the home of the celebrated late poet and counterculture luminary Charles Bukowski.

Information: San Pedro Chamber of Commerce | 390 W. 7th St., 90731 | 310/832–7272 | chamberinfo@sanpedrochamber.com | www.sanpedrochamber.com.

Attractions

Cabrillo Marine Aquarium. Thirty-five saltwater aquariums allow you to see and feel the marine life of Southern California at this institution at Cabrillo Beach, between Pt. Fermin and the port of Los Angeles. The aquarium sponsors seasonal events like grunion and whale-watching tours. The tidepools of the Pt. Fermin Marine Life Refuge, a salt marsh, sandy beaches, and fossil-rich cliffs are all within walking distance. | 3720 Stephen White Dr. | 310/548–7562 | www.cabrillo.org | Free, $2 donation suggested, $6.50 parking | Tues.–Fri. noon–5, weekends 10–5.

Los Angeles Maritime Museum. An 18-ft-long model of the *Titanic,* pre-iceberg, is a high point here. Local nautical artifacts and memorabilia, including historical photographs and a 21-ft-long scale model of the *Queen Mary,* make up the rest of the exhibits. | Berth 84 at the foot of 6th St. | 310/548–7618 | By donation | Tues.–Sun. 10–5.

Ports o' Call Village. Shops, restaurants, and a museum fill this waterfront complex on Sampson Way, east of Harbor Boulevard, at the foot of 6th Street. | 310/732–7996 | Free | Daily.

Vincent Thomas Bridge. Named after a San Pedro street orphan who went on to become a state assemblyman, this is the first bridge of its kind to be constructed on pilings. Completed in 1963 and nicknamed "San Pedro's Golden Gate," the 6,050-ft suspension bridge welcomes visitors to Los Angeles and connects the Harbor and Long Beach freeways. | Hwys. 110 and 117 | 310/832–7272 | www.sanpedrochamber.com | Free | 24 hrs.

ON THE CALENDAR

JAN.–DEC.: *First Thursday.* Local artists, merchants, and chefs combine their creative energies to celebrate at this event, held—you guessed it—the first Thursday of every month. From 6 AM to 9 PM, artists give the town a jolt with open galleries and studios, painting events, and live music all over the city. | 310/832–7272 | www.sanpedro.com/first/happen/htm.

Dining

Babouch. Moroccan. Velvet couches, low brass tables, and colorful tapestries set the stage for dishes such as bastilla (lamb with honey and roasted almonds), and chicken with lemon. Kids' menu. | 810 S. Gaffey St. | 310/831–0246 | Closed Mon. No lunch | $8–$23 | AE, D, DC, MC, V.

22nd St. Landing. Seafood. Windows overlook Cabrillo Marina at this harborside restaurant where you dine on cherrywood tables beneath prints of fishermen. Seafood grilled over applewood is the specialty. Ono sautée (sautéed Hawaiian fish with shrimp, tomatoes, green onion, and garlic butter), bouillabaisse, and Fisherman's Platter (grilled shrimp, scallops, and swordfish served on brochettes with rice and vegetables) are some of the favorites. You can eat on the deck in nice weather. | 141 W. 22nd St. | 310/548–4400 | $19–$30 | AE, D, DC, MC, V.

Lodging

Best Western Sunrise. One mi south of the harbor terminal, this is a good place to stay if you're embarking on a cruise. The hotel will shuttle you to the cruise terminal. Complimentary Continental breakfast. Refrigerators, cable TV. Pool. Hot tub. No pets. | 525 S. Harbor Blvd. | 310/548–1080 | fax 310/519–0380 | www.bestwestern.com | 110 rooms | $65–$70 | AE, D, DC, MC, V.

Hilton. Overlooking Cabrillo Marina, this Italian Riviera–style hotel is ½ mi south of Cabrillo Beach and 2 mi from the World Cruise Center. Restaurant, bar. Cable TV. Pool. Beauty salon, hot tub. Tennis. Exercise equipment. Business services. No pets. | 2800 Via Cabrillo Marina | 310/514–3344 | fax 310/514–8945 | www.hilton.com | 226 rooms | $129–$169 | AE, D, DC, MC, V.

Holiday Inn San Pedro L.A. Harbor. At the south end of the harbor freeway (I–110), less than 1 mi from the Los Angeles World Trade Center, the hotel has high-ceilinged rooms with Victorian-style furnishings. Restaurant, room service. In-room data ports, refrigerators, cable TV. Pool. Laundry facilities. Business services. No pets. | 111 S. Gaffey St. | 310/514–1414 | fax 310/831–8262 | 60 rooms | $99–$149 | AE, D, DC, MC, V.

Pacific Inn and Suites. With Cabrillo Beach and Friendship Park on the same street, within 1 mi, this family-owned hotel makes a convenient option if you (and the kids) want to get out and play. The hotel has several large suites. No air-conditioning, kitchenettes, cable TV. Laundry facilities. No pets. | 516 W. 38th St. | 310/514–1247 | fax 310/831–5538 | 24 rooms, 8 suites | $55–$90 | AE, D, MC, V.

Sheraton Los Angeles Harbor. Across the street from Ports o' Call Village and the Maritime Museum, this hotel has many rooms with harbor views. Restaurant, bar (with entertainment). Cable TV. Pool. Hot tub. Exercise equipment. Laundry facilities. Business services. No pets. | 601 S. Palos Verdes St. | 310/519–8200 | fax 310/519–8421 | www.sheraton.com | 244 rooms, 56 suites | $138–$148, $168–$500 suites | AE, D, DC, MC, V.

Tasman Sea Motor Hotel. This no-frills lodging is 5 mi west of Point Fermin Park and the beach. Laundry facilities. | 29601 S. Western Ave. | 310/833–4431. No fax | 20 rooms | $50 | No credit cards.

Vagabond Inn. This four-story, exterior corridor hotel is 1 mi west of Ports O' Call Village. Complimentary Continental breakfast. Cable TV. Pool. Pets allowed. | 215 S. Gaffey St. | 310/831–8911 | fax 310/831–2649 | www.vagabondinns.com | 72 rooms | $65–$80 | AE, D, DC, MC, V.

SAN RAFAEL

MAP 3, C7

(Nearby towns also listed: Berkeley, San Francisco, Vallejo)

For years, San Rafael (pop. 54,500) was the hard-working county seat of affluent Marin County, north of San Francisco. In the midst of communities sprouting jaw-dropping mansions, this city clung to its blue-collar roots. In fact, the main drag (4th St., off U.S. 101) remained so all-American, with mom-and-pop hardware stores next to five-and-dimes, that local boy George Lucas chose it as a backdrop for scenes in his classic coming-of-age film, *American Graffiti*. Just as George and his empire have grown (he now runs, among other things, Industrial Light and Magic, still in San Rafael), so has the city. And, inevitably, some of the county's astounding affluence has rubbed off on San Rafael, too. But instead of being swallowed by boutique chains, the city has welcomed an eclectic mix of locally owned shops and restaurants. Low-key Mexican eateries rub shoulders with white-linen restaurants; magic stores and coffee houses lure browsers from newly spruced sidewalks. In another melding of old and new, the original Art Deco cinema is now an elegant, three-screen film center, showing art films and independent productions.

Information: San Rafael Chamber of Commerce | 817 Mission Ave., 94901 | 415/454–4163 | fax 415/454–7039 | srcc@sanrafael.org | www.sanrafael.org.

Attractions

China Camp State Park. Where Chinese fishermen once hauled shrimp nets from the north end of San Francisco Bay back in the 1880s, you can now hike or pedal mountain bikes through oak and redwood forests, and watch wildlife along the shoreline of this 1,512-acre park. Take N. San Pedro Road exit off U.S. 101 and head east 3 mi to the park. | N. San Pedro Rd. | 415/456–0766; campsite reservations (April through Oct.), 800/444–7275 | parks.ca.gov/north/marin/ccsp202.htm | 30 sites, $12. $1 day-use fee | Daily 8–sunset.

Falkirk Cultural Center. This 1888 "painted lady," a restored Queen Anne Victorian, was once the home of a local shipping magnate. Now, the 17-room mansion displays contemporary works from Bay Area artists. You're welcome to spread out a picnic blanket on the center's 11 manicured acres. | 1408 Mission St., at E St. | 415/485–3328 | www.falkirkculturalcenter.org | By donation | Grounds open dawn to dusk, house open weekdays 10–5 (Thurs. till 9), Sat. 10–1.

Marin County Civic Center. Master architect Frank Lloyd Wright was known for his efforts to link buildings to their environment, and he did that here, in his last major work and the only completed public administration building in his canon. The blue-roofed structure, a designated national and state historic landmark and completed in 1959, has two wings—one 880 ft long, the other nearly 600 ft long—which span low, tree-dotted hills. At their apex is a dramatic, 75-ft-wide dome, the roof of the county library. Self-guided tour details are available at the information window, open weekdays 9–3. Guided tours are also offered, $3, Wed. at 10 or by appointment. The center is 2 mi north of downtown, off U.S. 101 at N. San Pedro Rd. | 3501 Civic Center Dr. | 415/ 499–6646 | Free | Weekdays 9–6.

Mission San Rafael Arcángel. Founded in 1817, this was the second-to-last mission (out of 21) built by the Spanish *padres* as they traveled north into what was then called *Alta California*. Named after St. Raphael, the angel of healing, the mission was used to treat sick Native Americans from the neighboring mission in San Francisco. The current mission building, built here in 1949, stands on the site of the original hospital. It houses a museum. A large Catholic church and school are also on the grounds. | 5th Ave. and A St. | 415/456–3016 | By donation.

ON THE CALENDAR

JUNE: *Italian Street Painting Festival.* Wielding chalk instead of paintbrushes, hundreds of artists, toddlers, and professionals take part in this vibrant festival, when downtown streets turn into canvases. Over 50,000 people ogle at the asphalt gallery at this weekend celebration. Music keeps things lively; Italian foods keep things smelling like garlic. | 5th and A Sts. | 415/457–4878 | yia@youthinarts.org | www.youthinarts.org/ispf.htm.

Dining

Bamyan. Afghan. Owner Wahid Maher keeps everyone happy at this handsome restaurant in an otherwise nondescript strip mall. His wife, Nadia, creates traditional dishes from their homeland, including succulent kebabs. Try some of the more unusual offerings, such as *mantu,* dumplings filled with onions, ground beef, and topped with a vegetable sauce, or *aushak,* tender ravioli filled with scallions and topped with a mint-scented meat sauce. Note the Afghani ceremonial robes on display. | 227 3rd St., near Grant St., in Montecito Plaza | 415/453–8809 | fax 415/453–8809 | No lunch weekends | $6.95–$11.95 | MC, V.

Kasbah. Moroccan. Two brothers, one in the kitchen, one with guests in the two dining rooms, run this exotic eatery. The two-story structure looks a bit like a mosque from outside; inside, you'll find vaulted ceilings and walls draped with Persian carpets. Sink into a long banquette and watch belly dancers perform (Thurs.–Sun.) while you eat. Moroccan offerings come à la carte or in five-course meals: lentil and tomato soup, vegetable salads, pastilla (phyllo-wrapped chicken, almonds, and spices), kebabs, seafood, or other slow-cooked meats, couscous, dessert, and mint tea. | 200 Merrydale Rd. | 415/472–6666 | Reservations advised | No lunch. Closed Mon. | $13–$17 | AE, MC, V.

Lodging

Embassy Suites. You have a separate living room with contemporary furnishings in this five-story all-suite hotel, 3 mi north of downtown San Rafael and ¼ mi north of the Frank Lloyd Wright-designed Marin Civic Center. A waterfall is a focal point in the atrium lobby. Restaurant, bar, complimentary breakfast. In-room data ports, microwaves, refrigerators, cable TV. Indoor pool. Exercise equipment. Business services. | 101 McInnis Pkwy. | 415/499–9222 or 800/362–2779 | fax 415/499–9268 | www.embassy-suites.com | 235 suites | $209–$299 suites | AE, D, DC, MC, V.

Panama Hotel. Built in 1910, this two-story Victorian sports a flamboyant collection of past and present antiques mingling with garage-sale finds. It's kind of a "Key West meets Queen Victoria" look, with rooms ranging from the elegant Venetian Room (French doors opening onto a private balcony and claw-foot tub in the bath) to Ken's Safari, where mosquito netting drapes the queen bed and a ceiling fan slowly spins. Mimi's is a separate bungalow. The hotel, five blocks west of downtown, is in a quiet, leafy neighborhood. Some rooms have balconies or patios. The adjacent restaurant has live jazz Tues. and Thurs., and Sunday brunch. Restaurant. Complimentary Continental breakfast. Kitchenettes, some microwaves, refrigerators. Pets allowed. | 4 Bayview St. | 415/457–3993 or 800/899–3993 | www.panamahotel.com | 17 suites | $75–$160 | AE, MC, V.

SAN SIMEON

(Nearby towns also listed: Cambria, Morrow Bay)

San Simeon is best known as the home of the publisher William Randolph Hearst's pleasure palace, Hearst Castle, perched high on the bluffs 3 mi northwest of town. La Cuesta Encantada ("enchanted hill") may have brought government and cultural leaders and movie stars to the region, but today everyone can enjoy the little community's crystal-clear air, dramatic vistas, and friendly atmosphere. The seaside town is a popular stop along California Highway 1 for people traveling to and from the Big Sur Coast, 57 mi to the north.

Information: San Simeon Chamber of Commerce | 9255 Hearst Dr., Box 1, 93452 | 805/927–3500 | www.caohwy.com/s/sansimeo.htm.

Attractions

★ **Hearst Castle.** It took nearly 30 years to create the 165 rooms and 127 acres of this estate's flamboyant main mansion, guest cottages, gardens, terraces, pools, and walkways—and they were never officially completed. The buildings, an extravagent mix of Spanish, Moorish, French, and Italian styling, house the exhaustive collections of publisher and newspaper magnate William Randolph Hearst, the creative force behind this one-of-a-kind complex on the 250,000-acre ranch he inherited from his father, George. Hearst's collections, donated to the state in 1958, are largely intact and on display—from valuable artworks, to massive antiques, to the ketchup bottle he used to use on his morning eggs. Once the hang-out of the movie elite, it's easy to imagine Tyrone Power slipping into the deep end of the statue-encircled outdoor pool. Reservations for the tours are a must. | 750 Hearst Castle Rd. | 805/927–2020 or 800/444–4445 | www.hearstcastle.org | $10 | 4 tours daily 8:20 AM–3:20 PM, evening hours vary.

William Randolph Hearst Memorial State Beach. This protected cove offers sunbathing, beach-combing, pier fishing, and deep-sea fishing from charter boats. The entrance is directly across from the Hearst Castle entrance off California Highway 1. | Rte. 1 | 805/927–2020 | cal-parks.ca.gov/central/sansimeon | Daily, dawn to dusk.

Dining

Cavalier Restaurant. American. Part of the Best Western Cavalier Resort, this eatery offers spectacular ocean views from large picture windows. A wide array of American cuisine is served, from steaks to baked snapper, served with Central Coast wines. | 9435 Hearst Dr. | 805/927–3276 | $15–$25 | AC, D, DC, MC, V.

El Chorlito Mexican Restaurant. Mexican. Decorated with Mexican paintings and artwork, this popular cantina has been in the same location for over two decades, serving up delicious Mexican food with a distinct California/New Mexico flare. Expect fresh ingredients and creative creations. Popular items include the fajitas and chiles rellenos. | 9155 Hearst Dr. | 805/927–3872 | $8–$15 | MC, V.

San Simeon Beach Bar and Grill. American. You can see the ocean from every table in this casual family-oriented eatery, and you can even hear the breakers from the outdoor patio. The wide-ranging menu includes pizza, pasta, lobster, and prime rib. Try a bottle of local wine. There's also a lively sports bar. Kids' menu. | 9520 Castillo Dr. | 805/927–4604 | fax 805/927–5840 | $16–$40 | AE, D, MC, V.

Lodging

★ **Best Western Cavalier Oceanfront Resort.** This family-owned resort offers the only oceanfront accommodations in the area. Most rooms have great ocean views and some have private patios, wood-burning fireplaces, and wet bars. Restaurant. In-room data ports, refrigerators, cable TV. Pool. Hot tub. | 9415 Hearst Dr. | 800/826–8168 or 805/927–4688 | fax 805/927–6472 | www.cavalierresort.com | $99–$135 | AE, D, DC, MC, V.

El Rey Garden Inn. Rooms are designed with a comfortable, country-style decor, and many have fireplaces and double whirlpool tubs, wet bar, and free movies. Comfortable beds, coffee makers, and tables and chairs provide a homey touch. Restaurant. Refrigerators. Pool. Hot tub. | 9260 Castillo Dr. | 805/927–3998 or 800/821–7914 | www.elreygardeninn.com | $69–$179 | AE, D, DC, MC, V.

Sands by the Sea. This family-operated motel offers friendly, personalized service. Rooms are spacious and modern, and can be linked to create family suites. There's easy beach access. Complimentary Continental breakfast. Indoor pool. | 9355 Hearst Dr. | 800/444–0779 or 805/927–3243 | www.sandsmotel.com | 33 rooms | $75–$129 | AE, D, MC, V.

SAN YSIDRO

MAP 4, K17

(Nearby towns also listed: Chula Vista, Coronado, San Diego, Tijuana)

This somewhat forlorn bordertown, gateway to Tijuana, is 14 mi from San Diego and home to the San Diego Factory Outlet, which includes more than 30 brand-name stores and two duty-free shops near the border.

In the early 20th century, San Ysidro was called the Little Landers Colony after a "back to the land" settlement begun by William Smythe, which eventually included 150 inhabitants. The town was renamed San Ysidro in honor of the patron saint of farmers. According to legend, the saint was a virtuous farmer whose fields were plowed by angels.

Information: **San Ysidro Chamber of Commerce** | 663 E. San Ysidro Blvd., 92173 | 619/428–1281 | www.sanysidrochamber.org.

Attractions

San Diego Factory Outlet. This complex of 35 brand-name stores, with goods up to 70 percent off retail, is on I–5. It's a few hundred feet from the U.S./Mexico border, and the steady traffic from both sides of the border translates to about 35 million customers a year. | 4498-B Camino de la Plaza | 619/690–2999 | Free | Weekdays 10–8, Sat. 10–7, Sun. 10–6.

ON THE CALENDAR

MAY: *Dia de San Ysidro.* A day to celebrate the city and its culture, with food, entertainment, and games. | 619/428–1281.

Dining

Guadalajara de Noche. Mexican. You're not going to get more authentic Mexican food without passing through customs. Try carne asada and the assorted burritos. | 111 W. Olive Dr., #50 | 619/428–2623 | $6–$14 | No credit cards.

Lodging

Americana Inn and Suites. This two-story motel is 5 blocks southeast of the Iris San Diego trolley stop. Complimentary Continental breakfast. Refrigerators, cable TV. Pool. Hot tub. Laundry facilities. | 815 W. San Ysidro Blvd. | 619/428–5521 or 800/553–3933 | fax 619/428–0693 | 125 rooms, 15 suites | $48, $75 suites | AE, D, DC, MC, V.

Economy Motel. This two-story motel is 1 mi from the Mexican border. Cable TV. Pool. Pets allowed. | 230 Via de San Ysidro | 619/428–6191 | fax 619/428–0068 | 120 rooms | $39–$47 | AE, D, MC, V.

International Motor Inn. This motor inn is 1 mi from the Mexican border. Some kitchenettes, refrigerators, cable TV. Pool. Hot tub. Laundry facilities. Business services. Pets allowed. | 190 E. Calle Primera | 619/428–4486 | fax 619/428–3618 | 127 rooms, 35 suites | $65, $75 suites | AE, D, DC, MC, V.

Ramada Limited. This three-story standard hotel has a shopping center adjacent, and Mexican and fast-food restaurants ½-mi away. In-room data ports, cable TV. Pool. Exercise equipment. Laundry facilities. Pets allowed (fee). | 930 W. San Ysidro Blvd. | 619/690–2633 or 888/298–2054 | fax 619/690–1360 | www.ramada.com | 68 rooms | $60–$90 | AE, D, DC, MC, V.

Travelodge. This four-story chain hotel is 11 mi from San Diego airport, 7 mi from Tijuana airport, just off I–5. Cable TV. Laundry service. Pets allowed (fee). | 643 E. San Ysidro Blvd. | 619/428–2800 or 888/515–6375 | fax 619/428–8136 | www.travelodge.com | 68 rooms | $40–$60 | AE, D, DC, MC, V.

SANTA ANA

MAP 4, J15

(Nearby towns also listed: Anaheim, Irvine, Mission Viejo)

On July 26, 1769, Don Gaspár de Portolá, a Spanish expedition party leader, came across a picturesque valley and river in southern California, which he christened Santa Ana in honor of Saint Anne. Originally developed as an agricultural area, Santa Ana has grown into the largest city in Orange County, with a population nudging toward 300,000. For a taste of the Old World, check out the South Coast Plaza at Bear Street, as well as Sunflower Avenue, with its Euro-style marketplace.

Information: Santa Ana Chamber of Commerce | 1055 N. Main St., Ste. 904, 92701 | 714/541–5353 | saccinfo@santaanacc.com | www.santaanacc.com.

Attractions

The Bowers Kidseum. Interactive exhibits encourage kids to explore art and different cultures, next to the Bowers Museum of Cultural Art. | 1802 N. Main St. | 714/480–1520 | fax 714/480–0053 | www.bowers.org | $8 | Weekends 10–4.

The Bowers Museum of Cultural Art. Art from the Pacific Rim, Africa, and the Americas fills the galleries in this Mission-style building. | 2002 N. Main St. | 714/567–3600 | www.bowers.org | $6 | Tues., Wed., Fri.–Sun. 10–4, Thur. 10–9.

Discovery Cube. "The amusement park for your mind," where you can lie on a bed of 3,500 steel nails, take a picture of yourself with an infrared camera, feel an earthquake, and make your hair stand on end with the Van de Graaf generator. The "look but don't touch" rule doesn't apply here. | 2500 N. Main St. | 714/542–CUBE | www.discoverycube.org | $9.50, parking $3 | Daily 10–5.

Santa Ana Zoo at Prentice Park. Monkeys, mountain lions, exotic birds, and iguanas are some of the animals you can see in re-created natural habitats here. | 1801 E. Chestnut

Ave. | 714/835–7484 | $3.50 | Memorial Day–Labor Day, daily 10–5; Labor Day–Memorial Day, daily 10–4.

ON THE CALENDAR

JAN.–DEC.: *Artists Village Open House*. On the first Saturday of every month, downtown Santa Ana comes alive at art galleries, theaters, and restaurants. A large number of local artists open their studios to the public and serve snacks and wine. | 714/571–4229 | www.santaanacc.com.

Dining

Antonello. Italian. Beneath vine frescos and chandeliers, the staff of this white-linen restaurant serves Northern Italian classics like saltimbocca alla Romana (veal scaloppine topped with sage and prosciutto in a white wine demiglace) and raviolletti di Mamma Pina (mini-veal raviolis in homemade bolognese sauce). | 1611 Sunflower Ave. | 714/751–7153 | Reservations essential | Jacket required | Closed Sun. | $13–$35 | AE, DC, MC, V.

★ **Gustaf Anders.** Swedish. Across from the South Coast Plaza Village, this elegant restaurant serves gravlax, herring, and filet of beef prepared with Stilton cheese, a red-wine sauce, and creamed morel mushrooms. Next door is the more casual, less expensive Gustaf Anders' Back Pocket, where a wood stove and rotisserie turn out simpler fare. | 3851 Bear St., Ste. B | 714/668–1737 | $18–$25 | AE, DC, MC, V.

Olde Ship. English. This British-owned and operated pub proudly flies the Union Jack. Get the fish and chips and a pint, or a ploughman's lunch. | 1120 W. 17th St. | 714/550–6700 | www.theoldeship.com | $7–$12 | MC, V.

Topaz Cafe. Southwestern. A Zuni Indian influence dominates the menu at this eatery in the Bowers Museum. In an open kitchen, chefs prepare spicy and imaginative dishes, like sweet corn chicken tamale and salmon wrapped in corn husk with cilantro pesto. Live entertainment on Sundays. Sunday brunch. Kids' menu. | 2002 N. Main St. | 714/835–2002 | $14–$25 | AE, DC, MC, V.

Lodging

Best Western Orange County Airport North. This three-story motel, 3 mi from the South Coast Plaza Shopping Mall, has a free shuttle to Disneyland. Restaurants, bars, complimentary breakfast. In-room data ports, some microwaves, refrigerators, cable TV. Pool. Exercise equipment. Laundry service. Business services, airport shuttle, free parking. | 2700 Hotel Terrace Dr. | 714/432–8888 or 800/432–0053 | fax 714/424–6228 | www.bestwestern.com | 148 rooms | $70–$90 | AE, D, DC, MC, V.

Comfort Suites John Wayne Airport. Off U.S. 55 N., this hotel is 1½ mi northeast of John Wayne/Orange County Airport and 12 mi south of Knott's Berry Farm. Complimentary Continental breakfast. In-room data ports, refrigerators, cable TV. Pool. Hot tub. Laundry facilities. Business services, airport shuttle. | 2620 Hotel Terrace Dr. | 714/966–5200 | fax 714/979–9650 | www.comfortinn.com | 130 suites | $59–$69 suites | AE, D, DC, MC, V.

Doubletree Club–Orange County Airport. In the Hutton Centre Business Park, this hotel is beside a small lake 1½ mi north of John Wayne/Orange County Airport and 1⅓ mi east of the South Coast Plaza Shopping Center. Restaurant, bar, room service. In-room data ports, refrigerators, cable TV. Pool. Hot tub. Exercise equipment. Business services, airport shuttle. | 7 Hutton Centre Dr. | 714/751–2400 | fax 714/662–7935 | www.doubletree.com | 167 rooms | $109–$129 | AE, D, DC, MC, V.

Embassy Suites–Orange County Airport North. Suites, each with two rooms and at least 500 square ft, open onto a 10-story atrium at this hotel, off U.S. 55 N., 1½ mi north of John Wayne/Orange County Airport. Restaurant, bar (with entertainment), room service. In-room data ports, microwaves, refrigerators, cable TV. Pool. Hot tub, sauna. Laundry facilities, laundry service. Business services, airport shuttle. | 1325 E. Dyer Rd. | 714/241–3800 | fax 714/662–1651 | www.winhotel.com | 300 suites | $99–$154 suites | AE, D, DC, MC, V.

Holiday Inn at Orange County Airport. Off U.S. 55, this three-story white hotel is 1½ mi north of John Wayne/Orange County Airport. Restaurant, bar, room service. In-room data ports, some refrigerators, cable TV. Pool. Hot tub. Exercise equipment. Laundry facilities. Business services, airport shuttle. | 2726 S. Grand Ave. | 714/966–1955 | fax 714/966–1889 | www.holiday-inn.com | 175 rooms | $109–$129 | AE, D, DC, MC, V.

Quality Suites. A stone fountain, fireplace, and cathedral ceilings distinguish the lobby of this three-story, all-suites hotel, off U.S. 55-N, 1½ mi north of John Wayne/Orange County Airport. Bar, complimentary breakfast. In-room data ports, microwaves, refrigerators, cable TV, in-room VCRs (and movies). Pool. Hot tub. Laundry facilities. Business services, airport shuttle. | 2701 Hotel Terrace Dr. | 714/957–9200 | fax 714/641–8936 | www.qualityinn.com | 177 suites | $89–$150 suites | AE, D, DC, MC, V.

Radisson Suite Hotel–Santa Ana. This four-story, all-suites hotel is 10 mi south of Disneyland and 3 mi north of Newport Beach. The restaurant is open for breakfast only. Restaurant, complimentary breakfast. Some in-room hot tubs, cable TV. Pool. Outdoor hot tub. Laundry service. Business services, airport shuttle, free parking. | 2720 Hotel Terrace Dr. | 714/556–3838 or 800/333–3333 | fax 714/241–1008 | www.radisson.com | 122 suites | $99–$219 suites | AE, D, DC, MC, V.

SANTA BARBARA

MAP 4, G14

(Nearby towns also listed: Ojai, Solvang, Ventura)

Santa Barbara has long been an oasis for Los Angeles residents, a quick R&R escape less than 100 mi north of the City of Angels. From ocean waves along the waterfront to the south, to soft light in the Santa Ynez range to the northeast, the city is cradled by natural splendor. Add to that a dynamic mix of history (a mission and early California buildings), boutique shopping, stunning homes, and a lively arts community, and you've got an exceptional destination, no matter where you're coming from.

Information: **Santa Barbara Conference and Visitors Bureau** | 12 East Carrillo St., 93101 | 805/966–9222 or 800/549–5133 | tourism@santabarbaraca.com | www.santabarbaraca.com.

Attractions

El Presidio State Historic Park. Founded in 1782, the Presidio was one of four military strongholds established by the Spanish along the California coast and served that purpose until 1846. The guardhouse, *El Cuartel*, one of the two original structures that remain of the complex, is the oldest building owned by the state. | 123 El Cañon Perdido St. | 805/965–0093 | www.sbthp.org/home.htm | Free | Daily 10:30–4:30.

★ **Mission Santa Barbara.** The architecture and layout of this "Queen of Missions," established in 1786, evolved from adobe-brick buildings with thatched roofs to more permanent structures as its population ballooned. An 1812 earthquake destroyed the third church built on the site. Its replacement, which has stood since then, is a still-working Catholic church, though it also served a stint as a boys school and seminary since mission times. Cacti, palms, and succulents flourish in the gardens. | 2201 Laguna St. | 805/682–4713 | www.californiamissions.com/cahistory/santabarbara.html | $4 | Daily 9–5.

★ **Santa Barbara County Courthouse.** Hand-painted tiles and a spiral staircase infuse the courthouse with the grandeur of a Moorish palace. Ride the elevator to an arched observation area in the courthouse tower to get a panoramic view of the city. | 1100 Anacapa St. | 805/962–6464 | Free | Daily 8:30–4:45; free 1-hr guided tours, Fridays at 10:30, Mon.–Sat. at 2.

Santa Barbara Zoological Gardens. More than 600 animals, a carousel, and a miniature train ride cover 30 acres overlooking East Beach. | 500 Ninos Dr. | 805/962–6310 | www.santabarbarazoo.org | $7 | Daily 10–5.

ON THE CALENDAR

JUNE: *Lompoc Valley Flower Festival.* This five-day event, 50 mi north of Santa Barbara, comes at the height of the blooming season, in a town known for its extensive flower fields. Enjoy a parade with bands, horses, drill teams, clowns, and flower floats. There are also carnival rides, tours of the fields, and a plethora of food booths. | 805/735–8511 | www.flowerfestival.org | Free.

Dining

Andria's Harborside Restaurant. Seafood. Go for a superb view of the harbor, creamy clam chowder, and fresh oysters. There's nightly entertainment at the piano bar. | 336 W. Cabrillo Blvd. | 805/966–3000 | $16–$23 | AE, D, DC, MC, V.

Arigato Sushi. Japanese. The chef makes 25 kinds of sushi rolls at this tiny, hip eatery, where changing art exhibits adorn the walls. Try the seaweed salad and local sea urchin. | 11 W. Victoria St. | 805/965–6074 | Reservations not accepted | $8–$20 | AE, MC, V.

Bouchon. Continental. Bouchon means "cork," and this intimate, upscale restaurant showcases a large selection of wines. The open kitchen lets you watch as chefs prepare dishes including braised rabbit, veal chops with asparagus, and the trademark choice, molasses-glazed pork tenderloin. | 9 W. Victoria St. | 805/730–1160 | No lunch | $18–$30 | AE, MC, V.

Brigitte's. Contemporary. This lively café serves local wines at affordable prices. The individual pizzas are popular, as are the pastas, grilled fresh fish, and roast lamb. | 1325–1327 State St. | 805/966–9676 | No lunch Sun. | $9–$19 | AE, D, DC, MC, V.

Brophy Bros. Seafood. The outdoor tables at this casual restaurant have unimpeded views of the harbor and fishing vessels. The seafood plates are enormous, with fish fresh off the boats. Great for lunch. | 119 Harbor Way | 805/966–4418 | Reservations not accepted | $8–$19 | AE, MC, V.

Cafe Buenos Aires. Argentine. Salads, sandwiches, pastas, and traditional *empanadas* (turnovers filled with chicken, beef, or vegetables) are on the lunch menu at this downtown eatery. Dinner includes potato omelettes, Spanish red sausage in beer, octopus stewed with tomato and onion, and grilled rib-eye steak, imported from Argentina. | 1316 State St. | 805/963–0242 | $13–$20 | AE, DC, MC, V.

★ **Citronelle.** French. At this offspring of chef Michel Richard's Citrus in Los Angeles, the lamb loin with couscous and cumin sauce and the seared ahi tuna with an Anaheim chili sauce showcase his bold approach to flavor. You can watch the sunset from the dining room's picture windows with views of the Pacific. For dessert try the chocolate truffle surprise or the chocolate hazelnut bars. | 901 E. Cabrillo Blvd. | 805/966–2285 or 800/231–0431 | Reservations essential | $23–$28 | AE, D, MC, V.

D'Angelo. Café. The bread served by many of Santa Barbara's best restaurants comes from the ovens of this bakery, which has a few indoor and outdoor tables. Come for breakfast—try the brioches—or for a sandwich or afternoon pastry break. | 25 W. Gutierrez St. | 805/962–5466 | Weekdays 7–6, weekends 7–3 | No dinner | $1–$10 | MC, V.

Emilio's Ristorante and Bar. Italian. Ravioli stuffed with butternut squash and potato gnocchi with rock shrimp share the menu with other northern Italian dishes at this harborside restaurant. During the week two prix-fixe wine-tasting menus are available. | 324 W. Cabrillo Blvd. | 805/966–4426 | No lunch | $15–$35 | AE, D, MC, V.

Harbor Restaurant. American. A place on the pier with great views, the bar and grill upstairs serves sandwiches, large salads, and finger-lickin' appetizers; on a sunny day the outdoor terrace is a glorious spot. Downstairs you can get seafood, prime rib, and steaks. | 210 Stearns Wharf | 805/963–3311 | $16–$40 | AE, MC, V.

★ **La Super-Rica.** Mexican. This food stand with a patio serves some of the spiciest Mexican dishes from LA to San Francisco. Fans drive for miles to dig into soft tacos and incredible beans. | 622 N. Milpas St., at Alphonse St. | 805/963–4940 | $4–$8 | No credit cards.

Montecito Cafe. Contemporary. Contemporary paintings decorate the dining area of this casual spot. The menu includes fresh fish, grilled chicken, steak, pasta, salads, and lamb dishes. | 1295 Coast Village Rd. | 805/969–3392 | $15–$25 | AE, MC, V.

Nepenthe. American. You can just imagine the view from this place atop an 800-ft-high cliff overlooking lush meadows and the ocean on California Highway One. Orson Welles once called this home. Fare is straightforward—roast chicken, sandwiches, and hamburgers. | Rte. 1 | 831/667–2345 | $11–$26 | AE, MC, V.

Palace Grill. Cajun/Creole. Hardwood tables and Caribbean-style paintings decorate the Palace. The chef has won acclaim for blackened redfish, jambalaya with dirty rice, and Caribbean fare like delicious coconut shrimp. Be prepared to wait as long as 45 min on weekends. | 8 E. Cota St. | 805/963–5000 | $9–$25 | AE, MC, V.

Palazzio. Italian. The ceiling in this restaurant, where generous portions of pasta standards are the rule, has been embellished with a replica of the Sistine Chapel. On Saturday nights, the staff sings "That's Amore." Wine consumption is on the honor system—you keep a crayon tally on your paper tablecloth. | 1026 State St. | 805/564–1985 | No lunch Sun. | $9–$16 | AE, MC, V.

Roy. Contemporary. Owner-chef Leroy Gandy serves a $15 prix-fixe dinner that includes a small salad, fresh soup, and a tempting roster of main courses in this downtown storefront restaurant. Expect a 20-min wait on weekends. | 7 W. Carrillo St. | 805/966–5636 | $15 | AE, D, DC, MC, V.

Stonehouse Restaurant. Contemporary. What was, in 1889, a citrus packing house has been transformed into an elegant and bright eatery boasting the imaginative touch of executive chef Jamie West. Entrées like grilled swordfish served over ginger risotto or citrus-braised Maine lobster on sweet corn risotto are vibrant enough to rival the astonishing beauty of the San Ysidro Ranch, in which the restaurant is located. | 900 San Ysidro La. | 805/969–4100 or 800/368–6788 | Breakfast also served | $21–$39 | AE, D, DC, MC, V.

Trattoria Mollie's. Italian. Ethiopian-born chef-owner Mollie Ahlstrand spent several years in Italy refining the subtly flavored seafood and pasta preparations served in this dining room filled with potted plants. | 1250 Coast Village Rd. | 805/565–9381 | Reservations essential | Closed Mon. | $16–$27 | AE, MC, V.

★ **Wine Cask.** Continental. Sautéed swordfish and Colorado lamb sirloin, each prepared with a wine-based sauce, are among the most popular entrées in this dining room with exposed beams and abstract art on the walls. The outdoor patio, lush with plants and a water fountain, is one of the most romantic dining spots in town. | 813 Anacapa St. | 805/966–9463 | Reservations essential | $14–$27 | AE, DC, MC, V.

Lodging

Cabrillo Inn at the Beach and Spanish Vacation Cottages. The second-floor sundecks have great views, and you're a half-block from East Beach and 1 mi from Stearns Wharf and downtown. A bike path runs in front of the inn, and the zoo is 1 mi east. Cottages are also available week by week. Complimentary Continental breakfast. No air conditioning, some kitchenettes, some refrigerators, cable TV, some in-room VCRs. Pool. | 931 E. Cabrillo Blvd. | 805/966–1641 or 800/648–6708, cottage rental 805/963–6774 | fax 805/965–1623 | www.cabrillo-inn.com | 39 rooms, 2 cottages | rooms $109–$179, $189–$249 suites, $2,520 per week for cottages | AE, D, MC, V.

Casa del Mar Inn. Terra-cotta tile roofs and a leafy courtyard highlight this inn, a half-block from the beach and harbor and two blocks from Stearns Wharf. Lodgings include some family-size units with fireplaces and kitchens. Complimentary Continental breakfast. In-room data ports, some kitchenettes, cable TV. Hot tub. Business services. Pets allowed (fee). | 18 Bath St. | 805/963–4418 or 800/433–3097 | fax 805/966–4240 | www.casadelmar.com | 21 rooms | $119–$249 | AE, D, DC, MC, V.

Cheshire Cat. Fireplaces, hot tubs, and private decks complement the period antiques and Laura Ashley prints that fill the rooms of this Victorian inn, surrounded by gardens and patios. Shops and restaurants are four blocks south. Complimentary breakfast. Microwaves, some in-room hot tubs, some in-room VCRs (and movies). Hot tub. Business services. | 36 W. Valerio St. | 805/569–1610 | fax 805/682–1876 | cheshire@cheshirecat.com | www.cheshire-cat.com | 18 rooms, 3 cottages | $140–$300 rooms, $300–$350 cottages | AE, D, MC, V.

Coast Village Inn. In the seaside community of Montecito, 1 mi east of Santa Barbara, this two-story inn is two blocks from the ocean. Rooms, some of which have views of the water, have pine furniture. Complimentary Continental breakfast. No air-conditioning, some kitchenettes, cable TV. Pool. Business services. No smoking. | 1188 Coast Village Rd., Montecito | 805/969–3266 or 800/257–5131 | fax 805/969–7117 | cvi@mi.com | www.coastvillageinn.com | 29 rooms | $135–$225 | AE, D, DC, MC, V.

Days Inn. This one-story chain motel is one block north of West Beach, the yacht harbor and wharf, three blocks from the State Street shopping district. Complimentary Continental breakfast. Cable TV. Hot tub. Laundry facilites. Pets allowed. | 116 Castillo St. | 805/963–9772 or 800/329–7466 | fax 805/963–6699 | www.daysinn.com | 25 rooms | $85–$160 | AE, D, DC, MC, V.

Eagle Inn. This white Spanish-style hotel two blocks from the beach has frilly rooms with canopy beds and ceiling fans. Complimentary Continental breakfast. No air conditioning, in-room data ports, in-room safes, some kitchenettes, cable TV. Beach. Free parking. No smoking. | 232 Natoma Ave. | 805/965–3586 | fax 805/966–1218 | www.theeagleinn.com | 27 rooms | $79–$164 | AE, D, DC, MC, V.

El Encanto Hotel and Garden Villas. Actress Hedy Lamarr and President Franklin Roosevelt both stayed at this 10-acre wooded property. Choose from Spanish Colonial and Craftsman-style cottages, all outfitted with brick fireplaces, hardwood floors, and over-stuffed furniture. Restaurant, bar (with entertainment). Cable TV. Pool. Tennis. Laundry facilities. Business services, airport shuttle. | 1900 Lasuen Rd. | 805/687–5000 or 800/346–7039 (CA) | fax 805/687–3903 | elencanto@aol.com | www.srs-worldhotels.com | 84 cottages | $239–$469 | AE, DC, MC, V.

El Prado Inn. Two blocks from shops and restaurants, this three-story motor inn, where some rooms overlook the pool, is ½ mi south of the Santa Barbara Mission. Complimentary Continental breakfast. In-room data ports, refrigerators, cable TV. Pool. Beauty salon. Business services, free parking. | 1601 State St. | 805/966–0807 or 800/669–8979 | fax 805/966–6502 | www.elprado.com | 68 rooms, 6 suites | $95–$200, $200 suites | AE, D, DC, MC, V.

Fess Parker's Doubletree Resort. Surrounded by the Santa Ynez Mountains, this two-story hotel, where suites have patios or decks overlooking the ocean, is on 24 acres eight blocks east of the downtown area. Restaurants, bar (with entertainment), room service. In-room data ports, cable TV. Pool. Beauty salon, massage. Putting green, tennis. Basketball, exercise equipment. Laundry facilities. Business services, airport shuttle, free parking. Pets allowed. | 633 E. Cabrillo Blvd. | 805/564–4333 | fax 805/564–4964 | www.fpdtr.com | 337 rooms, 23 suites | $235–$285 rooms, $455–$855 suites | AE, D, DC, MC, V.

★ **Four Seasons Biltmore.** Adobe archways and terra-cotta roofs characterize the Spanish Colonial architecture of this 1927 hotel, on 23 acres of gardens and palm trees, where some rooms have ocean views. 3 restaurants, bar (with entertainment), room service. In-room data ports, cable TV, in-room VCRs. 2 pools, wading pool. Beauty salon, hot tub, massage. Putting green, tennis. Gym, bicycles. Kids' programs. Business services, airport shuttle. Pets allowed.

| 1260 Channel Dr. | 805/969–2261 | fax 805/969–4682 | www.fshr.com | 234 rooms | $450–$610 | AE, DC, MC, V.

Franciscan Inn. Rooms in this 1920s Spanish Colonial inn a block from the beach have floral patterns and some have fireplaces. Complimentary Continental breakfast. Some kitchenettes, refrigerators, cable TV. Pool. Hot tub. Beach. Laundry facilities. Business services, free parking. | 109 Bath St. | 805/963–8845 | fax 805/564–3295 | www.franciscaninn.com | 32 rooms, 21 suites | $95–$145; $155–$260 suites | AE, DC, MC, V.

★ **Glenborough Inn and Cottage.** Three houses make up this B&B. Each room has its own distinctive details; the Craftsman room, for instance, has dark wood paneling and a tile fireplace, while the Nouveau Suite has white walls and glass cabinets. Several rooms have hot tubs outside on a patio. Complimentary breakfast. No air-conditioning in some rooms, some refrigerators, some in-room hot tubs, cable TV. Hot tub. Business services. No smoking. | 1327 Bath St. | 805/966–0589 or 800/962–0589 | fax 805/564–8610 | glenboro@silicom.com | www.silcom.com/~glenboro | 7 rooms, 7 suites, 1 cottage | $110–$200; $175–$295 suites; $300–$360 cottage | AE, D, DC, MC, V.

Hotel Santa Barbara. The top-floor rooms have ocean views in this four-story hotel on State Street. Complimentary Continental breakfast. In-room data ports, cable TV. Laundry service. | 533 State St. | 888/259–7700 | fax 805/962–2412 | www.hotelsantabarbara.com | 72 rooms, 3 suites | $119–$169; $139–$189 suites | AE, D, MC, V.

Inn By The Harbor. Tropical gardens surround this hotel, three blocks from the beach and harbor. Rooms, appointed with pine furniture, overlook a pool and spa. Family suites have full kitchens. Complimentary Continental breakfast. No air-conditioning, some kitchenettes, microwaves, some refrigerators, cable TV. Pool. Hot tub. Laundry facilities. Business services, free parking. No smoking. | 433 W. Montecito St. | 805/963–7851 or 800/626–1986 | fax 805/962–9428 | www.sbhotels.com/harbor.htm | 20 rooms, 23 suites | $88–$108, $108–$138 suites | AE, D, DC, MC, V.

Marina Beach. Surrounded by flowers, this one-story white motel with French doors is less than a block from the beach, and 15 min west of the city center. Complimentary Continental breakfast. Some kitchenettes, cable TV. Business services. | 21 Bath St. | 805/963–9311 | fax 805/564–4102 | marinabeachmotel.com | 50 rooms | $81–$266 | AE, D, DC, MC, V.

Montecito Inn. When Charlie Chaplin built this three-story inn in 1928, he spared no expense: marble floors, marble columns, chandeliers, hand-painted tiles, and wood window frames. Chaplin posters adorn the walls of every room, which are done in floral prints. Restaurant, complimentary Continental breakfast, room service. Some in-room hot tubs, cable TV, in-room VCRs (and movies). Pool. Exercise equipment. Bicycles. Laundry facilities. Business services. | 1295 Coast Village Rd. | 805/969–7854 or 800/843–2017 | fax 805/969–0623 | info@montecitoinn.com | www.montecitoinn.com | 60 rooms | $285–$350 | AE, D, DC, MC, V.

Motel 6. This two-story motel is a half-block from the beach. Cable TV. Pool. Laundry facilities. Pets allowed. | 443 Corona del Mar | 805/564–1392 or 800/466–8356 | fax 805/963–4687 | 51 rooms | $60–$80 | AE, D, DC, MC, V.

Ocean Palms Hotel. This ocean-front property, with red tile roof, patios, and flowering courtyards is across the street from the beach, and two blocks from shops, and restaurants. Complimentary breakfast. No air conditioning, some kitchenettes, some microwaves, some refrigerators, cable TV. Pool. Spa. Beach. Laundry service. Pets allowed. | 232 W. Cabrillo Blvd. | 805/966–9133 or 800/350–2326 | fax 805/965–7882 | www.oceanpalms.com | $55–$185 | AE, D, MC, V.

Old Yacht Club Inn. Rooms at this Craftsman-style home, the area's first B&B, have century-old antiques and oriental rugs. Five rooms are in the adjacent Hitchcock House. Complimentary breakfast. No air-conditioning, some in-room hot tubs. Bicycles. Business services. No smoking. | 431 Corona del Mar Dr. | 805/962–1277, 800/549–1676 or 800/676–1676 (outside CA) | fax 805/962–3989 | oyci@aol.com | 12 rooms | $110–$190 | AE, D, MC, V.

Pacifica Suites. Among 7 acres of exotic gardens, this inn is off U.S. 101, near the Patterson Avenue exit. All suites have one bedroom with a separate living room. Complimentary breakfast. In-room data ports, microwaves, refrigerators, cable TV, in-room VCRs (and movies). Pool. Hot tub. Business services, airport shuttle, free parking. Pets allowed. | 5490 Hollister Ave. | 805/683–6722 or 800/338–6722 | fax 805/683–4121 | www.pacificasuites.com | 87 suites | $139–$169 suites | AE, D, DC, MC, V.

Radisson. Across from East Beach, this 1931 hotel, made up of four Spanish Colonial buildings spread across three acres, is steps from the zoo. Most rooms have balconies or patios, which overlook the water or mountains. Restaurant, bar (with entertainment), room service. In-room data ports, cable TV. Pool. Beauty salon, massage. Exercise equipment. Shops. Business services. | 1111 E. Cabrillo Blvd. | 805/963–0744 | fax 805/962–0985 | www.radisson.com | 174 rooms | $189–$315 | AE, D, DC, MC, V.

★ **San Ysidro Ranch.** The views across 500 acres of orange groves and west to the sea and Channel Islands were enough to entice John and Jackie Kennedy here on their honeymoon. You, too, can enjoy luxury fit for a future president in this 1893 lodge, with rooms warmed by wood stoves or fireplaces. Dining room, bar (with entertainment), room service. In-room data ports, refrigerators, some in-room hot tubs, cable TV, in-room VCRs (and movies). Pool, wading pool. Massage. Driving range, tennis. Gym, hiking. Playground. Business services. Pets allowed (fee). | 900 San Ysidro La. | 805/969–5046 or 800/368–6788 | fax 805/565–1995 | www.sanysidroranch.com | 23 rooms, 15 suites | $375–$575, $675–1750 suites | AE, DC, MC, V.

Santa Barbara Holiday Inn. Off U.S. 101, this two-floor hotel, where rooms overlook the pool, is less than 1 mi northeast of the Santa Barbara Municipal Airport. Restaurant, room service. In-room data ports, cable TV. Pool. Shops. Business services, airport shuttle, free parking. Pets allowed. | 5650 Calle Real, Goleta | 805/964–6241 | fax 805/964–8467 | www.holiday-inn.com | 160 rooms | $120–$137 | AE, D, DC, MC, V.

Santa Barbara Inn. From the balconies of this three-story inn, where beige rooms recall the beach beyond the inn's doors, you have views of either the ocean or mountains. Restaurant, bar, room service. Some refrigerators, cable TV. Pool. Hot tub, massage. Babysitting. Laundry service. Business services. | 901 E. Cabrillo Blvd. | 805/966–2285 or 800/231–0431 | fax 805/966–6584 | www.santabarbarainn.com | 71 rooms | $249–$359 | AE, D, DC, MC, V.

Santa Barbara Ramada Limited. Water lillies, ducks, turtles, and koi fill a small lagoon that you can see from many of the peaked-ceiling rooms in this two-story hotel, near biking and jogging trails, north of U.S. 101 off Turnpike Road. Complimentary Continental breakfast. Cable TV. Pool. Hot tub. Laundry facilities. Business services, airport shuttle, free parking. | 4770 Calle Real | 805/964–3511 or 800/654–1965 | fax 805/964–0075 | www.sbramada.com | 126 rooms | $67–$100 | AE, D, DC, MC, V.

Tiffany Country House. Some rooms in this Victorian mansion surrounded by a garden in a residential neighborhood a short walk from downtown, have fireplaces, hot tubs, and views of the mountains. Tea is served every afternoon. Complimentary breakfast. Some in-room hot tubs, no TV in some rooms, some in-room VCRs. Business services. No smoking. | 1323 de la Vina St. | 805/963–2283 or 800/999–5672 | fax 805/962–0994 | www.tiffanycountryhouse.com | 7 rooms, 3 suites | $135–$175; $200–$285 suites | AE, D, MC, V.

Travelodge Santa Barbara Beach. A half-block from the beach and harbor and close to downtown, this single-story motel is across the street from a park. Some refrigerators, cable TV. Business services. | 22 Castillo St. | 805/965–8527 | fax 805/965–6125 | bchtrvl@west.net | www.travelodge.com | 19 rooms | $75–175 | AE, D, DC, MC, V.

Tropicana Inn and Suites. Sundecks overlook the mountains at this two-story inn, two blocks from the beach. The rooms here have pine furniture. Complimentary Continental breakfast. Microwaves, refrigerators, cable TV. No air-conditioning. Pool. Hot tub. Bicycles. Laundry facilities. Business services, free parking. No smoking. | 223 Castillo St. | 805/966–2219 or 800/468–1988 | fax 805/962–9428 | 31 rooms, 17 suites | $124–$154; $144–$240 suites | AE, D, DC, MC, V.

Upham Hotel. Southern California's oldest continuously operating accommodation opened in 1872 as a boarding house. The lodging is surrounded by a garden and is filled with period antiques. Restaurant, complimentary Continental breakfast. No air-conditioning, some in-room hot tubs, cable TV. Business services. | 1404 de la Vina St. | 805/962–0058 or 800/727–0876 | fax 805/963–2825 | www.uphamhotel.com | 50 rooms, 5 cottages | $145–$195; $245–$395 cottages | AE, D, DC, MC, V.

Villa Rosa. Some of the rooms in this Spanish Colonial inn less than 100 steps from the ocean have fireplaces. Complimentary Continental breakfast. Some kitchenettes, some refrigerators, cable TV. Pool. Hot tub. Business services. No kids under 14. No smoking. | 15 Chapala St. | 805/966–0851 | fax 805/962–7159 | 21 rooms | $110–$230 | AE, MC, V.

West Beach Inn. A gardenside pool anchors this inn, one of the few in town with air-conditioned rooms, where wine and cheese are served each evening. Complimentary Continental breakfast. Cable TV. Pool. Spa. Laundry service. | 306 W. Cabrillo Blvd. | 805/963–4277 or 800/423–5991 | fax 805/564–4210 | www.westbeachinn.com | 44 rooms and suites | $81–$175, $156–$255 suites | AE, D, DC, MC, V.

SANTA CRUZ

MAP 4, D9

(Nearby towns also listed: Aptos, Los Gatos, Palo Alto, San Jose, Saratoga, Watsonville)

People have been drawn to the stunning natural beauty of the Santa Cruz area for more than 8,000 years. The first permanent inhabitants of the northern end of Monterey Bay were the Ohlone people, who fished the waters and hunted game in the towering redwood forests that dominated the countryside in their time. The village of Santa Cruz was established in 1791 as the 12th Franciscan mission in California. The tiny settlement survived political turmoil and the threat of pirate attacks and was incorporated shortly after the Gold Rush of 1849. The natural resources of the Monterey Bay area have played a part in fueling the local economy of Santa Cruz; the town has been supported in turn by the lumber and fishing industries, limestone quarrying concerns, and finally, as the area developed a reputation for scenic beauty and laid-back living, the tourist trade. Thousands come to Santa Cruz every year for hiking, kayaking, mountain-biking, and to surf some of the best waves anywhere. Today, Santa Cruz is home to nearly 50,000 permanent residents, scores of restaurants, shops, and hotels, as well as a major state university and a number of up-and-coming corporations. Santa Cruz prides itself on a high standard of living, a vibrant arts-and-culture community, and a down-to-earth sense of civic and global responsibility. Many of the political and social movements that swept the nation in the 1960s had their genesis here, and the memory of those times remains today.

Information: Santa Cruz County Conference and Visitor Council | 701 Front St., 95060 | 831/425–1234 or 800/833–3494 | www.scccvc.org.

Attractions

Natural Bridges State Beach. On the western end of West Cliff Drive, this stretch of sand is dotted with tidal pools and vegetation. The naturally formed rock bridge for which the beach is named is a few hundred yards down, and perhaps best of all, from October to early March, a huge colony of monarch butterflies settles here. | 2531 W. Cliff Dr. | 831/423–4609 | $3 | Daily, dawn–dusk.

★ **Santa Cruz Beach Boardwalk.** This wooden walkway extends west from the San Lorenzo River and curves around public beaches, an amusement park with antique roller coasters and carousels, restaurants, and shops. | Beach St. | 831/423–5590 | Free. Amusement park day pass, $22 | Amusement park open Memorial Day–Labor Day 11–11; weekends only the rest of the year.

Santa Cruz Municipal Wharf. The barking din of dozens of sea lions lounging under the redwood pilings accompanies the sounds of music and the smells wafting out of a score of restaurants lining the street here. | Beach St. | 831/420–5273 | www.santacruzwharf.com | Free.

Surfing Museum. Housed in a historic, decommissioned lighthouse overlooking a popular surfing beach, this museum documents over 100 years of surfing history with its vast collection of surfboards, wet suits, and multimedia exhibits. | W. Cliff Dr. | 831/420–6289 | Free | Thurs.–Mon. noon–4.

Santa Cruz Museum of Art and History. Ever-changing exhibits at this gallery in the McPherson Center range from displays of the area's ecological heritage to photography retrospectives and installation art. The museum also hosts lectures and outreach programs throughout the year. | 705 Front St. | 831/429–1964 | www.santacruzmuseums.org | $3 | Tues.–Sun. 11–5; Thurs. 11–7.

University of California Santa Cruz. Established in 1965, the UC Santa Cruz is nestled in the redwood-covered hills above Santa Cruz proper. The school is home to the famed Lick Observatory and more than 11,000 students here work toward degrees in some 40 majors and 26 post-graduate programs. The four-year college has won accolades for its contributions to the fields of astronomy and linguistics, but perhaps the school's most abiding attribute is its mascot: the UCSC Banana Slug. | 1156 High St. | 831/459–0111 | www.ucsc.edu | Free | Daily.

On the 4,209-ft summit of Mt. Hamilton, the 1888 **Lick Observatory,** part of the University of California at Santa Cruz, perches high above Santa Clara Valley. The observatory offers guided tours of the Great Lick Refractor, and you can view the Shane Reflector from the Visitor's Gallery. For six weekends during the summer, the observatory allows limited telescope viewings. Locals love to head here when occasional snow shuts down the roadway; call ahead if winter weather looms. | Mt. Hamilton | 408/274–5061 | Free | Weekdays 12:30–5, weekends 10–4:30.

ON THE CALENDAR

FEB.: *Clam Chowder Cook-off.* Teams and individual chowder-masters converge on the Beach Boardwalk in downtown Santa Cruz every year for a frenzied day of chowder-making and tasting. Winners in several divisions take home trophies and T-shirts. Tasting kits for spectators are available for about $5. | 831/420–5273.

APR.: *Children's Day Downtown.* Dozens of activity booths crowd downtown Front Street, and dancers, storytellers, and costumed characters create a day-long celebration for families. | 831/429–8433.

JUNE: *Vintners' Festival.* Every summer, 35 area wineries open their doors to the public—and some of their barrels—for two weekends of music, art exhibits, food, and wine-tasting. | 800/211–6630.

AUG.: *Cabrillo Music Festival.* Conductors, composers, and accomplished musicians descend on several venues througout Santa Cruz for two weekends every summer to celebrate contemporary music in all its forms. There are concerts, operatic performances, juried art shows, wine tastings, and educational lectures. | 831/426–6966.

OCT.: *Sentinel Triathlon.* Hosted by a local newspaper and sponsored by local and national businesses, this grueling physical test puts participants through a mile-long swim around the Municipal Wharf, a 23-mi bike ride through Santa Cruz, and a 6-mi run along the waterfront. | 831/423–4242.

Dining

Benten. Japanese. The dining room and sushi bar here are illuminated by softly glowing lanterns and hung with calligraphic scrolls. The menu features the usual sushi, sashimi, and tempura offerings, as well as some more exotic delicacies, like sea-urchin eggs served over sticky rice. | 1541 Pacific Ave. | 831/425–7079 | $8–$13 | AE, MC, V.

Dolphin Restaurant. Seafood. This small, careworn restaurant's location on the Municipal Wharf makes it a great spot for taking in ocean views as well as some excellent chowder and fish and chips. If you're in a rush, order from the walk-up window and enjoy your meal on the beach. Breakfast available. | Beach St., at end of Municipal Wharf | 831/426–5830 | $6–$12 | MC, V.

El Palomar. Mexican. Housed in the Palomar Hotel, this restaurant has original Spanish Mission–era architecture with high ceilings, exposed wooden beams, and a central atrium that lets in sunlight. The menu features feisty options like chili verde, fish tacos, and tostadas. The restaurant's adjacent taco bar is open all day. | 1336 Pacific Ave. | 831/425–7575 | $10–$25 | AE, D, DC, MC, V.

Gabriella Café. Italian. The menu at Gabriella changes regularly to take advantage of the freshest local produce. The dining area is small and intimate, with light stucco walls and potted plants. Consider the steamed mussels, or the braised shank of lamb. | 910 Cedar St. | 831/457–1677 | $9–$22 | AE, D, MC, V.

India Joze. Eclectic. As the name might suggest, you can get curries and chutneys here to your heart's content, but the menu doesn't stop there. The kitchen at India Joze takes inspiration from the Middle East, Indonesia, and Asia, using exotic spices and familiar ingredients in creative ways to make everything from salads to homemade soups special. You can take your meal on the restaurant's tree-shaded patio amid flowers and tiny twinkling lights. | 1001 Center St. | 831/427–3554 | $8–$18 | AE, D, MC, V.

Oswald's. Contemporary. The dining area at this diminutive bistro is arranged around a central courtyard with tiles and plants. Mediterranean-inspired menu favorites include sherry-steamed mussels and sautéed beef livers. | 1547 Pacific Ave. | 831/423–7427 | Reservations essential | Closed Mon. | $29–$35 | AE, D, MC, V.

Pearl Alley Bistro. Eclectic. The interior of this popular restaurant is spare and artsy, with lots of blond wood and brushed metals. You can sit and sip a cocktail at the marble-topped bar while your table is prepared, and then sit down and experience a different globally inspired menu every week, ranging from Pacific Rim cuisine to old-fashioned Continental dishes. | 110 Pearl Alley | 831/429–8070 | Reservations essential | No lunch | $27–$39 | AE, MC, V.

Positively Front Street. Seafood. The mood here is distinctly laid-back, with beachcombers and sun-worshippers coming in from the sand for seafood chowder, steamed clams, and oysters on the half shell. There's also burgers and pizza. | 44 Front St. | 831/426–1944 | $6–$15 | AE, MC, V.

Vasili's. Greek. This café's festive frescoes and shelves of crockery serve as a fitting backdrop to a menu of hearty dishes straight from the Greek countryside. Always popular are the meat kebobs, which you can get with beef, pork, lamb, or any combination of the three. If you're feeling adventuresome, consider punctuating your meal with swigs of *retsina*, Greece's very piquant national white wine. | 1501-A Mission St. | 831/458–9808 | Closed Mon. | $9–$17 | No credit cards.

Zachary's. American. Very popular among Santa Cruz's young hipsters, this small, sometimes noisy café is known for its mean breakfast offerings. You can roll in early and get fluffy sourdough pancakes, artichoke frittatas, and the formidable Mike's Mess, a mound of eggs scrambled with bacon, mushrooms, and hash browns then doused with sour cream, melted cheddar cheese, and diced tomatoes. | 819 Pacific Ave. | 831/427–0646 | No dinner | $4–$8 | MC, V.

Lodging

Adobe on Green Street. A historic adobe house in a historic neighborhood, this modernized bed and breakfast sits on a half-acre of wooded hillside overlooking downtown Santa Cruz. The wharf and boardwalk are within a five block walk. Guest rooms are done in Mexican and Native American motifs, with exposed adobe walls, warm terra-cotta tilework, and wrought-iron beds and fixtures. Complimentary breakfast. Some in-room hot tubs. No TV in some rooms. Some in-room VCRs. Hot tub, steam room. | 103 Green St. | 831/469–9866 or 888/878–2789 | fax 831/469–9493 | adobeongreen@aol.com | www.santa-cruz-california.com | 4 rooms | $135–$165 | AE, D, MC, V.

Babbling Brook Inn. The running stream, lush gardens, and thick stands of trees on the grounds of this old mill and tannery-turned-inn might make you forget that you're right in the middle of Santa Cruz, mere blocks from the wharf, the boardwalk, and the shops and restaurants downtown. Guest rooms here have patios and fireplaces—some wood-burning, some electric. In the afternoon, the innkeeper serves wine, cheese, and fresh-baked cookies gratis. Complimentary breakfast. TV in common area. | 1025 Laurel St. | 831/427–2456 or 800/866–1131 | www.babblingbrookinn.com | 13 rooms | $135–$230 | AE, D, MC, V.

Best Western TorchLite Inn. This modest two-story grey stone motel is three blocks from the boardwalk and the beach and a mile from the UCSC campus and surrounding redwood forests. The motel itself is L-shaped and centers on a palm-shaded pool patio area with tables, lounge chairs, and canvas umbrellas. Some kitchenettes. Microwaves, refrigerators. Cable TV. Pool. Business services. | 500 Riverside Ave. | 831/426–7575 | fax 831/460–1470 | 38 rooms | $60–$190 | AE, D, DC, MC, V.

Compassion Flower Inn. It's probably safe to say you've never stayed anywhere quite like the Compassion Flower. This 1860s Gothic Revival mansion on a quiet residential street mixes Victorian antiques and modern-primitive art with New Age flourishes. It sounds discordant, yet it works. The house philosophy is liberal, laid-back, and eco-friendly —breakfast is organic, the hot tub out back is clothing-optional, and all the soaps, lotions, and linens are hemp-based. There's even a cannabis-leaf mosaic inlay in the entry hall. Complimentary breakfast. Some in-room hot tubs. No TV in some rooms. Outdoor hot tub. No pets. | 216 Laurel St. | 831/466–0420 | fax 831/466–1431 | www.compassionflowerinn.com | 5 rooms | $125–$175 | AE, D, MC, V.

Chateau Victorian. Built in 1885, this deep-violet Victorian home is just one block from the beach and within five blocks of downtown Santa Cruz. Guest rooms are equipped with antique cedarwood pieces, wood-burning fireplaces, and large windows with mountain views. A made-from-scratch breakfast is served every morning either in the gracious dining room or outside on the deck. Complimentary breakfast. No TV in some rooms. | 118 Front St. | 831/458–9458 | www.chateauvictorian.com | 7 rooms | $115–$145 | MC, V.

Inn at Depot Hill. Occupying an old railway depot about 4 mi east of Santa Cruz, this bed and breakfast is perhaps a refreshing change from the Victorian lace-doily theme of so many of its brethren. The rooms here are outfitted with feather beds and fireplaces, but each has a different destination theme ranging from the sun-drenched grandeur of Portofino, Italy, to the austere beauty of Kyoto, Japan. Some rooms also have private patios. Complimentary Continental breakfast. In-room data ports, some in-room hot tubs, cable TV, in-room VCRs. Hot tub. | 250 Monterey Ave., Capitola-by-the-Sea | 831/264–3376 or 800/572–2632 | fax 831/426–3697 | 6 rooms, 6 suites | $235–$265 rooms, $275–$325 suites | AE, D, MC, V.

Inn at Manresa Beach. Famed photographer Ansel Adams stayed at this 1867 neo-Georgian farmhouse just over a hill from the beach. The house, designed as a replica of Abraham Lincoln's home in Springfield, Illinois, is considered part of the little town of La Selva Beach, but it's less than 10 mi from Santa Cruz. Guest rooms are done in warm, earth-colored hues and set about with fresh flowers and growing plants. Some have gas fireplaces and whirlpool tubs. A short walk takes you to one of Northern California's longest stretches of unbroken beach. Complimentary breakfast. Cable TV, in-room VCRs. 2 tennis courts, volleyball. No smoking. | 1258 San Andreas Rd., La Selva Beach | 831/728–1000 or 888/523–2244 | fax 831/728–8294 | 6 rooms | $180–$205 | AE, D, MC, V.

Ocean Pacific Lodge. Though not right on the beach, this large, multi-story concrete lodging is four-block stroll from the action on the waterfront. What you forgo in views and bus-tle you make up for in peace and quiet. Guest rooms are spacious, and upper floors have some interesting views of the mountains east of town. Refrigerators. Cable TV, in-room VCRs. Pool. 2 hot tubs, exercise equipment. | 120 Washington St. | 831/457–1234 or 800/995–0289 | 44 rooms, 15 suites | $103–$150 rooms, $150–$209 suites | AE, D, DC, MC, V.

Pleasure Point Inn. Situated on some prime oceanfront property just across the street from the Pacific, this modern bed and breakfast is just the place if you like the idea of a morning run along the beach or listening to the waves as you drift off at night. The inn has a rooftop sun deck for basking, fireplaces, clawfoot bathtubs, and an eclectic blend of antique, modern, and antique-reproduction furniture. Complimentary Continental breakfast. Some in-room safes. No TV in some rooms. Massage. No pets. | 2–3665 E. Cliff Dr. | 831/469–6161 or 877/577–2567 | www.pleasurepointinn.com | 4 rooms | $210–$275 | MC, V.

West Coast Santa Cruz Hotel. Less than three blocks from the Beach Boardwalk and Municipal Wharf, this resort maintains its own private stretch of sandy beach. The building itself is an unremarkable concrete monolith, but guest rooms here all have private balconies or patios with views of the water. Restaurant, 2 bars, room service. Refrigerators. Cable TV. Pool. 2 hot tubs. Laundry service. | 175 W. Cliff Dr. | 831/426–4330 or 800/426–0670 | fax 831/427–2025 | www.westcoasthotels.com | 163 rooms | $175–$350 | AE, D, DC, MC, V.

SANTA MARIA

MAP 4, F13

(Nearby towns also listed: Lompoc, Los Olivos, Pismo Beach)

Santa Maria (pop. 71,000) lies 12 mi inland from California's Central Coast, between Santa Barbara and San Luis Obispo. The earliest inhabitants of the Santa Maria Valley were the Chumash Indians, who settled here long before Spanish explorers and Mission *padres* arrived in the area in the 1700s. Santa Maria was not always the lush agricultural zone it is today—the valley was dry and dusty before the advent of irrigation, coupled with the planting of some 40,000 eucaplytus trees as a wind break. Santa Maria is known by many as the "Barbecue Capital of the World"—wood from native red oak trees make for distinctive open-fire grilling.

Information: Santa Maria Valley Chamber of Commerce & Visitor & Convention Bureau | 614 S. Broadway, 93454 | 800/331–3779 or 805/925–2403 | www.santa-maria.com.

Attractions

Guadalupe-Nipomo Dunes Preserve. More than 200 bird species live in or migrate through this 3,000-plus-acre Nature Conservancy preserve. But you don't have to be an expert to enjoy the wildlife, or the dunes, some reaching 500 ft, the highest on the California coast, creating such landscape drama that Cecil B. DeMille filmed *The Ten Commandments* here. Hiking trails lace the preserve, and a boardwalk takes you to Oso Flaco Lake. Guided tours are offered several times monthly by docents from the Dune Center interpretive center. The preserve's two entrances are at Oso Flaco Lake, and W. Main Street/Route 166. West Main Street meets U.S. 101 in Santa Maria. | The Dunes Center, 951 Guadalupe St., Guadalupe | 805/343–2455 | fax 805/343–0442 | www.tnccalifornia.org/preserves/guadalupe | $4 | Daily dawn to dusk; Dunes Center, Fri. 2–4, weekends noon–4.

The Lost City of DeMille. In 1923 filmmaker Cecil B. DeMille built what was then the largest set in motion picture history, for his epic silent film *The Ten Commandments*. After completing filming, DeMille didn't have enough money to cart away the set, so he simply buried it in the sand. Sixty years later, working from enigmatic clues left by the filmmaker at his death, a team of movie buffs unearthed the legendary set in the Guadalupe Nipomo Dunes, 9 mi west of Santa Maria. Visit the Dunes Discovery Center to view some of the remains as well as photos and memorabilia from the movie. | Dunes Discovery Center, 951 Guadalupe St., Guadalupe | 805/343–2455 | www.lostcitydemille.com | $4.

Oso Flaco Lake. Apparently the big game hunting was a bit disappointing when the Spanish settlers first came through here—the lake's name translates to "skinny bear." It's one of a dozen fresh-water lakes in the dunes northwest of Santa Maria and Guadalupe, and is excellent for hiking and birdwatching. There's also a well-maintained boardwalk along the lakeside, perfect for a leisurely stroll. The lake is off Rte. 1, 2 mi west on Oso Flaco Rd. | Oso Flaco Rd. | 805/473–7220 | $4 | Daily, dawn–dusk.

Dining

Chef Rick's Ultimately Fine Foods. Steak. Voted as Santa Maria's best restaurant by the *Santa Maria Times*, it's hard to go wrong in this classy but casual watering hole. Specialties include blackened prime rib sandwich and tenderloin *andouille maquechow*—skillet steak covered in vegetable cream sauce. The dining room only has 13 tables and it is decorated with fresh flowers and paintings done by local artists. | 4869 S. Bradley Rd. | 805/937–9512 | www.chefricks.com | Closed Sunday | $15–$35 | AE, D, MC, V.

Shaw's Steakhouse. Steak. With its red-oak-stoked, open-fire grill in plain view, this restaurant lets you watch your steak sizzle from the dining room, which is dressed up with a mural and various pictures from the 1930s. It's been serving barbecue-savvy locals for almost a half-century, using beef, woodchips, and recipes all gleaned from the region; go for the baby back ribs and the rib-eye steak. Kids' menu. | 714 S. Broadway | 805/925–5862 | No lunch Sat.–Sun. | $15–$25 | AE, D, MC, V.

Lodging

Best Western Big America. One block north of U.S. 101, this comfortable hotel has rooms with rooms Early American–style furniture by Thomasville. Some rooms have king-size beds and separate dressing areas. Special touches include a free daily newspaper and fresh-baked cookies every afternoon. Restaurant, complimentary Continental breakfast. Refrigerators, cable TV. Pool Hot tub. | 1725 N. Broadway | 805/922–5200 or 800/426–3213 | fax 805/922–9865 | www.bigamerica.com | 106 rooms | $77–$99 | AE, D, MC, V.

Historic Santa Maria Inn. The Santa Maria Inn has been a Central Coast landmark since 1917. Restored in old English style, the original inn has casement windows, old brick fireplaces, dark polished wooden phone booths, stained-glass windows (with images taken from the inn's flower gardens), wainscoting, and staircases. The modern six-story tower has spacious rooms and modern amenities. The hotel is famous for its flower gardens and arrangements, which can be enjoyed from the patio. Pool. Hot tub, sauna. Shops. | 801 S. Broadway | 805/928–7777 or 800/462–4226 | fax 805/928–5690 | www.santamariainn.com | 166 rooms, 16 suites | $89–$119, $149–$259 suites | AE, D, DC, MC, V.

Holiday Inn Hotel and Suites–Mesquites. Granite floors and attractive murals at the reception desk give way to spacious units with modern decor and fully equipped kitchens in this four-story hotel off U.S. 101, at the Broadway exit. Restaurant. In-room data ports, cable TV. Pool. Hot tub, sauna. | 2100 N. Broadway | 805/928–6000 | fax 805/928–0356 | www.holidayinnsantamaria.com | 220 rooms | $79–$158 | AE, D, DC, MC, V.

SANTA MONICA

MAP 4, H15

(Nearby towns also listed: Culver City, Los Angeles, Marina del Ray, Pacific Palisades, Venice)

This developed beach community (pop. 86,900) is one of the most sought-after addresses on L.A.'s west side. Home to college students, actors, and young executives, it is known for its carousel and the carnival booths on its pier. But the real city is a few blocks away from the ocean, where coffee shops, yoga schools, and boutiques line Main Street. The 3rd Street Promenade, closed to traffic, has bustling stores, coffeehouses, bookstores, movie theaters, and restaurants. It's always packed with shoppers, in-line skaters, tourists, and street performers.

Back on the coast, the extraordinarily broad beach is one of the most popular in Southern California, not just with everyday sun-and-surf worshippers, but with movie and TV crews as well, who frequently use the wide expanse and bustling pier as backdrops.

Information: **Santa Monica Visitors Bureau** | 1400 Ocean Ave., 90401 | 310/393–7593 | smcvb@www.santamonica.com | www.santamonica.com.

Attractions

California Heritage Museum. Restored period rooms dating from the 1890s through the 1930s complement other changing exhibits illustrating California's history and culture. | 2612 Main St. | 310/392–8537 | fax 310/396–0517 | $3 | Wed.–Sun. 11–5.

Museum of Flying. On the site where Donald Douglas built the first DC3, the museum here houses more than 30 vintage aircraft and an interactive flight area. | 2772 Donald Douglas Loop N. | 310/392–8822 | fax 310/450–6956 | www.mof.org | $7 | Wed.–Sun. 10–5.

Palisades Park. This cliff-trimming park consists of a narrow strip bordering Ocean Avenue and overlooking Santa Monica's broad beachfront. | Ocean Ave., between Colorado and San Vicente Blvds | 310/458–8310 | www.santamonica.com | Free | Daily.

★ **Santa Monica Pier.** An antique carousel, roller coaster, amusement arcade, shops, restaurants and to-go eateries, a fishing deck, and plenty of gulls crowd this pier next to downtown. | Santa Monica beachfront, Ocean Ave. at Colorado Blvd. | 310/458–8900 | www.santamonicapier.org | Free | Daily.

Santa Monica State Beach. Santa Monica Beach is noted for its remarkable width—more than a football-field wide in places—as well as its bustling pier and lively boardwalk. Swimmers, surfers, and sunbathers come here on hot summer days, while in-line skaters, joggers, and walkers enjoy the paved boardwalk at the base of the cliffs, running between the Santa Monica Pier and Venice. | 310/458–8310 | Free | Daily dawn to dusk.

Third Street Promenade. A European-style mall in the heart of Santa Monica, with lots of cool shops and restaurants, street vendors, and performance artists. Exit I–10 at 4th St.

UCLA Ocean Discovery Center. Learn about Santa Monica Bay, watch sharks feed, look through microscopes, and try your hand at making fish puppets in this university-linked aquarium under the pier. | 1600 Ocean Front Walk | 310/393–6149 | www.odc.ucla.edu | $3 | Weekends 11–5, summer Tues.–Sun. 11–5.

SANTA MONICA

INTRO
ATTRACTIONS
DINING
LODGING

ON THE CALENDAR

APR.: *Santa Monica Festival.* Arts, interactive exhibits, workshops, storytelling, and international and organic foods emphasize the multicultural heritage of the city, along with a good dose of enviro-friendly information. | 323/962–1976 | www.santa-monica.org.

Dining

★ **Border Grill.** Mexican. Bright murals add color to this eatery where the menu includes Yucatan grilled-fish tacos, vinegar-and-pepper-grilled turkey, and grilled portobellos with guacamole, black beans, and cheese. | 1445 4th St. | 310/451–1655 | No lunch | $14–$24 | AE, D, MC, V.

★ **Broadway Deli.** Contemporary. Despite its name, this is a cross between a European brasserie and an upscale diner, rather than a New York–style deli. Smoked fish, Caesar salad, polenta with mushrooms, and broiled salmon with creamed spinach make up the menu. Kids' menu. | 1457 3rd St. Promenade | 310/451–0616 | $18–$26 | AE, MC, V.

Cézanne. Contemporary. The open dining room with oversized banquettes, large chandeliers, and a still life by the dining room's namesake, set the scene for an elegant dining experience, within Le Merigot hotel. The California menu has French overtones with entrées like medallions of veal with ravioli of sweetbreads and mushroom ragù and appetizers like organic greens with dried pears and goat cheese crostini in hazelnut vinaigrette. There is an extensive wine menu. Outdoor patio dining is available. | 1740 Ocean Ave. | 310/395–9700 or 800/926–9524 | fax 310/395–9200 | Breakfast also served | $20–$35 | AE, D, DC, MC, V.

★ **Chinois on Main.** Eclectic. A once-revolutionary outpost in Wolfgang Puck's repertoire, this is still one of LA's most crowded restaurants—and one of the noisiest. Asian and French influences yield seasonal dishes like grilled Mongolian lamb chops with cilantro vinaigrette, Shanghai lobster with spicy ginger-curry sauce, and Cantonese duck with fresh plum sauce. | 2709 Main St. | 310/392–9025 | Reservations essential | No lunch Sat.–Tues. | $43–$61 | AE, D, DC, MC, V.

★ **Drago.** Italian. Pappardelle with pheasant ragout, squid-ink risotto, and ostrich breast with red-cherry sauce are some of Celestino Drago's innovative Sicilian dishes served here amid stark, white walls and massive fresh-flower arrangements. | 2628 Wilshire Blvd. | 310/828–1585 | Reservations essential | $11–$23 | AE, D, DC, MC, V.

Jiraffe. Continental. The gleaming, wood-paneled, two-story dining room with ceiling-high windows is the stage for inventive entrées like roasted Chilean sea bass with a ragout of salsify, chanterelles, and pearl onions and toasted rack of lamb with truffled potato gnocchi. | 502 Santa Monica Blvd. | 310/917–6671 | Jacket required | No lunch Sat.–Mon. | $25–$35 | AE, DC, MC, V.

Ocean Avenue Seafood. Seafood. Low ceilings, dim lighting, and well-spaced tables set the tone at this cavernous restaurant with views of the ocean across the street. Cioppino, a fish stew made with Dungeness crab, clams, mussels, and prawns, and selections from the oyster bar are two popular dinner options. For dessert, the apple tart with caramel sauce is tops. | 1401 Ocean Ave. | 310/394–5669 | $25–$35 | AE, D, DC, MC, V.

Rockenwagner. Contemporary. In a Frank Gehry–designed building, the chef here serves up eclectic California and German-inspired fare like shrimp in a black bean sauce with snow peas, crab soufflé, and pork tenderloin with goat cheese and spaetzle. | 2435 Main St. | 310/399–6504 | Reservations essential | No lunch. Weekend brunch | $17–$30 | AE, DC, MC, V.

Teasers. American. It's a sports bar. No, it's a nightclub. No, it's a family restaurant. Well, it's all three. Sandwiches, burgers, quesadillas, antipasti, salads, and pastas fill the expansive menu that also includes many health-conscious options. A large outdoor patio allows you to watch all the action on 3rd Street Promenade. Kids' menu. | 1351 3rd St. Promenade | 310/394–8728 | $5–$10 | AE, DC, MC, V.

★ **Valentino.** Italian. An outstanding wine list complements dishes such as carpaccio with arugula and shaved parmesan and tagliolini sautéed with salmon and asparagus. And there's a lengthy list of daily specials. | 3115 Pico Blvd. | 310/829–4313 | Reservations essential | Jacket required | Closed Sun. No lunch | $22–$30 | AE, DC, MC, V.

Wolfgang Puck Cafe. Contemporary. Want to blend in with the hip crowd at this noisy, busy California-Italian bistro? Order a Perrier with a twist of lime and flip open the cell phone. Colorful tiles create a jumbled mosaic on the walls and floors. Savory entrées like mushroom tortellini and calzones are the menu choices. Kids' menu. | 1323 Montana Ave. | 310/393–0290 | $9–$22 | AE, DC, MC, V.

Lodging

Best Western Gateway Hotel. This four-story pink hotel, a little over a mile from the beach, provides free shuttle service to the ocean and promenade. Restaurant, room service. In-room data ports, cable TV. Exercise equipment. Business services. | 1920 Santa Monica Blvd. | 310/829–9100 | fax 310/829–9211 | www.bestwestern.com | 122 rooms | $104–$159 | AE, D, DC, MC, V.

Best Western Ocean View. The location is excellent for walking around downtown Santa Monica and to the Santa Monica Pier. The beach is across the street, and over 30 restaurants are within a five-block radius. Some rooms have ocean views; otherwise, the facilities are standard. Room service. Some microwaves. Gym. Beach. | 1447 Ocean Ave. | 310/458–4888 | fax 310/458–0848 | 65 rooms | $119–$229 | AE, DC, MC, V.

Channel Road Inn. Windows overlook the ocean or garden at this 1910 inn, one block from the beach. Four-poster beds combine with over-stuffed furnishings in the rooms, some of which have decks. Complimentary breakfast. In-room data ports, some in-room hot tubs, cable TV. Hot tub. Bicycles. Business services. | 219 W. Channel Rd. | 310/459–1920 | fax 310/454–9920 | channelinn@aol.com | www.channelroadinn.com | 14 rooms, 2 suites | $165–$285, $325–$335 suites | AE, MC, V.

Comfort Inn. This hotel is 2 mi northeast of the beach and 2 mi northwest of the Santa Monica Airport. Complimentary Continental breakfast. Refrigerators, cable TV. Pool. | 2815 Santa Monica Blvd. | 310/828–5517 | fax 310/829–6084 | www.comfortinns.com | 108 rooms | $99–$119 | AE, D, DC, MC, V.

Days Inn Santa Monica. This three-story chain hotel, 1 mi from the beach, sits in the middle of the city near popular restaurants. Complimentary Continental breakfast. Cable TV. Outdoor hot tub. Exercise equipment. Laundry facilities. Pets allowed. | 3007 Santa Monica Blvd. | 310/829–6333 or 800/591–5995 | fax 310/829–1983 | www.smdaysinn.com | 68 rooms | $79–$115 | AE, D, MC, V.

Doubletree Guest Suites. Three blocks from the pier and beach, Santa Monica's only all-suites hotel is south of I–10. Restaurant, bar, room service. In-room data ports, minibars, cable TV. Pool. Hot tub. Exercise equipment. Laundry facilities. Business services. | 1707 4th St. | 310/395–3332 | fax 310/458–6493 | 253 suites | $195–$220 suites | AE, D, DC, MC, V.

Fairmont Miramar. An 1889 mansion anchors this tree-filled property, which includes bungalows and a contemporary 10-story tower with ocean views. 2 restaurants, 2 bars (with entertainment), room service. In-room data ports, some minibars, cable TV. Pool. Beauty salon, hot tub, massage, sauna, steam room. Gym, beach. Baby-sitting. Laundry facilities. Business services. | 101 Wilshire Blvd. | 310/576–7777 | fax 310/458–7912 | www.fairmont.com | 302 rooms, 31 bungalows | $299–$339 rooms, $739 bungalows | AE, D, DC, MC, V.

Four Points Inn Santa Monica. Check out the ocean or mountains from many of the rooms of this nine-story hotel, four blocks from the beach, off I–10. Restaurant. In-room data ports, cable TV. Pool. Hot tub. Exercise equipment. Laundry facilities. Business services. | 530 W. Pico Blvd. | 310/399–9344 | fax 310/399–2504 | www.sheraton.com | 307 rooms, 7 suites | $199–$219; $360 suites | AE, D, DC, MC, V.

Georgian. Marble floors and arched entry ways complement the Art Deco facade of this 1931 landmark, across the street from the ocean. Rooms, many with views of the water, are appointed with custom-made furnishings. Restaurant. In-room data ports, cable TV. Business services. Pets allowed. | 1415 Ocean Ave. | 310/395–9945 or 800/538–8147 | fax 310/451–3374 | sales@georgianhotel.com | www.georgianhotel.com | 84 rooms, 28 suites | $210–$260, $325–$475 suites | AE, DC, MC, V.

Holiday Inn. Sand hues dominate the rooms, suggestive of the beach one block from the hotel. Restaurant, bar, room service. In-room data ports, some refrigerators, cable TV. Pool. Exercise equipment. Laundry facilities. Pets allowed (fee). | 120 Colorado Ave. | 310/451–0676 | fax 310/393–7145 | www.holidayinnsm.com | 132 rooms | $179–$219 | AE, D, DC, MC, V.

★ **Hotel California.** A small hotel with lots of charm, right on the ocean and four blocks south of shopping areas and eateries, Hotel California has private, gated beach access and large, airy rooms with hardwood floors. Reserve well in advance. Some refrigerators, some in-room VCRs. Beach, water sports. Laundry facilities. Free parking. | 1670 Ocean Ave. | 310/393–2363 | fax 310/393–4180 | 102 rooms, 8 suites | $140, $169–$250 suites | AE, DC, MC, V.

Hotel Carmel. Some of the rooms in this hotel have ocean views. Laundry service. | 201 Broadway | 310/451–2469 | fax 310/393–4180 | 102 rooms | $85–$125 | AE, D, DC, MC, V.

Hotel Casa del Mar. Sit on oversized chairs, enjoy a cocktail in the richly-colored lobby of this elegant recently renovated European-style boutique hotel, and appreciate the care given to preserve its 1920s history. Bathrooms have amenities such as bathrobes, Rainforest toiletries, and scented candles, and beds are made in imported linens. Some rooms and suites have ocean views, suites range in size from one to two bedroom. 1 Restaurant, 1 bar. Air conditioning, in-room data ports, minibars, in-room hot tubs, cable TV, in-room VCRs (and movies), room phones. 1 outdoor pool. Hot tub, massage, spa, outdoor hot tub, sauna, steam room. Gym. Shops. Laundry service. Business services, airport shuttle. | 1920 Ocean Front Way, | 310/581–5533 or 800/898–6999 | www.hotelcasadelmar.com | fax 310/581–5503 | 127 rooms, 8 suites | $345–$525 rooms, $825–$3000 suites | AE, D, DC, MC, V.

Hotel Oceana. The bright, whimsically stylish frescoes in the lobby lend a Mediterranean air to this contemporary all-suites hotel 8 mi north of Los Angeles International Airport. The pool area is intimate, and the gym sun-drenched. Some suites have ocean views; all have either a private lanai or a balcony set with interesting furniture. The feeling throughout is refreshingly residential, rather like your own southern California mansion. Room service at lunch and dinner comes from the Wolfgang Puck Café. Bar, complimentary Continental breakfast, room service. In-room data ports, kitchenettes, cable TV. Pool. Gym. beach. Laundry facilities, laundry service. Business services, parking (fee). | 849 Ocean Ave. | 310/393–0486 | www.hoteloceana.com | 63 suites | $235–$450 | AE, D, DC, MC, V.

Le Merigot Beach Hotel. Blending the flair of Europe's elegant hotels with the vibrance of Southern California, this luxury hotel has everything you need for business or pleasure travel: meeting planning services, spa treatments, and personal trainers are at your disposal. All rooms have Frette linens, down comforters, marble tile bathrooms, Bare Escentuals fine toiletries, oversized towels, and feather pillows; many have views of the ocean from private patios. The Catalina suite has a king-size bed, separate living area, and view of the southern coastline from a private balcony; the Malibu suite has an identical layout with the added perk of an oceanfront balcony view. The hotel is just one block south of the Santa Monica pier, five blocks north of the 3rd St. Promenade, and five blocks south of shopping and entertainment. Restaurant. Air conditioning, in-room data ports, minibars, cable TV, room phones. Massage, spa, beauty salon, sauna, steam room. Gym. Laundry service. Business services, parking (fee). | 1740 Ocean Ave., | 310/395–9700 or 800/926–9524 | www.lemerigotbeachhotel.com | fax 310/395–9200 | 175 rooms, 13 jr suites, 2 suites | $279–$399 rooms, $429 junior suites, $800 Catalina suite, $1200 Malibu suite.

Loews Santa Monica Beach Hotel. You can't stay any closer to the beach—the sand starts outside the door of this hotel. Most rooms open onto a five-story atrium and have views of the water or city. Restaurants, bar (with entertainment), room service. In-room data ports, cable TV, in-room VCRs (and movies). Indoor-outdoor pool. Beauty salon, hot tub, massage. Gym, beach, bicycles. Kids' programs. Business services. | 1700 Ocean Ave. | 310/458–6700 | fax 310/458–6761 | loewssantamonicabeach@loewshotels.com | www.loewshotels.com | 345 rooms, 35 suites | $240–$305, $590 suites | AE, D, DC, MC, V.

Pacific Shore Hotel. Some rooms have ocean views in this eight-story hotel 200 steps from the beach near many popular restaurants. A free shuttle runs to attractions within a 5-mi radius. Restaurant, bar. In-room data ports, in-room safes, some minibars, some refrigerators, cable TV. Pool. Hot tub. Exercise equipment, beach. Laundry facilities. Business services, parking (fee). | 1819 Ocean Ave. | 310/451–8711 | fax 310/394–6657 | 168 rooms | $135–$200 | AE, D, DC, MC, V.

Radisson Huntley. Many rooms at this 18-story hotel, two blocks from the beach and promenade, have ocean views. Restaurant. In-room data ports, refrigerators, cable TV (and movies). Exercise equipment. Business services. | 1111 2nd St. | 310/394–5454 | fax 310/458–9776 | www.radisson.com | 213 rooms | $179–$199 | AE, D, DC, MC, V.

Shangri-La. Rounded corners and sleek lines distinguish the facade of this hostelry built in the 1930s. Inside, Art Deco furnishings fill bedrooms and suites, and views take in the mountains or the ocean. Large terraces and tropical grounds surround the hotel, and it's two blocks from the beach. Complimentary Continental breakfast. Some kitchenettes, some microwaves, some refrigerators, cable TV. | 1301 Ocean Ave. | 310/394–2791 or 800/345–7829 | fax 310/451–3351 | www.shangrila-hotel.com | 19 rooms, 35 suites | $160, $205–$310 suites | AE, D, DC, MC, V.

★ **Shutters on the Beach.** Informal and elegant are the buzzwords at this pampering lodging, where comfortable deck chairs beckon you to bask on the deck overlooking the ocean, as in the unassuming beach homes that grew up along the Southern California shores in the 1920s. The rooms' floor-to-ceiling windows have ocean views, and suites have fireplaces and private decks. Restaurant, bar, room service. In-room data ports, cable TV, in-room VCRs (and movies). | 1 Pico Blvd. | 310/458–0030 or 800/334–9000 | fax 310/458–4589 | Sotb@earthlink.com | www.shuttersonthebeach.com | 184 rooms, 12 suites | $360–$560, $895–$2,500 suites | AE, D, DC, MC, V.

Travelodge. Picnic tables and a gas barbecue occupy a courtyard at this hotel, 2 mi from the beach. Picnic area, complimentary Continental breakfast. Some microwaves, some refrigerators, cable TV. Business services, airport shuttle. | 3102 Pico Blvd. | 310/450–5766 | fax 310/450–8843 | www.travelodge.com | 84 rooms | $79–$99 | AE, D, DC, MC, V.

SANTA NELLA

(Nearby town also listed: Merced)

Modest Santa Nella is not much more than a rest stop along I–5 in the Central Valley, 275 mi north of Los Angeles and 116 mi south of Sacramento. But even this humble hamlet has an interesting legend. The story goes that Santa Nella was established by developers hoping to capitalize on the construction of I–5, but they ran out of money and their early efforts sat, half-finished, for a decade. When new investors came along, they found a sign with the name of the never-realized town, St. Isabella, but time had faded all but the letters "S" and "Ella." With admirable thrift, they recycled the old sign and dubbed their enterprise "Santa Nella."

Information: **Los Banos Chamber of Commerce** | 503 J St., 93635 | 209/826–2495.

Attractions

Los Banos Grassland Wetlands. This region, 160,000 acres of publicly and privately owned wetlands, serves as a critical stopover point along the Pacific Flyway, an ancient bird migration route stretching 10,000 mi from Alaska to South America. Los Banos wetlands, accessible from Gustine, Los Banos, and Santa Nella, constitutes California's largest protected wetland ecosystem, providing seasonal and year-round habitat for roughly 550 species of plants, birds, mammals, and other creatures. To get oriented in this vast preserve, and to get directions to trails and driving routes, check out the displays at Los Banos Wildlife Area, and at the Merced and San Luis National Wildlife Refuge Areas. Ask for a schedule of guided tours. | 22759 S. Mercey Springs Rd., Los Banos | 209/826–5188 | fax 209/826–4984 | www.grasslandwetlands.com | Daily, dawn–dusk.

San Luis Reservoir State Park. Consisting of 65 mi of shoreline surrounding three lakes, this water system is the largest off-stream reservoir in the United States. A visitors center offers information on the region's history, from the days of the Northern Valley Yokut Indians through the Spanish Mission era and the reservoir's construction as an agricultural water source. You'll find boating, picnicking, hiking, water-skiing, and camping at three campgrounds, from primitive to developed, with hookups for RVs. It's 4 mi south of Santa Nella and 7 mi west of I–5. | 31426 Gonzaga Rd., Gustine; Rte. 152 | 209/826–1196 or 800/444–7275 for campsite reservations | www.cal-parks.ca.gov/DISTRICTS/fourrivers | $5/car day-use; campsites $10–$16 | Open ½ hr before sunrise to sunset.

Dining

Denny's. American. This is a convenient, kid-friendly chain restaurant with counter and table seating. Reliable American dishes, with breakfast, lunch, and dinner served at any time. Popular items the fajita steak skillet and the pot roast. Kids' menu. | 12820 S. Rte. 33 | 209/826–3723 | Daily, 24 hrs | $5–$10 | AE, MC, D, DC, V.

Mrs B's. American. Here's a homey, friendly truck stop–style restaurant in the Travel Center complex, which also has a convenience store, gas station, and vehicle repair shop. The extensive menu includes steak, pastas, and everything in between; don't miss the clam chowder on Fridays. | 12323 Rte. 33 | 209/826–0741 | Daily, 24 hours | Breakfast also served | $7–$12 | AE, MC, V.

Pea Soup Andersen's. American. This family-style restaurant with rustic Scandinavian decor, a branch of the famous Buellton original, is celebrated far and wide for its pea soup, and has been turning it out for more than 50 years. The menu also offers steaks, chops, and pasta dishes. Kids' menu. | 12411 S. Rte. 33 | 209/826–1685 | Breakfast also available | $6–$15 | AE, DC, MC, V.

Lodging

Best Western Andersen's Inn. This two-story, Danish-style inn with a real windmill overlooks a landscaped courtyard and pool. Restaurant, bar, complimentary Continental breakfast. Pool. Laundry service. Pets allowed. | 12367 S. Rte. 33 | 209/826–5534 | fax 209/826–4353 | www.bestwestern.com | 94 rooms | $61–$79 | AE, D, DC, MC, V.

Holiday Inn Express. This attractive, two-story Mission-style hotel surrounds a landscaped courtyard with fountain. Complimentary Continental breakfast. Refrigerators, cable TV. Outdoor pool. Spa. Laundry facilities. Pets allowed. | 28976 W. Plaza Dr. | 209/826–8282 | www.holidayinn.com | 100 rooms | $59–$79 | AE, D, DC, MC, V.

Ramada Inn. This two-story hotel surrounds an attractive, early California–style plaza. Complimentary Continental breakfast. In-room data ports, cable TV. | 13070 S. Hwy. 33 | 209/826–4444 or 800/546–5697 | www.ramada.com | 159 rooms | $55–$80 | AE, D, DC, MC, V.

SANTA ROSA

MAP 3, C7

(Nearby towns also listed: Guerneville, Healdsburg, Jenner, Petaluma, Sonoma)

Originally home to the Pomo, Miwok, and Wappo Indians, Santa Rosa was settled by the Spanish in the early 1800s. The City of Santa Rosa was founded in 1833 by General Mariano Vallejo, commander of the Mexican forces north of San Francisco. The Gold Rush later lured people into the vicinity. Many of the people realized that they would get rich faster by farming the region's rich soils. When the railroad reached Santa Rosa in 1870, the town became an agricultural center for the shipment of crops all over the country. Botanist Luther Burbank arrived five years later and spent the next half-century developing more than 800 varieties of vegetables, flowers, and fruits, including the deep-purple Santa Rosa plum.

The hub of Sonoma County and the largest city in the Wine Country, Santa Rosa (50 mi north of San Francisco) is now a thriving town of more than 130,000 people. Business and light industry have boomed here, but the area remains a land of natural riches. In surrounding county lands, there are 22 city, state, and county parks and 63 mi of Pacific Ocean coastline.

Santa Rosa is the gateway to an agricultural region known for apple orchards and other produce, and to more than 200 vineyards. Lucky for visitors that the result is a cornucopia of restaurants, celebrating the marriage of this local bounty.

Information: Greater Santa Rosa Convention and Visitors Bureau | 9 4th St., 95401 | 800/404–ROSE | www.visitsonoma.com.

Attractions

Annadel State Park. Hikers, mountain bikers, horseback riders, photographers, anglers, and joggers enjoy this preserve's 35 mi of trails, looping through nearly 5,000 acres of rolling hills, intermittent streams, meadows, and woodland. Keep your eyes and ears peeled for the park's burgeoning population of wild turkeys. The park spreads across the hills on the east side of town, off Route 12. | 6201 Channel Dr. | 707/539–3911 | www.parks.ca.gov/north/silverado/asp246.htm | $2 | Daily sunrise–sunset.

Howarth Park. In addition to a lake where you can fish and boat, this 152-acre park includes a softball field, picnic areas, miles of hiking and jogging trails, and an amusement area with train ride, carousel, animal farm, and pony rides. | 630 Summerfield Rd. | 707/543–3282 | Free | Nov.–Mar., daily 6AM–6PM; Apr.–Oct., daily 6AM–9PM.

Luther Burbank Home and Gardens. Luther Burbank, developer of more than 800 plant species, including the Santa Rosa Plum and the Burbank Rose, worked for more than 50 years in Santa Rosa. His home and gardens were renovated in 1990 to serve as an outdoor museum, complete with a greenhouse, cutting garden, wildlife garden, and Victorian-style orchard. | Santa Rosa Ave. | 707/524–5445 | www.santarosachamber.com | Free | Gardens daily 8–dusk; home Apr.–Oct., Tues.–Sun. 10–3:30; museum Apr.–Oct. 10–4.

Railroad Square. Browse this shopping district set in basalt stone buildings holding antiques shops, coffee houses, vintage clothing stores, and restaurants. | 4th and Wilson Sts.

Snoopy's Gallery and Gift Shop. Original artwork and collectibles capturing images of Charlie Brown, Lucy, Linus, and, of course, the inimitable beagle, are showcased at this gallery, opened in 1981. The site also houses and sells the largest collection of gift items related to Charles Schulz's beloved comic strip. Next door is the Redwood Empire Ice Arena, conceived and built by the cartoonist, who hailed from Santa Rosa and passed away in 2000. An expanded Charles Schulz museum, with galleries, and auditorium, classrooms, and gardens, is scheduled to open on the site in Fall 2001. | 1665 W. Steele La. | 707/546–3385 | www.snoopygift.com | Free | Daily 10–6.

Sonoma County Museum. Artifacts, documents, and photographs that touch on the area's history are on display in the 1910 Federal Post Office. In addition, an installation re-creates the facades of buildings from the early 1900s. Special exhibits for kids appear year-round. | 425 7th St. | 707/579–1500 | $1 | Wed.–Sun. 11–4.

Sonoma County Vineyards Tour. This self-guided road trip leads you on a tour of the valley, with details on more than 200 vineyards. Appellations include Dry Creek Valley, Alexander Valley, Russian River Valley, Sonoma Coast, and Sonoma Valley. | 9 4th St. | 800/404–ROSE | www.gosonoma.com | Free | Daily.

Sonoma Museum of Visual Art. Founded by local artists, the museum showcases local and internationally known artists who work in paint, wood, steel, film, and video. | 50 Mark West Springs Rd. | 707/527–0297 | fax 707/545–0518 | $2 | Wed., Fri. 1–4, Thurs. 1–8, weekends 11–4.

ON THE CALENDAR

JULY–AUG.: *Sonoma County Fair.* Flower and art shows, entertainment, horse racing, rides, exhibits of agricultural products and livestock keep everything hopping at the Sonoma County Fairgrounds. | 707/545–4200.

OCT.: *Sonoma County Harvest Fair.* Wine tasting and judging, art shows and sales, hayrides, sheep dog trials, and marathons are part of this festival, held at the Sonoma County Fairgrounds. | 707/545–4203.

Dining

Ca'Bianca. Italian. A metal fireplace, gas chandeliers, murals, and inlaid hardwood floors distinguish this 1876 Victorian house where you'll be served dishes such as monkfish in tarragon sauce, rack of veal, and eggplant-and-tomato-stuffed ravioli. | 835 2nd St. | 707/542–5305 | No lunch Sat.–Sun. | $11–$22 | AE, MC, V.

Capri. Italian. Beneath the high ceilings, soaring windows, and walls of glazed Venetian plaster are served imaginative entrées like pork chops beneath shiitake and cremini mushrooms, and salmon pasta in a vodka cream sauce. Kids' menu. | 115 4th St. | 707/525–0815 | Closed Sun. No lunch Sat. | $11–$18 | AE, MC, V.

Equus. Contemporary. Plush cushioned booths and large tables fill this restaurant where specialties include seared Dungeness crab cakes and summer truffle risotto primavera. | 101 Fountain Grove Pkwy. | 707/578–0149 or 800/222–6101 | Closed Sun. No lunch Sat. | $15–$30 | AE, D, DC, MC, V.

Gary Chu's. Chinese. With high ceilings and white-linen tablecloths, this restaurant offers a pretty setting for a long menu with many Mandarin and Szechuan Chinese favorites, including kung pao chicken and orange peel beef. | 611 5th St. | 707/526–5840 | Closed Mon. | $6–$10 | AE, D, DC, MC, V.

John Ash and Co. Contemporary. Arched windows open to lawns and vineyards beneath high-vaulted ceilings here, in the dining room of the Vintner's Inn. Ahi tuna seared and coated with sesame seeds, and sautéed duck breast with rice pancakes and asparagus are two examples of the imaginative cuisine. | 4350 Barnes Rd. | 707/527–7687 | No lunch Mon. | $17–$30 | AE, MC, V.

Josef's. Continental. A fireplace, glass cabinets, and original art distinguish this dining room at the Hotel La Rose, in Railroad Square. Rack of lamb, beef bourguignonne, and veau Zurichois (veal sliced thin and served with mushrooms and spaetzle) are some of the classic dishes that fill the menu. | 308 Wilson St. | 707/571–8664 | Closed Sun. No lunch Mon. | $16–$25 | MC, V.

Kenwood. Continental. Whimsical art warms the walls of this restaurant, in the Sonoma Valley vineyards, 10 mi south of Santa Rosa. Hardwood floors and bamboo chairs set the stage for poached salmon in a caper beurre blanc, crab cakes, and rack of lamb. Also dine outside looking over vineyards and fields. | 9900 Sonoma Hwy., Kenwood | 707/833–6326 | Closed Mon., Tues. | $15–$25 | MC, V.

LeGare. Continental. Stained wood chairs and booths complement the idyllic scenes of the Swiss countryside on the walls at this Railroad Square restaurant, serving dishes like braised duck in orange sauce, veal with mustard, and beef Wellington. Kids' menu. | 208 Wilson St. | 707/528–4355 | Closed Mon. No lunch | $15–$30 | AE, D, DC, MC, V.

Lisa Hemenway's. Contemporary. Bright paintings create a lively, upbeat environment in which to savor specialties like chicken and lemongrass hash and crab fritters accompanied by green papaya salad. | 1612 Terrace Way | 707/526–5111 | Closed Sun. | $20–$30 | AE, DC, MC, V.

Mark West Lodge. Contemporary. Entering through the gazebo gateway, you reach the ornately detailed dining room of this 1833 building. The dining ballroom has a stained-glass wall and fountain. Regulars come for seafood (including lobster) and steaks like beef Wellington, Chateaubriand, and pepper steak. | 2520 Mark West Springs Rd. | 707/546–2592 | Closed Tues. in Oct.–May and Mon., Sun. brunch | $20–$35 | AE, MC, V.

Mistral. Mediterranean. Matisse-like designs decorate booths inside, while outside, on a brick patio, a stone fountain purls beneath a wisteria-laden trellis. The menu changes daily but might include salmon in a basil-mint vinaigrette or pasta with olives, feta, artichoke hearts, and marinara sauce. Kids' menu. | 1229 N. Dutton Ave. | 707/578–4511 | $9–$17 | AE, D, DC, MC, V.

★ **Mixx.** Eclectic. A hand-carved bar, built in Italy in the late 1880s, stands at the center of this high-ceilinged dining room, lit by fluted chandeliers. Roasted salmon under a honey-miso glaze, basil-fettucine served with smoked chicken, and chicken pot pie are some of the menu's highlights. Kids' menu. | 135 4th St. | 707/573–1344 | Closed Sun. No lunch Sat. | $15–$25 | AE, DC, MC, V.

Old Mexico East. Mexican. The Mission-style building, surrounded by grass and palm trees, has a colorful interior with Aztec murals. Named after a city in Mexico, the Tostada Mazatlan, grilled chicken or prawns over a bed of rice topped with tropical fruit, and seafood enchiladas are two of the more popular dishes. Dine outside on the colorful tile patio next to a fountain. Kids' menu. | 4501 Montgomery Dr. | 707/539–2599 | $10–$20 | AE, D, DC, MC, V.

Syrah. Continental. Behind a curvy dining counter, watch the chef working in the open kitchen, preparing items from the always-changing menu. Selections might include foie gras with fruit preserve and molasses bread or tea-smoked pheasant in a blackberry sage sauce. There's an interior courtyard with fountain for outside dining. | 205 5th St. | 707/568–4002 | Closed Sun., Mon. | $20–$30 | DC, MC, V.

Third Street Aleworks. American. Burgers, fish and chips, and chili are some of the comfort-food mainstays at this high-energy restaurant in the Courthouse Square area. Of the 22 different beers brewed here, between 8 and 14 are always on tap. | 610 3rd St. | 707/523–3060 | $7–$15 | AE, D, MC, V.

The Villa. Contemporary. Beneath cathedral ceilings, enormous windows open onto panoramic scenes of the surrounding hills. The menu includes pizza, pasta, steaks, seafood, and chicken dishes. Fridays and Saturdays are prime rib nights. | 3901 Montgomery Dr. | 707/528–7755 | No lunch weekends | $9–$20 | AE, D, MC, V.

Lodging

Best Western Garden Inn. Attractively landscaped grounds surround this hotel east of U.S. 101 and less than 1 mi from the Sonoma County Fairgrounds and Luther Burbank Gardens. Some refrigerators, cable TV. 2 pools. Laundry facilities. Business services. Pets allowed (fee). | 1500 Santa Rosa Ave. | 707/546–4031 or 800/929–2771 | fax 707/526–4903 | www.bestwestern.com | 78 rooms | $80–$180 | AE, D, DC, MC, V.

Flamingo Resort. Many rooms overlook the Olympic-size pool on this 10-acre resort, opened in 1957, where a can't-miss-it neon flamingo tops a tower emblazoned with the resort's name. Restaurant, bar, room service. In-room data ports, refrigerators, cable TV. Pool, wading pool. Beauty salon, hot tub, massage, spa. 5 tennis courts. Health club. Business services. | 2777 4th St. | 707/545–8530 or 800/848–8300 | fax 707/528–1404 | info@flamingoresort.com | www.flamingoresort.com | 170 rooms | $99–$199 | AE, DC, MC, V.

Fountaingrove Inn. Oak, redwood, and stone accent the Frank Lloyd Wright–inspired buildings on landscaped grounds below the landmark Round Barn, once used to house horses. The spacious rooms have brass details, mirrored walls, and floor-to-ceiling windows. Restaurant (see Equus Restaurant), complimentary breakfast, room service. In-room data ports, refrigerators, cable TV. Pool. Hot tub. Business services, airport shuttle. | 101 Fountaingrove Pkwy. | 707/578–6101 or 800/222–6101 | fax 707/544–3126 | www.fountaingroveinn.com | 126 rooms | $119–$199 | AE, D, DC, MC, V.

Gables Inn. The name of this 1877 inn, on 3 landscaped acres, comes from the 15 gables that grace the roof. Italian marble fireplaces, chandeliers, and period furnishings complement the Victorian architecture. Picnic area, complimentary breakfast. Some in-room hot tubs, no room phones. | 4257 Petaluma Hill Rd. | 707/585–777 or 800/GABLESN | fax 707/584–5634 | innkeeper@thegablesinn.com | www.thegablesinn.com | 4 rooms, 2 suites, 1 cottage | $150–$175, $175–$195 suites, $225 cottage | AE, D, DC, MC, V.

Hilton. On a hill east of U.S. 101, this three-story hotel overlooks 11 landscaped acres. Restaurant, bar. Refrigerators, room service, cable TV. Pool. Hot tub. Exercise equipment. Business services, free parking. | 3555 Round Barn Blvd. | 707/523–7555 or 800/HILTONS | fax 707/569–5550 | www.hilton.com | 246 rooms | $199–$239 | AE, D, DC, MC, V.

Holiday Inn Express. This two-story motel east of U.S. 101 has rooms with balconies and patios. Complimentary Continental breakfast. Some in-room hot tubs, cable TV. Pool. Hot tub, sauna. Basketball, gym. Business services, airport shuttle. | 870 Hopper Ave. | 707/545–9000 or 800/533–1255 | fax 707/571–0145 | www.winecountryhotel.com | 96 rooms | $79–$179 | AE, D, DC, MC, V.

Hotel La Rose. The rooms of this hotel, built of local cobblestone in 1907, are appointed with antiques—two-poster beds and armoires that conceal large-screen TVs. You can relax in a garden courtyard. You can eat on the premises at Josef's. Restaurant, bar, complimentary breakfast. In-room data ports, cable TV. Laundry facilities. Business services. | 308 Wilson St. | 707/579–3200 | fax 707/579–3247 | concierge@hotellarose.com | www.hotellarose.com | 49 rooms, 11 suites | $114–$124, $295 suites | AE, D, DC, MC, V.

Kenwood Inn. The four vine-covered, Tuscan-style villas that make up this antiques- and featherbed-filled inn surround a garden and fountains in Kenwood, 35 min south of downtown Santa Rosa. Complimentary breakfast. No room phones. Pool. Hot tub, steam room. Business services. No kids under 16. | 10400 Sonoma Hwy., Kenwood | 707/833–1293 or 800/353–6966 | fax 707/833–1247 | www.sterba.com/kenwood/inn | 12 rooms | $285–$395 | AE, DC, MC, V.

Los Robles Lodge. Five acres of landscaped grounds surround this two-story lodge off U.S. 101. Restaurant, bar (with entertainment), room service. In-room data ports, refrigerators, cable TV. Pool, wading pool. Hot tub, steam room. Exercise equipment. Laundry facilities. Business services, airport shuttle. Pets allowed. | 1985 Cleveland Ave. | 707/545–6330 or 800/255–6330 | fax 707/575–5826 | www.losrobleslodge.com | 104 rooms | $96–$150 | AE, D, DC, MC, V.

Pygmalion House. Antiques from famed stripper Gypsy Rose Lee and colorful former Sausalito Mayor Sally Stanford complement the fireplaces and octagonal windows of this 1886 Queen Anne Victorian within two blocks of Old Santa Rosa and downtown. Complimentary breakfast. Cable TV, no room phones. Library. No smoking. | 331 Orange St. | 707/526–3407 | 5 rooms | $79–124 | MC, V.

Sandman Motel. Landscaped gardens and a pond surround this motel with quiet rooms set back from the street and close to restaurants, east of U.S. 101. Complimentary Continental breakfast. Refrigerators, cable TV. Pool. Hot tub. | 3421 Cleveland Ave. | 707/544–8570 | fax 707/544–8710 | www.sonoma.com/lodging/sandman | 112 rooms | $68–$118 | AE, D, DC, MC, V.

Super 8. This three-story, interior corridor motel is west of U.S. 101. Cable TV. Pool. Business services. | 2632 Cleveland Ave. | 707/542–5544 or 800/800–8000 | fax 707/542–9738 | 100 rooms | $35–$90 | AE, D, DC, MC, V.

Vintners Inn. Forty-five acres of vineyards and lush landscaping surround these four pine-furnished stone buildings. Upstairs rooms have vaulted ceilings and fireplaces, while downstairs rooms open onto a patio. Restaurant (*see* John Ash and Co.), bar, complimentary Continental breakfast, room service. In-room data ports, refrigerators. Outdoor hot tub. Business services. | 4350 Barnes Rd. | 707/575–7350 or 800/421–2584 | fax 707/575–1426 | www.vintnersinn.com | 44 rooms | $198–$278 | AE, DC, MC, V.

SARATOGA

MAP 6, E9

(Nearby towns also listed: Los Gatos, San Jose, San Mateo, Santa Cruz)

Saratoga is a charming village of 31,255 with coffeehouses, antiques dealers, and boutiques, at the foot of the Santa Cruz Mountains. A well-heeled crowd strolls the tree-lined streets, including many employees of Silicon Valley firms—Saratoga is on its western edge. The town got its name in 1865, after the village of the same name in upstate New York, because that town, too, had a mineral spring. Back then, town lots sold for $10 to $50. Apricot and cherry orchards spread out across adjacent open lands. A sawmill built in 1847 by William Campbell, for whom a nearby city is named, kicked off a lumber and paper-milling industry that thrived until the late 1800s. Today, paper has given way to computer chips, with high-tech firms mushrooming where the fruit trees once grew, and real estate values are about a hundred-fold higher than they were in 1865. Nevertheless, Saratoga retains a quaint, small-town ambience.

Information: Saratoga Chamber of Commerce | 20460 Saratoga–Los Gatos Rd., 95070 | 408/867–0753 | www.saratogachamber.org.

Attractions

Cooper-Garrod Estate Vineyards. Just one example of area wineries, this family-owned and operated enterprise produces Chardonnay, Cabernet Blanc, and Cabernet Sauvignon varietals. The 21-acre estate has an antique tasting room, the "Fruit House," open for tastings on weekends. | 22600 Mount Eden Rd. | 408/741–8094 | Free | Tasting room open weekends 11–4:30.

Hakone Gardens. Oliver and Isabel Stine created this serene Japanese-style garden in 1918. Its 18 acres include gazebos, a moon bridge, waterfalls, and ponds filled with silver-and-gold koi fish. Hakone Gardens is 1/4 mi from the main village of Saratoga. | 21000 Big Basin Way | 408/741–4994 | Parking, $5 | Weekdays 10–5, weekends 11–5.

Villa Montalvo. This Mediterranean-style villa sits on 175 acres 1/2 mi south of town just off Route 9. Senator James Phelan built it in 1912 and willed the property as a public park and center for the arts. It's home to the West's oldest artist-in-residence program, quarterly readings, and you can enjoy the open studios that contain the fruits of the program. A gallery has exhibitions by regional artists. There are classical music and theatrical concerts in summer in the 1,200-seat outdoor amphitheater. | 15400 Montalvo Rd. | 408/961–5800 | Grounds free | Gallery Wed.–Sun. 1–4.

Dining

The Basin. Contemporary. This eatery caters to Silicon Valley's tech crowd, with an open, light-filled dining room with sleek wood furnishings. The Atomic Lounge is a private dining room wired for high-tech presentations with projector screen, computer, DSL access, space for 30 guests and "a comfy couch." The bar offers Santa Cruz wines and 20 different martinis. Try the grilled chili-crusted prawns appetizer, mushroom pasta, braised lamb shanks, or pizza. | 14572 Big Basin Way | 408/867–1906 | www.thebasin.com | Closed Mon. | $10–$18 | AE, DC, MC, V.

La Mère Michele. French. The first French-style restaurant in the area, this is hung with Impressionist-style paintings, and there's a Bohemian crystal chandelier in the main dining room. The large windows of the Terrace Room overlook the street. Try the seared eastern scallops with prawns in puff pastry with lobster sauce, the filet mignon with lobster tails in garlic butter, or rack of lamb with honey and almonds. It's 2 mi west of the Saratoga Avenue exit on Route 85. Sunday brunch. | 14467 Big Basin Way | 408/867–5272 | fax 408/867–2011 | Reservations essential | No lunch Sat. Closed Mondays | $19–$48 | AE, D, DC, MC, V.

Plumed Horse. French. Built in 1883 as a stable, this is an elegant restaurant with seven private rooms, rich with mahogany and silk-paneled walls and paintings by local artists. Tables are set with chargers and crystal stemware, and the menu is filled with fresh local organic produce and fish, game birds, venison, and rack of lamb (a specialty of the house); the lobster tail with black truffle sauce is decadent, and the Grand Marnier soufflé is delicious for dessert. Jazz trio on weekends in the lounge. | 14555 Big Basin Way | 408/867–4711 | fax 408/867–6919 | Reservations essential | Closed Sun. | $20–$48 | AE, DC, MC, V.

Lodging

Inn at Saratoga. This four-story hotel offers a quiet setting in the center of downtown. All rooms are oversized, each overlooking Saratoga Creek and a wooded park. Rooms have taupe and teal appointments, with some balconies. The bathrooms are spacious. Junior suites may be connected with parlors, and suites have whirlpool baths. Complimentary Continental breakfast. In-room data ports, refrigerators, cable TV, in-room VCRs (and movies). Business services. No smoking. | 20645 4th St. | 408/867–5020 or 800/338–5020 | fax 408/741–0981 | 39 rooms, 7 suites | $210; $280–$495 suites | AE, DC, MC, V.

Saratoga Oaks Lodge. Old oak trees shade this one- and two-story lodge on the main street of Saratoga village, a one-and-a-half-block stroll from shops and restaurants. Some rooms have steam baths and fireplaces. Complimentary Continental breakfast. In-room data ports, refrigerators, microwaves, cable TV, in-room VCRs. Business services. | 14626 Big Basin Way | 408/867–3307 | fax 408/867–3307 | www.saratogaoakslodge.com | 15 rooms, 5 suites | $125–$160; $160–$175 suites | AE, DC, MC, V.

SAUSALITO

MAP 6, B4

(Nearby towns also listed: Corte Madera, Mill Valley, San Francisco, Tiburon)

Across the Golden Gate Bridge and accessible by ferry from San Francisco and the East Bay, Sausalito is a colorful, Mediterranean-style waterfront city. Originally home to the Miwok Indians, it was named in 1775 by the Spanish explorer Juan Manual de Ayala "Saucelito" or "little willow." For more than a century sailing ships docked at its waterfront. Until transformed by tourism in the 1970s, Sausalito was a fairly quiet little town filled with colorful residents. Beat poets, artists, and musicians rented the tiny houses clinging to its hills, and notorious madame Sally Stanford did a lively business—she even served as mayor in the 1960s. Eclectic houseboats and oceangoing yachts tie up at the waterfront. Downtown, a National Historical Landmark District is known for its street-side cafés, waterfront restaurants, artists' studios and galleries, and many shops and boutiques, most located along Bridgeway, Sausalito's main drag. Traffic can be congested on weekends, and parking is difficult (and the meter checkers relentless); plan to park away from downtown and stroll in. A good stop for the foot-weary is the No-name Bar on Bridgeway, an unpretentious place where you can often find a jazz jam session in progress.

Information: **Sausalito Chamber of Commerce** | 29 Caledonia St., 94965 | 415/332–0505 | www.sausalito.org.

Attractions

Bay Area Discovery Museum. A hands-on learning center for kids up to age 10, exhibits here include a simulated ocean environment where kids can "fish" from a boat, a home-building center, and a computer lab. Special events, performances, and exhibits occur year-round. The museum is in Fort Baker, a former military post at the south end of town, almost underneath the Golden Gate Bridge. | 557 McReynolds Rd., Fort Baker | 415/487–4398 | www.badm.org | $7 | Tues.–Thurs. 9–4, Fri.–Sun. 10–5; longer on some weekdays during school breaks.

Marine Mammal Center. Volunteers and staff at the this center rescue and rehabilitate sick, injured, or distressed seals and other marine mammals (and even a few sea turtles). You're welcome to take a self-guided tour. To reach the center, 4 mi west of U.S. 101, take the Alexander Avenue exit off U.S. 101 and head north ½ mi to Tunnel Road; turn left, continue through the tunnel for 3 mi, and follow the signs. | 1065 Fort Cronkhite Dr. | 415/289–SEAL | www.tmmc.org/ | Daily 10–4.

San Francisco Bay Delta Model. This is a three-dimensional, 3½-acre representation of San Francisco Bay and adjacent delta, complete with a mini–Golden Gate Bridge. A scale replica of the region's watery networks is capable of simulating tides, currents, and other variables affecting water quality and movement. In use since 1956, this model has helped scientists unravel the bay's secrets. It's now mostly retired for scientific uses, and is used to educate visitors about their environment. | 2100 Bridgeway | 415/332–3870 | free | Memorial Day–Labor Day, Tues.–Fri. 9–4, weekends and holidays 10–6, Sept.–May, Tues.–Sat. 9–4.

Dining

Mikayla. Contemporary. Artist Laurel Burch designed this bright, airy restaurant in Casa Madrona, which has a superlative view of Belvedere and Angel Islands. In good weather, a glass roof is rolled back, or when it's foggy, you can take a table by the fireplace. Beer and wine. Sunday brunch. | 801 Bridgeway | 415/331–5888 or 800/567–9524 | Reservations essential | $15–$20 | AE, D, DC, MC, V.

Ondine's. Seafood. A historic yacht club building houses this upscale, upstairs restaurant with picture windows on three walls overlooking the bay and an elegant, burnished-wood interior and curved bar. Try the seafood triangles or grilled tuna. | 588 Bridgeway | 415/331–1133 | Reservations essential | Jackets required | $25–$36 | AE, DC, MC, V.

Sushi Ran. Japanese. Here you can watch sushi being prepared and served with a flourish. Specials are sushi, sashimi, and hot Japanese dishes. The bar pours beer, wine, and 17 kinds of sake. | 107 Caledonia St. | 415/332–3620 | Reservations essential | $7–$15 | AE, D, MC, V.

Lodging

Casa Madrona. This landmark 1885 Victorian house, decorated with antiques, climbs up a hill overlooking the bay. Rooms are small and cozy, and some have views of the harbor, or you can stay in a cottage or casita, suitable for families. There's a terraced garden with a pond and an outdoor hot tub. Restaurant, complimentary breakfast, room service. Some kitchenettes, refrigerators, cable TV, in-room VCRs (and movies). Hot tub. Business services. | 801 Bridgeway | 415/332–0502 | fax 415/332–2537 | casa@casamadrona.com | www.casamadrona.com | 29 rooms, 5 cottages | $188–$340 | AE, D, DC, MC, V.

Gables Inn Sausalito. This elegant two-story 1869 bed and breakfast, on a hillside a half-block from Bridgeway in Sausalito's oldest commercial building, was the first in the city. The rooms have vaulted ceilings and antiques. Some have balconies, bay views, fireplaces, and bathrooms with deep claw-foot tubs or Jacuzzi tubs. Complimentary Continental breakfast. Cable TV, in-room VCRs. Business services. | 62 Princess St. | 415/289–1100 or 800/966–1554 | fax 415/339–0536 | gablesinnsausalito@aol.com | www.gablesinnsausalito.com | 9 rooms | $155–$325 | AE, D, MC, V.

Inn Above the Tide. This contemporary, three-story, brown-shingle building on the water makes a luxurious getaway just steps from the ferry terminal. All rooms have panoramic views of San Francisco and the bay, and most have water-level balconies with glass panels. The rooms are done in soft sea greens and blues, and the bathroom windows are port-hole-style. Complimentary Continental breakfast. In-room data ports, minibars, some in-room hot tubs, cable TV, some in-room VCRs. Business services. | 30 El Portal | 415/332–9535 or 800/893–8433 | 30 rooms | $195–$310 | AE, MC, V.

SEAL BEACH

MAP 9, G7

(Nearby towns also listed: Long Beach, Los Angeles, San Pedro, Torrance)

South of Long Beach, on San Pedro Bay, this mostly blue-collar town of 25,000 residents enjoys a beautiful, relatively unblemished stretch of shoreline.

Information: **Seal Beach Chamber of Commerce** | 311 Main St., Ste. 14A, 90740 | 562/799–0179 | www.sealbeachchamber.com.

Attractions

Pacific Electric Red Car Museum. This museum serves as a reminder of what was once the greatest public transportation system in Southern California. At one time, the aptly named Red Cars connected Balboa Peninsula and points north, including Long Beach and downtown Los Angeles. | Electric Ave. and Main St. | 562/683–1874 | Free | 2nd and 4th Sat. of month 1–4.

ON THE CALENDAR

SEPT.: *Sand Castle Contest.* Families love this big beach party, which brings out the kid in everyone. The creations are truly amazing—volcanoesque, formed, and drip-style alike. | 562/799–0179 | www.sealbeachchamber.com/scf.

Dining

Old Town Cafe. Café. Come in for homemade waffles, 21 kinds of omelets, breakfast quesadillas, or a salad or turkey breast sandwich for lunch. | 137 Main St. | 562/430–4377 | Closed for dinner | $4–$10 | No credit cards.

Walt's Wharf. American. You'll find fresh seafood and good beer at this place where locals gather over drinks and appetizers at the bar. No smoking. | 201 Main St. | 562/598–4433 | Reservations not accepted | $20–$37 | AE, DC, MC, V.

Lodging

Radisson Inn of Seal Beach. This three-story hotel is two blocks from the beach. Pool. Exercise equipment. Laundry facilities. Business services, airport shuttle. Pets allowed. | 600 Marina Dr. | 562/493–7501 | fax 562/596–3448 | 71 rooms | $118–$125 | AE, D, DC, MC, V.

Seal Beach Inn and Gardens. You'll have a canopied pre–Civil War plantation bed and an enormous armoire in this French Mediterranean–style bed and breakfast, the first in southern California. Built in the 1920s, it is entwined with vines and sits among rich, varied gardens embellished with a 200-year-old Parisian fountain and period street lamps; you can eat breakfast on the courtyard surrounded by colorful flowers. It is in a residential area, a block from the beach and four blocks from Seal Beach Pier. Some rooms have gas-burning fireplaces. Complimentary breakfast. Some kitchenettes, some refrigerators, some in-room hot tubs. Pool. Library. Laundry service. Business services. No smoking. | 212 5th St., | 562/493–2416 or 800/443–3292 | fax 562/799–0483 | www.sealbeachinn.com | 24 rooms | $175, $205–$225 suites, $350 penthouse | AE, D, DC, MC, V.

SELMA

MAP 4, G10

(Nearby towns also listed: Fresno, Hanford, Visalia)

This hub city of southern Fresno might be small (pop. 18,000), but nearly all of the world's raisins are grown within a 40-mi radius. It's also an economical stop to or from Yosemite (60 mi north) and Sequoia and Kings Canyon (25 mi south).

Information: **Selma Chamber of Commerce** | 1850 Mill St., 93662 | 559/896–3315 | www.selma.ca.us.

Attractions

Sun-Maid Visitors Center. A half-mile southeast of Selma on I–99, this 130-acre processing plant can store more than 300 million pounds of raisins. Shop for some natural goodness in the Grower's Store. Call ahead to schedule a tour. | 13525 S. Bethel Ave., Kingsburg

| 559/896–8000; store, 800/786–6243 | fax 559/897–6348 | www.sunmaid.com | Free | Weekdays 10–2, Mon.–Sat. 9:30–5:30.

ON THE CALENDAR

MAY: *Selma Raisin Festival.* We heard it through the grapevine that 90 percent of the world's raisins come from the Selma area. Arts and crafts, a baking contest, and plenty of activities show off the shrunken grape in style. | 559/896–3315 | www.selma.ca.us.

Dining

Archie's Place. American. The walls display old pictures of Selma. Order up burgers, fries, and steaks. | 2000 High St. | 559/896–0994 | $3–$15 | AE, MC, V.

Spike and Rail. American. This big, friendly-family restaurant serves steaks and a great split pea soup—perhaps a natural reflection of its former incarnation as a Pea Soup Andersen franchise (note the address, too). | 2910 Pea Soup Andersen Blvd. | 559/891–7000 | $8–$20 | AE, D, MC, V.

Lodging

Best Western John Jay Inn. This Federalist-style, three-story hotel is on landscaped grounds across the highway from convenience stores. Pool. Hot tub, sauna. Exercise equipment. Laundry facilities. Pets allowed. | 2799 Floral Ave. | 559/891–0300 | fax 559/891–1538 | 57 rooms | $50–$95 | AE, D, DC, MC, V.

Holiday Inn Swan Court. A windmill and a family of black swans in a pond can be found on the grounds of this hotel. Inside, look for exposed beams, flagstone floors, and a fireplace in the lobby. There's also a half-scale replica of an 1871 Porter locomotive, which you can ride. Restaurant. Pool. Exercise equipment. Laundry facilities. Business services. | 2950 Pea Soup Andersen Blvd. | 559/891–8000 | fax 559/891–9575 | 64 rooms | $67 | AE, D, DC, MC, V.

Microtel Inn and Suites. The Selma branch of this fast-growing chain is 3 mi from the Sun-Maid raisin factory. A trimmed-down approach keeps room rates down. In-room data ports, cable TV. Laundry facilities. Pets allowed (fee). | 2527 Highland Ave. | 888/771–7171 | www.microtelinn.com | 62 rooms | $55–$75, $69–$99 suites | AE, D, DC, MC, V.

Super 8 Motel. This one-story motel sits across from fast-food eateries. Pool. Pets allowed. | 3142 S. Highland Ave. | 559/896–2800 | fax 559/896–7244 | 40 rooms | $49 | AE, D, DC, MC, V.

Villager Inn Motel. This independent, no-frills establishment is very quiet and easily accessed from I-99. No air conditioning. Pool. | 1765 Young St. | 559/896–5500 | 33 rooms | $25–$40 | AE, D, DC, MC, V.

SEQUOIA AND
KINGS CANYON
NATIONAL PARKS

INTRO
ATTRACTIONS
DINING
LODGING

SEQUOIA AND KINGS CANYON NATIONAL PARKS

MAP 4, I10

(Nearby towns also listed: Bishop, Lone Pine, Three Rivers)

Disappear into the land that time forgot. The overlords of this land of rock, ice, and forest are the giant sequoias, which can tower more than 200 ft in the air and span the width of a city street. Sequoias may be the scene-stealers here, but great stands of sugar and ponderosa pine, white and red fir, and incense cedar also have their turns at the limelight in this expansive wilderness. Thousands of hikers, on day-long ambles or week-long treks, pass this way, many along the Pacific Crest Trail, which slices down the center of the park, following the Sierra ridge.

Beneath the earth are other marvels—caves dripping with stalactites and stalagmites. (Grab a sweater before you tour; cave temperatures hover around 55° F year-round.) And then there are the mountains, the burly beasts of the southern Sierra Nevada, many topping 10,000 ft. In fact, the tallest mountain in the continental U.S. casts its impressive shadow here—Mt. Whitney, at a sky-scraping 14,495 ft—rises just to the east of the park, in adjacent Sequoia National Forest.

Generals Highway connects the two parks. The 46-mi scenic route stretches from Route 198 at Ash Mountain—headquarters for both parks—to Route 180. Snow often closes the roads in winter; call ahead for conditions (in California, 800/427–7623).

Information: **Sequoia and Kings Canyon National Parks Visitor Information** | 47050 Generals Hwy., Three Rivers, 93271-9651 | 559/565-3341 | www.nps.gov/seki.

Attractions

Boyden Cavern. Take a guided tour through this chain of underground formations, at the bottom of Kings Canyon just north of Kings Canyon National Park, in Sequoia National Forest. The caves are on the south side of Route 180, 10 mi west of Cedar Grove Village. | 209/736–2708 | fax 209/736–0330 | www.caverntours.com | $8 | Oct.–May, daily 11–4, tours on the hour, last tour starts at 4; June–Sept., daily 10–5, tours on the hour, last tour starts at 5; additional evening tours available.

★ **Cedar Grove.** The best view of this region, in the bottom of Kings Canyon and named for the incense cedar that grows here along the south fork of the Kings River, is from the spectacular 30-mi descent along Kings Canyon Highway from Grant Grove to Roads End, where the highway ends, 6 mi east of Cedar Grove Village. | 559/565–3766 | www.nps.gov/seki | $10 per vehicle (park entrance fee good for 7 days) | Mid-Apr.–early Nov., daily sunrise to sunset.

Crystal Cave. Buy a ticket at Foothills or Lodgepole visitors centers, in Sequoia National Park, then hike the scenic ½ mi along Cascade Creek to the cave. It's 9 mi off Generals Highway. The 45-min tour takes you from room to room on paved and lighted pathways, while water drips and echoes in the eerie subterranean spaces. Bring a sweater—it's cool down there. | End of Crystal Cave Rd. | 559/565–3134 or 559/565–3782 | www.sequoia.national-park.com | $5 | June–Sept., daily 11–4.

Foothills, Lodgepole, and Grant Grove Visitors Centers. The visitors centers have displays on park history, birds and beasts, geology, etc., as well as maps and helpful rangers or park volunteers. Special talks and walks are offered year-round. Foothills is on Generals Highway, 1 mi from the Sequoia National Park entrance at Route 198. For Lodgepole, take Lodgepole Road off Generals Highway, 21 mi from Sequoia's park entrance on Route 198. For Grant Grove, go 4 mi east on Route 180 from the Big Stump Entrance Station. | Foothills, 559/565–4212; Lodgepole, 559/565–3782; Grant Grove, 559/565–4307 | www.nps.gov/seki | Free with park entrance, $10 per vehicle, good for 7 days | Daily 9–5 with seasonal variations.

General Grant Grove. Named for Ulysses S. Grant, this grove of trees on the north end of Generals Highway between the Giant Forest and Cedar Grove was the original grove designated as General Grant National Park in 1890. It's 4 mi from the Big Stump Entrance. | Kings Canyon Hwy./Rte. 180 | 559/565–4307 | www.nps.gov/seki | Daily.

Giant Forest. This grove of giant sequoia, in Sequoia National Park, encircles five meadows speckled with wildflowers mid-May through June. Go 4 mi south of Lodgepole on the Generals Highway. | 559/565–3782 | Daily.

Redwood Mountain Grove. This is the world's largest grove of *Sequoia giganteum,* or giant sequoia, the largest living things on earth. As you exit Kings Canyon on Generals Highway, a paved turnout lets you look out over the grove. There are also hiking trails accessing the grove, two 6-mi loops an a 10-mi out-and-bike hike along Redwood Creek. | 559/565–3782.

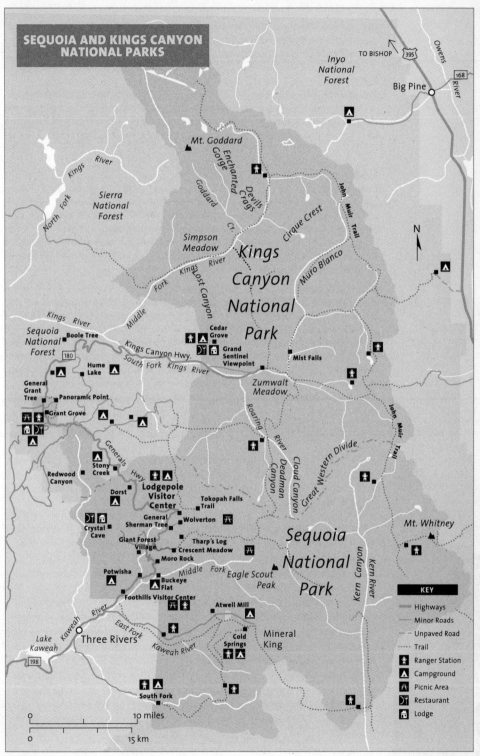

SEQUOIA AND KINGS CANYON
NATIONAL PARKS

Inyo
National
Forest

TO BISHOP
Big Pine

Owens River

Mt. Goddard

Enchanted Gorge

Devils Crags

Kings River

North Fork

Sierra
National
Forest

Goddard Cr

Simpson
Meadow

Cirque Crest

Kings Canyon National Park

John Muir Trail

Muro Blanco

Kings River

Middle Fork

Lost Canyon

Sequoia
National
Forest

Boole Tree

Cedar Grove

Grand Sentinel Viewpoint

Kings Canyon Hwy.

South Fork Kings River

Mist Falls

John Muir Trail

Hume Lake

General Grant Tree

Panoramic Point

Grant Grove

Zumwalt Meadow

Roaring River

Deadman Canyon

Cloud Canyon

Great Western Divide

Redwood Canyon

Stony Creek

Generals Hwy

Dorst

Lodgepole Visitor Center

Tokopah Falls Trail

Wolverton

Crystal Cave

General Sherman Tree

Giant Forest Village

Tharp's Log

Crescent Meadow

Moro Rock

Sequoia National Park

Mt. Whitney

Kern Canyon

Kern River

Potwisha

Buckeye Flat

Middle Fork

Eagle Scout Peak

Foothills Visitor Center

Atwell Mill

Lake Kaweah

Kaweah River

Three Rivers

East Fork

Kaweah River

Cold Springs

Mineral King

South Fork

KEY

Highways
Minor Roads
Unpaved Road
Trail
Ranger Station
Campground
Picnic Area
Restaurant
Lodge

0   10 miles
0   15 km

CA | 569

ON THE CALENDAR

DEC.: *Annual Christmas Tree Ceremony.* Check out the ultimate Christmas tree–these would suit the Jolly Green Giant. Bring the family to the base of the General Grant Tree for yuletide caroling and good cheer. | 559/335–2856.

Dining

Wuksachi Lodge Dining Room. Eclectic. Far from offering predictable park fare, this glass-enclosed restaurant serves creative food to match spectacular views of the giant trees and mountains. Try rock shrimp flautas with pepperjack cheese and cilantro and black bean chili filet mignon. | Sequoia National Park | 559/561–3314 | Breakfast also served | $14–$22 | D, MC, V.

Lodging

Cedar Grove Lodge. Although accommodations are close to the road, Cedar Grove manages to retain a quiet atmosphere. Book far in advance—the lodge has only 18 rooms. Each room is air-conditioned and has two queen-size beds, and three have kitchenettes. You can order trout, hamburgers, hot dogs, and sandwiches at the snack bar and take it to one of the picnic tables along the river's edge. Restaurant, picnic area. No room phones. Laundry facilities. No smoking. | Rte. 180 | 559/335–5500 | fax 559/335–5507 | www.sequoia-kingscanyon.com | 18 rooms | $90 | Closed Nov.–Apr. | D, MC, V.

Grant Grove Cabins. Clusters of cabins (some with private baths) and tent cabins (wooden structures with canvas roofs) are scattered through the sugar pines and other conifers at this family-friendly location. There's a central bath and shower facility. Ranger-led walks and talks are held daily in summer, on weekends in winter. Cabins are in Grant Grove Village, 4 mi east of the Big Stump entrance to Kings Canyon National Park. Restaurant, picnic area. No smoking. | Rte. 180 | 559/335–5500 | fax 559/335–5507 | www.sequoia-kingscanyon.com | 15 tent cabins, 24 rustic housekeeping cabins (no running water; 3 with electricity; wood-burning stove on porch for cooking, summer only), 9 housekeeping cabins with bath (heating, electricity; must provide own stove for cooking on outside deck) | $38 tent cabins, $45–$55 rustic cabins, $88 cabins with bath | D, MC, V.

GIANT SEQUOIAS

Giant sequoias are truly one of nature's marvels. These trees are the largest living things on earth, and only grow naturally on the western slope of the Sierra Nevada Mountains (at elevations between 5,000 and 7,000 ft). They can live for two or three thousand years; in that time, they grow almost 300 ft tall, 40 ft in diameter, and more than 100 ft around.

Sequoia National Park, where you're likely to get the best view of these beautiful wonders, is the second-oldest national park in the United States. It was created in 1890 for the giant trees, including the General Sherman tree, which is the world's largest living thing and is estimated to be between 2,300 and 2,700 years old. Its largest branch is about 7 ft in diameter.

The longevity of the sequoias is innate. Chemicals in their wood and bark offer resistance to insects and fungi. The oldest known sequoia lived for over 3,200 years. You can't help but wonder about the changes they've experienced.

John Muir Lodge. This new lodge is nestled in a wooded area near Grant Grove Village. The 30 rooms and six suites all have queen beds and private baths. There's a comfortable lobby with a stone fireplace, but no restaurant. Picnic area. Air-conditioning. No room phones. Laundry facilities. | Rte. 180 | 559/335–5500 | fax 559/335–5507 | www.sequoia-kingscanyon.com | 21 rooms | $93 | Closed Nov.–Apr. | D, MC, V.

Stony Creek Lodge. Pine beams and stone make up this lodge, in Sequoia National Forest between Sequoia and Kings Canyon national parks. The lodge is 14 mi southwest of Grant Grove Village. Restaurant. No air-conditioning, no room phones. | Generals Hwy. | 559/335–5500 | fax 559/335–5507 | www.nps.gov/seki | 11 rooms | $97 | Closed Nov.–Apr. | D, MC, V.

Wuksachi Lodge. You can't beat the rustic chic at this granite-and-cedar hotel, 2 mi south of Lodgepole Visitor Center, 22 mi from the Ash Mountain entrance. Named after a local tribe that used to migrate through this part of the Sierra, it has modern rooms with views of either nearby mountains or secluded forests. Rangers lead programs and guided walks in summer. Restaurant, bar. In-room data ports. Hiking. No smoking. | 64740 Wuksachi Way, Sequoia National Park | 888/252–5757 or 559/565–4070 | fax 559/565–4097 | www.visitse-quoia.com | 84 rooms, 18 suites | Mid–May–Oct., $120–$145, $165 suites; Nov.–mid–May, $75–$90, $105 suites | AE, D, DC, MC, V.

SHERMAN OAKS

MAP 9, C2

(Nearby towns also listed: Beverly Hills, Hollywood Studio City, Los Angeles, North Hollywood, Universal City, Van Nuys, Woodland Hills)

This upmarket hillside residential area overlooks the San Fernando Valley and is home to the famed Galleria Mall, birthplace of the "Valley Girl" phenomenon of big-haired, gum-popping teenage girls with a fondness for words like "totally" and "fer sure." Universal Studios and Rodeo Drive are within striking distance.

Information: Sherman Oaks Chamber of Commerce | 14827 Ventura Blvd., Ste. 207, 91403 | 818/906–1951 | ourchamber@aol.com | www.shermanoakschamber.org.

Attractions
Mulholland Drive. This sometimes winding road takes in spectacular views of the city and the houses in the Hollywood Hills. It runs east–west off the I–405 freeway. | Daily.

New Sherman Oaks Galleria. Rub elbows with real Valley Girls at this mall, straight out of the movie *Clueless.* It's complete with a 16-screen multiplex. Like, totally. | 15303 Ventura Blvd. | 818/382–4100 | Free | Daily 9–6.

ON THE CALENDAR
OCT.: *Street Fair.* For three days, arts and crafts, food, entertainment, and local comics transform the Valley into a carnival. | 818/906–1951 | www.shermanoakschamber.org.

Dining
★ **Cafe Bizou.** French. You can bring your own wine to this crowded, trendy eatery that serves all the classics with a California twist. | 14016 Ventura Blvd. | 818/788–3536 | Reservations required | $20–$35 | AE, MC, V.

Great Greek. Greek. Singing waiters bring you moussaka, grilled pita bread, stuffed grape leaves, and roasted lamb, while a fleet of fast-footed (yes, they're dancing) busboys clear the remains away. You might find yourself linked arm-in-arm with fellow diners, dancing to live music from a Greek band. No smoking. | 13362 Ventura Blvd., Sherman Oaks | 818/905–5250 | $21–$32 | AE, D, DC, MC, V.

Posto. Contemporary. Owner Piero Selvaggio, of Santa Monica's Valentino, has made this one of the most prestigious restaurants in the area, with creamy-pink walls, lavender table-cloths, and fresh flowers. Start with fried crab and potato chips or roasted rabbit and beets, then continue with pumpkin risotto with roasted quail or chicken and asparagus in marsala sauce. | 14928 Ventura Blvd. | 818/784–4400 | Reservations essential | Closed Sun. No lunch Sat. | $11–$25 | AE, D, DC, MC, V.

Lodging

Carriage Inn. Faux plants fill the rooms in this hotel 3 mi from Universal Studios and 5 mi from Rodeo Drive. Dining room. Pool. Hot tub. Exercise equipment. Laundry facilities. Business services. | 5525 Sepulveda Blvd. | 818/787–2300 | fax 818/782–9373 | 184 rooms | $85–$95 | AE, D, DC, MC, V.

Heritage Motel. A good place to stop when you just need a room, it's west of I–405 and within walking distance of many restaurants and bars. | 15485 Ventura Blvd. | 818/981–0500 | fax 818/907–8050 | 62 rooms | $50–$70 | AE, D, DC, MC, V.

Radisson Valley Center. Some of the rooms in this hotel 5 mi from Universal Studios have mountain views, and you'll find personal trainers in the gym ready to help you get California-buff. If this is too stressful, call upon the licensed masseuse. Dining room. Pool. Hot tub. Exercise equipment. Laundry facilities. Business services. | 15433 Ventura Blvd. | 818/981–5400 | fax 818/981–3175 | 201 rooms | $129 | AE, D, DC, MC, V.

SIMI VALLEY

MAP 4, H14

(Nearby town also listed: Oxnard)

Simi Valley and its 100,200 residents are the proud "parents" of the hilltop Ronald Reagan Presidential Library. Hidden away in the Santa Susanna Mountains on the eastern end of Ventura County, the town is consistently ranked as one of the safest cities in the U.S.

Information: Simi Valley Chamber of Commerce | 40 W. Cochran St., Ste. 100, 93065 | 805/526–3900 | webmaster@simivalleychamber.com | www.simivalleychamber.com.

Attractions

Ronald Reagan Presidential Library. This library and museum document Reagan's presidency and political life, with memorabilia, photographs, and exhibits of the actor-turned-world-leader at the Berlin Wall, in the Oval Office, and in other presidential poses. | 40 Presidential Dr. | 805/522–8444 | www.reaganlibrary.net | $5 | Daily 10–5.

Strathearn Historical Park and Museum. A Chumash Indian village and original Simi Valley houses, including an early 1800s adobe, a late 19th-century prefab "Colony House," and Simi Valley's first library, are displayed in this 6-acre park. | 137 Strathearn Pl. | 805/526–6453 | fax 805/526–6462 | $2 | Weekends 1–4.

ON THE CALENDAR

AUG.–SEPT.: *Simi Valley Days.* A horse show, parade, carnival, and chili cook-off highlight this event. | 805/581–4280 | www.simivalleydays.com.

Dining

Baja Fresh Mexican Grill. Tex-Mex. No lard or MSG goes into the large burritos and soft-shell tacos made up in this local chain restaurant. | 1464 Madera Rd. | 805/520–7301 | www.bajafresh.com | $2–$7 | MC, V.

Dakota's Mesquite BBQ and Steakhouse. Steak. There are views of the valley from the wrap-around outdoor patio at this eatery, where large portions of steak, pasta, barbecued chicken, and mesquite-smoked back ribs make up the menu. | 2525 Stow St. | 805/582–1700 | fax 805/582–1701 | www.dakotassteakhouse.com | No lunch | $10–$22 | AE, D, DC, MC, V.

Lodging
Clarion Posada Royale Hotel. Rooms have either inside or outside entrances at this two-story hotel built in 1987. It's furnished with glossy, dark-wood pieces and is ½ mi from the Reagan Library. In-room VCRs. Pool. Exercise equipment. Laundry facilities. Business services. | 1775 Madera Rd. | 805/584–6300 | fax 805/527–9969 | 120 rooms | $85–$160 | AE, D, DC, MC, V.

Grand Vista Hotel. In the foothills, this hotel has views of the valley and free shuttle transportation to area attractions within 10 mi. Some in-room hot tubs. Pool. Laundry facilities. | 999 Enchanted Way | 805/583–2000 | fax 805/583–2779 | 195 rooms | $145–$185 | AE, D, DC, MC, V.

Holiday Inn Express. This hotel, situated along a strip of similar properties, is notable for its cream-colored stucco facade and terracotta-tile roof. Rooms are done in dusty-pastel hues reminiscent of the high desert. A poolside patio is shaded by strategically placed potted greenery. Some in-room hot tubs. Pool. Exercise equipment. Laundry facilities. | 2550 Erringer Rd. | 805/584–6006 | fax 805/527–5629 | 96 rooms | $59–$89 | AE, D, DC, MC, V.

Radisson Hotel Chatsworth. This four-story hotel built in 1985 is across from a driving range on the edge of a residential neighborhood, 1 mi east of Simi Valley on Route 118. Restaurant, bar, complimentary Continental breakfast. In-room data ports, some kitchenettes, cable TV. Outdoor pool. Hot tub. Gym. Laundry facilities. Business services. | 9777 Topanga Canyon Blvd. | 818/709–7054 | fax 818/998–3573 | 147 rooms | $105–$150 | AE, D, DC, MC, V.

SOLVANG

MAP 4, F13

(Nearby towns also listed: Lompoc, Los Olivos, Santa Maria)

Forty-five miles northwest of Santa Barbara in the Santa Ynez Valley, Solvang originally hung out its shingle in 1911. That's when a handful of Danish teachers from the Midwest settled on this area as site for a folk school dedicated to Danish traditions. The settlers left their mark with still-intact Danish-style architecture—half-timbered buildings, gaslights, cobblestone walks, windmills, and artficial "good luck" storks perched on many rooftops. For outdoor pursuits, visit Nojoqui Falls County Park. After wet winters, the 164-ft waterfall booms over a mossy cliff.

Information: Solvang Conference and Visitors Bureau | Box 70, 93464 | 800/468–6765 | scvb@syv.com | www.solvangusa.com.

Attractions
Elverhoj Museum. Photographs, arts and crafts, period rooms, and fine-art galleries illustrate local history in this Danish heritage museum. | 1624 Elverhoj Way | 805/686–1211 | By donation | Wed.–Sun. 1–4.

Lake Cachuma Recreation Area. Lake Cachuma is a quiet lake and recreation area, a pleasant break from the Dutch-everywhere look of Solvang. Activities include boating, fishing, swimming, and picnicking. The lake is 15 min southeast of Solvang on Route 154. | 805/688–4658 or 559/565–3782, 559/565–3134 | $5 | Daily.

Nojoqui Falls County Park. This pleasant park (it's pronounced "No-ho-wee"), a local favorite for picnics and barbecues, has ball fields, barbecue pits, playgrounds, and volleyball courts. After rains, don't miss the 164-ft waterfall, reached by a ½-mi trail. Nojoqui Falls is 1½ mi east of U.S. 101, near Gaviota Pass. | 805/688–4217 | Free | Daily 8–sunset.

Old Mission Santa Inés. This 1804 site named for St. Agnes predates the Danish settlement by more than a century and includes a museum of religious texts, vestments, and church documents. | 1760 Mission Dr. | 805/688–4815 | fax 805/686–4468 | www.missionsan-taines.org | $3 | June–mid-Sept., daily 9–7; mid-Sept.–May 9–5:30.

ON THE CALENDAR

JUNE–OCT.: *Solvang Theaterfest.* The town's Danish heritage hits the boards at this summer-long theater festival. | 805/922–8313.

SEPT.: *Danish Days Festival.* This is a 3-day event celebrating Danish culture in the center of town. | 800/468–6765.

OCT.: *Oktoberfest.* Raise your steins and enjoy the wienerschnitzel while listening to live hofbrau music at this classic event. | 805/688–0298.

Dining

A.J. Spurs. Barbecue. This eatery in Buellton 3 mi west of Solvang, serves huge portions of oak-pit barbecue, steaks, chicken dishes, and surf-and-turf platters. | 350 E. Rte. 246 | 805/686–1655 | fax 805/688–3948 | No lunch | $16–$40 | AE, D, MC, V.

Bit o' Denmark. Danish. Perhaps the most authentic Danish eatery in town, this restaurant is in a beamed building that was a church until 1929. The outdoor dining area is spacious and shaded by large canvas parasols. Try the *Medisterpolse* (beef and pork sausage with red cabbage), or grab a fork and dig in to a *Frikadeller* (meatballs). | 473 Alisal Rd. | 805/688–5426 | $20–$30 | AE, D, MC, V.

Cafe Angelica. Contemporary. The open kitchen of this downtown café serves filet mignon stuffed with blue cheese and wild mushrooms topped with a sherry and mascarpone cheese sauce. Or try filet of sole finished with crabmeat, shrimp, asparagus, mushrooms, and piccata sauce. Local vintages highlight the wine list. | 490 1st St. | 805/686–9970 | $15–$20 | AE, MC, V.

Hitching Post. Contemporary. Ostrich burger, anyone? This boisterous eatery 3 mi west of Solvang serves them, along with other oak-grilled meats. No smoking. | 406 E Rte. 246, Buellton | 805/688–0676 | No lunch | $23–$49 | AE, MC, V.

Mollekroen. Danish. For a good Danish meal of an open-face sandwich and Danish pastry, join the local patrons in this cheerful upstairs dining room. | 435 Alisal Rd. | 805/688–4555 | fax 805/688–2335 | $9–$17 | AE, D, DC, MC, V.

Paula's Pancake House. Danish. Thin Danish pancakes are the specialty here, but waffles and omelets are also served all day. Sandwiches and homemade soups are on the lunch menu. | 1531 Mission Dr. | 805/688–2867 | Reservations not accepted | No supper | $3–$9 | AE, D, DC, MC, V.

River Grill at The Alisal. Contemporary. Generous portions of Colorado lamb loin chops, grilled Black Angus steak, and chicken piccata are served on the patio and in the Southwestern-style dining room with a fireplace overlooking the surrounding golf course. | 150 Alisal Rd. | 805/688–7784 | fax 805/688–8229 | www.alisal.com | Reservations essential | Closed Sun.–Mon. | $10–$24 | AE, D, DC, MC, V.

Lodging

Alisal Guest Ranch. Get your boots dusty, but then have someone else shine them clean at this luxe ranch, sprawling across 10,000 acres of the Santa Ynez Mountains 3 mi south of Solvang. Private studios and suites, all with wood-burning fireplaces and Western appointments, are clustered in groups of two to six. All guests use a common dining area, surrounded by the cottages and views of an expansive lawn. There's also a separate library, with data-port hookups, and plenty of volumes to take back to your room for a good read.

Activities include horseback riding, golf, tennis, in-room massage, hayrides, winery tours, and cookouts in summer. The ranch has a 100-acre lake for boating and fishing (boats and fishing gear available year-round), a pool ringed by a terra-cotta tile deck, and even a petting zoo. Both indoor and outdoor games are available, and guitar-strumming cowboys entertain regularly. Clark Gable, Doris Day, and Kevin Costner have all vacationed here. Restaurant, bar. No air-conditioning, refrigerators, no room phones. Pool, lake. Hot tub. Two 18-hole golf courses, putting green, tennis. Horseback riding. Water sports, boating, fishing, bicycles. Library. Kids' programs in summer and holidays. Laundry facilities. Business services. | 1054 Alisal Rd. | 805/688–6411 or 800/425–4725 | fax 805/688–2510 | www.alisal.com | 73 rooms | $375–$400 rooms, $425–$450 suites | Modified AP | AE, DC, MC, V.

Ballard Inn. A picket fence and wraparound porch front this rambling two-story building painted a delicate blue-gray. Each room reflects a different wine-country theme. The Mountain Room, done in shades of blue and gray, has an expansive view of the Santa Ynez Range. The Vineyard Room pays homage to the vintners of the valley with its deep green and maroon color scheme. The inn's Cafe Chardonnay serves California cuisine. Restaurant, dining room, complimentary breakfast. TV in common area. Bicycles. Business services. No smoking. | 2436 Baseline Ave., Ballard | 805/688–7770 or 800/638–2466 | fax 805/688–9560 | kelly@ballardinn.com | www.ballardinn.com | 15 rooms | $170–$250 | AE, MC, V.

Best Western Kronborg Inn. Floral-motif guest rooms have either patio access to the outdoor pool or balconies that overlook it. Complimentary Continental breakfast. Refrigerators, some in-room hot tubs, cable TV. Outdoor pool. Hot tub. | 1440 Mission Dr. | 805/688–2383 or 800/788–8932 | fax 805/688–1821 | info@kronborginn.com | www.kronborginn.com | 38 rooms | $60–$140 | AE, D, DC, MC, V.

Best Western Pea Soup Andersen's Inn. The architecture of the hotel was inspired by Solvang's Danish heritage. Rooms have a special charm, with lots of brightly painted wooden furniture and wall art. Some rooms overlook the large pool. There's a grill you can use, along with a picnic area and gazebo. The inn is within 5 mi of a pair of golf courses. Restaurant, bar, complimentary Continental breakfast. Refrigerators, cable TV. Pool. Hot tub. Putting green. Business services. | 51 E. Rte. 246, Buellton | 805/688–3216 | fax 805/688–9767 | pea@impulse.net | www.peasoup.wrkforyou.com | 97 rooms | $69–$99 | AE, D, DC, MC, V.

Chimney Sweep Inn. The thatched-roof lodge and the half-timbered cottages of this inn are 1/2 mi west of town. Complimentary Continental breakfast. Some kitchenettes, some in-room hot tubs, cable TV. Hot tub. Business services. | 1564 Copenhagen Dr. | 805/688–2111 or 800/824–6444 | fax 805/688–8824 | 50 rooms, 6 cottages | $100–$135, $275 cottages | AE, D, MC, V.

Country Inn and Suites. The loft spaces and Mission-style furniture in these spacious rooms give this hotel more character than the typical chain hotel. Complimentary breakfast. Microwaves, in-room refrigerators, cable TV, in-room VCRs. Outdoor pool. Hot tub. Business services. | 1455 Mission Rd. | 805/688–2018 | fax 805/688–1156 | cisolvang@rimcorp.com | www.countryinns.com | 82 rooms | $99–$110 rooms, $139 suites | AE, D, DC, MC, V.

Days Inn at the Windmill. A working windmill anchors this barn-like inn filled with blond-wood furniture, 3 mi west of town. Bar, complimentary Continental breakfast. Cable TV. Pool. Hot tub. Laundry facilities. Business services. | 114 E. Rte. 246, Buellton | 805/688–8448 or 800/946–3466 | fax 805/686–1338 | www.daysinn.com | 108 rooms | $75–$89 | AE, D, DC, MC, V.

Econo-Lodge. One of the two buildings has interior entrances and the other has exterior at this motel 3 mi west of town. Some microwaves, cable TV. Laundry facilities. Business services. Pets allowed. | 630 Ave. of Flags, Buellton | 805/688–0022 | fax 805/688–7448 | www.econolodge.com | 60 rooms | $64–$80 | AE, D, DC, MC, V.

Marriott Rancho Santa Barbara. This four-story Spanish Mission–style building with landscaped grounds is 1 mi east of an ostrich ranch and 3 mi east of Solvang. Restaurant, bar. In-room data ports, microwaves, cable TV. Pool. Hot tub. Tennis. Exercise equipment. Laundry facilities. Business services, airport shuttle. | 555 McMurray Rd., Buellton | 805/688–1000 | fax 805/688–0380 | www.marriott.com | 149 rooms | $126–$147 | AE, D, DC, MC, V.

★ **Petersen Village Inn.** This is one of Solvang's most luxurious lodgings. Its exterior is in keeping with the town's Danish theme, but the interior has dark, polished wood and soft golden lighting. All the rooms have four-poster canopy beds and are fitted out with reproductions of antiques. The three-level Tower Suite has a fireplace and its own hot tub. Breakfast consists of a Danish-style buffet, and there's piano entertainment with desserts and local wines in the courtyard lounge for guests each evening. The inn is in Solvang's Danish Village, within sight of shops, Danish bakeries, and cafés. Complimentary Continental breakfast. In-room data ports, some in-room hot tubs, cable TV. Business services. No kids under 7. | 1576 Mission Dr. | 805/688–3121 or 800/321–8985 | fax 805/688–5732 | www.peterseninn.com | 42 rooms | $145–$200 rooms, $255 suite | AE, MC, V.

Solvang Royal Scandinavian Inn. The rooms repeat the Scandinavian theme found in so many of the town's lodgings. The inn has a restaurant, with a champagne brunch on Sundays. Restaurant, bar with entertainment. Refrigerators, cable TV. Pool. Hot tub. Business services. | 400 Alisal Rd. | 805/688–8000 or 800/624–5572 | fax 805/688–0761 | sroyal@silicon.com | 133 rooms | $126–$171 | AE, D, DC, MC, V.

Storybook Inn. Hans Christian Andersen stories inspired the names of the rooms in this bed-and-breakfast. Suites have four-poster beds and marble whirlpool tubs. Restaurant, complimentary breakfast. Some in-room hot tubs, cable TV, some in-room VCRs. | 409 1st St. | 805/688–1703 or 800/786–7925 | fax 805/688–9555 | ortonstorybook@aol.com | www.solvangstorybook.com | 7 rooms, 2 suites | $139–$165, $205 suites | D, MC, V.

Svendsgaard's Danish Lodge. In this three-story hotel with a stone facade, some rooms have gas fireplaces. On the sun deck you can take in a view of downtown and nearby windmills. Complimentary Continental breakfast. Some kitchenettes, microwaves, refrigerators, cable TV. Pool. Hot tub. Business services. | 1711 Mission Dr. | 805/688–3277 or 800/733–8757 | fax 805/686–5616 | 52 rooms | $70–$95 | AE, D, DC, MC, V.

SONOMA

MAP 3, C7

(Nearby towns also listed: Kenwood, Napa, Petaluma, Santa Rosa)

Sonoma, the oldest town in the Wine Country, has the history to show for it: the last of the 21 missions established by Franciscan fathers from Mexico in the early 1800s is here, Mission San Francisco Solano. In fact, the town is a trove of Mission-era history. Many old adobe and false-front buildings, long since converted to hotels, restaurants, and shops, flank the eight-acre town plaza, where festivals and wine tastings are held throughout the year. The town is a favorite destination of wine lovers.

Information: **Sonoma Valley Visitors Bureau** | 453 1st St. E, 95476 | 707/996–1090 | info@sonomavalley.com | www.sonomavalley.com.

Attractions

Sonoma State Historic Park. Encompassing the collection of old adobe buildings surrounding the town plaza, this park includes the Sonoma Mission, the Sonoma Barracks, and the home of Sonoma's founder, Gen. Mariano Guadalupe Vallejo. Guided tours of the Vallejo house are offered weekdays and some weekends. | 20 E. Spain St. | 707/938–1519 | Free for park; $2 for mission, barracks, and house.

Mission San Francisco Solano is the heart of Sonoma's central plaza. The chapel and school were used to bring Christianity to the Native Americans; they now house a museum, with a fine collection of 19th-century watercolors. | 114 Spain St. E | 707/938–1519 | $2 | Daily 10–5.

Sonoma Cheese Factory. A combination factory, deli, restaurant, and store, this on-the-plaza favorite stays jam-packed most of the time. You can nosh on free samples—variations on the house specialty, Sonoma jack—while watching cheese being made behind a plate glass window in back. There's no set schedule, but no cheese is made on the weekends. | 2 Spain St. | 707/996–1931 or 800/535–2855 | fax 707/935–3535 | www.sonomajack.com | Free | Daily 8:30–6, weekends until 7.

Viansa Wetlands. Ducks, geese, tundra swans, and other migratory waterfowl (and attendant predators) flock to this 90-acre preserve; more than a million birds come here to feed each year—over 10,000 per day during peak migration periods. The land was set aside by Sam and Vicki Sebastiani; it shares the Carneros property with their winery, Viansa. You can get a broad view from the winery's hilltop or see it up close on occasional Saturday morning tours. | 25200 Rte. 12/121 | 707/935–4700, 800/995–4740 | fax 707/996–4632 | www.viansa.com | $7 | Tours Mar.–Oct., Sat.

Wineries. While the nearby Napa Valley is upscale and elegant, Sonoma Valley, to the west and separated by a small range of rugged mountains, is rustic and unpretentious. Here, family-run wineries treat visitors like friends, and tastings are usually free. Cool marine air from the Russian River gorge (which flows through the valley's northern reaches and empties into the Pacific) combined with the area's rocky soil helps vintners grow their intensely flavored wines, particularly the region's complex Zinfandels and other reds. Sonoma Valley's 145 wineries range from stately hilltop châteaux to converted caves, and most offer visitors free tastings and (not unbiased) advice on wine appreciation. A few notable wineries are listed below.

A grand white villa dominates the hub of the 400-acre **Bartholomew Park Winery.** The grounds are made up not only of vineyards, but also picnicking lawns, woodlands, and 3 mi of hiking trails through the neighboring hills. The main building houses a small museum devoted to area history and wine-making lore. | 1000 Vineyard La. | 707/935–9511 | Free | Tasting daily 10–4:30; tours by appointment.

For the Sonoma wine industry, it all started here, at the **Buena Vista Carneros Winery.** Hungarian count Agoston Harazthy, considered the grandfather of the California wine industry, founded Buena Vista in 1857. He planted the property with cuttings he imported from Europe, setting the stage for the state's ultimate domination of domestic wine production. Tours, tastings, and picnic tables are available. Every Sunday in August and September, there's "Shakespeare at Buena Vista" when you can spread out the picnic blanket, uncork a bottle, and enjoy a day with the Bard. | 18000 Old Winery Rd. | 707/938–1266 or 800/678–8504 | fax 707/939–0916 | www.buenavistawinery.com | Daily 10:30–5; Nov.–Mar. 10–5.

An 1850s farmhouse on the river provides a home for **Cline Cellars,** and the surrounding grounds abound with rose gardens, hot springs, and shady spots for picnicking. The winery, established in 1982, produces red, white, and rosé wines on 356 acres. | 24737 Arnold Dr. | 707/935–4310 | Free | Daily 10–6.

At **Favero Vineyards,** vintner Frank Favero dug his winery straight into the side of Monte di Sassi in 1994, creating a cool, dim cavern in which to produce and store his product. Beaten-copper wall sconces in the shape of grape leaves provide light, and huge metal doors lead into the tasting area. | 3939 Lovell Valley Rd. | 707/935–3939 | Free | Tastings and tours by appointment only.

At **Gloria Ferrer Champagne Caves,** arched windows and doorways, terra-cotta roofing tiles, and a wheat-colored stucco exterior give this stately winery the look and feel of a Spanish hacienda. Indeed, the Ferrer family, who founded the caves in the early 1980s, hail from the Catalonia region of Spain. The winery produces nearly 2,000 tons of grapes a year, and specializes in sparkling wines. The winery's specialty food shop purveys homemade cooking oils, vinegars, condiments, and champagne-filled chocolate truffles. | 23555 Carneros Hwy. (Rte. 121) | 707/996–7256 | Free | Tastings daily 10:30–5:30; tours by appointment.

Run by the same family for four generations, the **Gundlach-Bundschu Wine Company** (nicknamed "Gund-Bund") produces 11 different wines from its 400 acres at the southern reaches of Sonoma Valley. Though wine-making is taken very seriously here, a festive atmosphere prevails, with bright murals depicting the wine trade decorating outbuildings. Shakespeare productions are staged in summer. | 2000 Denmark St. | 707/938–5277 | Free | Tastings daily 11–4:30; tours on weekends only.

Just north of downtown Sonoma, 800 ft up in the Mayacamas Mountains, is secluded **Hanzell Vineyards,** which specializes in very robust, intense Pinot noirs and Chardonnays. The winery building was fashioned to resemble a centuries-old Burgundian country estate. The drive up to the winery leads through some 200 acres of vines and spectacular mountain views. | 18596 Lomita Ave. | 707/996–3860 | Free | Tastings and tours by appointment only.

The mantra at **Ravenswood** is "No wimpy wines!" and the hilltop winery stays true to its claim, specializing in robust, complex reds and a few hard-hitting whites. The vines here produce a hefty 300,000 cases of wine per year, and you're more than welcome to drop in for a tasting, a tour of the facility, or some good-natured tips on wine appreciation. | 18701 Gehricke Rd. | 707/938–1960 | Free | Daily 10–4:30.

Originally planted by Franciscans of the Sonoma Mission in 1825, the **Sebastiani Vineyards** were bought by Samuele Sebastiani in 1904. Red wines are king here. | 389 4th St. E | 707/938–1266 | Daily 10–5, tours daily 10–4:30.

Dining

Deuce. California. The chefs have injected new life into a hippie-era restaurant, leaving the massive oak bar and stained glass in place and introducing a contemporary menu. Specialties include rock shrimp rolls, dry-aged steak, and seafood dishes. | 691 Broadway | 707/933–3823 | fax 707/933–9002 | $13–$20 | AE, MC, V.

Girl and the Fig. French. This French bistro has seating in the colorful old bar, in a side room and, when weather permits, on the prettiest patio in town. | 110 W. Spain St. | 707/938–3634 | Dinner only | $10–$20 | AE, MC, V.

Piatti. Italian. Pastel yellow walls decorated with simple paintings of vegetables, plus an open kitchen, and windows on two sides make this the most attractive dining room on the plaza. Pastas, pizzas, and calzone vary with the season; an excellent variation is pappardelle with prawns and arugula. | 405 1st St. W | 707/996–2351 | fax 707/996–5863 | $12–$21 | AE, MC, V.

Lodging

El Dorado. Most accommodations are on the second floor of this renovated 1843 adobe. Steel-frame beds, nearly bare Mexican tile floors, and pocket closets make the undersized accommodations look uncluttered rather than spartan. Some rooms have a balcony overlooking the Sonoma plaza. Restaurant. | 405 1st St. W | 707/996–3030, or 800/289–3031 | fax 707/996–3148 | info@hoteldorado.com | www.hoteleldorado.com | 26 rooms | $185–$225 | AE, MC, V.

MacArthur Place. This luxury country inn opened in 1998 on the grounds of an old estate four blocks south of the plaza. Ten rooms are in the original 1857 Victorian house. Stylish rooms in clapboard quadriplexes come in Mediterranean colors like mustard and olive, with original artwork and faux-finished walls. Suites have their own hot tubs as well as wood-burning fireplaces, wet bars, and porches or balconies overlooking the central garden. DVD players are in every room and DVD movies are available to borrow. Restaurant. In-room data ports. Business services. Pool. Spa. | 29 E. MacArthur St. | 707/938–2929 or 800/722–1866 | fax 707/933–9833 | info@macarthurplace.com | www.macarthurplace.com | 64 rooms, 31 suites | $249–$325 rooms, $375–$750 suites | AE, D, MC, V.

Sonoma Mission Inn and Spa. Surrounded by 10 acres of gardens, bricked paths, fountains, and redwoods, this inn has seen many incarnations since it was founded in 1895; the original structure burned to the ground in the mid-1920s, was rebuilt, and was shut down entirely during the Depression. Now it is arguably the finest accommodation in the area. Guest rooms are outfitted with antique reproductions in warm, blond wood, and many have fire-places and private patios or balconies. All rooms have a view of the grounds and direct access to the inn's thermal mineral pool. If your vacation plans include dropping a few pounds or shedding months of urban stress, the spa facility can come to the rescue; there are personal trainers, nutritional consultants, and massage therapists. 2 restaurants, 2 bars. Cable TV. 2 pools. Hair salon, hot tub, massage, sauna, spa. 18-hole golf course. Gym, health club. Shops. Laundry services. Business services. No pets. No smoking. | 18140 Rte. 12 | 707/938–9000 or 800/358–9022 | fax 707/996–5358 | www.sonomamissioninn.com | 198 rooms, 30 suites | $249–$449, suites $429–$1200 | AE,D,DC,MC,V.

Vineyard Inn. The only lodging in the Carneros appellation claims a busy corner at the south end of Sonoma Valley. Adjoining Mission Revival–style bungalows face a landscaped courtyard. Pool. | 23000 Rte. 12/121 | 707/938–2350 or 800/359–4667 | fax 707/938–2353 | vineyard@vom.com | www.sonomavineyardinn.com | 24 rooms, 4 suites | $89–$189 | AE, MC, V.

SONORA

(Nearby towns also listed: Jamestown, Lodi, Oakdale, Stockton)

South-of-the-border miners who worked this stretch of the Gold Country named the town after their homeland in northern Mexico. Today this gracious city is the seat of Tuolumne County. Many well-preserved Victorian homes still stand as reminders of the area's history as one of the wealthiest Gold Rush communities.

Information: Tuolumne County Visitors Bureau | 55 W. Stockton Rd., Box 4020, 95370 | 800/446–1333 | tcvb@mlode.com | www.tcvb.com.

Attractions

Bear Valley. Fresh air and mountain views draw crowds to this resort town—for skiing in winter and spring, for hiking and mountain biking in summer and fall. There are lodgings, restaurants, and many activities. It's 67 mi northeast of Sonora via Route 49, then east on Route 4. | Rte. 4 at Rte. 207 | 209/753–2301 or 209/753–2308 | www.bearvalley.com | Nov.–Apr., daily.

Don Pedro Lake Recreation Area. There are 160 mi of shoreline at this lake and wooded area in the Sierra Nevada foothills 40 mi south of Sonora, Route 49 south to J59. | 31 Bonds Flat Rd. | 209/852–2396 | www.donpedrolake.com | $5 per vehicle | Daily.

Mercer Caverns. Since 1885 the caverns have been popular for their 10 rooms of crystalline formations. Guided tours are available. | 1665 Sheep Ranch Rd. | 209/728–2101 | fax info@mercercaverns.com | www.mercercaverns.com | $8 | Memorial Day–Labor Day, Sun.–Thurs. 9–6; Fri.–Sat. 9–8. Labor Day–Memorial Day, Sun.–Thurs. 10–4:30; Fri., Sat. 10–6.

Moaning Cavern. Miners discovered this cavern in 1851. It yielded no gold, but did hold pre-historic human remains. You can take a guided tour 165 ft down into the cavern along a 235-step spiral staircase that wraps around the perimeter of a room large enough to hold the Statue of Liberty. The more adventurous-minded can rappel down (ropes and instruction provided). The caves are 8 mi north of Sonora off Rte. 4. | 5350 Moaning Cave Rd. | 209/736–2708 | fax 209/736–0330 | www.longbarn.com/caverns.htm | $8.75 | Weekdays 10–5, weekends 9–5.

New Melones Lake Recreation Area. Lakeside attractions, including boating, fishing, hiking, and picnicking, are available at this reservoir. It's 12 mi north of Sonora on Route 49. | 209/536–9094 | Free | Daily.

Sierra Repertory Theater Company. The local professional company presents a full season of plays, comedies, and musicals at the Fallon House Theater. Productions are also staged in East Sonora. | 11175 Washington St. | 209/532–3120 | srt@mlode.com | www.sierrarep.com | Box office Mon.–Sat. 10–6.

Skiing. Cut your tracks off the beaten track at ski area near Sonora. These low-key, family-oriented destinations don't tend to get the throngs that pack resorts closer to Lake Tahoe.

Roads rarely close on the way to **Dodge Ridge,** a pleasant downhill resort but also a year-round access point for hikers in summer and backcountry skiers and snowshoers in winter into nearby Yosemite National Park and surrounding mountains. The resort is 30 mi east of Sonora off Route 108. | 1 Dodge Ridge Rd. | 209/965–3474 or 209/965–4444 (24–hr snow conditions) | fax 209/965–4437 | www.dodgeridge.com | Nov.–Apr., daily.

Stanislaus National Forest. This preserve covers nearly 900,000 acres on the northwest side of Yosemite. Deep river gorges, rugged terrain, and an absence of crowds make this an excellent backcountry destination for camping, rafting, canoeing, hunting, hiking, backpacking, mountain biking, and, in winter, cross-country skiing and snowshoeing. | 19777 Greenley Rd. | 209/965–3434 or 209/532–3671 | www.r5.fs.fed.us/stanislaus | Free | Daily.

Tuolumne County Museum and History Center. Here you can view a jail museum, vintage firearms, a case with gold nuggets, and the libraries of the local historical and genealogical societies. | 158 W. Bradford St. | 209/532–1317 | Free | Sun.–Mon. 9–4, Tues.–Fri. 10–4, Sat. 10–3:30.

ON THE CALENDAR

MAY: *Fireman's Muster.* History springs to life in this celebration in a Victorian gold-mine setting. | 209/536–1672.

MAY: *Mother Lode Roundup Parade and Rodeo.* On Mother's Day weekend the town of Sonora celebrates its gold-mining, agricultural, and lumbering history with a parade, rodeo, entertainment, and food. | Motherlode Fairgrounds, 220 Southgate Dr. | 209/532–7428 or 800/446–1333.

JULY: *Mother Lode Fair.* Sonora was settled by miners from Mexico and has never forgotten its gold-mining roots. The Mother Lode Fair celebrates this unique time in California history. | Motherlode Fairgrounds, 220 Southgate Dr. | 209/532–7428 or 800/446–1333.

Dining

Banny's Cafe. Contemporary. A sense of calm and a menu of hearty but refined dishes make this café a pleasant option. Try the grilled salmon fillet with spinach and red pepper aioli or the eggplant grilled with shiitake mushrooms, leeks, roasted-tomato pesto, and mozzarella. | 83 S. Stewart St. | 209/533–4709 | D, MC, V.

Garcia's Taqueria. Mexican. Murals of Yosemite and other California landscapes cover the walls of this eatery, serving Mexican and Southwestern fare with an emphasis on seafood dishes. The spicy roasted-garlic soup is popular. | 145 S. Washington St. | 209/588–1915 | Closed Sun. | $2–$6 | No credit cards.

Josephine's California Trattoria. Italian. Seared ahi tuna, duckling with polenta, Delta crayfish risotto, and angel-hair pasta with fresh seafood are among the dishes on the seasonal menu here. Single-portion pizzas are a staple, and musicians perform several evenings a week. | 286 S. Washington St. | 209/533–4111 or 800/533–4111 | fax 209/533–3835 | Closed Mon. No lunch | $13–$25 | AE, D, MC, V.

North Beach Cafe. Italian. This popular bistro doesn't bely its before-life as an auto parts store. Now it serves traditional Italian fare, including pastas and steaks, as well as fish, chicken, and veal dishes. At lunch, you can have a burger, soup, sandwich, or salad. No smoking. | 14317 Mono Way | 209/536–1852 | $19–$27 | No credit cards.

Lodging

Barretta Gardens Bed and Breakfast Inn. This inn is perfect for a romantic getaway or a special business meeting. Its elegant Victorian rooms vary in size, but all are furnished with period pieces. The three antiques-filled parlors carry on the Victorian theme. A French bakery on the property provides the fresh pastries at breakfast. Complimentary breakfast. TV in common area. Hot tub. | 700 S. Barretta St. | 209/532–6039 | fax 209/532–8257 | barettagardens@hotmail.com | www.barrettagardens.com | 5 rooms | $95–$110 | AE, MC, V.

Best Western Sonora Oaks. The larger rooms of this hotel off Route 108 on the east side of Sonora have outside sitting areas, and the suites have fireplaces, whirlpool tubs, and hillside views. (Rooms fronting the highway can be noisy.) Restaurant. Some in-room data ports, cable TV. Outdoor pool. Hot tub. Laundry service. Business services. | 19551 Hess Ave. | 209/533–4400 or 800/532–1944 | fax 209/532–1964 | www.bestwestern.com | 96 rooms, 4 suites | $74–$84, $94 suites | AE, D, DC, MC, V.

Days Inn. This 1896 Victorian hotel furnished in antique reproductions is downtown. Some refrigerators, cable TV. Pool. | 160 S. Washington St. | 209/532–2400; 800/580–4667 from CA | fax 209/532–4542 | becky@sonoradaysinn.com | www.sonoradaysinn.com | 64 rooms | $69–$79 | AE, D, DC, MC, V.

Lavender Hill. This 1900 Eastlake Victorian house has a view of downtown from the porch swings on the wraparound veranda. There's also a peaceful, year-round garden. The sunny rooms are filled with period antiques, and breakfast often includes fresh fruit from the property. Complimentary breakfast. Library. | 683 Barretta St. | 209/532–9024 | lavender@sonnet.com | www.lavenderhill.com | 4 rooms | $79–$99 | AE, D, MC, V.

Sterling Gardens. Ten woodland acres surround this Tudor-style house furnished with a mix of antiques and contemporary pieces, a backyard hammock, and a fireplace. Complimentary breakfast. In-room VCRs. Pond. No kids under 12. | 18047 Lime Kiln Rd. | 209/533–9300 | fax 209/536–1303 | www.sterlinggardens.com | 4 rooms | $105 | AE, D, MC, V.

SOUTH LAKE TAHOE

MAP 3, G6

(Nearby towns also listed: Lake Tahoe Area, Tahoe City, Tahoe Vista)

South Lake Tahoe has the setting of an incomparable destination—on the southern shore of cerulean-blue Lake Tahoe, surrounded by snow-capped mountains. But its look and tone is more like Las Vegas, with neon signs and huge hotels above 24-hour casinos. The city straddles the California/Nevada border, and while many people come here for the nearby recreation and the gorgeous views, casino traffic bound for "Stateline" can jam the main thoroughfare, U.S. 50. To avoid the crowds, head to the outskirts of town, where casinos and strip malls give way to state parks and national forests.

Information: **Lake Tahoe Visitors Authority** | 1156 Ski Run Blvd., 96150 | 530/544–5050 or 800/288–2463 | www.virtualtahoe.com.

Attractions

Emerald Bay State Park. Glaciers carved the 3-mi long and 1-mi wide bay, a natural divet on the shores of Lake Tahoe, that's the focal point of this park. Take a gander at the water and you'll know how it got its name. Stop at the lookout for breathtaking views, or hike 1 mi down to nearby Vikingsholm, the 1929 castle-like estate at the water's edge. The park is 9 mi west of South Lake Tahoe. | Rte. 89 | 530/525–7277 | www.cal-parks.ca.gov | Free; Vikingsholm, $1 | Daily; Vikingsholm open Memorial Day–Labor Day, daily 10–4.

★ **Heavenly Tram.** You'll be impressed by the view of Lake Tahoe from this 50-passenger tram which runs 2,000 ft, skimming the slopes of Heavenly Ski Resort to an elevation of 8,200 ft. Views are spectacular, with the Sierra ringing the turquoise blue of Tahoe. In summer, the tram accesses several hiking trails. There's a cafeteria-style restaurant. | U.S. 50 | 775/586–7000 | www.skiheavenly.com | $20 | June–Oct., daily 10–9; Nov.–May daily 9–4.

Hornblower's *Tahoe Queen*. Tour Lake Tahoe from this 500-passenger, glass-bottomed, paddle-wheel ship on a sightseeing or lunch- or dinnertime cruise. | Ski Run Marina, off U.S. 50 | 530/541–3364 or 800/238–2463 | fax 530/541–8685 | www.hornblower.com | $20, not including meals | Daily.

Lake Tahoe Visitor Center. The U.S. Forest Service operates this center, on Taylor Creek 3½ mi west of South Lake Tahoe on Route 89. Here you can visit the site of a Washoe Indian settlement and walk self-guided trails through meadow, marsh, and forest. There's also the Stream Profile Chamber, where windows built underground and below creek level let you spy on native salmon (in fall, you might see them digging shallow nests and laying eggs). In summer, naturalists lead discovery walks and nighttime campfires, with singing and marshmallow roasts. | Rte. 89 | 530/573–2674 (in season only) | June–Sept., daily 8–5:30; Oct., weekends, 8–5:30.

Sierra at Tahoe Ski Resort. Forty-six slopes and trails and a vertical drop of 2,212 ft make this resort popular among skiers, snowboarders, and snow tubers alike. Half the trails are intermediate, so it's a great place to learn to be a beginner. It's 12 mi south of South Lake Tahoe. | U.S. 50 | 530/659–7453 | sierra@boothcreek.com | www.sierratahoe.com | $48 lift tickets | Weekdays 8:30–4, weekends 9–4.

Dining

Red Hut Waffle Shop. American. Sit at the counter or slip into a booth at this vintage diner, and sample unusual preparations of waffles, like pecan or coconut, or any of the omelets. Basic lunch staples are also on the menu. | 2749 U.S. 50 | 530/541–9024 | No dinner | $4–$10 | No credit cards.

Scusa! Italian. Modern in design, though intimate in character, this restaurant serves a variety of pastas, steak, chicken, fish, and house-made pizzas and flatbread. | 1142 Ski Run Blvd. | 530/542–0100 | Closed Mon. from Sept.–Nov. and Apr.–Jun. Dinner only | $9–$20 | AE, D, MC, V.

Swiss Chalet. Swiss. Schnitzel, fondue, and sauerbraten are the specialties at this Old World–style Tahoe institution. The setting is pure Heidi, with cheerful flower boxes fronting the chalet-style building. In winter, it's especially cozy and convivial inside, a special après-ski destination, where the conversation gravitates toward moguls and powder. | 2544 U.S. 50 | 530/544–3304 | Closed late Nov.–early Dec. | $15–$23 | AE, MC, V.

Lodging

★ **Embassy Suites.** All guest rooms at this hotel are suites. A complimentary full breakfast and evening cocktails are served under the nine-story atrium in the lobby. 4 restaurants, bar with entertainment, complimentary breakfast. Indoor pool. Hot tub, sauna. | 4130 Lake Tahoe Blvd. | 530/544–5400 or 800/362–2779 | fax 530/544–4900 | www.embassytahoe.com | 400 suites | $199–$349 suites | AE, D, DC, MC, V.

★ **Inn by the Lake.** Across the road from a beach, all of the spacious rooms at this motel have balconies; some have lake views and kitchenettes. Pool. Hot tub, sauna. Bicycles. Laundry facilities. | 3300 Lake Tahoe Blvd. | 530/542–0330 or 800/877–1466 | fax 530/541–6596 | info@innbythelake.com | www.innbythelake.com | 87 rooms, 12 suites | $108–$198, $182–$372 suites | AE, D, DC, MC, V.

Ridgewood Inn. This single-story, mom-and-pop motel offers simple accommodations on the outskirts of town and makes a good jumping-off point for skiing or exploring the mountains. Every room has a fireplace. Hot tub. | 1341 Emerald Bay Rd. | 530/541–8589 | fax 530/

542–4638 | ridgewoodinn@aol.com | www.ridgewoodinn.com | 11 rooms, 1 suite | $68–$78, $125 suite | AE, MC, V.

Sorensen's Resort. In business since 1926, this resort is on 165 wooded acres at an elevation of 7000 ft 20 mi south of South Lake Tahoe. It's a great family place, with lots to do for every member of the family. In winter, everybody cross-country skis on the resort's network of trails or goes downhilling and snowboarding at Kirkwood ski area, 15 mi away. Cabins have wood furnishings and most have wood-burning stoves. Restaurant. Some kitchenettes, some microwaves, some refrigerators, some room phones, no TV. Sauna. Fishing. Cross-country skiing. Pets allowed. No smoking. | 14255 Hwy. 88, Hope Valley | 530/694–2203 or 800/423–9949 | fax 530/694–2271 | sorensensresort@yahoo.com | www.sorensensresort.com | 33 cabins | $105–$215 | AE, MC, V.

STOCKTON

(Nearby towns also listed: Livermore, Lodi, Modesto, Oakdale)

Between the Sacramento River Delta and the 60-mi-long Stockton Channel is this city of 210,900, which also happens to be the first of California's two inland seaports. Originally a gateway to the Mother Lode country, Stockton has become one of the fastest developing warehousing and distributing hubs in California and can boast one of the most lucrative agricultural centers in the country. The city also has a large and vibrant immigrant community; local festivals and restaurants reflect their culture.

Information: San Joaquin Convention and Visitors Bureau | 46 W. Fremont St., 95202 | 209/943–1987 or 800/350–1987 | ssjcvb@ssjcvb.org | www.ssjcvb.org.

Attractions

Children's Museum. This is a hands-on museum of permanent and temporary exhibits. | 402 W. Weber Ave. | 209/465–4386 | fax 209/465–4394 | www.sonnet.com/usr/children | $4 | Tues.–Sat. 9–4, Sun. noon–5.

★ **Haggin Museum.** Here's a museum of Asian artworks. | 1201 N. Pershing Ave. | 209/462–4116 or 209/462–1566 | www.askasia.org | By donation | Tues.–Sun. 1:30–5, tours by appointment.

Magnolia Historic District Walking Tour. You can take a self-guided or group tour to learn about the histories of Stockton's romantic mansions and distinguished old homes as well as the Hotel Stockton, built in the early 1900s. | 46 W. Fremont St. | 209/943–1987 or 800/350–1987 | fax 209/943–6235 | www.ssjcvb.org | Free | Weekdays 8–5.

Pixie Woods. This fanciful kids' playland has amusement rides, theater programs, and sets from stories and legends. | Mt. Diablo Ave. | 209/937–8206 | www.stocktongov.com/parks/pixie.htm | $1.75; rides 60 cents | June 5–Sept. 9, Wed.–Fri. 11–5, weekends 11–6; Feb. 26–June 4 and Sept. 10–Oct., weekends noon–5.

ON THE CALENDAR

APR.: *Asparagus Festival.* Here you can celebrate the agricultural and gastronomical benefits of the pointy vegetable. | Oak Grove Regional Park, I–5 and Eight-Mile Rd. | 209/943–1987.
JUNE: *San Joaquin County Fair.* This is a classic county fair representing rural California. | Fairgrounds, at Charter and Airport Ways | 209/466–5041.
JULY: *Obon Festival and Bazaar.* This one-of-a-kind local festival celebrates Japanese culture. | 2820 Shimizu Dr. | 209/466–6701.
SEPT.: *Dewey Chambers Storytelling Festival.* Nationally acclaimed and local storytellers spin yarns for all ages. | 209/546–8295.

SEPT.: *Greek Festival.* Delicious Mediterranean food and drink, as well as plenty of entertainment, help you celebrate Greek culture. | 920 W. March La. | 209/478–7564.

Dining

Le Bistro. Continental. The menu here, at one of the valley's most upscale restaurants, has lamb tenderloin, fillet of sole, sautéed prawns, and a Grand Marnier soufflé. Try the white veal or the grilled swordfish. The dining room, awash in soft, flattering light, is done in tones of pale apricot and cream. No smoking. | 3121 W. Benjamin Holt Dr. | 209/951–0885 | No lunch weekends | $24–$55 | AE, D, DC, MC, V.

On Lock Sam. Chinese. Draw the curtains for privacy—and a touch of intrigue—in some of the booths of this pagoda-style building run by same family since 1898. The Cantonese cuisine includes specials such as crab with ginger sauce. | 333 S. Sutter St. | 209/466–4561 | $5–$13 | AE, D, MC, V.

Lodging

City Center Days Inn. This downtown chain hotel has water views. Complimentary Continental breakfast. In-room data ports, cable TV. Outdoor pool. Business services. | 33 N. Center St. | 209/948–6151 | fax 209/948–1220 | www.daysinn.com | 93 rooms | $45–$55 | AE, D, DC, MC, V.

Redroof Inn. Marigolds and petunias surround this three-story white hotel. In-room data ports, refrigerators, cable TV. Pool. Hot tub. | 2654 W. March La. | 209/478–4300 or 800/633–8300 | fax 209/478–1872 | www.redroof.com | 123 rooms | $65 | AE, D, DC, MC, V.

STUDIO CITY

MAP 9, D2

(Nearby towns also listed: Hollywood, North Hollywood, Sherman Oaks, West Hollywood)

Studio City is a stylish, leafy San Fernando Valley hillside district over the hill from Hollywood. Sandwiched between Laurel and Coldwater canyons, Studio City is minutes from the studios (hence the name) and the happening Hollywood Hills.

Information: Studio City Chamber of Commerce | 4024 Radford Ave., 91604 | 818/769–3213.

Attractions

CBS Studios. Although there are no public tours here, you can still get a glimpse of the inner workings of TV shows as an audience member. To get free tickets to show tapings, contact Audiences Unlimited, Inc., either on-line or by phone. | 4024 Radford Ave. | 818/753–3470 | www.tvticket.com | Free | Call for show times.

ON THE CALENDAR

JULY: *4th of July Celebration.* CBS Studio Center is the place to be on the nation's birthday. There's picnicking on the back lots, you can tour the studio, and fireworks light up the skies once the sun goes down. | 818/655–5916 | www.studiocitychamber.org.

Dining

Art's Deli. Delicatessen. "Every sandwich is a work of art" is the tongue-in-cheek motto at this Jewish-style deli with bistro tables and chairs. You'll think you're in Manhattan, what with the corned beef and pastrami sandwiches and matzo-ball and sweet-and-sour cabbage soups on the menu. No smoking. | 12224 Ventura Blvd. | 818/762–1221 | Reservations not accepted | Breakfast also available | $8–$11 | AE, D, DC, MC, V.

Caioti. Pizza. The relaxed approach of the staff, patio seating, and delectable food are some of the charms of this country-style restaurant. Shrimp and oyster pizza with spinach and gruyère pleases both the eye and the palate. You can design your own pie for dessert. Beer and wine only. No smoking. | 4346 Tujunga Ave. | 818/761–3588 | $12–$18 | AE, D, DC, MC, V.

Perroche. French. A wrought-iron chandelier lights this minimalist Provençal dining room at night where two- and three-course meals begin with house-smoked trout, an airy parfait of chicken livers, or other delightful starter. For supper you might find linguine with house-smoked salmon or roast loin of pork with caramelized apples and mashed potatoes. No smoking. | 1929 Ventura Blvd. | 818/766–1179 | Closed Sun. No lunch Sat. | $17–$23 | AE, D, DC, MC, V.

Pinot Bistro. French. Butter-yellow walls, polished wood, and comfortable banquettes accent this Parisian bistro where fresh oysters, sautéed foie gras with caramelized apples, Basque-style bouillabaisse (Fri. only), pot-au-feu, and a grilled sirloin steak with a roasted potato cake fill the menu. No smoking. | 12969 Ventura Blvd. | 818/990–0500 | Reservations essential | No lunch weekends | $32–$40 | AE, D, DC, MC, V.

Lodging

Beverly Garland Holiday Inn Universal Studios. Balcony rooms have views of the Hollywood Hills, and there are free shuttles to Universal Studios. Restaurant, room service. In-room data ports, cable TV. Outdoor pool. Hot tub. Tennis. Gym. Laundry services. Business services, airport shuttle, free parking. | 4222 Vineland Ave. | 818/980–8000 or 800/238–3759 | fax 818/766–5230 | sales@beverlygarland.com | www.beverlygarland.com | 255 rooms | $149–$189 | AE, D, DC, MC, V.

Sportsmen's Lodge. The eight manicured acres of waterfalls and waterfowl at this hotel have attracted stars like Garth Brooks and Randy Travis. Restaurant, bar, room service. Cable TV. Pool. Beauty salon, hot tub. Exercise equipment. Laundry facilities. Business services, airport shuttle. | 12825 Ventura Blvd. | 818/769–4700 or 800/821–8511 | fax 818/769–4798 | www.slhotel.com | 198 rooms | $109–$122 | AE, D, DC, MC, V.

SUNNYVALE

MAP 3, D8

(Nearby towns also listed: Cupertino, San Jose)

Sunnyvale developed along stagecoach lines linking the area to San Jose and San Francisco. From the mid-1800s on, orchards and vineyards flourished in its rich soil and temperate climate. Following World War II, aerospace and electronics companies clustered among the research labs near Stanford University in Palo Alto. Plums and cherries began to give way to silicon chips, and Sunnyvale is now one of the hot spots of Silicon Valley.

Information: Sunnyvale Chamber of Commerce | 499 S. Murphy Ave., 94086 | 408/736–4971.

Attractions

Sunnyvale Historical Museum. Exhibits at this museum in Martin Murphy, Jr., Park depict local history. Exit U.S. 101 at Mathilda. | 235 E. California Ave. | 408/749–0220 | Free | Tues., Thurs. noon–3:30, Sun. 1–4, or by appointment.

Sunnyvale Community Center Theatre and Gallery. Theater presents music, children's plays, classics; the gallery has changing shows of work by local artists. | 550 E. Remington Ave. | 408/730–7343 theater, 408/730–7336 galery | Gallery free | Gallery, Tues.–Thurs. 11–5, Wed., Fri. 1–5, Sat. 10–2.

Dining

Kabul Afghan Cuisine. Afghan. This friendly, family-run place is spacious with bright tapestries and Afghan costumes on the walls. The authentic ethnic options include grilled lamb chops marinated in yogurt. Beer and wine only. To get there take the Lawrence Expressway exit off U.S. 101. | 833 W. El Camino Real | 408/245-4350 | No lunch weekends | $8-$16 | AE, MC, V.

Niccolino's Garden Cafe. Italian. Plants fill this airy, pastel dining room with arched windows. Signature dishes hail from the province of Puglia, but you'll also find pizza. There's usually live piano music; on Saturdays, singers perform Neapolitan arias and Broadway show tunes. Bar. Open-air dining. Exit U.S. 101 at Lawrence Expressway. | 1228 Reamwood Ave. | 408/734-5323 | No lunch Sat., closed Sun. | $15-$26 | AE, D, DC, MC, V.

Palace. American. This enormous restaurant-and-night-spot occupying a former movie theater. It is eclectically decorated with Italianate and Art Nouveau motifs, and serves an inventive tapas menu. Try the crayfish in spicy broth or the spring rolls, then take a turn on the dance floor. There are two bars and live entertainment. To get there exit U.S. 101 at Mathilda. | 146 S. Murphy Ave. | 408/739-5179 | Closed Mon. | $19-$30 | AE, MC, V.

Lodging

Four Points Hotel at Sheraton. This luxurious lakeside hotel has a vaguely California Mission-style look. It's on a lagoon with colorful landscaped gardens and a small beach. Access is off U.S. 101's Lawrence Expressway exit. Restaurants, bar, room service. In-room data ports, refrigerators, some in-room hot tubs, cable TV. Pool. Gym. Hot tub, sauna. Business services, airport shuttle. | 1250 Lakeside Dr. | 408/738-4888 | fax 408/737-7147 | www.fourpointssvl.com | 372 rooms | $269-$299 | AE, D, DC, MC, V.

Maple Tree Inn. This comfortable motel has attractive landscaping comes with health club privileges. Exit U.S. 101 at Lawrence Expressway. Complimentary Continental breakfast. In-room data ports, some refrigerators, cable TV. Pool. Laundry facilities. Business services. | 711 E. El Camino Real | 408/262-2624 or 800/262-2624 from CA, 800/423-0243 from outside CA | fax 408/738-5665 | www.mapletreeinn.com | 181 rooms | $125-$150 | AE, D, DC, MC, V.

Sheraton Sunnyvale. Rooms overlook a swimming pool at this elegant two-story hotel with an attractive garden patio and gazebo. Exit U.S. 101 at N. Mathilda Avenue. Restaurant, bar. In-room movies, cable TV. Pool. Hot tub. Exercise equipment. Business services, airport shuttle. | 1100 N. Mathilda Ave. | 408/745-6000 or 800/325-3535 | fax 408/734-8276 | www.sheraton.com | 174 rooms | $89-$269 | AE, D, DC, MC, V.

SUSANVILLE

MAP 3, F3

(Nearby town also listed: Chester)

When pioneer Isaac Roop founded this high-desert town on the eastern slope of the Sierra Nevada mountains in 1854, he named it after his daughter. Today, with 17,000 inhabitants, Susanville is Lassen County's county seat, its primary commercial center, and home to almost half its population.

Information: Lassen County Chamber of Commerce | 84 N. Lassen St., 96130-0338 | 530/257-4323 | info@lassencountychamber.org | www.lassencountychamber.org.

Attractions

Bizz Johnson Trail. From its starting point at the Susanville Depot Trailhead Visitor Center and Museum, this 25-mi trail follows a defunct line of the Southern Pacific railroad through canyons and upland forests along the Susan River. You can hike the trail, ride a mountain bike, or go on horseback; whichever way you choose, you'll find wonderful views of a wide variety wildlife (including beaver dams) and, in the fall, colorful autumn foliage. | Trailhead: 601 Richmond Rd. | 530/257–0456 | www.ca.blm.gov/eaglelake/biz-ztrail.html | Free.

Roop's Fort and the Lassen Historical Museum. Susanville's oldest building, a log trading post built by town founder Isaac Roop in the 1850s, is preserved next door to a small local history museum. Displays include early photographs, antique lumbering equipment, Native American handicrafts, and a quilt collection. | 75 N. Weatherlow St. | 530/257–3292 | Free | May–Oct., weekdays 10–4; Sat. 11–3. Closed Nov.–Apr.

Eagle Lake. This 22,000-acre natural lake, ringed by high desert on the north and alpine forests on the south, is one of the largest in the state. It's a popular destination for picnicking, hiking, boating, and above all fishing—the native Eagle Lake trout is highly prized. | 20 mi northwest of Susanville on Eagle Lake Rd. | shastacascade.org/blm/eagle/lake.htm | Free.

Dining

Grand Cafe. American. This downtown coffeeshop, under continuous family ownership since the 1920s, serves reliable, traditional breakfasts and lunches. The early 20th-century decor is all original, including the individual jukeboxes at every booth. | 730 Main St. | 530/257–4713 | Breakfast and lunch only. Closed Sun. | $4–$10 | No credit cards.

Josephina's. Mexican. A loyal clientele comes to this traditional Mexican restaurant for tacos, enchiladas, and chiles rellenos. It's open late on weekends. | 1960 Main St. | 530/257–9262 | Closed Mon. | $5–$12 | MC, V.

St. Francis Champion Steakhouse. Steak. On the ground floor of Susanville's oldest continuously operating hotel, this restaurant serves steaks, chops, and seafood in a dining room decorated in an Old West theme. The lighter lunch menu features sandwiches, salads, and burgers. | 830 Main St. | 530/257–4820 | fax 530/357–4195 | Closed Sun. | $14–$25 | AE, MC, V.

Lodging

Best Western Trailside Inn. This large, business-friendly motel, located ½ mi east of downtown Susanville, offers a meeting room and data lines for business travelers. Some rooms have wet bars. Restaurants nearby. Complimentary Continental breakfast. In-room data ports, some refrigerators, room phones, cable TV. Pool. No pets. | 2785 Main St. | 530/257–4123 | fax 530/257–2665 | www.bestwesterncalifornia.com/shastacascade/susanville/info.htm | 110 rooms | $49–$89 | AE, D, MC, V.

High Country Inn. Built in 1996, this two-story, colonial-style independent motel on the east edge of town. The spacious rooms open onto indoor corridors, and dining is available next door at a Country Kitchen chain restaurant. All rooms have hairdryers and coffeepots. Some microwaves, some refrigerators, cable TV, room phones. Pool. No pets. | 3015 Riverside Dr. | 530/257–3450 | fax 530/257–2460 | 56 rooms | $62–$79 | AE, D, MC, V.

St. Francis Hotel. Susanville's oldest continuously-operated guest house, this three-story brick hotel (built in 1913) in the heart of the Uptown district has been under enthusiastic new ownership since 2000. Rooms are furnished with wooden antiques, and public spaces include a sitting parlor and a rear courtyard patio. Bar and restaurant downstairs. Only 16 of the rooms have private bath. Complimentary breakfast. No air conditioning, no room phones, no TV. No pets. No smoking. | 830 Main St. | 530/257–4820 | fax 530/357–4195 | 34 rooms | $40–$65 | AE, MC, V.

TAHOE CITY

MAP 3, G6

(Nearby towns also listed: Lake Tahoe Area, South Lake Tahoe, Tahoe Vista)

In the 1860s, the Truckee River attracted gold miners and prospectors, but when the ore proved to be poor, many followed the river to present-day Tahoe City and purchased land. Today, Lake Tahoe's water level is controlled here by the Outlet Gates, where you can lean over the railing and watch trout.

Information: North Lake Tahoe Resort Association | Box 5578, 96145 | 530/583–3494 or 800/824–6348 | fax 530/581–4081 | www.tahoefun.org.

Attractions

North Tahoe Cruises. Sightseeing tours and mealtime cruises aboard a 19th-century-style paddle-wheel ship depart several times daily in the summer, with a diminished schedule in spring and fall. | 850 North Lake Blvd. | 530/583–0141 or 800/218–2464 | fax 530/583–3743 | www.tahoegal.com | $17–$25, not including meals | May–Oct.; call for departure times.

★ **Gatekeeper's Log Cabin Museum.** This museum preserves the area's past, with artifacts from Paiute and Washoe tribes, as well as pioneer memorabilia. | 130 West Lake Blvd. | 530/583–1762 | fax 530/583–8992 | $2 | June 15–Labor Day, daily 11–5; May 1–June 15, and Labor Day–Oct. 1, Wed.–Sun., 11–5.

Squaw Valley USA. Four thousand acres of skiable terrain, six different peaks, and an average of 300 sunny days per year make this huge facility in Olympic Valley a hot destination for slope-lovers. There are dozens of well-maintained runs for all levels of expertise, as well as half-pipes and dishes for snowboarders. If you'd rather not tackle the slopes, there are shops, restaurants, lounges, heated outdoor swimming pools, and even an indoor rock-climbing wall to explore. Olympic Valley is about 6 mi north of Tahoe City. | Off Rte. 89 | 800/403–0206 | www.squaw.com | half-day $35, full day $49 | 9–4 Mon.–Fri., 8:30–4 Sat.–Sun. Open til 9PM after Mid-Dec.

Watson Cabin Living Museum. Costumed docents lead tours through this 1909 cabin, which re-creates the life of a typical pioneer family. | 560 N. Lake Tahoe Blvd. | 530/583–8717 | fax 530/583–8992 | $2 | June 15–Labor Day, noon–4.

Dining

Fiamma. Italian. Urban in design, this modern northern Italian restaurant and wine bar offers seafood, meat, vegetarian dishes, and pizzas from a wood-burning oven; the menu changes seasonally. | 521 N. Lake Blvd. | 530/581–1416 | No lunch | $14–$23 | AE, MC, V.

Fire Sign Café. American. Everything from pastries to smoked salmon is made fresh at this outstanding roadside restaurant in a converted Tahoe-style house. | 1785 W. Lake Blvd., 2 mi south of Tahoe City | 530/583–0871 | fax 530/583–1422 | Breakfast and lunch only | $4–$8 | AE, MC, V.

★ **Wolfdale's.** Contemporary. Set inside a century-old house, this intimate restaurant serves Asian-inspired California cuisine in a romantic dining room. | 640 N. Lake Blvd. | 530/583–5700 | fax 530/583–1583 | Reservations essential | Closed Tues. No lunch | $18–$30 | MC, V.

Lodging

Cottage Inn. All rooms have gas fireplaces at this lakeside compound of cottages. Though they have been divided into two units each, the cottages retain their rustic charm. No air-conditioning, no room phones, some kitchenettes, some in-room hot tubs. Lake. Sauna. Beach. | 1690 W. Lake Blvd. | 530/581–4073 or 800/581–4073 | fax 530/581–0226 | cottage@sierra.net | www.thecottageinn.com | 17 rooms, 10 suites | $149–$245 | MC, V.

Mayfield House. Within walking distance to town, this fieldstone bed and breakfast has charming Tahoe-style rooms, all individually decorated. Complimentary breakfast, no air-conditioning, no room phones, no TV in some rooms. | 236 Grove St. | 530/583–1001 | fax 530/581–4104 | innkeeper@mayfieldhouse.com | www.mayfieldhouse.com | 5 rooms in main house, 1 cottage | $150–$210 | AE, MC, V.

★ **Sunnyside Lodge.** Across the street from Lake Tahoe, the rooms at this impressive lodge have private decks with lake or mountain views. Restaurant, complimentary Continental breakfast, room service. No air-conditioning. Beach. | 1850 W. Lake Blvd. | 530/583–7200 or 800/822–2754 | fax 530/583–2551 | www.sunnysideresort.com | 18 rooms, 5 suites | $165–$180, $190–$205 suites | AE, MC, V.

TAHOE VISTA

MAP 3, G5

(Nearby towns also listed: South Lake Tahoe, Tahoe City)

Founded in the 1930s as a summer vacation community, Tahoe Vista commands sweeping views southward over Lake Tahoe's turquoise waters.

Information: **North Lake Tahoe Resort Association** | Box 5578, Tahoe City, 96145 | 530/583–3494 or 800/288–2463 | fax 530/530/581–4081 | www.tahoefun.com.

Attractions

North Tahoe Regional Park. Encompassing 124 acres of recreational lands, the park offers hiking and bicycle trails in the summer and sledding and snowmobiling in the winter months. | 1 mi north of Hwy. 28 via National Ave. | 530/546–4212 | fax 530/546–2652 | www.north-laketahoe.net | Free | Daily 7–dusk.

Northstar-at-Tahoe Resort. This resort offers downhill skiing, mountain biking, horseback riding, and golfing. Chair lifts operate in the summer for mountain biking. | Off Hwy. 267, between Truckee and King's Beach | 530/562–1010 or 800/466–6784 | fax 530/562–2215 | www.skinorthstar.com | Summertime all-day lift pass, $13, in the winter $52 | Call for hrs.

Windsurf North Tahoe. Learn to skitter across the icy blue waters with one of Lake Tahoe's kindest instructors, or rent a board here if you're already experienced. | Register at the Holiday House, 7276 N. Lake Blvd. | 530/546–5857 or 800/294–6378 | fax 530/546–1438 | Private and group lessons available; call for prices | Open daily by reservation.

Dining

Jason's. American. Serving a range of dishes from steaks to sandwiches, this lakeside roadhouse has a lively bar scene and outdoor dining in the summertime. | 8338 N. Lake Blvd., King's Beach | Open daily | $7–$19 | AE, D, DC, MC, V.

Le Petit Pier. French. Views are superb at this lakeside contemporary French restaurant, where specialties include rack of lamb and New Zealand venison. | 7238 N. Lake Blvd. | 530/546–4464 | fax 530/546–7508 | Closed Tues. No lunch | $20–$30 | MC, V.

Spindleshanks. Contemporary. This handsome restaurant, decorated with knotty-pine walls and plank floors, serves a wide variety of fresh seafood, meats, and house-made pastas. | 6873 N. Lake Blvd. | 530/546–2191 | fax 530/546–9443 | Closed Mon. in winter. No lunch | $12–$23 | MC, V.

Lodging

Franciscan Lakeside Lodge. This lakeside resort offers individual cabins, condominiums, and motel-style units on well-tended grounds that extend from Lake Tahoe's edge to the forest on the other side of Hwy. 28. No air-conditioning, kitchenettes, some in-room VCRs.

Pool, lake. Volleyball, beach, dock. | 6944 N. Lake Blvd. | 530/546–6300 or 800/564–6754 | fax 530/546–0348 | franciscan@powernet.net | www.franciscanlodge.com | 25 rooms, 29 suites | $85–$119, $139–$290 cabins and suites | AE, MC, V.

Holiday House. All units have a living room, bedroom, and kitchenette, and all but one have a dramatic view of Lake Tahoe at this two-story lakeside inn. No air-conditioning, kitchenettes. Outdoor hot tub. Lake. | 7276 N. Lake Blvd. | 530/546–2369 or 800/294–6378 | fax 530/546–1438 | 7 suites | $175–$185 | AE, D, MC, V.

Rustic Cottages. Detached 1920s clapboard cottages encircle a central lawn across the road from Lake Tahoe; many have kitchenettes and fireplaces. No air-conditioning, some kitchenettes. Some pets allowed (fee). | 7449 N. Lake Blvd. | 530/546–3523 or 888/778–7842 | fax 530/546–0146 | www.rusticcottages.com | 18 cottages | $59–$95, $95–$189 suites | AE, D, DC, MC, V.

TEHACHAPI

MAP 4, I13

(Nearby town also listed: Bakersfield)

This 19th-century high-desert town (pop. 5,800, elev. 3,973 ft), once a railroading center, is now the site of a 21st-century renewable energy wind turbine center. The downtown historic district reveals the past, while the Tehachapi-Mojave Wind Resource Area shows you the power of the record-setting gusts borne of the surrounding Mojave Desert. The town is also known for its annual apple harvest.

Information: **Greater Tehachapi Chamber of Commerce** | 209 E. Tehachapi Blvd., 93561 | 661/822–4180 | chamber@tminet.com | www.tehachapi.com/chamber.

Attractions

Tehachapi Heritage Museum. Artifacts and photographs illustrate the history of the Tehachapi region and its surrounding railroad network. | 310 S. Green St. | 661/822–8152 | www.tehachapi.com | Free | Tues.–Sun. noon–4.

Tehachapi Loop. This loop was designed in 1876 by a railroad engineer faced with the problem of how to climb a steep grade. His seemingly simple loop design was a landmark in railroad innovation. It's at Route 58, north from Tehachapi to Woodford/Tehachapi Road. | 661/822–4180 | www.tehachapi.com | Free | Daily.

ON THE CALENDAR

JUNE: *Indian Powwow.* Dozens of tribes perform song and dance to celebrate and preserve Native American culture. | Indian Hills RV Park and Campground, Banducci Rd. | 661/822–1118, 661/822–6613 campground.

AUG.: *Mountain Festival and PRCA Rodeo.* This is a full-scale rodeo and festival celebrating Tehachapi's history as a railroad town, Wind Resource Area, and Native American community home. | 661/822–4180.

SEPT.: *Fall Fest.* Kick off the apple harvest here at this arts and crafts fair. You can tour local orchards. | 661/822–4180.

Dining

Apple Shed. American. Look for all 13 types of local apples in this eatery's stuffed French toast, turnovers, and pies. On Friday and Saturday nights, locals flock to the outdoor barbecue pit for platters of ribs, chicken, and tri-tip beef. | 333 E. Tehachapi Blvd. | 661/823–8333 | fax 661/823–1010 | www.tehachapi.com/appleshed | $4–$12 | AE, D, MC, V.

Village Grille. American. Portions are huge in this family-run restaurant where breakfast is served all day, and the weekend prime rib special draws crowds. For dessert, try the cream pies, berry pies, cobblers, and brownies. | 410 E. Tehachapi Blvd. | 661/822–1128 | $7–$11 | AE, D, MC, V.

Lodging

Best Western Mountain Inn. The buildings of this property form a huge rectangular enclosure around the pool. A panoramic mountain view rears up on the horizon. The town's shopping district is a block away. Restaurant. Refrigerators, cable TV. Pool. Laundry facilities. | 416 W. Tehachapi Blvd. | 661/822–5591 | fax 805/822–6197 | www.bestwestern.com | 74 rooms | $75–$105 | AE, D, DC, MC, V.

Quarter Circle U Rankin Ranch. This dude ranch in Caliente, 32 mi northwest of Tehachapi on Route 58, sits on 30,000 acres in the heart of the Tehachapi Mountains. Outdoor pool, pond. Tennis. Hiking, horseback riding, volleyball, fishing. | 23500 Walker Basin Rd. | 661/867–2511 | fax 661/867–0105 | www.rankinranch.com | AP | 7 cabins | $150–$175 | AE, D, MC, V | Closed Oct.–Mar.

Resort at Stallion Springs. You enter the resort, surrounded by an ancient oak forest at 4,000 ft, through a covered bridge across a small lake, then up to the lodge and its sweeping mountain views. Some of the cottages overlook the golf course and all have fireplaces. Dining room, bar with entertainment. Some kitchenettes, cable TV. Pool. Hot tub. Driving range, 18-hole golf course, putting green, tennis. Exercise equipment, hiking, bicycles. Kids' programs, playground. Pets allowed. | 18100 Lucaya Way | 805/822–5581 or 800/244–0864 | fax 805/822–4055 | www.stallionsprings.com | 63 rooms, 19 cottages | $75–$85, $160–$205 cottages | AE, D, DC, MC, V.

Tehachapi Summit Travelodge. This two-story lodging, with a 20-ft ceiling supported by large pillars in the lobby, is 15 mi north of the Mojave Airport. Restaurant, bar. In-room data ports, cable TV. Pool. Hot tub. Business services. | 500 Steuber Rd. | 805/823–8000 | fax 805/823–8006 | www.travelodge.com | 81 rooms | $59 | AE, D, DC, MC, V.

TEMECULA

MAP 4, K15

(Nearby towns also listed: Escondido, San Clemente, San Diego, San Juan Capistrano)

This former Butterfield stagecoach route and rail station, now a town of 27,100, is a bedroom community of both Riverside and San Diego counties. Old Town Temecula on Front Street between Moreno Road and 3rd Street, preserves the early character of the place and doubles as a hot spot among antiques lovers.

Information: Temecula Valley Chamber of Commerce | 27450 Ynez Rd., #104, 92591 | 909/676–5090 | info@temecula.org | www.temecula.org.

Attractions

Hot Air Balloon Rides. Several local companies will take you into the sky for unusual views of Wine Valley and parts of San Diego County. | Temecula Valley Chamber of Commerce, 27450 Ynez Rd., #104 | 909/676–5090 | www.temecula.org | $125–$135 | By appointment.

Temecula Museum. This museum is dedicated to the history of the area as a Native American community, stagecoach stop, and home of Perry Mason. | 28314 Mercedes St. | 909/676–0021 | Free | Tues.–Sat. 10–5, Sun. 1–5.

Temecula Shuttle Wine Country Tours. You can take a narrated tour of valley wineries, including Callaway, Mount Palomar, and Thornton. A light lunch is included. | 28464 Front St. | 909/694–0292 | fax 909/506–4472 | www.temeculatours.com | $52 | By appointment.

Temecula Valley Winegrowers Association. This nonprofit regional organization has details on wineries and wine tours throughout the region. | 800/801–WINE | www.temeculawines.org.

ON THE CALENDAR

JUNE: *Balloon and Wine Festival.* Views of horse ranches, wineries, and vineyards from the sky highlight this celebration. | June 9–11 | 909/676–4713 or 909/676–6713.
JUL.–SEPT. *Hot Summer Nights.* Every Friday night in Old Town Temecula you can listen to live music at a variety of outdoor venues. | Front St. between Moreno Rd. and 3rd St. | 909/694–6412 | www.temeculacalifornia.com.

Dining

Bailey Wine Country Cafe. Continental. This family-run eatery in a shopping center serves herb-macadamia-nut-crusted fresh mahi-mahi, crab cakes with aoli and gorgonzola sauce, or a steak Diane prepared tableside. It's also got the largest selection of Temecula Valley wines in the area. No smoking. | 27644 Ynez Rd. | 909/676–9567 | $25–$38 | AE, DC, MC, V.

Bank of Mexican Food. Mexican. Flautas—shredded beef or chicken rolled in a flour tortilla and deep fried, served with rice and beans—crab enchiladas, and other south-of-the-border dishes are served in this place that was a bank in 1913. There is a ceramic-tiled patio if you want to eat outside. Kids' menu. Beer and wine only. No smoking. | 28645 Front St. | 909/676–6160 | $11–$18 | AE, D, DC, MC, V.

Cafe Champagne. Contemporary. The Thornton Winery's restaurant, with big windows overlooking the vineyards, serves dishes like seafood pasta and mesquite-grilled fish to complement its wines. You can sit outside with a view of the vineyard's bubbling fountain and sweeping grounds. Sunday brunch. No smoking. | 32575 Rancho California Rd. | 909/699–0099 | $25–$40 | AE, D, DC, MC, V.

Temet Grill. Contemporary. Order rack of lamb, portobello mushrooms stuffed with crayfish, or coffee-crusted New York strip steak at this restaurant overlooking the Temecula Creek Inn's golf course. The warm bread pudding follows a recipe created by Vincent Price. | 44501 Rainbow Canyon Rd. | 909/587–1465 or 800/962–7335 | fax 909/676–3422 | $16–$24 | AE, D, DC, MC, V.

Lodging

Embassy Suites. This hotel is ½ mi from downtown Old Temecula and less than 5 mi from most of the area's vineyards. Restaurant, bar, complimentary breakfast, room service. In-room data ports, microwaves, refrigerators, cable TV, in-room VCRs. Pool. Hot tub. Exercise equipment. Laundry facilities. Business services. | 29345 Rancho California Rd. | 909/676–5656 | fax 909/699–3928 | www.embassysuites.com | 176 suites | $109–$149 suites | AE, D, DC, MC, V.

Guest House Motel. This 1984 motel is two blocks north of Old Town Temecula. Complimentary Continental breakfast. Cable TV. Outdoor pool. Outdoor hot tub. | 41873 Moreno Rd. | 909/676–5700 | fax 909/694–8520 | 24 rooms | $59–$69 | AE, D, DC, MC, V.

Loma Vista. This bed-and-breakfast in a contemporary home surrounded by citrus orchards and vineyards is 8 mi from the Murrieta Hot Springs. Complimentary breakfast. No room phones, TV in common area. Hot tub. No smoking. | 33350 La Serena Way | 909/676–7047 | fax 909/676–0077 | 6 rooms | $100–$150 | MC, V.

Ramada Inn. A half-mile from Old Temecula, this hotel with mountain views is in the Temecula Wine Country. Complimentary Continental breakfast. Refrigerators, cable TV. Pool. Hot tub. Business services. | 28980 Front St. | 909/676–8770 | fax 909/699–3400 | www.ramada.com | 70 rooms | $75–$99 | AE, D, DC, MC, V.

Temecula Creek Inn. A chalet-style lounge and restaurant overlook a reflecting pool in front of this hotel on 300 acres where most rooms have a balcony. Bar, dining room, picnic area. Minibars, refrigerators, cable TV. Pool. Hot tub. Driving range, golf courses, putting green, tennis. Bicycles. | 44501 Rainbow Canyon Rd. | 909/694–1000 or 800/962–7335 | fax 909/676–3422 | www.jcresorts.com | 80 rooms in 5 buildings | $125–$205 | AE, D, DC, MC, V.

Temecula Valley Inn. Downtown is less than 1 mi away from this large motor hotel on Temecula's "Restaurant Row." Complimentary Continental breakfast. In-room data ports, refrigerators, cable TV. Outdoor pool. Outdoor hot tub. Business services. | 27660 Jefferson Ave. | 909/699–2444 or 877/836–3285 | fax 909/695–4775 | reservations@temeculavalleyinn.com | www.temeculavalleyinn.com | 90 rooms | $89–$99 | AE, D, DC, MC, V.

THOUSAND OAKS

(Nearby town also listed: Simi Valley)

This suburb of 117,600 is 39 mi west of Los Angeles and 12 mi inland from the Pacific Ocean. It is heavily developed both residentially and commercially, but more than 13,000 acres have been designated as open space in an effort to maintain the natural environment that inspired the city's name.

Information: Thousand Oaks and West Lake Village Chamber of Commerce | 600 Hampshire Rd., 91360 | 805/370–0035 | info@towlvchamber.org | www.towlvchamber.org.

Attractions

Chumash Interpretive Center. Take a nature walk around a Chumash Indian village, enter a cave to look at ancient pictographs, and learn about the history of the area's Native Americans at this center. | 3290 Lang Ranch Pkwy. | 805/492–8076 | $5 | Tues.–Sat. 10–5.

Stagecoach Inn Museum Complex. The 1876 main building of this inn was originally a way station for travelers heading between Los Angeles and Santa Barbara. Also part of the complex are a pioneer house, one-room schoolhouse, Chumash hut, and an adobe building filled with Chumash artifacts and Victorian antiques. | 51 S. Ventu Park Rd. | 805/498–9441 | www.toguide.com/stagecoach | $3 | Wed.–Sun. 1–4.

ON THE CALENDAR

MAY: *Conejo Valley Days.* A huge outdoor barbecue, chili cookoff, parade, and rodeo are among the many highlights at this family-oriented community event. | 805/371–8730.

NOV.: *Fall Craft-a-Rama.* You'll find handicrafts of all kinds and food stands at the Thousand Oaks Community Center the first Sunday of the month. | 805/499–7526.

Dining

Corrigan's Steak House. Steak. This bare-bones roadhouse serves what management claims is the best slab of beef in town. | 556 E. Thousand Oaks Blvd. | 805/495–5234 | Breakfast also available weekends | $14–$25 | AE, D, DC, MC, V.

Fins Seafood Grill. Seafood. Live jazz on the weekends and new artists' work on the walls make this place 5 mi from downtown a local hotspot. Try the macadamia-crusted halibut, the bouillabaisse, or the grilled catch of the day. The chocolate fondue is served with fresh berries. | 982 S. Westlake Blvd., Westlake Village | 805/494–6494 | $10–$24 | AE, D, DC, MC, V.

Johnny Rockets. American. Don't forget your nickels. You'll need them to feed the tabletop jukeboxes at this 1950s-style burger and malt chain in the Thousand Oaks Mall. | 322 W. Hillcrest Dr. | 805/778–0780 | www.johnnyrockets.com | $5–$10 | AE, D, DC, MC, V.

Lodging

Best Western Oaks Lodge. Stained-glass windows add a little flair to this A-frame motel. Restaurant, complimentary Continental breakfast. In-room data ports, kitchenettes, cable TV. Outdoor pool. Outdoor hot tub. Laundry service. | 12 Conejo Blvd. | 805/495–7011 or 800/600–6878 | fax 805/495–0647 | 76 rooms | $70 | AE, D, DC, MC, V.

Hyatt Westlake Plaza. Flower beds and trees surround this five-story hotel, 3 mi south of Thousand Oaks. Meeting space for up to 500 people draws occasional big crowds. Restaurant, bar with entertainment. In-room data ports, cable TV (and movies). Pool. Hot tub. Exercise equipment, bicycles. Business services. | 880 S. Westlake Blvd., Westlake Village | 805/497–9991 | fax 805/379–9392 | www.hyatt.com | 262 rooms | $115–$214 | AE, D, DC, MC, V.

Thousand Oaks Inn. The Santa Monica Mountains are the backdrop to this four-story hotel with spacious rooms. Restaurant, complimentary Continental breakfast. In-room data ports, some microwaves, some refrigerators, cable TV, in-room VCRs (and movies). Outdoor pool. Outdoor hot tub. Library. Business services. | 75 W. Thousand Oaks Blvd. | 805/497–3701 or 800/600–6878 | fax 805/497–1875 | www.thousandoaksinn.com | 106 rooms | $100–$145 | AE, D, DC, MC, V.

Westlake Village Inn. Fountains flow all over this 17-acre property, which is 3 mi south of Thousand Oaks. Rooms are filled with Victorian reproductions. Restaurant, bar with entertainment, complimentary Continental breakfast, room service. In-room data ports, cable TV, in-room VCRs (and movies). Pool. Hot tub. 18-hole golf course, tennis. Exercise equipment. Business services. | 31943 Agoura Rd., Westlake Village | 805/496–1667 or 800/535–9978 from CA | fax 818/879–0812 | www.wvinn.com | 140 rooms | $132–$230 rooms, $300 suites | AE, D, DC, MC, V.

THREE RIVERS

MAP 4, H10

(Nearby towns also listed: Fresno, Porterville, Visalia)

Three Rivers is a leafy hamlet of 1,400 along the Kaweah River and Route 198. From here, the road becomes the southern end of the Generals Highway, the main access route through Sequoia National Park. The park's Ash Mountain entrance station is 5 mi east of town.

Information: Central Sierra Chamber of Commerce | 54120 Badger Rd., Miramonte, 93641 | 559/336–9076.

Attractions

Lake Kaweah. Fish, swim, hike, camp, or picnic on the shore of this lake 5 mi west of town, on Route 198. | 34443 Sierra Dr., Lemon Cove | 559/597–2301 | fax 559/597–2468 | Free; camping $14; boat launch $2 | Weekdays 7:45–4:30. Daily dawn to dusk.

Sequoia National Forest. Covering 1,139,500 acres in central California, this forest runs from the San Joaquin Valley foothills to the crest of the Sierra Nevada. The more northerly of its two section abuts Sequoia and Kings Canyon National Parks on the south and east; the southern section adjoins other public lands, among them the Inyo National Forest and the Tule River Reservation. Of the world's sequoia groves, more than half are here, and they're among the forest's most-visited attractions. There are five designated wilderness areas, and three National Recreation Trails and a section of the Pacific Crest Trail cross the landscape. Four streams are designated National Wild and Scenic Rivers; some of the nation's liveliest whitewater is found on the Forks section of the Kern. Anglers go for 10- to 12-inch trout on Hume Lake; 11,000-acre Lake Isabella is one of the area's largest reservoirs. There's cross-country skiing and snowmobiling in winter, hiking on 900 mi of trail, as well as camping and picnicking the rest of the year. | 900 W. Grand Avenue | 559/784–1500 | www.r5.fs.fed.us/sequoia/ | Free | Daily.

Dining

Cafe Raven. American. You can watch the chef prepare Australian lamb chops, chicken teriyaki, and vegetarian lasagna in the open kitchen of this bistro on the village green where the dense chocolate cake is named "Nevermore." | 40869 Sierra Dr. | 559/561–7283 | fax 559/732–4950 | Closed Sun.–Mon. in winter | $9–$16 | AE, DC, MC, V.

Gateway Restaurant and Lodge. American. The patio of this local favorite, which serves a half-rack of baby back ribs and a large portion of eggplant parmigiana, overlooks the Kaweah River. | 45978 Sierra Dr. | 559/561–4133 | fax 559/561–3656 | www.gateway-sequoia.com | $7–$15 | AE, D, MC, V.

Lodging

Best Western Holiday Lodge. The lobby of this two-story stucco lodge 8 mi from Sequoia National Park and 4 mi from Lake Kaweah has a stone fireplace and Navajo-print fabrics. Complimentary Continental breakfast. Refrigerators, cable TV. Pool. Hot tub. Playground. Pets allowed. | 40105 Sierra Dr. | 559/561–4119 | fax 559/561–3427 | www.bestwestern.com | 54 rooms | $85–$105 | AE, D, DC, MC, V.

Cinnamon Creek Ranch. The antiques-filled rooms on this 10-acre ranch with resident donkeys have mountain views—one also has a private terrace overlooking the river. Complimentary Continental breakfast. Some kitchenettes, some refrigerators, some in-room hot tubs, in-room VCRs. Hiking. | 45542 South Fork Dr. | 559/561–1107 | cinnamon@theworks.com | 2 rooms, 1 cabin | $85–$120 rooms, $115 cabin | MC, V.

Lazy J Ranch Motel. Some rooms in this single-story motel in the foothills of the Sierra Nevada have fireplaces, and the cabins are fully equipped. Picnic area. Refrigerators, cable TV. Pool. Cross-country skiing. Playground. Laundry facilities. Pets allowed. | 39625 Sierra Dr. | 559/561–4449 or 800/341–8000 | fax 559/561–4885 | www.bestvalueinn.com | 11 rooms, 7 cottages | $70–$78, $95–$160 cottages | AE, D, DC, MC, V.

Organic Gardens Bed and Breakfast. Organic fruit from the garden shows up at breakfast at this B&B, ½ mi off Route 198, in the Sierra foothills with views of Sequoia National Park. Complimentary breakfast. Outdoor hot tub. | 44095 Dinely Dr. | 559/561–0916 | fax 559/561–1017 | bandb@organicgardens-sequoia.com | www.organicgardens-sequoia.com | 1 room, 1 cottage | $115, $130 cottage (2–night minimum stay) | MC, V.

Sierra Lodge. This lodge with mountain views and a small library is near the entrance to Sequoia National Park, as well as Lake Kaweah. Complimentary Continental breakfast. Some kitchenettes, refrigerators, cable TV. Pool. Library. Business services. Pets allowed (fee). | 43175 Sierra Dr. | 559/561–3681 or 800/367–8879 | fax 559/561–3264 | 22 rooms, 5 suites | $68–$82, $110–$150 suites | AE, D, DC, MC, V.

TIBURON

MAP 6, B3

(Nearby towns also listed: Mill Valley, San Francisco, Sausalito)

Named after the Spanish Punta de Tiburon (Shark Point), peninsular Tiburon feels village-like despite the growth of its downtown. The harbor faces Angel Island across Raccoon Strait, and San Francisco is due south, 6 mi across the bay. Once a railroad town, it is now full of marinas, and beautiful homes climb the hills above the water; along the shore there are waterfront restaurants with fine views of Fog City and a brisk Sunday brunch business as well as galleries, boutiques, and antiques shops. Shady Ark Row,

TIBURON

INTRO
ATTRACTIONS
DINING
LODGING

where many of them are clustered, dates from the 1800s when houseboats were clustered on the lagoon, and many of the buildings there are actually former houseboats, now beached and transformed. Angel Island, where immigrants from the Far East were held while awaiting entry into San Francisco, is a short ferry ride away.

Information: **Tiburon Peninsula Chamber of Commerce** | 96B Main St., Box 563, 94920 | 415/435–5633 | tibcc@aol.com | www.tiburon.org.

Attractions

Angel Island State Park. The 740-acre "Ellis Island of the West" has served, by turns, as a Miwok hunting ground, a Civil War encampment, a Spanish-American War quarantine station, a World War I discharge depot and recruitment processing center, and a World War II POW camp as well as an immigration station between 1910 and 1940 and a Nike Missile Base from 1955 to 1962. Now a park accessible by ferry from San Francisco, Vallejo, and Tiburon, it offers hiking on 13 mi of trails and biking on 8 mi of roadways, as well as kayaking and camping. You can tour the historic Civil War Camp Reynolds and Fort McDowell as well as the Immigration Station at China Cove. Tram and kayaking tours are available, and bikes can be rented. | Park headquarters, 5757 A Sonoma Dr., Pleasanton | 415/897–0715, 925/426–3058, 800/444–7275 campground reservations | www.angelisland.com | $4, $11.50 tours | Daily 8–sunset; tours daily at 10:30, 12:15, and 1:30, weekends also at 3:15.

Lyford House. This 1876 fantasy is a study in Victoriana, with its period decor and furniture. It's the focal point for Audubon Society activities, and the grounds, which abut 900 acres of protected water and mud flats. Exit U.S. 101 at Tiburon/East Blithdale. | 376 Greenwood Beach Rd., off Tiburon Blvd. | 415/388–2524 | fax 415/388–0717 | $4 | Wed.–Sun. 9–5; house Nov.–Apr., Sun. 1–4.

Old St. Hilary's Landmark and Wildflower Preserve. A Victorian-era Carpenter Gothic church built in 1886 overlooks the town from a hillside perch. Operated by the Landmarks Society, the church is surrounded by a wildflower preserve that is spectacular in May and June, when the rare black jewel flower is in bloom. | Esperanza St., off Mar West St. | 415/435–2567 | $2 suggested donation | Apr.–Oct., Wed. and Sun. 1–4.

Tiburon Railroad-Ferry Depot. A museum is in the offing for this structure, the only dual-use terminal remaining west of the Hudson River. It's a relic of the days of railroad-ferry yards and piers at Point Tiburon. A museum is planned for the restored building. | 1920 Paradise Dr. | 415/435–1853 | Free | Wed. and Sun. 1–4.

Dining

Caprice. Contemporary. This stylish waterfront restaurant has a spectacular view of Golden Gate Bridge and Angel Island. A fire warms you up on foggy days, and fresh local ingredients go into every dish; the rack of lamb and seafood paella get kudos. | 2000 Paradise Dr. | 415/435–3400 | fax 415/435–8034 | No lunch | $18–$27 | AE, MC, V.

Guaymas. Mexican. Located on Tiburon Harbor at the ferry landing, this rooftop dining room with a fireplace and panoramic views was named for the fishing village of Guaymas, Mexico, and the menu of *cocina fresca regional,* or regional fresh cooking, reflects the ties. Try the ceviche, the hand-made tamales, or the mesquite-grilled meats. Mariachis Sun. Open-air dining. | 5 Main St. | 415/435–6300 | $12–$18 | AE, DC, MC, V.

Sam's Anchor Cafe. Seafood. This landmark restaurant was reportedly once the hub of a bootlegging operation which made a fortune for founder Sam Vella. Nowadays, it's better known for the spacious sundeck with great views of San Francisco, Angel Island, and the marina. Some diners sail right up to the private dock in order to tuck into cracked Dungeness crab, oysters, or cioppino. Worth knowing: If a seagull snatches your meal, the management will replace it gratis. Open until 2 AM, it's a good bet for late dinners. Open-air dining. | 27 Main St. | 415/435–4527 | fax 415/435–5685 | $16–$19 | AE, DC, D, MC, V.

Lodging

Tiburon Lodge. This attractively landscaped three-story hotel with large, comfortably furnished rooms is within walking distance of the Tiburon pier and offers a panoramic view of the San Francisco Bay. Some rooms have their own patio or balcony, and quarters on the top floor rooms have cathedral ceilings. A VCR and movies are available. Restaurant. Complimentary breakfast. In-room data ports, some in-room hot tubs, cable TV. Pool. Business services. | 1651 Tiburon Blvd. | 415/435–3133, 800/762–7770, 800/842–8766 from CA | fax 415/435–2451 | 107 rooms | $199–$309 | AE, D, DC, MC, V.

Water's Edge Hotel. This luxury boutique hotel occupies a century-old building on the water downtown, where ferries used to dock with their wares. Furnishings are simple and contemporary in gold and yellow tones with black accents; some rooms have views and many have balconies, though a few are tiny. Complimentary Continental breakfast. In-room data ports, cable TV, in-room movies. Laundry service. No smoking. | 25 Main St. | 415/789–5999 or 877/789–5999 | fax 415/789–5888 | www.marinhotels.com | 23 rooms, 2 suites | $195–$350 | AE, D, DC, MC, V.

TORRANCE

MAP 9, E6

(Nearby towns also listed: Long Beach, Los Angeles)

Torrance is just inland from Redondo Beach and south of I–405. This bedroom community of 133,100 started to take off in the late 1940s and early '50s, when the area became a center for the postwar aerospace industry.

Information: Torrance Chamber of Commerce | 3400 Torrance Blvd., Ste. 100, 90503 | 310/540–5858 | www.torrancechamber.com.

Attractions

Alpine Village. Every night you can come dance to the beat of live rock n' roll, swing, and country-western bands. It's the shops and restaurants, rather than the music, that have a touch of the Alps, especially in fall, when the venue hosts the annual Oktoberfest. | 833 W. Torrance Blvd. | 310/327–4384 | www.alpinevillage.net | Free | Daily.

ON THE CALENDAR
APR.: *Bunka Sai Japanese Cultural Festival.* Japanese heritage is the focus of this event with cultural presentations, food, and music, in Little Tokyo. | 310/618–2930.
OCT.: *Arts Alive Festival.* The Torrance Cultural Arts Center puts on this weekend-long program of art exhibits, performances of music, theater, and dance, and workshops. | 310/781–7150.

Dining

Aioli Restaurant and Tapas Bar. Eclectic. Spanish tapas and paella, French goat cheese cigars, and Italian roast pork share the menu in this downtown eatery, where murals of flamenco guitarists line the walls. | 1261 Cabrillo Ave. | 310/320–9200 | fax 310/320–9931 | Closed Sunday | $10–$29 | AE, D, DC, MC, V.

Depot. Contemporary. This dining room, where Asian and Californian influences inspire combinations like honey garlic chicken, smoked veal ribs, and Thai grilled shrimp, resembles the inside of a 1920s railroad dining car. No smoking. | 1250 Cabrillo Ave. | 310/787–7501 | Closed Sun. No lunch Sat. | $15–$30 | AE, DC, MC, V.

Lodging

Hilton–South Bay. Skylights, marble, and plants fill the atrium of this 12-story tower hotel 2 mi from the beach across from the Del Amo Fashion Center. All rooms have antique-replica furnishings and marble-tiled bathrooms. Restaurant, bar. In-room data ports, some refrigerators, cable TV. Pool. Hot tub. Exercise equipment. Laundry facilities. Business services. | 21333 Hawthorne Blvd. | 310/540–0500 | fax 310/540–2065 | www.hilton.com | 350 rooms, 18 suites | $89–$199 rooms, $299 suites | AE, D, DC, MC, V.

Marriott. Surrounded by palm trees, this 14-story hotel is across from the Del Amo Fashion Center, next to the beach, and 15 mi south of downtown L.A. Restaurant, bars. In-room data ports, cable TV. Indoor-outdoor pool. Beauty salon, hot tub. Exercise equipment. Laundry facilities. Business services. | 3635 Fashion Way | 310/316–3636 | fax 310/543–6076 | www.marriott.com | 476 rooms, 11 suites | $112–$159 rooms, $200–$600 suites | AE, D, DC, MC, V.

Residence Inn Torrance–Redondo Beach. All the rooms have fireplaces, and there are some two-bedroom, two-story rooms at this motorlodge 2 mi south of downtown. Complimentary Continental breakfast. Some kitchenettes, microwaves, refrigerators, cable TV. Outdoor pool. Hot tub. Exercise equipment. Baby-sitting. Laundry service. Business services. Pets allowed. | 3701 Torrance Blvd. | 310/543–4566 or 800/331–3131 | fax 310/543–3026 | www.marriott.com | 247 suites | $109–$259 suites.

Summerfield Suites. Choose from a one- or two-bedroom suite, each with its own work area and kitchen. Picnic area, complimentary Continental breakfast. Kitchenettes, microwaves, cable TV. Pool. Hot tub. Exercise equipment. Laundry facilities. Airport shuttle. Pets allowed. | 19901 Prairie Ave. | 310/371–8525 or 800/833–4353 | fax 310/542–9628 | www.wyndham.com/AboutWyndham/summerfield.cfm | 144 suites | $148–$178 suites | AE, D, DC, MC, V.

Torrance Travelodge. This two-story motel built in the 1980s is five blocks from downtown. Microwaves, refrigerators, cable TV. Outdoor pool. Laundry facilities. Business services. | 2448 Sepulveda Blvd. | 310/539–9888 or 800/578–7878 | fax 310/539–6420 | tortravel@aol.com | 53 rooms | $58–$65 | AE, D, DC, MC, V.

TRINIDAD

MAP 3, B2

(Nearby towns also listed: Arcata, Eureka)

Trinidad was named by the Spanish mariners who entered the bay on Trinity Sunday, June 9, 1775. The town became a prime trading post for mining camps along the Klamath and Trinity rivers. When mining, and then whaling, faded, so did the luster of this former boomtown. Development has bypassed this scenic spot for now, making it one of the quietest towns along the coast, yet still with a healthy complement of inns and dining spots. The looming rock formations jutting out of Trinidad Bay can look stark and raw on brilliant, windblown days, yet muted and haunting when cloaked by marine fog.

Information: Trinidad Chamber of Commerce | Box 356, 95570 | 707/677–1610 | trinchamber@humboldt1.com | www.trinidadcalifchamber.org.

Attractions

North Coast Adventures. Explore Trinidad Bay in a kayak for on-the-water looks at seals and sea birds on these guided tours. If you're lucky you might catch sight of a whale. Previous kayak experience is required. Call to make reservations and arrange a put-in site. | 707/677–3124 | fax 707/677–0603 | www.northcoastadventures.com | $50 for 2-hr trip, $60 ½-day, $90 full-day | Apr.–Oct. daily, 7–7.

Patrick's Point State Park. This 640-acre park, cloaked in fir, hemlock, red alder, and spruce, has trails to cliffs overlooking the Pacific. It's a great spot for whale-watching, rock hunting, or exploring tidepools. A reconstructed Indian village has a bookstore, campgrounds, rental cabins, and several picnic areas. | 4150 Patrick's Point Dr. | 707/677–3570 or 800/444–7275 (camping information) | www.cal-parks.ca.gov | Free | Daily.

Telonicher Marine Laboratory. Follow a self-guided tour, observe displays on marine science and environment, and check out the critters in the "touch tanks" at this marine and environmental science lab, part of Humboldt State University. | 570 Ewing St. | 707/677–3671 | www.humboldt.edu/~marinelb/ | Mid-Aug.–May, weekdays 9–5, weekends 10–5; June–mid-Aug., weekdays 9–5.

ON THE CALENDAR
JUNE: *Annual Trinidad Fish Festival.* Salmon and ocean whitefish, barbecued or deep fried, are some of the dishes you can sample at this fish and live music smorgasbord hosted by Trinidad Town Hall. | 707/677–1610.

Dining
★ **Larrupin' Cafe.** Contemporary. Mesquite-grilled ribs and fresh fish are served in this bright yellow-two-story house on a quiet country road 2 mi north of town. | 1658 Patrick's Point Dr. | 707/677–0230 | Reservations essential | Closed Tues. No lunch | $15–$22 | No credit cards.

Lodging
Turtle Rocks Oceanfront Inn. Each guest room has an ocean view at this bed and breakfast 4 mi north of town. You can watch the seals on the impressive Turtle Rocks off shore from a rocking chair on the two-tiered deck. Complimentary breakfast. Cable TV. | 3392 Patrick's Point Dr. | 707/677–3707 | trocks@northcoast.com | www.turtlerocksinn.com | 5 rooms, 1 suite | $185, $210 suite | D, MC, V.

TRUCKEE

MAP 3, F5

(Nearby town also listed: Lake Tahoe Area, Tahoe City)

History and natural grandeur fill this town north of Lake Tahoe, once a frontier town of the Old West. It's popular among skiers in winter; summer brings campers, golfers, and water sports enthusiasts. Saloons and boarding houses from the era have been well preserved.

Information: **Truckee Chamber of Commerce** | 10065 Donner Pass Rd., 96161 | 530/587–2757 | truckeechamber@thegrid.net | www.truckee.com.

Attractions
Donner Memorial State Park. Named for the party of pioneers who were stranded in the mountains and resorted to cannibalism, this Sierra Nevada park includes a pine forest, interesting geologic formations, and 3 mi of frontage on Donner Lake. The Pioneer Monument, Murphy family cabin site, and Emigrant Trail Museum depict the history of the area and its inhabitants. | 12593 Donner Path Rd. | 530/582–7892 | cal-parks.ca.gov/DISTRICTS/sierra/dmsp301.htm | $5 | Daily.

At **Donner Lake** you can boat, camp, picnic, fish, water-ski, and hike. It's 1 mi west of Truckee off I–80. | 530/587–2757 | cal-parks.ca.gov/districts/sierra/dmsp301.htm | Free | Daily.

Old Truckee Jail Museum. First opened in 1875, this was the longest-operating jail in California until 1964. Today, you can tour the cells and see local history exhibits and Native American artifacts. | 10142 Jibboom St. | 530/582–0893 | Free | May–Labor Day 11–4.

Skiing. Eight major ski resorts are in the Truckee vicinity. The season usually starts in late November. | Truckee Chamber of Commerce, 10065 Donner Pass Rd. | 530/587–2757 | www.truckeetahoe.com/truckeelinks.html.

At **Boreal,** the closest ski resort to the San Francisco bay area, you'll find lots of beginners trying out their snowplow on relatively gentle slopes. If you bundle up, you might try night-skiing on the resort's lighted runs. Boreal is off I–80 at the Castle Peak exit. | 530/426–3666 | www.skiboreal.com | Nov.–May (snow permitting), daily | $32.

Donner Ski Ranch is a low-key resort named after the ill-fated Donner Party, which tried (and failed) to make it over the Sierra crest here. | 19320 Donner Path Rd. (I–80 west 10 mi to Soda Springs exit; left over the bridge for 3 mi) | 530/426–3635 | www.donnerski-ranch.com/ | Nov.–May (snow permitting), daily | $28.

The base lodge at **Northstar** ski area was built to resemble an Alpine village. The resort is a favorite of families. | Rte. 267 and Northstar Dr. | 530/562–1010 or 800/533–6787 | www.skinorthstar.com | Nov.–Apr. (snow permitting), daily | $25.

Royal Gorge Cross Country Ski Resort has panoramic views of the gorge and surrounding mountains, plus 175 km of groomed trails, warming huts, and a café. It's a top spot for kick-and-gliders. The resort is on Hillside Road, 15 mi west of Truckee off I–80. | 530/426–3871 or 800/500–3871 | fax 530/426–9221 | www.royalgorge.com/ | Nov.–Apr. | $21.

Sugar Bowl ski resort, 13 mi west of town off I–80, gets its name from the foot upon foot of white stuff it receives—typically one of the heaviest accumulations of all the region's ski resorts. | 629 Sugarbowl Rd. | 530/426–9000 | fax 530/426–3723 | www.sugar-bowl.com | Nov.–Apr., daily.

Tahoe National Forest. Draped along the Sierra Nevada in northern California and surrounded by the Plumas, Eldorado, and Humboldt-Toiyabe national forests above Lake Tahoe, this preserve encompasses Donner Pass, the mountain pass that terrified California-bound emigrants during the mid-19th century. Scattered with alpine lakes and criss-crossed by trails, including sections of the Pacific Crest trail, it offers abundant outdoor recreation today. There's picnicking and camping in summer; heavy snows delight snow-shoers, skiers, and sledders. Although the forest headquarters are in Nevada City, the visitors center, a focal point for many forest visits, is at Big Bend, 18 mi west of Truckee just off I–80. | 631 Coyote St., Nevada City | 530/265–4531 | www.r5.fs.fed.us/tahoe/ | Free | Daily.

The **Big Bend Visitor Center** occupies a state historic landmark 10 mi west of Donner Summit. This area has been on major cross-country routes for centuries; Native Americans crossed through, trading acorns and salt for pelts, obsidian, and other materials. Between 1844 and 1860, more than 200,000 emigrants traveled to California along the Emigrant Trail, which passed nearby; you can see rut marks left by wagon wheels scraping the famously hard granite. Later the nation's first transcontinental railroad ran through here (and still does), as do U.S. 40, the old national road, and its successor I–80. Exhibits in the Visitor Center explore the area's transportation history. There are also occasional exhibits focusing on natural history. Take the Rainbow-Big Bend exit off I–80. | U.S. 40, Soda Springs | 530/426–3609 | www.r5.fs.fed.us/tahoe/big_bend/ | Free | Apr.–Oct., daily.

Tahoe Truckee Factory Stores. Search for great bargains at this outlet complex. Stores include Reebok, Van Heusen, and Villeroy & Boch. | 12047 Donner Pass Rd. | Mon.– Sat. 9:30–6.

ON THE CALENDAR

JUNE: *Truckee-Tahoe Air Fair.* This event at the Truckee Fairgrounds, 2 mi east of town on Route 267, includes aircraft displays, classic cars, food and beverage stands, and a USO dinner dance. | 530/587–4540.

AUG.: *Truckee Rodeo.* The rough and tumble character of the pioneer town is revived during rodeo season at the Truckee Fairgrounds. | 530/582–9852.

SEPT.: *Truckee Railroad Days.* At this celebration of new and old trains, you're invited to tour railroad cars, visit a model train exhibit, watch the National Handcar Races, and take in other goings-on around town. For all this and chili, too, turn off I–80 onto Route 267. | 530/546–1221 | www.truckee.com.

OCT.: *Donner Party Hike.* Guides from the Truckee Chamber of Commerce lead hikes through the surrounding mountains to commemorate the Donner Party's ill-fated trip west. | 530/587–2757.

Dining

Cafe Meridian. Contemporary. American standbys like hamburgers, and more unusual offerings, such as Caribbean (tangy and sweet) hanger steak, and mushroom and sage-walnut pesto ravioli, share the menu in this airy, downtown café. | 10118 Donner Pass Rd. | 530/587–0557 | $13–$20 | AE, D, DC, MC, V.

Cottonwood Restaurant. Contemporary. Sunset views from the patio of this hilltop restaurant, a fireplace in the dining room, and live jazz Saturday evenings complement signature preparations like prawns with sun-dried tomato and kalamata olive tapenade, served over pasta with feta cheese and fresh basil, or the garlic- and dijon-rubbed pork tenderloin medallions. | Rte. 267 and Old Brockway Rd. | 530/587–5711 | fax 530/587–3955 | www.cottonwoodrestaurant.com | No lunch | $16–$23 | MC, V.

OB's Pub and Restaurant. American. Barn wood, lace curtains, antique tables and chairs, and photos of Truckee in bygone days adorn this eatery where the menu includes burgers, wraps, salads, pasta, fish, pork, or the Harris Ranch slow-roasted prime rib of beef. No smoking. | 10046 Donner Pass Rd. | 530/587–4164 | $15–$30 | D, DC, MC, V.

Lodging

Best Western Truckee-Tahoe Inn. Between Truckee and the north shore of Lake Tahoe, this two-story hotel is 2 mi east of town. Complimentary Continental breakfast. Pool. Hot tub. Exercise equipment. Business services. | 11331 Rte. 267 | 530/587–4525 | fax 530/587–8173 | 100 rooms | $92–$135 | AE, D, DC, MC, V.

Donner Lake Village Resort. A family-friendly place if you want to keep busy—water sports on Donner Lake in summer, cross-country and downhill skiing at nearby resorts in winter. Or, do nothing at all. Rooms are styled with lots of wood and plaid flannel. The resort is 8 mi west of downtown Truckee. No air-conditioning, cable TV. Lake. Sauna. Business services. | 15695 Donner Pass Rd., Ste. 101 | 530/587–6081 or 800/621–6664 | fax 530/587–8782 | 66 rooms | $100–$225 | AE, D, DC, MC, V.

Hania's Bed and Breakfast Inn. Take a peek at the Sierra peaks from this 19th-century hillside inn with contemporary, Southwestern-style guest rooms. Come morning, have breakfast in bed, at the log table in the dining room, or, when weather obliges, outside on the deck. Complimentary breakfast. In-room data ports, cable TV, in-room VCRs. Outdoor hot tub. Airport shuttle. | 10098 High St. | 530/582–5775 or 888/600–3735 | fax 530/587–4424 | www.truckee.com/hania | 4 rooms | $95–$155 | AE, MC, V.

Northstar-at-Tahoe. A cedar lodge surrounded by pines and mountain vistas is at the heart of this sprawling resort. Places to stay include lodge rooms, condominiums, and three- to five-bedroom mountain homes overlooking the golf course. Bar, picnic area. No air-conditioning, cable TV. 2 pools, wading pool. Hot tub. Driving range, 18-hole golf course, putting green, tennis. Exercise equipment. Cross-country and downhill skiing. Video games. Playground. Laundry facilities. Business services. | Northstar Dr., off Rte. 267 | 530/562–1010 or 800/533–6784 | fax 530/562–2215 | www.skinorthstar.com | 30 rooms in lodge, 205 apartments, 27 houses | $129–$139 rooms, $99–$329 condos, $289–$489 houses | AE, D, MC, V.

Richardson House. On a hill overlooking downtown, this 1880s green-and-gold gingerbread Victorian filled with antiques, vintage fixtures, and plenty of period lace has views of the surrounding Sierra. Some rooms have four-poster canopy beds and claw-footed tubs. Two adjoining rooms share a bath, and can be rented together as a family-style suite. Complimentary breakfast. TV in common area. No kids under 10. | 10154 High St. | 530/587–5388 or 888/229–0365 | fax 530/587–0927 | innkeeper@richardsonhouse.com | www.richardsonhouse.com | 8 rooms (2 with shared bath) | $100–$180 | AE, D, MC, V.

Truckee Hotel. Charlie Chaplin's talkie, *The Gold Rush*, was filmed at this former stagecoach stop, which looks like an Old West saloon. Antiques and fine linens fill the rooms overlooking town; some have private bathrooms with claw-footed tubs. Bar, complimentary Continental breakfast. No air-conditioning, no room phones. Business services, airport shuttle. No smoking. | 10007 Bridge St. | 916/587–4444 or 800/659–6921 | fax 916/587–1599 | truckee.sierra@aol.com | www.truckeehotel.com | 37 rooms (29 with shower only) | $115–$125 | AE, MC, V.

TWENTYNINE PALMS

MAP 4, L1

(Nearby towns also listed: Desert Hot Springs, Joshua Tree National Park, Palm Springs, Yucca Valley)

"Two-nine," as it's known locally, is a high-desert hamlet bookended by the Marines Corps's sprawling (and off-limits) Air Ground Combat Center to the north and Joshua Tree National Park to the south. With the resurgence of Palm Springs as a desert hot spot some 40 mi southwest, the main drag along Route 62 has been spruced up a bit, embracing a smattering of hip coffeehouses, antiques shops, and new cafés.

Information: **Twentynine Palms Chamber of Commerce** | 6455-A Mesquite Ave., 92277 | 760/367–3445 | www.virtual29.com/chamber.

Attractions

The Old Schoolhouse Museum. Native Americans, miners, cowboys, and homesteaders are all represented here. The museum also houses the Twentynine Palms Historical Society. | 6760 National Park Dr. | 760/367–2366 | Free | Wed.–Sun. 1–4.

ON THE CALENDAR

OCT.: *Pioneer Days.* A pancake breakfast, parade, outhouse races (you have to see it to believe it), an arm-wrestling contest, and spirited dancing fill downtown the third weekend of the month. | 760/367–3445.

Dining

Jimmy the Greek's Deli and Grill. Delicatessen. A good bet for a quick meal of generous portions, with filling fare including huge gyros and grilled sandwiches. | 73501 Twentynine Palms Hwy. | 760/367–3456 | fax 760/367–9644 | Closed Sunday. No supper Sat. | $2–$6 | AE, D, DC, MC, V.

29 Palms Inn. Contemporary. Original works by local artists are on display in this dining room. Look for grilled seafood, fresh sourdough bread, and vegetables grown in the inn's own garden. There's also pool-side, open-air dining. | 73950 Inn Ave. | 760/367–3505 | fax 760/367–4425 | www.29palmsinn.com | $11–$18 | AE, D, DC, MC, V.

Lodging

Best Western Gardens Inn and Suites. This hotel is an oasis in the clear, high desert 7 mi from Joshua Tree National Park and 4 mi from the marine base. Some rooms open directly onto the pool. Cable TV. Pool. Hot tub. Exercise equipment. | 71487 Twentynine Palms Hwy. | 760/367–9141 | fax 760/367–2584 | 84 rooms, 12 suites | $69–$100 rooms, $109 suites | AE, D, DC, MC, V.

Circle C Lodge. You'll have panoramic views of the Mojave desert from this secluded hotel in the rugged, mountainous Morongo Basin. Rooms are positioned around an attractively landscaped garden and poolside courtyard with fountains and decorative sculpture. Joshua Tree National Park and the U.S. Marine Corps Air Ground Combat Center are nearby. Restaurant, picnic area, complimentary Continental breakfast. Kitchenettes, microwaves, refrigerators, cable TV, in-room VCRs. Pool. Hot tub, spa. Business services. | 6340 El Rey Ave.,

| 760/367–7615 or 800/545–9696 | fax 760/361–0247 | www.circleclodge.com | 12 rooms | $85 | AE, D, MC, V.

Homestead Inn Bed and Breakfast. Rock paths and palm trees punctuate the grounds of this Mission-style downtown bed-and-breakfast, with red terra-cotta roof tiles, white-washed stucco walls, and turquoise-hued rooms 1 mi north of Joshua Tree National Park. Some in-room hot tubs. Massage. No smoking. | 74153 Two Mile Rd. | 760/367–0030 | fax 760/367–1108 | 7 rooms | $95–$150 | AE, MC, V.

Roughley Manor. A pioneer built this stone inn and guest house with maple floors, intricate woodwork, and huge stone fireplaces surrounded by palm gardens. The rooms have marble dressers, and some have canopy beds and fireplaces. Complimentary breakfast. Some kitchenettes. Outdoor hot tub. | 74744 Joe Davis Dr. | 760/367–3238 | fax 760/367–2584 | themanor@cci-29palms.com | www.virtual29.com/themanor | 8 rooms, 1 cottage | $75–$125 | AE, MC, V.

29 Palms Inn. Adobe and wood-frame cottages make up this 70-acre estate on the Oasis of Mara, a tree-shaded watering hole that's home to assorted wildlife. Restaurant, complimentary Continental breakfast. Outdoor pool. Outdoor hot tub. | 73950 Inn Ave. | 760/367–3505 | fax 760/367–4425 | info@29palmsinn.com | www.29palmsinn.com | 15 rooms, 4 suites | $100–$125 rooms, $200–$285 suites | AE, D, DC, MC, V.

UKIAH

MAP 3, C5

(Nearby towns also listed: Boonville, Hopland)

As the seat of Mendocino County, Ukiah is more of a working town than its coastal cousins. Most attractions and restaurants cluster downtown west of the highway, but there are wineries as well.

Information: Greater Ukiah Chamber of Commerce | 200 S School St., 95482 | 707/462–4705 | info@ukiahchamber.com | www.ukiahchamber.com.

Attractions

Grace Hudson Museum and Sun House. Pomo Indian baskets and other tribal artifacts are the highlights of this collection, which also includes photographs and paintings by Grace Hudson, who lived with her husband, a scholar of basketry, in the adjacent house. The museum also mounts exhibits of work by local artists. | 431 S Main St. | 707/457–2836 | fax 707/467–0468 | www.gracehudsonmuseum.org | Closed Sun.–Mon.

Lake Mendocino. When the Russian River was dammed in 1958, this 1,822-acre recreational lake was the result. Accessible from three points roughly 10 mi north of Ukiah, it is popular for water sports, picnicking, hiking, and camping. Anglers go for striped bass, large- and smallmouth bass, bluegill, and catfish, or fish nearby streams for trout. A visitors center designed to resemble a Pomo roundhouse has exhibits on the lake as well as on Native American traditions. Access to the south end of the lake is off U.S. 101, 2 mi northeast of Ukiah; to the north end via Route 20, 5 mi north of Ukiah. | Rte. 20 and Marina Dr. and Lake Mendocino Dr. | 707/462–7581, visitors center 707/485–8285 | www.spn.usace.army.mil/mendocino.html | Daily; visitors center Apr.–Sept., Wed.–Sun., and Oct.–Mar., Sat.-Sun.

Wineries. Several of the county's 38 wineries can be found in nearby Redwood and Potter valleys as well as along Route 128, the route linking Ukiah with the coast.

Parducci Wine Cellars, founded in 1931 by Adolph Parducci, is known for its moderately priced white and red wines, including Chardonnay and several Zinfandels. A white, Spanish-style building houses the tasting room, which is just off the beaten track north of Ukiah. | 501 Parducci Rd. | 707/462–9463 | www.parducci.com | Mon.–Sat. 10–5, Sun. 10–4.

Dining

Dish. California. Generously sized sandwiches, pastas, and salads are so good here that this place is Ukiah's top caterer. Dinner is served only occasionally but is available for takeouts most nights from a menu that may include chicken, seafood, and a vegetarian choice. | 109 S School St. | 707/462–5700 | No dinner Sat., closed Sun. | $6–$10 | MC, V.

Ruen Tong. Thai. More than 100 choices, ranging from soft spring rolls, grilled eggplant, and pad Thai to rich dishes like sliced duck breast in peanut sauce, are served in snappy order at this restaurant, the best ethnic specialist for miles around. Outside, it's a California bungalow; inside, it's a trip to Southeast Asia. | 801 N State St. | 707/462–0238 | $6–$12 | D,MC,V.

Ukiah Brewing Co. and Restaurant. American. Everything is organic at this spacious corner restaurant, including the house-made beer and all the wines. Depending on the changing menu, you might order Flemish pot roast, pasta, or salmon cakes. | 102 S State St. | 707/468–5898 | fax 707/468–5898 | Closed Sun. | $7–$14 | MC,V.

Lodging

Discovery Inn. Several two-story C-shaped buildings wall out the drab surroundings at this north side motel. Glossy dark-wood desks and tables and bordered wallpaper give the accommodations a semblance of a residential appearance. The best rooms have balconies overlooking an Olympic-size pool where a waterfall drowns out highway noise. Some rooms have a queen bed plus a sofabed. Some kitchenettes. Pool, hot tubs. | 1340 N. State St. | 707/462–8873 | fax 707/462–1249 | 179 rooms | $65–$81 | AE, CB,D,MC,V.

Sanford House. Only two blocks from downtown Ukiah, this 1904 Queen Anne–style Victorian fits right in with the neighborhood of carefully tended homes and gardens. Five upstairs rooms have family antiques and pastel wallpaper; one has a bathtub facing out over the treetops. The house, built by a former state legislator, has a lush garden out back, complete with reading chairs and a koi pond. Complimentary breakfast. | 306 S Pine St. | 707/462–1653 | fax 707/462–8987 | dorsey@sanfordhouse.com | www.sanfordhouse.com | 5 | $75–$100 | AE, DC, MC, V.

Vichy Springs Resort. Mark Twain, Robert Louis Stevenson, and Jack London all slept at this 700-acre retreat about 3 mi east of U.S. 101. And probably slept well, at that, having taken advantage of the warm, soothing, effervescent spring water that fills its intimate outdoor grotto and soaking pools. In fact, people have been coming here since 1854. Accommodations include cottages, arranged in a little horseshoe above a greensward, as well as motel-style rooms (some on the creek, some with mountain views). Complimentary breakfast. Pool, massage. | 2605 Vichy Springs Rd. | 707/462–9515 | fax 707/462–9516 | vichy@vichysprings.com | www.vichysprings.com | 22 rooms, including 4 cottages and 1 suite | $105–$175 rooms, $235–$270 cottages, $205 suite | AE, DC, MC, V.

UNIVERSAL CITY

MAP 9, D2

(Nearby towns also listed: Beverly Hills, Burbank, Glenville, Los Angeles, North Hollywood, Sherman Oaks, Studio City)

While primarily residential, Universal City is best known as the home of Universal Studios Hollywood, a theme park that gives you a behind-the-scenes glimpse at motion picture and TV productions, along with rides, shows, and entertainment. There's also plenty of shopping around town as well.

Information: **Universal City/North Hollywood Chamber of Commerce** | 11335 Magnolia Blvd., Ste. 2-D, North Hollywood, 91601-3706 | 818/508–5155 | info@noho.org | www.noho.org.

Attractions

Universal CityWalk. Street performers keep things lively in this three-block shopping-and-nightlife complex just outside the gates of Universal Studios Hollywood. There are movie theaters, more than a dozen restaurants, some three dozen shops, and night spots including a dueling piano bar called Howl at the Moon, a Latin dance club, a dinner theater with magicians as entertainment, a state-of-the-art bowling alley with rock-and-roll music, an ice rink, and a blues club bearing the name of no less than B. B. King. | 100 Universal City Plaza | 818/622–4455 | www.citywalkhollywood.com | Free | Daily.

Universal Studios Hollywood. Universal Studios Hollywood is the world's largest movie studios and theme park. Hour-long tram rides traverse the 420-acre property, where you can see a Charlton Heston–style parting of the Red Sea; experience an avalanche, earthquake, and flood; meet King Kong; fend off *Jaws* and a pack of aliens; and rumble through a killer earthquake, among other experiences. Carl Laemmle first invited the public to tour his 230-acre chicken-ranch-turned-movie-studios in 1915, and it has been going strong every since. More than 8,000 films have been produced here since then, including scenes from *Apollo 13, Liar, Liar, Charlie's Angels, Annie,* and *The Wedding Singer.* | 100 Universal City Plaza | 818/508–9600 | $43 | Oct.–May, weekdays 9–7, weekends until 8; June–Sept., daily 8–10.

Universal TV Production Studios. Here you can tour the production facilities or watch a sitcom being taped. | 100 Universal City Plaza, Bldg. 3153 | 818/753–3470 or 818/753–3476 | www.tvtickets.com | Free | Weekdays 9–6.

Lodging

Hilton and Towers–Universal City. This hotel is adjacent to Universal Studios and 12 mi northeast of downtown LA. The exterior has impressive marble and black mirror glass. Restaurant, bar. Minibars, room service, cable TV. Pool. Hot tub. Exercise equipment. Business services. | 555 Universal Terrace Pkwy. | 818/506–2500 | fax 818/509–2058 | www.hilton.com | 483 rooms | $190–$210 | AE, D, DC, MC, V.

Sheraton Universal Hotel at Universal Studios. A fountain lit with multicolored underwater lights in the center of a circular drive welcomes you to this hotel, where rooms have floor-to-ceiling windows to take in the action at the studio back lots which share the same hill. The hotel is 9½ mi southeast of downtown. There's a free shuttle to take you to the studios. Restaurant. Pool. Hot tub. Exercise equipment. Laundry facilities. | 333 Universal Terrace Pkwy. | 818/980–1212 | fax 818/985–4980 | 442 rooms | $250–$375 | AE, D, DC, MC, V.

Universal City Hilton and Towers at Universal Studios. This hotel on 6½ acres across from Universal CityWalk has oversize rooms and suites with views of the Hollywood Hills and San Fernando Valley. There's a complimentary sightseeing shuttle. Restaurant. Pool. Exercise equipment. Laundry facilities. Business services. | 555 Universal Terrace Pkwy. | 818/506–2500 | fax 818/509–2058 | 483 rooms, 8 suites | $150–$245 rooms, $275–$625 suites | AE, D, DC, MC, V.

VACAVILLE

(Nearby towns also listed: Fairfield, Napa)

Vacaville, which means "cow town," was named for the original Spanish land grantee, Manuel Vaca. Vacaville was incorporated on September 8, 1892. For many years people moved here for the peace, quiet, and country living; for excitement, residents went north to Sacramento or south to San Francisco (Vacaville is about halfway in between). Downtown you can stroll along the Ulatis Creek Walk, take in local flora, and learn a bit about the city's history. It's certainly a pleasant way to take a break before continuing on a journey to elsewhere.

Information: **Vacaville Chamber of Commerce** | 300 Main St., 95688 | 707/448–6424 | www.vacavillechamber.com.

Attractions

Stars Recreation Center. Arcade games, darts, big-screen TVs, and live music keep this 40-lane bowling alley hopping. There's a restaurant here with regular family specials, such as Taco Tuesdays. Take Interstate 80 to Allison exit. | 155 Browns Valley Pkwy. | 707/455–7827 | www. starsrecreation.com/city.htm | Daily 24 hrs.

Dining

Black Oak. American. The menu is varied and there are plenty of choices at this popular roadside restaurant near Interstate 80 and Interstate 505. Go for the all-day breakfast menu choices, or lunch on monte cristos or burgers, or try a dinner special such as beef stroganoff or ginger stir-fry. Kids' menu. | 320 Orange Dr. | 707/448–1311 | $6–$17 | AE, MC, V.

Outback Steakhouse. Steaks. Stuffed koala bears fill this busy, sprawling Aussie-theme restaurant where the servings are large. Choose from steaks and chops to cream-sauced pizzas and fried shrimp. Exit Interstate 80 at Davis Street. | 521 Davis St. | 707/452–9200 | No lunch | $17–$25 | AE, D, DC, MC, V.

Vaca Joe's. Italian. Seafood and pastas are the specialty at this restaurant at the Leisure Town Road exit off Interstate 80. Try calimari with peppers, fresh-broiled salmon, or a steak and lobster special. Kids' menu. | 980 Leisure Town Rd. | 707/447–4633 | Closed Mon., breakfast also served | $8–$22 | AE, D, DC, MC, V.

Lodging

Best Western Heritage Inn. This simple two-story motel is at the Monte Vista exit off Interstate 80. Complimentary breakfast. Pets allowed. | 1420 E. Monte Vista Ave. | 707/448–8453 or 800/552–2124 | fax 707/447–8649 | www.bestwestern.com | 41 rooms | $66–$80 | AE, MC, V.

Courtyard Vacaville. Interior corridors lead to rooms in this two-story hostelry. Each room has a sitting area with a desk, two phones, and a coffeemaker. Take the Nut Tree Parkway exit off Interstate 80. Restaurant, complimentary breakfast, room service. In-room data ports, cable TV. Pool, Outdoor hot tub. Gym. Laundry service. Business services. | 120 Nut Tree Pkwy. | 707/451–9000 | fax 707/449–3952 | www.marriott.com | 117 rooms | $79–$109 | AE, D, DC, MC, V.

Quality Inn Vacaville. This well-landscaped two-story hotel is at the Leisure Town Road exit off Interstate 80. Complimentary breakfast. In-room data ports, cable TV. Hot tub. Laundry facilities. Business services. Pets allowed (fee). | 950 Leisure Town Rd. | 707/446–8888 | fax 707/449–0109 | www.qualityinn.com | 120 rooms | $54–$99 | AE, D, DC, MC, V.

VALENCIA

MAP 4, I14

(Nearby towns also listed: Los Angeles, Palmdale)

Thirty miles north of downtown Los Angeles, Valencia is a meticulously planned community. One of the town's most distinctive features is its 21-mi lattice of pedestrian walkways know as "paseos."

Information: **Santa Clarita Valley Chamber of Commerce** | 23920 Valencia Blvd., Ste. 100, Santa Clarita, 91355-2175 | 661/259–4787 | webmaster@santa-clarita.com | www.santa-clarita.com.

Attractions

Pyramid Lake Recreation Area. Pre-historic fossils and artifacts from the Paiute Indians have been found at this ancient lake. Today, the recreation area attracts anglers going after huge trout and the unusual cui-cui fish. Boats and fishing gear can be rented. | 43000 Pyramid Lake Rd. | 661/295–1245 | $6 per vehicle | Daily.

Six Flags Magic Mountain. Go crazy at this park's 10 theme areas packed with rides and attractions. Six Flags is known for its thrill rides, like Batman the Ride (an upside-down roller-coaster), Riddler's Revenge (the world's tallest and fastest stand-up roller-coaster), and Colossus, one of the world's largest wooden roller coasters. Next door to Six Flags is Hurricane Harbor, an immense water park. | 26101 Magic Mt. Pkwy. | 661/255–4100 | www.sixflags.com/magicmountain | $37 | Mid-May–late Sept.; call for hours.

Lodging

Best Western Ranch House Inn. This low-rise, four-building complex, across the street from the Six Flags amusement complex, has common areas and rooms laden with Navajo blankets, equestrian tack, and cowboy paraphernalia. Restaurant, bar, room service. Cable TV. 2 pools, wading pool. Hot tub. Laundry facilities. Business services. | 27413 N. Tourney Rd. | 661/255–0555 | fax 661/255–2216 | rhi@scvnet.com | www.bestwestern.com | 185 rooms, 2 suites | $62–$72, $175 suites | AE, D, DC, MC, V.

Hampton Inn. This hotel is just west of I–5, near Six Flags, 4 mi southeast of Valencia. It's also convenient to restaurants and shopping, and is 2 mi northeast of downtown Los Angeles. Complimentary Continental breakfast. In-room data ports, refrigerators, cable TV. Pool. Hot tub. Laundry facilities. Business services. | 25259 Old Rd., Santa Clarita | 661/253–2400 | fax 661/253–1683 | www.hampton-inn.com | 130 rooms | $69–$109 | AE, D, DC, MC, V.

Hilton Garden Inn–Six Flags. This hotel, adjacent to Six Flags has Southwestern details that reflect the area's history. Restaurant, bar, room service. In-room data ports, microwaves, cable TV. Pool. Hot tub. Exercise equipment. Laundry facilities. Business services. | 27710 Old Rd. | 805/254–8800 | fax 805/254–9399 | www.valencia.gardeninn.com | 152 rooms | $128–$149 | AE, D, DC, MC, V.

VALLEJO

MAP 3, D7

(Nearby town also listed: San Rafael)

Vallejo (pronounced vuh-LAY-oh) was named after General Mariano Guadalupe Vallejo. A number of beautifully restored Victorian homes cluster in the 20-block Washington Park neighborhood in central Vallejo, bounded by Tennessee Street on the north, Broadway Avenue on the east, Florida Street on the south, and Sonoma Boulevard on the west. Local redevelopment efforts have earned it a Main Street designation. Waterfront revitalization is an ongoing community effort, and its ferry dock has become a regional model. For many, though, the main draw is the town's proximity to the bay— it's an hour away from San Francisco via high-speed catamaran—and to the region's biggest theme park, Six Flags Marine World, the nation's only combination wildlife park, oceanarium, and theme park.

Information: Vallejo Convention and Visitors Bureau | 495 Mare Island Way, 94590 | 707/642–3653 or 800/482–5535 | vjocvb@visitvallejo.com | www.visitvallejo.com.

Attractions

Six Flags at Marine World. A combination theme park, animal park, and oceanarium, this sprawling center has sea lion, killer whale, and dolphin shows, elephant and seal exhibits, and thrill-a-minute rides with names like Medusa, Kong, Roar, and Boomerang. See the swimming Bengal tigers, and check out the butterfly area and animal nursery. | Marine World Pkwy. | 707/643–6722 | www.sixflags.com | $40 | Memorial Day–Labor Day, Easter week, and Dec. 15–Jan. 1, daily; Mar.–Apr., Sept.–Oct., Fri.–Sun.

Mare Island Historic Park. This 5,000-acre park was the West Coast's first shipyard when it opened in 1854; it closed in 1996. As legend tells, the island was named after a herd of horses was driven by General Vallejo across the Carquinez Strait. Tours are available with one day's notice. | 328 Seawind Dr. | 707/557–1538 or 707/644–4746 (tours) | Daily.

Dining

Cha Am. Thai. In a shopping center next to Six Flags Marine World, the restaurant has three dining areas with piped-in Thai music. On the menu you'll find pad Thai and tom-ka-gai, a chicken soup redolent of lemongrass and coconut, and sautéed squid, roast duck, and marinated barbecued salmon. Best starter: deep-fried vegetarian rolls with chili-peanut sauce. | 153 Plaza Dr. | 707/648–8066 | No lunch Sat.-Sun. | $6–$12 | AE, DC, MC, V.

Remark's Harbor House. American. Two 1930s houses were moved here and joined at the lobby to create this waterfront restaurant with a fireplace in the lounge. The menu offers salmon and tilapia, baby-back ribs, and chicken saltimbocca. | 23 Harbor Way | 707/642–8984 | fax 707/642–2456 | No lunch Sun. | $11–$19 | MC, V.

Sardine Can. Seafood. No fancier than its name, this ultra-casual bayside spot with picnic tables inside and outside serves old-style fast food like fish and chips, fried prawns, Cajun jambalaya, salads, and grilled sandwiches. Large windows inside overlook the bay. | Harbor Way | 707/553–9492 | No dinner | $6–$10 | MC, V.

Lodging

Comfort Inn. A well-kept, slate-gray building with a clapboard-style exterior, this two-story motel has simple rooms in pastel colors. It's at the rear of a shopping center close to Six Flags, although it's relatively quiet here. Refrigerators. Pool. Hot tub, sauna. | 1185 Admiral Callaghan La. | 707/648–1400 | fax 707/552–8623 | 80 rooms | $79–$94 | AE, D, MC, V.

Holiday Inn at Six Flags Marine World. You'll have to cross your fingers if you request one of the rooms facing the roller coaster across the road; they are much in demand. Restaurant, bar. In-room data ports. Pool. Exercise equipment. Laundry facilities. Business services. | 1000 Fairgrounds Dr. | 707/644–1200 or 800/533–5753 | fax 707/643–7011 | www.rimcorp.com | 170 rooms | $89–$129 | AE, D, MC, V.

Ramada Inn. Easily recognizable with its gray-and-burgundy exterior, this three-story hotel is in the middle of a shopping mall, close to Six Flags, and within walking distance of restaurants. Room service. Some in-room safes, some minibars, microwaves, refrigerators. Pool. Laundry facilities, laundry service. Pets allowed. | 1000 Admiral Callaghan La. | 707/643–2700 | fax 707/642–1148 | www.ramada.com | 130 rooms | $78–$145 | AE, D, MC, V.

VAN NUYS

MAP 9, C2

(Nearby towns also listed: Beverly Hills, Burbank, Glendale, Hollywood, Los Angeles, North Hollywood, Sherman Oaks, Universal City, West Hollywood, Woodland Hills)

Van Nuys is a wide-flung San Fernando Valley suburb of Los Angeles. It's primarily middle-class and residential and has lost the country flavor that brought Angelenos into the area more than a half century ago.

Information: **Van Nuys Chamber of Commerce** | 14540 Victory Blvd., Ste. 100, 91411 | 818/989–0300.

Attractions

Japanese Garden at the Tillman Water Reclamation Plant. This 6½-acre garden has decorative stones, bonsai trees, and a zigzag bridge. Reservations are required for tours. | 6100 Woodley Ave. | 818/756–8166 | www.thejapanesegarden.com/ | $3 | Mon.–Thurs., noon–4, Sun. 10–4; guided tours Mon.–Thurs. at 9:30, 10, and 10:30, Sat. at 10:30.

Dining

Matterhorn Chef Restaurant. German. This restaurant looks like a Bavarian chalet on the outside and an Alpine beerhall within. Blue-and-white banners and costumed staff bolster the Ocktoberfest theme. You'll find a wurstplatte and wienerschnitzel along with duckling à l'orange on the menu. On weekends, there's yodelling and polka-dancing. Kids' menu. No smoking. | 13726 Oxnard St. | 818/781–4330 | No lunch Sun. | $8–$20 | AE, D, DC, MC, V.

Lodging

Airtel Plaza Hotel and Conference Center. This glass-walled behemoth is lit up like a chandelier at dusk. Rooms look out onto rock gardens, manicured lawns, a man-made brook, and the Van Nuys airport. 2 restaurants, bar with entertainment room service. In-room data ports, some refrigerators, cable TV. Pool. Hot tub. Exercise equipment. Business services. | 7277 Valjean Ave. | 818/997–7676 | fax 818/785–8864 | www.airtelplaza.com | 267 rooms | $99–$149 | AE, D, DC, MC, V.

Travelodge. This standard motel is ½ mi west of the Van Nuys airport. Complimentary Continental breakfast. Refrigerators, cable TV. Pool. | 6909 Sepulveda Blvd. | 818/787–5400 | fax 818/782–0239 | www.travelodge.com | 74 rooms | $55 | AE, D, DC, MC, V.

VENICE

MAP 9, C4

(Nearby towns also listed: Beverly Hills, Manhattan Beach, Santa Monica)

Venice is an offbeat, counter-culture, beachside enclave founded in 1905. The city of 37,700 was once defined by a miles-long lattice of canals; today, only six remnant waterways remain, fronted by both historic and newer homes. The Venice Boardwalk is unmatched as a people-watching venue. Cyclists, barbell-pumping boys, bodacious bikini-clad roller babes, street merchants, and legions of homeless converge here. Add to this great steet theater, a wild panoply of headshops, artisan booths, piercing/tattoo studios, and alfresco dining, and whatever you're looking for, you'll find it here.

Information: Venice Area Chamber of Commerce | Box 202, 90294 | 310/396–7016 | vcc@venice.net | www.venice.net/chamber.

Attractions

★ **Venice City Beach and Boardwalk.** Surf and sand are fine for tossing Frisbees with the kids, but, if it's real action you want, hang out on the 1½-mi-long boardwalk, where everything and then some passes the time of day. Be forewarned: pickpockets abound. Around 18th Avenue, look for the infamous (and still active) "Muscle Beach," where oil-slicked body builders pump iron. | West of Pacific Ave. | 310/394–3266.

Canal Tours. In 1905 Venice was established with a series of interconnected canals. Only a small portion of those remain today but the Visitors Bureau has a nice walking map of the area. It's a peaceful little stroll in stark contrast to the bold beach area. | 6541 Hollywood Blvd. | 213/689–8822 | www.lacvb.com | Free | Daily, Visitors Bureau, Mon.–Sat. 9–1 and 2–5.

Dining

The Firehouse. American. In a 1902 Venice firehouse (near the border of Santa Monica), healthy diner fare is served to the young and hip amid antique firetrucks. The Cajun mahi mahi burger, vegetable burger, and turkey burger are some of the popular menu options. | 213 Rose Ave. | 310/396–6810 | Breakfast also available | $16–$24 | AE, MC, V.

Joe's Restaurant. Contemporary. The name might be plain, but the setting for the savory cuisine is surprisingly modern. Joe's menu includes inventive grilled fish, chicken, and roast pork dishes. Favorites include a crisp chicken with creamy twice-baked parmesan potatoes and saffron risotto with scallops and a frizz of carrots. Weekend brunch. No smoking. | 1023 Abbot Kinney Blvd. | 310/399–5811 | Closed Mon. | $18–$25 | AE, MC, V.

Lodging

Holiday Inn Express–Marina Del Rey/Venice. Keeping pace with the neighborhood, this Holiday Inn is a bit different from its other chain entries. Rooms are done in shades of taupe and caramel and the furnishings are faux-cane. Between Venice and Marina Del Rey, the inn is two blocks from the beach. Complimentary breakfast. In-room VCRs (and movies). Pool. Hot tub. Laundry facilities. | 737 Washington Blvd. | 310/821–4455 | fax 310/821–8098 | 68 rooms | $89–$99 | AE, D, DC, MC, V.

Lincoln Inn. This inn is between Venice and Washington Boulevard, ½ mi from Venice beach and Marina Del Rey. Rooms are pictures of breezy California beach-culture style with big windows to let in plenty of sunlight and ocean air. Refrigerators, cable TV. Hot tubs. | 2447 Lincoln Blvd. | 310/822–0686 | fax 310/822–3136 | 30 rooms | $85–$89 | AE, D, DC, MC, V.

Venice Beach House. This Craftsman-style beach house is filled with one-of-a-kind antiques from a variety of periods. You can relax at the piano in the sitting room or stroll through the rose garden. The hotel is right on the beach. Complimentary breakfast. No air-conditioning, cable TV. Beach. No smoking. | 15 30th Ave. | 310/823–1966 | fax 310/823–1842 | 9 rooms (4 with shared bath) | $95–$165 | AE, MC, V.

VENTURA

MAP 4, G14

(Nearby towns also listed: Oxnard, Port Hueneme, Santa Barbara)

Like many of the communities in this area, the original inhabitants here were the Chumash Indians, a self-contained agricultural society. Spanish missionaries were followed by white Americans and Europeans, who established bustling towns, intense agricultural operations, and transportation advancements. From the 1920s onward, non-farm industries like oil—and now tourism—have replaced agriculture as Ventura's main business. Today, Ventura enjoys the gorgeous weather and beaches that LA is famous for, without the smog and congestion.

Information: **Ventura Visitors and Convention Bureau** | 89 South California St., Suite C, | 800/333–2989 | www.ventura-usa.com.

Attractions

Beaches. Ventura boasts mile upon mile of beautiful uncrowded beaches, with picnic areas, barbecues, restrooms, snack shops, and umbrella rentals. The beaches are also a favorite destination for athletes of all levels, with everything from body surfing and boogie boarding, to scenic paths for walking and biking. | Ventura Visitors and Convention Bureau, 89 South California St., Suite C | 800/333–2989 | www.ventura-usa.com | Free.

Channel Islands National Park and National Marine Sanctuary. Often referred to as "America's Galapagos," this park includes five of the eight Channel Islands, and 6 nautical mi of ocean. It's a magnificent nature preserve, home to wildlife unique to the islands, such as the island scrub-jay, the island fox, and the Anacapa deer mouse. The channel waters are also teeming with life, including dolphins, whales, seals, sea lions, and thousands of sea birds. Sunrise over the water from Smuggler's Cove, an inlet on Santa Cruz Island, is spectacular. Various outfits have boat and hiking tours of the islands—call the Visitor Center for information. | 1901 Spinnaker Dr. | 805/658–5730 | fax 805/658–5799 | www.nps.gov/chis | 8:30–4:30, later on weekends and summer.

Lake Casitas Recreation Area. Some lunker largemouth bass, rainbows, crappie, red-ears, and channel catfish live in the waters of this impoundment of the Ventura River, one of the country's best bass fishing areas, and anglers come from all over the United States to test their luck. You can row or motor across the reservoir, cast a line, pitch a tent, or enjoy a picnic. Rowing and canoeing events were held here during the 1984 Olympics. Nestling below the Santa Ynez Mountains' Laguna Ridge to the Los Padres National Forest, it's very scenic as well. It's 13 mi northwest of Ventura. | Rte. 33 | 805/649–2233 or 805/649–1122 (campground reservations) | www.ojai.org/casitas.htm | $6.50 per vehicle, $11.50 per boat | Daily.

Whale Watching. California gray whales migrate through the Santa Barbara Channel off the Ventura shore from late December through March; giant blue and humpback whales feed here mid-June through September. In fact, the channel is teeming with marine life year-round, so tours include more than just whale sightings. Contact the Chamber of Commerce for a list of tour operators. | 89 South California St., Suite C | 800/333–2989 | www.ventura-usa.com.

Dining

Andrea's Seafood. Seafood. Place your order at the counter, then sit at the large tables inside, or outside on a patio where you can overlook the harbor and marina at this casual family-oriented restaurant. Specials are fish and chips (with angel shark) and homemade clam chowder. | 1449 Spinnaker Dr. | 805/654–0546 | $8–$20 | No credit cards accepted.

Christy's. American. You can get breakfast all day—try the breakfast burrito—at this greasy spoon across the water from the Channel Islands which also serves burgers, sandwiches, and soup. | 1559 Spinnaker Dr. | 805/642–3116 | Breakfast also available | $5–$8 | AE, V.

Jonathan's at Peirano's. Mediterranean. The main dining room here has a gazebo where you can eat surrounded by plants and local art work. The menu has dishes from Spain, Portugal, France, Italy, Greece, and Morocco. Stand-outs are the Moroccan-inspired chicken penne checca pasta, and the halibut de almendras (halibut with almonds). | 204 E. Main St. | 805/648–4853 | No lunch Sun., closed Mon. | $18–$35 | AE, D, DC, MC, V.

71 Palm Restaurant. French. In a 1910 house, this classy restaurant has wood floors and trim, lace curtains, and a working fireplace. For an appetizer, try the innovative potato caviar (boiled red potatoes hollowed out and filled with caviar); for dinner there's the grilled salmon on a potato pancake, or the New Zealand rack of lamb provençal. Indoor and outdoor seating. | 71 Palm Dr. | 805/653–7222 | No lunch Sat., closed Sun. | $18–$30 | AE, D, DC, MC, V.

Lodging

Best Western Inn of Ventura. A block off Highway 101 in the historic district, this hotel has been welcoming guests for nearly 40 years. Large rooms with oversize beds come with free local calls, and some rooms have ocean views. Beaches, restaurants, and theaters are within walking distance. Restaurant, complimentary Continental breakfast. Pool. Hot tub. Laundry service. | 708 E. Thompson Blvd. | 805/648–3101 or 800/648–1508 | fax 805/648–4019 | www.bestwestern.com | 75 rooms | $59–$79 | AE, D, DC, MC, V.

Clocktower Inn. In the heart of downtown, this inn is next to Mission San Buenaventura, the Historical Museum, and the area's many boutique shops. Rooms are decorated in soft Southwest colors, and many have private patios, fireplaces, carved headboards, desks, leather chairs, and armoires. | 181 E. Santa Clara | 805/652–0141 or 800/727–1027 (CA) | 50 rooms | $66–$169 | AE, D, DC, MC, V.

Fern Oaks Inn. Colorful tiles, crown molding, and antiques accent this two-story 1929 Spanish Revival home, a gracious pink structure with arched windows 12 mi east of Ventura on Route 126. Don't miss the Arts and Crafts–era fireplace in the common living room. Seasonal fruits from the inn's own orchard are served with breakfast. Complimentary breakfast. Outdoor pool. Massage. No-room phones. No TV in rooms; big-screen TV and VCR in common area. No smoking. Business services. | 1025 Ojai Rd., Santa Paula | 805/525–7747 | fax 805/933–5001 | info@fernoaksinn.com | www.fernoaksinn.com | 4 rooms | $95–$130 | No credit cards.

Motel 6. This two-story motel is 2 mi from the ferry to the Channel Islands. Cable TV. Pool. | 2145 E. Harbor Blvd. | 805/643–5100 | fax 805/643–4519 | www.motel6.com | 200 rooms | $50–$70 | AE, D, DC, MC, V.

Victorian Rose. This inn is a Victorian Gothic Church turned Bed & Breakfast. (The 96-ft steeple is a good clue.) Carved beam ceilings reach dizzying heights and are adorned with elaborate stained-glass panels. The former sanctuary now holds several cozy rooms, each with gas burning fireplaces and newly appointed baths. Wine and cheese hour. Complimentary breakfast. Hot tub. | 896 E. Main St. | 805/641–1888 | fax 805/643–1335 | www.victorian-rose.com | 5 rooms | $99–$175 | AE, MC, V.

VICTORVILLE

MAP 4, J13

(Nearby town also listed: Barstow)

Before Victorville became less of a speck and more of a sizable dot on the map, a seemingly endless forest of Joshua trees sloped down from the gusty Cajon Pass below the San Gabriel and San Bernardino mountains, studding the Victor Valley with their whimsically top-knotted trunks. Back then, that "typical" Western backdrop of stark mountains and seer landscape provided the backdrop for countless cowboy movies. Today, there are still some wide-open spaces, but pink-tiled subdivisions, fast-food outlets, and malls are quickly transforming the landscape. Roughly 40,700 residents call it home.

Information: **Victorville Chamber of Commerce** | 14174 Green Tree Blvd., 92392 | 760/245–6506 | vvchamber@vvchamber.com | www.vvchamber.com.

Attractions

California Route 66 Museum. Exhibits chronicle the famous American highway. | 16849 Route 66 D St. | 760/261–8766 or 760/951–0436 | www.national66.com/victorville | Free | Thurs.–Mon. 10–4.

Mojave Narrows Regional Park. Nature trails in this 200-acre park take you up close to unique rock formations and the region's varied plant life. Picnic grounds. | 760/245–2226 | $3.50 per vehicle | Daily 10–4.

Roy Rogers–Dale Evans Museum. Check out the personal and professional memorabilia of these two stars who helped shape the romantic vision of the American West. | 15650 Seneca Rd. | 760/243–4547 or 760/243–4548 | www.royrogers.com | $7 | Daily 9–5.

ON THE CALENDAR

JUNE: *Huck Finn Jubilee.* Father's Day weekend celebrates the high-spirited pioneer atmosphere of the Mark Twain novel with games, live music, a fishing derby, and more. The events are held at Mojave Narrows Regional Park, 3 mi off Bear Valley Road on Ridgecrest Avenue. | 909/780–8810 | www.huckfinn.com.

MAY OR JUNE: *San Bernardino County Fair.* This county fair has games, food, rodeo demonstrations, and agricultural contests. The fair is held at various sites annually. | 760/951–2200 or 760/261–1854.

Lodging

Best Western Green Tree Inn. This inn five blocks from downtown has views of the high desert and the mountains. Restaurant, bar, room service. Refrigerators, cable TV. Pool, wading pool. Hot tub. Business services. | 14173 Green Tree Blvd. | 760/245–3461 | fax 760/245–7745 | www.bestwestern.com | 168 rooms | $68–$85 | AE, D, DC, MC, V.

Howard Johnson Express Inn Apple Valley. This hotel is 3 mi from the Roy Rogers Museum. It's often busy as travelers heading to either LA or Las Vegas stop here to rest. Cable TV. Pool. Laundry facilities. Business services. | 16868 Stoddard Wells Rd. | 760/243–7700 | fax 760/243–4432 | www.howardjohnson.com | 96 rooms | $44–$55 | AE, D, DC, MC, V.

VISALIA

(Nearby towns also listed: Hanford, Porterville, Selma)

Founded in 1852, Visalia is the elder statesman among California cities between Stockton and Los Angeles. With its 155 acres of grasslands dotted with valley oaks and palms trees, Mooney Grove Park reflects the early undeveloped ranch look of the area. The area's successful agricultural industry has given rise to a number of lovely homes and estates.

Information: Visalia Convention and Visitors Bureau | 301 E. Acequia St., 93291 | 559/738–3435 or 800/524–0303 | cvb123@ci.visalia.ca.us | www.cvbvisalia.co.

Attractions

Chinese Cultural Center. This center for the Chinese community educates and holds events to commemorate the Asian influence on the area. | 500 S. Akers Rd. | 559/625–4545 | Free | Daily 10–4.

Tulare County Museum. Exhibits trace the history of Tulare County in the 1800s through pioneer memorabilia and American Indian artifacts. | 27000 Mooney Blvd. | 559/733–6616 | $2 | Mon., Thurs., Fri. 10–4, weekends 1–4.

Dining

★ **Vintage Press.** Contemporary. Built in 1966, the Vintage Press has an extensive antiques collection and cut-glass doors to adorn the dining room. The California-Continental cuisine includes dishes such as baby abalone in champagne-butter sauce, wild mushrooms in puff pastry, and sturgeon in caviar butter. The wine list boasts more than 900 choices. Open-air dining is available in the garden. Kids' menu. No smoking. | 216 N. Willis | 559/733–3033 | $20–$50 | AE, DC, MC, V.

Lodging

Econo Lodge. There is a golf course 2 mi away and a gym and health spa two blocks down the street from this hotel. Mooney Grove Park is 1 mi south. Restaurant, complimentary Continental breakfast. Cable TV. Pool. | 1400 S. Mooney Blvd. | 559/732–6641 | fax 559/739–7520 | www.basshotels.com | 49 rooms | $59–$65 | AE, D, DC, MC, V.

Radisson. This massive white-concrete tower houses a beautiful main lobby with checkered marble-tile floors and huge urns full of fresh-cut flowers. Rooms are spacious and decorated in deep blues and grays. Restaurants in downtown Visalia are two blocks away. Restaurant. In-room data ports, refrigerators, cable TV. Pool. Hot tub. Exercise equipment. Business services, free airport shuttle to Visalia Airport. | 300 S. Court St. | 559/636–1111 | fax 559/636–8224 | www.radisson.com | 201 rooms | $89–$99 | AE, D, DC, MC, V.

Spalding House. This inn is a two-story, Colonial Revival–style house fronted by huge trees and a wraparound porch. The interior is softened by scores of Persian carpets and authentic antiques. Once you've steeped yourself in the old-fashioned ambience of the inn, head to one of the three antique malls that operate less than 5 mi from Spalding House. Complimentary breakfast. No room phones, TV in common area. Library. No smoking. | 631 N. Encina | 559/739–7877 | fax 559/625–0902 | www.spaldinghouse.qpg.com | 3 suites | $65– $85 suites | AE, MC, V.

WALNUT CREEK

MAP 6, F3

(Nearby towns also listed: Berkeley, Oakland, San Francisco)

There really were walnut trees here, and a creek, once upon a time. Buried beneath Civic Drive downtown are countless shells from the nut industry that once thrived in the area, and parts of the creek run in culverts under the asphalt. The post–World War II building boom turned farmland into suburbs, and Walnut Creek was one of the first communities where gray-suited commuters from San Francisco moved to raise families and coach Little League baseball teams. A big slice of the population fills Rossmoor, a retirement community built in the mid-1960s. Still, the small-town feeling has touches of big-city shine: There are many restaurants and ethnic eateries (a sign of the region's changing demographics), a lively downtown shopping area, and plenty of cultural offerings, including a gleaming civic arts facility, art galleries, a ballet, and several small theaters.

Attractions

The Bedford Gallery. This gem of a public gallery brings thoughtful, challenging art to the suburbs. It's at the Dean Lesher Center for the Arts, which also has a theater. | 1601 Civic Dr. | 925/295–1417 | Free | Tues.– Sun. noon–5, Thurs., Fri., Sat., 6–8PM.

The Blackhawk Automotive Museum. The Art Deco building houses 120 restored classic cars. No reservations are required for the guided tours. | 3700 Blackhawk Plaza Cir | 925/ 763–2777 | $8 | Wed.–Sun. 10–5; guided tours weekends at 2.

Lindsay Wildlife Museum. In addition to displaying local wildlife, this facility cares for injured animals and birds. You can see feedings and watch the animals going through rehab exercises and also borrow nature objects or even a live rabbit, hamster, or guinea pig from the pet library. | 1931 1st Ave. | 925/935–1978 | $4.50 | Tues.–Fri. noon–5, weekends 10–5.

Dining

Abernathy's. Continental. Here's a no-frills watering hole favored by locals as a welcoming spot for everyone from pin-striped suits to students. The restaurant has homemade Greek and Italian specialties and barbecue. At night the bar rocks with music by local acts. | 1411 Locust St. | 925/934–9490 | fax 925/934–0962 | $10 | MC, V.

Lark Creek Inn. Contemporary. "You can close your eyes and pick just about anything on the menu, and you'll like what you get," noted readers of a local magazine survey about this restaurant in an old white house in a shady grove in Larkspur, a few miles from Walnut Creek. Chef Bradley Ogden calls his products "farm-fresh American fare"—but although you will find steaks, chicken, and biscuits, it's always cooked perfectly and presented with a special twist that you seldom find down on most farms. Sunday brunch. | 1360 Locust St., Larkspur | 925/256–1234 | fax 925/256–1811 | Reservations essential | $12– $20 | AE, DC, MC, V.

Spiendini. Italian. Marin County diners consistently vote the food here the "Best Italian" in the area. Try the duck, pheasant, pancetta-wrapped rabbit, and tiramisu. The pasta is homemade, and much of the roasting goes on in a wood-fired rotisserie oven. | 101 Ygnacio Valley Rd. | 925/939–2100 | fax 925/939–1706 | $15–$28 | AE, D, DC, MC, V.

Lodging

Embassy Suites Pleasant Hill–Walnut Creek. In this all-suite, eight-story hotel, most rooms have a sitting area as well as a bedroom plus two telephones, two TVs, and kitchen facilities. Restaurant, bar, complimentary breakfast. In-room data ports, microwaves, refrigerators, cable TV, in-room VCRs (and movies). Indoor pool. Sauna. Exercise equipment. Laundry service. Business services, airport shuttle. No pets. No smoking. | 1345 Treat Blvd. | 925/934–2500 or 800/362–2779 | fax 925/256–7233 | www.embassywc.com | 249 rooms | $135–$169 | AE, D, DC, MC, V.

Walnut Creek Marriott Hotel. The six-story multi-level hotel with a large covered entranceway is two blocks from a rapid transit station. On the executive floor there are suites. Restaurant, bar, room service. In-room data ports, refrigerators, cable TV, in-room VCRs (and movies). Outdoor pool. Spa. Exercise equipment. Laundry service. Business services, airport shuttle. No pets. No smoking. | 2355 N. Main St. | 925/934–2000 | fax 925/934–6374 | www.marriott.com | 338 rooms, 15 suites | $149–$169, $219–$380 suites | AE, D, DC, MC, V.

Walnut Creek Motor Lodge. One block from a rapid transit station, this two-story motel has some rooms with kitchenettes. It's at the Ygnacio Valley Road exit off I–680. In-room data ports, refrigerators, cable TV, in-room VCRs (and movies). Hot tub. Pets allowed. No smoking. | 1960 N. Main St. | 925/932–2811 | fax 925/932–5989 | wcmotorlodge@hotmail.com | 71 rooms | $69–$79 | AE, DC, MC, V.

WATSONVILLE

MAP 4, D10

(Nearby towns also listed: Hollister, Monterey, San Jose)

Watsonville is apple, strawberry, and flower-growing country, with peak harvest time in late summer and fall. This agricultural town of 31,100, with a heavy Mexican influence from resident and migrant field workers, sits above Monterey Bay, between Salinas and San Jose.

Information: Pajaro Valley Chamber of Commerce | 444 Main St., 95076 | 831/724–3900 | commerce@pvchamber.com | www.pvchamber.comco.

Attractions

Elkhorn Slough National Estuarine Research Reserve. These 1,400 coastal acres, 10 mi south of Watsonville on Route 1, are devoted to protecting hundreds of species of birds, fish, marine mammals, and other animals. Walking trails wind along the salt marsh, through eucalyptus groves and live oaks. | 1700 Elkhorn Rd., Moss Landing | 831/728–2822 | inlet.geol.sc.edu/elk/home.html | $2.50 | Wed.–Sun. 9–5.

A great way to tour the extensive slough network, and to get close-up views of dozens of sea otters, harbor seals, herons, egrets, and other sea birds, is to take a 2-hr ride on a safe and steady, 27-ft pontoon-boat run by **Elkhorn Slough Safaris.** Tours run regularly, year-round. | Moss Landing Marina, Moss Landing | 831/633–5555 | www.elkhornslough.com | $26 | Daily.

Lodging

Best Western Inn. This two-story inn in downtown Watsonville is 1 mi from shopping and a movie theater. There is a 24-hr restaurant across the street. Complimentary Continental breakfast. In-room data ports, microwaves available, refrigerators, cable TV. Outdoor pool, outdoor hot tub. Laundry facilities. Business services. No pets. | 740 Freedom Blvd. | 831/724–3367 | fax 831/761–1785 | www.bestwestern.com | 43 rooms | $150–$250 | AE, D, DC, MC, V.

WEAVERVILLE

MAP 3, C3

(Nearby towns also listed: Redding)

Set in a mountain valley in the Trinity Alps and partly surrounded by the Shasta-Trinity National Forest, Weaverville was settled in 1850 during the first wave of California's gold rush. Though better known today for logging and sport fishing, the town of 3,500 still shows evidence of its colorful past, when prospectors from as far away as China washed gold from the nearby Trinity River.

Information: **Trinity County Chamber of Commerce** | 211 Lakes Blvd., 96093 | 530/623–6101 | www.trinitycounty.com.

Attractions

★ **Joss House State Historical Park.** This colorful, ornate Taoist temple was built and decorated in 1875 by Chinese gold miners. Although now run as a California Historical Landmark and museum, it's still a place of worship, and the oldest continuously used Chinese temple in the state. It also hosts a Lion Dance festival every February to celebrate Chinese New Year. | 404 Main St. | 530/623–5284 | cal-parks.ca.gov/districts/nobuttes/wjhshp/wjhshp127.htm | $1 | Call for hrs.

J. J. Jackson Museum and Historical Park. Artifacts on Trinity County's pioneer and prospector past fill this museum, among them a functioning steam-powered stampmill used to extract gold from ore. Connected to the museum is a research center with public records for historical and genealogical study. | 508 Main St. | 530/623–5211 | www.trinitycounty.com/museum | By donation | May–Oct. 10–5 daily; Apr. and Nov. noon–4 daily; Dec.–Mar. Tues., Sat. noon–4.

Trinity Lake. As the third-largest reservoir in California, this impound of the Trinity River has 16,500 acres and 145 mi of shoreline in a dramatic mountain setting at 2,387 ft; it's part of the Whiskeytown-Shasta-Trinity National Recreation Area. Lake waters shelter kokanee salmon, large- and smallmouth bass, and German brown, rainbow, and eastern

YOUR FIRST-AID TRAVEL KIT

- ❏ Allergy medication
- ❏ Antacid tablets
- ❏ Antibacterial soap
- ❏ Antiseptic cream
- ❏ Aspirin or acetaminophen
- ❏ Assorted adhesive bandages
- ❏ Athletic or elastic bandages for sprains
- ❏ Bug repellent
- ❏ Face cloth

- ❏ First-aid book
- ❏ Gauze pads and tape
- ❏ Needle and tweezers for splinters or removing ticks
- ❏ Petroleum jelly
- ❏ Prescription drugs
- ❏ Suntan lotion with an SPF rating of at least 15
- ❏ Thermometer

*Excerpted from *Fodor's: How to Pack: Experts Share Their Secrets*
© 1997, by Fodor's Travel Publications

brook trout. The bass angling is some of the best west of the Mississippi with 1-pounders the average and some running to 4 or 5 lbs; the largest smallmouth bass caught in California was reeled in here. There are private marinas and public boat ramps as well. It's 18 mi northeast of Weaverville. | Rte. 299W and Rte. 3 | 530/623–2121 | www.recreation.gov/detail1.cfm? | Daily.

Dining

La Grange Cafe. Contemporary. Weaverville's most talked-about restaurant serves a regularly updated menu of game, fresh fish, inventive pastas, and seasonal produce. It occupies the two oldest buildings downtown (both dating from 1851), and is appointed with antique tables, a century-old carved wooden bar, and local artwork. | 226 Main St. | 530/623–5325 | No lunch Sunday | $8–$21 | AE, D, MC, V.

Noelle's Garden Cafe. Contemporary. At this remodelled wooden house in the center of town, healthy California lunches (chicken, fish, pasta, quiche, and salads) are the rule. If you have a bigger appetite, try the strudel, filled with shrimp or cheese, or visit for weekend dinner, when hearty red meat dishes are served. Outdoor patio seating available. | 252 Main St. | 530/623–2058 | Reservations essential | No lunch weekends | $13–$22 | No credit cards.

Pacific Brewery Restaurant and Bar. American. In a former brewery dating back to 1855, this two-story restaurant near the center of town serves meals all day long, from hotcakes at breakfast to steaks at dinner. Patio seating is available. | 401 S Main St. | 530/623–3000 | $8–$15 | MC, V.

Lodging

49er Gold Country Inn. A dozen rooms in this one-story motel have whirlpools and gas fireplaces, and the grounds include a re-creation of a 49er cabin and gold mining machinery. It's in the center of town, within walking distance of restaurants. Complimentary Continental breakfast. Some microwaves, refrigerators, some in-room hot tubs, cable TV. Outdoor pool. Pets allowed. | 718 Main St. | 530/623–4937 | www.49ermotel.random.net | 25 rooms | $61–$85 | AE, D, MC, V.

Red Hill Motel. Among two acres of ponderosa pines and fruit trees, these eclectic 14 units (cabins, duplexes, and a porched motel) are painted red with green trim. Most units come with car ports, the bigger cabins with kitchenettes. It's two blocks from the center of town. Picnic area. Cable TV, room phones. | 2 Red Hill Rd. | 530/623–4331 | fax 530/623–4341 | redhill@snowcrest.net | www.redhillresorts.com | 14 units | $35–$75 | AE, D, MC, V.

Weaverville Hotel. This Old West survivor—a hotel since 1861—is in the heart of town, across the street from the courthouse and next to the town bandstand. The hotel's simplicity and faded charm (and the sporting goods store downstairs) make it a popular destination for European backpackers. There are full baths in all rooms, two with antique claw-foot tubs. No room phones. Pets allowed. No smoking. | 201 Main St. | 530/623–3121 | 8 rooms | $39.50–$42.50 | MC, V.

WEST COVINA

MAP 9, I3

(Nearby towns also listed: Arcadia, Glendora, Los Angeles)

Traversed by I–10, this city of 96,100 residents is midway between Los Angeles and San Bernardino. The largest shoehorn collection in the country in private hands is here in a building painted with the largest continuous Route 66 mural west of the Mississippi on a wall; call the City Council before visiting to see if it's on display when you visit.

Information: **West Covina City Council** | 1444 West Garvey Ave., 91790 | 626/814–8400 | www.westcov.org.

Dining

Monterey Bay Canners. Seafood. Nautical artifacts and marine oddities decorate the two levels and bar area of this restaurant with a menu of smoked salmon, teriyaki mahi-mahi, and penne pasta with garlic, basil, and grilled shrimp, among other dishes. Raw bar. Kids' menu. No smoking. | 3057 E. Garvey Ave. | 626/915–3474 | $20–$32 | AE, D, DC, MC, V.

Lodging

Comfort Inn. This motel is across the street from the Eastlake Mall. Complimentary Continental breakfast. Some refrigerators, in-room hot tubs, cable TV. Pool. Hot tub. | 2804 E. Garvey Ave. S | 626/915–6077 | fax 626/339–4587 | www.comfortinn.com | 58 rooms | $68–$89 | AE, D, DC, MC, V.

Holiday Inn. The rooms in this downtown motel have printed carpet, vertical window-blinds, and modular furniture. A breezy white gazebo dominates the courtyard area, and bright flowerbeds add color. Restaurant, bar, complimentary breakfast, room service. Refrigerators, cable TV. Pool. Laundry facilities. Business services. | 3223 E. Garvey Ave. N | 626/966–8311 | fax 626/339–2850 | www.holiday-inn.com | 135 rooms | $89–$119 | AE, D, DC, MC, V.

Sheraton Industry Hills Resort and Conference Center. This hotel sits on 650 acres, three blocks southwest of West Covina off I–605, at the base of the San Gabriel range. All rooms have floor-to-ceiling windows with panoramic views. Restaurants, bars with entertainment. Some refrigerators, cable TV. 2 pools. Hot tubs. Driving range, 2 18-hole golf courses, 17 tennis courts. Exercise equipment. Business services. | 1 Industry Hills Pkwy., City of Industry | 626/810–4455 | fax 626/964–9535 | www.sheraton.com | 294 rooms, 3 suites | $170–$185, $285–$375 suites | AE, D, DC, MC, V.

WEST HOLLYWOOD

MAP 9, D3

(Nearby towns also listed: Beverly Hills, Burbank, Glendale, Hollywood, Los Angeles, North Hollywood, Santa Monica)

West Hollywood was known exclusively as a gay community in the 1980s. Today it has replaced Hollywood as the center of wealth and celebrities. Luxury hotels, high-end and theme restaurants, and Art Deco landmarks punctuate its swank, cosmopolitan Sunset Strip. Some of the best cafés, bars, and dance clubs in the area can be found here. Be prepared for some beautiful people–watching. The area remains a focal point of the gay and lesbian community in Los Angeles, and it retains its eclectic, hip, bohemian airs. Both diverse and relaxed, it is home to piercing shops, tattoo parlors, and coffee bars.

Information: **West Hollywood Convention and Visitors Bureau** | Pacific Design Center, 8687 Melrose Ave., Ste. M25, 90069 | 310/289–2525 or 800/368–6020 | whcvb@visitwesthollywood.com | www.visitwesthollywood.com.

Attractions

Paramount Film and Television Studios. On walking tours of Paramount's facilities here, you'll see the *Hard Copy* production room and historic buildings and landscapes, including the *Forrest Gump* bench and the *Clueless* court. You can also sign up to attend TV show tapings on occasion. | 5555 Melrose Ave. | 323/956–5575 or 323/956–5000 | www.paramount.com | $15 | Tours weekdays at 9, 10, 11, 12, 1, and 2.

Melrose Avenue. A unique collection of galleries, fashion boutiques, restaurants, and antique shops show off the newest and best of fashion, trendy design, and art deco.

Dining

Cava. Spanish. Tapas and sangria star along with barbecued shrimp in this dark bistro with deep velvet booths, golden chandeliers, and a swirling staircase. Separate bar and outdoor patio. Jazz Thurs.–Sat. No smoking. | 8384 W. 3rd St. | 323/658–8898 | Breakfast also available | $15–$25 | AE, D, DC, MC, V.

Dan Tana's. Northern Italian. Established in 1964, this show biz hangout hasn't changed its heavy, dark, New York styling since it opened. A great Italian restaurant, but a lot of the old guard come here for the big NY prime steaks and martinis. No smoking. | 9071 Santa Monica Blvd., Los Angeles | 310/275–9444 | Reservations essential | Jacket required | No lunch | $28–$35 | AE, D, DC, MC, V.

Le Dome. French. Hollywood players still frequent this classy, Art Nouveau restaurant for the fresh fish and prime beef. An enclosed patio with operable windows brings the outdoors inside. No smoking. | 8720 Sunset Blvd., Los Angeles | 310/659–6919 | Closed Sun., No lunch Sat. | $28–$35 | AE, D, DC, MC, V.

Lola. Contemporary. Although the 50 different martinis tend to blur this hipster hangout with skylights and chandeliers, this downhome place dishes up tasty meals such as pork chops, fish, and barbecued steak. A large lounge with colorful couches, dining area, bar, and pub absorb the natural and candle light. No smoking. | 945 N. Fairfax Ave., Los Angeles | 213/736–5652 | No lunch | $18–$29 | AE, DC, MC, V.

The Palm. Steak/Lobster. The original Palm restaurant opened in the 1920s in New York; the same family created the Los Angeles version. Hundreds of Hollywood celebrity caricatures cover the walls above traditional white clothed tables that hold some of the biggest steaks in town. You don't have to be "somebody" to get a good seat, but it doesn't hurt. Steak, lobster, veal, and chops dominate the old school menu handled by old school waiters. No smoking. | 9001 Santa Monica Blvd., Los Angeles | 310/550–8811 | Reservations essential | No lunch weekends | $35–$48 | AE, D, DC, MC, V.

Spago. Contemporary. Wolfgang Puck's first restaurant, and arguably Los Angeles' most famous. Tourists and celebrities alike come here to see and be seen and eat the famed pizza and homemade pasta. Casual yet elegant, Spago's colors reflect the seasoned dishes, such as the smoked goat cheese and roasted corn ravioli with grilled baby chicken, grilled rare tuna with wasabi-potato puree, and roasted Cantonese duck with Bing cherries. No smoking. | 8795 Sunset Blvd., Los Angeles | 310/652–4025 | Reservations essential | Closed Mon. No lunch | $22–$35 | AE, D, DC, MC, V.

Yujean Kang's. Chinese. This restaurant serves some of the most innovative and most elegantly prepared fusion fare in town, exemplified by the chicken with silk squash in plum wine, the tofu bamboo braised with wild mushrooms, the spicy steamed veal with crispy fava beans and crispy baby bok choy, and the poached plum with watermelon ice and chocolate sauce. No smoking. | 8826 Melrose Ave. | 310/288–0806 | $12–$18 | AE, D, DC, MC, V.

Lodging

The Argyle. Mythological creatures, zeppelins and many other images commingle above the street entrance and along the building setbacks of this Art Deco restoration. Now listed on the National Register of Historical Places, this 15-story hotel withstood several earthquakes and near demolition since its 1929 construction. Each suite is unique in its Art Deco interior, including some original works of art, and equipped with everything from two-line phones to marble baths. Restaurant, bar, room service. In-room data ports, in-room safes, minibars, refrigerators, some in-room hot tubs, cable TV, in-room VCRs (and movies). Pool. Massage. Gym. Business services. | 8358 Sunset Blvd., Los Angeles | 323/654–7100 or 800/225–2637 (for reservations) | fax 323/654–9287 | rez@argylehotel.com | www.argylehotel.com | 20 rooms, 44 suites | $260, $300–$1,200 suites | AE, DC, MC, V.

Hyatt West Hollywood. This posh establishment is popular with music-industry types. Burnished metal with exotic hardwood accents deck the lobby, and rooms follow suit in neo-Deco style. The famous Whisky-a-Go-Go is seven blocks southwest. Pool. Exercise equipment. Laundry facilities. Business services. | 8401 Sunset Blvd. | 323/656–1234 | fax 323/650–7024 | 262 rooms | $199–$274 | AE, D, DC, MC, V.

Le Parc Hotel. A tree-bordered residential street is the setting for this hotel. Accommodations are all roomy suites, with sunken living rooms, fireplaces, high ceilings, and eclectic furnishings. CBS Television City is 1 mi east and Rodeo Drive 2 mi southwest. Pool. Outdoor hot tub. Tennis. Exercise equipment. Business services, airport shuttle. Pets allowed. | 733 N.W. Knoll Dr. | 310/855–8888 | fax 310/659–7812 | 44 suites | $225–$275 suites | AE, D, DC, MC, V.

Le Montrose Suite Hôtel de Grand Luxe. A contemporary exterior leads into the Art Nouveau lobby of this hotel noted for its excellent service. You can take in a game of tennis or relax by the pool, on the rooftop, five stories up. Rooms have sunken living rooms and fireplaces; suites have upgraded amenities such as fax machines, copiers, printers, and furnishings, and the lobby displays an elaborately polished marble floor. Restaurant, room service. In-room data ports, kitchenettes, refrigerators, cable TV. Pool. Hot tub, massage. Tennis. Gym. Business services. Some pets allowed. | 900 Hammond St., West Hollywood | 310/855–1115 or 800/776–0666 | fax 310/657–9192 | www.lemontrose.com | 132 suites | $260–$390 suites | AE, DC, MC, V.

Le Reve. This charming hotel, near Sunset Strip, has a rooftop garden with a pool and a hot tub with a 360° panoramic view. All accommodations are suites, with large baths, separate living rooms, and multi-line touch tone telephones and fax machines; most come with fireplaces, and some with fitness equipment. Room service. In-room data ports, some kitchenettes, minibars, cable TV. Pool. Laundry service. Business services. | 8822 Cynthia St. | 310/854–1144 | fax 310/657–2623 | 80 suites | $120–$220 | AE, DC, MC, V.

Park Sunset Hotel. This Georgian-style, all-suites lodging provides a respite from the massive chain properties that dominate the West Hollywood landscape. Antiques and reproductions furnish the rooms. The Comedy Store and House of Blues are less than a block away. Restaurant. In-room VCRs. Pool. Laundry facilities. Business services. | 8462 Sunset Blvd. | 323/654–6470 | fax 323/654–5918 | 82 suites | $110 suites | AE, D, DC, MC, V.

Ramada Plaza–West Hollywood. A cool contemporary design distinguishes this four-story hotel in a West Hollywood commercial district. Restaurant, bar. Some microwaves, refrigerators, cable TV. Pool. Shops. Laundry facilities. Business services, airport shuttle. | 8585 Santa Monica Blvd., Los Angeles | 310/652–6400 | fax 310/652–2135 | info@ramada-wh.com | www.ramada-wh.com | 175 rooms, 44 suites | $155, $175–$279 suites | AE, D, DC, MC, V.

Summerfield Suites. A courtyard with a landscaped outdoor dining area is a focal point of this six-story all-suites. All units have a fireplace and a balcony. It's 11 mi west of downtown. Complimentary Continental breakfast. In-room data ports, kitchenettes. Cable TV, in-room VCRs (and movies). Pool. Exercise equipment. Laundry facilities. Some pets allowed. Parking (fee). | 1000 Westmount Dr. | 310/657–7400 or 800/833–4353 | fax 310/854–6744 | www.summerfieldsuites.com | 111 suites | $155–$258 | AE, D, DC, MC, V.

★ **Wyndham Bel Age.** Original artwork fills this all-suites luxury hotel. The spacious rooms have separate dressing areas, with marble counters and mirrors and rosewood furnishings. It's 15 mi west of downtown and 1 mi north of the Beverly Center. Diaghilev restaurant is on site. 2 restaurants, bar, room service. In-room data ports. Cable TV. Pool. Beauty salon. Exercise equipment. Video Games. Business services, parking (fee). | 1020 N. San Vicente Blvd. | 310/854–1111 | fax 310/854–0926 | www.wyndham.com | 200 suites | $229 | AE, D, DC, MC, V.

WHITTIER

(Nearby towns also listed: Brea, Fullerton, Los Angeles)

South and east of downtown Los Angeles, Whittier is a residential community of 77,700 and a former citrus empire. It was founded in the 1880s as a Quaker community and named for the poet John Greenleaf Whittier.

Information: Whittier Chamber of Commerce | 8158 Painter Ave., 90602 | 562/698–9554 | staff@whittierbiz.com | www.whittierbiz.com.

Attractions

Richard Nixon Library and Birthplace. This privately supported, non-profit institution is dedicated to educating the public about the life and times of the 37th President. The facility, covering nine acres, is a three-dimensional walk-through memoir with a 52,000-square-ft museum, 22 high-tech galleries, movie and interactive video theaters, the First Lady's Garden, the President's 1910 birthplace, and the memorial sites of Richard Nixon and his wife, Pat. | 18001 Yorba Linda Blvd. | 714/993–5075 or 714/993–3393 | www.nixonlibrary.org | $6 | Mon.–Sat. 10–5, Sun. 11–5.

Rose Hills Memorial Park. This is one of the world's largest memorial parks and is graced by the 3½-acre Pageant of Roses Garden. Some 1,000 bushes of 600 varieties grow here. | 3888 S. Workman Mill Rd. | 562/692–1212 or 562/699–0921 | Free | Daily 8 AM –7PM.

Dining

Seafare Inn. Seafood. A low-key nautical theme is the backdrop for seafood specialties here, served since 1961. Fish 'n chips, salmon, oysters, and lobster tails are on the daily "fresh list." Kids' menu. Beer and wine only. No smoking. | 16363 E. Whittier Blvd. | 562/947–6645 | Closed Mon. | $7–$20 | MC, V.

Lodging

Hilton. This Hilton property is steps from Historic Uptown Village. Some guest rooms have poolside patios. Restaurant, bar with entertainment. Some microwaves, refrigerators. Pool. Hot tub. Exercise equipment. Business services. | 7320 Greenleaf Ave. | 562/945–8511 | fax 562/693–651 | whithilt@gte.net | www.hilton.com | 202 rooms | $139–$$185 | AE, D, DC, MC, V.

Vagabond Inn. This three-story property is built around a sparkling outdoor pool surrounded by live palm trees and faux-tropical rock outcroppings. Complimentary Continental breakfast. Cable TV. Pool. Pets allowed (fee). | 14125 E. Whittier Blvd. | 562/698–9701 | fax 562/698–8716 | www.vagabondinn.com | 49 rooms | $60–$70 | AE, D, DC, MC, V.

WOODLAND

(Nearby towns also listed: Davis, Sacramento)

Woodland's downtown core, 20 min north of Sacramento, lies frozen in a quaint and genteel past. In its heyday, it was one of the wealthiest cities in California, established in 1861 by gold-seekers and entrepreneurs. Once the boom was over, attention turned to the rich surrounding land, and the area became an agricultural gold mine. The memories of the old land barons are in the Victorian homes, many of them restored and surrounded by lavish gardens that line Woodland's wide streets.

Information: **Woodland Chamber of Commerce** | 307 First St., 95695 | 530/662–7327, 888/843–2636.

Attractions

Heidrick Ag History Center. Ancient trucks and farm machinery seem to rumble to life within this shed-like museum. You can see the world's largest collection of antique agricultural equipment, plus interactive exhibits, a food court, gift shop, and a kids' play area. | 1962 Hays La. | 530/666–9700 | fax 530/666–9712 | www.aghistory.org | $6 | weekdays 10–5, Sat. 10–6, Sun. 10–4.

The Woodland Opera House. More than 300 touring companies, including Frank Kirk, the Acrobatic Tramp, and John Philip Sousa's marching band, appeared at this opera house built in 1885 (and rebuilt after it burned in 1892). Now restored, the building hosts a season of musical theater from September to July every year in addition to concerts. Weekly guided tours reveal old-fashioned stage technology. | Main and 2nd Sts. | 530/666–9617 | Tours free | Mon. and Tues. 10–2, weekends 2–4; tours Tues., noon–4.

Yolo Country Historical Museum. The former 10-room Classic Revival home of settler William Byas Gibson was purchased by volunteers and restored as a county museum. You can see collections of furnishings and artifacts from the 1850s–1930s. Old trees and established lawn cover the 2-acre site off Route 113. | 512 Gibson Rd. | 530/666–1045 | $2 | Mon.–Tues. 10–4, weekends noon–4.

Dining

Club Satay. Pan-Asian. This small, bright downtown restaurant has authentic Southeast Asian food. In addition to Thai red and green curries and skewered grilled meat (satay), try Indonesian rice dish nasi-goreng or vegetarian laksa, made with seasonal greens and coconut milk. | 534 Main St. | 530/669–3242 | $6–$8 | MC, V.

Ludy's Main Street BBQ. Barbecue. Here's a big, casual restaurant next door to the Opera House that looks like something out of the "Beverly Hillbillies." You can tuck into huge portions of ribs, beef, chicken, fish and chips, or have a half-pound burger slathered in red sauce. On the patio, water misters cool you in summer and heaters keep you toasty in winter. Kids' menu. | 667 Main St. | 530/666–4400 | $5–$14 | AE, MC, V.

Morrison's Upstairs. American. A Victorian building registered as a State Historic Landmark houses this restaurant. Downstairs is a bar, deli, and patio. The top floor, once the attic, is full of nooks and alcoves where you can have your meal. It's furnished throughout with polished wood tables that suit the style of the house. The menu lists burgers and sandwiches, scampi, Chinese chicken salad, pasta, and prime rib, with some vegetarian choices. | 428½ 1st St. | 530/666–6176 | $8–$28 | AE, D, DC, MC, V.

Lodging

Best Western Shadow Inn. Palm trees wave over the landscaped pool area at this two-story hotel. Some rooms have wet bars and kitchenettes. Complimentary Continental breakfast. Cable TV. Pool. Hot tub. Laundry facilities. Business services. | 584 N. East St. | 530/666–1251 | fax 530/662–2804 | www.bestwestern.com | 120 rooms | $60–$78 | AE, D, DC, MC, V.

Cinderella Motel Woodland. The basic rooms at this two-story motel have combination or shower baths. Refrigerators, cable TV, in-room VCRs (and movies). Pool. Hot tub. Pets allowed (fee). No smoking. | 99 W Main St. | 530/662–1091 | fax 530/662–2804 | 30 rooms | $49–$58 | AE, D, DC, MC, V.

Valley Oaks Inn. Rooms in this two-story motel have basic furnishings and amenities. Refrigerators, cable TV. Pool. | 600 N East St. | 530/666–5511 | 62 rooms | $46–$56 | AE, D, DC, MC, V.

WOODLAND HILLS

(Nearby towns also listed: Glendale, Los Angeles)

It was in this area that the treaty to end the Mexican War was signed, clearing the way for California to be admitted to the union in 1850 as the 31st state. In later years, Harry Warner of Warner Brothers Pictures was a major landholder in Woodland Hills; he used his 1,100 acres to breed thoroughbred horses. Today, part of that acreage has become the Warner Center, considered the hub of San Fernando Valley business, much like Century City is to Los Angeles. Nearby Warner Park, also on the old horse ranch, is home to the Valley Cultural Center's "Concerts in the Park" series.

The city's 62,700 residents don't have to hunt for shopping. Topanga Plaza and The Promenade shopping mall, with its 16-screen theater complex, will keep any shopaholic happy.

Information: Woodland Hills Chamber of Commerce | 22025 Ventura Blvd., Ste. 203, 91364 | 818/347–4737 | whcc@sfvalley.org | www.woodlandhillscc.net.

Attractions

Warner Park. This leafy refuge from L.A.'s crush is a popular place for office workers and residents to spread out the picnic blanket. Arts and craft shows fill the park regularly. | 5800 Topanga Canyon Blvd. | 818/883–9370 | Daily dawn to dusk.

Valley Cultural Center. This bandshell facility in Warner Park presents a wide range of musical performers—from country and rock headliners to classical talents to swingin' big bands. | 5800 Topanga Canyon Blvd. | 818/704–1358 | Free | June–August, Sundays at 5.

Dining

Cheesecake Factory. Eclectic. Started as a bakery in 1978, this casual spot with marble floors and tabletops serves more than 30 varieties of cheesecake and more than 200 appetizers and entrées. Try the jambalaya or the spicy cashew chicken. Kids' menu. | 6324 Canoga Ave. | 818/883–9900 | $8–$24 | AE, D, DC, MC, V.

Cosmos Grill and Rotisserie. Contemporary. Locals are crazy about this vibrant restaurant based in a mini-mall, 2 mi west of Woodland Hills. The menu has fresh pastas, chicken, steak, seafood, burgers, and salads, joined by dishes such as the Atlantic salmon steamed in parchment with a julienne of leek, spinach, and lime. Kids' menu. Beer and wine only. No smoking. | 23631 Calabasas Rd., Calabasas | 818/591–2211 | No lunch Sun. | $10–$17 | AE, DC, MC, V.

Lodging

Hilton and Towers–Warner Center. The hotel is 1 mi north of the Ventura Freeway in the heart of Warner Center. Restaurant, bar. Cable TV. Pool. Hot tub. Tennis. Business services, airport shuttle. | 6360 Canoga Ave. | 818/595–1000 | fax 818/596–4578 | 318 rooms | $154–$199 | AE, D, DC, MC, V.

Marriott–Warner Center. This 16-story structure is in the heart of the San Fernando Valley. Topanga Plaza and the Promenade Mall are both across the street. Restaurant, bar. In-room data ports, cable TV. Indoor-outdoor pools. Hot tub. Exercise equipment. Business services, airport shuttle. | 21850 Oxnard St. | 818/887–4800 | fax 818/340–5893 | wcmarriott@aol.com | www.marriott.com/marriott/cao15.htm | 463 rooms | $107–$159 | AE, D, DC, MC, V.

Red Lion Suites–Warner Center. The lobby of this hotel is walled with glass and lush with live plants and trees. All rooms have parlor areas, bar seating, and work areas. Complimentary Continental breakfast. In-room data ports, some kitchenettes, microwaves, refrigerators, cable TV, in-room VCRs (and movies). Pool. Tennis. Laundry facilities. | 20200 Sherman Way,

Canoga Park | 818/883–8250 | fax 818/883–8268 | www.redlion.com | 99 rooms, 98 suites | $79, $89–$149 suites | AE, D, DC, MC, V.

YOSEMITE NATIONAL PARK

MAP 3, G8

(Nearby towns also listed: June Lake, Lee Vining)

It's tough to find anyone who isn't moved by Yosemite's spectacular beauty, especially in 7-mi-long Yosemite Valley, where trademark Half Dome and El Capitan rock formations loom. While steps are underway to reduce traffic and overuse problems, particularly in that jaw-dropping valley, sometimes it seems like everyone in the world is ogling at those looming rock walls with you. Best bet is to avoid peak summer periods; April through Memorial Day can be outstanding, with mild temperatures and snow melt setting the waterfalls to booming, while fall finds maples and other deciduous trees trimming the valley with color. If you can't dodge summer, try heading for lesser-used corners of the 1,169-square-mi park—Tuolumne Meadows (accessible when snows melt), Glacier Point, and Wawona (near Mariposa Grove).

Yosemite National Park is 214 mi southeast of San Francisco. Route 120 (Tioga Road), which joins I–395 to the east and Route 99 to the west, roughly divides the park in half—and is usually closed in winter. Access routes on the west side are Route 120 (enter at Big Oak Flat/Crane Flat and Arch Rock/El Portal), and Route 41 (South Entrance/Wawona). On the east side of the Sierra Crest, access is just south of Lee Vining. To reduce traffic impacts in Yosemite Valley year-round, cars park in designated lots, and free shuttle buses take you to specific drop-off points along a paved loop road. These points access dozens of sites and hiking paths.

Information: Yosemite National Park | Box 577, Yosemite, 95389 | 209/372–0200; camping reservations, 800/436–7275; road conditions, 800/427–7623 from California | www.nps.gov/yose | $20 per vehicle (park entrance fee, good for 7 days).

The **Yosemite Association** sells the 77-page *Yosemite Road Guide*, which tells the story behind each road marker in the park. | Box 230, El Portal, 95318 | 209/379–1906.

Yosemite Concession Services runs park facilities and offers scheduled activities year-round, including free and fee-based educational and interpretive programs ranging from fly-fishing demonstrations to guided bus tours to astronomy classes. | 209/372–1240 | www.yosemitepark.com.

Badger Pass Ski Area has information on winter programs and sports. | 209/372–8430 or 209/372–1000 | www.yosemitepark.com/activities.

Attractions

Fishing. Brown, rainbow, golden, and Lahontan cutthroat trout live in the waters of Yosemite. Lakes and reservoirs are open for fishing year-round, while most stream and river fishing runs late April through mid-November. Frog Creek is the exception. Its delayed, mid-June opening aims to protect spawning trout. A California fishing license is required. California Department of Fish and Game | 3211 S St., Sacramento | 916/227–2244 | $10 per day for license. can be ordered by phone, or check local sporting goods stores.

Forests. Yosemite is a land where you can lose your perspective—everything's big. Really big. Big rocks, big waterfalls, even big trees. Dense stands of incense cedar, Douglas fir, and assorted pines cover much of the park, but the stellar standouts, quite literally, are the *Sequoia sempervirens*, "sequoia evergreen," the giant sequoia.

At **Mariposa Grove** you'll find these trees, the largest living things on earth, some nearly three millennia old, towering overhead. Self-guided trails lead uphill through the massive cinammon-red trunks, with interpretive signs explaining the ecology and threats to the sequoia ecosystem. There's also a guided, 1-hour Big Trees Tram Tour; you can ride it all the through the grove, or disembark at any point to hike back to the parking lot. | 209/372–0200 | Grove May–early Oct., weather permitting; tram tour late spring through August, daily 9–4 | $8.50 for tram tour.

Geological Sites. The truth is, all of Yosemite is a geology lesson. Much of it, most notably the incomparable Yosemite Valley and its rock formations, consists of remnants of glacial ice that chiseled through these mountains thousands of years ago. Here are some of the best known, most accessible sites.

With its summit 3,593 ft above the floor of Yosemite Valley, **El Capitan** might well be the largest single block of exposed granite in the world. Intrepid hikers can take the 8-mi trail to the top. Plan to stick closer to *terra firma*? Spring through fall, just make sure you bring the binoculars—from down below, look for brightly colored clothes and gear of climbers tackling the vertical face.

★ **Glacier Point,** 3,214 ft above Yosemite Valley, offers sweeping, bird's-eye-views of the granite massifs below. The Glacier Point Road leaves Wawona Road (Route 41) about 23 mi southwest of the valley; then it's a 16-mi drive, with fine views, into higher country. From the parking area walk a few hundred yards and you'll see waterfalls, Half Dome, and other peaks. Glacier Point is also a popular hiking destination either to or from the valley floor, especially since it doesn't have to be an up-and-back-route, thanks to the Glacier Point Hikers' bus, June through October weather permitting. | $10.

Although it is on countless postcards and calendars, it's still a shock to see the real **Half Dome,** the valley's most recognizable formation, topping out at an elevation of 8,842 ft. You don't have to scale its 2,000-ft face to make it to the top, though you will have to eat your Wheaties: the John Muir trail accesses the summit from the valley, a nearly 17-mi round-trip.

Hiking and Backpacking. From paved rambles to multi-day scrambles, Yosemite's 840 mi of trails have a hike for you. Detailed guides and topographic maps are on sale in park stores and visitors centers. Overnight stays in the backcountry require a wilderness permit, available during the off-season at permit stations throughout the park. In summer, permit reservations are highly recommended and can be made through the Wilderness Center. Staff there provide trail-use reservations (recommended for popular trailheads on weekends and between May and September) as well as permits, maps, and advice on backcountry treks. When the center is closed, try the Valley Visitor Center. Need some hand-holding or want to explore or rock-climb with knowledgeable guides? They're available through the Yosemite Association or Yosemite Mountaineering. | Yosemite Village | 209/372–0200 for information, 209/372–0740 for permit reservations; 209/379–2646 for the Yosemite Association, or 209/372–8344 for Yosemite Mountaineering | www.yosemitepark.com | $3 per person for permit reservations | April–Oct., daily 8–5.

High Country. This part of Yosemite, the above-treeline, high-alpine region east of Yosemite Valley—land of alpenglow and top-of-the-world vistas—is often missed by those only focusing on the valley's more publicized splendors. If you've never seen Sierra High Country, go. If you've already been there, you know why it's not to be missed. Summer wildflowers, usually mid-July through August, can be spectacular.

Tioga Road, also known as Route 120, is the scenic route to the most accessible parts of Yosemite's High Country, most notably **Tuolumne Meadows.** The largest subalpine meadow in the Sierra, at 8,575 ft, is a popular way station for backpack trips along the Sierra-scribing Pacific Crest and John Muir trails. Camping is allowed. A small store sells a limited selection of expensive provisions, and there's a gas station, stables for pack animals, a lodge, and a visitors center, which is open in summer. The highway closes when snow piles up, usually in mid-October.

Rafting. Rafting is permitted only on designated areas of the Middle and South Forks of the Merced River. Check with the Visitor Center for current river closures and other restrictions. | 209/372–8341 | www.yosemitepark.com | $12.50 | Memorial Day–early July, depending on water flow.

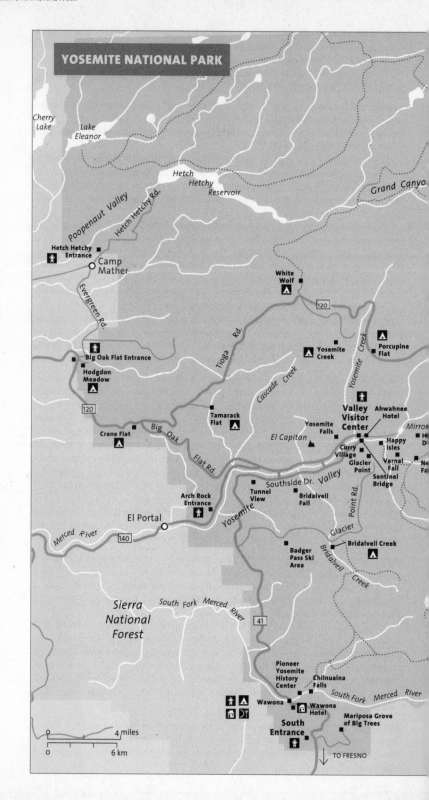

YOSEMITE NATIONAL PARK

Cherry Lake

Lake Eleanor

Poopenaut Valley

Hetch Hetchy Reservoir

Grand Canyo

Hetch Hetchy Rd.

Hetch Hetchy Entrance

Camp Mather

Evergreen Rd.

White Wolf

120

Big Oak Flat Entrance

Hodgdon Meadow

Tioga Rd.

Yosemite Creek

Porcupine Flat

120

Cascade Creek

Yosemite Creek

Tamarack Flat

Valley Visitor Center

Ahwahnee Hotel

Mirror

Crane Flat

Big Oak

Yosemite Falls

El Capitan

Happy Isles

H D

Curry Village

Glacier Point

Vernal Fall

Ne Fa

Flat Rd.

Southside Dr. Valley

Sentinel Bridge

Arch Rock Entrance

Tunnel View

Bridalveil Fall

Glacier Point Rd.

El Portal

140

Merced River

Yosemite

Glacier

Bridalveil Creek

Bridalveil Creek

Badger Pass Ski Area

Sierra National Forest

South Fork Merced River

41

Pioneer Yosemite History Center

Chinquapin Falls

South Fork Merced River

Wawona

Wawona Hotel

Mariposa Grove of Big Trees

South Entrance

4 miles

6 km

TO FRESNO

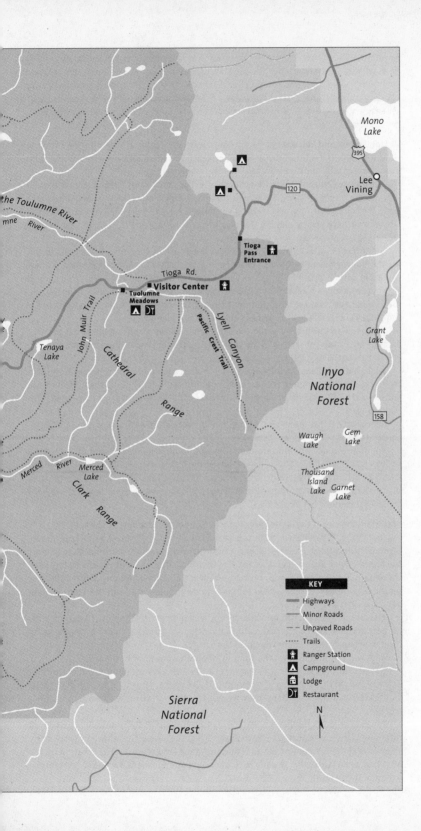

Mono
Lake

Lee
Vining

the Toulumne River

mne River

Tioga Rd.

Tioga
Pass
Entrance

Visitor Center

Tuolumne
Meadows

John Muir Trail

Tenaya
Lake

Cathedral

Range

Lyell Canyon

Pacific Crest Trail

Grant
Lake

Inyo
National
Forest

Waugh
Lake

Gem
Lake

Merced River

Merced
Lake

Clark

Range

Thousand
Island
Lake

Garnet
Lake

KEY

Highways
Minor Roads
Unpaved Roads
Trails
Ranger Station
Campground
Lodge
Restaurant

Sierra
National
Forest

N

Swimming. The Merced River at the eastern end of Yosemite Valley has several swimming holes with small sandy beaches. You can also swim at the Curry Village and Yosemite Lodge swimming pools. If you head for the river, remember that water can be very cold, and may cause hypothermia. Also, never swim above or below waterfalls, or in or near rapids. | 209/372–0299 | www.yosemitepark.com | Free for river, $3 for pools | Mid-July–mid-Sept. for swimming pools.

Visitor Centers and Museums. It's hard not to learn something at Yosemite. The excellent nature centers and interpretive information teach you about all kinds of features—from Indian lore to why granite cleaves in such seemingly perfect lines.

The **Nature Center at Happy Isles,** named after the pair of little islands where the Merced River enters Yosemite Valley, has exhibits on the natural features of the park. Hikers take note: the John Muir Trail and treks to Vernal and Nevada Falls, Merced Lake, and Half Dome begin here. Happy Isles is a short walk from Shuttle Stop #16. | 209/372–0200 | Free | June–Sept., daily 10–4.

A number of 19th-century buildings have been gathered together in Wawona to create the **Pioneer Yosemite History Center.** Here, as part of the living-history program, interpreters in period costumes introduce you to some of the people and events that shaped Yosemite's history—blacksmiths, bankers, and more. Ranger-led walks leave from the covered bridge, Saturdays at 10 in summer. | Rte. 41 near the South Entrance, Wawona | 209/379–2646 | Free | Daily year-round; hrs change seasonally.

In the **Indian Cultural Museum** you can learn the ways of the region's native peoples. Exhibits are housed next door to the Valley Visitor Center (shuttle bus stops #6 and #9). | 209/379–2646 | Free | Daily 9–5.

At the **Indian Village (Ahwahnee)** speakers impart a unique and informative story relating a sense of the economic and social changes in America in 1872 and their effect on the culture of the Ahwahneechee people of Yosemite. | Off Northside Dr. | 559/252–4848 | Free | Daily 9–5.

Special art exhibits are shown frequently at the **Yosemite Fine Arts Museum.** | Off Northside Dr. | 209/372–0299 | Free | Daily 9–5.

For maps, guides, and information from park rangers, be sure to stop at the helpful **Valley Visitor Center,** which also has exhibits on the history of Yosemite Valley. A 1-mi paved loop trail, "A Changing Yosemite," charts the park's natural evolution. There is also a Sierra Visitors' Bureau here. | Off Northside Dr. | 209/372–0299 | www.yosemitepark.com | Free | Daily 9-5 (extended hrs in summer).

Waterfalls are one of the distinctive characteristics of the Yosemite landscape, especially Yosemite Valley. When the snow starts to melt (usually peaking in May), almost every rocky lip or narrow gorge becomes a sluiceway for streaming snowmelt churning down to meet the Merced River. But even in drier months (barring a drought year, which can happen), the waterfalls can still take your breath away. If you choose to hike any of the trails to or up the falls, be sure to wear shoes with good, no-slip soles; rocks can be extremely slippery. Stay on trails at all times.

★ Blowing as much as 20 ft one way or the other depending on the wind, filmy (and aptly named) **Bridalveil Fall** is the first sight that catches your eye as you drive into the valley from Wawona. Native Americans called the 620-ft cascade Pohono, "spirit of the puffing wind." A ¼-mi trail leads from the parking lot off Wawona Road to the falls.

Nevada Fall (594 ft) is the first major fall as the Merced River plunges out of the High Country toward the eastern end of Yosemite Valley. A strenuous 2-mi section of the Mist Trail leads from Vernal Fall to the top of Nevada Fall. Allow 6 to 8 hrs for the full 7-mi round-trip hike.

You walk through rainbows when you visit 317-ft **Vernal Fall.** The hike on a paved trail from the Happy Isles Nature Center to the bridge at the base of the fall is only moderately strenuous and less than 1 mi long. It's another steep (and often wet) ¾-mi grind up the Mist Trail, open late spring to early fall (depending on snowmelt). Allow 2 to 4 hrs for the 3-mi round-trip hike.

KODAK'S TIPS FOR PHOTOGRAPHING LANDSCAPES AND SCENERY

Landscape
- Tell a story
- Isolate the essence of a place
- Exploit mood, weather, and lighting

Panoramas
- Use panoramic cameras for sweeping vistas
- Don't restrict yourself to horizontal shots
- Keep the horizon level

Panorama Assemblage
- Use a wide-angle or normal lens
- Let edges of pictures overlap
- Keep exposure even
- Use a tripod

Placing the Horizon
- Use low horizon placement to accent sky or clouds
- Use high placement to emphasize distance and accent foreground elements
- Try eliminating the horizon

Mountain Scenery: Scale
- Include objects of known size
- Frame distant peaks with nearby objects
- Compress space with long lenses

Mountain Scenery: Lighting
- Shoot early or late; avoid midday
- Watch for dramatic color changes
- Use exposure compensation

Tropical Beaches
- Capture expansive views
- Don't let bright sand fool your meter
- Include people

Rocky Shorelines
- Vary shutter speeds to freeze or blur wave action
- Don't overlook sea life in tidal pools
- Protect your gear from sand and sea

In the Desert
- Look for shapes and textures
- Try visiting during peak bloom periods
- Don't forget safety

Canyons
- Research the natural and social history of a locale
- Focus on a theme or geologic feature
- Budget your shooting time

Rain Forests and the Tropics
- Go for mystique with close-ups and detail shots
- Battle low light with fast films and camera supports
- Protect cameras and film from moisture and humidity

Rivers and Waterfalls
- Use slow film and long shutter speeds to blur water
- When needed, use a neutral-density filter over the lens
- Shoot from water level to heighten drama

Autumn Colors
- Plan trips for peak foliage periods
- Mix wide and close views for visual variety
- Use lighting that accents colors or creates moods

Moonlit Landscapes
- Include the moon or use only its illumination
- Exaggerate the moon's relative size with long telephoto lenses
- Expose landscapes several seconds or longer

Close-Ups
- Look for interesting details
- Use macro lenses or close-up filters
- Minimize camera shake with fast films and high shutter speeds

Caves and Caverns
- Shoot with ISO 1000+ films
- Use existing light in tourist caves
- Paint with flash in wilderness caves

From *Kodak Guide to Shooting Great Travel Pictures* © 2000 by Fodor's Travel Publications

★ Two-tiered **Yosemite Falls** drops 2,425 ft total and is the highest waterfall in the U.S.; it tumbles down to the valley floor just west of Yosemite Village. The Upper Yosemite Fall Trail, a strenuous 3½-mi climb rising 2,700 ft, takes you all the way up and beyond. It starts at Sunnyside Campground.

Winter Sports. Want Yosemite to yourself? Come in winter, when snow and mysterious morning mist not only keep crowds low, but cast a stunning hush on the valley floor. This is often the favorite time of year for seasoned Yosemite visitors in-the-know. Access is limited; call ahead for latest road conditions (800/427–7623 from California) and be prepared for mountain storms at all times.

There are many ways to explore Yosemite in winter. Snow rarely piles up for long on the valley floor, but higher elevations are usually cloaked in thick layers of white stuff well into spring.

Badger Pass Ski Resort, the oldest operating ski area in the state, is a low-key, family-oriented winter destination with nine downhill runs. The season generally runs from Thanksgiving through early April. Badger Pass Day Lodge has a ski rental shop, a general store, restaurants, a bar, and sun deck. It's 6 mi east of Route 41. | Glacier Point Rd. | 559/252–4848 or 209/372–1000 (ski conditions) | www.yosemitepark.com | $17–$28 for daily lift ticket | Nov.–Apr., daily 10–4 (snow permitting).

Yosemite's trails and unplowed roads make for splendid **cross-country skiing or snow-shoeing.** Most of the park's 90 mi of marked trails begin from Badger Pass Ski Area, 23 mi south of Yosemite Valley on Route 41. There are also overnight treks to Glacier Point Hut and guided treks into the park. Instruction and rentals are available from Yosemite Cross-

© Artville

MONO LAKE

When you're driving through California, particularly the northern half of the state, you'll notice the bumper sticker: "Save Mono Lake." That's because Mono Lake is an example of natural beauty, poor political planning, and grass-roots activism—all in one place.

Mono Lake's problems began in 1941 when the City of Los Angeles bought the Mono Lake basin and the Los Angeles Department of Water and Power redirected four of the five streams that fed Mono Lake to the California Aqueduct to feed L.A.'s growing demand for water. This feat of engineering deprived the lake of its fresh-water source and led to a drop in the lake's water level. By 1962 the water level had dropped by 40 ft and its salinity had doubled.

Islands in the lake, used as safe nesting sites for millions of migratory birds, became peninsulas open to predators. Lack of water ruined the stream ecosystems, and the air quality dropped because of the chemicals in the exposed lakebed.

In 1978 a Stanford University teaching assistant named David Gaines formed the Mono Lake Committee and started telling anyone who would listen why this lake was important and how it was endangered. Thanks to much hard work and some positive legal findings, water levels are beginning to rise again. There are beautiful high-desert views, and tufa towers—calcium carbonate formations that look like castle turrets—rise from the lake. The best place to view them is at the south end along the mile-long South Tufa Trail.

Country Ski School next to Badger Pass Day Lodge. | 209/372–8444 (Cross–Country School) | www.yosemitepark.com/activities/badger | $16 adults, $10 kids 12 and under, for all-day rental of cross-country skis | Nov.–Apr. (snow permitting), daily 10–4.

Spin and twirl (or just fall down a lot) at the **Curry Village Ice-Skating Rink** in Yosemite Valley. The outdoor rink has spectacular views of Half Dome and Glacier Point. | 209/372–8319 | www.yosemitepark.com/html/ice.html | $5 for 2½ hours; rental skates, $2 | November through March, weather permitting, weekends 8:30AM–9:30PM; weekdays noon–9:30PM.

Dining

★ **Ahwahnee Dining Room.** American. The dining room of this noble lodge is just as spectacularly enormous, and elegant, as the rest of the hotel. Like everywhere else in Yosemite Valley, this is a place where you can't help but look up. The 34-ft tall trestle-beam ceiling isn't supported by just any lumber; those are complete tree trunks up there. Full-length windows, wrought-iron chandeliers, and snappily dressed waitstaff scurrying about the room complete the scene. Leave the shorts, jeans, hiking boots, and tennis shoes back in your room; jackets are requested for men. The classic American specialties include New York steak, broiled swordfish filet, and prime rib. Sunday brunch. | Ahwahnee Rd. | 559/372–1489 | Breakfast also available | $13–$28 | Reservations essential | AE, D, DC, MC, V.

Mountain Room Restaurant. American. The food becomes secondary when you see Yosemite Falls, the world's fifth largest waterfall, through the enormous, floor-to-ceiling wall of windows in this dining room in the Yosemite Lodge. Baked shrimp, sautéed blackened Cajun catfish, steak, and pasta are a few of the menu choices. Kids' menu. No smoking. | Northside Dr. | 209/372–1281 | No lunch. Closed weekdays from Thanksgiving–Easter except for holiday periods | $18–$30 | D, DC, MC, V.

Sierra Restaurant. Contemporary. A freestanding stone fireplace warms this casually elegant dining room, with open-beam, 30-ft ceilings, and French doors opening onto a heated patio. Much of the patio is covered for protected al fresco dining spring, summer, and fall. Inside, Native American accents lend a rustic look. Try the Rainbow trout with almond-roasted potatoes and caper butter, or the Burgundy-roasted pork tenderloin with cinnamon-apple potatoes. The Sunday brunch is extremely popular. Kids' menu. No smoking. | Tenaya Lodge, 1122 Rte. 41, Fishcamp | 800/635–5807, ext. 2 | tenaya_restaurant@destinationhotels.com | www.tenayalodge.com/dining.htm | No lunch | $15–$30 | Reservations essential | AE, D, DC, MC, V.

Wawona Dining Room. Contemporary. Watch deer graze on the meadow while dining in the romantic, candlelit dining room of the whitewashed Wawona Hotel, which dates from the late 1800s. The American style cuisine favors California ingredients and flavors. Trout is a menu staple. Sunday brunch. | Rte. 41, Wawona | 209/375–1425 | Closed weekdays Nov.–Easter except at holidays | $9–$23 | Reservations essential | D, DC, MC, V.

Lodging

★ **Ahwahnee.** To say this is a lodging is like saying the White House is just a house. This grande dame of the National Park system, one of a handful of Great Lodges built in the 1920s, is all granite boulders and exposed timbers, built with a grandness to match the spectacular surroundings. The main common area has a pair of massive stone fireplaces, an irresistible place to settle into enormous chairs and sofas—you'll never feel so Lilliputian—done in colors and styles that echo native Miwok and Paiute tribes. Artifacts abound. If you're lucky enough to book one of the polished-wood and earth-tone rooms, there's a good chance your neighbors will be honeymooners—this is a popular destination for weddings. Some rooms have fireplaces; all have extraordinary views. Restaurant, bar (with entertainment), room service. Pool. Tennis. | Ahwahnee Rd. | 559/252–4848 | fax 559/456–0542 | www.yosemitepark.com | 99 rooms, 4 suites, 24 cottages | $292, $565–$800 suites, $292 cottages | AE, D, DC, MC, V.

Camping in Yosemite. There are lots of sites in Yosemite (nearly 2,000 in summer, 400 year-round)—but there are also lots of people who want them. Reservations at most of Yosemite's campgrounds are required, especially in summer. Most of the park's 15 campgrounds are in Yosemite Valley and along the Tioga Road (Route 120). Glacier Point and Wawona have one each. None of the campgrounds has water or electric hookups, but there are dump stations and shower facilities in the valley area year-round. You can sometimes find a site on the spur of the moment by stopping at the Campground Reservations Office in Yosemite Valley, but don't bank on it. Summer reservations are strongly recommended for Tuolumne Meadows, Hogdon Meadows, Wawona, Crane Flat, Lower Pines, North Pines, and Upper Pines campgrounds. On the 15th of each month you can reserve a site up to five months in advance. Sites at the Sunnyside campground in the valley are available on a first-come basis year-round. | Box 1600, Cumberland, MD | 800/436–7275 | reservations.nps.gov/ | $6–$15 per site | D, MC, V | Reservations office 7–7, PST.

Tenaya Lodge At Yosemite. You could hang a canoe from the four-story, vaulted lobby and lounge area of this hotel—and, in fact, that's exactly what's up there. This contemporary take on the High Sierra lodge has rustically upscale touches—iron chandeliers, exposed timbers, and a huge stone fireplace with plenty of soft seating nearby. Native American rugs add warm earth tones to the mix. The main lodge and wing of rooms and suites looks out across heavily wooded parklands. This lodge books a lot of corporate conferences off-season. In summer, it's a prime spot for families, especially for touring Yosemite's southern sites—the Mariposa Grove and Glacier Point. A nearby stable leads trail rides through the mountain terrain (ask for details at the Activity Desk, in the lobby.) The hotel is 2 mi

© Artville

WATCH OUT

Man meets wilderness in Yosemite. To conserve this great national treasure—and for your own safety—it's important to obey park regulations.

Please don't litter. Discard trash in the proper receptacles—or carry it with you until you can do so. Every tiny candy wrapper is an eyesore in the woods.

Beware of bears. Bears are a very real problem in Yosemite. Wherever you pitch your tent, store all items with a scent (food, coolers, toiletries, water bottles, film canisters, baby wipes) in designated metal bear-proof boxes, or in portable bear canisters (for rent at park stores or at camping supply stores outside the park). If you don't, expect a 300-pound visitor, day or night. Violators will be fined—and Yogi and Boo-Boo may trash your car or tent.

Obey fire regulations. Yosemite Valley may seem pristine, but at times, woodsmoke from thousands of crackling campfires cast an ugly pall and obscure views. To limit pollution, campfires are permitted in Yosemite Valley only between 5PM and 10PM, from the first of May through mid-October. Collecting firewood of any kind is prohibited in the valley. Avoid smoky pine needles and cones; use newspaper as a starter instead. Outside the valley, wood may not be gathered at elevations above 9,600 ft or in sequoia groves. Cutting standing trees or attached limbs, alive or dead, is prohibited, as is the use of chain saws. Campfires are permitted only in established fire rings.

south of Yosemite's South Gate entrance. 2 restaurants, bar. In-room data ports, room service. Cable TV. 2 pools (1 indoor). Hot tub. Exercise equipment, hiking, horseback riding, water sports, boating, bicycles. Cross-country skiing, downhill skiing. Kids' programs (ages 3–12). Laundry facilities. Business services. Pets allowed (fee). | 1122 Rte. 41, Fish Camp | 559/683–6555 or 800/635–5807 | fax 559/683–8684 | www.tenayalodge.com | 244 rooms, 20 suites | $159–$279, $409–$529 suites | AE, D, DC, MC, V.

Wawona Hotel. This 1879 National Historic Landmark is at the southern entrance of the park, near the Mariposa Grove of Big Trees. It's an old-fashioned Victorian hotel with wraparound verandas. Rooms are small and furnished with antiques. Horseback riding trips through surrounding trails are available. Dining room. No air-conditioning, no room phones. Pool. Horseback riding. Golf courses, putting green, tennis. | Rte. 41, Wawona | 209/375–6556 | fax 209/375–6601 | 104 rooms (54 with shared bath) | $94–$120 | AE, D, DC, MC, V.

Yosemite Lodge. This lodge on the Valley floor, near Yosemite Falls, was the former headquarters of the U.S. Cavalry when it protected and maintained the park prior to World War II. Built in 1915, the lodge has glass and wood detailing, designed to blend with the surrounding wilderness. Lodge rooms are larger than standard rooms, and have patios or balconies. Restaurant, bar. No air-conditioning. Pool. Kids' programs. | Northside Dr. | 559/252–4848 | fax 559/456–0542 | www.yosemitepark.com | 226 rooms | $100–$126 | AE, D, DC, MC, V.

Yosemite Valley Tent Cabins and Housekeeping Cabins. More than 400 tent cabins (rough wood frames and canvas walls and roofs) are also available in the valley at Curry Village. Just be forewarned that you'll be cheek-by-jowl with your neighbors and no cooking is allowed. Another option is the rustic—and very popular—housekeeping cabins in the valley. You can book these ahead—up to a year in advance is a good idea. | 559/252–4848 | www.yosemitepark.com | $62–$82 | D, DC, MC, V | Late May–early Oct.; reservations office daily 7–7.

YOUNTVILLE

MAP 3, D7

(Nearby towns also listed: Napa, Rutherford/St. Helena, Sonoma)

Founded by George Yount, the first European settler in Napa Valley, this town retains its quaintness despite a frenzy of development since the mid 1990s. In addition to Napa's biggest museum and most famous maker of sparkling wine, the town is the site of outstanding shops and galleries, several bed and breakfasts, and excellent restaurants—including the renowned French Laundry. Most everything is within walking distance of everything else.

Information: Yountville Chamber of Commerce | 6516 Yount St., 94599 | 707/944–0904 | info@napavalley.com | www.napavalley.com.

Attractions

Adventures Aloft. Drifting high above the Napa Valley is the best way to get a bird's-eye view of the northern California wine country. Balloons take off at sunrise every day (weather permitting) for 1-hr flights that culminate in a champagne breakfast. | 6525 Washington St. | 707/255–8688 | $185 | Daily.

Wineries. A number of wineries make their home in and around Yountville.
★ **Domaine Chandon** makes California's best-known sparkling wine. The guided tour is one of Napa's best as well, taking in the champagne-making process from fermenting the wine to getting that big cork inside the bottle. The winery also has an acclaimed restaurant. | 1 California Dr. | 707/944–2280 | fax 707/944–1123 | www.dchandon.com | Free; fee for tasting | Daily 10–6; tours on the hour.

Dining

Diner. Mexican. The outside of this one-story eatery is pink with an overhang and patio in front. Inside, you can eat at a countertop, a booth, or table. From huevos rancheros and walnut pancakes with fresh fruit to quesadillas, burritos, and burgers, this restaurant skillfully mixes Mexican and California cooking. At dinner the chef tosses in a few seafood specials. | 6476 Washington St. | 707/944–2626 | fax 707/944–0605 | Closed Monday | $8– $13 | MC, V.

★ **French Laundry.** French. You'll have to plan ahead if you want to eat in this restaurant in a two-story, stone-and-timber house—superstar Thomas Keller's work been acclaimed by food lovers nationwide as among the best in the country. Every meal consists of many tiny superbly conceived and sparklingly executed courses; over the hours it all adds up to a major feast that's at once surprising, sophisticated, and intelligent. Ingredients are the freshest and the imagination quotient at work in the kitchen is high. | 6640 Washington St. | 707/944–2380 | Reservations essential | No lunch Mon.–Thurs. | $100–$125 prix fixe | AE, MC, V.

Livefire. American. Earthy colors like those painted on this terra-cotta building underscore the cooking style in this unusual restaurant. There's a fireplace in the main dining room, an exhibition kitchen as you walk in, and outdoor eating on the patio. Chicken, fish, and ribs are prepared in a Chinese smoker or a rotisserie fired by almond, cherry, and walnut wood chips, and then served in generous portions. | 5518 Washington St. | 707/944–1500 | fax 707/944–1504 | www.livefireyountville.com | $22–$33 | AE, D, DC, MC, V.

Lodging

Maison Fleurie. Rooms are small in the ivy-covered 19th-century brick building that's one of three in the inn, but they're filled with Victorian-style furnishings. The inn's within walking distance of the best restaurants in town. Pool. Hot tub. Bicycles. | 6529 Yount St. | 707/ 944–2056 or 800/788–0369 | fax 707/944–9342 | info@foursisters.com | www.foursisters.com | 13 rooms | $110–$260 | AE, DC, MC, V.

Petit Logis. At this inn tucked into a courtyard in the heart of town you and a significant other can relax in a double hot tub, or share a bottle of wine in front of the fireplace. Furnishings vary from room to room but the feeling is generally European and there's art, high ceilings, and pastel murals. Transformed in 1997 from a collection of shops, it's a cross between a bed and breakfast and a motel, with luxurious quarters yet total privacy. Refrigerators, in-room hot tubs, cable TV. | 6527 Yount St. | 707/944–2332 | fax 707/944–2388 | www.petitlogis.com | 5 rooms | $150–$195 | MC, V.

Vintage Inn. Terrycloth robes, a bottle of wine, afternoon snacks, and champagne with breakfasts warm the welcome at this inn, one of three upscale sister properties on 23 acres, and every room has a ceiling fan and a wood-burning fireplace. The coffee in in-room coffeemakers is Starbucks. Complimentary Continental breakfast. In-room data ports, cable TV. Outdoor pool. Spa. Gym. 2 tennis courts. Laundry service. | 6541 Washington St. | 800/351–1133 | fax 707/944–1617 | www.vintageinn.com | 68 rooms, 8 suites, 4 villas | $250–$385.

YREKA

MAP 3, C1

(Nearby towns also listed: Dunsmuir, Mt. Shasta)

In 1851 some of the richest mines of the California gold rush turned the northern end of the Shasta Valley into a teeming boomtown. Today the gold is mostly tapped out, but the 7,000 residents of Yreka (pronounced "Why-reeka") have lovingly restored more than 75 Victorian-era wooden buildings in its downtown Historic District, making this a worthy destination for anyone interested in California history and architecture.

Information: Yreka Chamber of Commerce | 117 West Miner St., 96097-2917 | 530/842–1649 | a-yreka@inreach.com | www.yrekachamber.com.

Attractions

Siskiyou County Courthouse. The centerpiece of Yreka's downtown Historic District is the Siskiyou County Courthouse, a three-story neo-Classical structure completed in 1857. The building is one of the oldest courthouses in the state, and its lobby has the largest display of natural gold nuggets south of Alaska. | 311 4th St. | Free | Weekdays 8–5.

Siskiyou County Museum. The museum brings to life the story of Yreka's settlement, with indoor and outdoor exhibits, including re-creations of pioneer cabins, stores, and a schoolhouse. | 910 S. Main St. | 530/842–3836 | $1 | Tues.–Sat., 9–5, outdoor exhibits closed in inclement weather.

Yreka Western Railroad. Known to locals as "The Blue Goose," this vintage steam-powered train departs from Yreka's 1910 depot on a 3-hr round-trip excursion across the Shasta Valley to the Old West rail terminal of Montague. Views along the way include 1850s cattle ranches, a working lumber mill, the Shasta River, and the 14,000-ft summit of Mount Shasta (30 mi to the south). | 300 E Miner St. | 800/973–5277 | $12.25 | June–Aug. Wed.–Sun. 11AM departure, Sept.–Oct. weekends only 11AM departure, closed Nov.–May.

Dining

Boston Shaft. Continental. This large restaurant at the south end of town is named for the former gold mine on which it's built. Its owners are Swiss, and are praised locally for the European spin they put on hearty meat dishes like prime rib, veal, and pork. | 1801 Fort Jones Rd. | 530/842–5768 | $9–$18 | AE, D, DC, MC, V.

Casa Ramos. Mexican. This noisy, family-style restaurant at the north end of town is particularly popular with locals, who come in search of specialties like *molcajete* (mortar-and-pestle) soup. | 715 N Main St. | 530/842–7172 | $5–$9 | AE, D, MC, V.

Purple Plum. American. Near the central I-5 off-ramp in the heart of downtown, this casual restaurant serves up family-oriented American fare 24 hrs a day. The dinner menu has a number of fish entrées. | 105 E. Miner St. | 530/842–0640 | $9–$15 | AE, D, MC, V.

Lodging

Amerihost Inn Yreka. This 1997 hostelry is off I-5 on the south edge of town. Complimentary breakfast. Some in-room hot tubs, cable TV. Indoor pool. Sauna. Business services. Pets allowed. | 148 Moonlit Oaks Ave. | 530/841–1300 or 800/434–5800 | fax 530/841–0399 | amerihostyreka@snowcrest.net | www.amerihostinn.com | 61 rooms | $64–139 | AE, D, MC, V.

Klamath Motor Lodge. This one- and two-story motel with a brick and stucco facade has been owned by the same family since it was built in 1962. It's five blocks south of the Historic District on a 1-acre lot landscaped with flowers and a towering shade tree. Picnic area. Microwaves, refrigerators, cable TV. Pool. No pets. | 1111 S Main St. | 530/842–2751 | fax 530/842–4703 | 28 rooms | $55–58 | AE, D, MC, V.

Wayside Inn. This single-story white brick motel, ½ mi south of downtown, was built in the 1950s and remodeled in 1988. The lawn behind the motel is available for picnicking. Some kitchenettes, refrigerators, cable TV. Outdoor pool. Hot tub. Pets allowed (fee). | 1235 S. Main St. | 530/842–4412 or 800/795–7974 | 44 rooms | $45–$78 | AE, D, MC, V.

YUCCA VALLEY

(Nearby towns also listed: Desert Hot Springs, Joshua Tree National Park, Palm Springs, Twentynine Palms)

Yucca Valley, one of the high-desert communities north of Palm Springs, proudly points to its own three-star Oasis of Eden Inn on the south side of town as a place just as eye-popping as its posh Palm Springs neighbors. If you're a space case, you'll be especially happy in this town, home of the 35-ft-high, 50-ft-diameter domed Integratron. Built in the 1940s by George Van Tassel, the unfinished device was intended to reverse human aging and serve as a conduit to extraterrestrials. In the 1950s Van Tassel held Giant Rock Spaceshift Conventions in an attempt to contact UFOs; the gatherings drew crowds topping 10,000 (spectators, not aliens). New Age workshops still take place there today.

Information: Yucca Valley Chamber of Commerce | 55569 Twentynine Palms Hwy., 92284 | 760/365–6323 | fax 760/365–0763 | chamber@yuccavalley.org | www.yuccavalley.com.

Attractions

Hi-Desert Nature Museum. Live animal displays, a rock and mineral collection, and Native American artifacts are on display. | 57116 Twentynine Palms Hwy. | 760/369–7212 | www.yuccavalley.com/organization/museum | By donation | Tues.–Sun. 10–5.

Integratron. Only in the desert, some might say. Former Lockheed designer and extraterrestrial-seeker George Van Tassel, who built this dome-shape structure in the late 1940s, believed it would not only contact E.T., but "recharge energy into living cell structure, to bring about longer life with youthful energy." Today's consortium of owners, who offer tours and rent the building out for special events, still believe the Integratron offers "a very powerful vortex for physical and spritual healing." Certainly, there is nothing else like it. The dome is 12 mi north of town off Route 247. | End of Belfield Rd. at Linn Rd. | 760/364–3126 | $5 | First three Sundays of the month, 2–4 PM.

Lodging

Desert View. Budget-minded travelers will find that this small hotel is peaceful, well-maintained, and close to restaurants. Complimentary Continental breakfast. Cable TV. Pool. Business services. | 57471 Primrose Dr. | 760/365–9706 | fax 760/365–6021 | 14 rooms | $42–$45 | AE, D, DC, MC, V.

Oasis of Eden Inn and Suites. An unusual inn ½ mi from the Joshua Tree National Park, 14 of the rooms here with in-room spas have names like Orient, Ancient Rome, Deep South, New York New York, and Persian. The "Safari" has a big four-poster bed with gauzy canopy and huge urns filled with palm fronds. Complimentary Continental breakfast. Some kitchenettes, refrigerators, some in-room hot tubs, cable TV, in-room VCRs (and movies). Pool. Hot tub. Business services. Pets allowed. | 56377 Twentynine Palms Hwy. | 760/365–6321 or 800/606–6686 | fax 760/365–9592 | www.desertgold.com/eden/eden.html | 20 rooms | $70–$200 | AE, D, DC, MC, V.

Super 8 Motel. This hotel is 14 mi west of Twentynine Palms and 10 mi north of Desert Hot Springs. Restaurant. Pool. Pets allowed. | Rte. 62 at Barberry Ave. | 760/228–1773 | fax 760/365–7799 | 48 rooms | $44–$56 | AE, D, DC, MC, V.

Index

Hilton Beach and Tennis Resort (San Diego, CA), 463
Hilton Del Mar (Del Mar, CA), 146
Hilton Garden Inn (Cupertino, CA), 135
Hilton Garden Inn (Gilroy, CA), 181
Hilton Garden Inn (Roseville, CA), 420
Hilton Garden Inn–Six Flags (Valencia, CA), 607
Hilton Harbor Island (San Diego, CA), 458
Hilton Inn–Sacramento Arden West (Sacramento, CA), 436
Hilton Irvine/Orange County Airport (Irvine, CA), 219
Hilton Mission Valley (San Diego, CA), 458
Hilton Newark–Fremont (Fremont, CA), 171
Hilton Plaza at Fisherman's Wharf (San Francisco, CA), 521
Hilton Pleasanton at the Club (Pleasanton, CA), 398
Hilton Suites (Orange, CA), 353
Hilton Waterfront Beach Resort (Huntington Beach, CA), 207
Hilton–Burbank Airport (Burbank, CA), 81
Hilton-South Bay (Torrance, CA), 597
Historic City Cemetery (Sacramento, CA), 426
Historic D Street (Marysville, CA), 293
Historic Fort Ross (Jenner, CA), 224
Historic Judge C.F. Lott House (Oroville, CA), 354
Historic Santa Maria Inn (Santa Maria, CA), 552
Historic Templeton (Atascadero, CA), 39
Hitching Post (Solvang, CA), 574
Hob Nob Hill (San Diego, CA), 450
Hofsas House (Carmel, CA), 101
Holbrooke Hotel (Grass Valley, CA), 184
Holiday House (Tahoe Vista, CA), 590
Holiday Inn (Auburn, CA), 42
Holiday Inn (Barstow, CA), 49
Holiday Inn (Chico, CA), 110
Holiday Inn (Laguna Beach, CA), 237
Holiday Inn (Modesto, CA), 306
Holiday Inn (San Clemente, CA), 438
Holiday Inn (Santa Monica, CA), 555
Holiday Inn (West Covina, CA), 618
Holiday Inn Anaheim at the Park (Anaheim, CA), 31
Holiday Inn at Orange County Airport (Santa Ana, CA), 541
Holiday Inn at Six Flags Marine World (Vallejo, CA), 608
Holiday Inn Bayside (San Diego, CA), 458
Holiday Inn Big Bear Chateau (Big Bear Lake, CA), 65
Holiday Inn Brentwood-Bel Air (Los Angeles, CA), 276
Holiday Inn Carlsbad by the Sea (Carlsbad, CA), 95
Holiday Inn City Center (Los Angeles, CA), 276

Holiday Inn Downtown (Los Angeles, CA), 275
Holiday Inn Express (Anaheim, CA), 31
Holiday Inn Express (Chula Vista, CA), 111
Holiday Inn Express (Half Moon Bay, CA), 191
Holiday Inn Express (Los Angeles, CA), 276
Holiday Inn Express (Madera, CA), 284
Holiday Inn Express (Manhattan Beach, CA), 290
Holiday Inn Express (Marina Del Rey, CA), 292
Holiday Inn Express (Mill Valley, CA), 303
Holiday Inn Express (Monterey, CA), 312
Holiday Inn Express (Mountain View, CA), 320
Holiday Inn Express (Palm Desert, CA), 366
Holiday Inn Express (San Mateo, CA), 533
Holiday Inn Express (Santa Nella, CA), 558
Holiday Inn Express (Santa Rosa, CA), 562
Holiday Inn Express (Simi Valley, CA), 573
Holiday Inn Express Dana Point Edgewater (Dana Point, CA), 137
Holiday Inn Express–Marina Del Rey/Venice (Venice, CA), 610
Holiday Inn Fresno–Airport (Fresno, CA), 174
Holiday Inn Hotel and Suites–Mesquite (Santa Maria, CA), 552
Holiday Inn Mission Valley/Stadium (San Diego, CA), 458
Holiday Inn on the Bay (San Diego, CA), 463
Holiday Inn Rancho Bernardo (Rancho Bernardo, CA), 406
Holiday Inn Rancho Bernardo (San Diego, CA), 459
Holiday Inn San Francisco Bay Bridge (Emeryville, CA), 156
Holiday Inn San Pedro L.A. Harbor (San Pedro, CA), 534
Holiday Inn Select (Fairfield, CA), 164
Holiday Inn Select–Riverside Convention Center (Riverside, CA), 419
Holiday Inn Select–Union Square (San Francisco, CA), 518
Holiday Inn South San Jose (San Jose, CA), 529
Holiday Inn Swan Court (Selma, CA), 567
Holiday Inn–Airport (Oakland, CA), 345
Holiday Inn–Beverly Garland (North Hollywood, CA), 336
Holiday Inn–Capitol Plaza (Sacramento, CA), 434
Holiday Inn–Conference Center (Buena Park, CA), 79
Holiday Inn–Costa Mesa (Costa Mesa, CA), 128
Holiday Inn–Fisherman's Wharf (San Francisco, CA), 517
Holiday Select Inn (Fullerton, CA), 176
Hollywood and Vine (Hollywood [L.A.], CA), 201

Hollywood Bowl (Hollywood [L.A.], CA), 201
Hollywood Entertainment Museum (Hollywood [L.A.], CA), 201
Hollywood Heritage Museum (Hollywood [L.A.], CA), 201
Hollywood Memorial Park Cemetery Mortuary (Hollywood [L.A.], CA), 202
Hollywood Orchid Suites Hotel (Hollywood [L.A.], CA), 205
Hollywood Wax Museum (Hollywood [L.A.], CA), 202
Holman Ranch Trail Rides (Carmel Valley, CA), 103
Homemade Café (Berkeley, CA), 57
The Homestead (Carmel, CA), 101
The Homestead (Oakhurst, CA), 338
Homestead B&B (Julian, CA), 230
Homestead Inn B&B (Twentynine Palms, CA), 603
Homestead Village (Brea, CA), 77
Homestead Village Guest Studios (Glendale, CA), 182
Hong Kong Flower Lounge (San Francisco, CA), 494
Honor Mansion (Healdsburg, CA), 197
Hope–Merrill House (Geyserville, CA), 180
Horizon Inn (Carmel, CA), 101
Horn of Zeese (Boonville, CA), 74
Hornblower Dining Yachts (San Francisco, CA), 482
Hornblower's *Tahoe Queen* (South Lake Tahoe, CA), 582
Horseback Riding (El Centro, CA), 153
Horton Grand (San Diego, CA), 459
Horton Plaza (San Diego, CA), 447
Hot Air Balloon Rides (Napa, CA), 325
Hot Air Balloon Rides (Temecula, CA), 591
Hotel Arcata (Arcata, CA), 38
Hotel Atwater (Catalina Island, CA), 105
Hotel Bel-Air (Los Angeles, CA), 278
Hotel Beresford (San Francisco, CA), 512
Hotel Beresford Arms (San Francisco, CA), 512
Hotel Bohème (San Francisco, CA), 513
Hotel California (Santa Monica, CA), 555
Hotel Carmel (Santa Monica, CA), 556
Hotel Carter (Eureka, CA), 163
Hotel Casa del Mar (Santa Monica, CA), 556
Hotel de Anza (San Jose, CA), 529
Hotel Del Capri (Los Angeles, CA), 275
Hotel Del Coronado (Coronado, CA), 124
Hotel Del Sol (San Francisco, CA), 509, 513
Hotel Diva (San Francisco, CA), 518
Hotel Durant (Berkeley, CA), 59
Hotel Figueroa (Los Angeles, CA), 275
Hotel Hermosa (Redondo Beach, CA), 417
Hotel Huntington Beach (Huntington Beach, CA), 207
Hotel Inverness (Inverness, CA), 217
Hotel La Jolla (La Jolla, CA), 243

Notes

Notes

Notes

Notes

Notes

Notes

Notes

Notes

Notes

TALK TO US

Fill out this quick survey and receive a free *Fodor's How to Pack* (while supplies last)

1 Which Road Guide did you purchase?
(Check all that apply.)

- ❏ AL/AR/LA/MS/TN
- ❏ AZ/CO/NM
- ❏ CA
- ❏ CT/MA/RI
- ❏ DE/DC/MD/PA/VA
- ❏ FL
- ❏ GA/NC/SC
- ❏ ID/MT/NV/UT/WY
- ❏ IL/IA/MO/WI
- ❏ IN/KY/MI/OH/WV
- ❏ KS/OK/TX
- ❏ ME/NH/VT
- ❏ MN/NE/ND/SD
- ❏ NJ/NY
- ❏ OR/WA

2 How did you learn about the Road Guides?

- ❏ TV ad
- ❏ Radio ad
- ❏ Newspaper or magazine ad
- ❏ Newspaper or magazine article
- ❏ TV or radio feature
- ❏ Bookstore display/clerk recommendation
- ❏ Recommended by family/friend
- ❏ Other:_____

3 Did you use other guides for your trip?

- ❏ AAA
- ❏ Compass American Guide
- ❏ Fodor's
- ❏ Frommer's
- ❏ Insiders' Guide
- ❏ Mobil
- ❏ Moon Handbook
- ❏ Other:_____

4 Did you use any of the following for planning?

- ❏ Tourism offices   ❏ Internet   ❏ Travel agent

5 Did you buy a Road Guide for (check one):

- ❏ Leisure trip
- ❏ Business trip
- ❏ Mix of business and leisure

6 Where did you buy your Road Guide?

- ❏ Bookstore
- ❏ Other store
- ❏ On-line
- ❏ Borrowed from a friend
- ❏ Borrowed from a library
- ❏ Other:_____

7 Why did you buy a Road Guide? (Check all that apply.)

- ❏ Number of cities/towns listed
- ❏ Comprehensive coverage
- ❏ Number of lodgings   ❏ Driving tours
- ❏ Number of restaurants ❏ Maps
- ❏ Number of attractions ❏ Fodor's brand name
- ❏ Other:_____

8 Did you use this guide primarily:

- ❏ For pretrip planning   ❏ While traveling
- ❏ For planning and while traveling

9 What was the duration of your trip?

- ❏ 2-3 days
- ❏ 4-6 days
- ❏ 7-10 days
- ❏ 11 or more days
- ❏ Taking more than 1 trip

10 Did you use the guide to select

- ❏ Hotels
- ❏ Restaurants

11 Did you stay primarily in a

- ❏ Hotel
- ❏ Motel
- ❏ Resort
- ❏ Bed-and-breakfast
- ❏ RV/camper
- ❏ Hostel
- ❏ Campground
- ❏ Dude ranch
- ❏ With family or friends
- ❏ Other:_____

12 What sights and activities did you most enjoy?

- ❏ Historical sights
- ❏ Sports
- ❏ National parks
- ❏ State parks
- ❏ Attractions off the beaten path
- ❏ Shopping
- ❏ Theaters
- ❏ Museums
- ❏ Major cities

13 How much did you spend per adult for this trip?

- ❏ Less than $500
- ❏ $501-$750
- ❏ $751-$1,000
- ❏ More than $1,000

14 How many traveled in your party?

___ Adults   ___ Children   ___ Pets

15 Did you

- ❏ Fly to destination
- ❏ Drive your own vehicle
- ❏ Rent a car
- ❏ Rent a van or RV
- ❏ Take a train
- ❏ Take a bus

16 How many miles did you travel round-trip?

- ❏ Less than 100
- ❏ 101-300
- ❏ 301-500
- ❏ 501-750
- ❏ 751-1,000
- ❏ More than 1,000

17 What items did you take on your vacation?

- ❏ Traveler's checks
- ❏ Credit card
- ❏ Gasoline card
- ❏ Phone card
- ❏ Camera
- ❏ Digital camera
- ❏ Cell phone
- ❏ Computer
- ❏ PDA
- ❏ Other

18 Would you use Fodor's Road Guides again?

- ❏ Yes
- ❏ No

19 How would you like to see Road Guides changed?

❐ More ❐ Less Dining
❐ More ❐ Less Lodging
❐ More ❐ Less Sports
❐ More ❐ Less Activities
❐ More ❐ Less Attractions
❐ More ❐ Less Shopping
❐ More ❐ Less Driving tours
❐ More ❐ Less Maps
❐ More ❐ Less Historical information
❐ Other: ____________________

20 Tell us about yourself.

❐ Male ❐ Female

Age:

❐ 18-24 ❐ 35-44 ❐ 55-64
❐ 25-34 ❐ 45-54 ❐ Over 65

Income:

❐ Less than $25,000 ❐ $50,001-$75,000
❐ $25,001-$50,000 ❐ More than $75,00

Name: ____________________ E-mail: ____________________

Address: ____________________ City: ____________ State: ____ Zip: ______

Fodor's Travel Publications
Attn: Road Guide Survey
280 Park Avenue
New York, NY 10017

The information herein will be treated in confidence. Names and addresses will not be released to mailing-list houses or other organizations.

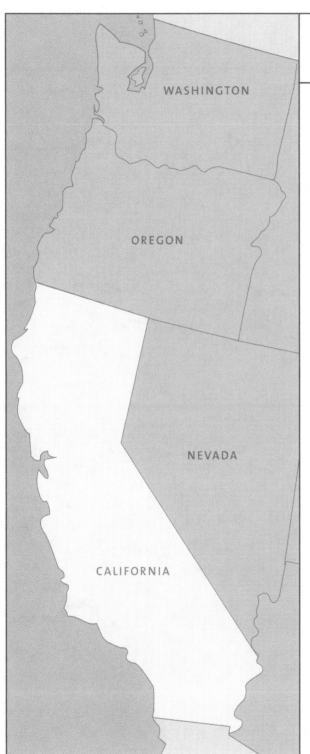

Atlas

WASHINGTON

OREGON

NEVADA

CALIFORNIA

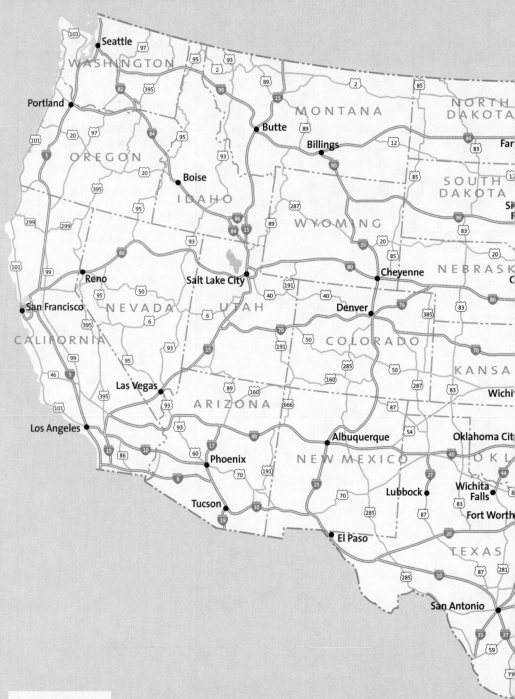

U. S. Highways

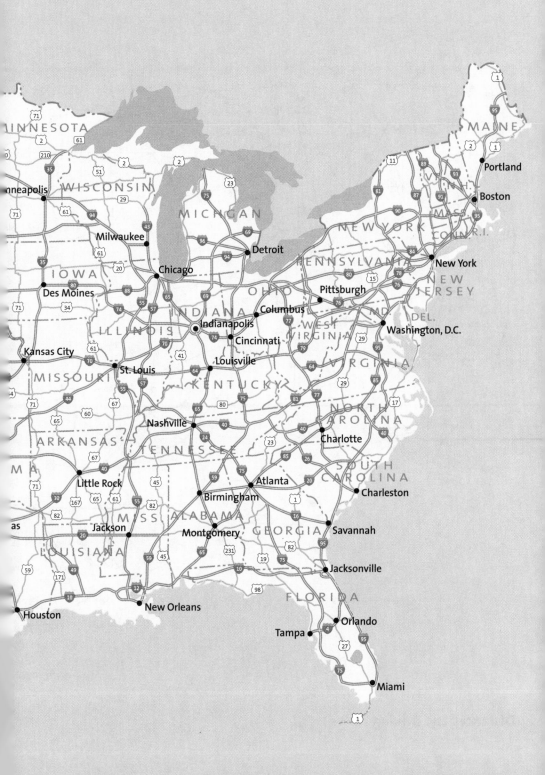

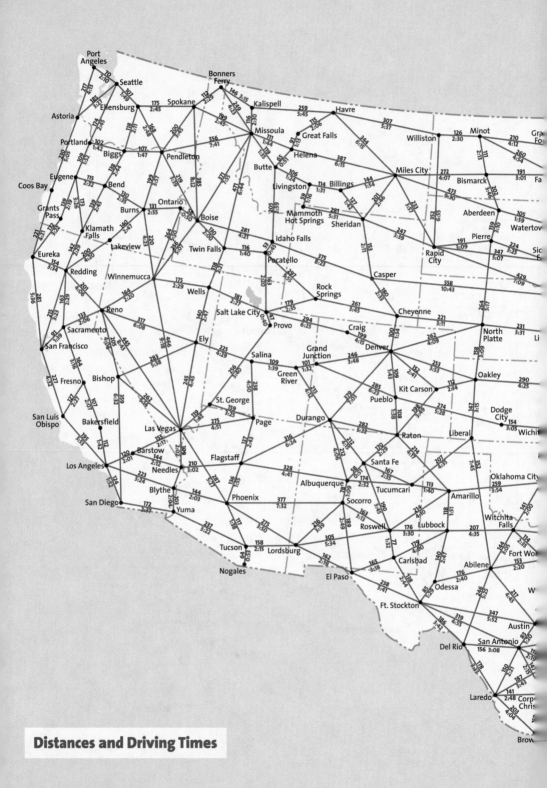

Distances and Driving Times

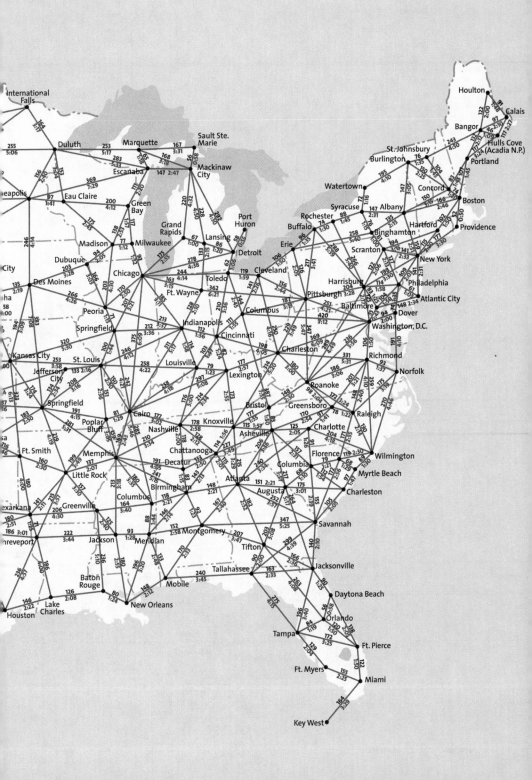

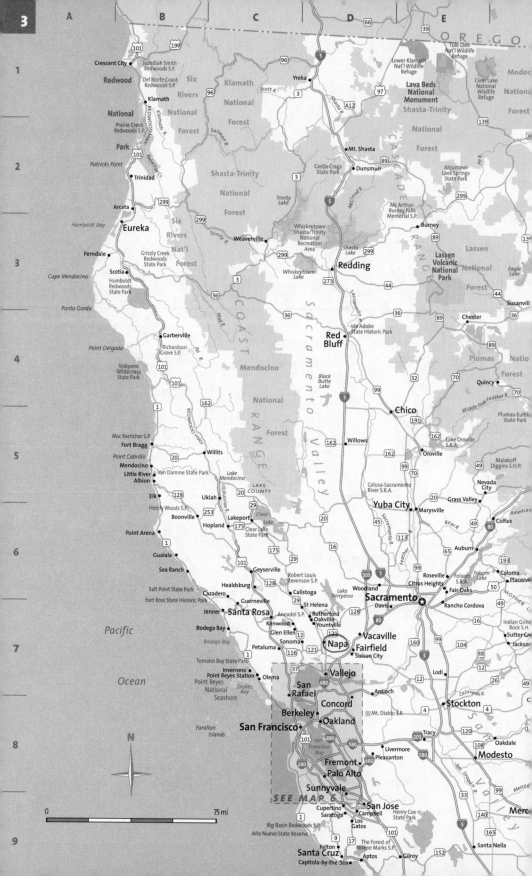

California – Cities and Towns

Albion	B5
Alturas	F2
Anaheim	J15
Antioch	D7
Aptos	D9
Arcadia	See Map 9
Arcata	B2
Atascadero	F12
Auburn	E6
Avalon	I16
Baker	L12
Bakersfield	H12
Barstow	J13
Beaumont	K15
Benicia	See Map 6
Berkeley	C8
Beverly Hills	See Map 9
Big Bear Lake	K14
Big Sur	D11
Bishop	I9
Blythe	N15
Bodega Bay	B7
Boonville	B6
Borrego Springs	L16
Brea	See Map 9
Bridgeport	H7
Buena Park	See Map 9
Burbank	H7
Burlingame	See Map 6
Burney	E3
Calabasas	See Map 9
Calexico	M17
Calistoga	C6
Camarillo	H14
Cambria	E12
Campbell	D9
Capitola	D9
Carlsbad	J16
Carmel	D10
Carmel Valley	D10
Cazadero	C6
Cerritos	See Map 9
Chester	E4
Chico	E5
Chula Vista	K17
Citrus Heights	E6
Claremont	See Map 9
Coalinga	F11
Colfax	E6
Coloma	F6
Columbia	F8
Concord	D8
Corona	J15
Corona Del Mar	I15
Coronado	J17
Corte Madera	See Map 6
Costa Mesa	See Map 9
Crescent City	B1
Crestline	J14
Culver City	See Map 9
Cupertino	See Map 6
Dana Point	J15
Davis	D7
Del Mar	J16
Desert Hot Springs	K15
Dunsmuir	D2
El Cajon	K17
El Centro	M17
Elk	B5
Emeryville	See Map 6
Encinitas	J16
Encino	See Map 9
Escondido	K16
Essex	M13
Eureka	B3
Fair Oaks	E6
Fairfield	D7
Fallbrook	J16
Felton	D9
Ferndale	A3
Fort Bragg	B5
Foster City	See Map 6
Fremont	D8
Fresno	G10
Fullerton	See Map 9
Garberville	B4
Garden Grove	See Map 9
Geyserville	C6
Gilroy	E9
Glendale	See Map 9
Glendora	See Map 9
Glen Ellen	C7
Grass Valley	E5
Gualala	B6
Guerneville	C7
Half Moon Bay	See Map 6
Hanford	G11
Hayward	See Map 6
Healdsburg	C6
Hemet	K15
Hollister	E10
Hollywood	I14
Hopland	C6
Huntington Beach	See Map 9
Idyllwild	K15
Indian Wells	L15
Indio	L15
Inverness	C7
Irvine	I15
Jackson	F7
Jamestown	F8
Jenner	C7
Julian	K16
June Lake	H8
Kenwood	C7
Kernville	I12
King City	E11
Klamath	B1
Lafayette	See Map 6
Laguna Beach	J15
La Habra	See Map 9
La Jolla	J17
Lake Arrowhead	J14
Lakeport	C6
Lancaster	I13
La Quinta	L15
Larkspur	See Map 6
Lee Vining	H8
Little River	B5
Livermore	D8
Lodi	E7
Lompoc	F13
Lone Pine	I10
Long Beach	I15
Los Altos	See Map 6
Los Angeles	I15
Los Gatos	D9
Los Olivos	F13
Madera	F9
Malibu	See Map 9
Mammoth Lakes	H8
Manhattan Beach	See Map 9
Marina del Rey	See Map 9
Martinez	See Map 6
Marysville	E6
Mendocino	B5
Menlo Park	See Map 6
Merced	F9
Millbrae	See Map 6
Mill Valley	See Map 6
Milpitas	See Map 6
Mission Viejo	J15
Modesto	E8
Monterey	D10
Morro Bay	E12
Mountain View	See Map 6
Mt. Shasta	D2
Murphys	F7
Napa	D7
Needles	N13
Nevada City	E5
Newport Beach	See Map 9
North Hollywood	See Map 9
Oakdale	F8
Oakhurst	G9
Oakland	D8
Oakville	D7
Oceanside	J16
Ojai	H14
Olema	C7
Olympic Valley	F6
Ontario	J15
Orange	See Map 9
Oroville	E5
Oxnard	H14
Pacific Beach	J17
Pacific Grove	D10
Pacific Palisades	See Map 9
Palm Desert	K15
Palm Springs	K15
Palmdale	I14
Palo Alto	D8
Pasadena	I14
Paso Robles	F12
Pebble Beach	D10
Petaluma	C7
Pine Valley	K17
Pismo Beach	F13
Placerville	F6
Pleasanton	D8
Point Arena	B6
Point Reyes Station	C7
Pomona	J14
Porterville	H11
Port Hueneme	H14
Quincy	E4
Rancho Bernardo	K16
Rancho Cordova	E7
Rancho Cucamonga	J14
Rancho Mirage	K15
Rancho Santa Fe	J16
Red Bluff	D4
Redding	D3
Redlands	K14
Redondo Beach	See Map 9
Redwood City	See Map 6
Riverside	J15
Roseville	E6
Rutherford	D7
Sacramento	D7
St. Helena	D7
Salinas	E10
San Bernardino	J14
San Clemente	J16
San Diego	J17
San Fernando	I14
San Francisco	C8
San Gabriel	See Map 9
San Jose	D9
San Juan Bautista	E10
San Juan Capistrano	J15
San Luis Obispo	F12
San Marino	See Map 9
San Mateo	See Map 6
San Pedro	See Map 9
San Rafael	C7
San Ramon	See Map 6
San Simeon	E12
San Ysidro	K17
Santa Ana	J15
Santa Barbara	G14
Santa Clara	See Map 6
Santa Cruz	D9
Santa Maria	F13
Santa Monica	H15
Santa Nella	E9
Santa Rosa	C7
Saratoga	See Map 6
Sausalito	See Map 6
Scotia	B3
Sea Ranch	B6
Seal Beach	See Map 9
Selma	G10
Sherman Oaks	See Map 9
Simi Valley	H14
Solvang	F13
Sonoma	C7
Sonora	F8
South Lake Tahoe	G6
Squaw Valley	F5
Stockton	E8
Studio City	See Map 9
Siusun City	D7
Sunnyvale	D8
Susanville	F3
Sutter Creek	F7
Tahoe City	G6
Tahoe Vista	G5
Tehachapi	I13
Temecula	K15
Thousand Oaks	H14
Three Rivers	H10
Tiburon	See Map 6
Torrance	See Map 9
Tracy	E8
Trinidad	B2
Truckee	F5
Twentynine Palms	L14
Ukiah	C5
Universal City	See Map 9
Vacaville	D7
Valencia	I14
Vallejo	D7
Van Nuys	See Map 9
Venice	See Map 9
Ventura	G14
Victorville	J13
Visalia	H11
Walnut Creek	See Map 6
Watsonville	D10
Weaverville	C3
West Covina	See Map 9
West Hollywood	See Map 9
Westwood Village	See Map 9
Whittier	See Map 9
Willits	C5
Woodland	D6
Woodland Hills	See Map 9
Yountville	D7
Yreka	C1
Yuba City	D6
Yucca Valley	K14

Copyright ©2001 by Maps.com and Fodors LLC

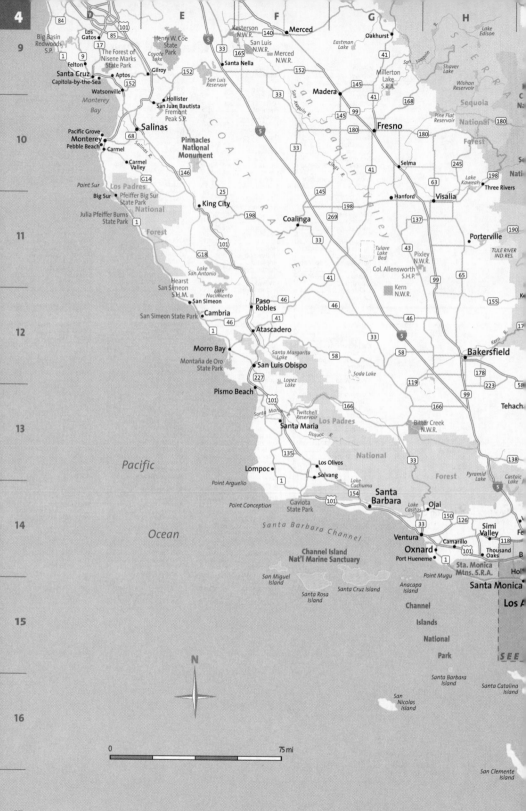

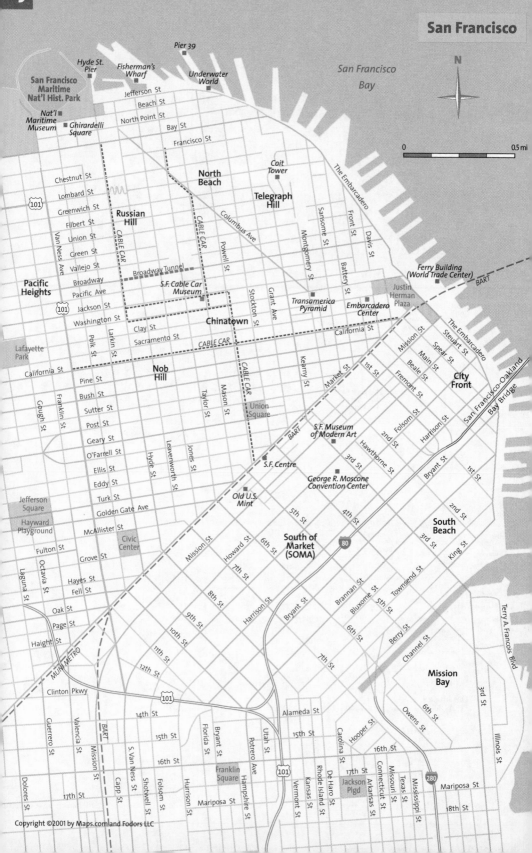

San Francisco

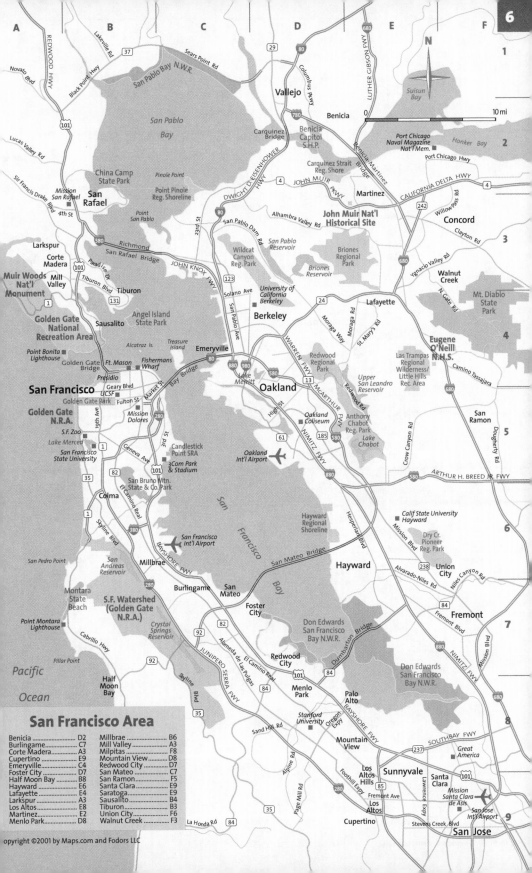

A B C D E F

1

2

3

4

5

6

7

8

9

N

0   10 mi

REDWOOD HWY
Lakeville Rd
Black Point Hwy
37
Sears Point Rd
29
Columbus Pkwy
80
780
LUTHER GIBSON FWY
580

Novato Blvd

San Pablo Bay N.W.R.

Vallejo

Benicia

Suisun Bay

Port Chicago Naval Magazine Nat'l Mem.
Honker Bay
Port Chicago Hwy

Lucas Valley Rd
101
San Pablo Bay

Carquinez Bridge

Benicia Capitol S.H.P.

CALIFORNIA DELTA HWY
4

Sir Francis Drake Blvd
Mission San Rafael
China Camp State Park
Pinole Point
Point Pinole Reg. Shoreline
Carquinez Strait Reg. Shore
DWIGHT D. EISENHOWER HWY
JOHN MUIR PKWY
Martinez
Benicia-Martinez Bridge
Willow Pass Rd
242
Concord

San Rafael
4th St
Point San Pablo
80
Alhambra Valley Rd
John Muir Nat'l Historical Site
Clayton Rd
3

Larkspur
580
Richmond
San Rafael Bridge
23rd St
San Pablo Dam Rd
Wildcat Canyon Reg. Park
San Pablo Reservoir
Briones Regional Park
Briones Reservoir
680
Ygnacio Valley Rd
Walnut Creek
N. Gate Rd
Mt. Diablo State Park

Corte Madera
Paradise Dr
JOHN KNOX FWY
123
Solano Ave
University of California Berkeley
24
Lafayette
Moraga Way
Moraga Rd
St. Mary's Rd
Camino Tassajara

Muir Woods Nat'l Monument
101
Mill Valley
Tiburon Blvd
131
Tiburon
San Pablo Ave
Berkeley
Redwood Regional Park
Las Trampas Regional Wilderness/ Little Hills Rec. Area
680
4

1
Sausalito
Angel Island State Park
Treasure Island
Emeryville
WARREN FWY
13
Upper San Leandro Reservoir
San Ramon

Golden Gate National Recreation Area
Alcatraz Is.
880
980
80
Lake Merritt
Oakland
Redwood Rd
Anthony Chabot Reg. Park
Lake Chabot
Camino Tassajara

Point Bonita Lighthouse
Golden Gate Bridge
Ft. Mason
Fishermans Wharf
Bay Bridge
High St
Oakland Coliseum
185
580
Crow Canyon Rd
Dougherty Rd

Presidio
Geary Blvd
UCSF
Market St
NIMITZ FWY
MacARTHUR FWY
San Ramon

San Francisco
Golden Gate Park
Fulton St
61
5

Golden Gate N.R.A.
19th Ave
Mission Dolores
I-280
Candlestick Point SRA
Oakland Int'l Airport
880
ARTHUR H. BREED JR. FWY
580

S.F. Zoo
Lake Merced
I-5 Dr
3Com Park & Stadium
Hesperian Blvd

San Francisco State University
Geneva Ave
Hayward Regional Shoreline
Calif State University Hayward
Mission Blvd
Dry Cr. Pioneer Reg. Park
6

Colma
82
El Camino Real
101
San Bruno Mtn. State & Co. Park
Hayward
Alvarado-Niles Rd
238
Union City

1
35
Skyline Blvd
San Andreas Reservoir
BAYSHORE FWY
San Francisco Int'l Airport
San Mateo Bridge
Niles Canyon Rd
NIMITZ FWY
Mission Blvd

San Pedro Point
380
Millbrae
Fremont Blvd
84
Fremont
680
7

Montara State Beach
S.F. Watershed (Golden Gate N.R.A.)
280
Burlingame
San Mateo
Foster City
San Francisco Bay
Don Edwards San Francisco Bay N.W.R.
Dumbarton Bridge
880

Point Montara Lighthouse
Cabrillo Hwy
Crystal Springs Reservoir
92
82
Redwood City
101
Don Edwards San Francisco Bay N.W.R.
680

Pillar Point
92
JUNIPERO SERRA FWY
Alameda de las Pulgas
El Camino Real
Menlo Park
84
Palo Alto
BAYSHORE FWY
SOUTHBAY FWY
Great America
237

Pacific Ocean
Half Moon Bay
35
Skyline Blvd
84
Sand Hill Rd
Stanford University
Oregon Expy
Mountain View
Lawrence Expy
Santa Clara
101

La Honda Rd
Alpine Rd
Page Mill Rd
Los Altos Hills
Sunnyvale
Mission Santa Clara de Asis
San Jose Int'l Airport

35
Foothill Expy
280
Fremont Ave
85
Los Altos
Stevens Creek Blvd
San Jose
9

Cupertino

San Francisco Area

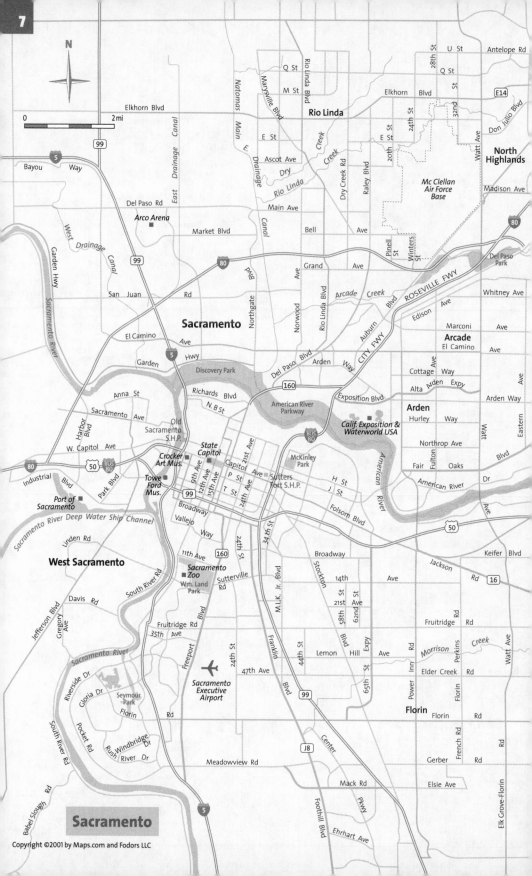

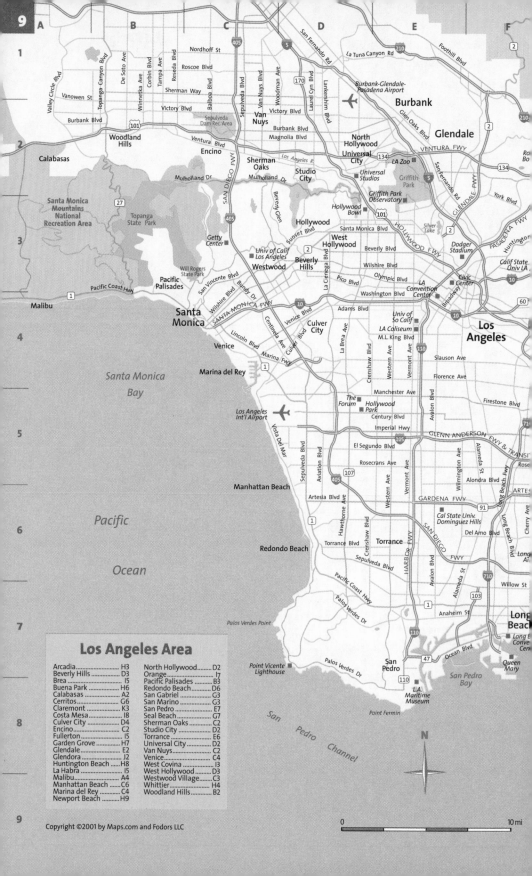

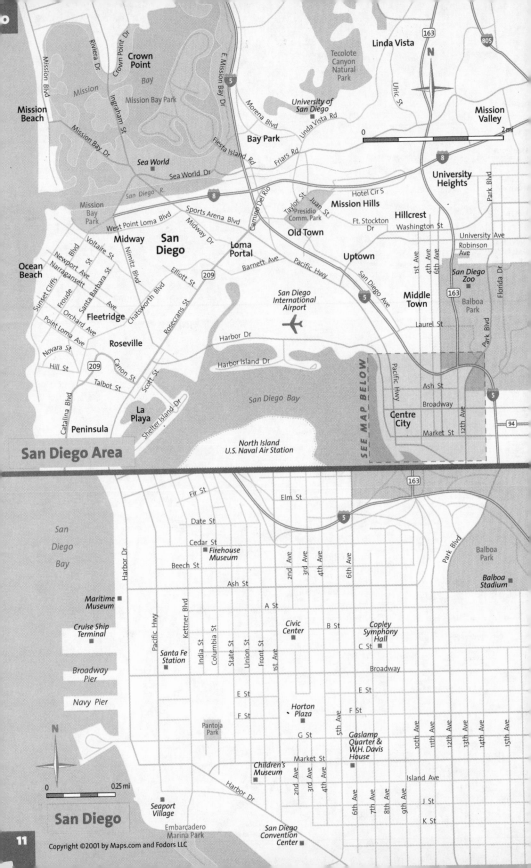

San Diego Area

North Island
U.S. Naval Air Station

San Diego

San Diego Bay

Copyright ©2001 by Maps.com and Fodors LLC